# THE HISTORIANS' HISTORY
# OF THE UNITED STATES

# The Historians' History
# of the United States

### Edited by

## ANDREW S. BERKY

### and

## JAMES P. SHENTON

VOLUME I

*G. P. Putnam's Sons   New York*

© 1966 BY ANDREW S. BERKY AND JAMES P. SHENTON

Library of Congress Catalog
Card Number: 66-20295

PRINTED IN THE UNITED STATES OF AMERICA

# Acknowledgments

Atlantic-Little, Brown and Company for pp. 144-169, *The Uprooted*, copyright 1951, Oscar Handlin.

Blaisdell Publishing Company for pp. 216-222, 223-233, *The Great Plains*, copyright 1931, 1959, Walter Prescott Webb.

Brandt & Brandt for pp. 220-230, 298-311, *The Incredible Era*, copyright 1939, Samuel Hopkins Adams.

The Arthur H. Clark Company for pp. 195-219, *The Repeal of the Missouri Compromise*, copyright 1908, 1935, P. Orman Ray.

Coward-McCann, Inc. for pp. 426-446, *The Age of Hate*, copyright 1930, 1958, George Fort Milton.

Dodd, Mead & Company for pp. 1-16, 46-57, *Twenty Years of the Republic*, 1885-1905 by Harry Thurston Peck, copyright 1906, Dodd, Mead & Co., renewed 1934, Constance Peck Beatty.

Doubleday and Company for pp. 11-37, *Mr. Lincoln's Army*, copyright 1951, Bruce Catton; pp. 619-631, *Experience of War*, © 1965, Kenneth S. Davis.

Mrs. Bernard DeVoto for pp. 5, 13, 20, 23, 25-27, 126-127, 225-230, 276-280, 286-291, *1846—Year of Decision*, copyright 1942, 1943, Bernard DeVoto.

Farrar, Straus & Giroux, Inc. for pp. 57-81, *The History of The New Deal*, copyright 1944, Basil Rauch.

Harcourt, Brace and World, Inc. for pp. 461-478, *Roosevelt: The Lion and the Fox*, © 1956, James MacGregor Burns; pp. 122-134, 141-148, *The Robber Barons*, copyright 1934, 1962, Matthew Josephson; pp. 7-22, 26-31, *The Beginnings of Critical Realism in America* by Vernon L. Parrington, copyright 1927, 1930, Harcourt Brace & Company, renewed 1955, 1958, Vernon L. Parrington, Jr., Louise P. Tucker, Elizabeth P. Thomas; pp. 279-302, *Theodore Roosevelt*, copyright 1931, 1956, Henry F. Pringle. All reprinted by permission of Harcourt, Brace and World, Inc.

Harper and Row, Publishers for pp. 507-527, *The Growth of American Thought* by Merle Curti, copyright 1943, Harper and Brothers; pp. 18-41, *Reconstruction, Political and Economic*, 1865-1877 by William A. Dunning, copyright 1907, Harper and Brothers, renewed 1935, Edward S. Cole; pp. 29-62, *America As a World Power* by John Holladay Latané, copyright 1907, Harper and Brothers, renewed 1935, Elinor Cox Latané; pp. 127-132, 136-137, 143-147, 149, 264-275, *Grover Cleveland, The Man and the Statesman*, Vol. I, by Robert McElroy, copyright 1923, Harper and Brothers, renewed 1951, Robert McElroy; pp. 1-26, *The Peacemakers*, © 1965, Richard B. Morris. All reprinted by permission of Harper and Row, Publishers.

Holt, Rinehart and Winston, Inc. for pp. 617-636, *A Diplomatic History of the United States* by Samuel Flagg Bemis, copyright 1916, 1942, 1950, 1955, © 1965, Holt, Rinehart and Winston, Inc.; pp. 2-6, 12-19, 247-254, 273-275, *The*

*Frontier in American History,* copyright 1920, Frederick Jackson Turner, renewed 1948, Caroline M. S. Turner.

Houghton Mifflin Company for pp. 101-125, 133-143, *The Life of John Marshall,* Volume III, Conflict and Construction, 1800-1815, copyright 1919, A. J. Beveridge, renewed 1947, Catherine Spencer Beveridge; pp. 486-510, *Jefferson and Hamilton,* copyright 1925, 1953, Claude G. Bowers; pp. 411-443, *Road to War; America,* 1914-1917, copyright 1935, 1962, Walter Millis; pp. 220-240, *History of the American Frontier, 1763-1893,* copyright 1924, F. L. Paxson, renewed 1952, Helen J. Paxson; pp. 173-197, *The Causes of the War of Independence,* copyright 1922, C. H. Van Tyne, renewed 1950, Jesselyn Van Tyne.

Indiana University Press for pp. 160-179, *The Old Northwest, Pioneer Period, 1815-1840,* Vol. II, copyright 1950, R. Carlyle Buley.

Alfred A. Knopf, Inc. for pp. 3-6, 8-12, 143-144, 303-313, 467-468, *Cities in the Wilderness,* copyright 1938, © 1966, Carl Bridenbaugh; pp. 213-225, 236-254, *The Age of Reason,* copyright 1955, Richard Hofstadter.

Little, Brown and Company for pp. 21-26, 28-32, 54-56, *A History of the Monroe Doctrine,* copyright © 1941, 1955, 1963, Dexter Perkins; pp. 661-689, *The Supreme Court in United States History* by Charles Warren, copyright 1922, 1926, Little, Brown and Company.

The Macmillan Company for pp. 254-277, *Wilson and the Peacemakers,* copyright 1944, 1945, 1947, Thomas A. Bailey; pp. 275-296, *The Rise of American Civilization,* Volume I by Charles A. and Mary R. Beard, copyright 1927, 1930, 1933, The Macmillan Company, renewed 1955, 1958, Mary R. Beard, 1961, William Beard and Miriam B. Vagts; pp. 556-582, *A History of the United States,* Volume II, A Century of Colonial History, 1660-1760 by Edward Channing, copyright 1908, The Macmillan Company, renewed 1936, Alice Channing and Elizabeth C. Fuller; pp. 281-284, 286-303, *The Irrepressible Conflict, 1850-1865* by Arthur Charles Cole (Volume VII of A History of American Life Series, Edited by A. M. Schlesinger, D. R. Fox and A. H. Thorndike), copyright 1934, The Macmillan Company, renewed 1962, Arthur Charles Cole; pp. 81-109, *The Quest for Social Justice, 1898-1914* by Harold Underwood Faulkner (Volume XI of A History of American Life Series), copyright 1931, The Macmillan Company, renewed 1959, Harold Underwood Faulkner; pp. 31-49, *The Emergence of Modern America, 1865-1875* by Allan Nevins (Volume VIII of A History of American Life Series), copyright 1927, The Macmillan Company, renewed 1955, Allan Nevins; pp. 53-60, 64-65, 66-77, *The Rise of the City, 1878-1898* by Arthur Meier Schlesinger (Volume X of A History of American Life Series), copyright 1938, The Macmillan Company, renewed 1961, Arthur M. Schlesinger; pp. 287-319, *The Great Crusade and After, 1914-1928* by Preston William Slosson (Volume XII of A History of American Life Series), copyright 1930, The Macmillan Company, renewed 1958, Preston William Slosson; pp. 68-90, *The Nationalizing of Business, 1878-1898* by Ida M. Tarbell (Volume X of A History of American Life Series), copyright 1936, 1964, The Macmillan Company; pp. 1-24, *The Age of the Great Depression* by Dixon Wecter (Volume XIII of A History of American Life Series), copyright 1948, The Macmillan Company.

John C. Miller for pp. 337-352, *Origins of the American Revolution,* copyright 1943, John C. Miller.

Mrs. Rachel Baker Napier for pp. 236-264, *Woodrow Wilson, Life and Letters*, Volume IV, copyright 1931, Ray Stannard Baker, renewed 1958, Jessie B. Baker.

New York University Press for pp. 1-17, 151-158, *The Golden Age of Colonial Culture* by Thomas J. Wertenbaker, copyright 1942, 1949, New York University.

W. W. Norton & Company for pp. 23-33, 50-59, *The Continental Congress* by Edmund Cody Burnett, copyright 1941, The Macmillan Company.

Princeton University Press for pp. 3, 4, 28-47, 109-112, *Japan Subdued: The Atomic Bomb and the End of the War in the Pacific* by Herbert Feis, copyright 1961, Princeton University Press; pp. 13-38, *The American Revolution Considered as a Social Movement* by J. Franklin Jameson, copyright 1926, Princeton University Press.

Henry Regnery Company for pp. 584-615, *Back Door to War*, copyright 1952, Charles Callan Tansill.

Charles Scribner's Sons for pp. 21-37, *The March of Democracy*, Volume I, The Rise of the Union, copyright 1932, 1933, James Truslow Adams, renewed © 1960, 1961, Kathryn Seely Adams; pp. 68-77, 114-128, *R. E. Lee*, Volume III by Douglas Southall Freeman, copyright 1935, Charles Scribner's Sons, renewed 1963, Inez Goddin Freeman; pp. 4-46, *Our Times*, Volume I, The Turn of the Century by Mark Sullivan, copyright 1926, Charles Scribner's Sons, renewed 1954, Mark Sullivan Jr.

Peter Smith, Publisher, for pp. 261-279, *American Negro Slavery* by Ulrich Bonnell Phillips, copyright 1918, D. Appleton and Company, renewed 1946, Lucie M. Phillips.

United States Publishers Association, Inc. for pp. 125-153, *The Agrarian Crusade: a Chronicle of the Farmer in Politics* by Solon J. Buck, copyright 1920, 1947, Yale University Press (Volume 47 of Yale Chronicles of America Series); pp. 1-34, *The Cotton Kingdom: a Chronicle of the Old South* by William E. Dodd, copyright 1919, 1922, 1946, Yale University Press (Volume 27 of Yale Chronicles of America Series); pp. 70-98, *The Masters of Capital: a Chronicle of Wall Street* by John Moody, copyright 1919, 1946, Yale University Press (Volume 41 of Yale Chronicles of America Series).

The University of Chicago Press for pp. 12-34, *The Perils of Prosperity* by William E. Leuchtenburg, copyright 1958, University of Chicago.

University of Minnesota Press for pp. 351-379, *The Populist Revolt* by John D. Hicks, copyright 1931, University of Minnesota, renewed 1959, John D. Hicks.

W. L. White for pp. 239-265, *A Puritan in Babylon* by William Allen White, copyright 1938, The Macmillan Company.

Yale University Press for pp. 421-443, *The American Mind* by Henry Steele Commager, copyright 1950, Yale University Press; pp. 192-210, *The Framing of the Constitution of the United States*, copyright 1913, 1940, Max Farrand; pp. 426-448, *Royal Government in America* by Leonard Woods Labaree, copyright 1930, Yale University Press; renewed 1958, Leonard Woods Labaree.

Samuel Yellen for pp. 44-65, *American Labor Struggles*, copyright 1936, S. Yellen, renewed 1963, Samuel Yellen.

# Contents

## III. A NEW COMMONWEALTH

## IV. THE MIDDLE YEARS

# THE HISTORIANS' HISTORY
# OF THE UNITED STATES

# Introduction

OF ALL ANIMALS, the human alone is probably aware of his existence in a time dimension, conscious that other humans have preceded him in time, and by their actions have determined in some manner his present condition. It is not surprising, given this awareness, that humans have evinced an interest in men and their works. The individual man who has obviously either dominated an era or served as an agent, perhaps unconsciously, of larger forces which determine the drift of events has exerted a peculiar fascination for his fellow man. But the observant commentator of the human scene will readily note that every human acts his role against a larger stage, that of society. Inevitably, any discussion of the individual's role requires an effort to differentiate between how free a man is to act without reference to his fellows and how much of his actions are determined by his presence in society. It has been the function of the historian to attempt that differentiation and to achieve, in the words of the French historian Fustel de Coulanges, "the science of human societies," remembering in the process the medievalist Marc Bloch's injunction that "man in society, and societies, are not precisely equivalent ideas."

From the beginning, man, controlled as he is by the biological facts of birth, life, and death, perceiving the existence in the space beyond earth of other entities, and ever conscious of powers larger than himself, has struggled to understand the unknown. In the absence of readily ascertainable fact, he has resorted to myth, one inhabited by gods, demigods, and other creatures of fantasy. Yet, the poetry of myth exists within a mind that is capable of reason, an attribute of mankind that permits him to subject his origins to the scrutiny of evidence. Where mankind once accepted his life as the result of the capricious decisions of inscrutable but homey gods, he entered the realm of history when he concluded that past events were explicable as the actions of men in a specific time location behaving as they did for ascertainable reasons. Within the framework of extant evidence, the investigator could both pose and answer questions about the past. It was the Greek Herodotus who gave the effort to understand the past its name "history," the Greek word for investigation, the findings of which would have lasting usefulness.

Herodotus' conclusion reveals what has been one of the abiding debates among historians: how final is the investigation of any single historian or group of historians? Can a historian, no matter how dedicated, achieve an "objective" truth, so total in its revelation that he can be said to have recreated the past as it was? Or must he accept the conclusion that our knowledge of the past, passing as it does through the mind of another time and again, is ever changing. The inadequacy of language alone severely hampers efforts to formulate exactly the meaning of a given idea, at least as it was understood by those who originally formulated it. The historian is further confined to conclusions that are supportable within the framework of available evidence. Obviously, what constitutes evidence is a major concern of the historian, for though written documentation is his primary source, as our knowledge of human behavior has been broadened by psychologists, anthropologists, sociologists, and economists among others, the historian has implemented their findings in his own researches to explain better past events. Thus as our medical knowledge grows and the effects of disease on personality are understood, the historian seeks to understand more fully the behavior of key figures in history through posthumous diagnosis, and with recent psychoanalytical knowledge has even indulged in cautious posthumous psychoanalysis. But in every instance the word is caution against stretching the evidence to support more than is justified. `

Historians have also been concerned with trying to determine whether` the course of human history is determined by large forces which dominate the course of individual and collective behavior. To discern the nature of these forces has occupied a central place in the attention of historians. A whole generation of historical research was dominated by the scholarly endeavor of Frederick Jackson Turner. It hardly matters that his frontier thesis has been severely modified since he first proposed it in 1893; it is sufficient to know that it contained a germ of truth which every investigator of the American experience recognizes as critical to our understanding of the United States. And though no one thesis is likely to dominate all history for all time, it is correct to conclude that no explanation of history which discounts a thesis which had as profound an impact as did Turner's is likely to be correct.

But beyond the search for forces and the emphasis upon interpretation is a further task. Any historian worth his salt must have a gift for telling a story. The unexpected nuance, the illuminating incident, the incisive phrase, when combined gives the touch of life to the dead past. What has been lives again. And in this effort, the historian reveals himself as an artist vested with the task of re-creating from imperfect evidence an imperfect image of what was, but nonetheless an image large enough to compel an understanding of a bygone time and of its vanished inhabitants. His success is proportional to his ability to convince the reader that no matter how distant the time and how great the change since then, the mankind represented retains a constant humanity. The link between then and now is the genius of the historian in convincing us that the response of man then touches a primal awareness that were we to be catapulted back in time to join him we would so respond. It is this ability that makes the historian an artist: we have been led by him to accept and understand the truth of the conclusions he has drawn from his exploration of the past. He has made us as one with our predecessors in the human journey through life. Though the grave may have silenced those we have visted, we leave them thinking we knew them and knowing that we will remember them.

It is the ability to tell a story that has distinguished the historians contained within these volumes. In a goodly number of instances their findings have been qualified by the discovery of new evidence and the application of new techniques of analysis, but in each instance, the period or incident they have written about remains strikingly alive and vivid. In a sense, they have taken a moment of American history and made it come alive. Names registered on tombstones have been restored to life and the society through which they move has been re-created in its complex subtleties and various manifestations. In addition, most historians presently working in the discipline recognize them as men who vitally affected or are affecting our understanding of the American past. Whatever new knowledge we have of that past is in some measure built or will be built upon their scholarship. In some instances, the historian is, as is Francis Parkman, long dead, himself the subject of biography, while in other instances, he is, as is Richard Hofstadter, actively exploring the outer edges of historical research.

This fusion of the old and new historian provides insight into the constants of the art of history. Each of them has been profoundly concerned with the re-creation of American history as accurately as their evidence will allow. The conclusions they have drawn have been rightly challenged, but the fact that they have drawn conclusions has provided subsequent historians with a framework within which to guide their own research. So as the reader progresses, he will frequently recognize the indebtedness of later historians to his predecessors. He will also recognize that the art of narrative is essentially unchangeable. Though historians have progressed far beyond the primitive techniques of Homer, they still retain the ability to tell a story so well that we are as transfixed by their written word as Homer's listeners were by his spoken words.

And through the whole of this complex recitation of the American experience is the unyielding fact that the history of the United States is one of the most extraordinary of human adventures. In the less than five centuries that have elapsed since Columbus stumbled upon the New World in his quest for the Orient, Europe, Asia, and Africa have disgorged a human cargo to populate the last wilderness frontier left to mankind. Within the boundaries of the better third of the North American continent, a nation has been founded, shaped by a various inherited tradition that made the legacy of western civilization the national birthright, but also unique. Within its boundaries mankind opened his final struggle to prove that self-government is a workable proposition and that poverty and deprivation is not the natural lot of most men. The energy which drew aside the mystery that had originally cloaked Columbus' discovery went on to tame a continent and mobilize its resources. The result has been a veritable material paradise which the world without may mock but also struggles to emulate. Out of the welter of peoples and races that have found their way to American shores a new nationality has been formed, one that is still incomplete but one still agitated by unfulfilled expectations. Here on a but recently unknown continent mankind has experienced a release of energy so extraordinary that it can be said to bid fair to revolutionize the world and, some uneasily fear, the universe.

The magnitude of the experience has attracted a legion of historians. Some have been the systematically trained social scientists of the university; others have been educated, liberally oriented amateurs; others have been journalists trying to make sense out of their immediate world; and others have been concerned citizens who wanted to know their country and its makers better. All are represented here. Together they form a most catholic company, and together they tell a coherent history. Whether they be soldier, admiral, senator, teacher, journalist, or scholar, they have informed their treatment with compassion and love for their subject. In their effort to understand the meaning of American history they have rarely revealed a cramped view or a narrow judgment. Rather they have reflected something of the vast openness which visitors from afar have found so characteristic of American life. When the reading is complete, one has seen the American past through American eyes, and one has sampled the diversity of men and women who in telling the American story have given it the shape and form in which we embed our previous experience.

# I

# Discovery and Colonization

THE *journey to America has been an overriding fact of world history since that fateful October 12, 1492, when Columbus beheld a new world without realizing it. Whether subsequent journeys were to be the long, lonely ones made by countless nameless millions from every continent or the one of imagination made by artists such as Franz Kafka, they have seared themselves onto the pages of history.*

*Yet, of all of these journeys, none has had quite the sense of high adventure as that of Columbus. It had the drama of being first, and humanity being what it is, the first, whether it be Hiroshima or the future first voyage to the moon, is remembered. It makes no difference to point out that legend has an Irish saint reaching the New World in the twilight of the misnamed Dark Ages or that considerable evidence supports the conclusion that a full five centuries before Columbus Vikings ranged along the northern shores of North America. These voyages generally lack a firm documentary basis, they rest betwixt myth and history, like an uncertain memory that fears it recalls not fact but a dream. But the journeys of Columbus are fact, fully documented, and his discovery sent a chill of expectation across western Europe, setting into motion a folk migration the end of which still has not come.*

*Columbus, a Genoese, recorded in his extraordinary journals his four voyages, but only slowly perceived the extent of his discovery. It was not until the third journey that he finally suspected that he beheld "a very great continent, which until today has been unknown." Beyond that suspicion, Columbus did not go. It remained for subsequent travelers to define the dimensions of the Admiral of the Ocean Sea's achievement. None of his successors faulted the accuracy of the words spoken by Columbus in a malarial fever on his fourth and final voyage in 1502: "Of those barriers of the Ocean Sea, which were closed with such mighty chains, he gave thee the keys." In the minds of man, Columbus alone discovered America.*

*The achievement of the Great Italian Navigator has captured countless imaginations. More than one historian has dealt with his voyages and each has found a new meaning and given new insight into their significance. The first American whose account achieved international recognition was the author Washington Irving (1783-1859). After an illustrious career as the author of comic accounts of early Knickerbocker history, he left the United States to reside in Europe between 1815 and 1832. While there he wrote a number of historical works, among them the history of Columbus that revealed Irving's flair for narrative history. In his classic account, Irving emphasized that the master of the Santa Maria had been searching for a*

*western route to the Orient when he stumbled upon the Western Hemi-*
*sphere. It is a conclusion that informs the most recent biography of Colum-*
*bus, that of Samuel Eliot Morison (1887-     ).*

# THE LIFE AND VOYAGES OF
# CHRISTOPHER COLUMBUS

## by Washington Irving

Whether in old times, beyond the reach of history or tradition, and in some remote period of civilization, when, as some imagine, the arts may have flourished to a degree unknown to those whom we term the Ancients, there existed an intercourse between the opposite shores of the Atlantic; whether the Egyptian legend, narrated by Plato, respecting the island of Atalantis was indeed no fable, but the obscure tradition of some vast country, ingulfed by one of those mighty convulsions of our globe, which have left traces of the ocean on the summits of lofty mountains, must ever remain matters of vague and visionary speculation. As far as authenticated history extends, nothing was known of terra firma, and the islands of the western hemisphere, until their discovery towards the close of the fifteenth century. A wandering bark may occasionally have lost sight of the landmarks of the old continents, and been driven by tempests across the wilderness of waters long before the invention of the compass, but never returned to reveal the secrets of the ocean. And though, from time to time, some document has floated to the shores of the old world, giving to its wondering inhabitants evidences of land far beyond their watery horizon; yet no one ventured to spread a sail, and seek that land enveloped in mystery and peril. Or if the legends of the Scandinavian voyagers be correct, and their mysterious Vinland was the coast of Labrador, or the shore of Newfoundland, they had but transient glimpses of the new world, leading to no certain or permanent knowledge, and in a little time lost again to mankind. Certain it is that at the beginning of the fifteenth century, when the most intelligent minds were seeking in every direction for the scattered lights of geographical knowledge, a profound ignorance prevailed among the learned as to the western regions of the Atlantic; its vast waters were regarded with awe and wonder, seeming to bound the world as with a chaos, into which conjecture could not penetrate, and enterprise feared to adventure. We need no greater proofs of this than the description given of the Atlantic by Xerif al Edrisi, surnamed the Nubian, an eminent Arabian writer, whose countrymen were the boldest navigators of the middle ages, and possessed all that was then known of geography.

"The ocean," he observes, "encircles the ultimate bounds of the inhabited earth, and all beyond it is unknown. No one has been able to verify any thing concerning it, on account of its difficult and perilous navigation, its great obscurity, its profound depth, and frequent tempests; through fear of its mighty fishes, and its haughty winds; yet there are many islands in it, some peopled, others uninhabited. There is no mariner who dares to enter into its deep waters; or if any have done so, they have merely kept along its coasts, fearful of departing from them. The waves of this ocean, although they roll as high as mountains, yet maintain themselves without breaking; for if they broke, it would be impossible for ship to plough them."

* * * * *

On the 14th of September, the voyagers were rejoiced by the sight of what they considered harbingers of land. A heron, and a tropical bird called the Rabo de Junco, neither of which are supposed to venture far to sea, hovered about the ships. On the following night they were struck with awe at beholding a meteor, or, as Columbus calls it in his journal, a great flame of fire, which seemed to fall from the sky into the sea, about four or five leagues distant. These meteors, common in warm climates, and especially under the tropics, are always seen in the serene azure sky of those latitudes, falling as it were from the heavens; but never beneath a cloud. In the transparent atmosphere of one of those beautiful nights, where every star shines with the purest lustre, they often leave a luminous train behind them which lasts for twelve or fifteen seconds, and may well be compared to a flame.

The wind had hitherto been favorable, with occasional, though transient, clouds and showers. They had made great progress each day, though Columbus, according to his secret plan, contrived to suppress several leagues in the daily reckoning left open to the crew.

They had now arrived within the influence of the trade wind, which, following the sun, blows steadily from east to west between the tropics, and sweeps over a few adjoining degrees of ocean. With this propitious breeze directly aft, they were wafted gently but speedily over a tranquil sea, so that for many days they did not shift a sail. Columbus perpetually refers to the bland and temperate serenity of the weather, which in this tract of the ocean is soft and refreshing without being cool. In his artless and expressive language he compares the pure and balmy mornings to those of April in Andalusia, and observes that they wanted but the song of the nightingale to complete the illusion. "He had reason to say so," observes the venerable Las Casas; "for it is marvellous the suavity which we experience when half way towards these Indies; and the more the ships approach the lands, so much more do they perceive the temperance and softness of the air, the clearness of the sky, and the amenity and fragrance sent forth from the groves and forests; much more certainly than in April in Andalusia."

They now began to see large patches of herbs and weeds drifting from the west, and increasing in quantity as they advanced. Some of these weeds were such as grow about rocks, others such as are produced in rivers; some were yellow and withered, others so green as to have apparently been recently washed from land. On one of these patches was a live crab, which

Columbus carefully preserved. They saw also a white tropical bird, of a kind which never sleeps upon the sea. Tunny fish also played about the ships, one of which was killed by the crew of the *Niña*. Columbus now called to mind the account given by Aristotle of certain ships of Cadiz, which, coasting the shores outside of the straits of Gibraltar, were driven westward by an impetuous east wind, until they reached a part of the ocean covered with vast fields of weeds, resembling sunken islands, among which they beheld many tunny fish. He supposed himself arrived in this weedy sea, as it had been called, from which the ancient mariners had turned back in dismay, but which he regarded with animated hope, as indicating the vicinity of land. Not that he had yet any idea of reaching the object of his search, the eastern end of Asia; for, according to his computation, he had come but three hundred and sixty leagues since leaving the Canary islands, and he placed the main land of India much farther on.

On the 18th of September the same weather continued; a soft steady breeze from the east filled every sail, while, to use the words of Columbus, the sea was as calm as the Guadalquiver at Seville. He fancied that the water of the sea grew fresher as he advanced, and noticed this as a proof of the superior sweetness and purity of the air.

The crews were all in high spirits; each ship strove to get in the advance, and every seaman was eagerly on the look-out; for the sovereigns had promised a pension of ten thousand maravadis to him who should first discover land. Martin Alonzo Pinzon crowded all canvas, and as the Pinta was a fast sailer, he generally kept the lead. In the afternoon he hailed the admiral and informed him, that, from the flight of a great number of birds, and from the appearance of the northern horizon, he thought there was land in that direction.

There was in fact a cloudiness in the north, such as often hangs over land; and at sunset it assumed such shapes and masses that many fancied they beheld islands. There was a universal wish, therefore, to steer for that quarter. Columbus, however, was persuaded that they were mere illusions. Every one who has made a sea voyage must have witnessed the deceptions caused by clouds resting upon the horizon, especially about sunset and sunrise; which the eye, assisted by the imagination and desire, easily converts into the wished-for land. This is particularly the case within the tropics, where the clouds at sunset assume the most singular appearances.

On the following day there were drizzling showers, unaccompanied by wind, which Columbus considered favorable signs; two boobies also flew on board the ships, birds which, he observed, seldom fly twenty leagues from land. He sounded, therefore, with a line of two hundred fathoms, but found no bottom. He supposed he might be passing between islands, lying to the north and south; but was unwilling to waste the present favoring breeze by going in search of them; besides, he had confidently affirmed that land was to be found by keeping steadfastly to the west; his whole expedition had been founded on such a presumption; he should, therefore, risk all credit and authority with his people were he to appear to doubt and waver, and to go groping blindly from point to point of the compass. He resolved, therefore, to keep one bold course always westward, until he should reach the coast of India; and afterwards, if advisable, to seek these islands on his return.

Notwithstanding his precaution to keep the people ignorant of the distance they had sailed, they were now growing extremely uneasy at the length of the voyage. They had advanced much farther west than ever man had sailed before, and though already beyond the reach of succor, still they continued daily leaving vast tracts of ocean behind them, and pressing onward and onward into that apparently boundless abyss. It is true they had been flattered by various indications of land, and still others were occurring; but all mocked them with vain hopes: after being hailed with a transient joy, they passed away, one after another, and the same interminable expanse of sea and sky continued to extend before them. Even the bland and gentle breeze, uniformly aft, was now conjured by their ingenious fears into a cause of alarm; for they began to imagine that the wind, in these seas, might always prevail from the east, and if so, would never permit their return to Spain.

Columbus endeavored to dispel these gloomy presages, sometimes by argument and expostulation, sometimes by awakening fresh hopes, and pointing out new signs of land. On the 20th of September the wind veered, with light breezes from the south-west. These, though adverse to their progress, had a cheering effect upon the people, as they proved that the wind did not always prevail from the east. Several birds also visited the ships; three, of a small kind which keep about groves and orchards, came singing in the morning, and flew away again in the evening. Their song cheered the hearts of the dismayed mariners, who hailed it as the voice of land. The larger fowl, they observed, were strong of wing, and might venture far to sea; but such small birds were too feeble to fly far, and their singing showed that they were not exhausted by their flight.

On the following day there was either a profound calm, or light winds from the south-west. The sea, as far as the eye could reach, was covered with weeds; a phenomenon often observed in this part of the ocean, which has sometimes the appearance of a vast inundated meadow. This has been attributed to immense quantities of submarine plants, which grow at the bottom of the sea until ripe, when they are detached by the motion of the waves and currents, and rise to the surface. These fields of weeds were at first regarded with great satisfaction, but at length they became, in many places, so dense and matted, as in some degree to impede the sailing of the ships, which must have been under very little headway. The crews now called to mind some tale about the frozen ocean, where ships were said to be sometimes fixed immovable. They endeavored, therefore, to avoid as much as possible these floating masses, lest some disaster of the kind might happen to themselves. Others considered these weeds as proofs that the sea was growing shallower, and began to talk of lurking rocks, and shoals, and treacherous quicksands; and of the danger of running aground, as it were, in the midst of the ocean, where their vessels might rot and fall to pieces, far out of the track of human aid, and without any shore where the crews might take refuge. They had evidently some confused notion of the ancient story of the sunken island of Atalantis, and feared that they were arriving at that part of the ocean where navigation was said to be obstructed by drowned lands, and the ruins of an ingulfed country.

To dispel these fears, the admiral had frequent recourse to the lead; but though he sounded with a deep sea line, he still found no bottom. The minds of the crews, however, had gradually become diseased. They were full of vague terrors and superstitious fancies: they construed every thing into a cause of alarm, and harassed their commander by incessant murmurs.

For three days there was a continuance of light summer airs from the southward and westward, and the sea was as smooth as a mirror. A whale was seen heaving up its huge form at a distance, which Columbus immediately pointed out as a favorable indication, affirming that these fish were generally in the neighborhood of land. The crews, however, became uneasy at the calmness of the weather. They observed that the contrary winds which they experienced were transient and unsteady, and so light as not to ruffle the surface of the sea, which maintained a sluggish calm like a lake of dead water. Every thing differed, they said, in these strange regions from the world to which they had been accustomed. The only winds which prevailed with any constancy and force, were from the east, and they had not power to disturb the torpid stillness of the ocean; there was a risk, therefore, either of perishing amidst stagnant and shoreless waters, or of being prevented, by contrary winds, from ever returning to their native country.

Columbus continued with admirable patience to reason with these fancies; observing that the calmness of the sea must undoubtedly be caused by the vicinity of land in the quarter whence the wind blew, which, therefore, had not space sufficient to act upon the surface, and heave up large waves. Terror, however, multiplies and varies the forms of ideal danger, a thousand times faster than the most active wisdom can dispel them. The more Columbus argued, the more boisterous became the murmurs of his crew, until, on Sunday, the 25th of September, there came on a heavy swell of the sea, unaccompanied by wind. This phenomenon often occurs in the broad ocean; being either the expiring undulations of some past gale, or the movement given to the sea by some distant current of wind; it was, nevertheless, regarded with astonishment by the mariners, and dispelled the imaginary terrors occasioned by the calm.

Columbus, who as usual considered himself under the immediate eye and guardianship of Heaven in this solemn enterprise, intimates in his journal that this swelling of the sea seemed providentially ordered to allay the rising clamors of his crew; comparing it to that which so miraculously aided Moses when conducting the children of Israel out of the captivity of Egypt.

The situation of Columbus was daily becoming more and more critical. In proportion as he approached the regions where he expected to find land, the impatience of his crews augmented. The favorable signs which increased his confidence, were derided by them as delusive; and there was danger of their rebelling, and obliging him to turn back, when on the point of realizing the objects of all his labors. They beheld themselves with dismay still wafted onward, over the boundless wastes of what appeared to them a mere watery desert, surrounding the habitable world. What was to become of them should their provisions fail? Their ships were too weak and defective even for the great voyage they had already made, but if they were still to press forward, adding at every moment to the immense expanse behind them, how should they ever be able to return, having no intervening port where they might victual and refit?

In this way they fed each other's discontents, gathering together in little knots, and fomenting a spirit of mutinous opposition: and when we consider the natural fire of the Spanish temperament and its impatience of control; and that a great part of these men were sailing on compulsion; we cannot wonder that there was imminent danger of their breaking forth into open rebellion and compelling Columbus to turn back. In their secret conferences they exclaimed against him as a desperado, bent, in a mad fantasy, upon doing something extravagant to render himself notorious. What were their sufferings and dangers to one evidently content to sacrifice his own life for the chance of distinction? What obligations bound them to continue on with him; or when were the terms of their agreement to be considered as fulfilled? They had already penetrated unknown seas, untraversed by a sail, far beyond where man had ever before ventured. They had done enough to gain themselves a character for courage and hardihood in undertaking such an enterprise and persisting in it so far. How much further were they to go in quest of a merely conjectured land? Were they to sail on until they perished, or until all return became impossible? In such case they would be the authors of their own destruction.

On the other hand, should they consult their safety, and turn back before too late, who would blame them? Any complaints made by Columbus would be of no weight; he was a foreigner without friends or influence; his schemes had been condemned by the learned, and discountenanced by people of all ranks. He had no party to uphold him, and a host of opponents whose pride of opinion would be gratified by his failure. Or, as an effectual means of preventing his complaints, they might throw him into the sea, and give out that he had fallen overboard while busy with his instruments contemplating the stars; a report which no one would have either the inclination or the means to controvert.

Columbus was not ignorant of the mutinous disposition of his crew; but he still maintained a serene and steady countenance, soothing some with gentle words, endeavoring to stimulate the pride or avarice of others, and openly menacing the refractory with signal punishment, should they do anything to impede the voyage.

On the 25th of September, the wind again became favorable, and they were able to resume their course directly to the west. The airs being light, and the sea calm, the vessels sailed near to each other, and Columbus had much conversation with Martin Alonzo Pinzon on the subject of a chart, which the former had sent three days before on board of the *Pinta*. Pinzon thought that, according to the indications of the map, they ought to be in the neighborhood of Cipango, and the other islands which the admiral had therein delineated. Columbus partly entertained the same idea, but thought it possible that the ships might have been borne out of their track by the prevalent currents, or that they had not come so far as the pilots had reckoned. He desired that the chart might be returned, and Pinzon tying it to the end of a cord, flung it on board to him. While Columbus, his pilot, and several of his experienced mariners were studying the map, and endeavoring to make out from it their actual position, they heard a shout from the *Pinta*, and looking up, beheld Martin Alonzo Pinzon mounted on the stern of his vessel, crying "Land! land! Señor, I claim my reward!" He pointed at the same time to the southwest, where there was indeed an appearance of land at about twenty-five leagues' distance. Upon this Columbus threw himself on his knees and returned thanks to God; and Martin Alonzo repeated the *Gloria in excelsis*, in which he was joined by his own crew and that of the admiral.

The seamen now mounted to the mast-head or climbed about the rigging, straining their eyes in the direction pointed out. The conviction became so general of land in that quarter, and the joy of the people so ungovernable, that Columbus found it necessary to vary from his usual course, and stand all night to the southwest. The morning light, however, put an end to all their hopes, as to a dream. The fancied land proved to be nothing but an evening cloud, and had vanished in the night. With dejected hearts they once more resumed their western course, from which Columbus would never have varied, but in compliance with their clamorous wishes.

For several days they continued on with the same propitious breeze, tranquil sea, and mild, delightful weather. The water was so calm that the sailors amused themselves with swimming about the vessel. Dolphins began to abound, and flying fish, darting into the air, fell upon the decks. The continued signs of land diverted the attention of the crews, and insensibly beguiled them onward.

On the 1st of October, according to the reckoning of the pilot of the admiral's ship, they had come five hundred and eighty leagues west since leaving the Canary islands. The reckoning which Columbus showed the crew, was five hundred and eighty-four, but the reckoning which he kept privately, was seven hundred and seven. On the following day, the weeds floated from east to west; and on the third day no birds were to be seen.

The crews now began to fear that they had passed between islands, from one to the other of which the birds had been flying. Columbus had also some doubts of the kind, but refused to alter his westward course. The people again uttered murmurs and menaces; but on the following day they were visited by such flights of birds, and the various indications of land became so numerous, that from a state of despondency they passed to one of confident expectation.

Eager to obtain the promised pension, the seamen were continually giving the cry of land, on the least appearance of the kind. To put a stop to these false alarms, which produced continual disappointment, Columbus declared that should any one give such notice, and land not be discovered within three days afterwards, he should thenceforth forfeit all claim to the reward.

On the evening of the 6th of October, Martin Alonzo Pinzon began to lose confidence in their present course, and proposed that they should stand more to the southward. Columbus, however, still persisted in steering directly west. Observing this difference of opinion in a person so important in his squadron as Pinzon, and fearing that chance or design might scatter the ships, he ordered that, should either of the caravels be separated from him, it should stand to the west, and endeavor as soon as possible to join company again: he directed, also, that the vessels should keep near to him at sunrise and sunset, as at these times the state of the atmosphere is most favorable to the discovery of distant land.

On the morning of the 7th of October, at sunrise, several of the admiral's crew thought they beheld land in the west, but so indistinctly that no one ventured to proclaim it, lest he should be mistaken, and forfeit all chance of the reward: the *Niña*, however, being a good sailer, pressed forward to ascertain the fact. In a little while a flag was hoisted at her mast-head, and a gun discharged, being the preconcerted signals for land. New joy was awakened throughout the little squadron, and every eye was turned to the west. As they advanced, however, their cloud-built hopes faded away, and before evening the fancied land had again melted into air.

The crews now sank into a degree of dejection proportioned to their recent excitement; but new circumstances occurred to arouse them. Columbus, having observed great flights of small field-birds going towards the southwest, concluded they must be secure of some neighboring land, where they would find food and a resting-place. He knew the importance which the Portuguese voyagers attached to the flight of birds, by following which they had discovered most of their islands. He had now come seven hundred and fifty leagues, the distance at which he had computed to find the island of Cipango; as there was no appearance of it, he might have missed it through some mistake in the latitude. He determined, therefore, on the evening of the 7th of October to alter his course to the west-southwest, the direction in which the birds generally flew, and continue that direction for at least two days, After all, it was no great deviation from his main course, and would meet the wishes of the Pinzons, as well as be inspiriting to his followers generally.

For three days they stood in this direction, and the further they went the more frequent and encouraging were the signs of land. Flights of small birds of various colors, some of them such as sing in the fields, came flying about the ships, and then continued towards the southwest, and others were heard also flying by in the night. Tunny fish played about the smooth sea, and a heron, a pelican, and a duck, were seen, all bound in the same direction. The herbage which floated by was fresh and green, as if recently from land, and the air, Columbus observes, was sweet and fragrant as April breezes in Seville.

All these, however, were regarded by the crews as so many delusions beguiling them on to destruction; and when on the evening of the third day they beheld the sun go down upon a shoreless ocean, they broke forth into turbulent clamor. They exclaimed against this obstinacy in tempting fate by continuing on into a boundless sea. They insisted upon turning home-ward, and abandoning the voyage as hopeless. Columbus endeavored to pacify them by gentle words and promises of large rewards; but finding that they only increased in clamor, he assumed a decided tone. He told them it was useless to murmur; the expedition had been sent by the sov-ereigns to seek the Indies, and, happen what might, he was determined to persevere, until, by the blessing of God, he should accomplish the enter-prise.

Columbus was now at open defiance with his crew, and his situation became desperate. Fortunately the manifestations of the vicinity of land were such on the following day as no longer to admit a doubt. Beside a quantity of fresh weeds, such as grow in rivers, they saw a green fish of a kind which keeps about rocks; then a branch of thorn with berries on it, and recently separated from the tree, floated by them; then they picked up a reed, a small board, and, above all, a staff artificially carved. All gloom and mutiny now gave way to sanguine expectation; and throughout the day each one was eagerly on the watch, in hopes of being the first to discover the long-sought-for land.

In the evening, when, according to invariable custom on board of the admiral's ship, the mariners had sung the *salve regina*, or vesper hymn to the Virgin, he made an impressive address to his crew. He pointed out the good-ness of God in thus conducting them by soft and favoring breezes across a tranquil ocean, cheering their hopes continually with fresh signs, increasing as their fears augmented, and thus leading and guiding them to a promised land. He now reminded them of the orders he had given on leaving the Canaries, that, after sailing westward seven hundred leagues, they should not make sail after midnight. Present appearances authorized such a precaution. He thought it probable they would make land that very night; he ordered, therefore, a vigilant lookout to be kept from the forecastle, promising to whomsoever should make the discovery, a doublet of velvet, in addition to the pension to be given by the sovereigns.

The breeze had been fresh all day, with more sea than usual, and they had made great progress. At sunset they had stood again to the west, and were ploughing the waves at a rapid rate, the *Pinta* keeping the lead, from her superior sailing. The greatest animation prevailed throughout the ships; not an eye was closed that night. As the evening darkened, Columbus took his station on the top of the castle or cabin on the high poop of his vessel, ranging his eye along the dusky horizon, and maintaining an intense and un-remitting watch. About ten o'clock, he thought he beheld a light glimmering at a great distance. Fearing his eager hopes might deceive him, he called to Pedro Gutierrez, gentleman of the king's bed-chamber, and inquired whether he saw such a light; the latter replied in the affirmative. Doubtful whether it might not yet be some delusion of the fancy, Columbus called Rodrigo Sanchez of Segovia, and made the same inquiry. By the time the latter had ascended the round-house, the light had disappeared. They saw it once or twice afterwards in sudden and passing gleams; as if it were a torch in the bark of a fisherman, rising and sinking with the waves; or in the hand of some person on shore, borne up and down as he walked from house to house. So transient and uncertain were these gleams, that few attached any importance to them; Columbus, however, considered them as certain signs of land, and, moreover, that the land was inhabited.

They continued their course until two in the morning, when a gun from the *Pinta* gave the joyful signal of land. It was first descried by a mariner named Rodrigo de Triana; but the reward was afterwards adjudged to the admiral, for having previously perceived the light. The land was now clearly seen about two leagues distant, whereupon they took in sail, and laid to, waiting impatiently for the dawn.

The thoughts and feelings of Columbus in this little space of time must have been tumultuous and intense. At length in spite of every difficulty and danger, he had accomplished his object. The great mystery of the ocean was revealed; his theory, which had been the scoff of sages, was triumphantly established; he had secured to himself a glory durable as the world itself.

It is difficult to conceive the feelings of such a man, at such a moment; or the conjectures which must have thronged upon his mind, as to the land before him, covered with darkness. That it was fruitful, was evident from the vegetables which floated from its shores. He thought, too, that he perceived the fragrance of aromatic groves. The moving light he had beheld proved it the residence of man. But what were its inhabitants? Were they like those of the other parts of the globe; or were they some strange and monstrous race, such as the imagination was prone in those times to give to all remote and unknown regions? Had he come upon some wild island far in the Indian sea; or was this the famed Cipango itself, the object of his golden fancies? A thousand speculations of the kind must have swarmed upon him, as, with his anxious crews, he waited for the night to pass away; wondering whether the morning light would reveal a savage wilderness, or dawn upon spicy groves, and glittering fanes, and gilded cities, and all the splendor of oriental civilization.

It was on Friday morning, the 12th of October, that Columbus first beheld the new world. As the day dawned he saw before him a level island, several leagues in extent, and covered with trees like a continual orchard. Though apparently uncultivated, it was populous, for the inhabitants were seen issuing from all parts of the woods and running to the shore. They were perfectly naked, and as they stood gazing at the ships, appeared by their attitudes and gestures to be lost in astonishment. Columbus made signal for the ships to cast anchor, and the boats to be manned and armed. He entered his own boat, richly attired in scarlet, and holding the royal standard; whilst Martin Alonzo Pinzon, and Vincent Janez his brother, put off in company in their boats, each with a banner of the enterprise emblazoned with a green cross, having on either side the letters F. and Y., the initials of the Castilian monarchs Fernando and Ysabel, surmounted by crowns.

As he approached the shore, Columbus, who was disposed for all kinds of agreeable impressions, was delighted with the purity and suavity of the atmosphere, the crystal transparency of the sea, and the extraordinary beauty of the vegetation. He beheld, also, fruits of an unknown kind upon the trees which overhung the shores. On landing, he threw himself on his knees, kissed the earth, and returned thanks to God with tears of joy. His example was followed by the rest, whose hearts indeed overflowed with the same feelings of gratitude. Columbus then rising drew his sword, displayed the royal standard, and assembling around him the two captains, with Rodrigo de Escobedo, notary of the armament, Rodrigo Sanchez, and the rest who had landed, he took solemn possession in the name of the Castilian sovereigns, giving the island the name of San Salvador. Having complied with the requisite forms and ceremonies, he called upon all present to take the oath of obedience to him, as admiral and viceroy, representing the persons of the sovereigns.

The feelings of the crew now burst forth in the most extravagant transports. They had recently considered themselves devoted men, hurrying forward to destruction; they now looked upon themselves as favorites of fortune, and gave themselves up to the most unbounded joy. They thronged around the admiral with overflowing zeal, some embracing him, others kissing his hands. Those who had been most mutinous and turbulent during the voyage, were now most devoted and enthusiastic. Some begged favors of him, as if he had already wealth and honors in his gift. Many abject spirits, who had outraged him by their insolence, now crouched at his feet, begging pardon for all the trouble they had caused him, and promising the blindest obedience for the future.

The natives of the island, when, at the dawn of day, they had beheld the ships hovering on their coast, had supposed them monsters which had issued from the deep during the night. They had crowded to the beach, and watched their movements with awful anxiety. Their veering about, apparently without effort, and the shifting and furling of their sails, resembling huge wings, filled them with astonishment. When they beheld their boats approach the shore, and a number of strange beings clad in glittering steel, or raiment of various colors, landing upon the beach, they fled in affright to the woods. Finding, however, that there was no attempt to pursue nor molest them, they gradually recovered from their terror, and approached the Spaniards with great awe; frequently prostrating themselves on the earth, and making signs of adoration. During the ceremonies of taking possession, they remained gazing in timid admiration at the complexion, the beards, the shining armor, and splendid dress of the Spaniards. The admiral particularly attracted their attention, from his commanding height, his air of authority, his dress of scarlet, and the deference which was paid him by his companions; all which pointed him out to be the commander. When they had still further recovered from their fears, they approached the Spaniards, touched their beards, and examined their hands and faces, admiring their whiteness. Columbus was pleased with their gentleness and confiding simplicity, and suffered their scrutiny with perfect acquiescence, winning them by his benignity. They now supposed that the ships had sailed out of the crystal firmament which bounded their horizon, or had descended from above on their ample wings, and that these marvelous beings were inhabitants of the skies.

The natives of the island were no less objects of curiosity to the Spaniards, differing, as they did, from any race of men they had ever seen. Their appearance gave no promise of either wealth or civilization, for they were entirely naked, and painted with a variety of colors. With some it was confined merely to a part of the face, the nose, or around the eyes; with others it extended to the whole body, and gave them a wild and fantastic appearance. Their complexion was of a tawny or copper hue, and they were entirely destitute of beards. Their hair was not crisped, like the recently-discovered tribes of the African coast, under the same latitude, but straight and coarse, partly cut short above the ears, but some locks were left long behind and falling upon their shoulders. Their features, though obscured and disfigured by paint, were agreeable; they had lofty foreheads and remarkably fine eyes. They were of moderate stature and well shaped; most of them appeared to be under thirty years of age: there was but one female with them, quite young, naked like her companions, and beautifully formed.

As Columbus supposed himself to have landed on an island at the extremity of India, he called the natives by the general appellation of Indians, which was universally adopted before the true nature of his discovery was known, and has since been extended to all the aboriginals of the New World.

❧ ☙

*The Europe from which Columbus sailed was a continent in tumultuous transition. Some historians have treated it as a Renaissance, while others have seen it as the waning of the Middle Ages. Despite the disagreement, historians have viewed it as a time of great events which, in words applied by Herodotus of Thurii to an earlier time, "should not lose their radiance."*

*Once again the arts flourished to remind western man that he had never fully lost touch with the classic harmony and simplicity of antiquity. Humanism, a touching philosophy which preached belief in mankind's fundamental goodness, pointed the way to the conversion of "the vicious into the virtuous, the corporal into the spiritual, the worldly into the divine." State and society seemed ready to renounce brutality; the individual could command that government existed for his own fulfillment. The land of Europe was increasingly divided into nation-states. United by language, custom, and common history, the European peoples, each in their turn, defined not only homelands but also created organized power designated the state. Even as humanism gave lyric wings to the human spirit, the state asserted its sovereignty, a definition of power which embodies the ultimate ability to negate spirit, soul, and existence.*

*It was the power of the Spanish state allied with human inspiration that propelled first Columbus and then those who traveled in his wake into the discovery and exploration of an unknown world. The men who ranged the seas and continents laid claim to what they found for their sponsors and as a result further expanded the power of the state. They also threw open the world to the West, precipitating worldwide upheavals as western ideals, institutions, and techniques gained sway.*

*A curious alliance of individual initiative and state enterprise combined to shape the economic system called mercantilism. It made patriotism and profits synonymous. So as the first stages of capitalism were laid, man and state entered into an alliance which triggered a ruthless and brutal struggle for the assumed limited wealth of earth. In the process, the original inhabitants of the New World, the Indians, were victimized, foreshadowing all future confrontations between non-whites and the imperial-minded western man. Often the Indian was enslaved, but since the Christian separated soul from body, he also aimed to convert the heathen to his own true faith. In the eyes of more than one explorer God and Mammon were one.*

*The conquest of the Indian took almost four centuries. The Spaniards and the Portuguese fused their blood with their subdued foes but in British America, as each tribe lost its struggle against the newcomer, he was expelled to the West. By mid-nineteenth century, the American Indian had reached the end of his journey. He would be confined to his reservations, out of all but the occasional sight of his conqueror. But the Indian bequeathed to his successor the most provocative of all American legends: the conquest of the last frontier. He also reminds us in the words of his poetry that the strident triumph of western man was underscored by the tragedy of the Indian. "I lift my voice in wailing. I am afflicted, as I remember that we must leave the beautiful flowers, the noble songs; let us enjoy ourselves for a while, let us sing, for we must depart forever, we are to be destroyed in our dwelling place." So as Europe knew a rebirth, the Indian faced death.*

*Edward Potts Cheyney (1861-1947) focused most of his long scholarly career on an analysis of the European roots of American life. He was greatly influenced by the "germ theory" of Herbert Baxter Adams (1850-1901) which emphasized that Teutonic institutions were the origin of what is distinctively American. Cheyney expanded Adams' emphasis to include generally European institutions as the seedbed from which American equivalents sprang. He looked away from the frontier as the shaping influence in American life and contended instead that America was formed by a transplanted European heritage.*

# EUROPEAN BACKGROUND
# OF AMERICAN HISTORY
## 1300-1600

### by Edward Potts Cheyney

The priority of Portugal and Spain in distant adventure did not secure them from the competition of the other nations of Europe, whose awakening activity, ambition, and enterprise perceived clearly the advantages of the

New World and of the new routes to the south and east. Almost within the first decade of the sixteenth century an Englishman cries out: "The Indies are discovered and vast treasures brought from thence every day. Let us, therefore, bend our endeavors thitherwards, and if the Spaniards or Portuguese suffer us not to join with them, there will be yet region enough for all to enjoy." Soon England, France, and the Netherlands were sending exploring and trading expeditions abroad, and somewhat later they all aimed at Colonial empires comparable with that of Spain. These colonial settlements were chiefly made for commercial profit and depended closely on a new and peculiar type of commercial organization, the well-known chartered companies. It was these companies which established the greater number of American colonies, and the ideals, regulations, and administrative methods of corporate trading were interwoven into their political fabric.

\* \* \* \* \*

A complete contrast exists between international trade in 1400 and 1600. The type of commerce characteristic of the earlier period was carried on by individual merchants; that belonging to the later period by joint-stock companies. Under the former, merchants depended on municipal support and encouragement; under the latter they acted under charters received from national governments. The individual merchants of the earlier period had only trading privileges; the organized companies of the later time had political powers also. In the fifteenth century the merchants from any one city or group of cities occupied a building, a quarter, or fondaco, in each of the foreign cities with which they traded; in the seventeenth they more usually possessed independent colonies or fortified establishments of their own on the coasts of foreign countries. In the earlier period trading operations were restricted to Europe; in the later they extended over the whole world.

The essential elements of the organization of trade at the period chosen for this description are its individual character, its restriction to well-marked European limits, and its foundation upon concessions obtained by town governments.

At the beginning of the fifteenth century there were five principal groups of trading cities, whose merchants carried on probably nine-tenths of the commerce of Europe. These groups were situated: (1) in northern Italy; (2) in southern France and Catalonia; (3) in southern Germany; (4) in northern France and Flanders; (5) in northern Germany. Two of them were in the south of Europe; the Hanse towns of northern Germany, at the other extremity of Europe, carried the productions of the Baltic lands to the centre and south; the Flemish and south German groups, intermediate between the two, exchanged among themselves and transmitted goods from one part of Europe to another. There were, of course, vast differences of organization among the trading towns. Venice and Cologne, Barcelona and Augsburg, Bruges and Lübeck were too far separated in distance, nationality, the nature of their trade, and the degree of their development to have the same institutions. And yet there were many similarities.

\* \* \* \* \*

The union among the merchants of any one city or league was one for joint trading privileges only, not for corporate investment or syndicated business. Each merchant or firm traded separately and independently, simply using the warehouse and office facilities secured by the efforts of the home government, and enjoying the permission to trade, exemption from duties, and whatever other privileges might have been obtained for its merchants by the same power. The necessity for obtaining such concessions arose from the habit of looking at all international intercourse as to a certain degree abnormal, and of disliking and ill-treating foreigners. Hence the Germans in London, the Venetians in Alexandria, the Genoese in Constantinople, for instance, needed to have permission respectively from the English, the Mameluke, and the Greek governments to carry on their trade. Although they found it highly desirable for many reasons to hold a local settlement of their own in those cities, such a possession was not a necessary accompaniment of the individual and municipally regulated commerce of the thirteenth, fourteenth, and fifteenth centuries. Where but a few traders made their way to any one market, and that only irregularly, they lodged with natives, sold their goods in the open market-place, organized no permanent establishment, and had no consulate. On the other hand, where trade was extensive and constant, the settlement was like a part of the home land located in the midst of a foreign population.

As the fifteenth century progressed many influences combined to bring about a change in this system. The most important one of these influences was the growth of centralized states in the north, centre, and west of Europe. As Russia, Denmark, Sweden, England, Burgundy, and France became strong, the self-governing cities within these countries necessarily became politically weak; and the trading arrangements they had made among themselves became insecure. Strong nationalities were impatient of the claims of privilege made by foreigners settled or habitually trading in their cities; the interests of their own international policy often indicated the desirability of either favoring or opposing bodies of merchants, which in the time of their weakness the governments had treated with exactly the opposite policy; finally the desire of their own citizens for the advantages of their own foreign trade often commended itself to the rulers as an object of settled policy. In other words, national interests and municipal interests were often opposed to one another.

Internal difficulties in many cities and internal dissensions in the leagues of cities helped to weaken the towns as guarantors of the trade of their citizens. As a result of these political influences, before the fifteenth century was over the distribution of commerce was much changed and municipal control was distinctly weakened. The Italian and the German cities became less active and wealthy, while London, Lisbon, Antwerp, and many other centres grew richer. Individual cities and even leagues of cities ceased to be able to negotiate with other municipalities or with potentates to obtain trading privileges for their citizens, since such matters were now provided for by commercial treaties formed by national governments. One of the main characteristics of earlier commerce, its dependence on city govern-ments, thus passed away.

Then came the opening up of direct commerce by sea with the East Indies, the discovery of America, and the awakening of ambition, enter-prise, and effort on the part of new nations to make still further explora-tions and to develop new lines of commerce. The old organization of com-merce was profoundly altered when its centre of gravity was shifted west-ward to the Atlantic seaboard, and Europe got its Oriental products for the most part by an ocean route. Cities which had for ages had the advantage of a good situation were now unfavorably placed. Venice, Augsburg, Col-ogne, and a hundred other towns which had been on the main highways of trade were now on its byways. Many of these towns made strenuous, and in some cases and for a time successful, efforts to conform to the new condi-tions. Vigorous industry, trade, and commerce continued to exist in many of the old centres, and some of the most famous "merchant princes" of history, such as the Fuggers and the Medici, built up their fortunes in the old commercial cities in the fifteenth and sixteenth centuries. Nevertheless, these were the exception rather than the rule; and such successes were due to financial rather than commercial operations. In a general sense the old commerce of Europe, so far as it followed its accustomed lines, suffered a grievous decline.

More important than the decay of the old method was the growth of the new. A vast mass of new trade came into existence; spices and other Oriental products, now that they were imported by the Portuguese and afterwards by Spanish, Dutch, French, and English, by direct routes and by water car-riage, were greatly cheapened in price, and thus made attainable by many more people and much more extensively consumed. The early explorers of America failed to find either the route to the East or the Eastern goods which they sought, but they found other articles for which a demand in Europe either already existed or was ultimately created. Sea-fish abounded on the northeastern coasts of America to a degree that partially made up their loss to the disappointed seekers for a northwest passage. Whale oil and whalebone were obtained in the same waters. Dye-woods, timber, and ship stores were found on the coasts farther south. Furs became one of the most valued and most permanent imports from America. Gradually, as habits in Europe changed, other products came to be of enormous production and value. Sugar stands in the first rank of these later products; tobacco, cocoa, and many others followed close upon it. As colonists from Europe became estab-lished in the New World they must be provided with European and Asiatic goods, and this gave additional material for commerce.

Besides creating an increased commerce with the East and a new commerce with the West, the awakened spirit of enterprise and the new discoveries widened the radius of trade of each nation. Men learned to be bold, and the merchants of each European country carried their national commerce over all parts of Europe and far beyond its limit to the newly discovered lands. English, Dutch, French, and Danish merchants met in the ports of the White Sea and in those of the Mediterranean, and competed with one another for the commerce of the East and the New World. Trading to a distance was the chief commercial phenomenon of the sixteenth century, and was more influential than any other one factor in the transformation of commerce then in progress. Distant trading proved to have different requirements from anything that had gone before: it needed the political backing of some strong national government; it needed, or was considered to need, a monopoly of trade; and it needed the capital of many men.

*     *     *     *     *

In contrast both with government-controlled commerce and with purely private trading and enterprise, the chartered companies of England, Holland, France, Sweden, and Denmark arose. They were by no means self-controlled and independent companies; they were dependent on their governments for many rights and privileges and for constant support, protection, and subsidy. On the other hand, the governments expected them not only to develop a profitable trade but to furnish certain advantages to the nation, such as the creation of colonies, the increase of shipping, the provision of materials for use in the navy, the humiliation of political rivals, the preservation of a favorable balance of trade, and ultimately the payment of imposts and the loan of funds. They stood, therefore, midway between unregulated individual trading, in which the government took no especial interest, and [that] complete government organization and control of trade [which has been described as characterizing the policy of Portugal and Spain].

Some fifty or sixty such companies, nearly contemporaneous, and on the same broad lines of organization, are recorded as having been chartered by the five governments mentioned above, a few in the second half of the sixteenth century. Of course, some of these companies were still-born, never having gone beyond the charter received from the government; some existed only for a few years; and some were simply reorganizations. The formation of these companies marks a distinct valuable clew to the foundation and early government of European colonies in America.

England, Holland, France, Sweden, and Denmark, as well as Scotland and Prussia, each had an "East India Company"; Holland, France, Sweden, and Denmark each had a "West India Company"; England, Holland, and France each had a "Levant" or "Turkey Company"; England and France each had an "African Company"; and a date might readily be found in the seventeenth century when all these were in existence at the same time.

*     *     *     *     *

It was not likely that the two most vigorous, free, and commercially enterprising states of Europe would allow themselves long to be excluded from the most attractive and lucrative trade in the world. After England, in her resistance to the Armada in 1588, applied the touchstone to the naval prestige of Spain and showed its hollowness, her merchants and mariners took heart and pressed directly to the East. In 1591 an English squadron of three ships, under Captains Raymond and Lancaster, with the queen's leave, sailed down the western coast of Africa, rounded the Cape of Good Hope, followed the east coast to Zanzibar, and then passed across to Cape Comorin, Ceylon, and the Malay peninsula. They had mixed fortune, but one vessel returned home laden with pepper, obtained for the most part from the hold of a Portuguese prize. In 1595 the first direct Dutch voyage was made along much the same route. Other English and Dutch voyages followed; and in 1600 and 1602, respectively, the English and Dutch East India companies were chartered. The following analysis of the charter of the former of these companies will give the main characteristics of the new commercial system.

1. The charter, granted by Queen Elizabeth on December 31, 1600, was addressed by name to the earl of Cumberland and two hundred and fifteen knights and merchants, whom it created a corporation and a body politic under the name of "The Governor and Company of Merchants of London Trading to the East Indies."

2. The territory to which they were given privileges of trade consisted of all continents and islands lying between the Cape of Good Hope and the Straits of Magellan—that is to say, the east coast of Africa, the southern shore of Asia, the islands of the Indian Ocean, and the west coast of America; so long as they made no attempt to trade with any port at the time of the charter in the possession of any prince in league with Elizabeth, who should protest against such trade.

3. The corporation was for all time; but the privileges of trade under the charter were granted for fifteen years, with a promise, if they should seem profitable to the crown and the realm, to extend them for fifteen years more; and with a reservation, on the other hand, of the power to terminate them on two years' notice.

4. The powers of the company were those of an ordinary corporation and body politic. The members of the company and their employees possessed a complete monopoly of trade in the regions described, so far as English subjects were concerned, having, moreover, the right to grant licenses to non-members to trade within their limits.

5. They could buy land without limitation in amount, and as a matter of fact the company gained its first foothold in each of its stations in the East by buying a small piece of land from the native government.

6. The company could send out yearly "six good ships and six pinnaces with five hundred mariners, unless the royal navy goes forth," and these ships should not be seized even in times of special naval restraint, unless the queen's need was extreme and was announced to the company three months before the ships were impressed.

7. They had the right, in assemblies of the company held in any part of the queen's dominions or outside of them, to make all reasonable laws for their government not in opposition to the laws of England, and they could punish by fine and imprisonment all offenders against these laws.

8. Nothing is said in the original charter of the powers of offence and defence, alliance and military organizations; but these were probably taken

for granted, as they were so generally used by merchants and navigators at the time, and were, as a matter of fact, exercised without limitation by the company from its first voyage.

9. Especial privileges and exemptions were granted to the company by freeing its members from the payment of customs for the first four voyages, by giving them from six to twelve months' postponement of the payment of subsequent import duties, and by allowing them re-export of Indian goods free from customs duties. The laws against the export of bullion were also suspended in their favor to the extent of allowing them to send out on each voyage £30,000 in coin.

10. The organization of this company was comparatively simple, consisting of a governor, deputy governor, and twenty-four members of a directing board, "to be called committees," all to be elected annually in a general assembly or court of the company. The governor and committees must all take the oath of allegiance to the English sovereign.

The East India Company remained for some years a somewhat variable body, as each voyage was made on the basis of a separate investment, by different stockholders, and in varying amounts. But in 1609 the charter was renewed, and in 1612 a longer joint-stock investment fixed the membership more definitely. By this time the company had become, in fact, as permitted by its charter, a closely organized corporation, with well-understood and clearly defined rights and powers, and it was soon started on its career of trade, settlement, conquest, and domination. A new type of commercial organization had become clearly dominant.

An exactly typical chartered commercial company, which combined all the characteristics of such companies, of course did not exist. The countries with which they expected to trade ranged all the way from India to Canada; the political services which their governments imposed upon them varied from the production of tar, pitch, and turpentine to the weakening of naval rivals; while the personal qualities of the founders of the companies and the sovereigns or ministers who gave the charters differed widely. Moreover, the later development of many of these companies had but little to do with the settlement of America. Nevertheless, three companies may be chosen which exerted a deep influence on American colonization, and which, with the English East India Company described in the last chapter, are fairly typical of the general system. These are the English Virginia Company, the Dutch West India Company, and the French Company of New France.

The charter of 1606 granted to the London and Plymouth companies was of an incomplete and transitional character; the second Virginia charter, however, which was granted at the request of the company, May 23, 1609, created a corporate trading and colonizing company closely analogous to the East India Company, as will appear from the following analysis:

1. The company was chartered under the name, "The Treasurer and Company of Adventurers and Planters of the City of London for the First Colony in Virginia." It was fully incorporated, with a seal and all legal corporate powers and liabilities. In the charter itself were named some twenty-one peers, ninety-six knights, eighty-six of the lesser gentry, a large number of

citizens, merchants, sea-captains, and others, and fifty-six of the London companies—in all, seven hundred and fifteen persons and organizations. They included a large proportion of the enlightenment, enterprise, and wealth of the capital, and, indeed, of all England. The grant was made to the company in perpetuity, although, as will be seen, some of its special exemptions and privileges were for a shorter term only.

2. The region to which the grant applied was the territory stretching four hundred miles along the coast, north and south from Chesapeake Bay, and "up into the land from sea to sea westward and northward."

The possession of the soil was given to the company by the most complete title known to the English law, but with the requirement that it be distributed by the company to those who should have contributed money, services, or their presence to the colony.

3. Its commercial powers extended to the exploitation of all the resources of the country, including mines, fisheries, and forests, as well as agricultural products; and to the requirement that all Englishmen not members of the company should pay a subsidy of five per cent of the value of all goods brought into or taken out of the company's territory, and all foreigners ten per cent of the value of the goods. The company might send to Virginia all shipping, weapons, victuals, articles of trade, and other equipment that might be necessary, and also all such colonists as should be willing to go.

4. Powers of government in its territory were granted to the company with considerable completeness, the charter declaring that it might make all orders, laws, directions, and other provisions fit and necessary for the government of the colony, and that the governor and other officers might, "within the said precincts of Virginia or in the way of sea thither and from thence, have full and absolute power and authority to correct, punish, pardon, govern, and rule" all the inhabitants of the colony, in accordance with its laws already made.

As to offensive and defensive powers, it had the right to repel or expel by military force all persons attempting to force their way into its territories and all persons attempting any hurt or annoyance to the colony. The governor might exercise martial law in the colony, and was provided with the general military powers of a lord-lieutenant of one of the English counties. Thus the company and its colony were organized not exactly as an *imperium in imperio*, but at least as an outlying *imperium*.

5. As for special subsidies and privileges, the government of King James was scarcely in a position to make money contributions for such an enterprise, or to give to it ships such as the continental governments might give to their companies; but for seven years the company was allowed to take out all that was necessary for the support, equipment, and defence of its colonists, and for trade with the natives, free of all tax or duty; and for twenty years it should be free from customs on goods imported into Virginia, and should forever pay only five per cent import duty on goods brought from Virginia to England. Among privileges of less material value, but long after remembered for other reasons, the charter promised to the company that all the king's subjects whom it should take to inhabit the

colony, with their children and their posterity, should have and enjoy all liberties, franchises, and immunities of free-born Englishmen and natural subjects of the king just as if they had remained or been born in England itself.

6. The duties to be performed by the company as respects the government were very few. In recognition of the socage tenure on which the land was held, a payment of one-tenth of all gold and silver was required; and the members of the council of the company were required to take an oath of allegiance to the king in the name of the company. The main requirement from the company was colonization. It was fully anticipated, and in the preamble expressed, that the process of taking out settlers should be a continuous one; and a failure to transport colonists by the company's efforts would certainly have been a failure to fulfill the conditions of its charter.

7. Although there was no requirement of absolute conformity with the established church of England, yet on the ground of the desire to carry only true religion to the natives it was made the duty of the officials of the company to tender the oath of supremacy to every prospective colonist before he sailed, and thus to insure the Protestantism of the settlers.

8. The form of government of the company in England received much attention in the charter, as well it might, after the failure of the arrangements of the former charter. The membership, quarterly assemblies of the general body of the members, more frequent meetings of a governing council of fifty-three officers, and their duties, were all minutely formulated; and the supremacy of this council, so consonant with the ideas of King James, and so opposed to the needs and the tendencies of the times, was carefully but, as it proved, unsuccessfully provided for.

\*     \*     \*     \*     \*

For the history of America, the most important characteristic common to the chartered companies of the seventeenth century is the territorial foothold they obtained in the regions where they possessed their monopolies. It might be only a few acres of ground used for a fort, storehouses, and dwellings, which was all the English East India Company possessed for the first century and a half of its existence; or it might be the almost limitless domains of the Canada or Virginia Company. There was no distinction between two kinds of companies, one for commerce, the other for colonization, but simply one of relative attention given to the two interests, according to the character of the regions for which the companies had obtained their concessions. All the companies expected to carry on commerce; all expected to plant some of their fellow countrymen on the soil of the country with which they meant to trade. If the region of their activity was the ancient, wealthy, thickly settled, and firmly governed coast of India, the settlers were only a few servants of the company. If, on the other hand, the region for which the monopoly of the company was granted was a broad and temperate tract, occupied by a sparse population of savages, and offering only such objects of trade or profit as could be collected slowly or wrested by European labor from the soil or the forest, the quickest way to a commercial profit was the establishment on the distant soil of a large body of colonists from the home land.

This necessity for colonization in order to carry out their other objects makes the chartered commercial companies of the seventeenth century fundamental factors in American history. The proprietary companies of Virginia, Massachusetts, New Netherland, Canada, and other colonies were primarily commercial bodies seeking dividends, and only secondarily colonization societies sending over settlers. This distinction, and the gradual predominance of the latter over the former, is the clew to much of the early history of settlement in America. The commercial object could only be carried out by employing the plan of colonization, but new motives were soon added. The patriotic and religious conditions of the times created an interest in the American settlements as places where men could begin life anew with new possibilities. Hence the company, the home government, dissatisfied religious bodies, and many individuals, looked to the settlements in America with other than a commercial interest. The policy of the companies was modified and eventually transformed by the influence of these non-commercial interests.

As financial enterprises, the chartered commercial companies were subject to such great practical difficulties that few of them survived for any great length of time or repaid their original investment to the shareholders. Some were reorganized time and again, each time on a more extensive scale, and each time to suffer heavier losses. They experienced much mismanagement and some speculation and fraud on the part of their directors; in some cases false dividends were declared for the purpose of temporarily raising the value of the stock. Their credit was bad, and they sometimes had to borrow money at fifty and even seventy-five per cent interest.

They encountered other difficulties quite apart from the incompetency or dishonesty of their directors. Parliaments and States-General were opposed to monopolistic and privileged companies, and threw what obstacles they could in their way; and political exigencies often forced even the sovereigns who had given them their charters to disavow and discourage them. Their greatest difficulties, however, arose from the very nature of the problem which they were trying to solve. Distant commerce with barbarous races, amid jealous rivals, carried on with insufficient capital; the persuasion of reluctant emigrants to establish themselves in the wilderness at a time when the mother-country was not yet overcrowded; the long waiting for returns and the failure of one dream after another—it was these difficulties in the very work itself that led to the failure of most of the companies and the scanty success of the others.

Nevertheless, the companies played a very important part in the advancement of civilization during the period of their existence. They enriched Europe with many products of the New World and the more distant Old World, which could hardly have reached it, or reached it in such abundance, except for the organized voyages of the chartered companies. The formation of chartered companies relieved certain nations of their dependence upon other nations for some of the necessities and many of the luxuries of life.

National independence was furthered, at the same time that foreign products were made much cheaper. Spices, sugar, coffee, tea, chocolate, tobacco, cotton, silk, drugs and other articles were made accessible to all. New shipping was built by the companies and additional commercial intercourse created. New territories were made valuable and new centres of activity created in old and stagnant as well as in new and undeveloped countries. Above all, the chartered companies were the actual instruments by which many colonies were founded, and a strong impress given to the institutions of these colonies through all their later history.

SPAIN *led the way into the New World, and briefly she dominated the western seas and the adjacent lands. But the newly emergent nation-states farther north in Europe first marauded upon Spanish treasure fleets and then openly staked out vast claims to the uncharted wilderness of the western hemisphere. No country proved more vigorous and ultimately more successful in her challenge than England. Two cultures, that of the Iberian and that of the English, were destined to shape most profoundly the new American societies. Of the two, the future United States drew its institutions, language, and creed from England.*

*The emergence of England as a major nation-state could hardly have been foreseen in 1485 when Henry VII laid claim to the English throne in the final days of the War of Roses. The Tudor dynasty which he founded produced five monarchs—all but one, the boy King Edward VI, of stunning vitality—and endured for 118 years. The Tudor genius climaxed in Elizabeth the Great, a woman who wedded her destiny to a people, treated their gains as her gains, humbled the Spanish Armada, and uniquely among major European rulers shared governance with her Parliament. She also ruled as the great Christian schism, the Reformation, divided western Europe into a Catholic and Protestant world.*

*The energetic islanders embraced mercantilism and propelled their country into commercial capitalism. Unwilling to remain bound to the ancient but tenuous loyalties that bound England to Rome, the English merchant embraced first the halfway house of Anglicanism, but then drank of the headier wine of Calvinism. No longer had they to do penance for indulging in usury as Calvin preached election and God's beneficence toward his chosen. To the elect would come Mammon, a sign of God's favor, as the Book of Job told.*

*Within England as Elizabeth's reign drew to its end, there arose a Calvinistic sect called Puritan. It meant to purify the English church and to assert its God-ordained right to rule. Its instrument would be Parliament; its target the Stuart monarchy. Convinced of their righteousness, without awe of the royal pretension, the Puritan would within forty-six years of Elizabeth's death behead a king, establish a dictatorship, and launch a great mi-*

*gration into the rock-strewn wilderness of New England. There in the Massa-
chusetts Bay Colony they founded a Bible State. The peculiar nature and the
distinctive strengths of the Puritan experiment were soon revealed. But the
logic of a successful challenge to authority, as the Puritan soon discovered,
is to provide precedent for further challenge. The seeds of that prospect
existed in the first New England settlement at Plymouth. There the Pilgrim
fathers not only embraced election but also flirted with separation of church
and state.*

*John Fiske (1842-1901) upon his death was described by the* American
Historical Review *as "without doubt deservedly the most popular historical
writer in America." It was a candid description of a historian who conveyed
in vivid color the heroic struggles, a modern reader might think heroic pose,
of the founding fathers from colonial times to the ratification of the Constitution. His* The Critical Period of American History *(1888) embedded in
the mind of his generation the proposition that the founders of the federal
republic were near demigods. The American achievement was made all the
more impressive by his pen sketches of the mighty obstacles they had overcome. Influenced as he was by Herbert Spencer, it is not surprising to learn
that the early Americans in Fiske's eyes were unquestionably the fittest survivors.*

# THE BEGINNINGS OF
# NEW ENGLAND

## by John Fiske

Scarcely ten months had James been king of England when he invited the
leading Puritan clergymen to meet himself and the bishops in a conference
at Hampton Court, as he wished to learn what changes they would like to
make in the government and ritual of the church. In the course of the discussion he lost his temper and stormed, as was his wont. The mention of
the word "presbytery" lashed him into fury. "A Scottish presbytery," he
cried, "agreeth as well with a monarchy as God and the Devil. Then Jack
and Tom and Will and Dick shall meet, and at their pleasures censure me
and my council, and all our proceedings. . . . Stay, I pray you, for one
seven years, before you demand that from me, and if then you find me pursy
and fat, and my windpipes stuffed, I will perhaps hearken to you. . . . Until
you find that I grow lazy, let that alone." One of the bishops declared that
in this significant tirade his Majesty spoke by special inspiration from
Heaven! The Puritans saw that their only hope lay in resistance. If any
doubt remained, it was dispelled by the vicious threat with which the king
broke up the conference. "I will *make* them conform," said he, "or I will
harry them out of the land."

These words made a profound sensation in England, as well they might, for they heralded the struggle which within half a century was to deliver up James' son to the executioner. The Parliament of 1604 met in angrier mood than any Parliament which had assembled at Westminster since the dethronement of Richard II. Among the churches non-conformity began more decidedly to assume the form of secession. The key-note of the conflict was struck at Scrooby. Staunch Puritan as he was, Brewster had not hitherto favoured the extreme measures of the Separatists. Now he withdrew from the church, and gathered together a company of men and women who met on Sundays for divine service in his own drawing-room at Scrooby Manor. In organizing this independent Congregationalist society, Brewster was powerfully aided by John Robinson, a native of Lincolnshire. Robinson was then thirty years of age, and had taken his master's degree at Cambridge in 1600. He was a man of great learning and rare sweetness of temper, and was moreover distinguished for a broad and tolerant habit of mind too seldom found among the Puritans of that day. Friendly and unfriendly writers alike bear witness to his spirit of Christian charity and the comparatively slight value which he attached to orthodoxy in points of doctrine; and we can hardly be wrong in supposing that the comparatively tolerant behaviour of the Plymouth colonists, whereby they were contrasted with the settlers of Massachusetts, was in some measure due to the abiding influence of the teachings of this admirable man. Another important member of the Scrooby congregation was William Bradford, of the neighbouring village of Austerfield, then a lad of seventeen years, but already remarkable for maturity of intelligence and weight of character. Afterward governor of Plymouth for nearly thirty years, he became the historian of his colony; and to his picturesque chronicle, written in pure and vigorous English, we are indebted for most that we know of the migration that started from Scrooby and ended in Plymouth.

It was in 1606—two years after King James's truculent threat—that this independent church of Scrooby was organized. Another year had not elapsed before its members had suffered so much at the hands of officers of the law, that they began to think of following the example of former heretics and escaping to Holland. After an unsuccessful attempt in the autumn of 1607, they at length succeeded a few months later in accomplishing their flight to Amsterdam, where they hoped to find a home. But here they found the English exiles who had preceded them so fiercely involved in doctrinal controversies, that they decided to go further in search of peace and quiet. This decision, which we may ascribe to Robinson's wise counsels, served to keep the society of Pilgrims from getting divided and scattered. They reached Leyden in 1609, just as the Spanish government had sullenly abandoned the hopeless task of conquering the Dutch, and had granted to Holland the Twelve Years Truce. During eleven of these twelve years the Pilgrims remained in Leyden, supporting themselves by various occupations, while their numbers increased from 300 to more than 1000. Brewster opened a publishing house, devoted mainly to the issue of theological books. Robinson accepted a professorship in the university, and engaged in the defence of Calvinism against the attacks of Episcopius, the successor of Arminius. The youthful Bradford devoted himself to the study of languages,—Dutch, French, Latin, Greek, and finally Hebrew; wishing, as he said, to "see with his own eyes the ancient oracles of God in all their native beauty." During their sojourn in Leyden, the Pilgrims were introduced to a strange and novel spectacle,—the systematic legal toleration of all persons, whether Catholic or Protestant, who called themselves followers of Christ. Not that there was not plenty of intolerance in spirit, but the policy inaugurated by the idolized William the Silent held it in check by law. All persons who came to Holland, and led decorous lives there, were protected in their opinions and customs. By contemporary writers in other countries this eccentric behaviour of the Dutch government was treated with unspeakable scorn. "All strange religions flock thither," says one; it is "a common harbour of all heresies," a "cage of unclean birds," says another; "the great mingle mangle of religion," says a third. In spite of the relief from persecution, however, the Pilgrims were not fully satisfied with their new home. The expiration of the truce with Spain might prove that this relief was only temporary; and at any rate, complete toleration did not fill the measure of their wants. Had they come to Holland as scattered bands of refugees, they might have been absorbed into the Dutch population, as Huguenot refugees have been absorbed in Germany, England, and America. But they had come as an organized community, and absorption into a foreign nation was something to be dreaded. They wished to preserve their English speech and English traditions, keep up their organization, and find some favoured spot where they might lay the corner-stone of a great Christian state. The spirit of nationality was strong in them; the spirit of self-government was strong in them; and the only thing which could satisfy these feelings was such a migration as had not been seen since ancient times, a migration like that of Phokaians to Massilia or Tyrians to Carthage.

It was too late in the world's history to carry out such a scheme upon European soil. Every acre of territory there was appropriated. The only favourable outlook was upon the Atlantic coast of America, where English cruisers had now successfully disputed the pretensions of Spain, and where after forty years of disappointment and disaster a flourishing colony had at length been founded in Virginia. The colonization of the North American coast had now become part of the avowed policy of the British government. In 1606 a great joint-stock company was formed for the establishment of two colonies in America. The branch which was to take charge of the proposed southern colony had its headquarters in London; the management of the northern branch was at Plymouth in Devonshire. Hence the two branches are commonly spoken of as the London and Plymouth companies. The former was also called the Virginia Company, and the latter the North Virginia Company, as the name of Virginia was then loosely applied to the entire Atlantic coast north of Florida. The London Company had jurisdiction from 34° to 38° north latitude; the Plymouth Company had jurisdiction from 45° down to 41°; the intervening territory, between 38° and 41° was to go to whichever company should first plant a self-supporting colony. The local government of each colony was to be entrusted to a council resident in America and nominated by the king; while general supervision over both colonies was to be exercised by a council resident in England.

In pursuance of this general plan, though with some variations in detail, the settlement of Jamestown had been begun in 1607, and its success was now beginning to seem assured. On the other hand all the attempts which had been made to the north of the fortieth parallel had failed miserably. As early as 1602 Bartholomew Gosnold, with 32 men, had landed on the head-land which they named Cape Cod from the fish found thereabouts in great numbers. This was the first English name given to any spot in that part of America, and so far as known these were the first Englishmen that ever set foot there. They went on and gave names to Martha's Vineyard and the Elizabeth Islands in Buzzard's Bay; and on Cuttyhunk they built some huts with the intention of remaining, but after a month's experience they changed their mind and went back to England. Gosnold's story interested other cap-tains, and on Easter Sunday, 1605, George Weymouth set sail for North Virginia, as it was called. He found Cape Cod and coasted northward as far as the Kennebec river, up which he sailed for many miles. Weymouth kidnapped five Indians and carried them to England, that they might learn the language and acquire a wholesome respect for the arts of civilization and the resistless power of white men. His glowing accounts of the spacious harbours, the abundance of fish and game, the noble trees, the luxuriant herbage, and the balmy climate, aroused general interest in England, and doubtless had some influence upon the formation, in the following year, of the great joint-stock company just described. The leading spirit of the Plymouth Company was Sir John Popham, chief-justice of England, and he was not disposed to let his friends of the southern branch excel him in promptness. Within three months after the founding of Jamestown, a party of 120 colonists, led by the judge's kinsman George Popham, landed at the mouth of the Kennebec, and proceeded to build a rude village of some fifty cabins, with storehouse, chapel, and block-house. When they landed in Au-gust they doubtless shared Weymouth's opinion of the climate. These Eng-lishmen had heard of warm countries like Italy and cold countries like Russia; harsh experience soon taught them that there are climates in which the summer of Naples may alternate with the winter of Moscow. The presi-dent and many others fell sick and died. News came of the death of Sir John Popham in England, and presently the weary and disappointed settlers aban-doned their enterprise and returned to their old homes. Their failure spread abroad in England the opinion that North Virginia was uninhabitable by reason of the cold, and no further attempts were made upon that coast until in 1614 it was visited by Captain John Smith.

The romantic career of this gallant and garrulous hero did not end with his departure from the infant colony at Jamestown. By a curious destiny his fame is associated with the beginnings of both the southern and the northern portions of the United States. To Virginia, Smith may be said to have given its very existence as a commonwealth; to New England he gave its name. In 1614 he came over with two ships to North Virginia, explored its coast minutely from the Penobscot river to Cape Cod, and thinking it a country of such extent and importance as to deserve a name of its own, rechristened it New England. On returning home he made a very good map of the coast and dotted it with English names suggested by Prince Charles. Of these names Cape Elizabeth, Cape Ann, Charles River, and Plymouth still remain where Smith placed them. In 1615 Smith again set sail for the New World, this time with a view to planting a colony under the auspices of the Plymouth Company, but his talent for strange adventures had not deserted him. He was taken prisoner by a French fleet, carried hither and thither on a long cruise, and finally set ashore at Rochelle, whence, without a penny in his pocket, he contrived to make his way back to England. Perhaps Smith's life of hardship may have made him prematurely old. After all his wild and varied experience he was now only in his thirty-seventh year, but he does not seem to have gone on any more voyages. The remaining sixteen years of his life were spent quietly in England in writing books, publishing maps, and otherwise stimulating the public interest in the colonization of the New World. But as for the rocky coast of New England, which he had explored and named, he declared that he was not so simple as to suppose that any other motive than riches would "ever erect there a commonwealth or draw company from their ease and humours at home, to stay in New England."

In this opinion, however, the bold explorer was mistaken. Of all migrations of peoples the settlement of New England is preëminently the one in which the almighty dollar played the smallest part, however important it may since have become as a motive power. It was left for religious enthusiasm to achieve what commercial enterprise had failed to accomplish. By the summer of 1617 the Pilgrim society at Leyden had decided to send a detachment of its most vigorous members to lay the foundations of a Puritan state in America. There had been much discussion as to the fittest site for such a colony. Many were in favour of Guiana, which Sir Walter Raleigh had described in such glowing colours; but it was thought that the tropical climate would be ill-suited to northern men of industrious and thrifty habit, and the situation, moreover, was dangerously exposed to the Spaniards. Half a century had scarcely elapsed since the wholesale massacre of Huguenots in Florida. Virginia was then talked of, but Episcopal ideas had already taken root there. New England, on the other hand, was considered too cold. Popham's experience was not encouraging. But the country about the Delaware river afforded an opportunity for erecting an independent colony under the jurisdiction of the London Company, and this seemed the best course to pursue. Sir Edwin Sandys, the leading spirit in the London Company, was favourably inclined toward Puritans, and through him negotiations were begun. Capital to the amount of £7000 was furnished by seventy merchant adventurers in England, and the earnings of the settlers were to be thrown into a common stock until these subscribers should have been remunerated. A grant of land was obtained from the London Company, and the king was asked to protect the emigrants by a charter, but this was refused. James, however, made no objections to their going, herein showing himself less of a bigot than Louis XIV in later days, who would not suffer a Huguenot to set foot in Canada, though France was teeming with Huguenots who would have been glad enough to go. When James inquired how the colonists expected to support themselves, some one answered, most likely by fishing. "Very good," quoth the king, "it was the Apostles' own calling." He declared that no one should molest them so long as they behaved themselves properly. From this unwonted urbanity it would appear that James anticipated no trouble from the new colony. A few Puritans in America could not do much to annoy him, and there was of course a fair chance of their perishing, as so many other colonizers had perished.

The congregation at Leyden did not think it wise to cut loose from Holland until they should have secured a foothold in America. It was but an advance guard that started out from Delft haven late in July, 1620, in the rickety ship *Speedwell*, with Brewster and Bradford, and sturdy Miles Standish, a trained soldier whose aid was welcome, though he does not seem to have belonged to the congregation. Robinson remained at Leyden, and never came to America. After a brief stop at Southampton, where they met the *Mayflower* with friends from London, the Pilgrims again set sail in the two ships. The *Speedwell* sprang a leak, and they stopped at Dartmouth for repairs. Again they started, and had put three hundred miles of salt water between themselves and Land's End, when the *Speedwell* leaked so badly that they were forced to return. When they dropped anchor at Plymouth in Devonshire, about twenty were left on shore, and the remainder, exactly one hundred in number, crowded into the *Mayflower* and on the 6th of September started once more to cross the Atlantic. The capacity of the little ship was 180 tons, and her strength was but slight. In a fierce storm in mid-ocean a mainbeam amidships was wrenched and cracked, and but for a huge iron screw which one of the passengers had brought from Delft, they might have gone to the bottom. The foul weather prevented any accurate calculation of latitude and longitude, and they were so far out in their reckoning that when they caught sight of land on the 9th of November, it was to Cape Cod that they had come. Their patent gave them no authority to settle here, as it was beyond the jurisdiction of the London Company. They turned their prow southward, but encountering perilous shoals and a stiff head-wind they desisted and sought shelter in Cape Cod bay. On the 11th they decided to find some place of abode in this neighbourhood, anticipating no difficulty in getting a patent from the Plymouth Company, which was anxious to obtain settlers. For five weeks they stayed in the ship while little parties were exploring the coast and deciding upon the best site for a town. It was purely a coincidence that the spot which they chose had already received from John Smith the name of Plymouth, the beautiful port in Devonshire from which the *Mayflower* had sailed.

There was not much to remind them of home in the snow-covered coast on which they landed. They had hoped to get their rude houses built before the winter should set in, but the many delays and mishaps had served to bring them ashore in the coldest season. When the long winter came to an end, fifty-one of the hundred Pilgrims had died,—a mortality even greater than that before which the Popham colony had succumbed. But Brewster spoke truth when he said, "It is not with us as with men whom small things can discourage or small discontentments cause to wish themselves at home again." At one time the living were scarcely able to bury the dead; only Brewster, Standish, and five other hardy ones were well enough to get about. At first they were crowded under a single roof, and as glimpses were caught of dusky savages skulking among the trees, a platform was built on the nearest hill and a few cannon were placed there in such wise as to command the neighbouring valleys and plains. By the end of the first summer the platform had grown to a fortress, down from which to the harbour led a village street with seven houses finished and others going up. Twenty-six acres had been cleared, and a plentiful harvest gathered in; venison, wild fowl, and fish were easy to obtain. When provisions and fuel had been laid in for the ensuing winter, Governor Bradford appointed a day of Thanksgiving. Town-meetings had already been held, and a few laws passed. The history of New England had begun.

This had evidently been a busy summer for the forty-nine survivors. On the 9th of November, the anniversary of the day on which they had sighted land, a ship was descried in the offing. She was the *Fortune*, bringing some fifty more of the Leyden company. It was a welcome reinforcement, but it diminished the rations of food that could be served during the winter, for the *Fortune* was not well supplied. When she set sail for England, she carried a little cargo of beaver-skins and choice wood for wainscoting to the value of £500 sterling, as a first instalment of the sum due to the merchant adventurers. But this cargo never reached England, for the *Fortune* was overhauled by a French cruiser and robbed of everything worth carrying away.

For two years more it was an anxious and difficult time for the new colony. By 1624 its success may be said to have become assured. That the Indians in the neighbourhood had not taken advantage of the distress of the settlers in that first winter, and massacred every one of them, was due to a remarkable circumstance. Early in 1617 a frightful pestilence had swept over New England and slain, it is thought, more than half the Indian population between the Penobscot river and Narragansett bay. Many of the Indians were inclined to attribute this calamity to the murder of two or three white fishermen the year before. They had not got over the superstitious dread with which the first sight of white men had inspired them, and now they believed that the strangers held the demon of the plague at their disposal and had let him loose upon the red men in revenge for the murders they had committed. This wholesome delusion kept their tomahawks quiet for a while. When they saw the Englishmen establishing themselves at Plymouth, they at first held a powwow in the forest, at which the new-comers were cursed with all the elaborate ingenuity that the sorcery of the medicine-men could summon for so momentous an occasion; but it was deemed best to refrain from merely human methods of attack. It was not until the end of the first winter that any of them mustered courage to visit the palefaces. Then an Indian named Samoset, who had learned a little English from fishermen and for his own part was inclined to be friendly, came one day into the village with words of welcome. He was so kindly treated that presently Massasoit,

principal sachem of the Wampanoags, who dwelt between Narragansett and
Cape Cod bays, came with a score of painted and feathered warriors and
squatting on a green rug and cushions in the governor's log-house smoked
the pipe of peace, while Standish with half-a-dozen musketeers stood quietly
by. An offensive and defensive alliance was then and there made between
King Massasoit and King James, and the treaty was faithfully kept for a
century. Some time afterward, when Massasoit had fallen sick and lay at
death's door, his life was saved by Edward Winslow, who came to his wigwam and skilfully nursed him. Henceforth the Wampanoag thought well
of the Pilgrim. The powerful Narragansetts, who dwelt on the farther side
of the bay, felt differently and thought it worth while to try the effect of
a threat. A little while after the *Fortune* had brought its reinforcement, the
Narragansett sachem Canonicus sent a messenger to Plymouth with a bundle
of newly made arrows wrapped in a snake-skin. The messenger threw it
in at the governor's door and made off with unseemly haste. Bradford understood this as a challenge, and in this he was confirmed by a friendly Wampanoag. The Narragansetts could muster 2000 warriors, for whom forty
or fifty Englishmen, even with firearms, were hardly a fair match; but it
would not do to show fear. Bradford stuffed the snake-skin with powder
and bullets, and sent it back to Canonicus, telling him that if he wanted
war he might come whenever he liked and get his fill of it. When the
sachem saw what the skin contained, he was afraid to touch it or have it
about, and medicine-men, handling it no doubt gingerly enough, carried
it out of his territory.

It was a fortunate miscalculation that brought the Pilgrims to New England. Had they ventured upon the lands between the Hudson and the
Delaware, they would probably have fared worse. They would soon have
come into collision with the Dutch and not far from that neighbourhood
dwelt the Susquehannocks, at that time one of the most powerful and
ferocious tribes on the continent. For the present the new-comers were less
likely to be molested in the Wampanoag country than anywhere else. In
the course of the year 1621 they obtained their grant from the Plymouth
Company. This grant was not made to them directly but to the joint-stock
company of merchant adventurers with whom they were associated. But
the alliance between the Pilgrims and these London merchants was not altogether comfortable; there was too much divergence between their aims.
In 1627 the settlers, wishing to be entirely independent, bought up all the
stock and paid for it by instalments from the fruits of their labour. By 1633
they had paid every penny, and become the undisputed owners of the
country they had occupied.

Such was the humble beginning of that great Puritan exodus from England to America which had so much to do with founding and peopling the
United States. These Pilgrims of the *Mayflower* were but the pioneers of a
mighty host. Historically their enterprise is interesting not so much for what
it achieved as for what it suggested. Of itself the Plymouth colony could
hardly have become a wealthy and powerful state. Its growth was extremely

slow. After ten years its numbers were but three hundred. In 1643, when the exodus had come to an end, and the New England Confederacy was formed, the population of Plymouth was but three thousand. In an established community, indeed, such a rate of increase would be rapid, but it was not sufficient to raise in New England a power which could overcome Indians and Dutchmen and Frenchmen, and assert its will in opposition to the crown. It is when we view the founding of Plymouth in relation to what came afterward, that it assumes the importance which belongs to the beginning of a new era.

*THE development of sectionalism in the nineteenth century and the savage bloodletting of 1861-65 has tended to make Americans think in terms of North and South. It is only natural that in seeking to understand the present the historian has searched out the roots of it in the past. But to understand the divergences that led to the development of distinct American regions, it must be remembered that the original settlements of English America were united by the common bond of an English heritage. No less emphatic a bond of union was that imposed by their having to come to grips with a wilderness environment. Whatever the motives that had led to settlement, all paled before the omnipresent need to survive. For without survival, profits or Bible State would prove only a chimera.*

*Once survival was assured, the English colonies retained for all their differences the overriding identity of English, and even so distinctive a group as the Puritan remained essentially English. A subtle quality that set apart the colonist, one that eludes precise definition, was a quality which led them to risk the hazardous journey, to endure the wrenching that comes with abandoning the familiar home, and then to tame the new land. Perhaps it is best defined as a contentious courage.*

*All that distinguished and challenged the colonist was amply demonstrated in the first successful colony, Jamestown. There, in 1607, Virginia began, and with it the First British Empire. It is the theme of Empire, the commonalty of home folk and colonial settler, upon which Charles M. Andrews (1862-1943), onetime Yale historian, focused his studies. His work in colonial history, particularly his monumental Pulitzer Prize-winning* The Colonial Period of American History, *emphasized the imperial relations of colonies and mother country. Andrews broadened the perspective of colonial history and reminded his reader that the distinctiveness of American life cannot be treated as solely the product of a unique environment. He insisted that American history before the Revolution must be seen as part of a larger world scene. To believe that one can isolate the part from the whole is to do injustice to the truth, but Andrews did subscribe to the idea that in the part, if properly analyzed, the whole will be revealed. One cannot help*

*as one reads him agreeing with the pointed words of the seventeenth-century*
*Virginian, William Byrd, which read: "In the beginning, All America was*
*Virginia."*

# THE COLONIAL PERIOD
# OF AMERICAN HISTORY

## *by Charles M. Andrews*

In the meantime the Virginia Company of London had been forwarding
its own plans for establishing a settlement in the southern part of the great
"Virginia" tract. Raising its funds in a manner probably similar to that
employed by the Plymouth Company, it despatched three vessels, the
*Sarah Constant*, the *Goodspeed*, and the *Discovery*, on December 20, 1606,
under Captain Christopher Newport, in sole charge and command "until
such time as they shall fortune to land upon the said coast of Virginia."
These vessels are believed to have been hired of the Muscovy company,
and, as was the case with many another sea captain of the day, Newport was
a sort of sailor of fortune, ready to enter the service of any group of
men that wanted him. During the years from 1606 to 1611, first in the
employ of the Virginia Company and later in that of the East India Company, he made five voyages to Virginia, thus laying the foundation of a
distinguished career.

The vessels took the southern route by the way of the Azores and Canary
Islands, cruised for some time among the West Indies from Martinique to
Porto Rico, and then bore northward, as many a later vessel was accustomed
to do, through the Mona Channel to the Capes. On the 26th of April, the
voyagers "descried the land of Virginia" and the same day entered the
Chesapeake. Shortly afterward they set up a cross at a point which they
named Cape Henry, in honor of the king's eldest son, whose lamentable
death five years later deprived the throne of its ablest successor. After many
strange experiences with the natives, they entered the James River, at the
head of which they set up another cross and proclaimed King James of
England "to have the most right unto it"; and then on May 24, having
after some discussion decided on a site—that of the future Jamestown—
they disembarked, only one hundred and five out of the one hundred and
forty-four who started on the voyage. Immediately these men began the
erection of a fort, within which eventually they built dwellings and a
church, just as the other company was to do at Sagadahoc. Then too, as
was done at Sagadahoc, following the custom established by the East India
Company, they opened the sealed box containing their instructions and
learned for the first time the names of their council—Captain Newport,
Captain Gosnold, Edward Maria Wingfield, John Smith, John Ratcliffe,
John Martin and George Kendall. Later Wingfield was chosen president

and Gabriel Archer, secretary or recorder. Fortunately the instructions for the Virginia colonists have been preserved, though those for Sagadahoc have been lost, but there can be little doubt that *mutatis mutandis* the two documents were the same, and that the plans for the two settlements were in all respects identical. Under these instructions the colony was governed for the first two years. They provided for a local council with a president, who had no other prerogatives than to preside and cast a double vote in case of a tie. The council could depose the president and expel any member by a majority vote, and at the very beginning it exercised this privilege by excluding John Smith, because he was charged with having been mutinous on the voyage. Thus before the settlement was fairly under way trouble began to brew, and it was only by the intercession of the preacher, the Rev. Mr. Hunt, that Smith, on June 20, was finally restored to his place.

The circumstances attending the settlement of Virginia differed in no essential particular from those attending the attempts at settlement on the Amazon, in Guiana, in Newfoundland and at Sagadahoc. The contemporary idea of colonization had advanced no further than to conceive of settlement in terms of ships, reasonably well equipped and captained, of hardy men sufficient in number but of any class or quality, drawn together in part by the prospect of gold or plunder and in part by need of employment, and of supplies adequate for the purpose in hand. The early desire to obtain wealth from mythical mines or Spanish plate fleets, though far from spent, was yielding place to the wiser design of promoting trade in the commodities of the country, fish and furs chiefly, and of creating a legitimate barter. The first Virginia settlers had hardly progressed beyond this point. They were not above gold and plunder and were interested in barter with the Indians, but neither they nor the company in England had yet learned in the hard school of experience the fundamental lesson that a colony to be successful and permanent must be self supporting, that it must raise its own food and render itself independent of supplies furnished by the promoters at home. The men who settled Jamestown were not of the kind to plough and cultivate the soil, and before the first supply had come from England in January, 1608, they had exhausted their provisions, already heavily depleted by the five months' voyage, and were obliged to live on what the natives provided and the woods furnished. Captain Newport went back to England five weeks after his arrival, and from that time until his return with additional men and provisions, the settlement was the scene of endless quarrels, bickerings, and plots, which culminated finally in the execution of Captain Kendall for hatching a mutiny. Sickness and death prevailed and before the end of the year there were only thirty-eight men alive in the colony. The tale of these seven months is a ghastly epic of misfortune.

After the arrival of the first "supply" on January 4, 1608, conditions improved, owing in part to Smith's presidency of the council, from September, 1608, to July, 1609, and in part to a second "supply" which came in October, 1608, with more immigrants, among whom were artisans and laborers, and one gentlewoman and her maid. Buildings which had been burned down the previous year—the storehouse, church, and probably some of the dwellings—were rebuilt and attempts were made to manufacture glass, pitch, tar, and potash, to split lumber for clapboards, and to dig and plant some forty acres of ground. The colonists also began to raise chickens and livestock; but it was only by threatening to drive the slackers out of the fort to starve in the wilderness that Smith compelled the drones among them to bear their share of the burden.

However at best the experiment was not succeeding and the company in England became convinced from the reports of Newport, who was back from this third voyage, and also from the accounts of the returned councillors, Wingfield, Archer, and Ratcliffe, that if the colony were to prosper its government would have to be radically changed. It saw that placing control of the colony in the hands of a group of councillors, liable to faction and dispute, was leading to continued mismanagement, and it did not want a repetition of the failure at Sagadahoc. In the winter of 1608 and 1609 the company carefully considered the whole situation and reached the conclusion that there were two causes of trouble: first, the length and danger of the voyage by way of the West Indies; and secondly, the form of government both at home and in the colony. To meet the first difficulty, the company determined to find a shorter way to Virginia, and to meet the second, decided to renew the charter and to obtain "such ample and large priviledges and powers" as to make it possible "to reform and correct these [inconveniences] already discovered and to prevent such as in the future might threaten [the settlers]." Once vested with the necessary authority, it would be able to "set and furnish out, under the conduct of one able and absolute governor, a large supply of five hundred men, with some number of families, of wife, children and servants, to take fast holde and roote in that land." Here for almost the first time appears the idea of a true colony, at least so far as the personnel, though not the government, is concerned, marking a noteworthy advance over the older notion of a settlement made up of adventurers, standing in constant need of relief from home, and profitable only as far as it could return to the company sufficient shiploads of marketable products.

But to change the personnel was not enough, the company concluded, the form and character of the government at home too must be changed. The new charter, it is supposed, was written by Sir Edwin Sandys, and, if so, then to him more than to anyone else must be credited the inception of an idea that marks a distinct (though not, as events were to show, a sufficient) improvement in the method of governing a distant plantation. Sandys—the name is pronounced Sands—was at this time forty-eight years old and had already been employed by the king in affairs of great trust and importance. He was a member of parliament, having entered at the early age of twenty-five as the member first for Andover in Hampshire, then for Plymouth, Devon, and finally for Stockbridge in Hampshire, and as leader of the opposition had taken a vigorous stand in 1601 against monopolies. In 1607 he had spoken with great determination against the reincorporation of the Spanish Company, because of the outrages committed by

Spain against English shipping, in which the offenses against Challons and his men played a conspicuous part. He had travelled widely on the Continent and was well known for his tolerant attitude in religious matters and for his progressive views on some of the leading issues of the day. He had advocated the abolition of feudal tenures and the granting to all prisoners the right to employ counsel in their own defense. He was a member of the royal council under the charter of 1606 and of the council of the company under that of 1609 and was destined to remain one of its leaders to the end of his career. He had a house in Aldergate, London, not far from that of the Ferrars, who were also closely identified with the company's affairs, and there at times (certainly after 1619) the company held its quarter courts. The petition for the charter was probably written in February, 1609, and the charter itself, after passing through the various offices and being delayed for the insertion of the names of subscribers to the joint-stock, finally received the great seal on May 23, of that year.

The new corporation, established by the charter of 1609, was known as the Treasurer and Company of Adventurers and Planters of the City of London for the first colony of Virginia, and is commonly known as the Virginia Company. Its head was called a treasurer instead of a governor, for what reason is not clear, unless it be to avoid the use of the same term for both company and colony. This official was first nominated by the crown, but afterward was elected by a majority vote of the members. Eventually the corporation consisted of fifty-six companies of London and six hundred and fifty-nine individuals—many of whom were of the Plymouth company resident in London and elsewhere—and the number and distribution of those who subscribed are a witness to the widespread interest which the affairs of the company aroused in England. The charter created a joint-stock company, which that of 1606 had not, with one notable difference from the type of organization perfected three years later by the charter of 1612, in that the powers of government were lodged with the treasurer and council and not with the company as a whole, meeting in a general court. Thus the system of 1609 stands midway between royal control on one side and generality control on the other. The royal council of 1606 had been eliminated, but the body of the company was not yet entrusted with governing powers. The latter was not expected to meet except at the call of the treasurer and then only for the purpose of choosing its head or of electing members to fill vacancies in the council. The treasurer and council were empowered to establish "all manner of orders, laws, directions, instructions, forms and ceremonies of government and magistracy, fit and necessary, for and concerning the government of the said colony and plantation, also they were to have full and absolute power and authority to correct, pardon, govern and rule" all inhabiting in the colony, according to such ordinances as they should lay down, or, in default of such, then according to the "good discretions" of those whom they shall appoint to govern in the colony, only provided that such ordinances be not contrary to the "laws, statutes, government and policy of England." The territory provided for was enlarged to extend north and south two hundred miles instead of fifty, and thus the company not only came into possession of an area six times as large as that granted by the previous charter, but now for the first time had direct and complete control of it.

At the head of the company as treasurer was placed Sir Thomas Smith, a man fifty-one years of age, who was among the most active commercial promoters of his day. He had been one of Raleigh's assignees in 1589; governor of the East India Company for more than twenty years, and of other companies, either actually or nominally, for shorter periods; and an ambassador to Russia; one of the four principal officers of the navy; and a member of parliament for fourteen years. At the time he was made treasurer of the company he was a working member of many of the important trading companies of London and no one of greater prominence could have been selected to fill this important post. Now that the reorganized company was facing its first great opportunity, he threw himself into the enterprise with enthusiasm and unbounded energy, giving heavily of his time and money, in order that the new venture should be an unqualified success. For the next fourteen years he was indefatigable in his work for commerce and colonization, carrying for many years weighty responsibilities and burdens and furthering expeditions into many other parts of the world than Virginia. He was the leading business man of his time and his house in Philpot Lane, London, was the office of the Virginia Company, the place of meeting of many a general and special court of both the Virginia and the Bermuda companies, and the headquarters at which every prospective colonist was expected to present himself for inspection. Smith himself was the accepted and recognized head and forefront of all important commercial operations in London for a quarter of a century.

The promoters of the company now made a wide appeal for financial support, fixing each share of stock or bill of adventure at £12 10s, with special inducements for those willing to contribute £25 and £50. Letters were sent to the members of the Plymouth Company, many of whom entered their names, probably on the £25 basis, and to the London gilds and liveries, fifty-six of which responded favorably. Broadsides and prospectuses were issued and scattered widely and even the clergy were called upon to spread the news. The plan was for a single voyage, on a large scale and with ample resources, and the enthusiasm and energy of the company was centered on the one great effort, for which alone the money was raised. In the same month of February Alderman Johnson, later sheriff of London, a man actively interested in mercantile affairs and a member of the Virginia, Bermuda, and other companies, issued, on his own responsibility and unofficially, the *Nova Britannia*, a pamphlet designed to arouse the interest of "all such as be well affected to further the [enterprise]." On March 10, 1610, Sir Walter Cope (probably) drew up a circular letter in the name of the company, which contains the following pious appeal. "The eyes of all Europe are looking upon our endeavors to spread the Gospell among the Heathen people of Virginia, to plant an English nation there, and to settle a trade in those parts, which may be peculiar to our nation, to the end we may thereby be secured from being eaten out of all profits of trade by our more industrious neighbors." Though the interest was great and the hopes high, the drive for funds did not bring in the desired amount, and in December a new appeal was made. The results were still unsatisfactory. As many of the subscribers defaulted on their second or third payments or on both, the sums paid in were never adequate for so elaborate an undertaking. It would look as if those with money to invest were none too sanguine as to the future of the Virginia colony, and it may be that a reason may lie in the plan of government which the council had drawn up for the settlement and the long period of time (seven years) that was to elapse before any subscriber could receive a return on his money.

As by the charter of 1609 the royal council resident in England was abolished and the right of control vested in the council of the company, so the decision was reached, probably toward the end of 1609, to alter fundamentally the manner of governing the colony in Virginia, and instead of a local president and council, which had been the form of organization until this time, to appoint a single head entrusted with exceptionally large powers. The company made up its mind to try a new experiment by sending to America a single and absolute governor, with authority so extensive as to make him almost a dictator for life. It was a dangerous experiment. On February 28, 1610, the treasurer and council revoked "the power and authority of the president and council," and "vested for life all authority in one principal governor, commander, admiral and captain general over all colonies to be planted within the limits of the patent. He was to be called lord governor and captain general of Virginia and to govern according to such instructions as should be sent him by the council in London or any two of them." He might, if he wished, "take unto him" as many persons of the colony as he should think "fit and meete" to aid him in the making of laws and ordinances, or he might govern "by his own discretion," with as full and absolute power, authority, and command as the company possessed itself. He could appoint and control all officers in the colony, except such as might be named by the council in England, and he could name his own deputy, should he be obliged to leave the colony at any time.

Fears of misrule were stilled for the moment by the selection as lord governor and captain general of Lord De la Warr, a high-minded gentleman and one of the council. Unfortunately he was unable to sail for his post at once, and as it was necessary for the expedition to start at the earliest possible moment, Gates, Newport, and Somers were sent on ahead. On May 15, 1609 (as is stated in Sir Stephen Powle's diary), "Oure 6 shippes lying at Blackwell [Thames dock, quite far down the river, at the east end of Poplar] wayed anker and fell downe to beginne their Viage toward Virginia. Sr. Thomas Gates being the deputye governour, until the Ld. De la Warre doth comme thiather, which is supposed shall be about a month hence. Captayne Newport [Vice-admiral], Sr. George Somers [Admiral] and 800 people of all sorts went in these six shippes, besides 2 moare that attend the fleet at Plymouth, and ther be inhabitauntes already at Virginia about 160. God bless them and guide them to his glory and our good." It was a great expedition, the greatest that was to go to America until the sailing of the Massachusetts Bay Company in 1630, and many who watched it depart may well have echoed Sir Stephen Powle's pious wish.

But the nine ships, six from London and three from Plymouth, though taking the shorter way according to instructions—to leave the Canaries (100 leagues) to the East and from thence to run in a straight western course (for Virginia)—fell on evil times. "A most terrible and vehement storme, which was the taile of the West Indian Horacano," drove the vessels apart and that particular ship which carried Gates, Newport, and Somers, the leaders of the expedition, foundered on one of the Bermuda islands. Though all lives were saved, supplies and equipment were lost, and the three most important men, in whom alone authority was vested, were compelled to remain in Bermuda until May 10, 1610, not arriving in Virginia until the 23rd. In the meantime the others reached the colony safely and there found John Smith, president of the council, obdurate in his refusal to resign his post, on the ground that the newcomers had no sufficient credentials. He was morally and technically right, but weakened at the moment by an accident, in which he was seriously injured, he gave up the contest, after considerable wrangling, and returned to England in the same vessel that brought the new colonists. Captain George Percy, eighth son of the Earl of Northumberland, was chosen president in his stead, and the old method of government continued, disastrously, for another year. Not until March 5, 1610, was Lord De la Warr able to leave England. Then "The Ld. De la Warr took his leave of all the company on Monday at Sr. Thomas Smiths in Fillpot Lane, Treasurer of the Virginia Co., and on Satterday following, 10 Martii departed toward his house in Hampsheere and from thence he went to meet his shippes at Southampton ready furnished with plantes, seedes, and all other provisions and grayne as well to sowe and to victule 1000 men for one year. He had 3 shippes, one of 200T, one a fly boate of 400 tunnes and a pinnace of 120t. His style was Lord Governor and Captaine of Virginia." He sailed from Cowes on April 1 and, after a fairly good voyage by way of the Azores, reached the colony on June 16, 1610.

There he found conditions reduced to the last extremity and the colonists on the eve of deserting the settlement. Jamestown had been strongly palisadoed, and contained some fifty or sixty houses, a fort, and a church, but it was a failure as the site of a permanent colony. It was located on low and marshy ground, liable to fogs and mists, possessing but a scant supply of water, and that bad, and subjecting its inhabitants to all the evils and miseries of malaria and dysentery—agues and fluxes, as they were called— cramps, gout, and death from famine, the starvation disease, scurvy, and Indian attacks. When Gates finally reached the colony from Bermuda, May 23, 1610, seven weeks before the arrival of De la Warr, he found a town "which appeared rather as the ruins of some antient fortification, than that any people living might now inhabit it. The palisadoes he found tourne downe, the portes open, the gates from the hinges, the church ruined and unfrequented, empty houses (whose owners untimely death had taken newly from them) rent up and burnt, the living not hable, as they pretended, to step into the woodes to gather other fire wood; and it is true the Indian as fast killing without as the famine and pestilence within. Only the blockhouse was the safetie of the remainder that lived; which yet could not have preserved them now many days longer from the watching subtle and offended Indians." This was the "Starving Time" for Virginia, just as there were to be starving times for Bermuda, Plymouth, and Barbados, when men suffered and died, because they had not yet learned the art of colonization, and had come to America inadequately supplied and equipped and unfamiliar with the method of wresting a living from the wilderness. In that one year the colony lost more than half its number and the rest were in a state of decrepitude and despair.

Gates could do little to relieve the situation, for having expected to find the colony flourishing and contented he had brought no more supplies than were enough for the voyage. With food remaining for only sixteen days, with all their hogs killed by the Indians, with not a hen or a chick in the fort, and with all the horses and mares killed for meat, with no seines or a sufficient number of boats for fishing, and with no assurance of aid from the hostile Indians they decided to abandon the settlement, and make for Newfoundland, where they hoped to meet with fishing vessels that would either give them employment or take them back to England.

But events turned out otherwise than they had feared and Jamestown was not to prove another Sagadahoc. As Gates with his company of dejected colonists fell down the river, they met the advance guard of the incoming De la Warr fleet and were ordered to return. It was a memorable event in our history when Gates "bore up the helm again and that night (the wind favorable) re-landed all his men at the Forte," and when De la Warr following, anchored his ship before the town, listened to a sermon by the preacher, who may well have dwelt on the miraculous intervention of God, and causing his commission to be read, took charge of the settlement." He first made a speech, "laying some blame on [the colonists] for many vanities" and their "idleness," and threatening if necessary "to draw the sword of Justice," and then began to organize the government, selecting a council, and dividing the men into bands of fifteen, each under a captain. New energies, new supplies, and new leadership brought new courage and hope. Sir George Somers and Captain Samuel Argall went off to Bermuda for hogs and fish, and others, in order to save their scanty stores of peas and oatmeal, turned again to fishing in the river and adjacent waters and began to consider once more the neglected cornfields, the kitchen gardens, and the wild grapes of the hedges and woods. De la Warr realized, as he wrote to the company, that no permanent success could be attained unless colonists of a better quality were sent out, worthy to be "the carpenters and workers in this so glorious a building."

But the crisis was not yet passed. Though De la Warr brought order and outward improvement to the town, restoring the church, renewing the palisades, and introducing a measure of dignity and display into all his official actions, he could not stem the tide of sickness and death. During the ensuing few months one hundred and fifty colonists, not yet inured to the conditions of Virginia climate and life, died of disease or at the hands of the Indians. De la Warr himself became dangerously ill and to save his life was obliged to quit the colony, March 28, 1611, leaving less than one hundred and fifty settlers behind under the charge of Captain Percy as deputy governor. He reached England in June and immediately sent a report to the company extolling the fertility of the country and endeavoring so to present conditions in the colony as to check the "coldnesse and irresolution" felt by the subscribers to the funds of the company.

But the promoters in England had no intention of deserting the colony. They had already decided that success depended on the right ordering of affairs there "by some industrious person" and planned to send aid in two installments, one under Sir Thomas Gates, who had returned from Virginia in September, 1610, and the other under Sir Thomas Dale, both of them soldiers of experience and for some years comrades-in-arms in the service of the States General of Holland. They also called for further contributions, and in order to stimulate payments issued "A True Declaration of the Colony of Virginia," designed to encourage the faltering souls, who must have watched with dismay the tragic failure of the great fleets that had started out so hopefully in 1609 and 1610. The money was raised, either by new subscriptions or the meeting of unpaid installments, and at the beginning of March, 1611, Dale sailed from London, reaching Jamestown May 23, two weeks before the arrival of De la Warr in England. He had three ships, carrying three hundred people and ample stores of provisions and livestock, increasing thereby the population to four hundred and fifty and materially adding to the number of horses, cows, and goats in the plantation.

Little sowing and harvesting had thus far been done, but the outlook was promising, for Dale had taken hold with a firm hand and for the first time was bringing the lives and activities of the settlers into a state of order and regularity. He made peace with the Indians, repaired and restored the buildings, and, most important of all, founded Dale's Town (Henricus, Henrico, Henricopolis, named after Prince Henry) fifty miles up the river, where he built a fort, a watch house, a church, a storehouse, and dwellings for himself and his men. The site was higher and more healthful than that of Jamestown and Dale had been impressed, as had all the earlier settlers who have left records of their experiences, with the fertility and attractiveness of the up country. When finally Sir Thomas Gates arrived in August with two hundred men, nearly all artisans, "fewer gallants to escape evil destinies," and twenty women, including his own wife and daughters, he found things in a fairly prosperous condition. The quality of the settlers, however, was still far from satisfactory, for as the company said those who went during the first years were far too often "lascivious sonnes, masters of bad servants, and wives of ill husbands," an idle crew who clogged the business and would rather starve than lay their hands to labor. Dale himself wrote home in 1613, "I protest unto you before the Livinge God, put them altogether, this country wilbe equivalent to [the best countries in Europe], if it be inhabited with good people."

\*     \*     \*     \*     \*

For a decade Sir Thomas Smith had been the treasurer of the company and in that time had accomplished a colossal task, promoting the settlement of Virginia and nursing it along, under most discouraging circumstances, to a successful rooting in the soil of the New World. When we realize how much else he was doing at the same time, we can but wonder how he was able to find energy and opportunity to devote himself to such a multiplicity of interests. To him more than to any one else in England is due the success attained in the face of heart-breaking disasters that threatened the existence of the colony in those embryo years. By 1616 things were looking more hopeful in many ways, and despite what to many was an undesirable form of government, under a sole and absolute governor, real accomplishment was full of promise and encouragement. The end of the joint management of land and stock, begun in 1609 and lasting seven years, had now come, and the opportunity was at hand for establishing private ownership and of making it possible for the colonists themselves to obtain a profit from the work of their own hands. Joint ownership, which in no sense of the word resembles communal ownership, may have been necessary as a device for promoting colonization at the beginning, but the time of its usefulness had passed. John Smith in Virginia and William Bradford in Plymouth both condemned it. Said the former, "When our people were fed out of the common store and laboured jointly together, glad was he could slip from his labour, or slumber over his taske, he cared not how, nay the most honest among them would hardly take so much true paines in a week, as now for themselves they will doe in a day; neither cared they for the increase, presuming that howsoever the harvest prospered, the general store must maintaine them, so that wee reaped not so much corne from the labours of thirtie, as now three or four doe provide for themselves." Bradford is equally explicit.

In 1613-1614 Dale had allotted to every man in the old settlement three acres of "cleare ground," in the nature of a farm, exempt from all payments, except one month's service to the colony (at other times than the sowing and harvesting seasons) and two barrels and a half of ears of corn, paid into the magazine—obligations similar to those of a tenant paying "gafol" on an English estate. In fact, the holders of these farms were tenants of the company. This arrangement worked well, for in 1616 the company could say that the colony was in a very good and prosperous condition. "They sow and reape their Corne in sufficient proportion, without want or impeachment; their Kine multiply already to some hundreds, their Swine to many thousands, their Goates and Poultry in great numbers; every man hath house and ground to his own use, and now being able to maintain themselves with food, they are also prepared and ready, once having the meanes, to set upon the minerals, whereof there are many sorts; as also to plant and how [hoe] such severall kinds of Seeds and Fruits, as may best befit the

Soyle and Climate, to make the Land profitable to themselves and the Adventurers." Therefore the company proposed to offer to everyone who had subscribed or would subscribe £12 10s fifty acres of land to be confirmed as an estate of inheritance to him and his heirs forever and to be held as of the manor of East Greenwich in free and common socage, that is, by fealty and fixed rent. In 1618, as a part of Sandys' elaborate scheme for the advancement of the colony, which, as we shall see later, touched nearly every phase of its organization and was designed to transform it from a struggling settlement into a thriving, populous, and self-sustaining community, the company apportioned unoccupied lands for public purposes —so much for the ministry, so much for the college which it hoped to found, and so much for the company itself. Upon these lands additional tenants and servants were to be located at the expense of the company, that the lands might yield a profit to those for whose benefit they had been laid out. Grants were now made to others than subscribers, either to those who had done some special service to the company, or to private persons—at the rate of fifty acres for every one transported—who would go to the colony with family and servants. This, the famous "adventure of the person" or "headright" system, became a characteristic form of land distribution not only in Virginia, but in many of the other colonies as well. In Virginia, after the fall of the company, it became a right inherent in the colony, as far as distribution was concerned, and continued to be used until its frequent abuse led to its modification and practical abolition toward the end of the century.

This introduction of private ownership in land and the profits of cultivation was accompanied with a change in the activities of the people of the colony. They no longer spent their time in searching for mines or in trafficking with the Indians, but became farmers and planters, and under the encouragement of the company, made strenuous efforts to produce a variety of staples—grain, grapes, licorice, silk-grass—and to promote industry by setting up saw-mills and by producing naval stores, potash, glass, and iron. From the beginning the company had tried to bring about such results as these, but had made so little impression upon the London mercantile world that in 1615 a writer could say, "I cannot find [for commercial enterprise] any worthy place of forraine anchorage; for the Bermudas we know not yet what they will do; and for Virginia we know not well what to do with it, the present profit of those not employing any store of shipping." In truth neither Virginia nor any other colony at so early a date was ready, even on a small scale, to enter a manufacturing stage, which above all things required what the colonists lacked, capital, labor, and skill. Later the company endeavored to meet the difficulty and did so, in part, by sending over not only English artisans, but also skilled workmen from other countries—Poles, Germans, Swedes, French, and Italians. But it was impossible to suppress the lure of tobacco raising which required little capital, any man's labor, and no great amount of skill. Practically anybody could raise tobacco, but not anybody could make glass, iron, potash, and naval stores.

John Rolfe in 1612 seems to have been the first to experiment with tobacco raising, and with sufficient success to send a consignment to England in March 1614, by the ship *Elizabeth*, thus beginning the first export of what was destined to become the great staple of Virginia in colonial times. We may well believe that it was the discovery of this new and profitable commodity that had something to do with the company's decision to make a general division of the colony's lands, for the formation of a subordinate company at this time, to deal in certain Virginia commodities (chief among which were tobacco and sassafras) and known as the Society of Particular Adventurers for Traffique with Virginia in a joint-stock, shows that the members were interested once more in profits from the colony. This new company, located of course in England, was under the direction of Alderman Johnson and was called the "magazine," a name formerly given to the store-house established in the colony under the seven year plan. The new "magazine" was, however, quite a different institution from the old. It had its court and its separate accounts, an arrangement which caused a great deal of pother during the years of its existence and was not settled for some time after it had ceased to function. It must have been badly mismanaged for eventually it showed a serious loss to the adventurers and went bankrupt. The first magazine ships arrived in Virginia in 1616, bringing provisions, clothing, utensils, and the like, and similar consignments continued to be sent for a number of years, but the goods do not appear to have been always chosen wisely. On one occasion the store keeper in the colony complained that the magazine in England sent needles when it ought to have sent ploughs! But the business began well and in 1617 20,000 pounds of tobacco were despatched to England. The colonists, however, complained that the adventurers charged too much for their goods, and the adventurers, in their turn, complained that the farmers of the customs levied too high a duty on the tobacco imported. Then the society suffered from the quarrels in the company, for its members were in the main supporters of the Smith party. An attempt at reorganization took place in 1620 and a new magazine was formed, but in 1621 that was already spoken of as having suffered heavily from the high price and poor quality of tobacco and from other causes. Of its later history we know almost nothing. In 1625 it was spoken of as "the late Magazine."

The colony was growing very slowly. The resources of the company, even with the aid of the lotteries, were inadequate to meet the cost of development and expansion. It was realized, as early as 1617-1619, that a variety of ways would have to be contrived to enlarge the population and to increase the agricultural output. Among these aids were the subsidiary joint-stocks or private ventures of one kind or another that were set up under the auspices of the company; the free admission to the company of those who would promise to take up land in the colony and seat it with families and servants; and, most important of all, the encouraging of small groups or associations of men, organized on a joint-stock basis, to settle particular plantations or private colonies within the boundaries of the company's patent. These associates were to provide tenants, servants, and equipment from their own resources, and to engage in agriculture, Indian trade, or fishing, as they preferred, in order that they might increase the staple output of the colony as a whole. The practice, a common one at the time and one frequently indulged in, was adopted by all the colonizing corporations—The Council for New England, which was the reorganized Plymouth Company, the Bermuda Company, and the Massachusetts Bay Company.

\*     \*     \*     \*     \*

While the company was thus encouraging private settlements for the purpose of increasing the population and economic strength of the colony, it was also doing as much as it could to promote immigration on its own account. Despite the accumulation of men and women, who had been sent over before 1616, the number of inhabitants did not increase. In that year there were fewer men, women, and children, taken altogether, in Virginia, than there had been in 1611, three hundred and twenty-four as against four hundred and fifty. In 1618 there were only six hundred. Efforts were now made to increase this number and to enlarge the occupied area by sending three hundred tenants for the company's land and gardens, the governor's land, and the college land at Henrico, all of which were under the company's direct control. These tenants were to hold their tenements at a yearly rental and thus benefit the company, the governor, and the college, whenever that should be set up. The company shipped also one hundred apprentices and servants and a hundred "young and uncorrupt to make wives to the inhabitants and by that means to make the men more settled and less movable." In all cases where maids married "public farmers," that is, tenants on the company's lands, the company promised to pay all charges of transportation; otherwise the husbands were to recompense the company for its outlay, at one hundred and fifty pounds of tobacco each, an amount which would certainly net a profit to the company. It persuaded the City of London to furnish one hundred children in 1618 and another hundred in 1619 for the better supply of the colony, which the mayor and aldermen did "fearing lest the overflowing multitude of inhabitants should, like too much blood, infect the whole city with plague and poverty." In the next two years the company received from the city an appropriation of £500 for the same purpose. In 1621 it tried to obtain the introduction of a bill into parliament requiring the "cities and towns corporate" in England to send the poor "with whom they were pestered" into Virginia, but the attempt failed, though a number of the corporate towns took advantage of the opportunity to get rid of their indigent population. The usefulness of Virginia in this bloodletting process was widely appreciated, as, except for Ireland and Bermuda, it was the only available place for undesirables outside of England. We read of the "citty boys and citty maids" carried over in the ship *City* in 1618 and of the "Duty boys," carried over in the ship *Duty* in 1619. The latter, fifty in number, were despatched at the command of King James, constituting the "divers young people" of whom the king wrote to Sir Thomas Smith, January 13, 1619, "who wanting imployment doe live idle and followe the Court," which at the time was at the Newmarket races.

These boys and girls were generally put to service in the colony, either as apprentices or domestic servants of the tenants on the company's lands. Some of the later arrivals were spoken of as "weak and unserviceable people, ragged, and not above a fortnight's provision," who frequently died and occasionally ran away to the Indians. But doubtless many grew up to be useful members of the colony, justifying England's efforts to rid herself, by just so much, of her vagrant population.

Convicts from the jails of Middlesex and other counties joined the procession to America, the first being transported as early as 1617, thus inaugurating a long line of these unfortunates, saved from the gallows in England, in order to "yeilde a profitable service to the Commonwealth in parts abroad." But they were unwelcome additions to the population in Virginia and by 1663 had become so numerous as to engage in a desperate conspiracy in September of that year, which fortunately, however, was discovered and circumvented. On April 16, 1670, the Virginia counties of York, Gloster, and Middlesex petitioned the council of Virginia regarding the great number of "fellons and other desperate villanes sent hither from the prisons of England," begging that body to prevent the barbarous designs and felonious practices of these wicked men and to forbid any one engaged in trade with the mother country from bringing in "jailbirds." The matter was referred to England, where the Privy Council issued an order prohibiting the practice.

But still the population did not increase. Death took its toll as remorselessly as it had done in the early years of the colony. From Easter, 1619, to March, 1620, the numbers decreased from 1000 to 867, and in March, 1621, though ten ships had gone across the ocean in the meantime with 1051 emigrants, only 843 remained. In one year 1095 had died, either on the way over or in the colony. No wonder "some of the children designed by the City [of London]" refused to go. To die from epidemics or in the process of getting acclimated or "seasoned" was not a pleasant prospect even for the vagrant and the criminal, and transportation acquired some of the horrors of prison life and the gallows.

But the company was not to be daunted. Sandys had become the treasurer in 1619 and was determined to carry forward the elaborate plans for the advancement of the colony that had been formulated and in great part executed while Sir Thomas Smith was in office. These plans . . . covered almost every phase of the colony's organization and life. Already in 1618 and 1619 a beginning had been made, but in the summer of 1620 reinforcements were considered on a larger scale than before. The company proposed to send 800 "choyce persons"—500 tenants, 100 young maids, 100 boys for apprentices, and 100 indentured servants—to be procured partly by advertising and partly through the cooperation of "noble friends." The sending of these "apprentices, servants and wives" was estimated in the summer of 1621 to have cost £2000 and it must have discouraged the promoters, at that time facing bankruptcy, to be informed by Robert Bennet, of "Bennett's Welcome," that "vittles being scarce in the country noe man will tacke servants."

The severest blow that the company suffered at this juncture, was the loss of the lottery. The attempts made since 1612 to raise money by this means had stirred up a good deal of opposition. The first great lottery, held at the west end of St. Paul's in the summer of 1612, lasted for a month, and a London tailor won the first prize of "four thousand crownes in fayre plate, which was sent to his house in a very stately manner." The records of the London guilds show that those companies as well as private individuals speculated in tickets, the Grocers Company, for example, paying £62 10s for five lots and other companies doing the same. The virtues of the lotteries were spread broadcast throughout southern England by various forms of propaganda, including among other methods of publicity, the issuing of ballads, extolling the benefits sure to accrue to all sorts of people—"maydes that have but small portions," "knights and gallant gentlemen," "merchants of the western partes," "farmers and countrymen"—all of whom would find prizes awaiting them, if they would but subscribe. In 1619 Gabriel Barbour was appointed manager and for his efficiency in raising money he was thanked on account of his "true and honest carriage of that buissinesse."

But Barbour's way of conducting the lottery wrought its evils, for the people of the towns in which his agents were at work complained of the demoralizing effects upon trade and industry that were caused by the popular excitement which the lottery aroused. The complaints were brought to the attention of parliament, where the master of the wards and later lord treasurer, Lionel Canfield, reported from the king that the latter had never liked the idea of the lottery and had only agreed to it because he was informed that the colony could not subsist without it. He was prepared to suspend the privilege if its exercise was found to be a grievance. Therefore, in March, 1621, at the request of the House of Commons, the Privy Council ordered "that the further execution of these lotteries be suspended." This was done by proclamation four days later, March 8, on the ground that "the sayd Lotteries doe dayly decline to more and more inconvenience, to the hinderance of multitudes of our Subjects," and that their suspension was necessary "for the general good." How far the suppression of the lottery was a political measure it is hard to decide, but the fact that the king and council acted on the recommendation of the House of Commons would seem to preclude such an assertion.

The overthrow of the lottery was little short of a crushing blow to the company, and as further expenditure from the common stock was impossible, because the treasury was empty, the device of the subordinate and voluntary joint-stock was resorted to on a scale larger than ever before. Companies or associations were created for "the sole making of Glasse and Beades," for "Apparell and other necessary provisions such as the Colony stood in great need of," for "sending of 100 mayds to be made wives," for "the setting out of a voyage to trade with the Indians in Virginia for furs," and for "sending Shipwrights and other principall workmen for making Ships, Boats and other Vessells." The new magazine, formed in 1620, was to provide not only cows, mares, goats, asses from France, and a large quantity of staple commodities, but also maids and apprentices. Continuing the work of earlier years, plans were set on foot for making salt, silk, oil, wines, hemp, and flax, for engaging "Dutch carpenters from Hamborough, skillful for the erecting of Sawing Mills," pushing forward the "iron worke so long and earnestly desired," and furnishing fishing tackle and other necessities and a grist mill. This courageous programme, largely the work of Sandys and Southampton, was carried out in part at least during the years 1620 and 1621 in the face of increasing financial difficulties, with the result that in 1622 when the great massacre by the Indians took place, there were 1240 people in the colony, and the outlook for the iron works, salt works, the breeding of silkworms and the making of silk, the manufacture of glass beads for trading with the Indians, and the increase of English and Irish cattle seemed reasonably bright.

While it is very unlikely that any of these industrial enterprises could have been successful, even under the most favorable circumstances—partly because of the seductive influence of the tobacco culture and partly because of the want of capital and the right kind of labor—yet more might have been accomplished had it not been for the attack of the Indians on the colony in 1622. This hideous tragedy cost the settlement about 400 lives, mostly of "seasoned men," the mainstays of the colony, and brought great discouragement in England, strengthening the opposition which had already been aroused against the policy of the company. But this setback did not cause immediately any cessation of effort. Patents of land continued to be issued and colonists to be sent over, even while the company's troubles were increasing and the members were warring among themselves. A year after the annulment of the charter, the population had risen to nearly 1100. The colony already possessed all the essentials of a permanent settlement— family and agricultural life, men, women, and children, artisans, hired laborers, and indentured servants, and a few Negroes. Its numbers were increasing from within and without; its stock in oxen, cows, swine, and goats was growing rapidly; forty-two sail of ships were reported in 1623 as plying back and forth between England and Virginia; and in the main the people were peaceful and contented. It looked as if the Virginia colony had actually taken root.

❧ ☙

*At the heart of mercantilist doctrine existed the belief that the wealth of the world was limited. The power of a nation-state, it was further believed, had a precise proportion to the wealth of the world it could successfully claim. Thus the establishment of a colony represented a credit claim in a nation's power balance. It is hardly surprising, therefore, that in the aftermath of the discovery of America, the major European powers scrambled to claim the newfound lands. Since the basis of a successful claim was not only discovery and exploration but also of settlement, by the seventeenth century the western hemisphere was a hodgepodge of competing claims and colonies.*

*In Europe, the struggle for empire triggered numberless wars, each of which spilled over into the colonies. The taxing demands of a new environment were complemented by the omnipresent threat of attack by a marauding enemy. The major target of the sixteenth-century colonial wars was Spain whose early arrival had given her a vast wealth that stirred envy among the other European powers. Even as the Spaniards continued to explore their new domain, they fought to repel challenges to their dominance. Even as they succeeded in holding their claims, the illusion of Spanish omnipotence faded, and not infrequently they retained a claim without being able to exploit it.*

*Edward Gaylord Bourne (1860-1908) spent most of his academic career at Yale. His main interest was in historical criticism and in early American history with a particular emphasis on the trans-Mississippi West. His narrative style has the virtue of terse directness unimpeded by complex analysis.*

# SPAIN IN AMERICA
## 1450-1580

## by Edward Gaylord Bourne

Hernando de Soto was born in Xerez de Badajos about the year 1500, and upon reaching manhood had gone to the isthmus to seek his fortune. Starting with nothing but his sword and shield, he displayed such qualities that he was sent to Peru with Pizarro, where he greatly distinguished himself. He returned to Spain with a fortune of over one hundred thousand pesos of gold—roughly equal to three hundred thousand dollars—and was rewarded by the emperor of Cuba and adelantado of Florida, and was commissioned to conquer and settle at his own expense the whole region now included in the southern part of the United States. Among those who joined De Soto were several Portuguese from Elvas. To one of these we owe the best account of the expedition that has come down to us.

A prosperous voyage across the Atlantic, an inspection of his new province of Cuba, and the replenishing of his stores occupied the months from April, 1538, to May, 1539, when De Soto left Havana with nine vessels, over six hundred and twenty men, and two hundred and twenty-three horses. On May 30 a landing was effected in Tampa Bay. By a strange coincidence they soon picked up a survivor of Narvaez's force, one Juan Ortiz, who had been living among the Indians twelve years. Ortiz at one time was on the point of being put to death, when his life was saved by the cacique's daughter in a way which may have suggested to Captain John Smith the romantic incident of his rescue by Pocahontas.

During the first summer various short reconnoissances were made, and the main force marched up the west coast of Florida to that same region of Apalachee where Narvaez gave up his march and turned seaward. There De Soto wintered. A large number of the Indian carriers died during the winter from exposure and lack of food. In the spring De Soto resumed the march towards the northeast across the present state of Georgia, in search of the land which the Indians told him was on another sea. Reaching the Savannah River, he turned northwestward, passed through the Blue Mountains nearly to the border of Tennessee, then went nearly southwest through Georgia and Alabama to a large Indian village, Mauvilla, a little above the head of Mobile Bay, where he arrived the middle of October.

We are not to think of this expedition as being always on the march. From time to time longer or shorter stops were made to recruit the strength of the men and to fatten the horses. The severest battle with the Indians occurred at Mauvilla, in which a large number of Indians were killed, eighteen Spaniards lost their lives, and one hundred and fifty were wounded. A less resolute and heroic spirit would have yielded at this point, for De Soto knew that his lieutenant, Malonado, was waiting for him at Ochuse, some six days journey distant, but he did not reveal this opportunity of escape to his men, and "determined to send no news of himself until he had found some rich country." That in the year and a half that he had spent in the southern forests he had lost only one hundred and two men from sickness or attacks by the Indians is a brilliant proof of De Soto's abilities as a leader and explorer.

Turning his back again on the world outside, De Soto marched northwest for a month until he came to the Indian village of Chicasa, in northern Mississippi, where he set up winter quarters December 17. Here in March, 1542, the worst disaster thus far experienced fell upon him. The Indians attacked the village suddenly about midnight and set it on fire. In this calamity eleven Spaniards were killed and most of the survivors lost their clothes, substitutes for which must now be devised from skins. Fifty horses and several hundred of the great drove of pigs, which accompanied the expeditition to serve in emergencies (for provisions), were burned.

Resuming the march, De Soto proceeded in a northwesterly direction until, on May 8, 1541, they "saw the great river." "The river was almost halfe a league broad. If a man stood still on the other side, it could not be discerned whether he were a man or no. The river was of great depth, and of a strong current; the water was alwaies muddie; there came downe the River continually many trees and timber." Such are the words of the earliest description of the Mississippi by a companion of its discoverer.

A month was spent in building barges to make a crossing, which was finally effected some distance south of Memphis, June 8. The identification of De Soto's route west of the Mississippi is very uncertain, but apparently his marchers were within the bounds of the present State of Arkansas. They came upon the nomadic Indians of the plains, heard of the buffalo, and procured buffalo robes, but did not see the animals, and they gathered from the Indians that to the west they could find guides to "the other sea." A long march in that direction was made, but in vain. They then turned back to the southeast and went into winter quarters early in November.

Such was the indomitable spirit of De Soto that he was still ready after an exploration of two years and a half to send word to Cuba and to New Spain for new supplies with which to prosecute discoveries and conquest, for he had not yet got as far west as Cabeca de Vaca. The losses among the Spaniards now numbered two hundred and fifty men. A winter of great severity followed, and the deep snow kept them housed most of the time. In the spring De Soto started towards the south to reach the gulf in pursuance of his plan, but the way was arduous and the men and horses had been weakened by the winter; De Soto became much depressed by the outlook, "his men and horses every day diminished, being without succor to sustain themselves in the country, and with that thought he fell sick."

The end was near, and the great explorer knew it. In a dignified and pathetic speech he bade farewell to his followers, and named Luis do Moscoso to succeed him in command. "The next day, being the 21st of May, 1542, departed of this life, the valorous, virtuous, and valiant Captain, Don Fernando de Soto, Governour of Cuba, and Adelantado of Florida, whom fortune advanced, as it useth to doe others, that he might have the higher fal." He was first buried, and then at Moscoso's order his body was taken up, wrapped in mantles with much sand, "wherein he was carried in a canoe, and thrown into the midest of the River."

The new leader and his followers were ready to return to civilization, but thought it best to go overland to Mexico, and they proceeded southwesterly into Texas, perhaps as far as the Trinity River; but the scarcity of provisions and the hostility of the Indians compelled them after some months to seek the Mississippi again. Early in 1543 they began to construct seven brigantines, which with difficulty were built and equipped. All the pigs and all but twenty-two of the horses were killed and their flesh dried for provisions. Some five hundred Indian slaves, men and women, were liberated, and about one hundred others carried along, but these were subsequently emancipated by royal orders.

The Spaniards embarked July 2, 1543, and floated down the river, with many perils from the stream and from Indians, for they no longer had firearms. In sixteen days they reached the sea, and then coasted along the gulf shore towards Mexico for fifty-two days, arriving at the river Panuco, September 10, 1543, four years, three months, and eleven days from the landing in Tampa Bay. Out of the six hundred and twenty people who started, three hundred and eleven survived, a favorable result, if one remember that half of the one hundred colonists at Jamestown died the first winter, and over four hundred out of five hundred died in the winter of 1609-1610. Thus ended the most remarkable exploring expedition in the history of North America. Its only parallel is the contemporary enterprise of Coronado, which did for the southwest what De Soto did for the eastern and central belt.

\*     \*     \*     \*     \*

As a term in the political geography of Spanish America, the name "Florida" was equivalent to the eastern half of the present United States, or the country from Mexico to Newfoundland. In 1558, Philip II authorized Luis de Velasco, viceroy of New Spain, to undertake the settlement of Florida. After a preliminary reconnoissance Velasco despatched, in the summer of 1559, an expedition of fifteen hundred soldiers and settlers to make a beginning at Pensacola Bay. The site selected was unfavorable, but attempts to find a better one were not successful; a winter of privation followed, and during the following summer the colony was much reduced. The second summer most of the settlers went off with Angel de Villafane to the Atlantic coast, to Santa Elena, Port Royal Sound. When he arrived there late in May 1561, Villafane, disappointed at the unsuitableness of the region for a colony, continued his explorations to Chesapeake Bay and then returned to Espanola. The unhappy experience of these colonists convinced Philip II that the region was not likely to be occupied by the French, and hence he decided that no future attempt at colonization should be made.

The very next year the unexpected happened. Jean Ribaut, of Dieppe, under the patronage of Coligny, the leader of the Huguenots in France, led a party of soldiers and young nobles to the east shore of Florida, whence they coasted as far north as Port Royal Sound. Here Ribaut left thirty men and returned to France. Want, lonesomeness, and contentions drove them to the desperate expedient of building a vessel to escape from the desolate continent, but only at the cost of such privations as reduced them to cannibalism before they were picked up by an English ship.

In 1564 the plans for a colony in Florida of French Huguenots were matured by Coligny; and the expedition set out in June under the command of René de Laudonnière, a French officer and gentleman who had been with Ribaut in the first voyage. The site selected was at the mouth of the St. John's river, Florida. Here a fort was built and parties were despatched to explore the country. There were few if any tillers of the soil in the company, and when the first novelty wore off, restlessness and ennui led to quarrels, insubordination, and plots.

Thirteen of the sailors seized one of the vessels and set off on a buccaneering cruise against the Spaniards. Want finally brought them up in Havana, where, to save themselves, they gave information in regard to the colony. Their example was soon followed by sixty-six others, tempted by the chances of wealth in plundering Spanish ships and settlements. At first successful, they came to grief, and less than half returned to the fort, where Laudonnière overpowered them and put to death four of the ringleaders for mutiny.

In August, 1565, after a summer of extreme want, the wasted garrison were preparing to leave the country, when Ribaut arrived with several hundred colonists, soldiers, and young gentlemen, with some artisans and their families. Ribaut also brought orders to Laudonnière to resign his command and return to France.

Contemporaneous with this effort of the French Huguenots to occupy

Florida was a new project to colonize the country for Spain. Pedro Menendez de Aviles, who had served as commander of the fleet to New Spain, secured a patent in March, 1565, erecting Florida into a government and constituting him adelantado, governor and captain-general. Menendez on his part was to take five hundred men, one hundred of them farmers, to explore and conquer Florida, to transport settlers thither, some of whom were to be married, support twelve friars as missionaries, and supply domestic animals for the settlements. This task Menendez undertook with great energy and zeal. The hazy ideas of the width of the continent, still prevalent even after De Soto's expedition, led him to think Florida near enough to the silver-mines of Zacatecas and St. Martin, in Mexico, to be substituted for Vera Cruz as the place of export, thus avoiding the dangers to health in that town and enabling traffic to escape the perilous and tedious navigation of the gulf by an overland journey of perhaps a hundred leagues longer than that to Vera Cruz. In reality it was over one thousand miles farther from Zacatecas to Florida than to Vera Cruz.

While Menendez was making his preparations the news first reached the Spanish court of the projects of the French. The king immediately gave orders that Menendez should be granted three vessels, two hundred cavalry, and four hundred infantry in the islands to drive out the French. That the Spanish government should allow a French settlement in so important a strategic point in relation to their commerce with New Spain was inconceivable, and one wonders why the French promoters of the enterprise expected that it would be regarded as anything but a declaration of hostilities. The islands were already exposed to the ravages of the French buccaneers. The corsair French Jacques de Sorie had sacked and burned Havana ten years before and killed thirty-four prisoners in cold blood. To furnish a basis for attacks of this sort, it was naturally believed by the Spanish authorities, was the motive of Ribaut and Laudonnière; and the conduct of the two detachments of mutineers only confirmed their supposition.

That the intruders were heretics intensified their exasperation. Carefully shielding the purity of the faith in the New World by excluding all Spaniards whose progenitors had been tainted with heresy, they would regard an enterprise which combined plunder of their colonies and fleets and a corruption of the Indians with diabolical heresy as an extraordinary provocation, excluding the guilty plotters from any claim to mercy.

Menendez, with a company of over two thousand six hundred persons, all maintained at his own expense, except one ship and about three hundred soldiers paid by the king, left Cadiz, June 29, about the time Ribaut must have left Dieppe. On the night of September 4, off the coast of Florida, Menendez fell in with some of Ribaut's ships, and in response to inquiries announced his instructions to hang and burn the Lutheran French to be found there. The French ships escaped in the darkness, and Menendez continued on his way to his new domain. September 6, 1565, a landing was made and a fort begun which may be considered the foundation of St. Augustine, the oldest town in the United States. Two days later Menendez landed and took formal possession of the territory.

His forces were not so superior to Ribaut's as to prevent his situation being one of peril. A storm, however, scattered Ribaut's ships, and Menendez decided to attack the French by land. A stealthy march, a desperate assault on a sleeping garrison just before daybreak amid a pouring rain, and soon all was over. One hundred and thirty men lay dead in and around the fort. The women and children under fifteen Menendez ordered to be spared. Of them he wrote to the king, "There were, between women, infants, and boys of fifteen years and under, some fifty persons, whom it gives me the greater pain to see in the company of my men, by reason of their wicked sect, and I have feared that our Lord would chastise me if I shall deal cruelly with them, for eight or ten children were born here."

About fifty persons escaped the slaughter by swimming across the river or by taking boats to the ships. One of the ships was sunk by the guns of the fort. The other slipped down the river a few miles where there were two more. Menendez determined to capture them if possible. In his absence word was brought that some twenty Frenchmen had come in from the woods, and he gave orders to execute justice upon them. A few days later, after Menendez had returned to St. Augustine, he heard of a party of Frenchmen some twenty miles distant to the south. He set out immediately with a small force against them. From their spokesman he learned that Ribaut's fleet, consisting of four galleons and eight pinnaces with four hundred picked men and two hundred sailors, which had put out in search of the Spaniards, had been struck by a hurricane, that three of the galleons had gone down with over two hundred persons, and that Ribaut's flag-ship had been dismasted.

In reply to a request for safe passage to the fort Menendez told him: "We held their fort, having taken and put to death those who were in it for having erected it there without the leave of your majesty, and because they were planting their wicked Lutheran sect in these your majesty's provinces, and that I made war with fire and blood as governor and captain-general of these provinces upon all who might come to these parts to settle and to plant this evil Lutheran sect, seeing that I came by your majesty's command to bring the gospel into these parts, to enlighten the natives thereof with that which is told and believed by the holy mother church of Rome for the salvation of their souls; that therefore I should not give them passage, but, on the contrary, should pursue them by sea and by land until I had their lives."

The Frenchmen, through a lieutenant of Laudonnière, then offered to surrender if their lives would be spared. "I answered," writes Menendez, "that they might give up their arms and place themselves at my mercy; that I should deal with them as our Lord should command me, and that he [i.e., the envoy] had not moved me from this nor could move me, unless God our Lord should inspire in me something different." According to Solis, the brother-in-law of Menendez, who was a witness, his reply was that "if they wished to surrender their arms and banners and put themselves at his mercy they might do so and he would do with them as God should give him grace, they might do as they liked; other truce or friendship they could not have."

It is possible that the translation of this reply into French made it seem to give grounds for a hope that did not exist. Today, in view of what Menendez had declared to the first envoy, he does not seem to have committed himself to any mercy. Their offer of fifty thousand ducats as a ransom he promptly declined, saying "that although he was poor he would not do that weakness; when he wanted to be liberal and merciful he would be so without self-interest." After consultation the Frenchmen decided to surrender. All of them, over a hundred in number, except twelve Breton sailors who had been kidnapped and four carpenters and caulkers, were put to the knife in cold blood. Ever since the spot has borne the name Matanzas ("Slaughters").

Next came the turn of Ribaut and those with him. October 10, Menendez received news of their approach, and went out to meet them with a body of one hundred and fifty men. The French asked for a parley, which was granted, and Menendez was then informed that it was Ribaut with some three hundred and fifty men, and that they desired safe passage to their fort. Again came the unrelenting answer that "I was his enemy and waged war against them with fire and blood, for that they were Lutherans, and because they had come to plant in these lands of your majesty their evil sect and to instruct the Indians in it." Ribaut himself desired an interview, which was granted. It was hard for him to believe that his fort was captured, the garrison slain, and that the other party of refugees from the wreck had been killed, but the sight of the dead bodies on the sands convinced him. In response to his request for terms, if they should surrender, Menendez made the same answer that he had made a fortnight earlier.

Ribaut consulted his men and found them divided. He returned and explained the situation to Menendez. Some wished to throw themselves on his mercy and others not. Menendez answered it made no difference to him; they might all come or part of them or none, they might do as they liked. Ribaut then said that half of them would pay one hundred and fifty thousand ducats ransom and that the other half would pay more, as there were rich men among them. Menendez replied that it was hard to lose such a sum, as he was in need of it. This answer gave an encouragement to Ribaut, for which one sees little ground, for if Menendez had intended to deceive him it would have been as easy to say "he should be glad to have it."

Grasping at the chance, whatever it was, Ribaut and one hundred and fifty of his men gave themselves up. They were led by tens back of the sand dunes and then asked whether they were Catholics or Lutherans, "and then John Ribaut replied that he and all that were there were of the new religion, and began to repeat the Psalm, 'Domine, memento Mei,' and when he had finished he said that they were of the earth and to the earth must return. Twenty years more or less, it was all the same thing." Then all were put to the knife save two young gentlemen about eighteen years of age and a drummer, a fifer, and a trumpeter. Menendez wrote to King Philip: "I hold it the chief good-fortune that he (Ribaut) is dead, because the King of France would do more with him with five hundred ducats than with others and five thousand, and he would do more in one year than another in ten, since he was the most expert sailor and corsair known, and very skillful in this navigation of the Indies and coast of Florida."

Three weeks later Indians brought information that the rest of Ribaut's party, who refused to surrender, were building a fort and a ship. Menendez set forth against them by forced marches with three hundred men. This time, affected perhaps by adverse criticism at St. Augustine, or because he saw that it would be impracticable to capture them and felt "that it would not be proper that so wicked a sect should remain in the land," and possibly because his own heart had softened, he offered them their lives if they would surrender. One hundred and fifty did so and were well treated. The captain and about twenty rejected the offer, sending word "that he would be eaten by the Indians rather than surrender to the Spaniards."

The story of this tragedy has been told from the Spanish side, for the accounts of Menendez and Solis bear upon them the marks of truth so far as these are discoverable. They do not blink the facts, nor do they show signs of consciousness that there was need of concealment or apology. The accounts of the French who escaped accuse Menendez of having promised on oath to save the lives of those who surrendered. This it is difficult to believe in view of the whole tone of Menendez's correspondence with the king. That a man of honor and religion would have done such a deed seems impossible today. Yet if the perplexed student will read Oliver Cromwell's account of the massacre at Drogheda, and if he will read Carlyle's comments, he may be able to understand why the historian Barcia accorded admiration to Menendez.

The French king, Charles IX, and his stronger mother, Catherine de' Medici, demanded reparation urgently and repeatedly; but Philip II only said that he was sorry for what had happened, and insisted that Admiral Coligny was responsible for having authorized the French to occupy Spanish territory, and that he ought to be punished; redress he refused to give. To Menendez, however, he expressed his approval of his conduct. In the state of politics and religion in France a breach with Spain seemed to the leaders of the Catholic party out of the question; they did not venture beyond protests.

A private adventurer, Dominic de Gourgues, so the accepted story runs, then took upon himself the responsibility of avenging his countrymen, setting out from France in the summer of 1567 with three vessels, under a commission to capture slaves in Africa. After selling his cargo in Espanola, when off the western end of Cuba he revealed his project to his men. They soon fell in with the plan, and De Gourgues made his way to the St. John's River to attack the Spanish fort San Mateo, which was the successor of Laudonnière's Fort Caroline. First two outposts lower down the river, then the fort itself, were taken by assault. All the Spaniards that escaped the sword were hanged, with the inscription placed above them: "Not as Spaniards, but as traitors, robbers, and murderers." He then razed the forts, and returned to France, hoping for a recognition which only the Huguenots gave.

It is a singular fact that a most careful search in the Spanish archives failed to find "the slightest allusion to any such capture of San Mateo and the two adjacent forts"; nor do the papers of the Menendez family appear to have contained any material on this incident, since the Spanish historian Barcia, who utilized those papers, had no sources save the French narrative. That account says nothing of the existence of St. Augustine, and, on the other hand, the existence of two forts besides San Mateo is unknown to the contemporary Spanish sources. To these perplexities may be added the fact that Juan Lopez de Velasco, the cosmographer of the Council of the Indies, writing in 1571-1574, in his account of Florida, knows nothing of De Gourgues raid in 1568, but says that Fort San Mateo was abandoned in 1570.

Historians have told the tale as one of poetic justice, and religious sympathies have naturally been enlisted on the side of the avenger. Yet it should not be forgotten that, merciless and cruel as was Menendez's deed—the nearest parallel to the bloody massacres of the Crusades or of the religious wars in Europe that ever happened in our country's history—he was the constituted authority in Florida, and was acting in general pursuance of instructions from his king. He looked upon the French colonists as corsairs, which, in fact, at least some of them were. That the French had a right to establish a colony in Florida can hardly be maintained; their own claim was based on a purely fictitious discovery in the fifteenth century. De Gourgues, acting as a private adventurer, had no color of law on his side.

The tragedy was the end of French colonization on the southern mainland for nearly a century and a half; and the end forever of the attempts to establish a Huguenot refuge and power on this side of the sea. Their contribution to American life was to be made as individuals, a sturdy leaven in a congenial though foreign society. On the other hand, neither Menendez nor his heirs or descendants succeeded in founding a flourishing Spanish community in Florida. Equally without permanent success were the repeated efforts of missionary bands to convert the Indians.

كچ ڇے

As *Spain's power in the New World declined, that of Great Britain steadily grew. But unlike Spain who insisted on concentrating the decision-making power in Madrid, Britain permitted the rise of a colonial system in which autonomy prevailed. London set forth the guidelines of policy but left the specific application of policy to the authorities on the spot. And since the colonials thought of themselves as Englishmen, they accepted the permissiveness of the mother country as an encouragement to develop self-government.*

*The erratic tendencies of British colonial policy were manifested in the divergent bases of colonial settlement. They ranged from the charter of Massachusetts Bay to the proprietary charter of Pennsylvania. The former implied royal underwriting of a mercantilist enterprise, while the latter signaled a mark of royal favor. Despite the absence of a single form of colonial organization, British authorities had committed themselves by 1650 to fostering representative governments in their North American colonies.*

*The result was the development of a system of self-government that ac-
centuated among colonials a sense of their independence of outside control.
It also created among the overseas Englishmen a vigorous sense of their
equality with their island brethren.*

*Ironically, a self-government fostered under royal auspices undermined
royal authority. For as one of the last royal officials of South Carolina noted:
"From the great religious and Civil indulgences granted by the Crown to
encourage Adventurers to settle in America, the Government of the Colonies
has gradually inclined more to the democratical than regal side."*

*James Truslow Adams (1879-1949), like many other historians, came to it
as an amateur. A highly successful Wall Street broker and railroad executive, he developed an increasing aversion for his original profession. Once
he turned to the writing of history, he revealed a vigorous tendency to demolish time-honored myths. This combined with an epigrammatic prose
style made him one of the most widely read of historians from the publication of his Pulitzer Prize-winning* The Founding of New England *(1922)
until his death. In the skeptical roaring twenties and turbulent thirties, he
touched a responsive chord among Americans who preferred their history
straight.*

# THE MARCH OF
# DEMOCRACY

## by James Truslow Adams

The period . . . from 1634 to 1690, was notable for the gradual evolution of a colonial system out of the scattered beginnings made at haphazard
by the commercial ambitions of a few groups of capitalists or needy
courtiers, partly assisted in the process of colonization by the religious hopes
or fears of particular groups. The evolution proceeded in two directions—
first, the actual peopling of the American coast and the Caribbean islands in
a vast semicircle extending from Maine to Barbadoes, and, secondly, in the
attempt to develop in England a theory of imperial needs, obligations, and
government. We shall speak of the second point later, and with regard to
the first our attention must be almost wholly directed to the continental half
of the semicircle. We may note, however,—to get the proper perspective
from the imperial point of view,—that in addition to the greater importance
of her natural products, the island of Barbadoes alone in 1642 had a larger
English population than all the New England colonies combined.

The New England population, however, had increased rapidly from the
Puritan settlement until about 1640, when the prospects for Puritans in
England altered completely, and for the better, with the Puritan revolution
there. After that, the stream of emigration to New England dried up almost
completely for well on to two centuries. Within eight years after the arrival

of Winthrop the number of settlers in the section had increased to perhaps seventeen thousand, and besides the colonies of Plymouth and Massachusetts four new ones had been founded—Rhode Island and Connecticut in 1636, New Haven in 1638, while there had been settlements in New Hampshire since 1622, and a number in Maine. The date of "founding" of many of the colonies is somewhat vague, for in many of them there were occasional stray single settlers or even small groups who had squatted on lands or more lawfully preceded larger bodies sent out after legal possession had been secured by charter or otherwise. There is no advantage in waxing too hot over what is often a verbal quibble. The settlement of a solitary, like the interesting Blackstone, for example, removing to live to Rhode Island, can scarcely be called the founding of a new colony, the term being better applied to the establishment of a permanent and fairly strong body of citizens with established forms of local government.

We may note that the establishment of New Hampshire, Rhode Island, and Connecticut was owing in each case to the opposition aroused in the minds of many by the narrow and tyrannical ruling Puritan oligarchy in control of Massachusetts. Just as the leaders of that colony had fled or been forced from England, so now many were fleeing or being forced from their colony in the new world to seek for greater liberty, as well as for new and well-located lands. As we have pointed out, resistance to intellectual or religious authority and insistence upon private judgment do not, unfortunately, necessarily result in tolerance. Indeed, the exaggerated importance given to his own views by the protesting individual seems rather to be likely to result in an aggressive *in*tolerance.

Moreover, there is no intolerance more overbearing than that springing from the belief by persons of rather narrow experience in their own superior morality or brand of religious truth. The local Massachusetts leaders had been people of no importance whatever in England when they suddenly found themselves ruling a commonwealth. They had also taken heavy risks to find a place where they not only could worship as they chose but could raise themselves in the social and economic scales. Having found it, they had no intention of allowing affairs to slip from their grasp. This was all quite human but militated strongly in some ways against the best interests of Massachusetts.

For many generations there were to be two strands in the history of that commonwealth,—resistance by the colony as a whole to any encroachments by England, and resistance by the more liberal elements among the colonists themselves to the ruling oligarchy, who believed not that the people should rule but that they should be ruled by the specially elect of God.

For a while, the leaders refused to allow the people even to see the charter, and carried matters with a high hand. In 1631 the men of Watertown protested against paying a tax levied on them, claiming that only the freemen could tax themselves. It was in that year the oligarchy ruled that only church members could be freemen. In 1634 two representatives elected from each town were finally granted a sight of the charter, when they found that they had been deprived of the rights under it. It was then decided, after a mild uprising against Winthrop and the other leaders, that the General Court, made up of delegates from the towns, should meet four times a year, and that it alone should have the power to pass laws, elect and remove officials, lay taxes, and grant lands.

Almost from the beginning, the Congregational form of church had been adopted in Massachusetts. By this system each church was independent of all others, chose its own pastor, and was composed of only such persons as could satisfy the rest of the congregation of their regenerate state. They were bound together by a covenant, and this church group and the political organization of the town became the two cells from which the New England social organism was built up. Adding the village or town school, soon introduced, the three ideas are to be found throughout our history wherever New England influence has penetrated. The tendency of all three was profoundly democratic, but this in no way altered the attempt of the leaders, such as even Winthrop and Cotton, who were opposed to democracy, to prevent its application to civil government.

Many complaints had been made in London about affairs in the colony when its peace in America was disturbed in 1635 by the ideas of Roger Williams. Williams had a gentle and winning personality, and soon fell foul of the bigotry of the Massachusetts lay and clerical leaders. Unfortunately besides preaching religious toleration he added certain dangerous doctrines, claiming, for example, that title to American soil was vested in the Indians and not in the King. After a trial, in which both religious and political motives bore their part, he was sentenced by the Massachusetts authorities to be banished the following spring. Escaping from home in midwinter, after having heard he was to be shipped to England, he made his way through the snows and bitter cold of a New England January to Narragansett Bay where he founded the new colony of Rhode Island, for which he obtained a charter in 1644.

Meanwhile others wished, voluntarily, to emigrate from Massachusetts, and the beautiful valley of the Connecticut attracted some of these. In 1635 a law was enacted that no one could leave Massachusetts without consent of the authorities, but it was finally decreed that the Rev. Thomas Hooker and a band of settlers might go. By the end of the following year there were probably 800 people at Hartford and neighboring places, and thus our endless western migration from the "settled East" had begun.

The government of Massachusetts, as we have said, as much as the rich Connecticut meadows, was probably the cause of the exodus. When the form of government of the new settlements was under consideration in 1638, the settlers having no charter, Hooker preached his famous sermon, arguing for fixed laws and popular control of the government and magistrates. Those who have the power to elect, he claimed, have the power to control, and "the foundation of authority is laid, firstly, in the free consent of the people." When the "Fundamental Orders" were accepted as the basis of government, they contained no reference to the King, and, probably as a reaction against conditions in Massachusetts, provided that the governor should not be eligible for re-election and that there should be no religious qualification for the franchise.

In the same year, 1638, in which Hooker was preaching his liberalism at Hartford, New Hampshire received its most important early accession to population in a group of refugees from Massachusetts. This emigration was consequent upon the trial of Ann Hutchinson, followed by her banishment, and the fining or disenfranchisement of many of her followers. Just when this affair was at its height an important body of intending settlers arrived in Boston from England headed by the Reverend John Davenport and several wealthy laymen. Resisting entreaties to remain in Massachusetts, they decided on New Haven as the site for their rather rigid democracy, and settled there in 1638. Like Hooker and his followers, they had no charter, but unlike them they entered into a reactionary covenant, making church membership essential for freedom and entrusting all government to an elected body and governor who for many years were restricted in authority only by the laws of Moses. For various reasons, the colony, although it grew, never prospered, and in 1661 was absorbed by Connecticut.

### NEW ENGLAND MAKES PROGRESS

New England was thus rapidly expanding, and it was able to do so in comparative safety as a result of the terrible Pequot War in 1637. It was the story of white aggression and racial hatred which was unhappily to be repeated on almost all of our frontiers for two and a half centuries. The chief incident of this first New England war was the surprise by the Puritans, under the lead of Captain John Mason, of the main village of the savages. In the dark, with a strong wind blowing, the two entrances to the stockade were guarded to prevent any escape, and then a torch was applied. Five hundred Indian men, women, and children were burned to death, the Puritan leader merely remarking that by the Providence of God there were 150 more than usual at home that awful night.

The fear of a general Indian uprising in 1642 led to a league among the four colonies of Massachusetts, Plymouth, New Haven, and Connecticut. Under the name of the New England Confederation, this league functioned rather feebly for forty years, and was of slight importance. Its chief significance is in showing how easily these colonies, which were beginning to plant themselves without charters or thought of King or Parliament, were slipping toward a belief in entire political independence in managing all their own affairs.

A step toward intellectual independence also was taken by Massachusetts in 1636 when Harvard College was established to train up a godly ministry. Much used to be made of this event, but when we contrast the courses of study and the scholarship produced in our first "college" with what the Spaniards had achieved long before at such universities as those in Mexico City or Lima, perhaps a more modest estimate of this event in our educational history may be preferable. It tended, moreover, to increase the provincialism of New England by encouraging it to keep students at home for an inferior training instead of sending them, as the other colonies later did, to enjoy the better opportunities in the universities of Europe.

By the mid-century, Massachusetts was hardening into the most cruel and narrow period of its long, and in many ways glorious, history. Winthrop died in 1649, and Cotton in 1652. Such mild restraining influences as there had been of gentleness, charity, and toleration appear for a while to have lost their power. Civil and ecclesiastical control passed to men of the type of Endicott. New England may well be proud of four such founders of her States as Bradford, Winthrop, Williams, and Hooker, but by 1657 only Williams remained, and his colony of Rhode Island was alone to play a noble part in refraining from the persecutions of the Quakers which blotted New England history between 1656 and 1663.

In the earlier of these years, a few weeks after the Massachusetts government had hung Ann Hibbens as a witch, two Quaker women, from England by way of Barbadoes, arrived in Boston. At once persecution began, and as others came it was increased in severity. The penalties, which included besides the selling of Quaker children into slavery in the West Indies, the imprisonment, beating, and torturing of their elders, culminated in the hanging of three men and one woman. At the request of Massachusetts all the other New England colonies, with the exception of Rhode Island, passed severe laws against the sect, though none tortured or killed them as did the leading Puritan State, then largely under the influence of Endicott and the Reverend John Norton.

Williams replied to the request of Massachusetts (though his colony was threatened with dangerous reprisals if it did not comply), that the Rhode Islanders had no laws against any one declaring by words only their religious beliefs, whatever they might be, and that although he conceived the doctrines of the Quakers tended to the subversion of civil government, nevertheless it would be found always that if Quakers were allowed to preach in peace and were not persecuted, they would gain fewer adherents by their sayings than they would by suffering martyrdom. The General Assembly of Rhode Island added that the colony prized freedom of conscience "as the greatest happiness that men can possess in this world."

In the forty years since the passengers of the *Mayflower* had unexpectedly been landed on the shores of Massachusetts instead of Virginia, New England must have seemed to its old inhabitants to have made astounding progress. In spite of the terrible conflict with the savages yet in store,— King Philip's War of 1676,—the older settlements were now as safe as shire towns in England, though the frontier, that ever present factor in American life, was open and liable to sudden attack and massacre. It would be a mistake to think even of Massachusetts as a land only of dour countenances, and hangings of witches or Quakers. Our first woman poet, Anne Bradstreet, had penned her love verses there, students ragged each other at Harvard, children played around school doors. Literature had begun in New England, and though much of it is musty theology that no one reads today, Bradford and Winthrop had written valuable histories, and Williams in Rhode Island and Hooker in Connecticut had wrought out the ideals of the rule of the people, and of intellectual toleration.

The ordinary citizen, living on his farm, owned in fee simple, untroubled by any relics of feudalism, untaxed save by himself, saying his say to all the world in town-meeting, had gained a new self-reliance. Wrestling with his soul and plough on week days, and the innumerable points of the minister's sermon on Sundays and Meeting days, he was coming to be a tough nut for any imperial system to crack. All were not farmers, though most were, and a merchant class of larger or smaller traders was springing up in seaports and in villages along navigable rivers, carrying on a commerce with the mother country, the Wine Islands, Africa for slaves, the West Indies, and their own fellow continental colonists to the south. For part of the century, however, between the English of New England and those of Maryland and Virginia lay colonies of Dutch and Swedes.

### THE DUTCH AND THE QUAKERS

From 1610, the year following Hudson's discovery of the river named for him, Dutch traders had frequented its mouth to traffic with the Indians, and in 1614 had founded a fort and small trading post on the site of what is now Albany. In 1623 the Dutch West India Company, a trading company such as we have become familiar with, planted a small settlement on Manhattan Island, where a few huts had been built some years before. The Dutch claim to New Netherland, with its principal town of New Amsterdam, was more or less indeterminate but included New York and Long Island, New Jersey, and Delaware. Of course it was not recognized by the English.

The Dutch were in fact rather late claimants, though their brief history in America was picturesque enough, and many prominent New York families like to trace their ancestry back to them. Their stay was a troubled one for they were in almost constant dispute not only with the advancing New Englanders in Connecticut and eastern Long Island, and the Virginians in Delaware, but also with colonies of Swedes which had been planted at Wilmington and surrounding points. The latter were finally conquered by the Dutch in 1655, but nine years later an English fleet arrived at the mouth of the Hudson and forced the Dutch governor, the redoubtable Peter Stuyvesant, to surrender. In honor of the Duke of York, the King's brother, to whom the territory had been granted, the colony and town were renamed New York, and the Dutch sway within the present United States came to an end. The two favorites to whom the Duke of York granted the land between New York and Delaware Bay founded East and West, now New, Jersey, the two colonies soon coming largely under the control of the Quakers, Berkeley, who had received West Jersey, selling out his rights to them almost immediately.

The Dutch had not believed in self-government by their colonists, and the history of New Amsterdam had been turbulent. The small town early acquired its modern cosmopolitan aspect, and it is said that eighteen languages were spoken on its streets in the Dutch period. Except for a few words adopted into our language, some social customs locally, and many romantic legends, the Dutch influence, however, has been almost negligible in the development of our institutions and culture in spite of much written to the contrary.

Charles II, who had returned to the English throne in 1660, after the Cromwellian interregnum, was only too willing to use the vast lands of America as grants to noblemen for his own or their benefit, and just as he granted the Dutch territories to his brother, so he also granted to a group of eight nobles the lands south of Virginia which are now included in North and South Carolina. Colonization was rather slow, but Charleston was settled in 1670, and grew fairly rapidly, a large accession of French Huguenots arriving ten years later. Rice growing, which was introduced in 1693, resulted in a great increase in slavery, rapid fortunes, and a basis of wealth and leisure which was to make South Carolina, within a few generations, perhaps the leading American colony in aesthetic culture and social charm.

The last colony founded in the period of this chapter was Pennsylvania, a charter for which was granted to the Quaker William Penn in 1681. Planting his chief town of Philadelphia on the bank of the Delaware, he expressed the wish that each house should always be surrounded by a garden so that the city might remain "a green country town," and "always be wholesome," an ideal of city planning which, until too late, we have most unhappily forgotten. Notable also in Pennsylvania under the leadership of Penn, alone among all the colonies, was the benevolent and honorable attitude adopted and maintained toward the Indians. Treaties were not only made, but kept, and the relation of Penn to the savages forms one of the few episodes in the long annals of our treatment of the native which honest Americans would not wish to have blotted out.

Although . . . there was soon to be a large influx of Germans into Pennsylvania, the colony had been founded mainly as a retreat for Quakers, and thus one more sect found refuge among us, adding to the fast growing complexity of our life even in this early period. In the neighboring colony of Maryland, in order to protect the Catholics, a law had been passed in 1649 by the colonial assembly (in which Catholics were in the majority at the time), providing that no person professing to believe in Jesus Christ should in any way be troubled or molested. Maryland and Rhode Island thus led the way toward complete toleration, at least for professing Christians.

Before proceeding to consider the second point of which we spoke at the beginning of this chapter as characterizing the period,—that is, the development in England of a colonial theory and practice,—we may note briefly one or two aspects of American development thus far.

First of all, in the colonies, as contrasted with England itself or with the French and Spanish empires in America, there was the great diversity in both race and religion. Within two generations from the gaining of a permanent foothold by the dominant English, we have already found large groups of Dutch, Germans, Swedes, and Huguenot French coming to make homes here for the purpose either of bettering themselves socially and economically, or to escape from persecution.

## THE NEW COUNTRY BECOMES THE HOPE OF MANY RACES

This diversity was greatly to increase in the future, but at its very inception the United States became both a hope and a refuge for those of many races, and not merely of a single one. There was also the marked variety in religion. Although all the colonies were under English rule, Catholics, Congregationalists, Lutherans, Church of England adherents, Quakers, and others could all find rapidly growing and prosperous communities in which they could make their homes, and be unmolested. The intolerance of individual colonies should not obscure the remarkable religious freedom that had come to exist within a group of colonies of a single European power. It could have been found at that time under neither French nor Spanish rule, but only under English.

Owing chiefly to soil, topography, and climate, there had also come about a rapid but clearly marked differentiation in the social and economic life of the various colonies. In New England all the physical factors in agriculture tended toward small farms which could most profitably be tilled by the head of a family with little help other than that of sons or a hired man. The system of small holdings tended to emphasize that compact type of settlement which naturally developed from the New England form of migration, which was that of a group closely knit together by being members of the church which was their chief concern. The small holding, the church, and the town meeting in New England all militated in that section against a loosely scattered mode of settlement.

New York had been started purely as a trading post. For more than a century, the policy of huge land grants adopted by both Dutch and English rulers; the importance of the fur trade for the only colony which (by the Hudson-Mohawk Valley route) had easy access to the interior of the continent; and the magnificent harbor the colony possessed, were all to determine its character as mainly commercial in a group of colonies that were otherwise dominated by agriculture.

Passing southward to Maryland, Virginia, and the Carolinas, we find agriculture again holding sway. In them the staple and exhausting crop of tobacco (except for rice to the far south) demanded larger landholdings than in New England, and brought about a more scattered way of living, as well, eventually, as a seemingly imperative demand for that black slave labor which was economically unprofitable on the much broken and stony surface of the Puritan colonies. These effects were not all felt in the south during its earlier and economically struggling period, but were to be of great importance after 1700.

Another characteristic of the English colonies as contrasted with those of any other nation at that time was the extraordinary amount of liberty granted to the individual colonist. Looking back from the vantage ground of a different era, we are too apt to think that the colonists were naturally entitled to this, and that in their constant struggles for ever greater liberty they were fighting against a tyrannical government. This was far from the case. As well as we can, we have to judge each age by the ideas dominant in it and not in our own. Neither France, Spain, nor even liberty-loving Holland dreamed of giving their colonists when they left the mother country anything like the freedom which England granted to hers.

Charles II was assuredly no lover of democracy or the liberty of the common man, yet although the charters which he granted for the colonies of New York, the Jerseys, Pennsylvania, and Carolina were of the type known as proprietary, and were based on the model of the Bishopric of Durham, they all contained, like that granted by the first Charles on the same model for Maryland, the clause we have noted, that the proprietor, unlike the Bishop, could make laws only "by and with the consent of the freemen."

All Americans under the proprietary charters were thus given much more liberty in self-government than was enjoyed by their fellows in England in the Durham Bishopric. The circumstances of distance and the inability to be properly represented in Parliament were to raise special and difficult problems for our ancestors in America, as well as for the government in England. Nevertheless, in studying the story of our incessant struggle against the English government, it is only fair to bear in mind that ours were the freeest colonies in the world during all of our colonial period.

Charles II, as we have said, was no lover to a too-great liberty of the subject, and the restoration of the Stuarts in his person in 1660 brought troublous times for the Americans in many colonies. According to the generally accepted theory of that day, which seemed not at all tyrannical but only natural to all statesmen in Europe, colonies existed chiefly for the benefit of the mother country. Following the breakdown of the unified world of the Roman Empire and the long incubation period of the Middle Ages, the modern theory and emotions of nationality were fast emerging.

Politics, religion, and commerce, which had been decentralized, were beginning to be considered as essentially clustering around each national State for its own inhabitants. According to the economic theory of the time, real wealth was believed to consist in a store of the precious metals. That State was thought to be best off which accumulated the largest store, either by mining or favorable trade balances. Thus developed the "Mercantile Theory,"—by no means dead today,—which demanded that a country should always have a balance in its favor to be settled by imports of gold.

When Europe broke its barriers and the period of overseas empires was inaugurated, the theory of empire was naturally based on this theory of wealth. In order that an empire should owe others as little as possible, each sought to be as nearly self-contained as might be, in both the supplies of its needed raw materials and the markets for its finished products, so as to absorb as much as might be of the profits throughout all the economic scale and be as independent as possible of others. Speaking generally, the colonies, plantations, and trading posts of the British Empire were supposed to supply the raw materials for British manufactures and such other materials, for food or other needs, as could not be produced in the British Isles. Thus, for example, England had its fisheries on the Newfoundland coast, the tobacco and rice colonies of our South, the sugar islands of the West Indies (to which the valuable island of Jamaica had been added in 1655), its fort in Guinea protecting its slave trade, and its settlements in India, Sumatra, Java, and the Celebes for the products of the Far East.

On the other hand, the colonists were supposed to increase the market for British manufactured goods, and to buy these with the money which they received from the sale of their raw materials. The increase of colonial population, beyond what was necessary merely for producing and shipping home the lumber, sugar, tobacco, and other raw materials, was considered of value solely from the standpoint of increasing the number of consumers of British goods.

According to this elaborate scheme, England was to remain the centre of manufactures, banking, and military resources, while the colonists were to confine themselves to the roles of producers of raw materials and consumers of English manufactures. In a world of empires competing for over-sea territories, the duty of protecting colonies against, so to say, being kidnapped by another empire, and also to guard the trade routes, fell to the navies of the home countries in Europe. When in 1650 and 1651, under Cromwell, and in 1660 and 1663, under the returned Stuarts, England passed Navigation Acts placing certain restrictions on the freedom of colonial trade with the outside world, this was not deemed tyranny but only reasonable regulation in exchange for protection and the smooth working of the imperial trade machinery. This theory of empire was not simply English. It was universal at the time, and on the whole England applied it with a far more enlightened and generous spirit than did either France, Spain, or Holland.

This far-flung empire, which had come into existence almost haphazard, and in scarcely more than fifty years when Charles II came to the throne, had no co-ordinated system of government. Especially during the troubled years of the Cromwellian Commonwealth, the American colonies in particular had been left much to themselves, and had got in the habit, even more than usual, of going their own way with little or no thought of the governing power at the center of empire. Massachusetts had even dropped the King's name from its legal writs. The years between the restoration of the Stuarts in 1660 and their fall in 1688 were marked in America by constant efforts to reassert royal authority and increase royal control over the colonists.

Some of the efforts were logical and reasonable in theory but all proved irritating in practice. Many of the royal governors were incompetent or venal, and in 1676 the people of Virginia finally broke into revolt against Governor Berkeley under a leader named Nathaniel Bacon. Tobacco was not only the staple crop of Maryland and Virginia but also served as currency in the absence of coin, and frequent trouble arose from fluctuations in value. Before 1675 there had been for some time much distress in the colony owing to the low prices of what was at once crop and currency. This was due in part to over-production and in part to the fact that the navigation laws cut the settlers off from all markets save those of England, and it was said that the planters were merely the slaves of the English merchants.

In all times of economic maladjustment the poor and weak are the worst sufferers, so there was a good deal of grumbling against the bad government of the colony and the richer classes allied to the governor's set.

Matters finally came to a head when the governor and the tidewater gentry declined to make any move to protect the frontier settlements against serious attacks by the Indians, and the poor people found a leader for armed revolt in Bacon. Although the rebellion collapsed in a few months with Bacon's death from fever, it was not unsuccessful. The King recalled Berkeley in disgrace, appointed one of the "rebels" governor, and remedied some of the grievances. The uprising has a special interest as indicative of the many minor cleavages beginning to appear between rich and poor, old settlement and frontier, in the several colonies.

New England never fitted into the scheme of empire based on the Mercantile Theory. With the exception of some timber she produced no raw material needed by England. Her fishing fleets competed with those of the home country. Having no staple crop and always driven to find means of paying for her imports from the mother country, she tended to encroach on English manufacturing to supply her own needs, and to trade not only with the West Indies within the empire but illegally with islands and countries outside it. Many complaints reached the King that the New Englanders were disobeying the laws of trade, that they were persecuting the Quakers and others, and that they were beginning to consider themselves as practically independent. These charges were mainly true.

At first it had seemed as though Charles II might prove liberal. In 1660 he had despatched a special messenger to Massachusetts to restrain that colony from further persecution, and the next year he granted charters to both Rhode Island and Connecticut which were so satisfactory to the people that they continued to be used as State constitutions until well into the nineteenth century. In 1676, however, he sent as Collector of Customs at the port of Boston and special investigator to Massachusetts a certain Edward Randolph to report on conditions. From the standpoint of efficient imperial administration, these were bad enough but Randolph was also almost insanely prejudiced against the colonies, particularly the Puritan ones, and his reports for many years painted the colonists in the blackest colors to the home authorities. By 1684 he had succeeded in having the Massachusetts charter forfeited in England and the commonwealth transformed into a royal colony. Writs were also issued against the charters of Connecticut, Rhode Island, the Jerseys, and Delaware. Pennsylvania narrowly escaped, but although Stuart rule was nearing its end and these cases were never determined against the colonies, another scheme was put into execution.

❧ ☙

ROYAL *policy helped foster self-government but it is doubtful whether an alternate policy would have worked. The far-flung settlements, remote from the metropolis, could rarely wait for decisions from home. Distance alone served to erode the pretensions to authority of the crown. The "democratical" spirit that visitors to the colonies commented on drew its strength in no small measure from the self-confidence bred by the colonist's successful confrontation with a hostile environment. The world of Europe rarely had solutions for the problems of the New World; the American, as the colonial was coming to describe himself, viewed with increasing impatience the effort of royal authority to decree law from afar. The makings of a rift existed but a larger necessity compelled temporary accommodation. For on all sides, the English colonies were surrounded by enemies. The certainty of British protection against external attack proved to be the glue of empire; once the danger was gone, the empire would come apart.*

*No si le enemy provoked greater fear than France whose empire stretche from the St. Lawrence into the Mississippi Valley. They and their Indian lies constantly harassed outlying English settlements, creating even in the bsence of formal war a condition of constant guerrilla warfare. The monumental struggle for a continent between the British and the French provided a theme for Francis Parkman (1823-1893). His evocation of this century-long war was made particularly graphic by his intimate knowledge of the land upon which the events occurred. The complex enigmatic Parkman saw history as literature. The colorful touch, the telling phrase, the description that evoked a sense of being on the scene, were part of the magic of Parkman. But there was something else: a total submersion in the documents and the scene of the history of which he wrote. His objective was a simple determination to recapture the past. The measure of Parkman's success is perhaps best defined by the simple statement that if his history were to die, it would continue to live as literature.*

# FRANCE AND ENGLAND IN NORTH AMERICA

## by Francis Parkman

About midwinter the governor of Canada sent another large war-party against the New England border. The object of attack was an unoffending hamlet, that from its position could never be a menace to the French, and the destruction of which could profit them nothing. The aim of the enterprise was not military, but political. "I have sent no war-party towards Albany," writes Vaudreuil, "because we must do nothing that might cause a rupture between us and the Iroquois; but we must keep things astir in the direction of Boston, or else the Abenakis will declare for the English." In short, the object was fully to commit these savages to hostility against New England, and convince them at the same time that the French would back their quarrel.

The party consisted, according to French accounts, of fifty Canadians and 200 Abenakis and Caughnawagas,—the latter of whom, while trading constantly with Albany, were rarely averse to a raid against Massachusetts or New Hampshire. The command was given to the younger Hertel de Rouville, who was accompanied by four of his brothers. They began their march in the depth of winter, journeyed nearly 300 miles on snow-shoes through the forest, and approached their destination on the afternoon of 28 February 1704. It was the village of Deerfield, which then formed the extreme northwestern frontier of Massachusetts,—its feeble neighbor, the infant settlement of Northfield, a little higher up the Connecticut, having been abandoned during the last war. Rouville halted his followers at a place now called Petty's Plain, two miles from the village; and here, under the shelter of a pine forest, they all lay hidden, shivering with cold;—for they dared not makes fires,—and hungry as wolves, for their provisions were spent. Though their numbers, by the lowest account, were nearly equal to the whole population of Deerfield,—men, women, and children,—they had no thought of an open attack, but trusted to darkness and surprise for an easy victory.

Deerfield stood on a plateau above the river meadows, and the houses—forty-one in all—were chiefly along the road towards the villages of Hadley and Hartfield, a few miles distant. In the middle of the place, on a rising ground called Meeting House Hill, was a small square wooden meeting house. This, with about fifteen private houses, besides barns and sheds, was enclosed by a fence of palisades eight feet high, flanked by "mounts" or blockhouses, at two or more of the corners. The four sides of this palisaded enclosure, which was called the fort, measured in all no less than 202 rods, and within it lived some of the principal inhabitants of the village, of which it formed the centre or citadel. Chief among its inmates was John Williams, the minister, a man of character and education, who, after graduating at Harvard, had come to Deerfield when it was still suffering under the ruinous effects of King Philip's War, and entered on his ministry with a salary of sixty pounds in depreciated New England currency, payable, not in money, but in wheat, Indian-corn, and pork. His parishioners built him a house, he married, and had now eight children, one of whom was absent with friends at Hadley. His next neighbor was Benoni Stebbins, sergeant in the county militia, who lived a few rods from the meeting house. About fifty yards distant, and near the northwest angle of the enclosure, stood the house of Ensign John Sheldon, a framed building, one of the largest in the village, and, like that of Stebbins, made bullet-proof by a layer of bricks between the outer and inner sheathing, while its small windows and its projecting upper story also helped to make it defensible.

The space enclosed by the palisade, though much too large for effective defence, served in time of alarm as an asylum for the inhabitants outside, whose houses were scattered,—some on the north towards the hidden enemy, and some on the south towards Hadley and Hatfield. Among those on the south side was that of the militia captain, Jonathan Wells, which had a palisade of its own, and, like the so-called fort, served as an asylum for the neighbors.

These private fortified houses were sometimes built by the owners alone, though more often they were the joint work of the owners and of the inhabitants, to whose safety they contributed. The palisade fence that enclosed the central part of the village was made under a vote of the town, each inhabitant being required to do his share; and as they were greatly impoverished by the last war, the General Court of the province remitted for a time a part of their taxes in consideration of a work which aided the general defence.

Down to the Peace of Ryswick the neighborhood had been constantly infested by scalping parties, and once the village had been attacked by a considerable force of French and Indians, who were beaten off. Of late there had been warnings of fresh disturbances. Lord Cornbury, governor of New York, wrote that he had heard through spies that Deerfield was again to be attacked, and a message to the same effect came from Peter Schuyler, who had received intimations of the danger from Mohawks lately on a visit to their Caughnawaga relatives. During the autumn the alarm was so great that the people took refuge within the palisades, and the houses of the enclosure were crowded with them; but the panic had now subsided, and many, though not all, had returned to their homes. They were reassured by the presence of twenty volunteers from the villages below, whom, on application from the minister, Williams, the General Court had sent as a garrison to Deerfield, where they were lodged in the houses of the villagers. On the night when Hertel de Rouville and his band lay hidden among the pines there were in all the settlement a little less than 300 souls, of whom 268 were inhabitants, twenty were yeomen soldiers of the garrison, two were visitors from Hatfield, and three were Negro slaves. They were of all ages,—from the Widow Allison, in her eighty-fifth year, to the infant son of Deacon French, aged four weeks.

Heavy snows had lately fallen and buried the clearings, the meadow, and the frozen river to the depth of full three feet. On the northwestern side the drifts were piled nearly to the top of the palisade fence, so that it was no longer an obstruction to an active enemy.

As the afternoon waned, the sights and sounds of the little border hamlet were, no doubt, like those of any other rustic New England village at the end of a winter day,—an ox sledge creaking on the frosty snow as it brought in the last load of firewood, boys in homespun snow-balling one another in the village street, farmers feeding their horses and cattle in the barns, a matron drawing a pail of water with the help of one of those long well-sweeps still used in some remote districts, or a girl bringing a pail of milk from the cow-shed. In the houses, where one room served as kitchen, dining-room, and parlor, the housewife cooked the evening meal, children sat at their bowls of mush and milk, and the men of the family, their day's work over, gathered about the fire, while perhaps some village coquette sat in the corner busy at the spinning-wheel, and ears intent on the stammered wooings of her rustic lover. Deerfield kept early hours, and it is likely that by nine o'clock all were in their beds. There was a patrol inside the palisade, but there was little discipline among these extemporized soldiers; the watchers grew careless as the frosty night went on; and it is said, towards morning they, like the villagers, betook themselves to their beds.

Rouville and his men, savage with hunger, lay shivering under the pines till about two hours before dawn; then, leaving their packs and their snow-shoes behind, they moved cautiously towards their prey. There was a crust on the snow strong enough to bear their weight, though not to prevent a rustling noise as it crunched under the feet of so many men. It is said that from time to time Rouville commanded a halt, in order that the sentinels, if such there were, might mistake the distant sound for rising and falling gusts of wind. In any case, no alarm was given till they had mounted the palisade and dropped silently into the unconscious village. Then with one accord they screeched the war-whoop, and assailed the doors of the houses with axes and hatchets.

The hideous din startled the minister, Williams, from his sleep. Half-wakened, he sprang out of bed, and saw dimly a crowd of savages bursting through the shattered door. He shouted to two soldiers who were lodged in the house; and then, with more valor than discretion, snatched a pistol that hung at the head of the bed, cocked it, and snapped it at the breast of the foremost Indian, who proved to be a Caughnawaga chief. It missed fire, or Williams would, no doubt, have been killed on the spot. Amid the screams of his terrified children, three of the party seized him and bound him fast; for they came well prepared with cords, since prisoners had a market value. Nevertheless, in the first fury of their attack they dragged to the door and murdered two of the children and a Negro woman called Parthena, who was probably their nurse. In an upper room lodged a young man named Stoddard, who had time to snatch a cloak, throw himself out of the window, climb the palisade, and escape in the darkness. Half-naked as he was, he made his way over the snow to Hatfield, binding his bare feet with strips torn from the cloak.

They kept Williams shivering in his shirt for an hour while a frightful uproar of yells, shrieks, and gunshots sounded from without. At length they permitted him, his wife, and five remaining children to dress themselves. Meanwhile the Indians and their allies burst into most of the houses, killed such of the men as resisted, butchered some of the women and children, and seized and bound the rest. Some of the villagers escaped in the confusion, like Stoddard, and either fled half dead with cold towards Hatfield, or sought refuge in the fortified house of Jonathan Wells.

The house of Stebbins, the minister's next neighbor, had not been attacked as soon as the rest, and the inmates had a little time for preparation. They consisted of Stebbins himself, with his wife and five children, David Hoyt, Joseph Catlin, Benjamin Church, a namesake of the old Indian fighter of Philip's War, and three other men,—probably refugees who had brought their wives and families within the palisaded enclosure for safety. Thus the house contained seven men, four or five women, and a considerable number of children. Though the walls were bullet-proof, it was not built for defence. The men, however, were well supplied with guns, powder, and lead, and they seem to have found some means of barricading the windows. When the enemy tried to break in, they drove them back with loss. On this, the French and Indians gathered in great numbers before the house, showered bullets upon it, and tried to set it on fire. They were again repulsed, with the loss of several killed and wounded; among the former a Caughnawaga Chief; and among the latter a French officer. Still the firing continued. If the assailants had made a resolute assault, the defenders must have been overpowered; but to risk lives in open attack was contrary to every maxim of forest warfare. The women in the house behaved with great courage, and moulded bullets, which the men shot at the enemy. Stebbins was killed outright, and Church was wounded, as was also the wife of David Hoyt. At length most of the French and Indians, disgusted with the obstinacy of the defence, turned their attention to other quarters; though some kept up their fire under cover of the meeting-house and another building within easy range of gunshot.

This building was the house of Ensign John Sheldon, already mentioned. The Indians had had some difficulty in mastering it; for the door being of thick oak plank, studded with nails of wrought iron and well barred, they could not break it open. After a time, however, they hacked a hole in it, through which they fired and killed Mrs. Sheldon as she sat on the edge of a bed in a lower room. Her husband, a man of great resolution, seems to have been absent. Their son John, with Hannah his wife, jumped from an upper chamber window. The young woman sprained her ankle in the fall, and lay helpless, but begged her husband to run to Hatfield for aid, which he did, while she remained a prisoner. The Indians soon got in at a back door, seized Mercy Sheldon, a little girl of two years, and dashed out her brains on the door-stone. Her two brothers and her sister Mary, a girl of sixteen, were captured. The house was used for a short time as a depot for prisoners, and here also was brought the French officer wounded in the attack on the Stebbins house. A family tradition relates that he lay in great torment, he begged for water, and that it was brought to him by one of the prisoners, Mrs. John Catlin, whose husband, son, and grandson had been killed, and who, nevertheless, did all in her power to relieve the sufferings of the wounded man. Probably it was in recognition of this charity that when the other prisoners were led away, Mrs. Catlin was left behind. She died of grief a few weeks later.

The sun was scarcely an hour high when the miserable drove of captives was conducted across the river to the foot of a mountain or high hill.

Williams and his family were soon compelled to follow, and his house was set on fire. As they led him off he saw that other houses within the palisade were burning, and that all were in the power of the enemy except that of his neighbor Stebbins, where the gallant defenders still kept their assailants at bay. Having collected all their prisoners, the main body of the French and Indians began to withdraw towards the pine forest, where they had left their packs and snow-shoes, and to prepare for a retreat before the country should be aroused, first murdering in cold blood Marah Carter, a little girl of five years, whom they probably thought unequal to the march. Several parties, however, still lingered in the village, firing on the Stebbins house, killing cattle, hogs, and sheep, and gathering such plunder as the place afforded.

Early in the attack, and while it was yet dark, the light of burning houses, reflected from the fields of snow, had been seen at Hatfield, Hadley, and Northampton. The alarm was sounded through the slumbering hamlets, and parties of men mounted on farm horses, with saddles or without, hastened to the rescue, not doubting that the fires were kindled by Indians. When the sun was about two hours high, between thirty and forty of them were gathered at the fortified house of Jonathan Wells, at the southern end of the village. The houses of this neighborhood were still standing, and seem not to have been attacked,—the stubborn defence of the Stebbins house having apparently prevented the enemy from pushing much beyond the palisaded enclosure. The house of Wells was full of refugee families. A few Deerfield men here joined the horsemen from the lower towns, as did also four or five of the yeoman soldiers who had escaped the fate of most of their comrades. The horsemen left their horses within the Wells fence; he himself took the lead, and the whole party rushed in together at the southern gate of the palisaded enclosure, drove out the plunderers, and retook part of their plunder. The assailants of the Stebbins house, after firing at it for three hours, were put to flight, and those of its male occupants who were still alive joined their countrymen, while the women and children ran back for harborage to the house of Wells.

Wells and his men, now upwards of fifty, drove the flying enemy more than a mile across the river meadows, and ran in headlong pursuit over the crusted snow, killing a considerable number. In the eagerness of the chase many threw off their overcoats, and even their jackets. Wells saw the danger, and vainly called on them to stop. Their blood was up, and most of them were young and inexperienced.

Meanwhile the firing at the village had been heard by Rouville's main body, who had already begun their retreat northward. They turned back to support their comrades, and hid themselves under the bank of the river till the pursuers drew near, when they gave them a close volley and rushed upon them with the war-whoop. Some of the English were shot down, and the rest driven back. There was no panic. "We retreated," says Wells, "facing about and firing." When they reached the palisade they made a final stand, covering by their fire such of their comrades as had fallen within range of musket-shot, and thus saving them from the scalping-knife. The French did not try to dislodge them. Nine of them had been killed, several were wounded, and one was captured.

The number of English carried off prisoners was 111, and the number killed was according to one list forty-seven, and according to another fifty-three, the latter including some who were smothered in the cellars of their burning houses. The names, and in most cases the ages, of both captives and slain are preserved. Those who escaped with life and freedom were, by the best account, 137. An official tabular statement, drawn up on the spot, sets the number of houses burned at seventeen. The house of the town clerk, Thomas French, escaped, as before mentioned, and the town records, with other papers in his charge, were saved. The meeting-house also was left standing. The house of Sheldon was hastily set on fire by the French and Indians when their rear was driven out of the village by Wells and his men; but the fire was extinguished, and "the Old Indian House," as it was called, stood till the year 1849. Its door, deeply scarred with hatchets, and with a hole cut near the middle, is still preserved in the Memorial Hall at Deerfield.

Vaudreuil wrote to the minister, Ponchartrain, that the French lost two or three killed, and twenty or twenty-one wounded, Rouville himself being among the latter. This cannot include the Indians, since there is proof that the enemy left behind a considerable number of their dead. Wherever resistance was possible, it had been of the most prompt and determined character.

Long before noon the French and Indians were on their northward march with their train of captives. More armed men came up from the settlements below, and by midnight about eighty were gathered at the ruined village. Couriers had been set to rouse the country, and before evening of the next day (the first of March) the force at Deerfield was increased to two hundred and fifty; but a thaw and a warm rain had set in, and as few of the men had snow-shoes, pursuit was out of the question. Even could the agile savages and their allies have been overtaken, the probable consequence would have been the murdering of the captives to prevent their escape.

In spite of the foul blow dealt upon it, Deerfield was not abandoned. Such of its men as were left were taken as soldiers into the pay of the province, while the women and children were sent to the villages below. A small garrison was also stationed at the spot, under command of Captain Jonathan Wells, and thus the village held its ground till the storm of war should pass over.

We have seen that the minister, Williams, with his wife and family, were led from their burning house across the river to the foot of the mountain, where the crowd of terrified and disconsolate captives—friends, neighbors, and relatives—were already gathered. Here they presently saw the fight in the meadow, and were told that if their countrymen attempted a rescue, they should all be put to death. "After this," writes Williams, "we went up the mountain, and saw the smoke of the fires in town, and beheld the awful desolation of Deerfield; and before we marched any farther they killed a sucking child of the English."

The French and Indians marched that afternoon only four or five miles,— to Greenfield meadows,—where they stopped to encamp, dug away the snow, laid spruce-boughs on the ground for beds, and bound fast such of the prisoners as seemed able to escape. The Indians then held a carousal on some liquor they had found in the village, and in their drunken rage murdered a Negro man belonging to Williams. In spite of their precautions, Joseph Alexander, one of the prisoners, escaped during the night, at which they were greatly incensed; and Rouville ordered Williams to tell his companions in misfortune that if any more of them ran off, the rest should be burned alive.

The prisoners were the property of those who had taken them. Williams had two masters, one of the three who had seized him having been shot in the attack on the house of Stebbins. His principal owner was a surly fellow who would not let him speak to the other prisoners; but as he was presently chosen to guard the rear, the minister was left in the hands of his other master, who allowed him to walk beside his wife and help her on the way. Having borne a child a few weeks before, she was in no condition for such a march, and felt that her hour was near. Williams speaks of her in the strongest terms of affection. She made no complaint, and accepted her fate with resignation. "We discoursed," he says, "of the happiness of those who had God for a father and friend, as also that it was our reasonable duty quietly to submit to his will." Her thoughts were for her remaining children, whom she commended to her husband's care. Their intercourse was short. The Indian who had gone to the rear of the train soon returned, separated them, ordered Williams to the front "and so made me take a last farewell of my dear wife, the desire of my eyes and companion in many mercies and afflictions." They came soon after to Green River, a stream then about knee-deep, and so swift that the water had not frozen. After wading it with difficulty, they climbed a snow-covered hill beyond. The minister, with strength almost spent, was permitted to rest a few moments at the top, and as the other prisoners passed by in turn, he questioned each for news of his wife. He was not left long in suspense. She had fallen from weakness in fording the stream, but gained her feet again, and drenched in the icy current, struggled to the farther bank, when the savage who owned her, finding that she could not climb the hill, killed her with one stroke of his hatchet. Her body was left on the snow till a few of her townsmen, who had followed the trail, found it a day or two after, carried it back to Deerfield, and buried it in the churchyard.

On the next day the Indians killed an infant and a little girl of eleven years; on the day following, Friday, they tomahawked a woman, and on Saturday four others. This apparent cruelty was in fact a kind of mercy. The victims could not keep up with the party, and the death-blow saved them from a lonely and lingering death from cold and starvation. Some of the children, when spent with the march, were carried on the backs of their owners,—partly, perhaps, through kindness, and partly because every child had its price.

On the fourth day of the march they came to the mouth of West River, which enters the Connecticut a little above the present town of Brattleboro. Some of the Indians were discontented with the distribution of the captives, alleging that others had got more than their share, on which the whole troop were mustered together, and some changes of ownership were agreed upon. At this place dog-trains and sledges had been left, and these served to carry their wounded, as well as some of the captive children. Williams was stripped of the better part of his clothes, and others given to him instead, so full of vermin that they were a torment to him through all the journey. The march now continued with pitiless speed up the frozen Connecticut, where the recent thaw had covered the ice with slush and water ankle-deep.

On Sunday they made a halt, and the minister was permitted to preach a sermon from the text, "Hear, all people, and behold my sorrow: my virgins and my young men are gone into captivity." Then amid the ice, the snow, the forest, and the savages, his forlorn flock joined their voices in a psalm. On Monday guns were heard from the rear, and the Indians and their allies, in great alarm, bound their prisoners fast, and prepared for battle. It proved, however, that the guns had been fired at wild geese by some of their own number; on which they recovered their spirits, fired a volley for joy, and boasted that the English could not overtake them. More women fainted by the way and died under the hatchet,—some with pious resignation, some with despairing apathy, some with a desperate joy.

Two hundred miles of wilderness still lay between them and the Canadian settlements. It was a waste without a house or even a wigwam, except here and there the bark shed of some savage hunter. At the mouth of White River, the party divided into small bands,—no doubt in order to subsist by hunting, for provisions were fast failing. The Williams family were separated. Stephen was carried up the Connecticut; Samuel and Eunice, with two younger children, were carried off in various directions; while the wretched father, along with two small children of one of his parishioners, was compelled to follow his Indian masters up the valley of White River. One of the children—a little girl—was killed on the next morning by her Caughnawaga owner who was unable to carry her. On the next Sunday the minister was left in camp with one Indian and the surviving child,—a boy of nine,—while the rest of the party were hunting. "My spirit," he says, "was almost overwhelmed within me." But he found comfort in the text, "Leave thy fatherless children, I will preserve them alive." Nor was his hope deceived. His youngest surviving child,—a boy of four,—though harshly treated by his owners, was carried on their shoulders or dragged on a sledge to the end of the journey. His youngest daughter—seven years old—was treated with great kindness throughout. Samuel and Eunice suffered much from hunger, but were dragged on sledges when too faint to walk. Stephen nearly starved to death; but after eight months in the forest, he safely reached Chambly with his Indian masters.

Of the whole band of captives, only about half ever again saw friends and home. Seventeen broke down on the way and were killed; while David Hoyt and Jacob Hix died of starvation at Coos Meadows, on the upper Connecticut. During the entire march, no woman seems to have been subjected to violence; and this holds true, with rare exceptions, in all the Indian wars of New England. This remarkable forbearance towards female prisoners, so different from the practice of many western tribes, was probably due to a form of superstition, aided perhaps by the influence of the missionaries. It is to be observed, however, that the heathen savages of King Philip's War, who had never seen a Jesuit, were no less forbearing in this respect.

The hunters of Williams's party killed five moose, the flesh of which, smoked and dried, was carried on their backs and that of the prisoner whom they provided with snow-shoes. Thus burdened, the minister toiled on, following his masters along the frozen current of White River till, crossing the snowy backs of Green Mountains, they struck the headwaters of the stream then called French River, now the Winooski, or Onion. Being in great fear of a thaw, they pushed on with double speed. Williams was not used to snow-shoes, and they gave him those painful cramps of the legs and ankles called in Canada *mal à la raquette*. One morning at dawn he was waked by his chief master and ordered to get up, say his prayers, and eat his breakfast, for they must make a long march that day. The minister was in despair. "After prayers," he says, "I arose from my knees; but my feet were so tender, swollen, bruised and full of pain that I could scarce stand upon them without holding on the wigwam. And when the Indians said, "You must run today," I answered I could not run. My master, pointing to his hatchet, said to me, "Then I must dash out your brains and take your scalp." The Indian proved better than his word, and Williams was suffered to struggle on as he could. "God wonderfully supported me," he writes, "and my strength was restored and renewed to admiration." He thinks that he walked that day forty miles on the snow. Following the Winooski to its mouth, the party reached Lake Champlain a little north of the present city of Burlington. Here the swollen feet of the prisoner were tortured by rough ice, till snow began to fall and cover it with a soft carpet. Bending under his load, and powdered by the falling flakes, he toiled on till, at noon of Saturday, lean, tired and ragged, he and his masters reached the French outpost of Chambly, twelve or fifteen miles from Montreal.

Here the unhappy wayfarer was treated with great kindness both by the officers of the fort and by the inhabitants, one of the chief among whom lodged him in his house and welcomed him to his table. After a short stay at Chambly, Williams and his masters set out in a canoe for Sorel. On the way a Frenchwoman came down to the bank of the river and invited the party to her house, telling the minister that she herself had once been a prisoner among the Indians, and knew how to feel for him. She seated him at a table, spread a table-cloth, and placed food before him, while the Indians to their great indignation, were supplied with a meal in the chimney corner. Similar kindness was shown by the inhabitants along the way till the party reached their destination, the Abenaki village of St. Francis, to which his masters belonged. Here there was a fort, in which lived two

Jesuits, directors of the mission, and here Williams found several English children, captured the summer before during the raid on the settlements of Maine, and already transformed into little Indians both in dress and behavior. At the gate of the fort one of the Jesuits met him, and asked him to go into church and give thanks to God for sparing his life, to which he replied that he would give thanks in some other place. The priest then commanded him to go, which he refused to do. When on the next day the bell rang for mass, one of his Indian masters seized him and dragged him into the church, where he got behind the door, and watched the service from his retreat with extreme disapprobation. One of the Jesuits telling him he would go to hell for not accepting the apostolic traditions, and trusting only in the Bible, he replied that he was glad to know that Christ was to be his judge, and not they. His chief master, who was a zealot in his way, and as much bound to the rites and forms of the Church as he had been before his conversion to his "medicines," or practices to heathen superstition, one day ordered him to make the sign of the cross, and on his refusal, tried to force him. But as the minister was tough and muscular, the Indian could not guide his hand. Then, pulling out a crucifix that hung at his neck, he told Williams in broken English to kiss it; and again being refused, he brandished his hatchet over him and threatened to knock out his brains. This failing of the desired effect, he threw down the hatchet and said he would first bite out the minister's finger-nails,—a form of torture then in vogue among the northern Indians, both converts and heathen. Williams offered him a hand and invited him to begin; on which he gave the thumb-nail a grip with his teeth, and then let it go saying, "No good minister, bad as the devil." The failure seems to have discouraged him, for he made no further attempt to convert the intractable heretic.

The direct and simple narrative of Williams is plainly the work of an honest and courageous man. He was the important capture of the year; and the governor, hearing that he was at St. Francis, despatched a canoe to request the Jesuits of the mission to send him to Montreal. Thither, therefore, his masters carried him, expecting, no doubt, a good price for their prisoner. Vaudreuil, in fact, bought him, exchanged his tattered clothes for good ones, lodged him in his house, and, in the words of Williams, "was in all respects relating to my outward man courteous and charitable to admiration." He sent for two of the minister's children who were in the town, bought his eldest daughter from the Indians, and promised to do what he could to get the others out of their hands. His youngest son was bought by a lady of the place, and his eldest by a merchant. His youngest daughter, Eunice, then seven or eight years old, was at the mission of St. Louis, or Caughnawaga. Vaudreuil sent a priest to conduct Williams thither and try to ransom the child. But the Jesuits of the mission flatly refused to let him speak to or see her. Williams says that Vaudreuil was very angry at hearing of this; and a few days later, he went himself to Caughnawaga with the minister. This time the Jesuits, whose authority within their mission seemed almost to override that of the governor himself, yielded so far as to permit the father to see his child, on condition that he spoke to no other English prisoner. He talked with her for an hour, exhorting her never to forget her catechism, which she had learned by rote. Vaudreuil and his wife afterwards did all in their power to procure her ransom; but the Indians, or the missionaries in their name, would not let her go. "She is still there," writes Williams two years later, "and has forgotten to speak English." What grieved him still more, Eunice had forgotten her catechism.

While he was at Montreal, his movements were continually watched, lest he should speak to other prisoners and prevent their conversion. He thinks these precautions were due to the priests, whose constant endeavor it was to turn the captives, or at least the younger and more manageable among them, into Catholics and Canadians. The governor's kindness toward him never failed, though he told him that he should not be set free till the English gave up one Captain Baptiste, a noted sea-rover whom they had captured some time before.

He was soon after sent down the river to Quebec along with the superior of the Jesuits. Here he lodged seven weeks with a member of the council, who treated him kindly, but told him that if he did not avoid intercourse with the other English prisoners he would be sent farther away. He saw much of the Jesuits, who courteously asked him to dine; though he says that one of them afterwards made some Latin verses about him, in which he was likened to a captive wolf. Another Jesuit told him that when the mission Indians set out on their raid against Deerfield, he charged them to baptize all children before killing them,—such, he said, was his desire for the salvation even of his enemies. To murdering the children after they were baptized, he appears to have made no objection. Williams says that in their dread lest he should prevent conversion of the other prisoners, the missionaries promised him a pension from the King and free intercourse with his children and neighbors if he would embrace the Catholic faith and remain in Canada; to which he answered that he would do so without reward if he thought their religion was true, but as he believed the contrary, "the offer of the whole world would tempt him no more than a blackberry."

To prevent him more effectually from perverting the minds of his captive countrymen, and fortifying them in their heresy, he was sent to Chateau Richer, a little below Quebec, and lodged with the parish priest, who was very kind to him. "I am persuaded," he writes, "that he abhorred their sending down the heathen to commit outrages against the English, saying it is more like committing murders than carrying on war."

He was sorely tried by the incessant efforts to convert the prisoners. "Sometimes they would tell me my children, sometimes my neighbors, were turned to be of their religion. Some made it their work to allure poor souls by flatteries and great promises; some threatened, some offered abuse to such as refused to go to church and be present at mass; and some they industriously contrived to get married among them. I understood they would tell the English that I was turned, that they might gain them to change their religion. These their endeavors to seduce to popery were very exercising to me."

After a time he was permitted to return to Quebec, where he met an

English Franciscan, who, he says, had been sent from France to aid in converting the prisoners. Lest the minister should counteract the efforts of the friar, the priests had him sent back to Chateau Richer; "but," he observes, "God showed his dislike of such a persecuting spirit; for the very next day the seminary, a very famous building, was most of it burnt down, by a joiner letting a coal of fire drop among the shavings."

The heaviest of all his tribulations now fell upon him. His son Samuel, about sixteen years old, had been kept at Montreal under the tutelage of Father Meriel, a priest of St. Sulpice. The boy afterwards declared that he was promised great rewards if he would make the sign of the cross, and severe punishment if he would not. Proving obstinate, he was whipped till at last he made the sign, after which he was told to go to mass, and on his refusal, four stout boys of the school were ordered to drag him in. Williams presently received a letter in Samuel's handwriting, though dictated, as the father believed, by his priestly tutors. In this was recounted, with many edifying particulars, the deathbed conversion of two New England women; and to the minister's unspeakable grief and horror, the messenger who brought the letter told him that the boy himself had turned Catholic. "I have heard the news," he wrote to his recreant son, "with the most distressing, afflicting, sorrowful spirit, Oh, I pity you, I mourn over you day and night. Oh, I pity your weakness that, through the craftiness of men, you are turned from the simplicity of the gospel." Though his correspondence was strictly watched, he managed to convey to the boy a long exposition, from his own pen, of the infallible truth of Calvinistic orthodoxy, and the damnable errors of Rome. This, or something else, had its effect. Samuel returned to the creed of his fathers; and being at last exchanged, went home to Deerfield, where he was chosen town-clerk in 1713, and where he soon after died.

Williams gives many particulars of the efforts of the priests to convert the prisoners, and his account, like the rest of his story, bears the marks of truth. There was a treble motive for conversion; it recruited the Church, weakened the enemy, and strengthened Canada, since few of the converts would peril their souls by returning to their heretic relatives. The means of conversion varied. They were gentle when gentleness seemed likely to answer the purpose. Little girls and young women were placed in convents, where it is safe to assume that they were treated with the most tender kindness by the sisterhood, who fully believed that to gain them to the faith was to snatch them from perdition. But when they or their brothers proved obdurate, different means were used. Threats of hell were varied by threats of a whipping, which, according to Williams, were often put into execution. Parents were rigorously severed from their families, though one Lelande, who had been sent to watch the elder prisoners, reported that they would persist in trying to see their children, till some of them were killed in the attempt. "Here," writes Williams, "might be a history in itself of the trials and sufferings of many of our children, who, after separation from grown persons, have been made to do as they would have them. I mourned when I thought with myself that I had one child with the Maquas

[Caughnawagas], a second turned papist, and a little child of six years of age in danger to be instructed in popery, and knew full well that all endeavors would be used to prevent my seeing or speaking with them." He also says that he and others were told that if they would turn Catholic their children should be restored to them; and among other devices, some of his parishioners were assured that their pastor himself had seen the error of his ways and bowed in submission to Holy Church.

In midwinter, not quite a year after their capture, the prisoners were visited by a gleam of hope. John Sheldon, accompanied by young John Wells, of Deerfield, and Captain Livingston, of Albany, came to Montreal with letters from Governor Dudley, proposing an exchange. Sheldon's wife and infant child, his brother-in-law, and his son-in-law had been killed. Four of his children, with his daughter-in-law, Hannah, the same who had sprained her ankle in leaping from her chamber window—besides others of his near relatives and connections, were prisoners in Canada; and so also was the mother of young Wells. In the last December, Sheldon and Wells had gone to Boston and begged to be sent as envoys to the French governor. The petition was readily granted, and Livingston, who chanced to be in the town, was engaged to accompany them. After a snow-shoe journey of extreme hardship they reached their destination, and were received with courtesy by Vaudreuil. But difficulties arose. The French, and above all the clergy, were unwilling to part with captives, many of whom they hoped to transform into Canadians by conversion and adoption. Many also were in the hands of the Indians, who demanded payment for them,—which Dudley had always refused, declaring that he would not "set up an Algiers trade" by buying them from their pretended owners; and he wrote to Vaudreuil that for his own part he "would never permit a savage to tell him that any Christian prisoner was at his disposal." Vaudreuil had insisted that his Indians could not be compelled to give up their captives, since they were not subjects of France, but only allies—which, so far as concerned the mission Indians within the colony, was but a pretext. It is true, however, that the French authorities were in such fear of offending even these that they rarely ventured to cross their interests or their passions. Other difficulties were raised, and though the envoys remained in Canada till late in spring, they accomplished little. At last, probably to get rid of their importunities, five prisoners were given up to them,—Sheldon's daughter-in-law, Hannah; Esther Williams, the oldest daughter of the minister; a certain Ebenezer Carter; and two others unknown. With these, Sheldon and his companions set out in May on their return; and soon after they were gone, four young men,—Baker, Nims, Kellogg, and Petty,—desperate at being left in captivity, made their escape from Montreal, and reached Deerfield before the end of June, half dead with hunger.

Sheldon and his party were escorted homeward by eight soldiers under Courtemanche, an officer of distinction, whose orders were to "make himself acquainted with the country." He fell ill at Boston, where he was treated with much kindness, and on his recovery was sent home by sea, along with Captain Vetch and Samuel Hill, charged to open a fresh negotiation. With these, at the request of Courtermanche, went young William Dudley, son of the governor.

They were received at Quebec with a courtesy qualified by extreme caution, lest they should spy out the secrets of the land. The mission was not very successful, though the elder Dudley had now a good number of French prisoners in his hands, captured in Acadia or on the adjacent seas. A few only of the English were released, including the boy, Stephen Williams, whom Vaudreuil had bought for forty crowns from his Indian master.

In the following winter John Sheldon made another journey on foot to Canada, with larger powers than before. He arrived in March, 1706, and returned with forty-four of his released countrymen, who, says Williams, were chiefly adults permitted to go because there was no hope of converting them. The English governor had by this time seen the necessity of greater concessions, and had even consented to release the noted Captain Baptiste, whom the Boston merchants regarded as a pirate. In the same summer Samuel Appleton and John Bonner, in the brigantine "Hope," brought a considerable number of French prisoners to Quebec, and returned to Boston at the end of October with fifty-seven English, of all ages. For three, at least, of this number, money was paid by the English, probably on account of prisoners bought by Frenchmen from the Indians. The minister, Williams, was exchanged for Baptiste, the so-called pirate, and two of his children were also redeemed, though the Caughnawagas, or their missionaries, refused to part with his daughter Eunice. Williams says that the priests made great efforts to induce the prisoners to remain in Canada, tempting some with the prospect of pensions from the King, and frightening others with promises of damnation, joined with predictions of shipwreck on the way home. He thinks that about one hundred were left in Canada, many of whom were children in the hands of the Indians, who could easily hide them in the woods, and who were known in some cases to have done so. Seven more were redeemed in the following year by the indefatigable Sheldon, on a third visit to Canada.

The exchanged prisoners had been captured at various times and places. Those from Deerfield amounted in all to about sixty, or a little more than half the whole number carried off. Most of the others were dead or converted. Some married Canadians, and others their fellow-captives. The history of some of them can be traced with certainty. Thus, Thomas French, blacksmith and town clerk of Deerfield, and deacon of the church, was captured, with his wife and six children. His wife and infant child were killed on the way to Canada. He and his two eldest children were exchanged and brought home. His daughter Freedom was converted, baptized under the name of Marie Françoise, and married to Jean Daulnay, a Canadian. His daughter Martha was baptized as Marguerite, and married to Jacques Roy, on whose death she married Jean Louis Menard, by whome she became ancestress of Joseph Plessis, eleventh bishop of Quebec. Elizabeth Corse, eight years old when captured, was baptized under her own name, and married to Jean Dumontel. Abigail Stebbins, baptized as Marguerite, lived many years at Boucherville, wife of Jacques de Noyon, a sergeant in the colony troops. The widow, Sarah Hurst, whose youngest child, Benjamin, had been murdered on the Deerfield meadows, was baptized as Marie Jeanne. Joanna Kellogg, eleven years old when taken, married a Caughnawaga Chief, and became, at all points, an Indian squaw.

She was not alone in this strange transformation. Eunice Williams, the namesake of her slaughtered mother, remained in the wigwams of the Caughnawagas, forgot, as we have seen, her English and her catechism, was baptized, and in due time married an Indian of the tribe, who thenceforward called himself Williams. Thus her hybrid children bore her family name. Her father, who returned to his parish at Deerfield, and her brother Stephen, who became a minister like his parent, never ceased to pray for her return to her country and her faith. Many years after, in 1740, she came with her husband to visit her relatives in Deerfield, dressed as a squaw and wrapped in an Indian blanket. Nothing would induce her to stay, though she was persuaded on one occasion to put on a civilized dress and go to church; after which she impatiently discarded her gown and resumed her blanket. As she was kindly treated by her relatives, and as no attempt was made to detain her against her will, she came again in the next year, bringing two of her half-breed children, and twice afterwards repeated the visit. She and her husband were offered a tract of land if they would settle in New England, but she positively refused, saying that it would endanger her soul. She lived to a great age, a squaw to the last.

One of her grandsons, Eleazer Williams, turned Protestant, was educated at Dartmouth College at the charge of friends in New England, and was for a time missionary to the Indians of Green Bay, in Wisconsin. His character for veracity was not of the best. He deceived the excellent antiquarian, Hoyt, by various inventions touching the attack on Deerfield, and in the latter part of his life tried to pass himself off as the lost Dauphin, son of Louis XVI.

Here it may be observed that the descendants of young captives brought into Canada by the mission Indians during the various wars with the English colonies became a considerable element in the Canadian population. Perhaps the most prominent example is that of the Gill family. In June, 1697, a boy named Samuel Gill, then in his tenth year, was captured by Abenakis at Salisbury in Massachusetts, carried to St. Francis, and converted. Some years later, he married a young English girl, said to have been named James, and to have been captured at Kennebunk. In 1866 the late Abbé Maurault, missionary to St. Francis, computed their descendants at 952, in whose veins French, English, and Abenaki blood were mixed in every conceivable proportion. He gives the tables of genealogy in full, and says that 213 of the prolific race still bear the surname of Gill. "If," concludes the worthy priest, "one should trace out all the English families brought into Canada by the Abenakis, one would be astonished at the number of persons who today are indebted to these savages for the blessings of being Catholic and the advantage of being Canadians,"—an advantage for which French-Canadians are so ungrateful that they migrate to the United States by myriads.

THE *settlement of America resembled a geological formation; by simply traveling from east to west during the first three centuries of American development, one was able to move from the most advanced growth to the original wilderness. Even in the earliest stages of colonial settlement, the process was apparent. The commercial basis of the English colonies stimulated the growth of ports. And as the wealth of the interior poured forth, these ports flourished, expanding into small cities where the amenities of civilized society were readily available.*

*Within the cities scattered along the Atlantic coasts, a distinctly American culture took form. It was in Philadelphia that America's philosophe, Benjamin Franklin, pursued his career as pragmatic intellectual, providing both an example and a foreshadowing of the direction in which the American intellect would move. It was also in the city that the growing strength of the American economy became manifestly obvious. The American merchant, motivated by an unashamed self-interest, increasingly declined to take a back seat to his British counterpart. Within his seaport base, the merchant shaped his challenge to British authority.*

*The city defined the American identity and asserted the American interest. It was the city that gave promise of a more complex world than the primitive simplicity of the wilderness. It also served as an arena within which a revolution was born. For although Americans have only within the recent past come to recognize the city as the characteristic expression of American life, the sum of history instructs us that a society without cities is a life of incomplete civilization.*

*Carl Bridenbaugh (1903-    ), long interested in American social and intellectual history, has made his particular specialty the urban society of the colonies. He recognized as few previous historians had the seminal role the cities made in both shaping and giving direction to colonial life before the Revolution. It was in this small urban society that the men who made the American Revolution were shaped. It was the city that provided the institutions which gave common threads to thirteen divergent colonies and set them on the road to union.*

## CITIES IN THE WILDERNESS

### by Carl Bridenbaugh

Cities rise and flourish in proportion as their natural advantages correspond with the demands of a particular age. This correspondence may be either accidental or the result of preconceived purpose, but history provides many instances of towns which, lacking this harmony between physical and economic environment, have despite artificial efforts of founders or promoters remained condemned to comparative unimportance, outdistanced by more fortunate rivals. In the seventeenth century material greatness was commercial, not industrial. Those towns prospered, therefore, whose sites commanded certain vital trading advantages—the possession of good natural harbors, the control of avenues of trade and communication, or the domination of a productive countryside. When in this period the Old World began to plant its colonial settlements on the North American continent, commercial considerations such as these largely dictated their locations. Design rather than accident endowed the principal offspring of seventeenth century colonizing impulses with situations favoring the pursuit of trade and navigation.

First in point of time, New Amsterdam on Manhattan Island enjoyed the finest harbor on the continent. Its site was the deliberate choice in 1625 of the engineer, Cryn Fredericksen, for the New World trading post of the Dutch West India Company. Five years its junior, Boston, at the mouth of the Charles, possessed a natural landlocked port open for most of the year, so that the capital of John Winthrop's Bible commonwealth was destined too to reap prosperity from its seaborne trade. Similarly, when William Coddington and his friends separated from the Portsmouth, Rhode Island, settlement in 1639, they chose an excellent year-round harbor, the best on Narragansett Bay, as setting for the town of Newport; not liberal politics so much as maritime adventure guaranteed its future increase. Nature thus formed the destiny of these island villages; good harbors and a command of prevailing trade routes characterized all three.

Another burst of colonizing activity a generation later produced two settlements of slightly different character but equally conditioned by considerations of commercial advantage. Proprietary interests, ever watchful for returns from an investment not yet proved profitless, dictated the founding of a settlement at Albemarle Point in South Carolina in 1670, but fear of the Spaniard and the "sickliness of the coast" led ten years later to its transfer to the tongue of land between the Ashley and Cooper Rivers, where it received the royal name of Charles Town. Here a fine harbor behind Sullivan's Island fostered exportation of the exotic produce of this semi-tropical land. Shortly after this another proprietor appropriated a protected site which promised security for the domestic and commercial development of an emigrating people. Philadelphia never knew the savage warfare of a wild frontier, for Dutch and Swedish settlers as well as many Englishmen had already established homes on the banks of the Delaware when Thomas Holme first surveyed the city bounds for William Penn in 1682. Though one hundred miles from the sea, the Quaker town found in the placid Schuylkill and the broad Delaware ready highways to the world markets and their profitable trade.

Coeval with the founding of these five settlements appeared certain factors and influences which in large measure conditioned their future growth and development. All were situated in the temperate zone and enjoyed its advantage of climate, although the semi-tropical location of Charles Town in a swampy region made it less healthy than the four northern ports. Moreover, the early villages were all similarly and strikingly isolated. From Boston on the north to Charles Town on the south stretched eleven hundred miles of wilderness, broken only by rare and occasional settlements. The four northern towns lay comparatively close together. The distance overland from Boston to Newport was seventy miles, from thence to New Amsterdam, one hundred and eighty, and from Manhattan to Philadelphia, ninety-five miles; but, seven hundred and fifty miles separated Charles Town from the Quaker village. This element of distance was multiplied many times by the difficulty of communication in a new country, and the villages were thus denied any great interchange of experience during most of the seventeenth century. The one notable exception was Newport, which as an offshoot from Boston and with easy access to it by land and sea developed in many ways similar to the Bay town. The factor of distance diminished in importance as the villages progressed. Although overland connections were practically non-existent, the fact that each village was a seaport made possible communication by water, and the presence of the ocean highway was a circumstance that tended with the passage of years to link the villages together economically and culturally, and thus to give them an advantage over the more isolated settlements of the interior.

The geographic position of the villages largely determined the form of their economic life. As seaports they became the focal points for trade between Europe and the colonies, and life within them was in consequence strongly commercial. But the character of the commercial development in each settlement depended chiefly upon the nature of its hinterland. The Appalachian mountain chain, which lies close to the sea in New England, extends in a south-westerly direction, forming an ever widening coastal plain to the south. The back country of Boston and Newport was consequently very limited. Such, too, would have been the case at New Amsterdam had not the Hudson and Mohawk Rivers provided an avenue through the barrier to the interior. Philadelphia and Charles Town, on the other hand, possessed seemingly unlimited hinterlands, which, when settled and connected with these centers by roads, promised wide territory for economic exploitation. Considerable diversity in the agricultural and industrial produce of the regions served by each of the five settlements resulted as the century passed in a coastwide exchange of goods, and the merchants of these villages became the agencies through which the first intercolonial contacts were effected. Seaborne trade made for the first intercourse between port and port.

The distantly separated villages were further united by the common national origins of the early settlers. The Dutch of New Amsterdam constituted the only non-English group of any size, and by 1690 this strain was becoming diluted by the steady infiltration of Englishmen. In like manner, the religious beliefs of the villages, heterogeneous as they were, exhibited more common elements than divergencies. All were Protestant; nearly all, save the ruling class of Charles Town, radically so. The social complexion of each town was further fashioned by persons whose economic and cultural roots, whether English or Dutch, lay for the most part in the rising middle class of the Old World.

The political institutions of the colonial villages derived from common European sources, and despite varying applications in the New World, their similarities were more striking than their differences. English and Dutch local institutions had much in common, and after 1664, when New Amsterdam became New York, the last vestiges of non-English political life all but disappeared from the American urban scene.

These various influences, geographic, economic, social and political, conditioned the early development of the five villages. Save for the factor of distance they made in general for the formation of a uniform type of society. Just as rural regions and colonial frontiers developed their distinguishing characteristics, so also did the urban centers. By 1690 a distinct village society was appearing in the American colonies. The five settlements had by that time outgrown most of the crudities of their village state and were emerging on the American scene as prosperous provincial towns. Collectively they harbored nine per cent of the colonial population. Boston, with seven thousand inhabitants, had attained a size which made it comparable with some of the cities of the Mother Country. In 1680 there were only four cities in England whose population exceeded ten thousand; Bristol, the second city, contained only about twenty thousand inhabitants in 1690. Boston was about as large as Gloucester at this time; Philadelphia and New York, with populations of approximately four thousand, paralleled Derby. The New World towns had thus passed well beyond the stages of colonial experiment or frontier outpost, and an examination of their physical properties reveals much that was to characterize urban America throughout its early history.

\*　　\*　　\*　　\*　　\*

The villages advanced in this period from the crudest of frontier settlements to the dignity and comparative comfort of established towns. Because of peculiar local conditions and varying degrees of age the rate of growth, especially at Charles Town and Philadelphia, was uneven. By 1690, however, the village physiognomy was easily distinguishable from that of the countryside. As in all pioneer countries the erection of temporary shelters had been the first concern of the colonial townsfolk, but soon these "hovels and holes, in which they huddled rather than dwelt," gave way to more permanent abodes. The bark houses of Manhattan, the wattle huts of Boston and Newport, and the famous caves of the Delaware were rapidly replaced by substantial homes of wood, brick or stone. The character of the buildings erected in each village was largely determined by the Old World traditions of the inhabitants and by the nature of the materials at hand. The features of the terrain whereon it was located further conditioned the appearance of each community. Thus by the close of the period each little seaport exhibited its own already perceptive individuality, while a suggestion of urban compactness was common to them all.

With the exception of New Amsterdam all the towns were decidedly English in appearance. The local stone of Massachusetts was unfit for building purposes, and since Boston Neck was almost entirely devoid of timber, the inhabitants were forced to procure their building materials by water from islands in the harbor. Their early homes were one-story structures, covered with thatch, and flung at random over the peninsula. By mid-century larger abodes were being raised; built around a single chimney, they had high-pitched, shingled roofs, and were lighted by small windows with leaded casements and diamond panes. In 1663 Josselyn noted that "the houses were for the most part . . . close together on each side of the streets as in London." The Paul Revere house, built in 1676, with its unlighted side walls, indicates that domestic architecture was already beginning to conform to town conditions. The prevailing architecture of Boston, like that of medieval England, which it so greatly resembled, was still essentially Gothic. Buildings of brick and stone, like Richard Wharton's triangular warehouse, became more common after the disastrous fire of 1679. Boston, wrote a nameless Huguenot refugee near the end of the period, "is built on the slope of a little Hill, and is as large as La Rochelle. . . . The Town is almost wholly built of Wooden Houses; but since there have been some ravages by Fire, building of Wood is no longer allowed, so that at this present writing very handsome Houses of Brick are going up."

The early buildings of Newport did not differ greatly from those of Boston, though the Rhode Islanders were more fortunate in finding a ready supply of timber in the woods surrounding their town. The relative security of life on the island led many of the more wealthy citizens to lay out large estates on which they built fine mansions, and although some maintained town houses as well, the result was the slow development of any thickly settled district in Newport. By 1670 the old one-room, end-chimney pioneer home had been supplanted by the central chimney type with either two or four rooms on a floor. Of such construction was the large town house built in 1641 by the Founder, William Coddington; the Wanton-Lyman-Hazard house, erected in 1675 and still standing, is another example of this more developed style. Newport was reported to contain four hundred houses in 1675; probably two thirds of these were located within the village proper, and represented the limits to which the town was to expand for several decades.

The other two English towns were founded late in the century and experienced a more mushroom growth. The problem of adequate housing for the vast numbers of immigrants who crowded over with William Penn confronted the town of Philadelphia from the beginning. It was solved with great rapidity; in ten years' time the Quaker City was as large as its oldest neighbor, New York. Penn wrote in July, 1683, that "within less than a Year" there had been erected "about four score Houses and Cottages," while in December he noted an increase of seventy more. The next year saw the total rise to 357 dwellings, sheltering a population of about twenty-five hundred. In 1685 the number doubled. Brick construction was said to be as cheap as wood, and the Proprietor was boasting of the great rise in the value of town lots—four times the original price, "and over!" "As to the Town," reported Robert Turner in 1686, "Building goeth on. Now many brave brick houses are going up, with good Cellars. . . . We build most houses with balconies." Construction had so far progressed by April, 1687, that the Provincial Council ordered the remaining denizens within a month "to provide for themselves other habitations, in order to have the Said Caves Distroy'd." In 1690 most of the inhabitants were well housed, and John Goodson was finding "rents toward the river high." Penn's dream of a great town had become a reality, and there seems reason in the enthusiasm of William Rodney's review of the eight years' progress: "Philadelphia is mightily improved, (for its famous Buildings, Stone-brick and Timber-Houses of very great Value, . . .) the most of any settlement in the World for its time."

At Charles Town over a hundred houses were built in 1680 in the small area which had been "regularly laid out," with places reserved for a church, town house, and other "publick structures." Two years later Thomas Newe was able to write proudly that "The Town which two years since had but 3 or 4 houses, hath now about a hundred houses, all of which all wholly built of Wood, tho there is excellent Brick made, but little of it." Unfortunately, after this auspicious beginning, there is little record of the early progress of building at Charles Town.

By 1636 the Dutch West India Company had constructed five large stone houses to be used as shops, and numerous other buildings outside the Fort, which added to private dwelling houses thus early gave to New Amsterdam, as it nestled complacently in the shadow of Fort and windmill, the appearance of a Dutch town. Prior to 1650 most houses were built of wood and covered with thatch, like that provided for the town schoolmaster in 1642, but by the time of the first English occupation Dutch brick "alla moderna" had largely supplanted wood as a building material. New Amsterdam was then a "brave place" containing about three hundred and fifty houses, "the meanest house therein being valued at one hundred pounds, and an ordinary dwelling yielding an annual rent of 120 to 180 guilders." English rule in the seventeenth century wrought little visible change in the Dutch Town. More houses were erected, some of wood, but the majority as in the past "built of brick and stone and covered with red and black tile." Placed gable-end to the street and surrounded by gardens and fruit trees, these homes were indeed "after the manner of Holland."

After the first desperate shortage townsfolk in the seventeenth century succeeded in providing themselves with shelter sufficient for their immediate needs. Constant building had by 1690 begun to invest the villages with an urban appearance. Save at Newport the houses of each community were set close together and usually directly upon the streets. A Massachusetts law of 1684, allowing half of a party wall to be placed upon the adjoining property, is evidence of the growing compactness of Boston. Since the first necessity of the colonists was for shelter, and their means limited, we cannot look for much architectural distinction prior to 1690. Most buildings were small, one- or two-story dwellings, but here and there appeared an occasional fine residence with its gardens and fruit trees. The severe, unpainted frame structures, grayed by the weather, that were the rule in Boston, Newport and Charles Town, gave to these settlements a more somber aspect than the colorful brick and stone houses with stepped gables and tiled roofs at New York, or the slightly Flemish bond of the balconied homes of the Philadelphians. Yet, despite the considerable progress of this period the problem of housing in the colonial villages was a continuous one, which grew larger rather than diminished as they expanded into towns and their enlarged populations came to include the poor and indigent as well as the enterprising and self-sufficient.

An adequate and inexpensive supply of firewood was indispensable to the life of the towns. Wood was the only fuel used for heating, and in the homes of the poor pine knots and "lightwood" were often also the sole means of illumination. The country was so well forested in the early years that there was seldom any necessity for townsfolk to go far afield for this commodity; an ample supply could be cut in the nearby woods and brought into the villages to be sold. The only town threatened with a fuel shortage in this period was Boston, for though the shores of Massachusetts Bay were well wooded no timber grew on the peninsula itself. During the winter of 1637 this scarcity became so acute that the inhabitants considered for a time abandoning the settlement. Wood was brought by sledge from the mainland in wintertime, and by boat from islands in the harbor during the rest of the year. As roads were opened up fuel from Muddy River and Roxbury could be carried into Boston, but the poor, who multiplied as time passed, annually suffered from its scarcity and high cost. Manhattan Island furnished sufficient firewood for New Amsterdam in its early years. When the supply began to fail, about 1680, a space was set aside on the Strand, near Smith's Fly, for the measurement and sale of cordwood brought by water from Long Island and New Jersey. In 1684 the General Assembly of New York, to protect people from "great abuses . . . by them that make their profession to sell firewood," ordered that no wood should be sold until officially corded by the standard measure.

\*       \*       \*       \*       \*

In the three decades, 1690-1720, the five colonial communities put away forever their village aspects and took on the appearance of sizable towns. Their social and economic problems multiplied, and the events of town life were enacted on a constantly widening stage. Although urban development in the New World continued to be ordered by the same factors as in the seventeenth century, the existence of abnormal conditions throughout much of this period is of utmost significance. During nineteen of these thirty years England and France were at war, and the American colonies now assumed their historic role as pawns on the chessboard of European diplomacy. The wars both stimulated and retarded town development. Common danger made for increased communication between settlements and with the Mother Country; opportunities arose for the sale of military supplies, privateering, smuggling, and clandestine trade with the enemy;

and in general the social and cultural activities of the towns expanded. On the other hand, the inevitable demoralizing effects of the conflict,— financial depression, moral decline, social unrest, and the increased burden of the poor,—shook the economic structure of the towns and severely strained the resources of their inhabitants.

Notwithstanding the ravages of war, urban population generally increased, with the result that only a few English provincial cities, like Bristol and Norwich with about twenty-five thousand inhabitants, exceeded Boston or Philadelphia in these years. Boston maintained its early lead, but Charles Town and Philadelphia showed remarkable gains, the former trebling its population, and the latter nearly equalling the Bay Town by the close of the period. Despite their growth, however, the increase in the towns did not keep pace with that of rural regions, and in 1720 dwellers in the five towns constituted only eight per cent of the colonial population.

＊　　＊　　＊　　＊　　＊

As the towns approached or attained their centuries, two long decades of peace and expanding trade consolidated the gains and intensified the character of the development of preceding years. In physical appearance raw youth was yielding rapidly to settled maturity. Increased age and experience were evident in the firmer handling of growing urban problems and in the deepening of public consciousness concerning its collective responsibilities. Moreover, the peace that permitted unprecedented commercial prosperity and material expansion was also more than ever making of the New World a haven for land-hungry and underprivileged citizens of the Old. These newcomers, scattered throughout the colonies, but many of them remaining in the towns, contributed to the physical and economic growth and left a mark upon the social and cultural complexions of these communities.

Twenty years of peace and continuous immigration greatly increased urban populations in the New World. At the close of the period Boston was still the largest community, but its population had begun to decline,— a phenomenon which continued until after the American Revolution. Philadelphia, on the other hand, rapidly growing, would soon pass the Bay Town in numbers. Even more significant for the development of urban America was the extraordinary expansion of New York, Charles Town and Newport, the more noteworthy when compared with the practically stationary populations of English cities prior to 1760. At the same time, however, colonial population in general expanded so rapidly that the proportion of persons living in the towns declined from 8 per cent in 1720 to 5.4 per cent in 1742.

Although urban growth everywhere bred conditions requiring the assumption of more authority by town governments, very little change in municipal political institutions took place in this period. The one notable exception was the new charter granted the Corporation of New York in 1731. By the discreet disposition of £1,000 the Mayor and Common Council secured from Governor James Montgomerie, who, it was well known, hoped to recoup his fortune in America, a confirmation of former privileges and a grant of additional concessions. But, though the city obtained an extension of its boundaries and a lucrative ferry monopoly, and the Corporation received augmented executive and judicial powers, the governor retained the right of appointing the mayor and other municipal officers. Thus, in spite of increased authority, the aristocratic nature of the Corporation became rather intensified than otherwise.

Elsewhere attempts to alter existing forms of government proved abortive. They are significant, however, in uncovering the three most important municipal needs,—popular control, administrative efficiency, and financial independence. Under the influence of Governor Francis Nicholson, the South Carolina Assembly in June, 1722, passed "An Act for the Good Government of Charles Town," which erected "Charles City and Port" into a municipal corporation modelled after that of New York. Unhappily for the future of the town, a "faction" of planters and merchants, claiming to represent a majority of the citizens, secured the disallowance of this act in England the next year on the grounds that "the town's people were surprised into the Law." Francis Yonge, colonial agent, held that the "whole complaint against the Corporation is only a Cavill stirred up by some designing persons who are angry they were not placed in the Magistracy." It also appears probable that much of the opposition came from the planter group, which did not wish to see the city made independent of the Assembly wherein it enjoyed complete control. All that Charlestonians achieved by way of self-government in these years was the right to elect parish firemasters, workhouse commissioners and measurers in 1737-1738, and road commissioners after 1742. Had the charter been allowed, Charles Town, thus made competent to deal with local problems, might not have remained the community of unrealized projects that it was.

The aristocratic nature of the Philadelphia Corporation, coupled with its financial ineptitude and its failure to cope adequately with the town's problems, aroused widespread public distrust. In 1740 dissatisfied inhabitants petitioned the Assembly for a law placing the collection of taxes and certain other powers of the Corporation in the hands of elected "Commissioners and Assessors," in accordance with current English practice. The Assembly passed the bill, but the Mayor and Common Council persuaded Governor Thomas to reject it on the grounds that it infringed rights granted by the charter of 1701.

The two New England towns were, on the whole, well governed. Boston's principal problem came from the smaller villages of Suffolk County, which resented economic control by the capital of the nearby countryside. In 1735 these communities made an unsuccessful attempt to have Boston separated from the County, and three years later Rumney Marsh failed in its effort to detach itself from the town. A similar demand came in 1742 from "freeholders of the woods part of Newport," who wanted independence from the "merchants and tradesmen" of the "compact part" of the town, but a committee of the Assembly rejected the petition after a public hearing. In both of these communities the town meetings, while ostensibly democratic, were in reality controlled year after year by the same group of merchant aristocrats, who secured most of the important offices, and it was only natural for inhabitants of rural districts to desire release from this overlordship.

The problem of adequate housing for the townsfolk intensified in this period, for despite considerable building in each town construction failed to keep pace with increase in population. Yet the operations of builders were constantly changing the face of each community; new public structures lent an air of distinction and civic maturity, and elaborate mansions for the rich gave evidence of accumulating wealth and taste, while in some of the towns overcrowding caused a subdivision of building lots and the appearance of multi-family houses.

Philadelphia experienced the greatest expansion. The settled area now reached west past Tenth Street, north beyond Vine, and south along the Delaware to Society Hill. In older sections large, three-storied brick houses and other buildings began to replace the "mean and low" frame or brick structures of earlier years. A sign of overcrowding in these areas was the gradual appearance of tenement houses; in 1722 four of them were erected on Front Street and two on Second. "House rent is high," wrote Christopher Saur two years later, "because the houses are all built of bricks. . . . According to appearances, plainness is vanishing pretty much." Even humble artisans, like Ebenezer Robinson, brazier, lived in brick houses, though many dwellings sheltered two or more families, and some people had to walk "up one Pair of Stairs" to their lodgings.

A large amount of construction took place between 1720 and 1742. With the erection of many new shops and warehouses in the business section real estate there rose in price. Mulberry Street, on the northern side of town, began to be a popular residential area at about this time. Land along the Delaware south of Walnut Street was opened up after 1728, and had by 1740 become a well-peopled residential district.

A unique development in Philadelphia was the appearance of suburbs. South of the town lay Society Hill, where the Shippen brothers owned a large tract of land which they began to sell off in house lots in 1739. Their advertisements made much of the accessibility of the site of a proposed new market. Another suburban development was opened up in the Northern Liberties in 1741, when Ralph Assheton disposed of his eighty-acre estate in small building lots. Fine rural estates, belonging to wealthy merchants who aspired to the life of country gentlemen, still characterized the countryside around Philadelphia. Among those most noted for their splendid architecture and formal Italian gardens were James Logan's lovely home at Stenton, Andrew Hamilton's palatial residence at Bush Hill, and the buildings of the Wharton estate on the road to Moyamensing.

Philadelphia owed the growing beauty of its public architecture to the talent and skill of its master builders and accomplished gentlemen amateurs, who in adapting the classicism of Palladio and Vitruvius improved upon their British contemporaries by their refusal to sacrifice practical comfort on the symmetrical altar of eighteenth century taste. In 1724 James Porteus,

Samuel Powell, Ebenezer Thompson, John Harrison and six other master builders formed the Carpenters' Company of Philadelphia "for the purpose of obtaining instruction in the science of architecture." Their studies soon bore fruit. Porteus designed the new Christ Church, completed in 1731, the most ambitious and ornate expression of the Georgian style in America. In 1730 the Pennsylvania Assembly, long in need of a suitable meeting place, appropriated funds and purchased a lot on Chestnut Street between Fifth and Sixth, and a beautifully proportioned Georgian building, of which the plans had been drawn by the gifted speaker, Andrew Hamilton, was ready for use by 1735. The State House, though incomplete in 1742, was the largest and most elaborate formal public building in the colonies, and its lovely interior, with its grand staircase and rich carvings, the work of Gustavus Hesselius, is a monument to the city's artistic coming of age. From the Delaware River in 1742 the pleasing prospect of Philadelphia, with its brick houses, gentlemen's estates and public buildings, revealed a city in most respects full grown, and comparable with similar communities in the Mother Country.

New York and Boston did not greatly extend their bounds, and became in consequence more compact, in places even congested. The Corporation of New York clung tenaciously to its property, seldom leasing or selling save from dire necessity. But the growth of population stimulated building activity and made the subdivision of large properties a profitable business to the original owners. In 1729 the Weems property was broken up and sold for small building lots, as was also land at the Fresh Water belonging to William Janeway. In 1731 to finance the acquisition of the Montgomerie Charter, the Corporation disposed of two large tracts, which thus became available for building. Other dispositions of city lands in this period were the grant of seventy acres to Alderman Rutgers in 1730 and the sale of ten lots to Jacobus Roosevelt in 1734. Nevertheless, the town continued to suffer a shortage of land and houses, and in 1732 the constables received orders to evict certain squatters from city property in the North Ward, and to "Cause their Hutts to be demolished . . . as public nuisances."

When real estate did become available, enthusiastic building often produced a glut of new properties. In 1735 reports circulated at Boston that "because trade is very dull by reason of heavy Taxes," one hundred and fifty houses were for rent at New York. John Symmenses' dwelling in Broadway, with "a small kitchen, a Grass-Plat, Wood Yard, several Fruit Trees and other conveniences," was advertised for many weeks without finding a buyer. But this situation appears to have been only temporary. The market for real estate soon picked up, and building was proceeding apace by 1739. The auction became the popular means of selling many of these newly erected houses.

New York dwelling houses still followed the Dutch architectural tradition, differing greatly from those of Philadelphia, where the current modes of Wren's London were known and copied. "The houses are . . . compact and regular; . . ." Dr. Alexander Hamilton described them in 1744; "there are a few built of wood, but the greatest number of brick, and a great many covered with pantile and glazed tile with the year of God when built figured out with plates of iron upon the fronts of several of them." The only public edifice to elicit his approval was Trinity Church, a stone building with a fine interior but a "clumsey Steeple." Despite some expansion, and the absence of many civic buildings, New York remained crowded at the southern tip of Manhattan, which explains why Dr. Hamilton thought it made "more of an urban appearance than Philadelphia."

Although much building took place, the limits of Boston were not greatly enlarged in these years. Many frame dwellings were demolished to be replaced by brick, and the central business district about the Town House became thickly populated. Near here the "poorer sort" lived in tiny quarters, and seldom enjoyed the luxury of a brick house unless it were a tenement. Many dwelt, like Edward Grater, carter, in a small "Wooden" two-family house down near the wharves, or in the "end of a house" up in town. Middle class artisans, living in the center of Boston, occupied "convenient" houses having two lower rooms, a kitchen, wood house and back yard. In this district also were several large double houses with pumps, renting at £40 to £50 per year. The North End, too, was becoming more crowded, and fine old residences occasionally had to give way to buildings like Martha Grover's "Brick Tenement" in Fish Street.

The greatest activity in real estate took place at the South End. Here larger lots, sometimes 65' x 120', were available for homes for the well-to-do. Long Lane, in this locality, was a pleasant street, lined with attractive houses renting for around £98 per year. Yet tenements had made their appearance here, too, by 1734. West Boston, toward Barton's Point, also filled up at this time, becoming, like the South End, a region of large and substantial residences. An English gentleman, surveying the town in 1740, concluded that Boston contained "a great many good houses, and several fine streets, little inferior to some of our best in London."

The building energies of Boston citizens seem to have confined themselves to domestic structures, for, as the town was already well supplied in this respect, no new public buildings appeared in these years. The spires of its fourteen churches still in 1742 dominated the view of the town from the harbor, and the crowding together of all its buildings, domestic and commercial, in the older sections, gave it a distinctly urban aspect. The most "elegant prospect" that the town afforded was still that from the lower end of Long Wharf for a half a mile up King Street to the Town House.

After recovering from the shocks of war, hurricane and fire, Charlestonians embarked upon an extended building program, which included the replacing of old structures and the erection of many new ones. The town expanded beyond its walls, and by 1739 had more than doubled in area. Within the old limits, where houses stood close together upon the streets, much of the rebuilding had taken place before 1730. The principal obstacle to adequate housing at Charles Town was shortage of labor. At far-away Boston in 1722 newspapers carried the notice that carpenters and bricklayers going to Charles Town would "find employment enough . . . by reason of the great want of such Artificers there." This scarcity probably accounted for the prevalence of cheaply built timber houses, which were "neither comfortable nor well constructed." Heavy immigration from New England and New York in the 1730's also raised the price of town sites to "four times the Value in 4 or 5 Yeares time."

The prevailing high price of real estate did not, however, prevent people from acquiring new homes, and after 1730 a veritable building boom took place. The marked improvement in construction and design of Charles Town dwellings can be attributed to the advent of trained carpenters and to men like Peter Chaffereau, a London architect who arrived in 1735. In addition to such skillful adaptations of West Indian and classical elements as Robert Brewton's home on Tradd Street, there appeared in newer sections show places like Joseph Shute's "Summer Houses" with their beautiful gardens, and Francis La Brasseur's elegant residence and orange grove, known as Petit Versailles. Several hundred dwellings, kitchens, warehouses, coach houses, and stables were built during this decade in newly opened areas west and south of the old lines. In 1737 choice lots, part of "Number 36, situate in Eliott Street," measuring 28′ x 88′ were being offered for sale. Another popular residential district was "Archdale's Square, near the Presbyterian Church."

As new residential areas opened up, older sections of Charles Town became consigned largely to business and to sheltering non-householders and members of the poorer classes. Here signs of congestion appeared, necessitating the erection of multi-family houses. In 1735 John Laurens advertised a house in Market Square, "divided into four commodious Tenements"; soon after James St. John offered one "to be let in several Apartments." Here also in 1727 was completed St. Philip's Church, as much the pride of the inhabitants as the present edifice which occupies its site. In the estimation of visitors Charles Town, with its predominance of frame buildings, made "a fine Shew at a Distance in the Sea," and suited the prevailing taste because "very regularly built."

For the first time in its hundred years of existence, Newport began to develop a closely settled area. By 1730 frame buildings, used chiefly for business purposes, crowded one another along Thames Street for half a mile, and homes on Mary, Marlborough and Spring Streets nestled close like those of other towns. For the most part, however, residents owned large plots of ground, and nearly every house had a garden at its back, so that the town still retained much of its earlier rural flavor. As well as shops and warehouses, new buildings included many homes, and the residential district expanded into favorable locations at the Point across the Cove from Thames Street. After the erection of Trinity Church, Spring Street, running parallel with Thames, became a fashionable place to live. The principal real estate operator of these years was "Augustus Lucas, Esq., Merchant," who advertised his ventures in Boston as well as Rhode Island newspapers. He generally built his houses with the proceeds of a lottery, and in 1732 a lucky Bostonian drew first prize of £50 in the lottery for his "new House and Shop over against the Market House in King Street."

In 1720 the Baptist Church and Quaker Meeting House had been the only large buildings at Newport, but during this period the town acquired some of the most beautiful public structures in the colonies. In 1726 Richard Munday completed Trinity Church, adapting plans possibly drawn in England by Christopher Wren. Few colonial churches can claim such simple beauty and proportion as this lovely edifice. Three years later, in collaboration with Henry Collins, Munday designed and executed the Seventh Day Baptist Church, whose exquisite interior and delicate carvings constitute the supreme monument to the maturity of colonial taste in this period. The carpenter-architect's success with Trinity Church led to his employment by the Assembly as architect and builder of the Colony House in 1739. Standing at the head of Queen Street in a direct line from the end of Long Wharf, and dominating the older section of the town, this handsome brick structure, finished in 1741, was the most complete public building in any of the towns. Munday was also responsible for the building of many fine homes for the wealthy merchant families of Newport. The impression gathered from a tour of the town's streets today is that the painted frame houses of Rhode Island grandees were surpassed by none in any town for classic proportion and exquisite detail.

By 1742 each of the towns presented a distinctly urban appearance. Increasing demand for houses and rising real estate values led to the subdivision of properties and growing compactness of dwelling houses in older sections. Boston, Charles Town and Philadelphia enforced strict regulations concerning construction of party walls. In the last named town special "Regulators of Party Wall and Partition fences" issued permits for such building, specified thickness of walls, and levied fines for non-compliance with their orders. Every town had further developed an individuality of its own, which found expression in types of architecture and building materials employed, and especially in the nature of its public buildings.

By 1720 the forests adjacent to the towns had everywhere so far receded that firewood had to be transported from distant points at an ever-increasing expense. Fuel prices rose steadily throughout the period, occasioning much real hardship for the poor. The problem was most acute at Boston, where inhabitants yearly consumed enormous amounts of wood, and where the original supply had early shown its insufficiency. In the winter of 1726 it was estimated that "during the uninterrupted sledding" over five hundred loads a day, or twenty-four thousand loads came across Boston Neck into the town; at fifty-one shillings a cord, this represented an outlay of about £17,000. Yet even this amount proved insufficient, and the Town Meeting sought other methods of providing the townspeople with fuel. In summer lighters carrying about twelve cords each brought wood to the wharves for measurement and sale. Here those who could afford to lay in an advance supply could purchase it far more cheaply than in winter, but this procedure obviously did not come within the means of the poor. This scarcity and high cost of firewood tempted many corders to perpetrate "frauds," and the authorities repeatedly passed orders to prevent such cheating. They met with scant success, until an elaborate set of regulations and penalties devised in 1740 brought an end to the abuse.

In 1736 and 1737 the Town Meeting chose committees to study plans for improving the fuel supply of Boston, but both times all action was postponed. Consequently, the bitter winter of 1740-41 found the community unprepared. The price of firewood mounted to forty shillings by March, and many of the poor had to go entirely without. Spurred to action by necessity, the Town spent £700 for fuel for the poor, and provided a warehouse where wood given for charity might be stored and dispensed.

After 1730 the use of imported coal by wealthy Bostonians became more general. Frequent advertisements of "choice" Newcastle, Scots', Welsh or Swansea coal appear in all the public prints. In 1735 New England imported seventeen hundred caldrons of English coal, most of which was consumed at Boston; two years later whole shiploads of coal were arriving from Bristol. Though some of the new fuel was used by smiths and braziers, advertisements increasingly stressed its suitability for "Private-Houses."

The poor of New York also suffered greatly from scarcity of firewood in winter, but here the authorities showed less concern over the problem. In 1721 the Corporation did permit gathering of felled timber lying on its common lands. During the winter of 1732 suffering was intense. On February 22 a resident wrote that "Firewood is so very scarce in this City, that it was sold yesterday for 32 shillings per Cord, and some for 36 shillings." Again, in 1737, humble folk became desperate, and rather than pay the high prices asked stole at least one boatload of wood from the North River. Every winter came complaints that the rich bought up the available supply of fuel and left the poor to freeze. As at Boston, conditions became intolerable in 1741, when even the Hudson froze over. Cord wood brought fifty shillings in January, and widespread suffering forced the Corporation to act. It distributed a "large Quantity of Coals" to the needy, and took up a collection of £500 for charity. But within a month this fund was exhausted, and so long as the cold hung on the price of fuel did not drop below forty shillings.

The rapid growth of Newport, and the clearing of Rhode Island and the Narragansett country for farms created a fuel shortage that became acute by 1733. At this time what was probably the first American proposal for conservation appeared in the *Rhode Island Gazette*. "When I consider," said the writer, "how much the Price of Wood for Firing has advanced in this Town for thirty Years past, it puts me to some Apprehensions for Posterity." He proposed a reforestation law requiring every farmer to plant a certain number of trees, and an act to prevent waste in the cutting and selling of firewood. Newport itself took no action until 1738, when the Town Meeting "weighed the deplorable condition the town will be in if the Small pox should prevail," and countrymen refuse to bring wood into town. Provision was then made for a loan to purchase fuel in case of possible emergency. When a genuine crisis occurred in December 1740, the Town Council spent £40 on firewood, and arranged with the "Principal Gentlemen" of Newport to reimburse Jahleel Bronton for wood which he allowed the poor to cut on his property.

The fuel problem was less perplexing at Philadelphia and Charles Town. The ready access to wooded regions afforded by numerous small creeks and inlets in both localities, quite as much as the gentle climate of the latter town, prevented suffering from shortage in either place.

\*    \*    \*    \*    \*

The first hundred years of town history on the American continent witnessed the foundation and gradual development of a truly urban society. The story of American life is customarily regarded as a compound of sectional histories, and in the early colonial period the two sections are commonly considered,—the tidewater and the frontier. Yet the tidewater was itself divided, and if we consider the sections as social and psychological rather than as purely geographical entities, it is possible to distinguish three of them,—the rural, agricultural society of the countryside; the restless, advancing society of the frontier; and the urban, commercial society of the larger seaports. Beginning as small specks in the wilderness, the five communities grew from tiny villages into towns, and finally attained the status of small cities. With other village communities of similar interest and outlook which multiplied and grew in the eighteenth century, they emerged as a social and economic "section" extending the length of the Atlantic seaboard, and exhibiting definite urban characteristics in striking contrast to rural farming districts and wilder regions of the frontier. Life in urban areas produced its own peculiar problems to be faced, and the urban viewpoint, based on continuous close contacts with Europe, derived less from agriculture than from trade. Commercially minded town society looked to the East rather than the West, and was destined from the first to serve as the connecting link between colonial America and its Old World parents.

The future of the colonial towns became immediately evident from the conditions surrounding their birth. Designed as trading communities, they were established on sites most favorable for the pursuit of commerce. They were the western outposts of European commercial expansion in the seventeenth century. City-dwellers from the Old World formed the larger proportion of early town populations, and from the start commercial relations with England or Holland were maintained. Most significantly, the founding process occurred at a time when western Europe, under Dutch and English leadership, was gradually outgrowing and casting off the limitations of medieval feudal economy. Colonial towns grew to maturity in the era of world expansion attending the emergence of modern capitalism, and being new communities, with few irrevocably established customs or traditions, they frequently adapted themselves to the economic drift with more ease and readiness than did the older cities of England. Moreover, the colonizing movement was itself an expression of early capitalistic activity. It called forth organized rather than individual efforts and resources, created new and wider markets for economic development, and opened up seemingly unlimited territories for imperialistic exploitation. It thus produced a marked effect upon Old World economy, accelerating the breakdown of local units of business, and facilitating the formation of larger and more complex organizations of commerce and finance.

❧ ☙

THE *wilderness city turned a civilized face to the outside world, but in the mid-eighteenth century, the probing frontier preoccupied the attention of Paris and London. Along the ridges of the Alleghenies and in the valleys of the Ohio, Mississippi, and St. Lawrence, the final stages of the Anglo-French struggle for control of North America was opening. More fundamentally, two distinct societies prepared for a final clash. One, the French, had spread a thin population through the largely desolate wilderness of the west and north and had allied itself to the Indian tribes; the other, the English, had established homes for millions, farmed the land, developed a far-ranging commerce—in fact, had planted the seed of a new nation.*

*Sooner or later, as the energetic American colonial pushed westward, the contest for the prevalence of France or Britain in North America raised the more fundamental question, would the fate of the better third of this vast continent be determined by the European or his transplanted cousin, the American? The particularistic tendencies of the British colonies alone remained as obstacles to the emergence of the American identity. Not even the danger of a French conquest was sufficient goad to the creation of an American union. At best, the colonists were either "indifferent or positively adverse . . . to the erection of a second superior body which, in addition to the imperial government might restrict their liberties."*

*So as the colonial wars continued through the eighteenth century, and as the English appeared the likely victor, the prospect grew that once the danger of France was eliminated, the struggle for the North American continent would cast colonies and mother country as the new protagonists. For in the long years that had elapsed since the first settlements, the colonials, despite their European heritage, had diverged sufficiently to become different persons. The distinctive features of colonial life and how they emerged occupied the attention of Herbert L. Osgood (1855-1918), professor of history at Columbia University for the last twenty-eight years of his life, and found their way into the multi-volume study he did not live to complete. His work was marked by "great accuracy, thoroughness of research, and clearness and precision of statement." He achieved what modern historians seek to achieve, an accuracy beyond challenge. No one interested in colonial history can neglect Osgood: factually his accounts of seventeenth- and eighteenth-century colonial America are definitive.*

# THE AMERICAN COLONIES
# IN THE EIGHTEENTH CENTURY

## *by Herbert L. Osgood*

In the process of colonization, expansion, or empire building, by whatever name it is described, land and trade are the two impersonal objects
sought, while increase in the number of the populations involved, with their
physical and spiritual improvement, and that of the world at large, is the
only justifiable and ultimate goal of the effort. A treatment of the subject
which throws any one of these three elements into the foreground, to the
neglect or undue obscuring of the others, is one-sided and inadequate. In
tracing the development of the Anglo-American colonies during the eighteenth century we have now reached a point where the influence resulting
from the slow but steady expansion of more than a century began to make
itself decisively felt upon the question of the balance between the French
and the British on the continent. The colonies of both nations had been
expanding, but in different ways, and by virtue of this the character of the
two movements had been made apparent. The expansion of the French had
been the result of exploration and trade, following the river and lake systems of the St. Lawrence and Mississippi and extending through vast spaces
in the interior of the continent. It had started from the lower St. Lawrence and extended westward through the region of the Great Lakes and
thence down the Ohio and Mississippi to the Gulf of Mexico. There the
province of Louisiana had been founded, and from Mobile and New
Orleans as centres a reflex movement up the Mississippi and northeastward
toward the Carolinas had been started. The two had met in the Illinois
country and as the result a chain of trading posts had been established connecting Canada and Louisiana. The process had been a quiet and a rapid
one and its effect seemed to be to block the westward advance of the British and to preempt the interior of the continent for the French. Such was
the hope of the French, when, by the middle of the century, this stage in
the process had been reached. It was also the fear of the leaders among the
British when, at the same time, they awoke to a sense of what had been
accomplished.

Viewed superficially, the achievement of the French was brilliant and
impressive. It had been carried to success by means of the fur trade with
the Indian tribes of the Great Lakes and upper Mississippi. With an irresistible passion for the wild and lawless life of the forest the most active
and adventurous part of the male population of Canada rushed into the fur
trade and spread themselves in small and widely detached bodies throughout the interior of the continent. Neither the restraints of the Church or
the government, nor the monopoly of trading companies, could control

or regulate their action. Wherever they went they spread among the natives the blighting influence of French brandy and lust, and with a total disregard of the conditions of the market cooperated with the savages in the rapid reduction or exhaustion of the stock of fur-bearing animals throughout large sections of the west. A few priests and soldiers followed in the wake of the *coureurs de bois* and a chain of trading posts, located at strategic centres, was established. In this way, and by means of such treaties and alliances with the Indians as accompanied the process, the claims of the French were extended over vast areas, but such occupation of the soil or spread of population as to give a firm support to the claims was not effected. The agriculturists, the substantial part of the Canadian population, were confined to the lower St. Lawrence Valley and there they remained. Scarcely any foreign trade developed, furs and certain minor products being exported to France. The population never even reached a hundred thousand in number and their rate of increase, rapid though it was, was never such as to enable them to spread very far into the interior. Above Montreal settlements were very scattering. The European French have never been a migrating people and, after the Huguenots had been excluded from New France, there was no longer a chance for a large influx of people from the Old World. The portals of New France were even more closely barred against the victims of old world persecution than were those of New England, and it was from this class that America received its largest and most valuable reinforcement. It therefore follows that French colonization in North America, romantic, daring, bold in conception and execution though it was, favored also by certain great natural advantages, as a political and social fabric was weak and unsubstantial. The government of the French possessed the military strength resulting from autocracy; such strength as comes from perfect unity and the exclusion or repression of all dissent belonged to its religion. But notwithstanding these, Canada found its chief protection in its inaccessibility, in the frigid cold of its long winters, and in the almost impregnable strength of the citadel at Quebec. Louisiana and the Illinois country did not seriously count. For military purposes their imposing array of Indian allies, though necessary, were quite as much a source of weakness as of strength. When it came to the final test, the chief contribution of the west was the *coureurs de bois*, who came back to fight for the lilies of France.

The propriety, reason or necessity for the long struggle between the French and British for supremacy in Europe and in the world outside . . . need not detain us here. What concerns us now is the position of the British colonies on the North American continent as compared with the dependencies of France. The word "type" has been borrowed from the natural sciences to indicate what is characteristic in social and political organization. So far as that term is applicable, it may be used here, though in a very general sense, briefly and upon a subject the general nature of which is well known. No fact is more familiar than this, that in all important respects the British colonies were the opposite of the French. They were situated along the Atlantic seaboard, within a temperate region as to climate, exposed to approach from abroad and dominated by no single river system. They had been settled at a variety of different centres along a coast a thousand miles in length, and by colonists who were moved by a variety of motives. A multiple system of colonies, instead of a single province, had resulted. The settlers became mainly agriculturists on a large or small scale. Certain trade centres developed, through which an active commerce not only with Great Britain but with other parts of the world was carried on. The fur trade was also prosecuted in various degrees in all the colonies.

From those regions which lay adjacent to the frontier large numbers of fur traders were continuously sent into the wilderness and the morals which they exhibited and the methods which they pursued were not essentially different from those of the French, except that they usually failed to conceal in any manner their brutality or dishonesty by the *bonhommie* which made the Gaul so attractive. The grossness of the Englishman or Dutchman was not usually relieved by a show of wit or manners. With the British, as with the French, Indian relations were closely connected with the fur trade, especially so far as they affected the remoter tribes. The alliance with the Iroquois also rested to a large extent on this trade. But in the case of nearly all the colonies the extension of settlement and pressure of population, steadily encroaching on the hunting grounds of the natives, constituted the most important element in the problem. The British advanced slowly but steadily, like an organized army, toward the west, and only now and then planted a trading post like Oswego, some distance in advance of the main line of settlement. Until a late period they had little knowledge of the interior, and showed little curiosity concerning it. They were not bold explorers, but rested their claims on the original sea to sea charters rather than on expeditions along the waterways of the west and the planting of trading posts at remote points.

To a certain extent the principles on which their government rested were autocratic, but these as time went on were more and more obscured by the influence of the representative assemblies and the policies of self government which in all the colonies emanated from them. Though the English, Scotch and Scotch Irish, with other components which made up the mass of the colonists, were combative by nature, made so by their religion and their inherited ideas and qualities in general, they were also strongly individualistic and frugal. They had not been reared under the military monarchies of the continent of Europe and, unlike the French, were not accustomed to move at the word of command. Their assemblies controlled the purse and in the great majority of cases, where the assemblies did not control the government, strained relations existed between them and the colonial executives. The pressure exerted by the imperial government in support of its executives was weak and ineffective. Therefore the forces which tended toward military efficiency were not strong, and the crude militia systems which were established when the colonies were founded continued essentially unchanged. The particularism of the different colonies, as directly expressed through the assemblies, made it very difficult, if not impossible, for them to unite in joint measures of offence or even of defence, unless they were directly imperilled. No machinery for securing joint action among them had yet been devised, and in time of need the only resort was to exhortations by the British government, requisitions in the form of quotas, and occasionally direct military assistance from the same quarter. In no respect was the difference between the French and the British in North America greater than in the adaptability of their political systems to the effective prosecution of war. So far inferior were the British to the French in this respect that, though in natural combativeness the two peoples were not unlike, it went far to counteract a superiority on the part of the British in population of about fifteen to one.

As the middle of the eighteenth century approached, the expansion of these two peoples had reached a point where they became fully conscious of each other's presence. As they believed themselves to be natural enemies, and that, as it were, by divine degree fitly reflected in the terrestrial order, the only natural relation between them was one of hostile rivalry, and each began to protect itself according to the approved methods of the time against its opponent. This method involved rapid and decisive advance or aggression at pivotal points or along lines where frontiers approached most closely. The object of this was to seize desirable territory, confirm the hold on trade routes, favorably influence the Indian tribes and thus confirm and extend trade relations and treaties of alliance with them. All this was done with about equal rapidity by both the British and French during the years which immeditely followed the treaty of Aix la Chapelle. While commissioners at Paris were vainly trying to find an adjustment of boundaries which might be permanent, soldiers and traders under authority from their governments were pushing forward and upsetting previous arrangements. As events rapidly succeeded one another, it became evident that, though the last war had been sluggish, the peace which concluded it was likely to be only a brief truce, and the slow gathering of forces in the wilderness and along the frontier, as well as in Europe, was preparing for a more decisive struggle than any which had preceded. The place of Indian relations in this crisis, including those of trade and territory combined, together with the move toward colonial unity which they helped to induce, it is now our duty to trace.

The stream of immigrants which for more than a quarter of a century had been pouring into Pennsylvania and thence spreading westward and southward, had now carried the line of the British frontier well up to the Appalachians. In the region of Pennsylvania and Virginia, this was a fact of great and immediate significance, because just opposite on the west lay the valley of the Ohio, the central line of approach to the Illinois country and the Mississippi. Into that region, as scouts despatched on ahead of the main line, British fur traders were being sent in unusually large numbers. The Indian tribes of the Ohio region, among whom these traders now sought an increasing influence, were Delawares, Shawnees and Wyandots. Among them were also fragments of other tribes from Canada. West of them, on the Miami and Wabash, lived the confederacy of the Miami or Twightwees, and still further west the Illinois, left after their defeat by the Iroquois. The native population of this region was of mixed origin, tribes and fragments of tribes which had been brought together by wars and recent migrations. The Shawnees in particular were newcomers after extended and somewhat mysterious wanderings up and down the interior of the continent. Over the Ohio region and its peoples the Iroquois claimed, by virtue of their earlier conquests, a vague right of control, and this the British insisted had been transferred to them by the treaties of 1701 and later. The long and bloody feud between the Illinois and the Iroquois, however, had proved indecisive and the former confederacy still retained considerable strength. Traders from Pennsylvania and Virginia, however, were now crowding into this region, and it was these colonies, rather than New York, which were forcing the question of the Ohio country and its Indians to the front. The plans which Spotswood had suggested, when he wrote about building a fort on Lake Erie and thus giving life to the claim of Virginia to a vast extension northwestward, were now beginning to come to fruition. Among the Indians of the Ohio the one who was most devoted to the British interest was Old Britain, called by the French La Demoiselle, the head of the Miami confederacy, whose town on Loramie Creek was called by the English Pickawillany. This was fortified with a stockade in 1750 and became the centre of the British trading interest for the entire region. The pushing of English trade interests in this region irritated the French, who came down from Detroit, and murders were not infrequently committed by both parties in the brutal fashion of attack and reprisal familiar to the wilderness. In 1748 Pennsylvania sent George Croghan with presents to the Twightwees and those Indians in turn sent deputies to Lancaster, where they agreed to have nothing more to do with the French. Later in the year Weiser visited Logstown, about eighteen miles below the fork of the Ohio, where a general treaty on behalf of Pennsylvania and Virginia was held with the various tribes of the Ohio region. As a result of this treaty it was hoped that the trade of those tribes had been secured for the British and that Pennsylvania would reap the chief benefit from it.

In 1747 and 1748, moved perhaps by the activity of Pennsylvania, a number of prominent Virginians took what was intended to be a decisive step toward opening up the Ohio valley for settlement, by forming a partnership and applying to the crown for a large grant of land west of the mountains. The application was made through Governor Gooch, not long before the end of his administration, and among the petitioners were John Hanbury, a London merchant, and Thomas Lee, Thomas Nelson, Colonel Cresap, William Thornton, John Carlisle, Lawrence and Augustine Washington, and George Fairfax. George Mason subsequently became an active member. The board of trade reported favorably upon the plan, and the committee of the council ordered that the governor of Virginia be instructed to issue the grant as desired. It was to be located on both sides of the Ohio River between the Monongahela and the Kanawba. A tract of 200,000 acres was to be first surveyed on condition that, within seven years, one hundred families be settled upon it and a fort built, all at the expense of the company, and that the usual conditions as to quit rents be observed.

When these terms should be complied with, 300,000 acres additional should be granted, making a total of 500,000. This was the origin of the famous Ohio Company. In applying for its grant express reference was made to the concession made by the Indians of that territory at Lancaster in 1744, and in the grant the promotion of trade with the western tribes was mentioned as a leading object, as well as settlement and defence.

The first important step taken by the Ohio Company was to employ Christopher Gist, in September, 1750, a frontiersman of English descent who lived in western North Carolina, to make a tour of exploration as far as the falls of the Ohio. Dinwiddie had then become governor of Virginia and a member of the company, and by him Gist's instructions were issued. Gist was to note the passes through the mountains, observe the courses of the rivers and report in particular upon tracts of fertile and accessible land which should be large enough for a settlement. In successive journeys during the next two years, of which he kept brief journals, Gist explored large parts of the present states of Ohio, Kentucky and West Virginia, with parts also of western Maryand and southwestern Pennsylvania.

In the course of his first and most important journey Gist traversed the route from Colonel Thomas Cresap's, at Old Town on the Potomac River in western Maryland, by the way of Indian paths and the Juniata River to Shannopin's Town, later Pittsburgh, at the junction of the Allegheny and Monongahela Rivers. At Logstown he met a parcel of traders from Pennsylvania whom he found "reprobate" and too inquisitive about his business in that region. Gist quieted them by referring to himself as the bearer of a message from the king and by inquiring for the half-breed Andrew Montour who, with George Croghan, was busily employed as agent of Pennsylvania in that region. Passing westward through what is now southern Ohio, he came to an important town of the Wyandots near the Muskingum, where Croghan had a trading house. There Gist met both Croghan and Montour and learned of recent captures of English traders by the French and of the building of a fort to the northward. A Protestant service was held and by presents and speeches an effort was made to promote friendly relations with the natives. Croghan and Montour accompanied Gist westward, and on the Scioto further conferences were held with Delawares and Shawnees. At Pickawillany the most important series of councils were held by Gist and his companions, and treaties of friendship concluded. But the harmony was interrupted by the arrival of four Ottawas with a French flag, a gift of brandy and tobacco and an invitation to the Indians to visit Detroit. But the French envoys were at once dismissed by the chief with a message of defiance, and festivities in honor of the British were continued with the special feature of an Indian feather dance. But owing to the fear of the French Indians to the westward, Gist did not continue as far as the falls of the Ohio, but turned southward and crossed to the southern bank of the river, whence he returned through the rugged and mountainous region of what is now West Virginia and submitted his report to Dinwiddie and his fellow partners.

The company had now imported goods from England, and had built a trading house on the south bank of the Potomac, opposite the mouth of Wills Creek, on which is located the present city of Cumberland in Maryland. In 1751 Gist was sent from this point on another journey through the region to the south of the Ohio and as far as the Big Kanawha. This lasted into the following year and was accompanied with invitations to a conference at Logstown, which it was intended to hold in 1752. It was the intention of the company to construct a road from Wills Creek to the fork of the Monongahela, and to build a fort in the neighborhood of its western terminus as an outpost for defence and a centre for Indian trade. A town, it was expected, would grow up around it. Thus it was proposed, by means of a private company organized directly under the authority of the British government, to extend the territory of Virginia and the crown and plant the British flag permanently beyond the Alleghanies—a method of expansion so effectively used by the English, to say nothing of other nations, in all quarters of the globe. The object of the conference at Logstown, which was held in May, 1753, by Joshua Fry and two other Virginians, and attended by Gist, Croghan and Montour, was to secure from the Indians a confirmation of the grant of western territory made to Virginia in the treaty of Lancaster in 1744. Since that date the concession had been disowned, but now in a private conference with Half King and other chiefs of the Six Nations its validity was acknowledged. All of these proceedings had the support of the board of trade and apparently also of the privy council, including an application for a number of small cannon for the company's projected fort on the Ohio.

After the conclusion of the conference at Logstown, Fry, Lomax, and Patten, as commissioners of Virginia, accompanied by Captain William Trent, left for the country of the Miamis to deliver to them the present which, at the instance of Governor Dinwiddie, was to be made to them also in the name of the king further to bind them in friendship to the English. When Trent and his companions reached the Miami country they learned that a body of French and Indians under Langlade had just surprised and destroyed the post at Pickawillany, killing Old Britain, one Englishman and a few Indians and carrying off others as prisoners. This attack not only led to more urgent solicitation of the Indians for their support but hastened the decision of the British to build a fort at the fork of the Ohio and also revealed more clearly the need of opening a road from Wills Creek to that point and building other posts on the way thither. These measures, as yet, lay within the sphere of Indian relations and the fur trade.

\* \* \* \* \*

Of the provinces along the western frontier those, if any, which must lead in preparing for active defence against the French must be Virginia and New York. Of the intense factional conflict which was still in progress in New York, incapacitating it for vigorous aggressive measures, an account has elsewhere been given. It grew out of conditions which were present in all the provinces, but which were intensified by personal and party rivalries that were peculiar to New York. Though it reacted upon the conduct of Indian relations, as upon everything else, the executive was still left with the means of making a show of activity in that department. Clinton could still correspond with neighboring governors, send agents among the Six Nations, hold conferences at Albany, plan joint conferences at which a semblance of united action on the part of the English could be exhibited before the Indians. All this he did with the efficient aid of Johnson throughout. But for the time the most valuable support of English interest among the savages lay in the advantages of their trade. They could undersell the French and furnish a better class of goods in exchange for the furs which the Indians brought than could the French. Their alliance with the Iroquois also continued, though the French were making serious inroads on the fidelity of the western tribes. Oswego was an outpost of great value and, as long as it remained in British hands, it was clear that active trade between Albany and the far Indians through the Iroquois country would be continued, and that insured the permanence of the alliance. The Iroquois had always coquetted with the French and would continue to do so, but English rum and woolens were a stronger attraction than French brandy. And yet the English were steadily encroaching on the lands of the Mohawks; and in the last war, it had been observed, they had made a woefully poor showing in all their military ventures along the frontier.

\* \* \* \* \*

In making the early preparations for the conference at Albany, the predominant idea was that it should result in an unusually inclusive and important treaty with the Indians. It was to be the outgrowth of Indian relations as just described, and was to have as its outcome a general alliance between the British colonies and the Indian tribes south of the Great Lakes, bringing to an end inter-tribal wars, convincing them that common opposition to the advance of the French was necessary to the proper interests of the Indian trade, and that to promote this general movement concerted measures should be taken by the English for building forts at certain points in the Indian country. It was a counter stroke to the French, a plan of the same kind as theirs, only as yet with less emphasis on the military as a compelling force, and was to be carried into execution by the joint action of a pseudo-confederation of colonies rather than by the prompt initiative of a single autocratic government. When the governors of the provinces along the western frontier brought the subject under discussion before their councils and assemblies, this aspect of it was the one predominantly considered. Virginia, as Dinwiddie wrote De Lancey in January, 1754, could not participate becauses of the expense she was incurring for the defence of the frontier, and because of a meeting with the southern Indians and the Six Nations which they had planned to hold at Winchester on May thirtieth. From the Maryland assembly Governor Sharpe with difficulty secured an appropriation of £3000 for the support of the neighboring colonies against any hostile troops which should attack or invade his majesty's continental territories. The Pennsylvania assembly made the necessary appropriation for the sending of commissioners, but its attention was greatly occupied with the claim of Connecticut to the Wyoming country, with the Virginia boundary question, which seemed connected with every event in the Ohio region, and with the demand for further issues of bills of credit. New Jersey was still divided by its internal disputes over land titles; the relations between the assembly and Governor Belcher were strained; while the boundary dispute with New York was at its height. Like Maryland, New Jersey had no exposed frontier and had never shared in treaties with the Indians. Therefore no commissioners were appointed and only a vague resolution was passed by the assembly, that they were ready to assist the neighboring colonies according to their ability against the French in any well concerted scheme for that purpose, whenever it should be laid before them. This resolution was passed on the day when the congress was appointed to meet. In December, 1753, the New York assembly voted unanimously that the next year, as soon as the weather should permit, the governor should meet the Indians and renew the "antient Treaty" with them, and upwards of £1000 was appropriated for presents. In New Hampshire the question of paper money affected, but did not prevent, action. Connecticut passed a resolution which referred both to Indian relations and the adoption of proper measures for general defence and safety. In the instructions to its delegates it laid stress on the large sums in excess of the meagre support from the southern colonies which it had spent on defence, while they received great benefit from the Indian trade and Connecticut nothing. Therefore it was a limited and temporary support which this colony proposed to give, while it looked with disfavor on the proposal of making presents to the Indians. If troops were to be raised, they desired that those of Connecticut should be joined with the eastern and not the western troops, while it was to be understood that nothing agreed to at Albany should be binding on the colony until approved of by its assembly.

\*　　\*　　\*　　\*　　\*

At the opening session, in addition to the submission of the credentials of the members, and the reading of a letter from the board of trade to the late governor, Sir Danvers Osborne, enforcing the necessity of a joint treaty with the Six Nations which should result in a renewal of the alliance with them and the redress of all their grievances, the minutes of the two meetings of the Indian commissioners were also read in which they suggested that the tribesmen should be urged to live more compactly together and that the British should build two forts, one at Onondaga and another in the country of the Senecas. A protest from the traders to Oswego was also read, which furnished evidence of the ill will with which they were regarded by the Mohawks. A general speech to the Indians was drafted by a committee and approved after extended debate by the whole conference. The speech was delivered by De Lancey, and was accompanied by the giving of a chain belt which signified that the colonies were acting jointly in the name of the king with the entire body of the Six Nations, together with such other tribes as could be brought into the general alliance. The question of their attitude toward French encroachments was the all important one submitted to them.

Before the Indians made answer to the general speech, very frank talks were held by the Mohawks with the New York delegates, at which the chiefs aired again the grievances of the previous year, and expressed their liking for Johnson and their feeling that in recent years the New York government had turned its back upon them. The fraudulent land patents, among them the great Kayadarosseras patent along the Hudson above Half Moon, came in for sharp criticism.

When the reply of the Indians to the general speech was made, the orators were chosen from the Mohawks, and Hendrick again held the chief place. His proud, though impotent, contempt for the British again found full expression. "You ask us," he said, "why we live so dispersed. The reason is, your neglecting us these three years past (then taking a stick and throwing it behind his back); you have thus thrown us behind your back and disregarded us, whereas the French are a subtle and vigilant people, ever using their utmost endeavors to seduce and bring our people over to them." The Indians could not find that they had sold land to the French for any of the posts they had built, but they had simply taken it without consent. The same course had been followed by the English; Virginia and Pennsylvania had "made paths through our Country to Trade and built houses without acquainting us with it." Virginia and Canada were "quarrelling about lands which belong to us, and such a quarrel as this may end in our destruction." Referring sarcastically to the Indian commissioners, Hendrick declared that the Six Nations had never been invited to smoke with them, but for the sake of their beaver the Canadian Indians were frequently invited to conference. "Look about you and see all these houses full of Beaver, and the money is all gone to Canada; likewise powder, lead and guns, which the French now make use of at Ohio. The goods which go from thence to Oswego, go from thence to Ohio, which further enables the French to carry on their designs at the Ohio." Turning from land and trade to defence, Hendrick told the commissioners that it was the fault of the English that Crown Point had not been taken. "When we were ready to go and take it, we were told it was too late, that the ice would not bear us. . . . But instead, you burned your own forts at Sarayhtoga and run away from it, which was a shame and a scandal to you. Look about your Country and see, you have no Fortifications about you, no, not even to this City; 'tis but one step from Canada thither, and the French may easily come and turn you out of your doors. . . . We are ashamed to say it, you are all like women." Another chief concluded the talk with a demand that Colonel Johnson be reinstated in the management of Indian affairs, for they had lived happily under him and knew that he was their good and trusty friend. He desired that the Indian commissioners would duly observe what he said.

The reply which the commissioners made to the charge that the English frontiers were open and defenceless was contained in the articles of union, of which nothing in detail was said to the Indians. Conrad Weiser was brought in to reply to the charge that Virginia and Pennsylvania had been unwarrantably invading Indian territory, and he reviewed at length the course of trade and negotiations since, thirty years before, Delawares and

Shawnees had removed into the Ohio country. He showed that no hostile steps had been taken against the Indians and only now, as the result of French encroachment, had Virginia begun to build a house at the mouth of the Monongahela, from which they had just been driven by the enemy. As to Johnson, De Lancey told the Indians that he would make trial of commissioners for another year, and if they did not give satisfaction, effectual means would be taken to secure it. By the release of certain claims which the Livingstons had to lands about Canajoharie and a promise of better regulation of the rum trade some steps were taken toward quieting the complaints of the Indians concerning local evils. But as to the defenceless state of the frontier, the Indians at the close of the conference were as emphatic as ever, and begged that some improvement might be resolved upon speedily. In this was revealed their abject fear of French attack and their instinctive reliance on Johnson as the only Englishman who they thought could bring them protection. The River Indians, of whom a few still remained, were also included in the conference and in the pious exhortations to peace and friendship with which it closed.

While the talks with the Indians had been in progress, a committee had drafted a representation on the present state of the colonies, which was debated and adopted by the conference. This set forth the territorial claims of the British in North America, especially as stated in the treaty of Utrecht, and denounced the encroachments which since the time of the treaty the French had been making. It then went on to indicate, in terms really as strong as the Indians had used, the divided and defenceless condition of the British colonies, the unjustifiable neglect of the affairs of the Iroquois, the evils of the rum traffic and the fraudulent grants and surveys of land. These evils, so far as they affected the Indians directly, it was resolved should be checked and, to this end, that reliable persons should be appointed to reside with each tribe and report to the superintendents all complaints and questions which needed adjustments; forts should be built in the Indian country and trade and the granting of land should be regulated in the public interest. The western boundaries of existing colonies should be limited by the Appalachian mountains, and from time to time inland colonies should be settled west of those mountains. And, finally, there should be a union of the several British colonies on the continent, so that their counsels, treasure and strength might be employed in due proportion against the common enemy.

It was the devotion of a large share of the attention of the commissioners to the line of policy indicated in the last sentence which made this assembly more than a mere Indian conference, large and important though it was in that connection, and gave to it its chief fame as a Congress of the American Continental Colonies, the first which in any large sense is entitled to that designation. We have seen that Shirley had urged that a plan of union be worked out. Franklin's mind was already working on the same problem. In his "Gazette," under date of May 9, he had drawn from the capture by the French of Captain Trent's party, who were building a fort at the fork of the Ohio, the moral that the colonies must unite in order to resist successfully the French aggression, and had enforced it by the famous picture of the snake divided into thirteen parts, with the motto at the bottom "Join or Die." He drew up some "Short Hints towards Uniting the Northern Colonies," and on his way to Albany showed them to James Alexander, Archibald Kennedy and Cadwallader Colden for their criticism. When the commissioners had met at Albany, private discussion of this subject at once began among them and, in view of the well known political weakness of the colonies, it was generally agreed that a union was absolutely necessary to their security and defence. On June 24, the subject was first brought forward, probably by Franklin in the conference and a resolution embodying the above sentiment was unanimously passed. A proposal of De Lancey to build two forts in the Indian country was postponed until some method of effecting colonial union had been considered. Each colony then chose one of its own commissioners to make up a committee to formulate and report a plan, De Lancey being asked to designate one of the council of New York to a place on the committee. Its members, as thus chosen, were Thomas Hutchinson, Theodore Atkinson, William Pitkin, Stephen Hopkins, William Smith, Benjamin Franklin and Benjamin Tasker. The representation on the state of the colonies was also drafted by this committee. On July 2 the board passed the decisive vote to form a plan of union, to be established by act of parliament. Aside from the fact that the inauguration of a scheme of colonial union without authority from the imperial government would be an almost revolutionary innovation, it was considered that only by act of parliament could the union be made permanent and colonies be prevented from withdrawing at pleasure. The Connecticut commissioners were opposed to the plan and did not vote for it. De Lancey and Murray, of New York, also refused to vote for the plan. Some dissatisfaction was also expressed with the plan as already drafted, and Franklin was asked to prepare a new draft. This he did, and on the tenth of July, the day after the representation on the state of the colonies had been accepted, this also was approved and the members were desired to lay it before their constituents for consideration, while the secretary was ordered to send a copy to the governor of each of the colonies which was not represented in the Congress. It was then voted that a fort ought to be built at Irondequoit, in the Seneca country, and papers on French and Indian relations, submitted by Johnson and John Pownall, were accepted with thanks.

The Plan of Union, as drafted, was a statesmanlike document, and by his connection with it Franklin laid the foundation of his intercolonial reputation; but, as events soon proved, it struck a note to which as yet there was no favorable response either in the colonies or Great Britain. It was the first impression of the constitution-making instinct, which was to become so active both in Europe and America before the close of the century. Had it been put into operation, not only would a federation of the colonies have been established, but a long step would have been taken toward freeing them from the maze of ill defined or undefined relations in which they existed under the charters and royal instructions. The new constitution was to be established by act of parliament, each colony retaining its existing government except so far as it might be changed by the said act.

\*     \*     \*     \*     \*

The unanimity with which the Plan of Union was either ignored or rejected by all on both sides of the ocean whom it was supposed to concern, shows how little diffused was the real feeling of danger from the French and how indifferent or positively adverse the great mass of the colonists were to the erection of a second superior body which, in addition to the imperial government, might restrict their liberties. The two corporate colonies, Rhode Island and Connecticut, were especially outspoken in opposition to it, on the ground that it tended to infringe on the privileges which they enjoyed by charter. In Rhode Island the fact that Hopkins had shared in drafting the plan and had submitted it to the legislature, was made the subject of a bitter attack on him. By the assemblies of these two colonies, and especially by that of Connecticut, strong opposition to the plan was expressed and both of them instructed their agents to oppose it in England. The only response made by a colony which failed to send commissioners was from the provincial council of New Jersey, in the form of a resolution that union was necessary but the colonial councils should be given a place in the federal legislature. The assemblies and executives either took no notice whatever of the plan or, like Dinwiddie, waited to see how it was received in England. A report of the proceedings of the Congress, together with its journal and Plan of Union, was sent by Governor De Lancey to the board of trade, but this was not accompanied by an address, and no attempt was made either in the colonies or in England to promote the acceptance of the plan.

◦◦ ◦◦

BETWEEN *1689 and 1763, Britain and France fought four wars in the New World. The first three, King William's War (1689-1697), Queen Anne's War (1702-1713), and King George's War (1740-1748), began in Europe and then spilled over into North America; but the last war, the French and Indian War (1754-1763) reversed the process. The westward expansion of Virginian and Pennsylvanian provoked the French to fortify their positions in the Ohio Valley. It was George Washington's report to Virginian authorities that the French could only be removed by force that accounts for Braddock's disastrous campaign against French positions around Fort Duquesne (modern Pittsburgh).*

*Swiftly the war spread northward as New Englanders invaded French Acadia. Once both sides realized that the final phase of their seven-decade-long struggle for dominance was coming to a close, they escalated their effort and in 1756, the American war changed into a European war as Britain and Prussia entered into an alliance against France and Austria. The confronta-*

*tion begun in the desolate reaches of the American frontier now extended across the world wherever the interests of France and Great Britain conflicted. The first American stages of this conflict are described by Channing. Perhaps the most significant aspect of this stage of the war was the extent to which Britain committed her best forces to expel the French from their fortifications. A war that started with the intention to secure colonial territorial claims to western lands had become a war to exclude France once and for all from North America.*

*Edward Channing (1856-1931), long a member of the Harvard staff, devoted much of his scholarly life to an exploration of local political institutions during the colonial era and to the Jeffersonian system. He helped mark the shift away from literary history to the heavily documented monograph. Where his predecessors sought to capture the broad sweep of history, he devoted his energy to a microcosmic analysis of events. In his final multivolume study of American history which was incomplete at his death, Channing attempted successfully to capture the sweep of American history in a systematic analysis of its events. The result was a detailed account that remains a landmark of history.*

# A CENTURY OF COLONIAL HISTORY
## 1660-1760

### by Edward Channing

On the 15th of June, 1749, Celoron de Bienville sent by the Marquis de la Galissonière, governor of Canada, set out from Montreal to take possession of the Ohio Valley for France. He had with him two hundred and fourteen white men, soldiers, and Canadians, and a body of Indians in twenty-three canoes. Leaving Lake Erie, they carried their canoes overland to Chautauqua Lake in Southwestern New York, less than ten miles away. This led them to the Allegheny, down which they floated, stopping every now and then to warn off a group of English Indian traders, to palaver with the natives, or to deposit a leaden plate suitably inscribed. On they went past the confluence of the Monongahela and down the Ohio to the Great Miami and up this stream and back to Canada by the way of the Maumee and Lake Erie. This ceremonial taking possession was a favorite way with the French. By itself, it conferred no rights, but when followed by settlement, it did not in any way diminish the right conferred by the latter.

For years traders had passed over the Alleghanies from Will's Creek, where Cumberland now stands, and also through central Pennsylvania to the junction of the Monongahela and Allegheny rivers, and thence westwardly. At this time it was uncertain whether this part of the Ohio Valley was within the limits of Pennsylvania or Virginia, and this doubt interfered with the English occupation either by traders or more permanent settlers.

In 1749, however, leading Virginia gentlemen, among them Lawrence and Augustine Washington and George Mason, determined to take the initiative. They procured from the king a grant of two hundred thousand acres, to be picked out and settled south of the Ohio and between the Monongahela and the Kanawha rivers, with a promise of three hundred thousand more if a hundred families were settled within seven years and a fort built and maintained. In 1750 the company dispatched Christopher Gist, an Indian trader, to explore the Ohio country and select lands for them. He reached Logstown, on the Ohio, in November; he went as far north as Pickawillany on the Great Miami, not very far from the site of the present Bellefontaine, Ohio. In the following spring he returned to the Ohio River and, following up the Kanawha, regained the settled parts of Virginia. At about the same time the Loyal Land Company was given eight hundred thousand acres west of the mountain by the Virginia Assembly. It sent Dr. Thomas Walker across the mountain, by way of Cumberland Gap, to select and survey the lands. He built a house somewhere on the upper waters of the Cumberland River, and, if we may believe the maps, lived there for some time. Nothing more was done by either of these land companies, the activity of the French shortly afterward discouraging them. Such was the condition of affairs when, in 1752, the Marquis Duquesne de Menneville became Governor of Canada and proceeded to carry out a more aggressive policy in the Ohio Valley.

The new governor was instructed to build whatever forts on the Ohio he might think were absolutely necessary, but he was informed that the expense of the French colonies in America was already enormous. In the spring of 1753 he sent a thousand men to the Ohio Valley. Passing by the landing place of Celoron, the expedition occupied Presque Isle on the southern shore of the lake, where the city of Erie now stands. Thence they cut a road to the Riviere aux Boeufs, where they built a fort which they named Fort Le Boeuf. This stream led to the Allegheny and thence to the Ohio. Much more was intended, but disease and discouragement prevented. Three hundred men remained to garrison the two forts; the rest returned to the settlements on the St. Lawrence.

The governor of Virginia at that time was Robert Dinwiddie, a Scotsman and a man of ability and patriotism, although perhaps given to over-energetic action. Being informed by the traders of the presence of the French, he determined to send a written protest and warning and to demand their retirement from the Ohio Valley. The person whom he selected for this dangerous mission was George Washington, a young surveyor who was already favorably known to many influential persons.

Of all men in history, not one so answers our expectations as Washington. Into whatever part of his life the historian puts his probe, the result is always satisfactory. Washington was a strong, vigorous human being, with a strong, vigorous mind, and an amount of will power which was always equal to the task of compelling his mind and body to perform the part to which Providence set them. He grew up with the expectation of making his own way in the world, and in youth enjoyed the inestimable advantage of close contact with the wilderness. He was trained as a surveyor and was also taught the rudiments of the military art. Descended from Robert and Lawrence Washington of Sulgrave Manor in Northamptonshire, England, he possessed that fairness of mind which had led them in the early years of James's reign to sign a petition in favor of certain Nonconformist ministers who had been driven from their cures. Coming to Virginia, we find his grandfather, John Washington, of so fiery a disposition that he was known to the Indians as the "Devourer of Villages," from the completeness of the way in which he did his appointed work. The young surveyor came honestly by that fair-mindedness and military capacity which were forever his distinguishing characteristics. Accompanied by Christopher Gist and six other white men, Washington followed the well-known trading route from Will's Creek to Logstown, and thence to Venango at the confluence of the Allegheny and French Creek; here was an English trading house which the French had seized with its occupants and converted into Fort Machault. Washington was well received at the conquered post and at Fort Le Boeuf. The French commander sent Dinwiddie's letter to Duquesne, and Washington returned to Virginia. This journey occupied the months of November to January, 1753-54.

Dinwiddie now decided to send a force of Virginia militia to the forks of the Ohio to seize and fortify that strategic point and also to incite the Indians to oppose the French. His activity, in turn, induced the Frenchmen to renewed exertions. An English fur trader, Captain Trent, had already gone to the forks of the Ohio in February, 1754, to build a fort there and thus forestall the French; but before the post had been made defensible, the Canadians appeared in much larger numbers than the English and compelled the latter to evacuate the unfinished post. They themselves constructed on the same spot a much more important work, which they named Fort Duquesne. Meantime Dinwiddie had been setting on foot an expeditionary force to cross the mountains and garrison the fortification which Captain Trent had begun. He now redoubled his efforts, but without much result. Virginia had no efficient military force, and Pennsylvania with its Quaker majority in the assembly was worse off in this respect than Virginia. The best that Dinwiddie could do was to raise a few hundred men who pressed to the point of danger under the command of Colonel Joshua Fry and Washington, the latter commanding the advance. The traders' routes across the Alleghanies and in the western country were bridle paths used by pack trains, but not suitable for artillery and wagons. To move any considerable number of men it was necessary to cut a road from Will's Creek, and this took time. It was thus that Washington found himself at a place called Great Meadows on the western slope of the Alleghanies (May, 1754). Understanding that there was a party of Frenchmen in the vicinity, Washington with a detachment set out to oppose them. He came across the Frenchmen suddenly in the forest and ordered his men to fire. The commander of the French force, Coulon de Jumonville, and a score of his men, were killed, and the remainder, twenty or more in number, were captured. This conflict is generally regarded as the beginning of hostilities, but the first blow had been struck when the French seized the English trading house at Venango.

Washington returned to Great Meadows and ultimately constructed a rude fortification at that point, which he called Fort Necessity. There on July 3, 1754, he was attacked by a larger French force, commanded by Jumonville's brother, Coulon de Villiers. After defending himself for a time until some of his men were killed and all were disheartened, Washington surrendered upon condition of marching out with the honors of war. The articles of surrender also contained the words "Passassinat du Sieur de Jumonville," which Washington is supposed to have understood to have signified "death of Jumonville," but which French writers have regarded as an acknowledgement on his part of the assassination of the French commander. The articles were signed about midnight of July 3-4, 1754, but the actual surrender was made on the latter date. In this way in the forests of Virginia began the imperial war between Great Britain and France that was to end with the expulsion of the French from the eastern half of North America.

The conflict which began in the American wilderness in 1754 spread to Europe and became merged in the world-wide struggle for existence and power that is known to English historians as the Seven Years' War. In America the contest was denominated the French and Indian War and cannot be thoroughly understood apart from the contest in Europe, for, as Pitt observed, "America was conquered in Germany." The strength of the combatants cannot be gauged from an American continental colonial standpoint; but regard must be had to the fact that the forces of both England and France were directed more especially to the eastern side of the Atlantic, to the West India Islands, and to the lands bordering on the Indian Ocean. Thus Pitt was obliged to provide an extensive fleet to keep the French within their harbors of Brest, Rochefort, and Toulon, or, in military phrase, to "contain" them, while combined naval and military expeditions seized Canada, Guadeloupe, Martinique, Pondicherry, and Havana. The great fleets of Hawke, Boscawen, Saunders, and Keppel in the Bay of Biscay and Straits of Gibraltar were as truly fighting for the possession of Canada as the smaller squadrons in the St. Lawrence; the armies which England gave to Frederick in Germany were fighting the battles of England in America as were the armies of Amherst and Wolfe at Louisbourg and Quebec. The English colonists on the mainland outnumbered the French and Canada and Louisiana many times; but France was relatively much stronger in the West Indies, where she possessed Grenada, Dominica, Guadeloupe, Martinique, and Haiti, or the western half of the island of Santo Domingo, besides many smaller islands advantageously situated for commerce protection. In the later years of the contest, Spain brought into the conflict besides Mexico and the lands of the Spanish Main the island of Cuba and the rest of Santo Domingo. The armies of France were large and admirably trained, her navies were supplied with splendid ships, excellently armed. Whenever matters seemed unusually grave, projects of invasion of the British Islands at once served to divert formidable portions of England's military and naval forces from the conquest of the colonial possessions of the French king in America and India to the defense of Great Britain and Ireland. The fact that the contest was prolonged for eight or nine years, notwithstanding the brilliancy of England's war minister and the victories of her forces in America and India, shows that the combatants were more evenly matched than the outcome of the war in America when taken by itself would indicate.

The military capacities of the colonists of France were out of all proportion to their numbers and wealth as compared with the English settlers. Possibly because the French colonists had never been self-sustaining, the home government had been more liberal in furnishing them with defenders than had been the English government with its colonists on the continent. The Indians of New France also for generations had been accustomed to fight in company with their white neighbors. Finally, the government of New France was a feudal military oligarchy directed from Paris. Fortunately, the administration in Canada was honeycombed with corruption and was weakened by the lack of harmony among the higher officers. The English continental colonies had taken care of themselves from the beginning. Ordinarily, they had provided for their own military necessities, although from time to time England had sent out expeditions or had reimbursed the colonists for their expenses. The English Government had taken a direct interest in the frontier warfare of Georgia, providing both men and money for that purpose; but up to this time the protection of the continental colonies had not come into the system of imperial defense, and the conquest of Canada and Louisiana had not been thought of by English statesmen as being within the realm of practical international policy. On the other hand, the islands of the West Indies had long been looked upon as being within the imperial system; the protection of English sugar plantations and the conquest of foreign sugar islands had been regarded as next in importance to the protection of the shores of England and the acquisition of European naval stations like Gibraltar and Minorca. These tasks absorbed the larger portion of British military and naval strength and deducted just so much from that which was applicable to the conquest of French possessions on the American continent.

The soldiers engaged in the contest in America were necessarily drawn mainly from the home countries; the naval armaments entirely so, and the military forces to a greater and greater extent as the conflict assumed more formidable proportions; thus Wolfe's Quebec expedition comprised eight thousand English soldiers and possible five hundred colonial rangers; the naval force and the transports being entirely drawn from England. The colonists often performed notable service, as in Bradstreet's campaign, but their chief contribution was providing the means for fitting out naval fleets and land expeditions. At first sight it would seem that the English colonies should have given England an overwhelming advantage; and had it been possible strictly to blockade the American possessions of France, the strength of the English colonists as providers of food would have worked greatly against the French.

None of the French colonies produced enough for the needs of their inhabitants; their sugar islands, like those of England, depended almost entirely upon the Northern Colonies for the food consumed by the servants and slaves who labored on their plantations. Of course in time the people of these islands could divert a part of their strength and time from the making of sugar to the production of bread and meat, but even then they would not have been able to fit out and supply the expeditions and fleets which used their harbors. Had the British government been able to stop all trade between the English continental colonies and Canada and the French sugar islands, their conquest would have been greatly simplified; but this proved to be impossible. For fifty years and more, in defiance of law, the continental colonists had traded with the French West India Islands; perhaps it was the fact that this commerce was always illegal that made it seem not so heinous and unpatriotic in wartime as it really was—and trade with the enemy has gone on unchecked in every great war. This traffic was contrary not only to English law, but was also illegal under the statutes of Pennsylvania, New York, South Carolina, and other colonies.

The commerce between the bread colonies and the French sugar islands at first was carried on as it always had been by means of certificates and bills of lading which were not true to the fact. When this commerce became dangerous, vessels engaged in supplying the enemy's islands with food were provided with licenses to sail to St. Pierre or some other French port for the purpose of exchanging prisoners. Governor Denny of Pennsylvania sold these licenses for twenty pounds or even less, so it is said. On the other hand, Governor Fauquier of Virginia informed Pitt that four hundred guineas had been offered him if he "would license a Flag of Truce"; prisoners under these circumstances had a commercial value. When this commerce was suppressed the colonists traded indirectly through some neutral port, especially by way of the roadstead of Monte Christo, off the northern coast of Santo Domingo, not far from the boundary of the French part of the island. Sometimes there were as many as fifty vessels lying at anchor there—most of them from the continental colonies, but a few were from the British islands. In 1760 Pitt directed the governors of the English colonies to "put the most speedy and effectual stop to such flagitious Practices."

While the French colonies formed an excellent military engine so far as their strength permitted, the power of the English plantations was distributed between twelve or thirteen separate governments, all of which were unfitted for the performance of strenuous military tasks and were jealous of one another. This weakness of the English colonies was due to the ascendency over the executive branch which the assemblies had gained in them. The voting of the smallest sum of money or the authorizing the mobilization of the militia always resulted in days and weeks spent in debate and often in constitutional controversies between the two branches of the administration. The strength of these governments for the solution of the peace problems was unfavorable to the transaction of military business. Moreover, the several colonies were jealous of one another and indisposed to united effort. The New Englanders habitually acted together, but they were very suspicious of the New Yorkers, and this feeling was fully reciprocated. It originated in differences in settlement and institutions and was intensified by long-continuing commercial rivalries. The passiveness of Pennsylvania angered the New Yorkers, Marylanders, and Virginians, who felt that the great Quaker-German colony was not doing its part. The Carolinas had grown rapidly in population and resources, but possessed little military strength, owing to the prevalence of slavery in an intensive form in South Carolina and to the dispersal of the settlements in North Carolina. The Carolinians also had their own problems to face in the shape of threatened Indian war and probable conflict with the Spaniards in Florida. Taking everything into consideration, the strength of the English colonies, save under exceptional circumstances, should be rated at only about one half of its nominal value.

In the approaching contest, the attitude of the Iroquois was of great importance, fully as much as it had been in the earlier French wars. In September, 1753, therefore, The Lords of Trade directed the governors of New Hampshire, Massachusetts, New York, New Jersey, Pennsylvania, Maryland, and Virginia to hold a conference with representatives of the Six Nations in order that a joint agreement might be made between all the English colonies, north of Carolina, and the Iroquois. Accordingly, on June 19, 1754, commissioners from these colonies, excepting New Jersey and Virginia, and from the two other New England colonies of Rhode Island and Connecticut, met at Albany. The commissioners proceeded to discuss not merely the conduct of Indian Affairs, but a union of all the colonies for their security and defense. Among the commissioners was Benjamin Franklin, and the document which is known as the Albany Plan of Union came from his pen. He was not the only one to propose plans of union at that conference or Congress, as it is usually termed. Indeed, the idea of intercolonial union seems to have been widespread at that time. Thomas Hutchinson of Massachusetts, Meshech Weare of New Hampshire, and the Rev. John Peters of Pennsylvania have also left plans of union in their handwriting. The consideration of the subject at Albany appears to have been due to Governor Shirley of Massachusetts, but it is not clear that he acted on the initiative of the English government. The plan that was agreed to demanded so great a surrender of power by the several colonies that none of them adopted it, although it had received the vote of every one of their commissioners. As the scheme was unacceptable to the colonists, it never came before the royal government for action; but there is no reason to suppose that the authorities in England would have approved it. They preferred a scheme which the Lords of Trade prepared in August, 1754, and presented to the king for his consideration. This plan provided that a circular of instruction should be sent to all the governors of the continental colonies, setting forth the necessity of a union for military purposes. Each colony was to appoint one person to represent it at a conference, at which the general defense of the colonies should be considered and the quota of troops and the amount of money to be raised by each colony should be settled. The king would appoint a commander-in-chief, who was to have the expenditure of the money so raised; but the colonial assemblies might make representations as to military affairs to the commander-in-chief as occasion arose. These commissioners also were to formulate a project of a General Convention for joint colonial action of military subjects, which, with the approbation of the assemblies, should be submitted to the king for his confirmation. Nothing was done in furtherance of this scheme, probably because the adoption of Franklin's plan of colonial union by the commissioners at Albany convinced the authorities in England that further agitation of the subject was not advisable at the moment. Later, in appointing Governor Shirley of Massachusetts commander-in-chief of all the forces on the continent, the English government may be regarded as acting in conformity with the project of the Lords of Trade.

The British government regarded the French aggressions in the interior as justifying reprisals on land and sea, and this without giving any just cause for war. An elaborate plan of action was proposed for 1755; one army operating from Virginia was to capture Fort Duquesne; other expeditions from New York and from New England were to attack Crown Point and Niagara and dispossess the French of their posts in Acadia. To add to the chance of success, a fleet under Boscawen was sent to the Gulf of St. Lawrence to seize a French fleet convoying troops and supplies to Canada. Boscawen bungled his part of the business in capturing only one or two of the French ships; but this was enough to induce the French government to look upon war as existing, although they probably would have endured the inconvenience of many attacks upon their land forces in America before proceeding to that extremity.

For the enterprise against Fort Duquesne, two regiments of British regulars were sent out from England under the command of General Edward Braddock, an Englishman, who was assisted by a staff of English officers. Braddock was a trained soldier of experience in warfare and of undoubted courage. His age of sixty years and his lack of tact are sufficient to account for his refusal to respect colonial conditions, but he also appears to have been deficient in administrative ability. The expedition proceeded through the unsettled portions of western Virginia, which was almost inevitable, since it may be said to have grown out of the policy of Virginia's governor in attempting to forestall the French on the Ohio. It is useless to speculate upon the might-have-beens, and England has almost always suffered defeats in the beginnings of wars and has almost as invariably succeeded in the end; it was with the British as it was with Washington—failure was necessary to bring forth the highest effort.

In the conditions of ocean transport and wilderness road cutting, Braddock made commendable speed. He sailed from England in December, 1754, reached Virginia in the following February, held a council with the colonial governors in April, was at Will's Creek on May 10th, on July 9, 1755, fought the battle in which his expedition was wrecked and himself mortally wounded. The English soldiers and their brave officers were done to death in an open space on the east side Monongahela, some seven or eight miles from Fort Duquesne. Braddock's only thought was to keep his soldiers in line and compact formation and send them thus against the enemy, mostly Indians sheltered behind trees and partly protected by some sort of defensive works. Some of the Virginia soldiers essaying to fight the enemy frontier-fashion broke ranks and deployed in skirmish line, utilizing every bit of cover; but Braddock with many a good military oath called them back to the ranks; some of the regulars also trying to do the same thing, he beat them back to their close formation with his sword. Attacked on three sides, the Englishmen stood this treatment as long as human nature permitted and then fled. The most gratifying thing about the whole affair was the bravery and utter disregard of self shown by the old general in this his last fight on earth. For the time being this was the end of attempts to seize Fort Duquesne. The interest of the war now turns to the North.

For a quarter of a century the French had occupied a post at Crown Point, where Lake Champlain narrows into riverlike proportions, and thus held a firm grasp on the route from the Hudson to the St. Lawrence. Even earlier the French had built a fort at Niagara, which gave them a certain measure of control of the lake route from Montreal to the West. On the other hand, the English had for many years held a post at Oswego at the southeastern corner of Lake Ontario. For the possession of these important points of strategic advantage, and the English forts between Lake George and the Hudson River, the contest was prolonged. Up to 1758 the course of events was generally in favor of the French.

With the signing of the Treaty of Aix-la-Chapelle in October, 1748, the English government for the first time displayed an active interest in the affairs of the Acadian peninsula. Having restored Louisbourg to France, the English ministry determined to build a stronghold and establish a naval base at Chebucto Bay, where Halifax now stands. Thither in June, 1749, came twenty-five hundred settlers, who laid out a town to which other colonists were attracted, so that in 1752 it numbered four thousand inhabitants. This settlement of Halifax in Nova Scotia was also memorable for being the only English colony founded by direct royal endeavor on the North American continent. In addition to this fortified town there were a few scattered posts in the peninsula and a feeble garrison at Annapolis near its southwestern end; but away from Halifax and its immediate vicinity there was no effective English occupation of Acadia. The French inhabitants of the peninsula numbered about nine thousand. They were agriculturists, were devoted to their religion, and were strong in their racial prejudices. Unfortunately for them, they lived in one of the most important strategic points on the Atlantic coast, holding the southern entrance to the Gulf of St. Lawrence. Moreover, the French authorities in Canada refused to accept the cession of Acadia as a finality. They disputed as to its boundaries and stationed a force at the most northerly point of the Bay of Fundy in a fort which they named Beauséjour. Not far to the east at Beaubassin the English established a fortified post which they named Fort Lawrence, in honor of the governor of Nova Scotia.

One part of the general scheme of offensive operations against the French in 1755 was the expulsion of the garrison at Beauséjour, which the English held to be wrongfully occupied. Lieutenant Colonel Monckton commanded the expedition, which was composed in part of two thousand Massachusetts troops enlisted for one year and led by Colonel John Winslow. No effective resistance was made and the French fort was surrendered by its commander, Duchambon de Vergor, in June, 1755. Before the month was out all the other French posts on the mainland east of the St. Croix were abandoned by their garrisons.

The French Acadians had taken the side of their compatriots and co-religionists in these preliminaries. The English resented their conduct and stood in fear of them—not without reason—considering their numbers and the nearness of the French garrison at Louisbourg. These communities might prove a serious menace to any expedition to the St. Lawrence that was conducted from Halifax as a base unless a considerable garrison was left at that post. The Acadians could be neutralized by seizing and holding as hostages the leading men among them, or by settling an overwhelming number of English colonists in their country; they could be eliminated from the military problem by distributing them throughout the old English settlements to the southward. The last was likely to be the most efficacious solution of the difficulty, as well as the easier and cheaper from a military point of view. So it seemed to Governor Lawrence and his advisers, among whom was Commodore Boscawen. The deportation of the Acadians was ordered and such papers as have survived do not contain any suggestion that Lawrence's action was disapproved by his superiors in England. The Acadians were unfortunate in living within the field of military operations; had their homes been a hundred miles farther south or north, they might have lived placidly and died peacefully where they were born.

The deportation was conducted under Lawrence by Monckton and Murray and Winslow, but the chief part fell to the last named, who had charge of sending the settlers away from Grand Pré and the Basin of Minas. He left a detailed journal of his doings and of the impression which the sad business made on his mind. The Acadians had already been disarmed, but they were so numerous that Winslow thought it necessary to place as many of the men as possible on five vessels, which he had at his disposal, while awaiting the arrival of transports to carry the exiles to their new homes. There were delays inevitable to such operations, and the Acadians did not assist Winslow to make easier his difficult and distasteful duty. While awaiting the arrival of the transports those who were confined on shipboard were fed by their families by means of boats, which came to the shore and collected supplies. "When the wind blows, the people on board are starving," so wrote Winslow on September 20, 1755. At last the transports arrived. In the harsh autumn weather there was much confusion, families were not kept together, and, no doubt, there was loss of property, but these accidents were inseparable from the circumstances of the case. The Acadians were carried to the colonies from Massachusetts to Georgia. The English settlers were not at all rejoiced at their coming, and, in some cases, were as frightened at the apparition of an Acadian as they would have been at the sight of a wild Indian in full war paint. Many of the exiles escaped from their new abodes, some of them going to Louisiana, others to Canada. A good many of them found their way back to Acadia and rejoined those of their former neighbors who had been fortunate enough to elude capture.

In 1757 a new chapter opened in the history of England and America, for it was then that William Pitt became the ruler of England, which position he held for four eventful years. This remarkable man had begun official life by refusing to handle the nation's money as his own when he occupied the office of Paymaster of the Forces. With a tendency toward theatricalism, William Pitt possessed the imaginative enthusiasm which marks the great statesman. He also was fearless of criticism when he felt that what he was doing was for the benefit of king and country, which is one of the attributes of the man of power. He now infused some of his own faith and energy into military and naval commanders. Acting on the initiative of others, he completely changed the policy of the empire as to America. Up to this time the idea had been simply to hold back the French; now, the plan was to expel them from the continent, and the difference was great. In carrying out this policy, Pitt also departed from tradition. He sought out the best men in military and naval life, regardless of their years, and gave them responsibility and stood behind them. He concentrated English military and naval forces in America upon one field of activity at a time, abandoning for the moment the conquest of the West India Islands for the occupation of Canada. He recognized that the colonists could supply men and food, but could not unaided withdraw much labor and what was equivalent to capital from ordinary occupations. He provided, therefore, that the colonists should pay the wages of the soldiers raised by them and supply them with arms and with clothing, but that all other expenses should be borne by the crown. In later campaigns the home government also provided arms, ammunition, tents, and part of the other expenses. The first result of the new policy was the capture of Louisbourg in 1758.

Since its restoration to them in 1748 the French had reconstructed and extended the fortifications of Louisbourg until it deserved the title of "the Dunkirk of America"; it was now a much more formidable fortress than when Pepperell and his New Englanders had captured it in 1745. In place of the small force which then defended it, more than three thousand disciplined soldiers now formed its garrison, while twelve warships, carrying over five hundred guns and three thousand men, lay at anchor in the harbor. For the conquest of Louisbourg, Pitt provided a fleet of twenty-three warships of the line and eighteen frigates under Admiral Boscawen and eleven thousand regular soldiers, besides a few hundred provincials, under the command of Jeffrey Amherst with whom as brigadiers were Charles Lawrence and James Wolfe. Of these the last was to win the greatest fame. Born in 1727, James Wolfe was now thirty-one years of age, but already he had had a long military career, since he entered the army at the age of fourteen; at eighteen he was a brigade major, and at twenty-two commanded a regiment. In person he was tall and slight and in health the reverse of robust, but he possessed a spirit as enthusiastic as Pitt's own. Landing at almost the same spot at which the New Englanders had gained the shore thirteen years earlier, the English advanced overland while Boscawen with his powerful fleet held open their communications. Once on shore and with his base secure, Amherst pushed the siege with vigor and success. The descriptions of life within the fortress are among the most vivid that we have. Ere long the French ships were set on fire, buildings within the walls destroyed or greatly damaged, and a breach opened through which an assault could be made. Then, on the 26th of July, 1758, Louisbourg finally passed out of the hands of France into those of England. The defense had been admirably conducted by Drucour and his subordinates, and the surrender at last was made at the intercession of the civil governor. While the siege of Louisbourg was drawing to a close, Brigadier General Forbes, commanding a new expedition against Fort Duquesne, lay ill at Carlisle on the frontiers of Pennsylvania.

Braddock's defeat was the signal for the Delawares and Shawanoes to attack the frontier settlements of Pennsylvania, which were utterly unprotected, the settlers lacking even powder and lead, although they had frequently petitioned the Assembly for supplies of these and other warlike stores. The sufferings of the frontier families became so intense that in 1755 the Assembly voted fifty-five thousand pounds for the king's use, to which the proprietors added five thousand pounds more. These funds were used to build a chain of forts on the Blue Mountains between the Delaware and the Susquehanna, to which the settlers could resort, and the garrisons of which would afford them protection in their houses. In the next year the Quakers retired from the Assembly and thereafter Pennsylvania took a more active part in the conflict. Besides the capture of Louisbourg, the plan of operations for 1758 included the sending of an expedition against Fort Duquesne and extensive warfare on the northern frontier.

The command of the Duquesne expedition was given to Brigadier General John Forbes, who had begun life as a physician, but had now been in the military service for some years. He had twelve hundred Highlanders besides colonial troops from Pennsylvania and the colonies to the southward, numbering in all about six thousand men. His leading subordinate was Lieutenant Colonel Henry Bouquet, a Swiss from Canton Berne. Contrary to Washington's advice, Forbes decided to proceed through Pennsylvania, Braddock's road being circuitous and overgrown with brush. He advanced by short stages, everywhere fortifying as he went. This slow rate of progression turned out to be in favor of his success, for the Indian allies of the French, disgusted at having nothing to do, deserted their employers. What made most in Forbes's favor, however, was a treaty of peace, which the Pennsylvanians were able to make with the Delaware and Shawanoe Indians who had been attacking the frontier settlements for several years. During the whole campaign Forbes was so ill that he had to be carried in a litter. The command of the advance fell to Bouquet. Unfortunately he permitted one of his subordinates, Major Grant, to reconnoitre out of supporting distance from the main body. This detachment was set upon by the French and Indians and badly defeated. So slow was Forbes's advance that November found the army still at some distance from the fort and a decision was reached to stop further progress for the year. Information then came to Forbes that the French were

in a critical condition. With twenty-five hundred men he now pushed
rapidly foward, Washington being in command of his right wing. When
they reached the vicinity of the fort, explosions were heard and a reconnoissance showed that the French had blown up their defenses and abandoned
their stronghold (November 24, 1758). In this way the French possession of
western Pennsylvania came to a close.

❦

THE *heart of New France was in the St. Lawrence valley, at the point where
the cliffs of Quebec towered above the river. Here the final stand of France
in the New World was made and here the confrontation between Britain
and her American colonials opened. For the union that joined England and
her colonies was more a marriage of convenience than a love match. So long
as the colonies faced the threat of France, they accepted the need for British
protection. But the long tradition of self-government precluded the possibility that the colonies would accept a tightening of the bonds between
themselves and the mother country. Thus once Britain found herself in possession of North America, reason dictated the establishment of an imperial
system that would simplify the processes of colonial administration. To the
colonial mind such an effort violated their most treasured rights, not the least
of which was to dwell in a commonwealth of equals.*

*The climactic battle on the Plains of Abraham proved Pyrrhic for the
British. It presented the victor with an empire, but it also provided the spark
which would ignite the concealed differences between Britain and her
colonies. It would not be too much to say that above the cliffs of Quebec
New France died but that also American independence was born.*

*William Milligan Sloane (1850-1928) brought a catholic range to his his-
torical research. After graduating from Columbia College (1868), he served
as private secretary to George M. Bancroft, the great historian-politician
of the mid-nineteenth century. Inspired by this contact, he went on to obtain
his Ph.D at the University of Leipzig (1876), where he was exposed to the
discipline of the seminar system. He concentrated his major interest on
France in the eighteenth century and particularly in the era of the French
Revolution. But he also found time to deal with the problem of party
government in the United States and, if that were not enough, also with the
Balkans. His treatment of American history cast it into the perspective of
the larger world scene. Unlike many of his contemporaries, Sloane rejected
the inward-looking perspectives of the disciples of Frederick Jackson Turner,
and settled instead for the broad ranging view that understands the agony of
one man, no matter where he dwells, is the agony of all.*

# THE FRENCH WAR
# AND THE REVOLUTION

## by *William Milligan Sloane*

Affairs in Canada had come to a crisis. The quarrel between Vaudreuil and Montcalm was so bitter that it was carried home to the court. The latter was supported, himself and friends were loaded with new honors, but substantial aid in men and supplies was withheld. A few hundred recruits and some absolutely essential munitions were embarked and reached Quebec in safety, but the condition of the province was no less desperate. The officials were so recklessly dishonest that even the scanty supplies afforded never reached those for whom they were intended. From Bigot, the intendant, down to the meanest commissary in Fort Duquesne, not excepting the commander Ligneris, every man through whose hands they passed stole a portion, until the troops, half-starved and revengeful, grew mutinous as well. The Indians, too, found the articles they wanted few and dear, and became so disaffected that the example of the powerful Delawares in abandoning the French grew more and more contagious. The Canadians themselves had thus far been deceived in every respect by the gasconade of Vaudreuil, and having sustained their courage by faith in a glory which was fictitious, suddenly found themselves with half-tilled fields and scanty crops, large contributions from which were often exacted for the king, while an angry and licentious soldiery were quartered in their cabins at the munificent rate of fifteen francs a man per month. It was evident that the rottenness and intrigue so successfully imitated from Paris and Versailles would quickly finish their work in Montreal and Quebec. Montcalm lost the buoyant cheerfulness natural to his southern blood, and with a secret desperation, but half-veiled by his assumed and pathetic courage, prepared to obey the instructions from home, to confine operations for the coming season to posts close together and with easy intercourse one with the other. And all the time Vaudreuil blustered, threatened, and plotted; nor was the tide of official corruption stayed even for an instant. Many expected and some desired the overthrow of New France, hoping to escape detection and punishment.

The course of the Seven Years' War on the Continent was far from uniform. In the west the able and determined Ferdinand defeated the French at Crefeld, forcing them across the Rhine. Frederick spent much time at Olmutz, where he was unsuccessful. But in August he won a fierce and bloody battle over the Russians at Zorndorf. Hastening thence to aid his brother Henry against the Austrians, he was in turn beaten at Hochkirch by Marshal Daun. At the opening of 1759 Ferdinand likewise suffered a reverse at the hands of De Broglie, but on August 1st he took summary vengeance at the battle of Minden. The day was a signal victory, and would have been an utter rout for the enemy, if Lord George Sackville had used the turn of affairs by hurling the English cavalry against the faltering lines of his opponents. It was not a mere error of judgment, and he was punished later for cowardice. On that day a new revelation was made to the student of the art of war. Six English infantry regiments, through a mistake in interpreting an order, charged the French cavalry opposite them, and regardless of a raking artillery fire, successfully broke through the lines. Twelve days later Frederick was defeated by the combined Austrians and Russians at Kunersdorf. The possible consequences were averted by the dissensions of his foes. The road to Berlin was open, but they did not take it. Dresden, however, surrendered and a part of Saxony was lost. Yet this, his darkest hour, was marked by the same unsurpassable qualities of greatness which illuminated his whole career. The winter found him still master of Silesia and much of Saxony.

The year 1759 seemed in England to atone for the past. Her career of victory both by land and by sea was almost unbroken. To herself and to others she seemed to be a world power of the first importance, and in the sphere of general history she has never since outdone the achievements of that wonderful time. France, in the last effort of exhaustion, made a feint of invading England, and began ostentatious preparations in the harbors of Toulon and Havre. In July Rodney bombarded Havre, and rendered ineffective whatever had been done there; Boscawen fell upon the Toulon fleet off Lagos, and scattered it; while Sir Edward Hawke gained a decisive victory over Admiral de Conflans, near Quiberon. A little British squadron during the same summer conquered Senegal. Keppel after a short struggle seized Goree. Pococke kept the upper hand in East Indian waters; and although the West Indian fleet failed against Martinique, it nevertheless captured Guadeloupe. Byng's defeat at Minorca had stung the nation to hasty injustice, for they saw themselves stripped of naval supremacy. It was felt that Quiberon had restored that mastery. There was in all English history no agreement so pusillanimous as that of Closter-Seven. Men saw in Minden the restoration of England's military honor. No less than twelve millions of supplies was voted by parliament during the year.

But the highest lustre shines on Pitt's ministry for none of these things. It is remembered in the story of the world for deeds quite as illustrious in another quarter of the globe, and more lasting in their influence on human destinies than any of these. The American campaign was again laid out on a complete and farsighted plan. The frontier between the newly founded Pittsburgh and Lake Erie was to be secured and held by Stanwix; Sir William Johnson and Prideaux were to collect Indians and provincials, and advance by Niagara and Lake Ontario on Montreal. Amherst had been appointed commander-in-chief. With the main army he was to march as far as Lake Champlain, and there seize the chance, if it offered, to unite with the army of the St. Lawrence for the capture of Quebec. Into this latter purpose the moral strength and nervous vitality of the whole movement were thrown. Admiral Saunders, in command of the fleet, was a thorough officer, a man of noble and generous personality, great enough to co-operate without jealousy or to rise independently to the height of an emergency.

Of Wolfe, Pitt's general, as he was called, we have already spoken. His form was feeble and his face uncomely, but the fire of his energy glowed in his fine eyes. After the dashing exploits of the preceding year he had spent the winter in London, where he won the affections of a noble woman whom he was destined never to see again. He was a devotee of that learning which is its own end and reward, and though a soldier at heart, often found refuge from the throng of camp and court in the avocation of quiet study. He had from the beginning been assigned to posts not ordinarily given to youth, and now, in the zenith of his power, he was but thirty-two years old. He fully realized the confidence placed in him, and the importance of the command which had been given to him. To one of his friends he had used these words: "I feel called upon to justify the notice taken of me by such exertions and exposures of myself as will probably lead to my fall."

The colonies were inferior to no other part of the British dominions in self-denying enthusiasm. In some of them, as in Massachusetts, fifteen per cent of all able-bodied men were under arms; in others, as in New Jersey, taxes amounting to five dollars for every man, woman, and child, were imposed in support of the war. Provincials and regulars together, there were about fifty-two thousand effective men in the field; Montcalm's forces were upward of twelve thousand, excluding the savages.

The campaign opened by the successful execution of the plan regarding Niagara. Prideaux had two regiments of English troops with artillery, a battalion of royal Americans, and two of New York provincials. Sir William Johnson brought his quota of Iroquois. A large garrison was left at Fort Stanwix, on the great carrying place, and still another considerable body was detached at Oswego to rebuild the fort. Early in July the small remainder sailed from Oswego, and reached Niagara in safety. The fort stood on the promontory where the river sweeps into Lake Ontario, and as befitted its importance, had been entirely rebuilt and strengthened by its commanding officer, Pouchot. But after some blunders, it was invested in due form and the English batteries set. Almost at the first discharge Prideaux was killed by the bursting of a small mortar. But Johnson took command immediately, and pursued the work so successfully that in a short time the works were breached. Meantime the French along the frontier had gathered the largest possible force to retake Fort Pitt, as the English had named the reconstructed Fort Duquesne. The force contained but few soldiers, being chiefly bush-rangers and Indians. Such as it was, however, its leaders, Aubrey and Ligneris, were ordered to bring it up for the aid of the beleaguered garrison at Niagara. They arrived, eleven hundred whites and two hundred Indians, on the twenty-fourth, but were almost at once engaged by the British forces and Johnson's Indians. The conflict was short but decisive. Many of the French forces were killed, and the rest fled, most of the fugitives continuing their retreat as far as Detroit. The leaders were all taken prisoners. There was nothing left for the brave garrison but surrender. Johnson made honorable terms for them, and though his Indians were permitted to plunder the fort, no massacre revenged the unforgotten slaughter at Fort William Henry.

By this success Stanwix was enabled to occupy the entire frontier, and the whole upper valley of the Ohio passed into undisputed English possession. The posts of the French as Presque Isle, Venango, and Leboeuf had been destroyed by the fugitives, and those further distant in the wilderness were entirely cut off from their eastern support. The only outlet for them was to Louisiana. The colony of New York claimed the hitherto debatable lands about the river and lakes. Amherst hoped to gain still further advantage by sending General Gage to take Prideaux's command and secure the upper St. Lawrence. Levis had been sent by Montcalm to prevent just such a movement. He had but eight hundred men, a number insufficient for his purpose. Gage would have had still fewer in all probability, if he had sufficiently garrisoned Niagara and Oswego. In any case he made no effort to carry out his orders, and reported that the plan was not feasible.

Holding Ticonderoga only as an outpost, the French had established themselves for real resistance on the Isle-aux-Noix, in the middle of the river Richelieu below Lake Champlain. Bourlamarque was in command, "intrenched," as he said, "to the teeth, and armed with a hundred cannon." His garrison numbered thirty-five hundred, and behind him was Levis, whose very name was a tower of strength to the Canadians. Nothing was more desired than an attack by Amherst. The English army was entirely disproportionate to its task, five thousand seven hundred and forty-three regulars and as many provincials with artillery and perfect equipments. By June they were assembled at Lake George, on July 21st they sailed down the lake, next day there was a skirmish under the walls of Ticonderoga, and the French retreated finally from that famous spot on the twenty-sixth, and from Crown Point on August 1st.

It is useless to speculate on the motives of Amherst, or to call him dull and slow, for the sequel seems incomprehensible on any hypothesis. He at once began a costly and massive fortress, and spent the remaining months of the season, August, September, and part of October in its construction, while a little navy of three vessels was building. The four French vessels made no stand, and three of them were rendered useless by their crews. Thereupon the regulars embarked in open boats, but a wintry storm arose and after five days the expedition returned to Crown Point. In August the general had sent a messenger, promising effectual assistance, who reached Wolfe by a long detour after a month's journey; a second letter was despatched in September by the directer route of the Abenakis on the St. Francis River, but the messengers were seized by them and carried to Montreal. In revenge Robert Rogers, with a party of rangers, destroyed the village, but the generals remained ignorant of each other's movements. This was the end of Amherst's campaign, and the result of all his extravagant preparation. The decisive blow was struck elsewhere, with fewer men and less expenditure of money, but with a lavish consumption of energy and brains. There was to be no co-operation, and Wolfe had therefore, after waiting in vain, dauntlessly undertaken his task, the most difficult hitherto assigned to any of the English generals.

In pursuance of the policy of concentration, Montcalm had gathered into the army around Quebec what was substantially the effective fighting force of Canada, between sixteen and seventeen thousand men, exclusive of the Indians, who were by this time disheartened and worthless. The city stands on a promontory formed by the great river of the St. Lawrence on the southwest, and the St. Charles, which directs its current into the main stream in a direction almost due east, on the north side of the town. At short intervals along the north shore, minor rivers, as the Larry and the Beaufort, flow down from the highlands of the interior, until the rushing torrent of the Montmorency with its famous waterfall is reached at a distance of about seven miles. Quebec itself had two parts, the lower town on the alluvium of the St. Charles, and the upper on a cliff, the slopes of which were crowned by the ramparts; and these in turn were overtopped on the riverside by the citadel. The majestic flood is here crowded into a narrow strait thirteen hundred yards in width. The left bank on the north is the more precipitous, and on its summit, level with the upper town, lie the Plains of Abraham, the end of a tableland which stretches southwest some eight miles to Cape Rouge.

Montcalm had done everything to deserve success. There were one hundred and six pieces of artillery on the walls of the stronghold. Above the place as far as Cape Rouge, batteries and mortars were disposed on the heights, and off the low shores lay fire rafts. Below the confluence of the rivers the low shores, as far as the intervals of Beaufort, were defended by earthworks, behind which were the headquarters of Vaudreuil. Beyond Beaufort the land was much higher, and along the natural escarpment strong ramparts were thrown up as far as the falls of Montmorency. At the upper end of these Montcalm had his quarters, at the lower Levis. Within this long and strong line the troops were placed to the best advantage, two thousand in the city, the remainder in camps stretching up and down the river. The channel at the mouth of the St. Charles was closed by a chain and guarded by armed hulks.

The English fleet, with Wolfe and his army of eight thousand men, had reached Louisburg in May, and on June 26th they anchored below the isle of Orleans, some miles from their objective point. There were many men on board whose names were to become either famous or notorious, among them Cook, the navigator, Monckton, George Townshend, Isaac Barre, William Howe, and Guy Carleton. The army was safely disembarked. Much time must, of course, be spent in reconnoitring, some arrangements were made only to be changed, and there were occasional skirmishes of no importance. The fleet commanded the waters; batteries were accordingly posted on the eastern point of the Isle of Orleans, and across the south channel of the river, at Point Levy, were built redoubts protected and strengthened by frigates at anchor; the shore guns were able to throw red-hot balls into the lower town, which they burned. The citadel was beyond range.

The chief camp was established on the left bank of the Montmorency, where the land is higher than that occupied by the French across the river, and to the northeast of them. Higher up the stream, four miles in the interior, a ford was found, but there was a strong entrenchment on the French side which rendered its passage impossible. Such, in short, had been the vigilance and capacity of the coolly desperate Montcalm, that from the Montmorency on one side to the St. Charles on the other, every possible means of approach from either one of the three rivers had been examined and fortified. His confidence that the citadel would be found impregnable was, moreover, not ill-founded. It must have appeared to him that his most dangerous foe was starvation. July was spent by Wolfe and the officers of the fleet in industrious but unavailing examination of the ground.

The French had begun, as early as June 21st, to use their favorite device of fire-ships. They tried it again on the twenty-eighth, and on July 27th despatched an ingeniously constructed raft consisting of numerous vessels against the fleet. This last infernal engine consisted, according to their own account, of over seventy different boats and rafts together, on which were erected old cannon, swivels, muskets, and mortars, all loaded to the muzzle with powder, ball, and grapeshot. The whole was daubed with pitch and fired. In this, as in every other case, however, the effort was nugatory, because, while the flames roared and the worthless firearms exploded and burst, the brave English sailors grappled the craft from small boats, and as the blaze lighted the sky either towed them into channels through which they passed picturesquely furious but harmless on toward the sea, or else ran them ashore.

The long month was not without exciting events. Day and night the heavens were torn by hissing bombs and the thunder of artillery. The camp on the heights of the Montmorency shelled the French under Levis across the intervening chasm; a portion of the fleet bombarded the French works below Beaufort; the batteries of Point Levy sent ruin and havoc into the lower city; another part of the squadron ran the batteries of Quebec citadel in safety, and compelled Montcalm to send troops for the defence of the highlands above the town; a sharp, short fight occurred at the ford of the Montmorency between Canadian Indians and provincial rangers, and there was scarcely a day without an encounter between savages and soldiers in the precincts of the various English camps, either on the north side, or on the island, or on the point opposite the city. This long line of six miles or more, with two great arms of a mighty river crossing it, was further lengthened when the squadron of Admiral Holmes passed the strait and anchored above. A land force followed and made the British position even more scattering and weak, although their raids rendered a still greater expanse of country unsafe and greatly weakened the moral courage of the Canadians, who were unable to appreciate the Fabian policy of Montcalm.

\*    \*    \*    \*    \*

The prospect of action revived Wolfe's failing powers for a time. "To be without pain for a few days and able to do my duty," such was his desire. On

August 31st he was able to be abroad once more, and once again, as of old, he passed from post to post rallying the ebbing spirits of his men. On September 3rd began the evacuation of the fortified camp above the Montmorency, a difficult feat, only accomplished by a feigned attack on Beaufort which drew off the enemy from his rear; on the fourth the stores were safely floated up the current. Brigadier Murray, with four battalions, forced his way under the fire of batteries on the opposite side, farther up the south shore than the English had yet gone, beyond the Etchemins River; next day three battalions followed under Monckton and Townshend, and that night the entire body of men were safely embarked on the vessels of Holmes's squadron with Wolfe himself in command.

The movement was not unknown, of course, to the enemy, but they believed it was preliminary to the embarkation of the whole army and the departure of the fleet. Nevertheless their vigilance was not relaxed. The steep sides of the plains above the city seemed insurmountable, but at every little cove a force was set in extraordinary precaution. The shores farther up were less inaccessible, and larger bodies of troops under Bougainville were sent to guard the places where attack was therefore more possible. Montcalm, with the residue of his men, who were a motley assemblage which neither he nor his enemies would dignify by the name of army, confronted Saunders behind the old earthworks of Beaufort.

Immediately the plan adopted by Wolfe began to unfold. An attack was made on September 7th, at Cape Rouge, but it was only to excite and mislead his opponents. For the next five days the entire fleet passed backward and forward on the tide opposite the plateau which stretched between that point and Quebec, as if ready at any moment to detach a landing party. The French dashed hither and thither by land to forefend a surprise, and thus exhausted their strength. Although they were untrained men, many of them but "disorderly peasantry," they yet outnumbered Wolfe's army two to one, including the reinforcement of twelve hundred which was coming up under Burton from Point Levy.

On the twelfth the climax was to come. With his acute mind and keen eyesight, Wolfe had discerned what neither friend nor enemy suspected, that it was feasible not merely to scale the heights higher up but those of Abraham near the city and surprise the foe. While reconnoitring he had found and chosen as his landing the little cove, since known by his name, from which a zigzag path on which but two men could climb abreast wound to the top. He had fortunately learned that French supply-boats were ordered to pass down in the darkness under the north shore that very night. Accordingly the fleet as usual floated above Cape Rouge, and although boats for the leaders of the desperate enterprise were lowered in full sight of the French, Bougainville thought nothing of it, expecting a repetition of the usual barren events of the past few days. It so happened also that the commanders on the plains above had carelessly given furlough to a considerable number of their scanty force, and that a Guienne regiment, which was to have encamped there, had inexplicably remained in its old quarters on the St. Charles River. Down below Admiral Saunders showed an ostentatious activity in taking soundings off Beauport and in other meaningless preparations for attack, which completely deceived Montcalm.

As the evening hours slowly passed, Wolfe proceeded from ship to ship to assure himself that everything was ready, and to inspire his troops with courage. A presentiment of death had overpowered him. Before leaving the cabin of the flag-vessel he had given to his friend and schoolmate, Jervis, a miniature of his affianced bride, Miss Lowther, and a farewell message. In the boat, during one of the intervals of inspection, he spoke of Gray's Elegy, quoting with deep pathos the verse:

> "The boast of heraldry, the pomp of power,
>     And all that beauty, all that wealth e'er gave,
>   Await alike the inexorable hour.
>   The paths of glory lead but to the grave."

It needs little imagination to realize the solemnity with which he repeated the last line. According to the midshipman who was present and told the touching story, he said he would rather have written that poem than take Quebec on the morrow. It has been suggested by his greatest historian that perhaps the hero is greater even than the poet.

Toward two in the morning the tide turned, and as the ships began to move downstream the signal was given and the boats were made ready. Soon the advance left the fleet behind and moved more swiftly under the north shore, the larger vessels following. Sentries hailed from the strand, but were deceived into a belief that the French supply-boats were passing. Soon the appointed bay was reached, but in the darkness the rowers grounded their prows a little below. Through the steep, pathless forest the vanguard climbed noiselessly, others following by the path, which had to be cleared of obstructions, and some even farther up the stream by ravines and water-courses. So precipitous was the hill that going was possible only on hands and knees. At length the top was reached. Quickly the weakened posts were seized, and as the firing of muskets gave the expected signal to the forces who were now waiting below on the narrow beach, the swarms of men began first to clamber and then more regularly to move up the path. The roads and outposts above having been seized by the volunteer adventurers, there was no resistance, and in the dawn Wolfe with his five thousand men stood safely on the long-expected field where the enemy must fight or surrender, within a mile of the prize to which he was pressing on.

The surprise was successful and complete, but the danger was immediate and great; on one side Quebec and Montcalm, on the other Bougainville and his troops. A hasty examination showed the most advantageous ground to be a narrow plateau, known as the Plains of Abraham, somewhat higher than the upland on which they stand. It was really a portion of the level on which upper Quebec stood. To the north were the abrupt steeps falling to the meadows of the St. Charles, to the south the cliffs just scaled, the width was about a mile, and the English forces in proper array for fighting could not reach across when the right wing rested on the brow toward the St. Lawrence. At the other end, therefore, a flanking party was set perpendicular to the rest and facing the north. In the main line were about thirty-two hundred men, the remainder, some sixteen hundred in all, were divided between the left flank, the guard of the landing-place, and the reserve. Two field-pieces had been dragged up from the cove.

All night long the guns of Saunders's fleet had thundered while his boats had skirted the shore as if to land. Montcalm had been thoroughly deceived, and was not disabused until in the early dawn he heard the artillery of his southern outposts just before their capture. After waiting in vain for an explanation, he set out on horseback to discover the cause. At the bridge of the St. Charles the close red ranks of the English became visible. An adjutant was quickly despatched for troops. The Guienne regiment had come up in the dawn, it was soon reinforced by other regulars as well trained as itself, but all told they numbered less than two thousand. Intermixed with them were about twenty-five hundred more, Indians and Canadian militia. Others were expected, but Vaudreuil retained them, still fearing an attack by the apparently watchful and busy fleet, and Ramesay, the commander of the garrison, refused both men and cannon on the plea of defending himself. At last three guns were extorted from him.

Capable, vigilant, and indefatigable as he had ever been, Montcalm was stunned. His subordinates, with criminal neglect, had virtually forfeited the natural strength of their position in the desperate game. His well-considered plan of delay, long and carefully carried out, was in a moment overthrown. Where he expected at the most "a small party come to burn a few houses and retire," stood an army of veterans. Corruption, selfishness, and incapacity environed him. For a time his auxiliaries harassed the English by the familiar tactics of bush fighting, and the cannon did serious execution. He might have postponed an action until the forces from Cape Rouge could make an attack in the rear. But he was overpowered by the unexpected crisis and emphasized the possibility of an English fortification which could repel Bougainville and cut off all the supplies of his army. Yielding to the passionate ardor of his men, he at last gave the fatal order toward ten o'clock of the cloudy, rainy morning.

The British had waited during these trying and seemingly interminable hours with the calmness and self-control to be expected of veterans. Wolfe was everywhere, encouraging, soothing, ordering. As the French came on, his little battery opened fire. Their evident aim was to flank and drive the columns back over the precipice. The onset was impetuous but irregular, and the English reserved their fire. The slow moments passed and but forty paces separated the lines. At the centre the quick order, the simultaneous volley thrice repeated, the groans of killed and wounded, the charge and rout, followed in the swift succession of but a few minutes. On the right the general himself led. Owing to fences and cornfields his ranks were broken and the charge less impetuous, but there, as all along the line, the rout of the French was complete.

Amid the awful clash death overtook the two conspicuous figures of the hour. Wolfe was wounded in the charge, twice as he pressed on and the third time fatally, when he fell and was carried by his own orders to the rear, anxious lest the forces should be discouraged by his fall. Knowing he would die surgical assistance was refused, but as the cry "They run; see how they run!" he rallied to ask "Who run?" Hearing the answer: "The enemy give way everywhere," he roused himself fully to the necessary decision. "Go, one of you, to Colonel Burton; tell him to march Webb's regiment down to Charles River and cut off their retreat from the bridge." Then in apparent resignation, and with his last breath, he murmured "Now, God be praised, I die happy." Montcalm, too, by a sad coincidence of fate, had been once struck by a musket-ball, but persisted in the duty of conducting his flying squadrons as they retreated toward the city gates. While rallying them to protect the other fugitives he received a mortal wound. Carried within the town, he survived to hold a council of war and write a letter to his conquerors, commending his brave men to their clemency. His last hours were spent in the consolations of religion, and he was buried the day he died, September 14th, in the chapel of the Ursuline Convent. It is believed that the grave was in large part a hollow formed by the bursting of a bomb. "Valor gave a united death, History a united fame, Posterity a united monument," runs the fit inscription on the monument in the governor's garden at Quebec, which bears on one side the name of Wolfe and on the other that of Montcalm.

On the eighteenth Quebec surrendered, and was occupied by a British garrison. In the mournful council over which the French general presided on the last day of his life, he gave it as his opinion that the forces must rally and fight again, or there would be an end of New France. But the governor was a poltroon as well as a backbiter and defamer. Consternation first, and chaos afterward, so utterly demoralized the conquered people that he lost the very semblance of braggadocio, and even Levis when he arrived could produce no order.

That officer's tenacity was as great as his courage, and during the long and bitter winter, while England, both sides of the Atlantic, was ringing with the pious hallelujahs of the people and on one with the premature jubilations of the sinking aristocracy, he conceived and prepared a daring and yet reasonable design. From time to time rumors of attack reached the incredulous garrison, and they therefore established outposts at Ste. Foy in a forest five miles distant, and at Lorette. French grenadiers, Canadians, and Indians further appeared in considerable numbers, and it was found that strong posts had been established at inconvenient points in the neighborhood. Skirmishes, some of them serious, were not infrequent, and the commander of Quebec, Murray, a just and gallant man, became uneasy toward the spring, as he saw disease and death at work among troops not inured to such a severe climate. By April his able-bodied, serviceable men did not number three thousand, although there had been seven thousand in the autumn; seven hundred were dead, the rest were victims of a pestilence, scurvy, and dysentery.

The same month found Levis's preparations complete. Starting in boats from Montreal on the twentieth, with seven thousand men, new reinforcements were added at every town on the way, and he appeared, after a wild and stormy night, on the twenty-seventh, at Ste. Foy with a force of between eight and nine thousand. The youthful and undaunted Murray made a sortie and drew in his outposts. Next day he resolved to fight, disparate as the numbers were, and at the head of three thousand men, engaged the enemy on the very ground which had been drenched with blood in the previous September. His first onset was apparently successful, and the enemy withdrew to the shelter of the forest. But the French rallied, and two desperate struggles ensued at a windmill made famous as the Mill of Dumont. In the first the English prevailed, but were raked by a flanking fire; in the second they were routed. After two hours of unsurpassed bravery, they were finally overpowered by numbers and forced to retreat behind the city walls. They lost one man in every three, and their opponents about eight hundred in all. The situation of Quebec was desperate. At once the French drew up their six war vessels in the river, and on shore began the lines for a siege. The fire from the town was so hot and incessant that they could with difficulty mount a gun. But undaunted to the last, their hope might not have been forlorn if vessels with munitions from France had reached them in season, as Levis had prearranged.

The event was otherwise; it was not a French, but an English fleet, which, in the third week of May, sailed up the St. Lawrence. It promptly engaged the French ships. Their admiral fought obstinately to the end, but was captured and his fleet destroyed. Levis awaited the decision and then retreated precipitately with his entire force, leaving sick, wounded, and all his guns to fall into Murray's hands. This was the real end of resistance, the gallant and ill-starred struggle of New France was over. All Canada below Three Rivers was lost, for the inhabitants had not repeated the conduct of the Acadians, but swore allegiance to Great Britain. There was nothing left but to concentrate farther away and make the final stand at Montreal.

Amherst at last began to show some mettle. Murray was to advance up the river from Quebec. He himself, with his large force, was to make the long detour by Lake Ontario, and descend the river so as to cut off a retreat toward Detroit. Haviland was to force the passage by Isle-aux-Noix and the Richelieu River, from which Bourlamaque had retreated to consolidate his troops with those of Levis, leaving seventeen hundred men under Bougainville. The last hope of the French was that the English expeditions might arrive separately, and in that event they hoped to defeat each one in turn. But the complicated plan of the commander-in-chief was perfectly executed, and by September 7th the city was surrounded. The next day it surrendered. By Amherst's leniency, honorable but decisive terms were made, and though the peace of Paris was not signed until three years later, that portion of the Seven Years' War fought in America, and known to us as one of the great turning points of our history, was over.

DANIEL BOORSTIN *has written:*

> AMERICA *began as a sobering experience. The colonies were a disproving ground for utopias. . . . Dreams made in Europe—the dreams of the zionist, the perfectionist, the philanthropist, and the transplanter—were dissipated or transformed by the American reality. A new civilization was being born less out of plans and purposes than out of the unsettlement which the New World brought to the ways of the Old.*

*Britain learned to her sorrow between 1763 and 1775 that the colonies she had thought tributary had matured and developed their own identity. Without anyone quite understanding the process, the English colonials had been transmuted into Americans. To believe as Parliament did that the colonies had no relation to each other but through the parent country was to miss the point: a remote people had met the wilderness and subdued it. The land upon which they dwelt was marked with their sweat, their tears, and their blood. Where once nothing existed but emptiness, there now stood flourishing towns whose ships crowded the harbors of the world, and the abundance of an agriculture that had freed all Americans from hunger. The affluence of American life had emancipated a whole people. In the words of de Crèvecoeur: "There is room for everybody in America." It was only a matter of brief time before the newcomer "begins to feel the effects of a sort of resurrection; . . . begins to forget his former servitude and dependence."*

*The new society had kept the best of Europe and added a pervasive hope. Though not possessed of the intellectual achievement of the Old World, the American on the eve of revolution did not doubt that in time even this would come. But for the moment, it was a land which the poet Philip Freneau described as "a continent . . . , abounding with a hardy and active race of inhabitants, producing everything within itself proper for its own maintenance and defense." One cannot but join with Freneau in his conclusion that it was beyond reason for Britain ". . . to entertain a serious thought of reducing by force of arms, this immense continent to their absolute sway." The time for colonial dependence had passed; the time for independence had come.*

*Thomas Jefferson Wertenbaker (1879-1966) briefly served as editor of the Baltimore* News *after his graduation from the University of Virginia (1902). He returned to his alma mater where he received his Ph.D. in 1910 and then went to Princeton where he taught until 1947. His interest in colonial history is wide-ranging, covering both the Southern and Northern colonies with particular emphasis upon social and intellectual history. His greatest achievement has been the synthesis of those colonial interpretations that have emphasized the imperial or the internal constitutional perspective. Wertenbaker saw them not as antithetical but complementary. The interaction of colonial deviations from the European norm and the needs of an imperial policy dictated from afar brought first conflict and then revolution. It was his genius to understand that the emergence of a distinctively American heritage*

*did not constitute a secession from western civilization but rather a further*
*proof that western genius had shaped a new variant within a common mold.*

# THE GOLDEN AGE
# OF COLONIAL CULTURE

## by *Thomas J. Wertenbaker*

The American colonies produced no Shakespeare, no Michelangelo, no Beethoven, no Pasteur; they could boast of no great accomplishment in music, or painting, or literature, or sculpture, or architecture; their only noted scientist was Benjamin Franklin. While Newton was discovering the laws of gravity, Harvey was studying the circulation of the blood, Milton, Jonson, Defoe, Pope, and others were writing their immortal works, Americans were busy chiefly with the axe, the hoe, and the saw. And this is as it should have been. The task which confronted them was not to make new contributions to civilization, but to extend its borders, to win for it a vast continent. A mighty task it was, a noble task, and right well was it accomplished.

The America of colonial days has been likened to a banquet, where the first comers, finding a feast awaiting them prepared by nature, had only to help themselves. It is true that theirs were the riches of a continent, but only on condition that they wrest it from stubborn Mother Nature. They had to risk the dangerous voyage across the ocean in the tiny vessels of the day, make their clearings in the forest, build their little cabins unaided by carpenters or bricklayers, put out their crops of wheat and corn, face the peril of the tomahawk, of hunger, of dreaded diseases. Their life was full of unremitting toil and severe hardships; it was not to be expected that they should create musical masterpieces or add to the world's knowledge of chemistry or botany. "No thing new and extraordinary in literature from this part of the world is to be expected," wrote Cadwallader Colden, "but as we are improving this wilderness and have in some measure in some places given it the appearance of cultivated grounds in Europe, so we make some small attempts for improvement in learning."

And when the sturdy pioneer, resting after a day of strenuous labor, reflected upon the need for educating his children, he was faced with discouraging difficulties. He could unite with his nearest neighbors to build a crude schoolhouse, but their meager means might not suffice to secure a teacher, while within a five-mile radius were seldom more than a handful of boys and girls. There were no hard-surfaced roads in the colonial period, no school buses, and erudition often bogged down in the mud. Yet, even in Virginia and Maryland it was common to see children, hornbook and luncheon in hand, trudging through the woods or riding over the rolling roads to the "old-field" schoolhouse, while in New England, where most of the people lived in the agricultural villages, there was a really effective educational system.

As with the school child, so with the artist, the musician, the poet, the scientist. If one were interested in botany, one would have to pursue its study alone, with no stimulus from others of like interest save through an occasional letter. It required indomitable spirit and burning inspiration for a poet or an essayist to pursue his work amid the isolation of the forest or the tobacco fields. A William Byrd or a Robert Carter might surround himself with books, interest himself in music, architecture, and the classics, but he was not, could not be, a creative artist, scientist, or poet. It was only with the development of cultural centers, where men of like interests could meet to discuss the latest productions of Dr. Johnson, or the discoveries of Boyle, or the design of the restored St. Paul's Cathedral, that the interest in cultural matters began to bear fruit.

With the growth of Boston, New York, Philadelphia, Annapolis, Williamsburg, Charleston, and other towns, came an increase in wealth which was all important for the development of intellectual and cultural interests. The day laborer, the field hand, the small merchant, the yeoman have neither the time to spare for music, art, and literature nor the means to indulge their fancies. It is only when one can build a beautiful residence that one's mind turns to the study of architecture; the ability to adorn a residence with family portraits creates an interest in painting and painters; the necessity of acquiring the polish and grace of the gentleman leads to a study of the classics and of current authors. The Boston merchant, the Virginia tobacco aristocrat, the rice millionaire of South Carolina, although by no means leading the life of leisure often ascribed to them, had the time and the inclination to turn from the counting room or the management of slaves or the disposing of crops to the higher things of life.

That this was clear to at least one great thinker of the colonial period is shown by Benjamin Franklin's plea for the founding of a college in Philadelphia, published in his *Pennsylvania Gazette* in 1749. "In the settling of new countries, the first care . . . must be to . . . secure the necessaries of life, this engrosses their attention and affords them little time to think of anything further. . . . Agriculture and mechanic arts were of the most immediate importance; the culture of minds by the finer arts and sciences was necessarily postponed to times of more wealth and leisure. Since these times are come . . . it is thought a proposal for establishing an Academy in this province will not now be deemed unreasonable."

Colonial culture, then, was crude in the seventeenth century under frontier conditions; it reached its full growth in the eighteenth century, especially in the decades just preceding the American Revolution. In these decades it was centered not in the newly settled Piedmont or the Appalachian valleys, but in the older communities of the East. It is true that the newer regions had distinctive cultures of their own—the peasant culture of the Pennsylvania Germans, the Scotch-Irish culture of the upper Valley of Virginia, southwest

Pennsylvania, and elsewhere—but they were still crude, still hampered by frontier conditions. To these regions the refined East, with its cities, its colleges, its handsome churches, its gazettes, its theaters, was what England in the seventeenth century had been to Charleston or Annapolis or Boston. To the Lancaster farmer who halted his Conestoga wagon in the streets of Philadelphia to gaze at Christ Church, the building must have seemed the epitome of beauty and costliness; the Scotch-Irish delegate from Rockbridge who came to Williamsburg to take his seat in the House of Burgesses was struck with awe by the Capitol and the Palace and the Wren Building at William and Mary.

Americans have been slow to recognize the extent and importance of the culture of their ancestors of the colonial period. There have been apologies for the meagerness of the literary output, for the absence of great painters, the lack of distinctive American music, and little emphasis upon the excellent work done in architecture, the artistic crafts, and the widespread appreciation of cultural things—the drama, poetry, music, painting, the sciences. It is within the past few decades that R. T. H. Halsey and others have awakened our interest in old American highboys, tables, and sofas, in the beautiful work of Paul Revere and other silversmiths, in American pewter, in the correct proportions and quiet dignity of Mount Pleasant at Philadelphia, or the Hammond House at Annapolis, or Drayton Hall near Charleston. Today, the thousands of visitors who wander through the quiet streets of the restored Williamsburg, visit the shop of the cabinetmaker or the silversmith, walk in the Palace gardens, view the handsome Georgian buildings, listen to eighteenth-century music produced by eighteenth-century instruments, have a new appreciation of the elegance, the good taste, the charm of colonial life in one of the chief centers of culture.

Culture in the colonies was shaped by the four great factors upon which all American civilization is based—foreign inheritance, local conditions, continued contact with Europe, and the melting pot.

The peoples who came to the shores of the New World brought with them the cultures of the Old. They continued in the American forests to speak the same languages, the same dialects, which they had spoken in Kent or Essex or Ulster or Switzerland or the Palatinate. They tried to establish schools and colleges modeled on those of the homelands, to erect houses just like those in which they had been born and had spent their youth, to wear clothes like those to which they were accustomed, to worship God after the tenets of their various faiths, to carry on the old industries and cultivate the soil after the European manner and with European tools. In short, colonial civilization was European civilization transplanted in the wilds of a new continent.

But this does not mean that each colonial culture had the same inheritance. We may speak broadly of European civilization, but we are conscious that there were many civilizations in Europe, many different cultures even in England. The immigrant who came from Devon spoke with a different accent from a Yorkshireman, was accustomed to a different type of rural cottage, possibly had different ideas of the proper way to worship God. But when settled side by side in Boston or Norfolk or Philadelphia, their differences seemed of minor importance when contrasted with those of the Scotch merchant next door or with the Huguenot silversmith down the street.

New England, more than the other colonies, had a uniform inheritance, for most of the settlers came from one class, having one religious faith, from one section of England. Yet we are reminded that they were not entirely East Anglicans by such Devon, Cornwall, and Somerset place names as Plymouth, Barnstable, Exeter, Falmouth, Truro, and Taunton. Nor was East Anglia itself homogeneous in population, made up as it was of Anglo-Saxons, Danes, Flemings, and other elements. Yet the Puritans brought with them a well-established and distinct culture, which they planted upon the shores of Massachusetts Bay, with its Calvinistic faith, its East Anglian architecture, its modified manorial system, its dialect.

Very different were conditions in New York and the country tributary to it. Even in the days of crabbed Peter Stuyvesant, when the town was called New Amsterdam, it was peopled by a heterogeneous group, mostly Dutch, but also Walloons, Flemings, English, Huguenots, Germans. After Colonel Nicolls took possession for the Duke of York, English culture slowly superseded Dutch, but it was the process of a century. It is said that in the seventeenth century one might hear no less than eighteen languages spoken along the canal or on Coenties Slip. Thus the colonial culture of New York was a mixed culture with some of its main roots extending to England, to the shores of the Zuider Zee, with minor roots in Flanders, France, and the Rhine Valley.

In the Philadelphia region the early inheritance, like that of New England, was chiefly English, but unlike that of New England it was not drawn from any one part of England. Not only did Quakers flock to Pennsylvania from many English shires, but they were joined there by foreigners of similar faith —Dutch, Germans, Swiss, Welsh. And since William Penn made his colony an asylum for the oppressed of all peoples and all religions, it soon became a medley of races and religions. The farming country immediately around Philadelphia remained Quaker, the fertile belt of limestone soil stretching from the Lehigh Valley in a great arc to the Mason and Dixon's line was almost solidly German and Swiss, and all southwest Pennsylvania predominantly Scotch-Irish and Irish and Presbyterian. Philadelphia, itself, though newcomers of various faiths eventually outnumbered the original settlers there, remained under the culture and political control of the Quaker aristocracy throughout the colonial period.

Further south, in the great tobacco region which extended from the Pennsylvania line to Albemarle Sound and from the eastern shore of the Chesapeake Bay to the Blue Ridge, the people were chiefly, although not exclusively, English. More than in any other region they represented various parts of England, various strata of English society, and various groups within the English Church. In Maryland and Virginia that Church was established by law and the great mass of the people were loyal to it, but it embraced within its congregations not only high church Anglicans but thousands of Puritans as well. Nor was the tobacco region entirely English, for there was a sprinkling of Scotch merchants, here and there a group of Huguenots or a pocket of Germans. In the main, however, its civilization was English, with its tongue, customs, architecture, and religion as unchanged as local conditions permitted.

Somewhat different was the situation in the rice and indigo region. The first group of settlers who set out for South Carolina under the patronage of Anthony Ashley-Cooper, later Earl of Shaftsbury, was a mixed company of English, Irish, and Welsh. Blown out of their course, they stopped at Barbados and took on additional settlers, the first of many from that island. In fact the migration from the Antilles grew to such proportions that Charleston was often regarded as a West Indian city. In 1680, however, two new streams set in, a stream of Huguenots fleeing the wrath of Louis XIV, and a stream of English dissenters who chose not to live in England under the Roman Catholic James. At the same time came Scotch Covenanters, Baptists from Massachusetts, a few Quakers, a few Irish Catholics, a large group of Dutch.

If the origins of different colonial cultures were diverse, the local conditions to which they were subjected and which changed them and molded them were more so. One wonders to what extent history would have been different had the Puritan fathers founded their Wilderness Zion on the banks of the Chesapeake Bay rather than in Massachusetts. Could they have established their towns amid the tobacco fields? Would their church system have disintegrated because of a sparseness of population, the great distances, and bad roads? Would a tobacco aristocracy have sprung up among them to dispute the leadership with the clergy? Whatever the answer to these questions, it is clear that the culture of colonial New England was profoundly affected by the soil, the climate, the harbors of the region; that Virginia and Maryland were shaped in large part by their great rivers, their mountain ranges, their rich soil; that South Carolina would have had a very different history had it not been for rice and indigo.

It was the rather sterile soil of New England which gave her a small farmer class instead of a planter aristocracy, her forests which made possible her shipbuilding industry, the great schools of cod and herring which made Gloucester, Salem, and Marblehead fishing centers; her many fine harbors stimulated trade and created her merchant aristocracy. This aristocracy it was which was so largely responsible for much of what is distinctive and charming in colonial New England culture.

In Philadelphia it was the broad Delaware, bringing the largest ocean ships to her wharves, together with the rich agricultural back country, which built up the merchant aristocracy. William Penn had planned a society of severe plainness, in which not only was the theater to be banned, but even music, costly furniture, and fine dress. But Quakerism could not prevent the development of a distinctive Philadelphia culture or even dictate its form. When John Adams visited the city to attend the Continental Congress, he found the Friends wearing their traditional plain clothes and broad-brimmed hats, yet dwelling in stately mansions, many of them filled with Chippendale furniture and elegant silver, and fitted out with libraries. One traveler as he approached the city was surprised to see the suburbs "covered with villas, gardens and luxuriant orchards." This region, like every other part of colonial America, could not escape the molding effect of local conditions.

In Virginia and Maryland some of the old families are fond of tracing their lineage back to the English gentry, yet nothing is clearer than the fact that the planter aristocracy was not part of the English aristocracy transplanted to America. It was created in America, was the product of the rich soil, the vast network of inland waterways, and of the sunny climate which made the region suitable to the culture of tobacco, with slave labor and extensive methods of production; and this in turn created the wealth of a Burwell, a Byrd, a Carter, or a Wormeley. The Virginia aristocrat, despite his conscious imitation of the English squires, despite the tenacity with which he clung to English traditions, was not really an Englishman at all, but an American.

In the Carolina low country it was the character of the soil, the long and hot summers, and the inland waterways which favored the culture of rice and indigo, and rice and indigo were the chief factors in creating a highly cultured aristocracy, for they brought wealth not only to the planters, but to the merchants who traded from Charleston to Barbados and Antigua or across the Atlantic to England.

In Virginia and Maryland, also, the soil was the chief source of wealth, for it gave those colonies their staple tobacco. But there was no such alliance of planter and merchant in the Chesapeake Bay region as existed in Charleston, even though some of the most prominent families came originally from the merchant class. In the seventeenth century, it is true, we find Robert Beverley taking part in the slave trade and William Byrd I sending out his pack horses to the southwest for skins and furs, but gradually the tobacco planter confined himself chiefly to agriculture, leaving commerce to the English and Scotch merchants. This was perhaps inevitable since Norfolk, the chief mart of the province, was remote from the tobacco fields, was never the political and cultural capital, never became a refuge from malaria. The Virginia planter aristocrat, despite some family alliances, in time began to consider the merchants a somewhat inferior class and the mercantile pursuit not entirely in keeping with the character of a "gentleman."

The various colonial cultures, had they been able to shake off the dominance of the mother country, would have become more and more distinctive. The American regional architectures which had sprung into being in the seventeenth century in time would have become more American, more expressive of the life of Massachusetts, or Pennsylvania, or South Carolina. The American dialects would have grown less like the English dialects, less like each other. It is probable, even, that each region, had it been cut off from the works of contemporary English writers, would have developed a literature of its own.

But the colonies continued to look to England for guidance in cultural things and constantly reshaped their ideas in conformity with changes there. If in the mother country Chippendale furniture began to replace the tables and chairs of the Queen Anne style, it was certain that within a few years it would find its way also into the houses of the merchants of Boston and Philadelphia and the planters of Virginia and South Carolina. The lady who attended a ball in a gown outmoded in London, or who was unfamiliar with the latest English dance step, subjected herself to ridicule; the gentleman whose clothes were out of style, who had not read the latest English books, or who was unfamiliar with the gossip of the London coffee houses was considered behind the times. Thus while local conditions acted as a centrifugal force within the British Empire, the cultural dominance of England was a centripetal force, tending to prevent each section from flying off the orbit.

Although all the colonies were subject to the influence of the mother country, it was especially strong in the tobacco region. Here the great fleets of tobacco ships which each year moved down from the rivers and creeks of Virginia and Maryland to the mouth of the Chesapeake Bay to head out through the Capes for England, returning a few months later with all kinds of manufactured goods, proved an iron link with the mother country. The planter, on his estate on the Potomac or the York, was in closer touch with London than with Philadelphia or Charleston, knew more of what was going on there. When the English ship drew up to his wharf he invited the master to dine with him, and, to the accompaniment of good food and rare wine, quizzed him upon the latest happenings at Court. This done, he would repair to his wharf to open his newly arrived crates and examine their precious contents—the latest books by Swift or Addison or Smollett, recent numbers of *The Spectator*, silver bowls, tankards, candlesticks for his dining-room cupboard, gowns, stockings, shoes for his wife and daughters, a set of new Chippendale chairs, kitchen utensils, farm implements, carpenter's tools.

In South Carolina, as well as in Virginia and Maryland, the cultural influence of England was strengthened by the Established Church, for a very large part of the ministers were English born and English educated. Not only did these men militate against the development of separate religious practices and tenets, but they constantly renewed and strengthened the cultural ties. Many added to their meager incomes by opening private schools or acting as tutors in the homes of the rich, and it was their influence in part which sent so many southern boys across the Atlantic to enter the English schools and universities.

In the northern colonies the tie with England was weaker. At the end of the seventeenth century, imports to New England from the mother country were about one eighth as large as those to Maryland and Virginia; in 1769, despite a considerable increase, less than a third. In fact, the commercial ties of this region were stronger with the West Indies than with England. If the wealthy Bostonian needed a silver teapot, he found Paul Revere and other Boston silversmiths quite capable of the finest workmanship; his clothes, his wig, his pewter dishes, his clocks, he could buy in the local shops as cheaply as from the importers.

New England was more independent, also, in religion and education. The Puritans, when they set up their Zion in the New World, claimed that it was the true Church of England, yet it differed from the established order not only when controlled by high churchmen, but by the reformers under the Commonwealth. The New Englanders set up their own colleges for the training of ministers and their own school system to prepare youths for them. Cotton Mather could boast that in its first century of existence New England had educated more ministers for England than England for New England. No doubt, Massachusetts and Connecticut kept in touch with the dissenting academies in the mother country, received inspiration from Philip Doddridge and other great educators, but on the whole they went their own way. Of the various "declarations of independence" which have gradually broken the ties between this country and England, the New England declaration of religious and educational independence was the first.

Nonetheless New England was by no means free from the cultural influence of England. The books which lined the walls in the minister's library were printed in England, most of them. Every educated man read his Tillotson, his Milton, and his Locke; the gazettes reprinted extracts from *The Spectator* and *The Rambler*. The cabinetmaker who defied the changing styles in England and continued to make Queen Anne chairs after Chippendale had published his book of designs soon found himself without patrons. The simple four-square meetinghouses of the seventeenth century gave way to Wren churches; the plain residence with its overhang and dew drop, its central chimney and multiple gables, to the formal Georgian mansion. The tailor, or silversmith, or architect, or coachmaker who could boast that he had learned his trade in London regarded his American-trained rival with contempt.

Conditions in the Middle Colonies were similar. Both Philadelphia and New York developed groups of artistic craftsmen second to none in the excellence of their work, yet they followed submissively in the wake of the great English designers. Philadelphia discarded her early Quaker architecture, and New York her Dutch traditions, at the command of the Georgian school of architects. Princeton, the first college to be established in the Middle Colonies, was patterned after the Calvinist academies of the mother country. Yet here too there was greater cultural independence than in the South, for trade relations with England were less extensive and there were fewer English ministers and teachers.

Of the great forces which shaped colonial civilization, none was more important than the melting pot. Even though culture was predominantly English, though the mass of the people spoke the English language, read English books, accepted English styles, lived under English institutions, were ruled by English common law, the influence of foreign populations, religions, tongues, literature, agriculture, industry, customs, traditions was also great. At one time Benjamin Franklin expressed the fear that the Germans of Pennsylvania might impose their culture upon the entire colony. "Few of their children . . . know English," he said. "They import many books from Germany, and of the six printing houses in the province, two are entirely German, two half German half English, and but two entirely English. . . . Unless the stream of importation could be turned from this to other colonies . . . they will soon [so] outnumber us that all the advantages we will have, will in my opinion, not be able to preserve our language."

Although Franklin's fears proved groundless and the Germans of Pennsylvania, Maryland, Virginia, North Carolina, and elsewhere have either been absorbed into the population or are far advanced in the process, they have made deep imprints not only upon the culture of the regions where they settled but upon the nation. The colonies were much the richer for German thrift, German agricultural methods, German folk art, German craftmanship, German music. The thousands of German barns scattered over southeastern Pennsylvania, western Maryland, the Valley of Virginia, and elsewhere remind us that there are still strong ties between the United States and central Europe.

The Scotch-Irish, more than the Germans, have melted into the population, yet they too have made invaluable contributions. Gone is the Scotch accent, gone the whirring bagpipe, gone even their skill as weavers, gone the quaint old costumes, the superstitions and customs, but their influence upon religion and education is attested today by thousands of Presbyterian congregations and scores of schools, colleges, and universities. For a century Princeton was the religious and educational capital of Scotch-Irish America, sending forth hundreds of ministers and teachers to southwestern Pennsylvania, Virginia, and North Carolina, and even to far-off Tennessee and Kentucky.

In New York the story is the same. When one visits lower Manhattan and wanders through the narrow streets beneath the towering buildings, he can hardly believe that for a century and a half a Dutch town occupied this space. New Amsterdam has vanished from the face of the earth. Yet the days of Peter Stuyvesant are brought back in imagination when we meet a Roosevelt or a Van Dyke or a Cowenhoven, when we walk along the Bowery or Cortlandt Street, when we purchase a "cookie" or step over a "stoop" or read the latest baseball "dope." The distinctive Dutch haystack, with its sliding roof, is still in use in the farming regions of eastern New Jersey and southern New York; the Dutch barn can be recognized at a glance as different from the English barn or the German barn.

It is clear that colonial culture follows a very complex pattern. There was no one uniform culture, but a dozen or more, not only the cultures of New England, the Middle Colonies, and the South, but of subdivisions in these major sections. In the South alone one must differentiate between the tobacco region, the rice region, the mercantile region, the pine belt, and the great back country. In Pennsylvania the German and Swiss belt differed radically from the Quaker region, which in turn was quite unlike the Scotch-Irish southwest. Moreover, within these various districts different groups had different cultures; the life of the wealthy tobacco planter was different from that of the yeoman farmer nearby, that of the great merchant from that of the cabinetmaker a few doors down the street. Finally, seventeenth-century culture, when the colonies were still in the pioneer stage, was very different from the more sophisticated culture of the mid-eighteenth century.

Any consideration of colonial culture should make a sharp distinction between creative work and mere interest in cultural things. Of the former comparatively little was done that was worth while, but the latter proved a powerful force in shaping the thought and life of the people. There was a colonial literature which reflects the spirit of the times, introduces us to the fears, the strivings, the joys, the sorrows of this interesting period. But it consists not of the dreary poetry of Urian Oakes or of Michael Wigglesworth, not of the sermons of the Puritan ministers, but of the letters of merchants, planters, officials, teachers, clergymen, of diaries, reports, and local histories. The *Journal* of the Reverend Robert Rose and the *Diary* of Judge Samuel Sewall are more revealing, are more interesting than a dozen poems.

Moreover, the culture of the period expressed itself not only in literature, but in architecture, music, the artistic crafts, the theater, and science. The wealthy man who pored over the pages of Gibbs's *A Book of Architecture* in quest of ideas for his own residence, who attended productions of *Othello* or *Macbeth* at Kean's Theater in New York or the old theater in Williamsburg, who experimented with foreign plants in his garden, who furnished his house with the exquisite tables and chairs of Thomas Affleck or William Savery, who enjoyed the music of Bach or Handel was doing his part in molding the cultural life of the colonies.

\*     \*     \*     \*     \*

Eighteenth-century American culture was the culture of contemporaneous England transplanted in America and superimposed upon the various civilizations that had developed there. It had, therefore, a degree of uniformity which was lacking in earlier days. The architecture of Boston in the decades preceding the Revolution had much in common with the architecture of Philadelphia, Annapolis, and Charleston because the English Georgian house, expressed in the books of Gibbs, or Halfpenny, or Ware, was the model for them all. Theatrical productions in one colony were like those in others, since they were produced by the same company of itinerant English actors. There was a uniformity in the work of the colonial cabinetmakers, because they all conformed to the English styles, whether Queen Anne, or Chippendale, or Sheraton.

Yet it was inevitable that the stream of English culture beating against the American shore should be deeply affected by that shore itself, and affected differently in each section. The warm welcome accorded the English theater in the South, the bitter opposition of Philadelphia, the complete ban laid down by New England were but expressions of the different traditions and concepts of these communities. The difference between a Georgian residence on Beacon Hill and on Capitol Green, Williamsburg, was the difference between the climate of Boston and Virginia, building materials, the life of the Bostonian and Virginian. In Massachusetts reading directed itself into the more serious literary channels; in Annapolis the modern novelists enjoyed a great popularity.

Throughout the colonies Georgian culture, with all its elegance, its display of wealth, its beautiful houses, its costly furniture, its growing libraries, was based upon the improvement in education. In the pioneer civilization of the seventeenth century education suffered not only because of the sparseness of the population, but because of the duplication which resulted from the insistence of each religious denomination upon having its own educational system. When a rural community of a hundred or so scattered families tried to set up four or five schools, one run by the Quakers, another by the Episcopalians, another by the Presbyterians, another by the Dutch Reformed, none would be efficient.

But with the growth of population and wealth, and the development of commercial cities in the eighteenth century, the situation became more favorable. Private schools were established which were nondenominational. The famous William Penn Charter School, the two town grammar schools in Boston, the Annapolis Free School, and many others were equal to some of the best in England. As for the various Presbyterian academies, modeled upon the dissenting academies of England, which were a combination of classical school and theological seminary, their work was remarkably thorough. Out from Samuel Blair's academy at Flagg's Manor, Pennsylvania, from Samuel Finley's academy at Nottingham, Maryland, from Jonathan Dickinson's school at Elizabeth, and especially from the so-called Log College went some of the ablest ministers in America.

With the multiplying of the preparatory schools, there came a demand for the founding of additional colleges. In New England Harvard and Yale had long monopolized the field, while William and Mary was the only college west and south of the Hudson. But in the mid-eighteenth century one new college after the other opened its doors—Princeton, the University of Pennsylvania, Columbia, Rutgers, Brown, Dartmouth, Hampden-Sidney, etc. These institutions, most of them, were founded by various denominational sects, chiefly for the purpose of training young men for the ministry, but they also sent out hundreds of laymen to take leading roles in the social, economic, and political life of the colonies. Despite the stream of wealthy boys from America to the English universities, life in Williamsburg, or Boston, or Philadelphia would have been less polished had it not been for the rapid expansion of education at the college level which marked the third quarter of the century.

At the same time, one wonders whether reading was not an even more important factor. For one youth who went to college there were scores who had the opportunity to purchase books or to join one of the circulating libraries. The increase in reading was the result of the accumulation of wealth and of better schools rather than of cheaper books, for modern printing presses had not been invented and the type was set by hand. It is true that paper-back novels could be had for one shilling, sixpence, but an edition of Shakespeare cost as much in 1775 as in 1700. Yet the ships from England each year brought thousands of volumes to the colonies and the bookstores in all the larger towns were crowded with works on religion, history, science, medicine, law, philosophy, architecture, agriculture, as well as the classics, drama, poetry, and fiction.

The centers of colonial culture had no way of shaping the character of English literature except in so far as they added to the purchasing public, but they expressed their individuality by their selections. The Annapolis gentlemen, taking their reading rather lightly, steeped themselves in fiction and the drama, shied off from works on theology, and searched Cicero and Horace chiefly for quotations for witty sallies; the Bostonian, wincing under the warnings of the clergy that fiction was a harmful mental dissipation, read his Fielding or his Richardson with a guilty conscience, to be atoned for only by more copious doses of theology or books on piety; the Virginian read the classics to round out his education as a gentleman and Coke and Locke to equip himself for a place in the colonial government, salving his conscience with Bishop Tillotson's works or perhaps *The Whole Duty of Man*.

In architecture, even more than in reading, the individuality of American centers expressed itself. If one transplants the seed of Havana tobacco in the Connecticut valley, in Pennsylvania, and in North Carolina, one will get a different leaf in each place, each differing also from the parent leaf. So it was with the Georgian architecture which conquered America in the eighteenth century and in turn was conquered by America. When Robert Smith and Dr. William Shippen sat down together to plan Nassau Hall, they certainly spread out before them various English books of architecture and decided upon one design which they considered most suited to their needs. But they then so modified it as to make it almost unrecognizable— by removing marble balustrades and pediments, since marble was not available at Princeton, substituting rough stone for cut stone or brick, adding a simple cupola taken from the tower of St. Mary-le-Strand. When the building was completed there was no difficulty in recognizing it as Georgian in style, yet there was nothing like it in England, nor even in Boston or Charleston. It belonged to New Jersey, or possibly Pennsylvania, as unmistakably as the Delaware River.

The colonial stage, on the other hand, was far more uniform, since it was almost entirely in the hands of English companies who traveled from town to town. One year they might present a series of plays in New York, the next in Philadelphia, the next at Charleston, the same actors taking the same roles. Had these places developed their own talent, had their literary lights written plays for local presentation, the colonial theater might have been as diverse as architecture, might have reflected the individuality of each cultural center. As it was, tradition expressed itself only in hostility or cordiality to the stage. Whereas Williamsburg and Annapolis welcomed the drama and feted the actors and actresses, Boston turned a cold shoulder on all that pertained to the stage.

In painting, the cultural dominance of the mother country tended not only to shape the work of native Americans, but actually to convert them into Englishmen. When West, Copley, and Peale went to England for study, they should have confined their efforts to mastering the technique of their art, while clinging stubbornly to their American tradition, with its simplicity, democracy, optimism, and even crudeness. But West and Copley were induced to turn their backs on America and devote themselves to becoming English artists, painting in the current English style, and taking subjects sanctioned by English critics. As a result, West lost his chance for permanent fame and Copley steadily deteriorated. On the other hand, Peale, whose independent spirit would not bow to dictation, probably left England too soon, for he never mastered the technique which might have made him a great painter.

We can only regret that the spirit of colonial America failed to find reflection on the canvases of its native artists. There was an unlimited opportunity. The Indians—their life, their habits, their wars; the vast forest with its wild life, hunters, and silent majestic beauty; the great tobacco fields of the South, the slaves at work, the English ships at anchor in the rivers or tied up at the wharves, the shallow boats laden with tobacco hogsheads, hastening down the upper courses of the streams, the gay assemblages at Westover or Tulip Hill; the busy scenes in the northern harbors, the rapt assemblages that listened to Whitefield and Tennent. Instead, the colonial heritage consists of little more than portraits, some of them invaluable for their revelation of the men and women who lived in America two centuries ago, but most of them lifeless and wooden.

In music there was both uniformity and diversity; both independence and servility. In the cultural centers, where sophisticated audiences assembled in concert halls to listen to trained soloists, or to the opera, or to orchestras, there was a strict conformity to European standards. It was the music of Handel or Bach or Corelli, rendered upon instruments popular in Europe, which was in vogue in Boston as well as Charleston or Williamsburg, and one listened in vain for a song expressive of the American spirit. Yet when the concert was over and the fashionably dressed men and women reached home, they might hear truly American music, perhaps from the cook who sang at her work, perhaps from the stable boy, perhaps from the nurse who sang the children to sleep.

Like other phases of American culture, the ballad came originally from Europe. It is probable that some arrived at Jamestown with Captain Newport in 1607, the others found their way to New England with the Pilgrims; we know that they were brought in by indentured workers, by artisans, by merchants, that they were sung by the Maine fisherman as well as the planter in the tobacco field, by the humble servant maid, and the proud dame. From the master or mistress or from poor whites the Negro slave took up the ballad, adding much of his own distinctive spirit, and giving it a new flavor instantly recognizable, a flavor perhaps leading back to Africa itself. But the whites, too, transformed the ballads, adding here, eliminating there, until they became more American than European. They became expressive, also, not only of life in the New World, but of life in distinctive colonies or sections.

In the artistic crafts we have the same story. From Boston to Charleston there was a uniform subserviency to the dictates of the English masters. When Chippendale was in vogue in London, the American cabinetmaker who dared to make a table or a chair in some other style was apt to have it left on his hands. A highboy made in Philadelphia would fit perfectly into the Hammond House in Annapolis, while a secretary made by Shaw in Annapolis would not have been out of place in Boston, on the other hand, or Charleston, on the other. Nonetheless, any one who knew furniture could have identified the Hammond House highboy as the work of Savery or Randolph, or the secretary as a Shaw piece, even in far-off South Carolina or New England. Had the colonies been suddenly cut off from England, had no more books on cabinetmaking been available, had there been no further imports of furniture, each colonial cultural center would probably have developed styles of its own; instead of a Philadelphia Sheraton or a Newport Chippendale, we might have had pure Philadelphian, or pure Newport. As it was, what we had was Queen Anne, or Chippendale, or Sheraton, or Hepplewhite, with a Newport, or a New York, or a Philadelphia flavor.

One could wish that colonial culture as expressed in literature, music, the theater, the artistic crafts had been more democratic and less aristocratic, more American and less English. But it was wealth that made it possible, so it is natural that it should be expressive of the life of the wealthy. The recent awakening of America to the richness of its cultural heritage has been accompanied by a commendable effort to preserve what time has left to us of old buildings, books, furniture, silverware, pewter, etc. Today a Philadelphia highboy is worth a small fortune; Stratford, Carter's Grove, the Hammond House, Mount Pleasant have been restored; in Williamsburg a whole village, with its buildings, gardens, furniture, music, has been brought back to life as by the touch of a magician's wand; the American wing of the Metropolitan Museum of Art has been a revelation to many thousands of the good taste of our ancestors as well as of the luxury with which some of them surrounded themselves.

# II

# *The Drive for Independence*

PRIOR *to 1763, the British imperial system revealed full-blown the British traditional genius for muddling through. Never was a great empire ruled with less system, but it worked. The explanation for this result was not difficult to ascertain; the complete novelty of the circumstances facing the colonials left the British without precedents to which reference for solutions could be made. The Westminster government settled for improvisations, the test of their worth was utilitarian; if they worked, that settled the issue.*

*But there existed one underlying assumption in British colonization that shaped the political system which evolved in the colonies. Colonials were defined as Englishmen abroad, and as such possessed of the rights owned by Englishmen. It followed that the colonials were entitled to some form of representative government. The assumption granted, all of the colonies developed elected Assemblies, vested with the power to impose taxes. Since the colonials accepted the Whig proposition that liberty and property were synonymous—that is, that without property no man truly possessed liberty —the Assemblies were viewed as the political cornerstone of colonial freedom. No Assembly was likely to dissent from the conclusion of South Carolina's Assembly that the people ". . . have . . . delegated to us alone the power of determining what Taxes, Assessments or Impositions they are able to bear." Nor were they likely to surrender "this fundamental and inherent right."*

*The complicated and subtle system of colonial government provided a formidable political antagonist when Parliament chose to challenge it between 1763 and 1775. Within the framework of this system, the men who made the American Revolution made their stand. When the freeholders of Albemarle County, Virginia, permitted Thomas Jefferson to assert in their name, "that the Inhabitants of the several states of British America are subject to the laws which they adopted at their first settlement, and to such others as have been since made by their respective legislatures, duly constituted and appointed with their own consent; that no other legislature whatever may rightfully exercise authority over them, and that these privileges they hold as the common rights of mankind, confirmed by the political constitutions they have respectively assumed, and also by several charters of compact from the Crown," they were stating the common sense of the matter. Under the colonial political system, the colonists were free both in fact and in theory. When they finally rebelled, it was to maintain rights that were, rather than rights that ought to be.*

*Leonard Woods Labaree (1897-     ) has concentrated his interest on colonial history. His long career at Yale University is culminating with his editorship of the* Papers of Benjamin Franklin. *It is part of a massive program to make available the papers of the founding fathers in definitive editions. At the moment, the* Jefferson Papers *are being published at Princeton; the* Hamilton Papers *at* Columbia; *the* Adams Papers *at* Harvard; *and the* Madison Papers *at the University of Chicago. When these volumes are completed, any affluent citizen can possess in his own library a miniature of the Library of Congress holdings.*

# ROYAL GOVERNMENT
# IN AMERICA

## by Leonard Woods Labaree

The inhabitants of the royal provinces lived under a system of "government by instruction," which underwent no fundamental change during the century before the American Revolution. Details of the system were modified from time to time and from place to place. But these changes lay on the surface. At bottom the system was fixed, static, and unchanging, an expression of what the Board of Trade loved to call "the true principles of a provincial constitution." In keeping with these principles, the British officials provided that the governor should exercise in the province all those broad powers which various officials exercised in England in the name of the king; that the governor should be assisted in his duties by a group of councillors chosen for their loyalty, ability, and standing in the community; that the assembly, even though modelled on the House of Commons, should be sharply limited in its powers; that a "balance" should always be kept between the executive and the legislature, whereby the improper aspirations of the assembly might be checked at all times; that the judiciary should be efficient but subject to the control of the crown rather than of the popular assembly; and that the interests of the province should be subordinated to the interests of the mother country whenever the two came into conflict. Drafted with these ends in view and issued in the spirit of government "by royal grace and favor," the commissions and instructions for all the royal provinces maintained their uniformity throughout the century.

But however uniform the commissions and instructions were and however proper in British eyes were the principles upon which they were drawn up, the actual constitution of the royal provinces underwent great changes in this century. Members of the old Lords of Trade set up under Charles II would have approved all the articles of a set of instructions signed by George III, could those men have been brought back to life in 1775. But they would not at first have understood why some of the more restrictive clauses were necessary. Upon further investigation of conditions in America they would have been aghast at the number of instructions that the assemblies were coolly ignoring. These English Rip Van Winkles would have felt—and rightly—

that the system of government which they had so carefully worked out for the four little royal provinces of their time, though spread to many other colonies, had lost most of its vitality and force through the rise of an institution which they themselves had feared and fought—the provincial assembly. And indeed, could they have but realized it, their own defeat in 1680 at the hands of the Jamaica assembly on the issue of the initiative in legislation marked the beginning of a movement which, within a hundred years, had substituted government "by the consent of the governed" for government "by royal grace and favor" as the controlling principle in the actual working of the provincial constitution. The prohibitions which were added in the later instructions bear witness to the fact that a new spirit was abroad in the land, a spirit which changed the balance of power in the colonial government from the prerogative to the assembly thereby greatly modifying the actual constitution of the royal provinces.

Undoubtedly the assembly leaders were largely responsible for their own success in the contest with the prerogative. At the start the assemblymen were mere novices at the parliamentary game, holding good cards, if they only knew it, but inexpert at their play. However, they proved quick to learn. Practice and experience soon developed masters among them who showed themselves able and willing to outmaneuver their opponents in ways made famous by the House of Commons. Delays, evasions, claims of privilege, short-term revenue acts, detailed and specific appropriations, "riders" attached to money bills—these were among the trumps which the provincial leaders learned to play so skilfully that the champions of the king were forced to the defensive in the hope of staving off complete defeat.

The assemblymen had certain advantages on their side which helped them greatly in their efforts to take from the governors the direction of provincial affairs. For one thing, they had the undisputed right, after 1680, to initiate all laws. The right to determine what bills should be brought forward for passage, what undertakings should be financially supported, and what governmental policies should be sanctioned by legislation was an essential part of the authority of the lower house and gave to the leaders of that body a positive voice in all important decisions. An able and popular governor might, and sometimes did, have a good deal to do with the shaping of legislation, but in the last analysis the chief executive's authority was limited to the approval or rejection of such bills as were laid before him. As compared with the governor's negative voice in lawmaking, the assemblymen's right of initiative gave them an advantage of great strategic importance.

A second advantage to the assemblymen grew out of the fact that the assembly was modelled on the House of Commons. Because the assembly was similar in structure to the lower house at Westminster, its leaders naturally claimed for it a position in local affairs similar to that which the elective branch of parliament occupied in England. Whenever a controversy arose over privilege or procedure, the assemblymen were able to cite English precedents which put the governor at once upon the defensive. Instead of attacking his opponents for their "unwarranted" innovations, he had to take the less convincing position of declaring that English precedents did not apply to the case in hand. Even more important in the minds of the colonial leaders than the practices of the House of Commons in such matters of detail as freedom from arrest and the approval of the speaker was the fact that parliament had, through a period of many years, gradually but effectively taken from the king the personal exercise in England of most of his pre-rogatives. The royal officials, on the other hand, were trying to keep the prerogative unimpaired in the colonies. As Governor Colden of New York once said, they believed that "the prerogative cannot be limited in these new countries by usage and custom." The instructions to the governors were drafted in accordance with this principle and the whole system of royal government gave to the crown a much more important place in the provincial constitution than it occupied in the British constitution in the eighteenth century. In combating this situation the assemblymen felt themselves sup-ported by common sense. They took the position that "the king can do nothing in the colonies which he cannot in England." They used English precedents as weapons not only in defending themselves against the demands of the governors but in launching their own attacks against the authority of the prerogative. England's own history was thus one of the most effective aids to the assemblymen in their opposition to the system of royal govern-ment.

A third advantage on the side of the assembly was its control of provincial finance. Except in a few cases, the English officials conceded the principle that the colonies could be properly taxed only by parliament or by their local assemblies. The home authorities did not set up a comprehensive pro-gram of parliamentary taxation while the provincial system was still develop-ing. They allowed the assemblies to raise their own revenues until the colo-nies had fully established the principle of self-taxation. By failing to use the taxing power of parliament during most of the colonial period, the minis-ters left in the hands of the assemblymen a powerful instrument which was destined to do great injury to the prerogative and at the same time to in-crease enormously the assemblymen's sense of their own importance. Instead of trying to get parliament to impose the necessary taxes, the royal officials adopted the policy of the local permanent revenue; that is, they urged the passage by the assemblies of perpetual laws for raising enough revenue to take care of the ordinary needs of local government. This policy proved entirely mistaken. Only a few of the provinces ever passed such laws, and in those that did, the taxes levied soon proved inadequate to support the governments. Sooner or later the assemblies of all the provinces were called upon to grant sums for ordinary as well as for extraordinary services. The financial supremacy of the assembly was thus established throughout the British colonial world. The harmful effects of this situation were of course apparent to the royal authorities, but they did not fall back upon the other alternative, that of taxation by parliament, until nearly the end of the period. By then the time for such action had long since passed. The assemblies had grown too strong to submit tamely to parliamentary interference with their fiscal affairs. The measures commonly associated with the names of Gren-ville and Townshend proved to be dismal blunders. The century-old policy with regard to colonial taxation could not be even partially reversed without calling forth a serious protest.

In the meantime the assemblymen had learned how to use their control of finance to reduce the influence of the prerogative to a minimum. By passing revenue laws for short periods only, by making detailed and specific appropriations, by refusing to accept amendments from the council, by controlling the appointment of the treasurer, and by arranging as far as possible that money should be paid on their authority rather than on that of the governor and council, the members of the lower house of every royal province placed themselves in a position from which they could dominate the administration and safely defy the orders of the home government. They became especially adept at picking the right moments for their maneuvers, as Governor Benning Wentworth of New Hampshire explained: "The prerogative of the crown, his Majesty's instructions, and the passing of laws inconsistent therewith are matters that the assemblies are exceedingly averse to submit to, and therefore upon every occasion when the necessity of the government calls for an immediate supply of the treasury, they never fail of invading the one or the other, and the greater the necessity or emergency is, the greater they esteem their advantage." This control of finance, whereby the assemblymen gain their ends, was not limited to one or two issues or details of local administration. Every field of governmental activity, civil, military, or judicial, which needed financial support, was fertile ground for controversy, and sooner or later, in one province or another, yielded its crop of discord. In many provinces the British authorities were measurably successful in placing the governor's salary out of the assembly's reach, but even where the lower house kept control, the salary issue was only one of many paths to legislative supremacy. The ultimate effect of the assembly's financial power was well summed up by Governor Knowles of Jamaica in 1752:

> Your Lordships is sensible of the difficulties most of the governors of this island have labored under to execute his Majesty's instructions, by the balance of power being constantly in the House of Representatives (an error, I am inclined to believe, in its first concoction).
>
> One who is thought to have understood the nature of government as well as any who ever wrote on that subject (James Harrington), says "That national or independent empire is to be executed by them who have the proper balance of dominion in the nation; wherefore provincial or dependent empire is not to be exercised by them who have the balance of dominion in the province, because that would bring the government from provincial and dependent to national and independent." Now as the assembly of this island have long (though contrary to his Majesty's instructions) assumed to themselves the sole power of raising and appropriating money exclusive of the council (for they will not so much as receive or admit of a literal amendment from them in any money bill) they are indeed the government.

Certainly the assembly's "sole power of raising and appropriating money" was second to nothing in importance as a means of making that body actually "the government" of the royal province.

The three great advantages that the assembly enjoyed in its contest with the prerogative—the initiative in legislation, the historical example of parliament, and the control of finance—were not the only causes of the final outcome. In addition, there were certain features of the system of "government by instruction" itself which weakened the authority of the governors and contributed to the decline of the prerogative.

Uncertainty as to how much discretion the governor might use in interpreting and enforcing his instructions was one factor tending toward the decay of the royal authority. The opinion has been held by some historians that the Board of Trade and the privy council considered the instructions as merely formal guides which the governors were not expected to obey too literally. Nothing could be farther from the truth. Again and again a provincial act was disallowed, not because it was a bad law in itself, but because it failed to comply with some detail of the instructions. Again and again the board wrote to one governor or another expressing in the strongest possible terms their disapproval of his failure to obey orders. They felt so keenly on this subject that they sent a circular letter to all the governors in 1752 in which they pointed out that "the experience of late years furnishes too frequent instances in which many of those instructions have been dispensed with and neglected upon slight and unwarrantable pretenses." They urged the governors to "have a proper regard to the regulations contained in your instructions" especially in the passing of laws. In self-protection the Board of Trade told the privy council in 1767 that they did not believe the neglect of the governors to protect British interests in colonial legislation was "owing to the want of frequent admonitions from this board to the said governors, who have been from time to time called upon by our predecessors in office to a more regular observance of their instructions relative to the passing and assenting to laws." There can be little doubt but that the home authorities intended the instructions to be literally obeyed.

Of course, there were times when the interests of the crown and of the colony would have been ill served by too strict an application of one or another of the formally worded instructions. Even the Board of Trade admitted this fact in their circular letter of 1752, when they cautioned the governors "strictly to adhere to your instructions and not to deviate from them in any point but upon evident necessity justified by the particular circumstances of the case." At such times the governors were to explain their reasons at once, and, if time allowed, to ask for directions from England before taking action. But who was to decide when a deviation from the instructions was immediately necessary? It was well enough for the duke of Portland to say that he believed he ought not to disobey his instructions "but on such emergencies as, when told, carry their reasons along with them, so that my behavior may be justified and my honor and integrity not called in question." But several governors found to their sorrow that emergencies which seemed very real and pressing to them in the colonies often appeared quite the reverse to the officials in England, and that their letters explaining their violations of instructions proved much less convincing to the readers in England than the writers had hoped. The slowness of ocean transportation in those days prevented easy consultation between the king's officers in England and America. Governors had a hard time getting the home authorities to understand the true state of affairs in the colonies and persuading them to excuse the occasional violation of an instruction. The colonial executives seldom knew just how far they dared go in disregarding their orders without being brought sharply to book. An easy-going governor was likely to have his acts publicly repudiated in Great Britain and even to find himself ignominiously recalled if he interpreted his instructions too liberally. On the other hand, a conscientious governor was likely to hesitate so long before disregarding an instruction that the assembly would look upon any indulgence that he finally showed them as a forced surrender rather than a voluntary act of generosity. His concession, therefore, would weaken rather than strengthen his position in the province. The uncertainty of the governor's discretionary power made difficult the game of give and take, which every successful politician must play, and seriously handicapped the royal governor in his contests with the assembly.

An even more important reason for the decline of the system of government by instruction was the fact that the governor had the sole responsibility for the enforcement of the instructions. They were directed to him alone and related almost exclusively to the manner in which he was to exercise the authority given to him by his commission. The Board of Trade made this fact clear in a letter to Governor Knowles, written in 1754 during the dispute over the use of the suspending clause in certain types of legislation. The board declared that the instruction in question was "not directory to the assembly as to the manner of framing their bills, . . . but to you only, as to the manner in which you are to apply your assent or negative to the bills which they have so framed." On the other hand, the home authorities repeatedly insisted that the instructions were to be accepted as an essential part of the constitutional system of the province. If the instructions were to receive the attention and respect which they deserved as a constitutional document of the highest importance, they should have been issued, as was the commission, in the form of a public document. They should have been openly read at the governor's installation and recorded in the office of the provincial secretary. They should have contained, as the commission did, a clause calling upon all officers, ministers, and other inhabitants to assist the governor in the execution of their provisions. They should have been "directory to the assembly as to the manner of framing their bills," and not simply to the governor as to his use of the veto. Instead the instructions were issued as a private paper for the eyes of the governor alone. Although he was told to show some of the articles to the council and was allowed to lay extracts before the assembly when occasion required, everyone was made to feel that the governor alone was responsible for their enforcement. In this sense, then, the instructions were a very narrow type of constitutional document.

If any moral or legal obligation rested upon any officers of the province to assist the governor in executing the instructions, it surely rested most of all upon the royally appointed councillors. Sometimes, especially when their own interests coincided with those of the crown, the members of the council took an active part in supporting the governor and in resisting the encroachments of the assembly. But even they often stepped aside when a crisis occurred and left the governor to uphold the prerogative alone. The councillors repeatedly showed their willingness to evade responsibility, especially on the frequent occasions when, in their legislative capacity, they passed a bill because it was desired in the province and then, in their executive capacity, solemnly advised the governor to veto the measure because it was contrary to his instructions. One Jamaica concillor frankly wrote a member of the Board of Trade that when certain very improper bills came up during a period of distress in the island, he and his colleagues "chose to give way to the necessity of the times and leave the supporting the king's instructions to the king's ministers, who had the framing of them, and who have sufficient power to do it, had they the leisure for such remote considerations; and the visible want of that encourages these men in their insolence." When councillors were so indifferent, assemblymen could hardly be expected to show greater loyalty.

Actually, the representatives paid no more attention to the instructions than they absolutely had to. Probably all the royal governors, in the West Indies as well as on the continent, would have agreed with Benning Wentworth of New Hampshire when he wrote: "In this government, and I believe in some other of the northern colonies, for want of a more perfect understanding of the intention and use of the king's instructions and the royal prerogative, they are esteemed by the assemblies as burdensome and useless and therefore they take every advantage to force acts contrary to both as opportunity offers; from which behavior it appears to me that nothing less than an act of parliament will be binding on the assemblies to pay a due obedience to his Majesty's instructions. I have laid before the present assembly, which I deem as well disposed as any I have had, a paragraph in your Lordships' letter wherein I am commanded to adhere to my instructions and not to deviate from them on any occasions. It had no effect upon them. They say among themselves that the instructions are binding on the governor but not on them."

Ten years before this letter was written, the Board of Trade had tried to get parliament to pass a bill which, among other things, would have required all governors, lieutenant governors, councils, and assemblies "to pay strict obedience to such orders and instructions as shall from time to time be transmitted to them or any of them by his Majesty or his successors or by any under his or their authority." The bill would have automatically made invalid all "acts, orders, votes, or resolutions" contrary to the instructions. The opposition of the colonial agents and the jealousy in the Commons of the prerogative prevented any such sweeping measure from being enacted by parliament. But even if such a bill had become law in 1744 it would have come too late to accomplish its purpose. The members of the Board of Trade must have been optimistic, indeed, if they thought the assemblies would accept with docility as late in their development as this, any constitutional change so revolutionary as the proposal to give the instructions the binding force of law. The assemblies had already taken the position that the instructions related to the governor alone and that under the constitution the legislatures could not be bound by royal orders. When news of the bill of 1744 reached New York, a committee of the assembly reported that the measure would, if enacted, "establish such an absolute power of the crown in all the British plantations as would be inconsistent with the liberties and privileges inherent in an Englishman whilst he is in a British dominion." By this time two full generations of colonists had grown up with the belief that the governor alone was responsible for carrying out the instructions. The proposed act of parliament would hardly have changed this belief, and although it might have increased the apparent power of the crown in the colonies, it would hardly have led the assemblies to give the governors more sympathetic support.

As matters stood, the royal governor to whom the instructions were addressed could count on very little certain support from any quarter in carrying out his orders. A few administrative officials whose appointment and removal he controlled, here and there an officer directly appointed from England, some members of the council nearly always, and others less frequently, and such friends as he might have made among the assemblymen, could be relied upon to give him a helping hand. But none of them had the same sense of responsibility that the governor had. No wonder that he found the task of enforcing the instructions so difficult; no wonder that his powers proved so often quite unequal to that task.

A third feature of the instructions which made them hard to enforce was their evident partiality. In drafting instructions on controversial points, the Board of Trade nearly always favored British rather than colonial interests. Emphasis has been placed . . . on the influence of the merchants in preparing orders for the royal governors. The assemblymen could not fail to understand this influence. They realized that whenever a law was passed in a province designed to protect local interests against those of the British merchants, the latter could nearly always get the law disallowed and could often persuade the Board of Trade and privy council to send an instruction to the governor forbidding him to approve any similar bills in the future. Such realization hardly increased the assemblymen's respect for the instructions or their willingness to obey such prohibitions as seemed to be harmful to the colonists as a whole. The representatives of Jamaica, for example, knew that the article restricting the duties on slaves was continued for seventeen years at the instigation of the British traders, in spite of the protests of every royal governor and their assertions that the slave trade as carried on was bad for the island. Such knowledge was not likely to make the Jamaica assemblymen respect the instructions in general; rather would it suggest to them the necessity of evasion at every possible point. The colonists knew that their local interests were not the foremost consideration of the British officials who prepared the instructions. Had it been otherwise, they might have felt differently about the whole system of government by instruction. But the number of cases in which the representatives of the prerogative completely disregarded the colonial point of view was so great as not only to increase the difficulty of enforcing the instructions, but, in the end, to lower the influence of the crown in controlling the affairs of the royal provinces.

The last and undoubtedly the most important feature of the instructions that contributed to the decline of the royal authority in America, was their inflexibility. In theory the commission and instructions were easily adjustable tools with which to build the constitutional system of the provinces. A new commission and set of general instructions were prepared for every province on an average of once in every five and a half years, and changes in detail were made during the intervals by the very simple method of issuing additional instructions. Even a radical alteration in the draft of a commission or instruction from the form previously in force needed only the recommendation of the Board of Trade and the approval of the privy council on the advice of its committee, and the privy council could dispense with the recommendation of the Board of Trade if it so wished. Few constitutional documents in all of history have offered such frequent opportunities for, or such easy means of, amendment. With the two hundred and more commissions and sets of general instructions which were issued during the century before the American Revolution, the British authorities had a magnificent opportunity to experiment in colonial government. They could modify the constitutional system almost at will; introduce new principles whenever such seemed desirable; try out some new feature in a single province and later apply it to the others if it proved successful. In short, they could do anything to keep the colonial constitution up to date so long as they did not violate the acknowledged liberties of the colonists. The colonial world was a splendid laboratory for the contemporary student of political science, and the commissions and instructions were almost perfect instruments for the experimenter.

But in Great Britain the eighteenth century was not an age of conscious experimentation in constitutional government, as the seventeenth century had been or as the nineteenth and twentieth centuries were destined to be. Between the collapse of the Dominion of New England and the passage of the Stamp Act the British officials showed no inclination to change the constitutional system of a single royal province, except in the case of Massachusetts whose special privileges they would have gladly destroyed. Their only contributions to the theory of colonial government during this time are to be found in their partly successful efforts to royalize the proprietary and corporate colonies, in the half-hearted and abortive attempts to bring the various colonies into closer union for defense, and in their ill-timed suggestion that parliament give the royal instructions the force of law in all the colonies. As far as the internal affairs of the royal provinces themselves were concerned, the Board of Trade and privy council made no fresh experiments after the late seventeenth century when the principle was established that each province was to have a local assembly endowed with the right to initiate legislation. Even in setting up the vice-admiralty courts in the continental colonies after the passage of the act of 1696, the home authorities merely extended and enlarged the powers of an institution which had existed in the West Indies for a generation. The parliamentary measures which the Board of Trade advocated, such as the Hat Act, the Molasses Act, and the Paper Currency Act, all dealt primarily with trade and commerce. None of them was passed for purposes of constitutional revision. Parliament passed no laws directly relating to colonial government before 1763, and even the measures enacted after that date were signs that the royal officials had failed to maintain their long-established system rather than proof of any particular effort to improve the system of colonial government. In their attitude toward royal government in America the Board of Trade and privy council showed an almost fanatical reverence for the *status quo*.

In letter and in spirit the commissions and instructions reflect this fundamental conservatism. The similarity of these documents from province to province and from governor to governor shows the lack of originality in the minds of their authors. Only two noteworthy changes in the organization of the provincial governments were made during the period before the Stamp Act. These two were the removal of the governor's right to give orders to officers commanding vessels of the royal navy in provincial waters and the substitution of the senior councillor for the whole council as the successor in administration to the governor and lieutenant governor. These were minor matters after all. Although the assemblies were growing in maturity and in ability to handle their own affairs, the Board of Trade modified the governors' instructions in favor of the assemblies only three times— once when they permitted the Jamaica assembly to lay a "reasonable duty" on slaves purchased in the island, again when they let Governor Belcher of Massachusetts accept an annual salary, and lastly when they allowed Governor Hardy of New York to approve temporary appropriation acts because of the impending war with France. Not one of these reversals of policy was made willingly; each was wrung from the board only after the most convincing evidence had been given that the concession was absolutely necessary. In a few other cases the board gave way when they found that acts had previously been passed and inadvertently approved by the king which made illegal the instructions the board had issued. With such exceptions as these, the changes in the instructions were all made with the intent of tightening the royal grip upon the colonies rather than of loosening it, and of counteracting the growing power of the assemblies rather than of conforming to it. The British authorities had no intention of experimenting with colonial government or of changing the commissions and instructions in the direction of greater liberality and freedom.

One incident deserves to be mentioned, however, because it stands so completely apart from the normal attitude of the English authorities toward the situation in the colonies. When the Quebec Act was passed in 1774, a new commission and new instructions were necessary for the governor of the province, Guy Carleton. This act was in considerable measure the work of Carleton himself, and, as he was in England while the new instructions were being prepared, the Board of Trade naturally called upon him for assistance. Carleton was a man of common sense and vision. The results of his activity are striking. He was unquestionably responsible for the omission of many of the usual paragraphs of the instructions and the inclusion of many new ones based on the recent act of parliament. Thanks to him the new orders were phrased in fresh and unhackneyed language. The meaningless formulae of the past century were discarded. Provincial problems were presented in a simple and informal manner. Throughout the document there flow a current of liberalism and a spirit of adventure. Confronted with a vast domain and an alien population, the British officials at last seemed bent on a great experiment. The instructions show the desire of these officials to give the governor the soundest advice possible and yet to allow the utmost freedom and discretion possible that he might bring order out of what must have seemed like chaos. Whatever may or may not have been the merits of the governmental plan laid down, whatever the success or failure of the administration in Quebec, the freshness and vigor of Carleton's instructions are a welcome contrast to the staleness and ineptitude of the orders given to the governors of the other provinces.

The inflexibility and uniformity of the instructions contributed directly to the failure of the royal system of government in America. No constitutional system can long survive the conditions which called it into being, unless the necessary steps are taken to adapt the system to changes in the community. In the case of the British colonies the constitutional system as embodied in the commissions and instructions was established in the seventeenth century when most of the provinces concerned were small and undeveloped. Even in those communities, such as the West Indies, which were foremost in wealth and population, the inhabitants had very limited political experience and the assemblies had not yet had time to establish strong traditions of self-government. The commissions and instructions then issued were based upon principles of government by royal grace and favor which, although distasteful to some individuals, were not entirely out of keeping with the immaturity of the colonies. A hundred years later conditions were wholly changed. In the continental colonies, population had increased enormously, territorial expansion had been continuous, and wealth had accumulated. Both in the West Indies and on the continent, the assemblies had created precedents, had established fixed rules of procedure, and had won recognition of their parliamentary privileges in fact if not in theory; they had gained control of finance and by these means they had come to dominate provincial affairs. The propertied classes, to whom the franchise was extended, had gained not only familiarity with political methods, but the habit of self-government. But during these hundred years the instructions had undergone no fundamental change; they still rested on the principle of government by royal grace and favor; they continued to give the governor, as the representative of the prerogative, the same large powers that he had received when the assembly was first created. The officials in Whitehall who drafted these documents were as unmoved by the changes in America as they would have been if those changes had taken place on another planet. Inevitably, therefore, the system of government by instruction proved more and more unworkable the longer it was in force.

The British authorities remained blind to the causes which underlay the decline of royal authority. They never offered a workable solution for the problem before them. They were suspicious and critical whenever a governor exercised any real discretion in applying his instructions. They made only futile and half-hearted attempts to help him share responsibility for observing the instructions with the council and assembly. They never receded from the position that the colonies existed primarily for the benefit of Great Britain and that the instructions ought to protect British rather than colonial interests when these came into conflict. And the royal officials never saw any need for liberalizing or modernizing the instructions, which they repeated from governor to governor with monotonous regularity. Instead of modifying the system from time to time so as to preserve the influence of the crown and insure the cooperation of the assemblies, they rejected all proposals of this sort as contrary to "the true principles of a provincial constitution." For the new wine of colonial conditions and ideals they offered only the old wineskins of an ancient and inflexible system. Responsibility for the catastrophe that followed must rest primarily upon the shoulders of those who prepared the commissions and instructions and who failed to see that the system of "government by instruction" was no longer suitable as the foundation of the colonial constitution. For they thought only in terms of the past and of government "by royal grace and favor," ignoring the new principle of government "by the consent of the governed," which not only was soon to become the cornerstone of a republic in America, but was in time to have an important place in the reconstruction of the British Empire itself.

GEORGE III *lives in history as a tyrant bent on restoring royal absolutism. It is a reputation that is ill-deserved. In his own eyes, he saw himself the victim of "his scrupulous attachment to the rights of Parliament." He was no less certain that the conflicts which developed between himself and his American colonies after 1763 resulted from his effort to restrain the pretensions of the colonial legislatures to supremacy. The stubborn tenacity with which he defended the rights of the Westminster Parliament persuaded the colonials that their king supported the claims of "subjects in one part of the King's dominions to be sovereigns over their fellow-subjects in another part of his dominions." But throughout the growing crisis agitating British-colonial relations, the young king never doubted that he was a Whig defending both the doctrines of parliamentary supremacy and separation of power. What he did not understand was that his colonial subjects believed that their legislatures were autonomous and that their sole link with the London government was through the crown. A more subtle intellect than that of George III might have grasped the significance of Benjamin Franklin's assertion, "The sovereignty of the Crown I understand, the sovereignty of Britain I do not understand. . . . We have the same King, but not the same legislature."*

*The substance of a large dispute between Britain and the colonies existed, but so long as the colonies faced the presence of a hostile France along their borders, the need for British protection kept in check their differences with the mother country. Once the Peace of Paris was concluded in 1763, Britain and her colonies moved on to a collision course. At the heart of the worsening relations was the British desire to make more rational the administration of the new empire and to find ways to reduce the burden of taxation in the home islands. Yet every step taken to implement either purpose was interpreted by the colonials as an impingement on their inherent rights. With the passage of the Stamp Act in 1765, an act which asserted the right of Parliament to tax the colonies, the battle between Parliament and the colonial Assemblies was joined. The position of the colonials was pungently stated by the Connecticut Assembly when it proclaimed: "For if the Privilege of not being taxed without their Consent be taken from them, Liberty and Freedom are certainly gone with it." The point, once made, required little further elaboration for the American common folk. The issue for them was not representation in Parliament, it was the retention of their right to be taxed as in the past by representatives of their own choice sitting in their own legislatures.*

*To the Stamp Act and all other subsequent efforts to implement parliamentary tax efforts, the colonials replied with a campaign of civil disobedience. The struggle so far as the colonials were concerned was not with Parliament but with their king who was trying to foist an alien rule upon them. Slowly but steadily, in their eyes, George III too appeared more alien. Without ever quite realizing it, the last American king placed his American crown in jeopardy. Sixteen years after he ascended his throne, he found himself indicted in the Declaration of Independence as the enemy of American liberty. His overthrow followed logically from the charge.*

*Carl L. Becker (1873-1945) was born in a German-American farm community near Waterloo, Iowa. He was subsequently educated at Cornell and the University of Wisconsin. He revealed a catholic range of interests doing extensive work in American Revolutionary history as well as in the French Enlightenment. Oddly enough, although the bulk of his written work dealt with American history, he chiefly taught European history at Cornell, Dartmouth and several other universities. The one characteristic that set his work apart was a preoccupation with style. He worked it over until each of his essays was an incisive, lucid gem whose brevity concealed a compact but dense scholarship.*

# THE DECLARATION OF INDEPENDENCE

## by Carl L. Becker

When the controversy with Great Britain began in 1764, the preconceptions of the Natural Rights philosophy lay quiescent in colonial minds, ready to be drawn upon in case of need, but never yet having been called forth in the service of any concrete issue. With a possible exception here and there, the colonists had never even contemplated the idea of independence. They were, on the contrary, proud to be counted British subjects and citizens within the empire, the burdens of which, such as they were, had never rested heavily upon them. Each colony had its own government, consisting of a governor, appointed by the Crown in most cases, and a legislature of which the lower house was in all cases elected by certain defined classes of people resident in the colony. Before 1764 the British Parliament had in the main confined its supervision to the regulation of colonial trade, so that each colony had long been accustomed to exercise, in respect to all internal affairs, a pretty full measure of self-government. Laws passed by the colonial legislatures were often vetoed by the governors, or disallowed by the Crown; but the British government had rarely intervened with regulations of a positive sort, and it had never, with some slight and negligible exceptions, laid a tax on the colonies by act of Parliament.

With this situation the colonies were in the main well satisfied; and when they thought of the constitutional relations by which the colonies were connected with the British empire, they thought of them as relations which permitted the colonists, and doubtless would always permit them, to regulate their own affairs in their own way: the immunities which they in fact enjoyed, they thought of as "rights" which they ought constitutionally to possess. The truth is, however, that the colonists had not given a great deal of thought to these matters. They had thought a good deal about the respective "rights" of their assemblies as against the "rights" of their governors; but there had been no great occasion to ask what were the rights of the assemblies as against the rights of Parliament. The Sugar Act suddenly raised this question; and suddenly called upon to define their rights as colonies within the empire, called upon to say what constitutional barriers there were, if any, against an unlimited parliamentary control of the colonies, they could immediately find at hand no elaborate or very convincing answer. What most men were thinking was doubtless well enough expressed by two men who committed their opinions to writing in this year of 1764—Stephen Hopkins, afterwards one of the signers of the Declaration of Independence, and Thomas Hutchinson, afterwards a self-exiled Loyalist.

In a pamphlet entitled *The Rights of the Colonies Examined*, Hopkins argued that all colonies, in ancient and modern times, have always enjoyed "as much freedom as the mother state," and it could hardly be supposed, he thought, that the British colonies were an exception to that rule. Until now, at all events, the British Parliament had understood the rights of the colonies in this sense. Why then should the ancient practices be changed?

> The parliament, it is confessed, have power to regulate the trade of the whole empire; and hath it not full power, by this means, to draw all the wealth of the colonies into the mother country at pleasure? What motive, after all this, can remain to induce the parliament to abridge the privileges and lessen the rights of the most loyal and dutiful sub-jects,—subjects justly entitled to ample freedom, who have long en-joyed, and not abused or forfeited, their liberties, who have used them to their own advantage in dutiful subserviency to the orders and in-terests of Great Britain? Why should the gentle current of tranquility, that has so long run with peace through all the British states, and flowed with joy and happiness in all her countries, be at last obstructed, be turned out of its true course into unusual and winding channels, by which many of those states must be ruined, but none of them can pos-sibly be made more rich or more happy?

Hopkins does not really define the rights of the colonies; he raises questions about them. Have we not rights? We have always enjoyed rights and privi-leges, why should we not continue to enjoy them? We have been very dutiful.

Thomas Hutchinson, writing to a friend in England, speaks of the rights claimed by the colonies a little more precisely, but still in much the same sense.

> The colonists claim a power of making laws, and a privilege of ex-emption from taxes, unless voted by their own representatives. . . . Not one tenth part of the people of Great Britain have a voice in the elections to Parliament; and, therefore, the colonies can have no claim to it; but every man of property in England may have his voice, if he will. Besides, acts of Parliament do not generally affect individuals, and every interest is represented. But the colonies have an interest dis-tinct from the interest of the nation; and shall the Parliament be at once party and judge? . . .
>
> The nation treats her colonies as a father who should sell the services of his sons to reimburse what they had cost him, but without the same reason; for none of the colonies, except Georgia and Halifax, occasioned any charge to the Crown or kingdom in the settlement of them. The people of New England fled for the sake of civil and re-ligious liberty; multitudes flocked to America with this dependence, that their liberties should be safe. They and their posterity have en-joyed them to their content, and therefore have endured with greater cheerfulness all the hardships of settling new countries. No ill use has been made of these privileges; but the domain and wealth of Great Britain have received amazing addition. Surely the services we have rendered the nation have not subjected us to any forfeitures?

Such were the first, tentative steps in the effort to find a theory that would meet the emergency—a kind of timid groping about in the dark in search of the half-forgotten British Constitution. During the year 1765, as a result of the discussion which was accompanied by the passage and the practical nullification of the Stamp Act, the conception of colonial rights began to take on a more definite form. Forcible resistance to the Stamp Act, which few people anticipated, proved to be singularly easy, because the act could not take effect without the use of stamped papers, and the bundles of stamped papers, when they were once landed, could be easily destroyed without any one in particular being held responsible for their destruction. The colonists therefore found themselves facing a new emergency. They had to find good and sufficient reasons for having ventured to violate, by open and forcible means, an act of Parliament. They had to have a definition of colonial rights which would make the Stamp Act out to be, not merely an inexpedient measure, but an unconstitutional measure, a measure which the British Parliament had no "right" to pass.

To meet this emergency, the colonists seized upon the well-established tradition that British liberty had originally been won, and had always been maintained, by a stubborn and persistent parliamentary opposition to arbitrary taxation. This opposition, as a matter of sober historical fact, had never been more than intermittently effective until the seventeenth century; but the parliamentary party of that time, in defense of *their* rights, maintained that the parliamentary control of taxation was as old as Magna Carta. And so in the eighteenth century it was commonly accepted as a principle of the British Constitution that no Englishman could be legally taxed except by his own consent, that is, by his representatives in Parliament. This being so, the colonists reasoned, we, being British subjects with all the rights of Englishmen born within the realm, cannot be legally taxed except with our consent; and therefore, we cannot be legally taxed by the British Parliament since we are not represented in it.

Thus stated, the argument was open to attack at two points: it could be affirmed that Parliament had as a matter of fact taxed the colonies in the past without any opposition on their part; and it could be said that the colonies were represented in Parliament in the same sense that Englishmen were. Soame Jenyns, in a pamphlet widely read in England, pointed out that many English communities, such as Manchester and Sheffield, were taxed without being privileged to send representatives to Parliament, so that the colonies were represented as much or as little as these English communities; either Manchester is not represented in Parliament, in which case Parliament can and does tax Englishmen without their consent, or else Boston is represented in Parliament, in which case she has no grievance. In other words, it was held that relatively few Englishmen had a right to vote for their representatives in Parliament; that they were nevertheless "virtually represented" by the members of Parliament chosen by those who had a right to vote; and that accordingly the people residing in the colonies were also "virtually represented" in Parliament in the same way as the non-electors residing in Great Britain.

This argument was most effectively answered by Daniel Dulany, of Maryland, in a pamphlet entitled *Considerations on the Propriety of Imposing Taxes in the British Colonies for the Purpose of Raising a Revenue by Act of Parliament*. The people of the colonies, says Dulany, are in a very different situation from the non-electors residing in Great Britain, because in the latter case the interests of

> the non-electors, the electors, and the representatives, are individually the same, to say nothing of the connection among neighbors, friends, and relations. The security of the non-electors against oppression is that their oppression will fall also upon the electors and the representatives. . . . Further, if the non-electors should not be taxed by the British Parliament, they would not be taxed at all. . . . Under this constitution, then, a double or virtual representation may be reasonably supposed. The electors, who are inseparably connected in their interests with the non-electors, may be justly deemed to be the representatives of the non-electors, at the same time they exercise their personal privilege in their right of election, and the members chosen, therefore, the representatives of both.

The situation of the colonists was manifestly different. If every inhabitant of America possessed the necessary freehold "not one could vote, but upon the supposition of his becoming a resident of Great Britain." Besides, the colonists already pay taxes levied by their own legislatures, and therefore they would not be exempt from taxation if not taxed by the British Parliament, as the non-electors in Great Britain would be. Most important of all,

> there is not that intimate and inseparable relation between the electors of Great Britain and the inhabitants of the colonies, which must inevitably involve both in the same taxation. On the contrary, not a single actual elector in England might be immediately affected by a taxation in America. . . . Even acts oppressive and injurious to an extreme degree, might become popular in England, from the promise or expectation that the very measures which depressed the colonies, would give ease to the inhabitants of Great Britain.

Dulany's refutation of the doctrine of "virtual representation" was complete—almost too complete. The inference from it was, either that the colonies should be permitted to send representatives to the Parliament, or that the Parliament had no right of taxing the colonies in any way whatever. Sending representatives to Parliament was a perfectly possible thing to do; but the colonists commonly rejected this solution, because it was obvious that sending a few representatives to England would serve only to justify parliamentary taxation without doing anything to prevent it. But, on the other hand, could the colonists stand uncompromisingly on the ground that Parliament had no right to tax them in any way whatever? The Sugar Act was a tax. The Parliament had for over a century imposed trade duties. These were in some sense taxes; and at this early date almost no one was ready to deny that Parliament had the right to impose taxes of this sort. In face of this difficulty, certain writers drew a distinction between "internal" and "external" taxes, denying the right of Parliament to lay the former but admitting, by implication at least, its right to impose the latter. This was no doubt a dangerous admission, and many were inclined to avoid the difficulty by ignoring it. That, for example, is substantially what the Stamp Act Congress did in framing its resolutions of protest against the Stamp Act and the Sugar Act. Expressly affirming that the colonists owed the same allegiance to the Crown of Great Britain as subjects residing in England, the Resolutions declared that "no taxes . . . can be constitutionally imposed upon them but by their respective legislatures"; but without explicitly drawing a distinction between "internal" and "external" taxes, the wording of the Resolutions is such as to imply that distinction; the Stamp Act is mentioned as "imposing taxes" which have "a manifest tendency to subvert the rights and liberties of the colonies," while the Sugar Act is only vaguely referred to as among "several late acts" which imposed "duties" that "will be extremely burthensome and grievous."

Thus at the time of the repeal of the Stamp Act in 1766, the colonies did not deny that the British Parliament possessed of right a general legislative jurisdiction over them; they maintained only that this jurisdiction did not include the right of laying taxes upon them without their consent; and that at least direct internal taxes, such as the Stamp Tax, were not only contrary to custom but were a violation of constitutional rights.

The repeal of the Stamp Act was greeted with general rejoicing and thanksgiving, and was accepted for the most part as an admission by the British government of the validity of the colonial contention. It is true, the Parliament categorically refused to admit, in principle, any such thing; on the contrary, the same day the king signed the Repeal bill he signed also the Declaratory Act, which affirmed that the king and Parliament "had, hath, and of right ought to have, full power and authority to make . . . laws and statutes . . . to bind the colonies and people of America . . . in all cases whatsoever." But the colonists were not, for the moment, oversensitive to the assertion of abstract rights, being well content to have won a practical victory. They felt that the Parliament, having repealed the Stamp Act, would be unlikely to pass a new one, or any similar measure laying direct or internal taxes. And if the Parliament in practice held to their distinction between internal and external taxes, what more could they ask, this being the ground on which they had elected, somewhat uncertainly and apprehensively to be sure, to stand in defense of their rights?

It presently appeared that their rights could not be defended on this ground. In 1767 Parliament passed the Townshend Acts. Townshend himself thought the distinction between "internal" and "external" taxes "perfect nonsense"; but since the colonists had made a point of it he thought it wise to humor them by laying only "external" taxes. Certain duties, to be collected in American ports, were accordingly laid upon the importation of various kinds of glass, lead, paper, and tea. The measure was avowedly a tax measure, and it was estimated that the duties might bring in some £40,000 of revenue if efficiently collected; and that these and other duties might be efficiently collected, Customs Commissioners were appointed and sent to Boston. Here was an emergency which the colonists had not anticipated. The Commissioners were as great a nuisance as the Stamp Collectors, and more effective, since they did not resign as the Stamp Collectors had done, under pressure, but called in British troops to support them, and actually collected the customs duties, something relatively unknown before. Under the circumstances, the colonists were disposed to agree with Townshend that the distinction between "internal" and "external" taxes was "perfect nonsense." After all, a tax was a tax; and the essence of the whole matter was that Parliament had no constitutional power to "take money out of their pockets," as Pitt said, without their consent, by any kind of tax whatever.

A more skilful dialectic was required to maintain this ground than to maintain the old one. It was a somewhat stubborn fact that Parliament had for more than a hundred years passed laws regulating colonial trade, and for regulating trade had imposed duties, some of which had brought into the Exchequer a certain revenue. The Americans could not well say at this late date that Parliament had no right to lay duties in regulation of trade. Must they then submit to the Townshend duties? Or was it possible to make a clear distinction between duties laid for the regulation of trade and duties laid for bringing in a revenue? John Dickinson, in a series of widely read and very influential essays, entitled *Letters from a Farmer in Pennsylvania to the Inhabitants of the British Colonies*, attempted to make this distinction. Arguing at length in the old manner that Parliament had no right to tax the colonies without their consent, he maintained that the sole question in respect to the Townshend duties was whether they were duties laid for revenue or for regulation of trade. A difficulty arose from the fact that any duties laid on trade might be both and were likely to be both. Well, said Dickinson, we must determine this question by the "intention" of the framers of the law. Did the British Parliament pass the Townshend Act primarily with the "intention" of raising a revenue, or primarily with the intention of regulating trade? Clearly the former, since the intention of raising a revenue was explicitly avowed in the act itself. Hence the Townshend duties were taxes, and as such unconstitutional.

The Townshend Act presented no difficulty on this score; but Dickinson was aware that his method might be difficult to apply in case, as might well be in the future, Parliament should lay duties on trade with the real intention of raising a revenue while openly professing the intention of regulating trade. How then? "It will be difficult for any person but the makers of the laws to determine which of them are made for regulation of trade, and which for raising a revenue." True enough! Well, in that case, since "names will not change the nature of things," the intention of the makers must be inferred from the nature of the law; and Dickinson hoped, for his part, that his countrymen "would never, to their latest existence, want understanding sufficient to discover the intentions of those who rule over them." To derive the nature of an act from the intention of its framers, and the intention of its framers from the nature of the act, was no doubt what logicians would call reasoning in a circle; but whatever the technical defects of the argument might be, the colonists could, and did, lay firm hold of the general conclusion that Americans have "the same right that all states have, of judging when their privileges are invaded."

Meantime, it appeared that their privileges were being invaded in other, and perhaps even more vital, ways than by parliamentary taxation. In 1768, after the Massachusetts Assembly had sent a circular letter to the other colonial assemblies asking for concerted action in defense of their liberties, the Earl of Hillsborough, speaking in the name of the king, categorically directed the Assembly "to rescind the resolution which gave birth to the circular letter from the Speaker, and to declare their disapprobation of, and dissent to, that rash and hasty proceeding." At an earlier date, Governor Colden of New York had been instructed to suspend the meetings of the Assembly of that province until it should have made provision, according to the terms of the Quartering Act, for the support of British troops stationed there. These were measures of ominous import. Of what value was it to safeguard the right of being taxed exclusively in their own assemblies, if the British government could by administrative order abolish their assemblies? If the British government could abolish colonial assemblies, it could destroy every vestige of colonial self-government. Clearly, therefore, the question which was now coming to include all others was the question of preserving the legislative independence of the colonies.

To meet this emergency, a theory which denied the jurisdiction of the British government in this or that particular matter, such as the taxing power, was inadequate; what was needed was a theory which would define the respective jurisdictions of the British and colonial governments in terms of some general principle. Dickinson had said that the colonies were "as much dependent on Great Britain as one free people could be on another." This might seem to be as indefinite as anything could well be; but the assumption on which it rests was to be the foundation upon which the colonists built up their theory from this time on. That assumption was that the Americans were one "people," the English another, and each a "free" people. No doubt an Englishman might have said that this was begging the question; the precise question at issue, he might have maintained, is whether the Americans *are* a "free" people. We maintain that they are subject to the British Parliament. The Parliament has always exercised jurisdiction over them in fact; and to prove this we point you to any number of statutes duly passed and recorded and submitted to. If positive law is any test, the colonies are not a "free" people, but a subject people; and any privileges which they may have are privileges granted or permitted by the British Parliament.

On this ground it was indeed difficult to meet the British contention. In order to maintain the rights of a free people, the colonists were accordingly forced to change the question; and from this time on we find them less disposed to ask, What are the rights which we possess as British subjects? and more disposed to ask, What are the rights which we possess as members of the human race? This latter question was one which Samuel Adams had been thinking about since the year 1743 when, upon receiving the degree of Master of Arts from Harvard College, he argued the thesis, "Whether it be lawful to resist the Supreme Magistrate if the Commonwealth cannot otherwise be preserved." In the present crisis, therefore, he was able to formulate a theory (best stated in a letter to Dennys De Berdt, January 12, 1769) designed to show that the colonies were "subordinate" but not "subject" to the British Parliament. Adams' theory of "subordination" may be taken as the first reasoned elaboration of Dickinson's general proposition that America is "as dependent on Great Britain as one free people can be on another."

For a major premise, Samuel Adams turned as a matter of course to the current philosophy of Natural Rights, familiar doctrine to him, and often enough expounded in newspaper articles or at the Caucus Club; and in bringing it in to solve a practical issue, he doubtless felt that he was only grounding the discussion upon commonly accepted axioms of political thinking. The delimitation of colonial and parliamentary jurisdictions, Adams achieved by subordinating all legislative authority to an authority higher than any positive law, an authority which no legislature could "overleap without destroying its own foundation." This higher authority was the British Constitution. The British Constitution, Adams said, "is fixed," having its foundation in "the law of God and nature." In the British empire there are many legislatures, all deriving their authority from, and finding their limitations in, the Constitution. Parliament has certainly a supreme or superintending legislative authority in the empire, as the colonial assemblies have a "subordinate" in the sense of a local, legislative authority; but neither the Parliament nor any colonial assembly can rightly extend its jurisdiction beyond the limits fixed by the Constitution. And therefore, since the Constitution is founded "in the law of God and nature," and since it is "an essential natural right that a man shall quietly enjoy and have the sole disposal of his property," the Americans must enjoy this right equally with Englishmen, and Parliament must be bound to respect this right in the colonies as well as in England; from which it followed that the consent of the colonies must be sought exclusively in their own assemblies, it being manifestly impossible for that consent to be "constitutionally had in Parliament."

Obviously, according to this reasoning, the authority of the British Parliament over the colonies would ultimately always have to stop where the "essential natural rights" of the colonies began. Adams had found at least one of these rights—the right which every man had of "quietly enjoying and having the sole disposal of his property." But perhaps there were other essential natural rights. What were they? Was there any sure way of finding out? Above all, in case there should be, as might well happen, between Britons and Americans any serious difference of opinion on this point, which opinion should prevail? Admitting that the British Parliament had a supreme or supervising jurisdiction in the empire, it might well be argued that in case of conflict the "supreme" rather than the "subordinate" jurisdiction should decide. Some authority would have to determine, in concrete cases, what were and what were not essential natural rights. If this authority were the British Parliament, the essential natural rights were likely to be few indeed; while if the colonial assemblies were to have this authority, the list of essential natural rights was likely in the end to be a long one.

Few men could go more directly to the heart of a question, once he gave his mind to it, than that shrewd old friend of the Human Race, Dr. Benjamin Franklin. Since 1764 he had been giving his mind more or less continuously to this question of colonial rights, and, without making much noise about it, had advanced farther than most men along the road that led to independence. In 1765 it did not appear to him that the Stamp Act was a measure beyond the constitutional jurisdiction of the British Parliament. An inexpedient measure it was certainly, highly burdensome to the colonies, and prejudicial to the true interests of Great Britain; but the only advice Franklin could give his countrymen at that time was to submit to the law as a legally valid act, while protesting against it as in effect an unwise one.

In the meantime Franklin had been reading and reflecting upon all that had been written, pro and con, about the respective rights and prerogatives of British and colonial legislatures. Among other things, he had read and reflected upon the writings of John Dickinson and Samuel Adams. The reasoning of these men seemed to him ingenious and interesting, but not altogether free from over refinement, a quality which was likely to prove a defect in the handling of practical questions. In the year 1768 he formulated the result of his reflections on the whole matter thus:

> I am not yet master of the idea these . . . writers have of the relation between Britain and her colonies. I know not what the Boston people mean by the "Subordination" they acknowledge in their Assembly to Parliament, while they deny its power to make laws for them, nor what bounds the Farmer sets to the power he acknowledges in parliament to "regulate the trade of the colonies," it being difficult to draw lines between duties for regulation and those for revenue; and, if the Parliament is to be the judge, it seems to me that establishing such a principle of distinction will amount to little. The more I have thought and read on the subject, the more I find myself confirmed in opinion, that no middle ground can be well maintained, I mean not clearly with intelligible arguments. Something might be made of either of the extremes: that Parliament has a power to make *all laws* for us, or that it has a power to make *no laws* for us; and I think the arguments for the latter more numerous and weighty, than those for the former. Supposing that doctrine established, the colonies would then be so many separate states, only subject to the same king, as England and Scotland were before the union.

Here at last was a clear-cut alternative—that Parliament had a power of making all laws for the colonies, or else that it had a power of making no laws for them. Which should it be? If it must be one or the other, the arguments for the latter contention would naturally seem to the colonists to be more numerous and weighty than for the former. From this time on Franklin at least assumed that the empire was composed of separate states all subject to the king, but each possessed of its own legislature outside the jurisdiction of the British Parliament. By 1770, Franklin felt that this was a position which should be taken for granted, and no longer argued.

❧ ☙

"POWER *is of a grasping, encroaching nature," the Congregationalist Jonathan Mayhew preached, "it aims at extending itself and operating according to mere* will *wherever it meets with no balance, check, control, or opposition of any kind." To have conceded the right of Parliament to institute a Stamp Act would have, in the eyes of the colonials, given license to a foreign legislature to do as it would to the colonies. Once an uninhibited legislature, one in which the colonials had no direct representation, had the power to tax, "like a cancer, it [would] eat faster and faster every hour." The Stamp Act crisis and the succeeding debates over parliamentary colonial legislation revealed the profound American suspicion of unchecked power. It was an attitude founded on the doctrines that permeated British political theory, reinforced by the American environment that had precluded "aristocratical families, courts, kings, bishops, ecclesiastical dominion, or an invisible power giving to a few a very visible one." A society of equals revealed a low tolerance for anything which threatened to overturn that condition.*

*A people who could entertain the idea that "Kings were . . . made for the good of the people and not the people for them," were by definition subversive of the eighteenth-century scheme of order. It made the concessions of London to the recalcitrant colonials not the substance of satisfaction, but the provocation for further demands to confine more securely the Parliamentary pretensions to power. The threat that Parliament could even contemplate unsettling the delicate system of checks and balances that permeated colonial government had touched the most sensitive of American fears: the claims to their domination by an external power. Once this fear was triggered, it was but a short step to decide to withhold from their rulers the traditional obedience and to consider the erection of a new authority which would derive its power from the governed and would be less master and more servant.*

*Claude Halstead Van Tyne (1870-1930) passed most of his academic career at the University of Michigan. A good deal of his academic training was obtained in Germany and France. He specialized in the period of the American Revolution and upon his death was working upon a projected history of the founding of the American Republic. The Causes of the War of Independence and The War of Independence, American Phase (1929) were the only parts completed at the time of his death.*

# THE CAUSES OF THE WAR OF INDEPENDENCE

*by Claude Halstead Van Tyne*

Besides the universal activities of merchants, lawyers, and printers in opposition to the Stamp Act and the ubiquitous riots of the rabble in the colonies, nothing more clearly proved the unanimity of distaste for the Stamp Act than the response to a circular letter sent out (June 8, 1765) by the Massachusetts House of Representatives urging the other colonies to send committees to New York in October to consult together on the evils of the late acts and to implore relief from the King and Parliament. A leader in bringing about this significant meeting with its augury of future union was James Otis, who, clogged with two conservative, unsympathetic colleagues, was chosen a delegate to the proposed Stamp Act Congress, a bearer of the sentiment of the Massachusetts radicals. An enemy saw in Otis "the first who broke down the barriers of government to let in the hydra of Rebellion," but it was John Adams' solemn judgement that he had never known a man whose love of his country was more ardent or sincere, whose services were so important and essential to the cause of his country. In one of Otis' early pamphlets (1762) was concentrated, Adams declared in after years, the Declaration of Independence, the liberal writings of Price and Priestley, Thomas Paine's "Common Sense," and the "Declaration of Rights" of the Congress of 1774. This pamphlet, though it was whimsical and even uncouth at times, and like most of his work hasty and unrevised, showing the impatience of a strong, turbulent mind, was filled with phrases prophetic of the ideas soon to dominate in American political thinking. "God made all men naturally equal," he asserted. "Kings were . . . made for the good of the people and not the people for them," he stoutly held, and he found most governments arbitrary, and therefore the "curse and scandal of human nature." He believed that "jealousy of political privilege is a godly jealousy," and he gloried in it. The ideas were not new, but Otis gave them new currency. In the "Sodalitas," a lawyers' club in which he and Adams were colleagues, the members read and discussed the great English law writers, and we know that Otis was also fully acquainted with Pufendorf, Grotius, Burlamaqui, and Vattel. The club members had great familiarity with Locke and Coke, and, as early as 1765, even dabbled in Rousseau. The free life in America created in its intelligent citizens a natural affinity for the writings of the liberal political philosophers of all ages. In knowledge of the history, common law and statute laws of England, Adams believed Otis had no superior—"at least in Boston," and he thought him well versed in Greek and Roman history, philosophy, and poetry. A treatise of his on Latin prosody is still in existence, and he was always ready with classical allusions. It is, perhaps, not wholly fanciful to attribute Otis' eloquence in part to his passionate admiration for Homer.

Though Otis came of an old family of high rank in Massachusetts, and though he was the head of his profession, "designed by nature for a genius," as even an enemy admitted, his great fame began with his speech (1761) against "Writs of Assistance." In the effort to enforce the Trade Acts the customs officials had found themselves helpless in the face of the almost universal sympathy with the smugglers. Juries refused to convict on the plainest evidence, and the British Government resorted to admiralty courts where the trial was without jury, but there still remained the difficulty of detecting the smugglers, where every neighbor sheltered them and informers feared for their lives. To overcome this impediment to justice, "Writs of Assistance" were issued authorizing the officers holding them to board ships lying in port or to enter warehouses, cellars, or garrets, by day or night, and search for dutiful goods. No special writ of search, issued on sworn testimony that the smuggled goods were concealed in a definite place, was needed. These general writs were offensive, because as Pitt declared, they interfered with "the immunity of an English home where the wind might blow through every cranny but the King's writ could not enter." They had been used in England since the days of Charles II, and the colonists had sullenly submitted to them until six months after the death of George II (1760) when the validity of old writs would cease, according to law, and new must be issued. In Massachusetts the application for them would be before the superior courts presided over by the new chief justice, Thomas Hutchinson, recently commissioned in spite of the fact that the father of James Otis had been promised the place. James Otis, senior, pleaded the merit of age and long legal practice, while Hutchinson frankly admits in his diary that it was "an eyesore to some of the bar" that he was not bred to the law, but explains that after becoming chief justice he "applied his intervals to reading" it. This was not quite so serious as though a would-be physician should begin reading medicine after he was in attendance upon a patient, but there was a similitude. As Hutchinson already had three other colonial offices, there might well have been criticism. Peter Oliver asserts that James Otis swore "if his father was not appointed a justice of the supreme court, he would set the province in a flame if he died in the attempt"; and Hutchinson sadly reflects that at this point Otis "veered his sails and steered into the troubled waters of republicanism." Both charges are fancies of bitter enemies and rather dubious as the springs of actions extending over at least a decade. Whatever his motives, however, Otis, "the favorite lawyer of smugglers," as an enemy dubbed him, and Oxenbridge Thatcher did appear before the court to represent the Boston merchants in the hearing against the writs.

The court scene set in the Council Chamber of the Town House is described by John Adams writing more than half a century after the event. "That council chamber was as respectable an apartment as the House of Commons or the House of Lords in Great Britain, in proportion, or that in the State House in Philadelphia. In this chamber, round a great fire, were seated five judges, with Lieutenant Governor Hutchinson at their head, as Chief Justice, all arrayed in their new, fresh, rich robes of scarlet English broadcloth; in their large cambric bands, and immense judicial wigs. In this chamber were seated at a long table all the barristers at law of Boston, and of the neighboring county of Middlesex, in gowns, bands, and tie wigs. They were not seated on ivory chairs, but their dress was more solemn and more pompous than that of the Roman Senate, when the Gauls broke in upon them. Two portraits, at more than full length, of King Charles the Second and of King James the Second, in splendid golden frames, were hung up on the most conspicuous sides of the apartment. If my young eyes or old memory have not deceived me, these were as fine pictures as I ever saw; the colors of the royal ermines and long flowing robes were the most glowing, the figures the most noble and graceful, the features the most distinct and characteristic, far superior to those of the King and Queen of France in the Senate Chamber of Congress—these were worthy of the pencils of Rubens and Vandyke. There was no painter in England capable of them at that time. They had been sent over without frames in Governor Pownall's time, but he was no admirer of Charles or James. The pictures were stowed away in a garret, among rubbish, till Governor Bernard came, who had them cleaned, superbly framed and placed in council for the admiration and imitation of all men—no doubt with the advice and concurrence of Hutchinson and all his nebula of stars and satellites."

Before this august body James Otis, with "a torrent of impetuous eloquence, hurried away everything before him." He had resigned the lucrative office of advocate general in order to oppose the Government, and he declared he took pleasure in arguing the cause, because it was in "opposition to a kind of power, the exercise of which, in former periods of English history, cost one king of England his head, and another his throne." If Patrick Henry uttered treason in 1765, he at least had an excellent model in this speech of 1761. Adams declares that Otis on this occasion was "a flame of fire." His own fever was contagious. Every hearer went away to take up arms against the writs. Then and there he sowed the seeds of patriots and heroes, and in that hour John Adams believed "the child of Independence was born." This oration against the writs "breathed into this nation the breath of life," declared Adams, and added that thereafter Otis was forever dedicated to the cause of American liberty. It was "like the oath of Hamilcar administered to Hannibal." Such a theory of individual responsibility for the Revolution is very pleasing to the eulogist, but in the larger view it is plain that James Otis was only the embodiment of New England's indomitable will to have its own way; just as Patrick Henry was only the frontier product of Virginia's high-strung spirit of liberty.

Despite John Adams' lifelong hero-worship of Otis, one must accept as true some part of his eulogy. His hero's articles, under the pseudonym of "Hampden," though in a style rugged and not elegant, are courageous, telling arguments for civil liberty and equality. There were curious seeming contradictions in his thinking which brought him much criticism, and even obloquy. Men thought him mad because being a champion of the popular cause he did not go the whole way. When in 1764 he held that it was the colonial duty to submit to the Sugar Act, and in 1765 said that it was the duty of all humbly and silently to acquiesce in all decisions of the supreme legislature, and when he admitted the Parliament had the "right to levy internal taxes on the colonies," he was frowned upon even by his friends. Yet, as the British Empire was then constituted, he was right, for, as he said, "there would be an end of all government if one or a number of subjects or subordinate provinces should take upon them so far to judge of the justice of an act of Parliament as to refuse obedience to it." That was but a forecast of the logic of the later opponents of "nullification." Besides, loyal as Otis was to the American cause, he was intelligent enough to realize the danger of opposition to Great Britain. Perhaps he reflected that the sword devours one as well as another. Moreover, he saw America's lack of unity. Independent America at that time (1765) would, he thought, become "a mere shambles of blood and confusion," a scene of mere "anarchy." Independence, he declared, "none but rebels, fools, or madmen will contend for." He was demanding justice, not revolution; he was urging the Government not to abuse its vast powers. If he believed that Parliament had "supreme, sovereign power," it was a "perfect Parliament" in which America would be represented. When his friends put before him the danger of such representation, he made it clear that the only kind he would accept implied "a thorough, beneficial union of these colonies to the realm . . . so that all parts of the empire may be compacted and consolidated," and the representation was to be real, not virtual. In truth, he was thinking of the best interests of the empire, not of a mere American province. It was a noble idea, too vast to be conceived by the ordinary mind, and not unlike that greater vision of a universal confederation among civilized nations.

It was not alone these views, however, which explain why his life "seemed all eccentricity." His rashness and excess of zeal made him enemies who watched him maliciously. When he opposed the Government, he estranged his aristocratic friends, who ascribed his action to ambition, and said he had adopted Satan's maxim, "better to reign in Hell than serve in Heaven." Moreover, he was not well balanced, but "fiery and feverous, . . . liable to great inequalities of temper"; obstacles, either men or facts, enraged him. The human vices of servility or venality chafed him, made him indignant. Though frank and arduous, he was irascible and lacked a saving sense of humor. His passionate spirit wore out his body, for, as a friend expressed it, "his imagination flames, his passions blaze; sometimes in despondency, sometimes in a rage." After the cowardly assault upon him (1769) in the British coffee-house by John Robinson and other enemies, his eccentricities greatly augmented. John Adams, who was much in his company, confided to his diary that Otis "grows the most talkative man alive; no other gentleman in company can find a space to put in a word." "He rambles and wanders like a ship without a helm." He feared Otis would "spoil the club." At the last, as an enemy wrote, he "became so frantic that he was frequently under the guardianship of the law." His noble mind, "overplied in liberty's defense," had been overthrown. His death by a stroke of lightning was as tragic as his life. No doubt John Adams and others exaggerated his effect on the nascent revolution, but to the extent that any individual furthered that spirit, James Otis, second to none, fired New England with the resolve to retain all of its liberties. It is significant that in the Stamp Act debates in Parliament both Lord Lyttleton and Lord Mansfield mention Otis by name as the preeminent champion of the American cause.

When the Stamp Act Congress, born in Otis' fertile mind, met (October, 1765) in the City Hall, New York, it was found that "ministerial monkery" had been practiced in New Hampshire, Virginia, North Carolina, and Georgia to prevent them sending delegates. A significant thing about the Congress is that the initiative came for the first time in colonial history, not from Crown officers, but from concerted action of provincial assemblies. Nevertheless, it is a curious fact that there is scarcely any mention of the Congress in the newspapers of that day, not even in the city of New York where it met. When differences began to appear among the twenty-seven men from nine colonies with varying interests and diverse charter rights, Christopher Gadsden urged all sections to harmonize by protesting on the broad common grounds of natural rights. As he expressed the idea in a letter, "a confirmation of our essential and common rights as Englishmen may be pleaded from charters safely enough; but any further dependence upon them may be fatal. We should stand upon the broad common ground of those natural rights that we all feel and know as men and as descendants of Englishmen." In the course of eleven days, the views and interests which jangled out of tune were harmonized, and though the chairman, Timothy Ruggles, of Massachusetts, would not sign the moderate and loyal "Declarations of Rights and Grievances" agreed upon, the delegates as a whole were content. A few days more sufficed to concur upon petitions to the King, the Lords and the Commons. With conscious purpose the several colonies had united for common interests and had given the world a united expression of American sentiment. It was the beginning of that union for which Otis hoped, a union that "should knit and work into the very blood and bones of the original system in every region, as fast as settled." American conviction was expressed in the assertion that they were entitled to all the inherent rights and liberties of natural-born subjects, born within the realm, and like them enjoyed the right to have no taxes imposed upon them but by their own consent, which could be given only in their own legislatures wherein alone they were or could be represented. Meaningless as the pet colonial phrases about "rights of Englishmen" and "taxation without representation" might be to a British constitutional lawyer, they expressed beliefs for which Americans would die. On those phrases hung all the colonial law and the prophets.

In England, meanwhile, political changes, little if any affected by American truculence, were taking place. Grenville's curtain lectures to George III upon his duties were not welcome, nor did the King relish his minister's habit of looking to Parliament rather than to him as the course of authority. Conflict over the Regency Bill, which aimed at excluding the King's mother from the list of regents, brought the climax. The King decided to be rid of Grenville even at the price of submission to the Old Whigs who had put the yoke upon his grandfather, which it was the life aim of George III to shake off. Failing to secure Pitt's leadership in forming a new ministry, the King's agent, the Duke of Cumberland, turned to the Marquis of Rockingham. English political parties in that day seem to have deserved Soame Jenyns' slur that principles did not divide them, but factions, which under the name of Whig or Tory were ready to support the Government if they enjoyed the administration of it, or to subvert it if they were excluded. A faction must have all power or no power, all posts or no posts. They did not worry about noble principles. During the reign of George III, true party government can hardly be said to have existed. Rockingham was the new leader of the Old Whigs, lately headed by the crafty Duke of Newcastle, whose aim was control of government by the aristocratic Revolutionary families like those of Robert Walpole's time. Pitt distrusted them, not merely because of an intense personal dislike of Newcastle, who was a member of the new ministry, but because they wished to conserve existing conditions while he wished to destroy parties and factions, shear special interests of their power, and keep no man of ability out of office; but, with a united country under "a patriot king," enter upon reform in every direction. His vision was a world empire on modern lines—an empire in all parts of the world bringing peace and good rule to mankind. To these effulgent visions Rockingham with his small talents could not rise. Though he had what Junius called "a mild but determined integrity," and had good ideals, he was a better horseman than politician. He believed in a predominant Parliament, but one guided by the Whig nobles. Lacking Pitt's hearty support, he could not command the best of Whig talent. Two reputed friends of America were included in the Ministry; one, General Conway, was a young man of good ideals and generous impulses, but without originality enough to give up the evil political practices of the past. Another was Lord Dartmouth, pious, mild, and honest, but wanting in force, "one who wears a coronet and prays," a Methodist Sir Charles Grandison, as Richardson dubbed him. Though the Ministry lacked in ability and cohesion, it was forced to carry out Pitt's strong policies by its very eagerness to place him at its head. Moreover, it was under pressure to repeal the Stamp Act, because in ports and factory towns, as a result of American non-importation measures, thousands were idle, exports had fallen to three fourths their normal values, and petitions from the sufferers flooded Parliament. It was of no use to denounce, as did some haughty members of the House of Lords, the American non-importation acts as "illegal and hostile combinations . . . to distress and starve our manufacturers and to withhold from our merchants the payment of their just debts." It did not comfort the manufacturers and traders that the former "measure had only been practiced in open warfare between two states, and the latter . . . not even in that situation . . . among civilized nations" of Europe in "modern times." Ruin faced these men, and they demanded relief, not moral precepts.

Early in 1766, Parliament took up the matter of enforcement or repeal of the Stamp Act. The first step was an examination of Benjamin Franklin before the bar of the House of Commons. No one can read in full that calm and dignified revelation of the colonial spirit without reaching the conviction that it must have profoundly moved all who were present. With an art of argumentation which, he was pleased to think he had learned from Socrates, he persuaded his hearers that even an army could not enforce the act, though it might, he admitted, cause a rebellion. Having answered with great simplicity and clarity a hundred questions about American political views and economic life, he closed with the subtle appeal to the English passion for trade, declaring that the American pride used to be "to indulge in the fashions and manufactures of Great Britain," but now it was their pride "to wear their old clothes over again, till they can make new ones."

Few more eloquent debates are recorded than that which followed in both houses of Parliament. Pitt, though feeling that he was "more fit for a lonely hill in Somersetshire than for the affairs of state," took up the American cause with spirit. He rejoiced that the Americans had resisted. For the welfare of the empire he would not have them so dead to the feelings of liberty as to become fit instruments to make slaves of the rest. Grenville was enraged that rebellion should be pronounced a virtue, that "even in this house, in this sanctuary of laws, sedition had found its defenders." He argued for the legal right to tax Americans, that the nation had run itself into immense debt to give them protection, that protection and obedience were reciprocal, Great Britain had protected, America owed obedience. It was this emphasis on legal right that did the mischief. England was in an age of strict legalism. Lawyers, dominated by a rigid legalism, were most influential in guiding the administration officers in their rule of the colonies. It was they who passed on the form and legality of the colonial charters and of instructions to governors, and as to the propriety of laws made in the American provinces.

Supporters of Grenville explained that the stamp tax would not pay a third of the expense of the troops stationed in America, but that "a pepper-corn in acknowledgment of right is of more value than millions without." Against this abstract right, which Burke later characterized as the "great Serbonian bog" into which whole armies had sunk, Pitt set himself. Legal right the Government might have, but a statesman would not use it. He intimated that Parliament might well take thought of the words of St. Paul, "All things are lawful unto me, but all things are not expedient." "The magnanimous Exertion of Power is often the Non-Exertion of it." He meant to waive it by silence. With a logic hard to follow, Pitt asserted British sovereignty over Americans; "we may bind their trade, confine their manufactures, and exercise every power, except that of taking their money out of their pockets without their consent." Having made that distinction, which was at least antiquated, Pitt went on to declare that America was right in her contention, and "if she fell would fall like a strong man. She would embrace the pillars of the state and pull down the Constitution along with her." Pitt was, as Grattan said, "very great and very odd," a mounte-bank, perhaps, but "a great mountebank, . . . a man of great genius and great flights of mind," but his logic would have carried him into embarrassing situations. In the House of Lords the American cause did not fare so well, perhaps because they had not heard Franklin's examination. Though opposed to the repeal, Lord Mansfield, one of the greatest lawyers of his age, who when he spoke was "dignity and reason itself," agreed that the colonial radicals were not to be disregarded, for many persons, like Otis, "who have entertained silly and mad ideas, have led people to rebellion and overturned empires." He was most fervent in hoping that it might "please God to open the understandings and better inform the minds of this poor, innocent, loyal, brave, but wickedly misled and deluded people." Though he had for them only the "greatest tenderness," he came "armed at all points" with legal precedents to prove that there was no difference between internal and external taxation, that there was no distinction between the authority of Parliament within or without the realm, that if it now abdicated its supreme power in this matter, the Government would be dissolved. In mere legal logic he was probably right. Precedent was with him, but he seemed to forget that the Constitution of England had come to its present state as the result of yielding to the changing needs of the people whose destinies it controlled. With him stood the profligate Earl of Sandwich, the Duke of Bedford, head of the "Bloomsbury Gang," and the Tory aristocracy in general.

In support of the repeal, Lord Shelburne, Lord Camden, and the Duke of Grafton bore the burden and heat of the debate. Lord Rockingham sat by "dumb and speechless." Though Rockingham was the head of the Ministry, the effort at repeal was a Pitt victory, for the eagerness of the Ministry to place Pitt at their head led them to yield to his policy. Rockingham wanted repeal with a declaratory act, but without Pitt's backing might not have ventured even that, faced as he was by Grenville's threat to regard any one who did that as "a criminal and a betrayer of his country." "He was bullied into it by Lord Chatham," his enemies declared, but Burke brilliantly defended his patron against that charge. None of the speakers in the Lords, if we may judge from the little that has come down to us in the "Parliamentary History," were very positive, but Camden, at least, did hold clearly that taxation and representation were inseparable, and therefore the British Parliament, as then constituted, had not the right to tax the colonies.

When the matter of repeal came to a vote, it is dubious whether it would have carried but for the Declaratory Act joined with it which asserted Parliament's right to make laws to bind the colonies in all cases whatsoever. In fact, the Lords at first resolved, fifty-nine to fifty-four, in favor of executing the Stamp Act, but after two formal protests against repeal they too joined the Commons, resolved to be content with the "Declaration"— "the peppercorn in acknowledgment of right." Pitt, ill with gout, was barely able to remain through the debate and "cry aye! to the repeal in no sickly voice." Though opposed to the Declaratory Act, "that barren tree, which cast a shade over the land but yielded no fruit," he quieted the fears of some by his own insistence upon Parliament's right to subordinate the colonists to all other legislation except that which took "money out of their pockets without their consent." The victory won, Pitt "hobbled out on crutches, gaunt, alone." The crowds, at first hushed and with hats in hand, then shouted in triumph. As for the hero, the joy of thousands was his, as Lady Chatham wrote. He found the scene of that glorious morning happy "when the sun of liberty shone once more upon a country too long benighted." He solemnly declared that he "never had greater satisfaction than in the repeal of this Act."

In spite of Pitt's doubt that "there would have been a minister to be found who would have dared to dip the royal ermines in the blood of the Americans," it was for military enforcement, if necessary, that Grenville and his followers had stood. There were two strong reasons for their eager defense of the act. The act had been originally approved by the King, and a repeal would weaken his prestige which it was Grenville's policy to build up. George III had preferred a mere modification of the act, but when that was out of the question, and the only issue was enforcement or repeal, he consented to Rockingham's demand that he support the repealers. The King was even forced to put his acquiescence in writing. Furthermore, an indirect result of the repeal of the Stamp Act was that the Imperial Government, by bending before the storm, had given up the source of money proposed to be expended in opening the Great Valley in America to settlement. A revision of the whole Grenville-Bedford imperial policy of expansion became necessary, and that faction, with whom the repeal went down heavily, became the supporters of all measures for subduing the colonists to obedience. Naturally, Rockingham did not wish to push a plan cursed with the brand of the Grenville Ministry, especially an expensive one for which they had not the funds. They must retrench, and this meant indifference to western expansion in the Mississippi Valley. Moreover, they had never understood the Proclamation of 1763, and thought it only a temporary measure to be followed by gradual opening of the West, and therefore had no idea except enforcement of the law at face value. Led by Barrington, they substituted a plan for maintaining "for ages" extensive Indian reservations in the heart of America. Such a programme, if successful, would stop settlement at the Appalachians.

To these ill-boding consequences America was blind. The universal joy over the repeal "composed every wave of popular disorder." America justified Pitt's noble tribute. "This country, like a fine horse, to use a beautiful expression of Job, whose neck is clothed in thunder—if you soothe and stroke it you may do anything; but if an unskilful rider takes it in hand, he will find that, though not vicious, yet it has tricks." An address of the Massachusetts House of Representatives attested the "general joy diffused among all his Majestie's loyal and faithful subjects throughout this extensive continent." They found the repeal a striking instance of their "most gracious sovereign's paternal regard," and because his royal ear was always open to the distresses of his people, they felt "the deepest sense of loyalty and gratitude." All of this might have revealed to a keen British statesman, that, though a colonist drank a health to George III "five fathoms deep," the act pledged him to nothing but loyalty as long as the King was not a tyrant.

The grateful colonists even found in the repeal the proof that they were the objects of the patronage and justice of Parliament. On a Day of Thanksgiving in Boston, Jonathan Mayhew preached from the text, "As cold waters to a thirsty soul, so is good news from a far country."

As late as 1774, the 18th of March, the anniversary of the repeal of the Stamp Act, was being celebrated by the ringing of bells, the discharge of cannon, and the display of colors on the liberty tree, but the next year (1775) it was "designedly neglected" because the colonists had learned that the repeal was not "done on generous fraternal principles." These celebrations were usually directed by the "Sons of Liberty," who seemed to assume that the repeal had been due to their activities. John Adams describes their plans for "illuminations, bonfires, pyramids, obelisks, such grand exhibitions and such fireworks as were never before seen in America."

One of the economic results of the repeal is suggested by Dr. Franklin's first letter from London to his wife Deborah whom he never could persuade to cross the sea. He was sending her "a fine Piece of Pompadour Sattin . . . A silk Negligee and Petticoat of Brocaded Lutestring," which he had not sent sooner, "as I knew you would not like to be finer than your Neighbors, unless in a Gown of your own spinning." It was a comfort to him to recollect, he declared, "that I had once been cloth'd from Head to Foot in Woollen and Linnen of my Wife's Manufacture." In general, commerce flowed again, non-importation ceased, plans for American manufactures vanished, the custom of expensive funerals and lavish mourning was resumed, homespun was given to the poor, and men once more wore suits ordered in London. Yet the merchants were not wholly content, and trade was not restored to the old basis before the trade laws of 1764 and 1765. Parliament proceeded, after the Declaratory Act and the repeal of the Stamp Act, to take off the three penny duty on foreign molasses, but replaced this with a duty of one penny per gallon on all molasses imported, British as well as foreign. It now gave no protection to the British sugar planters and was plainly a tariff for revenue, a taxation without representation, just as surely as was the Stamp Act. A new law arranged to collect the duty on foreign textiles at the English port rather than the American, but that was a mere disguising of the fact of taxation. In all this, and more which undid the concessions of the repeal, the followers of Rockingham and Pitt, believing fully in the legislative power of Parliament, heartily joined. Moreover, to the grievance of the paper money regulation, so warmly protested as a reason why the colonists could not pay the stamp tax, Parliament gave not the cold respect of a passing glance.

Nevertheless, America rejoiced and gave herself up to generous enthusiasms for her friends in Parliament. The Boston town meeting had already thanked Conway and Barre for their "noble and generous speeches," and ordered their portraits for Faneuil Hall. A group of Virginians subscribed nearly a hundred pounds to have Lord Camden's picture "limned," at full length in judge's robes, by either Reynolds or West, for a place of honor in Westmoreland County Court-House. New York voted a statue to Pitt in a toga, while George III, for no explicable reason except colonial ignorance, was cast in lead and brass on horseback and gilded. Lord Shelburne, too, was praised, and Lord Dartmouth who, all his life, was regarded as a friend of the colonies. On the other hand, the colonial heart hardened against Lord Mansfield, Lord Sandwich, and the Duke of Bedford. The Earl of Halifax was also in their bad graces, but among them all Grenville stood alone in his bad eminence. The whole group were reputed to wish to take away every charter and to unite all colonies under governors and councils appointed by the King and burdened with no assemblies. The ministerial mind was dumbfounded by the vast spaces of the earth which fate obligated it to rule; to centralize and unify seemed the only hope. Against these aims, as, indeed, against any loss of liberties already won, America had shown her spirit to be fixed. No wise statesman could thereafter ignore that fact, and yet some solution of Great Britain's imperial problem must be found. The truth now appeared that a constitution for the empire as distinguished from the realm had never been worked out. The imperial constitution was still a thing of shreds and patches. England had her constitution and it provided for the supreme power of Parliament. But, while this was being evolved, the East and West Indies had been added, continental American colonies founded, and finally an empire conquered from France. For all these world-wide dominions no settled constitution existed; all was fluid. Pitt, the materials for whose speeches were "great subjects, great empires, great characters, effulgent ideas and classical illustrations," declared he wished "this to be an Empire of Freemen; it will be stronger for it, and it will be the more easily governed." A very noble idea it was, but did he, did any one, in that trying hour have a definite plan by which the splendid vision could be realized?

COLONIAL *suspicions of Parliamentary intentions, incited by the Stamp Act, had barely subsided, when in 1767 a new act imposed duties on imports of glass, painters' colors, paper and teas. It had been preceded in the previous year by the Declaratory Act, which asserted the right of Parliament to legislate for the colonies "in all cases whatsoever." The Townshend Acts, as the 1767 measures were designated, provided evidence that the British legislature meant to have its "badge of parliamentary supremacy." The colonials responded with a boycott of the taxed products that proved so successful the British manufacturers of the items lobbied for revocation of the measures. In 1770, all were repealed but the tax on tea which, in the words of the New York Sons of Liberty, remained "as a test of the parliamentary right to tax us." There the matter rested until 1773 when Parliament decided to bail the East India Company out of near bankruptcy by removing all duties, except the colonial tea tax, from the company's surplus tea exported to the colonies. Suddenly, the East India Company was able to undersell both the legitimate importer and the smuggler and, by an act*

*of almost Machiavellian subtlety, Parliament seemed on the verge of gaining
its point. They had reckoned without the colonial merchant who presented
the issue to the public as "an important trial of our virtue."*

*With this act, the final rupture between Britain and her colonies pro-
ceeded as inevitably as the denouement of a Greek tragedy. The long preparation for independence was finally complete; the colonials were no longer
Englishmen abroad but Americans. They held their rights to be larger than
any authority and were prepared to defend them against all comers. Since
they assumed that liberty and property were obverse sides of the same coin,
they felt no embarrassment at defending their profits as synonymous with
freedom.*

*John C. Miller (1907-    ), a Harvard-educated historian, is Robinson
Professor of American History at Stanford University. He has concentrated
his interest as a historian on the Revolutionary and the Federalist eras. He
has viewed it as a time when the basis of American rights were firmly
founded within the framework of a liberal tradition. And since what exists
becomes the guideline within which men operate, it would not be incorrect
to note that a commitment to liberalism in the United States is the hallmark
of the true American conservative.*

# ORIGINS OF THE AMERICAN REVOLUTION

## by John C. Miller

It was not the colonists but the East India Company which disturbed
Lord North's slumbers and impelled him to take action. The East India
Company had again fallen on evil days and the British government was
obliged to come to its rescue. And, to the Prime Minister's consternation,
in his efforts to save the East India Company he blundered into a dispute
with the colonies from which the British government found it impossible to
retreat with honor.

The settlement of 1767 had not brought order into the tangled affairs of
the East India Company. The corporation continued to be plundered by its
officials and the natives remained at the mercy of ruthless and irresponsible
Englishmen who were bent upon getting rich in the shortest possible order.
By 1773, the plight of the company had become critical; it had no cash; it
could not pay bills drawn upon it; and its credit was almost exhausted. The
value of its stock fell from 280 to 160 while millions of pounds of unsold
tea and Indian goods rotted in its warehouses. The distress of the company
jeopardized the £400,000 which the British government since 1767 had
received annually from it and threatened the loss of England's foothold in
India. Accustomed as Lord North was to blink at trouble, he could not
close his eyes to the predicament into which the East India Company had
fallen.

The directors of the company feared that the government would seize this opportunity to strip it of its territorial revenues and put its affairs under the direct control of the Crown. They appealed to the Whigs for aid; and the Whigs rallied to the company's support as they had in 1767. They warned that interference by the government would establish the supremacy of the Crown over Parliament; Edmund Burke declared that Lord North was seeking to decorate the Crown "with the collected spoils of the East" in order to enable the King to rule without Parliament. The City of London protested against any infringement of the company's rights on the ground that it would be "a direct and dangerous attack upon the liberties of the people." The American colonists likewise expressed their sympathy with the East India Company in its efforts to stave off governmental control. Because it was a chartered corporation, the fate of the East India Company was believed to be bound up with that of the chartered colonies and hence with the defense of American liberty.

But Lord North had little interest in extending the authority of the Crown: his chief concern was to preserve the East India Company from bankruptcy and to save the government's equity. It was this consideration, rather than any deep-laid plot of depriving Parliament of control of the purse or enslaving the colonies, which influenced North when he set out in 1773 to make the American colonies safe for the East India Company's tea.

It was well known that the company's distress was partly owing to the refusal of the American colonists to buy British tea after it had been taxed by Charles Townshend. They drank instead smuggled Dutch tea in such quantities that the salvation of the East India Company seemed to require that the colonial tea market be regained by driving out the smugglers. But the directors were not eager to be thrust again into the thick of the dispute over taxation which troubled relations between Great Britain and the colonies. They believed that their business was to sell tea, not to uphold the rights of Parliament over the colonies; and they had little confidence that their tea could be sold to Americans until the issue of taxation without representation had been set at rest. The directors therefore urged the government to repeal the threepence duty paid into the customs on every pound of tea imported into the colonies. Only by this means, they reasoned, could the government be certain of driving the smugglers from the field and recovering the colonial market.

North refused to heed this advice: it was enough, he believed to give Americans cheap tea—they would drink it regardless of the tax. As in 1769, he insisted that the tea duty stand lest the right of Parliament to tax the colonists fall into disuse. North at no time lost sight of the importance of maintaining parliamentary sovereignty over the colonies; and he considered taxation to be the most vital element of sovereignty. He scoffed at warnings that Americans prized principle more than cheap tea and would spurn the East India Company's tea because it was taxed. He confidently expected Americans to set about contentedly brewing their tea, forgetting in its cheapness that they were helping the British government to raise a revenue which might be used against their liberties.

By the Tea Act of 1773, the threepence tax on tea imported into the colonies was retained; the British government made the East India Company a loan of £1,400,000 and renounced the £400,000 it had compelled the company to pay annually since 1767. Moreover, the company was no longer required to reimburse the government for any losses in revenue it might suffer as a result of its remission of duties paid upon importation into Great Britain. This, coupled with permission to export tea directly to America without putting it up for public sale in England, put the company in an excellent competitive position. By eliminating the middleman—the English merchants who bought tea at the company's auctions in London and then resold it to American merchants—the company was able to sell tea in the colonies cheaper than in England itself. More significantly, its tea now undersold that of the Dutch smugglers. Instead of twenty shillings a pound, tea now sold for ten shillings—a price which even the smugglers could not meet. There seemed excellent prospect, therefore, that this cheap tea would "overcome all the Patriotism of an American" and that the colonists would hail Lord North as one of the great benefactors of thirsty humanity.

Not without some misgivings on the part of the directors, the East India Company set about unloading its surplus tea upon the colonies. Two hundred and ninety-eight chests of tea—valued at £10,994—were dispatched to Boston; 257 chests to Charleston, South Carolina; and 698 chests to New York and Philadelphia. For the safe delivery of this tea, the British merchants trading to North America stood security.

At first, many Americans rejoiced in the prospect of slaking their thirst by drinking up the tea that filled to bursting the warehouses of the East India Company. There were some killjoys, however, who pointed out that tea, unlike wine, did not grow better "by sweating several years, in a warehouse"; and it even began to be whispered that the tea was rotten and the East India Company was trying to dispose of it in the colonies because it could find no market elsewhere. And sober second thought brought home to Americans the menace of this taxed tea: even if their constitutions were unimpaired, their political liberties and their economic well-being seemed certain to suffer.

The smugglers appeared destined to be the first victims of the Tea Act. Undersold by the East India Company, they could look forward only to ruin at its hands. Because their interests were more immediately threatened by the Tea Act than those of any other group, it was the smugglers—and not the slave drivers, as Dr. Johnson supposed—who raised the "loudest yelps" for liberty and took the lead in fomenting opposition to the East India Company.

The most active tea smugglers in the colonies in 1773 were the merchants of Rhode Island, New York, and Philadelphia. Although Englishmen supposed that Boston was a nest of smugglers, its citizens had long since lost their pre-eminence as runners of contraband. This reformation was owing not to any awakening of conscience to the sinfulness of smuggling but simply to the fact that there was stricter enforcement of the laws in Boston than in other colonial seaports. As the headquarters of the Commissioners of the Customs and with a British fleet stationed in its harbor, Boston felt the full force of the British government's war upon illicit trade. New York, on the other hand, was almost a wide-open town for smugglers: in 1774 there was not a boat of any kind belonging to the New York customhouse; the customs officers were still bribed by the merchants; and large quantities of contraband were brought into the port without interference. Much the same state of affairs prevailed in Philadelphia where the merchants salved their consciences with the argument that "every man has a natural right to exchange his property with whom he pleases and where he can make the most advantage of it."

It is significant that the first outcry against the Tea Act came from Philadelphia and New York, the smugglers' strongholds, while Boston remained relatively quiet—an unaccustomed role for the "metropolis of sedition." The merchants of Philadelphia and New York held meetings to protest against the importation of East India tea and to demand the resignation of the tea consignees several weeks before the Boston merchants took action. Indeed, in October 1773 it seemed far more probable that the tea would be destroyed in New York or Philadelphia than in Boston. The Philadelphia patriots had prepared a reception for Captain Ayres of the tea ship which might well have persuaded that sea dog to give the City of Brotherly Love a wide berth. The Whigs declared that they would "heave him keell cut, and see that his bottom be well fired, scrubbed and paid—His upper works too will have an overhauling." They had calculated, they said, "to a gill and a feather, how much it will require to fit him for an American exhibition."

Although the smugglers led the attack upon the Tea Act, the law-abiding merchants followed closely upon their heels. The menace of monopoly united virtually all businessmen—whether smugglers or honest traders—in opposition to the East India Company. The company had chosen to send its tea to a picked group of merchants—called "consignees"—who were directed to sell it to tea dealers in the colonies. The colonial importers saw in this measure a threat to free enterprise: once the East India Company had established itself firmly in the colonies, it would presumably eliminate the middlemen altogether and sell tea directly to the people through its agents. A monopoly of the tea market would be followed by a monopoly of wines, spices, silks, and other commodities, until the American merchants had been squeezed completely out of business.

Viewed in this light, the Tea Act was more inimical to the interests of American merchants than were the Townshend duties: in place of a tax that could be passed on to the consumer, there was now danger that all business would be swallowed up by the East India Company and its Tory favorites. John Hancock declared that if the Tea Act had gone into effect, "we soon should have found our trade in the hands of foreigners [i.e., Englishmen] . . . nor would it have been strange, if, in a few years, a company in London should have purchased an exclusive right of trading to America." It was supposed that one of the first acts of the East India Company, once its position was secure in the colonies, would be to ruin the Philadelphia china factory which competed with its wares; the promoters of the china factory warned that its destruction would "clip twenty Years from the Growth of *American* Improvements." No longer regarded as a helpless corporation in the grip of the British government, the East India Company now appeared to the colonists as the merciless exploiter of India seeking new worlds to conquer. "It is shocking to Humanity," said a New Yorker, "to relate the relentless Barbarity, practised by the Servants of the Body, on the helpless Asiatics; a Barbarity scarce equalled even by the most brutal Savages, or *Cortez*, the *Mexican* Conqueror." It was recalled that in India the company had "monopolized the absolute Necessaries of Life," with the result that "thousands perished by this black, sordid and cruel Avarice." And because the nabobs' rapacity knew no bounds, they were believed to have leagued themselves with the British government in order to pillage the colonies. "Thank GOD," exclaimed John Dickinson, "we are not Sea Poys, nor Marattas, but *British Subjects*," yet he urged watchmen as they made their rounds to call out, "*Beware of the East-India Company*."

But the peril uppermost in the minds of patriot leaders in 1773 was that the Tea Act threatened the foundations of American political liberty. The triumph of the East India Company over American merchants would in fact be a victory for the British government over colonial rights: "What the Parliament could not Fleece from us by Taxes," exclaimed the New York merchants, "the Crown will by Monopoly." The tea duty imposed by Townshend and retained by Lord North in 1773 was designed to raise a revenue for the purpose of maintaining armies and a civil list in the colonies —thereby nullifying the privileges of the colonial assemblies. The preamble to the Townshend duties still remained upon the statute books; and never before had the danger been greater that its ends would be achieved. The colonists were well aware that the tea duty had been retained because the British government wished to keep alive the right of taxation and that the successful collection of this tax would place them at the mercy of Parliament. Crediting Lord North with more duplicity than he was guilty of, they assumed that he was now striving to take by ruse what he could not capture by storm. Once the American defenses had been breached by the tea duty, it was expected that North and the King's Friends would "enter the Bulwarks of our sacred Liberties, and will never desist, till they have made a Conquest of the whole."

It was fortunate for the colonial merchants that the British government had not repealed the tea duty. If the East India Company's tea had not been taxed—if it had not been mixed with the question of Americans' political rights—the colonists would have been under strong temptation to make the most of their opportunity to buy cheap tea even though it meant the ruin of the American merchants. Under such circumstances they might have drunk the East India Company back to solvency; and the Boston Tea Party might have been an entirely decorous affair in which the Bostonians regaled themselves instead of the fishes with the East India tea.

The besetting fear of the patriots was that Americans, if they would not sell their liberties for a mess of pottage, would gladly do so for a dish of tea. The colonists' fondness for tea seemed to both the imperialists at Westminster and the patriots overseas to be the Achilles' heel of American patriotism. Per Kalm, the Swedish traveler, found that there was "hardly a farmer's wife or a poor woman, who does not drink tea in the morning," and he ascribed to excessive tea drinking the fact that American girls often lost their teeth before they were twenty years old. It was estimated that at least one million Americans drank tea twice daily; in Philadelphia, it was remarked that "the women are such slaves to it, that they would rather go without their dinners than without a *dish of tea*." The Whigs groaned that tea was the "Idol of America" and that its devotees were lost to reason. Since 1767, when tea was first taxed by Townshend, tea drinking had been under fire as an injurious unpatriotic habit. American physicians testified that tea caused spleen, and weakened "the tone of the stomach, and therefore of the whole system, inducing tremors and spasmodic affections." Tea drinkers were warned that they were in danger of becoming "weak, effeminate and valetudinarian for life." But it not only shortened Americans' lives: it destroyed their civil liberties because every dish of British tea brewed in the colonies paid tribute to the British government. "Do not suffer yourself to sip the accursed, dutied STUFF," exclaimed a colonist. "For if you do, the devil will immediately enter into you, and you will instantly become a traitor to your country."

As the chief tea drinkers in the colonies, women were certain to play a crucial part in the struggle. No matter how strictly the Sons of Liberty abstained from tea, if their wives and daughters continued to sip the "baneful weed" the enemies of colonial liberty would surely triumph. Patriots who had no fear of redcoats and men-of-war dreaded this attack upon Americans at their breakfast tables; in this war of the teacups, everything depended upon the hardihood of American women. An indignant patriot swore that Lord North was attempting "to damn half mankind by tempting *female weakness* with *empoisoned* TEA." Englishmen congratulated themselves upon their astuteness in attacking the patriots in their weakest spot. It was believed that even the stiff-backed Saints of New England would be overborne by their wives "for the New-England husbands however they may intimidate British merchants and the British administration, are, in their own houses, too much on the hen-pecked establishment, to be able to carry such a measure against the Sovereign and absolute authority of their fair helpmates." The Whigs, however, were far from giving up the fight for lost: "With the Ladies on our Side," they exclaimed, "we can make every Tory tremble."

But Lord North, less fortunate than the devil, his supposed boon companion, failed to tempt frail woman. On the contrary, the women of America spurned the taxed tea and drank home-grown "Labradore" in its stead, pronouncing it "vastly more agreeable" than anything out of China. When tea was found in the possession of a tea addict in Bedford, Massachusetts, he was given the alternative by the patriots of either surrendering his tea or being turned over to the ladies for punishment. The offender wisely chose to give up his tea, whereupon he received "three cheers from the sons and a glass of American wine from the daughters of liberty."

Deprived of these invaluable allies, the British government had little else upon which to depend for the enforcement of the Tea Act. Lord North anticipated no trouble in the colonies and, like George Grenville before him, made no preparations for overcoming resistance. Indeed, he was so certain there would be no mishap that instructions regarding the disposition of the tea were not even sent British officials in the colonies: the East India Company alone was expected to see to it that its tea was sold to Americans. As a result, most of the royal governors refused to touch the tea when it became apparent that, instead of tea, Americans were brewing trouble; almost without exception they pleaded want of instructions as an excuse for remaining safely on the side lines.

The tea consignees sorely needed the protection of the British government, for like the stamp masters they found themselves exposed to the full fury of the Sons of Liberty. In the opinion of their fellow colonists, they had been appointed to do the dirty work of the British Ministry; and, as in the case of the stamp officers, the patriots declared that it was "as great a grievance to be under the hands of monopolizers and extortioners among ourselves, as under foreign task-masters and tax-gatherers." When they were presented with the choice of resigning their posts or withstanding "the insults of many rascally Mobbs Convened in the Dark high charged with Liquor to do every act of Violence their mad Brain could invent," the consignees looked in vain to the British officials for aid. The only place of safety in the colonies was aboard a British man-of-war; but the chances of fighting one's way through mobs to this haven were not encouraging. The tea consignees, in short, had an excellent opportunity of making themselves martyrs to the cause of British authority in America; yet this prospect had little charm for them. As merchants, they wished to carry on their business in the colonies, not to ruin themselves for the sake of the East India Company or the British Parliament. Therefore they resigned their posts with little ado and thrust the problem of protecting the tea upon the reluctant Crown Officers.

The situation in Boston set that town apart from the other colonial seaports. There existed among the Saints a powerful, organized party prepared to go any length to strike a "Home Blow" at British tyranny. The heavy importations of taxed British tea into Boston from 1768 to 1773 while the other colonists were patronizing the Dutch smugglers made necessary, in the opinion of the patriots, a bold stroke which would wipe out the stain of Toryism. And lastly, Governor Thomas Hutchinson, smarting under the publication of his confidential letters, had resolved to make a decisive stand upon the Tea Act against the radicals; another retreat, he believed, would be fatal to British sovereignty over the colonies. Therefore, the tea consignees—among whom were Hutchinson's sons—were supported by the royal government in Massachusetts, whereas in most of the other colonies they were compelled to stand alone against the patriot mobs. Largely because of this aid, the Boston consignees refused to follow the example of their fellow consignees by resigning their posts. Instead, they took refuge at Castle William, where, surrounded by cannon and redcoats, they lived very cozily with the Commissioners of the Customs who had likewise found Boston too hot for comfort. Safe behind the ramparts, these much-harassed gentry passed their time drinking bumpers to Peggy Hutchinson and "the other Toasts of the Town" and hobnobbing with the army officers. The baffled patriots, finding the birds flown, were obliged to take drastic action to redeem Boston's reputation as a patriot stronghold.

Hutchinson's resolute stand gave the Boston Whigs little choice between submission and the destruction of the tea. Convinced that Adams and his "crew" would yield at the last moment and determined not to give an inch of ground to the patriots, Hutchinson refused to permit the tea ships in Boston Harbor to leave port with their cargoes. His obduracy convinced the patriots that they must dispose of the tea before December 17, 1773—last day of grace before it was liable to seizure by the customhouse authorities for nonpayment of duty. The patriots feared that once the tea was in the possession of the customs officers it would be sold secretly to the people in order to raise money to pay the salaries of the governor and judges. There- fore, on the night of December 16, after the citizens assembled at Faneuil Hall had made an eleventh-hour attempt to persuade Hutchinson to release the tea ships, the "Mohawks" struck. Three companies of fifty men, each led by a captain, had been appointed to board the three tea ships which lay under the guns of the British men-of-war in the harbor. Although the men masqueraded as Indians, their disguise would not have deceived a redskin—or, more important, a British Crown Officer. For example, George Hewes, one of the "Indians," had time only to darken his complexion with soot from a blacksmith's shop on Boylston's wharf and run to a friend's house to borrow a blanket before he joined his fellow Mohawks. More effective protection was afforded by the hundreds of spectators who covered the waterfront, making it impossible for any royal officer to see closely the men aboard the tea ships. No resistance was offered the Indians; on the contrary, the sailors aboard the ships helped hoist the tea chests from the hold, break them open, and heave them overboard. Neither the ships nor any other items of their cargo were damaged; the Whigs boasted that all that was found missing the next morning was the tea and one padlock.

The identity of the Indians was a well-kept secret; although the Attorney General of Massachusetts pronounced the destruction of the tea to be treason, he was unable to ferret out any culprits. Only one citizen of the hundreds who witnessed the destruction of the tea was willing to testify—and then only on condition that the trial take place in England, three thousand miles away from the Boston mob. A trial in Boston would serve no good purpose: as Hutchinson pointed out, the jury would certainly be composed of the Indians or their sympathizers. It was rumored, however, that the tea was destroyed by "King Hancock, and the damn'd sons of liberty" in blackface and feathers. Hancock and Sam Adams were alleged to have led the braves aboard the tea ships and to have assisted in throwing the tea into Boston

Harbor. Franklin ridiculed the story, pointing out "the Improbability that, when the lower Actors tho't it prudent to disguise themselves, any of the principal Inhabitants should appear in the Affair." Nevertheless, George Hewes declared many years later that Sam Adams and John Hancock were among those that poured at the Boston Tea Party, claiming that he helped Hancock heave a chest overboard. He recognized Hancock, he said, "by his ruffles" and exchanged with him the countersign: "an Indian grunt, and the expression *me know you.*" Certainly, the presence of Hancock and Adams would have bolstered patriot morale by demonstrating that the leaders were as deeply involved in the enterprise as were the rank and file.

Not all the East India Company's tea was dumped into Boston Harbor on the night of December 16, 1773. One of the ships carrying tea to Boston was wrecked on Cape Cod. Much of the tea aboard was washed ashore and burned by the patriots but part of it was saved and stored in Castle William by the British, to the great chagrin of Sam Adams, who declared that had he known that the "Indians" of Cape Cod were so "sick at the knees," the Boston braves would have "marched on snowshoes to do the business for them."

The Tories railed against "ye wicked Bostonians, who have given it to the fishes"; and Thomas Hutchinson declared that a full-fledged tyranny had been established in Boston. Hutchinson believed that the Sons of Liberty in disguising themselves as Mohawks did the Indians a grave injustice, for "such barbarity none of the Aboriginals were guilty of"—although the redskins had slain his great-grandmother, Anne Hutchinson. Daniel Leonard, the Massachusetts Tory, declared that the Tea Party was "a more unaccountable phrenzy, and more disgraceful to the annals of America, than that of the witchcraft." As always, however, the Whigs were prepared to justify their assault upon British authority. They contended that the villainy of that "damn'd arch traitor," Thomas Hutchinson, made the destruction of the tea imperative. Had the royal governor not encouraged the tea consignees to resist the people and had he permitted the tea ships to return to England, they argued that there would have been no necessity for the Tea Party. The Whigs pictured it as an act of self-defense; and since "the great Law of Nature and Reason has possessed every Society with a Right to defend itself from Ruin, without having Recourse to Books or Statutes, or recorded Customs," the destruction of the tea was legitimate resistance to tyranny within the definition laid down by John Locke. It was accordingly pronounced to be a "glorious illegality" perpetrated by "a band of virtuous patriots"—"an act of absolute moral and political necessity, and therefore exempt from even good laws."

Nevertheless, signs were not wanting that the Boston patriots had outrun public opinion even in New England. Many towns rebuked the Bostonians for their rashness and dissolved their Committees of Correspondence on the ground that they were "calculated to introduce anarchy, confusion and blood-shed among the people." Some committees, in their eagerness to clear their skirts of complicity in the acts of the mobbish metropolis, instructed their representatives in the General Court to bring the "Indians" to justice. Much of this alarm among the country people was owing, how-ever, less to moral indignation than to the fear that they would be obliged to pay for the tea; and the punishment meted out to Boston by the British government for the Tea Party, together with the refusal of the Bostonians to reimburse the East India Company, put an end to these recriminations.

In Charleston, South Carolina, there occurred what the Boston patriots had most feared might be awaiting them: the tea was seized by the custom-house officers for nonpayment of duty and stored. Although threats had been made to destroy the tea aboard ship in Charleston Harbor, the Whigs were restrained by the fear that violence against the East India Company would cost them their bounty upon indigo and the privilege of exporting rice to southern Europe. They therefore permitted the tea to be landed and to be taken into the custody of the customhouse. The subsequent events at Charleston refuted, at least to the Tories' satisfaction, the Bostonians' contention that if the tea were seized by the customhouse, the duty would be paid and it would be sold to unsuspecting citizens. No duty was ever paid upon the tea stored in Charleston nor was it sold until July 1776, when the South Carolina delegates to the Continental Congress petitioned Con-gress for permission to dispose of it. By the same token, said the Tories, had the tea at Boston fallen into the hands of the customhouse officers it "might have lain till doomsday, and would never have hurt you or your posterity." But the Whigs answered, with no small justification, that there was no powerful faction in Charleston, as in Boston, headed by the royal governor, which was determined to make the Tea Act a test case of British sover-eignty.

The Boston Tea Party was merely the first of a series of tea parties given by Americans at the expense of the East India Company and colonial tea importers. In March 1774 over a score of chests of tea arrived in Boston. This tea did not belong to the East India Company: it was the property of a New England merchant but it bore the hated tax and hence was fair game for the patriots. The Committees of Correspondence from the towns in the neighborhood of Boston were called into consultation by the Boston patriots. To the consternation of the radicals, a majority of the committee-men favored returning the tea to England unharmed; no violent solution was countenanced. But while the committeemen proposed, the "Indians" disposed: "His Majesty OKNOOKOTUNKOGOG King of the Narraganset Tribe of Indians, on receiving Information of the arrival of another Cargo of that Cursed Weed TEA immediately Summoned his Council at the Great Swamp by the River Jordan, who did Advise and Consent to the immedi-ate Destruction thereof."

In other colonies as well, Americans sang "Tea Deum." At Greenwich, New Jersey, the tea cargo of the ship *Greyhound* was burned by the local tribe of Indians; in November 1774, seven chests of tea were thrown into the Cooper River at Charleston, South Carolina, while crowds cheered from the wharves; and in Annapolis, Maryland, the ship and cargo of a tea importer were burned. The New York patriots could not be prevented from joining in this sport, despite the fact that the governor of New York was Tryon, the conqueror of the North Carolina Regulators. Tryon came to the colony with a formidable reputation as a fighting man and the Tories confidently expected him to cram the tea down the throats of the Sons of Liberty. He attempted to land the tea and store it pending instructions from the British government, but the citizens refused to permit it to be brought ashore. When Tryon ordered the tea ship convoyed by His Majesty's sloop *Susan* to the wharf at New York, two thousand citizens met in the New York City Hall to express their determination that the tea should never be landed. Committees were appointed to prevent the tea being removed from the ship. On December 16, the day the tea was destroyed at Boston, an outbreak of violence seemed inevitable at New York. Had the governor made a move to bring the tea ashore, thousands of patriots would have rushed to the waterfront with equally fatal results to the tea and any Crown Officers who stood in their way. A tea party was averted in New York at this time only because Governor Tryon decided not to run the risk of a mob uprising. But in March 1774, the New York Mohawks fell upon tea consigned to merchants in the city and—in the manner of the redskins at Boston—brewed it with salt water.

After 1773, the patriots insisted upon the complete proscription of tea throughout the colonies. They reasoned that only by abstaining altogether from tea could Americans be certain that they were not drinking dutied British tea. Even the smugglers were warned not to import tea lest they unwittingly aid the British government in its efforts to raise a colonial revenue. A close scrutiny was maintained by the patriots over the business affairs of the merchants; and for the first time in their careers, the Sons of Liberty found themselves suppressing smuggling. They did the job so thoroughly that they boasted that there was no longer need for the "tide-Waiters, Pimps, or Informers" of the customhouse. It is significant that it was the radicals who demanded the complete prohibition of tea—the merchants, whether Whig or Tory, were obliged to take orders from men whom they considered on a social level with their employees. Nevertheless, under patriotic pressure tea disappeared from the colonies: "You may ride days, nay weeks," a traveler observed, "and never get a drop." The women of Boston, "to their immortal honor," took a solemn oath never to drink another cup; and whole chests were burned upon village commons, thus sacrificing "the obnoxious Drug at the Shrine of American Liberty." Coffee drinking became patriotic in the colonies and Americans were weaned from the teacup to the coffee cup, where, for the most part, their devotion still rests.

THE *Boston Tea Party ended whatever remote chance remained that Parliament and the colonies might reach a compromise. Once the Americans had resorted to violence, the British authorities had to assert their power*

*or admit they had lost the game, that the American colonies were all but in name independent. George III and his ministers, unable to comprehend the depth of colonial alienation, concluded the time for discipline had come.*

*To the already unutterable indignities of a standing army in their midst, of writs of assistance, of a horde of civil servants sent to the colonies to administer the reorganized empire, London now added the Coercive Acts. These acts which closed Boston, shifted trials outside of their usual jurisdiction, suspended civil government in Massachusetts, and ordered civilians to quarter troops united as never before the colonies. What the colonials had long suspected was now translated into a conviction that London meant to enslave Americans. Jefferson set this conviction forth in 1774 when he concluded, "A series of oppressions begun at a distinguished period and pursued unalterably through every change of ministers too plainly prove a deliberate and systematical plan of reducing us to slavery." American revolutionists were convinced that a union of the American colonies alone could hope to check the plot.*

*To prepare to repulse the intention of London, the colonies convoked the first Continental Congress, bringing together, for the first time, the men who made the American Revolution. Once assembled, they revealed themselves as an extraordinary lot. Any one of them would have ornamented an era; the simultaneous presence in a single remote country of Thomas Jefferson, John Adams, Alexander Hamilton, James Madison, John Jay, Benjamin Franklin, and George Washington gave America a veritable galaxy of leaders. They assured that the American Revolution would be expressed with uncommon eloquence and be informed by astute political awareness. Two questions arise: What accounted for this confluence of talent? Where did the ideas that shaped the Revolution originate?*

*The answer to the first question requires an understanding of the narrow confines of pre-Revolutionary American life. Until the Revolution was over, few Americans lived more than one hundred miles from the sea. The isolation which so characterized American life in the nineteenth century had not yet cast deep roots. Rather, American eyes were riveted across the ocean to the imperial metropolis. The outlook of the American city, as Carl Bridenbaugh noted, "was eastward rather than westward." Consequently, "it was more nearly a European society in an American setting." The perspective, inevitably, within which the American intellectual operated was cosmopolitan, but the worth of ideas was determined by their applicability to the task of taming the frontier. The latest European wind of doctrine, upon its arrival in the New World, met immediately with skepticism. Until it had proven its utility, Americans were likely to consign a new theory to the category of the unproven. The result was a society which shared Benjamin Franklin's belief that "the right Road of Improvement" was "Experiments."*

*The empirical emphasis of American thinking was complemented by a profoundly conservative attachment to the traditional beliefs of seventeenth-century liberal doctrine. "Thus Hamilton, Adams, Paine, Barlow, Jefferson, and others were working with ideas and principles fifty to a hundred*

*years old," Russel Nye (1913-    ) has written, "in another time and place,
for new purposes, and occasionally with different meanings." The average
American was no less convinced that his word on any subject matched in
significance that of any gentleman or scholar. They anticipated that at
some near time the barriers that separated the rich from the poor would
crumble, and so they had small reverence for prestigious names but great
respect for large achievements. A generally literate population, the American provided an audience that put potential leaders on their mettle.*

*The Continental Congresses united all these crosscurrents of American
life. Once assembled, the delegates discovered that their parochial identities
as colonials had been infused by the catholic identity of Americans. They
also discovered a larger faith: the certitude that "the cause of America is
in a great measure the cause of all mankind." It informed the Revolution
with purpose. Edmund Cody Burnett (1864-1949) devoted most of his
scholarly life to a study of the Continental Congresses. In the process, he
edited an eight-volume collection of the* Letters of Members of the Continental Congress *(1921-1938). It remains the basic source to which all students interested in the subject have recourse.*

# THE CONTINENTAL
# CONGRESS

## by Edmund Cody Burnett

"The continent," now about to gather itself a congress, was in fact little
more than a slender strip along the Atlantic seaboard; yet, for the dozen
of small political communities, the problems involved in the gathering were
not simple and the labor was not light. Heavier they were by far than now
devolve upon their heirs and assigns, fourfold in number and far-flung
across the width of a continent in fact. Whether it be from New Hampshire
and Massachusetts at one extreme or South Carolina at the other, the journey
to Philadelphia was slow, dreary, and toilsome. For most of the delegates
to the congress it must be on horseback, with bulging saddlebags, or by
lumbering stagecoach. The South Carolinians did indeed find transportation
by wind and water more feasible, still not as swift as the winds.

Of the journeyings of the delegates from the southward not a great deal
is known. The southerners may not have been less conscious of posterity
than their New England compatriots, but they seem never to have contracted to the same degree the habit of communing with posterity through
the medium of a diary. Of the journey of the Massachusetts delegates, however, we have a circumstantial account, recorded by that indefatigable
diarist, John Adams—the journal of a veritable triumphal procession from
Boston, down through Connecticut, New York, New Jersey, and on into
Philadelphia.

"The Committee for the Congress," as Adams characterizes the Massachusetts delegation, set out from Boston on the 10th of August, and so leisurely was their journey that they did not arrive in Philadelphia until the 29th. They were bent on surveying the political landscape as they journeyed, therefore they lingered and tarried wherever the lingering and the tarrying offered them good mental and spiritual grazing. For one thing, they would take a measure of the depth and breadth of the sympathies with Boston, of the genuineness of those offers to make the cause of Boston their own. For another thing, they would have a look in advance at as many as possible of the men whom the colonies to the south of them had chosen for the great conclave, would discover what manner of men they would encounter in Philadelphia and what their views. They would have opportunities also to meet and to measure other men, men not destined to appear in the coming congress, but important figures in their own colonies. This eagerness to probe, to pry, to discover was not of course all on the part of the Massachusetts delegates; they, in turn, would be objects of interest, subjects for careful inspection.

In Hartford they encountered Silas Deane, one of the Connecticut delegates. Deane was to stand forth as one of the impressive figures in the congress, but destined to become a pathetic one before the contest had ended. "The Congress," declared Deane magniloquently, "is the grandest and most important assembly ever held in America, . . . *all* of America is intrusted to it and depends upon it." His enthusiasm however swept him over far, when he declaimed, "The resolutions of the congress shall be the laws of the Medes and the Persians." In New Haven they met and had converse with another of Connecticut's delegates, that "solid, sensible man," Roger Sherman, who then and there proved his right to the characterization by boldly offering the opinion that Massachusetts might well "have rescinded that part of their Circular Letter where they allow Parliament to be the supreme Legislature over the Colonies in any case."

Ten days of this leisurely browsing brought them to New York City, where the hobnobbing continued on an even more extensive scale. Isaac Low, one of New York's delegates-elect, would loudly profess attachment to the cause of liberty, but (so it was whispered) there were those who doubted his sincerity. (Many another man, during the succeeding months, would be pursued by interrogation points.) John Alsop, another delegate, was reputed to be "of a good heart," but "unequal to the trust in point of abilities." Adams thought him "a soft, sweet man." (Too soft and too sweet, no doubt, for such parlous times, Alsop went along cheerfully until they came to that parting of the ways called the Declaration of Independence; then he refused to follow the procession farther.) In contrast, Philip Livingston was "a downright, straight forward man," "a great, rough, rapid mortal," who "blusters away" in such a manner that "there is no holding any conversation with him." Evidently Livingston wished to do some of the talking himself. He did taunt Adams with a reminder that Massachusetts had once indulged in a bit of Quaker-hanging. More than that, he opened his mouth and shockingly prophesied: "If England should turn us adrift, we should instantly go to civil wars among ourselves, to determine which colony should govern all the rest." Of James Duane, with whom Adams would soon be engaged in a tough wrestling match on the floor of Congress, the first impressions were that he had "a sly, surveying eye, a little squint eyed . . . very sensible, I think, and very artful." Of John Jay, also to become one of the leading antagonists of the Adams program, the Bostonian learned little except that he was a bright young lawyer and a good speaker. All this round of "breakfasting, dining, drinking coffee, etc., about the city" was "very disagreeable on some accounts," still it had its uses.

Ambling on down through New Jersey they came to Princeton, where they met the president of the college, the Reverend Doctor Witherspoon, drank a glass of wine with him at his house, afterward shared a dish of coffee with him at their lodgings. Between the wine and the coffee Adams became convinced that Doctor Witherspoon was "as high a son of liberty as any man in America." The next day being Sunday, Adams also took the doctor's measure as a preacher: "Heard Dr. Witherspoon all day," he recorded. While Witherspoon would not be in the congress now gathering, he was destined to become, at a vital moment, a member of the subsequent congress and to prove his right to the title, "high son of liberty." Meanwhile, as he had taken an important part in the New Jersey proceedings, he could furnish the Massachusetts delegate much enlightenment respecting the state of mind in New Jersey in general, and more particularly of the state and the quality of mind of one of the New Jersey delegates, namely, William Livingston, whom he characterized as "very sincere and very able in the public cause, but a bad speaker, though a good writer." From a young lawyer named Jonathan Dickinson Sergeant, himself also destined to become a member of the so-called "Second Congress," they learned much respecting the delegates-elect of other states, particularly those of New York, Pennsylvania, and Virginia. Of two of their delegates, said Sergeant, the Virginians speak in raptures. Patrick Henry and Richard Henry Lee were the Demosthenes and Cicero of America. No doubt a feast of oratory would be spread when the congress assembled; but Adams, impatient for action, was to become "fed-up" on oratory.

On to Philadelphia. If for a time all eyes had been turned toward Boston, now all were focused on Philadelphia, about to become the dazzling center of the somewhat dazed American world. And Philadelphia was all primed to do its part nobly and effectively. For one thing, it would give these men of the other colonies the time of their lives. It would extend to them such a joyous welcome and spread before them such lavish entertainments that the memories thereof would be cherished to the closing days of their lives. For another thing, if the eastern delegates had been eager to take the measures of those of the other colonies, certainly the statesmen of Pennsylvania would be no less eager to discover what manner of men the New Englanders were, and more especially those two Bostonian fire-eaters, Samuel and John Adams. To begin the zestful welcome a goodly number of the notables of the city, together with a few of the recently arrived delegates from other colonies, journeyed out beyond the city limits to greet the cavalcade of eastern delegates, even as weary and sore they jogged along on this last lap of their pilgrimage, and to escort them into the city, where the welcome would be redoubled and entertainments multiplied. At the city tavern other notables, along with "a multitude" of the less notable, awaited them, "dirty, dusty, and fatigued" though they were, to engage them in conversation, then to offer them a supper, "as elegant as ever was laid on a table."

This was Monday, August 29, and, though the Congress was scheduled to assemble on the following Thursday, another Monday would come before there would be delegates enough to organize and get down to business. Perhaps it was just as well. The week could be profitably occupied in spying out the land and one another; for others than James Duane had eager ears, if not also sly, surveying eyes. And how better could all this be done than at sumptuous tables? Philadelphia could and did provide the sumptuous tables. Breakfasts, dinners, suppers, followed one another in unbroken procession; and even betwixt times groups might gather to drink punch and eat dried smoked sprats. There were "mighty feasts," "sinful feasts," every imaginable thing to eat, every desirable thing to drink. And if now and then some of the delegates became "very high" (it is open to question whether Adams uses the expression with a political or a bibulous connotation), it is not of record that any of them at any time became *very low*. Adams avers that for his part, unaccustomed though he was, he met the tests with a fair degree of success.

Strange to tell, however, the Pennsylvania delegates for the most part seem to have made themselves conspicuous by their absence from these tables, as they likewise for the most part failed to take conspicuous parts in the later contest. The chief exception was Thomas Mifflin, who practically kept open house for the visiting delegates—"a grand, spacious, and elegant house," Adams records. What was more, Quaker though he was, Mifflin proved himself militant enough to satisfy the Massachusetts men. Another Philadelphian who assiduously cultivated the men of the east was John Dickinson, author of the famous "Letters of a Pennsylvania Farmer." To make his first call on the Bostonians he drove from his country seat "in his coach with four beautiful horses." He hoped to make a good impression, and he did. "Mr. Dickinson," Adams confided to his Diary, "is a very modest man, and very ingenious as well as very agreeable; he has an excellent heart, and the cause of his country lies near it." Though not yet a delegate to the Congress he soon would be, and in due time he and Adams would find themselves crossing political swords and clashing sharp tongues. Fortunately Adams did not afterward turn back the pages of his Diary to erase the record of his first impressions. Rather, he dug deep into his vocabulary for other labels.

It was on the second morning of their sojourn in Philadelphia that Adams and his brethren "had much conversation" with a man named Charles Thomson, reputed to be "the Sam Adams of Philadelphia, the life of the cause of liberty, they say." They say! Could it be possible that the man who was the life of the cause of liberty in Philadelphia had remained wholly unknown to the men who had been playing similar parts in Boston, that "cradle of liberty"? Certainly the lusty cries of the Boston infant had been heard in Philadelphia. But this is only one of the many revelations of the profound ignorance of one another that prevailed amongst the colonies. No wonder that in such soil jealousies and suspicions should take root and grow. Anyway, all the delegates would soon know this Charles Thomson, for he was about to become the secretary of Congress, to remain the wedded spouse of that body until the demise of the Congress did them part.

Among the first to extend the welcoming hand to the Massachusetts delegation was Thomas McKean, essentially of the Philadelphia group, although actually a delegate from the "Three Lower Counties," already in business for themselves and presently to constitute themselves the state of Delaware. There seemed to be no reason why Adams should not be satisfied with McKean and McKean with Adams. But it was another delegate from the Three Lower Counties that actually set John Adams to gurgling. "Caesar Rodney," Adams wrote, "is the oddest looking man in the world; he is tall, thin and slender as a reed, pale; his face is not bigger than a large apple, yet there is sense and fire, spirit, wit, and humor in his countenance." Rodney himself was meanwhile measuring his associates in the Congress. "All the seven delegates appointed for Virginia are here," he wrote, "and more sensible fine fellows you'd never wish to see, in short it is the greatest assembly (in proportion to the number) that ever was collected in America." The Bostonians, he went on to say, had been condemned by many for their violence, but, compared to those from Virginia, South Carolina, and Rhode Island, they were moderate men.

Of the southern delegates Adams was less sure than was Rodney, but in characteristic manner he proceeded to measure them and to label them. Henry Middleton of South Carolina he found to be "silent and reserved"— evidently inclined to keep his own counsel. Of the two brothers Rutledge, the appearance of the elder, John, was "not very promising." "There is no keenness in his eye, no depth in his countenance; nothing of the profound, sagacious, brilliant, or sparkling." Later, when he found Rutledge and himself more in unison, he conceived a better opinion of him. Edward Rutledge was "high enough" (meaning evidently his political views); likewise he was "sprightly," "but not deep," "good natured though conceited." But the South Carolinian soon got on the New Englander's nerves. "Young Ned Rutledge," Adams later wrote, "is a perfect Bob-o-Lincoln—a swallow, a sparrow, a peacock; excessively vain, excessively weak, and excessively variable and unsteady; jejune, inane, and puerile." (Can it be that John Adams had exhausted his vocabulary?) Thomas Lynch is characterized as "a solid, firm, judicious man," with whom they were all "vastly pleased." At a dinner, "Mr. Lynch gave us a sentiment: 'The brave Dantzickers, who declare they will be free in the face of the greatest monarch in Europe.'" (Roll away a hundred and sixty-five years, and lo! Poland would again be undergoing dismemberment; but Danzig will have reversed the picture.) Silas Deane amplified in several particulars the portrait of Lynch, who, declared Deane, "carries with him more force in his very appearance than most powdered folks in their conversation. He wears his hair strait, his clothes in the plainest order, and is highly esteemed." Perhaps the best known of all the South Carolinians was the fiery Christopher Gadsden, of whom Deane wrote: "Mr. Gadsden leaves all New England Sons of Liberty far behind, for he is for taking up his firelock and marching direct to Boston." Indeed Gadsden had affirmed that, "were his wife and children all in Boston, and they were to perish by the sword, it would not alter his sentiment or proceeding for American Liberty." (Gadsden seems to have been unduly rash, even for times so raw.)

Inasmuch as Virginia had been most forward in support of Massachusetts, Adams was especially eager to meet the Virginia delegates, four of whom, Peyton Randolph, Benjamin Harrison, Richard Henry Lee, and Richard Bland, arrived in the afternoon of September 2. A little converse with them, and Adams declared, "These gentlemen from Virginia appear to be the most spirited and consistent of any. Harrison said he would have come on foot rather than not come. Bland said he would have gone, upon this occasion, if it had been to Jericho." After a breakfast-table talk with Lee next morning, Adams set Lee down as "a masterly man." Physically, Randolph was "a large, well looking man." Lee "a tall, spare man," Bland "a learned, bookish man." Silas Deane drew a better portrait of Randolph: "Of an affable, open, and majestic deportment, large in size, though not out of proportion, he commands respect and esteem by his very aspect." It was Deane who described Harrison as "an uncommonly large man . . . rather rough in his dress and speech"; but it was Adams who later characterized him as "an indolent, luxurious, heavy gentleman, of no use in Congress or committee, but a great embarrassment to both." This, however, was when enthusiasms had cooled and the wires of purposes had become crossed. As the other Virginia delegates, Edmund Pendleton, Patrick Henry, and George Washington, did not arrive until Sunday, they failed to get their portraits hung in the Adams gallery at this time. It was Deane again, who a few days later supplied sketches of them. Pendleton was "of easy and cheerful countenance, polite in address, and elegant if not eloquent in style and elocution." Henry was "the compleatest speaker" he had ever heard. (Congress had then had some "samples" of the celebrated Virginian's oratory.) Colonel Washington was a tall man, of a "hard" countenance, "yet with a very young look, and an easy, soldier like air and gesture . . . speaks very modestly and in determined style and accent." What particularly placed him high in the estimation of the New Englanders was the speech he was said to have made in the House of Burgesses, when he offered to raise and arm and lead one thousand men himself at his own expense for the defense of the country.

Came Saturday night, and all the delegates who had arrived gathered for one grand feast of reason and flow of soul. "We drank sentiments till eleven o'clock," says Adams, and among the toasts were: "Union of the Colonies"; "Unanimity to the Congress"; "Union of Britain and the Colonies on a Constitutional Foundation." The toasts were in fact prayers, and well might they pray, for their aims would be long in the attainment and not without many a hard wrestle.

Others than John Adams had no doubt been busy the while plying their political thermometers and stethoscopes, but Adams beyond all others had left charts of his tests and diagnoses. Fortunately one who was for the moment the chief of the rival school of political medicos has left some record of his probes and prognoses. Joseph Galloway, speaker of the Pennsylvania House of Representatives and delegate in Congress for that colony, was as eager as any man to discover what the Congress was like to do, and none more anxious to steer its course away from the vortexes of extreme measures. At the close of that busy week of dinings and winings and diplomatic maneuverings Galloway made a report of progress to Governor William Franklin of New Jersey, a man of like opinions and purposes. He had been endeavoring, he wrote, "to find out the Temper of the Delegates" and, after sounding them as best he could, he was of opinion that they would "behave with Temper and Moderation."

The Boston commissioners were "warm" (no one could have expected them to be cool), although "in their Behaviour and Conversation were modest, yet not so much so as not to throw out Hints, which, like Straws and Feathers, tell us from which Point of the Compass the Wind comes." One man he had found with views that marched side by side with his own (in so far as he had explained himself)—John Rutledge of South Carolina, who, beyond all others, had weighed the arguments pro and con and was keenly aware of the consequences that would flow from rash measures. To a number of the delegates Galloway had intimated his own idea of the moderate and tentative course that the Congress should adopt, such a course as could not, in his opinion, "fail to give Strength to our Cause, and, if not immediately, in the End bring the Government to attend to Reason and redress our Aggrievances."

John Adams would no doubt have been delighted to know that Galloway, of all men, had deemed him modest in his behavior and conversation. Midway the sitting of Congress he confided to William Tudor: "We have had numberless prejudices to remove here. We have been obliged to act with great delicacy and caution. We have been obliged to keep ourselves out of sight, and to feel pulses, and to sound the depths; to insinuate our sentiments, designs, and desires, by means of other persons, sometimes of one province, and sometimes of another." For the feeling of pulses, the sounding of depths, the insinuations of designs had not ceased with the preliminary week of amenities; skirmishing continued through the session, notwithstanding the frequent frontal attacks and the stanch defenses.

By Sunday, September 4, the majority of the delegates destined to the Congress had arrived, with only a few stragglers to make their belated appearance. The stage was set; the drama about to begin. Taking the Congress as a whole, it was a notable body of men; with a few exceptions, probably the pick of the colonies. Nine of them, namely, Eliphalet Dyer of Connecticut, Philip Livingston of New York, Thomas McKean and Caesar Rodney of Delaware, John Dickinson and John Morton of Pennsylvania, and Thomas Lynch, Christopher Gadsden, and John Rutledge of South Carolina, had been members of the Stamp Act Congress of 1765, constituting in fact one-third of that body. One of them, Stephen Hopkins of Rhode Island, had been a member of the Albany Congress of 1754. Of the fifty-six men who, first and last, attended the Congress of 1774, most of them would reappear in the succeeding Congress. On the other hand, many of them, as the years went by and the political winds shifted their courses, would be compelled to yield their places to others. A few indeed would of their own will and purpose slip away, to commune no more with the men on revolution bent.

From the beginning it was clear enough that the Congress would be divided into two main groups, conservatives, aiming at patching up the quarrel, and radicals, determined upon resistance. In the forefront of the conservative forces were Galloway of Pennsylvania and Duane and Jay of New York, whilst strenuously pressing for "vigorous measures" were the Massachusetts and Virginia delegations, each group with its allies. One of the first tests of strength came before ever their organization had been effected, and was over the apparently innocuous question where Congress should hold its sessions.

The question arose as of course when the delegates first drew together informally at the City Tavern. Galloway, as speaker of the Pennsylvania assembly, offered the use of the State House, the carpenters their own hall, the one a provincial chamber, the other a private house. Duane contended that acceptance of the speaker's offer was "a piece of respect" due to him; but the fact that the Galloway party preferred the State House was a good reason why the other party should not. The choice of Carpenter's Hall, they argued, would be "highly agreeable to the mechanics and citizens in general." Good politics. Travel might be slow, but minds were quick and keen. They would take a view of each; but first, to Carpenter's Hall. From the City Tavern to Carpenter's Hall therefore they proceeded, on foot. "The general cry was that this was a good room." For one thing, there was an "excellent library"; for another, there was "a long entry where gentlemen may walk." The library would be useful, and there would no doubt come times when gentlemen would do well to take a walk. A little walking sometimes served to cool mental heats, to promote calmer reflection. The vote, although not quite unanimous, was to stay. (Galloway afterward asserted that the question had already been "privately settled by an Interest made out of Doors.")

Proceeding then to organization, the choice of a chairman, Peyton Randolph, speaker of the Virginia House of Burgesses, was accomplished with complete unanimity; but when it came to the election of a secretary the two parties again found themselves at odds. The Galloway party wished to choose a member of the Congress, and they appear to have picked on Silas Deane of Connecticut. The froward faction, on the other hand, nominated Charles Thomson, leader of the radical movement in Pennsylvania, and elected him. (That matter also, Galloway declared, had been fixed out of doors.) Galloway, to whom Thomson was as rank poison, had in fact maneuvered the election of delegates in Pennsylvania so as to eliminate Thomson and was therefore greatly chagrined that his purpose to keep

Thomson out of Congress had been defeated. The majority for Thomson as secretary was, however, so large that opposition was withdrawn, and his election also was recorded as unanimous. (No need for straws and feathers to determine the direction of that wind.)

Between the election of the chairman and the election of the secretary came two other decisions, not even officially recorded (James Duane does, however, record them), namely, that the body should be called "The Congress," and the chairman should be styled "The President." Thus originated the two principal titles in our present governmental organization. The Congress provided for by the Constitution of 1787 is in a real sense the successor of the Congress of 1774; on the other hand, the President of the United States is scarcely in any sense the successor of the presidents of the old Congress. The presidents of Congress were almost solely presiding officers, possessing scarcely a shred of executive or administrative functions; whereas the President of the United States is almost solely an executive officer, with no presiding duties at all. Barring a likeness in social and diplomatic precedence, the two offices are identical only in the possession of the same title.

\* \* \* \* \*

Having now pretty effectually squelched all efforts toward conciliation and having decided upon the principal means to be adopted to obtain a restoration of colonial rights, Congress next appointed a committee "to bring in a plan for carrying into effect the non-importation, non-consumption, and non-exportation resolved on." At this juncture (October 1) the pacificators succeeded nevertheless in prevailing upon Congress to send a "loyal address" to his majesty; and a few days later (October 12) it was decided that it would be a good stroke of policy to send an address also to the people of Great Britain. Many of the people in the homeland, some of them in high authority, were sympathetic with the colonies in their contentions, and might do much to sweeten the temper of the ministry. Still later (October 21) Congress concluded that it would be wise to lay their case before those North American colonies that were not represented in the Congress—Quebec, St. John's in Nova Scotia, Georgia, and East and West Florida—particularly Quebec. These addresses were all prepared with great care and subjected to close scrutiny in Congress. That they were admirably drawn no less an authority than the Earl of Chatham gave testimony.

It was of course the petition to the king that gave Congress the greatest concern, and a carefully picked committee was assigned to the task of preparing it—Richard Henry Lee, John Adams, Thomas Johnson, Patrick Henry, and John Rutledge. The committee, for its part, chose the oratorical Mr. Henry to draft it. Apparently, however, Henry's pen did not prove itself the peer of his tongue and his voice, for his proposed address was so unsatisfactory Congress demanded that it be rewritten and added John Dickinson to the committee for the purpose (October 21). Dickinson, who had taken his seat in Congress only a few days before, had made a reputation as the wielder of a facile and a powerful pen; and Congress was not disappointed in the result. The petition as drawn by Dickinson was approved October 25.

With the first draft of the address to the people of England, Congress was more deeply disappointed than it had been even with that to the king. It was another instance of an orator having failed with his pen, for the drafting of that address had been entrusted to Richard Henry Lee. The story of that address comes to us from Jefferson, as related to him by Benjamin Harrison and Edmund Pendleton. When Lee's production was read, "every countenance fell and a dead silence ensued for many minutes." The consideration of the address was postponed until the following day (October 19). Probably William Livingston and John Jay, the other members of the committee, were not surprised at what had taken place, for Jay also had prepared an address, and at Livingston's suggestion it was read. As told to Jefferson and retold by him, "there was but one sentiment of admiration."

While Congress was mulling over these addresses, consideration was being given betwixt times to other matters, which, if not weightier, were at least more to the point of their immediate purpose. A statement of colonial rights having been postponed until the means for recovering them had been determined upon, it now behooved Congress to decide, if it could, what in particular were those rights they had so stoutly resolved to maintain. To be sure, they had, in that first tussle with the problem, scrubbed it all over the threshing floor, until the threshers themselves were all but worn to a frazzle; but they must needs thresh it over again. So once again the two main questions were raised and debated: should they plant their main batteries of Defense on the law of nature, and what authority, if any, should be allowed to Parliament in the regulation of their trade? Duane, Galloway, and their group had no very large idea of the law of nature as a defensive position, whereas John Adams and others of the philosophically minded members had a notion that, although some of the suggested positions might not be impregnable, the law of nature was one post they could defend against all the cohorts of the enemy.

Duane, for his part, had labored earnestly with the problem and had presented to the committee on rights a carefully reasoned statement of the case, as he conceived it, taking pains to preface his propositions with the general statement that "A firm Union between the Parent State and her Colonies ought to be the great object of this Congress." (This, be it remembered, was before Galloway had offered his plan of union, which Duane heartily espoused.) "It is this alone," he asserted, "which can ensure the permanent Stability of the british empire and the mutual Happiness of its respective Members." Therefore, he contended, "the Prerogatives of the Crown, the interest of Great Britain, and the Rights of the Colonies ought each to have their proper Influence" in any resolves that might be adopted, whereas the proceedings of Congress ought to be "tempered not only with a Regard to Justice but a desire of Reconciliation." Touching the supremacy of the crown he maintained that the same allegiance was due the king from the colonies as from his subjects within the realm of England. The rights of the colonies, Duane admitted, were derived from three sources: "1. From the Common Law of England and such ancient Statutes applicable to our local Circumstances, as existed at the time of our Colonization, which are fundamentals in our Constitution. 2. From our respective Charters confirming these Rights. 3. From our several Codes of provincial Laws." Those acts of trade that had been submitted to and recognized for more than a century "ought to be considered in the Light of an ancient Compact between the parent State and the Colonies." From the spirit of this compact, he went on to say, and because of the expediency of a controlling power over the general commerce of the empire, as well as for the protection the colonies had always derived from the mother country, the authority of Parliament in matters of trade "ought not to be questioned," provided that authority is "exercised bona fide for the Purposes of securing the Advantages of the Commerce of the whole Empire to Great Britain, with a Just Regard to the Interests of its respective Members."

A good deal of Duane's reasoning and phraseology was presently embodied in the so-called "Declaration of Rights," which, by the 14th of October, had been whipped into a shape sufficiently satisfactory to obtain a vote of approval. One sentence of especial significance (cited below) seemed to catch everybody's fancy, with the result that it was incorporated in the Declaration with only a few verbal changes. Taken as a whole, this Declaration, which includes a review of the measures of the British government which the colonies deemed to be obnoxious, is an admirable statement, in the form of ten resolutions, of the fundamental rights on which the colonies laid hold as indubitably theirs—rights derived from "the immutable laws of nature, the principles of the English constitution, and the several charters or compacts."

In view of the fact that "the violent party" was now in the ascendancy in Congress, it is little short of remarkable that the Declaration of Rights is so restrained in tone. Enumerating the rights of the colonists, the Declaration sets forth that they are entitled to life, liberty, and property, that these rights had never been ceded to any sovereign power whatever, and that neither these nor any other of the "rights, liberties, and immunities of free and natural born subjects, within the realm of England" had been forfeited by emigration. Next is posited what is termed "the foundation of English liberty, and of all free government," namely, "a right in the people to participate in their legislative council." This was an old bone of contention, and it was deftly disposed of thus: inasmuch as the colonies can not, "from their local and other circumstances," be represented in the British Parliament, "they are entitled to a free and exclusive power of legislation in their several provincial legislatures . . . subject only to the negative of their sovereign, in such manner as has been heretofore used and accustomed." Then follows the carefully phrased proviso, taken over almost verbatim from the proposition earlier laid down by Duane:

But from the necessity of the case, and a regard to the mutual interest of both countries, we cheerfully consent to the operation of such acts of the British parliament, as are bona fide, restrained to the regulation of our external commerce, for the purpose of securing the commercial advantages of the whole empire to the mother country, and the commercial benefits of its respective members; excluding every idea of taxation, internal or external, for raising a revenue on the subjects in America, without their consent.

Among the other rights specified were that the colonies were entitled to the common law of England, "and more especially to the great and inestimable privilege of being tried by their peers of the vicinage," the right of assembly and petition, and lastly the right to be free of a standing army in times of peace, unless by "the consent of the legislature of that colony, in which such army is kept." The tenth resolution is, in effect, a criticism of a principal feature of the Galloway plan of union. Good government and conformity to the English constitution rendered it indispensably necessary "that the constituent branches of the legislature be independent of each other; that, therefore, the exercise of legislative power in the several colonies, by a council appointed, during pleasure, by the crown, is unconstitutional, dangerous, and destructive of the freedom of American legislation."

Congress was now ready to take up the report, offered October 12, of the committee appointed to bring in a plan for carrying into effect the non-importation, non-consumption, and non-exportation agreements, which together now began to be called the plan of the Association. Both the name and the form appear to have been derived from the Virginia Association of August, 1774. It seems to have been generally supposed that the battle over the substance of the Association was at an end, that only the form and minor details would require further discussion. Those who thought thus had reckoned, however, without South Carolina. The resolution in favor of non-exportation (September 30) had in fact been carried only after some compromises to meet the demands of Virginia, Maryland, and North Carolina, and against the protests of the South Carolina delegation in particular; for the exportation of rice and indigo was essential to the commercial life of that colony. Now, upon a renewal of the discussion, that delegation (four of them at least, the Rutledges, Lynch, and Middleton; Gadsden seemed quite willing to yield) laid down an ultimatum that, unless the South Carolina staples, rice and indigo, should be excepted from the non-exportation provision, they would not sign the Association; and those delegates did in fact withdraw from Congress for the time being.

This was on the 20th of October. Thereupon, to prevent the break-up of the union, a compromise was effected whereby the South Carolinians yielded their contention with regard to indigo on condition that an exception be made of rice. Thus it came about that, at the end of the fourth article of the Association, were appended the words "except rice to Europe." For the moment at least the crisis had passed, and the delegates proceeded to append their signatures to the Association. That not all the delegates signed of their own free will, to say nothing of full accord, Joseph Galloway at least gave later testimony. He had signed the Association, partly in the hope of "preventing the Congress from proceeding to more violent measures," but partly also, it would seem, from fear of violent measures toward himself personally.

In form the Association is a solemn agreement on the part of the several colonies to pursue a rigid policy of non-intercourse with Great Britain until the grievances complained of should be redressed. The introductory paragraph, wherein are set forth the reasons for entering into the agreement, opens significantly with a pious avowal of loyalty to the king, although it does not fail in the close to point an accusing finger at a "wicked ministry."

Besides the non-intercourse resolutions already agreed upon but here somewhat elaborated, the Association embodies other mutual pledges, which at first glance might seem to have but little relation to the main objective. The associators enter into a pledge, for instance, that they will use their "utmost endeavors to improve the breed of sheep, and increase their number to the greatest extent"; and, if any should find themselves overstocked with sheep, they will dispose of them to their neighbors, "especially to the poorer sort, on moderate terms." Further, they pledge that, in their several stations, they will "encourage frugality, economy, and industry, and promote agriculture, arts and the manufactures of this country, especially that of wool." All of which was rational enough, when it is borne in mind that the population was like to find itself presently subjected to many deprivations. But the associators went further still, promising to "discountenance and discourage every species of extravagance and dissipation, especially all horse-racing, and all kinds of gaming, cock-fighting, exhibitions of shews, plays, and other expensive diversions and entertainments." Nor was this all. The pious associators even prescribe a severe simplification of the mourning customs. The conclusion is inescapable that some of these associated frowns were motivated by ethical rather than economical purposes. The ancient, if not always honorable, sport of cock-fighting, for instance, could scarcely have affected the commerce between Great Britain and her colonies or otherwise have thwarted the great common cause.

So far the Association was no more than a pledge, even if the pledge did include promises that, if any vendor of goods should by any device whatsoever violate this agreement, the colonies one and all would thereafter have no dealings with such a person. The associators did not for a moment deceive themselves into supposing that their covenant, however solemnly entered into, would enforce itself. There must be machinery for its enforcement, and in this manner was such machinery provided for:

> That a committee be chosen in every county, city, and town . . . whose business it shall be attentively to observe the conduct of all persons touching this association; and when it shall be made to appear . . . that any person within the limits of their appointment has violated this association, that [they] cause the truth of the case to be published in the gazette; to the end, that all such foes to the rights of British-America may be publicly known, and universally contemned as the enemies of American liberty.

Furthermore, if any colony should fail to accede to the Association or hereafter violate it, such colony would be held as "unworthy of the rights of freemen, and as inimical to the liberties of their country."

If there had ever been any doubt that the machinery devised would be efficient for its purpose, that doubt was speedily dispelled. Committees were everywhere set up and went to work with zeal to perform the duties assigned them. There was rioting and burning, tarring and feathering, until the story became monotonous. Nor did these valiant enforcement agencies limit their interest and their activities to the weightier matters of the Association; the injunctions respecting diversions and entertainments likewise received due attention. For instance, a lady was counseled to "decline" giving a proposed ball at her house, as contrary to the spirit of the Association; and some men who had taken part in a horse race were prevailed upon to express repentance and to promise "proper atonement" for their "enormity." Of course there were lamentations and groans from the victims. Growled one such: "If I must be enslaved, let it be by a KING at least, and not by a parcel of upstart lawless Committee-men. If I must be devoured, let me be devoured by the jaws of a lion, and not gnawed to deth by rats and vermin." What a pity we could not have escaped this sordid chapter of our "Glorious Revolution"!

The Association has nevertheless a much worthier place in the history of the American Revolution than this story of mobs gone wild and liberty run mad. As the Declaration of Rights was in an important sense a forerunner of the Declaration of Independence, so the Association stands out as an important step toward the creation of an organic union among the colonies. Though not a constitution, for it laid down no framework of government other than for its own enforcement, it was in a true sense an instrument of union and the first to be subscribed by all the colonies then participating.

The Association completed, there remained little to detain Congress except to put the finishing touches to the several memorials and addresses, including one to their own constituents, giving an account of their stewardship. Anticipating that all its labors in behalf of a restoration of rights might prove to have been in vain, Congress resolved on October 22 that, unless the desired redress of grievances had been obtained before the 10th of May, 1775, another congress of all the colonies should be convened in Philadelphia at that time. On the same day, because of the indisposition of Peyton Randolph, Henry Middleton of South Carolina was chosen president, and therefore it came about that most of the addresses were signed by Middleton as president. All the Virginia delegates except Washington and Richard Henry Lee took their departure October 23 to attend the House of Burgesses; accordingly Washington and Lee between them appended all the Virginia signatures to the petition to the king. Washington having subscribed those of Bland, Harrison, and Pendleton, while Lee wrote the name of Patrick Henry. Randolph's signature is not found on the petition. A letter to the colonial agents in London was then prepared, arrangements made for its despatch, and on October 26 the Congress adjourned itself.

That evening "all the Congress and several gentlemen of the town" gathered at the City Tavern for a last friendly communion and farewells. It is not recorded that the delegates fell upon one another's necks and wept, yet time was to reveal that many strong and lasting friendships had been formed during those eventful, if somewhat quarrelsome, weeks of discussion. Without doubt this mingling of minds from the separated colonies was fraught with consequences far surpassing any personal relationships. If it was the beginning of separation from the mother country, it was also the beginning of union among themselves.

As the delegates wended their several ways homeward, many a mind must have been weighted with serious reflections upon the probable outcome of this congress of the colonies—the weal or the woe, may be the woe and the weal. So, no doubt, the mind of John Adams, chief among the chroniclers, if not also chief among the actors in that drama. Yet, however somber may have been his reflections, it was a gladsome note that John Adams chanted as he began the jog back to his beloved Boston (pity that his chant was buried in his diary):

> Took our departure, in a very great rain, from the happy, the peaceful, the elegant, the hospitable, and polite city of Philadelphia. It is not likely that I shall ever see this part of the world again, but I shall ever retain a most grateful, pleasing sense of the many civilities I have received in it, and shall think myself happy to have an opportunity of returning them.

A few short but anxious months, nevertheless, and John Adams would find himself once more in Philadelphia, in the midst of its abounding and charming civilities—but not less amid redoubled perplexities.

❧ ☙

ONCE *the verbal argument had been exhausted, the shooting war commenced. The final blow to old friendships had been delivered, blood had been shed, and more than one American wrote, as did Benjamin Franklin, to an Englishmen: "You and I were long friends; you are now my enemy." For the men who sprang to arms at Lexington and Concord, the issue had the ring of the elemental; it would be succinctly said by an old veteran who recalled, "What we meant in going for those Redcoats was this: we always had governed ourselves, and we always meant to. They didn't mean we should." The struggle with the enemy from abroad was complemented with an internecine warfare between Tory and Whig. Before the war had ended, no less than 80,000 Tories fled into exile, leaving behind home and country.*

*Compared to a modern war, the Revolution proceeded at a leisurely pace. The British war effort remained divided until the end, and no less an eloquent voice than that of Edmund Burke defended the American cause on* the floor of Parliament. *Washington and his army fought a hit-and-run war that denied the British a ready target. As the war progressed, the redcoats learned the uncomfortable lesson that the particularistic tendencies of the colonies made it impossible to win a final battle. No one target served as the acknowledged heart of the new nation, the loss of which would convince Americans the war was lost.*

*The ragtag quality of Washington's army is captured in Fisher's lively account of its peregrinations across the Middle Colonies. When one has finished reading it, one wonders how the Revolution was ever won. Perhaps the answer in the end was that for the American revolutionary there was nowhere else to go should he lose. With such a prospect looming, he chose to endure.*

*Sydney George Fisher (1865-1927) complemented his career as a lawyer with one as an amateur historian. His range of interest was confined to subjects related to Pennsylvania and to the Revolutionary period. He took particular delight in the discovery of everyday details that are the substance of daily life. Much of his work has subsided into the realm of the antiquarian, but even so his books remain mines of information.*

# THE TRUE HISTORY OF THE
# AMERICAN REVOLUTION

*by Sydney George Fisher*

After the battle of Bunker Hill, June 17, 1775, there was, it is true, Arnold's and Montgomery's romantic dash at Canada the following autumn, but there was no fighting in the rebellious colonies, where we would naturally expect it, until the summer of 1776, when Clinton attacked Charleston, South Carolina, June 28; and the battle of Long Island was fought August 27. England would not in modern times allow such a long interval to elapse in the suppression of independence.

It was a great advantage to the patriots to hold themselves independent, unsuppressed, and even unattacked, for a whole year. It helped to prove the Whig position that the Tory ministry had raised a rebellion which they could not suppress; and it increased the possibility of that aid from France which was the dread of England and the best hope of the Americans.

The army, if we may call it by that name, which was besieging Boston was composed almost exclusively of New Englanders. But it was joined during the summer by a few troops from the frontiers of Pennsylvania and Virginia, who aroused much interest, because they were expected to make deadly use of the rifle at three hundred yards instead of using the smoothbore musket, which was useless at only half that distance.

Shortly before the battle of Bunker Hill the Congress passed a resolution for raising six companies of riflemen in Pennsylvania, two in Maryland, and two in Virginia. Subsequently, on June 22, they increased the number of Pennsylvania rifle companies to eight, which were to be formed into a battalion and join the patriot army at Boston.

During July these eight companies were rapidly recruited in the interior of the colony among the Scotch-Irish frontiersmen and hunters. No money had to be appropriated to buy their weapons, for, like the Boer of South Africa, each one of them procured his rifle by taking it down from the pegs on which it rested above his fireplace. He slung his own powder-horn across his shoulder and strapped his bullet-pouch around his waist.

As for his uniform, it consisted of a round hat, which could be bought for a trifle at any country store, and a garment made at home by his wife, and sometimes called a smock-frock, which was nothing more than a shirt belted around the waist and hanging down over the hips instead of being tucked into the trousers. It was the same sort of garment used by farm laborers, and it was made of the cotton cloth which is now used for overalls, or of ticking such as we use to cover mattresses and pillows. When used in the woods it was called a rifle-shirt or hunting-shirt, was sometimes ornamented with a fringed cape, and into its ample looseness above the belt were stuffed loaves of bread, salt pork, dried venison, a frying-pan, or a coffee-pot, until the hardy woodsman became most unsoldier-like in figure.

It may be said that our pictures of handsome Revolutionary uniforms are very misleading. It is pleasant, of course, to think of the Revolution as a great spontaneous uprising of all the people, without doubt, hesitation, or misgiving, and that each hero put on his beautiful buff and blue uniform, brought to him presumably by a fairy, or found growing on a tree, and marched, with a few picturesque hardships, to glorious victory. But the actual conditions were very different from what most of us have been led to believe. Some companies and regiments tried at the start to have uniforms. We find uniforms mentioned here and there, and boards of officers adopted fashion-plates of beautiful garments for all ranks; but there is many a slip between a fashion-plate and getting the beautiful garment on a rebel's back. Those who actually saw the patriot troops in the field describe them as without uniforms, very ragged, and at best clothed in home-made hunting-shirts. Many regiments stained their hunting-shirts with butternut, which was used for a similar purpose by the Confederates of the Civil War. The hunting-shirts were usually white, and butternut gave at once the color that the white cotton cloth would assume after a few weeks of dirt and smoke in camp.

Washington, in an order of July 24, 1776, recommended the hunting-shirt for all troops.

> The General, sensible of the difficulty and expense of providing clothes of almost any kind for the troops, feels an unwillingness to recommend, much more to order, any kind of uniform; but as it is absolutely necessary that the men should have clothes, and appear decent and tight, he earnestly encourages the use of hunt-shirts, with long breeches made of the same cloth, gaiter-fashion about the legs, to all those yet unprovided.—"Force," 5th series, vol. I, pp. 676, 677.

Lafayette has described in his memoirs the patriot army he found in this country on his arrival in the summer of 1777:

> About eleven thousand men ill-armed, and still worse clothed, presented a strange spectacle. Their clothes were parti-colored and many of them were almost naked. The best clad wore hunting shirts, large gray linen [cotton] coats which were much used in Carolina. As to their military tactics, it will be sufficient to say that, for a regiment ranged in battle order to move forward on the right of its line it was necessary for the left to make a continued counter-march. They were always arranged in two lines, the smallest men in the first line.—Vol I, p. 19, London, 1837.

At first the officers could not be distinguished from the men; but on May 3, 1776, they were ordered to wear colored cockades of ribbon. A major-general was marked by a purple or blue ribbon; a brigadier by pink or light red; the staff and the adjutant by green. When the French officers appeared among us after the alliance, our officers were often unable to entertain them from lack of decent clothes and food.

Many of us have, of course, seen scores of portraits of Revolutionary officers in very good uniforms, which do away with all appearance of rebellion. Those were uniforms for a picture, in order that our officers and men might appear as smart-looking as European troops; but they were not the garments worn by our ancestors in the war. Good uniforms could always be painted in a picture. Who would have an ancestor painted in a butternut rifle-shirt and labelled rebel, when an artist could paint a portrait and paint on it a uniform from the fashion-plate of the Board of War,—such a uniform as our ancestors would have worn had they had the time and money to obtain one.

The patriot army consisted for the most part of mere squads of militia, over whom Washington, and even their own chosen officers, had little or no authority except that of enthusiasm and persuasion. The army often melted away before their eyes without any power on their part to stop the disbanding. In 1777 the Continental line was formed of men who enlisted for three years or for the war, and they constituted a small but somewhat steady nucleus, round which the militia squads could rally. The militia served for six or three months, or a few weeks. It was a "come-and-go" army; and Graydon tells us that the officers as well as the men felt that they could leave with impunity when they were dissatisfied.

The rifle companies were rapidly recruited in Pennsylvania and Virginia during July, and as each company got ready it started for Boston, and for several weeks these hardy fellows were scattered along the beautiful route through the mountainous region of Pennsylvania and New York, crossing the Hudson above West Point, thence through another mountainous region by Litchfield, Connecticut, and on through Massachusetts. Their first destination was Reading, in Pennsylvania, where they received their blankets, knapsacks, and ammunition. These supplies were all they required from the patriot government, and when these were furnished they immediately sought the enemy.

Their expectations from the long range of their weapons were partially realized. The rifle companies did good service, their numbers were increased, and we hear of them in almost every battle. Besides those already mentioned, there was a corps of them under McCall, another under Wills, and there were numerous temporary organizations. The British also had a few riflemen, but the rifle was not generally adopted by the military profession until about one hundred years afterwards, when the breech-loader came into use. As a muzzle-loader it was too slow in reloading, and required more care and skill than could be had from the ordinary recruit. To insure accurate and long range the bullet had to be carefully wrapped in a leather patch and forced with difficulty into the muzzle, often aided by a little mallet. The weapon was also easily fouled by repeated firing, and would then lose its range and accuracy, and become almost useless.

At Boston the riflemen seem to have done little or nothing except to pick off an occasional regular who incautiously showed himself above the line of fortifications round Bunker Hill. For the rest of the time they were inactive with the others. One day they picked off an officer in his handsome uniform, and the report quickly spread that this man's income had been £10,000 a year. On another occasion William Simpson, who had accompanied the riflemen as a gentleman volunteer, was shot in the foot and died of his wound. They had a grand funeral over him, and eulogized and mourned for him as though he had been a statesman. Incidents were few in that long summer and autumn, and they had to make the most of anything that happened.

It must have been a rare sight to see that patriot army living in huts made of field stones and turf, or twisted green boughs, some in improvised tents made of sail-cloth or any stuff they could stretch over poles; some quartered in friendly houses, some sleeping in Massachusetts Hall of Harvard College; and all the supposed sixteen thousand scattered in this manner through Cambridge and half round Boston, with the patient Washington and the humorous Greene trying to coax them to submit to discipline. General Greene was a Quaker from Rhode Island; there were many jokes at his expense, and Washington made a point of referring to him all suggestions of peace.

There was cannonading almost every day from the British. Thousands of balls and shells were fired during the summer with the most trifling result. The ground was ploughed up, the apples came rattling down in the orchards as the big missiles thumped the trees and the shells spluttered among the limbs. Occasionally a ball would pass through a house, filling every room and the plates and dishes with a cloud of plaster-dust.

McCurtin tells us of a loyalist who, being, one evening, the only man in company with a number of young patriot women, began to abuse the Congress. The girls seized him, tore off his coat and shirt, and instead of tar, covered him to the waist with molasses, and for feathers took the downy tops of flags that grew in the garden.

Patriots deserted to the British, and regulars deserted from the army in Boston and came into the Cambridge camp in twos or threes. Sometimes they had to swim the water which surrounded Boston, and were not infrequently drowned in the attempt. McCurtin kept a steady record of their arrivals, and they were heartily welcomed to the patriot ranks, which were believed to be growing to such stupendous numbers that they would soon be able to overwhelm all the armies that could be sent from England.

There seems to have been a systematic exaggeration of numbers at this time, as well as later on, in the Revolution. It could not be very well prevented, because the officers were quite willing to have it so. There was much coming and going, and consequently an apparent increase, because some of the men were returning to their farms, and others were coming in to take their places.

The best instance of the exaggeration is a passage in McCurtin's "Journal," of September 20: "This day also our army is computed to be above 60,000, and that we have taken and killed of the regulars 2500." This was a very gross exaggeration. The army was never above 16,000, and as soon as autumn came it quickly decreased to less than 10,000.

It was an army in which, in most instances, you could not distinguish the captain or the colonel from his men; an army in which there were applications every day for leave to go home to help get in the hay, or to see how the wife was getting on; and, if leave were granted, the fellow always took his allotment of powder with him to shoot squirrels, and he seldom brought any of the powder back. Shaving was more universal than now, and the greatest fuss was made over it. It was believed that it could be made a good starting-point for regular discipline, and a colonel was sometimes seen shaving one of his men.

\*  \*  \*  \*  \*

It is always very easy, however, to ridicule the appearance of a rebel army. No army of freedom or independence was ever well dressed. There was plenty of good fighting material at Cambridge. Daniel Morgan, the commander of the Virginia riflemen, was one of those frontier characters of superb manhood and intelligence, of which we have, fortunately, had many specimens down into our own time; but with another generation they will have all passed away. He was not appreciated by the Congress, but at the close of the war he showed remarkable military capacity. He was a powerful-looking man, and capable of arousing the enthusiasm of his men.

General Putnam, or "Old Put," as they called him, the hero of the French War, was the life of the camps. In his shirtsleeves, which was his usual summer garb, with an old hanger slung by a broad strap across his brawny shoulders, he was to be seen everywhere, and he was clamorous to have a fight every day. People listened by the hour to the tales of his cutting-out expeditions and adventures. The troops who believed in levelling could have no objection to him as an officer, for he was a plain jovial farmer. When the Boston Port Bill went into effect he started from his farm in Connecticut with one hundred and thirty sheep, driving them before him to Boston to relieve the suffering of the people.

There is no mention of any colors or flags carried by the farmer troops at Cambridge, and possibly they had none. A flag for the patriot cause had been designed about this time, and was used soon afterwards. It had on it a pinetree and a coiled rattlesnake about to strike, with the motto, "Don't tread on me." It was a good enough pirate's or smuggler's flag, the loyalists said; a very proper red rag of rebellion, undignified, crude, with the snake as the emblem of low cunning, ingratitude, and treachery. Paul Jones was so disgusted with it that he was hardly willing to hoist it on his ship. The stars and stripes were not designed until nearly two years afterwards.

*     *     *     *     *

The patriot military forces at New York, when General Howe first arrived, were only about ten thousand. His delay of nearly two months allowed them the opportunity to increase this number. Enthusiasm and rumors soon had their numbers up to forty-five thousand or fifty thousand. It had seemed to both the patriots and their Congress that before long they must surely have that number. Many expected more. But by the actual returns made by Washington, his forces, all told, were only 20,275. Of these the sick were so numerous that those fit for duty were only about fourteen thousand. The large sick-list was apparently the result of shocking unsanitary conditions, which for long afterwards were characteristic of the patriot camps; and in winter they were always afflicted with the small pox. Besides disease which was so prevalent among them, they were a most badly armed, undisciplined, disorderly rabble, marauding on the inhabitants and committing all kinds of irregularities. Except a few troops, like Smallwood's Marylanders, they were for the most part merely a collection of squads of farmers and militia bringing with them the guns they had had in their houses.

It was no longer exclusively a New England army. It contained numerous troops from the middle and southern colonies, and its size may be said to have indicated the high-water mark of the rebellion, under the influence of the Declaration of Independence, and the belief that a great victory had been gained some months before by compelling Howe to evacuate Boston. It was the largest number of patriots that were collected in one army during the whole war. To handle such a disorganized mob so as to offer any respectable resistance to Howe's superb army was a task requiring qualities of homely, cautious patience and judgment which few men besides Washington possessed. John Jay, General Charles Lee, and others believed that no attempt should be made to hold New York. The risk of an overwhelming defeat was too great. In fact, the general patriot plan for that summer of 1776 was to wear it away with as little loss as possible.

It was a delicate question to decide, and no doubt a great deal could be said in favor of making a present of New York to the British without a battle; allowing them to lock themselves up there, and reserving the patriot force to check their subsequent expeditions. But Washington seems to have been influenced by a principle of conduct on which he frequently acted. He must make some sort of resistance to Howe's entering New York if the rebellion and its army was to retain any reputation. He also wished to delay Howe so that after settling in New York he could make but few expeditions into the country before winter.

Washington was obliged to use nearly half of his effective force in the fortifications and in guarding various points in the town. The most important place to defend was Brooklyn Heights, on the Long Island side of the East River, directly opposite New York, and commanding it very much as Bunker Hill or Dorchester Heights commanded Boston. If Howe took Brooklyn Heights, he had the city. Washington accordingly sent across to these heights some eight thousand of his men under Putnam, who made rough intrenchments of earth and fallen trees.

These eight thousand men were, of course, in a trap, for if Howe attacked them in front, their chance of escaping across the river was doubtful, and he could absolutely prevent it by sending the fleet into the river behind them. Military critics have commented on this risk, and the only answer is that, under all the circumstances, Washington thought himself justified in taking the chances rather than abandon New York without a blow.

General Howe proceeded to dispose of the patriots on Brooklyn Heights, and he showed the same perfect knowledge of the ground and of the enemy opposed to him which he afterwards displayed at Brandywine. He also showed his skill in winning easily so far as it suited his purpose to win.

He had remained on Staten Island from his arrival on the 30th of June until the 22nd of August, when he took across to Long Island about twenty thousand of his men, a force which was certainly ample for defeating the eight thousand Americans on Brooklyn Heights.

Between Brooklyn Heights and the place where Howe had landed on Long Island there was a wooded ridge, and a large part of the patriot force, leaving their breastworks at Brooklyn Heights, went out on this ridge to check the advance of Howe's army. Their right was commanded by William Alexander, of New Jersey,—or Lord Sterling, as he was called from a lapsed Scotch title which he had ineffectually claimed,—and their left was commanded by Sullivan, of New Hampshire. This movement in force to the ridge has been criticized as risking too much, because the army was not organized or officered, and had not the sort of troops necessary for advanced positions.

Several roads led directly from Howe's position to the ridge and to Brooklyn Heights. On the night of August 27 he sent nearly half his force by these roads,—Grant on the left along the shore and Heister with the Hessians on the right. Taking the rest of his force under his own personal command, Howe, with Clinton and Cornwallis, went by another road far to the eastward, and, making a long detour, came upon the American flank and rear just as the battle was beginning with the regulars and Hessians, who had come by the direct roads. The timing of the movement was most exact and successful, and the patriots, as usually happened, had no means of obtaining information or detecting a movement of this sort.

Sullivan's division, which had Howe on its flank and rear and the Hessians in front, were nearly all killed or taken prisoners. Sullivan was taken hiding in a field of corn. Alexander's division, composed of Delaware troops and Smallwood's famous Marylanders, made a most desperate and heroic stand for four hours against the regulars under Grant, and succeeded in escaping back to the fortifications at Brooklyn Heights, but with heavy loss in killed and prisoners, and Alexander was captured.

Among the prisoners, Graydon tells us, was one of the famous Connecticut cavalrymen armed with a long duckgun, who was compelled to amble about for the amusement of the British army. When asked what his duties had been, he is said to have replied, "To flank a little and carry tidings."

Clinton, Cornwallis, and Vaughan all urged Howe to pursue the rebels at once into their intrenchments, and the common soldiers were with difficulty restrained from pressing on. He admitted that the intrenchments might be easily taken, but declined to take them in that way. He thanked his officers for their zeal and advice, said enough had been done for one day, and that the intrenchments could be taken by regular approaches with less loss.

The battle was a curious one, because it now largely depended upon the direction of the wind. It had apparently been intended to use the men-of-war, and possibly send them into the East River behind Brooklyn Heights. But the wind was northeast, and after beating against it they were compelled to anchor when the tide turned; and only one vessel, the "Roebuck," exchanged shots with Red Hook.

Possibly Howe expected that in making his approaches the next day the fleet would co-operate with him, go around into East River, and entrap the force at Brooklyn. But the wind continued from the northeast with rain. Washington crossed over to Brooklyn Heights, raising the force there to possibly ten thousand men. He remained there all that day, evidently believing that as long as the wind blew northeast he was safe. The next day the wind and rain continued, but the British were pushing their approaches, and Washington was unwilling to trust to Providence any longer. He collected boats, and that night, although it became bright moonlight, he slipped all his men safely across to New York, although, according to Stedman, Howe knew of the movement in time to have prevented it.

Instead of following up his advantage, as a policy of severity would require, Howe now remained on Long Island for over two weeks. The patriots were astonished. When he finally entered New York he allowed the patriot army plenty of opportunity to evacuate the town, and made no attempt to hem them in on the narrow island. Landing near what is now Thirty-third Street, he occupied the high ground between Fifth and Sixth Avenues and Thirty-fifth and Thirty-eighth Streets. Most of the Americans had escaped northward, but Putnam was still within the town with four thousand men. He also escaped northward by the Bloomingdale road, passing within sight of the British right wing unmolested, while Howe and some of his officers were lunching with Mrs. Robert Murray at that part of New York still known as Murray Hill.

Mrs. Murray was a patriot, and, as the pretty story goes, invited Howe to lunch for the purpose of delaying him and saving Putnam's force; or, at any rate, her offer of lunch and entertainment, as we are solemnly informed by historical writers, is supposed to have had that effect. But that Howe and the officers with him and all the other officers who were not at the lunch were deceived in this way is absolutely incredible. There must have been an intention to move easily and give the patriots every chance. The lunch at the patriot house and the jokes that are said to have passed at the table were a part of the conciliatory method thus far adopted by the ministry or by Howe. They appear to have thought that under this method the movement for independence would finally collapse; but under modern British methods Mrs. Murray would have been captured and locked up in a reconcentrado camp.

But why detail all the extraordinary care and pains Howe took at this time? Must he do what the Whigs had said was impossible—namely, crush the rebellion? Had he not instructions from the ministry to be lenient and hold out the olive-branch? The peace negotiations were renewed by the admiral, and this time he addressed himself directly to the Congress through General Sullivan, who had been taken prisoner. The Congress allowed an informal committee to meet the admiral on Staten Island, where he entertained them at lunch in a rustic bower of branches. But as his peace powers extended no farther than the issuing of full pardon on return to allegiance and obedience, nothing could be accomplished. He afterwards issued a proclamation containing vague promises or intimations that in return for obedience all objectionable acts of Parliament would be repealed. As a Whig he undoubtedly intended to accomplish a settlement which would give him the reputation of having solved the American problem and be very advantageous both to the patriots and to his own party in Parliament. He seems to have believed that if the ministry had given him proper authority he could have settled the question by conversation with the leading patriots. He had tried hard to get from the ministry sufficient authority for that purpose, and delayed his departure from England for two months in the hope of obtaining it.

After escaping from New York, Washington's army went no farther than to the upper end of the island, where, at Harlem Heights, along the Harlem River, he fortified himself in a strong position. He could be forced from that position or entrapped within the narrow strip of land on which he was if a British force went round behind him to the north. Howe started to entrap him in this way, and both Lafayette and Stedman agree in saying that Washington would have remained in the trap had it not been for General Charles Lee, who urged him to go out to White Plains, from which it was easier to retreat.

Howe confronted him there on October 28 and took by storm a small American outpost on Chatterton Hill. But he would not attack Washington's main force, although, in the opinion of most people, he had a chance to inflict on it irreparable damage. He admitted in his "Narrative" that he could have inflicted some damage, but would not tell why he refrained, except to say that he had "political reasons and no other for declining to explain," and his confidential friend, Cornwallis, when questioned before the committee of inquiry, made the same enigmatical statement. We are therefore left to the inference that he was either trying to bring about a compromise by lack of severity or that he was determined to stop just short of crushing the rebellion and prove the Whig position that the rebellion was unconquerable.

The patriots still held Fort Washington, on the Hudson, two and a half miles below King's Bridge. Washington was in favor of abandoning it, but between the bungling of the Congress and General Greene it was retained and reinforced.

It was not really a fort, but an open earthwork without a ditch or outside obstruction of any consequence, and with high ground in its rear. It had no barracks, casemates, fuel, or water. The troops that were supposed to be holding it found that they could protect themselves better by remaining outside of it. But it was decided to retain it against the British for the sake of inspiriting the patriot cause, and the New Englanders, Graydon complains, were quite willing to see the Southern troops, some 3000 Pennsylvanians and Marylanders, sacrificed in the attempt.

There was desultory fighting round them for many days, and Graydon's descriptions are interesting. There was the patriot lad of eighteen who killed a regular and brought in his shining, beautiful arms, such a contrast to the brown and battered American weapons; and those shining arms were with much ceremony formally presented to the boy at evening parade. There was the sergeant who killed a British officer, stripped him of his uniform and wore it like a glittering peacock in the patriot camp. Graydon describes the British soldiers as absurdly bad marksmen. They threw up their guns with a jerking motion and pulled the trigger the instant the gun reached the shoulder. Ten of them fired at him within forty yards and missed him.

Fort Washington was practically within Howe's lines. He took it because it was almost thrust upon him, and he had also the advantage of one of its garrison deserting and revealing all its approaches. So he plucked the ripe plum, almost ready to drop into his lap, with trifling loss on either side, and had another large batch of ragged prisoners for the amusement of his officers.

Graydon, who was one of them, gives most vivid descriptions of the scenes. They were threatened with the butts of guns, reminded that they would be hung, and, cursing them for "damned rebels," mock orders were given to kill prisoners. The patriots had any sort of clothes and accoutrements they could get, and some of their equipments had once been the property of the British government. Graydon had a belt with the British army marks G.R. stamped upon it; and as soon as this was recognized it was wrenched from him with violence.

The officers surrounded them in crowds, and were as much amused as they had been in Canada at the inferior social condition of the patriot captains and lieutenants. As the names were written down there were shouts of laughter at each tattered farmer who announced that he was a captain, or "keppun," as one of them pronounced it. Young officers, insolent young puppies, anxious to show that they were soldiers, were continually coming up to curse the captives in affected Billingsgate, and to parade them over and over again under the pretence of looking for deserters.

Fort Lee, on the other side of the Hudson, was untenable, and the rebels abandoned it as they should have abandoned the so-called Fort Washington. It was a terrible clearing-out and wiping-up for the supporters of independence. In spite of all his restraint, Howe was accomplishing more than he intended. The great size of his army and the two battles it fought at Long Island and Fort Washington so demoralized the patriots that their force was cut in half and was melting away. Lee was on the east side of the Hudson, with 7000, soon reduced by desertions to 4000. He refused, though repeatedly requested, to join Washington, who, having retreated into New Jersey, was now falling back towards the Delaware.

Washington wished to keep himself between Howe and Philadelphia, which every one now supposed would be taken by the British. Washington, however, could not have offered any real resistance to a movement against Philadelphia, because as he kept retreating his force dwindled until, when he crossed the Delaware, he had only 3300 men.

This retreat through New Jersey brought another storm of abuse upon Howe from the loyalists and Tories. They could not understand why Washington and his handful of men were not all captured or destroyed long before they reached Trenton.

\*     \*     \*     \*     \*

Howe had gone so far in his plans as to conquer New York and New Jersey, and thousands of people who had been hesitating now came in and took the British oath of allegiance. They had been for the rebellion if it should succeed; but they could now see nothing but futile wickedness in prolonging such a struggle and the sacrifice of life and property to the patriotic sentiment that it was better to die than to live political slaves.

It seems probable that Howe expected some sort of voluntary peace or compromise which would show that the colonies could be retained without subjugation, as Burke and Chatham supposed was possible. His successes, as he afterwards put it in his "Narrative," "had very nearly induced a general submission."

But to loyalists like Galloway the waiting for peace seemed to give the rebels a chance to recuperate. It seemed as if Howe purposely refused to move again until Washington had a sufficient number of men to meet him. Months passed away before Washington was able to collect ten thousand men, and nearly a year after, and as late as September, 1777, he had only eleven thousand with which to fight the battle of the Brandywine. He never again got together as many as he had had at New York.

Settled down in New York with Mrs. Loring and cards for the winter, Howe made no effort to wear out the scattered patriot commands or to complete and make permanent his conquest. He never did anything in winter. The three winters he spent in repressing the rebellion were passed in great luxury in the three principal cities, Boston, New York, and Philadelphia, waiting for a voluntary peace. It would have been Charleston's turn next.

Before settling down in New York he sent, on December 8, some six thousand troops to occupy Newport, Rhode Island. His great army of nearly thirty thousand was larger than the population of New York, and filled the houses, churches, and public buildings, crowding out alike both the loyalist and the rebel, spreading out into the suburbs and cutting down the woodlands for miles in every direction to supply fuel. Fine old mansions, and the neat, pretty houses of the thrifty, where domestic morals had prevailed, were filled with trulls, doxeys, little misses, dulcineas, and all the other female followers of the armies in that age.

Before returning from Trenton, on December 13, he adopted a plan for keeping possession of his great conquest of New Jersey. He placed a cantonment of troops at Amboy, near New York, one at New Brunswick, another at Princeton, and two cantonments of fifteen hundred Hessians each at Trenton and Bordentown on the Delaware. The cantonments at Trenton and Bordentown were six miles apart; Trenton was twelve miles from the small force at Princeton, and New Brunswick eighteen miles from Princeton. Such weak outposts as Trenton and Bordentown, so far away from support and from the main army in New York on the other side of the Hudson, were tempting objects of attack, and Washington prepared to destroy them.

The Hessians at Trenton were under the command of Colonel Rall, who was drunk most of the time, could speak no English, had no fortifications for his men, and allowed them to plunder and disaffect the inhabitants. The fifteen hundred Hessians at Bordentown were under Count Donop, and seem to have been intended to cover the neighboring town of Burlington.

Washington collected the remains of Lee's force, which, together with his own and some sent down from Lake Champlain, gave him six thousand men, which represented all there was left of fighting enthusiasm in the patriot population. It was only by the greatest persuasion that he kept this small force together, for the enlistments of many of them were expiring. Artists and sculptors represent these troops as dressed in handsome uniforms. But those who saw them agree in describing them as dressed in ragged summer clothes, with their shoes so worn that the frozen roads cut their bare feet. Their camps along the Delaware were filled with loyalists and spies, for most of the people in that region were lukewarm or hostile, had given up the rebellion as hopeless, and thought that the best plan was to make some sort of peace with Howe.

Washington divided his force into three divisions, which were to cross the Delaware through the floating ice at about the same time. One under Cadwalader was to go against Donop at Bordentown, another under Ewing was to cross directly in front of Trenton, and the third, of 2500 men, which Washington himself commanded, was to cross above Trenton.

Crossing the Delaware through the floating ice was cold and unpleasant but not dangerous work. If the ice was floating loosely the passage could be made, but if the pieces were closely packed together by the tide, boats could not be forced through them. Where Washington himself crossed, above the influence of the tide, the ice appears to have been floating loosely. It was Christmas night, cold, and at eleven o'clock a northeast snow-storm began, which became sleet before morning. It was severe exposure for patriots with ragged summer clothes and worn-out shoes; but the darkness, the storm, and the Christmas carousing of the Hessians were well suited to Washington's purpose. He marched quietly down upon Trenton, where the drunken Rall, though warned through the numerous loyalists and spies of the intended attack, allowed himself to be taken by surprise, was mortally wounded, and most of his men were made prisoners.

The other divisions seem to have found the ice jammed by the tide, for they failed to cross that night. But the next day Cadwalader crossed at Burlington, to find that Donop had retreated. The Hessian prisoners were sent to Philadelphia to be paraded in triumph. It was a great success, and the first event which impressed upon Europeans the ability of Washington to seize an opportunity.

Washington immediately fell back to the Pennsylvania side of the river, but finding no vigorous movement made from New York, he recrossed and again occupied Trenton. The appearance, however, of Cornwallis with 8000 men compelled him to abandon Trenton and cross a creek immediately south of the town, where he encamped for the night. Cornwallis might have shut him in against the Delaware and the creek and captured him; but he postponed this until the next morning. It was a narrow escape for Washington, and as Clinton remarked, rather extraordinary conduct on the part of Cornwallis.

During the night Washington left his camp-fire burning and men working noisily on intrenchments, and with the rest of his little force, passing out through the way Cornwallis had left unguarded, performed the brilliant manoeuvre of marching to the rear of that general towards New York. He had made up his mind that he could penetrate into the interior of New Jersey, and attack Princeton and possibly New Brunswick without any interference from Howe. The men who now followed him were comparatively few, and not supported by the surrounding population, but they were the enthusiasts of the rights of man, the desperate and determined element of the patriot party; and the roads to Princeton were marked with blood from their naked, frost-bitten feet.

He reached Princeton about daybreak, where three regiments of British reinforcements were starting out to join Cornwallis at Trenton. One of them, under Colonel Mawhood, followed by part of another regiment, passed out of Princeton on Washington's left as he entered by another road. Seeing the Americans enter the village, Mawhood turned back and attacked Mercer's brigade. Mercer was mortally wounded, and the brigade in danger of retreating, when Washington rode to its head and led the men to within thirty yards of Mawhood's regiment, which was repulsed, and went on to join Cornwallis at Trenton. The other regiment and a half fought for a while in the streets of Princeton, but were compelled by the superior numbers of the Americans to retreat to New York.

The battle of Princeton was a small affair. The engagement with Mawhood is said to have lasted hardly twenty minutes; and the troops engaged in that affair and in the fighting in the streets of Princeton were only about 2000 British against some 4000 or 5000 Americans. But, coupled with Trenton as part of a sudden success in the midst of overwhelming defeat, it aroused great rejoicing among the friends of the patriots in Europe, and deserves all that has been said of it. It was brilliant work on the part of Washington, in a time of utter hopelessness, when the belief was becoming general that the only safe place for the patriot party was on the other side of the Alleghany Mountains.

Howe, with his army of 28,000, now quietly allowed Washington to reconquer New Jersey with 5000. After the battle at Princeton Cornwallis abandoned Trenton, Bordentown, and Princeton, removed all the British troops from them, and quietly returned to New Brunswick. Washington found that there would be too much risk in attacking New Brunswick immediately after Princeton, so he passed on northward into the heart of New Jersey, and took up a strong position at Morristown Heights, west of New York, and half-way between New York and Delaware. Putnam came from Philadelphia with a few troops and occupied Princeton, and Heath had a few more on the Hudson. In other words, Washington, with scarcely 10,000 men, made a line of cantonments through New Jersey and held it without opposition from Howe's 28,000 all that winter and the following spring until June, 1777.

He was constantly picking off stragglers from the British posts at New Brunswick and Amboy, and, as Galloway remarked, killed more regulars in that way than Howe would have lost by surrounding and defeating or starving him out at Morristown. In March Washington's force had sunk to less than 3000 effectives, and yet he remained undisturbed by the vast force in New York.

Washington had taken Howe's measure. For the rest of the British general's year and a half in America, the patriot general, no matter how low his force dwindled, always remained encamped within a few miles of the vast host of his Whig antagonist undisturbed and unpursued. There was no need of retreating among the Indians and the buffalo of the West.

When we think of the measures of relentless severity and slaughter, the persistent and steady hunting down of the men, the concentration camps for the gradual destruction of the women and children, which we have known England to use in our time to destroy all hope of independence, the extraordinary conduct of Howe is difficult to explain except by the method which his loyalist critics adopted.

That was a marvellous winter in New York with a gorgeously caparisoned army far outnumbering the population of the town, and crowding the poor, devoted loyalists out of their houses. Judge Jones was there, and he has left us a graphic and indignant description of what happened in this and the following year.

The commissaries, quartermasters, barrack-masters, engineers, and their assistants and followers, were making prodigious fortunes by the most wholesale fraud. The loyalists about New York had supplied the invading army with horses and wagons in the campaign of 1776, and were cheated out of their payment. In the campaign of 1777 they again supplied the horses and wagons, and were again defrauded. The quartermaster, Judge Jones says, netted for himself £150,000 out of that campaign and retired to England a rich man. His successor made another fortune. During the seven years of the war, our quartermasters in succession returned with fortunes varying from £150,000 to £200,000. These were enormous sums in those times, fully the equivalent of three million dollars in our own day. The fifth quartermaster was stopped half-way on his road to a fortune by the arrival of Sir Guy Carleton to take command in 1782.

Howe's favorite engineer received for merely levelling the rebel fortifications about New York a fortune, with which he retired and bought a town house and a country-seat. His successor was given greater opportunities. The barrack-masters seized private houses, public buildings, and churches, for which, of course, they paid nothing, and rented them to the army. They cut down the oak and hickory forests all round New York and for sixty miles along the Sound, selling two-thirds of a cord to the army at the price of a cord, sixteen to twenty-eight shillings, and selling the fraudulently reserved third to the loyalists at £4 and £5 for two-thirds of a cord. Like the quartermasters and engineers, they too became nabobs of the West. And then there were commissaries of forage, commissaries of cattle, and commissaries of artillery, not to mention the commissaries of prisoners, together with all their dependents, male and female, who enjoyed a perfect carnival of plunder and wealth.

❧ ☙

*It has been written that the pen is mightier than the sword. The American Revolution does not necessarily prove the accuracy of the aphorism, but it did produce a remarkable literature. The Revolutionary fathers seemed unable to dip their pens without producing a quotable phrase. Thus John Adams wrote in the aftermath of the Declaration of Independence, "Every Post and every Day rolls in upon us Independence like a Torrent." But no more eloquent summation of the structure of assumptions upon which American independence was constructed exists than Jefferson's preamble to his Declaration. The self-evident truths stated, as Jefferson remembered them almost half a century later, the accepted sense of the matter. Building their revolution on a set of fixed values, propositions that set forth the innate value of the individual, and the no less emphatic belief that governments are made to serve, not to master, these men committed the new republic to support the institution of "new governments," whenever the status quo impinged upon the happiness and welfare of the governed.*

*It is the Revolutionary tradition that Moses Coit Tyler wrote about. He described it as "literary history," and so it was, for the men who wrote about the American Revolution did so with a passion that transmuted deep-felt sentiments into a poetry that time has not dimmed. Long after the battles had been entombed in monuments, the words remained fresh, a goad to conscience when the heir of the Revolution strays from its path. For however the purpose of the Revolution is defined, no one has done it more eloquently than Thomas Paine. He wrote, "We fight not to enslave, but to set a country free, and to make room upon the earth for honest men to live in."*

*Moses Coit Tyler (1835-1900) was one of those nineteenth-century historians whose career reads as if he were a jack-of-all-trades. New England born, he graduated from Yale in 1857. During the Civil War, he served as a pastor of a Congregational Church in Poughkeepsie, New York. Afterward he was professor of English literature at the University of Michigan from 1867 to 1881, but in 1881, he accepted appointment as professor of American history at Cornell, a post he held until his death. In the decade before his death, he was active in the organization of the American Historical Association.*

# THE LITERARY HISTORY OF THE AMERICAN REVOLUTION
## 1763-1783

### by Moses Coit Tyler

Samuel Adams was, indeed, a man of letters, but he was so only because he was above all things a man of affairs. Of literary art, in certain forms, he was no mean master: of literary art for art's sake, he was entirely regardless. He was perhaps the most voluminous political writer of his time in America, and the most influential political writer of his time in New England; but everything that he wrote was meant for a definite practical purpose, and nothing that he wrote seemed to have had any interest for him aside from that purpose. Accordingly, as has been said by his latest biographer, "like cannon balls which sink the ship, and then are lost in the sea, so the bolts of Samuel Adams, after riddling British authority in America, must be sought by diving beneath the oblivion that has rolled over them."

Deep as is the obscurity which has fallen upon his literary services in the cause of the Revolution, the fame of those services was, at the time of them, almost unrivaled by that of any other writer, at least in the colonies east of the Hudson River. So early as the year 1765, John Adams spoke of him, among a group of brilliant and accomplished men, as having "the most correct, genteel, and artful pen" of any of them. In the year 1774, he again pointed out Samuel Adams as "the most elegant writer" who had figured in America in his time. In the year 1768, James Otis, with his usual amplitude of assertion, publicly declared "that there was not a person in England capable of composing so elegant, so pure, and so nervous a writing," as a certain state paper by Samuel Adams then recently given to the public. The one man among his contemporaries who had the most occasion to know and to dread the literary skill of Samuel Adams, bore witness to the fact that, though he was at first but an indifferent writer, yet "long practice caused him to arrive at great perfection, and to acquire a talent of artfully and fallaciously insinuating into the minds of his readers a prejudice against the character of all whom he attacked, beyond any other man I ever knew." "Damn that Adams," groaned Governor Bernard; "every dip of his pen stings like horned snake." A Loyalist writer in the year 1775 spoke facetiously of Samuel Adams as "a sachem of vast elocution," and then added with more seriousness—"what proceeds from the mouth of Adams, is sufficient to fill the mouths of millions in America."

Born in Boston in 1722, graduated at Harvard in 1740, he early showed an invincible passion and aptitude for politics. Though both orthodox and devout, he was disinclined to the ministry. Though fond of the discussion of politico-legal questions, he was easily dissuaded from the study of the law. Enrolled as a merchant's clerk in his native town, he had no difficulty, after a brief apprenticeship, in securing a release from his employer, who naïvely explained that young Adams "would never do for a merchant," as "his whole soul was engrossed by politics." Having been by his father set up in trade, with a capital of a thousand pounds, he proved himself to be so much more apt at parting with his goods than at getting pay for them, that he soon had nothing left of what his father had given him. Being then taken as a partner into his father's business—that of a brewer—and being upon his father's death in 1758 made his successor in the business, he continued to concern himself so much with the affairs of the state house and so little with those of the malt house, that even the petty revenue to be derived from the office of tax collector for the town of Boston,—an office which he held from 1756 to 1764,—became a matter of convenience to him.

In the meantime, the man whom his enemies had already nicknamed "Samuel the Maltster," and "Samuel the Publican," was far advanced in that line of activity which subsequently earned for him the additional titles of "Arch-Manager," "Man of the Town Meeting," "Father of Democracy," "Grand Incendiary," "Cromwell of New England," and "Man of the Revolution." The one title, however, which perhaps best describes him, as being free alike from sarcasm and from panegyric, is one which seems never to have been given to him—that of Citizen. It was simply as a citizen—it was in the exercise of the rights and duties of the free and fearless civic character—that he found his true vocation. Moreover, under the peculiar conditions of his time, the most important function of citizenship seemed to him to be that of criticism, opposition, destruction. For precisely that function he was supremely endowed,—he was the incomparable leader of his fellow-citizens in the development of astute, far-reaching, and masterly measures of destructive statesmanship. At the moment when the business of constructive statesmanship became the chief function in the emancipated commonwealth, the work of Samuel Adams was done.

Even his thrifty fellow-townsmen, who perhaps nodded their heads at his thriftless ways in all matters pertaining to his own business, could not fail to note his singular appetence for the business of the public—his readiness to think and write and speak and plot and otherwise to toil, in order that the interests of the public should receive no harm. And nothing that affected the public interests was too inconsiderable for him to engage in—

if the public so desired. In the records of the town of Boston—as we are told by a writer who has turned them over with this subject in view—one finds the name of Samuel Adams so early as 1753 as a patient plodder in town business; and "scarcely a year passes from that date until the town meetings cease, crushed out by the battalions of Gage, when his name does not appear in connections becoming constantly more honorable,"—from membership of committees to see that chimneys are properly inspected, and that precautions are taken against the spread of small-pox, to member-ship of committees to instruct the town's representatives in the assembly. Finally, in September, 1765, in the fever-heat of opposition to the Stamp Act, he himself became one of the town's representatives in the assembly; and from about that time, until 1774, when he was sent to represent Massa-chusetts in the Continental Congress, he was the real director of the policy of opposition in the eastern colonies. In the assembly of Massachusetts no other member could rival him in minute knowledge of the rules and business of the house, in laborious devotion to its work, in steadiness, endurance, tact, shrewdness, persuasiveness, and in the not very noble art of manipulat-ing committees and caucuses; and while some other men—notably James Otis and John Adams—were far more brilliant in debate, not even their dashing and dazzling speeches could win votes as did the brief, unadorned, informing, and convincing talks of Samuel Adams.

It is easy to see, also, that his political influence was vastly increased by the evident purity of his character, his disinterestedness as to pecuniary gain, and his unassuming ways. He began to illustrate democratic simplicity and democratic friendliness, long before Jefferson was old enough to know the meaning of those words. Seated on a log by the side of some caulker in the shipyard, or pausing on a street corner for leisurely and confidential discourse with any cobbler or hod carrier who should care to spend his time in that way, he won extraordinary affection from his fellow-townsmen by his evident willingness to impart to the humblest of them the political fears, and hopes, and aims, which possessed his own soul respecting the commonwealth. In his concern for the interests of the public, he was "for-getful of the ordinary pursuits which occupy the minds of men. . . . He was truly and really contented with poverty"; so that, in his old age, he could say, proudly, that "a guinea had never glistened in his eyes." Abste-mious, untiring, unswerving, he seemed never to care who had the credit of his measures—if only his measures had success. "He eats little," wrote his chief antagonist in the Congress of 1774, "drinks little, sleeps little, thinks much, and is most decisive and indefatigable in the pursuit of his objects." So great became his ascendancy over the people, that, as one of his biog-raphers declares, "in the stormiest days preceding the outbreak of the war, it was common among the vulgar and uneducated to assert that he was actually gifted with prophecy, and not a few believed that he held peace or war in his keeping." In 1771, Hutchinson reprobated this Boston politi-cian as "an incendiary equal to any at present in London." Two years afterward, in a private letter to Lord Dartmouth, Hutchinson explained at length the methods by which Samuel Adams had made himself so powerful and so dangerous: "Whenever there appears a disposition to any conciliatory measures, this person, by his art and skill, prevents any effect; sometimes by exercising his talents in the newspapers; . . . at other times by an open opposition, and this sometimes in the house, where he has defeated every attempt as often as any has been made. But his chief dependence is upon a Boston town meeting, where he originates his measures, which are followed of course by the rest of the towns, and of course are adopted or justified by the assembly." By the year 1774, his reputation had become so great in England that, according to Josiah Quincy, many people there considered him "the first politician in the world." It was not without reason that in the royal offers of amnesty to the American rebels in case of their repentance, no place for repentance was left for one who was probably the first to avow the doctrine of American Independence, and who, next to the British ministry itself, was probably the most influential in securing its adoption. Even though a disinterested student may abate somewhat from the extreme assertions made on his behalf by recent eulogists of Samuel Adams, it is a clear token of the immense influence he had upon political and military events in America, especially between 1765 and 1776, that it is now possible for reasonable men to claim for him that he was the first to deny all legislative authority of parliament over the colonies, as well as the first to suggest the leading measures made necessary by such denial,—intercolonial union, committees of correspondence, circular letters, the league for non-importation, and the establishment of an incipient national government under the title of the Continental Congress. Surely, of one who had an initial and a necessary part in the creation of a series of political devices so thorough-going and so epoch-making as were these, it is not altogether an extravagance to say—as has been said in our day by a masterly critic of those times—that, "in the history of the American Revolution," Samuel Adams "is second only to Washington."

It comports with the particular purpose of this book, to direct attention to the fact that one principal instrument by means of which Samuel Adams so greatly molded public opinion, and shaped political and even military procedure, was the pen. Of modern politicians, he was among the first to recognize the power of public opinion in directing public events, and likewise the power of the newspaper in directing public opinion. It was, therefore, an essential part of his method as a politician to acquire and to exercise the art of literary statement in a form suited to that particular end. He had the instinct of a great journalist, and of a great journalist willing to screen his individuality behind his journal. In this service, it was not Samuel Adams that Samuel Adams cared to put and to keep before the public,—it was the ideas of Samuel Adams. Accordingly, of all American writers for the newspapers between the years 1754 and 1776, he was perhaps the most vigilant, the most industrious, the most effective, and also, the least identified. Ever ready to efface himself in what he did, he realized that the innumerable productions of his pen would make their way to a far wider range of readers, and would be all the more influential, if they seemed to be the work, not of one writer, but of many. Therefore, he almost never published anything under his own name; but, under a multitude of titular disguises which no man has yet been able to number,—as "Alfred," "An American," "A Bostonian," "A Tory," "A Chatterer," "A Son of Liberty," "An Imperialist," "An Elector in 1771," "Valerius Poplicola," "A.," "A.B.," "E.A.," "Z.," "T.Z.," "Candidus," "Determinatus," "Sincerus," "Populus," "Cedant Arma Togae," "Principiis Obsta," "A Religious Politician," "A Layman," "Observation," "Shippen,"—this sleepless, crafty, protean politician, for nearly a third of a century, kept flooding the community with his ideas, chiefly in the form of essays in the newspapers,—thereby constantly baffling the enemies of the Revolutionary movement, and conducting his followers victoriously through those battles of argument which preceded and then for a time accompanied the battles of arms. "Some of his essays over one signature extend, in consecutive series, through several years,— the argument being maintained right and left with his various Loyalist assailants,—while, with different names, he kept up contests simultaneously with others of the crown writers on distinct subjects. All this time his pen was employed on the state papers of the legislature and other public bodies, and in his extensive correspondence with patriots in the other colonies and with gentlemen in England. . . . If published entire, together with the arguments of his antagonists, they would present a formidable array of controversial papers, embracing all the issues between Great Britain and the colonies, and showing the gradual progress of events which culminated in American Independence."

In the long line of his state papers—the official utterances of the several public bodies with which he was connected and which so long trusted him as their most deft and unerring penman—one may now trace, almost without a break, the development of the ideas and the measures which formed the Revolution. It was he who drafted, both in 1764 and in 1765, the instructions of the town of Boston to its representatives in the assembly; and in October, 1775, the assembly's answer to the governor's speech; and in 1768, the assembly's petition to the king, the assembly's letters to the chief members of the British ministry, the assembly's letter of instructions to its agent in London, and the assembly's circular letter to the Legislatures of the other colonies; in 1769, the remonstrance of the house of representatives to the governor, and the "Appeal to the World," sent forth by the town-meeting of Boston; in 1772, Boston's statement of the "Natural Rights of the Colonists as Men"; in 1773, the two answers of the house of representatives to the governor's speech on the authority of parliament, and the circular letter of the town of Boston to all its sister towns in Massachusetts; in 1774, the circular letter of the town of Boston and of its nearest neighbors to the committees of correspondence throughout all the colonies; in 1775, the address of the Continental Congress to the Mohawk Indians; in 1776, the resolves of Congress for the disarmament of the Tories; in 1778, the manifesto of congress against the barbarities practiced by their enemies in the conduct of the war; in 1779, an important portion of the new constitution of the State of Massachusetts, particularly the bill of rights, together with the address of the constitutional convention to the people of Massachusetts.

If we take into account the strain of thought and of emotional energy involved in all these years of fierce political controversy and of most perilous political leadership, we shall hardly fear to overestimate the resources of Samuel Adams in his true career of agitator and iconoclast;—especially the elasticity, the toughness, the persistence of a nature which could, in addition to all this, undertake and carry through, during the same long period, all the work he did in literary polemics,—work which alone might seem enough to employ and tire the strength even of a strong man who had nothing else to do. Some glimpse of the secret of his strength, and of his actual method while engaged in the forging of his politico-literary thunderbolts, is given us through a vivid picture of him as drawn by his great-grandson: "Frugal and temperate in his habits, his wants were few, and his powers of endurance fitted him for ceaseless industry. Most of his public papers were written in a study or library adjoining his bedroom; and his wife, after his death, related how, in the stillness of the night, she used, in the Revolutionary times, to listen to the incessant motion of the pen in the next room, whence the solitary lamp, which lighted the patriot in his labors, was dimly visible. Mr. Joseph Pierce, who personally knew Samuel Adams, and whose business obliged him for a long time to pass after midnight by the house, related, early in the present century, that he seldom failed to see the study lighted, no matter how far the night had gone, 'and he knew that Sam Adams was hard at work writing against the Tories.' "

The traits of Samuel Adams the writer are easily defined—for they are likewise the traits of Samuel Adams the politician, and of Samuel Adams the man. His fundamental rule for literary warfare was this—"Keep your enemy in the wrong." His style, then, was the expression of his intellectual wariness,—a wariness like that of the scout or the bush-whacker, who knows that behind any tree may lurk his deadly foe, that a false step may be his ruin, that a boldly-aimed shot may make it impossible for him ever to shoot again. Jefferson, who first became aware of the intellectual quality of Samuel Adams as it came out in the debates of Congress, long afterward described him as "truly a great man, wise in council, fertile in resources, immovable in his purposes. . . . As a speaker he could not be compared with his living colleague and namesake, whose deep conceptions, nervous style, and undaunted firmness, made him truly our bulwark in debate. But Mr. Samuel Adams, although not of fluent elocution, was so rigorously logical, so clear in his views, abundant in good sense, and master always of his subject, that he commanded the most profound attention whenever he rose in an assembly by which the froth of declamation was heard with the most sovereign contempt."

\*      \*      \*      \*      \*

Perhaps no long public career was ever more perfectly self-consistent than his. From boyhood to old age, his master principle was individualism.

As an undergraduate in college, having occasion to choose a subject for a public discussion, he revealed the bent of his mind by taking that of "Liberty." In 1743, for his master's degree at Harvard, he wrote a Latin thesis on the affirmative side of the question,—"Whether it be lawful to resist the Supreme Magistrate, if the Commonwealth cannot be otherwise preserved," —a mettlesome doctrine, which, as his latest biographer has graphically said, "he proceeded to discuss in the presence, not only of the college dignitaries, but of the new governor, Shirley, and the crown officials, who sat in state near the young speakers at commencement, as do their successors today. . . . No one knew that as the young man spoke, then, for the first time, one of the great Revolutionary group was asserting the right of resistance by the people to arbitrary oppressors. Shirley was perhaps lost in some far-away dream of how he might get at the French; and when thirty years after, in his retirement at Dorchester, he asked who the Sam Adams could be that was such a thorn in the side to his successors Bernard and Hutchinson, he was quite unconscious of the fact that he himself had had the benefit, close at hand, of the first scratch."

From the day of his graduation till his work as a political writer was done, he did but play variations on this robust doctrine and its corollaries. Men shall be talking much of liberty—no one more than he; but what is liberty? Broadly, it is a something which distinguishes "a society of wise and reasonable creatures from the brutal herd, where the strongest horns are the strongest laws." "The perfection of liberty, . . . in a state of nature, is for every man to be free from any external force, and to perform such actions as in his own mind and conscience he judges to be rightest; which liberty no man can truly possess whose mind is enthralled by irregular and inordinate passions,—since it is no great privilege to be free from external violence, if the dictates of the mind are controlled by a force within which exerts itself above reason." As "no man's life is his own in such a sense as that he may wantonly destroy it at his own pleasure, or submit it to the wanton pleasure of another, so neither is his liberty." "But, alas! in this exalted sense, liberty is rather admired in the world than truly enjoyed. What multitudes of persons are there who have not so much as the shadow of it; who hold their property and even their lives by no other tenure than the sovereign will of a tyrant, and he often the worst and most detestable of men, who, to gratify the least humor or passion in his nature, does not scruple to massacre them by thousands!"

So, too, in his time, men shall be talking much of loyalty—others, perhaps, much more than he. But what is loyalty? According to Samuel Adams, it is "the beauty and perfection of a well-constituted state. It cannot, indeed, subsist in an arbitrary government, because it is founded in the love and possession of liberty. It includes in it a thorough knowledge of our constitution, its conveniences and defects as well as its real advantages; a becoming jealousy of our immunities, and a steadfast resolution to maintain them. It delights in the quiet and thankful enjoyment of a good administration, and it is the scourge of the griping oppressor and haughty invader of our liberties." "Whoever, therefore, insinuates notions of government contrary to the constitution, or in any way winks at any measures to suppress or even to weaken it, is not a loyal man." "Whoever acquaints us that we have no right to examine into the conduct of those who, though they derive their power from us to serve the common interests, make use of it to impoverish and ruin us, is, in a degree, a rebel—to the undoubted rights and liberties of the people."

These definitions, put forth by Samuel Adams when he was but twenty-six years of age—seventeen years before the Stamp Act, twenty-eight years before the Declaration of Independence—mark the solidity and the clarity of the foundation which he thus early laid for that system of stalwart political philosophy which he was to continue to teach during all those years of storm and stress wherein he served as the inspirer and leader of his people. Moreover, while keeping full in view that side both of liberty and of loyalty which points toward rights, he did not forget that for both there was a side which points toward duties. "It is not unfrequent," said he, "to hear men declaim loudly upon liberty, who, if we may judge by the whole tenor of their actions, mean nothing else by it but their own liberty,—to oppress, without control or the restraint of laws, all who are poorer or weaker than themselves." "He that despises his neighbor's happiness because he wears a worsted cap or leather apron, he that struts immeasurably above the lower size of people, and pretends to adjust the rights of men by the distinctions of fortune, is not over loyal." Nor did Samuel Adams, like some other speculative democrats of that age, content himself with being a democrat chiefly in theory: his theory of democracy was also the gentle and faithful practice of his life. Not only were the lowliest and most helpless people made to feel in his presence that they were his brethren, but no man, no woman, however lowly and helpless, could be his slave. When one day, a full decade before the Declaration of Independence, his wife told him of the valuable present of a slave-girl she had just received, he said to her: "A slave cannot live in my house: if she comes, she must be free." And free she was.

On no other topic of the Revolution was his writing more trenchant or more characteristic, than on that of the due subordination of the military power,—a topic which to Americans became peculiarly interesting about the time of the entrance of the British regiments into the town of Boston in 1768. "Military power," said he at that time, "is by no means calculated to convince the understandings of men. It may in another part of the world affright women and children, and perhaps some weak men, out of their senses, but will never awe a sensible American tamely to surrender his liberty." "Are we a garrisoned town, or are we not? If we are, let us know by whose authority and by whose influence we are made so. If not—and I take it for granted we are not—let us then assert and maintain the honor, the dignity, of free citizens, and place the military where all other men are, and where they ought always and will be placed in every free country,—at the foot of the common law of the land! To submit to the civil magistrate in the legal exercise of power, is forever the part of a good subject; and to answer the watchmen of the town in the night, may be the part of a good citizen, as well as to afford them all necessary countenance and support. But to be called to account by a common soldier, or any soldier, is a badge of slavery which none but a slave will wear."

In 1773, in view of the colossal blunders in statesmanship presented by the farcical and galling policy of the British king and ministry, he wrote: "That Great Britain should continue to insult and alienate the growing millions who inhabit this country, on whom she greatly depends, and on whose alliance in future time her existence as a nation may be suspended, is perhaps as glaring an instance of human folly as ever disgraced politicians or put common sense to the blush." In 1774, in the midst of the labors of the first Continental Congress, he published these words of stern meaning: "If the British administration and government do not return to the principles of moderation and equity, the evil which they profess to aim at preventing by their rigorous measures, will the sooner be brought to pass, namely, the entire separation and independence of the colonies." "I wish for a permanent union with the mother country, but only on the terms of liberty and truth. No advantage that can accrue to America from such an union, can compensate for the loss of liberty." In February, 1776, when, in his opinion, no choice was left to Americans but that between servitude under Great Britain and separation from her, he wrote: "I account a state a moral person, having an interest and will of its own; and I think that state a monster whose prime mover has an interest and will in direct opposition to its prosperity and security."

\*     \*     \*     \*     \*

In the interval between the publication of his pamphlet, "Common Sense," in January, 1776, and the final determination of Congress, six months later, to take the very course recommended in that pamphlet, Thomas Paine followed up the lines of argument and appeal on which he had thus wrought, by writing for a Philadelphia journal a series of at least four articles over the signature of "The Forester." During this interval, also, appeared in Philadelphia a brochure which in our time has been confidently attributed to Paine, bearing the whimsical title,—"A Dialogue between the Ghost of General Montgomery just arrived from the Elysian Fields, and an American Delegate, in a Wood near Philadelphia,"—a well-managed political colloquy, in which the argument for Independence is developed with much of Paine's vigor, but perhaps with rather more accuracy, delicacy, and polish, than one expects to find in him.

But the man who had so brilliantly served the American cause by the pen, seems to have been eager to serve it by the sword also. Accordingly, in the summer of 1776, soon after the Declaration of Independence, he joined as a volunteer General Roberdeau's division of the Pennsylvania troops, called "the flying camp." With these troops he served at Perth Amboy, and at Bergen; and when, after a few weeks, their time expired and they returned home, Paine, unwilling at such a time to avail himself of such an excuse for leaving the field, "went to Fort Lee and served as aid-de-camp to General Greene, . . . and was with him during the whole of the black times of that trying campaign." Benjamin Rush mentions that during that period, Paine lived a good deal with officers of the first rank in the army, at whose tables his " 'Common Sense' always made him a welcome guest." General Greene himself, in a letter written at Fort Lee to his wife, on the second of November, gives a glimpse of the daily life of his military family, especially mentioning the curious fact that in that time of appalling distress, Paine was "perpetually wrangling about mathematical problems" with a certain other officer of the army.

Whoever served in the American army, in any capacity, in the autumn of 1776, had an employment full of discomfort and peril. On the twenty-seventh of August, Washington had suffered a shattering defeat in the battle of Long Island. Then had followed, in awful rapidity, a gloomy succession of disasters,—the abandonment of New York on the fifteenth of September, the defeat at White Plains on the twenty-eighth of October, the surrender of Fort Washington on the sixteenth of November, the stampede from Fort Lee on the eighteenth of November, finally, Washington's harassed retreat through New Jersey, and, on the eighth of December, his escape across the Delaware. In all these calamitous and distressing experiences,—defeats, retreats, marchings, and countermarchings, before a victorious and scornful foe,—Paine seems to have participated. A letter-writer in the British army, describing the capture of Fort Lee, connects Paine with the event in a somewhat grotesque manner: he relates that on the appearance of the British troops before that fortress, "the rebels fled like scared rabbits," leaving in their intrenchments "some poor pork, a few greasy proclamations, and some of that scoundrel 'Common Sense' man's letters, which we can read at our leisure, now that we have got one of the 'impregnable redoubts' of Mr. Washington's to quarter in."

It was in the midst of the dismay and disorder of this retreat across New Jersey, that Paine was inspired to begin that series of impassioned and invigorating pamphlets which at once became famous under the title of "The Crisis," and which continued to appear intermittently down to the close of the war. He has himself related how, on the scrambling retreat from Fort Lee, he began at Newark the first number of "The Crisis," "and continued writing it," as he says, "at every place we stop at," until it was finished, and issued from the press at Philadelphia on the nineteenth of December,— just four days before;that on which Washington announced to some of his officers his purpose to recross the Delaware and to strike the enemy at Trenton. Those were perhaps the darkest days of the Revolution. Even Washington had then written: "If every nerve is not strained to recruit the new army with all possible expedition, I think the game is pretty nearly up."

It was under such circumstances that the first number of "The Crisis," bearing the resounding signature of "Common Sense," greeted the American people with words that were electrical, and that soon became classic: "These are the times that try men's souls. The summer soldier and the sunshine patriot will, in this crisis, shrink from the service of his country;

but he that stands it now, deserves the love and thanks of man and woman. Tyranny, like hell, is not easily conquered; yet we have this consolation with us, that the harder the conflict, the more glorious the triumph."

As he passes on from paragraph to paragraph of this tremendous harangue, he touches with unfailing skill, with matchless power, the springs of anxiety, anger, contempt, love of home, love of country, fortitude, cool deliberation, and passionate resolve; and he closes with such a battle call as might almost have startled slain patriots from their new graves under the frozen clods: "Up and help us; lay your shoulders to the wheel; better have too much force than too little, when so great an object is at stake. Let it be told to the future world, that in the depth of winter, when nothing but hope and virtue could survive, the city and country, alarmed at one common danger, came forth to meet and repulse it. . . . It matters not where you live, or what rank of life you hold, the evil or the blessing will reach you all. . . . The heart that feels not now, is dead. The blood of his children will curse his coward-ice, who shrinks back at a time when a little might have saved the whole, and made them happy. I love the man that can smile in trouble, that can gather strength from distress, and grow brave by reflection. 'Tis the business of little minds to shrink; but he whose heart is firm, and whose conscience approves his conduct, will pursue his principles unto death. . . . It is the madness of folly to expect mercy from those who have refused to do justice. . . . By perseverance and fortitude, we have the prospect of a glorious issue; by cowardice and submission, the sad choice of a variety of evils,—a rav-aged country, a depopulated city, habitations without safety, and slavery without hope, our homes turned into barracks and bawdy-houses for Hes-sians, and a future race to provide for, whose fathers we shall doubt of. Look on this picture and weep over it; and if there yet remains one thought-less wretch who believes it not, let him suffer it unlamented."

From the day on which he finished this pamphlet onward to the very close of the war, Paine seems to have had his personal share in nearly every form of service or of privation which befell the American people. During the greater portion of this period, he gained his livelihood either by acting as secretary to the committee of Congress on foreign affairs, or as clerk in the commercial house of Owen Biddle, or as clerk to the general assembly of Pennsylvania. In September, 1777, while preparing at Philadelphia the dispatches of Congress for Franklin in Paris, he was interrupted by the booming of the cannon at Brandywine. Instantly dashing off a fresh number of "The Crisis," for the purpose of giving check to a popular panic, he threw aside his pen and by personal entreaty endeavored to induce the au-thorities to adopt some practicable plan for a volunteer defense of the city. Failing in this, he hurried away to the army, and as aid-de-camp to General Greene, and perhaps in other capacities as well, he partook to the full of the toils and perils of the troops during the remainder of that autumn, even standing by Washington's side in the grim retirement of Valley Forge. In February, 1781, at a time when further American resistance was in danger of collapsing through sheer lack of the means to carry on the war, Paine sailed out of Boston harbor on the frigate "Alliance," in the company of

Colonel John Laurens,—the latter going as minister extraordinary to France for the purpose of securing for Congress a special loan from the king. Just six months afterward, Paine and Laurens again appeared in Boston harbor, having with them, as the fruits of their expedition, 2,500,000 livres in silver, and in convoy a ship laden with clothing, ammunition, arms,—a most opportune supply, which had perhaps an essential part in the train of events which led, two months later, to the surrender of Cornwallis.

Noble-minded and important as were these various services rendered by Paine to the American cause, on sea and land, in office and field, they could in no way be compared, as contributions to the success of the Revolution, with the work which he did during those same imperiled years merely as a writer, and especially as the writer of "The Crisis." Between December, 1776, when the first pamphlet of that series was published, down to December, 1783, when the last one left the printer's hands, this indomitable man produced no less than sixteen pamphlets under the same general title, adapting his message in each case to the supreme need of the hour, and accomplishing all this literary labor in a condition of actual poverty,—poverty so great that on one occasion, shortly after his return from France, he was obliged to apologize to his friend Laurens, then at the siege of Yorktown, for some delay in forwarding to headquarters a pair of new boots which that gallant officer had ordered in Philadelphia, by the naïve confession that he had not then in hand money enough to pay the bootmaker.

The marvelous power which this untitled and impecunious penman wielded over the minds of men and over the course of events, during the entire period of our Revolution, was essentially the power of a great journalist. He had to the full the journalistic temperament,—its tastes, capacities, limitations. He had no interest in the past except so far as the past had a direct message for the present. His life was the life of today. He rose from his bed every morning to ask what was the uppermost thought, the keenest necessity, the most notable event, of that particular day. Books to him were of no vital account; his only library was a heap of pamphlets, and a pocket stuffed full of newspapers. All that he wrote was suggested by an occasion, and was meant for one. By some process of his own he knew just what the people thought, feared, wished, loved, and hated: he knew it better than they knew it themselves. The secret of his strength lay in his infallible instinct for interpreting to the public its own conscience and its own consciousness, and for doing this in language which, at times, was articulate thunder and lightning. The history of the long war may be read in the blazing light of these mighty pamphlets, in which with the confident look, with the unhesitating voice, of a leader born to lead, he rallied the people in many an hour of disaster and fright, pleaded with them, rebuked them, inspired them, and pointed out to them the path of duty and of victory, or, standing in front of them, on their behalf flung his jests, taunts, and maledictions at the foe. Thus, he addresses, on one occasion, the leading British officer just then in America, in order, as he says to him, "to expose the folly of your pretended authority as a commissioner, the wickedness of your cause in general, and the impossibility of your conquering us at any rate."

As regards the American people, he says, "my intention is to shew them their true and solid interest; to encourage them to their own good; to remove the fears and falsities which bad men have spread, and weak men have encouraged; and to excite in all men a love for union, and a cheerfulness for duty."

In those days, certainly, Thomas Paine represented, not only the faith of the people in themselves, but their faith in God and in God's guidance and mastery of the affairs of this world, and in the ultimate victory of God's cause against every possible league of men and of devils. Speaking always in the character of an avowed Christian, and to a nation of Christians, Paine declares: "God Almighty will not give up a people to military destruction, or leave them unsupportedly to perish, who have so earnestly and so repeatedly sought to avoid the calamities of war, by every decent method which wisdom could invent. Neither have I so much of the infidel in me as to suppose that He has relinquished the government of the world, and given us up to the care of devils." "If we believe the power of hell to be limited, we must likewise believe that their agents are under some providential control." "There has been such a chain of extraordinary events in the discovery of this country at first, in the peopling and planting it afterwards, in the rearing and nursing it to its present state, and in the protection of it through the present war, that no man can doubt but Providence hath some nobler end to accomplish than the gratification of the petty elector of Hanover, or the ignorant and insignificant king of Britain." We dare to believe that ours is the cause to which Providence will give the victory, because "we fight not to enslave, but to set a country free, and to make room upon the earth for honest men to live in."

And who is it, at this late day, who can any longer doubt the wisdom of our resolve to cast aside the colonial character, and to set up a national establishment for ourselves? "To know whether it be the interest of this continent to be Independent, we need only ask this easy, simple question: Is it the interest of a man to be a boy all his life?"

And you, my Lord Howe, in your so-called proclamation,—a preposterous compound of assumptions, promises, and threats,—you have the audacity to speak of our claim to Independence as something "extravagant and inadmissible." "Why, God bless me, what have you to do with our Independence? We ask no leave of yours to set it up; we ask no money of yours to support it; we can do better without your fleets and armies than with them; you may soon have enough to do to protect yourselves without being burdened with us. We are very willing to be at peace with you, to buy of you and sell to you, and, like young beginners in the world, to work for our living. Therefore, why do you put yourselves out of cash, when we know you cannot spare it, and we do not desire you to run into debt?"

And, moreover, what a ridiculous thing it is for a man in your circumstances to issue a proclamation at all! "Your authority in the Jerseys is now reduced to the small circle which your army occupies, and your proclamation is nowhere else seen, unless it be to be laughed at. The mighty subduers of the continent have retreated into a nut-shell; and the proud forgivers of our sins are fled from those they came to pardon. . . . In short, you have managed your Jersey expedition so very dexterously, that the dead only are conquerors, because none will dispute the ground with them."

As to those troops of yours, with which you have tried to overawe us, and from which the world has been taught to expect so much, what is their real condition? "Like a wounded, disabled whale, they want only time and room to die in; and though in the agony of their exit, it may be unsafe to live within the flapping of their tail, yet every hour shortens their date, and lessens their power of mischief." "Their condition is both despicable and deplorable: out of cash, out of heart, out of hope. A country furnished with arms and ammunition, as America now is, with three millions of inhabitants, and three thousand miles distance from the nearest enemy that can approach her, is able to look and laugh them in the face."

"Your cargo of pardons," he says contemptuously to the three British commissioners who came out in 1778, "will have no market. It is unfashionable to look at them—even speculation is at an end. They have become a perfect drug, and no way calculated for the climate." "You may plan and execute little mischiefs; but are they worth the expense they cost you, or will such partial evils have any effect on the general cause? Your expedition to Egg-Harbor will be felt at a distance like an attack upon a henroost, and expose you in Europe with a sort of childish phrenzy. Is it worth while to keep an army to protect you in writing proclamations, or to get once a year into winter quarters?"

As he had bestowed much frankness on Lord Howe, he is disposed to treat his brother, Sir William, with equal distinction: "Indolence and inability have too large a share in your composition, ever to suffer you to be anything more than the hero of little villainies and unfinished adventures."

"Let me ask, sir, what great exploits have you performed? Through all the variety of changes and opportunities which the war has produced, I know no one action of yours that can be styled masterly: You have moved in and out, backward and forward, round and round, as if valor consisted in a military jig. The history and figure of your movements would be truly ridiculous could they be justly delineated. They resemble the labors of a puppy pursuing his tail; the end is still at the same distance, and all the turnings round must be done over again." "The time, sir, will come when you, in a melancholy hour, shall reckon up your miseries, by your murders in America. Life with you begins to wear a clouded aspect. The vision of pleasurable delusion is wearing away, and changing to the barren wild of age and sorrow. The poor reflection of having served your king will yield you no consolation in your parting moments. He will crumble to the same undistinguishable ashes with yourself, and have sins enough of his own to answer for. It is not the farcical benedictions of a bishop, nor the cringing hypocrisy of a court of chaplains, nor the formality of an act of parliament, that can change guilt into innocence, or make the punishment one pang the less. You may, perhaps, be unwilling to be serious; but this destruction of the goods of Providence, this havoc of the human race, and this sowing the world with mischief, must be accounted for to Him who made and governs it. To us they are only present sufferings, but to Him they are deep rebellions."

Turning to his fellow-countrymen on the day after a harrowing defeat, his words go forth as a trumpet call to reassurance and to a renewal of the conflict: "Those who expect to reap the blessings of freedom, must like men undergo the fatigues of supporting it. The event of yesterday was one of those kind alarms which are just sufficient to rouse us to duty, without being of consequence enough to depress our fortitude. It is not a field of a few acres of ground, but a cause, that we are defending; and whether we defeat the enemy in one battle, or by degrees, the consequence will be the same. . . . We have always been masters at the last push, and always shall be while we do our duty. . . . Shall a band of ten or twelve thousand robbers, who are this day fifteen hundred or two thousand men less in strength than they were yesterday, conquer America, or subdue even a single State? The thing cannot be done, unless we sit down and suffer them to do it. Another such a brush, notwithstanding we lost the ground, would, by still reducing the enemy, put them in a condition to be afterwards totally defeated. . . . It is distressing to see an enemy advancing into a country, but it is the only place in which we can beat them, and in which we have always beaten them, whenever they have made the attempt. . . . You have too much at stake to hesitate. You ought not to think an hour upon the matter, but to spring to action at once. Other States have been invaded; have likewise driven off the invaders. Now our time and turn is come, and perhaps the finishing stroke is reserved for us. When we look back on the dangers we have been saved from, and reflect on the success we have been blessed with, it would be sinful either to be idle or to despair."

Near the close of the first three years of the war, he sums up the results in a single sentence: "It is now nearly three years since the tyranny of Britain received its first repulse by the arms of America,—a period which has given birth to a new world, and erected a monument to the folly of the old."

And when, at last, the final victory is come and actual peace draws on, this unfatigued prophet consents to pause long enough to chant, in sinewy prose, a virile song of congratulation; but almost before its close he begins to beckon his fellow-countrymen away from mere exultation, and from past success, to point toward the new dangers and the new duties which that very success is about to lay upon them: "The times that tried men's souls are over—and the greatest and completest Revolution the world ever knew, gloriously and happily accomplished. But to pass from the extremes of danger to safety—from the tumult of war to the tranquillity of peace—though sweet in contemplation, requires a gradual composure of the senses to receive it. Even calmness has the power of stunning, when it opens too instantly upon us. . . . In the present case, the mighty magnitude of the object, the various uncertainties of fate which it has undergone, the numerous and complicated dangers we have suffered or escaped, the eminence we now stand on, and the vast prospect before us, must all conspire to impress us with contemplation. To see it in our power to make a world happy, to teach mankind the art of being so, to exhibit on the theatre of the universe a character hitherto unknown, and to have, as it were, a new creation intrusted to our hands, are honors that command reflection, and can neither be too highly estimated, nor too gratefully received. In this pause, then, of reflection, while the storm is ceasing, and the long-agitated mind vibrating to a rest, let us look back on the scenes we have passed, and learn from experience what is yet to be done."

But just before us lie two immense dangers; the first, financial dishonor, the second, disunion. To guard against, to avert, these two dangers—this is the new duty which now summons us: "The debt which America has contracted, compared with the cause she has gained, and the advantages to flow from it, ought scarcely to be mentioned. . . . Character is much easier kept than recovered; and that man, if any such there be, who, from sinister views, or littleness of soul, lends unseen his hand to injure it, contrives a wound it will never be in his power to heal. As we have established an inheritance for posterity, let that inheritance descend, with every mark of an honorable conveyance. The little it will cost compared with the worth of the States, the greatness of the object, and the value of national character, will be a profitable exchange."

"But that which must more forcibly strike a thoughtful, penetrating mind, and which includes and renders easy all inferior concerns, is the union of the States. On this, our great national character depends. It is this which must give us importance abroad and security at home. . . . In short, we have no other national sovereignty than as United States. . . . Individuals, or individual States, may call themselves what they please; but the world, and especially the world of enemies, is not to be held in awe by the whistling of a name. Sovereignty must have power to protect all the parts that compose and constitute it; and as the United States, we are equal to the importance of the title, but otherwise we are not. Our union, well and wisely regulated and cemented, is the cheapest way of being great—the easiest way of being powerful, and the happiest invention in government which the circumstances of America can admit of. . . . I ever feel myself hurt when I hear the union, that great palladium of our liberty and safety, the least irreverently spoken of. It is the most sacred thing in the constitution of America, and that which every man should be most proud and tender of. Our citizenship in the United States is our national character. Our citizenship in any particular State is only our local distinction. By the latter we are known at home, by the former to the world. Our great title is AMERICANS."

THAT *the Revolution was won is remarkable. The odds against the colonials seemed insurmountable. There existed no consensus; rather, most historians have concluded that a bare third of Americans were firmly committed to the Revolution while an equivalent number were no less opposed. It was the middle third that vacillated in its loyalties and, as John Adams recalled, "united with the first or last third, according to circumstance." Only the division of British home sentiment, described by one contemporary as one in which "the bulk of the people of England and Ireland" strongly supported the American stand, explains the failure of Britain to exploit these divisions.*

*But the result nonetheless had painful consequences for Americans. It frequently seemed doubtful whether Washington would retain an army sufficiently large to keep in the field. The Continental Congress represented the narrow, parochial views of the states, rarely thinking of the larger interest of the whole. No one was more victimized than the soldier. Underfed, badly equipped, and rarely paid, they nonetheless remained remarkably loyal. As Bancroft indicates, Washington understood the need for a consolidated effort, but he deferred to the Congress, powerfully buttressing the tradition of military deference to civil authority.*

*The need for greater power in the central government was by Revolution's end firmly embedded in the minds of the men who had led the Revolutionary armies. It accounts for the willingness of Washington to lend his enormous prestige to the federal experiment. It also explains why he refused to play the autocrat and settled instead to rule through a government of men under law. For his refusal to usurp power under the provocation of the Continental Congress's incompetence established his trust with the American people. Upon the rock of that trust a republic would be built.*

*The American historian of the nineteenth century was nothing if he were not wide-ranging in his interests. Since the study and teaching of history was not yet professionalized, it was a discipline indulged in by self-taught amateurs. An excellent example of this tendency was George Bancroft (1800-1891). Massachusetts born, educated at Phillips Exeter Academy and Harvard University, he went on to obtain in 1820 his Ph.D. at the University of Göttingen in Germany. Upon his return to America, he both tutored at Harvard and delivered sermons, often from his father's pulpit. He identified himself with Jacksonian Democracy and in 1838 received appointment as Collector of the Port of Boston. He played a dominant role in the nomination of James K. Polk for the Presidency in 1844 and received as his reward first an appointment as Secretary of the Navy and then Minister to Great Britain. Between 1834 and 1874, he wrote a ten-volume* History of the United States *which still retains considerable value. At eighty-one, he wrote a* History of the Formation of the Constitution of the United States *(1882) and at eighty-nine, a biography,* Martin Van Buren *(1889). It was truly a busy and a productive life.*

# THE
# AMERICAN REVOLUTION

## *by George Bancroft*

When at last Washington was joined by troops from the northern army, a clamor arose for the capture of Philadelphia. Protected by the Schuylkill and the Delaware, the city could be approached only from the north, and on that side a chain of fourteen redoubts extended from river to river. Moreover, the army by which it was occupied, having been reenforced from New York by more than three thousand men, now exceeded nineteen thousand. Yet four American officers voted in council for an assault upon the lines of this greatly superior force; but the general, sustained by eleven, disregarded the murmurs of congress and rejected "the mad enterprise."

Ashamed of inaction, Sir William Howe announced to his government his intention to make a forward movement. Washington, with a quickness of eye that had been developed by his forest-life as a surveyor, selected in the woods of Whitemarsh strong ground for an encampment, and there, within fourteen miles of Philadelphia, awaited the enemy, of whose movements he received exact and timely intelligence. On the severely cold night of the fourth of December, the British, fourteen thousand strong, marched out to attack the American lines. Before daybreak on the fifth, their advance party halted on a ridge beyond Chestnut hill, eleven miles from Philadelphia, and at seven their main body formed in one line, with a few regiments as reserves. The Americans occupied thickly wooded hills, with a morass and a brook in their front. Opposite the British left wing a breastwork defended the only point where the brook could be easily forded. About noon, General Irvine, who led some Pennsylvania militia into a skirmish, was wounded and taken prisoner, and his party were dispersed. At night the British force rested on their arms, and the hills far and wide blazed with the innumerable fires of the two armies. Washington passed the hours in strengthening his position; and though from sickness, fatigue, and want of clothing, he had at most but seven thousand really effective men, he wished for an engagement. Near the end of another day Howe marched back to Germantown, and on the next, as if intending a surprise, suddenly returned upon the American left, which he made preparations to assail. Washington rode through every brigade, delivering in person his orders on the manner of receiving their enemy, exhorting to a reliance on the bayonet; and his words, and still more his example, inspired them with his own fortitude. All day long, and until eight in the evening, Howe kept up his reconnoitring, but found the American position everywhere strong by nature and by art. Nothing occurred during the day but a sharp action on Edge hill, between light troops under Gist and Morgan's riflemen and a British party led by General Grey. The latter lost eighty-nine in killed and wounded; the Americans twenty-seven, among them the brave Major Morris of New Jersey. On the eighth, just after noon, the British suddenly filed off, and marched by the shortest road to Philadelphia. Their loss in the expedition exceeded one hundred. Thus the campaign closed. Howe had gone out with superior numbers and the avowed intention of bringing on a battle, and had so respected his adversary that he would not engage him without some advantage of ground. Henceforward he passed the winter behind his intrenchments, making only excursions for food or forage; and Washington had no choice but to seek winter-quarters for his suffering soldiers.

Military affairs had thus far been superintended by congress, through a committee of its own members. After some prelude in July, 1777, it was settled in the following October to institute an executive board of war of five persons not members of congress.

Conway, a French officer of Irish descent, whom Greene and others describe as "worthless," had long been eager for higher rank. In a timely letter to Richard Henry Lee, a friend to Conway, Washington wrote: "His merits exist more in his own imagination than in reality; it is a maxim with him not to want anything which is to be obtained by importunity"; his promotion would be "a real act of injustice," likely to "incur a train of irremediable evils. To sum up the whole, I have been a slave to the service; I have undergone more than most men are aware of to harmonize so many discordant parts; but it will be impossible for me to be of any further service, if such insuperable difficulties are thrown in my way." These words might be interpreted as a threat of resignation in the event of Conway's promotion. Conway breathed out his discontent to Gates, writing in substance: "Heaven has been determined to save your country, or a weak general and bad counsellors would have ruined it." The correspondents of Gates did not scruple in their letters to speak of the commander-in-chief with bitterness or contempt. "This army," wrote Reed, "notwithstanding the efforts of our amiable chief, has as yet gathered no laurels. I perfectly agree with that sentiment which leads to request your assistance." On the sixth of November, Wilkinson, the principal aid of Gates, a babbling and unsteady sycophant praised by his chief for military genius, was made a brigadier. On the seventh, Mifflin, leaving his office of quartermaster-general, of which he had neglected the duties, yet retaining the rank of major-general, was elected to the board of war. The injurious words of Conway having through Wilkinson been reported to Washington, on the ninth he communicated his knowledge of them to Conway, and to him alone. Conway, in an interview, justified them, made no apology, and after the interview reported his defiance of Washington to Mifflin. On the tenth, Sullivan, second in rank in the army, knowing the opinion of his brother-officers and of his chief, and that on a discussion at a council of war about appointing an inspector-general Conway's pretensions met with no favor, wrote to a member of congress: "No man can behave better in action than General Conway; his regulations in his brigade are much better than any in the army; his knowledge of military matters far exceeds any officer we have. If the office of inspector-general with the rank of major-general was given him our army would soon cut a different figure from what they now do." On the same day Wayne expressed his purpose "to follow the line pointed out by the conduct of Lee, Gates, and Mifflin." On the eleventh, Conway, foreseeing that Gates was to preside at the board of war, offered to form for him a plan for the instruction of the army; and on the fifteenth, to advance his intrigue, he tendered his resignation to congress. On the seventeenth, Lovell of Massachusetts wrote to Gates threatening Washington "with the mighty torrent of public clamor and vengeance," and subjoined: "How different your conduct and your fortune; this army will be totally lost unless you come down and collect the virtuous band who wish to fight under your banner." On the twenty-first, Wayne, forgetting the disaster that had attended his own rash confidence, disparaged Washington as having more than once slighted the favors of fortune. On the twenty-fourth, congress received the resignation of Conway, and referred it to the board of war, of which Mifflin at that time was the head. On the twenty-seventh, they filled the places in that board, and appointed Gates its president. On the same day Lovell wrote to Gates: "We want you in different places; we want you most near Germantown. Good God, what a situation we are in! how different from what might have been justly expected!" and he represented Washington as a general who collected astonishing numbers of men to wear out stockings, shoes, and breeches, and "Fabiused affairs into a very disagreeable posture." On the twenty-eighth, congress declared themselves by a unanimous resolution in favor of carrying on a winter's campaign with vigor and success, and sent three of their members with Washington's concurrence to direct every measure which circumstances might require. On the same day, Mifflin, explaining to Gates how Conway had braved the commander-in-chief, volunteered his own opinion that the extract from Conway's letter was a "collection of just sentiments." Gates, on receiving the letter, wrote to Conway: "You acted with all the dignity of a virtuous soldier." He wished "so very valuable and polite an officer might remain in the service." To congress he complained of the betrayal of his correspondence to Washington, with whom he came to an open rupture. On the thirteenth of December, congress, following Mifflin's report, appointed Conway inspector-general, promoted him to be a major-general, made his office independent of the commander-in-chief, and referred him to the board of war for the regulations which he was to introduce. Some of those engaged in the cabal wished to provoke Washington to the resignation which he seemed to have threatened.

This happened just as Washington by his skill at Whitemarsh had closed the campaign with honor. The condition of his troops required repose. The problem which he must solve was to keep together through the cold winter an army without tents, and to confine the British to the environs of Philadelphia. There was no town which would serve the purpose. Valley Forge, on the Schuylkill, but twenty-one miles from Philadelphia, admitted of defence against the artillery of those days, and had more than one route convenient for escape into the interior. The ground lay sheltered between two ridges of hills, and was covered by a thick forest. From his life in the woods, Washington could see in the trees a town of log-cabins, built in regular streets, and affording shelter enough to save the army from dispersion.

As his men moved towards the spot selected for their winter resting-place, they had not clothes to cover their nakedness, nor blankets to lie on, nor tents to sleep under. For the want of shoes their marches through frost and snow might be traced by the blood from their feet, and they were almost as often without provisions as with them. On the nineteenth they arrived at Valley Forge, within a day's march of Howe's army, with no shelter till they could build houses for themselves. The order for their erection was received by officers and men as impossible of execution, and they were still more astonished at the ease with which, as the work of their Christmas holidays, they changed the forest into huts thatched with boughs in the order of a regular encampment. Washington's unsleeping vigilance and thorough system for receiving intelligence secured them against surprise; love of country and attachment to their general sustained them under their unparalleled hardships; with any other leader the army would have dissolved and vanished. Yet he was followed to Valley Forge by letters from congress transmitting the remonstrance of the council and assembly of Pennsylvania against his going into winter-quarters. To this senseless reproof Washington on the twenty-third, after laying deserved blame upon Mifflin for neglect of duty as quartermaster-general, replied: "For the want of a two days' supply of provisions, an opportunity was scarcely ever offered of taking an advantage of the enemy that has not been either totally obstructed or greatly impeded. Men are confined to hospitals or in farmers' houses for want of shoes. We have this day no less than two thousand eight hundred and ninety-eight men in camp unfit for duty, because they are barefoot and otherwise naked. Our whole strength in continental troops amounts to no more than eight thousand two hundred in camp fit for duty. Since the fourth instant, our numbers fit for duty from hardships and exposures have decreased nearly two thousand men. Numbers still are obliged to sit all night by fires. Gentlemen reprobate the going into winter-quarters as much as if they thought the soldiers were made of stocks or stones. I can assure those gentlemen that it is a much easier and less distressing thing to draw remonstrances in a comfortable room by a good fireside, than to occupy a cold, bleak hill, and sleep under frost and snow without clothes or blankets. However, although they seem to have little feeling for the naked and distressed soldiers, I feel superabundantly for them, and from my soul I pity those miseries which it is neither in my power to relieve or prevent."

While the shivering soldiers were shaping the logs for their cabins, the clamor of the Pennsylvanians continued; and the day after Christmas, Sullivan, who held with both sides, gave his written advice to Washington to yield and attack Howe in Philadelphia, "risking every consequence in an action." The press was called into activity. On the last day in the year, an anonymous writer in the "New Jersey Gazette," at Trenton, supposed to be Benjamin Rush, began a series of articles under the name of a French officer, to set forth the unrivalled glory of Gates, who had conquered veterans with militia, pointing out plainly Washington's successor.

The year 1778 opened gloomily at Valley Forge. To the touching account of the condition of the army, congress, which had not provided one magazine for winter, made no response except a promise to the soldiers of one month's extra pay, and a renewal of authority to take the articles necessary for their comfortable subsistence. Washington was averse to the exercise of military power, not only from reluctance to give distress, but to avoid increasing the prevalent jealousy and suspicion. Seeing no movement towards a reform in the administration, on the fifth of January he renewed his remonstrances with respect and firmness: "The letter from the committee of congress and board of war does not mention the regulations adopted for removing the difficulties and failures in the commissary line. I trust they will be vigorous or the army cannot exist. It will never answer to procure supplies of clothing or provision by coercive measures. The small seizures made of the former a few days ago, when that or to dissolve was the alternative, excited the greatest uneasiness even among our warmest friends. Such procedures may give a momentary relief, but, if repeated, will prove of the most pernicious consequence. Besides spreading disaffection, jealousy, and fear among the people, they never fail, even in the most veteran troops under the most rigid and exact discipline, to raise in the soldiery a disposition to plunder, difficult to suppress, and not only ruinous to the inhabitants, but, in many instances, to armies themselves. I regret the occasion that compelled us to the measure the other day, and shall consider it among the greatest of our misfortunes if we should be under the necessity of practising it again." Still congress did no more than on the tenth and twelfth of January appoint Gates and Mifflin, with four or five others, to repair to head-quarters and concert reforms.

While those who wished the general out of the way urged him to some rash enterprise, or, to feel the public pulse, sent abroad rumors that he was about to resign, Benjamin Rush in a letter to Patrick Henry represented the army of Washington as having no general at their head, and went on to say: "A Gates, a Lee, or a Conway, would in a few weeks render them an irresistible body of men. Some of the contents of this letter ought to be made public, in order to awaken, enlighten, and alarm our country." This communication, to which Rush dared not sign his name, Patrick Henry in his scorn noticed only by sending it to Washington. An anonymous paper of the like stamp, transmitted to the president of congress, took the same direction.

Meantime, the council and assembly of Pennsylvania renewed to congress their wish that Philadelphia might be taken and the British driven away. Congress hailed the letter as proof of a rising spirit, and directed the committee appointed to go to camp to consult on the subject with the government of Pennsylvania and with General Washington.

Nor was this all. The board of war was ambitious of the fame of great activity, and also wished to detach Lafayette, the representative of France, from the commander-in-chief. In concert with Conway, but without consulting Washington, they induced congress to sanction a winter expedition against Canada, under Lafayette, who was not yet twenty-one years old, with Conway for his second in command, and with Stark. Assured at Yorktown by Gates that he would have a force of three thousand men, and that Stark would have already destroyed the shipping at Saint Johns, Lafayette repaired to Albany, but not until he obtained from congress Kalb as his second, and Washington as his direct superior. There the three major-generals of the expedition met, and were attended or followed by twenty French officers. Stark wrote for orders. The available force for the conquest, counting a regiment which Gates detached from the army of Washington, did not exceed a thousand. For these there was no store of provision, nor clothing suited to the climate of Canada, nor means of transportation. Two years' service in the northern department cannot leave to Gates the plea of ignorance; his plan showed his utter administrative incapacity; it accidentally relieved the country of Conway, who, writing petulantly to congress, found his resignation, which he had meant only as a complaint, irrevocably accepted. Lafayette and Kalb were recalled.

Slights and selfish cabals could wound the sensibility but not affect the conduct of Washington. The strokes of ill-fortune in his campaigns he had met with equanimity and fortitude; but he sought the esteem of his fellowmen as his only reward, and now unjust censure gave him the most exquisite pain. More was expected from him than was possible to be performed. Moreover, his detractors took an unfair advantage, for he was obliged to conceal the weakness of his army from public view, and thereby submit to calumny. To William Gordon, who was seeking materials for a history of the war, he wrote freely: "Neither interested nor ambitious views led me into the service. I did not solicit the command, but accepted it after much entreaty, with all that diffidence which a conscious want of ability and experience equal to the discharge of so important a trust must naturally excite in a mind not quite devoid of thought; and after I did engage, pursued the great line of my duty and the object in view, as far as my judgment could direct, as pointedly as the needle to the pole." "No person ever heard me drop an expression that had a tendency to resignation. The same principles that led me to embark in the opposition to the arbitrary claims of Great Britain operate with additional force at this day; nor is it my desire to withdraw my services while they are considered of importance to the present contest. There is not an officer in the service of the United States that would return to the sweets of domestic life with more heartfelt joy than I should, but I mean not to shrink in the cause."

In his remonstrances with congress he wrote with plainness, but with moderation. His calm dignity, while it irritated his adversaries, overawed them; and nothing could shake the confidence of the people, or divide the affections of any part of the army, or permanently distract the majority of congress. Those who had been most ready to cavil at him soon wished their rash words benevolently interpreted or forgotten. Gates denied the charge of being in a league to supersede Washington as a wicked, false, diabolical calumny of incendiaries, and would not believe that any such plot existed; Mifflin exonerated himself in more equivocal language; and both retired from the committee that was to repair to head-quarters. In the following July, Conway, thinking himself mortally wounded in a duel, wrote to Washington: "My career will soon be over; therefore justice and truth prompt me to declare my last sentiments. You are in my eyes the great and good man. May you long enjoy the love, veneration, and esteem of these states, whose liberties you have asserted by your virtues." The committee which towards the end of January was finally sent to consult with Washington, was composed exclusively of members of congress, and the majority of them, especially Charles Carroll of Maryland, were his friends. But in the procrastination of active measures of relief, the departments of the quartermaster and commissary remained like clocks with so many checks that they cannot go. Even so late as the eleventh of February, Dana, one of the committee, reported that men died for the want of straw or materials to raise them from the cold, wet earth. In numerous and crowded hospitals the sick could not be properly cared for. Inoculation was delayed for want of straw and other necessaries. Almost every species of camp-transportation was performed by men, who, without a murmur, yoked themselves to little carriages of their own making, or loaded their fuel and provisions on their backs. Some brigades had been four days without meat. Desertions were frequent. There was danger that the troops would perish from famine or disperse in search of food.

All this time the British soldiers in Philadelphia were well provided for, the officers quartered upon the inhabitants. The days were spent in pastime, the nights in entertainments. By a proportionate tax on the pay and allowances of each officer, a house was opened for daily resort and for weekly balls, with a gaming-table which had assiduous votaries, and a room devoted to the game of chess. Thrice a week, plays were enacted by amateur performers. The curtain painted by André was greatly admired. The officers, among whom all ranks of the British aristocracy were represented, lived in open licentiousness. At a grand review, a beautiful English girl, mistress of a colonel and dressed in the colors of his regiment, drove down the line in her open carriage with great ostentation. The pursuit of pleasure was so eager, and Howe had on former occasions been so frequently baffled, that an attack in winter was not added to the trials of the army at Valley Forge.

The troops of Burgoyne remained in the environs of Boston. In violation of the word of honor of the officers, much public property had been carried off from Saratoga. As if preparing an excuse for a total disengagement from his obligations, Burgoyne, complaining without reason of the quarters provided for his officers, deliberately wrote and insisted that the United States had violated the public faith, and refused to congress descriptive lists of the non-commissioned officers and soldiers who were not to serve in America during the war. On these grounds, congress suspended the embarkation of the troops under his command till a ratification of the convention should be notified by the court of Great Britain to congress. Burgoyne sailed for England on his parole.

All the while, events illustrated the greatness of the struggle. In February, 1778, a detachment of men from Pittsburg, descending the Ohio and Mississippi, arrived on the evening of the nineteenth at Natchez. The next day they hoisted the flag of the United States, and took possession of the country in their name. The inhabitants, promising a strict neutrality, were admitted to parole as prisoners of war; and the liberty and property of actual residents were respected.

The parties of Indians which the English had let loose on the frontiers roused Virginia, and Saint Clair Clarke received from its governor the commission to carry the flag of independence through the country northwest of the Ohio to Detroit. To counteract the arts of the British emissaries among the Indians on the borders of Virginia and the Carolinas, Colonel Nathaniel Gist was commissioned to take into the public service two hundred of the red men and fifty of the white inhabitants of the neighboring counties. Care was taken to preserve the friendship of the Oneidas.

The American militia of the sea were restlessly active. In the night of the twenty-seventh of January, a privateer took the fort of New Providence, made prize of a British vessel of war of sixteen guns, which had gone in for repairs, and recaptured five American vessels. Biddle, in the "Randolph," a United States frigate of thirty-six guns on a cruise from Charleston, falling in with the "Yarmouth," a British ship of sixty-four guns, hoisted the stars and stripes, fired a broadside, and continued the engagement till his ship went down.

The country was weak only from being without a government. During the winter the members present in congress were sometimes only nine, rarely seventeen; and of former members Franklin, Washington, Jefferson, John Rutledge, Jay, and others, were employed elsewhere, and John Adams had recently been elected to succeed Deane as commissioner in France. The want of power explains and excuses the continuous inefficiency of congress. It proposed in January to borrow ten millions of dollars, but it had no credit. So in January, February, and March two millions of paper money were ordered to be issued, and in April six and a half millions more. These emissions were rapidly followed by corresponding depreciations. When the currency lost its value, congress would have had the army serve on from disinterested patriotism; but Washington pointed out the defect in human nature which does not permit practical affairs to be conducted through a succession of years by a great variety of persons without regard to just claims and equitable interests; and after months of resistance, officers who should serve to the end of the war were promised half-pay for seven years, privates a sum of eighty dollars.

As enlistments failed, Washington urged congress to complete the continental battalions of all the states except South Carolina and Georgia by drafts from their militia; congress, though not till the end of February, adopted the advice, limiting the service to nine months. The execution of the measure was unequal, for it depended on the good-will of the several states; but the scattered villages paraded their militia for the draft with sufficient regularity to save the army from dissolution. Varnum, a brigadier of Rhode Island, proposed the emancipation of slaves in that state, on condition of their enlisting in the army for the war. The scheme, approved by Washington, and by him referred to Cooke, the governor of the state, was accepted. Every able-bodied slave in Rhode Island received by law liberty to enlist in the army for the war. On passing muster he became free and entitled to all the wages and encouragements given by congress to any soldier. The state made some compensation to their masters.

The powerlessness of congress admitted no effective supervision over officers of their own appointment. Unable to force a defaulting agent to a settlement, in February they asked the legislatures of the several states to enact laws for the recovery of debts due to the United States; and they invited the supreme executive of every state to watch the behavior of all civil and military officers of the United States in the execution of their offices.

Driven by necessity, congress won slowly a partial victory over their pride and their fears; and on the second of March they elected Greene quarter-master-general, giving him two assistants that were acceptable to him and the power of appointing all other officers in his department. After more than another month, the same system was extended to the commissary department. The place of inspector-general fell to Baron Steuben, a Prussian officer, then forty-seven years of age, who had served during the seven years' war, and now adopted America for his country. The high rank which he assumed falsely but without question, the good opinion of Vergennes and Saint-Germain, the recommendation of Franklin, and his real merit, secured for him the place of a major-general, which he claimed, and on the fifth of February he was welcomed to Valley Forge. Setting an example to the officers by drilling squads of men, he wrought a reform in the use of the musket and in manœuvre.

Yet there remained a deeply seated conflict of opinion between congress and the commander-in-chief of questions of principle and policy. Washington would from the first have had men enlisted for the war; congress, from jealousy of standing armies, had insisted upon short enlistments. Washington was anxious to exchange prisoners; congress bore in mind that each British prisoner would resume his place in the army, while the American prisoner, from the system of short enlistments, would return home. Washington, by sudden interference, required a respect for the law of treason of each separate state. Washington would have one continental army; congress, an army of thirteen sovereignties. Congress was satisfied with the amount of its power as a helpless committee; Washington wished a government of organized vigor. Congress guarded separate independence; the patriotism of Washington took a wider range, and in return the concentrated public affections, radiating from every part of the United States, met in him. All this merit and this popularity, and the undivided attachment of the army, quickened the jealousy of congress, and made them more sensible of their own relative weakness. They could not have defended themselves against the mutiny of a single regiment. They felt that their perfect control over the general sprung in part from his own nature, and that could not be fully judged of before the end. Nor was it then known that the safety of the country against military usurpation lay in the character and circumstances of the American people, which had life in all its parts, and therefore a common life that was indestructible.

To allay the jealousy which congress entertained and some of its members labored to establish, Washington, on the twenty-first of April, wrote to one of its delegates: "Under proper limitations it is certainly true that standing armies are dangerous to a state. The prejudices of other countries have only gone to them in time of peace, and from their being hirelings. It is our policy to be prejudiced against them in time of war, though they are citizens, having all the ties and interests of citizens, and in most cases property totally unconnected with the military line. The jealousy, impolitic in the extreme, can answer not a single good purpose. It is unjust, because no order of men in the thirteen states has paid a more sacred regard to the proceedings of congress than the army; for without arrogance or the smallest deviation from truth it may be said, that no history now extant can furnish an instance of an army's suffering such uncommon hardships as ours has done, and bearing them with the same patience and fortitude. Their submitting without a murmur is a proof of patience and obedience which in my opinion can scarce be paralleled. There may have been some remonstrances or applications to congress in the style of complaint from the army, and slaves indeed should we be if this privilege were denied; but these will not authorize nor even excuse a jealousy that they are therefore aiming at unreasonable powers, or making strides subversive of civil authority. There should be none of these distinctions. We should all, congress and army, be considered as one people, embarked in one cause, in one interest, acting on the same principle and to the same end." In framing an oath of fidelity for all civil and military officers, congress, much as it avoided the expression, made them swear that the "people of the United States" owed no allegiance to the king of Great Britain. The soldiers serving under one common flag, to establish one common independence, and, though in want of food, of shoes, of clothes, of straw for bedding, of regular pay, of pay in a currency of fixed value, never suffering their just discontent to get the better of their patriotism, still more clearly foreshadowed a great nationality. The unity of the country was formally proclaimed in its relations to the rest of the world.

&§ §&

AMERICANS *date their independence from July 4, 1776, but it was not until September 3, 1783, that the Treaty of Paris officially confirmed the result. The result was preordained almost two years earlier at Yorktown. The British indicated their desire to have done with the hopeless struggle when on March 20, 1782, Lord North's government fell. Fifteen days earlier, the House of Commons had directed the crown to negotiate a settlement of the war. John Adams, who since September 27, 1779, had been authorized to negotiate a peace treaty, now shared the responsibility with such luminaries as Thomas Jefferson, Benjamin Franklin, John Jay, and Henry Laurens. These commissioners were directed to take their cues from the French government. It was hardly a condition destined to set well with the xeno-phobic John Adams.*

*The hallmark of American independence was made apparent when on April 19, 1782, the Dutch government recognized the new nation's in-dependence. By early autumn, The Hague had extended a loan to and signed a treaty of commerce and friendship with the Confederation. London gave tacit recognition to American independence when its commissioner agreed to open negotiations beginning on September 27, 1782, at Paris. At first, the two commissioners in Paris, Franklin and Jay, deferred to French wishes. But with the arrival of John Adams on the scene late in October, the com-missioners struck out on their own to reach an agreement with the British. They suspected, rightly, that the French hoped to play a devious game which would guarantee them large gains while circumscribing American in-dependence. On November 5, 1782, the basic articles of peace were agreed upon, and with only minor changes became the final Treaty of Paris. The French Foreign Minister, Count Vergennes, surprised at the American show of independence, protested, but the commissioners, well aware that the British wanted to minimize their own losses, turned his protest aside with a bland reply. Peace had been obtained and Paris had its first sign that the newly independent colonies did not mean to trade one master for another.*

*Richard B. Morris (1904- ), a prolific historian, whose* Government and Labor in Early America *(1946) is a classic, has explored the records of the peace negotiations again. The result is a brilliant narrative of a complex diplomacy that culminated in American independence. It also confirms the wisdom of John Adams' request: "Let posterity have all means of judging and let them judge." As he knew, the findings reflect well on himself and his fellow commissioners; they were in the finest sense of the word,* patriots.

# THE
# PEACEMAKERS

## by *Richard B. Morris*

In late October of 1779, the Continental frigate *Confederacy* weighed anchor and stood out into the Delaware Bay for the long voyage across the North Atlantic. Crowded on and below her decks was a complement of three hundred, mostly sailing and fighting men, but including a dozen passengers. Two of the latter were men of special distinction, and the captain of the thirty-six-gun warship, a Connecticut Yankee named Seth Harding, had been entrusted by the American Congress with the responsibility of ensuring their safe passage to Europe. They were Conrad Alexandre Gerard, the retiring French minister plenipotentiary to the United States, and John Jay, the newly appointed American minister plenipotentiary to Spain.

Over the past months Jay and Gerard had worked in close association. Though the latter was crowding fifty and sixteen years the American's senior, the careers of the ship companions ran somewhat parallel courses. Both came from upper-middle-class French backgrounds, Gerard from a family of Alsatian public servants and Jay was the son of a wealthy New York merchant of Huguenot descent. Both had been trained for the law and turned to diplomacy; Gerard had behind him a quarter of a century of experience as a career diplomat, while Jay stood at the threshold of a new career. One epitomized the diplomacy of the *ancien régime;* the other the untutored approach of a revolutionary government. To accept his assignment to Spain, John Jay had resigned both the Presidency of the Continental Congress and the Chief Justiceship of the State of New York. The persuasive and conscientious New York lawyer headed the first of three missions dispatched in the course of the fall and winter of 1779-80 to win friends and support for the cause of American independence and bring to a victorious conclusion the lengthening War of the Revolution. Gerard was returning home for reasons of health, and the achievements of his mission were still to be evaluated.

On departure John Jay and his vivacious young wife Sarah were showered with farewell gifts and the cordial good wishes of a host of friends. Robert Morris, the Patriot merchant prince, had promised a box of "seegars," if needed. From West Point General Washington sent Sally a lock of his hair enclosed in a note expressing the wish that "prosperous gales, unruffled seas, and everything pleasing and desirable, may sooth the path she is about to walk in." Unfortunately the General did not possess the kind of magic that could make this wish come true. Jay's boyhood friend, classmate, and former law partner, Robert R. Livingston, New York's Chancellor, delegate-designate to Congress replacing Jay, and an upstate feudal lord, wrote him a note admonishing the voyager to "omit no occasion of lessening the pain I feel in your absence by writing to me by every conveyance." Little did either man realize how distance and a divergent view of the way peace should be made were to bring about the first rift between the man who signed himself "Dear John, your friend," and the minister plenipotentiary, a rift which would widen with the passing years.

Sally would be missed, too. In a poignant letter her father, William Livingston, the Patriot Governor of New Jersey, a man pre-eminent among the Whig intellectual leadership, confessed the pain at parting with his daughter "across a wide ocean and to a foreign land." Considering his age and "the mortality of man," Livingston thought it probable that he would never see her again. Invoking God's protection for his "dear child," he enjoined her not to suffer "the gaieties and amusements of the world, and the particular avocations of what is called *high life*" and not to banish from her life a sense of religious obligation. In lighter vein, Sally's brother, William James, spoofed that neither the mountains nor the fleas of Spain should "terrify the mind of an American" and admonished his sister not to fail to report "every piece of knight errantry" she would experience on reaching "the land of the renowned Don Quixote." That "fine sensible woman," as

Richard Bache described Sally Jay in a letter to his father-in-law, Benjamin Franklin, was destined to see little chivalric behavior and even less of that hospitality for which Spain was proverbial.

Smothered by the attention of friends and armored with the cautions and prayers of relatives, the Jays, along with the motley ship's party, embarked for France en route to Madrid. Five days later Jay's private secretary and brother-in-law, Henry Brockholst Livingston, wrote his own mother that the ship was still becalmed in Delaware Bay and had covered a mere forty miles, with seventy more to go before reaching the Capes. The sea air proved a tonic for Sally's appetite, and seasickness had not yet struck. Jay took advantage of the motionless trip to send Robert Livingston a simple numerical cipher to be used in their personal correspondence.

On the sixth day out from Chester the becalmed ship underwent a dramatic change of fortune. Gale winds now pounded the *Confederacy*. "Who saith," Sally asked her mother, "unto the wave thus far shall thou go. And to the winds, peace, be still?" If most passengers henceforth were to suffer intermittent bouts of *mal de mer*, the American minister plenipotentiary seemed to be especially signaled out by Neptune. "My dear Mr. Jay suffered exceedingly at least five weeks and was surprizingly reduced," Sally wrote home. One consolation was that in the turbulent sea the *Confederacy* had managed to elude the British frigates *Roebuck* and *Romulus* believed to be standing off the coast to intercept her.

Other and severer trials were in store. "About 4 o'clock in the morning of the 7th November," Sally Jay wrote her mother, "we were alarmed by an unusual noise upon deck, and what particularly surprised me was the lamentations of persons in distress." Her brother Brockholst tried to calm her, but he had little reason for composure. When the passengers scrambled on deck they grasped the situation at once. A freak accident had befallen the frigate. As the *Confederacy* had moved out of the chill gray waters of the North Atlantic coast into the great indigo mass of the Gulf Stream the warm air had caused the taut rigging to slacken. The master ordered the watch into the shrouds, but before steps could be taken to fend off disaster, the mainmast crashed to the decks, followed almost immediately by mizzenmast, foremast, and even bowsprit. The groans of the injured heightened the terror of those first moments. Among those struck by the falling timber was a sailor whose hand was broken and a gunner whose injured leg required amputation. A few days later the amputee was buried at sea.

The ship was now rolling heavily in a high wind and rough sea. While all hands cleared away the wreckage, Captain Harding took a shot to get his bearings. The *Confederacy* lay like a log in the water south-southeast of Newfoundland, some eleven hundred miles from the Capes of the Delaware and under nine hundred from the Azores. A small mast with improvised sail was erected, but a south-southeast wind of gale proportions combined with a turbulent sea wrenched and split the shank of the rudder, which now began banging against the stern. To steady the ship into the wind a floating anchor was thrown off the bow. By heroic efforts the rudder was temporarily bolted in place and made to function after a fashion. More than two weeks of strong winds and heavy seas elapsed, however, before the jury masts were securely rigged. Still the rudder demanded daily attention, as the steering ropes would snap and the rudder's uncontrolled banging against the stern sent the ship's company into a constant state of alarm. To prevent further damage bags filled with oakum were hung on each side, but not before considerable water had leaked in through the stern and ruined the bread supply. By now the improvised sails were little more than rags. Splits had to be sewn every day, and the ship was virtually out of twine.

By November 23rd the weather had moderated and the frigate was in fair condition to proceed. But how far and where to were the big questions. A council of commissioned officers advised Captain Harding that the most prudent course now would be to head south for the first safe port in the West Indies. Harding concurred, and reported accordingly to Jay and Gerard, whose orders, by the instructions of Congress' Marine Committee, were to govern. Jay saw no other prudent course but to follow the captain's advice. The alternatives would have placed both ship and crew in jeopardy. Frigates, in the current state of the Continental Navy, were hardly expendable, and crews, as Harding himself had too recently found out, were hard to come by.

Notwithstanding hazards which made a winter crossing of the North Atlantic almost certain suicide, the Chevalier Gerard, impatient to return to France for reasons that were entirely personal, lost both his head and his temper. If France had to be ruled out, why not the Azores? he expostulated. The Portuguese islands were five hundred miles nearer than Martinique, and there the diplomats should have no difficulty in getting passage to the Continent on another ship. Harding patiently explained that an open roadstead, which was the best that the Azores could offer, would not provide safe anchorage for a ship in the condition of the *Confederacy*, nor the opportunity to repair and refit the vessel. Again Jay concurred. Furious that the American diplomat did not override the captain, Gerard now sulked apart. To add fuel to the flame, the secretary of Jay's mission, William Carmichael, appointed to that post by Congress in an ill-advised moment, openly took Gerard's part and began his systematic intrigues to undermine the authority which the American minister plenipotentiary jealously guarded. It was perhaps a small chink, but the dispute over the ship's course was the first of those differences with European diplomats which were in time to persuade John Jay, then one of America's foremost Francophiles, that the best course for America was to go it alone.

Jay was too much the responsible diplomat to let a private argument hamper his mission. To thaw the diplomatic ice the Jays arranged a birthday party for Madame Gerard. Despite the "intolerable" roll of the ship even in the smooth southerly sea, elaborate day-long festivities took place. Following a formal breakfast, the participants spent the day under a huge awning stretched out across the deck, playing chess, cards, and drafts, and ended with what was, considering the circumstances, described as an elegant dinner, culminating with numerous toasts, punctuated with the discharge of cannon. That same day the sailors insisted on shaving and ducking all voyagers who had never crossed the Tropic of Cancer before, not forgetting the Jays' twelve-year-old nephew, Peter Jay Munro, who did not entirely relish the initiation rites.

Any thought that the festivities would have mollified Gerard was quickly dissipated. As the *Confederacy* approached Martinique, Gerard suddenly resumed his belligerent posture. He insisted on making for St. Pierre on the north side of the island on the ground that if the ship went to the south side it would be in danger of running to leeward of the island, then be unable to get up to Fort Royal, and very likely fall to the British squadron operating out of St. Lucia. Astonished that Gerard should presume to direct the navigation of the ship, Jay again left the decision to the captain, who reserved judgment until they were in sight of the islands. On the fourteenth of December Sally wrote: "A land bird! a land bird! Oh! the pleasure of being near land." On the eighteenth she reported seeing "the most verdant, romantic country I ever beheld." This was the volcanic island of Martinique, and as its lush green Mont Pelée loomed on the horizon the ship's company distinctly heard the sound of cannon fire to the south. The decision had been made for them by Rear Admiral Parker, whose squadron from St. Lucia had slipped across and chosen that moment to attack a convoy heading for Fort Royal. For the *Confederacy* there was no choice but the northern port of St. Pierre, and the fact that Gerard was shown to be in the right only made him more unbearable. Had the southerly course been chosen, the *Confederacy* would almost surely have become a prize of the Royal Navy, and Mr. Jay's mission would have ended for him in the Tower of London.

The ten days spent at Martinique provided welcome diversion for the Jays. At gay, crowded St. Pierre, glistening white in the tropic sun at the foot of slumbering Mont Pelée, the Jays were the guests of William Bingham, Robert Morris' trading partner and one of the numerous tribe of international war profiteers. Bingham, then acting as agent of Congress in the French West Indies, was concerned with the procurement of supplies for the Continental Army. Accorded every politeness by the Marquis de Bouille, the island's Governor, including a military review in their honor, the Jays combined official business with pleasure. Mrs. Jay shopped, observed bee-keeping techniques, visited sugar mills, saw the wild *bal doudou*, and was fed every bit of gossip about the duel fought between an officer of the *Confederacy* and a lieutenant of a French frigate over a quarrel arising in a bagnio, with no harm to either participant. Mrs. Jay's husband, whose aversion to slavery was one day to culminate in his affixing his signature as Governor of New York to an emancipation act, saw at firsthand that system in its most degrading aspect. He saw slaves going about their duties, with iron collars around their necks and dragging fifty-pound chains. He saw canoes laden with hogsheads of sugar rowed by slaves chained by one leg to the boat and bearing on their backs the marks of the lash. These sights he would not soon forget.

With Gerard, Jay visited Fort Royal to have Admiral La Motte Piquet expedite the refitting of the *Confederacy* and arrange their own passage to Europe. Jay advised Harding that, once his ship was outfitted—and the French officials seemed to give that operation a rather low priority—he should proceed to an American port for supplies. On Christmas Day Jay drew against the meager funds allotted for his own salary and divided a hundred guineas among the officers of the *Confederacy* so that they would not be "obliged to sneak, as they phrase it, from the company of French officers for fear of running in debt with them for a bottle of wine, or a bowl of punch, because not able to pay for their share of the reckoning." Such a situation Jay considered "too humiliating to be tolerated, and too destructive to that pride and opinion of independent equality which I wish to see influence all our officers. . . . Indeed," he added, "it would have given me pleasure to have done something towards covering the nakedness of the crew, but the expence I have been put to by coming here, and the preparations for another voyage would not admit of it." Prideful of his position, Jay himself was soon to share the humiliating experiences of these ship's officers, when Congress, with its accustomed financial irresponsibility, overdrew against his accounts abroad and left him without resources until the Spanish government in a most grudging fashion came to his rescue.

Three days later the Jay and Gerard parties set sail from Martinique on the French frigate *Aurora*. How unlike the first phase of the journey was the "short passage" to Europe. "Sailing sweetly before the wind," was the way Sally headed a letter to Jay's father, dated January 9th, in which she reported that her spouse was enjoying perfect health, something that Jay seldom confessed to throughout a very long life. The *Aurora* may have seemed to Sally Jay to be a "dull sailor" after her previous adventure, but it did offer some excitement. A few days before coming in sight of land the *Aurora* was chased by a British man-of-war, and cleared for action, but managed to outsail her pursuer and reach the safe harborage of Cadiz on January 22nd. There it was learned that the naval superiority of the enemy in the Mediterranean rendered it unsafe to proceed to Toulon, the frigate's destination. "Admiral Rodney had saved us the necessity of going that round about way to Madrid," was the way Sally put it, little realizing how long the distance from Cadiz to the court of Spain would prove to be.

Before Jay left Philadelphia Virginia's elder statesman, Edmund Pendleton, volunteered advice which in retrospect was to take on an ironic note. "I cordially wish you may be able to heal the new-made breach between Spain and Britain," he wrote Jay, "since France appears disposed to peace, and I am mistaken if the Court of London are not ready to make up with us, if nothing respecting our allies hinder it. Indeed we want an honourable peace; but I hope there lives not a wretch who wishes it upon terms of dishonor to our noble allies." It was a piece of wishful thinking to suppose that Jay would be able to step into the role of peacemaker between France's ally and America's enemy and that he could secure a peace which would both satisfy Spain's honor and meet the necessities of the Thirteen United States. The American minister was too much of a realist to take so exalted a view of the role he was expected to play. It had taken the Jays three months to negotiate the waters between the Delaware and Cadiz, and they were still months away from Madrid.

Jay's selection by the Continental Congress had come as a climax to a great debate over foreign policy which almost completely monopolized the business of Congress for virtually the whole of the year 1779 preceding his appointment. What touched off the debates was the arrival early in 1779 of the Chevalier Gerard, designated by His Most Christian Majesty as minister to the United States, and charged with taking measures to implement the alliance between France and America. On reaching Philadelphia Gerard lost no time letting Congress know how urgent it was for that body to spell out its terms for peace. To make sure that the members of Congress could have the benefit of his expert knowledge, he took a residence within a stone's throw of Congress' meeting place, the State House at the eastern end of the town. There he wined and dined Congressmen nightly, and made his presence felt at Congressional committee meetings. A born meddler, Gerard never learned to let well enough alone.

The French minister proved an acute observer of the American scene. Though insensitive to the broader implications of the American Revolution, he quickly demonstrated a range of knowledge of the Thirteen United States and their delegates in Congress which would have gratified the omniscient French Encyclopedists had they been privileged to read his confidential reports. In weekly dispatches to the Comte de Vergennes, Gerard reported the intense factional struggle that was shaping up, and reassured his chief that he was throwing all his weight as well as his not insubstantial pecuniary resources on the side which he considered, if not openly pro-French, at least the more amenable to the wishes of Louis XVI.

Over the issues of peace an outsider like Gerard might have anticipated that there would be a rather clear-cut division in Congress along North-South lines, since the South was concerned about the West, to which its states had territorial claims under their old charters, and was equally concerned with having the Mississippi open to American shipping. In both these areas the vital interests of the North were not involved. Contrariwise, the New Englanders could be expected to insist on regaining the rights of fishing off the Grand Bank of Newfoundland which they had lost by Parliamentary reprisal for their contumacy, and the fisheries were a matter of indifference to Southerners.

This was not what Gerard found when he came to Philadelphia. For a very curious and special reason the evolving parties did not divide on strict geographic lines. Congress, and with it the country, was torn apart by an intense and savage personal feud between two of the three American commissioners to France, Silas Deane, Connecticut merchant and onetime schoolteacher, and Arthur Lee, scion of the aristocratic Virginia planter family. Prosecuted with a degree of acrimony that makes the later breach between Jefferson and Hamilton seem like a decorous spat at a vicarage garden party, the Deane-Lee dispute was to have a profound impact on both the conduct of the war and the objectives of the peace. The Deane faction, heartened by French support, believed in trimming peace demands to the realities of the sober military situation; the supporters of Lee, known as the anti-Gallican party, were outright expansionists.

Like its predecessors of ancient Rome, Congress' triumvirate of Deane,

Lee, and Franklin, named back in 1776 as commissioners to France, was destined to founder on the rock of mutual distrust. Arthur Lee, albeit a man of considerable abilities, knowledgeable about conditions abroad, and fluent in a number of foreign tongues, was bitten by ambition and envy, and these not uncommon traits were compounded by a frightening paranoidal streak. Lee begrudged Franklin his enormous popularity in France and ready access to the court at Versailles, and never forgave him for having outsmarted him in some big land deals. He suspected Deane of lining his own pockets by complex, secret, and highly irregular financial operations. As the first commissioner to come to Paris, Deane had originally performed yeoman feats in acquiring arms and supplies for the American cause, but he soon betrayed a lack of sound judgment in the associations he formed and the decisions he made, and showed himself utterly devoid of that sense of the proprieties that we have now come to expect of public characters.

The fact is that in the days of the Revolution the concept of conflict of interest had by no means crystallized. Men like Robert Morris and Nathanael Greene found no inconsistency in representing the government and private business interests simultaneously and in the same transactions. Government officials engaged in procurement, commissary, and quartermaster matters, intermingled the government's business with their own, bought goods for themselves or their partners and employed their own ships in the public service or public ships for private business. Robert Morris, who became the virtual manager of foreign procurement, once remarked to his protégé, "I shall continue to discharge my duty faithfully to the public and pursue my private fortune by all such honorable and fair means as the times will admit of, and I dare say you will do the same."

Benjamin Franklin, prince of pragmatists, chose to be ignorant or tolerant about the nature and extent of Deane's private speculations. If Franklin was associated with Deane in a great Western land speculation known as the Vandalia enterprise, which involved correspondence with British subjects in wartime, and if he allowed his own grandnephew Jonathan Williams to be set up by Deane as a shipping agent at Nantes, the third commissioner in Paris did not share the philosopher-statesman's complacency. Lee quickly became Deane's implacable enemy. Convinced that the original supplies France furnished America through the fictitious business house set up by that talented adventurer and past master of blackmail, Caron de Beaumarchais, were a gift from the French court, Lee denounced Deane's agreement to reimburse Beaumarchais as improper if not fraudulent. Since Lee had initiated the negotiations with Beaumarchais in London, much weight must be given to this accusation. Other accusations were not so well substantiated. Lee passed along to his friends in Congress every rumor, regardless of how slender, so long as it was discreditable to Silas Deane. In fact, he made so many charges that some of them could not have failed to have hit their mark.

One charge that Lee could not prove then, but was later substantiated, was the accusation that Deane, in association with Samuel Wharton, Philadelphia merchant and land speculator, and Dr. Edward Bancroft, had leaked news of the signing of the treaty of alliance with France in order to promote their speculations on the London Stock Exchange. The true character of Bancroft was unknown at the time, except to a select few. Of New England birth and once a student of schoolteacher Silas Deane, Bancroft had studied medicine in England and came to Franklin's attention during the latter's prewar residence in England. When war broke out he acted as a spy on Franklin's behalf, subsequently joined the doctor in France, and continued to make cross-Channel journeys from time to time. It did not take long before Bancroft, an amoral opportunist, became a double agent, furnishing secret and confidential data to the British under the name of Dr. Edward Edwards. In retrospect, Bancroft's close working relationship with Silas Deane, with whom he engaged in various dubious speculations, carries sinister overtones, and lends credence to, if it does not confirm, some of Arthur Lee's worst suspicions.

Lee found ready ears in Congress, including those of his influential brother, Richard Henry, and the New England contingent headed by Samuel Adams. Soon shrill voices were raised in the halls of Congress against Deane. Summoned home to give an accounting, Deane returned in July, 1778. Although he demanded a prompt hearing, he was kept waiting for months while his accusers held the floor. Finally, he blew the lid off the case himself, with a published account in the *Pennsylvania Packet* of December 5, 1778, in which he defended his own conduct and made countercharges against Lee. In quick rejoinder Tom Paine, secretary of the Committee of Foreign Affairs, entered the lists against Deane with an indiscreet letter to a newspaper exposing the nature of Louis XVI's secret aid to America prior to the alliance. Paine's admissions made mockery out of Vergennes' endless protestations of innocent neutrality, protestations which Britain's last minister to Paris, Lord Stormont, knew from British intelligence sources had to be taken with more than the proverbial grain of salt. With the battle transferred momentarily from Congress to the newspapers, Gerard stepped in, remonstrating that the honor of France was involved. In its first of many acts of obeisance to the French minister, Congress dismissed Paine from his post. Notwithstanding, the Lees and their New England allies pressed the attack against Deane, and secured a recruit in the person of Henry Laurens, the South Carolina merchant Patriot, whom age had not mellowed, but rather made increasingly quarrelsome, petulant, and, perhaps in some part because of his Huguenot father, critical of France. In protest against the Deane faction, Laurens resigned the Presidency of Congress on December 9th, and John Jay, a strong champion of Silas Deane, was elected in his place the very next morning. Congress, which had heard all Deane's accusers, permitted its Paris commissioner only to submit written answers to the charges. Enough was heard, however, to prove one or two irregularities, and to suggest countless others.

In assuming the mantle of virtue the Lee faction might have had a stronger case if its own operations had been aboveboard. But the Lees did not come into court with clean hands. On his return to America in the fall of '79 Dr. Lee shipped a cargo of his own merchandise on the Continental frigate *Alliance,* thereby providing his enemies with ground for court-martialing

Pierre Landais, the eccentric French captain of that naval vessel. Arthur's merchant brother, William, the only American to hold the post of alderman of London, was not above trying to capitalize on his inside knowledge of the approaching alliance with France. Employed by Congress on missions abroad, he charged Congress excessive commissions in his dual capacity of commercial agent and commissioner to Berlin. The older brother, Richard Henry Lee, who carried the gauntlet for his family in Congress until, worn down in body and spirit, he resigned his seat in May of '79, had only recently been involved in an ugly scandal. To protect himself from currency inflation he had changed the rents due from his tenants under leases from money to payments in wheat or tobacco, thereby bringing down upon his head the wrath of the tenantry and the condemnation of holier-than-thou Patriots.

It is only fair to observe that, if there was a conspicuous lack of self-restraint in high places, Congress and the states could not escape their share of the blame. The unchecked flow of printing-press money and the unwillingness of the states to invest Congress with adequate taxing power had fanned the flames of speculation. "The inundation of money appears to have overflowed virtue, and I fear will bury the liberty of America in the same grave," Richard Henry Lee confessed in June of '79, adding, "The demon of avarice, extortion, and fortune-making seizes all ranks."

The Deane-Lee imbroglio, despite its divisive impact, had two constructive effects on the peacemaking to come. The quarrel convinced Congress that it was now necessary to be represented abroad by ministers who could be counted on to put the public good above private gain or personal rancor, and it impelled Congress to spell out its peace aims. A committee consisting of one delegate from each state, appointed on January 20, 1779, to investigate the Deane affair, brought in its report on March 24th. It reinforced its revelations of imprudent conduct of public affairs abroad with the recommendation that, as a result of "suspicions and animosities . . . highly prejudicial to the honor and interests of the United States," the commissioners be removed and "but one plenipotentiary minister or commissioner" be appointed for each foreign court.

If Deane was sacked, Lee failed to escape the shake-up. One of the chief complaints against the latter was that, aside from his quarrelsome disposition, he had been unrestrained in his expressions of "contempt for the French nation." His supporters, chief among them Sam Adams, vainly sought to elicit from Gerard a statement to the effect that Lee enjoyed the confidence of the French court. Instead, the French minister showed Congressmen William Paca and William Henry Drayton a letter from Vergennes in which the foreign minister confessed: *"Je crains M. Lee et ses entours."* This was enough to bring about the downfall of that self-righteous troublemaker and to make Gerard forever *persona non grata* with the Lee faction. Franklin was now left in sole command of Congress' business in Paris.

Even after Lee's recall was voted, his partisans were determined to have him named minister to Spain to secure an alliance with that nation, and to have John Adams, an acknowledged friend of the cause of Lee, designated peace commissioner to treat with Great Britain once negotiations started. On

September 25th Adams was put up for the latter post by Henry Laurens. Meriwether Smith of Virginia countered for the Deane faction by proposing John Jay. On the first ballot Adams failed to win an absolute majority. On the second he shaded Jay by a vote of six states to five, but, with South Carolina still divided, he again failed of nomination.

To break the deadlock the Deane partisans now proposed that a minister plenipotentiary be appointed to the Spanish court in lieu of a commissioner, a post to which Arthur Lee had earlier been named. The negotiation of a treaty of alliance, they argued, involved duties quite different from those which Lee had been performing. Laurens promptly nominated Lee, but the anti-Lee forces, pursuing what Laurens recognized as the rule of "divide and conquer," put up the name of John Adams. Then, having split the Lee faction, the Gallican party put up a third name, the man they really wanted, John Jay, Congress' President. "Mr. Jay," as Laurens ungenerously put it, "squeezed in," helped by his own vote as a member of the New York delegation. Desperate to have Adams in Paris conducting the peace negotiations, the New Englanders were ready to strike a compromise, one which sent the President of Congress to Madrid, resulted in Adams being unanimously chosen for the post of peace commissioner, and made Arthur Lee the sacrificial goat.

The die-hard supporters of Lee took it hard. James Lovell denounced Jay's election "to take the post of a man murdered on purpose to make room" as "the crowning act of all Deane's base arts," and Henry Laurens wrote hopefully, "Our friend Arthur Lee will rise again." But after a little time for reflection most New Englanders put the best face on the results that they could. "Away with sackcloth and ashes when evitables become inevitables," Lovell wrote in more sensible vein in his very next letter to John Adams. As might have been expected, Gerard plumed himself on what he considered a victory for the pro-French party. "The choice of Jay leaves nothing to be desired," he wrote to Vergennes. "To much intelligence and the best intentions he joins an aimiable and conciliatory temper." If by "conciliatory" he really meant pliable, he was soon to find out that he had misjudged his man. The Spanish observer in America, Juan de Miralles, was equally exultant. Jay, with whom he had been on cordial relations, possessed in his eyes the background and temperament of the true aristocrat. In addition to his impeccable social standing, Jay had shown a sympathetic attitude toward Spain, which would make him, Miralles felt, most acceptable in Madrid.

In the long tedious months before Jay took up his duties at Madrid he could not have helped reflecting on the heated battle which had been fought over his selection, and, more to the point, on what Congress expected him to accomplish in Spain. The instructions binding Jay and Adams had been adopted only after extended debate, to which the Deane-Lee controversy had served as curtain raiser. The Congress had to consider the effect on America's peace objectives of two alliances, the one with France, which had been cemented in 1778, and the other between France and Spain, in which the United States was not even a junior partner. It was clear to Congress that America's peace objectives would have to be reconciled with those of their ally, His Most Christian Majesty, and their ally's ally, His Most Catholic Majesty. Should they for one moment forget it, the Chevalier Gerard, considered the representative of Spanish interests in America, was there to remind them of their duty.

So far as France was concerned, that nation had virtually renounced large territorial aspirations in America. Specifically, she had abandoned the idea of recovering Canada lost in the previous war, even secretly resolved that it remain in British hands. France was determined nonetheless to gain trade advantages from the war, advantages which England had commanded when the Thirteen Colonies were a part of her vast mercantile empire. France was immensely concerned about recovering the fishing rights she had once exercised, since the Seven Years' War, while allowing her to retain her right to fish the banks of Newfoundland and to retain the two tiny fishing islands of St. Pierre and Miquelon, deprived her of the right of fishing along the edge of the coasts and of curing fish except in specifically allotted places. To enhance her fishing opportunities France hoped to acquire Newfoundland and her old possessions around the Gulf of St. Lawrence. It must be borne in mind that eighteenth-century statesmen looked upon the fisheries as the nursery of seamen and as holding one of the keys to a powerful maritime and naval establishment. In the light of this traditional point of view the French national interest in the North Atlantic fisheries seems perfectly comprehensible. The issue had come up on two occasions, at the time of the treaty of alliance with America in 1778 and the following year, in the Franco-Spanish negotiations. Franklin and Arthur Lee failed to persuade France to insert a clause in her treaty with America renouncing the right of conquests "in the islands of Newfoundland, Cape Breton, St. John's Anticosti, and the Bermudas." Herein lay a potential source of trouble. The New England fishing fleet had enjoyed immemorial privileges of fishing and curing on the coasts of Newfoundland and Nova Scotia. Though Parliament, as a punitive measure, had canceled these privileges, the New Englanders had never conceded Parliament's authority to enact that repressive measure.

If the potential rivalry with France was in a fringe area, the brewing controversy with Spain struck at the heart of America's territorial aspirations as a nation. Until the spring of '79 Spain was a bystander, courted by France to enter the war on her side and by England to remain neutral. The Spanish court found itself in an excellent position to blackmail both sides, and it made the best of its opportunities. Spain had put pressure upon England to accept her mediation, but at a very high figure. Her price for compelling France to quit the war was the fortress of Gibraltar, facetiously described by her Principal Minister, the Conde de Floridablanca, as "that pile of stones," which was "only a matter of expense and trouble to them, disturbing to us, and an impediment to permanent friendship." The British government was unwilling to pay this kind of blackmail, and remained unbudgeable on the question of referring to outside mediation her private quarrel with the Thirteen Colonies.

On April 3, 1779, Spain issued an ultimatum to Great Britain, calling for an indefinite suspension of arms in England's wars with France and the United States and a peace congress at Madrid to settle boundaries. Significantly, the ultimatum suggested that the territorial limits be fixed on the basis of the ground held by each side at the time the truce went into effect (the *uti possidetis*, as it was called in the language of diplomacy).

The proposal for a truce came up again and again. Suspicious delegates in the American Congress recognized that it would "let the wolf into the sheep-fold," for it would have left America a badly truncated collection of states, hardly a viable nation. At the time of the Spanish ultimatum, it should be borne in mind, Great Britain held New York City as well as Long Island, Rhode Island, a substantial part of Georgia, and vast if indeterminate parts of the Northwest. The issue of the recognition of the United States was evaded in the ultimatum; at best Spain proposed *de facto* recognition during the negotiations. France, when notified of the ultimatum, bitterly protested the terms as humiliating and "fatal to the dignity of the King," but Great Britain prevented a breach between the two members of the Family Compact by flatly turning them down.

The ultimatum was in fact a brazen piece of deception, for, without waiting for England to reject it, Spain went ahead and signed a secret treaty with France at Aranjuez on April 12th, committing Spain to war. By its terms an invasion of the British Isles was to be undertaken. Every effort was to be made to recover for Spain Minorca, Pensacola, and Mobile, lost in the previous war, to expel the British from the Bay of Honduras, and revoke the privilege of British subjects to cut wood in the Bay of Campeche. For France the parties agreed to expel the British from Newfoundland, to recover Dominica, to secure liberty of trade with the East Indies, to get back Senegal, along with the liberty to trade on the coasts of Africa not pre-empted by English factories. Significantly, in the light of Spain's later concern about America's claim to fishing privileges off the Grand Bank, it was agreed that, were France to regain Newfoundland, she would admit Spanish subjects to the fisheries there, presumably no one else; and, reciprocally, French subjects were to be allowed a share in the woodcutting on the Campeche coast should the British be expelled from that area. The two courts bound themselves to make no peace or enter into any truce until Gibraltar should be restored to Spain and France's control over the port of Dunkirk fully achieved.

Vergennes had sought to win from Spain a pledge not to put down arms until the independence of the United States was recognized by England, since American independence was the ostensible cause of France's original entry into the war. The most he could secure by the secret treaty was a Spanish promise not to attempt to interfere in this matter or to conclude any understanding either with the United States or with another party regarding American independence without consulting France. The ostensible reason given for Spain's declination was that she had as yet not concluded any treaty with the United States, but Charles III of Spain let it be understood in the chancelleries of Europe that France's alliance with the insurgents had no bearing on Spain's decision to enter the conflict, that she had little interest in the new United States, and regarded a successful rebellion as a bad example to her own colonies.

The secret pact of Aranjuez seemed on its face to be a triumph for the combined diplomatic efforts of the Comte de Vergennes, France's respected Foreign Minister, and Spain's ambassador to Versailles, the Conde de Aranda, the prowar leader of the Aragonese faction critical of Floridablanca. All along Vergennes and Aranda had been pressing the Spanish court to join France in the war and thus fulfill the obligations of the Family Compact existing between the two branches of the Bourbon House. The fact is that cooperation between the two nations had virtually come to a dead end before the American Revolution had gotten under way, and at most there had persisted an outward show of intimate union. The cooling-off process began at least as far back as 1770, when Spain tried to force England to quit the Falkland Islands. Instead of rushing to Spain's support, Louis XV dismissed the Duc de Choiseul, his anti-British Foreign Minister, and informed a shocked Spanish court that it could not count upon military assistance from France. Forced to yield the Falklands, Spain suffered a public humiliation so proud a nation was unlikely to forget quickly. Deprived of French support, Spain was also obliged to take a more conciliatory stand toward Portugal, with whom she had been having a running feud.

What the insurgent Americans could not have known at the time Congress dispatched Jay to Europe, because of the secrecy with which the Franco-Spanish understanding was cloaked, was that France, by agreeing not to make peace without Spain and to continue the war until Gibraltar was obtained, had in effect modified her alliance with America and changed and enlarged the purposes of the war without America's consent and even without her knowledge. With America about to send a minister plenipotentiary to the court of Charles III it would not be long before Spain's objectives would be revealed as in fact incompatible with those of the Thirteen States. France's Minister to Spain was among the first to recognize that incompatibility of peace aims between an absolutist Catholic monarchy and a revolutionary republican and secular state. "Let us not conceal from ourselves," Montmorin warned Vergennes, "how little interest Spain takes in the United States of America. We shall certainly have evidence of this not only in the course of the war but more especially when the question comes up of concluding peace."

In view of her vast holdings on the North American Continent, Spain could hardly be expected to view with equanimity either the dangerous example which the Thirteen rebellious Colonies offered to her own restless possessions in the Americas or the threat that American expansionism posed to her interests in the Mississippi region. Vergennes sought to dispel Spain's suspicions and to reassure her that she had nothing to fear from the United States, since the new nation was bound by that "inertia that is characteristic of all constitutional democracies." Floridablanca, perhaps the greater realist of the two, quickly recognized the challenge to Spanish possessions that an independent America posed.

By the Convention of Aranjuez, France was obliged to watch over Spain's interests in her negotiations with the United States. Gerard had, even before the Convention went into effect, anticipated its mandate. Concerned about rumors of impending peace talks between the United States and Great Britain apart from France, he elicited from Congress the declaration "that as neither France or these United States may of right, so these United States will not consider either truce or peace with the common enemy, without the formal consent of their ally first obtained." In a communication to Congress on February 9th and in a private audience before that body the next week, Gerard declared that Spain had made her final offer of mediation to George III. Were it to prove fruitless, she would honor her commitments under the Family Compact. It was imperative, therefore, for the United States to prepare to take part in the impending peace negotiations planned for Madrid, to designate "a proper person" to participate, to furnish him with "ample powers," and allow him that discretion which the remoteness of the negotiations from America dictated. The United States, Gerard told Congress, should draw up instructions and decide upon its ultimata. Should these be moderate, there was a good chance that Britain would accept them, Gerard advised. The French Minister counseled that in drafting these peace objectives the states should consider "the peace in relation to Spain," and bear in mind that Spain wished some terminal limits placed on the territorial claims of the United States, and that she intended to close the navigation of the Mississippi to other powers, and to recover the Floridas. The diplomatic archives reveal that Spain was determined to control the entire Mississippi Valley, a claim which Vergennes considered "*gigantesque*," and viewed American expansionist activities in the West with grave concern. At first the French Foreign Minister saw no reason why Spain should not share the navigation of the Mississippi with the United States. That he was later to adopt a more inflexible and even unsympathetic position toward America's claims in that area seems in no small part to have been the result of Gerard's influence.

The committee to whom had been assigned the task of putting the several issues of the peace into form suitable for discussion brought in its report on February 23rd. In the handwriting of Gouverneur Morris of New York, a moderate who wished to put a brake on expansionist fever, the report recommended that, first of all, independence, absolute and unlimited, as well "in matters of government as of commerce," must be granted as a precondition to opening negotiations. Then followed six stipulations to be considered in the nature of ultimata—namely, securing minimum boundaries from Canada to the Floridas and west to the Mississippi, the evacuation of the country by the British forces, fishing rights on the banks and coast of Newfoundland, the navigation of the Mississippi River to the southern boundary of the United States, free commerce with some port or ports on the Mississippi below that boundary, and, lastly, the cession to the United States of Nova Scotia or the latter's independence, this last subject to the willingness of the Allies to support the claim.

Over these peace objectives debate waxed furious and unabated for the next six months despite constant prodding by Gerard. The French Minister took every occasion to warn Congress that the King of Spain would be alienated by delays and to oppose pressing claims to land west of the Appalachians, or to the fisheries. The Lee faction's response to Gerard's ill-concealed pressures and his readiness to exploit factional difference for France's ends was to bristle like a porcupine. "I am afraid," James Lovell wrote to General Horatio Gates, "of the arts [they] are using to hurry us into a rash ultimatum."

Of the six stipulations, three provoked sharp controversy. These were the boundaries, the fisheries, and the navigation of the Mississippi. Oddly enough, the first and the most important was in essence settled on March 19th, with a permissible modification of the northwest boundary if the ultimatum could not be obtained without continuing the war for that purpose (but not south of 45° NL), and a similar provision was later inserted in the instructions with respect to the northeast boundary.

While Congress was quickly united in setting national boundaries which would include what was later known as the Northwest Territory, assigned by Parliament to Canada under the Quebec Act, and the lands claimed by colonial charters from the Appalachians to the Mississippi, it was sharply divided over two issues which were to prove far less consequential to America's future. Over the fisheries and the free navigation of the Mississippi Congressmen split along Deane-Lee lines, with the Deaneites, mostly from the Middle States and the South, adopting the more moderate position on both demands that Conrad Gerard was nightly preaching.

The "long struggle about cod and haddock," as James Lovell, a manager of the Lee cause, described it, began early in February and continued virtually nonstop until the middle of August. On the twenty-second of March a resolution was adopted demanding the acknowledgment of the right of the fisheries provided that the Allies were so circumstanced as to be able to back the United States in continuing the war to obtain this concession. In no event, however, were the fishery rights to be abandoned in any treaty of peace. This was too weak an instruction to satisfy the cod-minded New England delegation. Two days later the Lee faction obtained a reconsideration of the question and the adoption of a substitute moved by Richard Henry Lee and designed to counter the French argument that the colonies by rebelling had forfeited their ancient rights to the fisheries which they had exercised as British subjects. Now, Gerard was not prepared to accept the fishing rights as an ultimatum, nor even to tie the King to a commitment as to specific boundaries for the United States. Working through his pro-Gallican supporters in Congress, he maneuvered to have the demand for the fisheries reduced to the negative assertion, "that in no case, by any treaty of peace, the common right of fishery be given up." Notwithstanding the Frenchman's best efforts, the New Englanders persisted in what one participant in the affray called their "pertinacious" efforts to put teeth into the fisheries articles. On June 3rd and again on the 19th Elbridge Gerry, speaking for his Marblehead fishing constituency, touched off a renewed debate on the question. Again Gerard came before Congress to press for moderation. Finally, on July 29th a resolution was adopted to the effect that, if after the treaty of peace Great Britain were to molest the inhabitants in taking fish on the banks, Congress would deem it a breach of the peace. Every state from New Hampshire to Delaware voted for this resolution; every state to the southward against it. The outcome was that the New Englanders were not able to insert into the instructions an affirmative acknowledgment of the fishery rights, but had to content themselves with the negative stipulation that the fishery rights be not yielded at the peace. Congress went even further in soft-pedaling the issue. Two weeks later, in preparing instructions for the minister who was to be charged with negotiating the peace, it inserted the sentence: "Yet a desire of terminating the war hath induced us not to make the acquisition of these objects an ultimatum on the present occasion."

The free navigation of the Mississippi, so consequential to states having territorial claims west of the Appalachians, was argued at great length, but with perhaps less vehemence than the right to catch cod. Gerard took it on himself to warn Congress that any attempt to treat directly with Great Britain for the navigation of the Mississippi might mean war with Spain. His lobbying paid dividends. Congress on March 24th overwhelmingly defeated an attempt to make the navigation of the Mississippi an ultimatum. The issue was not closed, for in midsummer an effort was made to have the minister to Spain instructed to secure cession of Canada, Nova Scotia, Bermuda, and the Floridas, along with the free navigation of the Mississippi. Again Gerard intervened. If Congress expected aid from Spain, Gerard advised, it would be prudent not to ask that power to yield two such cherished objects as the Floridas and Mississippi navigation. John Dickinson moved to make these demands conditional and to propose a number of *quid pro quo's*. There was even a proposal by Samuel Huntington that the United States should assist Spain in the conquest of the Floridas, but it gained few backers. Gerard found that he could not sit on the lid indefinitely. On September 17th, the very day that the retiring French Minister took his formal leave of Congress, that body resolved that, if Spain should join hands with France and the United States, Congress would make no objection to her acquiring the Floridas, provided "always, that the United States shall enjoy the free navigation of the river Mississippi into and from the sea." Although some members feared that even this was demanding too much of Spain, and it was proposed that the American minister to Spain be privately instructed to recede from the claim to navigate the river on condition that Spain grant America a free port, the majority stood by the proposition as adopted. In addition to this instruction to Jay to insist on the free navigation of the Mississippi, which was to prove the stumbling block to all negotiations, Jay was instructed to obtain a free port on the lower Mississippi for American commerce and to secure a loan of five million dollars "upon the best terms in your power not exceeding six per centum per annum, but before borrowing to try to get a subsidy in consideration of America's guaranteeing the Floridas to Spain if they were reconquered."

All this Jay had closely observed as presiding officer of the sessions of Congress. Now he was responsible in part for carrying out the instructions which Congress, despite the constant meddling of Gerard, had wrung from its steamy debates. Little wonder that Jay had remarked to Washington, "There is as much intrigue in this State House as in the Vatican but as little secrecy as in a boarding school." But when he wrote these words he had not enjoyed the privilege of witnessing at firsthand the operations of the court of Madrid.

Since the Lee-Deane feud had placed all of America's commissioners abroad under a cloud, John Adams took his appointment as peace commissioner to Great Britain as a vindication of his record. "There is no character in which I could act with so much pleasure as that of a peacemaker," he wrote the Chevalier de La Luzerne from his Braintree home on October 17th, but added this caution: "Alas! When I reflect upon the importance, delicacy, intricacy and danger of the service, I feel a great deal of diffidence in myself." Nevertheless, since he was technically the unanimous choice of Congress for the peace mission as a result of a compromise between the contending factions, Adams expressed the view that, considering how divided Congress had been "about most other characters," this was an honor he could not decline.

The clear-headed and forthright New Englander foresaw the pitfalls ahead. "Peace is an object of such vast importance," Adams wrote Samuel Huntington, who succeeded Jay in the Presidency of Congress, "the interests to be adjusted in the negotiations to obtain it are so complicated and so delicate, and the difficulty of giving even general satisfaction is so great, that I feel myself more distressed at the prospect of executing the trust, than at the thoughts of leaving my family and country; and again encountering the dangers of the seas and of enemies."

Adams' party of seven embarked at Boston on the French frigate *Sensible*. His companions included his two sons, the precocious John Quincy, then twelve years of age and destined to carry on notable missions abroad on his own, and Charles, nine, along with Francis Dana, a Boston lawyer who was serving as Adams' secretary and chargé d'affaires, and two servants. If in retrospect Adams dramatized the circumstances of his parting, events proved him a sound prophet. "On the thirteenth of November 1779," he later recorded, "I had again the melancholly tryal of taking leave of my family, with the dangers of the seas and the terrors of British men of war before my eyes, with this additional aggravation that I now knew by experience how serious they were, much better than I had when I embarked in Nantasket Road in 1778."

Adams' party had not been out to sea a full two days before the *Sensible*, hardly justifying its name, sprang a leak. Soon all hands were at the pumps, and a large stream of water was constantly flowing over the sides. The planks and timber were so decayed that another strong gust would have torn the old frigate to pieces. In the unhappy event of pursuit by a superior British foe she would have been forced to spread all sails. If that had occurred the leak would have become a deluge and the ship would have foundered.

So critical was the situation when they passed the Grand Bank that the captain determined to head for one of "the Western Islands." Missing all of them, the exhausted ship's company found themselves by the beginning of December within a hundred leagues of Corunna, off the coast of Spain. Adams and Company got into Ferrol on December 8th. Within an hour after coming to anchor the *Sensible* was found to have seven feet of water in her hold.

To render the frigate seaworthy would be a matter of weeks. Adams realized that it would be best for him to continue on to Paris overland. Traveling over mountainous Galicia through January frost, snow, and ice, Adams and his party observed the poverty and economic sluggishness of the Spanish countryside. He saw men, women, and children "with naked legs and feet, standing on the cold stones in the mud, by the hour together." Although the Inquisition had had some of its fangs removed by now, he found that the huge numbers of regular clergy encountered everywhere were "drones enough to devour all the honey of the hive." Journeying over mountainous roads where neither horse nor mule could be trusted, where carriage axles were frequent casualties, the Adams party spent their nights at filthy accommodations, windowless houses without chimneys. "Smoke, soot and dirt, everywhere, and in everything," John observed of the evil-looking taverns in which he was put up. Ragged and dirty people, fleas and lice, a land where nobody "appeared rich but the churches, nobody fat but the Clergy." Taking a southeasterly course over rugged mountains from Galicia to Leon, Adams found at the walled town of Astorga "clean beds and no fleas for the first time since we had been in Spain." At Leon's cathedral the Braintree Puritan drew the "eagle eye of the Bishop" when he failed to fall to his knees to receive the apostolic benediction. As he journeyed across the plain to Paredes de Nava he saw villagers dance the fandango. He also noted crumbling villages of mud and straw, an impoverished countryside exploited by "Church, State and Nobility." By the time he reached Burgos, a town "held by an army of ecclesiasticks," he had caught something of the spirit of Spain that he was unlikely soon to forget.

"I had never experienced anything like this journey," Adams confessed many years later. For the travelers, devoid of any knowledge of Spanish, there was no relief from rain, snow, sleet, fatigue, poor food, and want of sleep. Small wonder that everybody in the company was soon down with violent colds. Where to now? Should the party proceed to Madrid? The idea was quickly dismissed. Not only was Madrid the long way around to Paris, Adams' destination, but a visit at this time might well prove embarrassing to John Jay, who had not yet reached the Spanish court. Quitting Spain saved Adams some embarrassments, too, and the Comte de Vergennes some sleepless nights, for the New Englander's information about the attitude of the Spanish court toward America was derived almost entirely from conversations with naval officials and Irishmen resident in Spain. There friendly discussions fortified his "very sanguine hopes that a solid treaty will soon be concluded with Spain." He could not have been worse informed.

Having made the decision not to go on to Madrid, Adams set his course northeast toward Bilbao. The party accomplished the serpentine descent to the village of Orduna, set in the midst of a fertile valley crowded by monasteries and convents. Reaching Sugar Loaf, the pyramidal-shaped mountain before Bilbao, called by its denizens "a republic," the Yankee Patriot was impressed by a sense of liberty pervading the autonomous community. Thence across the border to St. Jean-de-Luz. "Never was a captive escaped from prison more delighted than I was, for everything here was clean, sweet and more comfortable in comparison of anything we had found in any part of Spain." On to Bordeaux and at long last the arrival in Paris on February 9th, almost three months since their embarkation at Boston. "We were more than twice as long in making the journey by land, as we had been in crossing the Atlantic Ocean," Adams observed.

Like Jay, Adams had plenty of time to ponder his instructions before getting down to work. In rereading the ultimata adopted by Congress after prolonged debate, the American peace commissioner could not help but be struck by a concluding caution. "You are to govern yourself by the Alliance between his Christian Majesty and these States; by the advice of our Allies, by your knowledge of our interests; and by your own discretion, in which we repose the fullest confidence." Those who knew their man would expect him to give at least as much weight to his own knowledge and discretion as he would to the advice of the French government.

Adams had few illusions about the difficult task ahead. A quick face-to-face confrontation with a peace emissary of the British government seemed unlikely to take place so long as "the English continue in their old ill humour and insolent language, notwithstanding their impotence grows every day more apparent," he reported to President Huntington. It should certainly have been clear to him, from his previous mission abroad, that Louis XVI was most reluctant to have the uninhibited American commissioner press peace talks with England, and, more serious, was unwilling to support American peace objectives which clashed head on with the avowed interests of France's own ally, Spain. If he had forgotten this, France's Foreign Minister, the Comte de Vergennes, was soon to give him a curt reminder. As the war continued its seesaw course, diplomatic intrigues burgeoned. To John Adams, who soon recognized that the American republic had the most to lose by outside mediation efforts, it appeared that the most perilous portion of his peace mission lay before him.

Still a third diplomatic mission was dispatched to Europe in the fall of '79. For the post of commissioner to the United Provinces Congress chose an ex-President, Henry Laurens, the Charleston merchant-Patriot, who along with the Virginia Lees had given a slight Southern coloration to the anti-Gallican faction. Laurens was instructed to secure a loan of ten million dollars from the Dutch and to negotiate a treaty of commerce and amity. The short, swarthy, cocksure Laurens, who had renounced slave trading after it had yielded him a fortune, was by temperament perhaps better suited for an executive role than a diplomatic assignment, although even in the former he had betrayed a spirit of intense partisanship hardly in keeping with his role as Congress' presiding officer.

Laurens was on the point of sailing from Charleston on the frigate *Ranger* in February, 1780, when news of the arrival of British transports and landings close by, within sixteen miles of South Carolina's capital, caused him to postpone his departure. "Were I to study my own private interests and desire, I should remain here and stand or fall with my country," Laurens declared, but he was persuaded by public duty to proceed to North Carolina to seek another passage. Abandoning his vast business interests and landed properties to the enemy converging on Charleston, Laurens did not find the opportunity to sail for Europe until August 13th, when he embarked at Philadelphia on the swift-sailing brigantine *Mercury*, commanded by Captain William Pickles. The *Mercury* was to be convoyed by the sloop-of-war *Saratoga*. However, at the Capes of the Delaware they encountered two frigates commanded by the celebrated Nicholson brothers. The Nicholsons promised to return to convoy them as soon as they had run up the bay to replenish their water supply. For four or five days Laurens and his party waited aboard the *Mercury* anchored off Port Penn. Hearing nothing further from the Nicholsons, Laurens ordered the *Mercury* to set sail without escort. Laurens justified his decision on the ground that in the Continental Navy "little regard was paid to orders inconsistent with the captain's own convenience." Furthermore a favorable wind and the advancing equinox suggested that it was perhaps now or never. For six days the *Saratoga* struggled to keep up with the *Mercury*, but the brigantine was obliged each night to shorten sail so as not to outdistance her escort. Laurens then made his second fateful decision. He advised Captain Young of the *Saratoga* to break off her escort duty and return to the Delaware.

On September 3rd, as dawn broke off Newfoundland, a sail was sighted far to leeward. Captain Pickles put the *Mercury* close upon the wind, and then, for reasons that are still not clear, he changed his mind and put her before the wind, her worst sailing, especially since she was badly ballasted with sand. The distant vessel obligingly altered her course, too, and about nine o'clock came within gun range. Two hours later a shot went over the *Mercury* and two more were fired between her masts. Captain Pickles hauled down the American flag.

All papers thought to be of importance were thrown overboard or burned, save a trunkful of Laurens' own papers, which, at his order, remained untouched. This was his third fateful decision. When he realized that there were confidential papers among them, he yielded to urgings to have them thrown overboard. The papers were put in a long bag and some twenty pounds of shot upon them. Unfortunately for both Laurens and his mission, the air inside buoyed up the bag, and seamen of the British frigate proceeded to hook it up. Among the papers was discovered a draft of a proposed treaty drawn up the year before by William Lee, as roving American agent abroad, with Engelbert Van Berckel, an agent of the burgomasters of Amsterdam. The treaty draft was never considered binding by anybody. Lee had no power to treat, and the burgomasters no authority to make treaties with foreign powers. It now served two purposes quite different from its original design. The British pounced upon the discovery and made it a convenient pretext to declare war upon the Netherlands and a ground for confining Henry Laurens in the Tower of London. There he remained from October 6, 1780, until New Year's Eve of the following year. His claims to diplomatic immunity were ignored, and his status as a state prisoner held on suspicion of high treason prevented his exchange as a military prisoner. Laurens' mission had ended in ignominious failure before it really got under way, and if blame was to be allotted, the South Carolinian, who had made a series of luckless decisions, deserved the lion's share of it.

Fortunately for the American cause, there was able John Adams ready and willing to take over. However much he may have commiserated with the South Carolinian in the latter's suffering and humiliation, the New Englander must have recognized that Laurens' capture was a providential stroke for him, if not for the country. Peace, as Adams would soon find out, seemed far removed when he arrived in France in early 1780. One could hardly expect so dynamic a personality to sit patiently offstage waiting for his cue, a call that might never come. Now he had a part to play, and he assumed his role with his accustomed zeal.

❦

THE *American Revolution has been described as "the shot heard round the world." Ill-managed though it might have been, the Revolution was for many Europeans proof "that North America is the country where reason and humanity will develop more rapidly than anywhere else." The inclination to equality, already strong, gained strength as ordinary Americans took up arms. Contemporary gentry conceded that "the spirit of independency was converted into equality, and everyone who bore arms esteemed himself on a footing with his neighbor." Once ordinary folk have shed their blood, they are hardly likely to give way to the pretensions of their ostensible superiors, and once the roughhewn yeoman has humbled King and Parliament, he may think to govern himself rather than allow others to do the job.*

*Independence was not the work of the American alone; it required the substantial assistance of France and the other European powers. They saw a chance to humble the pretensions of the tight little isle and took it. And as the Beards indicate, the uncertain British war effort prevented an exploitation by the crown of the deep-rooted differences that divided their distant empire. Once peace and independence were achieved, the new nation was faced with the task of fusing out of diversity a single nationality. The real Revolution came after the battles had ended. It was the success in broadening the scope of individual freedom that made the new America a signal of the impending changes that would rock the world in the centuries to come.*

*A nation born in revolution, as James Madison noted, is hardly in a position to question the revolution of others lest it place its own legitimacy in doubt. But as the time that separates us from our own revolution steadily increases, Americans have revealed an increasing tendency to forget their origins. The equation of liberty and property has tended to make Americans view any threat to private property as a repudiation of the fundamental premises of a legitimate revolution. And as we have come to differentiate between the legitimate and illegitimate revolution, some historians have come to scrutinize how genuine was the American Revolution. Observing present realities, they have wondered whether the preoccupation with individual rights and possessions has not obscured the larger question of the rights of the whole society. The first extensive questioning of the traditional view of American history came during the Progressive Era.*

*No historian was more active in this challenge than Charles Austin Beard (1874-1948), whose wife Mary R. Beard (1876-1958) was his frequent collaborator. Born in Indiana, he taught at Columbia University between 1904 and 1917, but resigned when a colleague was dismissed because of his pacifist leanings. He had already gained both fame and notoriety when he authored* An Economic Interpretation of the Constitution *(1913), a work that sought to explain through history how the American economy had come into the possession of a few great capitalists. It suggested inconclusively that the men who made the Constitution were governed by economic considerations. He placed particular emphasis upon the economic motives of humans, a point which was thoroughly developed in his* The Economic Basis of Politics *(1922).*

*After his departure from Columbia, he helped found the New School for Social Research and for a time was an adviser to the Tokyo Institute of Municipal Research. His interest shifted toward foreign policy during the 1930's and 40's. He drew the conclusion in his* President Roosevelt and the Coming of War *(1948) that Roosevelt had deliberately maneuvered Japan into war. It was a reflection of his deep-rooted hostility to the New Deal and his no less profound commitment to isolation. Although much of his work has been sharply challenged, it would not be inappropriate to note that the sum of his work has been one from which other historians have been obliged to depart. For as Max Lerner noted, Beard "cut through the whole tissue of liberal idealism and rhetoric to the economic realities in American history."*

# THE RISE OF AMERICAN CIVILIZATION

## by Charles A. Beard and Mary R. Beard

Against the contentious governments which rose on the ruins of British dominion in America and against the small and badly supported forces of the American army was pitted the might of the greatest empire in the world. Unlike the Continental Congress, the British political system was powerfully organized, the Parliament at Westminster commanding the purses and allegiance of its subjects. The British navy, ruling the sea, could transport men and supplies across the ocean or along the coast with comparative ease. Moreover, King George, besides having at his disposal a substantial body of regular soldiers disciplined in the arts of war, could also summon to his aid a number of high officers who, if they were not supreme masters of strategy, had at least seen more serious fighting than Washington and his subordinates. How then was it possible for the thirteen states, weak and divided in councils, to effect their independence in the test of arms?

In the enumeration of the items that go to make up the answer, all historians agree in assigning first rank to the personality of Washington, commander of the weary and footsore Continental army that clung to the cause to the bitter end. Mythology, politics, and hero-worship did their utmost to make a solemn humbug of that amazing figure but his character finally survived the follies of his admirers and even the thrusts of his detractors made in their reaction to idolatrous adulation. Washington was a giant in stature, a tireless and methodical worker, a firm ruler yet without the ambitions of a Caesar or a Cromwell, a soldier who faced hardships and death without flinching, a steadfast patriot, a hard-headed and practical director of affairs. Technicians have long disputed the skill of his strategy; some have ascribed the length of the war to his procrastinations; others have found him wanting in energy and decision; but all have agreed that he did the one thing essential to victory—he kept some kind of an army in the field in adversity as well as in prosperity and rallied about it the scattered and uncertain forces of a jealous and individualistic people.

Fortunately for Washington and for the cause of independence there were elements of weakness in the armed might of Great Britain. The English landed gentry and the mercantile classes that shouted for "strong measures in America" did not rush to the standard to fight the battles for which they had called. Long protected against invasion by means of the navy, the British people had not been nourished on the martial spirit. For generations, therefore, the Crown had found it imperative to employ brusque methods in order to secure enough men to fill the ranks of its regular army.

Theoretically it relied mainly on volunteers; practically the statutes and the common law sanctioned a disorderly kind of conscription, two expedients which yielded soldiers of about the same type. The volunteers were drawn chiefly from a miserable proletariat; while the men who were dragooned into the uniform by compulsion, drink, and violence came from what the English historian, Lecky, called "the dregs of the population." The laws pertaining to conscription specifically authorized the snatching of sturdy beggars, fortune tellers, idle, unknown, and suspected fellows, incorrigible rogues, poachers, and convicts. Criminals were pardoned "on condition of their enlistment in His Majesty's army," three British regiments being composed entirely of lawbreakers released from prison.

But all these methods failed to produce enough men for the task of saving America for the landlords and merchants of England. Six months after the battle of Lexington, the British government confessed that its efforts to fill the ranks had failed. Thereupon "the King went into the open market for troops on the continent," and hired from German princes several thousand fighting men—peasants dragged from their fields, mechanics snatched by crimps, and wretches raked up from the highways and byways.

In the wake of the British army followed the usual rearguard of wastrels. Burgoyne's forces were accompanied by approximately two thousand women, some of them the wives of officers, three hundred "on the strength of the regiments," the remainder "fed and maintained by the soldiers themselves." Although there were good fighting men in the British ranks, although some of the criminal regiments distinguished themselves for valor, the most friendly historian of the British army had to admit that it was not inspired by an intense desire to overwhelm the American rebels at any cost of life and limb.

The British officers, of course, were drawn from a different class but for one reason or another those placed in command in America were lacking in skill or energy or both. Sir William Howe, on whom a large part of the burden fell, though a general of experience and distinction, suffered from many disabilities. He had strenuously opposed the coercive measures which brought on the war and he had publicly declared that he would not fight the Americans if called upon to take up arms. And yet, after making such professions, he had yielded to the appeal of his sovereign and accepted the command. Just why he was chosen for the important post in view of his attitude has never been made clear but it was hinted at the time that he owed the honor to his "grandmother's frailty," that is, to the fact that he was the grandson of George I through an illegitimate connection.

However that may be, Howe was a gay man of the world, loving ease, wine, gambling, and the society of ladies. "In Boston," as the Americans were fond of saying, "this British Anthony found his Cleopatra." Competent critics ascribed his final discomfiture to the "baneful influence" of "this illustrious courtesan." Enamored of indolence, drink, and high living, eager to effect peace by conciliation, Howe shrank from ruthless, swift, persistent, punitive measures. He proceeded on the theory that, by the continued possession of New York and Philadelphia and by the blockade of the coast, he could wear out the patriots. If the French had not intervened with their navy, he might have succeeded in his plan and been hailed as one of the far-seeing statesmen and warriors of his age. But events sank his fortunes beyond recovery. Sir Henry Clinton, who succeeded Howe as Commander-in-chief in 1778, if more active in war, was not much happier in the display of military talents; and of Lord Cornwallis, the less said the better.

Among the other factors favorable to the American cause were advantages due to the geographical situation. The British had to cross three thousand miles of water and then fight on a field that stretched almost a thousand miles north and south merging in the west into a wilderness. With the aid of the navy they could readily seize the ports and strike at the seaboard commerce; although they were definitely forced out of Boston in 1776— in spite of their costly victory at Bunker Hill—they occupied, in the course of the war, New York, Philadelphia, Charleston, and Savannah. All these places, except Philadelphia, they continued to hold until Cornwallis' surrender at Yorktown and their grip on that city was only broken by the menace of the French fleet.

When, however, they ventured far into the interior they met reverses or achieved only temporary victories. Burgoyne was compelled to surrender at Saratoga because he was surrounded, harassed, and cut off from his base of supplies. The British captured Charleston in 1780 and, after beating Gates at Camden, overran most of the state, were assailed and worried by militiamen. Cornwallis could ravage the coasts of North Carolina and Virginia almost at will; he could even strike far into the interior and give Greene a drubbing at Guilford, but he could not hold the hinterland over which he had raised his flag. As soon as his troops were withdrawn, revolutionary forces took possession of the abandoned territory. In short, the conquest of the American continent by arms called for continuous occupation and for regular government by military process—a gigantic task to which the British forces dispatched to America were not equal.

In reckoning the elements that brought victory to the United States, the aid afforded by France must be given great weight. Money received from the treasury of Louis XVI paid for supplies that were desperately needed and buoyed up the sinking credit of the young republic. After the fashion of adventurous military men, French officers with the Marquis de la Fayette and Baron de Kalb in the lead joined Baron Steuben of Prussia, Count Pulaski, and Thaddeus Kosciusko of Poland, in helping to furnish inspiration and discipline for the raw recruits from American farms and shops. French regulars dispatched to American camps and fields, besides giving heart to the discouraged forces under Washington's command, rendered a good account of themselves in the business of warfare. At Yorktown, the last scene in the grand enterprise, the French soldiers, almost equal to the Americans in number, stood like a rock against the attempts of Cornwallis to break the cordon of besieging armies. On the sea, as on the land, the power of France, in spite of England's superior strength, counted heavily on the side of victory for America. French captains united with American naval commanders headed by Paul Jones and John Barry in preying upon British commerce, in cutting off ships bearing fresh troops and supplies to Yorktown, and in blockading Cornwallis on the side of the sea. Thus when the final blow was delivered—the blow which brought the British cabinet to terms—the honors were shared by the French and American arms. Once more the balance of power had been utilized, this time in ushering a young republic into the family of nations.

In trying to explain the outcome of the war for independence many writers, old and new, have laid great stress on the argument that the English nation showed little zeal for the fighting throughout the long contest. Some have gone so far as to represent the efforts to coerce the colonies by arms as the labors of an arrogant king and subservient ministers who enjoyed little support among the English people at large. Indeed, the Whig historians in England and their copyists in America have laid the main responsibility for the conduct of the war, as well as the measures that led to it, upon George III himself. Sir Thomas Erskine May, a Whig of the Whigs, in his *Constitutional History of England* issued in 1871, represented the King as managing Parliament during all the contest, distributing patronage, dictating domestic and foreign policies, directing debates, conferring titles and honors, and settling the fate of ministers, in the grand and arbitrary fashion of Louis the Great. "It is not without reason," he concluded, "that this deplorable contest was called the king's war." John Richard Green, describing the North administration in his *Short History of the English People*, published in 1874, declared that "George was in fact the minister through the twelve years of its existence, from 1770 till the close of the American war."

Many years later another English Liberal, Sir George Trevelyan, a nephew of the great Whig apologist, Macaulay, made a special effort to collect proofs that "the war itself was disliked by the nation." From the evidence assembled he showed that the members of the Commons from London were opposed to the war, that several officers in the British army and navy refused to take part in it, that an open opponent was almost elected to Parliament in Newcastle at a by-election held in 1779 while the conflict was raging, that British consols fell in price, and that there was a great deal of outspoken criticism of the government which would hardly have been tolerated if armed coercion of America had been popular.

Without attempting to traverse that general argument, it is appropriate to recall certain facts equally significant which point to a contrary conclusion. It is true that George III displayed a lively interest in the proceedings of Parliament, that he indulged in high-flown language about his prerogatives, that he used his power to penalize men who opposed measures on which his heart was set, that he appointed his friends to high offices, and that on one occasion with a somewhat childish gesture he pointed to his sword and threatened to use it if a dissolution of Parliament was forced upon him. But the Whig historians who have raked over every word of the king's correspondence have found no passage showing that George III used his authority to force the enactment of a single coercive law directed against the American colonies.

In reality no such course on his part was necessary for, as the judicious Lecky shows, "all the measures of American coercion that preceded the Declaration of Independence were carried by enormous majorities in Parliament." And he might have added that all the war measures passed after that event were likewise carried by enormous majorities. As a matter of fact the one conspicuous use of royal power over Parliament during the conflict was in the case of Lord North's conciliatory resolution offering "the olive branch" to America in 1775: the proposal was so hotly resisted in the Commons that the king's influence was invoked to push it through. No doubt George III was outspoken in vindicating the course of his government. He once declared that he would accept no minister who favored stopping the war or granting American independence; but a year before he uttered these emphatic words he had actually offered to accept a ministry of peace and independence. So it would seem that the verdict of the Whig historians needs revising; the responsibility for the war, as far as England was concerned, rested mainly on the governing classes, not upon George III alone.

How far the English "nation" approved the prosecution of the war was never determined by anything like a referendum. The general election of 1774, held while the controversy with the colonies was raging, sustained the ministry of Lord North and gave him a thumping majority. Normally, in the course of the conflict, he could muster in the House of Commons about two hundred and sixty votes against the ninety arrayed on the side of the opposition. Beyond all question the landed gentry were solidly entrenched in support of the government and, if Edmund Burke is to be taken as an authority, the industrial and mercantile groups were almost equally stanch in their loyalty. "The mercantile interest," he lamented in January, 1775, "which ought to have supported with efficacy and power the opposition to the fatal cause of all this mischief, was pleaded against us, and we were obliged to stoop under the accumulated weight of all the interests of this kingdom."

Later in the same year Burke made again the same complaint: "The merchants are gone from us and from themselves. . . . The leading men among them are kept full fed with contracts and remittances and jobs of all descriptions and are indefatigable in their endeavours to keep the others quiet. . . . They all, or the greatest number of them, begin to sniff the cadaverous *haut gout* of lucrative war." Burke also found "the generality of the people of England" aligned with the ministers in the prosecution of the war—deluded no doubt by "the misrepresentations and arts of the ministry, the Court, and its abettors," but still loyal to the government in its hour of battle. Long after Burke, Lecky, on reviewing a huge mass of testimony, rendered a similar judgment: "It appears to me evident that in 1775 and 1776 the preponderating opinion, or at least the opinion of the most powerful and most intelligent classes in the community, on the American question was with the King and his ministers."

Certainly the bishops of the Established Church sustained the government and the Universities proclaimed their unquestioning fealty, while the lawyers as a class found historic and constitutional grounds for supporting the proceedings of the ministry. To give verbal expression to official policy, a large group of editors, clergymen, economists, historians, and men of letters devoted their talents, either through conviction or for a consideration, to fanning the temper of those determined to bring the revolutionists to the ground at all costs. Dr. Samuel Johnson, a royal pensioner, hurled against the Americans a weighty diatribe, Taxation no Tyranny; according to the faithful Boswell, "his inflammable corruption" burst into horrid fire whenever the Americans were mentioned; he breathed out threatenings and slaughter, calling them rascals, robbers, pirates, and exclaiming that he would burn and destroy them—this safely in a tavern corner in front of a roast and a pot of ale.

John Wesley, whose varied and dubious career in America had taught him the nature of American emotions, joined the ministerial hosts in condemning the Revolution, and attributing colonial resistance to the writings of wicked Englishmen, such as Burke, who were encouraging rebellion and striving to overturn the perfect English constitution. With serene assurance, Wesley informed the Americans that they had no case at all, waving aside the issues of taxation and representation with a short fling: "You are the descendants of men who either had not votes or resigned them by migration. You have therefore exactly what your ancestors left you; not a vote in making laws nor in choosing legislators but the happiness of being protected by laws and the duty of obeying them." The great Edward Gibbon, then at work on his history of the Roman tragedy, though inclined at first to criticize Lord North's policy, after gazing a while upon the contemporary game with a stately amusement, went over to the support of the government, receiving in the going a sinecure of a thousand pounds a year, which helped to eke out his slender income and enabled him to enjoy fine wine while finishing off his immortal pages. Yet he was good natured about the business and, as he said, laughed and blushed at his own inconsequence when he heard himself lashed by Burke for drawing public money in return for nothing but mischief.

On the other side of the controversy in England there was, no doubt, a troublesome opposition that continued to bait the government until the close of the War for Independence. Among the leaders in this group Edmund Burke stood first in discernment, combining an accurate knowledge of American economy and American temper with a profound faith in the healing power of toleration and generosity—a faith that strangely contrasted with the scurrilous dogmatism manifest in his thunderous pamphlets on the French Revolution a little later. Unlike Chatham, who, as his sister often said, "knew nothing accurately except Spenser's Faery Queen," Burke had the statistics of American trade and the history of American progress always on the tip of his tongue. Repeatedly he pointed out in the House of Commons the magnitude of American commerce, the growth of population, the fierce spirit of liberty in the colonies, "the dissidence of dissent" in matters religious, the rise of lawyers "acute, inquisitive, dexterous, prompt in attack, ready in defense, full of resources," the growth of popular government through local assemblies, the feebleness of the Established Church, and the high proud spirit of Southern slaveholders. Having described the power of America, he told his countrymen that coercion would bring nothing but resistance and revolt.

The burden of Burke's grand argument flowed from reason and moderation. The relations of nations, he urged, must be considered in the same fashion as personal relations with respect to sensibilities; generosity will call forth generosity; human affairs cannot be twisted to fit any dogmatic scheme of black and white; great good can come out of liberty unbidden by tyrannical rule and systematic policy; the "unsuspecting confidence of the colonists" is the best hope of prosperous connections; refined, hair-splitting policy is always the parent of confusion; government must be based on barter and compromise; plain, good intention is a great force in the management of mankind; wise governments take into account the nature of the circumstance of those who are governed; prudent negotiation is better than force; if force you must have, let it be for some defined object worthy of the sword, not the outcome of foolish arrogance; reverence for black letter learning, for precise constitutional rights, is reverence for a Serbonian bog where whole armies have sunk; "it is not what a lawyer tells me I may do; but what humanity, reason, and justice tell me I ought to do." In such noble words was expressed the serene, friendly, tolerant spirit in which Burke begged the British government to turn back upon its course to the old ways that were followed before Grenville and Townshend started their "systematic imperial policy."

Outside Parliament, Burke had some literary support. David Hume, philosopher and historian, objected to "mauling the poor unfortunate Americans in the other hemisphere." At the beginning of the conflict, Catherine Macaulay, sister of the mayor of London and a historical writer, then the vogue in England and the subject of "flattering attentions" in Paris, lauded the American cause and sent a letter to Washington encouraging him in the course he had chosen. In another quarter, the celebrated Dr. Richard Price, nonconformist clergyman, whose sermon on constitutional reform later called forth Burke's *Reflections on the French Revolution*, defended the Americans in a powerful tract that quickly passed through eight editions and made a profound impression on the British public, especially on the dissenting elements.

In the houses of Parliament, Burke's attacks on ministerial policies were applauded by a small but distinguished body of Whigs. Whether their contrariety of opinion flowed principally from resentment at exclusion from office or from a confirmed belief in the injustice of war on America, it was impossible to determine. Indeed, there was no unanimity of doctrine among them. Chatham, for example, declared that Parliament had no constitutional right to impose internal taxes on the colonies and favored the repeal of the coercive measures; but he was dead set against granting independence after the armed conflict had begun. Rockingham, on the other hand, upheld with decided vigor the right of Parliament to tax, assailing the measures of Lord North on grounds of expediency.

Great as it was intrinsically, the confusion of the Whigs was increased by the demands of the colonists. Committed by a long tradition to the creed that the power of the Crown should be reduced and the authority of the legislature exalted, the Whigs found themselves invited by American agitators to condemn acts of Parliament in the name of royal prerogative. Not only that, they were called upon by Benjamin Franklin to treat parliamentary interference with America as sheer usurpation—an invasion of the king's undoubted sphere of power—and then they were asked by the authors of the Declaration of Independence to lay the blame for the disaster on George III.

Although a few Whigs made a clean cut through this legal verbiage by discarding the niceties of logic and advocating peace with America on terms of independence, the majority employed it chiefly with reference to the tactics of defeating the ministry and restoring their party to its old control over government and patronage. Of this, there was indisputable proof. In

1778, in the midst of the war, George III was ready to give up; in his name the Whigs were offered "the majority in a new cabinet under Lord Weymouth, on the basis of a withdrawal of the troops from America and a vigorous prosecution of the war with France."

Then and there the Whigs could have ended the armed conflict with America. Fox begged them to do it but they refused, thus taking on their own heads responsibility for the war which they denounced, allowing it to go on to the conclusion so bitter for England. On no simple theory of devotion to American principles, therefore, could the course of Whig politics during the American Revolution be explained, and yet the generous peace of 1783 was in the main their work. In the end it was they who drove Lord North from office, urged George III to yield to necessity, and closed the unhappy quarrel by accepting the United States as one of the free nations of the earth.

The negotiation of the treaty of peace, when the moment came, was a delicate task for Franklin and his colleagues at Paris, as well as for the British government. Under instructions from the Congress and the terms of the French alliance, the American agents were bound to consult Louis XVI's ministers at every stage of the transaction. Had nothing intervened, Franklin, easy-going and fond of the French, might have obeyed to the letter the canons of strict propriety, but John Jay, fresh from the intrigues of Madrid, and John Adams, who had learned new tactics at The Hague, were too canny for the diplomacy of Versailles. They knew that France and Spain had not shed blood and spent treasure merely to erect a powerful republic in the western hemisphere. It was no dark mystery that France, still cherishing imperial dreams, hoped to recover the Mississippi Valley and enlarge her fishing rights in western waters. It was no secret that Spain also had irons in the fire. In any event, both powers agreed that the Americans should be satisfied with the seaboard and were prepared to block American designs upon the hinterland.

Called upon to favor the United States, on the one hand, or the French and Spanish, on the other, the British ministry chose to patronize the rebellious provinces. Moreover, the new colonial secretary in London sincerely desired "reconciliation with America on the noblest terms and by the noblest means." Quick to grasp the realities of the problem thus presented, the American commissioners artfully disregarded the decorum of the occasion. Besides holding secret conversations with the British agent, they actually agreed upon the general terms of peace before they told the French foreign minister about their operations. For this furtive conduct, Louis XVI's minister, Vergennes, on hearing the news at last, reproached Franklin, only to receive from the aged gentleman the suave reply that, although the Americans had been guilty of bad manners, they hoped that the great work would not be ruined by "a single indiscretion." Doubtless the French were angry; perhaps, technically, they had a right to be; but those who practiced the arts of diplomacy in those days were usually prepared to accept the rules of the game and the hazards of the combat.

In the end, the shrewd maneuvers of the American commissioners and the liberality of the English cabinet made the general settlement at Paris in 1783 a triumph for the United States. Independence was specifically recognized by the mother country; and the coveted territory west of the Mississippi, north to Canada, and south to the Floridas was acknowledged as the rightful heritage of the young republic. Spain won Minorca and the Floridas but not Gibraltar. For her sacrifices in blood and treasure, France gained practically nothing in territory and commerce, but had the satisfaction of seeing the British Empire dismembered and the balance of power readjusted. In spite of her defeat in America, England retained Canada, Newfoundland, and her islands in the West Indies, made gains in India, and held her supremacy on the sea.

Clear as it was in bold outline, the grand adjustment at Paris left many issues clouded. Not unnaturally, the Tories demanded a return of their sequestered estates and English merchants insisted on the payment of debts owed by American citizens. These were sore points with the patriots and nothing but a compromise was possible. In its final form, the treaty provided that the Congress should advise the states to restore the property they had confiscated and stipulated that no lawful impediment should be placed in the way of collecting just debts—smooth promises difficult to fulfill. In a counter-claim, the Americans demanded a restoration of all goods and slaves seized by the English army during the war, and in the terms of the treaty their exactions were conceded. Here, too, was a pledge easier to make than to discharge; for some of the English were horrified at the idea of sending human beings back to bondage and the recovery of the other property claimed by the patriots proved to be impossible in practice. For good measure, the question of fishing rights off the coast offered irritating problems; issues which vexed the two countries for more than a hundred years.

Many a patriot grumbled when he heard that the treaty promised a return of Tory property and a payment of debts but all such laments were lost in the universal rejoicing that greeted the close of the war. Nothing dampened the ardor of the demonstration. Orators exhausted their forensic powers in portraying the benefits of independence and in framing taunts to the despotisms of the Old World. One preacher, climbing an Alpine peak, summoned his countrymen to look upon the fair opportunity now presented "for converting this immense northern continent into a seat of knowledge and freedom, of agriculture and commerce, of useful arts and manufactures, of Christian piety and virtue; and thus making it an inviting and comfortable abode for many millions of the human species; an asylum for the injured and oppressed in all parts of the globe; the delight of God and good men; the joy and pride of the whole earth; soaring on the wings of literature, wealth, population, religion, virtue, and everything that is excellent and happy to a greater height of perfection and glory than the world has ever yet seen!"

The fair prophecy of the preacher, to be fulfilled in a surprising measure in the long reach of time, seemed at the moment to rest on a slender basis. The "America" to which the orator paid tribute was only in the process of making. Politically, it consisted of thirteen independent states, each jealous of its rights, fiercely claiming the loyalty of its citizens, and dominated by ambitious men. The union that bound them together, such as it was, had no guarantee of permanence in the affections of the people. It was new. It had been a product of necessity, long debate, and grudging consent. The idea of an enduring association, raised in the Continental Congress many months before the Declaration of Independence, was not given a concrete form in the Articles of Confederation until more than a year after that event. The autumn of 1777 was far advanced when the Congress, after tedious argument, finally agreed on the document and sent it to the states for ratification. Though all the local legislatures were aware that their common fate seemed to hang upon prompt and united action, a long time passed before the last of them signed and sealed the instrument of federation. The year that saw the surrender of Cornwallis at Yorktown had opened when Maryland, the remaining laggard, gave her approval. It was March 1, 1781, that thundering guns from ships of war in the Delaware announced that the Union "begun by necessity" had been "indissolubly cemented."

The Articles of Confederation, wrung from reluctant delegates in the Congress and from still more reluctant states, in fact made little difference in the system which had been established for revolutionary purposes. It did not materially alter the structure or powers of the continental government created provisionally in 1774. Management of the general interests of the United States was still vested, under the Articles, as before, in a Congress composed of delegates from each state, appointed as the legislature might direct, subject to recall at any time, and paid from the local treasury.

If this system seemed strangely inadequate to the requirements of a potential nation, it corresponded with marked fidelity to the ideas of the radicals who had engineered the Revolution. In their several colonies, they had revolted against the financial, commercial, and political control exercised by the government of Great Britain; by war they had destroyed deliberately that dominion; and they wanted no strong and effective substitute in the form of a central government—even one controlled by Americans. In this sense a fundamental transformation had been wrought in the higher ranges of continental politics.

Within each state, no less than in external relations, the Revolution started a dislocation of authority—a phase of the eventful years which the historians, too long concentrating on spectacular episodes, have just begun to appreciate. The shifts and cracks in the social structure produced by the cataclysm were not all immediately evident; half a century passed before the leveling democracy proclaimed in Jefferson's Declaration of Independence came flooding into power. But still the states of the confederation differed as much from the colonial provinces of Governor Shirley's time as the France of Louis Philippe, hero of the green umbrella, did from the regime of Louis XV. Just as the French Revolution sent émigrés fleeing into Germany and England, so that American Revolution drove out about one hundred thousand high Tories of the old school. By breaking the grip of English economic and political adventurers on the spoils of America, it brought into power new men with new principles and standards of conduct.

It is true that, in the severe and sometimes savage contests between the conservative and radical supporters of the Revolution, the former were generally the victors for the moment and were able to write large their views of economic rights in the first state constitutions. Broadly speaking, only taxpayers or property owners were given the ballot as in colonial times and only men of substantial wealth were made eligible to public office. But in many cases the qualifications were lowered and the structure of the old social system seriously undermined.

Above all, the spirit of domestic politics, especially in the royal provinces, was distinctly altered by the sudden removal of the British ruling class— a class accustomed to a barbarous criminal code, a narrow and intolerant university system, a government conceived as a huge aggregation of jobs and privileges, a contempt for men and women who toiled in field and shop, a denial of education to the masses, an Established religion forced alike on Dissenters and Catholics, a dominion of squire and parson in counties and villages, callous brutality in army and navy, a scheme of primogeniture buttressing the rule of the landed gentry, a swarm of hungry placemen offering sycophancy to the king in exchange for offices, sinecures, and pensions, and a constitution of church and state so ordered as to fasten upon the masses this immense pile of pride and plunder. From the weight of this mountain the American revolutionists delivered the colonial subjects of the British Crown. Within a decade or two after that emancipation they accomplished reforms in law and policy which required a hundred years or more of persistent agitation to effect in the mother country—reforms which gave to the statesman who led in the agitation their title to immortality in English history.

Naturally the American Revolution, a movement carried to its bitter end by the bayonets of fighting farmers, even though it was started by protesting merchants and rioting mechanics, wrought a far-reaching transformation in the land system that had been developed under British inspiration and control. With engaging conciseness, these changes have been summarized in J. Franklin Jameson's admirable little book on the American Revolution Considered as a Social Movement. First of all, royal limitations on the seizure and enjoyment of vacant lands—notably the prohibition upon the free settlement of regions beyond the Alleghenies contained in the proclamation of 1763—were swept away; and at the same time the "vast domains of the Crown" were vested in the hands of the state legislatures to be dedicated to the uses of their constituents.

Secondly, the quitrents paid to the king and to proprietary families, the Penns and the Baltimores, by farmers and planters according to their acreage were simply abolished, relieving Americans of an annual charge approximating a hundred thousand dollars a year. Thirdly, the rule and the practice of reserving for the royal navy white pine trees suitable for masts were abrogated without ceremony, releasing landowners from an irksome restriction. In the fourth place, there was a smashing confiscation of Tory estates, including Sir William Pepperell's Maine holdings extending thirty miles along the coast, the Phillipse heritage in New York embracing about three hundred square miles, the property of the Penn family worth in round numbers five million dollars, and the Fairfax estate in Virginia stretching out like a province. All in all, the Tories reckoned their losses at no less than forty million dollars and the British Parliament, after scaling their demands to the minimum, granted the claimants fifteen million dollars by way of compensation.

In harmony with their principles, the Revolutionists who made this huge sequestration of property distributed the land by sales in small lots on generous terms to enterprising farmers. The principality of Roger Morris in New York, for example, was divided into no less than two hundred and fifty parcels, while a still larger number of farms were created out of the confiscated holdings of James De Lancey.

Finally, among the effects of the Revolution on agricultural economy, must be reckoned the abolition of the system of entails and primogeniture. Whereas it took a century of debate and then the corroding taxes of a World War to drive a wedge into the concentrated land monopoly of England, the American Revolutionists brought many an ancient structure to earth by swift and telling blows. Three months after he penned the Declaration of Independence, Jefferson opened a war on the entailed estates of the Old Dominion, to the horror of the best people; and before the lapse of a year he pushed through the legislature an act which accomplished his radical design, releasing from entail "at least half, and possibly three-quarters of the entire 'seated' area of Virginia." Within ten years "every state had abolished entails excepting two, and those were two in which entails were rare. In fifteen years every state, without exception, abolished primogeniture"—all save four placing daughters on an equality with sons in the distribution of landed inheritances.

Considered relatively, therefore, the destruction of landed privilege in America by the forces unchained in the War for Independence was perhaps as great and as significant as the change wrought in the economic status of the clergy and nobility during the holocaust of the French Revolution. As in France country lawyers and newly rich merchants swarmed over the seats of the once proud aristocracy, so in the United States during and after the cataclysm a host of groundlings fresh from the plow and counting house surged over the domains of the Jessups, De Lanceys, and Morrises. When members of the best families of France turned to tutoring and translating in London for a livelihood or to teaching dancing and manners in America, in the days of Danton, Marat, and Robespierre, they found ladies and gentlemen who sighed for good old colonial days ready to join them in cursing the rights of man.

The clergy as well as the landed gentry felt the shocks of the American Revolution. When the crisis opened, nine of the thirteen colonies had established churches. In New Hampshire, Massachusetts, and Connecticut it was the Congregationalists that enjoyed this legal privilege, while in Virginia, Maryland, New York, the Carolinas, and Georgia it was the Episcopalians who claimed a monopoly on religion supported by taxes. Before the echoes of Lexington and Concord had died away, an attack on ecclesiastical establishments was launched, and in five of the states where the Anglican clergy possessed privileges and immunities under the law, the dissenters, outnumbering their opponents, were quickly victorious. In Virginia, however, where the Anglican party was strong, and in New England, where the Congregationalists enjoyed a supremacy, every clerical redoubt was stubbornly defended.

It took a struggle of more than half a century in the mother country to win political equality for Catholics and Dissenters, and to sweep away tithes for the support of an official religion. The twentieth century opened before France, going beyond England in her evolution, could put asunder Church and State. Only ten years sufficed to carry through the legislature Jefferson's "Statute of Virginia for Religious Freedom," and before the nineteenth century had far advanced, the Congregationalists were finally disestablished— in New Hampshire in 1817, in Connecticut the following year, and in Massachusetts in 1833. So before Jefferson's death Episcopalians could enjoy in Connecticut liberties they had once withheld in Virginia.

In law as in religion the light of reason was being turned on ancient customs. During this stirring period of intellectual and spiritual awakening, the British government was making its penal code more and more savage; when George III came to the throne in 1760 there were about one hundred and sixty offenses for which men, women, and children were put to death; before the end of his reign nearly one hundred new offenses were added to this appalling list.

Although the American colonists had never been so sweeping in their vengeful passions as English lawmakers, they too had adopted penal codes of shocking brutality—codes that loomed black and ominous against the new faith in the common run of mankind. Deeply moved by this incongruity, the impetuous Jefferson, to whom at least his Declaration was no mere mass of glittering generalities, hastened away from Philadelphia soon after independence to start the revolution in the legal system of Virginia. On his arrival he announced that the law must be reformed root and branch "with a single eye to reason and the good of those for whose government it was framed," so alarming the bench and bar by his rashness that it took him twenty years to gain his principal points. In the other states a similar campaign was waged against the barbarities of the statute books, now swiftly, now tardily casting into oblivion great fragments of the cruel heritage. Even at the worst the emancipated colonists were in most matters respecting criminal legislation half a century ahead of the mother country.

Indeed, in nearly every branch of enlightened activity, in every sphere of liberal thought, the American Revolution marked the opening of a new humane epoch. Slavery, of course, afforded a glaring contrast to the grand doctrines of the Revolution, but still it must be noted that Jefferson and his friends were painfully aware of the anachronisms; that Virginia prohibited the slave trade in 1778—a measure which the British Crown had vetoed twenty years before; that a movement for the abolition of slavery appeared among the new social forces of the age; and that it was the lofty doctrines of the Revolution which were invoked by Lincoln when in the fullness of time chattel bondage was to be finally broken. If a balance sheet is struck and the rhetoric of the Fourth of July celebration is discounted, if the externals of the conflict are given a proper perspective in the background, then it is seen that the American Revolution was more than a war on England. It was in truth an economic, social, and intellectual transformation of prime significance—the first of those modern world-shaking reconstructions in which mankind has sought to cut and fashion the tough and stubborn web of fact to fit the pattern of its dreams.

GEORGE BANCROFT *described the American Revolution as having been "achieved with such benign tranquillity that even conservatism hesitated to censure." The absence of systematic terror, the comparatively small bloodshed, and the failure to overturn American society has led many historians to wonder whether a revolution had actually occurred. Accustomed to think in terms of the upheavals which shook France, Russia, and China subsequently, they concluded as bland an affair as the American Revolution hardly fits the definition of a revolution. Such a conclusion overlooks the revolutionary premises upon which the Americans justified their resort to arms. To be specific, the ideas were drawn from the Puritan Revolution and its confirmation in the Glorious Revolution. The American Revolution fulfilled these earlier revolutions.*

*The social changes that resulted from the American Revolution were such as would have heartened the Levellers of the Puritan Revolution. Among a people instinctively democratic, the aftermath of the Treaty of Paris was an acceleration of the drive for equality. The sovereignty of the people written of in other countries was embedded in the new state constitutions. The underlying prop of the American system was neatly summarized by the Massachusetts General Court when it declared: "It is a general maxim in every government, there must exist, somewhere, a supreme, sovereign, absolute and uncontrollable power; but this power resides always in the body of the people; and it never was, or can be delegated to one man, or a few." The social implications of this commitment were truly revolutionary; it guaranteed that the American Revolution would not simply be a change of the political guard but the beginning of a process that would terminate only in the emergence of a society firmly set on the path to equalitarianism.*

*J. Franklin Jameson (1859-1937) had a distinguished academic career at Johns Hopkins, Brown, and the University of Chicago, this prior to his appointment in 1905 to serve as Director of the Department of Historical Research in the Carnegie Institution. He held this post until 1928 when he became chief of the Division of Manuscripts of the Library of Congress. He had a productive scholarly career in colonial and revolutionary history although all of it pales beside the work whose title belies its length. The brevity of* The American Revolution Considered as a Social Movement *is an inverse measurement of its subsequent impact upon historical research. Jameson played large roles in the establishment of such projects as the* Dictionary of American Biography, *the* Atlas of the Historical Geography of the United States, *and the* American Historical Review. *He also led the campaign that finally persuaded Congress to set up the National Archives. To a whole generation and more of historians, he served as a guide and adviser. By the time of his death, he had achieved the place of sage without peer among historians. It is an achievement few other historians can claim.*

# THE AMERICAN REVOLUTION
# CONSIDERED AS
# A SOCIAL MOVEMENT

## *by J. Franklin Jameson*

A popular revolution usually consists in the transfer of political power from the hands of a smaller into those of a larger mass of the citizens, or from one great section of the population to another. As the result of such a revolution, we expect to see the new group exercising its new-found power in accordance with its own interests or desires, until, with or without fixed intention of so doing, it alters the social system into something according better with its own ideals. After the peaceful English revolution known as the passing of the Parliamentary Reform Act of 1832, we look to see the new Parliament, chosen by a wider suffrage and representing now the middle classes, passing a mass of legislation that brings the social state of England into better conformity with middle-class ideals. After the American Civil War, which shifted the seat of political power from the planting aristocracy of the South to the manufacturing and commercial classes of the North, we look to see legislation and the growth of custom whereby the American social system takes on forms congenial to the minds of the new possessors of power. But indeed we do not need to look farther into the past than the last nine years, to observe how the greatest of all revolutions, the one destined evidently to be the most momentous in its consequences, beginning with the overthrow of a tsar and the substitution of a republic, speedily escapes from the control of those who would keep it purely or mainly political, and transforms Russian society by 1925 to an extent which no one would in 1913 have dreamed to be possible.

If then it is rational to suppose that the American Revolution had some social consequences, what would they be likely to be? It would be natural to reply that it depends on the question, who caused the Revolution, and that therefore it becomes important to inquire what manner of men they were, and what they would be likely, consciously or unconsciously, to desire. In reality, the matter is not quite so simple as that. Allowance has to be made for one important fact in the natural history of revolutions, and that is that, as they progress, they tend to fall into the hands of men holding more and more advanced or extreme views, less and less restrained by traditional attachment to the old order of things. Therefore the social consequences of a revolution are not necessarily shaped by the conscious or unconscious desires of those who started it, but more likely by the desires of those who come into control of it at later stages of its development.

You know how it was with the English Revolution of the seventeenth century. At first it was the affair of moderate statesmen, like Pym and Hampden, or moderate generals like Essex or Manchester, earls, who would not push the king too hard, but before long it fell into the hands of men like Cromwell, whose spirit is shown by his bold declaration, "If I should meet the king in battle, I would as soon fire my pistol at him as at any man." Now when we examine the interesting mass of constitutional and social legislation enacted by the parliaments of the Commonwealth, we see in it the work of men of far more advanced views than those of Pym and Hampden, to wit, of radicals who had come into control of the movement in its latest stages.

Or again, take the French Revolution. Everyone knows how its history is marked by distinct successive periods, in each of which the control is exercised by a group more radical and extreme than its predecessors; and the same has been true of the great Russian revolution. Now, widely as our American Revolution differed from these, do not let us suppose that it escaped every trait of conformity to the natural history of such movements. Certain it is that, in some of our states at least, it fell ultimately into quite other hands than those that set it in motion.

Well, then, we may ask, who were in favor of the Revolution, and who were against it? The answer of course varies with the different stages of its development. In 1774 the partisans of American independence were very few, though there had long been those who thought, in an academic way, that it would soon take place. In most years after 1776 the partisans of American independence were the great majority. But what sort of man became a Tory as it gradually became necessary to take sides? What sort of man became a Whig? As a matter of course, almost all persons who enjoyed office under the Crown became Tories, and these were a large number. In an age when the king's turnspit was a member of Parliament, and under a king whose chief means of political action was the distribution of offices, officeholders were certain to be numerous, and their pay was, in proportion to the wealth of the country and the work they had to do, much greater than it is now. If the natural desire of all mankind to hold on to a lucrative office (a desire which is said sometimes to influence political action even in this age) did not make an office-holder a Tory, there was another motive arising from the fact that he had been appointed and had sworn to execute the laws, and might therefore feel in duty bound to obey the instructions of the ministers in England. As for the merchants, many, who had extensive interests that were imperilled by rebellion, adhered to the royal cause. But on the whole the great body of the merchants of the thirteen colonies were Whigs, for of the deep underlying causes, which for a generation had been moving the American mind in the direction of independence, none was so potent, according to all the best testimony, as the parliamentary restrictions on the trade of the colonies. Among farmers many of the richest took the royalist side. Probably most Episcopalians did so, except in the South. Everywhere the debtor class was, as was natural, and as has been true the whole world over, mainly on the side of revolution.

If we speak of professions, we should note that probably most of the clergy were Whigs, with the exception of nearly all the clergymen of the Church of England in the northern colonies. Most lawyers were Whigs, but most of the most eminent and of those enjoying the largest practice were Tories. John Adams says that, of the eight lawyers who had an important practice before the Superior Court of Massachusetts at the time of the Stamp Act, only Otis and he were Whigs ten years later. One of the others had died, and the remaining five were Tories. Among physicians the proportion of Tories was quite as large as among lawyers.

A word as to race and nationality. Colonists who had very recently arrived from England were likely to take the Tory side. Immigrants from Scotland, also, were usually Tories. A hundred and fifty years ago the Scots at home were among the warmest of Tories; Hume's *History of England* is typical of their feelings. Perhaps, too, their well-known clannishness gave them, in America, the position of aliens who held together, and would not assimilate with the rest of the population. Of the Irish, on the other hand, and those of the Scotch-Irish stock, Protestants from the north of Ireland, it is customary to hold that they were warmly and by vast majority on the side of revolution. It is not so certain. Industrious efforts have been made to show that they formed the backbone of the Revolutionary army—efforts partly based on a misinterpretation of a single passage in Joseph Galloway's testimony before a committee of the House of Commons. On the other hand, I have observed that, in the two large lists of Loyalist claimants that gave the country of birth, 146 out of 1358 claimants, or eleven per cent, say that they were born in Ireland— a larger number than were born in England. Yet in Pennsylvania, where the proportion of Irish or Scotch-Irish population was greatest, it was unquestionably their influence that carried the state for independence, at the same time breaking the power in state affairs of the Philadelphia conservatives, and bestowing upon the state a radically democratic constitution. In all the colonies the Germans generally adhered to the party of independence, but not with great ardency.

As is usually the case, the revolutionary side was more frequently espoused by young men, the conservative cause by their elders. There were not a few conspicuous cases, such as that of Sir John Randolph, the king's attorney-general in Virginia, and his son Edmund Randolph, in which the son adopted the former, the father the latter cause, and other cases, like that of Samuel and Josiah Quincy, in which an elder and a younger brother were thus divided. Among all the leaders of the Revolution, very few were forty-five years old in 1775; most were under forty. But think for a moment of the leaders of the French Revolution—Robespierre thirty-one years old when the Revolution began, Danton thirty, Camille Desmoulins twenty-seven, Collot d'Herbois thirty-nine, Couthon thirty-three, Lebas twenty-four, Saint-Just twenty-one—and we shall see cause to be glad that our Revolution was carried through by men who, though still young, had at any rate reached their full maturity of thought and of character.

If we should investigate the Tory party in the several colonies in detail, we should be forced to the conviction that, in New England, it comprised in 1775 a very great share, probably more than half, of the most educated, wealthy, and hitherto respected classes. In March 1776, when Howe evacuated Boston, eleven hundred refugees sailed away with him. These eleven hundred, and the thousand or more who subsequently followed them, bore away perhaps a majority of the old aristocracy of Massachusetts. The act of banishment which the state legislature passed in 1778, to punish the Tories, includes among its three hundred-odd names some representatives of most of the families which had been distinguished in the earlier days of the colony. The loss of this important element, cultivated, experienced, and public-spirited, was a very serious one. It is true that many Tories returned after the war, but their fortunes were usually much broken, and they could never regain their influence. In New England, in short, it appears that the Revolution brought new strata everywhere to the surface.

In New York it seems probable that, in the height of the war at least, the bulk of the property-owners belonged to the Tory party, and it was strong also among the middle classes of the towns and among the country population. On the large manorial estates the tenant farmers sided with their landlords if they took sides at all. The city of New York and the county of Westchester were strongly Tory during at least the period of the British occupation, and Westchester very likely before. So were Staten Island and the three counties of Long Island.

In Pennsylvania it is probable that during the critical years of the war, at least, the majority of the population was on the side of the Crown, and that majority seems to have included many persons of eminence, and many Quakers. On the other hand, as is well known, the Virginian aristocracy in general, living somewhat remote from the influence of the royal officials, upon their secluded estates, were full of the spirit of local independence. Quite unlike their New England compeers, they took the Whig side, and that almost unanimously. It was the Virginian planters who formed the local committees, seized from the outset the control of the movement, and made it impossible for loyalty to show itself in concerted or effective action. And it is well known how numerous and active were the Tories in the Carolinas. But, says Dr. Ramsay, speaking of South Carolina, "Beside their superiority in numbers, there was an ardour and enthusiasm in the friends of Congress which was generally wanting in the advocates for royal government." Is not this a most significant touch? After all the evidence as to classes and numbers—for perhaps there were a hundred thousand Loyalist exiles, to say nothing of the many more who did not emigrate—the ultimate success of the American cause might well seem to us a miracle. But the fact remains that the Revolutionary party knew what they wanted. They had a definite programme, they had boldness and resolution, while those averse to independence were divided in their counsels, and paralyzed by the timidity which naturally cleaves to conservative minds. The first scientific observer of political revolutions, Thucydides, pointed out, and every subsequent revolution has accentuated his words, that in such times boldness and energy are more important requisites to success than intelligence or all other qualities put together. This is the secret of the whole matter. "There was an ardour and enthusiasm in the friends of Congress which was generally wanting in the advocates for royal government."

All things considered, it seems clear that in most states the strength of the revolutionary party lay most largely in the plain people, as distinguished from the aristocracy. It lay not in the mob or rabble, for American society was overwhelmingly rural and not urban, and had no sufficient amount of mob or rabble to control the movement, but in the peasantry, substantial and energetic though poor, in the small farmers and frontiersmen. And so, although there were men of great possessions like George Washington and Charles Carroll of Carrollton who contributed a conservative element, in the main we must expect to see our social changes tending in the direction of levelling democracy.

It would be aside from the declared purpose . . . to dwell upon the political effects which resulted from the victory of a party constituted in the manner that has been described. There are, however, some political changes that almost inevitably bring social changes in their wake. Take, for instance, the expansion of the suffrage. The status in which the electoral franchise was left at the end of the Revolutionary period fell far short of complete democracy. Yet during the years we are considering the right of suffrage was much extended. The freeholder, or owner of real estate, was given special privileges in four of the new state constitutions, two others widened the suffrage to include all owners of either land or personal property to a certain limit, and two others conferred it upon all tax-payers. Now if . . . we are considering especially the status of persons, we must take account of the fact that the elevation of whole classes of people to the status of voters elevates them also in their social status. American society in the colonial period had a more definite and stable organization than it ever has had since the Revolution. It had been like that English county society of which the poet speaks,

> Where Aylmer followed Aylmer at the hall,
> And Averill Averill at the rectory.

Now, multitudes of squires had been driven into exile or dethroned from their high position of dominance over the community. Multitudes of other Loyalists had been disfranchised, or impoverished by confiscations. Rip Van Winkle, whose sleep bridged just these years, found the atmosphere of his village radically altered. Jeremy Belknap of New Hampshire, writing in 1792, after remarking on the effect of the Revolution in calling the democratic power into action and repressing the aristocratic spirit, confesses that in the new state "the deficiency of persons qualified for the various departments in the Government has been much regretted, and by none more than by those few who know how public business ought to be conducted." In that entertaining Virginian autobiography, the *Life* of the Reverend Devereux Jarratt, after speaking of the habit in that writer's youth, among the plain people with whom he grew up, of regarding gentlefolk as beings of a superior order, he says in 1794:

> But I have lived to see a vast alteration in this respect and the contrary extreme prevail. In our high republican times there is more levelling than ought to be, consistent with good government. I have as little notion of oppression and tyranny as any man, but a due subordination is essentially requisite in every government. At present there is too little regard and reverence paid to magistrates and persons in public office; and whence do this regard and irreverence originate but from the notion and practice of levelling? An idea is held out to us that our present government and state are far superior to the former, when we were under the royal administration; but my age enables me to know that the people are not now by half so peacefully and quietly governed as formerly; nor are the laws, perhaps by the tenth part, so well executed. And yet I know the superiority of the present government. In theory it is certainly superior; but in practice it is not so. This can arise from nothing so much as from want of a proper distinction between the various orders of the people.

Similar voices come from North Carolina, where one stout conservative laments the "extension of that most delicate and important right [of suffrage] to every biped of the forest," and another declares that: "Anyone who has the least pretence to be a gentleman is suspected and borne down *per ignobile vulgus*—a set of men without reading, experience, or principle to govern them." In fact, the sense of social change pervaded the country. A writer in South Carolina says . . . "There is nothing more common than to confound the terms of the American Revolution with those of the late American war. The American war is over, but this is far from being the case with the American revolution. On the contrary, nothing but the first act of the great drama is closed."

The workings of the popular sentiment in favor of equality may of course be plainly seen in the legislation abolishing rights of primogeniture and distributing more or less equally the estates of persons dying intestate, but this movement may perhaps be more conveniently considered in a lecture devoted to the Revolution and the Land. We might also expect the equalitarian or humane spirit to show itself in alterations of the laws respecting redemptioners or indented servants. Those laws, however, seem not to have been changed in the Revolutionary period. We may infer that the laws protecting the interests of such persons, a very numerous class in the years just preceding the Revolution, either were, or were deemed to be, adequate for their humane purpose, and that the status of the indented, who after all had but a few years to serve and then would have all the rights of other poor people, was not regarded as seriously unsatisfactory.

A far more serious question, in any consideration of the effect of the American Revolution on the status of persons, is that of its influence on the institution of slavery, for at this time the contrast between American freedom and American slavery comes out, for the first time, with startling distinctness. It has often been asked: How could men who were engaged in a great and inspiring struggle for liberty fail to perceive the inconsistency between their professions and endeavors in that contrast and their actions with respect to their bondmen? How could they fail to see the application of their doctrines respecting the rights of man to the black men who were held among them in bondage far more reprehensible than that to which they indignantly proclaimed themselves to have been subjected by the King of Great Britain?

At the time when the Revolution broke out there were about a half-million of slaves in the Thirteen Colonies, the figures probably running about as follows: 200,000 in Virginia, 100,000 in South Carolina, 70,000 or 80,000 each in Maryland and in North Carolina, 25,000 perhaps in New York, 10,000 in New Jersey, 6,000 in Pennsylvania, 6,000 in Connecticut, 5,000 in Massachusetts, 4,000 in Rhode Island. Slavery in the continental colonies at that time was no doubt less harsh than in the West Indies, and milder than it has been in many other countries and times. An English parson, preaching to a Virginian congregation in 1763, says: "I do you no more than justice in bearing witness, that in no part of the world were slaves ever better treated than, in general, they are in the colonies." But slavery is slavery, and already before the Revolution many hearts had been stirred against it. It is of course true that other influences than those of the American Revolution were abroad in the world at the same time which would surely work in some degree against the institution of human slavery. On the one hand Voltaire had raised a powerful, if at times a grating, voice in favor of a rational humanitarianism, and Rousseau had poured upon time-worn institutions the active solvent of abounding sentimentality. Quite at another extreme of human thought from them, Wesley and White-field had stirred the English nation into a warmth of religious feeling of which Methodism was only one result, and with it came a revived interest in all varieties of philanthropic endeavor.

There is no lack of evidence that, in the American world of that time, the analogy between freedom for whites and freedom for blacks was seen. If we are to select but one example of such evidence, the foremost place must surely be given to the striking language of Patrick Henry, used in 1773, when he was immersed in the struggle against Great Britain. It is found in a letter which he wrote to one who had sent him a copy of Anthony Benezet's book on slavery.

Is it not amazing [he says] that at a time, when the rights of humanity are defined and understood with precision, in a country above all others fond of liberty, that in such an age and in such a country we find men professing a religion the most humane, mild, gentle and generous, adopting a principle as repugnant to humanity as it is inconsistent with the Bible and destructive to liberty? . . . Would anyone believe I am the master of slaves of my own purchase! I am drawn along by the general inconvenience of living here without them. I will not, I can not justify it. However culpable my conduct, I will so far pay my devoir to virtue, as to own the excellence and rectitude of her precepts, and lament my want of conformity to them. I believe a time will come when an opportunity will be offered to abolish this lamentable evil. Everything we can do is to improve it, if it happens in our day, if not, let us transmit to our descendants, together with our slaves, a pity for their unhappy lot, and an abhorrence of slavery. . . . It is a debt we owe to the purity of our religion, to show that it is at variance with that law which warrants slavery.

Along with many examples and expressions of individual opinion, we may note the organized efforts toward the removal or alleviation of slavery manifested in the creation of a whole group of societies for these purposes. The first anti-slavery society in this or any other country was formed on April 14, 1775, five days before the battle of Lexington, by a meeting at the Sun Tavern, on Second Street in Philadelphia. The members were mostly of the Society of Friends. The organization took the name of "The Society for the Relief of Free Negroes unlawfully held in Bondage." In the preamble of their constitution they point out that "loosing the bonds of wickedness and setting the oppressed free, is evidently a duty incumbent on all professors of Christianity, but more especially at a time when justice, liberty, and the laws of the land are the general topics among most ranks and stations of men." The New York "Society for Promoting the Manumission of Slaves" was organized in 1785, with John Jay for its first president. In 1788 a society similar to these two was founded in Delaware, and within four years there were other such in Rhode Island, Connecticut, New Jersey, Maryland, and Virginia, and local societies enough to make at least thirteen, mostly in the slave-holding states.

In actual results of the growing sentiment, we may note, first of all, the checking of the importation of slaves, and thus of the horrors of the trans-Atlantic slave trade. The Continental Congress of 1774 had been in session but a few days when they decreed an "American Association," or non-importation agreement, in which one section read: "That we will neither import nor purchase any slave imported after the first day of December next, after which we will wholly discontinue the slave trade, and will neither be concerned in it ourselves, nor will we hire our vessels nor sell our commodities or manufactures to those who are concerned in it"; and the evidence seems to be that the terms of this agreement were enforced throughout the war with little evasion.

States also acted. Four months before this, in July 1774, Rhode Island had passed a law to the effect that all slaves thereafter brought into the colony should be free. The influence under which it was passed may be seen from the preamble. "Whereas," it begins, "the inhabitants of America are generally engaged in the preservation of their own rights and liberties, among which that of personal freedom must be considered as the greatest, and as those who are desirous of enjoying all the advantages of liberty themselves should be willing to extend personal liberty to others," etc. A similar law was passed that same year in Connecticut. Delaware prohibited importation in 1776, Virginia in 1778, Maryland in 1783, South Carolina in 1787, for a term of years, and North Carolina, in 1786, imposed a larger duty on each Negro imported.

Still further, the states in which slaves were few proceeded, directly as a consequence of the Revolutionary movement, to effect the immediate or gradual abolition of slavery itself. Vermont had never recognized its existence, but Vermont was not recognized as a state. Pennsylvania in 1780 provided for gradual abolition, by an act which declared that no Negro born after that date should be held in any sort of bondage after he became twenty-eight years old, and that up to that time his service should be simply like that of an indented servant or apprentice. Now what says the preamble of this act? That when we consider our deliverance from the abhorrent condition to which Great Britain has tried to reduce us, we are called on to manifest the sincerity of our professions of freedom, and to give substantial proof of gratitude, by extending a portion of our freedom to others, who, though of a different color, are the work of the same Almighty hand. Evidently here also the leaven of the Revolution was working as a prime cause in this philanthropic endeavor.

The Superior Court of Massachusetts declared that slavery had been abolished in that state by the mere declaration of its constitution that "all men are born free and equal." In 1784 Connecticut and Rhode Island passed acts which gradually extinguished slavery. In other states, ameliorations of the law respecting slaves were effected even though the abolition of slavery could not be brought about. Thus in 1782 Virginia passed an act which provided that any owner might, by an instrument properly attested, freely manumit all his slaves, if he gave security that their maintenance should not become a public charge. It may seem but a slight thing, this law making private manumission easy where before it had been difficult. But it appears to have led in eight years to the freeing of more than ten thousand slaves, twice as great a number as were freed by reason of the Massachusetts constitution, and as many as there were in Rhode Island and Connecticut together when the war broke out.

That all was not done that might have been done for the removal or amelioration of slavery we cannot deny, nor that there was in many places a glaring contrast between the principles avowed by the men of the Revolution and their acts respecting slavery; yet very substantial progress was made, and that more was made in this period than in any other until a much later time may be taken as clear evidence of a pronounced influence of the Revolution upon the status of persons in the realm where that status stood most in need of amelioration.

Thus in many ways the successful struggle for the independence of the United States affected the character of American society by altering the status of persons. The freeing of the community led not unnaturally to the freeing of the individual; the raising of colonies to the position of independent states brought with it the promotion of many a man to a higher order in the scale of privilege or consequence. So far at any rate as this aspect of life in America is concerned, it is vain to think of the Revolution as solely a series of political or military events.

# III

# A New Commonwealth

CORNWALLIS *laid down his arms; the band played* "The World Turned Upside Down," *on October 19, 1781, at Yorktown, Virginia. Two years later, the Treaty of Paris of 1783 confirmed the independence then secured. Less than eight months before Yorktown, Maryland signed the Articles of Confederation, and with that the first experiment in American union was launched. It proved of brief duration, lasting only to the ratification and implementation of the Constitution on March 4, 1789.*

*Since the Articles were so quickly superseded by the Constitution, it has generally been assumed that they were unworkable. They have usually been indicted as too weak in the powers they assigned to the central government. The period of the Confederation has also been described as one of increasing social upheaval. State after state was swept by social disorders, the most famous of which was Shays's Rebellion of 1786 in Massachusetts. The object of these disorders was to protest the heavy tax burdens, the financial instability of many states, and the general inability of the states to provide both internal and external security. The classic account of the period is that given by John Fiske,* The Critical Period of American History *(1888); it set forth the proposition that the Founding Fathers in drawing up the Constitution saved the new nation from degenerating into squabbling Balkanized states.*

*This image overlooks the fact that several states, notably Virginia, had achieved considerable success in putting their economic needs in order. It also overlooks the fact that the Confederation successfully launched through the Northwest Ordinance a land policy of unusual liberality. It encompassed the proposition that the unorganized western lands should be "formed into distinct republican states, which shall become members of the federal union, and have the same rights of sovereignty, freedom and independence, as the other states." Indeed, the Founding Fathers took care to justify the Constitution, not as an indictment of the Articles, but rather as a step to form "a more perfect Union." A particularly cogent defense of the Confederation is contained in Merrill Jensen,* The New Nation *(1950). Andrew C. McLaughlin (1861-1947), onetime President of the American Historical Association, sets forth an able synthesis of the earlier view, although he concedes that the Articles provided the basis of a model confederation. The work also marked his emergence as a major constitutional historian whose* Constitutional History of the United States *(1935) won a Pulitzer Prize.*

# THE CONFEDERATION
# AND THE CONSTITUTION
## 1783-1789

### by *Andrew Cunningham McLaughlin*

The important process of making state constitutions was pretty well completed four years after the Declaration of Independence, but the formation of a national system was not so simple. For some years after the Declaration the affairs of the Union were conducted by a Congress of delegates on whose discretion or authority there were no constitutional restraints; hence Congress did, not what was needed to be done, but what it was able to do or thought it wise to attempt, at times showing energy and intelligence, again sinking into sloth and incompetence. During these years America was acting under an unwritten constitution, and, in spite of the inability of Congress, establishing precedents of some weight and importance.

On March 1, 1781, Maryland, the last of the thirteen states, signed by its delegates the Articles of Confederation, and henceforward the powers of Congress were clearly outlined. The first form of imperial organization was that of a "perpetual Union," a "league of friendship" between states. To care for the interests of the Confederation, a Congress was provided, to be made up of delegates annually chosen in the states. Each delegation was entitled to one vote; Rhode Island had as much influence in the affairs of America as Massachusetts or Virginia. Congress had authority to decide on peace and war, to carry on hostilities, to manage all diplomatic matters, to build and equip a navy, to borrow money and emit bills of credit, to make requisitions on the states for men and money, to appoint naval officers and superior military officers, to establish and regulate post-offices, to determine the alloy and value of coin, and to perform some other duties supposed to be of general interest. This was a generous allotment of authority, but its exercise was carefully guarded, since no vote, except to adjourn from day to day, could be carried except by a majority of all the states, while the consent of nine states was required to carry any measure of special importance. Unless nine states agreed, Congress could not engage in war or enter into treaties or alliances, or coin money or borrow money, or make appropriations, or appoint a commander-in-chief, or, indeed, even determine on the sums of money for which it would ask the states.

The better to secure mutual friendship and intercourse, it was especially provided that the free inhabitants of each state should be entitled to all the privileges and immunities of citizens in the several states. Sundry restraints were placed upon the states; they were not to enter into treaties,

confederations or alliances, interfere in foreign affairs, or engage in war
without the consent of Congress, unless actually invaded. These and similar prohibitions marked with some clearness the line of demarcation between the reserved power of the states and the authority granted to Congress. Congress was the final resort on appeal in all disputes between the
states, its authority to be exercised by the establishment of a special court
or board of arbitration whose decision was decisive of the question at
issue. The Articles were in many ways dissimilar to the state constitutions;
in fact, there is no evidence that their framers intended to follow the
examples of the states. There was no effort to establish a government with
distinct branches; all the authority granted was in the hands of Congress,
which was, however, authorized to appoint an executive committee to sit
when Congress itself was not in session.

This simple arrangement, a confederation of sovereign states, performing
certain functions through a body of delegates, proved in the course of a
short time so inadequate that it is easy to pass these Articles by with an
amused smile at their utter unfitness for the work at hand. As a matter of
fact, they were in many respects models of what articles of confederation
ought to be, an advance on previous instruments of like kind in the world's
history. Their inadequacy arose from the fact that a mere confederacy of
sovereign states was not adapted to the social, political, and industrial needs
of the time.

In one important particular the Articles were of profound significance:
with remarkable care they separated the particular or local powers from
those of general character; and let us notice that on the wisdom and the
accuracy with which this division is made must depend the permanence of
any plan of imperial organization. Under no conditions, of course, would
the states surrender all political authority to any central government; but
by the Articles of Confederation they granted nearly every power that
was really of a general or national character. Two powers that the central
authority much needed were withheld: the power to raise money and the
power to regulate commerce—the very ones about which there had been
so much discussion before the war. "Let the king ask for money," the
colonists had said to Parliament, "and we will pay it." This plan of imperial organization was to prove a very lame one when applied on this
side of the Atlantic; Congress was to try this plan, to call for money, plead
for it, implore attention, and remain penniless. But few years were needed
to show the necessity for general control of commerce if the Confederation
were to be more than a name, or if the states were not to change from
rivals into open enemies. In spite of all this, as far as the mere division
of powers was concerned, the Articles were not far from perfection, and
in any plan for a broader and better system this allotment of authority
would be of the utmost service.

Of course the Congress of the Confederation, made up of delegates from
the states, could not pass effective laws or enforce its orders. It could ask
for money but not compel payment; it could enter into treaties but not
enforce their stipulations; it could provide for raising of armies but not

fill the ranks; it could borrow money but take no proper measures for repayment; it could advise and recommend but not command. In other words, with some of the outward seemings of a government, and with many of its responsibilities, it was not a government.

The Articles, as we have seen, provided for no executive department. They did provide for the appointment of a member of Congress to preside over its sessions; but in fear of kingly authority, it was stipulated that no one person should serve as president more than one year in any term of three years. They also provided for the appointment of civil officers for managing the general affairs of the United States under the direction of Congress. And yet the course of the war had already proved how unfit for general administrative duties were the whole body of delegates or committees of members, and as a result a movement for the establishment of executive departments began even before the Articles went into effect.

\* \* \* \* \*

The year 1786 was, as we have already seen, one of discouragement. The country was filled with the discontented, who had succeeded in the majority of states in getting possession of the government. The dangerous restlessness of the people, the absurd extravagances of Rhode Island, and, above all, the insurrection in Massachusetts cast deep gloom over conservative men. Congress, begging for power and money, placed solemnly before the people their choice of life or death as a nation; but there was no indication of willingness on the part of the states to give up money to save the country from disgrace.

Everywhere there was great cause for despondency: disorder within the states, plots and threatenings on the border, loud laments over commercial distress and heavy taxes, and, worst of all, a reckless disregard of political obligations. But in this year of despair there were some men who still worked for real government, and we may now turn our attention to the efforts to amend the Articles of Confederation and to establish the necessary authority; we shall see that these efforts, reaching a climax in 1786, had in reality begun some years before.

Almost from the time of their adoption there had been dissatisfaction with the Articles and little hope of their success. No one saw the situation more clearly than Washington, who did not hesitate at the very outset to say that the affairs of the nation could not be well conducted by a Congress with only power of recommendation. As early as 1781 he declared that a mere nominal head would no longer do, and that a real controlling power and the right to regulate all matters of general concern should be given to Congress. He saw with his accustomed simplicity and directness that the states could not be relied on to do what Congress asked, and he pointed out that the Articles provided no means of compelling states to furnish men and money, and that for want of such coercive power the war would necessarily be prolonged. Like others who were to work over this problem in the succeeding years, he wondered how the states could be forced to do their duty, but he was confident that some means must be found. Thus, even before the war was over, Washington had stated what was the most evident fact and the most trying problem of the anxious days of political reorganization.

*     *     *     *     *

In this dreary year of 1786, while men were writing and arguing, and the liberal-minded among them were almost in despair, a movement which had results of unexpected magnitude was already under way. It grew out of the need of some sort of understanding between Maryland and Virginia concerning the navigation of the Potomac; and back of the plan of agreement and accommodation were Washington and Madison. As early as 1777 three commissioners had been appointed from each of the two states. Nothing having been accomplished at the first convention, Virginia, in 1784, again appointed commissioners, and in January, 1785, Maryland, willing to co-operate, took like action. On the invitation of Washington, who was then greatly interested in projects for opening up routes of communication between the east and the west, five of the commissioners met in the spring of 1785 at Mount Vernon, drew up resolutions to be submitted to their states, and asked the co-operation of Pennsylvania in their plans. This report was accepted by each of the states, but Maryland was prepared to go further; she asked for a new conference on commercial questions and proposed the concurrence of Pennsylvania and Delaware.

Those who were anxiously scanning the horizon saw hope in the suggestion; if two more states were to come into the conference they would "naturally pay the same compliment to their neighbors." Madison, hard at work in the legislature, was ready to do what he could to further the movement; but he had to contend with a vehement anti-nationalist party, who were "bitter and illiberal against Congress . . . beyond example," and in their narrow dread of northern commercial power actually considered whether it would not be well to encourage British shipping in preference to that of the eastern states. When resolutions granting Congress authority to regulate commerce were brought before the legislature, they were long discussed, but were at length so hopelessly mutilated that friends of the measure lost interest in their passage; and on the last day of the session another resolution, which had been lying peacefully on the table, was taken up and passed almost without opposition (January, 1786). This resolution appointed commissioners to meet such commissioners as might be appointed by other states to take into consideration the trade of the Union, and "to consider how far a uniform system in their commercial regulations may be necessary to their common interest and their permanent harmony." The commissioners, of whom, of course, Madison was one, being instructed to make the necessary arrangements, invited the other states to send delegates to a convention at Annapolis to be held the first Monday in September, 1786.

During the summer before the meeting Madison was doing what he could, but had not much hope. "I almost despair of success," he wrote.

And yet he believed that something must be done quickly, for delay added to the peril; the introduction of new states might add new elements of uncertainty and perhaps of discord, and there was, moreover, so much selfishness and rascality abroad in the land that any one looking about him might well have feared that the game by which Philip managed the confederacy of the Greeks would be played on the American states. "I saw eno'," Madison said, "during the late Assembly of the influence of the desperate circumstances of individuals on their public conduct to admonish me of the possibility of finding in the council of some one of the states fit instruments of foreign machinations."

The convention met at Annapolis, but delegations from only five states were in attendance. Evidently nothing could be done in the way of carrying out the express purpose of the meeting, and it was therefore decided to take another bold step forward and to hope for better results. A report, written by Hamilton, was unanimously adopted. It pointed to the critical situation of the states, which called for the exercise "of the united virtue and wisdom of all the members of the confederacy," and it proposed a convention of delegates from all the states to meet at Philadelphia the second Monday in May (1787) "to take into consideration the situation of the United States, to devise such further provisions as shall appear to them necessary to render the constitution of the federal government adequate to the exigencies of the Union; and to report such an act for that purpose to the United States Congress assembled, as, when agreed to by them, and afterwards confirmed by the legislatures of every state, will effectually provide for the same."

\*   \*   \*   \*   \*

As the delegates chosen to the convention began coming together in Philadelphia in May, it was apparent that the crises had produced an assembly of capable men; many of them had already won distinction; most of them had had experience in political affairs. They represented on the whole the conservative elements of the nation, who were dismayed by the appearance of discord and lawlessness, and who appreciated the national danger. They were more than practical politicians; they were men of education as well as of experience; about half of them had had college education; many of them were learned in law and history.

Washington and Franklin, the most famous members, were without the advantages of university training; but they had the wisdom which is not gleaned from books or absorbed from teachers—rare judgment, wide knowledge of men, profound insight into human motives, remarkable sanity, and a capacity for generous appreciation of the sentiments of their fellows. Franklin did not play a very conspicuous part in the convention, but his kindly humor and his national spirit were of value. Washington had hoped that he would be excused from attending; his friends persuaded him to come, however, and no one better realized the gravity of the movement—he saw the best men of the country chosen as delegates; the convention was the end for which earnest men had long been toiling; if it failed, what hope of reformation or the saving of national credit and reputation? "My wish is," he wrote, "that the convention may adopt no temporizing expedients, but probe the defects of the constitution to the bottom, and provide a radical cure, whether they are agreed to or not." He did not take an active part in the debates of the convention; there is no evidence of his having spoken more than once; but by sheer weight of character he did what much volubility and streams of sonorous language could not have accomplished. Of the more active members of the convention Madison deserves chief consideration. We have already seen how anxious he was to better the federal government; he had been waging continuous warfare against the paper-money men and the forces of disorganization within his state. He prepared carefully for the work of the convention: he bought and read books; he studied the confederacies of the ancient world and the combinations of modern states; he noted carefully the characteristics of each and dwelt on the sides that were pertinent to American problems. He saw that the Amphictyonic Council could employ the "whole force of Greece against such as refused to execute its decrees." In the Lycian League he found that "the number of votes allotted to each member was proportioned to its pecuniary contributions." Before the convention met he draughted an indictment of the vices of the political system of the United States. The first and most significant of the faults of the Confederation was the failure of the states to comply with the constitutional requisitions. This he declared to be exemplified in every confederacy and fatal to the objects of the American Union. The other vices he enumerated serve to show how clearly Madison saw the situation and what he deemed the task of the convention: encroachments by the states on the federal authority; violations of the law of nations and of treaties; trespasses of the states on one another's rights; want of concert in matters of common interest; absence of a guaranty for state constitutions and laws against domestic violence; no sanction to the laws and no coercive powers in the central government; ratification of the Articles by the legislatures and not by the people; multiplicity, mutability, and injustice of state laws. "A sanction," he declared, "is essential to the idea of law, as coercion is to that of Government." For want of real power the Confederation had been a failure; the confidence which the framers of the Articles had shown in the good faith of the state legislatures only did honor to the "enthusiastic virtue of the compilers" of the instrument.

By such careful methods of study and by accurate thinking Madison had fitted himself to take a leading part in the convention's work. Quiet and unobtrusive, his knowledge gave him an advantage over more eloquent members. "In the management of every great question," wrote a delegate from Georgia, "he evidently took the lead in the Convention. . . . From a spirit of industry and application which he possesses in a most eminent degree, he always comes forward the best informed Man of any point in debate."

\*     \*     \*     \*     \*

Of all the problems of the convention not one caused greater perplexity than determining the powers of the president and the method of his election. This fact should not surprise us if we stop to consider how difficult the task of providing for an executive head of a nation, who should have dignity and authority and yet be not overpowerful; who should work harmoniously with the other branches of government, and yet not be the creature of the legislature or of either chamber; who should be so hemmed about by republican restrictions as not to affright the populace when the veil was lifted from the work of their delegates.

The convention was bent on carrying into effect the principle that the three departments of government should be separate and independent. With more or less accuracy that principle had already found its formulation in state constitutions, but to apply it to the natural government was, nevertheless, not easy, chiefly, perhaps, because there was difficulty in discovering a suitable method of choosing the president. In fact the convention had on its hands a delicate task; it must hit on a method of adjusting the departments so nicely and yet with such strength that each could maintain itself for years to come, while the government performed its functions smoothly, safely, and efficiently. The result was, as we know, the establishment of what publicists now call the presidential form of government, one of the two great and successful forms of popular national government now in use in the civilized world. We need not wonder, then, that the problem was perplexing almost beyond compare, and that the delegates debated long and passed many resolutions, only to rescind them again.

On twenty-one different days the general subject of executive office was under discussion; and on the method of election alone over thirty distinct votes were taken. If the executive were to be chosen by Congress, or by either branch, there was a likelihood that he would be yielding and dependent in his relations with those to whom he owed his position. To trust the main body of the people seemed impossible. How could the common man judge who was fit to be president of the United States? To give the right to the legislatures of the states had its most obvious dangers. Moreover, any plan which took into consideration the size of the respective states gave the large states an advantage over their smaller neighbors. Here, in other words, came up the old antagonism; here in the effort to decide the most difficult and delicate of questions, and to adjust a complex piece of political mechanism, the delegates were harassed by an imaginary antithesis between big and little states and by temporary or trivial considerations.

After long consultation a committee was appointed, which reported (September 4) in favor of having the president chosen by electors, a plan that had been several times discussed. Each state was to appoint, in such manner as its legislature might direct, a number of electors equal to the whole number of its senators and representatives in Congress. Each elector was to vote for two persons, the one receiving the highest number, if a majority, to be president, the one receiving the next highest to be vice-president. This method gave an evident advantage to the large states, but the report of the committee also provided that, in case the electors should not by their votes give a majority to any one person, the choice of president from the five highest on the list should devolve upon the Senate; likewise the Senate should choose one of two receiving a majority and an equal number of votes. By this plan it was supposed the election, in the first instance, would devolve on persons qualified to have opinions and express them, and yet would not magnify the authority of any official body in the states or of either house of Congress. In this way also the power of the large states was in a measure recognized, for the larger the state the greater the number of electors. The plan, moreover, was not without its advantages for the small states, since the alternative choice might devolve on the Senate, where the states were equally represented; and the delegates seemed actually to have believed that the electors in many, if not in the majority of cases, would not be in sufficient agreement to give any person a majority.

This power of ultimate choice would, however, greatly increase the influence of the Senate, which had enough without it, and this was a real objection. Wilson, not generally fearful of authority, pointed to the Senate's power over appointments and the making of treaties and its right to try impeachments. "According to the plan as it now stands," he said, "the President will not be the man of the people as he ought to be, but the minion of the Senate. He cannot even appoint a tide-waiter without the Senate." Apparently influenced by such considerations as these, the right to select the president, in case the electors failed to choose, was transferred from the Senate to the House of Representatives, with the proviso that in the House each state should have one vote. Of the ignorance of the fathers concerning political parties, this naïve compromise with all its complexities stands as a golden example. It did not occur to them that in a few years men from New Hampshire to Georgia would be deciding on candidates for party purposes, that the party reins would reach into the remotest corner of the land, and that before long these electors would be but men of straw, mere pieces of machinery, to register the will of the people or their political masters.

As the convention neared the end of its labors its perplexities did not diminish. The summer had gone and the early days of September passed, and yet, after four months of toil and of remarkable patience, the delegates found themselves dissatisfied. No one seemed wholly content, and those who labored most earnestly could only say that the instrument before them was the result of their best efforts and ought to be adopted by the people. They might all have said, with Touchstone, "An ill-favored thing, Sir, but mine own." Franklin urged unanimity of action, even if the Constitution did not suit everybody in all its parts. "The older I grow," he said, "the more apt I am to doubt my own judgment," and he pleasantly told of "a certain french lady"—perhaps one of the many who had listened to his own wisdom in his conquering days in France—who in a dispute with her sister said, "I don't know how it happens, Sister, but I meet with nobody but myself, that is always in the right—*Il n'y a que moi qui a toujours raison.*"

Franklin's pleasantry was of possible service, but it did not win all the discontented. The new Constitution must go forth to be criticized by some who had helped to make it. Most of the delegates, it is true, were ready to sign the finished instrument and advocate adoption, although not entirely satisfied. Even Hamilton, who had not taken an important part and who openly expressed his dislike of the system, was ready to acquiesce, declaring that it was impossible "to deliberate between anarchy and Convulsion on one side, and the chance of good" on the other.

But some of the delegates were not so reasonable. Martin, who had stayed till near the end, went home to attack the Constitution with his customary vehemence. Mason remained to the end, but, vigorously protesting against the powers of Congress by a mere majority to pass navigation acts, a power which "would enable a few rich merchants" of the northern cities to monopolize the staples of the southern states, refused to accept the Constitution or to advocate its adoption. Randolph and Gerry also protested and declined to sign. Altogether seventy-three delegates had been appointed to the convention. Of these, fifty-five were at one time or another in attendance; but only thirty-nine signed the finished instrument. Of the twelve regular members, not counting Martin, who were not in attendance at the end and did not sign, seven are known to have approved of the Constitution and three are known to have disapproved.

For the purpose of sending out the Constitution supported by apparent unanimity, and also if possible to win the hesitant, Franklin proposed as a form of ratification by the convention, "Done in Convention by the unanimous consent of *the States* present." This equivocal expression was adopted and the work of the convention finished on September 17. Incomplete and inadequate as the men believed it to be, there was hope in its lines, and the best among them could honestly ask the people to establish the work of their hands.

The document to which the framers attached their names with mingled hopes and misgivings that September day in the old state-house in Philadelphia has come to be looked on as one of the great documents of the world's history; it is now the fundamental law of the oldest republic on earth; the government which it established has outlived dynasties and seen ancient governments totter; it has stood without destruction while England was abandoning her old-time aristocratic government, while France was making and remaking a series of constitutions, while Italy was unified and the German people were founding a national organization, while the pope himself was deprived of his ancient temporal authority, while Spain, who at one time claimed nearly the whole of the New World, was losing her dominions and shrinking back into the old limits of the Iberian peninsula.

The Constitution has sometimes been spoken of as if it were in all respects the creature of the men at Philadelphia, or as if it were, as Mr. Gladstone once said, "the most wonderful work ever struck off at a given time by the brain and purpose of man." That in one sense the Constitution was made in four months' time is true; in four months a series of articles and sections were pieced together. In another sense it is not true; time made the American Constitution as it has made others of any moment. An artificial constitution, not the product of a people's life, can never have vitality, strength, or usefulness. The delegates at Philadelphia did not sit brooding over the chaos of the Confederation to bring forth by their fiat a new government. The idea that they created institutions out of nothingness loses sight of the manner and the conditions of their work. Neither is it true that they copied European institutions, borrowing scraps here and there to patch up a system suited to their tastes. Some of them were students of law, familiar with Vattel, Locke, Montesquieu, and Blackstone. Some of them had read history to a purpose, and could cite the failures of past confederacies or draw illustrations from the experiences of European states. But there is no evidence of borrowing or of slavish copying; for, while they were students and readers of history and knew that their own little experience was not the sum of knowledge, they were practical political workers, had for years studied the problems of forming governments, and had been acquainted with the great process of making state constitutions. The men of the generation that declared independence and formed new states were steeped in political theory as their great-grandfathers had been in theology, and for years they were engaged in the difficult process of adapting old institutions to new ideas, framing governments and laws that suited the economic, social, and moral conditions which the New World had produced.

We might, therefore, expect to find from these experienced craftsmen, not a document hurriedly patched together, nor one taken in part from distant ages or strange climes, but an American document, in its entirety new, but made up of parts that had found their places in the state organizations. If we look, then, for the origin of the Constitution, we find much of it in the failures of the Confederation, in the tribulations of eleven confused years when the nation was without a proper government and when distress and disorder and incompetence were showing the way to success; and much of it, too, in the state constitutions which had been drawn up by men familiar with colonial governments and administration. This old-fashioned colonial practice was not thrown aside when independence was declared, any more than a man throws aside his body or his brains when he emerges from boyhood to manhood. The work of constitution-making for the states was a work of adaptation, of enlargement, of emphasis, not of creation; it registered growth.

And thus it may be said that colonial history made the Constitution. Even in the division of authority between the states and the national government we see a readjustment of the old practical relationship between colonies and mother-country, a readjustment which was based in part on the imperfections of the old system but carried out the teachings of the Revolution. Even the essentially American notion, the notion that government is the agent of the people and must not transcend the law set by the people was an outgrowth of the free society of a new world, had found its expression in the theory of the Revolution, and had arisen in a country in which from time immemorial there had been no government possessed of all political power. And this only means, of course, that the Constitution of the United States took its root in the history of England; it was not borrowed by conscious imitation from England, it was a product of the forces of English history; but it was shaped by American necessities, was framed by men who could learn lessons and use the material the tide of history washed to their feet.

*THE Federal Constitution established a stable, enduring government. It would be, for that reason alone, a subject of more than lasting interest, but it also created a government of unusual complexity. It deliberately divided power to prevent its concentration in the hands of any one person or groups of persons. It also created a semantic impossibility: dual sovereignty. It intended to provide a central government of large but specific powers while reserving remaining power to the individual states. But it also employed language broad enough to allow for an extensive expansion of federal power. A good deal of American history has involved, as a result, complex, frequently long-winded debates over the precise meaning of a phrase or a clause. Not infrequently, Americans have spent much energy trying to divine the original intent of its authors. It is a game that might well be entitled, "Getting right with the Founding Fathers."*

*The motives of the men who met at the Philadelphia Convention in 1787 have excited considerable historical scrutiny. The conclusions drawn have varied. Historians during the nineteenth century were prone to treat the Founding Fathers as divinely inspired if not themselves demigods. This interpretation received a rude shock in 1913 when Charles Austin Beard, responding as much to the contemporary Progressive concern with "malfactors of wealth" as with a concern for the Founding Fathers' motives, treated them as men whose actions were determined by their interest in unredeemed paper issued during the Revolution. When Beard had finished, the Constitution emerged as a document designed to protect the property interests of the privileged against the claims of a hard-pressed democracy. This view permeated the thinking of a whole generation. Recently Beard's interpretation has come under sharp scrutiny. Robert Brown,* Charles A. Beard and the Constitution *(1956) and Forrest McDonald,* We the People *(1958) have between them raised not only serious questions about Beard's conclusions but, more damaging, have also cast grave doubts on his uses of evidence.*

*As is likely to happen, historians have moved toward a golden mean, arguing that though the Founding Fathers were hardly demigods, as they would have been the first to admit, they were men concerned with founding a government that would secure the rights, among them property, for all white men. They also informed their endeavor with a large enough spirit to create a government that has endured despite many trials, a result which would hardly have been true if amongst them only narrow self-interest had prevailed. Such is the view set forth in the classic account of the Philadelphia Convention composed by Max Farrand (1869-1945). It is a treatment which has the benefit of a commonsensical lucidity, an attribute which is eminently suitable in explaining the actions of the Founding Fathers. For those who knew them well noted that they always had a large concern for the common sense of a question. A point which received sharp underscoring in Federalist Paper No. 51 when James Madison commented in defense of the Constitution, "But what is government itself, but the greatest of all reflections on human nature? If men were angels, no government would be necessary."*

# THE FRAMING OF THE CONSTITUTION
# OF THE UNITED STATES

## by Max Farrand

On Monday, the 17th, the convention met for the last time. The engrossed constitution was read and in order to disguise the fact that a few of the delegates present were unwilling to sign the document, Gouverneur Morris devised a form that would make the action appear to be unanimous: "Done in Convention, by the unanimous consent of the States present the 17th of September. . . . In Witness whereof we have hereunto subscribed our names." Thinking that the idea would meet with a better reception if it came from some one else than himself, Morris persuaded Franklin to present the proposed form of approval, which Franklin did in a speech urging harmony and unanimity. Franklin himself was rather proud of this effort, and he made several copies of the speech which he sent to various friends. It was not long before the speech found its way into print, and was very favorably received. Another point of view with regard to it, however, which also throws some light upon the contemporary opinion of Franklin, is represented by the note made by McHenry: "It was plain, insinuating persuasive—and in any event of the system guarded the Doctor's fame."

Just before the question was to be put upon the adoption of the engrossed constitution, Gorham said that if it was not too late he would like to see the ratio of representation in the lower house changed from one for every 40,000 inhabitants to one for every 30,000. He was supported by King and Carroll, but there is no reason for supposing that this suggestion would have met with any different fate now than when previously made in the convention, especially as it was so irregular to bring it up at this stage of the proceedings, unless the motion was "inspired." When Washington arose to put the question he said that although he recognized the impropriety of his speaking from the chair he felt this amendment to be of so much consequence that "he could not forbear expressing his wish that the alteration proposed might take place." Without a single objection being made, the change was then unanimously agreed to. This was another concession made to forestall popular criticism, but it may have originated in a suggestion from Washington and under any circumstances its adoption was a striking testimony to his influence.

The constitution was then signed by all the members present, except Gerry, Mason, and Randolph. "Whilst the last members were signing it Doctor Franklin looking towards the Presidents Chair, at the back of which a rising sun happened to be painted, observed to a few members near him, that Painters had found it difficult to distinguish in their art a rising from a setting sun. I have, said he, often and often in the course of the Session, and the vicissitudes of my hopes and fears as to its issue, looked at that behind the President without being able to tell whether it was rising or setting: But now at length I have the happiness to know that it is a rising and not a setting Sun."

It was agreed that the papers of the convention should be turned over to Washington for safe keeping subject to the order of congress if ever formed under the new constitution. The convention then adjourned *sine die.* According to the local papers, the work was completed about four o'clock on Monday afternoon, and from the diary of Washington we know that the "members adjourned to the City Tavern, dined together and took a cordial leave of each other." The next day's edition of the *Pennsylvania Packet and Daily Advertiser* consisted of nothing but the new constitution printed in large type. In those days of limited journalism, there could be no better indication of contemporary opinion as to the importance of what the federal convention had accomplished.

The convention was over; it had completed its work. In the achievement of its task James Madison had been unquestionably the leading spirit. It might be said that he was the masterbuilder of the constitution. This is not an overvaluation of his services derived from his own account of the proceedings in convention, for Madison laid no undue emphasis upon the part he himself played; in fact, he understated it. Nor is it intended to belittle the invaluable services of many other delegates. But when one studies the contemporary conditions, and tries to discover how well the men of that time grasped the situation; and when one goes farther and, in the light of our subsequent knowledge, seeks to learn how wise were the remedies they proposed,—Madison stands pre-eminent. He seems to have lacked imagination, but this very lack made his work of peculiar value at the moment. His remedies for the unsatisfactory state of affairs under the confederation, were not founded on theoretical speculations, they were practical. They were in accord with the historical development of our country and in keeping with the genius of our institutions. The evidence is also strong that Madison not only took an important part in the debates but that he was actually looked up to by both friends and opponents as the leader of those in the convention who were in favor of a strong national government.

In these respects, he was in marked contrast to Alexander Hamilton, who was a stronger man intellectually, and suggested a more logical and consistent plan of government than the one which was followed. But Hamilton was out of touch with the situation. He was aristocratic rather than democratic, and while his ideas may have been excellent, they were too radical for the convention and found but little support. At the same time, being in favor of a strong national government, he tried to aid that movement in every way that he could. But within his delegation he was outvoted by Yates and Lansing, and before the sessions were half over he was deprived of a vote altogether by the withdrawal of his colleagues. Finding himself of little service he went to New York and only returned to Philadelphia once or twice for a few days and to sign the completed document in September.

Second to Madison and almost on a par with him was James Wilson. In some respects he was Madison's intellectual superior, but in the immediate work before them he was not as adaptable and not as practical. Still he was Madison's ablest supporter. He appreciated the importance of laying the foundations of the new government broad and deep, and he believed that this could only be done by basing it upon the people themselves. This was the principal thing for which he contended in the convention, and with a great measure of success. His work on the committee of detail was less conspicuous but was also of the greatest service.

Next to these two men should come Washington. Not that he ever spoke in the convention, beyond the one recorded instance at the close of the sessions. But as previously pointed out, personal influence must have been an important factor in the outcome of the convention's work, and Washington's support or opposition would be of the greatest importance. He voted with the Virginia delegation, his views were known, and it is therefore a matter of no little moment that Washington's support was given to Madison. Madison's ideas were the predominating factor in the framing of the constitution and it seems hardly too much to say that Washington's influence, however it may have been exerted, was important and perhaps decisive in determining the acceptance of those ideas by the convention.

Gouverneur Morris was a conspicuous member, brilliant but erratic. While he supported the efforts for a strong national government, his support was not always a great help. His best work in the convention was as the member of the committee on style and arrangement to whom was entrusted the final drafting of the constitution. Charles Pinckney also took a conspicuous part in the convention, but his work is not to be classed with that of other and larger minds. It is undoubtedly true that he suggested a great many things that were embodied in the constitution, but they were minor points and details rather than large, constructive features.

Other members of the convention who deserve notice, though hardly to be classed with the names already mentioned, were Rufus King, General Charles C. Pinckney, John Rutledge, Nathaniel Gorham and, in spite of their refusal to sign the completed constitution, Edmund Randolph and George Mason. It may seem surprising that no particular mention is made of Benjamin Franklin, but it must be remembered that Franklin was at that time a very old man, so feeble that Wilson read all of his speeches for him, and while he was highly respected his opinions do not seem to have carried much weight. For instance, Madison recorded with regard to one of Franklin's motions: "It was treated with great respect, but rather for the author of it, than from any apparent conviction of its expediency or practicability."

Thus far the men who have been considered were all supporters to a greater or less extent of a strong national government. On the other hand were men such as William Paterson, John Dickinson, Elbridge Gerry, Luther Martin, and the three Connecticut delegates, Oliver Ellsworth, William Samuel Johnson, and Roger Sherman. They were fearful of establishing a too strongly centralized government, and at one time or another were to be found in the opposition to Madison and his supporters. They must none the less be given great credit for the form which the constitution finally assumed. They were not mere obstructionists and, while not constructive to the extent that Madison and Wilson were constructive, it is certain that the constitution would not have assumed so satisfactory a form if it had not been for the part taken by them. Their best service was rendered in restraining the tendency of the majority to overrule the rights of states and individuals, in endeavoring to establish a thoroughly strong government.

The document which the convention presented to congress and to the country as the proposed new constitution for the United States was a surprise to everybody. No one could have foreseen the processes by which it had been constructed, and no one could have foretold the compromises by which the differences of opinion had been reconciled, and accordingly no one could have forecast the result. Furthermore, the construction of the document was unusual. Wilson and the committee of detail, and Gouverneur Morris and the committee of style had done their work remarkably well. Out of what was almost a hodge-podge of resolutions they had made a presentable document, but it was not a logical piece of work. No document originating as this had and developed as this had been developed could be logical or even consistent. That is why every attempted analysis of the constitution has been doomed to failure. From the very nature of its construction the constitution defies analysis upon a logical basis.

There would seem to be only one way to explain and only one way to understand the "bundle of compromises" known as the constitution of the United States. John Quincy Adams described it when he said that it "had been extorted from the grinding necessity of a reluctant nation." The constitution was a practical piece of work for very practical purposes. It was designed to meet certain specific needs. It was the result of an attempt to remedy the defects experienced in the government under the articles of confederation.

A statement has been made as to what the delegates to the federal convention probably considered those defects of the confederation to be. We have seen that in the speech with which he opened the main business of the convention, Randolph pointed out the most glaring of these defects, and that he presented the Virginia plan as a basis of procedure in providing a remedy for those defects. We have seen how the Virginia plan developed step by step into the constitution. At every stage, suggestions for further remedies were made from one or another delegate, until every defect recorded as known to the members of the convention had been under consideration.

In the completed constitution: the president had been given the power of veto instead of establishing a council of revision; the federal courts instead of congress were to be relied upon to check improper state legislation; and no specific powers had been vested in congress to establish a national bank, to make internal improvements, or to legislate upon the subject of education. With these few exceptions, every known defect of the confederation had been provided for.

On the other hand, there is practically nothing in the constitution that did not arise out of the correction of these specific defects of the confederation. The completed constitution necessarily included many details that would not be mentioned in any enumeration of defects. Compromises had been necessary at every point, and those compromises in some cases produced unforeseen results. With those two qualifications, it would seem to be a safe statement that the only new element in the constitution, that is, the only thing not originating in the correction of the defects noted, was the provision regarding impeachment. This was such a natural result when a powerful executive had been established, that it is hardly worthy of record. It was as inevitable as it was to place limitations upon the extensive powers of congress in order to prevent abuse. When once prescribed for the president, it was but a step to include the "Vice President and all civil Officers."

It has been recognized that the framers of the constitution were indebted to the constitutions of the individual states for many of the specific provisions in the federal instrument. But this becomes more significant in the light of the present study. However much the members of the federal convention may have prepared themselves by reading and study, and however learnedly they might discourse upon governments, ancient and modern, when it came to concrete action they relied almost entirely upon what they themselves had seen and done. They were dependent upon their experience under the state constitutions and the articles of confederation. John Dickinson expressed this very succinctly in the course of the debates, when he said: "Experience must be our only guide. Reason may mislead us." In fact, making allowance for the compromises and remembering that the state constitutions were only a further development of colonial governments, it is possible to say that every provision of the federal constitution can be accounted for in American experience between 1776 and 1787.

The lack of power to establish a national bank was one of the weaknesses charged against the government of the confederation. It was not specifically provided for in the new constitution, because its importance had not yet been realized. Hamilton's genius, within a year or two, was able to wrest its concession from a reluctant congress, but it required the disastrous financial situation in the war of 1812 to awaken the nation to the necessity of some such institution. In the same way, it was the unexampled spread of population beyond the Alleghanies, and the consequent necessity of better means of transportation, that brought the opposition to acquiesce in national support of internal improvements, which Washington had advocated long before the federal convention met. Gouverneur Morris claimed to have foreseen the acquisition of Louisiana and Canada and to have embodied in the constitution a guarded phrase which would permit of their retention as "provinces, and allow them no voice in our councils." He claimed that "had it been more pointedly expressed, a strong opposition would have been made." Whether or not the people of the United States in 1803 would have accepted Morris' point of view and granted the power he had advocated in 1787, the incident shows the subterfuges to which a far-sighted member of the federal convention resorted in order to provide for possible contingencies beyond the ken of his fellow delegates.

If, then, the federal constitution was nothing but the application of experience to remedy a series of definite defects in the government under the articles of confederation, it must needs be that in the short space of time the confederation had existed experience could not have covered the whole range of governmental activities. Reference is not made here to contingencies impossible to foresee, such as the introduction of steam and electricity, but there were matters that it would seem inexplicable not to have provided for in an instrument of government, if the attempt had been made to frame a logical and comprehensive constitution.

The embargo of 1807 and the protective tariff of 1816 afford illustrations of matters outside the experience of the confederation and not having been expressly provided for in the new instrument raised many doubts as to their constitutionality. The great issue of states rights came forward most dramatically in the concrete cases of nullification and secession. It would have been inexpedient to have forced this issue in 1787, when the fate of any sort of a central government was doubtful. But these subjects were probably not even seriously considered at that time; there certainly is no record of their being mentioned in the convention. Yet it is inconceivable that if Madison, or Wilson, or Hamilton had been permitted to frame a logical or consistent instrument of government, a constitution would have resulted which would not have covered such contingencies. It would seem, then, that the omissions in the constitution furnish a striking proof of its immediately practical character.

Robert Morris took no active part in the proceedings of the convention, but having followed everything that was done with the keenest interest, he wrote to a friend: "This paper has been the subject of infinite investigation, disputation, and declamation. While some have boasted it as a work from Heaven, others have given it a less righteous origin. I have many reasons to believe that it is the work of plain, honest men, and such, I think, it will appear."

It was this compelling feature, its simplicity, its practical character, that was responsible for the final adoption of the constitution when it was laid before the people of the various states. Here was a document which every one could understand. There were differences of opinion, of course, for such differences are inevitable in human nature, and convictions were as strong then as they are now. "In Halifax, Virginia, it is reported that a preacher on a Sunday morning had pronounced from the desk a fervent prayer for the adoption of the federal constitution; but he had no sooner ended his prayer than a clever layman ascended the pulpit, invited the people to join a second time in the supplication, and put forth an animated petition that the new scheme be rejected." Moreover, there is no doubt that the same class of men who may be regarded as responsible for the calling of the federal convention are also to be credited with getting the new constitution adopted. But public opinion, at least so far as it was represented in the state conventions, was divided, and some had to be won over. The substance of the argument which prevailed was: Reform is necessary; the new constitution proposes remedies with which all are familiar; and if the government does not work well, provision is made for changes at any time and to any extent.

Once adopted, the constitution succeeded beyond the hopes of its most ardent advocates. This of course was attributed to virtues inherent in the instrument itself. Respect and admiration developed and quickly grew into what has been well termed "the worship of the constitution." It was this attitude that for so long obscured the insight into the real character of the document. And yet, soon after the federal convention was over, Madison himself had stated in the *Federalist*: "The truth is, that the great principles of the Constitution proposed by the convention may be considered less as absolutely new, than as the expansion of principles which are found in the Articles of Confederation. . . . If the new Constitution be examined with accuracy and candor, it will be found that the change which it proposes consists much less in the addition of *New Powers* to the *Union*, than in the invigoration of its *Original Powers*."

The articles of confederation had failed; the constitution succeeded. The former worked through the medium of the state governments; the latter by virtue of the power of taxation and of control over commerce, dealt directly with the people. But changes of that sort might have been engrafted upon the old confederation, without so essentially altering its character. Something more was necessary, and something more had been achieved.

A fundamental objection to the old confederation was the inability of congress to enforce its decrees. To remedy this had been one of the chief concerns of the federal convention. The most obvious provision was the power granted to congress "to provide for calling forth the Militia to execute the Laws of the Union." But the most significant provision was the clause originating with Luther Martin and modified by the committee of style to read, "This Constitution . . . shall be the supreme Law of the Land." Not a treaty, nor an agreement between sovereign states, but a law. It was a law enacted by the highest of all law-making bodies, the people; and in its enforcement the government was backed by all the armed power of the nation; but the significance is that it was a law, and as such was enforceable in the courts.

Still this was not enough. Over one hundred years before, in the preface to the *Frame of Government of Pensilvania*, William Penn had quaintly said: "Governments, like clocks, go from the motion men give them; and as governments are made and moved by men, so by them they are ruined too. Wherefore governments rather depend upon men than men upon governments." However radical the differences between the federal constitution and the articles of confederation, however sweeping the provisions of the later document and however carefully they might be worded, the most potent factor in rendering the new instrument of government effective was the changed attitude of the American people. When the federal convention had been called, trade was already improving though it was almost unnoticed. By the time the constitution was adopted and put into operation, the improved conditions were plainly felt. And so it came about that in place of opposition or distrust, commercial confidence caused welcome and support to be extended to the new government.

Neither a work of divine origin, nor "the greatest work that was ever struck off at a given time by the brain and purpose of man," but a practical, workable document is this constitution of the United States. Planned to meet certain immediate needs and modified to suit the exigencies of the situation, it was floated on a wave of commercial prosperity, and it has been adapted by an ingenious political people to meet the changing requirements of a century and a quarter.

*THE American government launched in 1789 was one without precedent. It inherited from the Confederation a foreign office administered by John Jay and a handful of clerks who communicated with Thomas Jefferson at his legation in Paris and John Adams at his post representing the new country at the Court of St. James. The military establishment of the nation consisted of an army of 840 men. The Treasury was empty, a circumstance that made the dozen or so clerks who were visible proof of the Confederation's existence decidedly unhappy as payless days succeeded one another. All in all, few Americans could then argue, as their Jacksonian descendants would, "The World is too much governed."*

*Without means, almost naked to the world, the new nation was born. A bare eight years later, it had been firmly secured. No man lent greater service to the result than George Washington. An unbending, incorruptible man, he lent his aegis, as Hamilton admitted, to the necessary institutions and legislation of new government. In a time of sharp political passions, he moderated disputes by simply choosing between competing claims. Always aware that each of his acts, by their originality, set a precedent for the future, he took care to act with caution lest he waste his prestige. His decision to step down after eight years in the Presidency assured later generations that power in the future would be transferred without violence. His charisma had legitimatized a new government. And for these services, his nation held him in reverence, one so total that Auguste Beaumont, the companion of Tocqueville on his memorable visit to America in the early 1830's, concluded, "Washington in America is not a man but a God." But gods do not lend themselves easily to history; thus Washington remains a curiously cold and austere figure, one that inspires in his biographer near-reverence. It took the English historian Marcus Cunliffe to define in his* George Washington, Man and Monument *(1960) the dilemma facing a Washington biographer when he wrote: "For America, he was originator and vindicator, both patron saint and defender of the faith, in a curiously timeless fashion, as if he were Charlemagne, Saint Joan and Napoleon Bonaparte telescoped into one person."*

*No less a difficult subject for the historian has been the Federal Congress. As yet, no history of it has been written. The task facing the historian who chooses to make the effort is awesome. Within the chambers that house the two legislative bodies and in the committees that perform the task of drawing up legislation or of seeking out information, much of the drama, the pathos, and the critical substance of history has been shaped. The complexity of its tasks has been an accurate index of the expanding complexity of the nation it helps govern. In the beginning, however, Congress reflected the simple needs of a far-flung nation whose sparse population dwelt close to the original wilderness.*

*The first Congresses were without well-defined parties. The long debate between Hamilton and Jefferson provided some of the momentum of party, but it took the Jay Treaty and America's seeming capitulation to the pretensions of its old British masters to convert finally Mr. Madison's faction into the Democratic-Republicans, a coherent opposition to the Federalists of Washington, Hamilton, and Adams. In the process, Congress groped its way toward defining its future role, fully aware, as was Washington, that its acts were precedents for the future. Bound by the Constitution to provide the funds of government, it expended budgets in the low millions. Its membership revealed the diversity of American life, but in coming together, it also provided an awareness of national similarities. Although it was a far cry from the modern Congress, its 26 Senators and 65 Representatives responded to the needs of their time. In so doing, they established a lasting precedent: each Congress governs for the present. It is the legislative attachment to the living that has made Congress a durable institution.*

*The historian who chooses to come to grips with a history of Congress would be well advised to begin with Ralph Volney Harlow (1884-1956),* The History of Legislative Methods in the Period Before 1825 *(1917). Alone in its field, it has achieved the rank of a classic, indispensable not because it is solitary, but because it handles a complex subject with enduring and lucid insights.*

# THE HISTORY OF LEGISLATIVE
# METHODS IN THE PERIOD BEFORE 1825

## by Ralph Volney Harlow

On the whole, the first House of Representatives would compare favorably with other bodies of its kind. It could apparently be depended upon to accomplish the work for which it was elected, and in so doing it would very likely waste as much time in debating trifles and in overemphasizing imaginary difficulties as its contemporaries were in the habit of doing. Such is the way of democracy. Those who expected more of it, who were inclined to idealize it and to hope for great and even spectacular achievements were disappointed, for when it finally settled down to work it proved to be very legislature-like in its movements. At the end of his first eight weeks in Congress, Ames wrote: "I felt chagrined at the yawning listlessness of many here, in regard to the great objects of the government; their liableness to the impression of arguments *ad populum;* their state prejudices; their overrefining spirit in relation to trifles; their attachment to some very distressing formalities in business, and which will be a curse to all despatch and spirit in transacting it. I compared these with the idea I had brought here, of demi-gods and Roman Senators, or at least, of the first Congress. The objects now before us require more information, though less of the heroic qualities, than those of the first Congress. I was sorry to see that the picture I had drawn was so much bigger and fairer than the life. . . . But since, I have reflected coolly, that in all public bodies, the majority will be such as I have described—I may add, ought to be such; and if a few understand business, and have, as they will, the confidence of those who do not, it is better than for all to be such knowing ones; for they would contend for supremacy; there would not be a sufficient principle of cohesion. . . . The House is composed of very good men, not shining, but honest and reasonably well informed, and in time they will be found to improve, and not be much inferior in eloquence, science, and dignity, to the British Commons. They are patriotic enough, and I believe there are more stupid (as well as more shining) people in the latter, in proportion." Two days later he wrote again: "We are not in haste, or at least, have not learned to be in a hurry to advantage. I think it is the most dilatory assembly in the universe."

In constructing the national legislature, the Federal Convention did little beyond laying down the broad outlines. It provided for the Speaker of the House, but it left practically all other matters of organization and all the details of procedure to the House itself. With the wealth of precedents available in the journals of contemporary state legislatures, there was really no definite reason why the first Representatives should not have formulated rules of procedure which would enable them to go ahead smoothly and rapidly in the transaction of business. They all knew, or could easily discover, how laws were made by their friends at home. And yet, in spite of all their experience, and their really remarkable opportunities for observation, they wasted time for want of good methods. At the end of two months, Madison wrote that "in every step the difficulties arising from novelty are severely experienced, and are an ample as well as just source of apology. Scarcely a day passes without some striking evidence of the delays and perplexities springing merely from the want of precedents. Time will be a full remedy for this evil; and will I am persuaded, evince a greater facility in legislating uniformly for all the States than has been supposed by some of the best friends of the Union."

The cause of that uncertainty, or lack of sure-footedness, was probably the fact that the members looked upon themselves as parts of an entirely new system. They seem to have preferred to adopt a very few familiar principles, just enough to make possible the transaction of business, and to wait for further rules until time and experience should reveal their exact needs. It is not strange that the members should be impressed with the importance of their position, and should go slowly in order to avoid possible errors.

The outstanding feature of procedure in the House was the important part played by the committee of the whole. Much of the business in the House of Delegates of Virginia was transacted in that way, and the Virginians were influential enough to impose their methods upon the federal House, in spite of the grumbling opposition on the part of members from other sections. The rules were so framed as to permit almost unrestricted freedom of debate, and every member was given unlimited opportunity to satisfy his own craving to talk, and incidentally to convince his watchful constituents at home that he was not neglecting their interests. As a matter of fact, this extensive use of the informal session was not wholly bad from the democratic point of view. The House was so small that it was a genuine deliberative assembly, in which national questions could be discussed and considered from every possible angle. It was in committee of the whole that Congress worked out the first tariff bill, and also the main outlines of such important measures as the laws organizing the executive departments. After the general principles were once determined, select committees would be appointed to work out the details, and to frame bills in accordance with the decision already agreed upon in committee of the whole.

The chief weakness in the system was that it presupposed a higher general level of intelligence among the members than was actually to be found. There were a few leaders, but only a few, who could carry on a profitable and illuminating discussion of general principles; the rank and file were speedily lost in a fruitless if not inane debate over minor details. Naturally the more brilliant members were disgusted at the waste of time necessarily attendant upon the process. To quote Ames again, it was "certainly a bad method of doing business. Too little use is made of special committees.

Virginia is stiff and touchy against any change of the committee of the whole. . . . They are for watching and checking power; they see evils in embryo; are terrified with possibilities, and are eager to establish rights, and to explain principles, to such a degree, that you would think them enthusiasts and triflers."

The same active commentator also described a session of the committee of the whole at work on a bill. "We consider it in committee of the whole, and we indulge a very minute criticism upon its style. We correct spelling, or erase *may* and insert *shall,* and quiddle in a manner which provokes me. A select committee would soon correct little improprieties. Our great committee is too unwieldly for this operation. A great, clumsy machine is applied to the slightest and most delicate operations—the hoof of an elephant to the strokes of mezzotinto. I dislike the committee of the whole more than ever. We could not be so long doing so little, by any other expedient."

In view of their prominence in the state legislatures, it might naturally be supposed that standing committees would be called into being to transact much of the routine work of Congress. Such, however, was not the case. To be sure there was a committee of elections, appointed to inspect the credentials of members, and to investigate facts in connection with contested elections, but strictly speaking it performed no legislative work. Then, about two months before the end of the first session, a standing committee of ways and means was appointed, but its career was exceedingly brief. Finance committees in many of the states were familiar institutions, and naturally members who were acquainted with them suggested that the federal House would do well to provide itself with similar machinery. The question arose during the debate on the bill for organizing a treasury department. Livermore was opposed to giving any single official authority to submit plans for raising revenue. If the House itself was not in a position to do all such work, it ought to appoint a committee for that purpose. Gerry agreed that a committee of ways and means would be of great value in the transaction of financial business. A month later Fitzsimons urged definite action in the matter. "If we wish to have more particular information on these points," he suggested while speaking of the revenue, "we ought to appoint a Committee of Ways and Means, to whom, among other things, the estimate of supplies may be referred, and this ought to be done speedily." His suggestion met with approval, and a committee of ten was appointed. This appointment was made on July 24, 1789. On September 11, Alexander Hamilton entered upon his work as Secretary of the Treasury. On September 17, the committee of ways and means was "discharged from further proceeding on the business referred to them," and it was "referred to the Secretary of the Treasury, to report thereon." Henceforth there was hardly a mention of such a committee in Congress until December, 1795, when Gallatin secured the appointment of the permanent committee.

This transfer of authority from a committee of the House to Alexander Hamilton suggests the theory that Congress may have considered the newly created heads of departments as instruments not only of the president, but of the legislature as well. If that was the case, standing committees would of course be superfluous, because there was no particular need for a duplication of machinery.

In the case of the departments of Foreign Affairs, or of State, as it was called shortly after, and of War, the statutes creating them contain nothing to warrant such an assumption. The secretaries of those departments were executive officials, required to perform whatever duties the president might entrust to them. The laws nowhere suggest that Congress enjoyed any authority to give them orders, or to assign any of their duties.

Because of the intimate relationship between Hamilton and Congress, the status of the Treasury department merits a more careful examination. The Constitution itself conferred upon the House alone full power to originate revenue bills, and that privilege was very jealously guarded by thoroughgoing democrats. The establishment of the department gave rise to a lengthy debate. Boudinot of New Jersey brought up the question in the House, and recommended a law providing for a "Secretary of Finance," whose duties should be to superintend the treasury and finances of the country, and in particular to look after the public debt, revenue, and expenditure. With reference to revenue, Boudinot advised that the new official be given authority to "form and digest plans for its improvement." In the mass of argument called forth by this seemingly sound recommendation two different points of view stand out very clearly. The Federalists, if the name may be applied to them as early as this, approved of Boudinot's recommendation. They pointed out the manifest advantages in having a single, expert official in charge, who would be ready at any time to lay carefully matured plans before Congress.

The opponents of the measure argued that in permitting the secretary to "report" plans, the House would be guilty of giving up power definitely conferred upon it by the Constitution, and also that it would make the official altogether too powerful. One of Madison's colleagues, Page, thought the secretary might be permitted to prepare estimates, "but to go any further would be a dangerous innovation upon the constitutional privilege of this House. . . ." It would establish a precedent, which might be extended until all the "ministers of the Government" might be admitted to the floor to explain and support their plans, "thus laying the foundation for an aristocracy or a detestable monarchy." Tucker agreed with Page. He thought that the granting of the proposed authority to report plans would "abridge the particular privilege of this House." Certainly revenue bills could not be said to originate in the House if they were reported by the "Minister of Finance." If the plans were to come from the executive at all, they should be sent in directly by the president, and not by a secretary.

Some of these fears were overcome by an amendment, which limited the secretary's authority to the preparation of plans. He was not given the right to "report" them. Moreover, in no part of the act was the term "executive" department used. Then, too, there seemed to be a general feeling that such an official could easily be held in restraint. Madison wrote that a finance department was under consideration, "to be under one head, though to be branched out in such a manner as will check the administration." Likewise Benson favored a single head, rather than a board, but he "would have the principal officer well checked in the execution of his trust."

As finally drawn, the statute was conspicuously different from those which created the other two departments. It required the Secretary of the Treasury "to digest and prepare plans for the improvement and management of the revenue, and for the support of the public credit; to prepare and report estimates of the public revenue, and the public expenditures; . . . to make report, and give information to either branch of the legislature, in person or in writing . . . respecting all matters referred to him by the Senate or House of Representatives, or which shall appertain to his office; and generally to perform all such services relative to the finances, as he shall be directed to perform."

It seems evident that Congress planned to create an agent, not for the executive, but for itself. Both by actual phraseology and by implication the head of this department was subject to the legislature, and nowhere does the statute confer upon the president authority to assign duties to the Secretary of the Treasury. Such being the case, it is easy to explain the disappearance of the committee of ways and means. A single official, properly controlled, would be far more useful and far more efficient than a committee, the personnel of which might be subject to change every two years. In a cabinet meeting Hamilton once observed "that as to his department the act constituting it had made it subject to Congress in some points, but he thot himself not so far subject as to be obliged to produce all the papers they might call for." That interpretation was one of Hamilton's own, not warranted by the wording, and certainly inconsistent with the general tone of the law itself.

\*     \*     \*     \*     \*

Although the departments of State and of War were not legally subject to Congressional orders, they together with the Treasury department were called upon to participate in the work of legislation. Instead of being referred to standing committees, as would have been the case in state legislatures, some routine business was turned over to cabinet officials. In dealing with certain matters recommended by Washington in one of his speeches to Congress, the House asked the Secretary of the Treasury to prepare and report plans for the encouragement of manufactures, while a similar request concerning a system of weights and measures was sent to the Secretary of State. Not long afterward Hamilton laid before the House a report from the Postmaster General, together with a bill drawn by the same official. Although one of the members took exception to this practice of receiving bills from the heads of departments, the custom was not abandoned. At about the same time Madison wrote that the chief measures before Congress were "the plans of revenue and the Militia, reported by Hamilton and Knox." Later, Jefferson as Secretary of State, drafted a bill "to promote the progress of the useful arts," which was introduced into the House on February 7, 1791.

In addition to depending upon the secretaries for the drafting of an occasional bill, the House also called upon them to deal with certain petitions. In the state legislatures such work would have gone to standing committees, but Congress seemed to feel that the head of a department would answer the purpose just as well as a committee. Surely if it could use the heads of departments in this way, the House might well dispense with standing committees.

Such a loose-jointed organization as this would work smoothly only under certain conditions, which are seldom found in any legislative body. If they expect to evolve the main outlines of important measures in committee of the whole, all the members must work together in a spirit of genuine cooperation and friendliness. Or, to put it in another way, for the successful operation of Congress under that kind of procedure, there must be a total absence of political parties.

These conditions prevailed for a time in the first Congress, so that there was very little factional bitterness or organized party effort. Such a striking peculiarity naturally attracted the attention of the members, some of whom felt impelled to report the phenomenon to their friends at home. One southern member wrote that he "received great pleasure from observing the liberality and spirit of mutual concession which appear to actuate every member of the House," and that he had "not observed the least attempt to create a party. . . ." Another reported that "Much harmony, politeness and good humor have hitherto prevailed in both houses—our debates are conducted with a moderation and ability extremely unusual in so large a body—consisting of men under the influence of such jarring interests." And even Fisher Ames, who allowed nothing to pass unnoticed, and who certainly would have mentioned party differences if there had been any, wrote that "There is less of party spirit, less of the acrimony of pride when disappointed of success, less personality, less intrigue, cabal, management, or cunning than I ever saw in a public assembly. . . . Measures are so far from being the product of caucussing and cabal, that they are not sufficiently preconcerted."

These statements, it should be noticed, refer to the early part of the session, before the Congressmen had fully recovered from the effects of a strange environment. The first actors on a new stage, mindful of the dignity of their position, and perhaps somewhat in awe of one another, would naturally display not only great consideration, but even mutual respect. Familiarity hardly gets time to breed contempt in the short space of two months.

It was not so much the fault of the individual members, however, as of the very nature of the federal Congress itself that this calm could not endure. Sectional differences, real and imaginary, to say nothing of widely divergent theories of government, were bound to produce dissensions, and from factional strife thus generated it is but a short step to party organization with all its accompanying cabals and intrigues. Men capable of drawing conclusions from very evident facts could not remain blind to approaching changes. It is not surprising to find that even while he was rejoicing at the absence of party quarrels, Fisher Ames was carefully analyzing the forces of disruption already at work. He found, it seems, that "Three sorts of people are often troublesome. The anti-federals, who alone are weak, and some of them well disposed. The dupes of local prejudices, who fear eastern influences, monopolies, navigation acts. And lastly the violent republicans, as they think fit to style themselves, who are new lights in politics; who would not make the law, but the people, king; who would have a government all checks; who are more solicitous to establish, or rather to expatiate upon, some high-sounding principle of republicanism, than to protect property, cement the union, and perpetuate liberty. 'This new Constitution,' said one Abner Fowler, in 1787, 'will destroy our liberties. We shall never have another mob in the world.' This is the republicanism of the aristocracy of the southern nabobs. It breaks out daily, tinctures the debates with the hue of compromise, makes bold, manly, energetic measures very difficult. The spectre of Patrick Henry haunts their dreams. They accuse the eastern people with despotic principles, and take no small consequence to themselves as the defenders of liberty." Ames' letter merely indicates that a change might be expected at any moment. Other accounts prove that differences soon made themselves evident. In the course of another month several members had complaints to make about party controversies. Senator Butler, for instance, of South Carolina, wrote that he was very much disappointed with the new government. "I find," he wrote, "locality and partiality reign as much in our Supreme Legislature as they could in a county court or State legislature. Never was a man more egregiously disappointed than I am. I came here full of hopes that the greatest liberality would be exercised; that the consideration of the *whole*, and the general good, would take the place of every other object; but here I find men scrambling for partial advantages, State interests, and in short, a train of those narrow, impolitic measures that must, after a while, shake the Union to its very foundation."

When the question of the permanent residence came up, intrigues began in earnest. One disconsolate member complained that "amendments in Congress are as much wanted as in the Constitution." A year later whatever regard the members may have had for each others' feelings had pretty much disappeared. By that time "violence, personality, low wit, violation of order, and rambling from the point" characterized at least one debate. Apparently the discussion took such a bitter turn that the papers did not venture to report in full, and we are again indebted to Ames for a vivid description. "The Quakers have been abused, the eastern States inveighed against, the chairman rudely charged with partiality. Language low, indecent, and profane has been used; wit equally stale and wretched has been attempted; in short, we have sunk below the General Court in the disorderly moment of a bawling nomination of a committee, or even of country (rather Boston) town meeting. The southern gentry have been guided by their hot tempers, and stubborn prejudices and pride in regard to southern importance and negro slavery . . . they have shown an uncommon want of prudence as well as moderation; they have teased and bullied the House out of their good temper, and driven them to vote in earnest on a subject which at first they did not care much about."

The later debate on the permanent residence exasperated the young member from Massachusetts. "I care little where Congress may sit. I would not find fault with Fort Pitt, if we could assume the debts, and proceed in peace and quietness. But this despicable grogshop contest, whether the taverns of New York or Philadelphia shall get the custom of Congress, keeps us in discord and covers us all with disgrace. . . . It is barely possible for any business to be more perplexed and entangled than this has been. We have fasted, watched, and prayed for the cause. I never knew so much industry and perseverance exerted for any cause. Mr. Sedgwick is a perfect slave to the business. Mr. Goodhue frowns all day long, and swears as much as a good Christian can, about the perverseness of Congress." Then with reference to finance he wrote: "We are passing the ways and means bill. We do so little and behave so ill in doing it that I consider Congress as meriting more reproach than has yet been cast upon it."

This comparatively sudden appearance of partisan differences made possible and even necessary the creation of a well-organized legislative machine. No faction could afford to sit idly by and rely upon a discussion in committee of the whole to evolve and formulate its favorite measures. Still less could it hope to secure the enactment of its policies without a concerted effort to win votes. The fear that their opponents might resort to those unparliamentary but extremely effective tactics already well known to the state legislatures compelled them all to resort to the same methods. Instead of waiting for action in committee of the whole, the party leaders would decide upon their policies and draft bills in accordance therewith in party councils. The scene of actual legislation would be shifted from Congress to the caucus.

The Federalists were the first to profit by this division of the House into party groups, partly because they were in the majority, but more especially because they enjoyed the tremendous advantage of able leadership. Temperamentally more of a philosopher than a general, Madison himself was never able really to command a majority, while Jefferson, the creator of the Republican party, was still laboring under the delusion that as an executive official he must keep clear of Congress. Opposed to him was the great Federalist chieftain, Alexander Hamilton, who stood without a peer as an organizer and director of party forces. His ready intelligence grasped the truth at once that Jefferson spent more than ten years in learning: that not even the Constitution of the United States could keep apart two such inseparable factors in government as executive and legislature. His official position naturally brought him into close contact with Congress, and enabled him to see that such a loosely organized body was simply waiting for a commander. The mere fact that he was not a member was not the slightest obstacle to him, because it was easier to dominate Congress indirectly, through the medium of a political party, than directly from the floor.

By the winter of 1790, Hamilton was attracting attention because of his influence over Congress. In March of that year in the course of a debate on an appropriation bill, one Jackson moved an amendment, providing for an appropriation for clearing the Savannah River. In reply to objections made to his amendment, he remarked that "according to the ideas of some gentlemen, the House had no right to add to the appropriations proposed by the Secretary," and that "according to this doctrine, the whole business of Legislation may as well be submitted to him, so in fact the House would not be the Representatives of their constituents, but of the Secretary."

In the diary of Senator Maclay there are several brief but pithy comments which reveal both the extent and the nature of Hamilton's power in Congress. "It really seems," he wrote, "as if a listlessness or spirit of laziness pervaded the House of Representatives. Anything which comes from a Secretary is adopted almost without any examination." Referring to the bank bill, he complained to the pages of his diary that "It is totally in vain to oppose this bill." "Nothing," he wrote, "is done without him." Sometimes the democratic senator seemed ready to throw up his hands in despair at the total inability of the opposition to stem the tide of Hamiltonian legislation. Some such state of mind must have been responsible for the following: "Were Eloquence personified and reason flowed from her tongue, her talents would be in vain in our assembly; . . . Congress may go home. Mr. Hamilton is all-powerful, and fails in nothing he attempts."

Such general assertions would not necessarily mean very much by themselves, but they are supplemented by occasional references both to specific instances of Hamilton's activity in Congress, and to his methods of operation. For instance, Maclay mentions four separate measures, the assumption, bank, and excise bills, and a resolution regarding the mint, all of which were passed in spite of opposition, largely through the influence and personal efforts of Hamilton himself.

His success was due in large measure to his careful oversight of the whole process of legislation. Maclay even went so far as to assert that "Hamilton prepares all matters for his tools." Then, in order to prevent his measures from falling into the hands of an ill-disposed select committee in Congress, the able secretary looked after the appointment of some committees himself. If the committee needed the benefit of his advice, he was ready to give it, of course, and in some cases he even went so far as to attend committee meetings, to guard against the danger of a slip at any stage.

After the preliminary steps had been taken, and the measure was on its way through Congress, Hamilton spared no pains to secure its passage. In case its success was doubtful, the measure would be held back, until the end of the session if necessary, or at least until a majority in its favor was certain. Referring to the resolution on the mint, Maclay charged that Hamilton "kept back this exceptionable business till there would be no time to investigate it," and that, finally, "it was foully smuggled through."

One or two more quotations throw interesting light on Hamilton's ceaseless vigilance and activity. "Mr. Hamilton is very uneasy, as far as I can learn, about his funding system. He was here early to wait on the Speaker, and I believe spent most of his time in running from place to place among the members."

Regarding the assumption measure, Maclay wrote: "I do not know that pecuniary influence has actually been used, but I am certain that every other kind of management has been practiced and every tool at work that could be thought of. Officers of Government, clergy, citizens, Cincinnati, and every person under the influence of the Treasury; Bland and Huger carried to the chamber of Representatives—the one lame, the other sick. Clymer stopped from going away, though he had leave, and at length they risked the question and carried it, thirty-one votes to twenty-six. And all this after having tampered with the members since the 22nd of last month, and this only in committee. . . ."

Again he wrote: "In Senate this day the gladiators seemed more than commonly busy. As I came out from the Hall, all the President's family were there—Humphreys, Jackson, Nelson, etc. They had Vining with them, and, as I took it, were a standing committee to catch the members as they went in or came out."

The facts described above do not necessarily prove that there was very much of a party organization in 1790; they merely show that the Secretary of the Treasury was the most important factor in Congress during its first session. Yet the main outlines of party organization were clearly visible even as early as that. In order to secure harmony and unanimity of action, it was customary for Hamilton's followers to hold meetings of their own. Although the word "caucus" was not applied to these party gatherings, they were caucuses in all but name. It was on these occasions apparently that policies were determined upon, and it was doubtless the assurances obtained in them that enabled Hamilton to estimate the probable vote with such exactness. Maclay refers to "the rendezvousing of the crew of the Hamilton galley," or to a "call of the gladiators this morning," or again to the statement of Speaker Muhlenberg that "there had been a call of the Secretary's party last night." These allusions are made in a perfectly matter-of-fact way, as though such meetings were already looked upon as familiar occurrences.

In view of these facts it is not surprising that Hamilton's financial policy was adopted in the face of bitter opposition. The Federalists were well organized and intelligently directed by a masterful leader, while at first the chaotic group of country gentlemen, the followers of Madison and Jefferson, could do nothing but growl and complain of corruption. From their point of view such success as Hamilton enjoyed could not be honestly won.

When he was complaining about the difficulties due to want of precedents, Madison was not aware of the actual nature of the trouble with Congress. The real need was not more rules, but more driving power. That was furnished by the Hamiltonian or Federalist party organization, and thus the gap in the Constitution was bridged over. The change that had taken place was of such nature as to fill with unpleasant forebodings the democratic minds of the "new lights in politics." One of their ideals was shattered before the new government was even two years old. Instead of being a forum, where every member was a peer and no man led, where great principles of government were evolved through the give and take of unrestricted discussion, Congress as such had become in effect a mere ratifying body. The real work of legislation was put in shape, not in the legislature, but in secret session of the majority party. In this organization, unknown to the Constitution and beyond the reach of the rules of either chamber, the executive could work with the party-following in Congress, and secure the adoption of a prearranged program.

This relationship between executive and Congress suggests the theory that the heads of departments may have considered themselves a cabinet similar in some respects to the English cabinet. If that was the case, their interest in drafting bills and in the course of legislative activity is very easily explained. If Hamilton was looked upon as a minister of finance he was not a self-seeking usurper, as Maclay considered him, a man interested in ruling the House partly from love of power, and partly from love of personal gain. Instead he was a part of the ministry, an executive official in charge of finance. Considering himself directly responsible for that department of the government, naturally he would exert himself to the utmost to secure the adoption of his policy. That conception of the heads of the departments as a ministry also explains the attitude of the Federalists toward their chief. If it was his duty to lead Congress, it was just as much its duty to follow. What was a party for if not to sanction and approve the carefully drawn plans of its leaders?

At that time, aside from the respectful manner in which the Federalists supported Hamilton, there was nothing to justify such a theory. In 1797, however, the views of the Federalists, as voiced by Fisher Ames, do permit such an interpretation. Referring to the Republican attempts to assert the power of the House at the expense of the executive, he wrote: "Our whole system is little removed from simple democracy. What we call *the government* is a phantom, as long as the democrats prevail in the House. The heads of departments are head clerks. Instead of being the ministry, the organs of the executive power, and imparting a kind of momentum to the operation of the laws, they are precluded of late even from communicating with the House, by reports. In other countries they may speak as well as act. We allow them to do neither. We forbid even the use of a speaking-trumpet; or, more properly, as the Constitution has ordained that they shall be dumb, we forbid them to explain themselves by signs. Two evils, obvious to you, result from all this. The efficiency of the government is reduced to its minimum—the proneness of a popular body to usurpation is already advancing to its maximum; committees already are the ministers; and while the House indulges a jealousy of encroachment on its functions, which are properly deliberative, it does not perceive that these are impaired and nullified by the monopoly as well as the perversion of information by these very committees. The silly reliance of our coffeehouse and Congress prattlers on the responsibility of the members to the people, &c., &c., is disgraced by every page of the history of popular bodies. We expect, confidently, that the House of Representatives will *act* out of its proper character—for if it should act according to it, we are lost.

"Our government will be, in fact, a mere democracy, which has never been tolerable nor long tolerated."

Evidently Ames believed that Congress needed a guide, and he would have had the executive act in that capacity. Harmony of purpose, unity of action, and fixed responsibility for measures passed, all these advantages could have been secured from the operation of such a system. But the Jeffersonians, before they controlled the administration, looked upon such a government as tyranny. Speaking of the House under democratic control, Ames ironically wrote: "We think the executive power is a mere pageant of the representative body—a custos rotulorum, or master of the ceremonies. We ourselves are but passive instruments, whenever the sovereign people choose to speak for themselves. . . ."

The totally opposite theories of government held by the Federalist and Jeffersonian parties were thus clearly brought out in their attitude toward the popular branch of Congress. One would give the balance of power to the executive, and make it the influential factor in legislation, while the other would subject the executive to Congressional control. This difference supplies the key to the history of Congress for several years to come.

*THE new American nation had been called an empire by the men who drew up its constitution. They meant to impose on its vast dimensions the conditions of a republic, although all of history seemed to militate against such an effort. The absence of historical precedent strengthened the American belief in the novelty of their efforts. It accentuated their sense of divorce from Europe; it turned their eyes inward and provided a basis for isolationism during the nineteenth century.*

*Distance also accentuated regional differences. The fully shaped civilizations of New England and Virginia provided a contrast that would sharpen as the first century of the American republic passed. But it would be a mistake to think of any part of the new nation as approaching modern conditions. The whole country remained close to the wilderness from which it originally sprang. Life was sustained by a rude abundance but, even under the most favorable of circumstances, it was harsh. Contemporaries invariably commented on the incompleteness of everything. Europeans were forever surprised by the intellectual isolation of even the largest American cities. And everyone noted Americans, surrounded as they were by a crude today, dreamed of a fruitful tomorrow.*

*The diversity of the nation tended to militate against its union. Only the curious balancing of national and state needs called* dual federalism *allowed for a range sufficiently large to keep the special identities and interests of state and region from coming until the 1850's into sustained conflict with the national interest. Within the* Federalist Papers, *John Jay stressed that "Providence had been pleased to give this one connected country to one united people—a people descended from the same ancestors, speaking the same language, professing the same religion, attached to the same principles of government, very similar in their manners and customs," but Alexander Hamilton, one of the* Federalist *co-authors, complained: "The great and radical vice in the construction of the existing Confederation is in the principle of Legislation for States or Governments, in their Corporate or Collective Capacities. . . ." The American was born a provincial; the task of the new government was to make him the citizen of a united nation, one that economically would in the mid-twentieth century be called underdeveloped.*

*Henry Adams (1838-1918), son of Charles Francis Adams, grandson of the sixth President, and great-grandson of the second President, took up history at thirty-two, and dropped it at fifty-three. His* History of the United States in the Administrations of Thomas Jefferson and James Madison *appeared in nine volumes between 1889 and 1891. Drawing upon the Adams family archives, written with a style rarely matched by other historians, and informed with a keen intellectuality, it was a work that until recently foreclosed research in the period. Its monumental bulk and its classic formulation presents both an obstacle and a necessary beginning for anyone who would understand the tumultuous events that stirred a nation between 1800 and 1817.*

# HISTORY OF THE UNITED STATES OF AMERICA DURING THE FIRST ADMINISTRATION OF THOMAS JEFFERSON

*by Henry Adams*

According to the census of 1800, the United States of America contained 5,308,483 persons. In the same year the British Islands contained upwards of fifteen millions; the French Republic, more than twenty-seven millions. Nearly one fifth of the American people were Negro slaves; the true political population consisted of four and a half million free whites, or less than one million able-bodied males, on whose shoulders fell the burden of a continent. Even after two centuries of struggle the land was still untamed; forest covered every portion, except here and there a strip of cultivated soil; the minerals lay undisturbed in their rocky beds, and more than two thirds of the people clung to the seaboard within fifty miles of tidewater, where alone the wants of civilized life could be supplied. The centre of population rested within eighteen miles of Baltimore, north and east of Washington. Except in political arrangement, the interior was little more civilized than in 1750, and was not much easier to penetrate than when La Salle and Hennepin found their way to the Mississippi more than a century before.

A great exception broke this rule. Two wagon-roads crossed the Alleghany Mountains in Pennsylvania,—one leading from Philadelphia to Pittsburg; one from Potomac to the Monongahela; while a third passed through Virginia southwestward to the Holston River and Knoxville in Tennessee, with a branch through the Cumberland Gap into Kentucky. By these roads and by trails less passable from North and South Carolina, or by water-ways from the lakes, between four and five hundred thousand persons had invaded the country beyond the Alleghanies. At Pittsburg and on the Monongahela existed a society, already old, numbering seventy or eighty thousand persons, while on the Ohio River the settlements had grown to an importance which threatened to force a difficult problem on the union of the older states. One hundred and eighty thousand whites, with forty thousand Negro slaves, made Kentucky the largest community west of the mountains; and about ninety thousand whites and fourteen thousand slaves were scattered over Tennessee. In the territory north of the Ohio less progress had been made. A New England colony existed at Marietta; some fifteen thousand people were gathered at Cincinnati; halfway between the two, a small town had grown up at Chillicothe, and other villages or straggling cabins were to be found elsewhere; but the whole Ohio territory contained only forty-five thousand inhabitants. The entire population, both free and slave, west of the mountains, reached not yet half a million; but already they were partly disposed to think themselves, and the old thirteen States were not altogether unwilling to consider them, the germ of an independent empire, which was to find its outlet, not through the Alleghanies to the seaboard, but by the Mississippi River to the Gulf.

Nowhere did eastern settlements touch the western. At least one hundred miles of mountainous country held the two regions everywhere apart. The shore of Lake Erie, where alone contact seemed easy, was still unsettled. The Indians had been pushed back to the Cuyahoga River, and a few cabins were built on the site of Cleveland; but in 1800 as in 1700, this intermediate region was only a portage where emigrants and merchandise were transferred from Lake Erie to the Muskingum and Ohio valleys. Even western New York remained a wilderness: Buffalo was not laid out; Indian titles were not extinguished; Rochester did not exist; and the county of Onondaga numbered a population of less than eight thousand. In 1799 Utica contained fifty houses, mostly small and temporary. Albany was still a Dutch city, with some five thousand inhabitants; and the tide of immigration flowed slowly through it into the valley of the Mohawk, while another stream from Pennsylvania, following the Susquehanna, spread toward the Genesee country.

The people of the old thirteen States, along the Atlantic seaboard, thus sent westward a wedge-shaped mass of nearly half a million persons, penetrating by the Tennessee, Cumberland, and Ohio rivers toward the western limit of the Union. The Indians offered sharp resistance to this invasion, exacting life for life, and yielding only as their warriors perished. By the close of the century the wedge of white settlements, with its apex at Nashville and its flanks covered by the Ohio and Tennessee rivers, nearly split the Indian country in halves. The northern half—consisting of the later

States of Wisconsin, Michigan, Illinois, and Indiana, and one third of Ohio —contained Wyandottes and Shawanese, Miamis, Kickapoos, and other tribes, able to send some five thousand warriors to hunt or fight. In the southern half, powerful confederacies of Creeks, Cherokees, Chickasaws, and Choctaws lived and hunted where the States of Mississippi, Alabama, and the western parts of Georgia, Tennessee, and Kentucky were to extend; and so weak was the State of Georgia, which claimed the southwestern territory for its own, that a well-concerted movement of Indians might without much difficulty have swept back its white population of one hundred thousand toward the ocean or across the Savannah River. The Indian power had been broken in halves, but each half was still terrible to the colonists on the edges of their vast domain, and was used as a political weapon by the Governments whose territory bounded the Union on the north and south. The governors-general of Canada intrigued with the northwestern Indians, that they might hold in check any aggression from Washington; while the Spanish governors of West Florida and Louisiana maintained equally close relations with the Indian confederacies of the Georgia territory.

With the exception that half a million people had crossed the Alleghanies and were struggling with the difficulties all their own, in an isolation like that of Jutes or Angles in the fifth century, America, so far as concerned physical problems, had changed little in fifty years. The old landmarks remained nearly where they stood before. The same bad roads and difficult rivers, connecting the same small towns, stretched into the same forests in 1800 as when the armies of Braddock and Amherst pierced the western and northern wilderness, except that these roads extended a few miles farther from the seacoast. Nature was rather man's master than his servant, and the five million Americans struggling with the untamed continent seemed hardly more competent to their task than the beavers and buffalo which had for countless generations made bridges and roads of their own.

Even by water, along the seaboard, communication was as slow and almost as irregular as in colonial times. The wars in Europe caused a sudden and great increase in American shipping employed in foreign commerce, without yet leading to general improvement in navigation. The ordinary sea-going vessel carried a freight of about two hundred and fifty tons; the largest merchant ships hardly reached four hundred tons; the largest frigate in the United States navy, the "line-of-battle ship in disguise," had a capacity of fifteen hundred and seventy-six tons. Elaborately rigged as ships or brigs, the small merchant craft required large crews and were slow sailers; but the voyage to Europe was comparatively more comfortable and more regular than the voyage from New York to Albany, or through Long Island Sound to Providence. No regular packet plied between New York and Albany. Passengers waited till a sloop was advertised to sail; they provided their own bedding and supplies; and within the nineteenth century Captain Elias Bunker won much fame by building the sloop "Experiment," of one hundred and ten tons, to start regularly on a fixed day for Albany, for the convenience of passengers only, supplying beds, wine, and provisions for the voyage of one hundred and fifty miles. A week on the North River or on the Sound was an experience not at all unknown to travellers.

While little improvement had been made in water-travel, every increase of distance added to the difficulties of the westward journey. The settler who after buying wagon and horses hauled his family and goods across the mountains, might buy or build a broad flat-bottomed ark, to float with him and his fortunes down the Ohio, in constant peril of upsetting or of being sunk; but only light boats with strong oars could mount the stream, or boats forced against the current by laboriously poling in shallow water. If he carried his tobacco and wheat down the Mississippi to the Spanish port of New Orleans, and sold it, he might return to his home in Kentucky or Ohio by a long and dangerous journey on horseback through the Indian country from Natchez to Nashville, or he might take ship to Philadelphia, if a ship were about to sail, and again cross the Alleghanies. Compared with river travel, the sea was commonly an easy and safe highway. Nearly all the rivers which penetrated the interior were unsure, liable to be made dangerous by freshets, and both dangerous and impassable by drought; yet such as they were, these streams made the main paths of traffic. Through the mountainous gorges of the Susquehanna the produce of western New York first found an outlet; the Cuyahoga and Muskingum were the first highways from the Lakes to the Ohio; the Ohio itself, with its great tributaries the Cumberland and the Tennessee, marked the lines of western migration; and every stream which could at high water float a boat was thought likely to become a path for commerce. As General Washington, not twenty years earlier, hoped that the brawling waters of the Cheat and Youghiogheny might become the channel of trade between Chesapeake Bay and Pittsburg, so the Americans of 1800 were prepared to risk life and property on any streamlet that fell foaming down either flank of the Alleghanies. The experience of mankind proved trade to be dependent on water communications, and as yet Americans did not dream that the experience of mankind was useless to them.

If America was to be developed along the lines of water communication alone, by such means as were known to Europe, Nature had decided that the experiment of a single republican government must meet extreme difficulties. The valley of the Ohio had no more to do with that of the Hudson, the Susquehanna, the Potomac, the Roanoke, and the Santee, than the valley of the Danube with that of the Rhone, the Po, or the Elbe. Close communication by land could alone hold the great geographical divisions together either in interest or in fear. The union of New England with New York and Pennsylvania was not an easy task even as a problem of geography, and with an ocean highway; but the union of New England with the Carolinas, and of the seacoast with the interior, promised to be a hopeless undertaking. Physical contact alone could make one country of these isolated empires, but to the patriotic American of 1800, struggling for the continued existence of an embryo nation, with machinery so inadequate, the idea of ever bringing the Mississippi River, either by land or water, into close contact with New England, must have seemed wild. By water, an Erie Canal was already foreseen; by land, centuries of labor could alone conquer those obstacles which Nature permitted to be overcome.

In the minds of practical men, the experience of Europe left few doubts on this point. After two thousand years of public labor and private savings, even despotic monarchs, who employed the resources of their subjects as they pleased, could in 1800 pass from one part of their European dominions to another little more quickly than they might have done in the age of the Antonines. A few short canals had been made, a few bridges had been built, an excellent post-road extended from Madrid to St. Petersburg; but the heavy diligence that rumbled from Calais to Paris required three days for its journey of one hundred and fifty miles, and if travellers ventured on a trip to Marseilles they met with rough roads and hardships like those of the Middle Ages. Italy was in 1800 almost as remote from the north of Europe as when carriage-roads were first built. Neither in time nor in thought was Florence or Rome much nearer to London in Wordsworth's youth than in the youth of Milton or Gray. Indeed, such changes as had occurred were partly for the worse, owing to the violence of revolutionary wars during the last ten years of the eighteenth century. Horace Walpole at his life's close saw about him a world which in many respects was less civilized than when as a boy he made the grand tour of Europe.

While so little had been done on the great highways of European travel, these highways were themselves luxuries which furnished no sure measure of progress. The post-horses toiled as painfully as ever through the sand from Hamburg to Berlin, while the coach between York and London rolled along an excellent road at the rate of ten miles an hour; yet neither in England nor on the Continent was the post-road a great channel of commerce. No matter how good the road, it could not compete with water, nor could heavy freights in great quantities be hauled long distances without extravagant cost. Water communication was as necessary for European commerce in 1800 as it had been for the Phoenicians and Egyptians; the Rhine, the Rhone, the Danube, the Elbe, were still the true commercial highways, and except for government post-roads, Europe was as dependent on these rivers in the eighteenth century as in the thirteenth. No certainty could be offered of more rapid progress in the coming century than in the past; the chief hope seemed to lie in the construction of canals.

While Europe had thus consumed centuries in improving paths of trade, until merchandise could be brought by canal a few score miles from the Rhone to the Loire and Seine, to the Garonne and the Rhine, and while her wealth and energy had not yet united the Danube with other river systems, America was required to construct, without delay, at least three great roads and canals, each several hundred miles long, across mountain ranges, through a country not yet inhabited, to points where no great markets existed,— and this under constant peril of losing her political union, which could not even by such connections be with certainty secured. After this should be accomplished, the Alleghanies must still remain between the eastern and the western states, and at any known rate of travel Nashville could not be reached in less than a fortnight or three weeks from Philadelphia. Meanwhile the simpler problem of bringing New England nearer to Virginia and Georgia had not advanced even with the aid of a direct ocean highway. In becoming politically independent of England, the old thirteen provinces developed little more commercial intercourse with each other in proportion to their wealth and population than they had maintained in colonial days. The material ties that united them grew in strength no more rapidly than the ties which bound them to Europe. Each group of States lived a life apart.

Even the lightly equipped traveller found a short journey no slight effort. Between Boston and New York was a tolerable highway, along which, thrice a week, light stage-coaches carried passengers and the mail, in three days. From New York a stage-coach started every week-day for Philadelphia, consuming the greater part of two days in the journey; and the road between Paulus Hook, the modern Jersey City, and Hackensack, was declared by the newspapers in 1802 to be as bad as any other part of the route between Maine and Georgia. South of Philadelphia the road was tolerable as far as Baltimore, but between Baltimore and the new city of Washington it meandered through forest; the driver chose the track which seemed least dangerous, and rejoiced if in wet seasons he reached Washington without miring or upsetting his wagon. In the Northern States, four miles an hour was the average speed for any coach between Bangor and Baltimore. Beyond the Potomac the roads became steadily worse, until south of Petersburg even the mails were carried on horseback. Except for a stage-coach which plied between Charleston and Savannah, no public conveyance of any kind was mentioned in the three southernmost States.

The stage-coach was itself a rude conveyance, of a kind still familiar to experienced travellers. Twelve persons, crowded into one wagon, were jolted over rough roads, their bags and parcels, thrust inside, cramping their legs, while they were protected from the heat and the dust of mid-summer and the intense cold and driving snow of winter only by leather flaps buttoned to the roof and sides. In fine, dry weather this mode of travel was not unpleasant, when compared with the heavy vehicles of Europe and the hard English turnpikes; but when spring rains drew the frost from the ground the roads became nearly impassable, and in winter, when the rivers froze, a serious peril was added, for the Susquehanna or the North River at Paulus Hook must be crossed in an open boat,—an affair of hours at best, sometimes leading to fatal accidents. Smaller annoyances of many kinds were habitual. The public, as a rule, grumbled less than might have been expected, but occasionally newspapers contained bitter complaints. An angry Philadelphian, probably a foreigner, wrote in 1796 that, "with a few exceptions, brutality, negligence, and filching are as naturally expected by people accustomed to travelling in America, as a mouth, a nose, and two eyes are looked for in a man's face." This sweeping charge, probably unjust, and certainly supported by little public evidence, was chiefly founded on the experience of an alleged journey from New York:—

"At Bordentown we went into a second boat where we met with very sorry accommodation. This was about four o'clock in the afternoon. We had about twenty miles down the Delaware to reach Philadelphia. The captain, who had a most provoking tongue, was a boy about eighteen years of age. He and a few companions despatched a dozen or eighteen bottles of porter. We ran three different times against other vessels that were coming up the stream. The women and children lay all night on the bare boards of the cabin floor. . . . We reached Arch Street wharf about eight o'clock on the Wednesday morning, having been about sixteen hours on a voyage of twenty miles."

In the Southern States the difficulties and perils of travel were so great as to form a barrier almost insuperable. Even Virginia was no exception to this rule. At each interval of a few miles the horseman found himself stopped by a river, liable to sudden freshets, and rarely bridged. Jefferson in his frequent journeys between Monticello and Washington was happy to reach the end of the hundred miles without some vexatious delay. "Of eight rivers between here and Washington," he wrote to his Attorney-General in 1801, "five have neither bridges nor boats."

Expense caused an equally serious obstacle to travel. The usual charge in the Northern States was six cents a mile by stage. In the year 1796, according to Francis Baily, President of the Royal Astronomical Society, three or four stages ran daily from Baltimore to Philadelphia, the fare six dollars, with charges amounting to two dollars and a quarter a day at the inns on the road. Baily was three days in making the journey. From Philadelphia to New York he paid the same fare and charges, arriving in one day and a half. The entire journey of two hundred miles cost him twenty-one dollars. He remarked that travelling on the main lines of road in the settled country was about as expensive as in England, and when the roads were good, about as rapid. Congress allowed its members six dollars for every twenty miles travelled. The actual cost, including hotel expenses, could hardly have fallen below ten cents a mile.

Heavy traffic never used stage routes if it could find cheaper. Commerce between one State and another, or even between the seaboard and the interior of the same State, was scarcely possible on any large scale unless navigable water connected them. Except the great highway to Pittsburg, no road served as a channel of commerce between different regions of the country. In this respect New England east of the Connecticut was as independent of New York as both were independent of Virginia, and as Virginia in her turn was independent of Georgia and South Carolina. The chief value of inter-State communication by land rested in the postal system; but the post furnished another illustration of the difficulties which barred progress. In the year 1800 one general mail-route extended from Portland in Maine to Louisville in Georgia, the time required for the trip being twenty days. Between New York and Petersburg in Virginia was a daily service; between New York and Boston, and also between Petersburg and Augusta, the mail was carried thrice a week. Branching from the main line at New York, a mail went to Canandaigua in ten days; from Philadelphia another branch line went to Lexington in sixteen days, to Nashville in twenty-two days. Thus more than twenty thousand miles of post-road, with nine hundred post-offices, proved the vastness of the country and the smallness of the result; for the gross receipts for postage in the year ending Oct. 1, 1801, were only $320,000.

Throughout the land the eighteenth century ruled supreme. Only within a few years had the New Englander begun to abandon his struggle with a barren soil, among granite hills, to learn the comforts of easier existence in the valleys of the Mohawk and Ohio; yet the New England man was thought the shrewdest and most enterprising of Americans. If the Puritans and the Dutch needed a century or more to reach the Mohawk, when would they reach the Mississippi? The distance from New York to the Mississippi was about one thousand miles; from Washington to the extreme southwestern military post, below Natchez, was about twelve hundred. Scarcely a portion of western Europe was three hundred miles distant from some sea, but a width of three hundred miles was hardly more than an outskirt of the United States. No civilized country had yet been required to deal with physical difficulties so serious, nor did experience warrant conviction that such difficulties could be overcome.

If the physical task which lay before the American people had advanced but a short way toward completion, little more change could be seen in the economical conditions of American life. The man who in the year 1800 ventured to hope for a new era in the coming century, could lay his hand on no statistics that silenced doubt. The machinery of production showed no radical difference from that familiar to ages long past. The Saxon farmer of the eighth century enjoyed most of the comforts known to Saxon farmers of the eighteenth. The eorls and ceorls of Offa and Ecgbert could not read or write, and did not receive a weekly newspaper with such information as newspapers in that age could supply, yet neither their houses, their clothing, their food and drink, their agricultural tools and methods, their stock, nor their habits were so greatly altered or improved by time that they would have found much difficulty in accommodating their lives to that of their descendants in the eighteenth century. In this respect America was backward. Fifty or a hundred miles inland more than half the houses were log-cabins, which might or might not enjoy the luxury of a glass window. Throughout the South and West houses showed little attempt at luxury; but even in New England the ordinary farmhouse was hardly so well built, so spacious, or so warm as that of a well-to-do contemporary of Charlemagne. The cloth which the farmer's family wore was still homespun. The hats were manufactured by the village hatter; the clothes were cut and made at home; the shirts, socks, and nearly every other article of dress were also home-made. Hence came a marked air of rusticity which distinguished country from town,—awkward shapes of hat, coat, and trousers, which gave to the Yankee caricature those typical traits that soon disappeared almost as completely as coats of mail and steel head-pieces. The plough was rude and clumsy; the sickle as old as Tubal Cain, and even the cradle not in general use; the flail was unchanged since the Aryan exodus; in Virginia, grain was still commonly trodden out by horses. Enterprising gentle-men farmers introduced threshing-machines and invented scientific ploughs; but these were novelties. Stock was as a rule not only unimproved, but ill cared for. The swine ran loose; the cattle were left to feed on what pasture they could find, and even in New England were not housed until the severest frosts, on the excuse that exposure hardened them. Nearly half a century afterward a competent judge asserted that the general treatment of cows in New England was fair matter of presentment by a grand jury. Except among the best farmers, drainage, manures, and rotation of crops were uncommon. The ordinary cultivator planted his corn as his father had planted it, sowing as much rye to the acre, using the same number of oxen to plough, and getting in his crops on the same day. He was even known to remove his barn on account of the manure accumulated around it, although the New England soil was never so rich as to warrant neglect to enrich it. The money for which he sold his wheat and chickens was of the Old World; he reckoned in shillings or pistareens, and rarely handled an American coin more valuable than a large copper cent.

At a time when the wealth and science of London and Paris could not supply an article so necessary as a common sulphur-match, the backwardness of remote country districts could hardly be exaggerated. Yet remote districts were not the only sufferers. Of the whole United States New England claimed to be the most civilized province, yet New England was a region in which life had not yet gained few charms of sense and few advantages over its rivals. Wilson, the ornithologist, a Pennsylvania Scotchman, a confirmed grumbler, but a shrewd judge; and the most thorough of American travellers, said in 1808: "My journey through almost the whole of New England has rather lowered the Yankees in my esteem. Except a few neat academies, I found their schoolhouses equally ruinous and deserted with ours; fields covered with stones; stone fences; scrubby oaks and pine-trees; wretched orchards; scarcely one grain-field in twenty miles; the taverns along the road dirty, and filled with loungers brawling about lawsuits and politics; the people snappish and extortioners, lazy, and two hundred years behind the Pennsylvanians in agricultural improvements." The description was exaggerated for Wilson forgot to speak of the districts where fields were not covered with stones, and where wheat could be grown to advantage. Twenty years earlier, Albert Gallatin, who knew Pennsylvania well, having reached Hartford on his way to Boston, wrote: "I have seen nothing in America equal to the establishments on the Connecticut River." Yet Wilson's account described the first general effect of districts in the New England States, where agriculture was backward and the country poor. The houses were thin wooden buildings, not well suited to the climate; the churches were unwarmed; the clothing was poor; sanitary laws were few, and a bathroom or a soil-pipe was unknown. Consumption, typhoid, scarlet fever, diphtheria, and rheumatic fevers were common; habits of drinking were still a scourge in every family, and dyspepsia destroyed more victims than were consumed by drink. Population increased slowly, as though the conditions of life were more than usually hard. A century earlier, Massachusetts was supposed to contain sixty thousand inhabitants. Governor Hutchinson complained that while the other colonies quadrupled their numbers, Massachusetts failed to double its population in fifty years. In 1790 the State contained 378,000 people not including the province of Maine; in 1800 the number rose to 423,000, which showed that a period of more rapid growth had begun, for the emigration into other States was also large.

A better measure of the difficulties with which New England struggled was given by the progress of Boston, which was supposed to have contained eighteen thousand inhabitants as early as 1730, and twenty thousand in 1770. For several years after the Revolution it numbered less than twenty thousand, but in 1800 the census showed twenty-five thousand inhabitants. In appearance, Boston resembled an English market town, of a kind even then old fashioned. The footways or sidewalks were paved, like the crooked and narrow streets, with round cobblestones, and were divided from the carriage way only by posts and a gutter. The streets were almost unlighted at night, a few oil-lamps rendering the darkness more visible and the rough pavement rougher. Police hardly existed. The system of taxation was defective. The town was managed by selectmen, the elected instruments of town-meetings whose jealousy of granting power was even greater than their objection to spending money, and whose hostility to city government was not to be overcome.

Although on all sides increase of ease and comfort was evident, and roads, canals, and new buildings, public and private, were already in course of construction on a scale before unknown, yet in spite of more than a century and a half of incessant industry, intelligent labor, and pinching economy Boston and New England were still poor. A few merchants enjoyed incomes derived from foreign trade, which allowed them to imitate in a quiet way the style of the English mercantile class; but the clergy and the lawyers, who stood at the head of society, lived with much economy. Many a country clergyman, eminent for piety and even for hospitality, brought up a family and laid aside some savings on a salary of five hundred dollars a year. President Dwight, who knew well the class to which he belonged, eulogizing the life of Abijah Weld, pastor of Attleborough, declared that on a salary of two hundred and twenty dollars a year Mr. Weld brought up eleven children, besides keeping a hospitable house and maintaining charity to the poor.

On the Exchange a few merchants had done most of the business of Boston since the peace of 1783, but a mail thrice a week to New York, and an occasional arrival from Europe or the departure of a ship to China, left ample leisure for correspondence and even gossip. The habits of the commercial class had not been greatly affected by recent prosperity. Within ten or fifteen years before 1800 three Banks had been created to supply the commercial needs of Boston. One of these was a branch Bank of the United States, which employed there whatever part of its capital it could profitably use; the two others were local Banks, with capital of $1,600,000, toward which the State subscribed $400,000. Altogether the banking capital of Boston might amount to two millions and a half. A number of small Banks, representing in all about two and a half millions more, were scattered through the smaller New England towns. The extraordinary prosperity caused by the French wars opened to Boston a new career. Wealth and population were doubling; the export and imports of New England were surprisingly large, and the shipping was greater than that of New York and Pennsylvania combined; but Boston had already learned, and was to learn again, how fleeting were the riches that depended on foreign commerce, and conservative habits were not easily changed by a few years of accidental gain.

Of manufactures New England had many, but none on a large scale. The people could feed or clothe themselves only by household industry; their whale-oil, salt fish, lumber, and rum were mostly sent abroad; but they freighted coasters with turners' articles, home-made linens and cloths, cheese, butter, shoes, nails, and what were called Yankee Notions of all sorts, which were sent to Norfolk and the Southern ports, and often peddled from the deck, as goods of every sort were peddled on the flat-boats of the Ohio. Two or three small mills spun cotton with doubtful success; but England supplied ordinary manufactures more cheaply and better than Massachusetts could hope to do. A tri-weekly mail and a few coasting sloops provided for the business of New England with domestic ports. One packet sloop plied regularly to New York.

The State of New York was little in advance of Massachusetts and Maine. In 1800 for the first time New York gained the lead in population by the difference between 589,000 and 573,000. The valuation of New York for the direct tax in 1799 was $100,000,000; that of Massachusetts was $84,000,000. New York was still a frontier State, and although the city was European in its age and habits, travellers needed to go few miles from the Hudson in order to find a wilderness like that of Ohio and Tennessee. In most material respects the State was behind New England; outside the city was to be seen less wealth and less appearance of comfort. The first impression commonly received of any new country was from its inns, and on the whole few better tests of material condition then existed. President Dwight, though maintaining that the best old-fashioned inns of New England were in their way perfect, being in fact excellent private houses, could not wholly approve what he called the modern inns, even in Connecticut; but when he passed into New York he asserted that everything suffered an instant change for the worse. He explained that in Massachusetts the authorities were strict in refusing licenses to any but respectable and responsible persons, whereas in New York licenses were granted to any one who would pay for them,—which caused a multiplication of dram-shops, bad accommodations, and a gathering of loafers and tipplers about every tavern porch, whose rude appearance, clownish manners, drunkenness, swearing, and obscenity confirmed the chief of Federalist clergymen in his belief that democracy had an evil influence on morals.

Far more movement was to be seen, and accumulation was more rapid than in colonial days; but little had yet been done for improvement, either by Government or by individuals, beyond some provision for extending roads and clearing water-courses behind the advancing settlers. If Washington Irving was right, Rip Van Winkle, who woke from his long slumber about the year 1800, saw little that was new to him, except the head of President Washington where that of King George had once hung, and strange faces instead of familiar ones. Except in numbers, the city was relatively no farther advanced than the country. Between 1790 and 1800 its population rose from 33,000 to 60,000; and if Boston resembled an old fashioned English market-town, New York was like a foreign seaport, badly paved, undrained, and as foul as a town surrounded by the tides could be. Although the Manhattan Company was laying wooden pipes for a water supply, no sanitary regulations were enforced, and every few years—as in 1798 and 1803—yellow fever swept away crowds of victims, and drove the rest of the population, panic stricken, into the highlands. No day-police existed; constables were still officers of the courts; the night-police consisted of two captains, two deputies, and seventy-two men. The estimate for the city's expenses in 1800 amounted to $130,000. One marked advantage New York enjoyed over Boston, in the possession of a city government able to introduce reforms. Thus, although still medieval in regard to drainage and cleanliness, the town had taken advantage of recurring fires to rebuild some of the streets with brick sidewalks and curbstones. Travellers dwelt much on this improvement, which only New York and Philadelphia had yet adopted, and Europeans agreed that both had the air of true cities: that while Boston was the Bristol of America, New York was the Liverpool, and Philadelphia the London.

In respect to trade and capital, New York possessed growing advantages, supplying half New Jersey and Connecticut, a part of Massachusetts, and all the rapidly increasing settlements on the branches of the Hudson; but no great amount of wealth, no considerable industry or new creation of power was yet to be seen. Two Banks, besides the branch Bank of the United States, supplied the business wants of the city, and employed about the same amount of capital in loans and discounts as was required for Boston. Besides these city institutions but two other Banks existed in the State,—at Hudson and at Albany.

The proportion of capital in private hands seemed to be no larger. The value of exports from New York in 1800 was but $14,000,000; the net revenue on imports for 1799 was $2,373,000 against $1,607,000 collected in Massachusetts. Such a foreign trade required little capital, yet these values represented a great proportion of all the exchanges. Domestic manufactures could not compete with foreign, and employed little bank credit. Speculation was slow, mostly confined to lands which required patience to exchange or sell. The most important undertakings were turnpikes, bridges such as Boston built across the Charles, or new blocks of houses; and a canal, such as Boston designed to the Merrimac, overstrained the resources of capital. The entire banking means of the United States in 1800 would not have answered the stock-jobbing purposes of one great operator of Wall Street in 1875. The nominal capital of all the Banks, including the Bank of the United States, fell short of $29,000,000. The limit of credit was quickly reached, for only the richest could borrow more than fifteen or twenty thousand dollars at a time, and the United States Government it-self was gravely embarrassed whenever obliged to raise money. In 1798 the Secretary of the Treasury could obtain five million dollars only by paying eight per cent interest for a term of years; and in 1814 the Government was forced to stop payments for want of twenty millions.

The precise value of American trade was uncertain, but in 1800 the gross exports and imports of the United States may have balanced at about seventy-five million dollars. The actual consumption of foreign merchandise amounted perhaps to the value of forty or fifty million dollars, paid in wheat, cotton, and other staples, and by profits on the shipping employed in carrying West India produce to Europe. The amount of American capital involved in a trade of fifty millions, with credits of three, six, and nine months, must have been small, and the rates of profit large.

As a rule American capital was absorbed in shipping or agriculture, whence it could not be suddenly withdrawn. No stock-exchange existed, and no broker exclusively engaged in stock-jobbing, for there were few stocks. The national debt, of about eighty millions, was held abroad, or as a permanent investment at home. States and municipalities had not learned to borrow. Except for a few banks and insurance offices, turnpikes, bridges, canals, and land-companies, neither bonds nor stocks were known. The city of New York was so small as to make extravagance difficult; the Battery was a fashionable walk, Broadway a country drive, and Wall Street an up-town residence. Great accumulations of wealth had hardly begun. The Patroon was still the richest man in the State. John Jacob Astor was a fur-merchant living where the Astor House afterward stood, and had not yet begun those purchases of real estate which secured his fortune. Cornelius Vanderbilt was a boy six years old, playing about his father's ferry-boat at Staten Island. New York city itself was what it had been for a hundred years past,—a local market.

As a national capital New York made no claim to consideration. If Bostonians for a moment forgot their town-meetings, or if Virginians overcame their dislike for cities and pavements, they visited and admired, not New York, but Philadelphia. "Philadelphia," wrote the Duc de Liancourt, "is not only the finest city in the United States, but may be deemed one of the most beautiful cities in the world." In truth, it surpassed any of its size on either side of the Atlantic for most of the comforts and some of the elegancies of life. While Boston contained twenty-five thousand inhabitants and New York sixty thousand, the census of 1800 showed that Philadelphia was about the size of Liverpool,—a city of seventy thousand people. The repeated ravages of yellow fever roused there a regard for sanitary precautions and cleanliness; the city, well paved and partly drained, was supplied with water in wooden pipes, and was the best-lighted town in America; its market was a model, and its jail was intended also for a model,—although the first experiment proved unsuccessful, because the prisoners went mad or idiotic in solitary confinement. In and about the city flourished industries considerable for the time. The iron-works were already important; paper and gunpowder, pleasure carriages and many other manufactures, were produced on a larger scale than elsewhere in the Union. Philadelphia held the seat of government until July 1800, and continued to hold the Bank of the United States, with its capital of ten millions, besides private banking capital to the amount of five millions more. Public spirit was more active in Pennsylvania than in New York. More roads and canals were building; a new turnpike ran from Philadelphia to Lancaster, and the great highway to Pittsburg was a more important artery of national life than was controlled by any other State. The exports of Pennsylvania amounted to $12,000,000, and the custom-house produced $1,350,000. The State contained six hundred thousand inhabitants,—a population somewhat larger than that of New York.

Of all parts of the Union, Pennsylvania seemed to have made most use of her national advantages; but her progress was not more rapid than the natural increase of population and wealth demanded, while to deal with the needs of America, man's resources and his power over Nature must be increased in a ratio far more rapid than that which governed his numbers. Nevertheless, Pennsylvania was the most encouraging spectacle in the field of vision. Baltimore, which had suddenly sprung to a population and commerce greater than those of Boston, also offered strong hope of future improvement; but farther South the people showed fewer signs of change.

The city of Washington, rising in a solitude on the banks of the Potomac, was a symbol of American nationality in the Southern States. The contrast between the immensity of the task and the paucity of means seemed to challenge suspicion that the nation itself was a magnificent scheme like the federal city, which could show only a few log-cabins and Negro quarters where the plan provided for the traffic of London and the elegance of Versailles. When in the summer of 1800 the government was transferred to what was regarded by most persons as a fever-stricken morass, the half-finished White House stood in a naked field overlooking the Potomac, with two awkward Department buildings near it, a single row of brick houses and a few isolated dwellings within sight, and nothing more; until across a swamp, a mile and a half away, the shapeless, unfinished Capitol was seen, two wings without a body, ambitious enough in design to make more grotesque the nature of its surroundings. The conception proved that the United States understood the vastness of their task, and were willing to stake something on their faith in it. Never did hermit or saint condemn himself to solitude more consciously than Congress and the Executive in removing the government from Philadelphia to Washington: the discontented men clustered together in eight or ten boarding-houses as near as possible to the Capitol, and there lived, like a convent of monks, with no other amusement or occupation than that of going from their lodgings to the Chambers and back again. Even private wealth could do little to improve their situation, for there was nothing which wealth could buy; there were in Washington no shops or markets, skilled labor, commerce, or people. Public efforts and lavish use of public money could alone make the place tolerable; but Congress doled out funds for this national and personal object with so sparing a hand, that their Capitol threatened to crumble in pieces and crush Senate and House under the ruins, long before the building was complete.

A government capable of sketching a magnificent plan, and willing to give only a half-hearted pledge for its fulfilment; a people eager to advertise a vast undertaking beyond their present powers, which when completed would become an object of jealousy and fear,—this was the impression made upon the traveller who visited Washington in 1800, and mused among the unraised columns of the Capitol upon the destiny of the United States. As he travelled farther south his doubts were strengthened, for across the Potomac he could detect no sign of a new spirit. Manufactures had no existence. Alexandria owned a bank with half a million of capital, but no other was to be found between Washington and Charleston, except the branch Bank of the United States at Norfolk, nor any industry to which loans and discounts could safely be made. Virginia, the most populous and powerful of all the States, had a white population of 514,000 nearly equal to that of Pennsylvania and New York, besides about 350,000 slaves. Her energies had pierced the mountains and settled the western territory before the slow-moving Northern people had torn themselves from the safer and more comfortable life by the seaboard; but the Virginia ideal was patriarchal, and an American continent on the Virginia type might reproduce the virtues of Cato, and perhaps the eloquence of Cicero, but was little likely to produce anything more practical in the way of modern progress. The Shenandoah Valley rivalled Pennsylvania and Connecticut in richness and skill of husbandry; but even agriculture, the favorite industry in Virginia, had suffered from the competition of Kentucky and Tennessee, and from the emigration which had drawn away fully one hundred thousand people. The land was no longer very productive. Even Jefferson, the most active-minded and sanguine of all Virginians,—the inventor of the first scientific plough, the importer of the first threshing-machine known in Virginia, the experimenter with a new drilling-machine, the owner of one hundred and fifty slaves and ten thousand acres of land, whose Negroes were trained to carpentry, cabinetmaking, house-building, weaving, tailoring, shoe-making, —claimed to get from his land no more than six or eight bushels of wheat to an acre, and had been forced to abandon the more profitable cultivation of tobacco. Except in a few favored districts like the Shenandoah Valley, land in Virginia did not average eight bushels of wheat to an acre. The cultivation of tobacco had been almost the sole object of land-owners, and even where the lands were not exhausted, a bad system of agriculture and the force of habit prevented improvement.

The great planters lavished money in vain on experiments to improve their crops and their stock. They devoted themselves to the task with energy and knowledge; but they needed a diversity of interests and local markets, and except at Baltimore these were far from making their appearance. Neither the products, the markets, the relative amount of capital, nor the machinery of production had perceptibly changed. "The Virginians are not generally rich," said the Duc de Liancourt, "especially in net revenue. Thus one often finds a well-served table, covered with silver, in a room where for ten years half the window panes have been missing, and where they will be missed for ten years more. There are few houses in a passable state of repair, and of all parts of the establishment those best cared for are the stables." Wealth reckoned in slaves or land was plenty; but the best Virginians, from President Washington downward, were most outspoken in their warnings against the Virginia system both of slavery and agriculture.

The contrast between Virginia and Pennsylvania was the subject of incessant comment.

"In Pennsylvania," said Robert Sutcliffe, an English Friend who published travels made in 1804-1806, "we meet great numbers of wagons drawn by four or more fine fat horses, the carriages firm and well made, and covered with stout good linen, bleached almost white; and it is not uncommon to see ten or fifteen together travelling cheerfully along the road, the driver riding on one of his horses. Many of these come more than three hundred miles to Philadelphia from the Ohio, Pittsburg, and other places, and I have been told by a respectable Friend, a native of Philadelphia, that more than one thousand covered carriages frequently come to Philadelphia market. . . . The appearance of things in the Slave States is quite reverse of this. We sometimes meet a ragged black boy or girl driving a team consisting of a lean cow and a mule; sometimes a lean bull or an ox and a mule; and I have seen a mule, a bull, and a cow each miserable in its appearance, composing one team, with a half-naked black slave or two riding or driving as occasion suited. The carriage or wagon, if it may be called such, appeared in as wretched a condition as the team and its driver. Sometimes a couple of horses, mules, or cows would be dragging a hogshead of tobacco, with a pivot or axle driven into each end of the hogshead, and something like a shaft attached, by which it was drawn or rolled along the road. I have seen two oxen and two slaves pretty fully employed in getting along a single hogshead; and some of these come from a great distance inland."

In the middle of these primitive sights, Sutcliffe was startled by a contrast such as Virginia could always show. Between Richmond and Fredericksburg—

"In the afternoon, as our road lay through the woods, I was surprised to meet a family party travelling along in as elegant a coach as is usually met with in the neighborhood of London, and attended by several gayly dressed footmen."

The country south of Virginia seemed unpromising even to Virginians. In the year 1796 President Washington gave to Sir John Sinclair his opinion upon the relative value of American lands. He then thought the valley of Virginia the garden of America; but he would say nothing to induce others to settle in more southern regions.

"The uplands of North and South Carolina and Georgia are not dissimilar in soil," he wrote, "but as they approach the lower latitudes are less congenial to wheat, and are supposed to be proportionably more unhealthy. Towards the seaboard of all the Southern States, and farther south more so, the lands are low, sandy, and unhealthy; for which reason I shall say little concerning them, for as I should not choose to be an inhabitant of them myself, I ought not to say anything that would induce others to be so. . . . I understand that from thirty to forty dollars per acre may be denominated the medium price in the vicinity of the Susquehanna in the State of Penn-sylvania, from twenty to thirty on the Potomac in what is called the Valley . . . and less, as I have noticed before, as you proceed southerly."

Whatever was the cause, the State of North Carolina seemed to offer few temptations to immigrants or capital. Even in white population ranking fifth among the sixteen States, her 478,000 inhabitants were unknown to the world. The beautiful upper country attracted travellers neither for pleasure nor for gain, while the country along the sea-coast was avoided except by hardy wanderers. The grumbling Wilson, who knew every nook and corner of the United States, and who found New England so dreary, painted this part of North Carolina in colors compared with which his sketch of New England was gay. "The taverns are the most desolate and beggarly imaginable; bare, bleak, and dirty walls, one or two old broken chairs and a bench form all the furniture. The white females seldom make their ap-pearance. At supper you sit down to a meal the very sight of which is sufficient to deaden the most eager appetite, and you are surrounded by half-a-dozen dirty, half-naked blacks, male and female, whom any man of common scent might smell a quarter of a mile off. The house itself is raised upon props four or five feet, and the space below is left open for the hogs, with whose charming vocal performance the wearied traveller is serenaded the whole night long." The landscape pleased him no better,—"immense solitary pine savannahs, through which the road winds among stagnant ponds; dark sluggish creeks of the color of brandy, over which are thrown high wooden bridges without railings," crazy and rotten.

North Carolina was relatively among the poorest States. The exports and imports were of trifling value, less than one tenth of those returned for Massachusetts, which were more than twice as great as those of North Carolina and Virginia together. That under these conditions America should receive any strong impulse from such a quarter seemed unlikely; yet perhaps for the moment more was to be expected from the Carolinas than from Virginia. Backward as these States in some respects were, they possessed one new element of wealth which promised more for them than anything Virginia could hope. The steam engines of Watt had been applied in England to spinning, weaving, and printing cotton; and immense demand had risen for that staple, and the cotton-gin had been simultaneously in-vented. A sudden impetus was given to industry; land which had been worthless and estates which had become bankrupt acquired new value, and in 1800 every planter was growing cotton, buying Negroes, and breaking fresh soil. North Carolina felt the strong flood of prosperity, but South Carolina, and particularly the town of Charleston, had most to hope. The exports of South Carolina were nearly equal in value to those of Mas-sachusetts or Pennsylvania; the imports were equally large. Charleston might reasonably expect to rival Boston, New York, Philadelphia, and Baltimore. In 1800 these cities still stood, as far as concerned their foreign trade, within some range of comparison; and between Boston, Baltimore and Charleston, many plausible reasons could be given for thinking that the last might have the most brilliant future. The three towns stood abreast. If Charleston had but about eighteen thousand inhabitants, this was the number reported by Boston only ten years before, and was five thousand more than Baltimore then boasted. Neither Boston nor Baltimore saw about them a vaster region to supply, or so profitable a staple to export. A cotton crop of two hundred thousand pounds sent abroad in 1791 grew to twenty millions in 1801, and was to double again by 1803. An export of fifty thousand bales was enormous, yet was only the beginning. What use might not Charleston, the only considerable town in the entire South, make of this golden flood?

The town promised hopefully to prove equal to its task. Nowhere in the Union was intelligence, wealth, and education greater in proportion to numbers than in the little society of cotton and rice planters who ruled South Carolina; and they were in 1800 not behind—they hoped soon to outstrip—their rivals. If Boston was building a canal to the Merrimac, and Philadelphia one along the Schuylkill to the Susquehanna, Charleston had nearly completed another which brought the Santee River to its harbor, and was planning a road to Tennessee which would draw the whole interior within reach. Nashville was nearer to Charleston than to any other seaport of the Union, and Charleston lay nearest to the rich trade of the West Indies. Not even New York seemed more clearly marked for prosperity than this solitary Southern city, which already possessed banking capital in abundance, intelligence, enterprise, the traditions of high culture and aristocratic ambition, all supported by slave-labor, which could be indefinitely increased by the African slave-trade.

If any portion of the United States might hope for a sudden and magnificent bloom, South Carolina seemed entitled to expect it. Rarely had such a situation, combined with such resources, failed to produce some wonderful result. Yet as Washington warned Sinclair, these advantages were counterbalanced by serious evils. The climate in summer was too relaxing. The sun was too hot. The sea-coast was unhealthy, and at certain seasons even deadly to the whites. Finally, if history was a guide, no permanent success could be prophesied for a society like that of the low country in South Carolina, where some thirty thousand whites were surrounded by a dense mass of nearly one hundred thousand Negro slaves. Even Georgia, then only partially settled, contained sixty thousand slaves and but one hundred thousand whites. The cotton States might still argue that if slavery, malaria, or summer heat barred civilization, all the civilization that was ever known must have been blighted in its infancy; but although the future of South Carolina might be brilliant, like that of other oligarchies in which only a few thousand freemen took part, such a development seemed to diverge far from the path likely to be followed by Northern society, and bade fair to increase and complicate the social and economical difficulties with which Americans had to deal.

A probable valuation of the whole United States in 1800 was eighteen hundred million dollars, equal to $328 for each human being, including slaves; or $418 to each free white. This property was distributed with an approach to equality, except in a few of the Southern States. In New York and Philadelphia a private fortune of one hundred thousand dollars was considered handsome, and three hundred thousand was great wealth. Inequalities were frequent; but they were chiefly those of a landed aristocracy. Equality was so far the rule that every white family of five persons might be supposed to own land, stock, or utensils, a house and furniture, worth about two thousand dollars; and as the only considerable industry was agriculture, their scale of life was easy to calculate,—taxes amounting to little or nothing, and wages averaging about a dollar a day.

Not only were these slender resources, but they were also of a kind not easily converted to the ready uses required for rapid development. Among the numerous difficulties with which the Union was to struggle, and which were to form the interest of American history, the disproportion between the physical obstacles and the material means for overcoming them was one of the most striking.

**⋙ ⋘**

THE *Constitution makes no provision for political parties. The men who shaped the early Republic viewed with unease the subsequent emergence of party. Historians attempting to explain their emergence have fastened upon the rivalry between Hamilton and Jefferson. It is undoubtedly true that both men provided the ideological cement for the competing Federalist and Jeffersonian Republican\* parties. But the Federalists were further fragmented by the diverging views between the great Treasury Secretary and John Adams, a split which became painfully apparent during the latter's administration.*

*Jefferson consistently opposed the creation of a powerful central government, while Hamilton was no less concerned lest the states prove too potent an obstacle to a strong national government. Jefferson feared debt; Hamilton welcomed a not too excessive national debt. Hamilton concerned himself with the creation of a stable government, one modeled on that of England. Jefferson dismissed the English system as utterly corrupt, and he accepted "a little rebellion now and then" as salutary to the health of the*

---

\* The party label Republican has had a checkered history. It was first used in Pennsylvania between 1780 and 1800 to describe those opposed to the Federalist party. The term gradually spread until it was understood to apply to the supporters of Jefferson and his policies. Since one of the most effective pressure organizations used to develop Jeffersonian support was known as the Democratic-Republican societies, the Jeffersonian party was designated the Democratic-Republican party. In 1824, the four candidates running were all drawn from the ranks of the old Democratic-Republican party, but by 1828, the supporters of Jackson were generally known as Democrats and those of both John Quincy Adams and Henry Clay as National Republicans. In 1834, opponents of Jackson allied with the National Republicans to form the Whig party. The collapse of the latter party in 1854 was followed by the organization of the modern Republican party. Their opponents retained the name Democratic. Thus both surviving major political parties in our time draw their names, if not their principles, from the original Democratic-Republican party of Thomas Jefferson.

*republic. On a wide range of subjects—the creation of the First Bank of the United States; the assumption of state debts; the institution of excise taxes; and the importance of manufacturing—the two men differed. But on one point the two men were in agreement, they wanted desperately to have the American experiment succeed.*

*Few historians have presented a more colorful account of the conflict between Jefferson and Hamilton in the republic's formative years than Claude G. Bowers (1879-1958). His formal education ended with high school but he had a lengthy career as both reporter and editorial writer for the New York* World *and* Journal. *His liberal inclinations led him to an active role in the Democratic party and he was prominent as a diplomat, serving as ambassador to Spain during its bitter Civil War between 1936 and 1939 and as ambassador to Chile during the Truman administration. His bias in favor of Jefferson led him to do less than justice to Hamilton. He used a technique that has an inherent drama: the confrontation of the forces of good (Jefferson) and the forces of bad (Hamilton). The result was exciting but less than accurate history. Yet, as Hamilton's role in the disputed election of 1800, which is treated in detail in the following selection, demonstrates, the division between the two men was not deep enough to obscure from each other their genius. Hamilton understood that Jefferson, in his own way, wanted to preserve and strengthen the republic. And Jefferson, in a memorable 1818 tribute to his long-dead rival, wrote: "Hamilton was indeed a singular character. Of acute understanding, disinterested, honest, and honorable in all private transactions, amiable in society, and duly valuing virtue in private life . . ." Nonetheless, Hamilton went to his grave convinced Jefferson was too bewitched by popular acclaim; and Jefferson ended his life believing Hamilton was "so bewitched and perverted by the British example as to be under thorough conviction that corruption was essential to the government of a nation."*

# JEFFERSON AND HAMILTON
## THE STRUGGLE FOR DEMOCRACY
## IN AMERICA

### by Claude G. Bowers

I

The final contest was staged in the new capital at Washington. It was as though destiny had arranged a new setting for the new drama on which the curtain was now rising. In the glamorous days of Federalist supremacy, Philadelphia, with its wealth, its fashion, and princely houses, harmonized with the spirit of government. The aristocratic party thrived in an atmosphere of luxury. Consistency called for a stage setting of more simplicity, in a wilderness suggesting the frontier, when the curtain rose on the triumph of democracy.

When that charming philosopher of cynicism, Gouverneur Morris, just elected to the Senate, reached the new capital in the clearing, after days of bumping and hardships on the woodsy road through Maryland, he looked about him with a smile and chuckled. Writing the Princesse de la Tour et Taxis, he poked gentle fun at the new seat of government. "We only need here houses, cellars, kitchens, scholarly men, amiable women, and a few other such trifles to possess a perfect city," he said, "for we can walk over it as we would in the fields and woods, and, on account of a strong frost, the air is quite pure. I enjoy it all the more because my room fills with smoke as soon as the door is closed. . . . I hasten to assure you that building stone is plentiful, that excellent bricks are baked here, that we are not wanting in sites for magnificent mansions . . . ; in a word, that this is the best city in the world to live in—in the future."

Ten days before Morris wrote, Mrs. Adams had reached the capital in the wilds looking older and graver, and without a ceremonious reception, due to jealousies among the socially ambitious over the choice of a master of ceremonies. After the well-traveled roads to Philadelphia, the journey to Washington had been quite enough to add to both her age and gravity. On the way from Baltimore her party had been lost in the woods, wandering aimlessly about for two hours until rescued by a wandering Negro. "Woods are all you see from Baltimore until you reach this city, which is only so in name," she wrote her daughter. "Here and there, a small cot, without a glass window, interspersed amongst the forest through which you travel miles without seeing a human being." Nor was the grandeur of the President's house entirely to her liking. From her windows she could see on the Potomac the "vessels as they pass and repass." But a rapid survey of the large mansion with its numerous draughty rooms, convinced her that it would require thirty servants "to attend and keep the apartment in order, and perform the ordinary business of the house and stables." Not a single apartment finished. "The great unfinished audience [East] room I have made a drying room of to hang up the clothes in!" she wrote glumly. But— added the tactful Abigail—"when asked how I like it, say that I wrote you the situation is beautiful, which is true." A few days later she wrote of the impatience of the ladies for a drawing-room, but "I have no looking glasses but dwarfs for this house, nor a twentieth part lamps enough to light it." Had the disgusted Abigail fared forth for a peep into the living arrangements of others, she might have thought herself more fortunate. But surveying the city from her point of vantage she would have found little to tempt to a tour of inspection.

Even then, it was a "city of magnificent distances," the houses separated by miles of mud roads, not entirely free from stumps. Travel by night was precarious. Blackness impenetrable, except when the moon was at its full, settled down over the homes and the frog ponds. Morris, having made an evening call, was forced to remain all night, for the road was "not merely deep but dangerous to drive in the dark." James A. Bayard and a party of Federalist leaders, venturing forth on a return to their lodgings from the home of a friend two miles from town, were caught in a storm, and the coachman losing his way, they drove about the waste lands throughout the night, threatened every moment by the ruts and ravines.

Pennsylvania Avenue, stretching from the President's house to the Capitol, bordered by miasmic swamps, did not at this time boast a single building; nor would it have been possible to have lived along this causeway "without devoting its wretched tenant to perpetual fevers." From the steps of the Capitol one could count seven or eight boarding-houses, one tailor's shop, one shoemaker's, one printing establishment, the home of a washwoman, a grocery shop, a stationery store, a dry-goods house, and an oyster market. And this was all. Three quarters of a mile away on the Eastern Branch stood five or six houses and an empty warehouse. At the wharf, not a single ship. From the President's house to Georgetown living conditions were better because of immunity from swamps, but the wretched roads made it all but prohibitive as a place of residence for members of Congress. Six or seven of the more fastidious braved the distance and found comfortable quarters; two or three found lodgings near the President's house; but the remainder crowded into the boarding-houses on Capitol Hill. In the best of these, by sharing a room one could have attendance, wood, candles, food, and an abundance of liquor for fifteen dollars a week. However, the fare was unsatisfactory, the beef not good, and vegetables hard to get. Such was the hair-trigger delicacy of the political situation that this packing of the politicians might easily have led to altercations and bloodshed had they not seen fit to herd together according to their political views. There was some gambling, some drinking, but Gallatin observed that for the most part the members "drank politics" instead of liquor.

How the dandies of the Federalist circle must have missed the royal hospitality at Mrs. Bingham's! Pathetic efforts were put forth to create something that might pass for society, but so limited were the resources that the lone church at the bottom of Capitol Hill, which had previously served as a tobacco house, was found alluring, and women donned their finery for worship. The Thomas Laws, who had one of the few pretentious houses, organized a "dancing assembly" to which many subscribed. Mrs. Law, related to both Lord Baltimore and Mrs. Washington, who aspired to the scepter of Mrs. Bingham, was a worldly woman, overfond of admiration and company, and finally there was a divorce. But at this time she drew the gayer element to her by her merry hospitality. "Lay down your hat, we have a fine roast turkey and you must stay and eat it," she would say to a caller, and soon others would casually appear, and an informal party would result. Callers in the old houses in Georgetown where Southern hospitality held sway, found "bread, butter, ham, and cakes set before them," and on leaving they would likely as not carry away cake and apples in their pockets, a bottle of milk in their hands. Great was the amusement of the fashionable men and women, who had been so elegantly served at the Binghams' by the French chef, on finding themselves jolting over the dirt roads to their lodgings with their pockets crammed with cake.

This was the Washington into which Jefferson was carried in a stage-coach for the decisive struggle of his career. Wishing to pay his respects to Adams, for whom he felt more respect than did the Hamiltonian wing of the President's own party, he wondered if the inordinate vanity of his defeated rival would interpret the call as an attempt to humiliate him. He determined to take the chance. Entering the President's house, he found Adams alone—the old man in those difficult days was all but isolated. One glance was enough to justify the caller's fears. In great agitation, and neglecting first to offer his visitor a chair, Adams burst forth: "You have turned me out; you have turned me out."

With the gentleness of an elder soothing a hurt child, Jefferson replied, drawing on his familiarity with the workings of the minds and hearts of men, "I have not turned you out, Mr. Adams; and I am glad to avail myself of this occasion to show that I have not and to explain my views. In consequence of a division of opinion existing among our fellow-citizens, as to the proper constitution of our political institutions, and of the wisdom and propriety of certain measures . . . that portion of our citizens that approved and advocated one class of these opinions and measures selected you as their candidate . . . and their opponents selected me. If you and myself had been inexistent, or for any cause had not been selected, other persons would have been selected in our places; and thus the contest would have been carried on, and with the same result, except that the party which supported you would have been defeated by a greater majority, as it was known that, but for you, your party would have carried their unpopular measures much further than they did." Suffering as he was under the treachery of the Hamiltonians, this softened the unhappy President's mood. Jefferson was offered a chair. The two men, who had been intimate in Revolutionary days and in Paris, engaged in a friendly discussion of the topics of the day, and parted with mutual expressions of respect.

Jefferson returned to Conrad's boarding-house, where he had taken a suite of rooms. It was a commodious house, standing on a hill, the precipitate sides of which were covered with grass and shrubs in a natural state. The windows of Jefferson's rooms commanded a beautiful view of the surrounding country—the level plain between the hill and the Potomac through which the tree-lined Taber wound its course; and the man of Monticello could look down from his windows on the tulip-poplar trees, the magnolia, the azalea, the wild rose, the hawthorn. Characteristically enough, he had gone to Conrad's because of the charms of the scenery. There the man of the hour lived like the other lodgers, with the exception of having a drawing-room for the reception of visitors; eating at the common table with the others, at the foot of the table nearest the door and most remote from the fire. When Mrs. John Brown, wife of the Kentucky Senator, insisted that he sit at the head of the table, as the oldest man if not as the Vice-President, he waved the suggestion aside with a smile of deprecation, and there, in the coldest part of the room, he continued until he moved into the President's house. But for Mrs. Brown and Mrs. Theodorus Bailey, wife of a Jeffersonian Congressman from New York, the mess table would have resembled "a refectory of monks." Living under the same roof during the hectic weeks that followed were Gallatin who shared his room with Varnum, a Democrat from Massachusetts, Senator John Langdon, General Sam Smith of Maryland, Senator Abraham Baldwin of Georgia, Senator Wilson Carey Nicholas of Virginia, his brother, the Virginia Representative, and the Browns and Baileys. In the impending crisis Jefferson could scarcely have surrounded himself with a better board of strategy. There we will leave him for a while to take up the threads of the Federalist conspiracy to prevent his election and thwart the public will.

II

While Jefferson was calmly observing the development of the conspiracy, and Gouverneur Morris was reflecting on the absurdity of the human comedy, Alexander Hamilton sat in his office in New York writing feverishly to the leaders of his party. If he wrote in bitterness it was because he was fighting for the last vestige of his prestige as a leader. It had been ominous enough when he lost control of the party caucus and the leaders of the second class deserted him for Adams, but now, to his horror, he found the leaders of the first class scheming for the election of Burr, his pet aversion, to the Presidency. This was too much. Through the latter part of December, the indignant sparks flew from his fast-flying pen as he sought desperately to dissuade the conspirators who had been his faithful servitors. On the 16th he wrote Wolcott of his hope that "New England at least will not so far lose its head as to fall into this snare." Jefferson was infinitely preferable, because "not so dangerous a man" and because he had "pretensions to character." But Burr was a "bankrupt beyond redemption except by the plunder of his country." He was "the Catiline of America." Would Wolcott communicate these views to Marshall and Sedgwick and reply speedily? The next day Hamilton and his erstwhile idolater, Otis, were both busy with their pens. The former, in an evident fever of anxiety, was writing again to Wolcott. It was incredible that Federalists should be considering Burr. Within the last three weeks at his own table he had toasted the French Republic, the commissioners on both sides who had negotiated the peace, Bonaparte and Lafayette. Could anything have been more monstrous? "Alas, when will men consult their reasons rather than their passions?" he asked. Elect Burr merely to mortify the Democrats by the defeat of Jefferson? "This disposition reminds me of the conduct of the Dutch moneyed man, who, from hatred of the old aristocracy, favored the admission of the French into Holland to overturn everything. Adieu to the Federal Troy if they once introduce this Grecian horse into their citadel."

While Hamilton was writing thus to Wolcott, Otis, in Boston, was writing to Hamilton. "It is palpable," he wrote, "that to elect Burr is to cover the opposition with chagrin and to sow among them the seeds of morbid division." But how open communication with Burr? "We in Massachusetts do not know the man. You do. Please advise us." Hearing a few days later that Sedgwick was deep in the plot, Hamilton wrote him with almost hysterical earnestness. "For heaven's sake, let not the Federalist party be responsible for the elevation of this man [Burr]." Two days more, and Hamilton was writing in New York; Harper, who had been his idolater, was similarly engaged in Baltimore. The former was writing Morris, seeking an understanding with Jefferson; Harper was writing Aaron Burr, proffering an alliance. "Jefferson or Burr? The former without all doubt," wrote Hamilton. "Let our situation be improved to obtain from Jefferson assurances on certain points—the maintenance of the present system, especially on the cardinal articles of public credit—a navy, neutrality. Make any discreet use you think fit with this letter." Alas, the flimsiness of political friendship! At that very hour Harper was writing Burr that the contest would be settled in the House. "The language of the Democrats is that you will yield your pretensions to their favorite. . . . I advise you to take no step whatever by which the choice of the House . . . can be impeded or embarrassed. Keep the game perfectly in your own hands, but do not answer this letter, or any other that may be written to you by a Federal man, nor write to any of that party."

No importunities from Hamilton were necessary in the case of Morris, who had taken the high ground "that since it was evidently the intention of our fellow citizens to make Mr. Jefferson their President, it seems proper to fulfill that intention." Such was his response to Hamilton, who responded gratefully to the loyalty of one follower. "If there is a man in the world I ought to hate," he wrote, "it is Jefferson. With Burr I have always been personally well. But the public good must be paramount to every private consideration." The next day Hamilton was bearing down hard on James A. Bayard, a Federalist Representative from Delaware, with an excoriation of Burr as liable to overturn the government to extend his power. Was it possible that Federalists were thinking of arrangements with a man of Burr's character? "No engagement that may be made with him can be depended upon. While making it, he will laugh in his sleeve at the credulity of those with whom he makes it; and the first moment it suits his views to break it he will do so." At the same time he was appealing to John Rutledge of South Carolina to assist in crushing the Federalists' conspiracy as "a service to your country." That month, too, Senator Ross of Pennsylvania heard from New York. "Mr. Burr is the last man in the United States to be supported by the Federalists," he read. Why not seek an understanding with Jefferson?

But as December faded from the calendar, the colossal genius of Federalism found himself in a position of pitiful impotency and isolation. Morris and Jay shared his views, but even the New York friends of his youth, like Troup, were unresponsive, and most of the leaders, who had once responded gladly to his nod, were ignoring his frantic efforts and proceeding with their plans. On the day he was writing Bayard, two men knocked at the lodgings of Morris, and Robert Goodhue Harper and Senator Henry Latimer of Delaware appeared to electioneer the delightful cynic whose cynicism held so much of wisdom. The voluble Harper was the spokesman. Burr, he said, was his "intimate friend." It was advisable, he thought, to elect Burr "without asking or expecting any assurances respecting his future administration." There was enough in Burr's temper and disposition to give ample security "for a conduct hostile to the democratic spirit." Morris listened patiently, and dryly suggested the wisdom of the House suspending its determination "until they can have more light as to the merit and probable conduct of the candidates." Unable to see with the majority of his party, Morris, who had touched life at so many points and in so many places, did not share in Hamilton's rage. "Indeed, my dear friend," he wrote Robert Livingston about this time, "this farce of life contains nothing which should put us out of humor." With Harper making a personal canvass for Burr, Judge Samuel Sewall, of the Essex Junto, was urging Otis to stand for "a steady and decided vote of the Federal party for Mr. Burr," because it might at any rate prevent an election—a consummation "most desirable."

Meanwhile Burr, pretending preoccupation with the approaching nuptials of his brilliant Theodosia, was suavely simulating, if he did not feel, a distaste for the plan of his "intimate friend" Harper. When the movement in his behalf was first launched, he wrote General Sam Smith that he would "disclaim all competition" with Jefferson, that the Federalists "could entertain no wish for such an exchange," and that his friends would dishonor his views and insult his feelings "by a suspicion that I would submit to be instrumental in counteracting the wishes and expectations of the United States." But eight days later, Harper had written him an encouraging letter on the prospects and he appears to have followed the admonition not to reply. After that—silence.

At Conrad's boarding-house the calmest man at the long table in the dining-room was Jefferson. He knew the plans of the opposition to prevent an election or to elect Burr, and noted the gloom among his friends and the exultation of his enemies. He was quite calm.

III

January found Hamilton still feverishly busy at his writing-desk. His worst fears had, by this time, been confirmed. His bosom friends had smiled incredulously upon his protests against Burr. The conspiracy was spreading ominously. His voice had lost its potency, his sword its shimmer. Grimly he fought against fate. McHenry had been impressed with the propaganda for Burr. A number of the Federalist leaders had escaped from the frog ponds of the capital to enjoy Christmas festivities in Baltimore, and from these he heard but one opinion—Burr should be supported. Burr's letter to Smith? These worldly Federalists laughed derisively. He would not resent being elected by Federalist votes. Even McHenry thought that with Burr elected "we may flatter ourselves that he will not suffer the executive power to be frittered away." Still, he had misgivings. "Can we promise ourselves that he will not continue to seek and depend upon his own party for support?" It was with these doubts in his mind that McHenry opened a letter from Hamilton, whom he worshiped. Here he found Burr denounced as "a profligate," as a "voluptuary," as "an extortionist" in his profession, as insolvent and dangerous. A word from Hamilton was enough, and McHenry joined his leader in combating the Federalist plans in Maryland—and not without effect. But with Senator William Hindman, who had been a supporter of Hamilton in the House, nothing could be done. He was aggressively for Burr. In early January, Pickering, still pitying himself, was not shocked at the idea of Burr's election. The suggestion that "the federalist interest will not be so systematically opposed under Mr. Burr as under Jefferson" impressed him. Then "in case of war with any European power there can be no doubt which of the two would conduct it with most ability and energy."

Meanwhile Bayard had sent a non-committal reply to Hamilton. He had found "a strong inclination of the majority" of the Federalists to support Burr with the disposition growing. He ought, therefore, to have strong grounds for separating himself from the others. While their action could not bind him, it would be a painful wrench to leave them. Still, "the magnitude of the subject forbids the sacrifice of strong conviction." As the pen of Bayard traveled over the page, the conspirators were moving about him, for he wrote in the House of Representatives. In truth, all Hamilton's advices were disturbing. Former Senator Gunn of Georgia, in sympathy with him, was afraid "some of our friends have committed themselves by writing improperly to Burr." Even John Rutledge, while disgusted at the idea of either Jefferson or Burr in the Presidency, found his party associates convinced that "Burr will be the least mischief," and that his election would be "prodigiously afflicting to the Virginia faction and must disjoint the party."

It is easy to imagine Hamilton laying down the letter of Rutledge with a frown, to open one which had arrived from Sedgwick in the same mail, to get a greater shock. It was a vigorous plea for Burr. The author found it "very evident that the Jacobins dislike Mr. Burr as President" and that "he hates them for the preference given to his rival." He had "expressed displeasure over the publication of his letter to General Smith." Would not "this jealousy and distrust and dislike . . . every day more and more increase and more and more widen the breach between them?" Would not the election of Burr by the Federalists cause "incurable" wounds? Then again, "to what evils should we expose ourselves by the choice of Burr, which we should escape by the election of Jefferson?" True, given an opportunity, Burr would be more likely to become a "usurper"—but what of that?

About this time, in the middle of the month, the Federalists met to determine on their course. The caucus was not entirely harmonious, but the Burr sentiment was overwhelming. Shocked and inwardly enraged at the disaffection of his friends, Hamilton now redoubled his efforts, and in a "very, very confidential" letter to Bayard dissected the character of Burr, demolished the arguments of his Federalist supporters, and pronounced Jefferson far superior in real ability. To this he gave a personal touch—something he had hitherto held back. "It is past all doubt," he said, "that he has blamed me for not having improved the situation I once was in to change the government; that when answered that this could not have been done without guilt, he replied, 'Les grandes âmes se soucient peu des petits moraux'; and when told that the thing was never practical from the genius and situation of the country, he answered, 'That depends on the estimate we form of the human passions, and of the means of influencing them.' Does this prove that Mr. Burr would consider a scheme of usurpation as visionary?" Four days after sending this letter to Bayard, Hamilton was writing Morris of the inability of the conspirators to get assurances from Burr, who complained that it would injure him with his friends. "Depend upon it," he warned, "men never played a more foolish game than will do the Federalists if they support Burr." But Hamilton was striving against the basest, lowest instincts of his party. One of his Boston followers was writing King at this very time that he favored Burr because "his opposition heretofore" had "arisen from ambitious motives," and because he was "not as honest in his politics as Jefferson." No one was a stouter contender against Hamilton's decent patriotic impulses than Sedgwick, who was moved by the motives just indicated. No one knew it better than Hamilton, but he persisted. "I never was so much mistaken," he wrote Sedgwick, "as I shall be if our friends in the event of their success do not rue the preference they will give to that Catiline." Fighting desperately, Hamilton looked clear-eyed upon the repudiation of his leadership of the party into which he had breathed the breath of life and given the dignity of power by the prestige of his genius. Among his friends he made no secret of his depression, admitting to them that his influence with the Federal party was wholly gone "and that he could no longer be useful." Had he created a Frankenstein to destroy not only himself but his policies and country? he wondered.

All through that month there was only serenity at Conrad's boarding-house in Washington. Thoroughly informed of every move made by the enemy, Jefferson discussed the situation in the evenings with Gallatin, the Nicholases, and General Smith. Such was his imperturbable temperament that in the midst of the intense excitement he was able to write to one friend of a meteorological diary from Quebec, and to another on a similar one from Natchez. His cause was in the keeping of Gallatin, who was quietly checking up on all members of the House, closing his own ranks, preparing for every possible contingency, and concluding that "the intention of the desperate leaders must be absolute usurpation and the overthrow of our Constitution." Thus January passed, and February came with its fateful possibilities.

IV

As the time for the contest approached, the village capital overflowed with visitors of stern visage. The boarding-houses packed with members of Congress, these onlookers found lodgment in Georgetown and in Alexandria. Notwithstanding the bitterness of the fight there was no trouble—due to stern repression. A little spark would have caused an explosion. The American people had determined on Jefferson, and it was no longer a secret that forces were at work to defeat the public will. Some of the Federalist papers deprecated the attempt to elect Burr with Federalist votes. The New York "Commercial Advertiser" made vigorous protest in denunciation of the conspirators. "They are now taking the ground which the Democrats have occupied and descending to the baseness of supporting their cause by railing, abuse and scurrility. Nothing can be less politic or honorable. It is the duty of good citizens to acquiesce in the election and be tranquil. It is proper that Mr. Jefferson should be made Chief Magistrate." The same note was struck by the New York "Gazette." "Many advocate the support of Mr. Burr," it said. "In matters of such importance it is idle to suffer our passions to get the better of our reason; and in statesmanship it would be particularly culpable from such puerile motives to risk the welfare of the nation. . . . Bad as both these men [Jefferson and Burr] are, there is no comparison between them." But the organ of the Essex Junto was openly advocating Burr's election. The "Centinel" of Boston teemed with Burr propaganda. "The people of New England have yet faith to believe that a good tree cannot bring forth bad fruit, nor vice versa," it said. "They think the stock from which Mr. Jefferson has sprung to be bad because his works are known to be so; and . . . that whatever Mr. Burr may be reported to be he will eventually turn out good; as he is the grandson of the dignified Edwards, the great American luminary of Divinity, and a son of President Burr who was also a burning and shining light in the churches." At times it fell into verse:

> "Stop ere your civic feasts begin;
>   Wait till the votes are all come in;
>   Perchance amidst this mighty stir
>   Your monarch may be Colonel Burr."

A correspondent from Washington was quoted approvingly on the plan to support Burr—"the expediency of which course is so palpable to common sense . . . that I am astonished any Federal man should hesitate upon the subject." And the "Centinel" expressed the hope that it would be able "by Saturday next to announce either that the people will have another opportunity to elect a Federal President; or that the House, rejecting a theoretical and experimental philosopher, will prefer, as a very respectable member of Congress describes Mr. Burr, 'a practical gentleman who will have judgment, taste and genius enough to appreciate the usefulness of our federal fabric, and nerve enough to preserve its integrity.' "

There was no longer any doubt that the Federalist hot-heads were ready for usurpation and revolutionary measures. It was known to every Democrat of any consequence in the country. Gallatin, counting noses, had no fear of desertions from the Jeffersonian ranks. The real danger, as the little conclave at Conrad's saw it, was the prevention of an election, and Gallatin was certain that, to prevent this calamity, a Federalist from Maryland and Morris of Vermont would go over to Jefferson. A plan to meet this contingency was drawn up by Gallatin and accepted by the chief. More sinister still was the threat, commonly heard, that should the Federalists succeed in preventing an election, they would pass a law placing the Presidency in the hands of Marshall or some other official. This the Democrats were prepared to resist by physical force. To prevent this usurpation, the Jeffersonians notified

Governor M'Kean of Pennsylvania and Governor Monroe of Virginia, who were prepared to march troops instantly upon the capital "for the purpose, not of promoting, but of preventing revolution and the shedding of a single drop of blood." A careful survey convinced Gallatin that this scheme of usurpation would not have mustered more than twenty votes among the Federalist members. Only Henry Lee, "a desperate character," and Roger Griswold of Connecticut, a bigot, appeared to Gallatin to be really favorable to such a monstrous measure. Even so the rumor spread, and it was said that fifteen hundred men in Virginia and Maryland had agreed in the event a usurper were placed in the Presidency to move on Washington to assassinate him.

Jefferson had other plans in view, which he conveyed only to Madison and Monroe—to call a convention to reorganize the Government and amend the Constitution, but he concealed this from Gallatin. The Gallatin plan, with its military feature, leaked out, causing some uneasiness among the conspirators, who proceeded, however, with their plans. The "Centinel" boasted that Federalists had no fear of Southern and Western fighters. "Our General [Burr] if called upon can assure them that he has seen southern regiments in former times and knows what they are composed of."

Meanwhile the Federalists proceeded with their plans. Burr, concealing himself in Albany, was maintaining a discreet silence, and on February 1st, Jefferson wrote him a letter. At no time had he any confidence in Burr's political honesty or reliability. During the two Federalist Administrations he had observed that, whenever a great military or diplomatic appointment was to be made, Burr had hurried to Philadelphia and was "always at market if they wanted him." Jefferson had thought it wise to remain rather distant. But he was too sagacious to reveal his distrust at this juncture. He had no thought of giving Burr any excuse for treachery, and enemies had been busy with a forged letter bearing Jefferson's signature setting forth uncomplimentary opinions. He wrote to call attention to the forgery and denounce it. "It was to be expected," he wrote, "that the enemy would endeavor to sow tares between us that they might divide us and our friends." If the letter was ever answered, the reply has been lost.

On the day Jefferson sat in his room at Conrad's writing Burr, Gouverneur Morris's morning slumber was interrupted by two visitors who wished to discuss with him the organization of Burr's Administration. "Laughable enough under the circumstances which now exist," chuckled the cynic. Two days later, still serene, Jefferson was writing Dr. Caspar Wistar of some bones recently discovered which the Doctor wished for the museum. The candidate had taken the trouble to write Chancellor Livingston, and the reply was inspired by the latter's letter in answer. With the village capital crowded, with talk of revolution, usurpation, assassination, he wrote at length. Perhaps it would be better to ask only for the bones missing from the museum's collection, as the town where they were found would probably be loath to part with them at all. Even then the philosopher and scientist was not wholly lost in the politician.

In New York, Hamilton, having gone his limit, was no longer writing letters. The indifference of his erstwhile followers had left him depressed and bitter. Then, one day at the Tontine Coffee-House, he had an opportunity to renew his warning in the most dramatic manner. Wolcott had resigned from the Cabinet, his treachery still unsuspected by Adams, to be wined and dined by the Federalist members of Congress in Washington, and toasted by the merchants of Philadelphia and New York. After the regular toasts had been given at the Tontine and volunteers were in order, Hamilton rose, and in his most impressive manner proposed: "May our government never fall a prey to the dreams of a Condorcet NOR THE VICES OF A CATILINE." "The vices of a Catiline" was the one expression remembered by the diners as they poured out into the streets.

The next day the balloting was to begin. On the day of the dinner at the Tontine the "Commercial Advertiser" predicted the election of Burr on the second ballot; and that same day Representative William Cooper was writing a friend of the determination of the Federalists "to run Burr perseveringly" and to "leave the consequences to those who have hitherto been his friends." At Conrad's boarding-house all was serene.

v

In a blinding snowstorm the lawmakers and spectators fought their way to the Capitol on Wednesday morning, the 11th. Nature spread a white mantle over the crudities of the village as though to dress it becomingly for the great day. The great plain between the foot of the hill and the river was covered with a spotless sheet, and even the shop of the shoemaker and the home of the wash-woman took on the appearance of beauty. No one minded the storm, not even Joseph H. Nicholson of Maryland, who, though bedridden with fever, insisted on being carried through the storm to cast his ballot for Jefferson. The electoral votes being counted in a joint session of the two houses, the members of the House retired to their own chamber to elect a President. The crowded gallery was ordered cleared. The visitors, grumbling loudly, filed out into the corridors. When Samuel Harrison Smith, editor of the "National Intelligencer," who had established his paper in the capital on the advice of Jefferson, insisted on remaining, he was angrily ordered out by Theodore Sedgwick, the Speaker. Arrangements were thereupon made by the Jeffersonians to keep Smith informed hourly of the fortunes of the fight. In a committee room off the chamber lay Nicholson on a bed, burning with fever, an anxious wife at his side to give him water and medicine. Even the conspirators could not restrain their admiration. "It is a chance that this kills him," wrote Otis. "I would not thus expose myself for any President on earth." The stricken Democrat was not there, however, against the wishes of his wife, who had the fighting spirit of a Spartan woman.

The first ballot found Jefferson with eight States—Burr with six—nine necessary to a choice. Another ballot immediately—the same result. A third, fourth, fifth, sixth, seventh—no change. As each ballot was taken, a teller from Maryland entered the little committee room where Nicholson lay fighting the fever, his head supported by the arm of his wife. He was awakened from his fitful sleep, a pencil was put in his trembling fingers, and with his wife's aid in guiding the pencil the name of Jefferson was written. The pencil fell from his hand—he slept again. At the end of the eighth ballot a motion to vote again in an hour prevailed. There was little election-eering—men's minds were made up. Only a buzz of conversation, some laughter.

The ninth ballot, the tenth, eleventh, twelfth, thirteenth, fourteenth, fifteenth ballots—and no change. Darkness had long since fallen on snow-covered Washington. Bed-clothing, blankets, pillows, had been brought in. The Federalists had determined to hold on without adjournment. At nine o'clock the sixteenth ballot brought no change. At ten o'clock the seventeenth, at eleven the eighteenth—and no change. The motion was made to adjourn until Thursday, only to be voted down. At midnight the nineteenth ballot was taken, with the lines unbroken. By this time the members were slipping off to cloak and committee rooms between ballots to sleep, and some slept in their chairs. As a ballot was called, it was "ludicrous to see them running from committee rooms with night caps on." The crowd in the corridors dwindled, a few stubbornly held on. Every hour a messenger waded laboriously through the heavy snow to the home of the editor of "The Intelligencer" with the results. No sleep in that house that night. When the knock at the door was heard, the editor's wife, her heart beating audibly, as she thought, could scarcely open to receive the paper.

At one o'clock another ballot—then at two. Nature was beginning to claim its toll when it was agreed not to vote again until four o'clock. After that the ballots were taken hourly throughout the night. When the twenty-seventh ballot was taken at eight o'clock and the motion was made to vote no more until noon, there were no protests. The vote at noon found the opposing lines unbroken. The House adjourned until eleven o'clock on Friday—the next day.

Friday: larger crowds about the Capitol. Nicholson still on his bed. When the twenty-ninth ballot showed no change, an adjournment was taken until noon on Saturday.

Meanwhile the participants in the struggle were sending out meager reports on the results. While the first ballots were being taken on Wednesday, Jefferson had written Tench Coxe: "For some time since, a single individual has said he would by his vote make up the ninth State. On Saturday last he changed, and it stands at present eight one way, six the other, and two divided. Which of the two will be elected, and whether either, I deem perfectly problematical; and my mind has long since been equally made up for either of the three events." Otis, writing his wife, was more interested in the scene at the sickbed than in conjectures. Gallatin wrote Mrs. Gallatin of the results without comment, other than that he had slept from eight o'clock until noon on Thursday morning. Saturday found the lines still holding, but with the conspirators subjected to a heavy and disturbing fire from outside. An imposing petition from Federalists in Maryland had been sent John Chew Thomas declaring that two thirds of his constituents favored Jefferson. Gallatin did "not know what effect they would have," and the thing that worried the Federalists was that they knew no better. Some of these were finding the back-fire distressing. Others were openly disgusted with Burr. "Had Burr done anything for himself, he would long ere this have been President," wrote Cooper of New York. It was clearly time to push the contest. Thus, on Saturday three ballots were taken without results, and the House adjourned until noon Monday.

Meanwhile, Jefferson, presiding over the Senate, surrounded by hatred and excitement, presented an unruffled front, an untouched temper. From time to time he could hear the angry discussions of his enemies, but he made no sign. His impartiality was beyond question. "A spectator," wrote a contemporary, "who watched his countenance would never have surmised that he had any personal interest in the impending event." From the Capitol he walked like one unconcerned back to Conrad's, enjoying the snow. Some of the politicians sought to wring concessions from him to gain support, but he was adamant. General Sam Smith, without his authority or knowledge, entered into a negotiation, which had no effect beyond furnishing the groundwork for the charge of his enemies in history that he had made arrangements. As far as we know he was openly approached by but one—and he was acting on the suggestion of Alexander Hamilton.

One day, as Jefferson was descending the steps of the Capitol, he met Gouverneur Morris and they paused to exchange compliments. Differing as widely as the poles, they had enjoyed their social contacts in Paris. The conversation turned naturally to the contest, and Morris observed, significantly, that the opposition to Jefferson's election on the part of some was the fear that he would turn all Federalists out of office, put down the navy, and wipe out the debt. All that was necessary to his election was the assurance that none of these steps would be taken. "I must leave the world to judge the course I mean to pursue by that which I have pursued hitherto," Jefferson replied. "I believe it my duty to be passive and silent during the present contest. I shall certainly make no terms, and shall never go into the office of President by capitulation, nor with my hands tied by any conditions which will hinder me from pursuing the measures which I shall deem for the public good." The two parted in the best of feeling.

The crisis was now approaching. Public sentiment was asserting itself unmistakably, and statesmen could hear afar off the cracking of the whips. The Jeffersonians would clearly not budge. Even Nicholson was recovering instead of sinking under the exposure and excitement. The Federalists in their caucuses were breaking up after stormy meetings. It was agreed that nothing was left but desperate measures, and, while but few urged their adoption, few openly disapproved. Burr was an ever-increasing torment. Only his cooperation was needed, said Bayard afterward, to have won. "By deceiving one man (a great blockhead) and tempting two (not incorruptible), he might have secured a majority of the States." But Burr was in Albany, silent as the sphinx and inactive as a mummy.

Over Sunday the leaders caucused and cursed. When the House met on Monday, Gallatin understood that Bayard was going to vote for Jefferson and end the fight. But on the one ballot taken on Monday, he remained with

Burr. "But it is supposed," wrote Gallatin to his father-in-law, "that the cause of delay is to make an attempt on his party and some others to prevail on the whole Federal party to come over."

The conferences continued on Monday and by night a decision had been reached. Nothing could be gained by fighting for a man who would not fight. The public was in an ugly mood. Hamilton's friends, like Bayard, were feeling a little ashamed of themselves. On Tuesday a crowd was packed in the corridors of the Capitol and in front of the building. Weary men in petulant mood pushed their way through these farmers, mechanics, and politicians to the House. A vote was immediately taken. Morris, Federalist from Vermont, withdrew, permitting Matthew Lyon to cast the vote of the State for Jefferson. The Maryland Federalists cast blank ballots—permitting the Democrats to put their State in the Jefferson column. Bayard, after much meandering, finally satisfied Hamilton by casting a blank, which, being the only vote to which his State was entitled, left Delaware out entirely. And Theodore Sedgwick, in a rage, was forced formally to announce the election of Thomas Jefferson. The throng in the corridors and in front of the Capitol gave way to noisy rejoicing, and the conspirators hurried to their lodgings to escape the scowls of the populace.

VI

While most of them hurried home, three members of the House, including two of the vanquished, with Thomas Pinckney as spokesman, made their way with many jests, we may be sure, up the slushy Avenue, between the frog ponds, to the President's house to notify John Adams that his successor had been chosen. No record of their reception remains, but the imagination can supply the want. Nor is there any record that Adams sent a note of congratulation to the victor. Those were the days when "The Duke of Braintree's" morbid vanity was suffering keenly the flings of outrageous fortune.

Two days later, the same committee formally notified Jefferson of his election and was asked to convey a gracious response to the House. Meanwhile, unflurried and unhurried, he went his way, appearing in the Senate, as usual to preside, and continuing to occupy the foot of the table at Conrad's boarding-house. He had long since determined upon Madison for the head of the Cabinet and Gallatin for the Treasury, gigantic figures compared with those who had occupied these posts after Jefferson and Hamilton had left them in the days of Washington. The other positions were filled during the two weeks intervening between the election and the inauguration.

On Saturday before his inauguration on Wednesday, Jefferson appeared for the last time in the Senate to withdraw from his post there in a farewell address. There before him sat men who hated him venomously, but the suave, serene victor took leave as though departing with sorrow from a cherished circle of congenial souls. Mistakes he had probably made, but he had sought to "observe impartial justice," and his measurable success had been due to the generosity and uniform courtesy of the members. Could he but carry to his new station such support as he had received from the Senate, he would "consider it as commencing under the happiest auspices." In tendering his "cordial and respectful adieux," he wished for all both health and happiness. With a courtly bow he descended from the rostrum, and passed out of the chamber.

On Monday, Gouverneur Morris, chairman of the committee named to make response, reported an answer matching the courtliness of Jefferson's farewell. It lamented "the loss of that intelligence, attention, and impartiality" with which Jefferson had presided, and expressed appreciation of the kindly expressions on the Senate. Then, as Morris proceeded, there was a savage wagging of heads among the die-hards, as he read: "In the confidence that your official conduct will be directed to those great objects (the honor and interests of the country)—a confidence derived from past events, we repeat to you, sir, the assurance of our Constitutional support in your future administration." Instantly an irreconcilable was on his feet with a motion to strike out the words, "derived from past events." The roll was called. The motion was lost by a vote of 9 to 19. The intolerant Tracy and Ross voted with the nine, but Morris carried some of his party with him. The next day Morris reported Jefferson's reply—a gesture of appreciation.

As the day of the inauguration approached, great crowds began to pour into the drab little capital from the surrounding country. In the President's house and in the Senate there was feverish activity. Early in the session, the Federalists, realizing that their power was over in the executive and legislative branches, sought to maintain themselves and provide for their favorites through the creation of many Federal judgeships. The purpose was transparent. The Democrats had fought the measure without avail. All that now remained was for Adams to pack the courts with partisans as narrow and intolerant as those who had for ten years been delivering common party harangues from the Bench. With the joyous visitors wading the muddy streets in holiday mood, with Jefferson closeted with his friends at Conrad's, the Senate was busy confirming these partisan Judges, and in the Executive Department they were busy signing the commissions. Night came—and John Marshall remained in his office making them out.

To this drama of hate, Adams gave a touch of irony in selecting the beneficiaries of his generosity. Wolcott had left him but a little while before. Through four years he had played the game of Adams's enemies, presenting all the while a smiling countenance to his chief. We have seen him lingering on in the citadel after Pickering and McHenry had been thrown from the battlements, to wig-wag secret messages to the enemy in New York. But Adams had suspected nothing. Moved by an impulse of gratitude, he offered Wolcott a life position on the Bench, and that consummate actor, smiling still, sent the assurance that "gratitude to benefactors is among the most amiable . . . of social obligations," and accepted. There is something of pathos to the Adams of the sunset. Something of pathos and inspiration, too— for, to the disgust of the inner circle of his party, he made John Marshall

Chief Justice of the United States, and thus, unwittingly, saved the better part of Federalism from the wreckage of the temple, to fight on through many years to come.

VII

The morning of inauguration day found the entire nation marching in the streets, exultant Democrats following the fife and drum, singing and shouting hosannas. Merchants locked their doors, mechanics left their work-benches, clerks laid down their pens, farmers deserted their homes for the towns, and from Boston to Savannah men and women celebrated with an enthusiasm not approached since the celebration of the peace in 1783.

In Washington, the thunder of artillery ushered in the day. As it shook the heavens, an embittered old man with a sour countenance sat far back in his coach as it bumped and splashed its way through the mire and over the stumps of the Baltimore road, for at four o'clock in the morning John Adams had slipped out of the house of the Presidents and hurried away, rather than remain to extend the ordinary courtesies to his successor. "You have no idea," wrote Gallatin to his wife, "of the meanness, indecency, almost insanity of his conduct, especially of late. But he is fallen and not dangerous. Let him be forgotten." Somewhere in hiding, or in flight, was Theodore Sedgwick, Speaker of the House, who could not bear to witness the triumph of a foe.

That morning Jefferson remained quietly at Conrad's, receiving friends. As he entered the dining-room for breakfast, the wife of Senator Brown rose impulsively and offered him her seat. With an appreciative smile he declined and sat down as usual at the end of the table near the door.

At ten o'clock there was a flurry among the men, women, and children standing reverently in front of Jefferson's lodgings, when, with a swinging stride, companies of riflemen and artillery from Alexandria paraded before the boarding-house. At noon, dressed plainly, with nothing to indicate the dignity of his position, Jefferson stepped out of Conrad's, accompanied by citizens and members of Congress, and walked to the Capitol. As he passed the threshold, there was a thunder of artillery. When he entered the little Senate Chamber, the Senators and Representatives rose, and Aaron Burr, now Vice-President, left his seat—all standing until Jefferson sat down in the chair he had occupied until a week before. On his right hand, Burr; on his left, Marshall. Only a little while, and Burr, arrested for treason at the instigation of Jefferson, would be tried by Marshall at Richmond.

After a moment, Jefferson rose and read a conciliatory address, in a tone scarcely audible in the tiny room. "We are all Republicans; we are all Federalists. If there be any among us who would wish to dissolve this Union, or to change its Republican form, let them stand undisturbed as monuments of the safety with which error of opinion may be tolerated where reason is left free to combat it." As he concluded, he turned to Marshall, his Hamilton of the future. The Chief Justice administered the oath. It was over. The festivities of '83 had celebrated the achievement of the right of the American people to form their own government and make their own laws. The roar of artillery as the new President emerged from the Capitol meant that the real American Revolution had triumphed, and definitely determined that this should be a democratic republic.

In the streets and public-houses that afternoon there was rejoicing, shouting, singing, laughing, drinking. Even the more tolerant of the vanquished fraternized with the victors, and the wife of the editor of the Jeffersonian organ poured tea for Gouverneur Morris, Jonathan Dayton, and James A. Bayard. For the moment "all were Republicans, all were Federalists." That night Washington saw its first illumination.

Lumbering along the wretched mud roads in his coach rode Adams, the reverberations of the artillery peal of the morning still hammering on his nerves, meditating bitterly on the treachery of men. . . . Somewhere in hiding, Sedgwick—cursing the fates. . . . And somewhere in New York, Alexander Hamilton was tasting the bitter fruits of the victory he had fought to win for his greatest opponent. From his window he could see the marching men and he could hear the paeans of triumph. The brilliant party he had moulded was in ruins—his leadership scorned by the crawling creatures who had shone only in the reflected light of his brilliance. He was alone—isolated. . . . A little while and he would write Morris, "What can I do better than withdraw from the scene? Every day proves to me more and more that this American world was not made for me." . . . A few months, and he would be describing himself as a "disappointed politician" in a letter to Pinckney requesting melon seeds for his garden and parroquets for his daughter. . . . Four years—and before Burr's pistol he would fall on the banks of the Hudson one tragic summer morning. . . . Some years more, and a visitor to the home of the retired sage of Monticello would see in the hall a marble bust of Hamilton—the tribute of one great man to another.

❧ ❧

THE *rivalry between Jefferson and Hamilton was succeeded in the great Virginian's presidency by a series of clashes with Chief Justice John Marshall. The genial Supreme Court chief proved more than a match for his fellow Virginian. With shrewd care, he shaped court decisions that advanced the two causes closest to his heart: the strengthening of the federal authority and the extending of the ill-defined power of the federal judiciary. But it is worth noting that he never operated outside of familiar judicial practice. Even when he asserted, in* Marbury v. Madison, *the power to pass upon the constitutionality of legislation, he did so with the knowledge that the authors of the Constitution as well as Jefferson assumed the judiciary possessed such power.*

*In his formidable decisions of* McCulloch v. Maryland (*1819*), *Dartmouth College* (*1819*), *and* Gibbons v. Ogden (*1824*), *Marshall decreed the supremacy of the federal power, the sanctity of contracts, and the exclusive-*

*ness of federal power over interstate commerce. The implications of all these assertions were to prove increasingly significant as the nation expanded and the role of the federal authority grew. The Marshall Court rendered decisions that cast long shadows across the future.*

*Marshall was fortunate in his major biographer. Senator Albert J. Beveridge (1863-1927) emphasizes a striking characteristic of American historians —some of the very best have been amateurs. Beveridge himself served as the Progressive Republican senator from Indiana (1899-1911). He fought the narrow conservatism of the Republican leadership as a Republican insurgent, and when he was defeated for reelection in 1911, he left office convinced that the need for economic reform continued. Departure from office also provided him with the time and leisure to compose his four Marshall volumes. In time, he wrote: "I consider it a Godsend that I am out of politics. . . . I now enjoy the opportunity of conversation and close intercourse with friends, among them the first scholars in America; the chance for investigation and undisturbed thinking; the normal living, the walks through the forests, . . . the new birth of mental and physical vigor which I feel every morning when I awake. . . . I would not exchange all this for the hectic, hurried, shallow, insincere life of politics."*

*The result of that tranquillity was a biography of Marshall that reflected the Hamiltonian bias of Beveridge, his support of a strong central government, his skepticism of democracy, and a sharp prejudice against Jefferson. But it also coated the dry bones of judicial decisions with the flesh of the human drama that lay behind each of them. It reminded the reader that the Supreme Court, despite its austerity, was an institution shaped by humans for humans.*

## THE LIFE OF JOHN MARSHALL

### by *Albert J. Beveridge*

"Rawleigh, Jan. 2, 1803

"My Dearest Polly

"You will laugh at my vexation when you hear the various calamaties that have befallen me. In the first place when I came to review my funds, I had the mortification to discover that I had lost 15 silver dollars out of my waist coat pocket. They had worn through the various mendings the pocket had sustained & sought their liberty in the sands of Carolina.

"I determined not to vex myself with what coud not be remedied & ordered Peter to take out my cloaths that I might dress for court when to my astonishment & grief after fumbling several minutes in the portmanteau, staring at vacancy, & sweating most profusely he turned to me with the doleful tidings that I had no pair of breeches. You may be sure this piece of inteligence was not very graciously receivd; however, after a little scolding I determined to make the best of my situation & immediately set out to get a pair made.

"I thought I should be a sans culotte only one day & that for the residue of the term I might be well enough dressd for the appearance on the first day to be forgotten. But, the greatest of evils, I found, was followed by still greater! Not a taylor in town coud be prevaild on to work for me. They were all so busy that it was impossible to attend to my wants however pressing they might be, & I have the extreme mortification to pass the whole time without that important article of dress I have mentiond. I have no alleviation for this misfortune but the hope that I shall be enabled in four or five days to commence my journey homeward & that I shall have the pleasure of seeing you & our dear children in eight or nine days after this reaches you.

"In the meantime I flatter myself that you are well & happy.

"Adieu my dearest Polly

I am your ever affectionate

J. Marshall"

With the same unfailing light-heartedness which, nearly a quarter of a century before, had cheered his comrades at Valley Forge, John Marshall, Chief Justice of the United States, thus went about his duties and bore his troubles. Making his circuit in a battered gig or sulky, which he himself usually drove, absent-minded and laughing at himself for the mishaps that his forgetfulness and negligence continually brought upon him, he was seemingly unperturbed in the midst of the political upheaval.

Yet he was not at ease. Rufus King, still the American Minister to Great Britain, had finally settled the controversy over the British debts, upon the very basis laid down by Marshall when Secretary of State. But Jefferson's Administration now did not hesitate to assert that this removal of one cause of conflict with Great Britain was the triumph of Republican diplomacy. Marshall, with unreserve so unlike him, reveals to King his disgust and sense of injury, and in doing so portrays the development of political conditions.

"The advocates of the present administration ascribe to it great praise," wrote Marshall to our Minister in London, "for having, with so much dexterity & so little loss, extricated our country from a debt of twenty-four million of dollars in which a former administration had involved it. . . . The mortifying reflection obtrudes itself, that the reputation of the most wise & skilful conduct depends, in this our capricious world, so much on accident. Had Mr. Adams been reelected President of the United States, or had his successor been [a Federalist] . . . a very different reception . . . would have been given to the same measure.

"The payment of a specific sum would then have been pronounced, by those who now take merit to themselves for it, a humiliating national degradation, an abandonment of national interest, a free will offering of millions to Britain for her grace & favor, by those who sought to engage in a war with France, rather than repay, in part, by a small loan to that republic, the immense debt of gratitude we owe her."

So speaks with bitter sarcasm the new Chief Justice, and pessimistically continues: "Such is, & such I fear will ever be human justice!" He tells King that the Federalist "disposition to coalesce" with the Republicans, which seemed to be developing during the first few months after Jefferson's inauguration, had disappeared; "but," he adds, "the minority [Federalist Party] is only recovering its strength & firmness. It acquires nothing." Then, with the characteristic misgivings of a Federalist, he prophesies: "Our political tempests will long, very long, exist, after those who are now toss'd about by them shall be at rest."

For more than five years Marshall had foreseen the complicated and dangerous situation in which the country now found itself; and for more than a year he had, in his ample, leisurely, simple manner of thinking, been framing the constructive answer which he was at last forced to give to the grave question: Who shall say with final authority what is and what is not law throughout the Republic? In his opinion in the case of Marbury vs. Madison . . . we shall see how John Marshall answered this vital question.

The philosophy of the Virginia and Kentucky Resolutions had now become the ruling doctrine of the Republican Party. The writer of the creed of State Rights sat in the Executive chair, while in House and Senate Virginia and her daughter Kentucky ruled the Republican majority. The two States that had declared the right and power of any member of the Union to pronounce a National law unconstitutional, and that had actually asserted a National statute to be null and void, had become the dominant force in the National Government.

The Federalist majority in the legislatures of ten States, it is true, had passed resolutions denouncing that anti-National theory, and had vigorously asserted that the National Judiciary alone had the power to invalidate acts of Congress. *But in none of these States had the Republican minority concurred.* In all of them the Republicans had vigorously fought the Federalist denial of the right and power of the States to nullify National laws, and had especially resisted the Federalist assertion that this power was in the National Judiciary.

In the New York Legislature, forty-three Republicans voted solidly against the Federalist reply to Virginia and Kentucky, while the Federalists were able to muster but fifty votes in its favor. In Massachusetts, Pennsylvania, and Maryland, the Republican opposition was determined and outspoken.

The thirty-three Republicans of the Vermont Legislature cited, in their protest, the position which Marshall had taken on the Sedition Law in his campaign for Congress: "We have ever been of an opinion, with that much and deservedly respected statesman, Mr. Marshall, (whose abilities and integrity have been doubted by no party, and whose spirited and patriotic defence of his country's rights, has been universally admired) that 'it was calculated to create *unnecessarily*, discontents and jealousies, at a time, when our very existence as a nation may depend on our union.' "

In Southern States, where the Federalists were dominant when Kentucky and Virginia adopted their famous Resolutions, the Republicans were, nevertheless, so strong that the Federalist majority in the Legislatures of those States dared not attempt to deny formally the new Republican gospel.

So stood the formal record; but, since it had been written, the Jeffersonian propaganda had drawn scores of thousands of voters into the Republican ranks. The whole South had now decisively repudiated Federalism. Maryland had been captured; Pennsylvania had become as emphatically Republican as Virginia herself; New York had joined her forces to the Republican legions. The Federalists still held New England and the States of Delaware and New Jersey, but even there the incessant Republican assaults, delivered with ever-increasing strength, were weakening the Federalist power. Nothing was plainer than that, if the Kentucky and Virginia Resolutions had been submitted to the legislatures of the various States in 1801-1803, most of them would have enthusiastically endorsed them.

Thus the one subject most discussed, from the campaign of 1800 to the time when Marshall delivered his opinion in Marbury vs. Madison, was the all-important question as to what power, if any, could annul acts of Congress. During these years popular opinion became ever stronger that the Judiciary could not do so, that Congress had a free hand so far as courts were concerned, and that the individual States might ignore National laws whenever those States deemed them to be infractions of the Constitution. As we have seen, the Republican vote in Senate and House, by which the Judiciary Act of 1801 was repealed, was also a vote against the theory of the supervisory power of the National Judiciary over National legislation.

Should this conclusion go unchallenged? If so, it would have the sanction of acquiescence and soon acquire the strength of custom. What then would become of the condition of the country? Congress might pass a law which some States would oppose and which they would refuse to obey, but which other States would favor and of which they would demand the enforcement. What would this entail? At the very least it would provoke a relapse into the chaos of the Confederation and more probably civil war. Or a President might take it upon himself to pronounce null and void a law of Congress, as Jefferson had already done in the matter of the Sedition Law, and if House and Senate were of a hostile political party, Congress might insist upon the observance of its legislation; but such a course would seriously damage the whole machinery of the National Government.

The fundamental question as to what power could definitely pass upon the validity of legislation must be answered without delay. Some of Marshall's associates on the Supreme Bench were becoming old and feeble, and death, or resignation enforced by illness, was likely at any moment to break the Nationalist solidarity of the Supreme Court; and the appointing power had fallen into the hands of the man who held the subjugation of the National Judiciary as one of his chief purposes.

Only second in importance to these reasons for Marshall's determination to meet the issue was the absolute necessity of asserting that there was one department of the Government that could not be influenced by temporary public opinion. The value to a democracy of a steadying force was not then so well understood as it is at present, but the Chief Justice fully appreciated it and determined at all hazards to make the National Judiciary the stabilizing power that it has since become. It should be said, however, that

Marshall no longer "idolized democracy," as he declared he did when as a young man he addressed the Virginia Convention of 1788. On the contrary, he had come to distrust popular rule as much as did most Federalists.

A case was then pending before the Supreme Court the decision of which might, by boldness and ingenuity, be made to serve as the occasion for that tribunal's assertion of its right and power to invalidate acts of Congress and also for the laying-down of rules for the guidance of all departments of the Government. This was the case of Marbury vs. Madison.

Just before his term expired, President Adams had appointed forty-two persons to be justices of the peace for the Counties of Washington and Alexandria in the District of Columbia. The Federalist Senate had confirmed these nominations, and the commissions had been signed and sealed, but had not been delivered. When Jefferson was inaugurated he directed Madison, as Secretary of State, to issue commissions to twenty-five of the persons appointed by Adams, but to withhold the commissions from the other seventeen.

Among the latter were William Marbury, Dennis Ramsay, Robert Townsend Hooe, and William Harper. These four men applied to the Supreme Court for a writ of mandamus compelling Madison to deliver their commissions. The other thirteen did not join in the suit, apparently considering the office of justice of the peace too insignificant to be worth the expense of litigation. Indeed, these offices were deemed so trifling that one of Adams's appointees to whom Madison delivered a commission resigned, and five others refused to qualify.

When the application of Marbury and his associates came before Marshall he assumed jurisdiction, and in December, 1801, issued the usual rule to Madison ordering him to show cause at the next term of the Supreme Court why the writ of mandamus should not be awarded against him. Soon afterward, as we have seen, Congress abolished the June session of the Supreme Court; thus, when the court again convened in February, 1803, the case of Marbury vs. Madison was still pending.

Marshall resolved to make use of this unimportant litigation to assert, at the critical hour when such a pronouncement was essential, the power of the Supreme Court to declare invalid acts of Congress that violate the Constitution.

Considering the fact that Marshall was an experienced politician, was intimately familiar with the political methods of Jefferson and the Republican leaders, and was advised of their purposes, he could not have failed to realize the probable consequences to himself of the bold course he now determined to take. As the crawling months of 1802 wore on, no signs appeared that the Republican programme for overthrowing the independence of the Judiciary would be relinquished or modified. On the contrary, the coming of the new year (1803) found the second phase of the Republican assault determined upon.

At the beginning of the session of 1803 the House impeached John Pickering, Judge of the United States District Court for the District of New Hampshire. In Pennsylvania, the recently elected Republican House had impeached Judge Alexander Addison, and his conviction by a partisan vote was assured. Already the Republican determination to remove Samuel Chase from the Supreme Bench was frankly avowed.

Moreover, the Republicans openly threatened to oust Marshall and his Federalist associates in case the court decided Marbury vs. Madison as the Republicans expected it would. They did not anticipate that Marshall would declare unconstitutional that section of the old Federalist Judiciary Act of 1789 under which the suit had been brought. Indeed, nobody imagined that the court would do that.

Everybody apparently, except Marshall and the Associate Justices, thought that the case would be decided in Marbury's favor and that Madison would be ordered to deliver the withheld commissions. It was upon this supposition that the Republican threats of impeachment were made. The Republicans considered Marbury's suit as a Federalist partisan maneuver and believed that the court's decision and Marshall's opinion would be inspired by motives of Federalist partisanship.

There was a particular and powerful reason for Marshall to fear impeachment and removal from office; for, should he be deposed, it was certain that Jefferson would appoint Spencer Roane of Virginia to be Chief Justice of the United States. It was well known that Jefferson had intended to appoint Roane upon the death of Chief Justice Ellsworth. But Ellsworth had resigned in time to permit Adams to appoint Marshall as his successor and thus thwart Jefferson's purpose. If now Marshall were removed, Roane would be given his place.

Should he be succeeded by Roane, Marshall knew that the great principles of Nationalism, to the carrying-out of which his life was devoted, would never be asserted by the National Judiciary. On the contrary, the Supreme Court would become an engine for the destruction of every theory of government which Marshall held dear; for a bolder, abler, and more persistent antagonist of those principles than Spencer Roane did not exist. Had he become Chief Justice those cases in which Marshall delivered opinions that vitalized the Constitution would have been decided in direct opposition to Marshall's views.

But despite the peril, Marshall resolved to act. Better to meet the issue now, come what might, than to evade it. If he succeeded, orderly government would be assured, the National Judiciary lifted to its high and true place, and one element of National disintegration suppressed, perhaps destroyed. If he failed, the country would be in no worse case than that to which it was rapidly tending.

No words in the Constitution gave the Judiciary the power to annul legislation. The subject had been discussed in the Convention, but the brief and scattering debate had arisen upon the proposition to make the President and Justices of the Supreme Court members of a Council of Revision with power to negative acts of Congress. No direct resolution was ever offered to the effect that the Judiciary should be given power to declare acts of Congress unconstitutional. In the discussion of the proposed Council of Revision there were sharp differences of opinion on the collateral question of the right and wisdom of judicial control of legislative acts. But, in the end, nothing was done and the whole subject was dropped.

Such was the record of the Constitutional Convention when, by his opinion in Marbury vs. Madison, Marshall made the principle of judicial supremacy over legislation as much a part of our fundamental law as if the Constitution contained these specific words: the Supreme Court shall have the power to declare invalid any act of Congress which, in the opinion of the court, is unconstitutional.

In establishing this principle Marshall was to contribute nothing new to the thought upon the subject. All the arguments on both sides of the question had been made over and over again since the Kentucky and Virginia Resolutions had startled the land, and had been freshly stated in the Judiciary debate in the preceding Congress. Members of the Federalist majority in most of the State Legislatures had expressed, in highly colored partisan rhetoric, every sound reason for the theory that the National Judiciary should be the ultimate interpreter of the Constitution. Both Federalist and Republican newspapers had printed scores of essays for and against that doctrine.

In the Virginia Convention of 1788 Marshall had announced as a fundamental principle that if Congress should pass an unconstitutional law the courts would declare it void, and in his reply to the address of the majority of the Virginia Legislature he had elaborately, though with much caution and some mistiness, set forth his views. Chief Justice Jay and his associates had complained that the Judiciary Act of 1789 was unconstitutional, but they had not had the courage to announce that opinion from the Bench. Justices Iredell and Paterson, sitting as circuit judges, had claimed for the National Judiciary the exclusive right to determine the constitutionality of laws. Chief Justice Jay in charging a grand jury, and Associate Justice Wilson in a carefully prepared law lecture, had announced the same conclusion.

Various State judges of the Federalist faith, among them Dana of Massachusetts and Addison of Pennsylvania, had spoken to like effect. At the trial of Callender Marshall had heard Chase deliver the opinion that the National Judiciary had the exclusive power to declare acts of Congress unconstitutional. Jefferson himself had written Meusnier, the year before the National Constitution was framed, that the Virginia Legislature had passed unconstitutional laws, adding: "I have not heard that in the other states they have ever infringed their constitution; . . . *as the judges would consider any law as void* which was contrary to the constitution."

Just as Jefferson, in writing the Declaration of Independence, put on paper not a single new or original idea, but merely set down in clear and compact form what had been said many times before, so Marshall, in his opinion in Marbury vs. Madison, did nothing more than restate that which had previously been declared by hundreds of men. Thomas Jefferson and John Marshall as private citizens in Charlottesville and Richmond might have written Declarations and Opinions all their lives, and today none but the curious student would know that such men had ever lived. It was the authoritative position which these two great Americans happened to occupy and the compelling emergency for the announcement of the principles they expressed, as well as the soundness of those principles, that have given immortality to their enunciations.

Learned men have made exhaustive research for legal decisions by which Marshall's footsteps may have been guided, or which, at least, would justify his conclusion in Marbury vs. Madison. The cases thus discovered are curious and interesting, but it is probable that Marshall had not heard of many of them. At any rate, he does not cite one of them in the course of this opinion, although no case ever was decided in which a judge needed so much the support of judicial precedents. Neither did he know anything whatever of what was said on the subject in the Constitutional Convention, unless by hearsay, for its sessions were secret and the Journals were not made public until 1819—thirty years after the Government was established, and sixteen years after Marbury vs. Madison was decided. Nor was Marshall informed of the discussions of the subject in the State Conventions that ratified the Constitution, except of those that took place in the Virginia Convention.

On the other hand, he surely had read the Judiciary debate in Congress, for he was in the Capital when that controversy took place and the speeches were fully reported in the Washington press. Marshall probably was present in the Senate and the House when the most notable arguments were made. More important, however, than written decisions or printed debates in influencing Marshall's mind was THE FEDERALIST, which we know he read carefully. In number seventy-eight of that work, Hamilton stated the principle of judicial supremacy which Marshall whole-heartedly adopted in Marbury vs. Madison.

"The interpretation of the laws," wrote Hamilton, "is the proper and peculiar province of the courts. A constitution is, in fact, and must be regarded by the judges, as a fundamental law. It therefore belongs to them to ascertain its meaning, as well as the meaning of any particular act proceeding from the legislative body. If there should happen to be an irreconcilable variance between the two, . . . the Constitution ought to be preferred to the statute, the intention of the people to the intention of their agents."

In this passage Hamilton merely stated the general understanding of nearly all the important framers of the Constitution. Beyond question, Marshall considered that principle to have been woven into the very fiber of the Nation's fundamental law.

In executing his carefully determined purpose to have the Supreme Court formally announce the exclusive power of that tribunal as the authority of last resort to interpret the Constitution and determine the validity of laws by the test of that instrument, Marshall faced two practical and baffling difficulties, in addition to those larger and more forbidding ones which we have already considered.

The first of these was the condition of the Supreme Court itself and the low place it held in the public esteem; from the beginning it had not, as a body, impressed the public mind with its wisdom, dignity, or force. The second obstacle was technical and immediate. Just how should Marshall declare the Supreme Court to be the ultimate arbiter of conflicts between statutes and the Constitution? What occasion could he find to justify, and seemingly to require, the pronouncement as the judgment of the Supreme Court of that opinion now imperatively demanded, and which he had resolved at all hazards to deliver?

When the Republicans repealed the Federalist Judiciary Act of 1801, Marshall had actually proposed to his associates upon the Supreme Bench that they refuse to sit as circuit judges, and "risk the consequences." By the Constitution, he said, they were Judges of the Supreme Court only; their commissions proved that they were appointed solely to those offices; the section requiring them to sit in inferior courts was unconstitutional. The other members of the Supreme Court, however, had not the courage to adopt the heroic course Marshall recommended. They agreed that his views were sound, but insisted that, because the Ellsworth Judiciary Act had been acquiesced in since the adoption of the Constitution, the validity of that act must now be considered as established. So Marshall reluctantly abandoned his bold plan, and in the autumn of 1802 held court at Richmond as circuit judge. To the end of his life, however, he held firmly to the opinion that in so far as the Republican Judiciary Repeal Act of 1802 deprived National judges of their offices and salaries, that legislation was unconstitutional.

Had the circuit judges, whose offices had just been taken from them, resisted in the courts, Marshall might, and probably would, have seized upon the issue thus presented to declare invalid the act by which the Republicans had overturned the new Federalist Judiciary system. Just this, as we have seen, the Republicans had expected him to do, and therefore had so changed the sessions of the Supreme Court that it could not render any decision for more than a year after the new Federalist courts were abolished.

Certain of the deposed National judges had, indeed, taken steps to bring the "revolutionary" Republican measure before the Supreme Court, but their energies flagged, their hearts failed, and their only action was a futile and foolish protest to the very Congress that had wrested their judicial seats from under them. Marshall was thus deprived of that opportunity at the only time he could have availed himself of it.

A year afterward, when Marbury vs. Madison came up for decision, the entire National Judiciary had submitted to the Republican repeal and was holding court under the Act of 1789. This case, then, alone remained as the only possible occasion for announcing, at that critical time, the supervisory power of the Judiciary over legislation.

Marshall was Secretary of State when President Adams tardily appointed, and the Federalist Senate confirmed, the forty-two justices of the peace for the District of Columbia, and it was Marshall who had failed to deliver the commissions to the appointees. Instead, he had, with his customary negligence of details, left them on his desk. Scarcely had he arrived at Richmond, after Jefferson's inauguration, when his brother, James M. Marshall, wrote him of the plight in which the newly appointed justices of the peace found themselves as the result of Marshall's oversight.

The Chief Justice replied: "I learn with infinite chagrin the 'development of principle' mentioned in yours of the 12th,"—sarcastically referring to the

Administration's conduct toward the Judiciary,—"& I cannot help regretting it the more as I fear some blame may be imputed to me. . . .

"I did not send out the commissions because I apprehended such as were for a fixed time to be completed when signed & sealed & such as depended on the will of the President might at any time be revoked. To withhold the commission of the Marshal is equal to displacing him which the President, I presume, has the power to do, but to withhold the commissions of the Justices is an act of which I entertaind no suspicion. I should however have sent out the commissions which had been signed & sealed but for the extreme hurry of the time & the absence of Mr. Wagner [Clerk of the State Department] who had been called on by the President to act as his private secretary."

Marshall, it thus appears, was thoroughly familiar with the matter when the application of Marbury and his three associates came before the Supreme Court, and took in it a keen and personal interest. By the time the case came on for final disposition the term had almost half expired for which Marbury and his associates had been appointed. The other justices of the peace to whom Madison had delivered commissions were then transacting all the business that required the attention of such officials. It was certain, moreover, that the Administration would not recognize Marbury and his associates, no matter what Marshall might decide. In fact, these appointees must have lost all interest in the contest for offices of such slight dignity and such insignificant emoluments.

So far, then, as practical results were concerned, the case of Marbury vs. Madison had now come to the point where it was of no consequence whatever to any one. It presented only theoretical questions, and, on the face of the record, even these were as simple as they were unimportant. This controversy, in fact, had degenerated into little more than "a moot case," as Jefferson termed it twenty years later.

\*     \*     \*     \*     \*

It was not, then, Marshall's declaring an act of Congress to be unconstitutional that was innovating or revolutionary. The extraordinary thing was the pretext he devised for rendering that opinion—a pretext which, it cannot be too often recalled, had been unheard of and unsuspected hitherto. Nothing but the emergency compelling the insistence, at this particular time, that the Supreme Court has such a power, can fully and satisfactorily explain the action of Marshall in holding this section void.

In his opinion the Chief Justice spoke of "the peculiar delicacy of this case, the novelty of some of its circumstances, and the real difficulty attending the points which occur in it." He would follow, he said, the points of counsel in the order in which they had been made. Did the applicants have a right to the commissions? This depended, he said, on whether Marbury had been appointed to office. If so, he was entitled to the commission which was merely the formal evidence of the appointment. The President had nominated him to the Senate, the Senate had confirmed the nomination, the President had signed the commission, and, in the manner directed by act of Congress, the Secretary of State had affixed to it the seal of the United States.

The President could not recall his appointment if "the officer is not removable." Delivery of the commission was not necessary to the consummation of the appointment which had already been effected; otherwise "negligence, . . . fraud, fire or theft, might deprive an individual of his office." But the truth was that "a copy from the record . . . would be, to every intent and purpose, equal to the original." The appointment of Marbury "vested in the officer legal rights . . . of his country," and "to withhold his commission is an act . . . not warranted by law, but violative of a vested legal right. . . .

"The very essence of civil liberty," continues Marshall, "certainly consists in the right of every individual to claim the protection of the laws, whenever he receives an injury. One of the first duties of government is to afford that protection." Ours has been "emphatically termed a government of laws, and not of men. It will certainly cease to deserve this high appellation, if the laws furnish no remedy for the violation of a vested legal right. . . .

"The act of delivering or withholding a commission" is not "a mere political act, belonging to the executive department alone," but a ministerial act, the performance of which is directed by statute. Congress had ordered the Secretary of War to place the names of certain persons on the pension rolls; suppose that he should refuse to do so? "Would the wounded veteran be without remedy? . . . Is it to be contended that the heads of departments are not amenable to the laws of their country?"

Would any person whatever attempt to maintain that a purchaser of public lands could be deprived of his property because a Secretary of State withheld his patent? To be sure, the President had certain political powers and could appoint agents to aid him in the exercise of them. The courts had no authority to interfere in this sphere of Executive action. For example, the conduct of foreign affairs by the Secretary of State, as the representative of the President, can never be examinable by the courts. But the delivery of a commission to an office or a patent to land was a different matter.

When Congress by statute peremptorily directs the Secretary of State or any other officer to perform specific duties on which "the rights of individuals are dependent . . . he cannot at his discretion sport away the vested rights of others." If he attempts to do so he is answerable to the courts. "The question whether a right has vested or not, is, in its nature, judicial, and must be tried by the judicial authority." The court therefore was empowered to decide the point; and held that Madison's refusal to deliver Marbury's commission was "a plain violation of that right, for which the laws of his country afford him a remedy."

But was this remedy the writ of mandamus for which Marbury had applied? It was, said Marshall; but could such an order be directed to the Secretary of State? This was a task "peculiarly irksome, as well as delicate," for, he observed, there were those who would at first consider it "as an attempt to intrude into the cabinet, and to intermeddle with the prerogatives of the executive." Far be it from John Marshall to do such a thing. He need hardly "disclaim all pretensions to such jurisdiction." Not "for a moment" would he entertain "an extravagance so absurd and excessive. . . . Questions in their nature political, . . . can never be made in this court." But if the case before him presented only questions concerning legal rights of an individual, "what is there in the exalted station" of the Secretary of State which "exempts him from . . . being compelled to obey the judgment of the law"? The only remaining question, therefore, was whether a mandamus could issue from the Supreme Court.

In such manner Marshall finally arrived at the examination of the constitutionality of Section 13, which, he said, fitted the present case "precisely"; and "if this court is not authorized to issue a writ of mandamus" to Madison, "it must be because the law is unconstitutional, and therefore absolutely incapable of conferring the authority." In reaching this point Marshall employs almost seven thousand words. Fifteen hundred more words are used before he takes up the principle of judicial supremacy over legislation.

The fundamental law of the Nation, Marshall explained, expressly defined the original jurisdiction of the Supreme Court and carefully limited its authority. It could take original cognizance only of specific cases. In all others, the court was given nothing but "appellate jurisdiction." But he omitted the words that immediately follow in the same sentence—"with such exceptions . . . as the Congress shall make." Yet this language had, for fourteen years, apparently been considered by the whole bench and bar as meaning, among other things, that while Congress could *not take from* the Supreme Court original jurisdiction in the cases specifically named in Article Three of the Constitution, Congress *could add* other cases to the original jurisdiction of the Supreme Court.

Marshall was quite conscious of all this, it would seem. In the argument, counsel had insisted that since "the clause, assigning original jurisdiction to the Supreme Court, contains no negative or restrictive words, the power remains to the legislature, to assign original jurisdiction to that court in other cases than those specified." But, reasons Marshall, in answer to this contention, if Congress could thus enlarge the original jurisdiction of the Supreme Court, "the subsequent part of the section is mere surplusage, is entirely without meaning, . . . is form without substance. . . . Affirmative words are often . . . negative of other objects than those affirmed; and in this case, a negative or exclusive sense must be given to them, *or they have no operation at all.*"

That is to say, when the Constitution conferred upon the Supreme Court original jurisdiction in specified cases, it thereby excluded all others—denied to Congress the power to add to the jurisdiction thus affirmatively granted. And yet, let it be repeated, by giving original jurisdiction in cases specifically named, the Constitution put it beyond the power of Congress to interfere with the Supreme Court in those cases; but Marshall asserted that the specific grant of jurisdiction has *"no operation at all"* unless "a negative or exclusive sense" be given it.

Marshall boldly held, therefore, that Section 13 of the Ellsworth Judiciary Act was "not warranted by the Constitution." Such being the case, ought the Supreme Court to act under this unconstitutional section? As the Chief Justice stated the question, could "an act, repugnant to the constitution . . . become the law of the land"? After writing nearly nine thousand words, he now reached the commanding question: Can the Supreme Court of the United States invalidate an act which Congress has passed and the President has approved?

Marshall avowed that the Supreme Court can and must do that very thing, and in so doing made Marbury vs. Madison historic. In this, the vital part of his opinion, the Chief Justice is direct, clear, simple, and convincing. The people, he said, have an elemental right to establish such principles for "their future government, as . . . shall most conduce to their own happiness." This was "the basis on which the whole American fabric had been erected." These "permanent" and "fundamental" principles, in the instance of the American Government, were those limiting the powers of the various departments: "That those limits may not be mistaken, or forgotten, the constitution is written. To what purpose are powers limited . . . if these limits may, at any time, be passed by those intended to be restrained?"

If Congress or any other department of the Government can ignore the limitations of the Constitution, all distinction between government of "limited and unlimited powers" is done away with. To say that "acts prohibited and acts allowed are of equal obligation" is to deny the very purpose for which our fundamental law was adopted. "The constitution controls any legislative act repugnant to it." Congress cannot alter it by legislation. All this, said Marshall, was too clear to admit of discussion, but he proceeded, nevertheless, to discuss the subject at great length.

There is "no middle ground." The Constitution is either "a superior paramount law" not to be changed by legislative enactment, or else "it is on a level with the ordinary legislative acts" and, as such, "alterable" at the will of Congress. If the Constitution is supreme, then an act of Congress violative of it is not law; if the Constitution is not supreme, then "written constitutions are absurd attempts, on the part of the people, to limit a power in its own nature illimitable." Three times in a short space Marshall insists that, for Congress to ignore the limitations which the Constitution places upon it, is to deny the whole theory of government under written constitutions.

Although the contention that the Judiciary must consider unconstitutional legislation to be valid was "an absurdity too gross to be insisted on," Marshall would, nevertheless, patiently examine it. This he did by reasoning so simple and so logical that the dullest citizen could not fail to understand it nor the most astute intellect escape it. But in the process he was tiresomely repetitious, though not to so irritating an extent as he at times became.

If two laws conflict, the courts must decide between them. Where the Constitution and an act of Congress apply to a case, "the court must determine which . . . governs [it]. This is of the very essence of judicial duty. . . . If, then, . . . the constitution is superior to any ordinary act of the legislature," the Judiciary must prefer it to a mere statute. Otherwise "courts must close their eyes on the constitution," and see only the legislative enactment.

But to do this "would subvert the very foundation of all written constitutions." It would be to "declare that an act which . . . is entirely void, is yet . . . completely obligatory," and that Congress may do "what is expressly forbidden." This would give to the legislature "a practical and real omnipotence, with the same breath which professes to restrict their powers within narrow limits." It would be "prescribing limits, and declaring that those limits may be passed at pleasure." This "reduces to nothing" both the letter and the theory of the Constitution.

That instrument expressly extends the judicial power to cases "'arising under the constitution." Must the courts decide such a case "without examining the instrument under which it arises?" If the courts must look into the Constitution at all, as assuredly they must do in some cases, "what part of it are they forbidden to read or to obey?"

Marshall cites hypothetical examples of legislation in direct conflict with the fundamental law. Suppose that Congress should place an export duty on cotton, tobacco, flour, and that the Government should bring suit to recover the tax. "Ought judgment to be rendered in such a case?" Or if a bill of attainer should be passed and citizens prosecuted under it, "must the court condemn to death those victims whom the constitution endeavors to preserve?"

Take, for example, the crime of treason: the Constitution emphatically prescribes that nobody can be convicted of this offense "unless on the testimony of two witnesses to the same overt act, or on confession in open court." The Judiciary particularly are addressed—"it prescribes, directly for them, a rule of evidence not to be departed from." Suppose that Congress should enact a law providing that a citizen might be convicted of treason upon the testimony of one witness or by a confession out of court? Which must the court obey—the Constitution or the act altering that instrument?

Did not these illustrations and many others that might be given prove that the Constitution must govern courts as well as Congress? If not, why does the Constitution require judges "to take an oath to support it"? That solemn obligation "applies in an especial manner to their conduct in their official character." How "'immoral" to direct them to take this oath "if they were to be used as the instruments, and the knowing instruments, for violating what they swear to support!" Such contradictions and confusions would make the ceremony of taking the oath of Judicial office "a solemn mockery" and even "a crime."

There is, then, said Marshall, no escape from the conclusion "that a law repugnant to the constitution is void," and that the judicial as well as other departments are bound by the Constitution. The application of Marbury and others must therefore be dismissed.

Thus, by a coup as bold in design and as daring in execution as that by which the Constitution had been framed, John Marshall set up a landmark in American history so high that all the future could take bearings from it, so enduring that all the shocks the Nation was to endure could not overturn it. Such a decision was a great event in American history. State courts, as well as National tribunals, thereafter fearlessly applied the principle that Marshall announced, and the supremacy of written constitutions over legislative acts was firmly established.

This principle is wholly and exclusively American. It is America's original contribution to the science of law. The assertion of it . . . was the deed of a great man. One of narrower vision and smaller courage never would have done what Marshall did. In his management and decision of this case, at the time and under the circumstances, Marshall's acts and words were those of a statesman of the first rank.

❧ ☙

AARON BURR *remains one of the enigmas of American history. Briefly in 1800-01, he had the Presidency in his grasp, as the House of Representatives, obliged by the Constitution to break the 73-73 electoral vote tie between himself and Jefferson, cast thirty-six ballots before the Virginian was chosen as the third President. In the long agonizing struggle, the Federalist Party, fully aware that it had been intended that Burr be Vice-President, had cast its vote in the House for the former Senator from New York. They had done so to the undisguised horror of Alexander Hamilton, who viewed Burr's use of Tammany to mobilize the city vote as the epitome of corrupt politics. And though no evidence exists to indicate Burr encouraged the Federalists, Jefferson and his supporters remembered long that he had done nothing to discourage them.*

*In 1804, aware that the Jeffersonians did not intend to back his Vice-Presidential candidacy, Burr bid for the governorship of New York, only to be defeated. Within him there rankled the memory of charges leveled against him by Hamilton. The result was a challenge, an acceptance, a duel, and death for the great Federalist. For Burr, there remained indictment for murder, flight to South Carolina, and the end of any chance for political preferment in the East. In 1805, he wandered west, some historians say to launch a new political career, others to detach the West from the United States to form a new nation, and others contend he wanted nothing other than to build a fortune in land speculation. Jefferson chose to believe his intent was to partition the Union and called for his trial for treason. Before Chief Justice Marshall, in August, 1807, he was tried and acquitted. Between 1808 and 1812, he lived abroad, returning in the latter year to practice law in New York. For the next twenty-four years, he sank into obscurity. Upon his death, he was taken to sleep beside his grandfather, Jonathan Edwards, at Princeton.*

*James Parton (1822-1891) has been called the father of American biography. His life of Andrew Jackson (1860) remains one of the finest biographies of the old general as his biography of Benjamin Franklin (1864) is a too neglected treasure. His bias was Whiggish but with the detachment of an intellectual. He never allowed his bias to obstruct his vision. The American future was a democratic future, and unless the American educated class*

*was prepared to accept this reality, they were foredoomed to pursue a life
of futility. His account of the Hamilton-Burr duel contains the vivid detail
which characterizes his biographies.*

# THE LIFE AND TIMES
# OF AARON BURR

## *by James Parton*

### THE DUEL

As habit is second nature, dueling must formerly have seemed a very
natural mode of settling personal disputes, for few public men passed through
life without being concerned in, at least, one "affair of honor." Gates, De
Witt Clinton, Randolph, Benton, Clay, Jackson, Decatur, Arnold, Walpole,
Pitt, Wellington, Canning, Peel, Grattan, Fox, Sheridan, Jeffrey, Wilkes,
D'Israeli, Lamartine, Thiers, and scores of less famous names, are found in
Mr. Sabine's list of duelists.

In all that curious catalogue, there is not the name of one politician who
received provocation so often-repeated, so irritating, and so injurious, as
that which Aaron Burr had received from Alexander Hamilton.

Burr was not a man to resent promptly a personal injury, even when what
he called his "honor" impelled him to do so. The infidelity of a comrade
cut him to the heart; to be doubted by a friend, was, as he once said, "to
have the very sanctuary of Happiness invaded"; the disapproval of his own
set he would have felt acutely. But, to the outcry of the outer world he
was comparatively indifferent, and the injurious attempts of enemies he
usually disregarded. Aaron Burr, whatever faults he may have had—and
he had grievous and radical faults—was *not* a revengeful man; there has
seldom lived one who was less so. He had to be much persuaded before
he would sue Cheetham for libel, and the suit was languidly prosecuted.
Cheetham himself, in January of this very year, 1804, had taunted him for
allowing Hamilton to speak and write of him as it was then notorious he was
in the habit of doing. "Is the Vice-President sunk so low," said this wretched
calumniator, "as to submit to be insulted by General Hamilton?"

At every step of Burr's political career, without a single exception, Hamilton, by open efforts, by secret intrigue, or by both, had utterly opposed
and forbidden his advancement. He had injured him in the estimation of
General Washington. He had prevented Mr. Adams from giving him a
military appointment. His letters, for years, had abounded in denunciations
of him, as severe and unqualified as the language of a powerful declaimer
could convey. From Burr's own table, he had carried away the unguarded
sallies of the host for use against the political opponent. The most offensive
epithets and phrases he had so habitually applied to Burr, that they had
become familiar in the mouths of all the leading Federalists; who, as the

reader may have observed, denounced Colonel Burr in Hamilton's own words. And, finally, he had just succeeded in frustrating Burr's keen desire for vindication at the people's hands; and, in doing so, had made it only too evident to all the influential politicians, that for the success of any plans of political advancement which Burr might in future form, it was, above all things else, essential that Hamilton's injurious tongue should be either silenced or bridled.

The two men had already been near collision. I think it was in 1802 that Colonel Burr, having obtained some imperfect knowledge of Hamilton's usual mode of characterizing him, had had a conversation with him on the subject. Hamilton (so said Burr in later years), had explained, apologized, satisfied Burr, and left upon his mind the impression, never effaced, that thenceforth Hamilton was pledged to refrain from speaking of him as he had been accustomed to do. They parted with cordiality, and had ever since been, apparently, very good friends. Burr considered then, and always, that he had made prodigious sacrifices, as a man of honor and a gentleman, for the sake of avoiding a hostile meeting that could not but injure both as candidates for the public confidence. From the hour Burr learned that Hamilton still used his former freedom, he ceased to respect him; he held him in contempt, as a man insensible to considerations of honor and good faith. Burr's new Federal friends, renegades from the Hamiltonian party, had given him new information respecting the *Burriphobia* under which their former leader labored, and the language in which it was accustomed to find vent.

Consider the force of another circumstance upon a mind like Burr's, whose religion was, fidelity to comrades. Men who proudly looked up to him as more than their political chief—as the preeminent gentleman, and model man of the world, of that age—had fought in his quarrel, and fought with a reckless courage which he had first inspired, and then commanded. If the occasion should arise, could chief decline the encounter with chief, after the subalterns had so gallantly contended? And this consideration had equal weight with Hamilton. Beside having sanctioned the practice of dueling, by serving as second to Colonel Laurens in his duel with General Lee, his own son had fallen, three years ago, in what the language of that day called the vindication of his father's honor. In short, *never*, since the duello was invented, were two men, if the requisite technical provocation should arise, so peculiarly and irresistibly bound to fight, as were Aaron Burr and Alexander Hamilton in the summer of 1804.

During the late election for governor, a letter from Dr. Charles D. Cooper to a friend, found its way into the papers, which contained two sentences relating to Colonel Burr. One was this:

"General Hamilton and Judge Kent have declared, in substance, that they looked upon Mr. Burr to be a dangerous man, and one who ought not to be trusted with the reins of government."

This was the other: "I could detail to you a still more despicable opinion which General Hamilton has expressed of Mr. Burr."

Six weeks after the election, the paper containing this letter was put into Colonel Burr's hands, and his attention called to the allusions to himself.

In the afternoon of June 17th, Mr. William P. Van Ness, one of Burr's staunchest friends, the *Aristides* of the pamphlet wars of 1802, received a note from Colonel Burr, requesting him to call at Richmond Hill on the following morning. He went. At the request of Burr, he conveyed Dr. Cooper's letter to General Hamilton, with the most offensive passage marked, and a note from Colonel Burr, which, as briefly as possible, called attention to the passage, and concluded with the following words: "You must perceive, sir, the necessity of a prompt and unqualified acknowledgment or denial of the use of any expressions which would warrant the assertions of Mr. Cooper."

Hamilton was taken by surprise. He had not, before that moment, seen Cooper's letter. Having read it, and the note of Colonel Burr, he said that they required consideration, and he would send an answer to Mr. Van Ness's office (Van Ness was a lawyer) in the course of the day. Late that evening he called at Mr. Van Ness's residence, and told him that a press of business had prevented his preparing a reply, and would prevent him for two days to come; but on the 20th he would give him a communication for Colonel Burr.

In that communication, which was very long, Hamilton declined making the acknowledgment or denial that Burr had demanded. Between gentlemen, he said, *despicable* and *more despicable* was not worth the pains of distinction. He could not consent to be interrogated as to the justice of the *inferences* which others might have drawn from what he had said of an opponent during fifteen years' competition. But he stood ready to avow or disavow explicitly any *definite* opinion which he might be charged with having expressed respecting any gentleman. He trusted that Colonel Burr, upon further reflection, would see the matter in the same light. If not, he could only regret the fact, and abide the consequences.

This letter was oil upon the flames of Burr's indignation. His reply was prompt and decided. Hamilton's letters can generally be condensed one half without the loss of an idea, Burr's compact directness defies abbreviation:

"Your letter of the 20th inst.," wrote he, "has been this day received. Having considered it attentively, I regret to find in it nothing of that sincerity and delicacy which you profess to value. Political opposition can never absolve gentlemen from the necessity of a rigid adherence to the laws of honor and the rules of decorum. I neither claim such privilege nor indulge it in others. The common sense of mankind affixes to the epithet adopted by Dr. Cooper the idea of dishonor. It has been publicly applied to me under the sanction of your name. The question is not, whether he has understood the meaning of the word, or has used it according to syntax, and with grammatical accuracy; but, whether you have authorized this application, either directly or by uttering expressions or opinions derogatory to my honor. The time 'when' is in your own knowledge, but no way material to me, as the calumny has now first been disclosed, so as to become the subject of my notice, and as the effect is present and palpable. Your letter has furnished me with new reasons for requiring a definite reply."

Hamilton seems to have read his doom in that letter. He said to Mr. Van Ness, who brought it, that it was such a letter as he had hoped not to receive; it contained several offensive expressions; and seemed to close the door to reply. He had hoped that Mr. Burr would have desired him to state what had fallen from him that might have given rise to the inference of Dr. Cooper. He would have done that frankly, and he believed it would not have been found to exceed justifiable limits. And even then, if Mr. Burr was disposed to give another turn to the discussion, he was willing to consider his last letter undelivered. But if that were not withdrawn, he could make no reply.

Mr. Van Ness detailed these ideas to Colonel Burr, and received from him a paper of instructions to guide him in replying, verbally, to General Hamilton. This paper expresses with force and exactness the view of this affair then taken, and always adhered to, by Colonel Burr. It read as follows:

"A. Burr, far from conceiving that rivalship authorizes a latitude not otherwise justifiable, always feels greater delicacy in such cases, and would think it meanness to speak of a rival but in terms of respect; to do justice to his merits; to be silent of his foibles. Such has invariably been his conduct toward Jay, Adams, and Hamilton; the only three who can be supposed to have stood in that relation to him.

"That he has too much reason to believe that, in regard to Mr. Hamilton, there has been no reciprocity. For several years his name has been lent to the support of base slanders. He has never had the generosity, the magnanimity, or the candor to contradict or disavow. Burr forbears to particularize, as it could only tend to produce new irritations; but, having made great sacrifices for the sake of harmony; having exercised forbearance until it approached to humiliation, he has seen no effect produced by such conduct but a repetition of injury. He is obliged to conclude that there is, on the part of Mr. Hamilton, a settled and implacable malevolence; that he will never cease, in his conduct toward Mr. Burr, to violate those courtesies of life; and that, hence, he has no alternative but to announce these things to the world; which, consistently with Mr. Burr's ideas of propriety, can be done in no way but that which he has adopted. He is incapable of revenge, still less is he capable of imitating the conduct of Mr. Hamilton, by committing secret depredations on his fame and character. But these things must have an end."

Upon meeting General Hamilton for the purpose of making the above explanation, Mr. Van Ness was informed by him, that he had prepared a written reply to Colonel Burr's last letter, and had left it in the hands of his friend Mr. Pendleton. The verbal explanation was therefore withheld, and General Hamilton's letter conveyed to Colonel Burr. It was as follows: "Your first letter, in a style too peremptory, made a demand, in my opinion, unprecedented and unwarrantable. My answer, pointing out the embarrassment, gave you an opportunity to take a less exceptionable course. You have not chosen to do it; but by your last letter received this day, containing expressions *indecorous* and improper, you have increased the difficulties to explanation intrinsically incident to the nature of your application. If by a 'definite reply' you mean the direct avowal or disavowal required in your first letter, I have no other answer to give, than that which has already been given. If you mean any thing different, admitting of greater latitude, it is requisite you should explain."

This letter, as might have been expected, produced no effect; as Mr. Van Ness hastened to inform General Hamilton's friend. Van Ness added, that what Colonel Burr demanded was this: a general disavowal of any intention on the part of General Hamilton, in his various conversations, to convey impressions derogatory to the honor of Burr. Pendleton replied, that he believed General Hamilton would have no objection to make such a declaration!

Hamilton, of course, declined making the disavowal. But he gave Van Ness a paper, in his own hand, the purport of which was that if Colonel Burr should think it proper to inquire of General Hamilton the nature of the conversation with Dr. Cooper, General Hamilton would be able to reply, with truth, that it turned wholly on political topics, and did not attribute to Colonel Burr any instance of dishonorable conduct, nor relate to his private character. And in relation to any other conversation which Colonel Burr would specify, a frank avowal or denial would be given.

A "mere evasion," said Burr, when he had read this paper.

Other correspondence followed, but it is too familar to the public, and too easily accessible, to require repetition here. Throughout the whole of it we see, on the one hand, an exasperated man resolved to bring the affair to a decisive and final issue; on the other, a man striving desperately, but not dishonorably, to escape the consequences of his own too unguarded words. Burr's final recapitulation, drawn up for the guidance of his second, was as follows:

"Colonel Burr (in reply to General Hamilton's charge of indefiniteness and inquisition) would only say, that secret whispers traducing his fame, and impeaching his honor, are at least equally injurious with slanders publicly uttered; that General Hamilton had, at no time, and in no place, a right to use any such injurious expressions; and that the partial negative he is disposed to give, with the reservations he wishes to make, are proofs that he has done the injury specified.

"Colonel Burr's request was, in the first instance, proposed in a form the most simple, in order that General Hamilton might give to the affair that course to which he might be induced by his temper and his knowledge of facts. Colonel Burr trusted with confidence, that, from the frankness of a soldier and the candor of a gentleman, he might expect an ingenuous declaration. That if, as he had reason to believe, General Hamilton had used expressions derogatory to his honor, he would have had the magnanimity to retract them; and that if, from his language, injurious inferences had been improperly drawn, he would have perceived the propriety of correcting errors, which might thus have been widely diffused. With these impressions, Colonel Burr was greatly surprised at receiving a letter

which he considered as evasive, and which in manner he deemed not altogether decorous. In one expectation, however, he was not wholly deceived,
for the close of General Hamilton's letter contained an intimation that, if
Colonel Burr should dislike his refusal to acknowledge or deny, he was
ready to meet the consequences. This Colonel Burr deemed a sort of defiance, and would have felt justified in making it the basis of an immediate
message. But as the communication contained something concerning the
indefiniteness of the request, as he believed it rather the offspring of false
pride than of reflection, and as he felt the utmost reluctance to proceed to
extremities, while any other hope remained, his request was repeated in
terms more explicit. The replies and propositions on the part of General
Hamilton have, in Colonel Burr's opinion, been constantly in substance the
same.

"Colonel Burr disavows all motives of predetermined hostility, a charge
by which he thinks insult added to injury. He feels as a gentleman should
feel when his honor is impeached or assailed; and, without sensations of
hostility or wishes of revenge, he is determined to vindicate that honor at
such hazard as the nature of the case demands."

The challenge was then given and accepted. Ten days had elapsed since
Colonel Burr had first sent for Mr. Van Ness, and it was now the 27th of
June. Mr Pendleton stated that a court was then sitting in which General
Hamilton had much business to transact; he would require also a little time
to arrange his private affairs; and, therefore, some delay was unavoidable.
This was assented to, and the next morning appointed for a meeting of the
seconds to confer further on time and place.

At that meeting Mr. Pendleton presented a paper which, he said, he had
received from his principal, and which contained some remarks upon the
matters in dispute. Van Ness replied that, if the paper contained a specific
proposition for an accommodation, he would receive it with pleasure; if
not, he must decline doing so, as his principal considered the correspondence completely terminated by the acceptance of the challenge. Pendleton
replied that the paper contained no such proposition, but consisted of remarks upon Van Ness's last letter. Mr. Van Ness, therefore, refused to
receive it, and Pendleton retired, promising to call again in a day or two
to make the final arrangements. The seconds conferred several times before
these were concluded; but, at length, July 11th, at seven in the morning,
was fixed upon as the time; the place, Weehawken; the weapons, pistols;
the distance, ten paces. Thus, between the time when Colonel Burr sent
for Van Ness and the day appointed for the meeting, twenty-four days
elapsed, during the greater part of which the secret was known, certainly,
to seven persons, and probably, to as many as ten.

During this long period, the principals went about their daily business
as usual. Hamilton, as was afterward fondly remembered, pleaded his causes
and consulted his clients, with all his wonted vigor, courtesy, and success.
Around his table at the "Grange," day after day, he saw his seven children
and his tenderly beloved wife, with a ceaseless consciousness of the blow

that was suspended over them all. A whisper could have saved him, and saved them, but how impossible it was to utter that whisper!

Burr was residing at cedar-crowned Richmond Hill, and found the great mansion there somewhat lone and chilly. On June 23rd (the very day upon which it became certain that the affair with Hamilton could only be terminated by a duel) Theodosia's birth-day came round again, a day on which Richmond Hill, for many a year, had known only the sights and sounds of happiness and mirth. Burr was an observer of fete days and family festivals. On this occasion, he invited a party to dinner, who, as he wrote the next day to Theodosia, "laughed an hour, and danced an hour, and drank her health." He had her picture brought into the dining-room and placed at the table where she was accustomed to sit. But, added he, "as it is a profile, and would not look at us, we hung it up, and placed Natalie's [his adopted daughter] at the table, which laughs and talks with us." The letter in which these particulars are given is remarkable for containing a suggestion which has since been admirably improved. "Your idea," wrote he, "of dressing up pieces of ancient mythology in the form of amusing tales for children is very good. You *yourself* must write them. Send your performances to me, and, within three weeks after they are received, you shall have them again in print. This will be not only an amusing occupation, but a very useful one to yourself. It will improve your style and your language, give you habits of accuracy, and add a little to your stock of knowledge. Natalie, too, must work at it, and I'll bet that she makes the best tale. I will be your editor and your critic." The reader is aware how well this "idea" has since been carried out by Mr. Kingsley and others.

His letters to his daughter, at this period, contain but a single allusion, and that a vague one, to the impending conflict. On the 1st of July, he began a letter with these words:

"Having been shivering with cold all day, though in perfect health, I have now, just at sunset, had a fire in my library, and am sitting near it and enjoying it, if that word be applicable to any thing done in solitude. Some very wise man, however, has exclaimed,

'Oh! fools, who think it solitude to be alone.'

This is but poetry. Let us therefore drop the subject, lest it lead to another on which I have imposed silence on myself."

The rest of the letter is cheerful enough. He says he is impatient to receive the "Tales," recommends her to subscribe for the *Edinburgh Review*, and to be forming a library for her son.

On the Fourth of July, Hamilton and Burr met, for the last time, at the convivial board. It was at the annual banquet of the Society of the Cincinnati, of which Hamilton was president and Burr a member. Hamilton was cheerful, and, at times, merry. He was urged, as the feast wore away, to sing the only song he ever sang or knew, the famous old ballad of *The Drum*. It was thought afterward, that he was more reluctant than usual to comply with the company's request; but after some delay, he said, "Well, you shall have it," and sang it in his best manner, greatly to the delight of the old soldiers by whom he was surrounded. Burr, on the contrary, was reserved, mingled little with the company, and held no intercourse with the president. He was never a fluent man, and was generally, in the society of men, more a listener than a talker. On this occasion, his silence was, therefore, the less remarked; yet it was remarked. It was observed, too, that he paid no attention to Hamilton's conversation, nor, indeed, looked toward him, until he struck up his song, when Burr turned toward him, and, leaning upon the table, looked at the singer till the song was done.

This difference in the behavior of the two men was doubtless owing partly to their different positions at the banquet. Hamilton, as the master of the feast, was in the eye of every guest, while Burr could easily escape particular observation. The object of both was, of course, to behave so as not to excite inquiry.

On the 9th of July, Hamilton executed his will, leaving his all, after the payment of his debts, to his "dear and excellent wife." "Should it happen," said he, "that there is not enough for the payment of my debts, I entreat my dear children, if they, or any of them, should ever be able, to make up the deficiency. I, without hesitation, commit to their delicacy a wish which is dictated by my own. Though conscious that I have too far sacrificed the interests of my family to public avocations, and on this account have the less claim to burden my children, yet I trust in their magnanimity to appreciate as they ought this my request. In so unfavorable an event of things, the support of their dear mother, with the most respectful and tender attention, is a duty, all the sacredness of which they will feel. Probably her own patrimonial resources will preserve her from indigence. But in all situations they are charged to bear in mind, that she has been to them the most devoted and best of mothers."

A few hours more brought them to the day before the one named for the meeting. In the evening, both the principals were engaged, to a late hour, in making their final preparations, and writing what each felt might be his last written words. The paper prepared by Hamilton on that occasion, in the solitude of his library, reveals to us the miserable spectacle of an intelligent and gifted man, who had, with the utmost deliberation, made up his mind to do an action which his intellect condemned as absurd, which his heart felt to be cruel, which his conscience told him was wrong. He said that he had shrunk from the coming interview. His duty to his religion, his family, and his creditors, forbade it. He should hazard much, and could gain nothing by it. He was conscious of no ill-will to Colonel Burr, apart from political opposition, which he hoped had proceeded from pure and upright motives. But there were difficulties, intrinsic and artificial, in the way of an accommodation, which had seemed insuperable; *intrinsic*, because he really *had* been very severe upon Colonel Burr; *artificial*, because Colonel Burr had demanded too much, and in a manner that precluded a peaceful discussion of the difficulty.

"As well," this affecting paper concluded, "because it is possible that I may have injured Colonel Burr, however convinced myself that my opinions and declarations have been well founded, as from my general principles and temper in relation to similar affairs, I have resolved, if our interview is conducted in the usual manner, and it pleases God to give me the opportunity, to reserve and throw away my first fire, and I have thoughts even of reserving my second fire, and thus giving a double opportunity to Colonel Burr to pause and to reflect. It is not, however, my intention to enter into any explanations on the ground. Apology, from principle, I hope, rather than pride, is out of the question. To those who, with me, abhorring the practice of dueling, may think that I ought on no account to have added to the number of bad examples, I answer, that my relative situation, as well in public as in private, enforcing all the considerations which constitute what men of the world denominate honor, imposed on me (as I thought) a peculiar necessity not to decline the call. The ability to be in the future useful, whether in resisting mischief or effecting good, in those crises of our public affairs which seem likely to happen, would probably be inseparable from a conformity with public prejudice in this particular."

Doing evil that good may come, though not the crime it is to do good that evil may come, is a dreadful error. It was the vice of Hamilton's otherwise worthy life. It proved fatal to him at last.

In the long letters which Burr wrote that evening, there are no signs that the gentle blood of Esther Edwards was revolting in the veins of her erring son against the morrow's deed. There is a tender dignity in his farewell words to Theodosia, but no misgivings. He gives her a number of minute directions about the disposal of his papers, letters, and servants. She was enjoined to burn all such letters as, if by accident made public, would injure any person. This, he added, was more particularly applicable to the letters of his female correspondents. To his step-son, "poor dear Frederic," to Natalie, to various friends, he requested her to give certain tokens of his remembrance. His faithful housekeeper, Peggy, was to have a lot of ground and fifty dollars, and the other servants Theodosia was urged to adopt as her own. His letter concludes with these touching words: "I am indebted to you, my dearest Theodosia, for a very great portion of the happiness which I have enjoyed in this life. You have completely satisfied all that my heart and affections had hoped or even wished. With a little more perseverance, determination, and industry, you will obtain all that my ambition or vanity had fondly imagined. Let your son have occasion to be proud that he had a mother. Adieu. Adieu."

In a postscript, he tells her, upon her arrival in New York, to open her whole heart to his step-son, Frederic, who loves him, he says, almost as much as Theodosia does, and loves Theodosia to adoration. He also gives her a seal of General Washington's, which he possessed, and says she may keep it for her son, or give it to whom she pleases.

He wrote a long letter to her husband, recommending to his regard and care the friends to whom he was most attached. "If it should be my lot to fall," he said, in conclusion, "yet I shall live in you and your son. I commit to you all that is most dear to me—my reputation and my daughter.

Your talents and your attachment will be the guardian of the one—your kindness and your generosity of the other. Let me entreat you to stimulate and aid Theodosia in the cultivation of her mind. It is indispensable to her happiness, and essential to yours. It is also of the utmost importance to your son. She would presently acquire a critical knowledge of Latin, English, and all branches of natural philosophy. All this would be poured into your son. If you should differ with me as to the importance of this measure, suffer me to ask it of you as a last favor. She will richly compensate your trouble."

Two very characteristic postscripts are appended to this letter. In the first, he commends to Mr. Alston's special regard, Frederic Prevost. "Under the garb of coarse rusticity you will find, if you know him, refinement, wit, a delicate sense of propriety, the most inflexible intrepidity, incorruptible integrity, and disinterestedness. I wish you could know him; but it would be difficult, by reason of his diffidence and great reluctance to mingle with the world. It had been a source of extreme regret and mortification to me that he should be lost to society and to his friends. The case seems almost remediless, for, alas! *he is married!*"

The other postscript was as follows: "If you can pardon and indulge a folly, I would suggest that Madame ———, too well known under the name of Leonora, has claims on my recollection. She is now with her husband at St. Jago, of Cuba."

Late at night Colonel Burr threw off his upper garments, lay down upon a couch in his library, and, in a few minutes, was asleep.

At daybreak, next morning, John Swartwout entered the room, and saw his chief still lying on the couch. Well as he knew Colonel Burr, he was astonished, upon approaching him, to discover that he was in a sound and tranquil slumber. He awoke the man who had better never again have opened his eyes upon the light of this world. Van Ness was soon ready. Matthew L. Davis and another friend or two arrived, and the party proceeded in silence to the river, where a boat was in readiness. Burr, Van Ness, Davis, and another embarked, and the boat was rowed over the river toward Weehawken, the scene, in those days, of so many deadly encounters.

Few of the present generation have stood upon the spot, which was formerly one of the places that strangers were sure to visit on coming to the city, and which the events of this day rendered for ever memorable. Two miles and a half above the city of Hoboken, the heights of Weehawken rise, in the picturesque form so familiar to New Yorkers, to an elevation of a hundred and fifty feet above the Hudson. These heights are rocky, very steep, and covered with small trees and tangled bushes. Under the heights, at a point half a mile from where they begin, there is, twenty feet above the water, a grassy ledge or shelf, about six feet wide, and eleven paces long. This was the fatal spot. Except that it is slightly encumbered with underbrush, it is, at this hour, precisely what it was on the 11th of July, 1804. There is an old cedar-tree at the side, a little out of range, which must have looked then very much as it does now. The large rocks which partly hem in the place are, of course, unchanged, except that they are decorated with the initials of former visitors. One large rock, breast-high, narrows the hollow in which Hamilton stood to four feet or less.

Inaccessible to foot-passengers along the river, except at low tide, with no path down to it from the rocky heights above, no residence within sight on that side of the river, unless at a great distance, it is even now a singularly secluded scene. But fifty years ago, when no prophet had yet predicted Hoboken, that romantic shore was a nearly unbroken solitude. A third of a mile below the dueling-ground there stood a little tavern, the occasional resort of excursionists; where, too, dueling parties not unfrequently breakfasted before proceeding to the ground, and where they sometimes returned to invigorate their restored friendship with the landlord's wine. A short distance above the ground, lived a fine-hearted old Captain, who, if he got scent of a duel, would rush to the place, throw himself between the combatants, and never give over persuading and threatening till he had established a peace or a truce between them. He was the owner of the ground, and spoke with authority. He never ceased to think that, if on this fatal morning, he had observed the approach of the boats, he could have prevented the subsequent catastrophe.

But, for the very purpose of preventing suspicion, it had been arranged that Colonel Burr's boat should arrive some time before the other. About half-past six, Burr and Van Ness landed, and leaving their boat a few yards down the river, ascended over the rocks to the appointed place. It was a warm, bright, July morning. The sun looks down, directly after rising, upon the Weehawken heights, and it was for that reason that the two men removed their coats before the arrival of the other party. There they stood carelessly breaking away the branches of the underwood, and looking out upon as fair, as various, as animated, as beautiful a scene, as mortal eyes in this beautiful world ever behold. The haze-crowned city; the bright, broad, flashing, tranquil river; the long reach of water, twelve miles or more, down to the Narrows; the vessels at anchor in the harbor; misty, blue Staten Island, swelling up in superb contour from the lower bay; the verdant flowery heights around; the opposite shore of the river, then dark with forest, or bright with sloping lawn; and, to complete the picture, that remarkably picturesque promontory called Castle Point, that bends out far into the stream, a mile below Weehawken, and adds a peculiar beauty to the foreground;—all these combine to form a view, one glance at which *ought* to have sent shame and horror to the duelist's heart, that so much as the thought of closing a human being's eyes for ever on so much loveliness, had ever lived a moment in his bosom.

Hamilton's boat was seen to approach. A few minutes before seven it touched the rocks, and Hamilton and his second ascended. The principals and seconds exchanged the usual salutations, and the seconds proceeded immediately to make the usual preparations. They measured ten full paces; then cast lots for the choice of position, and to decide who should give the word. The lot, in both cases, fell to General Hamilton's second, who chose the *upper* end of the ledge for his principal, which, at that hour of the day, could not have been the best, for the reason that the morning sun, and the flashing of the river, would both interfere with the sight. The pistols were then loaded, and the principals placed, Hamilton looking over the river toward the city, and Burr turned toward the heights, under which they stood. As Pendleton gave Hamilton his pistol, he asked,

"Will you have the hair-spring set?"

"*Not this time*," was the quiet reply.

Pendleton then explained to both principals the rules which had been agreed upon with regard to the firing; after the word *present*, they were to fire as soon as they pleased. The seconds then withdrew to the usual distance.

"Are you ready," said Pendleton.

Both answered in the affirmative. A moment's pause ensued. The word was given. Burr raised his pistol, took aim, and fired. Hamilton sprang upon his toes with a convulsive movement, reeled a little toward the heights, at which moment he involuntarily discharged his pistol, and then fell forward headlong upon his face, and remained motionless on the ground. His ball rustled among the branches, seven feet above the head of his antagonist, and four feet wide of him. Burr heard it, looked up, and saw where it had severed a twig. Looking at Hamilton, he beheld him falling, and sprang toward him with an expression of pain upon his face. But at the report of the pistols, Dr. Hosack, Mr. Davis, and the boatman, hurried anxiously up the rocks to the scene of the duel; and Van Ness, with presence of mind, seized Burr, shielded him from observation with an umbrella, and urged him down the steep to the boat. It was pushed off immediately, and rowed swiftly back to Richmond Hill, where Swartwout, with feelings that may be imagined, received his unhurt chief—a chief no more!

Mr. Pendleton raised his prostrate friend. Dr. Hosack found him sitting on the grass, supported in the arms of his second, with the ghastliness of death upon his countenance. "This is a mortal wound, doctor," he gasped; and then sunk away into a swoon. The doctor stripped up his clothes, and saw at a glance that the ball, which had entered his right side, must have penetrated a mortal part. Scarcely expecting him to revive, they conveyed him down among the large rocks, to the shore, placed him tenderly in the boat, and set off for the city. The doctor now used the usual restoratives, and the wounded man gradually revived. "He breathed," to quote the doctor's words; "his eyes, hardly opened, wandered without fixing upon any object; to our great joy, he at length spoke. 'My vision is indistinct,' were his first words. His pulse became more perceptible, his respiration more regular, his sight returned. Soon after recovering his sight, he happened to cast his eye upon the case of pistols, and observing the one that he had had in his hand lying on the outside, he said, 'Take care of that pistol; it is undischarged and still cocked; it may go off and do harm. Pendleton knows' (attempting to turn his head toward him) 'that I did not intend to fire at him.'

"Then he lay tranquil till he saw that the boat was approaching the wharf. He said, 'Let Mrs. Hamilton be immediately sent for; let the event be gradually broke to her, but give her hopes.' Looking up we saw his friend, Mr. Bayard, standing on the wharf in great agitation. He had been told by his servant that General Hamilton, Mr. Pendleton, and myself had crossed the river in a boat together, and too well he conjectured the fatal errand, and foreboded the dreadful result. Perceiving, as we came nearer, that Mr. Pendleton and myself only sat up in the stern sheets, he clasped his hands together in the most violent apprehension; but when I called to him to have a cot prepared, and he at the same moment saw his poor friend lying in the bottom of the boat, he threw up his eyes, and burst into a flood of tears and lamentation. Hamilton alone appeared tranquil and composed. We then conveyed him as tenderly as possible up to the house. The distress of his amiable family was such that, till the first shock had abated, they were scarcely able to summon fortitude enough to yield sufficient assistance to their dying friend."

By nine in the morning the news began to be noised about in the city. A bulletin soon appeared on the board at the Tontine Coffee House, and the pulse of the town stood still at the shocking intelligence. People started and turned pale as they read the brief announcement:

"GENERAL HAMILTON WAS SHOT BY COLONEL BURR THIS MORNING IN A DUEL. THE GENERAL IS SAID TO BE MORTALLY WOUNDED."

Bulletins, hourly changed, kept the city in agitation. All the circumstances of the catastrophe were told, and retold, and exaggerated at every corner. The thrilling scenes that were passing at the bedside of the dying man—the consultations of the physicians—the arrival of the stricken family—Mrs. Hamilton's overwhelming sorrow—the resignation and calm dignity of the illustrious sufferer—his broken slumbers during the night—the piteous spectacle of the *seven* children entering together the awful apartment—the single look the dying father gave them before he closed his eyes— were all described with amplifications, and produced an impression that can only be imagined. He lingered thirty-one hours. The duel was fought on Wednesday morning. At two o'clock, on Thursday afternoon, Hamilton died.

TWENTIETH-CENTURY *Presidents have been acutely aware of history. In the recent past, Harry S Truman, Dwight D. Eisenhower, and Herbert Hoover have composed their memoirs. We have it on the testimony of Arthur Schlesinger, Jr., that John F. Kennedy, if he had lived, intended to do the same. The assassinated Kennedy, however, belongs to that group of three Presidents—Theodore Roosevelt, Woodrow Wilson, and himself—who not only made but also wrote history. Of these historians, Theodore Roosevelt comes closest to revealing the roots of his character in his writings.*

*Theodore Roosevelt (1858-1919) took to the outdoors as a bird takes to*

*the skies. His passion for nature permeated his thinking and shaped pro-
foundly the conservation policies of modern America. Much of the beauty
of primeval America remains forever preserved because of his commitment.
His six-volume* The Winning of the West *is a mass of detail, a reflection of
his conviction that history was a record of consecutive public events, and
a joyous journey into an America that was rapidly disappearing even as he
wrote of it.*

*The Lewis and Clark expedition of which Roosevelt wrote resulted from
the earlier Louisiana Purchase. Then President Thomas Jefferson had seized
the vagrant opportunity to purchase the vast territory from Napoleon. He
had done so though he doubted the constitutionality of the effort. But he
had finally resolved the difficulty with the argument, "The laws of necessity, of self-preservation, of saving our country when in danger, are of a
higher obligation. To lose our country by a scrupulous adherence to written
law, would be to lose the law itself. . . ." It was a sentiment that the ever-
energetic Theodore would have described as "Bully good!" The story he
wove of the West remains a "bully good" narrative.*

# THE WINNING OF
# THE WEST

## by Theodore Roosevelt

The Far West, the West beyond the Mississippi, had been thrust on
Jefferson, and given to the nation, by the rapid growth of the Old West,
the West that lay between the Alleghanies and the Mississippi. The actual
title to the new territory had been acquired by the United States Government, acting for the whole nation. It remained to explore the territory
thus newly added to the national domain. The Government did not yet
know exactly what it had acquired, for the land was not only unmapped but
unexplored. Nobody could tell what were the boundary lines which divided
it from British America on the north and Mexico on the south, for nobody
knew much of the country through which these lines ran; of most of it,
indeed, nobody knew anything. On the new maps the country now showed
as part of the United States; but the Indians who alone inhabited it were
as little affected by the transfer as was the game they hunted.

Even the Northwestern portion of the land definitely ceded to the United
States by Great Britain in Jay's treaty was still left in actual possession of
the Indian tribes, while the few whites who lived among them were traders
owing allegiance to the British Government. The headwaters of the Mississippi and the beautiful country lying round them were known only in a
vague way; and it was necessary to explore and formally take possession of
this land of lakes, glades, and forests.

Beyond the Mississippi all that was really well known was the territory in the immediate neighborhood of the little French villages near the mouth of the Missouri. The creole traders of these villages, and an occasional venturous American, had gone up the Mississippi to the country of the Sioux and the Mandans, where they had trapped and hunted and traded for furs with the Indians. At the northernmost points that they reached they occasionally encountered traders who had traveled south or southwesterly from the wintry regions where the British fur companies reigned supreme. The headwaters of the Missouri were absolutely unknown; nobody had penetrated the great plains, the vast seas of grass through which the Platte, the Little Missouri, and the Yellowstone ran. What lay beyond them, and between them and the Pacific, was not even guessed at. The Rocky Mountains were not known to exist, so far as the territory newly acquired by the United States was concerned, although under the name of "Stonies" their Northern extensions in British America were already down on some maps.

The West had passed beyond its first stage of uncontrolled individualism. Neither exploring nor fighting was thenceforth to be the work only of the individual settlers. The National Government was making its weight felt more and more in the West, because the West was itself becoming more and more an important integral portion of the Union. The work of exploring these new lands fell, not to the wild hunters and trappers, such as those who had first explored Kentucky and Tennessee, but to officers of the United States Army, leading parties of United States soldiers, in pursuance of the command of the Government or of its representatives. The earliest and most important expeditions of Americans into the unknown country which the nation had just purchased were led by young officers of the regular army.

The first of these expeditions was planned by Jefferson himself and authorized by Congress. Nominally its purpose was in part to find out the most advantageous places for the establishment of trading stations with the Indian tribes over which our government had acquired the titular suzerainty; but in reality it was purely a voyage of exploration, planned with intent to ascend the Missouri to its head, and thence to cross the continent to the Pacific. The explorers were carefully instructed to report upon the geography, physical characteristics, and zoology of the region traversed, as well as upon its wild human denizens. Jefferson was fond of science, and in appreciation of the desirability of non-remunerative scientific observation and investigation he stood honorably distinguished among the public men of the day. To him justly belongs the credit of originating this first exploring expedition ever undertaken by the United States Government.

The two officers chosen to carry through the work belonged to families already honorably distinguished for service on the Western border. One was Captain Meriwether Lewis, representatives of whose family had served so prominently in Dunmore's war; the other was Lieutenant (by courtesy Captain) William Clark, a younger brother of George Rogers Clark. Clark had served with credit through Wayne's campaigns, and had taken part in the victory of the Fallen Timbers. Lewis had seen his first service when he enlisted as a private in the forces which were marshaled to put down the whiskey insurrection. Later he served under Clark in Wayne's army. He had also been President Jefferson's private secretary.

The young officers started on their trip accompanied by twenty-seven men who intended to make the whole journey. Of this number one, the interpreter and incidentally the best hunter of the party, was a half-breed; two were French voyageurs; one was a Negro servant of Clark; nine were volunteers from Kentucky, and fourteen were regular soldiers. All, however, except the black slave, were enlisted in the army before starting, so that they might be kept under regular discipline. In addition to these twenty-seven men there were seven soldiers and nine voyageurs who started only to go to the Mandan villages on the Missouri, where the party intended to spend the first winter. They embarked in three large boats, abundantly supplied with arms, powder, and lead, clothing, gifts for the Indians, and provisions.

The starting point was St. Louis, which had only just been surrendered to the United States Government by the Spaniards, without any French intermediaries. The explorers pushed off in May, 1804, and soon began stemming the strong current of the muddy Missouri, to whose unknown sources they intended to ascend. For two or three weeks they occasionally passed farms and hamlets. The most important of the little towns was St. Charles, where the people were all creoles; the explorers in their journal commented upon the good temper and vivacity of these *habitants*, but dwelt on the shiftlessness they displayed and their readiness to sink back toward savagery, although they were brave and hardy enough. The next most considerable town was peopled mainly by Americans, who had already begun to make numerous settlements in the new land. The last squalid little village they passed claimed as one of its occasional residents old Daniel Boone himself.

After leaving the final straggling log cabins of the settled country, the explorers, with sails and paddles, made their way through what is now the State of Missouri. They lived well, for their hunters killed many deer and wild turkey and some black bear and beaver, and there was an abundance of breeding water fowl. Here and there were Indian encampments, but not many, for the tribes had gone westward to the great plains of what is now Kansas to hunt the buffalo. Already buffalo and elk were scarce in Missouri, and the party did not begin to find them in any numbers until they reached the neighborhood of what is now southern Nebraska.

From there onward the game was found in vast herds and the party began to come upon those characteristic animals of the Great Plains which were as yet unknown to white men of our race. The buffalo and the elk had once ranged eastward to the Alleghanies and were familiar to early wanderers through the wooded wilderness; but in no part of the East had their numbers ever remotely approached the astounding multitudes in which they were found on the Great Plains. The curious prong-buck or prong-horned antelope was unknown east of the Great Plains; so was the blacktail, or mule deer, which our adventurers began to find here and there as they gradually worked their way northwestward; so were the coyotes, whose uncanny wailing after nightfall varied the sinister baying of the gray wolves;

so were many of the smaller animals, notably the prairie dogs, whose populous villages awakened the lively curiosity of Lewis and Clark.

In their note-books the two captains faithfully described all these new animals and all the strange sights they saw. They were men with no pretensions to scientific learning, but they were singularly close and accurate observers and truthful narrators. Very rarely have any similar explorers described so faithfully not only the physical features but the animals and plants of a newly discovered land. Their narrative was not published until some years later, and then it was badly edited, notably the purely scientific portion; yet it remains the best example of what such a narrative should be. Few explorers who did and saw so much that was absolutely new have written of their deeds with such quiet absence of boastfulness, and have drawn their descriptions with such complete freedom from exaggeration.

Moreover, what was of even greater importance, the two young captains possessed in perfection the qualities necessary to pilot such an expedition through unknown lands and among savage tribes. They kept good discipline among the men; they never hesitated to punish severely any wrong-doer; but they were never over-severe; and as they did their full part of the work, and ran all the risks and suffered all the hardship exactly like the other members of the expedition, they were regarded by their followers with devoted affection, and were served with loyalty and cheerfulness. In dealing with the Indians they showed good humor and common-sense mingled with ceaseless vigilance and unbending resolution. Only men who possessed their tact and daring could have piloted the party safely among the warlike tribes they encountered. Any act of weakness or timidity on the one hand, or of harshness or cruelty on the other, would have been fatal to the expedition; but they were careful to treat the tribes well and to try to secure their good-will, while at the same time putting an immediate stop to any insolence or outrage. Several times they were in much jeopardy when they reached the land of the Dakotas and passed among the various ferocious tribes whom they knew, and whom we yet know, as the Sioux. The French traders frequently came up river to the country of the Sioux, who often mal-treated and robbed them. In consequence Lewis and Clark found that the Sioux were inclined to regard the whites as people whom they could safely oppress. The resolute bearing of the newcomers soon taught them that they were in error, and after a little hesitation the various tribes in each case became friendly.

With all the Indian tribes the two explorers held councils, and distributed presents, especially medals, among the head chiefs and warriors, informing them of the transfer of the territory from Spain to the United States and warning them that henceforth they must look to the President as their protector, and not to the King, whether of England or of Spain. The Indians all professed much satisfaction at the change, which of course they did not in the least understand, and for which they cared nothing. This easy acquiescence gave much groundless satisfaction to Lewis and Clark, who further, in a spirit of philanthropy, strove to make each tribe swear peace with its neighbors. After some hesitation the tribe usually consented to this also, and the explorers, greatly gratified, passed on. It is needless to say that as soon as they had disappeared the tribes promptly went to war again, and that in reality the Indians had only the vaguest idea as to what was meant by the ceremonies, and the hoisting of the American flag. The wonder is that Clark, who had already had some experience with Indians, should have supposed that the councils, advice, and proclamations would have any effect of the kind hoped for upon these wild savages. However, together with the love of natural science inculcated by the fashionable philosophy of the day, they also possessed the much less admirable, though entirely amiable, theory of universal unintelligent philanthropy which was embodied in this philosophy. A very curious feature of our dealings with the Indians, not only in the days of Lewis and Clark, but since, has been the combination of extreme and indeed foolish benevolence of purpose on the part of the Government, with, on the part of the settlers, a brutality of action which this benevolent purpose could in no wise check or restrain.

As the fall weather grew cold the party reached the Mandan village, where they halted and went into camp for the winter, building huts and a stout stockade, which they christened Fort Mandan. Traders from St. Louis and also British traders from the North reached these villages, and the inhabitants were accustomed to dealing with the whites. Throughout the winter the party was well treated by the Indians, and kept in good health and spirits; the journals frequently mention the fondness the men showed for dancing, although without partners of the opposite sex. Yet they suffered much from the extreme cold, and at times from hunger, for it was hard to hunt in the winter weather, and the game was thin and poor. Generally game could be killed in a day's hunt from the fort; but occasionally small parties of hunters went off for a trip of several days, and returned laden with meat; in one case they killed thirty-two deer, eleven elk, and a buffalo; in another forty deer, sixteen elk, and three buffalo; thirty-six deer and fourteen elk, etc. The buffalo remaining in the neighborhood during the winter were mostly old bulls, too lean to eat; and as the snows came on most of the antelope left for the rugged country further west, swimming the Missouri in great bands. Before the bitter weather began the explorers were much interested by the methods of the Indians in hunting, especially when they surrounded and slaughtered bands of buffalo on horseback; and by the curious pens, with huge V-shaped wings, into which they drove antelope.

In the spring of 1805 Lewis and Clark again started westward, first sending downstream ten of their companions, to carry home the notes of their trip so far, and a few valuable specimens. The party that started westward numbered thirty-two adults, all told; for one sergeant had died, and two or three persons had volunteered at the Mandan villages, including a rather worthless French "squaw-man," with an intelligent Indian wife, whose baby was but a few weeks old.

From this point onward, when they began to travel west instead of north, the explorers were in a country where no white man had ever trod. It was not the first time the continent had been crossed. The Spaniards had crossed and recrossed it, for two centuries, further south. In British America

Mackenzie had already penetrated to the Pacific, while Hearne had made a far more noteworthy and difficult trip than Mackenzie, when he wandered over the terrible desolation of the Barren Grounds, which lie under the Arctic Circle. But no man had ever crossed or explored that part of the continent which the United States had just acquired; a part far better fitted to be the home of our stock than the regions to the north or south. It was the explorations of Lewis and Clark, and not those of Mackenzie on the north or of the Spaniards in the south which were to bear fruit, because they pointed the way to the tens of thousands of settlers who were to come after them, and who were to build thriving commonwealths in the lonely wilderness which they had traversed.

From the Little Missouri on to the head of the Missouri proper the explorers passed through a region where they saw few traces of Indians. It literally swarmed with game, for it was one of the finest hunting grounds in all the world. There were great numbers of sage fowl, sharp-tailed prairie fowl, and ducks of all kinds; and swans, and tall white cranes; and geese, which nested in the tops of the cottonwood trees. But the hunters paid no heed to birds, when surrounded by such teeming myriads of big game. Buffalo, elk, and antelope, whitetail and blacktail deer, and bighorn sheep swarmed in extraordinary abundance throughout the lands watered by the upper Missouri and the Yellowstone; in their journals the explorers dwell continually on the innumerable herds they encountered while on these plains, both when traveling upstream and again the following year when they were returning. The antelopes were sometimes quite shy; so were the bighorn, though on occasions both kinds seemed to lose their wariness, and in one instance the journal specifies the fact that, at the mouth of the Yellowstone, the deer were somewhat shy, while the antelope, like the elk and buffalo, paid no heed to the men whatever. Ordinarily all the kinds of game were very tame. Sometimes one of the many herds of elk that lay boldly, even at midday, on the sand-bars or on the brush-covered points, would wait until the explorers were within twenty yards of them before starting. The buffalo would scarcely move out of the path at all, and the bulls sometimes, even when unmolested, threatened to assail the hunters. Once, on the return voyage, when Clark was descending the Yellowstone River, a vast herd of buffalo, swimming and wading, plowed its way across the stream where it was a mile broad, in a column so thick that the explorers had to draw up on shore and wait for an hour, until it passed by, before continuing their journey. Two or three times the expedition was thus brought to a halt; and as the buffalo were so plentiful, and so easy to kill, and as their flesh was very good, they were the mainstay for the explorers' table. Both going and returning this wonderful hunting country was a place of plenty. The party of course lived almost exclusively on meat, and they needed much; for, when they could get it, they consumed either a buffalo, or an elk and a deer, or four deer, every day.

There was one kind of game which they at times found altogether too familiar. This was the grisly bear, which they were the first white men to discover. They called it indifferently the grisly, gray, brown, and even white bear, to distinguish it from its smaller, glossy, black-coated brother with which they were familiar in the Eastern woods. They found that the Indians greatly feared these bears, and after their first encounters they themselves treated them with much respect. The grisly was then the burly lord of the Western prairie, dreaded by all other game, and usually shunned even by the Indians. In consequence it was very bold and savage. Again and again these huge bears attacked the explorers of their own accord, when neither molested nor threatened. They galloped after the hunters when they met them on horseback even in the open; and they attacked them just as freely when they found them on foot. To go through the brush was dangerous; again and again one or another of the party was charged and forced to take to a tree, at the foot of which the bear sometimes mounted guard for hours before going off. When wounded the beasts fought with desperate courage, and showed astonishing tenacity of life, charging any number of assailants, and succumbing but slowly even to mortal wounds. In one case a bear that was on shore actually plunged into the water and swam out to attack one of the canoes as it passed. However, by this time all of the party had become good hunters, expert in the use of their rifles, and they killed great numbers of their ursine foes.

Nor were the bears their only brute enemies. The rattlesnakes were often troublesome. Unlike the bears, the wolves were generally timid, and preyed only on the swarming game; but one night a wolf crept into camp and seized a sleeper by the hand; when driven off he jumped upon another man, and was shot by a third. A less intentional assault was committed by a buffalo bull which one night blundered past the fires, narrowly escaped trampling on the sleepers, and had the whole camp in an uproar before it rushed off into the darkness. When hunted the buffalo occasionally charged; but there was not much danger in their chase.

All these larger foes paled into insignificance compared with the mosquitoes. There are very few places on earth where these pests are so formidable as in the bottom lands of the Missouri, and for weeks and even months they made the lives of our explorers a torture. No other danger, whether from hunger or cold, Indians or wild beasts, was so dreaded by the explorers as these tiny scourges.

In the plains country the life of the explorers was very pleasant save only for the mosquitoes and the incessant clouds of driving sand along the river bottoms. On their journey west through these true happy hunting grounds they did not meet with any Indians, and their encounters with the bears were only just sufficiently dangerous to add excitement to their life. Once or twice they were in peril from cloudbursts, and they were lamed by the cactus spines on the prairie, and by the stones and sand of the river bed while dragging the boats against the current; but all these trials, labors, and risks were only enough to give zest to their exploration of the unknown land. At the Great Falls of the Missouri they halted, and were enraptured with their beauty and majesty; and here, as everywhere, they found the game so abundant that they lived in plenty. As they journeyed upstream through the bright summer weather, though they worked hard, it was work of a kind which was but a long holiday. At nightfall they camped by the boats on the river bank. Each day some of the party spent in hunting, either along the river bottoms through the groves of cottonwoods with shimmering, rustling leaves, or away from the river where the sunny prairie stretched into seas of brown grass, or where groups or rugged hills stood, fantastic in color and outline, and with stunted pines growing on the sides of their steep ravines. The only real suffering was that which occasionally befell some one who got lost, and was out for days at a time, until he exhausted all his powder and lead before finding the party.

Fall had nearly come when they reached the headwaters of the Missouri. The end of the holiday time was at hand, for they had before them the labor of crossing the great mountains so as to strike the headwaters of the Columbia. Their success at this point depended somewhat upon the Indian wife of the Frenchman who had joined them at Mandan. She had been captured from one of the Rocky Mountain tribes, and they relied on her as interpreter. Partly through her aid, and partly by their own exertions, they were able to find, and make friends with, a band of wandering Shoshones, from whom they got horses. Having cached their boats and most of their goods they started westward through the forest-clad passes of the Rockies; before this they had wandered and explored in several directions through the mountains and the foothills. The open country had been left behind, and with it the time of plenty. In the mountain forests the game was far less abundant than on the plains and far harder to kill; though on the tops of the high peaks there was one new game animal, the white antelope-goat, which they did not see, though the Indians brought them hides. The work was hard, and the party suffered much from toil and hunger, living largely on their horses, before they struck one of the tributaries of the Snake sufficiently low down to enable them once more to go by boat.

They now met many Indians of various tribes, all of them very different from the Indians of the Western Plains. At this time the Indians, both east and west of the Rockies, already owned numbers of horses. Although they had a few guns, they relied mainly on the spears and tomahawks, and bows and arrows with which they had warred and hunted from time immemorial; for only the tribes on the outer edges had come in contact with the whites, whether with occasional French and English traders who brought them goods, or with the mixed bloods of the Northern Spanish settlements, upon which they raided. Around the mouth of the Columbia, however, the Indians knew a good deal about the whites; the river had been discovered by Captain Gray of Boston thirteen years before, and ships came there continually, while some of the Indian tribes were occasionally visited by traders from the British fur companies.

With one or two of these tribes the explorers had some difficulty, and owed their safety to their unceasing vigilance, and to the prompt decision with which they gave the Indians to understand that they would tolerate no bad treatment, while yet themselves refraining carefully from committing any wrong. By most of the tribes they were well received, and obtained from them not only information of the route, but also a welcome supply of food. At first they rather shrank from eating the dogs which formed the favorite dish of the Indians; but after a while they grew quite reconciled to dog's flesh; and in their journals noted that they preferred it to lean elk and deer meat, and were much more healthy while eating it.

They reached the rain-shrouded forests of the coast before cold weather set in, and there they passed the winter, suffering somewhat from the weather, and now and then from hunger, though the hunters generally killed plenty of elk, and deer of a new kind, the blacktail of the Columbia.

In March, 1806, they started eastward to retrace their steps. At first they did not live well, for it was before the time when the salmon came upstream, and game was not common. When they reached the snow-covered mountains there came another period of toil and starvation, and they were glad indeed when they emerged once more on the happy hunting-grounds of the Great Plains. They found their caches undisturbed. Early in July they separated for a time, Clark descending the Yellowstone and Lewis the Missouri, until they met at the junction of the two rivers. The party which went down the Yellowstone at one time split into two, Clark taking command of one division, and a sergeant of the other; they built their own canoes, some of them made out of hollowed trees, while the others were bull boats, made of buffalo hides stretched on a frame. As before they reveled in the abundance of the game. They marveled at the incredible numbers of the buffalo, whose incessant bellowing at this season filled the air with one continuous roar, which terrified their horses; they were astonished at the abundance and tameness of the elk; they fought their old enemies the grisly bears, and they saw and noted many strange and wonderful beasts and birds.

To Lewis there befell other adventures. Once, while he was out with three men, a party of eight Blackfeet warriors joined them and suddenly made a treacherous attack upon them and strove to carry off their guns and horses. But the wilderness veterans sprang to arms with a readiness that had become second nature. One of them killed an Indian with a knife thrust; Lewis himself shot another Indian, and the remaining six fled, carrying with them one of Lewis' horses, but losing four of their own, which the whites captured. This was the beginning of the long series of bloody skirmishes between the Blackfeet and the Rocky Mountain explorers and trappers. Clark at about the same time suffered at the hands of the Crows, who stole a number of his horses.

None of the party was hurt by the Indians, but some time after the skirmish with the Blackfeet Lewis was accidentally shot by one of the Frenchmen of the party and suffered much from the wound. Near the mouth of the Yellowstone Clark joined him, and the reunited company floated down the Missouri. Before they reached the Mandan villages they encountered two white men, the first strangers of their own color the party had seen for a year and a half. These were two American hunters named Dickson and Hancock, who were going up to trap the headwaters of the Missouri on their own account. They had come from the Illinois country a year before, to hunt and trap; they had been plundered, and one of them wounded in an encounter with the fierce Sioux, but were undauntedly pushing forward into the unknown wilderness toward the mountains.

These two hardy and daring adventurers formed the little vanguard of the bands of hunters and trappers, the famous Rocky Mountain men, who were to roam hither and thither across the great West in lawless freedom for the next three-quarters of a century. They accompanied the party back to the Mandan village; there one of the soldiers joined them, a man named Colter, so fascinated by the life of the wilderness that he was not willing to leave it, even for a moment's glimpse of the civilization from which he had been so long exiled. The three turned their canoe upstream, while Lewis and Clark and the rest of the party drifted down past the Sioux.

The further voyage of the explorers was uneventful. They had difficulties with the Sioux of course, but they held them at bay. They killed game in abundance, and went down-stream as fast as sails, oars, and current could carry them. In September, they reached St. Louis and forwarded to Jefferson an account of what they had done.

They had done a great deed, for they had opened the door into the heart of the far West. Close on their tracks followed the hunters, trappers, and fur traders who themselves made ready the way for the settlers whose descendants were to possess the land. As for the two leaders of the explorers, Lewis was made Governor of Louisiana Territory, and a couple of years afterward died, as was supposed, by his own hand, in a squalid log cabin on the Chickasaw trace—though it was never certain that he had not been murdered. Clark was afterward Governor of the Territory, when its name had been changed to Missouri, and he also served honorably as Indian agent. But neither of them did anything further of note; nor indeed was it necessary, for they had performed a feat which will always give them a place on the honor roll of American worthies.

꧁ ꧂

JEFFERSON *wrote in 1816 with obvious dismay, "We have experienced what we did not then believe, that there exists both profligacy and power enough to exclude us from the field of interchange with other nations." Then referred to the early days of independence, and the power to exclude to the long, bitter struggle between Great Britain and France that erupted in 1793 and closed with Napoleon's final defeat at Waterloo in 1815. The United States learned during those long years that the plight of the weak neutral in wartime is often a sad one. Without the military power to compel respect for its rights, it had to submit to search, seizure and impressment of its ships and seamen. The Jeffersonians committed to maintenance of peace struggled, as it turned out unsuccessfully, to keep the country at peace.*

*Denunciations of increasing British infringements on American maritime rights led in February of 1806 to a senatorial resolution denouncing these infringements as "an unprovoked aggression." The London government refused to heed the protests and in April Congress retaliated with the Non-Importation Act which placed extensive restrictions on British imports. Jefferson hoped to use it as an instrument of retaliation sufficiently strong to persuade the British to make concessions. The effort failed. As the war in Europe escalated, Britain and France, locked in a death struggle, struggled to impose blockades on one another which would undermine the other's power. By 1807, as both sides seized American ships with blithe abandon, Americans found it difficult to decide whether France or Britain was their more dangerous foe.*

*The British, masters of the sea, offended American pride more sharply than the French. They chose to sit outside American harbors in full view of the shore and exact their toll. When on June 22, 1807, the British frigate* Leopard *attacked the American warship* Chesapeake *to remove from its crew suspected British deserters, national pride welled up. The country stood on the brink of war, but Jefferson resorted instead to an embargo, hoping with it to coerce the British into respecting our rights. He succeeded only in ruining American commerce and creating sharp sectional grievances. As his final presidential act, Jefferson signed the repeal of the Embargo and into law the less burdensome Non-Intercourse Act which proved a feeble instrument for compelling respect for the advancement of American maritime rights. Even in London supporters of a less aggressive policy toward America had to concede with the liberal William Cobbett: "No triumph can be more complete than that of the [government] ministers."*

*The British added insult to injury. When their minister to Washington, David M. Erskine, assured Madison that London intended to modify its trade policies, the recently inaugurated President lifted the act's restrictions against British trade. George Canning, the British foreign secretary, promptly repudiated his minister, leaving Madison no choice but to resume Non-Intercourse with Britain. Americans, already aware that French depredations on American commerce exceeded those of Britain, were in a quandary, all the more exasperating since the Madison administration seemed wedded to a policy of aimless drift. But behind the drift was the government's knowledge that the only step left was war, a step that the policy of the previous ten years had struggled to forestall.*

*Since the termination of trade had not deterred either the British or French, Congress allowed the Non-Intercourse Act to lapse in 1810 and passed in its place the Macon's Bill No. 2. It offered to reopen trade with either Britain or France if one or the other agreed to cease its attacks upon American commerce before March 3, 1811. To increase the lure of the offer, Congress authorized the President to reinstitute Non-Intercourse with the power that continued its depredations. Some congressmen denounced the policy as holding up "the honor and character of this nation to the highest bidder." The French saw in it an opportunity to practice a piece of duplicity; they allowed the Americans to think they had revoked their Berlin and Milan decrees. Madison responded by restoring Non-Intercourse with Britain, only to learn subsequently that the supposed cancel-*

*lation of the decrees had been conditional on Madison terminating trade with Britain. The author of the Constitution had been thoroughly out-maneuvered by the French, and the British reacted with a blockade of New York and renewed the impressment of American seamen.*

*As American international relations worsened, the elections for the 12th Congress revealed renewed popular support for the Republicans as they increased their majority. The turnover as compared to previous Congresses was not particularly large. But a handful of energetically aggressive Republicans, whom John Randolph dubbed the "War Hawks," wore their nationalism on their sleeve, and obtained positions of power. Henry Clay gained the House Speakership; John C. Calhoun, Felix Grundy, and Peter B. Porter dominated the Foreign Relations Committee; and Langdon Cheves ruled the Naval Committee. Since most of these men came either from the New West or the older frontier areas, historians have tended to follow the lead of Julius W. Pratt, The Expansionists of 1812 (1925), to emphasize western land hunger for Florida and Canada as the dominant cause of the War of 1812. It is an interpretation further strengthened by the strong vote cast against the war by representatives from New England, New York, New Jersey, and Delaware. Their vote does not uphold Madison's stated reason for the war, the violations by Britain of American maritime rights.*

*Recent historians, among them Bradford Perkins (1925-    ) and Norman Rijsord (1931-    ) have reexamined the Pratt thesis. They have shifted to the older conclusion that national honor and self-regard explains the American decision for war. The words of numerous contemporary Americans support their position. John Quincy Adams, no mean expansionist himself, contended, "The principle for which we are now struggling . . . is the principle of personal liberty, and of every social right." More pointedly, John C. Calhoun declared, "This is the second struggle for our liberty." The opposition to war in the commercial regions of the country is well explained by remembering that patriotism exacts a price and that, in their case, a challenge to Britain enabled them to estimate quickly the cost of war. John Bach McMaster (1852-1932) emphasized national honor as central to the coming of the War of 1812. Though a gifted narrative historian, Mc-Master never informed his work with either a consistent theme or a coherent interpretation. The individual parts of his work still retain considerable value, but the whole is often reduced to pointlessness, a circumstance which is further aggravated by his habit of intruding extraneous matter into the easy flow of his presentation.*

# A HISTORY OF THE PEOPLE
# OF THE UNITED STATES
# FROM THE REVOLUTION TO THE CIVIL WAR

## by John Bach McMaster

Henry Clay was born, his campaign biographies, some of which passed under his own eye, assure us, on April twelfth, 1777, in Hanover County, Virginia. His father, John Clay, was a Baptist preacher who administered to the spiritual wants of the poor whites on the South Anna river in a region known as "the Slashes." In 1781 the good man died, leaving Henry, in the language of his campaign biographers, with poverty for his only inheritance and Providence for his only guide. But this is unjust to his mother. She indeed was a guide, and sent him regularly to the little log-cabin where the traditional wandering schoolmaster taught him to read, write, add, and spell. When not in school, his time was spent laboring on the patch of land which cannot be called a farm. Long afterward, when the country was ringing with his fame, when it became fashionable for men who had never distinguished him from hundreds of other boys to ransack their memories for anecdotes, one was told which is still repeated. In this he is represented as a hard-working lad dressed in a coarse cotton shirt and Osnaburg trousers, without hat and without shoes, straddling a bag of grain or corn thrown over the back of a horse which he guides with a rope to Daricott's mill on the Pamunkey. The story is quite probable, and his admirers, taking it up, won for him thousands on thousands of votes by dubbing him the "mill-boy of the Slashes."

At fourteen, his mother having married again, his step-father placed Henry in a small retail store kept by one Richard Denny near the market place in Richmond. There he remained till, a year later, his step-father secured for him a yet better place in the office of Peter Tinsley, Clerk of the High Court of Chancery. To the senior clerk in the office fell the duty many years after of describing the appearance of the lank, awkward, rawboned boy as he came to take his seat at the office desk, bearing all over him, in the arrangement of his hair, in the cut of his home-made clothes, in the uncommon stiffness of his shirt, the marks of the pride and undying love of his mother. Hardly was he settled in his new place when his step-father caught the rage for Western emigration, and the whole family moved into Kentucky, leaving the lad of fifteen to make his way as best he could at Richmond. Fortunately, he attracted the attention of George Wythe, the Chancellor, and was selected by him to write out and record the decisions of the Court of Chancery. During the four years he was so employed the Chancellor took a fatherly interest in his welfare, shaped his manners, formed his mind, prescribed his reading, and probably suggested that he should study law. Scanty knowledge was then required for admission to the bar, and after a twelvemonth in the office of the Attorney-General, Clay received his license and started west to begin practice at Lexington, Kentucky. He was still some months under age, and had, as yet, no higher ambition than to make each year one hundred pounds Virginia money. This wild hope was quickly realized. Prosperity attended him from the very start. His genial qualities won him friends. His friends brought him law-cases. His oratorical powers made him successful with juries, and his success with juries spread his fame over the whole State. Before he had been two years in Lexington his friends, his clients, and his local fame sufficed to send him to the State Constitution Convention of 1799. In 1803 he entered the Legislature. In 1806 he went to the Senate of the United States to fill the unexpired term of John Adair, the friend and confederate of Aaron Burr. There he rose at once into notice as a fine speaker, a ready debater, a strong friend to internal improvements, and was thought not undeserving of repeated mention in the diaries of John Quincy Adams and William Plumer. On the expiration of his term in 1807 he was again returned to the Kentucky Legislature, was made Speaker of the Assembly, once more distinguished himself as the steady advocate of internal improvements and American manufactures, and in 1809 went back to the United States Senate to fill the unexpired term of Buckner Thurston. To the roles he had played in his previous term a new one was now added. He was still the champion of better roads, better canals, better means of communication at Government expense. His voice was still raised, his vote was still cast, in behalf of every effort to encourage domestic manufactures. But he was, more than all, the mouth-piece of young America. In almost every speech of any length made by him during the sessions of the eleventh Congress the spirit which animated the young Republicans is easily discernible. In his speech on the occupation of West Florida it is expressed most fully.

A senator from Delaware had said that he feared that the occupation of West Florida would lead England as the ally of Spain to make war on us. The threat set Clay on fire, and at the close of a long reply he burst forth: "Sir, is the time never to arrive when we may manage our affairs without the fear of insulting his Britannic Majesty? Is the rod of British power to be forever suspended over our heads? Does Congress put on an embargo to shelter our rightful commerce against the piratical depredations committed upon it on the ocean: We are immediately warned of the indignation of offended England. Is a law of non-intercourse proposed: The whole navy of the haughty mistress of the sea is made to thunder in our ears. Does the President refuse to continue a correspondence with a minister who violates the decorum belonging to his diplomatic character by giving and deliberately repeating an affront to the whole nation: We are instantly menaced with the chastisement which English pride will not fail to inflict. Whether we assert our rights by sea or attempt their maintenance by land—whithersoever we turn ourselves this phantom incessantly pursues us. Already has it had too much influence on the councils of the nation. It contributed to the repeal of the embargo—that dishonorable repeal which has so much tarnished the character of our Government. Mr. President, I have said on this floor, and now take occasion again to remark, that I most sincerely desire peace and amity with England; that I even prefer an adjustment of all differences with her before one with any other nation. But if she persists in a denial of justice to us, or if she avails herself of the occupation of West Florida to commence war upon us, I trust and hope that all hearts will unite in a bold and vigorous vindication of our rights."

That Great Britain did persist in denying us justice was the firm belief of every Republican the land over. And when the people of the Lexington district sent Clay to the twelfth House of Representatives, and his associates in that House chose him Speaker, they did so because they were determined to have in the future a bold and vigorous vindication of our rights. From the moment he took his seat in the Speaker's chair a new era opens in our history. At last the Republicans had found, what had long been wanted, a leader; a man of the people, young, eloquent, intensely American. Hesitation, doubt, timidity, fear of England, now gave way to a bold and well-defined policy of peace or war. Peace if Great Britain did us justice; war if she did not.

When the President's Message had been read, it became necessary to appoint the select committees to whom the important paragraphs were to be referred. As Speaker, the appointment rested with Clay, who chose the members with strict regard to the new policy, and in two weeks' time listened to a report from one of them, every line of which was warlike. It came from the Select Committee of Foreign Relations. We will not, said they, encumber your Journal nor waste your patience with a history of the wrongs, the injuries, the aggressions known and felt by every one. The cold recital of them would deaden the national sensibility and make callous the public mind. The committee then passed in review the decrees of Berlin and Milan, the Embargo, the Non-intercourse and Non-importation Laws, the Erskine Agreement, the perfidious conduct of England since the repeal of the decrees by France, and the shameful indifference with which the impressment of our sailors had been treated. To wrongs so daring in character, the committee then continued, and so disgraceful in their execution, the people of the United States can no longer be indifferent. We must tamely submit or boldly resist. The time has now come when the national character, so long traduced by enemies at home and by enemies abroad, must be vindicated. If we have not rushed to arms like nations driven by the mad ambition of a single chief, like nations led by the avarice of a corrupted court, it has not been because we fear war, but because we love justice and humanity. The proud spirit of liberty and independence which sustained our fathers is not dead! The patriotic fire of the Revolution still burns and will yet lead the people to those high destinies which are not less the reward of dignified moderation than of exalted valor. But patience has now ceased to be a virtue. The day has come when, in the opinion of your committee, it is the duty of Congress to call out the resources and rouse the patriotism of the people. Then, with the blessing of God, we shall secure that redress hitherto denied to our remonstrances, our forbearance, our just demands. To this end the committee offered six resolutions. The six were: that the ranks of the regular army be filled up; that an additional force of ten thousand regulars be raised to serve for three years; that the services of fifty thousand volunteers be accepted; that the President order out from time to time such detachments of the militia as the public service may require; that all ships of the navy fit for sea be instantly put in commission; and that merchantmen be suffered to arm.

As soon as these resolutions were taken up in the Committee of the Whole, Peter Buell Porter rose to explain them. The Committee on Foreign Relations, said he, have no hope of a peaceful settlement of our differences with Great Britain. Her conduct toward us is not regulated by her sense of justice, but by the extent of our submission. For six years past she has been gradually and progressively encroaching on our rights. We have seen her one year advancing doctrines which the year before she denounced. We have seen her one day seizing our ships under pretexts which the day before she was ashamed or afraid to avow. Indeed, she has been steadily and carefully feeling our pulse that she might know what potions to administer, until, if we go on submitting, British subjects will soon be engaged, not only in taking our ships in the waters of our harbors, but in trampling on our citizens in the streets of our cities. Looking at the matter from this stand-point, the committee are strongly in favor of war. We cannot, indeed, cope with England's navy. She is mistress of the sea. But there were two ways in which we can greatly injure her. We can cover the ocean with privateers, we can destroy her fisheries to the north, harass her West India commerce as it passed our doors, annoy her trade along the coast of South America, and plunder her ships at the very entrances to her own ports. We can take from her Canada and the rich province to the eastward. Let such a warfare be begun—a war on land at the public cost, a war on sea at private cost—and we shall in a little while remunerate ourselves tenfold for six years of spoliation of our commerce. This is the kind of warfare contemplated in the resolutions. I entreat you, therefore, do not vote for the resolutions unless you will fight. Do not raise armies unless you are ready to use them. Those who heard him were ready to fight, and in a few hours the six resolutions were approved by the Committee of the Whole, reported, and the first passed by the House.

The second resolution called for an additional force of ten thousand regulars for three years, and provoked a debate on the evils and dangers of a standing army. Randolph began it. He declared that the resolution contained an unconstitutional proposition, because no money could be voted for a standing army for more than two years, and that such an army was unnecessary, because seven million free Americans had no idea of intrusting their defence to ten thousand mercenaries picked up at brothels and tippling-houses. He would like to know, moreover, what use it was proposed to make of the soldiers. Let the President say they were necessary to protect New Orleans, that they were needed to fight the Indians, that they were wanted to repel invasion from Canada, and he would vote for them. But he well remembered the reign of terror in 1798, and was as much in dread of a standing army now as he had been then. So far as the House was concerned, there was no necessity for answering Randolph. The majority for the resolution was eager in spirit and overwhelming in number. But the war party wished to be fair. They knew, moreover, that in answering Randolph they were speaking not to him and his few followers, but to all their countrymen, to England, to France, and to the whole world. The debate, if it may be so called, which thus sprang up and occupied the time of the House during six days, is interesting for many reasons. Twenty members spoke, yet but two—John Randolph and Richard Stanford—had a word to say against the resolution. The majority took their ground carefully, and stated their position over and over again. There had not, in their opinion, been an hour since 1806 when the United States would not have been fully justified in making war on England. But the prudence, the humanity, the patience, and long-suffering which had ever marked her dealings with foreign nations had prevailed. Congress and the President had tried every peaceful expedient known to man rather than attack England when she was stretching every nerve in her struggle with Napoleon. She, however, had attributed to fear what was due to humanity. Every offer had been rejected; every concession had been followed by a new indignity till from very shame the United States must strike back. This was the will of the people clearly expressed at the polls. No Congress had gone further in concessions than the eleventh, yet how many members of the eleventh had seats in the twelfth? Hardly one half. And what was the feeling of those chosen by the people to take the seats of the sixty-one men rejected? Was it to go on negotiating, go on submitting, go on indifferent to the cries of six thousand American sailors impressed into English service? No! The sentiment of these new members was for war. Let it be clearly understood, then, exclaimed one of the speakers, that these resolutions mean war, and in this lies the difference between the army which Republicans condemned in 1798 and the army Republicans are to raise in 1812. The old army was not for use; the new army is for use. The old army was to extend executive patronage; the new army is to take the Canadas. To contend with the navy of Great Britain is impossible. Happily, it is not necessary. Such is her condition that she can send but a few ships to attack us, and these we can drive from our coast with the frigates we have and a few that we can build. Our war will be chiefly on land. Before determining the force needed for such a war the committee consulted the Secretary of War, and, in accordance with his wishes, which are undoubtedly the wishes of the President, framed the resolution under debate. The result of a war cannot but be beneficial. The loss of the Canadas will end British power, influence, and intrigue in America. Then will the Indians cease the massacre of women and children. Then will the Canadian trade be secured, and the political equilibrium of the republic be made secure. When the vast plains of Louisiana shall be populated the Northern States will lose their power; they will be at the mercy of others. It is wise, therefore, to add the Canadas to the North at the same time that we add the Floridas and Louisiana to the South.

The people, said Randolph, will never submit to be taxed for such a war.

The Government of the United States was framed to provide for the common defence and general welfare. Whoever, therefore, plunges it into an offensive foreign war subjects the Constitution to a strain it will not bear. To the men of Tennessee, of Genesee, of Lake Champlain, a war may be of advantage. Their hemp will bring better prices; they will furnish the troops with supplies and grow rich. But, mark my word for it, the planters of Virginia will not be taxed to support a war in which they have not the slightest interest and which cannot but add to their present distress. His speeches were long and rambling, abounded in denunciation of England, of France, of John Adams, of General Wilkinson, of the administration, of the plan to take the Canadas, and of the call for a standing army. Such remarks carried no weight, and when the yeas and nays were taken, but twenty-one members voted with him. This was the highest number reached by the minority on any resolution in the series. Sixteen votes came from New England; four came from Virginia; North Carolina furnished two. All the resolutions having passed by handsome majorities, bills in accordance with them were ordered.

While the committee was at work on their tasks, a bill providing for an additional military force came down from the Senate. The author was William B. Giles, of Virginia, and his purpose was not to aid but embarrass the administration. Madison and the committee had asked for ten thousand men for three years, not because they believed that force sufficient to take Canada, but because they believed that the troops, if raised at all, should be raised at once, and because it was not likely that the recruiting officers could in one year find more than ten thousand men who would enlist for three years of service. Giles proposed to call for twenty-five thousand regulars, enlist them for five years, divide them into regiments of two thousand each, and, whether the ranks were filled or not, commission and keep in pay the entire staff of officers. His purpose was apparent; nay, he was told to his face that his aim was to drain the Treasury, embarrass the fiscal concerns, and paralyze the best-arranged measures of Government. Yet he persisted, and, by the help of every Federalist senator present, carried through the bill.

On reaching the House, it went at once to the Committee on Foreign Relations. That Madison was then consulted is quite likely, for, when it was reported, the number of troops was cut down from twenty-five to fifteen thousand. On this compromise every war Republican fell with vigor. Their views, however, were best stated by Henry Clay, who, as the House was in Committee of the Whole was out of the Speaker's chair, and seized the opportunity to attack the amendment.

It is admitted, he said, that the troops are to be raised for war purposes. It is also admitted that they are to be used against Canada. The question, then, is, Are they enough? All military men know that when any given number of troops is to be raised, from a quarter to a third must be deducted for sickness and desertion. Of the twenty-five thousand called for by the Senate bill, twenty-one thousand may be considered as fighting-men. Add to this the four thousand already in service, and there will be twenty-five thousand with which to garrison forts along the seaboard and make war. Canada is invaded. The upper province falls and the army moves on Quebec. There will indeed be no European enemy behind the troops, but it is a rule never to leave in the rear an undefended place of strength. As the army marches toward Quebec its ranks will therefore be thinned by drawing off men to hold the chief towns along the route. Much reduced, the invaders at last sit down before Quebec; the city falls, and the army, yet further diminished by the men left behind on garrison duty, moves on for Halifax. Is it not obvious that an army of twenty-five thousand men at least will be needed? The difference between twenty-five thousand and fifteen thousand is precisely the difference between a short war and a long war, between a war fought with vigor and a war of languor and imbecility. As a concession to such Republicans as still held to their old party traditions, hated a standing army, and dreaded to spend the public money, Clay moved an amendment. He would have the officers of eight regiments commissioned at once. When three fourths of the privates of these eight had been enlisted, he would have the officers of the five other regiments commissioned, and not before. In the end he carried the day, and the House, having changed the eight to six, and made a few other amendments, passed the bill and sent it to the Senate. Within eight-and-forty hours it came back with four important amendments stricken out almost unanimously. And now the less extreme Republicans began to waver, but the Federalists once more came to the help of Clay. The House receded from all its amendments save one, and on January eleventh Madison signed the bill. While the document was on its way to the President, Randolph once more returned to the attack. The great army about to be raised might, he said, never be used to wage war. In that event, as the President could not disband them, their time, so far as he could see, would be spent in shouldering their muskets on the south side of some range of buildings. Idleness of this sort led to depravity and dissoluteness of manners. He believed that regular and wholesome labor would preserve the health of the troops, and make the burden such an existence forced them to bear less heavy. If they were employed in digging the President's house or the war office from under ground, their appetites would be better both for their existence and their dinners. He moved, therefore, that, when not fighting, the army should be kept busy building roads, digging canals, laboring on works of public utility. Against this proposition every Republican cried out. Randolph was accused of seeking to degrade the army to the level of the criminals who in Maryland dug canals and in Virginia made shoes, nails, and clothing; of seeking to hinder enlistment; of wishing to embarrass public measures; and his motion, by a vote of one hundred and two to fifteen, was rejected.

This flurry over, the House went into committee, took up a bill to raise a volunteer corps, and soon plunged into a curious constitutional debate. The bill authorized the President to accept the services of fifty thousand volunteers, to be officered by the State authorities, and called into service by the President. Under the Constitution he could call them in service for either of three purposes—to execute the laws, to put down insurrection, to repel invasion. But these volunteers were to be used for no such purposes. They were to go with the regulars and invade Canada. The question then arose, May the militia be used without the limits of the United States? Almost everybody thought it could not. An amendment was therefore offered requiring each volunteer to sign an agreement to serve without the jurisdiction of the United States. Every variety of opinion was expressed. Some thought militia could be used to chase an invading enemy over the border. Some thought it could be marched into Canada if the States to which it belonged consented. Some thought that, as the Constitution provided for two kinds of troops, the regulars and the State militia, the regulars must be used for offensive war and the State militia for defensive. Others thought the amendment useless, for, said they, if the Constitution does not give the President power to use militia without the United States, how can Congress authorize him to do so? The question was not settled, and the bill when it reached Madison said not a word on the use of the volunteers beyond our borders.

\* \* \* \* \*

The plan proposed by Clay was an embargo for thirty days, and then a declaration of war if, meanwhile, good news did not come from England. Though Madison was ready to make an appeal to arms, he was not willing to accept an embargo. For a year past he had boldly asserted that the Berlin and Milan decrees were repealed, and that the United States was bound by a contract to trade with France. A general embargo meant the stopping of this trade, meant the placing of France on the same footing with England, and must, in the eyes of the President, have been a flagrant violation of his pretended contract. But his scruples were now removed by France. On the ninth of March an American brig called the *Thames,* from Portugal, reached New Haven, where her captain, Samuel Chew, appeared before a notary and made a statement under oath. He swore that about the middle of January, 1812, he set sail from St. Ubes for New Haven with a cargo of salt and fruit, and that when a fortnight out he fell in with a French squadron of two frigates and a sloop-of-war. The boarding-officer informed him the squadron had left Nantes early in January with orders to burn American ships trading with an enemy's ports; that, in obedience to these orders, the ship *Asia,* from Philadelphia to Lisbon, and the brig *Gershom,* from Boston to Oporto, both laden with flour and corn, had been burned at sea; and that the *Thames* should meet the same fate on the morrow. In the course of the night the French commodore changed his mind, and on the morrow sent the crews of the *Asia* and the *Gershom* on board the *Thames,* gave Captain Chew a document written in French, and dismissed him. The crews were landed at St. Bartholomew's, but the document and the sworn statement Chew sent to Washington, where, on the twenty-fourth of March, Timothy Pitkin, Jr., read them to the House of Representatives. To maintain the fiction of a repeal of the decrees was now impossible. Not a man in the whole country would believe it. Longing to be revenged for the exposure of the Henry letters, the Federalist press set upon the administration with

taunts, jeers, and, what was worse, with new affidavits from captains whose
ships had been burned by the French. Should these acts of piracy go on,
war with France would be inevitable. But the only way to stop them was
to keep American ships at home, and to keep American ships at home there
must be an embargo. The measure which, when Clay marked out his policy,
had seemed dangerous, thus came to seem necessary, and Monroe, having
sent for the Committee on Foreign Relations, informed them that Madison
was ready to recommend an embargo if the House would give it support.
The committee answered that the House would support it, and on April
first the secret message arrived, recommending a general embargo for sixty
days. Peter B. Porter brought in the bill; Clay made a strong appeal in its
behalf; the majority cut off debate with the previous question, and, rushing
the bill through all its stages, passed it at nine that night. As the Senate was
about to begin business the next forenoon two members of the House appeared, delivered it to the Vice-President, and asked for instant action.
Instant action was taken, and on the following morning two senators carried back the bill with two amendments to the House. And now the peace
party made one more desperate struggle for peace, and carried the Senate
amendment extending the embargo to ninety days. All manner of reasons
were given. Some were anxious that the ships of constituents might be
brought home before the war began. Some were eager to put off war. Some
wanted time for negotiation. Had the wishes of these men prevailed, James
A. Bayard would have been despatched to London, would have laid an
ultimatum before the Prince Regent, and the war for commercial independence would never have been fought. This scheme Clay defeated, and on the
fourth of April the embargo began.

Though the debates had gone on with closed doors, it was no secret that
an embargo was soon to be laid. For ten days past it was a matter of public
notoriety that a caucus had been held at Washington to discuss a declaration
of war; that the members from New York and New Jersey had bitterly
opposed such a measure; that a compromise had been effected, and the agreement reached that, when the New England election was over, an embargo
should be laid on ships and commerce. Many thought the rumor without
foundation. But the Baltimore merchants were so well informed that the
enormous shipments they made of flour attracted newspaper comment. So
openly and so positively was the assertion made that John Randolph, happening to be in Baltimore, heard it and hastened back to Washington, for,
as a member of the Committee of Foreign Relations, the report concerned
him deeply. At Washington he soon learned that the rumor was true. But
when the committee decided to recommend an embargo, and an attempt was
made to pledge the members to secrecy, Randolph refused to be bound. The
committee, he held, had no power to lay injunctions to secrecy. Even if
they had, it would do no good. To his knowledge, the people of Baltimore
already knew that an embargo was coming. This statement induced Calhoun, the moment the committee rose on March thirty-first, to inform
Quincy, Lloyd, and Emott, in order that one commercial city might not
be more favored than others. By Quincy and Emott an express was instantly

sent eastward. On April first he reached Philadelphia and showed the despatch to James Milnor, a Pennsylvania member then in the city. On April second the news reached New York, where in a few hours flour went up one dollar a barrel and freight twenty per cent. In three days' time seventy ships had been loaded, cleared, and were out of sight of Sandy Hook. By the almanacs of that day the post-road distance from Washington to Boston was four hundred and ninety-six miles. Yet this great space was covered in seventy-six hours.

Within the next eight-and-forty hours eighty-five ships left port. Some got off without hindrance, but twenty were detained by bad weather and head-winds in the outer bay till news of the passage of the law reached the Collector. Signals were instantly hoisted on Fort Hill; but the weather was thick, the warnings could not be seen, and, before the captains were aware of the danger, a revenue cutter was upon them demanding their sea-papers. Some slipped their cables and went out despite the fog. More than half were detained.

For a moment the gravity of the situation was lost sight of. The news had come in the closing hours of the most exciting campaign that had ever yet taken place in Massachusetts. A year of complete Republican control had almost produced a social revolution. By one law the inferior courts were reorganized; by another, the right to divert parish taxes from the Congregational minister to any other was secured to the tax-payer; by another, the franchise was extended, and the property qualification, which had existed since 1692, was ruthlessly swept away. Any man could now vote for town officers who was twenty-one years old and had lived one year in the town. In all other town affairs he could have a vote if he had paid a poll-tax. But the two laws which set the State aflame were the Districting Act and the act which made the pay of the representative a charge on the State Treasury.

Provision was made by the Constitution of Massachusetts for forty senators to be chosen by the people of such districts as the General Court should mark out. In using this power the General Court was to make not less than thirteen districts, nor give more than six senators to any one. Just how many any district should have was to depend on the proportion of public taxes that district paid. Until the General Court ordered otherwise, the Constitution further provided that each one of the thirteen counties of the State should be a senatorial district. As other counties were formed this principle of making each county a district was not departed from, and what was a temporary provision became an established usage with all the force of law. This usage the Republicans now laid hands on and destroyed. At last, after years of persistent effort, they controlled the Senate. That control must be kept, and to keep it they rearranged the senatorial districts without regard to county lines, overcame Federalist strongholds with Republican strongholds, cut Worcester County in two, joined Bristol and Norfolk, attached some of the towns of Suffolk to those of Essex, and in the next Senate had twenty-nine senators out of forty. The thing was not new in our politics, for it had some years before been tried in Virginia.

Having pulled down one time-honored custom in order to secure the

Senate, the Republicans pulled down another to secure the House. In that branch of the Legislature each incorporated town of one hundred and fifty ratable polls or less sent one representative, and for every two hundred and twenty-five ratable polls above one hundred and fifty, one representative more. Expenses incurred in going to and coming from the General Court were paid out of the State Treasury, but the daily pay of the member was borne by the town that sent him. Should a town fail to elect its delegates because of the cost, the House could fine it. In consequence of these things, it became customary for the poorer and smaller towns to elect representatives, send them to the General Court, have them remain till government was organized, and then come home. As many of these little places were Republican, their votes were lost, while the wealthy commercial towns, strongholds of Federalism, kept up a full delegation. To counteract this a law was passed by which the rich Federalist cities were taxed in order to pay the salaries of delegates from the poor Republican towns. In other words, the pay of members of the General Court was made a charge on the State Treasury, and the money needed was raised by increased taxation. In 1812 the sum required was over ninety-three thousand five hundred dollars, and, as apportioned among the towns, produced some curious contrasts. Thus in the town of Hull there were thirty-two ratable polls. Under the old system the member would probably have attended for a few days and no more. Under the new system he was present during the whole session, and received as salary three times as much as the town of Hull paid in State taxes. Salem was entitled to twelve members, yet it was compelled to pay a sum equal to the compensation of twenty-three members. The share of Roxbury was seven hundred and thirty-two dollars, yet the cost of its member the year previous was but two hundred and eighty-four dollars.

Innovations such as the Districting Law and the Salary Law would of themselves have been sufficient to make the campaign intensely exciting. But the two candidates for Governor, Elbridge Gerry and Caleb Strong, had hardly been nominated when every mail from Washington and every ship from abroad brought intelligence more and more exasperating. The new loan of eleven millions; the proposed new land-taxes, excises, and stamp duties; the story of the orders from the French admiralty to burn, sink, and destroy American vessels; the deposition of Captain Chew that the burning had begun; the Henry letters; and, on the very eve of the election, the embargo, roused the people and brought out almost every voter in the State. Never had there been such an election. One hundred and four thousand votes were cast. When they were counted, Strong was found to have sixteen hundred more than Gerry. Massachusetts was lost to Republicanism.

The exultation over the result of the elections had not subsided when the Federalists found new cause for rejoicing in the failure to place the eleven-million loan. Subscriptions were opened on the first and second of May in all the chief seaport cities from Portsmouth to Charleston. The advertisement of the Secretary of the Treasury and the comments by the newpapers had made the time and places of subscription well known to everybody. The terms were thought liberal. For every hundred dollars taken, twelve dollars and a half were to be paid down, and a like sum on the fifteenth of each month from June to December, both inclusive. Six per cent was to be the rate of interest, and twelve years the term of the loan. Republican journals vied with each other in urging the people to subscribe, to be liberal, and to take the bonds with the same eagerness with which they had so often competed for the stock of banks, turnpike companies, manufacturing companies, and companies to build bridges. When, however, the books were closed on May second, not quite two millions had been subscribed by the people, and but a little over four millions by the banks.

Small as was the amount purchased by individuals, it was, when judged by past experience, quite large. In 1796 one half of a five-million six-per-cent loan was offered to the people without one dollar's worth being taken for several weeks. Nor did the people ever buy more than eighty thousand of the two and a half millions of stock offered them. Again, in 1798, a six-per-cent loan was advertised. It ought to have been popular. Federalism was triumphant. All over the land Federalists were mounting the black cockade, associating, enlisting, voting addresses to Adams, and singing their national songs. Millions for defence, not a cent for tribute, was the cry, and this money was to be spent on the navy. Yet the total amount of stock subscribed for and issued was but a trifle over seven hundred thousand dollars. Now, in a day of great financial distress, the people had subscribed almost two millions. Nevertheless, the result was most discouraging, and carried with it a meaning not to be misunderstood. In New England the cry had been: "No commerce—no loan," "Let those who want war pay for the war," and in all New England, from Eastport to the New York border, not a million was obtained. The South had little to give; yet from that vast region between the Potomac and Florida but seven hundred thousand was collected. Failure to subscribe in New England was undoubtedly largely due to the bitter animosity felt toward the administration and its ways. But the small amount of the stock taken elsewhere was to be ascribed to the low rate of interest, to the great number of banks the people had formed and were about to form, and to the large profits they expected these institutions to make for them.

As the month began, so it went on, with one discouragement after another, to the close. In Massachusetts the Federalists carried the House of Representatives. In New York they secured the Assembly. Regions supposed to be warmly Republican broke out in open opposition to the embargo and besieged Congress with petitions for its repeal. The death of the Vice-President late in April, the caucus nomination of Madison and Gerry in May, and the excitement in the wheat-growing counties of New York over the embargo, encouraged the discontented Republicans to defy the administration and nominate De Witt Clinton for the presidency. Every mail from the South brought news of warfare on the Spanish border. The *Hornet* came back from France without evidence that the French decrees had been repealed, and the English Minister communicated to Monroe renewed assurances that England would not recall her orders.

Congress meantime seemed dazed. The warlike spirit which marked the opening weeks of the session had gone down. Indeed, it was with the utmost difficulty that the war party could prevent the House from agreeing with the Senate to take a recess from the twenty-ninth of April to the eighth of June. As it was, many of the members went home on leave with the understanding that no measures of a war nature should be taken during the month of May. As the month drew to a close, a rumor was current that on Monday, the first of June, the House would be asked to declare war. The rumor was well founded, and about noon on that day Madison's private secretary delivered at the table of the Speaker, and at the table of the President "pro tempore" of the Senate, a packet the contents of which, he said, were confidential. When opened and read, it proved to be the long-expected war message.

Going back to the year 1803, Madison charged Great Britain with a course of conduct insulting to the independence and neutrality of the United States, and arranged her hostile acts in four classes. Her cruisers had violated the sanctity of the American flag on the great highway of nations by seizing and carrying off persons sailing under it. Her cruisers had violated our maritime rights by hovering on our coasts, harassing our incoming and outgoing ships, and wantonly shedding the blood of our citizens. She had, under pretended blockades, without the presence of ships-of-war to make them valid, plundered our commerce in every sea. She had, not content with these occasional expedients for ruining our trade, resorted at last to the sweeping system of blockades known as orders in council, which she had moulded and managed as best suited her politics, her commercial jealousy, or the avidity of her cruisers. Whether the United States should remain passive under these progressive usurpations, or, meeting force with force, commit a just cause into the hands of the Almighty Disposer of events, was a solemn question which the Constitution wisely left with Congress. In urging Congress to an early decision, he did so in the happy assurance that, be the decision what it might, it would be worthy of the councils of a virtuous, free, and powerful people.

Obedient to this request, the House acted with great promptness. On the third of June, Calhoun, for the Committee on Foreign Relations, reported in favor of war, and on the fourth the bill making the declaration reached the Senate.

When the vote cast in the House on that memorable day is examined, it appears that not a representative from Ohio, Kentucky, Tennessee, South Carolina, or Georgia voted for peace, and that not a representative from Rhode Island, Connecticut, or Delaware voted for war; that in Massachusetts, New York, and New Jersey the majority was for peace; that in Pennsylvania, Maryland, Virginia, and North Carolina the majority was for war; that, in short, the Eastern and Middle States, with two exceptions, were against war, and the Southern and Western States were for it.

The deliberations of the Senate consumed two weeks, so that it was not till the eighteenth of June that the act was passed and approved by Madison. On June nineteenth the proclamation was issued. As the riders hurried from Washington to spread the news throughout the land, Madison visited the department of war and of the navy, "stimulating everything," said one who saw him, "in a manner worthy of a little commander-in-chief, with his little round hat and huge cockade."

&#8766;

ON *June 1, 1812, James Madison called for a declaration of war; two days later the House voted 79-49 for war; and on June 17, the Senate, by a vote of 19-13, completed the decision for war. A day earlier, London had repealed the objectionable Orders in Council. So began a war without an evident cause, one which faced from its inception a large body of dissident sentiment. Before it was over, the war provoked renewed threats of disunion, and also revealed the paucity of the American military establishment.*

*It had been a cardinal principle of Jeffersonian belief that a standing army and navy were "inconsistent with the principles of republican Governments, dangerous to the liberties of a free people, and generally converted into destructive engines for establishing despotism." Thus the United States entered war against the greatest naval power of the world with an army of 6,700 scattered across the vast reaches of the Republic. The call for volunteers to invade Canada produced only a fifth of the expected fifty thousand patriots. The result was the repulse of the Canadian invasion. Military matters were not improved by the ceaseless efforts of Secretary of State James Monroe to undermine the new Secretary of War John Armstrong. The disenchantment of the Northeast with the whole enterprise denied its fiscal resources to the Federal Treasury. The army bogged down in a welter of both administrative and military incompetence.*

*The navy showed the effects of Jefferson's emphasis upon economy; the gunboats constructed to defend coastal ports proved unable to do their assigned task. Naval weaknesses were further accentuated when the Secretary of the Navy Paul Hamilton persisted in practicing economy. His successor, William Jones, set to work building ships of the line, but these would meet future contingencies rather than the immediate need. The existing ships of the line, like the* Constitution, Essex, *and* Hornet, *won striking victories, and captured no less than 165 British craft; but freebooting privateers far exceeded the naval score: they hauled in more than 1,300 prizes. But America had chosen to go to war with Britain at an inauspicious moment. Napoleon in 1812 had invaded Russia, and with that act he had forged a Grand Alliance that by 1814 had broken his power. Once Britain turned its full naval might against the United States, American war craft were swept from the seas, the coast was completely blockaded, British war parties landed at will. Only in the far interior did the war take a more promising direction. There in the future American heartland, Captain Oliver Hazard Perry defeated British naval forces on Lake Erie; William Henry Harrison prevented our repulse in Canada from turning into a rout; and Andrew Jackson broke the power of the Creek Indian federation in the Southwest.*

*Captain Alfred T. Mahan (1840-1914) was the son of a West Point professor of engineering. He entered Annapolis in 1856, and here he developed an interest that matured into a profound concern for naval history. His first work,* The Influence of Sea Power Upon History, 1660-1783 *(1890), argued that world power was founded on control of the seas. Its impact was worldwide; in the widening race for military power at the outset of the twentieth century, his arguments were martialed by proponents of naval strength to support their case. His no less emphatic case for the use of military power to uphold the moral right lent itself to supporters of ethical uplift through force.*

*Mahan also foresaw in an 1897 essay, "A Twentieth Century Outlook," the day "when the vast mass of China—now inert—might yield to one of those impulses which have in past ages buried civilization under a barbaric invasion." To counteract this prospect, he viewed "the great armies of Europe . . . as a barrier to that great movement, if it come." And if China should "burst her barriers eastward as well as westward, toward the Pacific as well as toward the European Continent," Mahan expected the American navy to draw its shield. He concluded, "Sea Power will play in those days the leading part which it has in all history, and the United States by her geographical position must be one of the frontiers from which, as from a base of operations, the Sea Power of the civilized world will energize." In his* Sea Power in Its Relations to the War of 1812 *(1905), Mahan drew the lesson of unpreparedness on the sea; he also saw war as a healthy invigoration of American nationalism.*

# SEA POWER IN ITS RELATIONS TO THE WAR OF 1812

## *by Alfred T. Mahan*

At sunrise of September 10, the lookout at the masthead of the "Lawrence" sighted the British squadron in the northwest. Barclay was on his way down the lake, intending to fight. The wind was southwest, fair for the British, but adverse to the Americans quitting the harbor by the channel leading towards the enemy. Fortunately it shifted to southeast, and there steadied; which not only enabled them to go out, but gave them the windward position throughout the engagement. The windward position, or weather gage, as it was commonly called, conferred the power of initiative; whereas the vessel or fleet to leeward, while it might by skill at times force action, or itself obtain the weather gage by manoeuvring, was commonly obliged to await attack and accept the distance chosen by the opponent. Where the principal force of a squadron, as in Perry's case, consists in two vessels armed almost entirely with carronades, the importance of getting within carronade range is apparent.

Looking forward to a meeting, Perry had prearranged the disposition of his vessels to conform to that which he expected the enemy to assume. Unlike ocean fleets, all the lake squadrons, as is already known of Ontario, were composed of vessels very heterogeneous in character. This was because the most had been bought, not designed for the navy. It was antecedently probable, therefore, that a certain general principle would dictate the constitution of the three parts of the order of battle, the centre and two flanks, into which every military line divides. The French have an expression for the centre,—*corps de bataille*,—which was particularly appropriate to squadrons like those of Barclay and Perry. Each had a natural "body of battle," in vessels decisively stronger than all the others combined. This relatively powerful division would take the centre, as a cohesive force, to prevent the two ends—or flanks—being driven asunder by the enemy. Barclay's vessels of this class were the new ship, "Detroit," and the "Queen Charlotte"; Perry's were the "Lawrence" and "Niagara." Each had an intermediate vessel; the British the "Lady Prevost," the Americans the "Caledonia." In addition to these were the light craft, three British and six Americans; concerning which it is to be said that the latter were not only the more numerous, but individually much more powerfully armed.

The same remark is true, vessel for vessel, of those opposed to one another by Perry's plan; that is, measuring the weight of shot discharged at a broadside, which is the usual standard of comparison, the "Lawrence" threw more metal than the "Detroit," the "Niagara" much more than the "Queen Charlotte," and the "Caledonia," than the "Lady Prevost." This, however, must be qualified by the consideration, more conspicuously noticeable on Ontario than on Erie, of the greater length of range of the long gun. This applies particularly to the principal British vessel, the "Detroit." Owing to the difficulties of transportation, and the demands of the Ontario squadron, her proper armament had not arrived. She was provided with guns from the ramparts of Fort Malden, and a more curiously composite battery probably never was mounted; but, of the total nineteen, seventeen were long guns. It is impossible to say what her broadside may have weighed. All her pieces together fired two hundred and thirty pounds, but it is incredible that a seaman like Barclay should not so have disposed them as to give more than half that amount to one broadside. That of the "Lawrence," was three hundred pounds; but all her guns, save two twelves, were carronades. Compared with the "Queen Charlotte," the battery of the "Niagara" was as 3 to 2; both chiefly carronades.

From what has been stated, it is evident that if Perry's plan were carried out, opposing vessel to vessel, the Americans would have a superiority of at least fifty per cent. Such an advantage, in some quarter at least, is the aim of every capable commander; for the object of war is not to kill men, but to carry a point; not glory by fighting, but success in result. The only obvious dangers were that the wind might fail or be very light, which would unduly protract exposure to long guns before getting within carronade range; or that, by some vessels coming tardily into action, one or more of the others would suffer from concentration of the enemy's fire.

It was this contingency, realized in fact, which gave rise to the embittered controversy about the battle; a controversy never settled, and probably now not susceptible of settlement, because the President of the United States, Mr. Monroe, pigeonholed the charges formulated by Perry against Elliott in 1818. There is thus no American sworn testimony to facts, searched and sifted by cross-examination; for the affidavits submitted on the one side and the other were *ex parte*, while the Court of Inquiry, asked by Elliott in 1815, neglected to call all accessible witnesses—notably Perry himself. In fact, there was not before it a single commanding officer of a vessel engaged. Such a procedure was manifestly inadequate to the requirement of the Navy Department's letter to the Court, that "a true statement of the facts in relation to Captain Elliott's conduct be exhibited to the world." Investigation seems to have been confined to an assertion in a British periodical, based upon the proceedings of the Court-Martial upon Barclay, to the effect that Elliott's vessel "had not been engaged, and was making away," at the time when Perry "was obliged to leave his ship, which soon after surrendered, and hoist his flag on board another of his squadron." The American Court examined two officers of Perry's vessel, and five of Elliott's; no others. To the direct question, "Did the 'Niagara' at any time during the action attempt to make off from the British fleet?" all replied, "No." The Court, therefore, on the testimony before it, decided that the charge "made in the proceedings of the British Court Martial . . . was malicious, and unfounded in fact"; expressing besides its conviction "that the attempts to wrest from Captain Elliott the laurels he gained in that splendid victory . . . ought in no wise to lessen him in the opinion of his fellow citzens as a brave and skilful officer." At the same time it regretted that "imperious duty compelled it to promulgate testimony which appears materially to differ in some of its most important points."

In this state the evidence still remains, owing to the failure of the President to take action, probably with a benevolent desire to allay discord, and envelop facts under a kindly "All's well that ends well." Perry died a year after making his charges, which labored under the just imputation that he had commended Elliott in his report, and again immediately afterwards, though in terms that his subordinate thought failed to do him justice. American naval opinion divided, apparently in very unequal numbers. Elliott's officers stood by him, as was natural; for men feel themselves involved in that which concerns the conduct of their ship, and see incidents in that light. Perry's officers considered that the "Lawrence" had not been properly supported; owing to which, after losses almost unparalleled, she had to undergo the mortification of surrender. Her heroism, her losses, and her surrender, were truths beyond question.

The historian today thus finds himself in the dilemma that the American testimony is in two categories, distinctly contradictory and mutually destructive; yet to be tested only by his own capacity to cross-examine the record, and by reference to the British accounts. The latter are impartial, as between the American parties; their only bias is to constitute a fair case for Barclay, by establishing the surrender of the American flagship and the hesitancy of the "Niagara" to enter into action. This would indicate victory so far, changed to defeat by the use Perry made of the vessel preserved to him intact by the over-caution of his second. Waiving motives, these claims are substantially correct, and constitute the analysis of the battle as fought and won.

Barclay, finding the wind to head him and place him to leeward, arranged his fleet to await attack in the following order, from van to rear: The schooners "Chippewa," "Detroit," "Hunter," "Queen Charlotte," "Lady Prevost," "Little Belt." This, he said in his official letter, was "according to a given plan, so that each ship (that is, the "Detroit" and "Queen Charlotte") might be supported against the superior force of the two brigs opposed to them." The British vessels lay in column, in each other's wake, by the wind on the port tack, hove-to (stopped) with a topsail to the mast, heading to the southwest. Perry now modified some details of his disposition. It had been expected that the "Queen Charlotte" would precede the "Detroit," and the American commander had therefore placed the "Niagara" leading, as designated to fight the "Charlotte," the "Lawrence" following the "Niagara." This order was now reversed, and the "Caledonia" interposed between the two; the succession being "Lawrence," "Caledonia," "Niagara." Having more schooners than the enemy, he placed in the van two of the best, the "Scorpion" and the "Ariel"; the other four behind the "Niagara." His centre, therefore, the "Lawrence," "Caledonia," and "Niagara," were opposed to the "Detroit," "Hunter," and "Queen Charlotte." The long guns of the "Ariel," "Scorpion," and "Caledonia" supplied in measure the deficiency of gun power in the "Lawrence," while standing down outside of carronade range; the "Caledonia," with the rear schooners, giving a like support to the "Niagara." The "Ariel," and perhaps also the "Scorpion," was ordered to keep a little to windward of the "Lawrence." This was a not uncommon use of van vessels, making more hazardous any attempt of the opponent to tack and pass to windward, in order to gain the weather gage with its particular advantages.

The rear four schooners, as is frequently the case in long columns, were straggling somewhat at the time the signal to bear down was made; and they had difficulty in getting into action, being compelled to resort to the sweeps because the wind was light. It is not uncommon to see small vessels with low sails thus retarded, while larger are being urged forward by their lofty light canvas. The line otherwise having been formed, Perry stood down without regard to them. At quarter before noon the "Detroit" opened upon the "Lawrence" with her long guns. Ten minutes later the Americans began to reply. Finding the British fire at this range more destructive than he had anticipated, Perry made more sail upon the "Lawrence." Word had already been passed by hail of trumpet to close up in the line, and for each vessel to come into action against her opponent, before designated. The "Lawrence" continued thus to approach obliquely, using her own long twelves, and backed by the long guns of the vessels ahead and astern, till she was within "canister range," apparently about two hundred and fifty yards, when she turned her side to the wind on the weather quarter of the "Detroit," bringing her carronade battery to bear. This distance was greater than desirable for carronades; but with a very light breeze, little more than two miles an hour, there was a limit to the time during which it was prudent to allow an opponent's raking fire to play, unaffected in aim by any reply. Moreover, much of her rigging was already shot away, and she was becoming unmanageable. The battle was thus joined by the commander-in-chief; but, while supported to his satisfaction by the "Scorpion" and "Ariel" ahead, and "Caledonia" astern, with their long guns, the "Niagara" did not come up, and her carronades failed to do their share. The captain of her opponent, the "Queen Charlotte," finding that his own carronades would not reach her, made sail ahead, passed the "Hunter," and brought his battery to the support of the "Detroit" in her contest with the "Lawrence." Perry's vessel thus found herself under the combined fire of the "Detroit," "Queen Charlotte," and in some measure of the "Hunter"; the armament of the last, however, was too trivial to count for much.

Elliott's first placing of the "Niagara" may, or may not, have been judicious as regards his particular opponent. The "Queen Charlotte's" twenty-fours would not reach him; and it may be quite proper to take a range where your own guns can tell and your enemy's cannot. Circumstance must determine. The precaution applicable in a naval duel may cease to be so when friends are in need of assistance; and when the British captain, seeing how the case stood, properly and promptly carried his ship forward to support his commander, concentrating two vessels upon Perry's one, the situation was entirely changed. The plea set up by Cooper, who fought Elliott's battle conscientiously, but with characteristic bitterness as well as shrewdness, that the "Niagara's" position, assigned in the line behind the "Caledonia," could not properly be left without signal, practically surrenders the case. It is applying the dry-rot system of fleet tactics in the middle of the eighteenth century to the days after Rodney and Nelson, and is further effectually disposed of by the consentient statement of several of the American captains, that their commander's dispositions were made with reference to the enemy's order; that is, that he assigned a special enemy's ship to a special American, and particularly the "Detroit" to the "Lawrence," and the "Queen Charlotte" to the "Niagara." The vessels of both fleets being so heterogeneous, it was not wise to act as with units nearly homogeneous, by laying down an order, the governing principle of which was mutual support by a line based upon its own intrinsic qualities. The considerations dictating Perry's dispositions were external to his fleet, not internal; in the enemy's order, not in his own. This was emphasized by his changing the previously arranged stations of the "Lawrence" and the "Niagara," when he saw Barclay's line. Lastly, he re-enforced all this by quoting to his subordinates Nelson's words, that no captain could go very far wrong who placed his vessel close alongside those of the enemy.

Cooper, the ablest of Elliott's champions, has insisted so strongly upon the obligation of keeping the station *in the line*, as laid down, that it is necessary to examine the facts in the particular case. He rests the certainty of his contention on general principles, then long exploded, and further upon a sentence in Perry's charges, preferred in 1818, that "the commanding officer (Perry) issued, 1st, an order directing in what manner the line of battle should be formed . . . and enjoined upon the commanders to preserve their stations in the line" thus laid down. This is correct; but Cooper omits to give the words immediately following in the specification: "and in all cases to keep as near the commanding officer's vessel (the 'Lawrence') as possible." Cooper also omits that which next succeeds. "2d, An order of attack, in which the 'Lawrence' was designated to attack the enemy's new ship (afterwards ascertained to have been named the 'Detroit'), and the 'Niagara' designated to attack the 'Queen Charlotte,' which orders were then communicated to all the commanders, including the said Captain Elliott, who for that purpose . . . were by signal called together by the said commanding officer . . . and expressly instructed that 'if, in the expected engagement, they laid their vessels close alongside of those of the enemy, they could not be out of the way.'" An officer, if at once gallant and intelligent, finding himself behind a dull sailing vessel, as Cooper tells us the "Caledonia" was, could hardly desire clearer authority than the above to imitate his commanding officer when he made sail to close the enemy:— "Keep close to him," and follow up the ship which "the 'Niagara' was designated to attack."

Charges preferred are not technical legal proof, but, if duly scrutinized, they are statements equivalent in value to many that history rightly accepts; and, at all events, that which Cooper quotes is not duly scrutinized if that which he does not quote is omitted. He does indeed express a gloss upon them, in the words: "Though the 'Niagara' was ordered to direct her fire at the 'Queen Charlotte,' it could only be done from her station astern of the 'Caledonia,' . . . without violating the primary order to preserve the line." This does not correctly construe the natural meaning of Perry's full instructions. It is clear that, while he had laid down a primary formation, "a line of battle," he also most properly qualified it by a contingent instruction, and "order of attack," designed to meet the emergency likely to occur in every fleet engagement, and which occurred here, when a slavish adherence to the line of battle would prevent intelligent support to the main effort. If he knew naval history, as his quotation from Nelson indicates, he also knew how many a battle had been discreditably lost by "keeping the line."

With regard to the line, however, it is apt to remark that in fleet battle, unless otherwise specially directed, the line of the assailant was supposed to be parallel to that of the defence, for the obvious reason that the attacking vessels should all be substantially at the same effective range. This distance, equal for all in fleets as usually constituted, would naturally be set, and in practice was set, by the commander-in-chief; his ship forming the point through which should be drawn the line parallel to the enemy. This rule, well established under Rodney, who died in 1792, was rigidly applicable between vessels of the same force, such as the "Lawrence" and

"Niagara"; and whatever deductions might be made for the case of a lightframed vessel, armed with long guns, like the "Caledonia," keeping out of carronade distance of an opponent with heavy scantling, would not in the least apply to the "Niagara." For her, the standard of position was not, as Cooper insists, a half-cable's length from her next ahead, the "Caledonia"; but abreast her designated opponent, at the same distance as the "Lawrence" from the enemy's line. Repeated mishaps had established the rule that position was to be taken from the centre,—that is from the commander-in-chief. Ships in line of battle, bearing down upon an enemy in like order, did not steer in each other's wake, unless specially ordered; and there is something difficult to understand in the "Niagara" with her topsail sharp aback to keep from running on board the "Caledonia," although the fact is in evidence. The expression in Perry's report of the action, "at 10 A.M. . . . formed the line and bore up," would by a person familiar with naval battles be understood to mean that the line was first formed parallel to the enemy, the vessels following one another, after which they steered down for him, changing course together; they would then no longer be in each other's wake, but in echelon, or as the naval phrase then went, in bow and quarter line. Barclay confirms this, "At 10 the enemy bore up under easy sail, in a line abreast." Thus, when the distance desired by the commander-in-chief was reached,—a fact more often indicated by his example than by signal,—the helm would bring them again in line of battle, their broadsides bearing upon the enemy.

The technical point at issue is whether Perry, finding the long-gun fire of the "Detroit" more destructive than he had anticipated, and determining in consequence to shorten the period of its duration by changing his original plan, increasing sail beyond the speed of such slower vessels as the "Caledonia," had a right to expect that his subordinates would follow his example. In theory and practice of fleet battles; his transfer of his own position transferred the line of battle in its entirety to the distance relative to the enemy which he himself was seeking to assume. Were other authority lacking, his action was warrant to his captains; but the expression in his report, "I made sail, and directed the other vessels to follow, for the purpose of closing with the enemy," causes increased regret that the exact facts were not ascertained by cross-examination before a Court-Martial.

Elliott's place therefore was alongside the "Queen Charlotte," so to engage her that she could attend to nothing else. This he did not do, and for failure the only possible excuse was inability, through lack of wind. The wind was light throughout, yet not so light but that the "Lawrence" closed with the "Detroit," and the "Queen Charlotte" with her flag-ship when she wished. None of Elliott's witnesses before the Court of Inquiry state that he made sail before the middle of the action, but they attribute the failure to get down to the lightness of the wind. They do state that, after the "Lawrence" was disabled, a breeze springing up, sail was made; which indicates that previously it had not been. Again, it is alleged by the testimony in favor of Elliott that much of the time the maintopsail was sharp aback, to keep from running into the "Caledonia"; a circumstance upon which Cooper dwells triumphantly, as showing that the "Niagara" was not by the wind and was in her place, close astern of the "Caledonia." Accepting the statements, they would show there was wind enough to fan the "Niagara" to—what was really her place—her commodore's aid; for in those days the distance between under fire and out of fire for efficient action was a matter of half a mile. Perry's formulated charge, addressed to the Navy Department, and notified to Elliott, but never brought to trial, was that when coming into action an order was passed by trumpet for the vessels astern to close up in the line; that a few moments previously to the enemy's opening fire the "Niagara" had been within hail of the "Lawrence," and nevertheless she was allowed to drop astern, and for two hours to remain at such distance from the enemy as to render useless all her battery except the two long guns. Perry himself made sail at the time the hail by trumpet was passed. The "Niagara" did not.

There is little reason for doubt that the tenor of Perry's instructions required Elliott to follow the "Queen Charlotte," and no doubt whatever that military propriety imperiously demanded it of him. The question of wind must be matter of inference from the incidents above stated: the movement of the "Lawrence" and "Queen Charlotte," and the bracing aback of the "Niagara's" topsail. A sentence in Perry's report apparently, but only apparently, attenuates the force of these. He said, "At half-past two, the wind springing up, Captain Elliott was enabled to bring his vessel, the 'Niagara,' gallantly into close action." Alluding to, without insisting on, Perry's subsequent statement that he endeavored to give as favorable a color as possible to Elliott's course, it is clear enough that these words simply state that Captain Eliott at 2:30 reached the range at which the "Lawrence" had fought since a little after noon.

Quitting now the discussion of proprieties, the order of events seems to have been as follows: Perry having taken the initiative of bearing down, under increased sail, Elliott remained behind, governed by, or availing himself of—two very different motives, not lightly to be determined, or assumed, by the historian—the technical point, long before abandoned in practice, that he could not leave his place in the line without a signal. Thus his action was controlled by the position of his next ahead in the line, the dull-sailing "Caledonia," a vessel differing radically from his own in armament, having two long and for that day heavy guns, quite equal in range and efficiency to the best of the "Detroit's," and therefore capable of good service, though possibly not of their best, from the distance at which Perry changed his speed. Elliott's battery was the same as Perry's. He thus continued until it became evident that, the "Queen Charlotte" having gone to the support of the "Detroit," the "Lawrence" was heavily overpowered. Then, not earlier than an hour after Perry bore down, he realized that his commander-in-chief would be destroyed under his eyes, unless he went to his support, and he himself would rest under the imputation of an inefficient spectator. He ordered the "Caledonia" to bear up, in order that he might pass. Though not demonstrably certain, it seems probable that the wind, light throughout, was now so fallen as to impede the retrieval of his position; the opportunity to close, used by Perry, had passed away. At all events it was not till between 2 and 2:30 that the "Niagara" arrived on the scene, within effective range of the carronades which constituted nine tenths of her battery.

With this began the second stage of the battle. Perry's bearing down, receiving only the support of the long guns of the "Caledonia" and of the schooners ahead of him, had brought the "Lawrence" into hot engagement with the "Detroit," supported a half hour later by the "Queen Charlotte." By a little after two o'clock both flagships were well-nigh disabled, hull and battery; the "Lawrence" most so, having but one gun left out of ten on the broadside. "At 2:30," wrote Barclay, "the 'Detroit' was a perfect wreck, principally from the raking fire of the gunboats." Which gunboats? Evidently the "Ariel" and "Scorpion," for all agree that the rear four were at this hour still far astern, though not absolutely out of range. To these last was probably due the crippling of the "Lady Prevost," which by now had gone to leeward with her rudder injured. Up to this time, when the first scene closed, what had been the general course of the action? and what now the situation? Assuming, as is very probable, that Barclay did not open with his long 24's until Perry was a mile, two thousand yards, from him,—that distance requiring six degrees elevation for those guns,— an estimate of speeds and courses, as indicated by the evidence, would put the "Lawrence" in action, at two hundred and fifty yards, at 12:10. This calculation, made independently, received subsequent confirmation in consulting Barclay's report, which says 12:15. The same time, for the duller "Caledonia" and the "Niagara," would place them one thousand yards from the British line. This range, for the 32-pounder carronades of the "Niagara," and the 24's of the "Queen Charlotte," required an elevation of from four to six degrees. Coupling this with the British statement, that the carronades of the "Charlotte" could not reach the "Niagara," we obtain probable positions, two hundred and fifty yards and one thousand yards, for the principal two American vessels at quarter-past noon.

From the general lightness and occasional failure of the wind up to 2 P.M., it is more than likely that no great change took place before that hour. What air there was might touch all alike, but would affect least the "Lawrence," "Detroit," and "Queen Charlotte," because their sails were being rent; and also they were in the centre of the cannonade, which is believed usually to kill the breeze. The tendency of the "Caledonia," "Niagara," and American vessels in rear of them, between 12:30 and 2 P.M., during which period, to use Barclay's report, "the action continued with great fury," would therefore be to approach slowly the scene where the "Lawrence," supported by the long guns of the "Ariel," "Scorpion," and "Caledonia," maintained the day against the "Detroit" and "Queen Charlotte," backed by the schooner "Chippewa" and the 6 and 4 pounder popguns of the "Hunter." How near they drew is a mere matter of estimate. Taking all together, it may be inferred that the "Niagara" had then been carried as close as five hundred to six hundred yards to the British line, but it would appear also towards its rear; rather, probably, that the British had advanced relatively to her, owing to her course being oblique to theirs.

The situation then was as follows: The "Lawrence," disabled, was dropping astern of the "Detroit," "Queen Charlotte," and "Hunter." More than half her ship's company lay dead or wounded on her decks. Her loss, 83 killed and wounded out of a total of 142,—sick included,—was mostly incurred before this. With only one gun left, she was a beaten ship, although her colors were up. The "Detroit" lay in the British line almost equally mauled. On her lee quarter,—that is, behind, but on the lee side,— and close to her, was the "Queen Charlotte." Her captain, second to Barclay, had been killed,—the first man hit on board,—and her first lieutenant knocked senseless; being succeeded in command by an officer whom Barclay described as of little experience. The first lieutenant of the "Detroit" was also wounded mortally; and Barclay himself, who already had been once hit in the thigh, was now a second time so severely injured,— being his eighth wound in battle, though now only thirty-two,—that he was forced at this critical instant to go below, leaving the deck with the second lieutenant. The "Hunter" was astern of her two consorts. The "Lady Prevost," fifth in the British order, had fallen to leeward with her rudder crippled. The position of the leading and rear British schooners is not mentioned, and is not important; the reliance of each being one long 9-pounder gun.

Before this, taking advantage of the breeze freshening, the "Niagara" had gone clear of the "Caledonia," on her windward side, and had stood to the southwest, towards the "Detroit." She had not at first either foresail or topgallantsails set; and since she passed the "Lawrence" to windward, she was then almost certainly over two hundred and fifty yards from the British line, for there is no conclusive proof that the "Lawrence" was nearer than that. Combining the narrative of the British commodore with that of his second lieutenant, who now took charge, it appears that Barclay, before going below, saw a boat passing from the "Lawrence" to the "Niagara," and that the second lieutenant, Inglis, after relieving him, found the "Niagara" on the weather beam of the "Detroit." Perry, seeing the "Lawrence" incapable of further offensive action, had decided to leave her and go on board the "Niagara," and in this brief interval was making his passage from one vessel to the other. After leaving the "Lawrence" astern, the "Niagara" had made sail; the foresail having been set, and the topgallantsails "in the act of being set, before Captain Perry came on board." This necessarily prolonged the time of his passage, and may have given rise to the opprobrious British report that she was making off. Her making sail as she did indicated that she had suffered little aloft; she had been out of carronade range, while her consort, still in fighting condition, was bearing the brunt; it was natural to conclude that she would not alone renew the action, now that the "Lawrence" was hopelessly disabled. The wish, too, may possibly have helped the thought. The "Lawrence," in fact, having kept her colors flying till Perry reached the "Niagara," struck immediately afterwards. Had she surrendered while he was on board, he could not honorably have quitted her; and the record was clearer by his reaching a fresh ship while the flag of the one he left was still up.

What next happened is under no doubt, so far as the movements of the "Niagara" are concerned, though there is irreconcilable difference as to who initiated the action. Immediately after Perry came on board, Elliott left her, to urge forward the rear gunboats. Her helm was put up, and she bore down ahead of the "Detroit" to rake her; supported in so doing by the small vessels, presumably the "Ariel," "Scorpion," and "Caledonia." The British ship tried to wear, both to avoid being raked and to get her starboard battery into action; many of the guns on the broadside heretofore engaged being disabled. The "Charlotte" being on her lee quarter, and ranging ahead, the two fell foul, and so remained for some time. This condition gave free play to the American guns, which were soon after re-enforced by those of the rear gunboats; enabled, like the "Niagara," to close with the freshening breeze. After the two British vessels got clear, another attempt was made to bring their batteries to bear; but the end was inevitable, and is best told in the words of the officer upon whom devolved the duty of surrendering the "Detroit." "The ship lying completely unmanageable, every brace cut away, the mizzen-topmast and gaff down, all the other masts badly wounded, not a stay left forward, hull shattered very much, a number of guns disabled, and the enemy's squadron raking both ships ahead and astern, none of our own in a position to support us, I was under the painful necessity of answering the enemy to say we had struck, the 'Queen Charlotte' having previously done so." A Canadian officer taken prisoner at the battle of the Thames saw the "Detroit," a month later, at Put-in-Bay. "It would be impossible," he wrote, "to place a hand upon that broadside which had been exposed to the enemy's fire without covering some portion of a wound, either from grape, round, canister, or chain shot." Her loss in men was never specifically given. Barclay reported that of the squadron as a whole to be forty-one killed, ninety-four wounded. He had lost an arm at Trafalgar; and on this occasion, besides other injuries, the one remaining to him was so shattered as to be still in bandages a year later, when he appeared before the Court-Martial which emphatically acquitted him of blame. The loss of the American squadron was twenty-seven killed, ninety-six wounded; of whom twenty-two killed and sixty-one wounded were on board the "Lawrence."

Thus was the battle of Lake Erie fought and won. Captain Barclay not only had borne himself gallantly and tenaciously against a superior force, —favored in so doing by the enemy attacking in detail,—but the testimony on his trial showed that he had labored diligently during the brief period of his command, amid surroundings of extreme difficulty, to equip his squadron, and to train to discipline and efficiency the heterogeneous material of which his crews were composed. The only point not satisfactorily covered is his absence when Perry was crossing the bar. In his defence his allusion to this incident is very casual,—resembles somewhat gliding rapidly over thin ice; but the Court raised no question, satisfied, probably, with the certainty that the honor of the flag had not suffered in the action. On the American side, since the history of a country is not merely the narrative of principal transactions, but the record also of honor reflected upon the nation by the distinguished men it produces, it is proper to consider the question of credit, which has been raised in this instance. There can be no doubt that opportunity must be seized as it is offered; for accident or chance may prevent its recurrence. Constituted as Perry's squadron was, the opportunity presented to him could be seized only by standing down as he did, trusting that the other vessels would follow the example of their commander. The shifting of the wind in the morning, and its failure during the engagement, alike testify to the urgency of taking the tide as it serves. There was no lagging, like Chauncey's, to fetch up heavy schooners; and the campaign was decided in a month, instead of remaining at the end of three months a drawn contest, to lapse thence-forth into a race of ship-building. Had the "Niagara" followed closely, there could have been no doubling on the "Lawrence"; and Perry's confidence would have been justified as well as his conduct. The latter needs no apology. Without the help of the "Niagara," the "Detroit" was reduced to a "defenceless state," and a "perfect wreck," by the carronades of the "Lawrence," supported by the raking fire of the "Ariel" and "Scorpion." Both the expressions quoted are applied by the heroic Barclay to her condition at 2:30, when, as he also says, the "Niagara" was perfectly fresh. Not only was the "Detroit" thus put out of action, but the "Charlotte" was so damaged that she surrendered before her. To this the "Caledonia's" two long twenty-fours had contributed effectively. The first lieutenant of the "Queen Charlotte" testified that up to the time he was disabled, an hour or an hour and a quarter after the action began, the vessel was still manageable; that "the 'Niagara' engaged us on our quarter, out of carronade range, with what long guns she had; but our principal injury was from the 'Caledonia,' who laid on our beam, with two long 24-pounders on pivots, also out of car-ronade-shot distance."

Is it to Perry, or to Elliott, that is due the credit of the "Niagara's" action in bearing up across the bows of the "Detroit"? This is the second stage of the battle; the bringing up the reserves. An absolute reply is impossible in the face of the evidence, sworn but not cross-examined. A probable inference, which to the present writer amounts to conviction, is attainable. Before the Court of Inquiry, in 1815, Captain Elliott put the question to several of his witnesses, "Was not the 'Niagara's' helm up and she standing direct for the 'Detroit' when Captain Perry came up board?" They replied, "Yes." All these were midshipmen. By a singular fatality most of the "Niagara's" responsible officers were already dead, and the one surviving lieutenant had been below, stunned, when Perry reached the deck. It may very possibly be that this answer applied only to the first change of course, when Elliott decided to leave his position behind the "Caledonia"; but if it is claimed as covering also the subsequent bearing up eight points (at right angles), to cross the bows of the "Detroit," it is to be observed that no mention of this very important movement is made in a letter addressed to the Secretary of the Navy, October 13, 1813, one month after the battle, drawn up for the express purpose of vindicating Elliott, and signed by all the lieutenants of the "Niagara," and by the purser, who formerly had been a lieutenant in the navy. Their account was that Perry, on reaching the ship, said he feared the day was lost; that Elliott replied it was not, that he would repair on board the rear schooners, and bring them up; that he did so, and "*the consequence was* that in ten minutes the 'Detroit' and 'Queen Charlotte' with the 'Lady Prevost,' struck to us, and soon after the whole of the enemy's squadron followed their example." This attributes the victory to the half-dozen long guns of the four schooners, mostly inferior in caliber to the nine carronades on board a single vessel, the "Niagara," raking within pistol-shot of antagonists already in the condition described by Barclay. Such a conclusion traverses all experience of the tactical advantage of guns massed under one captain over a like number distributed in several commands, and also contravenes the particular superiority of carronades at close quarters. An officer of the "Detroit," who was on deck throughout, testified that the "Lawrence" had engaged at musket-shot, the "Niagara," when she bore down under Perry, at pistol-shot. Barclay, and his surviving lieutenant, Inglis, both lay most weight upon this action of the "Niagara," from which arose also the fouling of the two largest British ships.

Perry's charges of 1818 against Elliott formulated deliberate statements, under the responsible expectation of cross-examination under oath. This is his account: "When the commanding officer [Perry] went on board the 'Niagara,' Captain Elliott was keeping her on a course by the wind, which would in a few minutes have carried said vessel entirely out of action, to prevent which, and in order to bring the said vessel into close action with the enemy, the said commanding officer was under the necessity of heaving-to, stopping and immediately wearing said vessel, and altering her course at least eight points"; that is, perpendicular to the direction before steered. Against this solemn and serious charge is unquestionably to be placed the commendatory mention and letter given by Perry to Elliott immediately after the battle. Upon these also he had to expect the sharpest interrogation, to the mortification attendant upon which he could only oppose evidence extenuative of, but in no case justifying, undeniable self-contradiction. If the formal charge was true, no excuse can be admitted for the previous explicit commendation. As a matter of historical inquiry, however, such contradictions have to be met, and must be weighed in the light of all the testimony. The author's conclusion upon the whole is that, as Perry's action in first standing down insured decisive action, so by him was imparted to the "Niagara" the final direction which determined victory. The influence of the rear gunboats brought up by Elliott was contributive, but not decisive.

In short, the campaign of Lake Erie was brought to an immediate successful issue by the ready initiative taken by Perry when he found the British distant fire more destructive than he expected, and by his instant acceptance of necessary risk, in standing down exposed to a raking cannonade to which he for a long while could not reply. If, as the author holds, he was entitled to expect prompt imitation by the "Niagara," the risk was actual, but not undue. As it was, though the "Lawrence" surrendered, it was not until she had, with the help of gunboats stationed by Perry for that object, so damaged both her opponents that they were incapable of further resistance. In the tactical management of the "Lawrence" and her supports was no mere headlong dash, but preparation adequate to conditions. Had the "Niagara" followed, the "Lawrence" need never have struck. The contemporary incidents on Erie and Ontario afford an instructive commentary upon Napoleon's incisive irony, that "War cannot be waged without running risks." There has been sufficient quotation from Chauncey to indicate why the campaign on Ontario dragged through two seasons, and then left the enemy in control. Small as the scale and the theatre of these naval operations, they illustrate the unvarying lesson that only in offensive action can defensive security be found.

The destruction of the British naval force decided the campaign in the Northwest by transferring the control of the water. Its general military results were in this respect final. Nothing occurred to modify them during the rest of the war. Detroit and Michigan territory fell back into the hands of the United States; and the allegiance of the Indians to the British cause, procured by Brock's sagacious daring a twelvemonth before, but rudely shaken by the events narrated, was destroyed by the death of their great leader, Tecumseh, a month later in the battle of the Thames, itself the direct consequence of Perry's success. The frontier was henceforth free from the Indian terror, which had hitherto disquieted it from the Maumee to Cleveland.

A more far-reaching political issue was also here definitely settled. A sense of having betrayed the Indian interests in the previous treaties of 1783 and 1794 was prevalent in British official circles, and in their counsels a scheme had been circulated for constituting an independent Indian territory, under joint guarantee of the two nations, between their several dominions. This would be located within the boundaries of the United States; the sole jurisdiction of which was thus to be limited and trammelled, because open to continual British representation and reclamation, based upon treaty stipulations. This infringement upon the perfect sovereignty of the nation inside its own borders, in favor of savage communities and under foreign guarantee, was one of the propositions formally brought forward as a *sine qua non* by the British negotiators at Ghent. Although by that time the United States stood alone face to face with Great Britain, at whose full disposal were now the veterans of the Peninsular War, and the gigantic navy, which the abdication of Napoleon had released from all other opponents, the American commissioners refused with dignity to receive the proposition even for reference. "It is not necessary," they replied, "to refer such demands to the American Government for its instructions. They will only be a fit subject for deliberation when it becomes necessary to decide upon the expediency of an absolute surrender of national independence."

The envoys of the United States were able to be firm, because secure of indignant support by their people; but it is beyond question that two naval victories had arrayed upon their side, at the moment, the preponderance of military argument, which weighs so heavily in treaties of peace. New Orleans was yet in the future, with adverse chances apparent; but, owing to the victory of Perry, the United States was in firm military tenure of the territory, the virtual cession of which was thus demanded. A year after Perry, McDonough's equally complete success on Lake Champlain, by insuring control of the water route for invasion, rolled back the army of Peninsular veterans under Prevost, at a season of the year which forbade all hope of renewing the enterprise until another spring. Great Britain was too eager to end twenty years of continued war to brook further delay. The lake campaigns of 1813 and 1814 thus emphasized the teaching of history as to the influence of control of the water upon the course of events; and they illustrate also the too often forgotten truth, that it is not by brilliant individual feats of gallantry or skill, by ships or men, but by the massing of superior forces, that military issues are decided. For, although on a small scale, the lakes were oceans, and the forces which met on them were fleets; and as, on a wider field and in more tremendous issues, the fleets of Great Britain saved their country and determined the fortunes of Europe, so Perry and McDonough averted from the United States, without further fighting, a rectification of frontier—as it is euphemistically styled,—the effecting of which is one of the most fruitful causes and frequent results of war in every continent and at every period.

\*    \*    \*    \*    \*

A year after the conclusion of peace, a weighty opinion as to the effect of the War of 1812 upon the national history was expressed by one of the commissioners, Mr. Albert Gallatin. For fifteen years past, no man had been in closer touch with the springs of national life, national policy, and national action; as representative in Congress, and as intimate adviser of two consecutive Presidents, in his position as Secretary of the Treasury. His experience, the perspicuity of his intellect, and his lucidity of thought and expression, give particular value to his conclusions; the more so that to some extent they are the condemnation, regretfully uttered, of a scheme of political conduct with the main ideas of which he had been closely identified. He wrote: "The war has been productive of evil and of good, but I think the good preponderates. Independent of the loss of lives, and of the property of individuals, the war has laid the foundations of permanent taxes and military establishments, which the Republicans had deemed unfavorable to the happiness and free institutions of the country. But under our former system we were becoming too selfish, too much attached exclusively to the acquisition of wealth, above all, too much confined in our political feelings to local and state objects. The war has renewed and reinstated the national feelings and character which the Revolution had given, and which were daily lessening. The people have now more general objects of attachment, with which their pride and political opinions are connected. They are more Americans; they feel and act more as a nation; and I hope that the permanency of the Union is thereby better secured."

Such, even at so early a date, could be seen to be the meaning of the War of 1812 in the progress of the national history. The people, born by war to independence, had by war again been transformed from childhood, absorbed in the visible objects immediately surrounding it, to youth with its dawning vision and opening enthusiasms. They issued from the contest, battered by adversity, but through it at last fairly possessed by the conception of a national unity, which during days of material prosperity had struggled in vain against the predominance of immediate interests and local prepossessions. The conflict, indeed, was not yet over. Two generations of civic strife were still to signalize the slow and painful growth of the love for "The Union"; that personification of national being, upon which can safely fasten the instinct of human nature to centre devotion upon a person and a name. But, through these years of fluctuating affections, the work of the War of 1812 was continuously felt. Men had been forced out of themselves. More and more of the people became more Americans; they felt and acted more as a nation; and when the moment came that the unity of the state was threatened from within, the passion for the Union, conceived in 1812, and nurtured silently for years in homes and hearts, asserted itself. The price to be paid was heavy. Again war desolated the land; but through war the permanency of the Union was secured. Since then, relieved from internal weakness, strong now in the maturity of manhood, and in a common motive, the nation has taken its place among the Powers of the earth.

ঙ৳ ৳ঙ

THE *War of 1812 ended in a draw. The United States had met the world's greatest power in conflict, and had managed to survive. The memory of the burning of Washington was superseded by the postwar triumph at New Orleans, for though the war had been officially ended at Ghent on December 24, 1814, fifteen days later, the unaware forces of Jackson had met and bested England's Peninsular War veterans. The memory of the wartime divisions lingered to deliver the* coup de grâce *to the Federalist party. It could not overcome its reputation for treason in wartime. The Jeffersonian Republicans surged forward to achieve a one-party dominance. And the Republic freed from the distraction of the now-ended Napoleonic wars turned its gaze inward; its faith in itself restored.*

*James Madison rested secure in the knowledge that Americans were not to be colonists and vassals, but an independent people. The most triumphant of War Hawks, Henry Clay, a career of three and a half decades before him, crowed, "Let any man look at the degraded condition of this country before the war; the scorn of the universe, the contempt of ourselves. . . . What is our present situation? Respectability and character abroad—security and confidence at home . . . our character and Constitutions are placed on a solid basis, never to be shaken."*

*From a war that ended in a draw, there was achieved a positive result.*

*The infinite capacity of mankind to draw from his most abysmal failures a fruitful result was once again demonstrated. Since historians draw their inspiration from the past, they are likely to find themselves entrapped by the rationalizations of the past. Kendrick C. Babcock (1865-1932) so went astray, but, as a consequence, he gives us a portrait that with fidelity conveys an image of a people coming to terms with a fruitless war. He avoids, if he were ever aware of it, the question of whether the benefits that accrued after the war were not the logical result of an inherently rich nation being freed from external distractions, a result that would have followed from the end of the Napoleonic Wars whether or not we had fought the War of 1812.*

# THE RISE OF AMERICAN NATIONALITY
## 1811–1819
### by Kendrick Charles Babcock

Smarting under military defeat, the British ministry was moved strongly to continue the war, even though the cost for the year would be ten million pounds. The ministers, however, had to face several uncomfortable facts: negotiations at Vienna were not proceeding smoothly; the reports from America were unfavorable; the continuance of the war would prevent the reduction of taxation already oppressively high, a reduction which the taxpayers of Great Britain had a right to expect after the defeat of Napoleon. Wellington was asked to go to America to assume command in order to bring about such victories as would enable England to end the war with honor. Wellington on his side gave the ministry very cold comfort; he would go to America if ordered, but it was useless to attempt a land campaign without control of the lakes, and that seemed remote. He furthermore stated that Great Britain was not justified in insisting upon the *uti possidetis*. So the cabinet yielded, negotiations went on, and the British commissioners asked the Americans to submit a project of a treaty.

During the early summer of 1814 the question of impressments loomed up as an insuperable obstacle to peace. The original instructions of April, 1813, made the abandonment of impressments by Great Britain a *sine qua non* for a treaty; failing to secure this, wrote Monroe, "all further negotiations will cease and you will return home without delay." By the new instructions of February, 1814, abandonment was made "important" but not "indispensable"; finally, when the commissioners were assured that no treaty could be made if they insisted on a renunciation by Great Britain of the right to impress, and that as a matter of fact impressments must cease since the royal navy was to be reduced, they asked for new instructions. Under the date of July 27, 1814, Monroe yielded the whole matter by writing to the commission: "You may omit any stipulation of the subject of impressments, if found indispensably necessary to terminate it [the war]."

Still, the formulation of an acceptable treaty in response to the request of the British, developed almost irreconcilable differences among the American commissioners. Those from the east were interested in the preservation of the right to fish off the coasts of British America. The west, whose sentiments were voiced by Clay, desired the nullification of the present right of Great Britain, based on the treaty of 1783, to free navigation of the Mississippi. If the treaty of 1783 was of a nature to be terminated by the result of the breaking out of war between the parties, then the navigation of the Mississippi and the fishing privileges or rights, both had automatically ceased to be. If, on the other hand, the treaty of 1783 was of an extraordinary nature, not nullified by war, which was the contention of Adams, and probably sound in international law, then the right to the fisheries was unimpaired, but the navigation of the Mississippi was still open to Great Britain. It was in the violent discussions which took place upon these questions that Gallatin was especially helpful in harmonizing the differences between Clay and Russell on the one hand and Adams and Bayard on the other. A humorous allusion, a witty thrust, or a keen sally more than once produced a laugh and saved the commission.

The draught treaty as finally sent to the British commissioners, November 10, contained no stipulations either as to the Mississippi or to the fisheries. The British returned the document with many notes and modifications, including the addition of a specific provision conceding their right to navigate the Mississippi. Again protracted debates and sharp contentions between Clay and Adams required the services of Gallatin as peacemaker among peacemakers. But the anxiety of the British cabinet for peace steadily increased; the Americans refused to consent to a clause reserving for further negotiations all questions relating to the fisheries and the Mississippi, since such a wording might have unwelcome implications; and the two commissions mutually agreed to omit all reference to both these questions. The treaty was thus reduced to lowest terms; each party consented to the elimination of all clauses on the questions which had produced the war, and which at the beginning of the negotiations had been considered of vital importance.

The treaty in this expurgated form, as signed December 24, 1814, provided for a cessation of hostilities, for the release of prisoners, for the appointment of commissioners to settle the disputed boundary, for the restoration of all conquests, for the termination of Indian hostilities, and for steps looking towards the abolition of the slave-trade. Not a word about impressments, the right of search, blockades, neutral rights or indemnities; no mention of neutral Indian territories, the control of the Great Lakes, the navigation of the Mississippi, or the fisheries. It was peace in its simplest form, but no more dishonorable to one than the other. It was, as Gallatin wrote to Monroe, "as favorable as could be expected under existing circumstances, so far as they were known to us."

The news of the signing of the treaty reached New York, February 11,

1815; the effect was immediately seen on every hand. Federalists and Republicans alike welcomed the treaty with satisfaction more or less tempered with regret. The Republicans were humiliated at its terms, which fell so far short of their party boasts when the war began, but they solaced themselves with the bare fact of peace. Madison officially declared to Congress that the treaty terminated "with peculiar felicity a campaign signalized by the most brilliant successes," and a war which had "been waged with a success which is the natural result of the wisdom of the Legislative Councils, of the patriotism of the people, of the public spirit of the Militia, and of the valor of the military and naval forces of the country." Presidential euphemism could hardly go further, even in addressing Congress. The Republicans drew great lessons from the war and looked forward eagerly to the prosperity which would surely be realized with the coming of peace. The Federalists reluctantly admitted their gratification at the treaty—"bad as it is we hail it with delight." The stock market in New York and Philadelphia reflected the satisfaction, for stocks rose ten and even eighteen per cent during the week after the announcement of peace.

The treaty was submitted to the Senate on February 15, unanimously ratified, and by proclamation of the president on the 17th, it became the law of the land. "Perhaps at the moment the Americans were the chief losers; but they gained their greatest triumph in referring all their disputes to be settled by time, the final negotiator, whose decision they could safely trust."

When measured by any standard of material or immediate advantage, the results of the War of 1812 were all negative. For two years and a half the United States had waged war upon land and upon sea, yet had not added a square mile of territory nor a ton to her commerce; she had not settled one dispute as to boundaries nor obtained definite recognition for a single right for which she had contended. On the other hand, the losses of men, money, and property were positive and distinct, while the derangement of the finances was not outgrown for some years. But however great the material losses, they were temporary and soon forgotten. The immaterial or spiritual results upon the nation and national policy were not so immediately obvious, but in reality they were second only to those of the Revolution: the first war segregated the materials for an independent nation; the second gave them new form and effective unity.

The cost of the war in men, as wars go, was moderate. The population of the country was about eight and a quarter millions, yet the effectives in the army never exceeded thirty thousand, and the number actually engaged in any one battle never reached four thousand. The number killed in battle was estimated to be about fifteen hundred, the total of killed and wounded in land battles not far from five thousand, and the grand total of losses, including prisoners, nine thousand seven hundred. The most liberal estimate of the loss of men, in battle on sea and land, in camp, in hospital, and in prisons, places it at thirty thousand. In other words, the loss of men could not have exceeded two per cent of the military population, a loss which seems almost insignificant when compared with South Carolina's sacrifice of twenty-five per cent of her military population during the Civil War.

In terms of money, the cost of the war was about two hundred million dollars, which cannot be considered exceedingly burdensome. The issue of bonds and treasury notes had added over eighty millions to the previous debt, which thus rose to one hundred and twenty-seven millions, or about fifteen dollars a head for the population, as against about twenty dollars a head in 1791. Had the currency been in good order and taxation equalized, no one would have complained of the burden of the federal debt.

The people felt the war most severely in the high prices of such commodities as groceries and iron, and in the low prices of the staple products like wheat, flour, tobacco, and cotton, for which there was little or no market while the war lasted. The extent of these difficulties was illustrated by the sudden reversal of conditions after peace was proclaimed, when the price of sugar was cut in two and the price of flour rose fifty per cent. The figures of the export trade of the country told the same story: 1811, forty-five million dollars; 1813, twenty-five million dollars; 1814, seven million dollars. New England suffered least, because the British in the early stages of the war refrained from harassing that section, and because the New-Englanders defied the laws of the United States by trading with the armies of the enemy on the Canadian frontier and in Maine, and by taking advantage of British permits for trading at sea. Yet Boston's trade in foreign products, first imported, and then exported to Europe, fell from nearly six million dollars in 1811, to slightly more than three hundred thousand dollars in 1813. Virginia, on the other hand, suffered most from lack of market for her flour and for her tobacco, which, Jefferson declared, "is not worth the pipe it is smoked in." Coasting-trade was practically suspended and land transportation so difficult that flour, in August, 1813, was worth $4.50 a barrel in Richmond and $11.87 in Boston.

Considering the extent of the American seaboard and the lack of provision for defence, it is rather surprising that the United States escaped with so little damage to her coasts and cities. Washington was the only city of importance that suffered severely, while the shores of Chesapeake Bay and of Georgia, and the Niagara frontier, were the only regions plundered. The commercial and shipping interests were hardly in a different situation after the war began from that in which they had been for the greater part of the preceding five years. Their losses probably were no greater by capture in war than they had been by French sequestration and English prize courts. At the Boston docks in September, 1813, two hundred and forty-nine sea-going vessels were lying idle, ninety-one being of the largest class. When the war ended, one hundred and forty-four vessels sailed from Boston within a month, while the entries into Charleston, South Carolina, in three weeks of April, 1815, showed one hundred and fifty-eight vessels exclusive of coasters. That the year 1815 did bring great relief to American commerce is undeniable, but it cannot safely be asserted that this relief was a result of the war, though Clay, in a fine frenzy, in 1813, had said that the United States was "fighting for FREE TRADE AND SAILORS' RIGHTS."

After the war and the peace of Ghent, rather than because of these events, the United States was in a new sense free to work out her destinies. By a stroke of good-fortune and a rare combination of circumstances in Europe and America, comparable with those which existed in 1783 and 1793, the United States was free from entangling connections with England or France and from subserviency to their animosities. Save for the brief period between 1789 and 1793, she had known no such freedom before. Old things had passed away—questions of neutral rights, impressments, embargoes, orders in council, French decrees, Napoleonic treachery. The new world was to be a domestic world. Its questions would be too big for the states to solve alone; national settlement and national action would be required on such issues as the currency, banking, the tariff, internal improvements, public lands, the extension of slavery, immigration, and the development of the west.

All but unconsciously the nation at the close of the war heard and obeyed the call to face about. Hitherto it had looked towards the sea; for years it had scanned the horizon anxiously, lest the coming ship should be unfriendly or the bearer of ill tidings for merchant and statesman. Now its face was set towards the west and the frontier, of which the illimitable possibilities were beginning to dawn upon the national consciousness, as they had been borne in upon Washington and Jefferson in the days of the fathers. The breezy exuberance and the high optimism of the first products of this western life had been felt with vague and uncertain forebodings by the leaders of the old school, when the "war hawks" took it upon themselves in 1811 and 1812 to settle for the nation the long-threshed question of peace or war. Now that the war was over, the same energy and optimism were to be devoted freely for a generation to the new problems. Surely in land areas and in politics there was to be a new earth if not a new heaven.

In dealing with these new affairs, or old affairs on a vaster scale, the ideal and spirit of the nation were to be of vital importance. There was no body of traditions to guide, no solid backing of experience to which to appeal, no adequate conception of the magnificence of the future for which the foundations must be deeply laid. Experimentation, reorganization, readjustment, expansion—these were the processes by which the youthful fibre of the republic was to be hardened for its ever-enlarging work in the world. "We are great," exclaimed Calhoun in 1816, "and rapidly—I was about to say fearfully—growing. This is our pride and danger, our weakness and our strength."

The consciousness of nationality which came out of the second war with Great Britain was the chief political result, the one most far-reaching in its effects. Before the war the alignment of parties was determined quite as much by the sympathies of the voter with England or with France as by his attitude towards the Constitution or towards the rights of the states. The British party (Jefferson's Anglomen) and the French party (the Federalists' Mobocrats), could not, of course, change all their stripes in a single five years; but common pride in the navy and its achievements, exultation in the peace which brought with it such immediate prosperity, and the fact that the Republicans of 1815 had absorbed a good number of Federalist principles in their fourteen years of power, tended to soften, if not to obliterate, party lines.

Up to the declaration of war, the United States was practically still in colonial relation to Europe, and was treated accordingly by Great Britain and France. The war in America and the closing of an era in Europe changed all this, and made steady progress in nationalism possible. The narrowness of the escape from exactly the opposite condition—the collapse of the national government in 1815—has not been given proper emphasis. The historian who begins to spin from the distaff of what might have been, may spin forever; but it seems clear that Madison's administration, and with it the fate of the federal government, was in the balance in 1815. Men waited anxiously for news from New Orleans, anticipating defeat for Jackson at the hands of the veterans from the Continental wars; they were prepared to learn from the next packet from Europe that negotiations at Ghent had failed; the committee from the Hartford Convention, with its ominous suggestions, was already in Washington to treat with Congress and the administration. The shock of severe defeat at New Orleans, or complete rupture at Ghent, might have loosed even the slender ties holding the administration together, and sent the fragments of the discredited government flying from the capitol just as the march of the British had dispersed the president and his cabinet in the preceding summer. With victory favoring the United States at Ghent and at the mouth of the Mississippi, the Federalists might well believe that the stars in their courses fought for the Republicans; for it seemed that no degree of incapacity or imbecility in the government and no excess of incompetency in its generals could overbalance good fortune, the fortune of peace.

The government and party thus saved had come into power by the "revolution of 1801," strongly emphasizing democratic principles, state rights, and strict construction of the Constitution; it emerged from the war in 1815 greatly changed, if not greatly chastened, by fourteen years of experience in administration, including three years of war. Every deviation from the strict principles of 1801 had been in the direction of nationalism—the purchase of Louisiana, the embargo, the seizure of West Florida, and the imposition of a direct tax along with the revival of excises. Hamilton himself would have hesitated to take some of the steps which the Jeffersonian Republicans took trippingly. It was this new, nationalized democracy, purged of most of its impractical theories, which found itself triumphant as the result of the war, and apparently endowed with a long lease of power. Nationalism and democracy were to grow together, both reinforced by the development of the west, by the diversion of the attention of the east from commerce to manufacturing, and by the change from attachment to European interests to devotion to internal development.

In several respects the two parties had exchanged places. The Federalists threatened secession in 1811, because the party responsible for the Virginia and Kentucky resolutions of 1798 and 1799 was about to admit part of the Louisiana purchase as the state of Louisiana, without the consent of all the

original states. Later on, the Hartford Convention seemed to make preparations for breaking up the Union. The extent to which Republicans had
adopted Federalist positions is perhaps best illustrated by the suggestions in
Madison's annual message of 1815; for none but a strong government with
liberal endowment of powers could carry out his programme: liberal provisions for defence, an enlarged navy, protection to manufacturers, national
roads and canals, a national university, more military academies, and—very
cautiously—a national bank.

Even before this message was prepared, Congress gave evidence of the
conversion of the Republicans to better views regarding the army and navy.
The ratification of the treaty of Ghent made it necessary to put the two
services on a peace footing. Monroe, the secretary of war, recommended to
the Senate committee on military affairs the establishment of an army of
twenty thousand men, involving an annual expense of five million dollars.
But this was too much for either House; after various votes for ten, six,
and fifteen thousand men, ten thousand was agreed upon in conference, and
in this form the bill became a law. Though no large provision was made for
the future of the navy, the whole war establishment was maintained unre-
duced, and an appropriation of four million four hundred thousand dollars
made for its support.

A little war upon the dey of Algiers might be called one of the results of
the war against England. In almost the same breath by which Congress had
voted to continue the whole war establishment of the navy, it authorized
the use of that navy for punishing the dey for his depredations upon American commerce. In the annual tribute which the United States had paid for
seventeen years to the piratical Algerine, he alleged there was a deficiency
of twenty-seven thousand dollars, and, taking advantage of the war with
England, he captured American ships and enslaved American citizens. In
accordance with the act of Congress, Captain Decatur sailed with ten vessels
in May, 1815, to punish the dey and exact a new treaty. After destroying
a forty-six-gun frigate and a smaller vessel, he sailed boldly into the harbor
of Algiers, and finally extracted from the dey the renunciation of all tribute
for the future, the release of all American prisoners without ransom, and a
guarantee that the commerce of the United States should never again be
molested by the Algerians. "You told us," one of the dey's courtiers is reported as saying to the British consul, "that the American navy would be
destroyed in six months by you, and now they make war upon us with three
of your own vessels which they have taken from you." A visit to Tunis and
Tripoli with the same grim purpose resulted in similar guarantees of safety
to American commerce in the Mediterranean.

Not the least of the results of the war was the prominence gained by three
of the younger military commanders, each of whom, in consequence, eventually was nominated for the presidency, and two of them elected. The
American people, while essentially peace-loving and unmilitary by temperament, have shown a curious hero-worship of the successful military leader.
The "availability" of Jackson, Harrison, Taylor, and Grant for the presi-

dency rested almost entirely upon their records as military commanders. Ever after 1815 Andrew Jackson was known as the "Hero of New Orleans," and in a few years he became a presidential possibility. William Henry Harrison was a man of good family, education, and political experience, but except as the victor at Tippecanoe in 1811, and at the Thames in 1813, he would hardly have been a highly eligible candidate for the presidency at the age of sixty-seven. Winfield Scott entered the war as a young lieutenant-colonel, but at the close he bore the epaulets of a major-general and a gold medal voted by Congress; promotion and the opportunities of the Mexican War made him the logical Whig military candidate in 1852. Another presidential candidate, a civilian, was John Quincy Adams, whose advancement came as a result of his part in the negotiations at Ghent—a fine recognition of real merit, undiminished by any suggestion of personal or party "pull." Madison transferred him from St. Petersburg to London at the close of the war, and from that post he was called to be secretary of state in 1817 and president in 1825.

Social results of any particular event or series of events, like those of a war, are not easy to disentangle or measure. Such results cannot be traced like a nerve-fibre from the brain to a particular organ. What changes might have appeared in American society, even had there been no war with England, simply as a result of the expansion of the country, the development of slavery, and the pacification of Europe, are matters for infinite speculation. This much, however, may be set down as an effect of the war: a new, almost intoxicating sense of self-respect on the part of the people and the governing powers in state and nation. The young men of 1815, who had heard so much depreciation of American character during the years of depression and subservience to France and England, gloried in the demonstration of the courage—and good fortune—of the nation; nor did even the Federalists analyze too carefully the validity of the grounds for this personal and national uplift. All were quite ready to forget those things which were behind, and press towards the realization of a new high calling.

The effect of this fresh, free impulse, this fine sense of detachment and of opportunity, affected the literary and religious life of America almost as profoundly as it did the political and economic ideals and activities of the nation. It aided the "theological thaw" which had already begun before 1815. The emotional side of the revolt from the hardness of the old orthodoxy found its expression in the attempts of Campbell in the west and of Hosea Ballou in the east to reduce religion to a simpler and more inclusive matter, as over against the complex, severely logical exclusiveness of Calvinism and its modifications. The Unitarian movement in New England, centering about Harvard University, had been spreading for a decade when the peace of Ghent was made. Its strong emphasis on the worth of man and the naturalness of his living a loving, sober, righteous, and godly life, according to the dictates of a mind carefully instructed in the comprehensible things of the spirit and of doctrine, fell in with the new national sense of the political worth of the people of the nation. Even where these two movements did not cause organized changes in the churches, their influence was clearly felt, though the era of good feeling in the religious world was slow in succeeding the war of faction and doctrine.

In literature the new life began to manifest itself in this second decade of the century, but it seems to be rather a part of the large movement in the English-speaking race than a merely local or national affair, for the international ferment of the American Revolution and of the French Revolution and the Napoleonic period had not exhausted its influence at the end of the generation of those who took part in these mighty events. Still it was perhaps due in no small degree to the conditions of the time, that, within a period of twelve years following 1810, there were graduated from Harvard University alone a group of men whose achievements, each in his own field of activity, were to be great: Edward Everett, Henry Ware, William H. Prescott, John G. Palfrey, George Bancroft, Caleb Cushing, and Ralph Waldo Emerson. Bryant was beginning his literary career with the striking "Lines to a Waterfowl" and "Thanatopsis." Irving published his uniquely fresh *History of New York, by Diedrich Knickerbocker,* in 1809. The *North American Review* began its long and honorable career in 1815. The rise of a group of political and occasional orators of great power and of brilliant diction must not be forgotten in any estimate of the intellectual and social characteristics of the period after 1811; their efforts were as distinctly literary and stimulating as were the efforts of Ware or Irving. Clay, Calhoun, Webster, and Everett found their original inspiration in the national idea, and with one exception maintained it with cumulative power and grace.

# IV

## The Middle Years

FEW *historians more profoundly affected the interpretation of American history than Frederick Jackson Turner (1862-1932). In a single essay written in 1893, one that stirred hardly a ripple among historians when first presented, Turner formulated his frontier thesis. It set forth the proposition that "The existence of an area of free land, its continuous recession, and the advance of American settlement westward, explain American development." Free land had provided Americans with free opportunity, and this in turn had broken down the ancient European social rigidities. The result was an essentially individualistic, highly democratic people, conditioned to think in terms of social and economic mobility. The announcement contained in the 1890 Federal Census that the frontier was finally closed led Turner to ask what would be the next stage of American history, and what would be the key force shaping its development? He concluded it would be the formulation of a distinctly American type with the merging of sectional diversity into a national type.*

*The provocative implications of Turner's thesis soon became apparent. A whole generation of historians set to work developing the implications of the thesis. It provided the framework for writing a nationalistic history, one which would clearly set America apart. By 1920, the Turner thesis had gained almost universal acceptance. It was also in the 1920's that a comprehensive criticism of the frontier thesis began. As early as 1921, Charles A. Beard rejected the singular importance of the frontier, insisting instead it was only one of a number of influences, and that subordinate to the conflict between capital and labor, which shaped the American character. Subsequent criticism focused on Turner's tendency toward treating westward migration as too orderly, his overemphasis on geographical rather than cultural and ethnic factors, and his exaggeration of the Middle-Western role in shaping the American character. The foundation of Turner's hypothesis concerning the impact of free land received a damaging blow when such historians as Fred A. Shannon (1893-1963) demonstrated that the Homestead Act, the legislative epitomization of free land, had proved of small benefit to land-hungry migrants. The insularity of the frontier thesis provoked sharp criticism, particularly from Carlton J. H. Hayes (1882-1965), who contended the preoccupation with the frontier had led Americans dangerously to divorce the American experience from the larger framework of western history.*

*By mid-century, as the twentieth-century American, increasingly living in an urban technology, and enveloped in a world characterized by upheaval, reacted against the obvious inadequacy of traditional values, historians turned their scrutiny on the "agrarian myth" fostered by Turner. The equation of democracy and agriculture had tended to cast the transition of the United States into an industrial-urban nation into the shadows. By implication, as the United States had moved away from its rural base, it had also moved away from democracy. The underlying bias of American politics in favor of rural representation, unchallenged until the Supreme Court decisions of the mid-1960's proclaiming one man one vote, had obstructed the solution of urban problems. Thus the Turner thesis faced a growing challenge from all sides.*

*Nevertheless, the frontier hypothesis of American history had provoked a wide research; it would not be unfair to state that if the worth of an historical hypothesis is its stimulation of research, then Turner had achieved a masterpiece. It also remains true that the frontier did greatly influence in a variety of ways the American character. And if what people believe is true shapes their responses to the world around them, then the incontrovertible fact remains that Americans believed the frontier made them different. In this latter sense, Turner's thesis is beyond dispute.*

# THE FRONTIER
# IN AMERICAN HISTORY

## by Frederick Jackson Turner

Behind institutions, behind constitutional forms and modifications, lie the vital forces that call these organs into life and shape them to meet changing conditions. The peculiarity of American institutions is the fact that they have been compelled to adapt themselves to the changes of an expanding people—to the changes involved in crossing a continent, in winning a wilderness, and in developing at each area of this progress out of the primitive economic and political conditions of the frontier into the complexity of city life. Said Calhoun in 1817, "We are great, and rapidly—I was about to say fearfully—growing!" So saying, he touched the distinguishing feature of American life. All peoples show development; the germ theory of politics has been sufficiently emphasized. In the case of most nations, however, the development has occurred in a limited area; and if the nation has expanded, it has met other growing peoples whom it has conquered. But in the case of the United States we have a different phenomenon. Limiting our attention to the Atlantic coast, we have the familiar phenomenon of the evolution of institutions in a limited area, such as the rise of representative government; the differentiation of simple colonial governments into complex organs; the progress from primitive industrial society, without division of labor, up to manufacturing civilization. But we have in addition to this a recurrence of the process of evolution in each western area reached in the process of expansion. Thus American development has exhibited not merely advance along a single line, but a return to primitive conditions on a continually advancing frontier line, and a new development for that area. American social development has been continually beginning over again on the frontier. This perennial rebirth, this fluidity of American life, this expansion westward with its new opportunities, its continuous touch with the simplicity of primitive society, furnish the forces dominating American character. The true point of view in the history of this nation is not the Atlantic coast, it is the Great West.

\*    \*    \*    \*    \*

In this advance, the frontier is the outer edge of the wave—the meeting point between savagery and civilization. Much has been written about the frontier from the point of view of border warfare and the chase, but as a field for the serious study of the economist and the historian it had been neglected.

The American frontier is sharply distinguished from the European frontier—a fortified boundary line running through dense populations. The most significant thing about the American frontier is, that it lies at the hither edge of free land. In the census reports it is treated as the margin of that settlement which has a density of two or more to the square mile. The term is an elastic one, and for our purposes does not need sharp definition. We shall consider the whole frontier belt, including the Indian country and the outer margin of the "settled area" of the census reports. This paper will make no attempt to treat the subject exhaustively; its aim is simply to call attention to the frontier as a fertile field for investigation, and to suggest some of the problems which arise in connection with it.

In the settlement of America we have to observe how European life entered the continent, and how America modified and developed that life and reacted on Europe. Our early history is the study of European germs developing in an American environment. Too exclusive attention has been paid by institutional students to the Germanic origins, too little to the American factors. The frontier is the line of most rapid and effective Americanization. The wilderness masters the colonist. It finds him a European in dress, industries, tools, modes of travel, and thought. It takes him from the railroad car and puts him in the birch canoe. It strips off the garments of civilization and arrays him in the hunting shirt and the moccasin. It puts him in the log cabin of the Cherokee and Iroquois and runs an Indian palisade around him. Before long he has gone to planting Indian corn and plowing with a sharp stick; he shouts the war cry and takes the scalp in orthodox Indian fashion. In short, at the frontier the environment is at first too strong for the man. He must accept the conditions which it furnishes, or perish, and so he fits himself into the Indian clearings and follows the Indian trails. Little by little he transforms the wilderness, but the outcome is not the old Europe, not simply the development of Germanic germs, any more than the first phenomenon was a case of reversion to the Germanic mark. The fact is, that here is a new product that is American. At first, the frontier was the Atlantic coast. It was the frontier of Europe in a very real sense. Moving westward, the frontier became more and more American. As successive terminal moraines result from successive glaciations, so each frontier leaves its traces behind it, and when it becomes a settled area the region still partakes of the frontier characteristics. Thus the advance of the frontier has meant a steady movement away from the influence of Europe, a steady growth of independence on American lines. And to study this advance, the men who grew up under these conditions, and the political, economic, and social results of it, is to study the really American part of our history.

In the course of the seventeenth century the frontier was advanced up the Atlantic river courses, just beyond the "fall line," and the tidewater region became the settled area. In the first half of the eighteenth century another advance occurred. Traders followed the Delaware and Shawnese Indians to the Ohio as early as the end of the first quarter of the century. Gov. Spotswood, of Virginia, made an expedition in 1714 across the Blue Ridge. The end of the first quarter of the century saw the advance of the Scotch-Irish and the Palatine Germans up the Shenandoah Valley into the western part of Virginia, and along the Piedmont region of the Carolinas. The Germans in New York pushed the frontier of settlement up the Mohawk to German Flats. In Pennsylvania the town of Bedford indicates the line of settlement. Settlements had begun on New River, a branch of the Kanawha, and on the sources of the Yadkin and French Broad. The King attempted to arrest the advance by his proclamation of 1763, forbidding settlements beyond the sources of the rivers flowing into the Atlantic; but in vain. In the period of the Revolution the frontier crossed the Alleghanies into Kentucky and Tennessee, and the upper waters of the Ohio were settled. When the first census was taken in 1790, the continuous settled area was bounded by a line which ran near the coast of Maine, and included New England except a portion of Vermont and New Hampshire, New York along the Hudson and up the Mohawk about Schenectady, eastern and southern Pennsylvania, Virginia well across the Shenandoah Valley, and the Carolinas and eastern Georgia. Beyond this region of continuous settlement were the small settled areas of Kentucky and Tennessee, and the Ohio, with the mountains intervening between them and the Atlantic area, thus giving a new and important character to the frontier. The isolation of the region increased its peculiarly American tendencies, and the need of transportation facilities to connect it with the East called out important schemes of internal improvement, which will be noted farther on. The "West," as a self-conscious section, began to evolve.

\*    \*    \*    \*    \*

The Atlantic frontier was compounded of fisherman, fur-trader, miner, cattle-raiser, and farmer. Excepting the fisherman, each type of industry was on the march toward the West, impelled by an irresistible attraction. Each passed in successive waves across the continent. Stand at Cumberland Gap and watch the procession of civilization, marching single file—the buffalo following the trail to the salt springs, the Indian, the fur-trader and hunter, the cattle-raiser, the pioneer farmer—and the frontier has passed by.

Stand at South Pass in the Rockies a century later and see the same procession with wider intervals between. The unequal rate of advance compels us to distinguish the frontier into the trader's frontier, the rancher's frontier, or the miner's frontier, and the farmer's frontier. When the mines and the cow pens were still near the fall line the traders' pack trains were tinkling across the Alleghanies, and the French on the Great Lakes were fortifying their posts, alarmed by the British trader's birch canoe. When the trappers scaled the Rockies, the farmer was still near the mouth of the Missouri.

Why was it that the Indian trader passed so rapidly across the continent? What effects followed from the trader's frontier? The trade was coeval with American discovery. The Norsemen, Vespuccius, Verrazani, Hudson, John Smith, all trafficked for furs. The Plymouth pilgrims settled in Indian cornfields, and their first return cargo was of beaver and lumber. The records of the various New England colonies show how steadily exploration was carried into the wilderness by this trade. What is true for New England is, as would be expected, even plainer for the rest of the colonies. All along the coast from Maine to Georgia the Indian trade opened up the river courses. Steadily the trader passed westward, utilizing the older lines of French trade. The Ohio, the Great Lakes, the Mississippi, the Missouri, and the Platte, the lines of western advance, were ascended by traders. They found the passes in the Rocky Mountains and guided Lewis and Clark, Frémont, and Bidwell. The explanation of the rapidity of this advance is connected with the effects of the trader on the Indian. The trading post left the unarmed tribes at the mercy of those that had purchased fire-arms—a truth which the Iroquois Indians wrote in blood, and so the remote and unvisited tribes gave eager welcome to the trader. "The savages," wrote LaSalle, "take better care of us French than of their own children; from us only can they get guns and goods." This accounts for the trader's power and the rapidity of his advance. Thus the disintegrating forces of civilization entered the wilderness. Every river valley and Indian trail became a fissure in Indian society, and so that society became honeycombed. Long before the pioneer farmer appeared on the scene, primitive Indian life had passed away. The farmers met Indians armed with guns. The trading frontier, while steadily undermining Indian power by making the tribes ultimately dependent on the whites, yet, through its sale of guns, gave to the Indian increased power of resistance to the farming frontier. French colonization was dominated by its trading frontier; English colonization by its farming frontier. There was an antagonism between the two frontiers as between the two nations. Said Duquesne to the Iroquois, "Are you ignorant of the difference between the king of England and the king of France? Go see the forts that our king has established and you will see that you can still hunt under their very walls. They have been placed for your advantage in places which you frequent. The English, on the contrary, are no sooner in possession of a place than the game is driven away. The forest falls before them as they advance, and the soil is laid bare so that you can scarce find the wherewithal to erect a shelter for the night."

And yet, in spite of this opposition of the interests of the trader and the farmer, the Indian trade pioneered the way for civilization. The buffalo trail became the Indian trail, and this became the trader's "trace"; the trails widened into roads, and the roads into turnpikes, and these in turn were transformed into railroads. The same origin can be shown for the railroads of the South, the Far West, and the Dominion of Canada. The trading posts reached by these trails were on the sites of Indian villages which had been placed in positions suggested by nature; and these trading posts, situated so as to command the water systems of the country, have grown into such cities as Albany, Pittsburgh, Detroit, Chicago, St. Louis, Council Bluffs, and Kansas City. Thus civilization in America has followed the arteries made by geology, pouring an ever richer tide through them, until at last the slender paths of aboriginal intercourse have been broadened and interwoven into the complex mazes of modern commercial lines; the wilderness has been interpenetrated by lines of civilization growing ever more numerous. It is like the steady growth of a complex nervous system for the originally simple, inert continent. If one would understand why we are today one nation, rather than a collection of isolated states, he must study this economic and social consolidation of the country. In this progress from savage conditions lie topics for the evolutionist.

The effect of the Indian frontier as a consolidating agent in our history is important. From the close of the seventeenth century various intercolonial congresses have been called to treat with Indians and establish common measures of defense. Particularism was strongest in colonies with no Indian frontier. This frontier stretched along the western border like a cord of union. The Indian was a common danger, demanding united action. Most celebrated of these conferences was the Albany congress of 1754, called to treat with the Six Nations, and to consider plans of union. Even a cursory reading of the plan proposed by the congress reveals the importance of the frontier. The powers of the general council and the officers were, chiefly, the determination of peace and war with the Indians, the regulation of Indian trade, the purchase of Indian lands, and the creation and government of new settlements as a security against the Indians. It is evident that the unifying tendencies of the Revolutionary period were facilitated by the previous cooperation in the regulation of the frontier. In this connection may be mentioned the importance of the frontier, from that day to this, as a military training school, keeping alive the power of resistance to aggression, and developing the stalwart and rugged qualities of the frontiersman.

It would not be possible in the limits of this paper to trace the other frontiers across the continent. Travelers of the eighteenth century found the "cowpens" among the cane-brakes and peavine pastures of the South, and the "cow drivers" took their droves to Charleston, Philadelphia, and New York. Travelers at the close of the War of 1812 met droves of more than a thousand cattle and swine from the interior of Ohio going to Pennsylvania to fatten for the Philadelphia market. The ranges of the Great Plains, with ranch and cowboy and nomadic life, are things of yesterday and of today. The experience of the Carolina cowpens guided the ranchers of Texas. One element favoring the rapid extension of the rancher's frontier is the fact that in a remote country lacking transportation facilities the product must be in small bulk, or must be able to transport itself, and the cattle raiser could easily drive his product to market. The effect of these great ranches on the subsequent agrarian history of the localities in which they existed should be studied.

The maps of the census reports show an uneven advance of the farmer's frontier, with tongues of settlement pushed forward and with indentations of wilderness. In part this is due to Indian resistance, in part to the location of river valleys and passes, in part to the unequal force of the centers of frontier attraction. Among the important centers of attraction may be mentioned the following: fertile and favorably situated soils, salt springs, mines, and army posts.

The frontier army post, serving to protect the settlers from the Indians, has also acted as a wedge to open the Indian country, and has been a nucleus for settlement. In this connection mention should also be made of the government military and exploring expeditions in determining the lines of settlement. But all the more important expeditions were greatly indebted to the earliest pathmakers, the Indian guides, the traders and trappers, and the French voyageurs, who were inevitable parts of governmental expeditions from the days of Lewis and Clark. Each expedition was an epitome of the previous factors in western advance.

In an interesting monograph, Victor Hehn has traced the effect of salt upon early European development, and has pointed out how it affected the lines of settlement and the form of administration. A similar study might be made for the salt springs of the United States. The early settlers were tied to the coast by the need of salt, without which they could not preserve their meats or live in comfort. Writing in 1752, Bishop Spangenburg says of a colony for which he was seeking lands in North Carolina, "They will require salt & other necessaries which they can neither manufacture nor raise. Either they must go to Charleston, which is 300 miles distant. . . . Or else they must go to Boling's Point in Va. on a branch of the James & is also 300 miles from here. . . . Or else they must go down the Roanoke—I know not how many miles—where salt is brought up from the Cape Fear." This may serve as a typical illustration. An annual pilgrimage to the coast for salt thus became essential. Taking flocks or furs and ginseng root, the early settlers sent their pack trains after seeding time each year to the coast. This proved to be an important educational influence, since it was almost the only way in which the pioneer learned what was going on in the East. But when discovery was made of the salt springs of the Kanawha, and the Holston, and Kentucky, and central New York, the West began to be freed from dependence on the coast. It was in part the effect of finding these salt springs that enabled settlement to cross the mountains.

From the time the mountains rose between the pioneer and the seaboard, a new order of Americanism arose. The West and the East began to get out of touch of each other. The settlements from the sea to the mountains kept connection with the rear and had a certain solidarity. But the over-mountain men grew more and more independent. The East took a narrow view of

American advance, and nearly lost these men. Kentucky and Tennessee history bears abundant witness to the truth of this statement. The East began to try to hedge and limit westward expansion. Though Webster could declare that there were no Alleghanies in his politics, yet in politics in general they were a very solid factor.

The exploitation of the beasts took hunter and trader to the west, the exploitation of the grasses took the rancher west, and the exploitation of the virgin soil of the river valleys and prairies attracted the farmer. Good soils have been the most continuous attraction to the farmer's frontier. The land hunger of the Virginians drew them down the rivers into Carolina, in early colonial days; the search for soils took the Massachusetts men to Pennsylvania and to New York. As the eastern lands were taken up migration flowed across them to the west. Daniel Boone, the great backwoodsman, who combined the occupations of hunter, trader, cattle-raiser, farmer, and surveyor— learning, probably from the traders, of the fertility of the lands of the Upper Yadkin, where the traders were wont to rest as they took their way to the Indians, left his Pennsylvania home with his father, and passed down the Great Valley road to that stream. Learning from a trader of the game and rich pastures of Kentucky, he pioneered the way for the farmers to that region. Thence he passed to the frontier of Missouri, where his settlement was long a landmark on the frontier. Here again he helped to open the way for civilization, finding salt licks, and trails, and land. His son was among the earliest trappers in the passes of the Rocky Mountains, and his party are said to have been the first to camp on the present site of Denver. His grandson, Col. A. J. Boone, of Colorado, was a power among the Indians of the Rocky Mountains, and was appointed an agent by the government. Kit Carson's mother was a Boone. Thus this family epitomizes the backwoodsman's advance across the continent.

\*     \*     \*     \*     \*

From the beginning of the settlement of America, the frontier regions have exercised a steady influence toward democracy. In Virginia, to take an example, it can be traced as early as the period of Bacon's Rebellion, a hundred years before our Declaration of Independence. The small landholders, seeing that their powers were steadily passing into the hands of the wealthy planters who controlled Church and State and lands, rose in revolt. A generation later, in the governorship of Alexander Spotswood, we find a contest between the frontier settlers and the property-holding classes of the coast. The democracy with which Spotswood had to struggle, and of which he so bitterly complained, was a democracy made up of small landholders, of the newer immigrants, and of indented servants, who at the expiration of their time of servitude passed into the interior to take up lands and engage in pioneer farming. The "War of the Regulation," just on the eve of the American Revolution, shows the steady persistence of this struggle between the classes of the interior and those of the coast. The Declaration of Grievances which the back counties of the Carolinas then drew up against the aristocracy that dominated the politics of those colonies exhibits the contest between the democracy of the frontier and the established classes who apportioned the legislature in such fashion as to secure effective control of government. Indeed, in a period before the outbreak of the American Revolution, one can trace a distinct belt of democratic territory extending from the back country of New England down through western New York, Pennsylvania, and the South.

In each colony this region was in conflict with the dominant classes of the coast. It constituted a quasi-revolutionary area before the days of the Revolution, and it formed the basis on which the Democratic party was afterwards established. It was, therefore, in the West, as it was in the period before the Declaration of Independence, that the struggle for democratic development first revealed itself, and in that area the essential ideas of American democracy had already appeared. Through the period of the Revolution and of the Confederation a similar contest can be noted. On the frontier of New England, along the western border of Pennsylvania, Virginia, and the Carolinas, and in the communities beyond the Alleghany Mountains, there arose a demand of the frontier settlers for independent statehood based on democratic provisions. There is a strain of fierceness in their energetic petitions demanding self-government under the theory that every people have the right to establish their own political institutions in an area which they have won from the wilderness. Those revolutionary principles based on natural rights, for which the seaboard colonies were contending, were taken up with frontier energy in an attempt to apply them to the lands of the West. No one can read their petitions denouncing the control exercised by the wealthy landholders of the coast, appealing to the record of their conquest of the wilderness, and demanding the possession of the lands for which they have fought the Indians, and which they had reduced by their ax to civilization, without recognizing in these frontier communities the cradle of a belligerent Western democracy. "A fool can sometimes put on his coat better than a wise man can do it for him,"— such is the philosophy of its petitioners. In this period also came the contests of the interior agricultural portion of New England against the coastwise merchants and property-holders, of which Shays' Rebellion is the best known, although by no means an isolated instance.

By the time of the constitutional convention, this struggle for democracy had affected a fairly well-defined division into parties. Although these parties did not at first recognize their interstate connections, there were similar issues on which they split in almost all the States. The demands for an issue of paper money, the stay of execution against debtors, and the relief against excessive taxation were found in every colony in the interior agricultural regions. The rise of this significant movement wakened the apprehensions of the men of means, and in the debates over the basis of suffrage for the House of Representatives in the constitutional convention of 1787 leaders of the conservative party did not hesitate to demand that safeguards to the property should be furnished the coast against the interior. The outcome of the debate left the question of suffrage for the House of Representatives dependent upon the policy of the separate States. This was in effect imposing a property qualification throughout the nation as a whole, and it was only as the interior of the country developed that these restrictions gradually gave way in the direction of manhood suffrage.

All of these scattered democratic tendencies Jefferson combined, in the period of Washington's presidency, into the Democratic-Republican party. Jefferson was the first prophet of American democracy, and when we analyze the essential features of his gospel, it is clear that the Western influence was the dominant element. Jefferson himself was born in the frontier region of Virginia, on the edge of the Blue Ridge, in the middle of the eighteenth century. His father was a pioneer. Jefferson's "Notes on Virginia" reveal clearly his conception that democracy should have an agricultural basis, and that manufacturing development and city life were dangerous to the purity of the body politic. Simplicity and economy in government, the right of revolution, the freedom of the individual, the belief that those who win the vacant lands are entitled to shape their own government in their own way,—these are all parts of the platform of political principles to which he gave his adhesion, and they are all elements eminently characteristic of the Western democracy into which he was born.

In the period of the Revolution he had brought in a series of measures which tended to throw the power of Virginia into the hands of the settlers in the interior rather than of the coastwise aristocracy. The repeal of the laws of entail and primogeniture would have destroyed the great estates on which the planting aristocracy based its power. The abolition of the Established Church would still further have diminished the influence of the coastwise party in favor of the dissenting sects of the interior. His scheme of general public education reflected the same tendency, and his demand for the abolition of slavery was characteristic of a representative of the West rather than of the old-time aristocracy of the coast. His sympathy with the Western expansion culminated in the Louisiana Purchase. In short, the tendencies of Jefferson's legislation were to replace the dominance of the planting aristocracy by the dominance of the interior class, which had sought in vain to achieve its liberties in the period of Bacon's Rebellion.

Nevertheless, Thomas Jefferson was the John the Baptist of democracy, not its Moses. Only with the slow setting of the tide of settlement farther and farther toward the interior did the democratic influence grow strong enough to take actual possession of the government. The period from 1800 to 1820 saw a steady increase in these tendencies. The established classes in New England and the South began to take alarm. Perhaps no better illustration of the apprehensions of the old-time Federal conservative can be given than these utterances of President Dwight, of Yale College, in the book of travels which he published in that period:—

> The class of pioneers cannot live in regular society. They are too idle, too talkative, too passionate, too prodigal, and too shiftless to acquire either property or character. They are impatient of the restraints of law, religion, and morality, and grumble about the taxes by which the Rulers, Ministers, and Schoolmasters are supported. . . . After ex-

posing the injustice of the community in neglecting to invest persons of such superior merit in public offices, in many an eloquent harangue uttered by many a kitchen fire, in every blacksmith shop, in every corner of the streets, and finding all their efforts vain, they become at length discouraged, and under the pressure of poverty, the fear of the gaol, and consciousness of public contempt, leave their native places and betake themselves to the wilderness.

Such was a conservative's impression of that pioneer movement of New England colonists who had spread up the valley of the Connecticut into New Hampshire, Vermont, and western New York in the period of which he wrote, and who afterwards went on to possess the Northwest. New England Federalism looked with a shudder at the democratic ideas of those who refused to recognize the established order. But in that period there came into the Union a sisterhood of frontier States—Ohio, Indiana, Illinois, Missouri—with provisions for the franchise that brought in complete democracy.

Even the newly created States of the Southwest showed the tendency. The wind of democracy blew so strongly from the West, that even in the older States of New York, Massachusetts, Connecticut, and Virginia, conventions were called, which liberalized their constitutions by strengthening the democratic basis of the State. In the same time the labor population of the cities began to assert its power and its determination to share in government. Of this frontier democracy which now took possession of the nation, Andrew Jackson was the very personification. He was born in the backwoods of the Carolinas in the midst of the turbulent democracy that preceded the Revolution, and he grew up in the frontier State of Tennessee. In the midst of this region of personal feuds and frontier ideals of law, he quickly rose to leadership. The appearance of this frontiersman on the floor of Congress was an omen full of significance. He reached Philadelphia at the close of Washington's administration, having ridden on horseback nearly eight hundred miles to his destination. Gallatin, himself a Western man, describes Jackson as he entered the halls of Congress: "A tall, lank, uncouth-looking personage, with long locks of hair hanging over his face and a cue down his back tied in an eel-skin; his dress singular; his manners those of a rough backwoodsman." And Jefferson testified: "When I was President of the Senate he was a Senator, and he could never speak on account of the rashness of his feelings. I have seen him attempt it repeatedly and as often choke with rage." At last the frontier in the person of its typical man had found a place in the Government. This six-foot backwoodsman, with blue eyes that could blaze on occasion, this choleric, impetuous, self-willed Scotch-Irish leader of men, this expert duelist, and ready fighter, this embodiment of the tenacious, vehement, personal West, was in politics to stay. The frontier democracy of that time had the instincts of the clansman in the days of Scotch border warfare. Vehement and tenacious as the democracy was, strenuously as each man contended with his neighbors for the spoils of the new country that opened before them, they all had respect for the man who best expressed their aspirations and their ideas. Every community had its hero. In the War of 1812 and the subsequent Indian fighting Jackson made good his claim, not only to the loyalty of the people of Tennessee, but of the whole West, and even of the nation. He had the essential traits of the Kentucky and Tennessee frontier. It was a frontier free from the influence of European ideas and institutions. The men of the "Western World" turned their backs upon the Atlantic Ocean, and with a grim energy and self-reliance began to build up a society free from the dominance of ancient forms.

The Westerner defended himself and resented governmental restrictions. The duel and the blood-feud found congenial soil in Kentucky and Tennessee. The idea of the personality of law was often dominant over the organized machinery of justice. That method was best which was most direct and effective. The backwoodsman was intolerant of men who split hairs, or scrupled over the method of reaching the right. In a word, the unchecked development of the individual was the significant product of this frontier democracy. It sought rather to express itself by choosing a man of the people, than by the formation of elaborate governmental institutions.

\* \* \* \* \*

But quite as deeply fixed in the pioneer's mind as the ideal of individualism was the ideal of democracy. He had a passionate hatred for aristocracy, monopoly and special privilege; he believed in simplicity, economy and in the rule of the people. It is true that he honored the successful man, and that he strove in all ways to advance himself. But the West was so free and so vast, the barriers to individual achievement were so remote, that the pioneer was hardly conscious that any danger to equality could come from his competition for natural resources. He thought of democracy as in some way the result of our political institutions, and he failed to see that it was primarily the result of the free lands and immense opportunities which surrounded him. Occasional statesmen voiced the idea that American democracy was based on the abundance of unoccupied land, even in the first debates on the public domain.

This early recognition of the influence of abundance of land in shaping the economic conditions of American democracy is peculiarly significant today in view of the practical exhaustion of the supply of cheap arable public lands open to the poor man, and the coincident development of labor unions to keep up wages.

Certain it is that the strength of democratic movements has chiefly lain in the regions of the pioneer. "Our governments tend too much to democracy," wrote Izard, of South Carolina, to Jefferson, in 1785. "A handicraftsman thinks an apprenticeship necessary to make him acquainted with his business. But our backcountrymen are of the opinion that a politician may be born just as well as a poet."

The Revolutionary ideas, of course, gave a great impetus to democracy, and in substantially every colony there was a double revolution, one for independence and the other for the overthrow of aristocratic control. But in the long run the effective force behind American democracy was the presence of the practically free land into which men might escape from oppression or inequalities which burdened them in the older settlements. This possibility compelled the coastwise States to liberalize the franchise; and it prevented the formation of a dominant class, whether based on property or on custom. Among the pioneers one man was as good as his neighbor. He had the same chance; conditions were simple and free. Economic equality fostered political equality. An optimistic and buoyant belief in the worth of the plain people, a devout faith in man prevailed in the West. Democracy became almost the religion of the pioneer. He held with passionate devotion the idea that he was building under freedom a new society, based on self government, and for the welfare of the average man.

And yet even as he proclaimed the gospel of democracy the pioneer showed a vague apprehension lest the time be short—lest equality should not endure—lest he might fall behind in the ascending movement of Western society. This led him on in feverish haste to acquire advantages as though he only half believed his dream. "Before him lies a boundless continent," wrote De Tocqueville, in the days when pioneer democracy was triumphant under Jackson, "and he urges forward as if time pressed and he was afraid of finding no room for his exertions."

Even while Jackson lived, labor leaders and speculative thinkers were demanding legislation to place a limit on the amount of land which one person might acquire and to provide free farms. De Tocqueville saw the signs of change. "Between the workman and the master," he said, "there are frequent relations but no real association. . . . I am of the opinion, upon the whole, that the manufacturing aristocracy which is growing up under our eyes is one of the harshest which ever existed in the world; . . . if ever a permanent inequality, of conditions and aristocracy, again penetrates into the world, it may be predicted that this is the gate by which they will enter." But the sanative influences of the free spaces of the West were destined to ameliorate labor's condition, to afford new hopes and new faith to pioneer democracy, and to postpone the problem.

*PROPONENTS of the frontier thesis drew to its banner many defenders. Few proved more effective than Frederic L. Paxson (1877-1948), for long a professor of history at the University of Wisconsin where Turner had launched his original investigations into the frontier. But Paxson reflected a steady reaction to the developing criticisms of the original Turner thesis. Throughout his career he was convinced that the dominant force in American life prior to the twentieth century was the frontier; but he anticipated that during the second century of American independence, the preponderant forces would be industry and the "pressure of the outside world." In addition, his observations of the outside world led him to question Turner's assertion that the frontier had shaped democracy, for the evidence overwhelmingly indi-cated that non-frontier countries had made substantial progress toward de-mocracy in the nineteenth century.*

*The existence of a frontier had shaped the American experience. Even if it were not a sufficient explanation for democracy, an explanation that neg-lected the frontier would be as ineffective as cannon drawn up for battle without cannon balls. The possession of western territories had endowed the federal government with a vast property whose disposition whetted the appetite of legions of entrepreneurs. Although at first the government tried to sell its domain, it soon discovered that a popularly elected government is hard pressed to play creditor, particularly when its debtors happen to be its electoral master. Since settlement on the frontier required a capital stake, not infrequently the major purchasers of western lands were speculative syn-dicates prepared to sell on credit lands purchased for a relative pittance from federal land offices. The purchaser, often unable to meet his obligations, fre-quently expressed his sense of grievance at his threatened loss in general de-nunciations of credit agents, and more practically compelled state legislatures to pass stay laws. Thus one of the great themes of American history was rooted in the frontier: on the one side an entrepreneurial rage for gain and on the other the exploitation of democratic politics by entrepreneurial fail-ures to escape the consequences of their failings. The story of wealth vs. commonwealth was as much a tale of the entrepreneurial winner against the entrepreneurial loser as it was of privilege seeking to dominate the exploited masses.*

# HISTORY OF
# THE AMERICAN FRONTIER
## 1763-1893

### by Frederic L. Paxson

The creation of new States along the unsettled border is an excellent index to the shifts of population. The fact that six such commonwealths were added to the United States in the six years beginning with 1816, would of itself establish that period as one of marked migration. But even better than the States as an index are the figures that show the sales of public lands by the United States, for these figures measure not only the opening of new settlements, but the extent to which help had been found to finance the settlement.

In the first fifteen years of the public land system, that terminated with the passage of the Harrison Land Act in 1800, the total sales from the public domain were 1,484,047 acres. This total includes the operations under the three private sales to the Ohio Associates, Symmes, and the State of Penn-sylvania, as well as under the law of 1796. The Harrison Act brought the land office to the buyer, opening at the start four local offices in the Eastern Division of the Northwest Territory. From year to year these offices were closed, shifted, or increased in number, in order to follow the business. Before the Harrison Act was revised in 1820, there were or had been in operation fourteen such offices in Ohio, four in Indiana, three in Illinois, and one in Michigan. Outside the Old Northwest, in the same period, there were three in Alabama, three in Mississippi, four in Louisiana, and two in Missouri.

The distribution of these offices indicates the regions where government sales were most numerous; the annual sales reveal the flow of occupation. But until after the beginning of the War of 1812 the volume of business showed no startling changes. Until this date the business of the land sales was managed in a bureau of the Treasury Department; on April 25, 1812, this was reorganized as a General Land Office, under Edward Tiffin of Ohio as Commissioner. After this date the business increased rapidly, the figures in millions of acres running as follows:

| | | | |
|---|---|---|---|
| 1813 | .14 | 1818 | 2.38 |
| 1814 | .82 | 1819 | 5.11 |
| 1815 | 1.07 | 1820 | 1.08 |
| 1816 | 1.47 | 1821 | .78 |
| 1817 | 1.92 | | |

It is not to be supposed that the figures of sales of public land give a complete measure of the new settlement. Much of the land thus bought was held by speculators and was not cleared or farmed until these owners could find purchasers. There was still much land on the market from earlier grants, in which the emigrants could buy tracts. There were school lands for sale in most of the States. And in Kentucky and Tennessee, where there was no public domain, there was an abundance of private land for sale. No general study has yet been made to show how private land titles originated for any large tract along the frontier. The Wisconsin "Domesday Book," now under way, will show it for a single State; but for the present there is no better indication of the speed with which all lands were being used than the fairly accurate figures for the government-owned part of it. By 1820, according to Donaldson, the government had sold 19,399,158 acres; but nearly a third of this was beyond the power of the purchaser to pay for, and was eventually turned back into the public domain, to be sold again. The defects in the land law that Harrison had promoted as a reform were grievous and notorious before it had been in operation for ten years.

The minimum cost of making a farm under the Harrison Act cannot have been much different from that of making it on land purchased otherwise. This law provided for sale first at public auction, and then at private sale at two dollars an acre. The better lands were often bid up at the auctions to fancy prices, but Donaldson shows that the apparent sales of over nineteen million acres were for a total of only forty-seven million dollars. After the unpaid-for lands were surrendered, the United States received twenty-eight million dollars for thirteen million acres. The actual receipts averaged so nearly the minimum of two dollars an acre that it is clear that this price was not too low for unimproved land on the average frontier.

Under the Harrison Act the minimum amount sold to one buyer was half a section, or three hundred and twenty acres. In 1804 this was lessened to the familiar quarter section of one hundred and sixty acres, which was quite as much as the ordinary frontier farmer could operate, and more than he could expect to pay for. The government requirement for a quarter of the purchase price, or fifty cents an acre, to be paid within forty days of the purchase, meant that such a buyer needed eighty dollars in cash at the time he made his selection. The theory of the credit system, upon which the Harrison Act was based, was that payments after the first were to be earned from the produce of the land. The second quarter was not due until two years after the purchase; the other installments followed a year apart.

Most of the buyers of western lands were both poor and hopeful. Because they were poor, they found that the initial charge of eighty dollars was a large amount of money. Because they were hopeful, they were convinced that it would be easy to raise the later installments, and accordingly used all the ready money they could command in order to make the first payment on as large an acreage as they could get. This left many of them without cash, and the next two years saw few who were able to lay much aside. The number of defaulters at the second, third, and fourth payments increased progressively, and in the long run nearly a third of the lands contracted for were given up. By 1809 Congress began to pass relief acts extending the time of settlement for later installments; and in 1820 the twelfth such act was passed.

That the land system was vicious, was apparent by 1809, but the full extent of the injury it did has never been made clear. Its normal tendency was to create a region in which every citizen was in debt to the United States for a period of four years or more. The political consequence of such a situation, under a system of manhood suffrage, was an unavoidable tendency of public opinion to crystallize against the government. Every elector owed money, and voted to determine the policy of the government to which he owed it. No right of the government as a whole could stand out in his mind as clearly as did his own difficulties in making payments. Even if the whole frontier had been prosperous, there would have been an incentive to tinker with the law to reduce the payments and lighten the load. But the frontier was far from prosperous most of the time, and with every default on an installment, there was added to the electorate another voter in danger of having his farm taken away from him. The Harrison Act made it possible to reassert United States title to tracts that were not paid for, and the contractor was liable to lose his equity in the seizure. As the number of defaulters increased, the pressure increased upon congressmen to bring in acts to relieve their constituents. Even worse, as the number of defaulters increased because of inability to pay, it was further increased by unwillingness to pay. Nothing was actually done to dispossess the men who could not pay. The government threatened to exercise its right to seize the land, but did not do it. The successful farmer, who met his obligation and paid his debt when due, saw that the only difference between himself and his default-ing neighbor was that he had given up his hard earned money and his neigh-bor had not. He asked himself what use it was to pay, when nothing hap-pened to the man who did not pay. In many cases, when his next installment came due, he let it pass unpaid. The larger the proportion of settlers that were in default, the less it was possible for the General Land Office to use successful pressure upon any of them. By 1812 the condition was one of general scandal, with no remedy except in a modification of the Harrison Act, and the total abolition of the credit system. The measurement of the injury done by the system to frontier standards of commercial honor would make an interesting study in group psychology.

A new view of the public lands was rising in the West between 1810 and 1820 as the people questioned the success of the old land policies. The lead-ers began to ask by what right the United States demanded any payment for its land. They challenged the basic idea upon which the public domain had been brought into existence. Congress had believed in 1780 that the western lands could be made a source of public revenue that would ma-terially lessen the financial burdens left by the Revolution. The pressure from the smaller States for the cessions was based upon the belief that the lands were a source of wealth. But the experience since the United States took up their administration was that much money went into them and little came out. There was little net revenue, or none. When at first they were sold in competition with the lands still available in Pennsylvania and western Virginia they could not command either good market or strong price; and as these competitions lessened, the government found itself able to sell a considerable amount, at a nominal price of two dollars an acre, which it could not collect. Land legislation was a consistent source of busi-ness for Congress, and every western representative, as he took his seat, be-came a new obstruction in the way of making the public domain a source of profit. Towards 1820, the western congressmen began to lay stress upon the public services of the men who made new homes in the wilderness, and to demand that they be relieved from the financial burdens placed upon them. A new senator who took his seat from Missouri in 1821, Thomas Hart Benton, made free lands his objective; and after thirty years' service in the Senate, he lived to see his idea widely popular and brought to the verge of complete triumph.

So long as tidewater congressmen prevailed in Washington, there was no hope of victory for the notion that the United States ought to give free farms to the frontiersmen. The eastern desire for revenue was mingled with a genuine fear of the growth of the western States. There was a willingness to restrict the free settlement of the frontier that was more often effective than avowed. By 1820 Congress was convinced that the Harrison Act had broken down, but was not ready to give up the hope of revenue. The par-ticular weakness of the law of 1800 had been the relatively large unit of sale, the system of credit, and the price. The unit was reduced in 1804, and now was reduced still further to half a quarter, or eighty acres. The prin-ciple of credit was now abolished; and by a new law passed April 24, 1820,

sales were required to be made for cash. Upon the matter of price there was
a compromise at $1.25 an acre. The farmers who were still in trouble, hav-
ing defaulted upon installments and become liable to dispossession, were
given the opportunity to make a compromise, and surrender to the United
States the proportion of their lands that they could not pay for. They were
thus enabled to start free once more.

The land law of 1820 was passed after the crest of the great migration
had been reached. The year 1819, in which over five million acres of the
public lands were sold, was also the year of general economic distress and
panic. Not until 1834 was there another year in which the sales were nearly
so great. For a decade after 1820 the frontier was assimilating the land it
had acquired, and there was no strain that indicated special weakness in the
new land act. In the thirties, when wholesale shift of population was resumed once more, the weakness appeared at a different spot; this time in
the inability of the General Land Office to keep its surveys progressing as
rapidly as the people demanded. The generation that established itself between 1800 and 1820 was grounded in the belief that a government price
for land was one of the numerous financial extortions from which it had to
suffer. It was generally convinced that the newer portions of the country
were subject to financial exploitation by the older, and was more bitterly
distressed by the financial bonds that bound it to fellow citizens than by
those that were held by the lighter hand of government.

The need of the frontier citizen for credit was second in importance only
to his need for land. First and most fundamental of his problems was ever
that of acquiring a good title to the land he farmed. The contracts that had
to be made in getting land left a mark upon the first generation, at least, in
any frontier. The second need, to get the money to pay for the land, began
to impress financial traits upon the community; and these in the next generation were sometimes more significant than even the land economics. Land
was one of the occasions for cash and credit. But it was only one among a
shoal of necessities that pressed down upon the young homeseeker and restricted his freedom of action until their demands were met.

Any analysis of the financial requirements of the typical frontier family
will reveal the fact that lack of financial opportunity was one of the compelling causes of migration; and that with migration determined upon, there
were important financial necessities under at least three heads. The money
for the cash payment upon the land was one of the three, and second in
sequence in most cases. In point of time it was preceded by the fund to
cover the costs of transportation; it was followed by a fund for maintenance
until the new farm could become self-supporting.

The typical family on the agricultural frontier was young, poor, and ambitious. There were of course exceptions to the rule of poverty, but these
were not enough to weaken its general binding force. Most young people,
with either property or easy opportunity, were glad not to undertake the
risks and hardships of the frontier life. Those who had neither were likely
to make as short a migration as was consistent with finding cheap land and
desirable living conditions. The exceptions, and numerous they were, to this

rule, are to be found in colonies like that at Marietta or the Connecticut Reserve, or in the individual families who made the long trip from tidewater to the Ohio Valley. New England expanded into the West in some measure, but when a census of origin was taken in any of the western regions it was commonly found that most of the dwellers in a new community originated in the immediately adjacent States, and sought their new homes with the minimum of travel. Yet travel they must in any case. Every homeseeker needed means to get his wagon and team, to buy his simple outfit for operating the home and farm, and to maintain himself and family while on the journey. There is enough scattered evidence—it has never been assembled —to show that a large proportion of the travelers moved on borrowed money, and were unable even to start for their new homes until some obliging neighbor or relative took their notes and provided them with funds. In individual instances the amount was so considerable that many who desired to move were unable to raise the money for it; in the aggregate, the capital so invested became a heavy mortgage upon the future production of the new region.

After raising funds to cover the cost of migration and to make the initial payments upon the land, there still remained the necessity to support the family until crops could be extracted from the reluctant soil. The first harvest can rarely have done this, for the number of acres that could be cleared, planted, and cultivated in the first season was small. There are many estimates that show that the cost of getting a crop into the ground for the first time might be twice or thrice what the land itself would bring while unimproved. The average family lived in part upon the savings of some one else for a year or more. In many instances the newcomers made the first year partially supporting by working for wages for earlier arrivals who could use them on the farms. This naturally lessened, by the amount of the wages, the debt that otherwise must be incurred. But over the whole frontier, taking the average, the home maker continued to go into debt for a year or more after his arrival.

Under these three heads fall most of the debts that the frontiersman accumulated during the process of establishment. If there had been more capital available for loans, every region could have been developed more rapidly than it was. But the United States as a whole possessed little surplus capital for investment. The invasion of European capital had not yet begun on a large scale. There were few sums of eastern wealth that could be used for western development, no machinery for investing it if it had existed, and even less inclination to risk it there. "I have found no evidence that any eastern capital was invested in this way before 1815," said the late Professor Callender. "The settler moved out into the wilderness with his own little stock of household goods, farm implements, and cattle. No merchant with large credit in the East stood ready to advance supplies of food and other necessities to him, while he devoted his labor to the production of a crop to be sent to market, nor was he assisted to clear his land and prepare it for cultivation by loans of cash from individuals or mortgage companies." Professor Callender minimized too much the family loans that sent many an emigrant upon his way, and gives no recognition to the fact that the average distance of the migrant was not many miles—that his connections were not those of a westerner with the East, but of a frontier farmer with a former frontier community, fifty miles or so behind him. But he is right in suggesting that there were few sources from which the pioneer could borrow the funds necessary for the capitalization of his venture, even on the most modest scale.

The development of social institutions provided a new financial resource for the pioneer at the moment of the great migration, and for two decades banks played a double role upon the frontier stage. Cast as the hero in the first act, ready and able to save the heroine from distress, the bank in the second act became the detected villain on the verge of strangling the confiding victim, only to be foiled as the curtain fell by the protective efforts of a new wave of fundamental democracy. Each of the parts played by the banks were inevitable; together they form a contrast that reveals much of the western spirit in its two phases of hopefulness and despondency. And both prove beyond question the high significance of financial institutions in the forming of a new society.

Banks, in the modern sense, are largely the creation of the half century that followed the American Revolution. Great establishments, like the Bank of England, had long preceded this period, but had revealed banking as a detached activity of the state; not as an ordinary agent of commerce. The profits of the banker, and his special interests, have received more attention than the real contribution of banks as such to social finance. It was not that they lent money. Money lenders are so ancient that their origin is lost in antiquity, and they have continued to exist in every community with no perceptible change until today. They have been able to lend, however, only what they possessed, and the limits of their possible business has been the amount of savings that they have accumulated.

The banking idea added two conditions that together brought a fundamental change; these were currency and credit. As to currency, it was gradually learned that promissory notes, redeemable in coin on demand, were seized upon by every community as a convenient local currency. They were kept so busy that until the notes wore to rags they were not sent to the bank of issue for redemption. The world was currency-hungry during these early years of the industrial revolution and found the paper of solvent banks an excellent substitute for specie. The banks of issue soon learned of the long interval that would elapse between the issue of a promissory note and the date of its probable presention for redemption. They learned that the coin held for redeeming the notes would not be needed, all or soon, and that they could extend credit to customers, not only to the amount of their coin capital, but to the amount of promissory notes that they could keep in circulation. The size of a prudent coin reserve, to be held on hand to redeem note issues, was a matter of estimate that ranged from one third to one fifth; but at whatever ratio it was fixed by the operators of the bank, there was a profitable margin of notes above the amount of capital that could be safely lent to borrowers. In the use of this margin, the banker made his profits, above those of the ordinary money lender, who could lend only what he had. For society, the discovery of this margin made the existing capital threefold, or fivefold as fluid as it would otherwise have been. The capital of a community with banks went several times further than the capital of the community without banks. Hence their spread.

Between 1791 and 1811 the United States possessed the Bank of the United States with a charter voted by Congress, and a small but growing number of local banks whose right to do business was based upon acts of legislature in the various States. There were always a few informal banks that existed without legal sanction but because the men behind them deserved and held the confidence of the people to whom they lent their notes. There was no "free banking" in the sense that any group of men who complied with the provisions of the law could enter the business. Instead each institution was supposed to derive its right to exist by a special act of the law-making body. There were only three of these in the United States before the inauguration of George Washington; at the end of his century there were only twenty-six. In 1811 when the charter of the Bank of the United States expired, there were only eighty-eight. The profitable nature of this business and the useful social character of their service had been found out by this time. The refusal of Congress to recharter its own creation opened a period of wholesale extension of private facilities that coincides with the great migration, and gives special form to its financial obligations and opinions.

It was natural that the American banks should appear earliest in the eastern towns where financial transactions were largest and where there were more men of means to appreciate the advantages of pooling their capital in such companies. But shortly after the beginning of the new century they made their appearance in the West. As in the East this function was sometimes acquired by indirection. Most famous of the early banking subtleties was that of the Manhattan Company, chartered in New York in 1799 for providing the lower end of Manhattan Island with drinking water and for other purposes. It construed its "other purposes" into a right to operate a bank of issue which has today become one of the great financial institutions of the United States. There appears to have been a Lexington (Kentucky) Insurance Company, of 1802, that quietly began to issue notes and to do a banking business. The Miami Exporting Company of Cincinnati was chartered by the Ohio legislature at its first session in 1803, to trade up and down the river with New Orleans; but it soon abandoned its first intention and became a bank. The profits to be gained by lending at interest the flexible credit that a bank of issue could control tempted numerous imitators to experiment with the new institutions, and to approach legislatures to solicit charters.

Between 1803 and 1811, banks appeared in one form or other in most of the frontier regions. There was a short-lived one chartered in Michigan Territory in 1806, only to be closed by refusal of Congress to approve the territorial act. It had meanwhile flooded the Detroit region with its notes. There was a Bank of Kentucky in 1806, and a Nashville Bank chartered the following year. This latter, until its suspension during the panic of 1819, was among the most famous of the western establishments. But there was nothing in western banking until 1811 to indicate a "craze" or to suggest more than a reasonable adaptation of business to the tendencies of the times. In 1811 the charter of the Bank of the United States was refused continuance, it closed its doors, and the business it had done became a lure to tempt new ventures into the field.

There was more than the old business of the bank to attract new efforts. There disappeared with the bank a sort of control that had made every other bank in the United States somewhat more reliable than it would otherwise have been. Being the largest financial institution in the country it had occasion daily to do business with the notes of nearly all the eighty-eight other banks that were living independent lives. Each of these was under constant pressure from desirous borrowers to increase its issues beyond what it could safely redeem, and thus to lower its reserve below the danger line. Many of the weaker, or less experienced, or less honest did this; and took the chance of failure in case any holder of their notes should demand their instant redemption. The Bank of the United States was always a large holder of these notes, and was in a position at any moment, when it distrusted solvency, to test this by sending in for redemption a large amount of its notes. The smaller institutions resented this, but could not well avoid it. Their representations, spread among their borrowers, that it was the restrictive policy of the Bank of the United States that kept them from being as accommodating as they desired, did much to stir up in Congress a dislike for the national bank and to prevent its recharter. With it gone, there was not only its business to be struggled for by new banks, but there was an assurance of lack of supervision and restraint that tempted speculators and crooks into the business. A boom struck the United States, under whose influence the banks of the United States multiplied to 307 by 1820. In this the West had more than its full share.

Most famous, perhaps, among the new banks created to replace the Bank of the United States was the Bank of Tennessee, opened in Knoxville, under the presidency of Hugh L. White, with Luke Lea as its cashier. Indicative of the lack of experience among its officers is the fact that upon its chartering, White was sent east to have its notes engraved, and to learn the "forms of financiering." He evidently learned them well, for it was continuously solvent until it wound up its affairs in 1827. As years went on it had many competitors with varying degrees of intelligence and honor, but it never lost its grip on either. Ohio, in 1816, noted the increase in private banking, and sought to regulate and control it by passing a general act under which all such institutions should pay tribute to the State. The State became a partner in the ventures, and began to accumulate experience in the workings of State-owned business. Kentucky, in 1818, responded to the popular desire for easy credit and created a chain of over forty banks with an aggregate capital above eight millions. By law it authorized them to pay in their capital and to redeem their notes, not in coin, but in the notes of either the Second Bank of the United States or the earlier Bank of Kentucky. Before 1819, when panic brought on a general reconsideration of existing banking, there was a flood of paper money induced by the demands of the West for credit. The restraining influences were abolished. The War of 1812 produced a condition in the East that forced most of the banks south of New England to suspend specie payments. It was the British raid on the Chesapeake in 1814, with the burning of the public buildings of Washington, that brought about actual suspension by those that were fearful of either runs or seizure of coin by the enemy. When they refused to redeem their notes in coin the notes remained in use, for there was not much other money, but their value declined. The western banks suspended, to keep what coin they had from being drawn to the East. And with suspension general, there was no possibility that an exigent note holder would bring down the structure of speculation in a crash. "During this year [1814]," wrote a western clergyman, "a money mania, like an epidemic, seized the people. There were seven banking establishments in Jefferson County [Ohio], one of which is said to have been kept in a ladies' chest. But it did not stop here—merchants, tavern keepers, butchers, and bakers became bankers."

The available banking capital of the West nearly doubled between 1814 and 1818, and there is no way of determining with precision the ratio of issues to capital, or the amount of the ostensible capital that was real. In more than one case the subscribers to the stock of a new bank paid in a small fraction of the price of the stock in coin, and received their certificates. They then took the stock certificates to the bank, used them as collateral, to borrow back the coin and with the coin thus received paid the rest of the purchase price. The bank thus did business with a capital nominally of coin but really of notes of the stock subscribers, and was never in a condition to redeem any large portion of its notes.

The elements of strength for society in the new banking institutions lay in the provision of a convenient currency and the saving involved in making what capital there was several-fold more fluid. The dangers were in the inflation of currency that resulted, the inexperience and recklessness of the bankers, and the erroneous use to which nearly every bank devoted its capital. The inflation of currency was certain, with a resulting cheapening of the dollar, and a rise in prices. Economists are not agreed as to the amount of influence that quantity of money has upon its value; but most of them believe that a sudden increase in the volume of circulating medium is followed by a rise in prices. The sudden turning loose upon society of the extra credit made available by the banking circulation brought on such a period of inflation. To much of the United States, and to the West in particular, this rise in prices seemed one of the evidences of prosperity due to the banks, and stimulated the creation of more banks, to make more money.

The bankers of this period were mostly amateurs, who could not have had much knowledge of the institutions they were guiding because the institutions were so new. They learned their lessons as to amount of circulation that was safe, and as to kind of loan that was certain, at the expense of their customers; and when they made mistakes their customers paid. The business was dangerous enough in the hands of honest and careful men. But when banks were founded by speculators, or gamblers, or with deliberate intent to defraud, their notes were likely to gain wide currency before the error was detected, with resulting loss to every one who held them. The "saddlebag" bank appeared in many a community, when slick strangers came to town, opened an office, lent to patrons the clean, fresh money that had bulged their saddlebags on their arrival, disposed of the notes they took to local note-shavers, and disappeared by night with the loot. It was a common fraud to make notes that nearly resembled those of a well-known and solvent bank, and to pass them on confiding merchants fifty or a hundred miles away. Counterfeiting was easy because most of the notes were poorly engraved, and could be imitated by any skillful and dishonest printer. These were the defects that might have been inherent in even a perfect system; but they were present in such proportions as to endanger the future of the whole principle of banking.

Worse than either the inflation or the defects due to the inexperience or dishonesty of bankers, was the type of loan that prevailed. Commercial bankers know today that all their obligations are demand obligations, payable on sight. So it was with the early bankers who lent to the borrower their notes redeemable on demand. It is now a commonplace that sight obligations may return suddenly for fulfillment, and that the harder the times, and the more uncertain the commercial situation, the quicker they come. The only safeguard against bankruptcy brought about by a sudden run is in an adequate reserve, and a set of assets that can be realized in a short time. Best of all the assets is commercial paper, running for short periods of thirty, sixty, or ninety days. A bank confining its business to loans of this type is continually turning over its capital and is ever in a position to watch the markets and trend of business and curtail or expand its loans according to the financial weather. Unless it has a large part of its assets in short-time paper, it is liable to be caught in a financial stringency with "frozen assets" on its hands, perhaps entirely good in the long run, but not negotiable in time to prevent a run from producing bankruptcy. The eastern banks were helped because their customers included the commercial institutions that needed short-time loans. The western ones found among their customers a preponderance of farmers for whom a three-months note was worthless. The farmer who borrowed to cover the costs of transportation, land purchase, and maintenance, had no collateral to offer but his land title, and no means of repayment until he had completed his purchase from the government and earned the money from the land. He needed a long-time mortgage, for three, five, or seven years. He was willing, or could be compelled, to agree to pay a high rate of interest; but he must have time. The result was a pressure upon the frontier banks to lend on mortgage and tie up their capital in slow-moving securities that offered no resource against sudden financial storm. The more prosperous the western bank appeared to be, in good and certain loans outstanding, the worse it really was because of the immense amounts of its notes that were subject to presentation for immediate redemption. So long as the war-time period of suspension lasted, the frontier banks financed the frontier farms, unknowing or careless of the danger they incurred. With the approach of peace, deflation, and specie payments, they saw the danger, and their customers felt it. The bank ceased to be the agent of easy prosperity, and soon assumed the popular appearance of a devouring monster.

The financial crisis of 1819 marks the transition point between the two financial periods, but signs of anti-bank reaction appeared earlier than this. The chartering by Congress of a second Bank of the United States in 1816, and the efforts of this institution to bring about specie payments in 1817 started a new train of thought and action. There was no question at Washington but that the new bank was needed. After the disappearance of the first one, and the outbreak of war, even the Government of the United States had difficulty in maintaining solvency. There was no one bank on which it could rely. Its revenues were uncertain. Its credit was poor. The war loans were raised only in part, and even this only because of the heroic contributions of men of large private means, John Jacob Astor, Stephen Girard, and David Parish. When the war was over, Congress in its reconstruction session chartered a new bank, with the United States as a stockholder, and with power to run until 1836. It had the right also to open branches throughout the country, as opportunity offered, and to do the usual business of issue and discount.

This new bank, in its first two years, was nearly as reckless as the local banks with which it came into competition. It immediately opened sixteen branches, in addition to the main office in Philadelphia. Of these, five were east of Philadelphia and eleven were south and west. It never did a full share of business in New England. There were six distinctly southern branches, at Baltimore, Washington, Richmond, Norfolk, Charleston, and Savannah; and five western, at Pittsburgh, Chillicothe, Cincinnati, Lexington, and New Orleans. At all of these, loans were made and notes were issued. At one time the specie assets of the second bank were less than one ninth of its liabilities. In 1819, when the State banks suspended for a second time, the directors of the Bank of the United States became aware how greatly it had over-issued, and installed a new president with a stern command to curtail and save the institution. It did this at once, and by curtailing its issues increased the number of failures that the panic of 1819 had already made too large. It saved itself, but at the expense of forcing bankruptcy upon many of the smaller banks and weaker merchants, and thereby increasing the wave of resentment that was mounting up. The anti-bank movement became one against all banks, but specially against the Second Bank of the United States. The system of branches made it easy for local antipathies to merge in common attack upon the one symbol of monopolistic national banking.

Even before it curtailed in 1819, the Bank of the United States uncovered hostility to itself and its policies. It forced the local concerns to resume specie payments in 1817 by importing gold and maintaining them itself. Its refusal to do business with suspended banks created heavy pressure upon the latter to resume. As many of the local banks had yielded to the temptation to over-issue, they resumed with difficulty, or not at all. And as they made their own curtailments that were necessarily the price of resumption, they passed on to the disappointed customers as they refused them loans, the antipathy to the second bank.

The constitution of Indiana, framed in 1816, reveals an early phase of the suspicion of the Bank of the United States. It adopted two existing territorial banks, at Madison and Vincennes, as legal; and allowed the legislature to establish a State Bank, with one branch for every three counties in the State, but provided that other than these "There shall not be established or incorporated in this State, any bank or banking company, or monied institution for the purpose of issuing bills of credit, or bills payable to order or bearer." This would have prevented, had the prohibition possessed constitutional validity, the opening in Indiana of any branch of the Bank of the United States. The Illinois constitution, framed two years later, contained a similar prohibition of "banks or monied institutions" except those chartered by the State. The southern States, Alabama and Mississippi, and Missouri, that made constitutions during the great migration, provided for the creation of State banks, but omitted the prohibition against the existence of any others.

The coercive power of the Bank of the United States, that roused resentment against the first, roused it against the second. What Indiana and Illinois wrote into their constitutions, Ohio, Kentucky, Tennessee, Maryland, North Carolina, and Georgia wrote into their statutes between 1816 and 1819. The common statutory way of excluding the branches of the Bank of the United States was to impose heavy taxes upon branches of "foreign" banks—$15,000 a year in Maryland, $50,000 in Ohio and Tennessee, and $60,000 in Kentucky. Before long the new bank was forced to decide how it should treat this attempt at prohibition. Its reluctance to submit brought the matter before the Supreme Court of the United States, and gave John Marshall the occasion to hand down the definitive decision in the cases of McCulloch vs. Maryland, and Osborn vs. United States Bank.

It was the need of the public domain for a policy of government that forced Congress in 1787 to take the first steps in asserting a national authority. From the frontier now, in the resistance against the power of this national authority to charter a national bank, came the stimulus to assert and define the nature of that power. It was not the East or the older sections that gave the most incentive to declare the meaning of the United States, but the frontier with its clear and uniform interests, and its institutions in formative stage. John Marshall seized the occasion arising in this controversy to assert the superiority of the Federal Government for all time. "Let the end [of Federal legislation] be legitimate," he wrote, "let it be within the scope of the constitution, and all means which are appropriate, which are plainly adapted to that end, which are not prohibited, but consist with the letter and the spirit of the constitution, are constitutional." Upon this argument rests the whole doctrine of implied powers, without which the United States Government would have been incompetent to meet the changing conditions brought about by the revolutions in life since 1787. To it may be attributed the steadiness with which the American Constitution has weathered the generations and watched with tranquillity the upheavals that have upset the rest of the world. The conclusion reached by Marshall was inherent in the Constitution, and would doubtless have been reached eventually by another, under a different provocation; but to the historian there is much significance in that the immediate provocation for the doctrine was the frontier experience with the new institutions of finance.

Under the decision in the case of McCulloch vs. Maryland the States were denied the power to interfere in any way with the Bank of the United States, and it proceeded to extend its branches as it pleased. As the years elapsed after the depression of 1819, and as the debtors of that year became solvent again, the antipathies to the second bank dropped beneath the surface of opinion, until a casual observer might have believed that they had vanished. But the distrust for banks continued, and was shown in local struggles for relief in the years immediately following the panic.

Down to 1819 the western States generally encouraged the creation of local banks, and issued charters to them readily, under the belief that they made credit obtainable and were of general use. The result was a blanket of mortgage indebtedness over the region of new development, and a system of banks unable to meet financial stress. When hard times came, and the banks found it necessary to raise funds to meet their notes, they had only two options:—to require debtors as the debts came due to pay in cash; and to make new loans in smaller amounts than were needed by the borrowers. The result was general bankruptcy. The mortgagor was rarely able to raise the money to pay off the principal of his loan; often he could not even meet the high interest charges. When he became delinquent, the bank that owned the mortgage had to decide whether it was wise to foreclose and try to collect what was coming to it by legal process. If it failed to foreclose it drifted into trouble itself with worthless assets. If it foreclosed it made an enemy and terrified every debtor who feared similar treatment.

The uniformity of the burden of debt on the frontier made foreclosure there a more unpopular thing than it is in a mixed community where debtor and creditor rub elbows at every turn. At best it is an unlovely act to turn a debtor out of his property, and by forcing a sale compel him to risk and perhaps lose his equity. But in a mixed community there is a buyer at every sale, and the transaction speedily becomes *fait accompli*. On the frontier, however, with all the neighbors fearing similar treatment, foreclosure became not a regrettable necessity, but an act of malignity. The bank was blamed for an impossible interest rate, and for wanting its money. The buyer was criticized as a bloodless speculator, little better than a thief because he bought at forced and non-competitive sales, and acquired the former owner's equity for nothing. The bank that felt impelled to foreclose, needed to inquire whether it could find a purchaser brave enough to incur local hostility. Like-endangered neighbors often attended the foreclosure sales and by menace discouraged bidding. If no buyer could be found, the bank could not gain anything but odium by attempted foreclosure. The temper of the frontier made debt collection hard.

When the panic broke in 1819 there was the burden of heavy and uniform debt covering the new States and many regions of their elders. Often the farmer had no equity at all because in the enthusiasm of settlement he and the bank had marked his property far above its real value, and he owed on it more than its whole worth. Few frontier banks could adhere to the good rule of a fifty per cent mortgage on a conservative valuation. As money became scarce because of the curtailment, the western legislatures sought to ward off depression. Tennessee launched another Bank of Tennessee, and Kentucky incorporated the Bank of the Commonwealth. Each of these, in substance, lent the credit of the State to citizens.

The Kentucky attempt to fight panic with law deserved, and has received, much attention from historians. The Bank of the Commonwealth was intended to be a machine for note issue, and was relieved by law from the requirement to redeem its notes. Its loans were apportioned among the counties, and were meant to be granted to persons who could not borrow anywhere else. At the same time, in 1820 and 1821, Kentucky passed laws staying the legal action for collecting debts and placing obstacles in the road of foreclosure. The creditor who would not accept the notes of the Bank of the Commonwealth was required to postpone the forcible collection of his debt; foreclosed debtors were given a long period in which they could redeem their property; sales of land by execution were forbidden unless the property brought three quarters of an appraised value fixed by the neighbors —and these could be trusted to make the appraisals high enough. Public opinion fell away from the creditor who sought to protect his rights, as it had already fallen away from the United States when the General Land Office wanted to collect the installments due upon land purchases. The debtor community persuaded itself that it had been so badly treated that default was honorable. In Kentucky the legislature fairly represented the opinion of its constituents.

The Kentucky relief laws were forced to run the gauntlet of the courts, and in 1823 the highest court of the State declared them to be unconstitutional. The judges who handed down this decision were not greeted as courageous defenders of justice against passion, but were denounced as the friends of privilege. The State campaign of 1824 was fought over the issue of the decision, and the people won. The next legislature, finding it impossible to change the decision, repealed the judiciary act, and legislated the offending judges out of legal existence. It created a New Court, more accommodating to public opinion. But the Old Court refused to be abolished, kept up an extra-legal existence, and became the rallying point for the more conservative and the more far-sighted members of the State. As the years went on, the worst effects of the panic were outlived, and solvent farmers, with money coming to them, saw little good in preventing the collection of just debts. By 1826 the Old Court party carried the State, and its next legislature repealed the New Court law over the veto of the governor. Financial solvency had won in the long run, but its victory left permanent scars.

The West that was taking shape between 1819 and 1829 never entirely forgot its antipathy to banks, and its fear of financial institutions. It lost them for short periods, but the emotion was always potent in shaping western opinion, breeding a fear of privilege, and reinforcing the ideas of democracy that Jefferson had found so strong. Neither while the bank war was raging, nor after it subsided, can one understand the frontier States without taking this experience into full account.

&#8669; &#8670;

THE *West has held an especial allure for the American mind. It has provided the setting for a folk myth that has captivated the world. The cowboy and the Indian, no matter how disguised, are the leading proponents for what is essentially a modern-day morality play. In the passing vestiges of a vanishing frontier, elemental man met the elements and triumphed. It was as if Americans were trying to expose the inner workings of their acceptance of the frontier myth. Within the wilderness, an elusive Eden awaited conquest. To surrender belief in the frontier was to surrender finally innocence. The heart of the cowboy and Indian confrontation was the reassurance that good inevitably triumphed over evil. The age-old afflictions of mankind could be lost in a reclaimed primeval world, one that still bore the imprint of original creation. In the end, Americans would escape history.*

*But the great West had come in large part into American hands as a result of a war of aggression against Mexico. Congressman Abraham Lincoln had indicted President James K. Polk for the action contending that Polk was "deeply conscious of being in the wrong—that he feels the blood of this war, like the blood of Abel, is crying to Heaven against him." The entrance of mankind into the wilderness proved the thin sharp edge that cut away the voiceless innocence of primal creation. It was the repeated theme of the frontier interpretation. It accounts for the undercurrent of apprehension and fear for the future that underscored Turner's work. The end of the frontier marked the final loss of Eden. America in the twentieth century was doomed to meet the corrosive impact of history. When there was no longer the hope of beyond, the American would reclaim the past and with it the inescapable ills of humanity.*

*But for a brief period in mid-nineteenth century, Americans believed that the West was ordained to remain closed to settlement. A series of federally inspired explorations of the vast territorial accessions between 1803 and 1853 had fostered in the American mind the belief that the territory was a "Great American Desert," inhospitable and forbidding to settlement. The Long expedition of 1819 had concluded mistakenly "this extensive section of country . . . is almost wholly unfit for cultivation, and of course uninhabitable by a people depending upon agriculture for their subsistence." The belief took a curious direction when in the fifties, despite the conviction that neither Kansas nor Nebraska could support slave agriculture, the ravaging sectional dispute over slavery centered upon the disposition of a territory, at least in much of the popular imagination, unsuited for settlement.*

*How Americans came to doubt this description was first suggested by Turner when he wrote: "The trading posts became the nuclei of later settlement; the trader's trails grew into the early roads, and their portages marked out the location for canals. Little by little the fur-trade was undermining the Indian society and paving the way for the entrance of civilization." The Americans who journeyed across the Great Plains toward the Pacific noted the discrepancies between the popular belief and the observed reality. They chose to stop many times and chance their luck. Their success triggered the erosion of the myth of desert. The epic proportions of this experience has been most fully related by Hiram M. Chittenden (1859-1918). A graduate of the United States Military Academy (1884), he spent his adult career in the army mostly employed on federal engineering works in the West. His two classics,* The American Fur Trade of the Far West *(1901) and* History of Early Steamboat Navigation on the Mississippi River *(1903), have the evocative power that comes only from an intimate awareness of the land of which one writes. The result is more than history, it is an image of a West in which Americans believed even as it passed.*

# THE AMERICAN FUR TRADE OF THE FAR WEST

## by Hiram Martin Chittenden

The expedition whose history forms the subject of this chapter was everywhere popularly known in its day as the Yellowstone Expedition, but is now always spoken of as Long's Expedition. The enterprise was regarded as one of great possibilities for the public good, particularly in the West. The failure of Mr. Astor's project upon the Columbia; the disastrous fortunes of the Missouri Fur Company; the evidences of British influence with Indians residing in United States territory; and the necessity of protection to American trade in the more remote regions; these considerations had prevailed upon Congress to make a formidable showing of national authority along the upper course of the Missouri. Not a few hoped that the arms of the government would be carried to the Columbia, and that American rights upon that river would be restored, as the Treaty of Ghent required, to the status existing before the War of 1812.

The enterprise was a popular one in all parts of the country, and was a favorite measure of President Monroe, and of his Secretary of War, John C. Calhoun. In a letter to the Secretary during the progress of the enterprise, the President said: "The people of the whole Western country take a deep interest in the success of the contemplated establishment at the mouth of the Yellowstone river. They look upon it as a measure better calculated to preserve the peace of the frontier, to secure to us the fur trade and to break up the intercourse between the British traders and the Indians, than any other which has been taken by the government. I take myself very great interest in the success of the expedition, and am willing to take great responsibility to ensure it."

The object of the expedition is officially stated by Secretary Calhoun as follows: "The expedition ordered to the mouth of the Yellowstone, or rather to the Mandan village, is a part of a system of measures which has for its objects the protection of our northwestern frontier and the greater extension of our fur trade."

To the people of the West, and in fact of the whole country, the expedition promised results of which the official purpose above quoted was a very inadequate expression. Quotations might be given at great length from the press of the country and even of Europe, evincing the warmest interest in the enterprise; but it will suffice to notice a few from the Western press to show how great were the expectations of those most directly interested. In an editorial of April 21, 1819, the *Missouri Gazette* of St. Louis said: "The importance of this expedition has attracted the attention of the whole nation, and there is no measure which has been adopted by the present administration that has received such universal commendation. If the agents of the government who have charge of it fulfil the high expectations which have been raised, it will conspicuously add to the admiration with which the administration of James Monroe will hereafter be viewed. . . . In every point of view the Yellowstone Expedition will stand prominent. It will add to the security of the Western country, particularly the frontier settlements; it will keep in check the Indians and prevent their depredations; it will tend to destroy in some measure the influence that our British neighbors possess over the minds of the natives; it will throw additional light upon the geography of that noble river, the Missouri, and also the country on its banks now inhabited by the Indians; it will encourage Western emigration; it will protect and encourage the fur trade which is now productive of such important benefits to the country, and which can be made much more productive; it will conduce to open the communication which nature has ordained ought to exist between the Mississippi and the Pacific ocean. . . . If the expedition should succeed, as we fondly hope and expect, and the views of government should be carried into effect, the time will not be far distant when another nation will inhabit west of the Mississippi, equal at least, if not superior, to those which the ancient remains still found in this country lead us to believe once flourished here: a nation indeed rendered more durable by the enjoyment of that great invention of American freemen—a Federal Republic." The article then went on to state some of the dangers of failure which might arise if unpractical men were put in charge. It gave wise advice in regard to the treatment of the Indians, and throughout displayed a knowledge of the conditions of success which might well have indicated the writer as a fitting individual to form part of the personnel of the expedition.

*Niles' Register* of October 17, 1818, quoting the *St. Louis Enquirer*, said:

"The establishment of this post [at the mouth of the Yellowstone] will be an era in the history of the West. It will go to the source and root of the fatal British influence which has for so many years armed the Indian nations against our Western frontier. It carries the arms and power of the United States to the ground which has hitherto been exclusively occupied by the British Northwest and Hudson Bay Companies, and which has been the true seat of British power over the Indian mind. Now the American arms and the American policy will be displayed upon the same theater. The Northwest and Hudson Bay Companies will be shut out from the commerce of the Missouri and Mississippi Indians; the American traders will penetrate in safety the recesses to the Rocky mountains in search of its rich furs; a commerce yielding a million per annum will descend the Missouri, and the Indians, finding their wants supplied by the American traders, their domestic wars restrained by American policy, will learn to respect the American name.

"The name of the Yellowstone river will hereafter be familiar to the American ear."

The high expectations which were built on the possibilities of this expedition are in no way better illustrated than in the exaggerations to which they gave rise. One enthusiast seriously avowed his opinion that the expedition would open a "safe and easy communication to China, which would give such a spur to commercial enterprise that ten years shall not pass away before we shall have the rich productions of that country transported from Canton to the Columbia, up that river to the mountains, over the mountains and down the Missouri and Mississippi, all the way (mountains and all) by the potent power of steam. These are not idle dreams, rely upon it; to me it seems much less difficult than it was universally considered when I first came here to navigate the Missouri and sailboats." The writer of this letter was indeed a trifle "previous" in his forecast, but one can discern in his heated imagination a dim conception of the railroad yet to be. It was not to be for many years, but the time has come when the "potent power of steam" transports the goods of China over "mountains and all" to every mart where the needs of the people require them.

We can hardly realize now what visions of future greatness then filled the minds of our people. Steam had fairly entered upon its conquest of the navigable waters of the globe, and scarcely a day passed but that some new feat astonished the world and brushed aside another of the "impossibilities" of conservatism. All ranks of society felt the thrill of the new era, and even men of sober experience were swept along in the current. The following views, expressed by a man of long and distinguished public service, reflect the general enthusiasm of the time. Speaking of the Yellowstone Expedition he said: "See those vessels, with the agency of steam, advancing against the powerful currents of the Mississippi and the Missouri! Their course is marked by volumes of smoke and fire, which the civilized man observes with admiration, and the savage with astonishment. Botanists, mineralogists, chemists, artisans, cultivators, scholars, soldiers; the love of peace, the capacity for war, philosophical apparatus and military supplies; telescopes and cannon; garden seeds and gunpowder; the arts of civil life and the force to defend them—all are seen aboard. The banner of freedom which waves over the whole proclaims the character and protective power of the United States."

We have given somewhat at length, and in their own language, the views of the people at the time upon this important expedition, because a full understanding of their high expectations is necessary in order to appreciate their deep disappointment at their non-fulfillment. Unfortunately the very magnitude of the enterprise and its unbounded possibilities led to an elaboration of the means for carrying it into effect which, by its cumbersomeness, proved fatal to the undertaking.

The expedition was to be both military and scientific in character. The movement of troops was planned on a scale wholly beyond the requirements of the occasion, and it was at one time contemplated to send upward of a thousand men. Congress had been led to believe that the movement would actually result in a saving to the military establishment of upwards of forty thousand dollars a year, owing mainly to the diminished cost of subsistence in a country where game was so abundant and grazing free. Troops were moved from Plattsburg, Philadelphia, Detroit, and Bellefontaine near St. Louis. The military expedition was under command of Colonel Henry Atkinson, and so far as he was unhampered in his operations he seems to have conducted it with the practical good sense for which that officer was distinguished. He adopted a device of his own for propelling keelboats, consisting of paddle wheels similar to those of a steamboat, but operated by the soldiers who were on board. This arrangement worked well enough to justify its adoption in an expedition conducted by General Atkinson to the mouth of the Yellowstone in 1825. The movement of the troops began in the fall of 1818 and a considerable detachment under Captain Martin passed the winter near the mouth of the Kansas river at a cantonment christened Camp Martin. The general advance took place in the following spring.

The scientific part of the expedition was under the direction of Major Stephen H. Long, of the Corps of Engineers, U.S.A., an officer of high professional reputation. He was assisted by Major Biddle, who kept the journal; Dr. Baldwin, botanist; Dr. Say, zoologist; Dr. Jessup, geologist; Mr. Peale, assistant naturalist; Mr. Seymour, painter and sketcher, and Lieutenant Graham and Cadet Swift, topographical assistants. The instructions of the Secretary of War to Major Long stated that "the object of the expedition is to acquire as thorough and accurate knowledge, as may be practicable, of a portion of the country which is daily becoming more interesting, but which is yet imperfectly known. You will ascertain the latitude and longitude of remarkable points, with all possible precision. You will, if possible, ascertain some point in the 49th parallel of latitude which separates our possessions from those of Great Britain. A knowledge of the extent of our limits will tend to prevent collision between our traders and theirs.

"You will enter in your journal everything interesting in relation to soil, face of country, water courses, and productions, whether animal, vegetable, or mineral.

"You will conciliate the Indians by kindness and presents, and will ascertain as far as practicable the number and character of the various tribes, with the extent of country claimed by each."

The instructions of President Jefferson to Captains Lewis and Clark were also cited for guidance.

Such were the fond expectations in regard to this great undertaking and such the elaborate preparations for carrying it into effect. But the magnitude of the conception was in no wise sustained by the skill of its execution. The arrangement for the transportation of the troops disclosed a degree of folly, if nothing worse, which is a disgrace to the military history of the government. The conditions of travel up the Missouri were thoroughly understood at the time, and it was known that by the aid of keelboats the march to the mouth of the Yellowstone could be easily accomplished in a single season. Such was evidently Colonel Atkinson's idea. But the officials in St. Louis having the matter of transportation in charge thought otherwise. So great an enterprise as the Yellowstone Expedition must be conducted with becoming state. No keelboat transportation would answer. The steamboat, that new power on the Western rivers, was alone appropriate to the occasion. Although no steamboat had yet entered the Missouri river, and although a little practical reflection must have shown that some experience would be required to develop and overcome the difficulties of navigating that unruly stream, and that the first efforts must be largely failures, still the government decided to rely mainly upon steamboats. In putting into effect this plan it committed the always disastrous mistake of trusting itself, bound hand and foot, to the tender mercies of a contractor. Of those connected with this expedition, one Colonel James Johnson, contractor, emerges from its confused history with the glory of having accomplished all and more than he expected. Without competition he secured a contract, December 2, 1818, in which not only were the prices exorbitant, but some of them were left to future contingencies to be fixed by arbitration if agreement should fail between the principals. He was also to be allowed advances before services were performed, and that without adequate security to the government. Thus practically guaranteed against loss, the shrewd Colonel Johnson took little care to see that his equipment was of a character which should ensure a prompt fulfillment of the contract. He provided five steamboats, the *Jefferson, Expedition, Johnson, Calhoun,* and *Exchange.* There is no record that the last two were able to enter the Missouri at all. The *Jefferson* gave out and abandoned the trip thirty miles below Franklin. The *Expedition* and *Johnson* wintered at Cow Island, a little above the mouth of the Kansas, and returned to St. Louis in the following spring. In his entire arrangements Colonel Johnson failed to come up to the contract, and the expedition was thereby hopelessly delayed and its main purpose thwarted. In the disagreements that subsequently arose arbitrators had to be called in, and these sided with the contractor, allowing him over forty thousand dollars for loss occasioned by the very delays for which he alone was responsible. The matter was so scandalous that it led to an investigation by a committee of Congress, who reported against the justice and legality

of the award, and recommended the institution of legal proceedings to recover the amount wrongfully paid.

The expedition had not proceeded far before it became evident that its
management was hopelessly weak and that it must fall far short of its original
purpose. The whole summer was spent on the lower river and it was September 26th before the troops reached Council Bluffs. All thought of going
farther was abandoned for the time. A camp was established called Camp
Missouri, and here the troops remained for the winter. It proved to be one
of the most disastrous winter encampments in the history of the army. The
troops suffered terribly from the scurvy. Over three hundred were attacked
and of these about one hundred died. The disease prevailed to some extent
all winter, and by spring the situation had become "truly deplorable." As
soon as it was possible to navigate the river, many of the sick were sent to
Fort Osage.

The steamboat craze on this expedition was not confined to the military
portion, but extended to the scientific adjunct as well. For the use of Major
Long's party a special boat was constructed which appears in every way
to have been a decided novelty. It was called the *Western Engineer,* and was
probably the first stern-wheel steamboat ever built. It was launched in Pittsburg in the winter of 1818-19. The only description of this craft which
has come to our notice is the following from the *Missouri Gazette* of May
26, 1819, and a letter written about a month later: "The *Western Engineer*
is well armed and carries an elegant flag representating a white man and an
Indian shaking hands, the calumet of peace and the sword. The boat is 75
feet long, 13 feet beam and draws 19 inches of water. The steam passes off
through the mouth of a large figure-head (a serpent). . . . The wheels are
placed in the stern." Omitting the absurd attempts at ornamentation, the
boat was as much of a success as could have been expected at that early stage
of steamboat experience. It was far better adapted to the navigation of the
Missouri than were any of Colonel Johnson's boats, and although it did not
leave St. Louis until some time after the rest of the expedition had gone, it
passed them all before they reached the mouth of the Kansas, and was the
only boat that went through to Council Bluffs.

How this unusual craft impressed the popular eye may be inferred from
the following extract from a letter dated St. Louis June 19, 1819, ten days
after its arrival at that city: "The bow of this vessel exhibits the form of a
huge serpent, black and scaly, rising out of the water from under the boat,
his head as high as the deck, darted forward, his mouth open, vomiting
smoke, and apparently carrying the boat on his back. From under the boat
at its stern issues a stream of foaming water, dashing violently along. All
the machinery is hid. Three small brass field pieces mounted on wheel carriages stand on the deck. The boat is ascending the rapid stream at the rate
of three miles an hour. Neither wind nor human hands are seen to help her,
and, to the eye of ignorance, the illusion is complete, that a monster of the
deep carries her on his back, smoking with fatigue, and lashing the waves
with violent exertion. Her equipments are at once calculated to attract and
to awe the savages. Objects pleasing and terrifying are at once placed before

him—artillery, the flag of the Republic, portraits of the white man and the Indian shaking hands, the calumet of peace, a sword, then the apparent monster with a painted vessel on his back, the sides gaping with portholes and bristling with guns. Taken altogether, and without intelligence of her composition and design, it would require a daring savage to approach and accost her with Hamlet's speech: 'Be thou a spirit of health or goblin damned, etc.' "

The *Western Engineer* left St. Louis on the 9th of June, 1819, and proceeded by very leisurely stages up the Missouri. The little boat seems to have done very well and to have experienced but few breakages of machinery. There were no incidents of special importance en route. At St. Charles four of the party left the boat for the purpose of exploring the country along shore, but the experience was too rough for them and they were fain to seek the comforts of the boat before a week had passed. At Franklin a stop of a week was made. The people of this frontier town fairly outdid themselves in their extravagant celebrations, on the occasion of the visits of Colonel Atkinson and Major Long. Banquets were had and toasts proposed on a scale that would have done honor to the Capital or metropolis of the country. The record of these elaborate ceremonials may still be read in the files of the newspaper published in Franklin at the time.

Major Long was unfortunate in losing one of his party at Franklin. Dr. Baldwin who was in very ill health was left here and died on the 31st of August following. On the 19th of July four of the party left Franklin to go by land to Fort Osage and the boat left the next day. Fort Osage was reached on the 1st of August. On the 6th most of the party set out from this place by land with the intention of visiting the Kansas and Pawnee Indians and rejoining the expedition near Council Bluffs. The boat left Fort Osage on the 10th, and on the 18th arrived at Isle à la Vache, a few miles above the present site of Leavenworth, where Captain Martin had wintered with three companies of troops, expecting to proceed up the river early in the spring.

A delay of a week was made at Camp Martin for the purpose of treating with the Kansas Indians. The *Western Engineer* resumed her trip on the 25th of August, being accompanied by fifteen soldiers under a Lieutenant Field in the keelboat *General Smith*. Four days after their departure the land party, who were to have gone on to Council Bluffs, arrived at Isle à la Vache for the purpose of again availing themselves of the comforts of the boat. They had been pretty roughly handled by a small party of Pawnees and were satisfied with their taste of frontier experience. Two of them, Messrs. Say and Jessup, were quite ill. Finding the boat gone, the party, except the two sick men, set out by forced marches, and overhauled her on the 1st of September. No other incident of moment occurred until the 17th of September when the boat arrived at Fort Lisa, where it was received by the inmates of the fort with a salute of ordnance and a hospitable welcome. Although yet scarcely halfway to the mouth of the Yellowstone, the great objective point of the expedition, it was decided to go into winter quarters here. Major Long remained only two weeks when he set out for Washington.

The site of the camp for the scientific party was located "half a mile above Fort Lisa, five miles below Council Bluffs, and three miles above the mouth of the Boyer river." The place was christened the *Engineer Cantonment.*

The winter passed away pleasantly enough with the scientific party. They improved their time in securing information concerning the neighboring tribes and particularly the Omahas. They made a few short excursions into the surrounding country, obtained the latitude and longitude of their cantonment, and made some investigation into the geology and natural history of the Missouri valley.

The records of the expedition show that there were continuous and friendly relations subsisting between the military and the members of the Missouri Fur Company. Hospitalities were given and received. Manuel Lisa invited the officers to dinner at his house and the officers reciprocated in kind, and thus began that hospitable intercourse between the citizens of this locality and the officers of the army which has continued until the present day. There were two ladies present, one of them the wife of Lisa and daughter of Stephen Hempstead of St. Louis. The name of the other is not known, but these two women are presumed to be the first who had ascended the Missouri as far as to the present site of Omaha.

It must be apparent from the account just given of the operations of 1819 that the Yellowstone Expedition thus far had been an unqualified failure if not a huge fiasco. The whole enterprise had been smothered in elaboration of method. Although the troops could with ease have marched three times as far as the boats carried them, it was considered necessary to transport them in a manner becoming the dignity of so vast an enterprise. As a result it took an entire season to reach a point which ought to have been reached in two months at most, and the troops passed a frightful winter in a deadly situation when they might have been encamped in the salubrious country at the mouth of the Yellowstone.

The same spirit of absurd extravagance pervaded the scientific branch of the enterprise. If Major Long had been content with sensible field equipment transported on pack mules, or on a keelboat while along the Missouri, he could have kept his party in the field for five years, and have explored the entire region east of the mountains, for less money than his actual operations cost in the year 1819 alone.

The insignificant results of the first season's work and the scandal growing out of the transportation contract, disgusted Congress with the whole enterprise and that body declined to appropriate any further funds for it. The preface of Dr. James' report of the expedition says that the "state of the national finances during the year 1820 having called for retrenchments in all expenditures of a public nature—the means necessary for the further prosecution of the objects of the expedition were accordingly withheld." It is very well to have a plausible explanation for a great and mortifying failure, but the historian will not let the managers of this enterprise off so easily.

The Yellowstone Expedition was thus cut off before it was half completed, and as a half-hearted apology to the public for its failure, a small side show was organized for the season of 1820 in the form of an expedition to the Rocky mountains. It was placed under charge of Major Long, who returned to the Engineer Cantonment on the 28th of May of that year. The extent to which the great enterprise of the previous year had forfeited public confidence may be inferred from the niggardly assistance which the government lent to the present expedition. The party of Major Long consisted, besides himself, of Captain John R. Bell, Lieutenant W. H. Swift, Thomas Say, Edwin James, T. R. Peal, Samuel Seymour, H. Dougherty, D. Adams, three engagés, one corporal and six private soldiers. Of the horses and mules required for the party the government furnished only six, while the members of the party furnished the remaining sixteen. The stock of merchandise wherewith to treat with the Indians was ridiculously small, and the whole equipment was justly styled by Dr. James a "very inadequate outfit."

The immediate object in view on this expedition was to go "to the source of the River Platte and thence by way of the Arkansas and Red rivers to the Mississippi." The expedition left winter quarters on the Missouri June 6, and arrived, with no occurrence worth mentioning, at the Pawnee villages on the Loup fork of the Platte, June 11. To what degree the size and equipment of this expedition were calculated to command the respect of the Indians may be seen in the fact that the chiefs of the Grand Pawnees not only did not welcome the visitors to their camp, but, when invited to appear before the party, declined on the ground that they were otherwise engaged. Nothing was accomplished here beyond an abortive attempt to introduce the process of vaccination among the tribe.

The party left the Loup villages June 13th and the following day reached the Platte about at the present site of Grand Island, Nebraska. Their progress up this river was devoid of incident. They ascended the north bank to the forks of the Platte, both of which they crossed just above the junction, and then ascended the south bank of the South Fork. On the 30th of June they saw the mountains, and the peak which first attracted their attention now bears the name of Major Long. When they first saw it they thought it to be Pike's Peak. On the 5th of July they were encamped within or near the present limits of the city of Denver, and the next day they halted about noon at the point where the South Platte emerges from the mountains. Here the party encamped for the purpose of following the stream into the mountains. The 7th of July was spent in this work, but the small detachment who undertook it got into the foothills only five or six miles, far enough, however, so that some of them saw the junction of the two forks of the South Platte. Finding mountain climbing a pretty exhausting business they returned to camp. Thus terminated that part of the official instructions directing an exploration of the Platte to its source, and the famous Bayou Salade, or South Park, from which the river flows, remained unknown, except to the hunter, for more than twenty years thereafter.

On the 9th of July the party resumed its journey and on the 12th encamped on Fountain creek about twenty-five miles from the summit of Pike's Peak. Here some definite results were accomplished in the ascent of Pike's Peak and the measurement of its altitude. Dr. James with two men made the ascent, arriving at the summit at 4 P.M. on the 14th, and were presumably the first white men to perform that now popular feat. They remained only an hour, made part of the descent that night, and reached camp after dark on the 15th. Lieutenant Swift, in the meanwhile, had measured the height of the peak by a system of horizontal and vertical triangles, and had found its altitude above the plain where the measurement was made to be 8,507 feet. Major Long erroneously estimated the elevation of the plain at only 3,000 feet above sea level. His estimate was arrived at from assumed slopes of the Mississippi, Missouri and Platte rivers, and was naturally liable to great error. The actual elevation of the plain, where the measurement of the altitude of the peak was made, is probably about 5,700 feet, which would give 14,200 feet as the altitude of the peak, as against Long's recorded estimate of 11,507 feet. The trigonometric work seems therefore to have been very accurate.

The party resumed its march on the 16th and arrived that day at the Arkansas near the mouth of Turkey creek. Here another excursion was made to the mountains, very much like that on the Platte. Captain Bell and Dr. James ascended the river one day's march to the cañon of the Arkansas and returned next day to camp. Although it was yet only the middle of July, no further attempt was made to explore the source of either of these rivers, and on the morning of the 12th the party took up its march for the settlements. It arrived in the vicinity of the present town of La Junta, Colorado, on the 21st and spent the next two days in arranging a division of the party and plans for the homeward journey. It was decided that Captain Bell, Lieutenant Swift, three Frenchmen and five soldiers, with most of the horses and baggage, should descend the Arkansas, while Major Long, Dr. James, Mr. Peale, and seven men should proceed to the sources of the Red river and follow that stream to the settlements. A rendezvous was appointed at Fort Smith on the Arkansas. Both parties took up their respective journeys on the 24th of July, 1820.

There is almost nothing in these two journeys that need detain us. Captain Bell's party encountered several small bands of Indians, but had no trouble of moment with any of them. On the 7th of August, two days before arriving at the Great Bend of the Arkansas, two French interpreters who had been hired at the Pawnee villages, terminated their engagements and set out alone to return. These men had given very satisfactory service. On the night of August 30th Captain Bell's party suffered a genuine catastrophe in the loss of much of their camp property, including nearly all the notes and records of the expedition. They were stolen by three men who deserted that night. Captain Bell arrived at Fort Smith on the 9th of September after a march in which the greatest cause of suffering was the excessive heat.

Major Long's party took a course slightly east of south until they reached the valley of Purgatory creek, probably a little below Bent's Cañon. They ascended a fork of this stream which joined the main stream from the east a little above the cañon and made their way to the high land at the head of the stream. Continuing south across several of the sources of the Cimarron, they at length came to a valley which, from its general direction and appearance, they believed to be tributary to the Red river, and they resolved to follow it. This was July 30th. Their course for the next four days was southeast down the valley of this stream, until they came to its junction with the main Canadian, which they supposed to be the Red river.

The route from the time the party left the South Platte until they arrived at the Canadian is extremely difficult to follow except along the Arkansas. It would be scarcely possible to find in any narrative of Western history so careless an itinerary, and in a scientific report like that of Dr. James it is quite inexcusable. . . .

From the camp of August 4th on the Canadian the party descended that stream without any remarkable experience except considerable suffering from heat and lack of food. On the 10th of September they arrived at the Arkansas and found for the first time that they had been following the Canadian Fork of that stream and had not been on the Red river at all. On the 13th of September the party arrived at Fort Smith.

September 21st the re-united party left Fort Smith for Cape Girardeau. A portion of their number visited the noted hot springs of the Washita on the way, and all finally assembled at Cape Girardeau on the 12th of October. Major Long set out at once for St. Louis on the *Western Engineer*, which had arrived a few days before.

In reviewing this expedition and comparing its actual results with what it proposed and what the public expected, the impression left is one of disappointment. In scarcely any respect did it accomplish its purpose. In the movement up the Missouri the point reached was but little more than one-third of the distance to the mouth of the Yellowstone, the intended destination. The whole purpose of carrying the power of the United States to these remote regions and of rendering American trade secure there, fell to the ground. The cherished idea that the expedition might open the way to a resumption of the lost business on the Columbia received not the slightest encouragement.

The net result of the military expedition was to establish a post near the present site of Omaha. The position was occupied but a few years when the garrison was withdrawn to the new Fort Leavenworth near the mouth of the Kansas river. Except as to those Indians who visited Fort Lisa or who lived in that vicinity, no intercourse of importance was had with any of the tribes and the influence of the expedition upon the Indian question was very small. It should be said, however, that the position near Council Bluffs became the base of operations against the Aricaras in 1823 and of the expedition to the Yellowstone under Atkinson and O'Fallon in 1825.

The expedition of 1820, which was the insignificant finale of the great enterprise, was scarcely more satisfactory than the other operations had been. The party was wretchedly equipped, and as a consequence kept almost continuously on the move in order to avoid starvation until they could get back to the settlements, and they spent at the most but five or six days in exploration of the mountains. The only permanent addition which they made to geographical knowledge was in discovering the great western extent of the Canadian river. This stream, which takes its rise near the mountains east of Santa Fe and flows east, had heretofore been supposed to be the head of the Red river. Major Long's expedition showed this not to be the case. He did not, however, descend the main stream in the vicinity of the mountains, but a branch farther east, that formed a junction with the main stream more than a hundred miles from its source; but he saw enough to show that all of the watershed in that section was tributary to the Canadian.

The ascent of Pike's Peak by Dr. James and his companion is supposed to have been the first performance of that feat; and Lieutenant Swift's very excellent measurement of its altitude above the plain where his observations were made is likewise the first attempt in that line. His determination has been but slightly modified by later more accurate measurements. Major Long named the peak James Peak, but posterity has decreed that the name of its discoverer shall stand.

Captain Bell's expedition down the Arkansas, so far as it has been given us, is almost of no geographical consequence. So important a tributary as the Cimarron he missed entirely, and identified the small stream Squaw creek, as that river. He made other similar errors, although traveling in a country which even then was no longer unknown.

Major Long's description of the country, which appears as an appendix to Dr. James' work, is on the whole an accurate one. His astronomical determinations of latitude were correct within an error of five or six miles; his longitudes were too great by from thirty to fifty miles.

By some consideration which had weight in the earlier history of our government the results of this expedition were not published as an official report under the authorship of its leader. Major Long did not write the narrative of his own travels. The work was published under a private copyright by Dr. Edwin James, with an elaborate dedicatory to the Secretary of War which reminds one of the obsequious grovelings to royalty so characteristic of early English writers. The report is interesting and valuable. Its accounts of the Indian tribes and of the native fauna are among the best which we possess. Many incidents of historic importance have also been preserved.

To the public, however, the work was a disappointment. They had looked to it for information relating to the great questions of Western progress then agitating men's minds. It was not a geological survey report that they wanted, but a comprehensive view of the country from a practical standpoint. Long disquisitions upon the evidence found in the mounds about St. Louis, tending to show that our Indian races were of Asiatic origin, might be very interesting to the cause of science, but they did not satisfy the public who were seeking the wealth of the Rocky mountains and a route to the distant Pacific. The report, in short, was not fitted to its purpose; it belonged to the scientific explorations of later times.

Nothing is clearer than that the managers of this enterprise utterly failed to grasp the spirit of its conception; and, as if this were not bad enough, Major Long added in his report the strongest possible negation to the hope that good could ever flow from such a country. Read the summary of his views upon that region which had honored his name by fixing it upon those magnificent mountains, and has given the world an accession of wealth such as the followers of Cortez never dreamed of: "In regard to this extensive section of country, we do not hesitate in giving the opinion, that it is almost wholly unfit for cultivation, and of course uninhabitable by a people depending upon agriculture for their subsistence. Although tracts of fertile land, considerably extensive, are occasionally to be met with, yet the scarcity of wood and water, almost uniformly prevalent, will prove an insuperable obstacle in the way of settling the country. This objection rests not only against the immediate section under consideration, but applies with equal propriety to a much larger proportion of the country. Agreeably to the best intelligence that can be had, concerning the country northward and southward of the section, and especially to the references deducible from the account given by Lewis and Clark, of the country situated between the Missouri and the Rocky mountains, above the river Platte, the vast region commencing near the sources of the Sabine, Trinity, Brazos, and Colorado, and extending northwardly to the forty-ninth degree of north latitude, by which the United States territory is limited in that direction, is throughout, of a similar character. The whole of this region seems peculiarly adapted as a range for buffaloes, wild goats, and other wild game, incalculable multitudes of which find ample pasturage and subsistence upon it.

"This region, however, viewed as a frontier, may prove of infinite importance to the United States, inasmuch as it is calculated to serve as a barrier to prevent too great an extension of our population westward, and secure us against the machinations or incursions of an enemy that might otherwise be disposed to annoy us in that quarter."

Here is an essay in prophecy that would have done credit to that great man, Daniel Webster, who could with difficulty see anything of national greatness beyond the Mississippi. Did Major Long perceive no inconsistency in declaring with one breath that the country he had traversed was "uninhabitable by a people depending upon agriculture for their subsistence" and in the next that "incalculable multitudes" of grazing animals could "find ample pasturage and subsistence upon it"? And he did not confine his views to the region that fell under his immediate observation, but applied them to the entire sweep of country from the Spanish to the British possessions and westward from the meridian of Council Bluffs to and beyond the mountains—a country where now are several large cities, towns and villages without number, and a population of more than six million people. In that section which he traversed at the base of the Rocky mountains where he said "the scarcity of wood and water" would "prove an insuperable obstacle in the way of settling the country" is now to be found some of the best agricultural land in the United States from which products are annually exported to distant parts of the country.

It is hard for us to comprehend today how an officer of such signal ability and long experience should have seen in this country nothing better than a fortunate frontier "calculated to serve as a barrier to prevent too great an extension of our population westward, and to secure us against the machinations or incursions of an enemy that might otherwise be disposed to annoy us in that quarter." It is true that at that time there had been cause enough to apprehend annoyance from our traditional enemy in the southwest, and Major Long is certainly not to be criticized for not foreseeing the expulsion of that enemy from the greater part of the territory west of our own; but his fear of undue expansion of our population was no more justifiable than have been, and are still, the phantom fears of certain minds at every effort of their country to put off the vestments of infancy for the more appropriate clothing of maturer years.

And so it resulted that Major Long's report proved a veritable stumbling-block in the way of a just appreciation of the importance of our Western interests. Whenever any measure was urged in Congress looking to the more immediate occupation of that country, this report was a sufficient answer. Why waste the public treasure in establishing possession of a region which could never become the abode of civilized man. Here was an official government report, prepared by an able officer sent for the express purpose of spying out the land. Surely the statements of irresponsible adventurers and uninformed enthusiasts were not to stand against it? It thus became one of the most powerful weapons which men of the Webster type made use of whenever they felt called upon to resist "too great an extension of our population westward."

Thus the people of the West, who had hoped from this expedition to enlist government aid in the reclamation of a remote region, found themselves in a worse plight than before. Instead of the government becoming enthused with their own faith, its doubts were strengthened. But the people themselves did not lose faith. They continued to penetrate farther and ever farther—even to the shores of the Pacific—through the unknown places of that illimitable country. Government was finally compelled to follow where it had refused to lead, and within another generation it was glad enough to be the fortunate possessor of those very regions which were at this time not considered worth having.

WITH *the end of the War of 1812, Americans turned their energies inward. The fortuitous presence of two great ocean moats provided a security against foreign attack, one which reinforced the American commitment into the twentieth century to isolationism. But Americans in the Era of Good Feelings harbored doubts that they could unilaterally maintain their security. Particularly was this true so long as either Spain or other European powers sought to continue colonial domination over Latin America. The uprisings of Bolívar and San Martín against Spanish control were greeted with enthusiasm by Americans. As early as the spring of 1818, then Secretary of State John Quincy Adams, at the behest of James Monroe, was exploring the possibility of a British-American concert designed to achieve "the total independence of the Spanish South American provinces."*

*From such small beginnings, the American and the British governments, motivated by self-interest, moved toward "a more permanent and harmonious concert of public policy and community of purpose between our two countries, than has ever yet existed since the period of our independence." When the British proposed in 1823 a policy of mutual action to underwrite Latin-American independence, even so ancient an enemy of Britain as Jefferson saw in the proposal a chance to advance the American goal to make the western hemisphere a "domicile . . . of freedom." John Quincy Adams, ever the militant proponent of American expansion, took it as an opportunity to assert: "We shall assume distinctly the principle that the American continents are no longer subjects for any new European colonial establishments." It was but a short step to the unilateral declaration contained in Monroe's message to Congress of December 2, 1823, of what since 1852 has been called the "Monroe Doctrine."*

*It pronounced the end of colonization in the Western Hemisphere; declared American neutrality in conflicts involving European powers as outside the hemispheric political system; and pledged American power to prevent any outside intervention in the affairs of the hemisphere. So was born one of the major supports of American foreign policy. With it went a tacit awareness that British self-interest dictated a parallel policy, one which would if it were challenged be met with the weight of British naval power. But as Samuel Flagg Bemis has noted in his* John Quincy Adams and the Foundations of American Foreign Policy *(1949), "There was no treaty, no agreement, no unwritten understanding, not even a concert of policy between the United States and Great Britain to uphold the Monroe Doctrine." In a moment of supremely self-aware interest, the United States had martialed to the support of its aims the might of the world's greatest naval power without surrendering its neutrality.*

*No historian has traced with greater fidelity the complex interweavings of the Monroe Doctrine, both in its origins and in its subsequent accommodations to the changing needs of developing American power than Dexter Perkins (1889- ).*

*Long a professor at the University of Rochester, he made his specialty the American role in the Caribbean. And as is often the case with historians, he found the time to participate in diplomatic affairs, most particularly at the United Nations Conference held in San Francisco during the spring of 1945.*

# A HISTORY OF THE MONROE DOCTRINE

## *by Dexter Perkins*

In the hard, and as it proved the ineffectual, struggle of the Jefferson and Madison administrations to defend American neutral rights without recourse to war we hear nothing of any flirtations with European courts, and the historian who seeks to trace the development of the idea of non-entanglement finds the annals of these years short and simple indeed. And when English arrogance, and American ambition to make the conquest of the Canadas and Floridas, led to the declaration of war on Great Britain in June of 1812, no one proposed any association whatsoever with the France of Bonaparte. The war was unpopular enough in some parts of the country as matters stood; it produced the most violent political discontent in New England, and it was with difficulty that financial, military, or political support could be found there; nebulous projects that squinted at secession began to be entertained; and it was with almost universal relief that American opinion received the Peace of Ghent.

In the meantime, too, momentous events were happening in another quarter which operated to bring into still clearer relief the separation of the New World and the Old.

It was the Napoleonic invasion of Spain which provided the impetus for the outbreak of revolt in her American dominions. In the year 1810 juntas were set up at Buenos Aires, at Bogotá, at Caracas, at Santiago de Chile, ostensibly to hold the country for King Ferdinand, but undoubtedly with larger purposes in the background. What began as a movement ostensibly loyal was soon transformed into a struggle for independence. By the end of 1811 this fact was already clear; President Madison alluded sympathetically to the new states in his message to Congress, and in the House of Representatives a resolution was passed expressing "a friendly solicitude in the welfare of these communities, and a readiness, when they should become nations by the exercise of their just rights, to unite with the Executive in establishing such relations with them as might be necessary." Observing these events, the prescient Jefferson, always alive to the large philosophical implications of what was going on in the world, wrote to his friend Alexander von Humboldt words which state with crystal clearness the doctrine of the two spheres.

But in whatever governments they will end, they will be American governments, no longer to be involved in the never ceasing broils of Europe. The European nations constitute a separate division of the globe; their localities make them a part of a distinct system; they have a set of interests of their own in which it is our business never to engage ourselves. America has a hemisphere to itself. It must have its separate system of interests; which must not be subordinated to those of Europe. The insulated state in which nature has placed the American continent, should so far avail that no spark of war kindled in the other quarters of the globe should be wafted across the wide oceans which separate us from them and it will be so.

For a time, however, it seemed as if Jefferson's prophecy might be belied. With the ending of the war in Europe Spain made a tremendous effort to regain her American provinces. Mexico was reduced to order; in Venezuela and Colombia the army of the Spanish general, Morillo, won victory on victory, and drove Bolívar, the leader of the revolutionists, into exile; Chile fell before the royalist leader, Osorio. But in the year 1817 the tide began once more to turn; the republic of La Plata, which had successfully maintained its independence, dispatched its great general, San Martín, across the Andes, and with the victory of Chacabuco a great step was taken toward the liberation of Chile. Enthusiasm for the cause of Latin-American liberation began once more to express itself in the United States. President Monroe very early in his term sent a mission of inquiry to La Plata, on whose soil not a single Spanish soldier remained, and began to talk of the recognition of the independence of the new state. In Congress the nascent republics of the South found a sturdy and eloquent champion in Henry Clay, who saw the birth of an "American system" in the events that were taking place. The separation of the New World from the Old seemed to the more imaginative and poetic minds of the time to be in the way of becoming a reality, and on both sides of the Atlantic men began to talk as if it were a fact.

Nor was it merely the revolt of the colonies that in the first years of Monroe's administration sharpened the cleavage of the continents. There had been nothing very shocking to American opinion in the peace settlements that followed the Napoleonic Wars. The union of Great Britain, Austria, Prussia, and Russia to prevent a new outbreak of violence on the part of France was not illogical; the provisions of the treaty of November 20, 1815, calling for meetings at fixed intervals of the representatives of the great powers for "the examination of such measures as shall be judged most salutary for the peace and prosperity of Europe," were equally reasonable; nor could there be any objection in principle to the famous treaty of the Holy Alliance of September 26 of the same year, by which, under the leadership of the mystical Tsar Alexander, and in language as vague as it was pious, the sovereigns of Europe bound themselves to observe in their domestic and foreign policies "the duties which the Divine Saviour has taught to mankind." Amongst pacifists, untaught by the history of the race, there was even a disposition to hail this last-named document with positive enthusiasm. But events were soon to demonstrate that the association of the great powers contained ominous possibilities; as early as the Congress of Aix-la-Chapelle in 1818 projects were brought forward looking to the interposition of the members of the Alliance in the affairs of the Spanish colonies; and when in 1819 the Russian Minister at Washington, Mr. Poletica, sounded John Quincy Adams, the American Secretary of State, on the possibility of American adhesion to the compact of the Alliance he received very little encouragement indeed. In a remarkable dispatch to Middleton, our minister at St. Petersburg, the reasons for our attitude were clearly stated:—

> For the repose of Europe as well as of America [wrote the son of the arch-isolationist of 1783], the European and American political systems should be kept as separate and distinct from each other as possible. If the United States as members of the Holy Alliance could acquire a right to ask the influence of its most powerful members in their controversies with other states (as suggested by Alexander), the other members must be entitled in return to ask the influence of the United States for themselves or against their opponents. In the deliberations of the League they would be entitled to a voice and in exercising their right must occasionally appeal to principles which might not harmonize with those of any European member of the bond. This consideration alone would be decisive for declining a participation in that league, which is the President's absolute and irrevocable determination, although he trusts that no occasion will present itself rendering it necessary to make that determination known by an explicit refusal.

This was the language of Adams in 1820; the events of the fall and of the succeeding years made its cogency more and more apparent. For, in October, in the protocol of Troppau, the three Eastern courts, Russia, Prussia, and Austria, committed themselves to the doctrine that it was the sacred duty of the great states of Europe to put down internal movements of discontent by force of arms. In the course of the next year, movements looking to the establishment of constitutional government in Naples and Piedmont were summarily snuffed out, and there was already talk of similar action in Spain, where the worthless Ferdinand VII had been temporarily compelled to submit to a measure of constitutional control. Action such as this was a violation of the American faith in popular government; it underlined and emphasized in the most striking fashion the difference in point of view between the American republic and the principal states of the Old World.

The year 1822 was to carry still further this process of differentiation, with the recognition by the United States of the revolted colonies as independent nations. This step had been talked about as early as 1818, but for a variety of reasons it had been delayed. John Quincy Adams was no romantic; he did not share the popular enthusiasm for the cause of the

Latin-American states; he doubted (and time has, to some extent, confirmed his doubts) whether all the governments to spring from the ruins of the Spanish Empire would be democracies in the American sense of the term. He was restrained, too, by the feeling that recognition ought to be accorded only when the result of the struggle was no longer doubtful; more important still, he was negotiating with Spain for the cession of the Floridas, and feared to wreck these negotiations by recognizing the revolutionists. Recognition, moreover, would be a sort of defiance to the Old World autocrats; and isolationist that Adams was by inheritance, conviction, and temperament, he yet appears to have hesitated to act in such flagrant disregard of the opinion of the chancelleries of Europe. In 1818 and 1819 he seems still to have hoped that recognition might be brought about by an accord with one or more European governments, though he would not be drawn into the deliberations of the Congress of Aix-la-Chapelle. But by February 1821, the Florida treaty had been duly ratified; in May, under the leadership of Clay, the House of Representatives voted resolutions indicating readiness to support recognition; in June, Bolívar inflicted a crushing defeat upon the army of Morillo at Carabobo; in July, his great associate and rival, San Martín, entered Lima, bringing the revolution to Peru, the last and most faithful of Spain's South American provinces; in August, the Spanish viceroy in Mexico was compelled to acknowledge the independence of that province. The facts of the situation pointed toward the complete success of the revolutionists. In March of 1822, President Monroe sent to Congress a message recommending recognition, and asking that provision be made for the sending of ministers. The administration, when it acted, acted with the most striking independence. It consulted with no European power; it gave no warning to any European chancellery of what was coming; and it paid no attention whatsoever to the situation which existed in Spain. It reckoned not at all with the fact that Ferdinand was in the power of his revolutionary subjects, and that recognition under such circumstances would be particularly distasteful to the legitimists of the Old World; it reckoned no more with the fact that the Spanish constitutionalists were making, or at least professing to make, new efforts at the reconciliation of the colonies with the mother country. Its action was taken on a purely American basis, and from a purely American point of view. The thesis of an American system appeared to be one step nearer realization in actual fact; the separation of the Old World from the New appeared to be still further advanced. But momentous events were still to come; and the fall of 1822 and the year 1823 were to march toward a crisis, or at any rate what seemed to be a crisis, which led to the public and vigorous expression of the doctrine of the two spheres, and to a new expression of its pervading spirit. This was the solemn warning to European states to keep their hands off America; this was the Monroe Doctrine.

*     *     *     *     *

The famous message of December 2, 1823, with the possible exception of the Farewell Address, the most significant of all American state papers, contains two widely separated passages which have come to be known as the Monroe Doctrine. In discussing American relations with Russia, the President laid down the principle that "the American continents, by the free and independent condition which they have assumed and maintain, are henceforth not to be considered as subject for future colonization by any European power." This phrase occurs early in the document. In its closing paragraphs, on the other hand, Monroe turned to the subject of the Spanish colonies. In language no less significant than that just quoted, he declared that the political system of the allied powers, that is, of the Holy Alliance, was different from that of America. "We owe it, therefore, to candor, and to the amicable relations existing between the United States and those powers," he went on, "to declare that we should consider any attempt on their part to extend their political system to any portion of this hemisphere as dangerous to our peace and safety. With the existing colonies and dependencies of any European power we have not interfered and shall not interfere. But with the governments who have declared their independence and maintained it, and whose independence we have, on great consideration and just principles, acknowledged, we could not view any interposition for the purpose of oppressing them, or controlling in any other manner their destiny, by any European power in any other light than as the manifestation of an unfriendly disposition towards the United States."

These pregnant phrases express in unmistakable terms the ideological cleavage between the New World and the Old. We have already seen how this cleavage had become sharper and sharper in the years after 1815. To Americans European absolutism, in 1823, was a system as odious, as devoid of moral sanction, as that of Nazi Germany or Stalinist Russia seems to many citizens of the United States today. On the other hand, to many of the statesmen of Continental Europe, the buoyant republicanism and the democratic faith of the people of the United States were a vast dissolvent which threatened destruction to the existing order, and unknown and incalculable perils for the future. The message of Monroe had to do with specific situations which we must soon examine, but it was based on general principles which played an important part in the thinking of the President and his advisers.

That part of the message which was directed against Russia appears to have been the work of John Quincy Adams. There is, perhaps, no figure more remarkable in the lengthening list of the Secretaries of State. Acidulous, combative, suspicious, Adams was none the less a great personality, great in his unswerving and intense patriotism, great in his powerful and logical intelligence, great in his immense industry, great in his high integrity. No man who ever directed American foreign policy came to his post with a wider background of experience, with a better education, academic, linguistic, legal, with a broader conception of his task. Adams was hard-headed and practical; but he also recognized the importance of ideas and general principles. And this fact he was to make clear in his working out of the so-called noncolonization dogma. Long before 1823 the Secretary of State had begun to formulate his ideas with regard to the exclusion of European influence from the American continents. When he negotiated the Florida treaty in 1819, he took special satisfaction in the extension of American territory to the Pacific by Spain's renunciation of all rights north of 42 degrees. As early as November of 1819 he had declared in the cabinet that the world "must be familiarized with the idea of considering our proper dominion to be the *continent* of North America." In a heated dispute with Stratford Canning, the British Minister, in January of 1821, over the title to the Columbia River region, Adams stated, "We certainly did suppose that the British government had come to the conclusion that there would be neither policy nor profit in cavilling with us about territory on this North American continent." "And in this," asked Canning, "you include our northern provinces on this continent?" "No," said Adams, "there the boundary is marked and we have no disposition to encroach upon it. Keep what is yours, but leave the rest of this continent to us." These statements, compared with what followed, were remarkable only for their modesty. In July of 1822, in one of those Fourth of July addresses so dear to American national pride, the Secretary went on to attack the whole colonial principle, as applied to both North and South America. By November he was ready to confide to the British Minister that "the whole system of modern colonization was an abuse of government, and it was time that it should come to an end."

In part, the position so boldly taken was a matter of political theory. The United States was not yet half a century from the Declaration of Independence, from its own shaking off of the chains of colonial tutelage. But, in part, Adams' doctrine had an economic basis. Adams disliked colonialism not alone because it was a reminder of political subordination, but because it was connected in his mind with commercial monopoly, and the exclusion of the United States from the markets of the New World. A New Englander of New Englanders, the representative of the great mercantile section of the Union, and that at a time when the American shipping interests were more important in relation to other interests than at any time in our history, the Secretary was to do battle for the trade of the American people no less than for more abstract notions of political righteousness. It was, indeed, a commercial controversy that sharpened his pen for the famous declaration with regard to colonization that we have quoted. . . .

This controversy was one with Russia. In 1823 Russia still had colonial claims on the northwest coast of America. For more than a decade, indeed, there had been a Russian establishment, Fort Ross, at Bodega Bay on the coast of California, whose existence, though it had occasioned no diplomatic discussion, had been noted with some mild apprehension. But more important, in September of 1821 the Tsar Alexander, acting at the instigation of a corporation known as the Russian American Company, had issued an imperial decree which conferred upon this concern exclusive trading rights down to the line of 51 degrees and forbade all foreign vessels to come within one hundred Italian miles of the shore on pain of confiscation.

This imperial decree was, from the outset, challenged by the American government. In connection with it John Quincy Adams, with a boldness that excelled that of his cabinet colleagues, wished to deny the right of Russia to any American territory. And though he was overruled in a measure, since the instructions to Middleton at St. Petersburg, sent in July of 1823, were based on possible recognition of Russian claims north of *fifty-five*, the Secretary nevertheless would not give up his viewpoint in principle. To Tuyll, the Russian Minister at Washington, he declared on July 17, 1823, that "we should contest the right of Russia to *any* territorial establishment on this continent, and that we should assume distinctly the principle that the American continents are no longer subjects for any new European colonial establishments." Five days later he set forth the same theory in a dispatch to Richard Rush, our minister at London, and set it forth in some detail. In December, when he came to draft for the President the customary sketch of foreign policy to be used in the preparation of the annual message, he used almost the identical words that had been used five months before in speaking to Tuyll, and Monroe took them over bodily and inserted them in his message of December 2.

This, in essentials, is the origin of the noncolonization clause, one of the two important elements in the enunciation of the Monroe Doctrine.

It cannot be said that this clause was particularly important or particularly influential in its immediate effects. It was not enthusiastically received by the general public. It was rarely commented upon in the newspapers. It occasioned no favorable word in Congress. The Tsar had already determined upon concession long before the message, as early as July 1822, and in the discussions at St. Petersburg Monroe's language was politely thrust aside by Alexander's Foreign Minister, who declared "it would be best for us to waive all discussions upon abstract principles of *right*." The President's declaration was without effect upon the actual compromise which was worked out between the two governments, limiting Russian rights to the line of 54 degrees 40 minutes, and conceding American trading privileges north of this line for a period of ten years. It was not favorably received by official opinion in any European country. In France Chateaubriand, the Foreign Minister, asserted on first reading it that Monroe's declaration "ought to be resisted by all the powers possessing either territory or commercial interests in that hemisphere." In Great Britain Canning flatly challenged the new doctrine in an interview with Rush, our minister at London, early in January of 1824. Monroe's thesis, said the British Foreign Secretary, "is laid down broadly, and generally, without qualification or distinction. We cannot acknowledge the right of any power to proclaim such a principle, much less to bind other countries to the observance of it." Six months later, when Richard Rush attempted to introduce the Adams theory into the negotiations over Oregon, he was met with an "utter denial" of its validity, and with the categorical statement that "the unoccupied parts of America" were "just as much open as heretofore to colonization by Great Britain . . . and that the United States would have no right whatever to take umbrage at the establishment of new colonies from Europe in any such parts of the American continent." In the immediate sense, the assertion of the noncolonization principle accomplished nothing positive, and aroused resentment rather than respect. There is room to doubt its wisdom as a diplomatic move, and a harsh critic might even go so far as to describe it as a barren gesture.

\*      \*      \*      \*      \*

It is possible . . . to state with definiteness and with assurance that the powers of the Holy Alliance had no designs against the liberties of the New World at the moment when Monroe launched his famous declaration. The story that the President prevented a terrible danger is legend and nothing more; as legend it deserves to be recorded. It assumes a material strength on the part of the United States which closer examination reveals not to have existed; it assumes that the United States was a great power, in the modern sense of the word, in 1823. It assumes that this country was listened to then with the same respect which it commands today.

One of the striking facts, indeed, about the events we have been examining is the attitude of the Continental powers toward the American government. With one exception, that of Russia, they proposed entirely to ignore it in their projected Congress on the colonial question. When, for example, Canning suggested in the course of the Polignac conversations that the administration at Washington ought to be represented at any Congress on Latin-American affairs, Chateaubriand and Villele were nothing less than shocked. To the former the British proposal seemed "malevolent" and "short-sighted"; to the latter it seemed better to have no Congress at all than to admit a country "whose political principles are directly at variance with those of every other Power." In a later pronouncement Chateaubriand went even further; the exclusion of the United States from European gatherings "might serve in case of need as a supplementary article of the public law of Europe." Views such as these were welcomed in Vienna and Berlin. When Adams, in one of his dispatches to Rush, indicated that his government would refuse to participate in a Congress if invited to do so, his resolution was superfluous; it was a certainty from the beginning that no invitation would be extended.

It would be pleasant if with these last sentences we could terminate the deflation of the message of 1823, from the standpoint of its contemporary effect; but candor compels us to press on still further before turning to the more agreeable task of indicating the many strong points of Monroe's declaration. We shall have to examine its reception in the Old World and the New; we shall have to ask what were its effects upon the policy of Old World monarchies or New World republics.

First of all, then, how was it received by Europeans? How were its resounding periods judged by European statesmen?

On the continent of Europe, there were here and there individuals, the friends of liberty, who hailed it with delight. The venerable Lafayette thought it "the best little bit of paper that God had ever permitted any man to give to the World," and Barbe-Marbois, always well-disposed to the United States, thought it "not only the best but the best-timed state paper which he had ever read." But to most Continentals, the message came as a most unpleasant surprise. They knew, of course, nothing whatever of its background; innocent of nefarious designs, they could hardly be otherwise than resentful of the imputations of the President. Without any preliminary warning or exchange of views, without any effort to establish the facts, in a document intended only for the American national legislature, Monroe and Adams had laid down the principles on which they expected the policy of the Old World to be governed in relation to the New. These doctrines were nothing more nor less than a challenge to the monarchies of Europe; they were as odious to a Metternich or a Chateaubriand as the diatribes of Hitler or Mussolini are to a convinced friend of liberty today. "Blustering," "monstrous," "arrogant," "haughty," "peremptory"—these were some of the terms applied to the message. And veritably vitriolic criticism came from the pen of the great Metternich.

> These United States of America [wrote the Austrian Chancellor], which we have seen arise and grow, and which during their short youth already meditated projects which they dared not then avow, have suddenly left a sphere too narrow for their ambition, and have astonished Europe by a new act of revolt, more unprovoked, fully as audacious, and no less dangerous than the former. They have distinctly and clearly announced their intention to set not only power against power, but, to express it more exactly, altar against altar. In their indecent declarations they have cast blame and scorn on the institutions of Europe most worthy of respect, on the principles of its greatest sovereigns, on the whole of those measures which a sacred duty no less than an evident necessity has forced our governments to adopt to frustrate plans most criminal. In permitting themselves these unprovoked [*sic*] attacks, in fostering revolutions wherever they show themselves, in regretting those which have failed, in extending a helping hand to those which seem to prosper, they lend new strength to the apostles of sedition, and reanimate the courage of every conspirator. If this flood of evil doctrines and pernicious examples should extend over the whole of America, what would become of our religious and political institutions, of the moral force of our governments, and of that conservative system which has saved Europe from complete dissolution?

Yet though there was widespread irritation at the message of 1823, there was not, on the part of any Continental power, any protest against it. It may be that Chauteaubriand considered such action; he had, as we have seen, told Stuart that the noncolonization clause "ought to be resisted by all the powers possessing either territory or commercial interests in that hemisphere." But the idea, if held, was soon abandoned. It would not have been strange if the Tsar, with his passion for dialectic and high-sounding principles, had wished to answer the philippic of Monroe; but when Tuyll proposed such action to his August Master, he was answered that "the document in question enunciates views and pretensions so exaggerated, it establishes principles so contrary to the rights of the European powers, that it merits only the most profound contempt. His Majesty therefore invites you to preserve the passive attitude which you have deemed proper to adopt, and to continue to maintain the silence which you have imposed upon yourself." Alexander evidently believed that further discussion would serve only to dignify the American manifesto. And the cabinets of Madrid, of Vienna and Berlin, despite their irritation, emulated his silence.

This silence is not to be regarded as flattering to the United States. It proceeded from a sense of American weakness, rather than American strength. Following a habit which European ministers seem early to have developed in evaluating American foreign policies, there was a distinct disposition to set the message down to the exigencies of domestic politics. Menou, the French charge at Washington, believed it was part of John Quincy Adams' campaign for the Presidential succession in 1824. Stoughton, his Spanish colleague, took a similar view, and thought the pronouncement a mere *brutum fulmen*. And on every hand, in the diplomatic correspondence of the time, one becomes painfully aware of the low estimate in which the physical power of the United States was held. The charge of materialism, a hoary weapon in the European arsenal of criticism of the United States, was reiterated again and again. The Americans would not fight, because they were too much interested in making money. They could not be brought to any real sacrifices. Such was the judgment of Menou, of Stoughton, of Tuyll. And if, perchance, they did take up the sword, their power would be anything but formidable. Financially, Tuyll reported, the Union "would . . . find itself a prey to considerable embarrassment." Its army was small, nor was it possible to raise forces to cope with a powerful expedition. "The sluggishness inherent in the forms of a federal republic [mark well these words, reader of today], the scanty powers and means of which this government disposes, the lack of inclination of the inhabitants of this country to make pecuniary sacrifices which offer them no bait of considerable and direct gain, the irritation which would be aroused among the merchants by the cessation of their commercial relations with France, Spain and the North . . . will tend to make such a war . . . rather a demonstration which circumstances have rendered indispensable and which is entered upon reluctantly with the secret desire of seeing it ended as soon as possible, than one of those truly national enterprises sustained by every means, and with every bit of energy, which might make it a very embarrassing obstacle. The attitude which the government of the United States has assumed," the minister concluded, "is undoubtedly of such a nature as to demand in an American expedition undertaken by Spain and her Allies a considerable development of means and of military force. But once the decision is taken to attempt it, I should not think that the course taken by the United States, unsupported by Great Britain, would be of a nature to change such a decision."

One might set down remarks such as these, remarks which have their parallel in the language of Chateaubriand and many others, as nothing more nor less than wishful thinking. Yet one can but admit that an analysis of the naval strength of the United States in 1823 does something to sustain the view frequently expressed. In 1823 this country had a naval establishment which, numerically, was about a quarter that of France in ships and men, and less than an eighth that of Russia. These are crude figures, it is true; and even were we to accept them at face value, we should have to remember that, even with Havana and the French Antilles as bases, the Continental powers would have been at a severe disadvantage in waging war on this side of the Atlantic. We have to take account too, of the numerous American privateers which might have been unleashed had war come. But even making such allowances it still remains true that in all human probability a combined French and Russian intervention in American affairs would have constituted a considerable menace, and that the forces of the Allied powers would have outnumbered those of the United States. We shall be making a gross error if we attribute to the United States of 1823 the material strength of a later age.

We shall be making an error, also, if we imagine that the *policies* of the European powers were much influenced by the solemn warnings of Monroe. The plans for a Congress on the colonial question went forward none the less rapidly because of the message of the President; indeed, Chateaubriand and Metternich and many others were led to hope that the flaming republicanism of the American pronouncement would operate to bring Great Britain into line with the Continental powers. The idea of Bourbon monarchies in the New World, dissociated from the use of force, was fully as vital in 1824 as it had been in 1823; and in St. Petersburg the Tsar Alexander seems to have played with the idea of intervention for the first time after, and not before, December of 1823. If his thoughts on this subject never got beyond the point of nebulous conversation, the reason lay not in the attitude of the United States, but in the frigid indifference of the other Continental courts, and in the obvious and vigorous opposition of Great Britain. That opposition was underlined by Canning's refusal, at the end of January, to attend a Congress on the colonial question. Never really seriously entertained, the whole idea of intervention in the New World became little less than an absurdity by the spring of 1824.

Yet it will not do, because the peril to the independence of the new states was in large degree illusory, to depreciate unduly the significance of Monroe's message. To say nothing of its long-time importance, of its epoch-making character in the perspective of more than a century, there is still much to be said for it from the viewpoint of 1823. We should not assess the President's action in the light of the knowledge of today. We must obviously assess it in the light of its own time. Viewed from this angle, it must first of all be said that the Presidential declaration took a considerable amount of courage. The cabinet discussions make it clear that whether or not a serious danger existed, Monroe *thought* it existed. So, too, with the exception of Adams, did his advisers. It needed, therefore, a certain audacity for the young republic of the West to throw down the gauntlet to the great states of Europe. True, there seemed some reason to believe that if emergency arose the United States would be supported by the power of the British navy. But there could be no real confidence that this would be the case. There was always the possibility, as Adams and Wirt had both pointed out, that Great Britain was playing a double game. There was, indeed, something suspicious in the way in which Canning had handled the whole matter. The President himself and Richard Rush, as well as Adams, were quick to question his motives. They could not but remark that in September the overtures of the British Minister had suddenly ceased. The silence that followed might be easily interpreted as the sign of a shift in British policy. In such circumstances, to speak out boldly was no mere cheap and easy gesture, no mere *brutum fulmen,* launched in the secure knowledge that the step taken would be made good by the armed might of Britain. It was an act, if not of unmitigated audacity, at least of calculated courage.

Moreover, from one angle at any rate, it was an exceedingly skillful piece of diplomacy. Great Britain and the United States were inevitably rivals for the favor of the young republics of Latin America, rivals for their favor and their commerce. By the declaration of December 2, 1823, Monroe anticipated Canning in giving open expression to opposition to the reconquest of the new states, and in the public assurance of the will of another power to protect them. And the records of the time clearly indicate the chagrin of the British Minister at having been thus outplayed in the diplomatic game. True, it strengthened his hand in refusing the invitation to the projected Congress on the Latin-American question. "The Congress," he wrote joyfully to A'Court, British Minister to Spain, "was broken in all its limbs before, but the President's speech gives it the *coup de grâce.*" But this pleasurable reaction to Monroe's pronouncement was short-lived. From exultation Canning soon changed to suspicion and jealousy. Hard on the reception of the message, he communicated the Polignac correspondence to the agents of Great Britain in the New World, and labored to show (with some accuracy, it must be confessed) that his own country had been first in assuming the protection of the new states. There are clear signs, too, that he dreaded the extension of the American political system in the New World, and labored to circumvent it. "The great danger of the time," he wrote to one of his friends in 1825, "a danger which the policy of the European System would have fostered, was a division of the World into European and American, Republican and Monarchical; a league of worn-out Govts. on the one hand, and of youthful and strong Nations, with the U. States at their head, on the other." With this thesis in mind, Canning himself seems to have flirted with the idea of Bourbon monarchy in the winter of 1824. He bent his every effort to settle the dispute between Portugal and its revolted colony, Brazil, with a view to preserving the monarchical system in the latter country. And at the same time, never the doctrinaire, always the ardent servant of British commercial interests, he pressed harder than ever before in the cabinet and at Madrid for the recognition of the colonies. Indeed, he even went so far as to offer King Ferdinand the guarantee of the island of Cuba if that obdurate prince would come to some kind of understanding with his former subjects on the mainland. He sought to persuade his colleagues that "the ambition and ascendancy" of the United States made forthright action imperative. And at more than one American capital he sought to undermine the prestige and throw doubt upon the motives of the American government. The message of Monroe had struck home; and the activity of British diplomacy in seeking to counteract it demonstrates clearly enough with what shrewdness Monroe had acted in proclaiming independently, and in anticipation of the Court of St. James's, the opposition of the New World to invasion or penetration from the Old. From this angle alone, despite its false assumptions, the message was a brilliant diplomatic document.

Nor is this by any means all that ought to be said. The *method* of the warning to Europe is no less interesting than the matter. Monroe and his advisers might have confined themselves in 1823 to the ordinary courses of diplomatic correspondence. They might have contented themselves with an answer to Tuyll, perhaps with a similar communication to France. They chose instead the course of open diplomacy. And how, indeed, could they have chosen better? Granted the premises upon which they acted, what could have been more skillful? How much more effective the declaration to Congress than an unostentatious diplomatic protest; how much more gratifying to the national pride, how much more productive of prestige in South America, how much more disconcerting to Europe! No wonder that the British charge, Addington, could write as follows of its reception in the United States.

> The message seems to have been received with acclamation through-out the United States. . . . The explicit and manly tone, especially, with which the President has treated the subject of European inter-ference in the affairs of this Hemisphere with a view to the subjugation of those territories which have emancipated themselves from European domination, has evidently found in every bosom a chord which vibrates in strict unison with the sentiments so conveyed. They have been echoed from one end of the union to the other. It would indeed be dif-ficult, in a country composed of elements so various, and liable on all subjects to opinions so conflicting, to find more perfect unanimity than has been displayed on every side on this particular point.

Whatever else the President had or had not done, he had certainly inter-preted the sentiments of his countrymen, and aroused their enthusiasm and their loyalty.

And, indeed, he had done more. He had stated with remarkable force and clarity the divergence in the political ideals of the Europe and the United States of 1823. Absolutism and democracy, these were the opposing principles which the President made clear. To Alexander, to Pozzo, to Metternich, whatever practical obstacles might stand in the way of the re-conquest of the colonies, the fundamental postulates of the situation were perfectly clear. Sovereigns held their power by the will of God. No revolu-tion could divest them of these rights. In theory, then, they could naturally assist one another in the putting down of their rebellious subjects. In theory, the republics of Latin America were outside the pale, and their success the symptoms of the dissolution of world order itself. "The Christian World," wrote Pozzo di Borgo, "tends to divide into two parts, distinct from, and I fear, hostile to, one another; we must work to prevent or defer this terrible revolution, and above all to save and fortify the portion which may escape the contagion and the invasion of vicious principles." Against this Old World order, based on the doctrines of absolutism, Monroe opposed a new one, based on the right of the peoples of the world to determine their own destiny, and to govern themselves. The principles which he expressed were more than the principles of his own government; they were the principles of the nineteenth and early twentieth centuries. They were the principles that, in the main, were to triumph, in the years that lay ahead, to triumph not only in the New World, but in a large part of the Old. Framed only for the continents of the West, they were to have an ecumenical significance for several generations of men. The liberty which Monroe desired and defended for the republics of Latin America was, in the course of the century, to be diffused throughout no small part of Europe as well. The President of the United States spoke not only for his people, but for his age.

&§ §&

*Few men have come to the Presidency with a more meritorious record of service to the republic than John Quincy Adams. Few have, however, inherited the post under a darker cloud of criticism. By right, his performance as Secretary of State alone would have justified his selection as President, but as a latecomer to the Democratic-Republican party, he had never progressed much beyond the periphery of party management. Nor had his dour introspection, with the peculiar Adam's family penchant for flying in the face of popular sentiment, helped his presidential aspirations. No man wanted more to gain popular approval without surrender of his personal integrity than John Quincy Adams. The Presidency, if he had his own way, would have come to him as the unsolicited reward for well-done service.*

*Under the normal practices of Jeffersonian politics, the Presidency should never have come to Adams. The choice of the congressional caucus was the ruggedly ambitious William Crawford, Secretary of Treasury under Monroe, who had come surprisingly close in 1816 to disrupting the Virginia succession by taking the caucus choice from Monroe. Eight years later, although incapacitated by a stroke, a rump caucus chose him. But the party system inaugurated by Jefferson was in a state of decline. The long dominance of Virginia aristocrats and the collapse of the Federalist party even in its old New England citadel had set in motion both undercurrents of dissent and political shifts. In the resulting realignment of party allegiances, the election of 1824 revealed a politic in flux.*

*The four candidates who finally ran—Jackson, Adams, Crawford, and Henry Clay—failed to gain even a near popular majority. Denied an electoral*

*majority, the election was thrown into the House of Representatives, where
after complex maneuvers and suitable political accommodations, the aloof
Adams was elected President. As his Secretary of State he chose Henry Clay,
and the defeated Jackson's supporters, although their candidate had run a
weak first, promptly set to work charging a corrupt deal between Adams and
Clay. The newly elected President further complicated his task by espousing
a large policy for the federal government. His vision of a nation crisscrossed
by railroads and canals, of a national university, and other large programs
collided with a growing belief that "the world is too much governed." It
also ran afoul of a shrewd campaign mounted by supporters of Jackson that
called for the return of the nation to the pristine virtues of an abandoned
Jeffersonian democracy. The emphasis throughout in the words of Martin
Van Buren was a society of "strict economy and frugality" and of "retrenchment and reform." The struggle was joined in 1828 and Andrew Jackson
emerged victorious.*

*The triumph of Old Hickory in 1828 stirred a historical debate which still
continues. The surprising threefold increase of voters between 1824 and
1828 led to the conclusion that Jackson had inaugurated the democratic era.
It was an image further reinforced by the fact that Jackson was the first
President out of the old West. No historian better stated the case than
Frederick Jackson Turner when he argued that out of a "frontier democratic
society . . . came the Jacksonian democracy which governed the nation
after the downfall of the party of John Quincy Adams." But as has often
been the case with Turner, his generalization has been proven an overstate-
ment. R. Carlyle Buley (1893- ), in a Pulitzer Prize-winning two-volume
history of* The Old Northwest, *revealed how narrow a margin Jackson's
support over Adams had been in the 1828 count. And he demonstrated that
Jackson's victory left his party supporters far from secure. The triumph of
Jackson was personal rather than party in its origin. The fundamental
achievement of Jacksonian democracy during their Old Hero's eight-year
tenure was to establish the foundations of a political party that has endured
until the present.*

# THE OLD NORTHWEST

## PIONEER PERIOD 1815–1840

### by R. Carlyle Buley

The election of John Quincy Adams to the Presidency by the House of
Representatives in 1825 led to the formation of the Jacksonian party in the
Northwest and created party alignments which lasted for many years. The
"Old Hero" had been robbed of his rights, a minority candidate had been
elected, the will of the majority disregarded and defied; not only had the

people of the West been misrepresented but the spirit of the Constitution had been violated. Jackson men turned against Clay, and the story of the "black coalition" was told and retold. The campaign of vindication began even before the nomination of Jackson by the Tennessee legislature in the autumn of 1825. Aside from a rather general and deep-seated distrust of an "office-holding class," "government by aristocrats," there was no issue beyond the wrong to Jackson, the man of the people; and the rugged Westerner, to exonerate his hero, organized a personal prejudice into a political force that was positive, warlike, and powerful.

Sharp as this political warfare was, national and state politics were still largely separate affairs. This was illustrated not only by the election of James B. Ray, a Clay man, to the Indiana governorship in August, 1825, but also in the Congressional elections of the following year.

In Illinois the Jackson issue added another element to the shifting factional political alignments. Daniel Pope Cook's vote for Adams in the House received the general approval of the northern or anticonvention party, while the conventionists or Thomas-Kane-McLean group were thus naturally led to the Jackson camp. The majority of the old Edwards following also seems to have supported Jackson after 1825. Three parties were distinguishable in the state as a result of the convention struggle and the Adams-Jackson contest: the "whole hog" Jackson party, the "milk and cider" men, also for Jackson, and the anti-Jackson group of the northern antislavery elements. The first and last represented in embryonic form the later Democratic and National Republican-Whig parties, while the "milk and cider" men divided both ways. In 1826 Ninian Edwards was elected governor by a plurality vote, but Cook in his sixth race for Congress was defeated, his vote for Adams having caused him a general loss of votes throughout the state. In the next two years radical factional changes took place in state politics. The Crawford men went over to Jackson as did a majority of the Clay and Calhoun leaders. The Adams following was divided, some supporting and others opposing Edwards; included among them were many of the later Jackson leaders. In December, 1826, a resolution which declared Adams elected by a bargain and which endorsed Jackson was introduced into the Illinois legislature; finally, on the last day of the session, with five Adams men absent, a resolution declaring for Jackson was passed.

Generally speaking, the Jackson men in the Northwest gained a distinct advantage over their opponents in the business of organization. They began at the bottom and in every instance possible got control of township, county, and militia offices, but the administration might control the bank and land offices, but the local offices outnumbered these. The party of "the common man," which emphasized the individual's right to run for and serve in any office, was first to subordinate that right to party success in the practice of local convention nominations. In Indiana, for instance, an organization was perfected which began with the township assessors and culminated in a State Committee of General Superintendence, which directed the listing of voters, assigned stump speakers, and mapped personal solicitation campaigns. A state convention (Indiana's second) was held at Indianapolis on January 8,

1828, and delegates representing twenty counties selected the Jackson electors. It was organization such as this which made it possible for the Jackson party to carry most of the presidential elections in Indiana, regardless of the fact that the state, on national issues, was opposed to its aims.

The administration party could not boast such a well-developed organization; they depended largely upon the eloquence of their speakers, the support of strong newspapers, and the appeal of their platform to the "better classes." Some Adams men advised taking a leaf from their opponents' book —better organization and unified action. Ohio supporters of Adams held a meeting at Columbus on December 28, 1827, in which, despite the condition of the roads, sixty-six of seventy-three counties were represented. It selected electors, passed resolutions in support of the administration, condemned the "coalition" charges, and issued a long address to the voters.

The interest of the Northwest in internal improvements and the tariff was so great that discussion of these issues carried into the state legislatures. The Indiana legislature instructed Governor Ray to write a letter to Jackson to get the latter's views on Federal appropriations for roads and canals, the tariff, and other issues. In reply Jackson referred the Governor to the Coleman letter of 1824 and his advocacy of a "judicious tariff." On these questions the Adams men had believed that they had the advantage, and that their reiterated cry of "measurers, not men" had carried some weight. But now the Jacksonians could add to the personality of their candidate the plank of a "judicious tariff," and Adams men in numbers, including three of the Adams state committee in Indiana, satisfied with this term, whatever it meant, came over to Jackson.

The attack on Jackson centered around his rough character, the fact that he was a "military chieftain," and the charge that he had permitted the execution of six militiamen for desertion after their terms had expired. He was called a rowdy, a cockfighter, a gambler, and a duelist; he was said to possess no qualifications for office and a violent temper. Resenting the charge of being Federalists at heart, the Adams men hurled it back and accused Jackson of being a Federalist in disguise and having voted for a property qualification while in the Tennessee legislature and of padding his expense accounts.

The question of Jackson's Burrism (his connection with the Burr affair in 1805) was exploited in the Adams press, and the marital status and character of Mrs. Jackson were questioned by innuendo and loud whispers. Even Thomas Jefferson was called upon to testify vicariously that the popular furor for the military hero had caused him to doubt the future of republican institutions more than anything which had occured since the American Revolution. Besides the attacks on Jackson, the Adams party kept the American System well to the front. They emphasized particularly the value of the tariff and internal improvements—at Federal expense—to the economy and prosperity of the West. Friends of the Old Hero struck back with interest. "Adams the Aristocrat," "Adams the Federalist," "Adams the Unitarian" (the latter in the West equivalent to atheist or heathen), as well as the "Corrupt Bargain" headings ("pimp of the coalition—pimp of the palace") spotted the editorial columns and news articles, and were dilated upon by stump speakers.

That Adams was born "with a silver spoon in his mouth" was bad enough—but that he had no control over; that a billiard table had been added to other White House trappings (presumably at public expense) was too much in the minds of righteous voters.

State politics began to be affected seriously by the presidential contest in 1828. Members of the Ohio Jackson convention of January 8, which nominated electors, after adjournment nominated John W. Campbell for governor to run against Allen Trimble, administration candidate. The northern counties polled heavily for Trimble, and he was elected by 53,971 to 51,951 votes in the October election.

For the second time in Indiana the state and national elections came in the same year. Governor James B. Ray, who had carried the state in 1825 on his internal improvements platform, was a candidate for re-election, but he believed national and state politics should be separate affairs and refused to run as either a Jackson or administration man. Party lines were more closely drawn than in 1825 and both administration and Jackson parties brought out their own candidates, the former nominating Harbin H. Moore and the Jacksonian press informally nominating Isreal T. Canby. Governor Ray in his attempt to ride two horses muddled things badly. He informed the Jackson men that Jackson's reply to his letter had convinced him that the General's stand on internal improvements and the tariff was sound, and promised them to come out openly for Jackson after the election. At Brookville, among Adams men, Ray maintained his attitude of studied indecision, but the editor of the *Repository* in an interview got the Governor to declare that the opposition to the administration was an outrageous and violent faction which it was the duty of all good men from the Governor down to oppose. When this was reported to the Jackson state chairman, he called a meeting of the state committee; Governor Ray was promptly disowned and Canby formally nominated. The newspaper ridicule put the Governor in an impossible situation, but the election was so near that knowledge of his double-dealing did not become general. The returns stood Ray, 15,141; Canby, 12,315; Moore, 10,904. Governor Ray was the last Indiana governor who tried to maintain a position independent of national politics.

As the November election approached, the appeals of the Jackson press were broadcast; warnings of fraudulent tickets and forthcoming rumors of Jackson's death too late to deny before election were sent out. But the tide had definitely turned. The vote totaled: Ohio, Jackson 67,597, Adams 63,396, Indiana, Jackson 22,237, Adams 17,052, Illinois, Jackson 9,600, Adams 4,687. Adams' strength in the Western Reserve counties of Ohio could not hold even that state against the Jackson wing.

Conservative Ohioans were shocked by the outcome. Hammond of the *Gazette* wrote before the event:

> I had thought in political affairs I could be surprised at nothing. But the events of the last four months have filled me with both surprise and sorrow. The combination which has been formed against the administration, the parties that compose it, its principles of action, and the men who seem prepared to unite with it, taken all together, present

an extraordinary spectacle. And one well calculated to excite alarm for our future destiny as a people.

After the election the editor of the *Ohio State Journal* showed both his pique and astonishment:

> For an event as mortifying as it was unexpected, it would, perhaps, be impossible to account satisfactorily, otherwise than by attributing it to the momentary influence of one of those fits of political delirium, of which the history of the human race affords too many examples. . . . Where the Jackson votes came from is, in sober truth, a perfect mystery.

Congressman Elisha Whittlesey explained it thus: "Office seekers and the discontents of every party united on him [Jackson]. It is a remarkable fact, that so soon as a man became soured towards his neighbor, or towards his family, or towards his brethren in the church, he was sure to support General Jackson, the better to satisfy his revenge." And Clay consoled Hammond as follows: "You infidels in the virtue and intelligence of the people require too much. You require that the people should never err, but be always right. I require them only to be *generally* right. The late election I look upon as the exception . . . you make it the rule."

Indiana had in 1826 three congressmen, all Clay or Adams men; in 1828, despite the prevailing Jackson sentiment, the August election returned only one Jackson man, Ratliff Boon, from the first district. His majority was ninety-one. Jonathan Jennings, on his personal popularity, was re-elected by an overwhelming majority, as was Judge John Test, another administration man in the third. In Illinois Congressman Joseph Duncan ran for re-election, but the Edwards forces supported George Forquer, an administration man. Efforts to keep the presidential question out of the campaign failed, and Duncan was re-elected 10,447 to 6,158 votes.

Party lines were reaching into the state legislatures as well, and from the election of 1828 remained established. The Ohio legislature elected in October, 1827, was listed as 66 Adams and 41 Jackson men, with 2 "on the fence"; the legislature elected in 1828 retained enough Clay-Adams men to elect Judge Jacob Burnet, anti-Jacksonian, to the United States Senate to succeed William Henry Harrison who had resigned. The Indiana members had tried to ignore national issues, but the new legislature still contained enough Adams men to elect the speaker. The "whole hog" Jackson men predominated in the General Assembly of Illinois, but a number of Adams men were elected from the northern counties. These men, however, seemed to work with Edwards, and at his request aided in securing the senatorship for McLean by a unanimous vote.

The spirit which led to the triumph of Jackson in 1828 contained in itself the makings of a political party, but the policies which came with his election made possible the birth of an organized opposition. The widespread removals and filling of offices with friends began early in the new administration. No office was too small to be overlooked. General sentiment against such a system gave the Clay and Adams men a means of attack. Also the tariff and internal improvements which had been so prominently displayed in the campaign were found suddenly to have become forgotten by the new administration after the election. Interest in these questions had existed side by side with interest in Jackson in 1828, and Jackson's strength had varied inversely with the importance attached to them. Ohio, most concerned because most populous, nearer to the eastern markets, and further advanced economically, gave the smallest percentage of majority, and in Illinois the policies on public lands and Indians far outweighed either tariff or internal improvements at this time. The cohesion resulting from the spirit of enthusiasm for Jackson the man, combined with the change in policies on the part of Jackson as political leader, brought about a rearrangement of party lines. After 1828 the inherent strict constructionism of Jackson came prominently into play. From the "judicious tariff" and internal improvements stand of 1824, he came around to the Maysville Road veto and war on the Bank.

The Jackson or "whole hog" press tried hard to defend the Maysville Road veto, but it was not easy in the Northwest, where Federal aid to internal improvements was a matter of vital interest. The Cincinnati *Western Tiller*, ostensibly an agricultural paper, said: "The change in policy . . . is so opposed to what were generally considered the sentiments of the President . . . that it has surprised and bewildered us more than any circumstance of equal importance that has ever occurred in the history of our country." Opposition papers bore down heavily on the veto, which they maintained met with universal disapprobation in the West. In view of the fact that Indian removals might require twenty-five million dollars, they saw no hope for internal improvements for years to come. Clay's American System was emphasized as being the program for the West.

> The West is vitally concerned in the work of Internal Improvement. We have no other public expenditures, and the payment on our lands has constantly drawn from this section of country, a great portion of its resources. On the sea-board there are fortifications, light-houses, break-waters, navy-yards, and a hundred other sources of expenditure, which cause the public money to be disbursed; in the West we have no navy-yards, no fortifications, no break-waters, no light-houses. We have nothing but Internal Improvements, which can enable the Federal Government to return to us, a part of our monies which it annually withdraws. If this is to be cut off, we shall be poor indeed.

The Maysville veto disconcerted many Jacksonians and further muddled the pond of personal politics, particularly in Illinois. Most of the Crawford following in the Northwest, that is, in Illinois, took with them into the Jackson party the Jeffersonian ideals of 1798 and, led by Elias Kent Kane, William C. Kinney, Theophilus W. Smith, Shadrach Bond, and John McLean, were recognized by the administration as regular Jackson men. Edwards had been wavering between Jackson and the opposition, but was strongly urged by his brother-in-law, Duff Green, to prove to Jackson that his support was sincere. The Jackson spirit would tolerate no halfway position; the new Crawford adherents fitted in better than the "milk and cider" men and became more insistent on party regularity than the original Jackson men. In the state election of 1830 Kinney, a Baptist minister, was the candidate for governor of the "whole hog" party, and John Reynolds, who had said he was a "milk and cider" Jackson man but who sought support from the anti-Jackson party, was supported by Edwards. Reynolds succeeded in getting many votes, and by thus "playing to all the pockets" won the governorship. The "whole hog" party won the legislature by a large majority, however, and took their dig at Edwards by electing Kane and J. M. Robinson, two of his enemies, to the United States Senate. In the last election in which the whole state formed the Congressional district, held in August, 1831, Joseph Duncan defeated Sydney Breese, Edward Coles, and two other candidates by a clear majority.

The Ohio state elections of 1830 indicated that the hold of the Jackson party on the state was not too secure. The candidates for governor were Duncan McArthur, of New York Scottish descent, former scout, surveyor, and soldier, and Robert Lucas, Virginia Democrat, who also possessed a military record. At the October polling the anti-Jackson men gained throughout the state. Hamilton County, which had given Jackson a majority of 2,201 in 1828, gave Lucas a majority of only 406. The total vote was: McArthur 49,668, Lucas 49,186, with 226 scattered. Three more congressmen were lost by the Jackson party, which left them only five of fourteen representatives. In the new legislature the anti-Jackson men had a majority of nine to fourteen on joint ballot.

In Indiana Governor Ray had attempted to maintain his independent position, but the legislature, with its disposition to draw party lines, soon found cause for controversy over appointments to internal improvement jobs and the courts, and the Governor's work in codifying the laws. The struggle between the partisan legislature and the proud and not too tactful Governor lasted three years; it not only cut short Ray's political career but ended the period of personal politics with reference to the higher state offices in Indiana. By 1831 the newspapers and party organizations tried to maintain strict party division. The candidates for governor were judged largely on their stand on national issues, but the party alignment did not yet extend sufficiently far down among the voters to make the national issue the determining one, nor did the candidates run strictly and avowedly on party tickets.

Gen. Noah Noble, one of the best-known and most popular men in the state, the gubernatorial candidate of the anti-Jackson forces in 1831, was favored by the anti-Ray faction as well. When James G. Read announced himself as a candidate, he made no mention of national issues, but later decidedly approved of the general policy of the administration, of Jackson's message on the tariff and internal improvements, and declared himself against the doctrines of southern nullifiers. State questions he touched upon only in a general way. The pleas of the party press were unavailing, and though Indiana was safely Jacksonian on national issues, the personality of Noble drew heavily; he was elected by a vote of 17,959 to 15,168. Milton

Stapp, an independent candidate, received only 4,424 votes. The vote indicated little beyond the fact that Noble was the more popular with the voters for both candidates had supported Jackson and were internal improvements men.

The legislature elected in 1830 had been anti-Jackson by a majority of about twenty; it re-elected William Hendricks, a Clay man, to the Senate over Ratliff Boon, a Jackson candidate. The new legislature also had an anti-Jackson majority, but in a nonpartisan election sent Gen. John Tipton to the United States Senate to succeed James Noble who died in February, 1831.

On January 3, 1831, President Jackson was nominated for re-election by the General Assembly of Illinois by a large majority. Later in the same month fifty-two members of the Ohio legislature wrote him, "your course as the chief magistrate of the nation, observant of those principles [correct constitutional principles], and firm in adherence to them, we assure you is approved by a majority of the people of Ohio, although accident has given a different appearance," and assured him that no measure was more important than his re-election. Jackson in his reply on February 9, stated that he had hoped a constitutional amendment for direct election of president and one-term tenure, as recommended in his first message, would release him from further service, yet, considering the numerous declarations of friends, another term might be necessary to bring to completion measures already begun.

Concerted opposition to the National Democrats, as the Jackson men were now calling themselves, began in 1831 when on November 7 and 8 a convention of Clay men, now calling themselves National Republicans and claiming to be the party of Jefferson, met in state convention at Indianapolis. The spoils appointments, Indiana policy, attacks on the Bank, and failure of retrenchment of the administration were condemned. To preserve the vital interests of domestic industry and internal improvements as well as to remedy the evils of Jacksonianism, the delegates recommended the elevation of Henry Clay to the Presidency. Resolutions for a protective tariff and encouragement of internal improvements were passed, a state committee of correspondence was appointed, and three delegates selected for the convention of National Republicans to be held at Baltimore in December. In Indiana, party lines were drawn about the two western leaders, Jackson and Clay.

The Ohio opposition talked up the Young Men's National Republican Convention to be held at Washington in May and urged that each county send delegates. A general meeting at Columbus in February appointed a state central committee, and the latter issued its letter to the "Free and Independent Electors of the State" in July. The proposed direct-election amendment was attacked as contrary to the spirit of the Constitution, the spoils system and tampering with the courts were condemned, and the early retirement of Jackson recommended as a "consummation devoutly to be wished." Charles Hammond, of the *Cincinnati Gazette*, temporarily disgruntled at Clay's lack of recognition of his services, had flirted with the idea of promoting Judge John McLean for the Presidency. Circumstances did not break, however, and the McLean boom did not get very far at this time.

The Democrats in the Northwest did not enter into the campaign of 1832 with overconfidence. Since 1828 the opposition had elected the governors of both Ohio and Indiana and the legislatures of these states were in their control, while the contest in Illinois between the adherents of Martin Van Buren and Richard M. Johnson for the vice-presidency, which was carried into the national convention, threatened to split the party. The effects of the removals from office, the influence of the Bank of the United States with its great wealth, and the efficacy of the newly established organization of the National Republicans could not be foreseen with certainty. Moreover, the race would have to be made against Henry Clay, also a western man, a most skillful politician and campaigner with a personal following second only to that of Jackson.

The Bank issue had been precipitated into the campaign by Jackson's veto of the charter, which took even the Democrats more or less by surprise. About the only preparation for such a decisive move had been provided late in 1831 when western papers began copying anti-Bank articles from the *Albany Argus*. Some were inclined to place the blame upon Van Buren, who was never very popular in the West, but the party avoided the worst consequences by soft-pedaling the Bank and centering the attack on "Nick Biddle" and all the evils popularly associated with his name. With the President's statement that the people were to decide whether they would "have General Jackson and no Bank or the Bank and no General Jackson," the issue was made clear. This stand was generally acceptable to the Jackson men in Ohio and most attractive to the voters of Indiana, whose earlier approval of the Bank under Crawford had turned to hatred and distrust. The *Hamilton Intelligencer*, however, argued that unless the people rose and put down this "high-handed, domineering, egregious folly of the President, the Western country is ruined."

The *Illinois Advocate* spoke for Democrats of that state: "We hazard nothing in saying that three-fourths, perhaps many more, of the people of Illinois, hail the rejection of this chartered monopoly as the salvation of our country."

The National Republicans rallied to support the Bank and exposed the consequences of Jackson's antagonistic and destructive policies. In December preceding, a resolution was introduced into the Indiana legislature petitioning Congress for the extension of the charter. Refusal to recharter would leave the country without a circulating medium. Memorials from mass meetings were sent to the congressmen, and Jackson's opposition to the Bank was denounced as a political grudge. When news of the veto came, friends of the Bank called it an act of despotism, "defeating the legislation of Congress and the expressed will of the great majority of the American people. . . . The Bank of the United States is to be prostrated to gratify the malignity of Isaac Hill, Amos Kendall and Co. . . . Will the people of this country submit to this wide-spread ruin which is thus wantonly inflicted upon their country?" It was stated that withdrawal of nineteen millions of capital from the western country would bring distress and sacrifices unparalleled in its history. A "dark and endless train of disasters" would befall farmers, mechanics, merchants, and property holders; the depressing effects would come home to the fireside of every one execpt the capitalists who possessed means to take advantage of the distress of the less fortunate. Major Jack Downing's "Proclamation" was copied as a shrewd interpretation of the goings on. "The rich folks have pretty much all the money, but as we can outvote 'em they ought to shell out—and that's pretty much Mr. Van Buren's notion too. . . . We want money, and must have it. Some of our folks who have been workin' hard for us haint got any, and we have no more offices to give 'em." Mass meetings were held at Indianapolis by Democrats as well as by friends of the Bank. Much of the blame for the act was placed upon Martin Van Buren, but Richard M. Johnson in his western stumping tour condemned the Bank for its political work and strongly supported the veto.

In Illinois prior to 1832 the national issues had not so seriously influenced the political alignment, but in 1832 the Clay men drew together in attack against Jackson's tariff, internal improvements, and Bank policies, and Jackson men were no longer satisfied if their candidates expressed only a personal loyalty to the President. But it was not easy for the Jackson forces to stand solid on a platform, for there were many diverging views on leading questions. A Jackson meeting at Vandalia, December, 1831, had taken no definite stand on the tariff but emphasized rather the President's service in ousting vested interests and the Indians. The Democratic press did likewise. The National Republican Convention in October issued a long address to the voters which, while not questioning Jackson's patriotism or bravery, directly questioned his capacity for statesmanship.

The Anti-Masons appeared as a third party in 1831. They selected electors in Ohio and Illinois and a committee in Indiana to sound out the candidates on their views. They nominated William Wirt for president and Amos Ellmaker for vice-president. The committee wrote to Clay in September to find out whether he was a Mason. Clay evaded the direct question by stating that the question of Masonry was not a constitutional one, and that he would not express his personal opinion regarding it until he saw how the subject was one that the government should meet. Soon afterwards the Indianapolis *Indiana Journal* said that the Anti-Masons had decided to support Clay, and shortly before election it dropped Wirt and Ellmaker from its list of candidates. After Governor McArthur, renominated by the National Republicans of Ohio, withdrew his name and entered the race for Congress in the seventh district, the National Republicans united with the Anti-Masons in support of Darius Lyman against Robert Lucas, the Democratic candidate; the Anti-Masons withdrew their ticket and adopted that of the National Republicans. In the October election Lucas received 71,251 votes to 63,185 for Lyman. The Anti-Masonic state committee in a public address to the citizens stated that "of late the face of things had changed," that they had mistaken the character of the National Republican electoral ticket, that it was in reality unpledged, contained no Masons, and recommended that it be supported. A letter was sent to each Clay elector stating that he was understood to be unpledged and could vote for Wirt and Ellmaker if in his judgment it seemed for the best interests of the country.

The anti-Jackson papers featured the President's vetoes of internal improvements, his "broken promises" regarding the Bank, and his defiance of the Supreme Court. The policy of the administration was held to be so clear that he who runs may read: "It is hostile to Internal Improvements—to the National Bank—and to the manufacturing industry of the United States. We are sincerely of the opinion that on the success of the principles thus denounced by the present administration, depend the growth, the wealth, and the happiness of the Western Country." Since Van Buren was more vulnerable than Jackson, editors emphasized the developing "oppugnation" in the West to the Democratic vice-presidential candidate. They pretended that great numbers of voters were renouncing their allegiance to Caesar and pledging themselves to support the welfare of Rome; they were now going to "go for their country." The Democratic organization, however, proved more effective in vote getting than the appeal of the platform, strong leaders, and important newspapers of the National Republicans. The Democrats held most of the Federal offices and hence had all the advantages of easy access to the voters, while their opponents had to carry on their electioneering at a greater sacrifice of time and effort. Besides, there were many who voted merely for Andrew Jackson, a great personality. As Charles Hammond of the *Cincinnati Gazette* had said in 1829: "Men of honour and integrity" belonged to either the party which advocated a tariff and internal improvements, or to the opposite; but there was a third party of "Swiss politicians" who followed a mere personality.

The November presidential election showed a solid Democratic Northwest. In Ohio the vote stood, Jackson 81,246, Clay 76,539, and Wirt 509; in Indiana 31,552 to 25,472; and in Illinois 14,617 to 6,754, with 97 for Wirt. As in 1828 the percentage of Democratic majority increased from east to west. In Ohio in addition to the Western Reserve counties, Clay practically doubled the vote of Jackson in Champaign, Clark, Logan, Medina, Meigs, Miami, Portage, and Ross. Clay found it impossible to take his own defeat as philosophically as he had taken that of Adams four years earlier. Shortly after the election he wrote to his friend Hammond, though the latter had been seeking a new hero in Webster: "The dark cloud which has been so long suspended over our devoted country, instead of being dispelled, as we had fondly hoped it would be, has become more dense, more menacing, more alarming. Whether we shall ever see light, and law and liberty again is very questionable."

No *aspect of the Presidency of Jackson has proved more controversial than the Bank War. The Second Bank of the United States chartered in 1816 by that most eminent of Jeffersonians, James Madison, was a tacit confession by*

*the disciples of the great Virginian that Hamilton was right. But it was a grudging assent as indicated by Jefferson's surrender to manufacture, "Our enemy has indeed the consolation of Satan on removing our first parents from Paradise: from a peaceful agricultural nation he makes us a military and manufacturing one." Nonetheless, it had been a surrender. The Jacksonians meant to undo that capitulation by laying low the "Monster Bank," the consequence of which Jackson proclaimed would "do more to revive and perpetuate those habits of economy and simplicity which are so congenial to the character of republicans than all the legislation which has yet been attempted." The struggle was presented by the Jacksonians as one between privilege and democracy. Their portrayal was made easier by the patrician third President of the Second Bank, Nicholas Biddle, a gentleman whose subtle imagination and fiscal knowledgeableness made it impossible for him to take seriously Jacksonian pretensions. Unwittingly Biddle lent credibility to the argument that the destruction of the Bank restored the equalitarian impulse.*

*No historian explored with greater objectivity the implications of the Bank War than Ralph C. H. Catterall (1866-1914) in* The Second Bank of the United States. *A recognized masterpiece, it was particularly ironic that its author spent the last twelve years of his academic career as professor of modern European history at Cornell. Although regretting the economic dislocations that ensued from the attack upon the Bank, Catterall recognized, as James Parton, the earlier biographer of Jackson, had, the complete sincerity of Old Hickory. They also understood how out of sympathy and communication the business community was with the burgeoning democracy. Catterall understood also the delicate role the Bank played in regulating an underdeveloped economy.*

*The central bank function played by the Second Bank was further explored by Bray Hammond (1886-　), who rebelled against Arthur Schlesinger, Jr.'s presentation of the Bank War as final evidence of the Jacksonian struggle to subordinate the claims of Eastern capitalists to the needs of the common folk. Hammond argued that the Jacksonian attack was less a victory for democracy than a triumph for competing entrepreneurs on the make. The fall of Chestnut Street, the Philadelphia domicile of the Second Bank, and the humiliation of Biddle, marked the victory of Wall Street. The end of the Bank marked the end of a responsible fiscal leadership subordinate to the needs of the community and the opening of an "age of triumphant exploitation." The frontier had bred its own master and confirmed his triumph as one for onsurging popular democracy.*

# THE SECOND BANK OF THE UNITED STATES

## *by Ralph C. H. Catterall*

In July, 1832, Biddle announced to supporters of the bank that it would take no active part in the campaign, since such action was contrary to its principles. It aided, however, by the dissemination of publications in its favor. Meanwhile it devoted its energies to its own affairs, though not yet determined upon its final policy, which could not be settled until the issue of the campaign was known. If the two-thirds majority was secured, it would continue as before; if it was not secured, then a change in policy might be adopted. When at last it was known that Jackson had been triumphantly re-elected, the directory concluded, nevertheless, that no "change in the general system of operations" should take place. The bank would not "commence any systematic reduction of its loans with a view to winding up its affairs." The only change contemplated was "to give gently and gradually the loans of the Bank the direction of domestic bills, . . . which being payable at maturity" would "give the Institution a greater command over its funds." But there was no intention of beginning "to close its concerns." Evidently the directors still hoped that a new charter might be secured.

Their chances, however, had materially diminished. A necessary consequence of the struggle had been to embitter both parties and to increase the suspicion of base motives on both sides. The *Globe* did not hesitate to assert "that members of the defeated party were prompting the 'minions of the bank' " to assassinate the president, and the tone of the party newspapers became absolutely ferocious. Jackson shared in this spirit and was not content to rest satisfied with his signal victory. He longed, he said, "for retirement, and repose on the Hermitage. But until I can strangle this hydra of corruption, the Bank, I will not shrink from my duty, or my part." Having once entered the fray, he would be appeased with nothing less than the total annihilation of the bank, thoroughly convinced that the monster was unconstitutional, undemocratic, corrupt, subversive of liberty, dangerous to "the people."

In the message of 1832 he complained at length of the bank's behavior and recommended the sale of the government stock therein and an investigation by Congress to determine whether it was safe to leave the public funds in its control. Biddle was well aware of the president's feeling and for the first time was not surprised by the contents of the message. He indeed suspected that the executive would attempt the discredit of the bank by planning a run upon the Washington office. "I have tonight directed a reinforcement of specie to Washington to protect the Branch against the Officers of the Executive. Is not that a monstrous state of affairs?" What hurt and angered him still more was that McLane had supported his chief's insinuations of the bank's insolvency, declaring that its action in relation to the 3 per cents. and other matters had "tended to disturb the public confidence in the management of the institution," and had suggested "an inquiry into the security of the bank as the depository of the public funds." The message and report shook the credit which is the very life of such an institution and depressed the price of the stock. The bank might be broken as a consequence of the loss of confidence in its solvency, and Biddle bitterly denounced master and man as deserving impeachment.

The president, however, had no reason to dread impeachment, but pressed constantly forward. He was determined to deprive the bank of the deposits, basing his determination upon two opinions: first, that they were not safe in the bank; and secondly, that if they were allowed to remain in its custody, they would be employed to bribe the members of Congress to pass a re-charter over the veto. To a friend he wrote:

> This combination [of Clay and Calhoun] wields the U. States Bank, & with its corrupting influence they calculate to carry every thing, even its recharter by two thirds of Congress, against the veto of the Executive, if they can do this, they calculate with certainty to put Clay or Calhoun in the Presidency—and I have no hesitation to say, if they can recharter the bank, with this hydra of corruption they will rule the nation, and its charter will be perpetual, and its corrupting influence destroy the liberty of our country. When I came into the administration it was said, & believed, that I had a majority of seventy-five —since then, it is now believed it has bought over by loans, discounts, &c., &c., until at the close of last session, it was said, there was two thirds for rechartering it.

In this opinion he was most obstinately fixed, Blair, of the *Globe*, pressing it upon him constantly. He was, moreover, informed by James A. Hamilton that "a gentleman whose knowledge of the views of the United States Bank is only second to that of its President" had told him that the bank counted upon securing a re-charter in spite of the president. Even if it did not succeed now, he believed that it would attain its purpose after his retirement, and consequently it was necessary to precipitate another conflict and thus force the bank's hand. The idea of withholding the deposits was not a new one. Secretary Ingham in his acrid correspondence with Biddle in 1829 had pointed out such a possibility, and it had been suggested during the investigation of 1819. Moreover, attempts at a partial withdrawal of the deposits had been made several times, though without success. The authority to remove the public funds from the bank had been confided by the charter to the secretary of the treasury, to be exercised at his discretion. He must, however, give his reasons for the act to Congress as soon as possible after the removal.

The advisability of depriving the bank of the public deposits was apparently discussed by the president's intimates during the campaign of 1832, for the bank was warned of the likelihood of such action in August of that year. After the campaign, rumors of the president's resolution came thick and fast, and Biddle was informed "that the determination to take the deposits away is *final*." Other correspondents gave the same assurance in January, 1833. He was also informed that there was a project to create another bank to take the place of that already existing. A third plan was for the president of the United States to issue "a scire facias to ascertain if the charter had not been forfeited."

While these projects were being discussed the administration had taken hostile measures against the bank. McLane, during the interval between the sessions, had appointed an agent, a Jackson partisan, formerly a director of the bank and engaged in western business, to examine into its affairs, especially into the condition of the western debts. To the discomfiture of its enemies, his report declared that these debts in his opinion were safe and that the deposits might with confidence be allowed to remain in the custody of the corporation. The report was strengthened through the rejection by the House in February, 1833, of a motion to sell the government stock, by a report of the Committee of Ways and Means to the same effect, and still more by the emphatic declaration of the representatives, by a vote of 109 to 46, that in their opinion the deposits were perfectly safe in the keeping of the bank.

Though these acts certainly staggered Jackson's supporters, they did not affect his purpose in the least. On the contrary, he was all the more convinced that it was necessary to act in order to hinder the bank's securing a re-charter by bribery. The effect upon Biddle and his friends was cheering. The hope of securing a new charter had not perished. In January Jaudon opposed the sale of the government's stock in the bank because "it would weaken our chance of a re-charter." On the day that the House declared its belief in the safety of the deposits in the bank's custody, Sergeant said that he thought there was reason to hope for a new charter, while Clay informed Biddle that the prospects were not bad, though nothing could be done for the present. He hoped "that at the next session or the session after, the charter" would be renewed, while Biddle expressed his conviction "that the chances of a renewal have increased and are increasing." Jackson's conflict with the Nullifiers encouraged Biddle to believe that support could be secured in the South, while the momentary affiliation of Webster and Jackson against the Nullifiers gave hopes of influencing the president through the bank's great champion. The first expectation was justified; the second was not. In April Biddle wrote to Webster asking him to attempt a reconciliation with the administration, saying that "whatever is done in the way of pacification should be done soon, for if the deposits are withdrawn, it will be a declaration of war which cannot be recalled"; "the whole question of peace or war lies in the matter of the deposits." Webster did what he could but without avail.

Before acting Jackson took advice as to the probable effect of a removal of the deposits. James A. Hamilton convoked a meeting of bankers in New York city and obtained their opinion. It was decidedly averse. Mr. Gallatin was most determined in opposition. Isaac Bronson answered a number of queries at length. He said that the bank would not be placed in the power of the state banks by the removal of the deposits; that it would be compelled to "reduce its discounts by an amount equal to the average sum of public deposits withdrawn from it," since it could not otherwise pay them without reducing its specie, which it "could not do safely"; that if it reduced, the state banks would have to do likewise; that a contest between the bank and the state banks would necessarily result; that no combination of state banks could be formed to take its place; and that the withdrawal of the deposits would probably aid in securing a re-charter. With these assurances to guide him, Jackson persisted in his course, and knowing that a panic must in all probability result, according to the opinion of a competent banker who was a friend to him and an enemy to the bank, he must be held accountable, as the supporters of the bank asserted, for having precipitated the panic. Besides securing these opinions, the president on April 14, and again on August 3, instructed the government directors to make an examination into the situation and conduct of the bank. In their reports to him they detailed a number of acts which he considered conclusive proof of the corrupt interference of the corporation in politics and its settled hostility to the government.

Meanwhile, warnings that the deposits would be removed in spite of the action of Congress continued to reach the bank's president. Yet, at the same time, he was informed that "the question . . . about removing the deposits *is as far from being settled as ever*," and that the leading members of the cabinet were unalterably opposed to the policy. His own opinion was that the administration "would not *dare* to remove them." On the 15th of April he was informed that changes would be made in the cabinet; that McLane would be secretary of state, a Pennsylvanian secretary of the treasury, and that "*the deposits will not be removed*," McLane having "taken a decided stand" and won the day.

This information was partially correct. The changes in the cabinet were made in accordance with it, but they were made with the expectation of securing a more pliable secretary of the treasury than McLane. The man selected was William J. Duane, of Philadelphia. He had been asked to take the office as early as December 4, 1832, and agreed to do so on the 30th of January, 1833. It is therefore evident that the removal had been determined upon even as early as this. Duane was informed immediately by R. M. Whitney, who claimed to be acting for the president, that the deposits were to be removed. Soon after this he was visited by Kendall, who gave him the same information, while on the 3d of June Jackson in person communicated his intentions. On this occasion the president discovered to his dismay that Duane was unwilling to order the removal. He argued the question, he expostulated, he begged his secretary to be reasonable; but the stubborn subaltern would not yield. On the contrary, he argued the point against the president with equal strenuousness, ending by promising to resign if he could not see his way clear to giving the required order.

Hereupon Kendall was sent on a mission to the state banks to see if they could be persuaded to take the deposits on terms advantageous to the administration. In Duane's opinion the mission was a failure, and Jackson's plan was certain, if carried out, to plunge the "fiscal concerns" of the country "into chaos." Kendall himself is said to have admitted to Jackson that the "project of removing the deposits must be given up." Jackson agreed neither with the secretary nor with his agent. His purpose was not shaken in the slightest degree. On his return from the eastern trip taken in the summer of 1833 he told Duane that the deposits must be removed and that he would take the responsibility. On the 18th of September he read his famous "paper" to the cabinet, in which he gave his reasons for the removal and assured the cabinet, as he had assured Duane, that he would take the responsibility. Duane, however, refused to budge from his position. He then exasperated Jackson still further by recalling his promise to resign. This decision was taken after the publication of the president's paper, an act which Duane considered personally insulting. The publication was made on the 20th of September, and on the 21st Duane sent Jackson a long, querulous letter, giving twelve reasons why he would not remove the deposits, refusing to resign, and rather inconsequently subscribing himself "your obedient servant." Jackson returned the letter forthwith, whereupon Duane wrote a second, third, and then a fourth in quick succession. Jackson returned the third and fourth as "inadmissible," and then gave Duane an ignominious dismissal, concluding a curt, cutting letter to him with these words: "I feel myself constrained to notify you that your further services as secretary of the treasury are no longer required."

Biddle was thoroughly informed of the relations existing between the president and the secretary, and knew at last that the determination of the president was unalterable. On the 30th of July he wrote to Robert Lenox that "the gamblers are doing everything in their power to bend Mr. Duane to their purposes," but the secretary "will not yield an inch." Two days later he described the situation so correctly that there can be no doubt that he had confidential information: "Duane has been required to withdraw the deposits and has refused. This mission [*i. e.*, Kendall's] is now got up to prove that he can do without the Bank of the United States and then he will be again asked—and he will again refuse. Then he will either leave the Treasury, or have conquered the Kitchen Cabinet—in either case the triumph of the Bank will be signal." Biddle was therefore sufficiently forewarned of the president's purpose and took precautions accordingly.

Immediately after Duane's dismissal, Roger B. Taney, a consistent foe of the bank, who had all along urged upon the president the necessity of removing the deposits, was appointed secretary and executed the president's design. The bank's stock immediately declined 1½ per cent. The deposits were not actually removed. On the contrary, the administration did not touch the government funds held by the bank, hoping thus to deprive the directors of an excuse for contracting their business. It was a shrewd move, but had little effect. The mere withholding of further deposits, while those still in the bank were gradually withdrawn in the regular course of the government's use of the funds, was sufficient, in the opinion of most men, to force a contraction. Besides, the phrase "removal of the deposits" gained instant currency, and the assertion that they were not removed passed almost unheeded.

Besides Taney, the other thick-and-thin supporters of "removal" about Jackson were Kendall and Blair, Barry, and Reuben M. Whitney. The members of the cabinet, excepting Barry and Taney, were either hostile to the act or lukewarm in support. Cass allowed himself to be overruled; Woodbury said he was with the president now, though opposed earlier. Many close friends of the president supported the opinion of the majority of the cabinet, considering the act unjust, and above all impolitic. A large proportion of the Democrats were in the position of Duane, who had always been "opposed to the United States bank, and to all such aristocratic monopolies; but . . . considered the removal of the deposits, unnecessary, unwise, vindictive, arbitrary, and unjust." These opinions were sound, though it is conceivable that the president might secure for his act of overbearing mastery almost as many supporters as he would lose. His own belief that the policy was one of justice and self-defense would in the long run be that of the Democratic masses, for Jackson's mental processes were those of the average honest, ignorant man. As he thought, so they would think. How differently different men would feel is evidenced by the wish of Robert Lenox that the president would remove the deposits in order that the bank might be re-chartered, and the admiration of Benton when it was done.

In his paper read before the cabinet on the 18th of September, and prepared for him by Taney, Jackson gave a variety of reasons for the removal: The bank had increased its loans in 1832 in order to compel a re-charter; it was settled by the campaign of that year that the charter should not be renewed, and therefore the president thought that the removal could not, "with due attention to the interests of the people, be longer postponed"; Congress could not act with regard to the deposits until the secretary had first acted; the public funds were probably unsafe in the bank's custody; it had interfered to hinder payment by the treasury of the 3 per cent stocks; had mistreated the government in the matter of the French indemnity bill; had refused to allow the government directors their charter privileges; had conducted business with less than a quorum of seven directors; had spent immense sums for publications for political effect, and thus corrupted the press. Finally he declared that the responsibility had been assumed "as necessary to preserve the morals of the people, the freedom of the press, and the purity of the elective franchise." One would search the constitution in vain to find the clauses giving the president of the United States the guardianship of "the morals of the people, the freedom of the press, and the purity of the elective franchise," but it is certain that Jackson thoroughly believed himself endowed with such authority, and considered this a sufficient reason for his action.

Jackson's act precipitated a panic in a market already stringent on account of the reductions in bank accommodations due to the hostile relations between the administration and the bank. The withdrawal of the deposits necessarily had this result, because it left all moneyed interests in a condition of suspense and doubt, put monetary affairs on a new and uncertain basis, and gave a tremendous shock to public confidence, without which commercial dealings cannot continue. The commercial situation was further aggravated at this moment by the effects of the compromise tariff law, which introduced a new system of paying duties, the importers being compelled to pay at once and not, as heretofore, after six months' time. The consequence was that an increased demand for credit was occasioned, at the very moment that it could least be met.

The bank immediately answered the move of the president by increasing a contraction already begun. In this it was justified. The only question was how far the contraction was to go. The bank would certainly not be justified in contracting after its own safety was assured. Where this point was no one could say excepting the directors. The massing of statistics to prove that the bank went too far, or not far enough, is of little value, if taken alone, since the amount of contraction must be determined at each moment by the peculiar circumstances of that moment, and what might prove an ample reserve at one time would be totally insufficient at another. But supposing the directors to go beyond the point of safety, they would certainly be severely censurable, since, whether legally bound or not, they were morally bound to protect the business of the country from harsh shocks. It may be concluded, therefore, that though the president of the United States was responsible for the first contractions of the bank and for the sufferings resulting therefrom, the question of responsibility for later contractions and later sufferings remains open.

In attempting to determine in how far the board of directors was justified in its policy, the reader must remember that the unceasing hostility of the administration placed the bank in a very precarious position. The withdrawal of the deposits was intended to weaken it and put it in the power of the state banks. If the executive had shown willingness henceforth to let the bank alone, it would have been morally confined to more restricted limits in its contraction. But every fresh act of hostility necessitated a further reduction, in order to make the institution perfectly secure. As such acts continued, the task of dividing the responsibility for the panic of 1833-34 becomes more and more difficult. It is of importance, therefore, to determine just what further aggressive steps were taken by the administration, and what other events affected the judgment of the directors.

In the autumn of 1832 a run had been made on the Lexington branch, incited without doubt by political opponents. In the autumn of 1833 a demand for $350,000 in specie was suddenly made upon the branch at Savannah, which could be met only because, the suspicions of the board having been aroused by the failure of the bank to receive the notes of the Savannah branch, it had sent large supplies of specie there. Biddle had no doubt that the administration was behind this attack.

The dispute over the French Indemnity Bill aggravated the situation. The United States, in order to collect the first instalment of that claim, had on the 7th of February, 1833, sold to the bank a bill of exchange drawn upon the French government. The amount was $903,565.89. The bank presented the bill in Paris, where payment was refused, and the bill went to protest. The bank would have been dishonored if the firm of Hottinguer et C$^{ie}$, its continental agent, had not taken up the bill for it. The bill was returned and the bank sent it to the secretary of the treasury, with a claim for the principal, interest, cost of protest, re-exchange, and damages at 15 per cent. The claim of the bank to the damages was based upon a statute of Maryland, which was law in the District of Columbia.

Secretary McLane at once paid the principal, but not the other items. In answer to a letter from Biddle in June, Secretary Duane admitted the validity of all the other claims excepting that for damages, to which Attorney-General Taney declared that the bank had no claim either "in law or in equity." Having given this opinion, Taney was requested to give his reasons for it, but so long as he was attorney-general he refused to give them. Not only so, but after becoming secretary of the treasury he completely ignored the bank's claim. Woodbury when secretary followed Taney's example. Thus affairs stood from May 16, 1833, until July 2, 1834, on which date Secretary Woodbury finally declined to pay the damages. The bank thereupon notified the secretary that the sum claimed would be deducted from the government's part of the semi-annual bank dividend. On the 16th of July this was done, the amount plus interest to that date being retained. The sum was $170,041.18. The bank's action was the only one left to it, since the administration refused either to pay or to submit the question to a judicial decision, and could not be sued. Consequently the corporation was bound to retain the money if the claim was ever to be adjudicated. The directors justified the demand for the damages by the "universal and inflexible rule of the Treasury department," which had always compelled the payment of the damages in cases of this character. Their action was good business, but bad politics, for it gave the administration a chance to charge the corporation with seizing public funds, and thus increased its unpopularity.

The retention of the dividend, however, brought the desired response from the administration. Secretary Woodbury censured the act of the corporation in an acrimonious letter, while Attorney-General Butler drew up reasons in support of Taney's assertion that the bank's claim had "no foundation in law or in equity." The government then instituted suit to recover the dividend withheld, and in the circuit court for Pennsylvania won its case on the fine distinction that the bank was an indorser and not the holder of the bill. This decision was reversed by the Supreme Court in 1844, which expressed the opinion that the United States was bound, both by law and equity, to pay the damages. The case was retried in the lower court in 1847, but came again before the Supreme Court on a writ of error, the government claiming that as a sovereign power it was not subject to the law merchant. The court affirmed this view, and judgment was entered against the bank. This ended the matter. It is only necessary to add that the nation's honor was forfeit by the refusal to pay the damages. On precisely the same plea it might have refused to pay the principal and interest.

At the time of the withholding of the deposits, members of the administration naturally feared retaliatory measures. To avert any injury likely to accrue to the state banks, Taney resolved to protect them by intrusting to certain of the deposit banks drafts for large amounts on the public funds left in the Bank of the United States. These sums were to be drawn from if the institution called upon the state banks for payments of balances due in coin, or refused to receive branch notes given in payment of government dues at places where they were not made payable. The Union Bank of Maryland received three drafts for the sum of $100,000 each; the Girard Bank of Philadelphia, one draft for $500,000; and the Bank of America, the Mechanics Bank, and the Manhattan Company Bank of New York city, each one draft for $500,000. Thus fortified, it was calculated that any "superfluity of naughtiness" of which the Bank of the United States might be guilty in trying to draw specie from banks which owed specie but had no specie, could be met and turned to the discomfiture of the aggressor.

The Union Bank of Maryland received its three drafts on the 3d and 4th of October; on the 5th it concluded that the time for action had come, and presented two of them, one at Baltimore and the other at Philadelphia. The pretext for this astonishing action was that the Bank of the United States had demanded coin from the Baltimore banks. The truth was that the Union Bank was in straits. Its president admitted that he had departed from the secretary's instructions, having swelled his discount list enormously, but pleaded the justification of the necessity of helping the commercial interests. His action embarrassed Taney, but he did not hesitate to repeat it, and had the third draft cashed at Baltimore on the 4th of November, the Bank of the United States having drawn on the Union Bank for $125,000 owed to it by that institution.

The Girard Bank received its check on the 3d of October, and with this security against calls for specie boldly proceeded to expand its business. By the 10th of October the bank had done this to such a degree that it had "made a very sensible impression on the moneyed market"—such a "sensible impression," indeed, that it had placed itself in a position where the use of the draft was almost necessary for its own safety. In this state of affairs it besought permission to have the draft cashed if it thought circumstances demanded, without waiting for any decided attack on the part of "the monster." The president of the bank believed that it ought to continue to extend its operations and, if the Bank of the United States called for specie, present the check. On November 2 the Girard Bank owed the Bank of the United States $149,000, and the time for action had come. Biddle was given his choice: either to permit the Girard Bank to continue its course, by not calling for the payment of the balances in coin, or to pay the $500,000. He insisted that the draft be cashed. He feared that by chance or design these large sums might be called for at a time or at a place where they could not be paid.

The three banks in New York acted in concert. On the 16th of November they concluded that it was necessary to present one of the drafts for $500,000, the bank having at that date drawn on the banks of the city for over $100,000. The Manhattan Bank, therefore, presented its draft on the 18th and received prompt payment. Taney had now become anxious about the remaining drafts, and desirous of having them returned to him. On the 21st of November, therefore, one of them was remitted to Washington, and no further use was made of this means of protection or offense.

The particular atrocity of this mode of granting to deposit banks the means of drawing heavily upon the Bank of the United States lay in the fact that no notice was given that institution that these drafts were out; and a sudden call for sums ranging from $100,000 to $1,500,000 might have ruined it. Yet this was not all. The bank had always been furnished with a weekly list of treasury drafts issued and also from 1829 with a daily list of all warrants out. It had a right to expect that this would continue to be the case until notice annulling the arrangements was given. As a matter of course, the daily business of the institution was conducted with the lists of warrants and drafts always in view, and with the certainty that the bank was thus prepared for all calls from the government. Now in these lists no information had been given of the drafts issued by Taney. The treasurer, in answer to Jaudon's remonstrances, acknowledged that lists were furnished to the bank, but defended the action of Taney on the ground that these were special drafts. If they had been included in the lists, the sums would have been at once deducted from the treasurer's account, and it was hoped all along that no necessity would arise for their use. They were "contingent drafts." To a further communication of Jaudon's the treasurer answered that the agreement was to give daily notice of warrants drawn, but not of "transfer drafts." To this subterfuge Jaudon replied by showing that the drafts were not in any sense transfer drafts, but warrants. Admitting, however, the treasurer's contention that they were not warrants, and therefore not placed on the daily lists, yet all drafts appeared on the weekly lists. To this the treasurer had no reply, and so discreetly made none.

In January, 1834, the administration took another aggressive step. Congress, by an act of the 3d of March, 1817, had transferred to the bank the functions of the commissioners of loans, including the duty of paying all pensions in states where it had branches. Where it had no branches it was to designate the state banks which should act as pension agents. An attempt was now made to deprive the bank of the exercise of its functions in respect to certain pension laws. This was not the first time that something of the sort had been tried. In 1829 the transfer of the pension funds from the branch at Portsmouth had been attempted, but the effort failed. In 1831 a similar attempt was made to remove the pension agency at New York to Albany. The bank again remonstrated, and in March, 1832, Secretary Cass admitted that in his opinion the War Department was "not warranted in appointing a pension agent, in any State or Territory, where the United States Bank has established one of its branches." In 1834 the action was based on a new plea. The administration contended that the acts of May 15, 1828, and June 7, 1832, were not pension acts, strictly speaking, but that they were laws allowing *pay* to the old Revolutionary veterans. Of course, for the sake of convenience, these sums were treated as pensions; and the pension office had control of the payments, and the pension agencies disbursed them. But all this was simply because they were like pensions, not because they were pensions. Accordingly, on January 2, 1834, the commissioner of pensions ordered the bank to give up the books, accounts, and funds relating to pensions disbursed under the act of June 7, 1832. The bank bluntly refused to do so. President Jackson was in a towering rage, and on the 4th of February communicated to Congress his complaint. As a matter of course, the Senate decided that the bank was in the right and the House declared that the bank was in the wrong. In this state of affairs there was no means of compelling the corporation to accede to the demands of the administration, and it did not yield.

This issue was skilfully made so as to bring odium upon the bank. The commissioner of pensions had not only ordered the institution to deliver the books and papers, but also to pay no more pensions under the act of June 7, 1832. The secretary of war assenting to this order, no pensions were paid under the act. The result was that many poor veterans of the Revolution could not draw their meager allowances when they needed them. The blame for this deprivation fell entirely upon the bank, though the fault was with the government. It is easy to imagine that many people were much moved over an act which seemed oppressive to the aged soldiers, while the enemies of the bank made effective political capital out of the situation. It "will not spare the holy remnant of the officers and sires of the revolution," declared Senator Wilkins, with maudlin pathos. "So sweeping and unsparing are they determined to make the distress, that even a solitary soldier of the revolution cannot escape." The same tone of injured indignation was employed by all the Democrats.

Webster accordingly urged Biddle to surrender the funds. "The Attorney General's argument," he wrote, "is a weak one; it is easy to demolish it, as an argument. But, after all, it is a bad subject to dispute about. The pensioners will not believe that the 'Old Soldier' is the cause of keeping back their money," therefore it would be "better to give up the fund and the papers." In this opinion he was heartily supported by Representative Gorham. The advice fell upon deaf ears. The bank had the support of the law, and it would not yield. Woodbury, in his report of December 12, 1834, remarks that the bank is still employed to pay pensions, "under an impression that it had . . . a right to perform these duties, until relinquished by its own consent, or until the acts were repealed." He is careful to add that the two acts in dispute are not regarded in this light, and the administration persisted in paying these pensions, though under almost insurmountable difficulties.

Another cause of strife was found in the acts of the government directors. Jackson believed that these directors were designed by the charter to keep a watchful eye upon the acts of the bank in the interest of the public, and, since he was the representative and the custodian of the public's interests, to report to him if they had any reason for suspecting abuses or mismanagement. In 1833 Messrs. Gilpin, Wager, Sullivan, and McElderry, government directors, sharing his opinion, forwarded to him reports respecting those transactions of the bank of which they did not approve. Moreover, they systematically opposed the other directors in regard to the powers of the exchange committee, the authority of the president, the curtailments in the West, and the measures taken against the administration. Naturally they were not welcomed at the board in Philadelphia, nor taken into the complete confidence of Biddle and his coadjutors, nor appointed to the important committees of the bank.

In these circumstances, Jackson renominated all of them as government directors for the year 1834. Biddle was immediately in arms, and wrote long letters to all the senators friendly to him, urgently pressing the rejection of the nominations. "They are people unfit to be there [i.e., in the directorate]—unfit to associate with the other members—so that their colleagues will not confer with them—or act with them on committees." The board "having no confidence in them, they were not allowed to know anything." He also wanted Taney's nomination to the Treasury Department rejected. Webster remonstrated against these measures, advising as little opposition to persons as possible. Again his good advice went unheeded. The strong-willed president of the bank had his way, and the Senate finally rejected Taney's nomination, and refused by a vote of 20 to 25 to concur in the nominations for government directors. The president, inflexible as always, returned the names to the Senate, and again it refused by a vote of 11 to 30 to concur.

In the end, Jackson made other nominations. Two of the nominees, Messrs. Ellmaker and Tibbetts, were disqualified as not being stockholders, and were therefore refused seats at the board. Three other gentlemen declined appointments, and accordingly for the year 1834 the government had only two directors. On the 14th of October Jackson notified them that he wanted certain information regarding the expenses and profits of the bank. They at once made a call for the necessary books, adding that they sought information for the use of the president of the United States. Their right to examine the books was incontestable, yet the bank could not permit these to be used to secure information which would be employed to injure the institution, and Biddle wrote Jaudon that they must not be permitted "to look at any thing." Hence the cashier refused their request. They immediately sent in a complaint to Jackson. This again placed the bank in a bad light before the people. If there was nothing to conceal, nothing to fear, why this refusal? Besides, the refusal itself was an infringement of the rights of the government directors. To these arguments the bank had no adequate defense.

Then there were fresh difficulties created in reference to the branch notes and drafts. Benton declared that the bank had conspired to embarrass the state banks and the nation by refusing to receive the notes of distant branches. Nothing could be more inaccurate. It is true that the officers of the branches at New York, Mobile, and Baltimore had shown an inclination not to receive notes of other branches from the state banks. But they had never received all branch notes at par from these banks, and their only intention was to continue the usual custom. But a new face was put upon the matter since the "pet banks" now received the revenue and most of the revenue was paid in "uncurrent notes" of the bank of the United States. When the bank had received the revenue it necessarily took all its notes in payment of revenue at par, since they were offered on behalf of the government. Now, however, if the old plan of not accepting such notes at par from the state institutions was continued, the revenues collected by them would be redeemed by the Bank of the United States at a loss to the state banks. Again, such action might nullify one great purpose of a bank's establishment—the purification of the currency—for if the bank should refuse to receive its notes at par, from the state banks, they would depreciate to a considerable extent, since all the notes which used to come to it from the revenues came to it now from the state banks. Was not the bank bound to receive these notes as coming indirectly from the government? The state banks thought so, and the government concurred in the opinion. On the other hand, if it did receive them it threw down all restrictions on the receipt of the issues of its branches, for there was no method by which it could discriminate notes received by the state banks in payment of duties from those received in the ordinary course of business. Consequently it would have to redeem all notes offered by the state banks. This was the position which it was finally forced to take. It was actually compelled to give to its branch notes a greater currency than ever before, receiving them from everybody at their face value at all the Atlantic offices. It did this because it feared by doing otherwise to create a demand upon distant, unprotected branches.

In regard to the branch drafts, the president repeatedly threatened that he would prohibit their receipt in payment of government dues. A rumor that such action would be taken was current as early as February 8, 1833. The directory fully expected that orders to cease receiving them would be issued in January, 1834, and adverted to the fact as a reason for further contraction. The supporters of Jackson further justified the bank in contracting its business by "loudly calling upon those who" took "part with them to collect and present the notes of the bank of the United States, for payment in coin."

The foregoing acts of the administration must be kept clearly in mind in reviewing the action of the bank in 1833-34. These measures show the temper of Jackson and his allies, and they palliate, to some extent, whatever retaliatory measures the bank adopted. They furnished plenty of reason for taking steps to protect its interests. Indeed, there could be but one policy to follow in any case, for the institution expected to go out of existence in March, 1836. It ought, therefore, to diminish its operations.

*Few Presidents have excited greater antipathy from their contemporaries than did Andrew Jackson, but then few generated greater admiration than he did. As James Parton, his first biographer, noted: "During the last thirty*

*years of his life, he was the idol of the American people." He further concluded in a neat counterpoint that "his elevation to power was a mistake on the part of the people of the United States." The rugged individualism of the Old General appealed to historians such as John Fiske who praised him for ending "a tendency toward the mollycoddling . . . theory of government, according to which the ruling powers are to take care of the people." His vigorous uses of Presidential power have also been cited to support the conclusion that he enlarged the role of the Presidency. His forceful handling of the Nullification crisis is used to demonstrate that conclusion.*

*In retrospect, many historians have concluded that this crisis proved to be a meteoric warning of an impending civil war. It is also treated as evidence of the declining economic position of South Carolina. The Carolinians, suffering from a severe economic depression during the twenties, traced their dislocations to the protective tariffs instituted after the War of 1812. Finally, in desperation, the Palmetto State nullified the tariffs of 1828 and 1832, challenged Jackson to enforce them, and stepped back from the verge of civil conflict only at the last moment. Jackson prepared to use federal force but a last-minute Compromise Tariff formulated by Henry Clay and Calhoun assuaged the grievances of the Carolina planters. Though Jackson won a verbal triumph, his opponents in Carolina could contend they had triumphed by forcing a tariff compromise.*

*More recently historians have emphasized that the Nullification crisis also reflected growing Southern fears of the Northern anti-slavery crusade. They depicted themselves as defending the huge and growing multibillion-dollar investment in slaves and plantations upon which was erected the distinctive qualities of Southern civilization. Jackson, himself a slaveholder, even as he asserted federal power, granted the South had legitimate grievances and was prepared to go further to assure them more relief than that conceded in the Tariff of 1833. Whatever the appropriate interpretation, it is obvious that the road first taken by South Carolina during the crisis proved one day to be the route most of the South would follow.*

*John Spencer Bassett (1868-1928), long a professor of history at Smith College, broke with the prevalent critical view of Jackson that had prevailed in the nineteenth century. He conceded the Old General's limitations and then emphasized his greatness. Whatever else one concludes about the seventh President, Bassett concluded he gave a "brave, frank, masterly leadership of the democratic movement which then established itself in our life." The equalitarian impulse that Tocqueville concluded throbbed through American life found its natural leader in the Old General. He came to power as its spokesman and he remained faithful to it. Bassett understood this truth, and as a result, his interpretation of Jackson has guided most modern historical interpretations of both the man and his era.*

# THE LIFE OF ANDREW JACKSON

## *by John Spencer Bassett*

The tariff passed in July. South Carolina found it exceedingly objectionable and the nullifiers raised loud cries in the campaign then waging and demanded a convention to consider the state's relation to the new law. The results at the polls were favorable and the governor, an ardent nullifier, called a meeting of the legislature, which quickly ordered an election for a convention to meet on November 19th. This precipitancy was employed in order that the intended programme might be completed before the meeting of congress in December, 1832. Now appeared the effects of the powerful efforts of Calhoun. Nearly the whole state turned to his doctrine, and, November 24th, the convention passed the famous nullification ordinance. This instrument declared the tariff laws of 1828 and 1832 unconstitutional and not binding on the state, it prohibited appeals to the supreme court of the United States in cases arising under this ordinance, it ordered all state officials except members of the legislature to take an oath to obey the ordinance, and it fixed February 1, 1833, as the day when it would go into operation. It closed with a threat that an attempt of the federal government to oppose its enforcement would absolve South Carolina from allegiance to the union and leave it a separate sovereign state.

Three days later the state legislature met in regular session and passed laws to meet contingencies likely to arise. It enacted a replevin law and other bills to enable a person who refused to pay duties to recover damages from federal customs officers, who might seize his goods, it passed a law looking to armed resistance, and finally adopted a test for ridding the state of officials who would not accept nullification. Thus panoplied South Carolina marched to the contest with the nation, at whose head was Andrew Jackson, keenly alive to the situation.

September 11, 1832, before the South Carolina elections were held, Jackson, fully alive to the progress of nullification, sent a warning to Woodbury, secretary of the navy. Efforts were being made, he said, to win naval and army officers in Charleston from their loyalty to the union, and this must be prevented. There were plans, he asserted, to gain possession of the forts there in order to prevent a blockade of the place, and he directed that the naval authorities at Norfolk, Virginia, be in readiness to despatch a squadron if it were needed. October 29th, he ordered the commanders of the forts in Charleston harbor to double their vigilance and defend their posts against any persons whatsoever.

Early in November, he sent George Breathit to South Carolina ostensibly as an agent of the post-office department, but he carried letters to Poinsett and was instructed to visit various parts of the state observing the temper, purpose, and military strength of the nullifiers. "The duty of the Executive is a plain one," said Jackson, "the laws will be executed and the Union preserved by all the constitutional and legal means he is invested with, and I rely with great confidence on the support of every honest patriot in South Carolina."

When Jackson heard the news from South Carolina, he wrote in his fragmentary journal:

> South Carolina has passed her ordinance of nullification and secession. As soon as it can be had in authentic form, meet it with a proclamation. Nullification has taken deep root in Virginia, it must be arrested by the good sense of the people, and by a full appeal to them by proclamation, the absurdity of nullification strongly repudiated as a constitutional and peaceful measure, and the principles of our government fully set forth, as a government based on the confederation of perpetual union made more perfect by the present constitution, which is the act of the the people so far as powers are granted by them in the federal constitution.

Here we have the germ of the nullification proclamation. The ideas are not as clear as in that famous paper, but the note shows that he was on his own initiative throughly opposed to secession.

The position of the executive, however, had some serious difficulties. Legally he might interfere forcefully in state matters in two events: 1. If the governor of the state requested him to suppress an insurrection; but under existing circumstances in South Carolina this was not to be expected. 2. To enforce the laws of congress; but the laws provided no clear procedure for such intervention when the law was violated by a state. It was contemplated that in an ordinary case a federal officer could summon a *posse comitatus*, as a state officer might do, to aid him in his duty; but this could hardly be done against a whole people. It was an unforeseen contingency, and the executive branch of government must find a way to meet it. Jackson realized the deficiency and asked congress to enact a law to remedy it; but until that could be done, he fell back on the theory of the *posse*. He encouraged Poinsett and his friends to be ready to be summoned on such duty, he placed arms at convenient and safe places, some of them across the North Carolina border, and he promised that if necessary, he would march to the aid of the defenders of the union at the head of a large force from other states, itself a kind of augmented *posse comitatus*.

Such was Jackson's feeling: in practice, he could not go so far. Nullification, until the adoption of the ordinance of November 24th, was closely bound up with the general Southern opposition to the tariff, and the administration hesitated to press it lest the whole South should become nullifiers. The South Carolinians played earnestly for this wider cause, and sought particularly to win Virginia. To that end, they stressed the connection between nullification and the Virginia and Kentucky Resolutions, trying to convert the regular republicans in that state. But the old antipathy was too strong: Virginia republicans of the Crawford school disliked Calhoun and all he stood for too much to follow him into his new vagaries. All this did not appear on the surface, and when in July, 1832, Senator Tazewell, an extreme state rights doctrinaire, suddenly resigned his seat in the United States senate, it caused much apprehension in administrative circles which desired to avoid taking the initiative in a policy of repression.

But vigilance was not relaxed. Seven revenue cutters and the *Natchez*, a ship of war, were sent to Charleston with orders to be ready for instant action. They took position where their guns could sweep the "Battery," the fashionable water front, on which dwelt the most prominent families in the place. Troops were ordered from Fortress Monroe to reinforce the garrison, and General Scott was directed to take chief command of the defenses and to strengthen them as he found necessary. There was to be no relaxation of the customs regulations, and in all things the authority of the government must be unimpaired. But it was not desired to irritate the inhabitants, and the commander was directed to surrender all state property claimed of him, even to arms and military supplies.

November 18th Jackson pronounced the movement of the nullifiers a bubble, but admitted their recklessness might lead to worse. In the forthcoming message, he said, he would refer to the affair as something to be checked by existing law. He would only ask that the revenue laws be changed so that in states where the legislature sought to defeat them, the collector might demand duties in cash. By ceasing to give bonds to secure deferred payments, the payer of duties could not bring suit in which he disputed the legality of the duty. "This," declared Jackson, "is all that we want peacefully to nullify the nullifyers."

The quick and vigorous action of the nullifiers in the succeeding fortnight made him change his mind. In his annual message, December 4th, 1832, he referred to the danger which threatened, expressed the hope that the laws would prove sufficient for the crisis, and promised to communicate further information on the subject if it should be necessary. These words disappointed most friends of the union, and his opponents openly expressed their horror. "The message," said Adams, "goes to dissolve the Union into its original elements and is in substance a complete surrender to the nullifiers." Jackson was much embarrassed by the situation. The party was alarmed at the prospect of a contest which might involve the whole South. When the message was written, some days before it went to congress, he was not convinced that extreme measures would be necessary.

About this time he received a letter from Poinsett, written November 29th, which showed how dangerous the situation had become in the disaffected state. Sixteen thousand citizens, said the writer, were deprived of their rights by the recent action of the legislature and left without other source of help than the national government. Some unionists, Colonel Drayton among them, thought congress would acquiesce and let South Carolina go in peace: some despairing ones even talked of leaving the state for other homes. But Poinsett protested that he would remain and fight it out, whatever the consequences. Such a letter was calculated to arouse the deepest emotions in a man like Jackson, who on December 2nd, said in a letter of his own, "Nullification means insurrection and war; and the other States have a right to put it down." December 9th, he announced that congress would sustain him in a programme of force against nullification. "I will meet it," he said, "at the threshold and have the leaders arrested and arraigned for treason. I am only waiting to be furnished with the acts of your Legislature to make a communication to Congress, asking the means necessary to carry my proclamation into complete effect, and by an exemplary punishment of those leaders for treason so unprovoked, put down this rebellion and strengthen our happy Government both at home and abroad. . . . The wicked madness and folly of the leaders, the delusion of their followers, in the attempt to destroy themselves and our Union has not its parallel in the history of the world. The Union will be preserved. The safety of the republic, the supreme law, which will be promptly obeyed by me."

The proclamation, which he issued the day after he sent this message of support to the union men in South Carolina, was a warning to the nullifiers, an appeal to the patriotism of the nation, and a constitutional argument against the doctrines of Calhoun. The doctrine of a state veto on laws of congress, said the proclamation, is constitutionally absurd, and if allowed it would have dissolved the union when Pennsylvania objected to the excise law, when Virginia resented the carriage tax, or when New England objected to the War of 1812. A law thus nullified by one state must be void for all; so that one state could repeal an act of congress for the whole union by merely declaring it unconstitutional. Through the whole document, ran a strong vein of nationalistic philosophy, supporting the right of congress to establish protection, denying that the constitution is a compact of sovereign states, and announcing that a state has no right to secede. The proclamation closed with a fervid appeal to the "fellow-citizens of my native state" not to incur the penalty of the laws by following blindly "men who are either deceived themselves or wish to deceive you." "The laws of the United States must be executed," said the President, "I have no discretionary power on the subject; my duty is emphatically pronounced in the Constitution. Those who told you that you might peaceably prevent their execution, deceived you; they could not have been deceived themselves. They know that a forcible opposition could alone prevent the execution of the laws, and they know that such opposition must be repelled. Their object is disunion. But be not deceived by names. Disunion by armed force is *treason*. Are you ready to incur its guilt?"

The nullification proclamation is written with a charm of logic and nicety of expression worthy of John Marshall. There is a persistent and widely accepted tradition that it was the work of Edward Livingston, who as secretary of state signed it with Jackson. Both its literary quality and its subtlety of reasoning show that at least the part relating to constitutional matters was not the work of the President. The closing part—the appeal to the South Carolinians—has much of his fire and suggests that he wrote it originally, but that its style was remodeled by him who wrote the former part. As a whole, the proclamation is one of the best papers of an

American President and compares favorably with the inaugural addresses of Lincoln.

A letter to General Coffee, written December 14th, gives Jackson's views without Livingston's charm of statement. In it is the following:

> Can any one of common sense believe the absurdity that a faction of any state, or a state, has a right to secede and destroy this union and the liberty of our country with it, or nullify the laws of the Union; then indeed is our constitution a rope of sand; under such I would not live. . . . This more perfect union made by the whole people of the United States, granted the general government certain powers, and retained others; but nowhere can it be found where the right to nullify a law, or to secede from this union has been retained by the state. No amendment can be made to the instrument, constitutionally, but in the mode pointed out in the constitution itself, every mode else is revolution or rebellion. The people are the sovereigns, they can alter and amend, and the people alone in the mode pointed out by themselves can dissolve this union peaceably. The right of resisting oppression is a natural right, and when oppression comes, the right of resistance and revolution is justifiable, but the moral obligation is binding upon all to fulfil the obligations as long as the compact is executed agreeable to the terms of the agreement. Therefore, when a faction in a state attempts to nullify a constitutional law of congress, or to destroy the union, the balance of the people composing this union have a perfect right to coerce them to obedience. This is my creed, which you will read in the proclamation which I sent you the other day. No man will go farther than I will to preserve every right reserved to the people, or the states; nor no man will go farther to sustain the acts of congress passed according to the express grants to congress. The union must be preserved, and it will now be tested, by the support I get by the people. I will die for the union.

In this letter we find no mental subtlety and but the simplest ideas of constitutional law; but in strength of will and devotion to the union it is splendid.

The response of the states, about which he was anxious, was soon seen to be all that could be desired. One after another they sent assurances of support, and later came resolutions from states north and south condemning nullification as a doctrine and as an expedient. There could be do doubt that if the matter came to the worst, ample forces would be ready to suppress the nullifiers. In forty days, Jackson said, he could throw fifty thousand men into South Carolina and forty days thereafter as many more.

The attention of both the administration and South Carolina was especially directed toward Georgia and Virginia. Between the position of the former in regard to the Indians and that of the nullifiers there was much in common. Jackson feared that she would go over to the new heresy and foresaw that if he had a clash with her on that account, she would be ranged on the side of South Carolina in the larger quarrel. He urged the Georgia congressman and ex-Governor Troup to do all they could to avoid a clash and to Governor Lumpkins wrote, "My great desire is that you should do no act that would give to the Federal Court a legal jurisdiction, over a case that might arise with the Cherokee Indians"; and he begged Lumpkins to believe in "my continued confidence and respect, in which, you may always confide, until you hear otherwise from my own lips, all rumors to the contrary notwithstanding." Under the circumstances, Georgia owed it to Jackson to remain quiet, and her attitude in the crisis of the winter was all that could be expected. Her legislature was content to pass resolutions calling for a convention of the states to amend the constitution in regard to the point in question.

Virginia was important on account of her influence. To the earnest entreaties of South Carolina her reply was resolutions in which she professed entire loyalty to the resolves of 1798 and 1799, and the dispatch of an agent, B. W. Leigh, to urge the nullifiers to suspend their ordinance until congress adjourned. He arrived after February 1st, but what he asked had been done before that time. A group of prominent nullifiers, acting informally, in Charleston, on January 21st, approved certain resolutions advising the officers of government that it would not be well to enforce the ordinance at present and pledging themselves to fulfil the program of nullification if at the end of a reasonable time the demands of the state were not granted. The resolutions were extra legal, sensible, and effective. February 1st came and went without conflict, and the federal officers continued to collect duties in the Charleston custom-house without opposition.

Meantime, the state was greatly excited. The unionists were actively preparing for an encounter, though careful to do all in their power to prevent one through some rash deed. The nullifiers were equally self-restrained in regard to actual fighting. But each side prepared arms and ammunition, drilled its supporters, and kept watch on its antagonist. Jackson was kept informed of all that was done and was keen for a struggle. His fighting blood was up, and he threw aside all that caution which he displayed earlier in the movement. "The moment they are in hostile array in opposition to the execution of the laws," he wrote, "let it be certified to me, by the atty. for the District or the *Judge*, and I will forthwith order the leaders prosecuted and arrested. If the Marshall is resisted by twelve thousand bayonets, I will have a possee of twenty-four thousand." While the "force bill" was before congress, he wrote: "Should congress fail to act on the bill and I should be informed of the illegal assemblage of an armed force with the intention to oppose the execution of the revenue laws under the late ordinance of So. Carolina, I stand prepared forthwith to issue my proclamation warning them to disperse. Should they fail to comply with the proclamation, I will forthwith call into the field such a force as will overawe resistance, put treason and rebellion down without blood, and arrest and hand over to the judiciary for trial and punishment the leaders, exciters and promoters of this rebellion and treason." He had a tender of volunteers from every state in the union and could bring two hundred thousand into the field within forty days. Should the governor of Virginia, he said, have the folly to forbid the passage of troops through his state to the scene of treason "I would arrest him at the head of his troops and hand him over to the civil authority for trial. The voluntiers of his own state would enable me to do this."

When Jackson sent his proclamation to Poinsett in December, he said he was only waiting for certified copies of the acts of the South Carolina legislature putting nullification into force in order to ask congress for power to enforce the proclamation and punish the leaders of the rebellion. This information did not come, and unwilling to wait longer than January 16th, he sent to congress on that day, a special message asking for authority to alter or abolish certain ports of entry, to use force to execute the revenue law, and to try in the federal courts cases which might arise in the present contingency. Five days later, a bill in accord with these requests was introduced in the senate by Wilkins, of Pennsylvania. It was popularly called the "force bill," but the nullifiers expressed their horror by styling it the "bloody bill." There was much opposition to it; for many who were not nullifiers, were unwilling to coerce a state.

This situation brought genuine alarm to the managers of the Jacksonian democracy. It was not possible to tell how much the Calhoun defection would weaken the party. The last stages of the fight against the bank were approaching when the administration would need all its resources. Moreover, the tariff wave was receding. It had been partly due to the enthusiasm of the rural North and West for "the American system" through which, it was believed, cities, better transportation, and rich and prosperous farming communities would soon spring up. This was an unwarranted expectation, and the moment of elation was passing. Many politicians of the old republican school yielded to the tariff unwillingly and at the first intimation of recession supported the reaction. From all these causes the time favored compromise.

Before congress met the administration was prepared to take a milder position on the tariff. The approaching extinction of the public debt, which would give a surplus, made revision seem necessary. December 13th, in a letter in the Richmond *Inquirer*, a close friend of the government, probably Cass, secretary of war, suggested that Virginia propose a reduction of the tariff. This was better than a suggestion in the annual message, since such a course would tend to turn from the President the protectionist group. December 27th, the house committee of ways and means, through its chairman, Verplanck, of New York, introduced a new tariff bill, reducing the duties in two years to about half of the former rates. It was prepared by Cass, Verplanck, and other administration friends, but was especially supported by the New York school, who following suggestions from South Carolina, were willing to have their favorite appear as "pacificator." Its appearance aroused strong hostility from the protectionists, and not all the New York democrats could be got to vote for it. It was too drastic a reduction for the circumstances, and it stuck in the house so long that Van Buren's opponents had the opportunity to pass a bill less injurious to the manufacturers; and in doing so, they gave the honor of the compromise to another than he.

Clay came into the senate in December, 1831; early in January 1833,

Calhoun, resigning the vice-presidency, took the seat in that body made vacant by the election of Hayne to the governorship of his native state. Each new senator smarted from defeat at Jackson's hands, each felt that Jackson was leading the country to misfortune, and each was bent on impeding the course of the destroyer. Early in the year it was noised abroad that they were in alliance against the administration. In regard to the "force bill" the Kentuckian was chiefly silent. He would not fight the battles of the state rights advocates, not even to embarrass Jackson, nor would he help suppress nullification. In the final vote on the bill, he did not respond on either side. His energy was saved for the tariff.

But Calhoun was deeply engaged as soon as the "force bill" appeared in the senate. He offered resolutions in support of his theory of government, and when the senate brushed them aside, he plunged into the acrid debate with all his energy. In the beginning it was evident that the extreme state rights democrats found the bill very disagreeable. Jackson was forced to see a division in his own ranks. "There are more nullifiers here," he said, "than dare openly avow it," but he did not doubt they would be good Jackson men at home.

If his enemies had combined with the disaffected in his own party the bill might have been defeated. But they could no more combine in this way than the radical state rights men could support a bill to give the President the authority to suppress a state. Webster has been praised for coming to the defense of the bill. It would have been entirely captious for him to oppose it. He could hardly break down Hayne's nullification arguments in 1830 and refuse in 1833 to create the means necessary to put his own views into execution. But his aid was splendidly rendered and most effective. He brought the anti-Jacksonians with him, and these, with the loyal Jackson followers, made the bill safe in the senate.

Before it could pass Calhoun withdrew his opposition in consequence of Clay's concession on the tariff. February 12th the father of the "American system," while Verplanck's bill was still in the house, arose in the senate and offered a compromise tariff of his own. It proposed that for all articles which paid more than 20 per cent duty the surplus above that rate should be gradually reduced until in 1842 it should entirely disappear. Verplanck would have reduced duties within two years by half: Clay would do it in ten years to a 20 per cent basis. The latter plan was less violent than the former and was preferred by the manufacturers, if either must be taken. This was all that South Carolina contended for. Nullification was the club with which she sought to ward off a danger, and that danger gone she willingly threw the club away: she protested from the first that she disliked to use it. When the vote on the "force bill" was taken Calhoun and his followers left the chamber. Obstinate John Tyler would not run away, and he loved state rights too much to support the bill. He, therefore, remained in his seat and cast the only negative against thirty-two affirmative votes. In the house the bill passed in much the same manner, John Quincy Adams leading the anti-Jackson party in favor of the measure.

Clay's part of the compromise was adroitly played. His bill was opposed in the senate because it was unconstitutional for a revenue bill to originate in that chamber. He then arranged through much quiet work to have it substituted for the Verplanck bill in the other house, which through the opposition of the tariff party was not likely to pass at that session. February 25th, in the afternoon as the house was about to adjourn for dinner, Letcher, of Kentucky, Clay's fast friend, arose and moved the substitution of bills. After a short debate the change was made and the bill ordered engrossed for the third reading by a vote of one hundred and five to seventy-one. The tariff men were surprised, but the administration party were previously informed of the plan. They rallied to the proposition as part of the compromise by which the South Carolina crisis was to be removed from the stage of action. The thing was done so quickly, said Benton, that the hot dinners of the representatives were eaten before the food became cold.

Van Buren's friends were shocked. All the honors of pacification to which they looked through the Verplanck bill were suddenly snatched away by Clay. They thought a trick was played on them and Cambreleng complained that everybody seemed to be against New York. He was nearly right: except for Jackson himself, very few of the leaders in Washington seemed to care to help the New Yorker to the goal of his ambition.

Although the South Carolinians resisted the passage of the "force bill" to their uttermost, they accepted the compromise. Their convention re-assembled March 11th to consider the situation. It repealed the ordinance nullifying the tariff laws of the union and passed another nullifying the "force bill." The latter step was ridiculous, but it saved the face of the nullifying party and enabled it to claim complete victory. No one, within the state or out of it, was disposed to deny them this comfort. Most people were glad to be rid of an unpromising situation—the politicians because they had other affairs to arrange, and the people because they loved peace and feared disunion.

Jackson alone of his party seems to have looked beyond the political significance of the situation. In spite of his latent feeling of protest, he temporized along with the others until the nullification ordinance was passed. This action he took as a challenge, and leading his unwilling followers he committed his party to the cause of union. His letters to Poinsett and the replies to them show well the conditions in South Carolina. But the Van Buren correspondence at this period—the letters of party lieutenants to Van Buren and those which passed between him and Jackson—show the political side.

The nullification proclamation, as it was the first note of Jackson's more energetic programme, was the first sign for dissatisfaction among his followers. They disliked its national tone which Cambreleng pronounced "the metaphyics of the Montesquieu of the Cabinet." To the mass of people, he said, this would make no difference; they would see only an endangered union, whereas "the speculations are left for refinements of those who are only capable of transferring the special pleading of chancery into the councils of statesmen."

The listlessness of the party in the face of disunion is another illustration of the divergence between its attitude and that of the President. The day before the date of the proclamation Michael Hoffman, a New York congressman, described the situation to Van Buren. He thought the ways and means committee would be satisfactory on every bank question, and that on the tariff it would not adopt South Carolina's equalizing ultimatum; but "meanwhile South Carolina will rush on *in furorem*. The President will march against her, civil war will rage, and the poor fools who can see no danger now, will be frightened out, not of their wits, for they have none, but out of their folly. How they will behave then I cannot anticipate, for when their folly is gone, there will be nothing left of them." He added that General Scott thought the situation very delicate.

A week later so valiant a person as Benton wrote that everybody was concerned to prevent the beginning of bloodshed in South Carolina, that there was talk of an extra session of congress in the spring, and that all agreed peace would come if Jackson's suggestion in his message of a more moderate tariff were adopted, but the existing congress would not support this. This idea found support in Cambreleng's terse forecast: "We shall do nothing," he wrote, "but project tariffs this winter—while the Legislature will talk of a convention of states. We shall have some riots in Charleston, some bloodshed perhaps; some stormy debating in congress in February and the new congress will have to act and supersede the necessity of a convention." In no letter in either the Jackson or Van Buren correspondence is there evidence that any other leader in his party felt the same impulse that Jackson felt to crush resistance and enforce the authority of the union.

These alarms were poured into the ear of Van Buren, who as vice-president-elect remained decently at Albany until March 4th. With characteristic, and probably necessary, caution he approached Jackson on the subject. Our people are restive, he said, because the opposition try to interpret some parts of the proclamation as a condemnation of the state rights doctrine of the West and South. They find difficulty in holding meetings, and there is a disposition to say harsh things, which is unfortunate. Great discretion is necessary in New York on account of the diversity of tariff opinion and of feelings engendered in the late election. This he said in substance, closing with the assurance that he would do what he could to keep things on the right course.

Jackson's reply took little notice of Van Buren's warning but dwelt on the imminence of armed force. The moment the nullifiers raised an army, he said, he would issue a proclamation telling them to disperse and give the marshal troops enough to suppress them. He would arrest the leaders and turn them over to the United States courts for trial. He referred to Virginia's late reassertion of the doctrine of 1798, saying:

> The absurdity of the Virginia doctrine is too plain to need much comment. If they would say, that the state had a right to fight, and if she has the power, to revolution, it would be right but at the same time it must be acknowledged, that the other states have equal rights, and the right to preserve the union. The preservation of the union is the supreme law. To shew the absurdity—Congress have the right to

admit new states. When territories the[y] are subject to the laws of the union; The day after admission they have the right to secede and dissolve it. We gave five millions for Louisiana. We admitted her into the union. She too has the right to secede, close the commerce of six states, and levy contributions both upon exports and imports. A state cannot come into the union without the consent of congress, but it can go out when it pleases. Such a union as this would be like a bag of sand with both ends open—the least pressure and it runs out at both ends. It is an insult to the understanding of the sages who formed it, to believe that such a union was ever intended. It could not last a month. It is a confederated perpetual union, first made by the people in their sovereign state capacities, upon which we the people of these United States made a more perfect union, which can only be dissolved by the people who formed it, and in the way pointed out in the instrument, or by revolution.

Van Buren's anxiety was not allayed by this vigorous utterance and he wrote again. He agreed that there should be no faltering now, but warned his friend that merely passing an act to raise a military force was not treason and that constructive treason was unpopular in the United States. He advised Jackson to ask only for force to execute the laws. He knew the latter would say that this was the writer's old trick of saying, " 'caution, caution'; but my dear sir, I have always thought that considering our respective temperaments, there is no way perhaps in which I could better render you that service which I owe you as well from a sense of deep gratitude as public duty." He added that Virginia was much concerned over the proclamation, that he did not think South Carolina would secede but if such a thing happened Virginia would desire the remaining states to decide whether they would form a new union without the seceder or wage war to retain her in the union. The best solution he saw was the modification of the tariff.

Other letters followed from the same writer, but a fortnight passed before they were answered by the busy Jackson. This reply showed unexpected self-control. It was necessary, he said, to protect good citizens and federal officers in South Carolina who might fall under the state's laws of vengeance; and as to the tariff, it was necessary to think of both ends of the union; for New England, protected by the tariff, might be as willing to secede if protection was abandoned as the South if it was not abandoned. Nullification and secession must be put down once for all: he must give congress full notice of the danger so that it could act before February 1st, or he would be chargeable with neglect of duty. "I will meet all things with deliberate firmness and forbearance, but wo to those nullifiers who shed the first blood. The moment I am prepared with proof I will direct prosecution for treason to be instituted against the leaders, and if they are surrounded with 12,000 bayonets our marshal shall be aided by 24,000 and arrest them in the midst thereof. Nothing must be permitted to weaken our government at home or abroad. Virginia, except a few nullifiers and politicians, is true to the core. I could march from that State 40,000 men in forty days. Nay they are ready in North Carolina, in Tennessee, in all western States, and from good old democratic Pennsylvania I have a tender of upwards of 50,000; and from the borders of South Carolina in North Carolina I have a tender of one entire Regiment. The union shall be preserved."

On the day Jackson wrote this determined letter, Silas Wright wrote in another strain to Van Buren. Everything, he said, was at stake, even the union as well as "our most favorite political hopes and prospects." For the time he seems to have forgotten that all his hope consisted in sticking close to that leader who alone could carry into safety the head of the New York group. In consternation he demanded that Van Buren tell him how to vote on the Verplanck bill, he admitted that he had never voted from conviction on the tariff question, but from expediency, and declared himself willing to do it again. As to others, "the President is very well and cool, calm, and collected, but very firm and decided as to the use of force. As to the sustention of his position that a state cannot secede he is very sensitive, and even abuses mildly Mr. Ritchie." The secretary of war was "highly excited" and McLane in the treasury department, "is much more so."

Jackson's keen observation of the situation did not relax and for the next month the politicians tried to find a way out of the labyrinth. The postponement of the execution of the nullification ordinance seemed only to delay the day when he must strike rebellion. By this time he had lost most of his interest in the attempt to settle the tariff question; and when Clay's compromise was introduced he was quick to resent the prospect that it should take precedence of the "force bill." "I am just informed," he wrote hastily to Grundy on the night of April 13th, "that there will be another move to lay the judiciary ['force'] bill on the table until Mr. Clay's tariff bill is discussed. Surely you and all my friends will push that bill through the senate. This is due the country, it is due to me, and to the safety of this union and surely you and others of the committee who reported it will never let it slumber one day until it passes the senate. Lay all delicacy on this subject aside and compel every man's name to appear upon the journals that the nullifiers may *all* be distinguished from those who are in support of the laws, and the union." His efforts were not successful. His bill—in the letter to Grundy he calls it "my bill"—passed the senate before Clay's compromise tariff bill, but they both reached Jackson for signature on the same day. It must have made him feel that it was worth little to provide a means of checking the pretensions of a wilful state while giving it at the same time the object for which its wilfulness was exerted. Nullification was South Carolina's weapon. Using it successfully in 1833 showed how it could be used and established her prestige in the practice. Had the desires of Jackson been supported by a less timid group of politicians state rights might now have been broken and a sterner struggle in the succeeding generation might have been avoided.

It is difficult to give Clay and Calhoun their just places in this affair, so well are mingled selfish and apparently sincere motives; it is easier to praise Webster, although when he fought for the union he but stood where he stood before; but as regards the President there can be no such hesitation. He forsook his old position, cast aside the formulas of his party, and declared for the union when it was in danger. His political philosophy was a simple one, when put to the test. It embraced obedience to his authority, hatred of monopoly, and courage to carry out his purposes. The first and the third united to shape his course on nullification; the second and third united to direct it in the next great crisis of his career, the struggle against the Second United States Bank.

꧁ ꧂

THE *two decades preceding the Civil War were a time of great change in almost every aspect of American life. Long-established traditions crumbled as the ceaseless ebb and flow of life continued to erode accepted patterns of life. By 1830, New England, long the commercial heart of the union, entered into the take-off stage of industrial growth. The rocky landscape of Yankeedom was broken with increasing frequency by the looming mill chimney. The farms sent into factory dormitories their young women to work as operatives. The railroads feeding Boston and its expanding suburbs moved raw materials, finished products, and commuters swiftly and efficiently. The once wilderness swiftly contracted as some men and women regretted its passing. Among them, Henry David Thoreau complained from his cabin on Walden Pond, "The mass of men lead lives of quiet desperation." He begged men to restore their communication with nature and to remember that they were "all sculptors and painters, and our material is our flesh and blood and bones."*

*Ingrown Yankees complained as their ancient dream of a Bible State moved ever further from their grasp. In its place a sturdy republic arose that posed endless difficulty for the author as he tried to write "a romance about a country where there is no shadow, no antiquity, no mystery, no picturesque and gloomy wrong, nor anything but a commonplace prosperity in broad and simple daylight." Nathaniel Hawthorne further concluded that "ruin" was essential to the growth of romance. The American condemned to inhabit a temple called his body understood too well the awful cry of Melville's Ahab, "Oh, lonely death on lonely life." Surrounded by growing evidence of material wealth, Americans sensed that something had gone wrong with the American experiment. They did not doubt its success, but as a young Lincoln had declaimed, "The experiment is successful; . . . but the game is caught; and . . . with the catching, end the pleasures of the chase."*

*In the northern reaches of the country, the gulf between the American word and deed seemed to widen. The conviction steadily grew that the bargain sealed in the Constitution between slavery and freedom subverted the moral law. John Greenleaf Whittier, poet laureate of anti-slavery, protested, "the age is dull and mean. Men . . . keep six days to Mammon, one to Cant." It was as if Americans were yearning for a new sense of purpose, one commensurate to the ostensible purpose of American democracy—the extension of "Liberty to all." The thrust forward to expand the realm of freedom, united as it was with an abhorrence of slavery, cut ever more deeply into agitated consciences, exposing the deep unease at the patent hypocrisy of preaching on one hand equality while simultaneously keeping slaves. It took the Mexican war to focus and direct anti-slavery sentiment.*

*Few wars have more deeply divided the American public than the Mexican War. From its beginning in April of 1846, Democrats defended it as inescapable since Mexico left the United States no choice between war and dishonor, and Whigs denounced it as "Mr. Polk's War." No less a future personage than Abraham Lincoln, at the time a little-known Illinois congressman, accused Polk of diverting public scrutiny of his aggression by appeals to military glory—"that rainbow," as he put it, "that rises in showers of blood." Some contemporaries treated it as the only recourse left to the United States if it were to fulfill its national destiny to extend the national domain to the Pacific Ocean. Walt Whitman saw the war as proof to the world that "America knows how to crush, as well as how to expand!" And as the prospect of territorial expansion at Mexico's expense grew, anti-slavery forces charged the war was one of aggression designed to extend the domain of slavery.*

*The controversy over expansion of the peculiar institution took sharp focus when Congressman David Wilmot proposed in a request for funds to advance the war that any territory taken from Mexico be closed to slavery. So was born the free soil contention that the federal government should exclude involuntary servitude from territory under its jurisdiction. By 1854, the free soil position provided a rallying point for the coalition of divergent interests known as the Republican party. In the escalating debate preceding the Civil War, the Mexican War, as seen by Republicans, took on the hue of a Southern conspiracy to advance their sectional interests. In the aftermath of civil war, northern historians accepted the Republican claim, and generally concluded as did James Schouler (1839-1920) that the South had plotted "to let loose the demon of war, and under the smoke of defending the fourth part of Mexico (Texas) which we had just snatched from her, to despoil her of another (California and New Mexico)."*

*Other historians influenced by the assumptions of manifest destiny argued as did Edward Channing that even if the United States had no "moral right" to seize Mexican territory, "it must be said that the moral argument for the retention of these splendid lands by a people who did not and could not convert them to the benefit of humanity raises a strong presumption in favor of those who could make, and, as a matter of fact, have made, a good use of them." It remained for Justin H. Smith (1857-1930) to provide the most reasonable exculpation for American behavior during the war. He defended American efforts to settle the dispute through negotiation and contended that only the mulish stubbornness of the Mexicans prevented a peaceful resolution. He charged that "self-seeking [Mexican] politicians" had fed their people "on the ideas of despising, fearing, hating and fighting the United States." The Mexican government, Smith concluded, openly courted war in the expectation they would easily "beat the small and apparently* demoralized American army." Although he justified American action, he provided the focus within which recent historians have viewed the conflict, specifically as one that resulted from basic differences in the cultures of the two belligerents. No longer concerned with justifying results, the emphasis is now on trying to understand why the war happened as it did.

# THE WAR WITH MEXICO

## by Justin H. Smith

### THE PRELIMINARIES OF THE CONFLICT
### April, 1845-April, 1846

Strangely enough, although our diplomatic troubles with Mexico would almost certainly have led to hostilities, the war actually came about in a totally different way.

During the spring and early summer of 1845, in view of Mexican threats and of reports from trustworthy sources that an invasion of Texas might be expected, it was decided by our government that when her people should have accepted our annexation proposal, as they were almost sure to do, it would become the duty of the United States to defend her; and this decision made the question where her southern boundary lay a practical matter. It was a thorny subject. In 1834 Mexico herself did not feel sure about the line; and according to the chief technical officer in our state department, sole commissioner to negotiate the treaty of peace with Mexico, if an official demarcation had existed, the war between Texas and the mother-country nad rubbed it out. The former now claimed the territory as far as the Rio Grande, but she did not establish her title by occupying completely and effectively the region south of the Nueces. Only by an agreement with Mexico, indeed, could limits have been fixed. So far as it concerned the republic of Texas, this was in effect the situation.

For the United States, however, this was not the whole story. Down to 1819 our government had insisted that Louisiana extended to the Rio Grande. in other language, since the southern part of Louisiana was called Texas, the official view was that Texas bordered on that stream. Such, then, was in effect the contention of Jefferson, Madison, Monroe, John Quincy Adams, Pinckney, Livingston and Clay, who represented three administrations in upholding the claim. By the treaty of 1819 we did not withdraw from our position, but merely arranged to "cede" whatever possessions we had west of the Sabine for certain valuable considerations. From 1819 to 1845, Texas, considered under its geographical and historical aspects as a district of old Louisiana, appeared to border on the Rio Grande not less truly than before, for no other line became established. Hence it seemed evident from this point of view, that by annexing Texas we revived our old claim, our old official view, and the testimony of all those eminent statesmen. Our government so held. November 10, 1845, in explaining to Slidell the extent of Texas, Buchanan went back to Jefferson, Madison, Monroe, Pinckney and the discussion of the Louisiana boundary. Polk, as the head of our government, could not well repudiate, simply on his own authority, the solemn declarations of Presidents and other high officials, in which through a term of years the nation had acquiesced. The fact that for a considerable time the Texans, asserting the Rio Grande line, had maintained themselves against Mexico perhaps had some confirmatory value; and Polk was further bound, not only by his apparently sincere belief in our old claim, but by the pledge he had given to Texas and the pledge our official representative had given her, expressly to promote the cause of annexation, that he would maintain the claim as President. These were grips of steel.

To meet the responsibility thus incurred, we had eight regiments of infantry, four of "artillery" and two of dragoons, including about 7200 men. The "artillery" regiments, which were theoretically expected to serve in fortifications with heavy guns, were armed, equipped and drilled as infantry; but one company of each had a field battery, and under the instruction of excellent officers had reached a high state of skill in using it. The infantry and cavalry, drilled on the French system, were in a good condition generally, though division among coast and frontier stations, besides impairing discipline and efficiency, had prevented manoeuvring in large bodies; and the infantry soldiers in particular, inured on the border to hard service, felt now a reasonable confidence in themselves and their immediate superiors. The forty-five capable engineer officers understood their duties fairly well, except that a lack of men to execute operations had left them, as the head of the corps admitted, too much like theoretical mariners. A few well-trained topographical engineers, a small medical staff, and a quartermaster's department rounded out this miniature army. Nearly all the infantry carried flint-lock muskets, and numerous defects and deficiencies existed; but probably the forces were better equipped for service than has generally been supposed. In view of possible difficulties with Mexico, a disproportionate share of the troops were placed at or near Fort Jesup on the western border of Louisiana; and in June, 1845, these included the Third Infantry, eight companies of the Fourth Infantry, and seven companies of the Second Dragoons.

Their commander was Brevet Brigadier General Zachary Taylor. This child of destiny, born in 1784, had grown up and gained some rudiments of an education amidst the Indian troubles of the Kentucky border. At the age of twenty-three he had been commissioned first lieutenant in the Seventh Infantry, and after showing remarkable coolness and intrepidity in two small affairs during our second war with England and the Black Hawk War, he had won a stubborn fight in 1837 against the Seminoles at the head of some 1100 soldiers. Three years later he was assigned to a supervising command in the southwest, and this included Fort Jesup.

Personally Taylor possessed a strong character, a very strong character, neither exhausted by self-indulgence nor weakened by refinement and study. He was every inch a man, with a great heart, a mighty will, a profound belief in himself, and a profound belief in human nature. The makings of a hero lay in him, and to a large extent the making had been done. He was gifted, too, with solid common sense, not a little shrewdness and ambition, a thorough knowledge of men—the sort of men that he knew at all—a military eye, and a cool, resourceful intelligence that was always at work in its own rather ponderous fashion. The sharp gray eyes and the contraction of his brows that made the upper part of his face look severe were tempered by the benignity of the lower part; and the occasional glimmer of a twinkle betokened humor.

On the other hand, everything about him suggested the backwoodsman. His thickset and rather corpulent body, mounted on remarkably short legs, typified barbaric strength. In speech he was rough and ungrammatical, in dress unkempt and even dirty, and in every external of his profession unmilitary. He never had seen a real battle nor even a real army. Ignorance and lack of mental discipline made him proud of his natural powers and self-mastered attainments, and he saw very distinctly the weaknesses of school-taught and book-taught men. West Pointers, trim in person and in mind but inferior to him in strength, practical sense and familiarity with men and things, he felt strongly inclined to belittle; and this feeling went so far that he despised, or at any rate frequently seemed to despise, knowledge itself. He could not, however, fail to recognize on occasions the professional superiority of his trained officers, and no doubt found himself unable now and then to defend his opinions. In such cases, being by temperament extremely firm, he naturally took refuge in obstinacy; and sometimes he appears to have been positively mulish, holding to his own view after he must have seen its incorrectness.

From various logical results of these limitations Taylor was happily saved by Major General Winfield Scott, the head of the army, who purposely gave him Captain W. W. S. Bliss as adjutant general. Bliss was described by a good authority as the peer of any man alive in learning, statesmanship and military capacity; and he felt willing to give the General—later his father-in-law—the unstinted benefit of all his talents and attainments. With him at his elbow Taylor could be sure of trustworthy information, honest and competent advice, a friendly hand to supplement or subtract, and a skilful pen to report, explain and, if necessary, discreetly color the facts. Captain Williams, an able officer, wrote in 1848 that he could not imagine one man's being more indebted to another than Taylor was to his assistant. In other words, "Taylor" in the history of the Mexican War is the name of a double star, one partner in which was the dominating personality of the General, and the other a fine, trained intelligence known as Bliss.

Taylor, then, having been warned by a despatch of May 28, 1845, to hold the troops in readiness, was confidentially ordered on the fifteenth of June to place them at some port where they could readily embark for the Texas frontier, and, after learning that our annexation overture had been accepted, to occupy "on or near the Rio Grande del Norte" such a position, favorable to the health of the men, as would be "best adapted to repel invasion." Accordingly he concentrated his infantry at New Orleans, where official notice that annexation had been accepted by Texas reached him. Further orders from William L. Marcy, the secretary of war, enjoined upon him to "avoid any Acts of aggression," and in particular to refrain from disturbing any Mexican posts on the left bank of the river "unless an actual state of war should exist"; and under these instructions the forces left New Orleans toward the end of July for Aransas Bay, Texas. His troops—counting the dragoons, who set out by land for San Antonio, about 120 miles from the coast, a little later—numbered some 1500.

Taylor himself with a part of the command reached his destination on the twenty-fifth; landed his men, with such rapidity as meagre facilities and heavy surf would permit, on St. Joseph's Island; and then, with row boats and small sailing-craft, conveyed them some twenty-five miles farther to Corpus Christi, a hamlet on the south side of the Nueces River at its mouth. News that Mexico was on the point of beginning hostilities caused great alarm presently; but no enemy came, and by the end of August the General felt secure. The rest of the troops from Fort Jesup were then on the ground. Seven companies of the Seventh Infantry, collected laboriously from a number of points, had arrived. Two volunteer artillery companies from New Orleans had come to the rescue; and a party of Texan rangers were near him. The Mexicans, on the other hand, showed no signs of concentrating.

Naturally the public inquired whether the occupation of Corpus Christi, and especially the words "on or near" the Rio Grande, could be justified. But, as the London *Times*—a witness by no means prejudiced in our favor —observed, "When the United States Government, with the full sanction of the American people, consummated the annexation of Texas, . . . they should, according to all the usages of civilized Governments, have proceeded to take military means for the protection of their new frontier." The performance of this duty involved giving the commander a somewhat liberal discretion, for southern Texas was a region of which the Washington authorities knew very little, and what steps it would be proper for the General to take, should the Mexicans launch a raid at San Antonio, was known there even less. It would have required about a month to send information and receive orders based upon it. Authority to occupy such a post as might seem necessary, in view of the ground, the vicinity and the news, had to be given. Taylor understood that Corpus Christi, which belonged to Texas by the same right of effective occupation as Nacogdoches or Galveston, satisfied the terms of the order; the government accepted that interpretation; and the country acquiesced.

Gradually his forces assumed rather formidable proportions. Some of the troops had to come from Detroit, and some from Florida; but it was feared in all quarters that a heavy Mexican body might cross the Rio Grande any day, and the reinforcements made quick time. October 13 the army included General W. J. Worth's command, called the first brigade, which comprised the Eighth Infantry and twelve companies of the so-called artillery consolidated as a battalion; the second brigade, consisting of the Fifth and the Seventh Infantry under Lieutenant Colonel J. S. McIntosh; the third brigade under Colonel William Whistler, which included the Third and the Fourth Infantry; the Second Dragoons, commanded by Colonel D. E. Twiggs; some United States and New Orleans field artillery, and the Texas rangers. In all, officers and men, there were about 3900.

Taylor, accustomed to frontier conditions, described his troops as healthy, remarkably well-behaved and very comfortable. But in reality the tents could scarcely keep out a heavy dew; for weeks together every article in many of them was thoroughly soaked; and much of the time water stood three or four feet deep in some. The weather oscillated sharply between sultry heat and piercing northers, so that one lay down gasping for breath and woke up freezing. As hardly enough wood could be obtained for the cooks, camp-fires were usually out of the question; and only brackish drinking water could be had. At one time nearly twenty per cent of the men were on the sick list, and half of the others more or less ill. Taylor knew so little of military evolutions that he could not get his men properly into line, and few of his chief officers excelled him very much. Despite orders from the President, military exercises were given up after a time; a sullen torpor and silence reigned in the camp, and many deserted. Meanwhile a horde of gamblers and liquor-sellers opened booths near by; and the soldiers, driven to desperation, paid what little money they had to be drugged into insensibility or crazed into brawls and orgies. Some, if not many, of the officers gave up acting like gentlemen, and one at least even forgot how to be honest.

Then a dispute regarding precedence brought the camp to the verge of battle. Twiggs had the honor of seniority as colonel; but Worth, as a brevet brigadier general, insisted that should Taylor cease to hold the command, it would fall to him. The question was referred to Washington; and Scott, directed by Marcy to settle it, gave a ruling in favor of brevet rank. This decision did not, however, end the controversy. More than a hundred officers joined in an appeal to Congress, while Worth declared he would maintain his rights "to any extreme." Taylor, instead of using his personal and official strength to enforce a *modus vivendi* until the issue could be properly decided, or at least refraining from all accentuation of it, ordered a general review, and in spite of the ruling announced by his superior officer, assigned Twiggs to command on that occasion; and then, finding that serious trouble would ensue, proved himself, by countermanding the review, unable to maintain even his own authority. After all this, discipline could hardly be said to exist. Moreover, a general want of confidence in the commander prevailed. "Whether an idea, strategic or of any other description, has had the rudeness to invade the mind or imagination of our chief is a matter of doubt," said Worth. "We are literally a huge body without a head." If Taylor succeeds, it will be by accident, concluded Lieutenant Colonel Hitchcock, now commanding the Third Infantry, who had studied and taught at West Point.

Toward the end of August Marcy wrote: "Should Mexico assemble a large body of troops on the Rio Grande and cross it with a considerable force, such a movement must be regarded as an invasion of the United States and the commencement of hostilities." This declaration called forth protests, but was quite fair. By stationing troops peaceably in the "intermediate region" between the Nueces and the Rio Grande we only placed ourselves on an equality with Mexico; and, as we ordered Taylor to leave her posts undisturbed, we showed a friendly recognition of the principle of pacific joint-occupation during negotiations. Our forces, to be sure, outnumbered hers, but her attitude made it unsafe to despatch a smaller representation. Unlike us, Mexico had no occasion to send an army into that region for defensive purposes. The United States had shown every sign of desiring peace and none of desiring war, and at this time was endeavoring to bring about a friendly settlement. Such an army could not have prevented us from entering the intermediate region, for at Corpus Christi Taylor was already there; and it could not have saved the Mexican posts and citizens, for they were not menaced. Mexico, on the other hand, had threatened us and made open preparations to strike; it was now understood at Washington that no declaration of war should be expected to precede a blow; her generals had proclaimed that hostilities were on the point of beginning; and it was only common sense to assume that, should a Mexican army cross the Rio Grande, it would come to execute the announced intention of those who sent it.

During the evening of January 12, 1846, despatches from Slidell and Black arrived at Washington, and made the rejection of our pacific overture look almost certain. This unexpected turn of affairs gave new seriousness and fresh urgency to the Mexican issue; and the next day Taylor was ordered to encamp on the Rio Grande at whatever point he should consider most advantageous. He was cautioned, however, against regarding Mexico as an enemy, unless war should be declared or hostilities be undertaken by her, and against provoking a conflict by insistence upon the joint navigation of the river, which our claim implied.

February 3 the General received these instructions, and replied that he should lose no time. Three days later the army was formally ordered to "be prepared for a field movement at short notice." But, although Taylor had been on the ground for six months, he was "utterly ignorant"—said Hitchcock—of the way to Matamoros, and had now to investigate the matter. By February 24 he possessed the necessary data, and ordered the troops to be in readiness to set out "at forty-eight hours notice"; yet it was not until the eighth of March that his cavalry, let by the impetuous Twiggs and accompanied by Ringgold's handsome battery, actually moved off. The infantry brigades followed at intervals of a day with Duncan's and Bragg's field artillery; and transports prepared to remove the convalescents, extra baggage and Major Munroe's artillery company to Point Isabel, near the mouth of the Rio Grande.

Soon after receiving the instructions to advance, Taylor had given notice of his orders to influential citizens of Matamoros then at Corpus Christi, explaining that his march would be entirely pacific, and that he expected the pending questions to be settled by negotiation; and similar assurances were conveyed to the Mexican customhouse office at "Brazos Santiago," near Point Isabel. March 8 a more formal announcement appeared in General Orders No. 30. Taylor here expressed the hope that his movement would be "beneficial to all concerned," insisted upon a scrupulous regard for the civil and religious rights of the people, and commanded that everything required for the use of the army should be paid for "at the highest market price." These orders, which merely anticipated instructions then on their way from Washington, were translated into Spanish, and placed in circulation along the border.

To the troops the march proved a refreshing and beneficial change. The weather was now fine, the road almost free from mud, and the breeze balmy. Frequently the blue lupine, the gay verbena, the saucy marigold and countless other bright flowers carpeted the ground. The cactus and the cochineal excited and gratified curiosity. Ducks and geese often flew up from the line of advance. Many rabbits and many deer scampered across the plain; and occasionally wolves, catamounts and panthers were frightened from cover. Wild horses would gaze for an instant at their cousins in bondage, and then gallop off, tossing their manes disdainfully; and once a herd of them, spaced as if to allow room for cannon, were taken for Mexican cavalry. Innumerable centipedes, tarantulas and rattlesnakes furnished a good deal of interest, if not of charm. The boundless prairie had somewhat the fascination of the sea; and occasionally, when a mirage conjured up a range of blue mountains—clothed with forests and reflected in lakes—that melted presently into the air, one had a sense of moving on enchanted ground.

To be sure, the march was not entirely agreeable. For about 196 miles it stretched on and on, and most of the way it lay through deep, sandy plains, here glistening with salt, and there varied with briny marshes or sticky black dirt. In some places Mexicans had burned the herbage; and the light ashes, raised by the tramp of many feet, settled on the soldiers' faces till they could scarcely recognize one another. Tortured with thirst, they would occasionally break ranks pell-mell at the sight of water; but as a rule they found it brackish. All suffered alike; and we have a picture of Taylor himself breakfasting at the door of his tent with a mess-chest for a table, his rugged countenance flaming with sunburn, his long lips cracked and raw, and his long nose white with peeling skin. But the experience, even at its worst, proved a wholesome tonic after the degeneration of Corpus Christi.

March 20 the army came to the Arroyo Colorado, a salt lagoon about a hundred yards wide and three or four feet deep. Here General Mejia, the commander at Matamoros, who knew all about our troops and their movements, had intended to win a sheaf of laurels; but orders from his government, not quite ready for action, arrived in time to curb this ambition. He concluded then to try the effect of a ruse, and his officer convinced the Americans, with solemn warnings, bugle-calls here and there, and a clever showing of heads among the bushes and trees on the southern side of the lagoon, that a hard fight would result from attempting to cross it. But without the least hesitation Taylor prepared for battle. Ringgold's pieces were made ready. Worth dashed into the stream at the head of an advance party; and on gaining, unopposed, the opposite bank, he saw—dust in the atmosphere, and far away a dozen small black specks rapidly growing smaller. But morally it was a victory; and the troops, though cheated, felt encouraged.

March 23, after making fifteen miles across a clear, dry prairie, the army came to a road that led to Matamoros, about eighteen miles away on the right, and to Point Isabel, distant nine or ten on the other side; and Taylor, ordering Worth and the infantry to camp and watch for the enemy at a suitable place in the former direction, proceeded to the coast with his cavalry. There he found the transports in sight and the wind favorable. Defences were planned at once; and on the 27th, leaving an engineer, supported by a guard under Munroe, to superintend the construction of them, the General returned to the army, then some ten miles from Matamoros. The next morning all advanced, and soon came to rough defiles. On each side bristled what a soldier described as an irregular, impenetrable mass of "scraggly, scrubby, crooked, infernally illegitimate and sin-begotten bushy trees loaded with millions of thorn-pins"—that is to say, *chaparral*. Passing this and a few cabins in the midst of corn, cotton and pomegranates, the troops found themselves at the end of their march, Rio Bravo, the "Bold river of the North," brown with mud, rolled swift and boiling at their feet; and in plain view about half a mile distant—black with crowded housetops, gay with flags, and noisy with bugles and barking dogs—lay Matamoros. A rude pole was soon raised; to the music of our national airs the colors went up; and a small masked battery of field guns was planted near them.

A singular political game then took place between Taylor and Mejia. The former did everything possible to convince the Mexican general that his movement was entirely pacific, and offered to "enter into any arrangements to secure the peace and harmony of the frontier" during negotiations between the two governments; but the latter insisted over and over again that a state of war had been created by the American advance. In spite of this Taylor reminded his officers of the "essentially pacific" and "conciliatory" intentions of the army; yet at the same time he reported the Mexican attitude as distinctly hostile, asked for reinforcements, mounted four 18-pounders to command the city, and about April 7 began what came to be known as Fort Brown, a large, bastioned "field-work" opposite the lower end of the city.

On April 11 General Ampudia, the assassin of Sentmanat, arrived at Matamoros to assume the chief command, accompanied by cavalry and followed, as the Americans understood, by two or three thousand more troops. The next day he signalized his advent by ordering Taylor to decamp at once for the other side of the Nueces—a proposal to which a courteous negative was returned—and by compelling all the Americans in the city, "under open threats of violence," to leave town within twenty-four hours. Taylor retaliated by requesting our naval commander off the Rio Grande to stop the use of that stream. As the Mexican attitude made it impossible for us to have the joint navigation implied by our claim, this appeared reasonable; but essentially the measure was defensive, since without supplies coming by water a large force could not remain long at Matamoros. When Ampudia complained, the General pointed out that sealing up the river was only the "natural result of the state of war so much insisted on by the Mexican authorities as actually existing," and offered to reopen it if Ampudia would join him in maintaining an armistice during the negotiations of the two governments; but this led to no result.

Ampudia's orders and intention had been to attack the Americans as soon as possible, but his glorious prospects darkened immediately. Though given the place of Major General Arista, long at the head of military affairs in this quarter, because he supported the revolution of Paredes while Arista not only frowned upon it, but seemed to aim at making northeastern Mexico independent, Ampudia was detested and thought incompetent—an opinion he did not share—by not a few in the northern army, whereas Arista stood high in his caste, and, as a person of wealth and position, had strong friends well able to make trouble for the central government. Consequently an order dated April 4 made Arista commander-in-chief with Ampudia as lieutenant. The latter was immediately forbidden to shine on the field of glory, and, finding his officers would not support him in disobedience, he submitted.

Arista, however, bearing instructions dated April 4 to attack the Americans, reached the scene on the 24th, and ordered his cavalry general, Torrejon, to cross above Matamoros with about 1600 men. Hearing a rumor of this movement, Taylor sent Captain Thornton and about sixty dragoons late that afternoon to reconnoitre; and the next morning, some twenty-eight miles from camp, finding himself completely shut in by overwhelming forces, the Captain tried to break through, lost several men killed and wounded, and then with all the rest surrendered. This was war. "Hostilities have begun," announced Arista on the day of his arrival. "Hostilities may now be considered as commenced," reported Taylor on the 26th; and—besides advising Polk to organize twelve-months volunteers—he at once called upon Texas and Louisiana for about 5000 men.

It was a tragic and most regrettable denouement; yet, on a close review of all the data now accessible, one does not find it easy to censure Polk. If he had wished and meditated war from the first, why did he work for an amicable settlement through Parrott, Black and Slidell? For the sake of appearances, many said. But in the first place we have found that Polk was honest in those negotiations; and, in the second, had war been his aim and appearances his care, he would not have permitted the order of January 13 to be issued that day. On January 12 it looked at Washington as if the question of receiving Slidell would soon be decided. The President could afford to wait a little, and he would have done this, for it was clear that an unnecessary military step, taken while he was extending the olive branch, would needlessly make him appear either treacherous or ridiculous. Moreover if he sought a war, he knew on January 12 that matters were shaping themselves to his taste; that Mexico was almost sure to close the door of negotiation soon; and consequently that he would soon be able to demand of Congress the forcible redress of our grievances.

Here lay a *casus belli* amply endorsed by international law, the practice of civilized powers, and the general opinion of the world. It was a ground, too, that Polk himself, as we have seen, felt entirely satisfied to stand upon, and one that our people, feeling as they did, would almost certainly have accepted. Having, then, apparently within his reach a pretext for war that almost everybody thought good, he would not have exerted himself to obtain one that almost everybody thought bad; and in fact—evidently expecting no event of decisive importance to occur near the Rio Grande—he went on day after day with his plan to lay our grievances before Congress, until news of the attack on Thornton burst upon Washington like a rocket. On the hypothesis that he had wished and meditated war from the first and merely stuck at appearances, his conduct was therefore irrational; and, besides, we have seen adequate reasons for believing that he desired peace.

Discarding that hypothesis, however, leaves us the important question, How did the idea of sending Taylor forward present itself to Polk? First, then, from his point of view it seemed entirely permissible. A proprietor is not debarred from going where a squatter has built a cabin; and in the light of our official claim and arguments Mexican occupation above the Rio Grande was merely by sufferance. The so-called "provocative act" of pointing guns at Matamoros could not be charged against the government, for Marcy had suggested other points also for Taylor's camp, leaving the choice to him. It was a defensive measure adopted by the General for military reasons in conjunction with pacific assurances and proposals; and we learn from Arista and others that it had a sedative effect on the property owners of that flimsily built city and on the army authorities.

No encroachment upon the powers of Congress appeared to be involved. Had Polk's aim been, as Calhoun alleged, to establish a boundary, he could not have tolerated Mexican posts, for the troops of foreign states cannot be permitted to sojourn within our officially defined limits. Besides, Polk had sent Slidell to treat on this very question, and Slidell had not given up the task. Though it rested with Congress to declare war, a President could legally, in the exercise of his discretion, take steps liable to bring about hostilities. Moreover Congress appeared to have authorized Taylor's movement. Corpus Christi, claimed by Tamaulipas, had been made an American port of delivery. A collection district had been established in the intermediate region. The declaration of Polk's Message, December, 1845, that our jurisdiction had been extended to the Rio Grande, and Marcy's appended report, which announced that Taylor's instructions were to regard that stream as our boundary, had raised no storm. For six months, admitted the chief Whig organ, our doings in this field not only had appeared to be endorsed by the people, but had gone on openly without calling forth "a single question from any public authority." Officially notified of the military occupation of Corpus Christi, Congress, instead of protesting, had voted supplies for the troops. Finally, Congress had instructed the Executive, in the resolutions for annexing Texas, to reach an agreement with Mexico regarding the boundary; it was his duty to persevere in the attempt until convinced he could not succeed; and Taylor's advance, as will presently be seen, appeared to him a proper step in the discharge of this obligation.

Familiar precedents and principles were believed to sanction the movement of our troops. In 1794 Washington had ordered Wayne to conduct hostilities in disputed territory, and had threatened to destroy a British fort there. In accordance with a resolution of Congress, Madison had seized the "Florida parishes" claimed by Spain. Just before Taylor was ordered to move, Hilliard informed the House of Representatives that England had magistrates in the southern part of Oregon; and John Quincy Adams proposed to take military possession of that disputed territory before concluding negotiations. If such a method could be employed in dealing with countries willing to treat, very naturally—in the case of one that had pronounced for war—pacific occupation, leaving the competing jurisdiction undisturbed, seemed fully justifiable.

Taylor's advance appeared also to be highly expedient. For one thing, our claim upon the intermediate region would have been weakened, had we refrained from sharing with Mexico in the occupation of it. For another, it seemed wise to place ourselves in a strategic position that would be of great value, should Mexico's threat of war be carried into effect. And for a third it was believed that a bold military attitude, indicating that at last the United States had made up its mind, would count with Mexico as a strong argument for negotiation. Such was the opinion of Parrott, Slidell, Worth, Taylor, Scott, Archer, now chairman of the Senate committee on foreign relations, Brantz Mayer, formerly secretary of legation at Mexico, Polk himself, the administration circle in general, and well-informed persons outside it. January 17 Conner was ordered to assemble all his vessels and exhibit them off Vera Cruz—evidently in pursuance of this design. The government organ stated, and opposition writers conceded, that such a purpose was in view.

But essentially, as already has been suggested, Taylor's advance rested on the necessity of military defence; and indeed there is reason to consider Scott the prime factor in the business, for the order of January 13 was based upon, and in part verbally reproduced, a "projet" submitted by him, whereas Polk's diary for January 12 and 13 does not even allude to the subject. Now not only were defensive measures called for on general principles, as we have just been informed by the London *Times*, but the Texans actually and urgently needed a sheltering arm. During the latter part of 1845 the chief Mexican engineers drew detailed plans for crossing, not only the Rio Grande, but the Sabine. Merely the refusal of Paredes, growing out of his revolutionary designs, to reinforce the troops on the frontier with 2400 men prevented an attack at this time. Almonte, who had particularly recommended incursions into Texas, held the post of war minister in January, 1846. The Mexican troops were extremely mobile. Ampudia's main force, at the end of a long march, did 180 miles in four days. Screened by rancheros and living on a little corn and jerked beef carried in their pouches, a body of light cavalry could have reached San Antonio by way of Laredo, ruined the town, and been well on their way toward home before their movement would have been suspected at Corpus Christi. The government received warnings of this danger from Dimond and from Parrott in 1845; Marcy and Polk feared it; and the probable rejection of Slidell—which meant a triumph of the war party—seemed likely to accentuate the peril. In fact Mejia ordered irregulars into Texas on February 16 and March 17, though, as their commander aspired to execute a revolution with American aid, he did us no harm.

Nor were only such formal incursions to be guarded against. The war of 1836 in Texas had shown what outrages Mexicans were capable of committing, and similar affairs had now begun to occur. In one instance a party of fifteen, including women, after having been induced to surrender, were all butchered except a single person, who survived though seriously wounded. In April, 1846, the Mexicans opposite Matamoros confessed that bloodthirsty guerillas were abroad. Ampudia, whose murderous record had been his chief distinction, commanded there. May 13 the British consul in that city reported that licensed bands of assassins, "caressed, rewarded, and encouraged" by the authorities, were committing atrocities near the Rio Grande; and, had the way been open, such gangs might have robbed and murdered in the settlements of Texas.

The position selected by Taylor was admirably suited to this emergency. Scott, though a Whig, wrote out a long explanation, showing that on the Rio Grande the army had a more healthful camp than before, better drinking water, more abundant fuel, better grazing and a better port. Information could be obtained more quickly; the border watched more closely; and invading force pursued more promptly; and its line of retreat cut more certainly. Besides, the river amounted to a great breastwork, for this part of it could be crossed with safety at only certain points, and a body of men, even though comparatively small, could not cross anywhere on its lower course without peril. It was not, however, simply that the Rio Grande position seemed far the best. The nature of the region made it essential. Taylor had to be in that vicinity or else near Corpus Christi, and for purposes of defence the latter point could not be deemed satisfactory. Now the necessity of defence was entirely due to the threatening conduct of Mexico. Therefore she could not reasonably complain of our precautions; and if she could not complain, then no one could do so in her name.

But the challenge was triumphantly thrown out: Can it be denied that our taking a position on the river did in fact cause the war? In view of the data it can and should be denied. First, joint occupation of the disputed region might have gone on peaceably, as occupation of that character has continued elsewhere, but for a distinctly aggressive step on the part of Mexico; and, secondly, for her the Rio Grande had no particular significance. She claimed all of Texas, and intended to drive us from it, if she could. Furthermore, the crass vanity and ambition of Mexican generals and the exigencies of domestic politics would probably have led to an attack upon us, had Taylor remained at Corpus Christi, or even pitched his camp at San Antonio. In spite of express orders, Mejia actually attempted an offensive in the intermediate region. When the Mexican government gave formal notice to England and France in the summer of 1845 that war had become inevitable, our army lay far from the Rio Grande. Taylor's advance to the Bold River no more produced the war than Pitcairn's march to Lexington produced the American revolution. It was an effect and an occasion, but not a cause.

Finally, as a matter of fact, the hostilities were deliberately precipitated by the will and act of Mexico. The circumstances proved this and testimony illuminates them. In October, 1847, a pamphlet written by Mariano Otero, editor of *El Siglo XIX* and Senator from the state of Jalisco, appeared. His object was by no means to defend the United States, but he said: "The American forces did not advance to the Rio Grande until after the war became inevitable, and then only as an army of observation. . . . The military rebellion of San Luis [Potosi] gave rise to a government [that of Paredes] pledged to resist all accommodation [with the United States] . . . which government . . . began hostilities." Arista declared in December, 1847, "I had the pleasure of being the first to begin the war." In short, Polk told only the truth when he said the conflict was forced upon us. Mexico wanted it; Mexico threatened it; Mexico issued orders to wage it; and on April 18 her President, no doubt in view of his political difficulties, insisted upon those orders. "It is indispensable," he wrote urgently to Arista, "that hostilities begin, yourself taking the initiative."

"If in a litigious affair," declared Vattel, "our adversary refuses the means of bringing the right to proof, or artfully eludes it; if he does not, with good faith, apply to pacific measures for terminating the difference, and above all, if he is the first who begins acts of hostility, he renders just [even] the cause which was before doubtful." Every condition of this judgment fitted the course of Mexico.

꿏 ꙸ

*A* POLL *of historians in mid-twentieth century which evaluated Presidents as great, near-great, average, mediocre, or failures contained one major surprise. Among the near-great Presidents was James K. Polk. The basis of their designation of Polk was the fact that no President has fulfilled more completely his inaugural pledges than the Tennessean who took office in 1845. He called for the reannexation of Texas, a demand met in the last days of the Tyler administration; for the settlement of the Oregon controversy; for reform of the tariff; and for the restoration of the independent treasury system. By 1846, a compromise division of Oregon along the 49° parallel had been reached with Britain, the Tariff of 1846 instituting the revenue principle had been approved, and the Independent Treasury was restored. At the same time, the Mexican War moved toward a successful conclusion, and with its close came the annexation of the vast territories including California, Arizona, New Mexico, and substantial parts of Nevada, Utah, Colorado, and Wyoming. The huge land accessions created administrative problems which persuaded Polk to establish in the final days of his administration the Interior Department.*

*Curiously enough, the success of Polk's administration brought not praise, as one would expect, but disruption of his party. The supporters of Martin Van Buren, convinced that their patronage claims had been unjustly handled by Polk, viewed the nomination of his longtime rival Lewis Cass in 1848 as an indefensible blow. They took a walk and joined defecting Conscience Whigs, who had rebelled against their party's designation of the slaveholder Zachary Taylor as an intolerable affront to morality, in founding the Free Soil party. The coalition took its stand on the Wilmot Proviso which called for the closing of the territories to slavery. When the 1848 election returns were tabulated, the Whigs had elected a President but the Free Soil vote exceeded 291,000 and in numerous states they had gained the balance of power between Whigs and Democrats. Both major parties entered the decade of the fifties in a state of disarray, one which would worsen as the decade lengthened, and which would be traced to Polk, who would increasingly be designated by contemporaries as "Polk the Mendacious" or as "the Hangman of the Confederacy." And after his departure the issue of Free Soil grew until it dominated the national political scene. By 1860 it was the point upon which Lincoln would not budge and which the Southerners chose to use to justify their secession.*

*Bernard DeVoto (1897-1955), long a professor at Harvard University, made his specialty the history of western America, and particularly its impact upon the national scene. His* Across the Wide Missouri, *a brilliant study of western explorations, won a Pulitzer Prize in 1947. His trenchant use of language made of his essays, many of which appeared originally in Harpers, controversial excursions into aspects of history. It was DeVoto's analysis of the Polk administration in 1846 that provoked the reevaluation by historians of Young Hickory. The centrality of slavery in the welter of causes leading to the Civil War, an emphasis developed at greater length by Allan Nevins in his* Ordeal of the Union (1947), *he argued was determined by the decisions of 1846. His terse conclusion that "At some time between August and December, 1846, the Civil War had begun" refocused the historian's explanation of the coming of the Civil War. It also had the curious result of refurbishing Polk's reputation by reminding us of his achievement while also confirming the conclusion of his contemporaries that his achievement put the nation on the road to civil upheaval.*

# THE YEAR OF DECISION, 1846

## *by Bernard DeVoto*

The nation began the year in crisis. It was a crisis in foreign relations. The United States was facing the possibility of two wars—with Great Britain and with Mexico. But those foreign dangers had arisen out of purely domestic energies. They involved our history, our geography, our social institutions, and something that must be called both a tradition and a dream.

Think of the map of the United States as any newspaper might have printed it on January 1, 1846. The area which we now know as the state of Texas had been formally a part of that map for just three days, though the joint resolution for its annexation, or in a delicate euphemism its "re-annexation," had passed Congress in February, 1845. Texas was an immediate leverage on the possible war with Mexico. Texas had declared itself a republic in 1836 and ever since then had successfully defended its independence. But Mexico had never recognized that sovereignty, regarded Texas as a Mexican province, had frequently warned the United States that annexation would mean war, and had withdrawn her minister immediately on the passage of the joint resolution which assured it.

In the far northwestern corner our map would tint or crosshatch a large area to signify that it was jointly occupied by the United States and Great Britain. This area would include the present states of Oregon, Washington, and Idaho, and small parts of Montana and Wyoming lying west of the continental divide. It would also include a portion of Canada, extending northward to agree with the political sentiments of the map maker, perhaps as far north as a line drawn east from the southern tip of Alaska. The whole area was known simply as "Oregon" and it was an immediate leverage on the possible war with Great Britain. For the President of the United States had been elected on a platform which required him to assert and maintain the American claim to sole possession of all "Oregon," clear up to 54°40′, that line drawn eastward from southern Alaska, and on January 1 the British press was belligerently resenting his preparations to do so.

West of Texas and south of Oregon, from the Pacific Ocean to the continental divide and the Arkansas River, was a still larger area which our map would show as Mexican territory. This area included the present states of California, Nevada, Utah, Arizona, New Mexico, and parts of Wyoming and Colorado. It was composed of two provinces, "California" and "New Mexico," but no American map maker could have approximated the theoretical boundary between them. It too was a powerful leverage, though not often a publicly acknowledged one, on the possible war with Mexico.

It is of absolute importance that no map maker of any nationality, even if he had been able to bound these vast areas correctly, could have filled them in. Certain trails, certain rivers, long stretches of certain mountain ranges, the compass bearings of certain peaks and watersheds, the areas inhabited by certain Indian tribes—these could have been correctly indicated by the most knowledgeful, say Thomas Hart Benton and the aged Albert Gallatin. But there were exceedingly few of these and the pure white paper which the best of them would have had to leave between the known marks of orientation would have extended, in the maps drawn by anyone else, from the Missouri River and central Texas, with only the slightest breaks, all the way to the Pacific. That blank paper would almost certainly have been lettered: "Great American Desert."

The Great American Desert is our objective—"Oregon," "New Mexico," and "California"—the lands lying west of the Louisiana Purchase. Like the Americans who occupied them, however, we must also deal with Texas, the newly annexed republic. The sum of these four geographical expressions composed, on January 1, 1846, the most acute crisis in foreign relations since the Treaty of Ghent had ended the second war with Great Britain in December, 1814, and they were bound together in what can now be understood as a system of social energies. Just how they were bound together will (the hope is) be clear by the end of this book, and we must begin by examining some of the far from simple reasons why they had produced the crisis. It will be best to lead into them by way of the man who in part expressed and in part precipitated the crisis, the President, hopefully called by some of his supporters "Young Hickory," James K. Polk.

Two years before, in the summer of 1844, the first telegraph line brought word to Washington that the Democratic convention, meeting in Baltimore, had determined to require a two-thirds vote for nomination. The rule was adopted to stop the comeback of ex-President Martin Van Buren, who had a majority. That it was adopted was extremely significant—it revealed that Van Buren had defeated himself when he refused to support the annexation of Texas. The convention was betting that the spirit of expansionism was now fully reawakened, that the annexation of Texas was an unbeatable issue, that the Democrats would sweep the country if factionalism could be quelled. Smoke-filled rooms in boarding houses scorned President Tyler (whose renomination would have split the party in two), and would not take General Cass, John C. Calhoun, or Silas Wright, all of whom were identified with factions that were badly straining the party. Factionalism, it became clear, was going to be quelled by the elimination of every prominent Democrat who had ever taken a firm stand about anything. So presently the telegraph announced that George Bancroft, with the assistance of Gideon Pillow and Cave Johnson and the indorsement of Old Hickory in the Hermitage, had brought the delegates to agree on the first dark horse ever nominated for the Presidency, Mr. Pillow's former law partner, James K. Polk.

"Who is James K. Polk?" The Whigs promptly began campaigning on that derision, and there were Democrats who repeated it with a sick concern. The question eventually got an unequivocal answer. Polk had come up the ladder, he was an orthodox party Democrat. He had been Jackson's mouthpiece and floor leader in the House of Representatives, had managed the anti-Bank legislation, had risen to the Speakership, had been governor of Tennessee. But sometimes the belt line shapes an instrument of use and precision. Polk's mind was rigid, narrow, obstinate, far from first-rate. He sincerely believed that only Democrats were truly American, Whigs being either the dupes or the pensioners of England—more, that not only wisdom and patriotism were Democratic monopolies but honor and breeding as well. "Although a Whig he seems a gentleman" is a not uncommon characterization in his diary. He was pompous, suspicious, and secretive; he had no humor; he could be vindictive; and he saw spooks and villains. He was a representative Southern politician of the second or intermediate period (which expired with his Presidency), when the decline but not the disintegration had begun.

But if his mind was narrow it was also powerful and he had guts. If he was orthodox, his integrity was absolute and he could not be scared, manipulated, or brought to heel. No one bluffed him, no one moved him with direct or oblique pressure. Furthermore, he knew how to get things done, which is the first necessity of government, and he knew what he wanted done, which is the second. He came into office with clear ideas and a fixed determination and he was to stand by them through as strenuous an administration as any before Lincoln's. Congress had governed the United States for eight years before him and, after a fashion, was to govern it for the next twelve years after him. But Polk was to govern the United States from 1845 to 1849. He was to be the only "strong" President between Jackson and Lincoln. He was to fix the mold of the future in America down to 1860, and therefore for a long time afterward. That is who James K. Polk was.

The Whigs nominated their great man, Henry Clay. When Van Buren opposed the annexation of Texas, he did so from conviction. It was only at the end of his life, some years later, that Clay developed a conviction not subject to readjustment by an opportunity. This time he guessed wrong— he faced obliquely away from annexation. He soon saw that he had made a mistake and found too clever a way out of the ropes which he had voluntarily knotted round his wrists. Smart politics have always been admired in America but they must not be too smart. The Democrats swept the nation, as the prophets had foretold. It was clear that the Americans wanted Texas and Oregon, which the platform had promised them. Polk, who read the popular mind better than his advisers did, believed that the Americans also wanted the vast and almost unknown area called New Mexico and California.

They did. Polk's election was proof that the energy and desire known as expansionism were indeed at white heat again, after a period of quiescence. This reawakening, which was to give historians a pleasant phrase, "the Roaring Forties," contained some exceedingly material ingredients. Historians now elderly made a career by analyzing it to three components: the need of certain Southern interests and Southern statesmen to seize the empty lands and so regain the power which the increasing population of the North was taking from them, the need of both Northern and Southern interests to dominate the Middle West or at least maintain a working alliance with it, and the blind drive of industrialism to free itself to a better functioning.

Now all those elements were certainly a part of the sudden acceleration of social energies signified by the election of 1844. But society is never simple or neat, and our elder historians who thus analyzed it forgot what their elders had known, that expansionism contained such other and unanalyzable elements as romance, Utopianism, and the dream that men might yet be free. It also contained another category of ingredients—such as the logic of geography, which the map of January 1, 1846, made quite as clear to the Americans then as it is to anyone today. You yourself, looking at a map in which Oregon was jointly occupied by a foreign power and all the rest of the continent west of Texas and the continental divide was foreign territory, would experience a feeling made up of incompletion and insecurity. Both incompletion and insecurity were a good deal more alive to the 1840's than anything short of invasion could make them now. And finally, expansionism had acquired an emotion that was new—or at least signified a new combination. The Americans had always devoutly believed that the superiority of their institutions, government, and mode of life would eventually spread, by inspiration and imitation, to less fortunate, less happy peoples. That devout belief now took a new phase: it was perhaps the American destiny to spread our free and admirable institutions by action as well as by example, by occupying territory as well as by practicing virtue. . . . For the sum of these feelings, a Democratic editor found, in the summer of '45, one of the most dynamic phrases ever minted, Manifest Destiny.

In that phrase Americans found both recognition and revelation. Quite certainly, it made soldiers and emigrants of many men (some of them among our characters) who, without it, would have been neither, but its importance was that it expressed the very core of American faith. Also, it expressed and embodied the peculiar will, optimism, disregard, and even blindness that characterized the 1840's in America. As we shall see, the nation which believed in Manifest Destiny came only by means of severe shock and after instinctive denial to realize that Manifest Destiny involved facing and eventually solving the political paradox, the central evasion, of the Constitution—slavery. But it is even more indicative of the 1840's that those who rejected the innumerable statements of Manifest Destiny, repudiated its agencies, and denied its ends, believed in Manifest Destiny. Let Brook Farm speak for them—Brook Farm, the association of literary communists who had withdrawn from the world to establish Utopia a few miles from Boston.

For the Brook Farmers, certainly, did not speculate in Western lands and so cannot come under the economic interpretation of expansionism. Neither were they the spirit of industrialism: they had organized with the declared purpose of nullifying industrialism. Nor were they political adventurers, conspirators, or opportunists: they had formally announced their refusal to adhere to the American political system. But Manifest Destiny had no clearer or more devout statement, and the 1840's had no more characteristic expression, than the editorial which the Brook Farmers published in optimism's house organ, *The Harbinger,* when the curve of the year 1846 began to be clear:—

> There can be no doubt of the design being entertained by the leaders and instigators of this infamous business, to extend the "area of freedom" to the shores of California, by robbing Mexico of another large mass of her territory; and the people are prepared to execute it to the letter. In many and most aspects in which this plundering aggression is to be viewed it is monstrously iniquitous, but after all it seems to be completing a more universal design of Providence, of extending the power and intelligence of advanced civilized nations over the whole face of the earth, by penetrating into those regions which seem fated to im-

mobility and breaking down the barriers to the future progress of knowledge, of the sciences and arts: and arms seem to be the only means by which this great subversive movement towards unity among nations can be accomplished. . . . In this way Providence is operating on a grand scale to accomplish its designs, making use of instrumentalities ignorant of its purposes, and incited to act by motives the very antipodes of those which the real end in view might be supposed to be connected with or grow out of.

Thus the literary amateurs: it violates our principles but is part of a providential plan. As Providence's instrumentality Polk was much less woozy. Shortly after he was inaugurated, he explained his objectives to George Bancroft, the scholar, historian, and man of letters who had been a Democratic Brain-Truster since Jackson's time, and whom Polk would make acting Secretary of War, Secretary of the Navy, and finally Minister to Great Britain. His objectives were: the revision of the protective tariff of 1842, the re-establishment of the independent treasury, the settlement of the Oregon question, and the acquisition of California. He was to achieve them all.

\*     \*     \*     \*     \*

When Polk took office, in March, 1845, his narrow, clear mind harbored no doubts about Texas. He accepted the orthodox Democratic position. Our theoretical "right" to Texas rested on claims that ran clear back to La Salle —and may possibly have been clear once. We had ceded away our right in 1819, but that was a blunder in statesmanship. But, whatever the legal claim, Texas was independent; Mexico did not recognize the independence but it was a fact. Finally, by the time Polk was inaugurated all discussion of claims and rights and sovereignties had become academic. President Tyler had correctly interpreted the election of Polk as a mandate for annexation. He failed to get a two-thirds vote in the Senate by treaty, but, in the closing hours of his administration, he put it through by joint resolution. (The same difficulty is a fixed pattern of our history.) Though Texas did not ratify it until July and was not formally a state of the Union till December, Polk regarded it, on March 4, 1845, as a part of the United States and as such entitled to protection.

If Texas was in danger, and the warmth of Mexican resentment indicated that it was, then to defend it was certainly Polk's duty. Since we had annexed a boundary dispute as well, there remained the question of just what Texas was. Part of that intricate and ancient question involved a strip one hundred and twenty miles wide between the Nueces River, on the north, and the Rio Grande. Texas claimed this almost uninhabited strip but had made no attempt to occupy it. Mexico, which did not recognize Texas as either independent or annexed, claimed that the strip belonged to the states of Tamaulipas and Nuevo Leon. The Texas claim had no substance; it was purely metaphysical. But it had great value and high potentialities for Polk, who was thinking well beyond Texas. That claim could be used as a move in the game of high politics whose objective was the acquisition of California. The first thing to do was to assert it.

Therefore in mid-June, 1845, a month before Texas ratified annexation, six months before it became a state, Polk had William Marcy, his Secretary of War, order the army under Zachary Taylor to take a position south of the Nueces—cautioning him, however, to treat any Mexican troops he might encounter with punctilious courtesy. Between three and four thousand troops had been concentrated at Fort Jesup, Louisiana, for some time, with precisely this step in mind. By the end of July Taylor got his forces to Corpus Christi, a minute Mexican seacoast village just inside the disputed strip. Polk's intention was clear: this was a show of force intended to give the Mexicans a sense of reality in the settlement of various matters he now intended to take up, among them the purchase of California. But, though a show of force, it was not, in Polk's mind, an invasion. It was a protective occupation. Whatever the right term may have been, the army was at Corpus Christi still on January 1, 1846.

*     *     *     *     *

Polk, who intended to acquire California, and by war if necessary, knew little about it. He was the dream finding an instrument. . . . As he opened the great game, an anxiety hurried him. The tension over Texas might develop into war with Mexico, quite apart from the great game—and California remained bound to Mexico by a gossamer only, if at all. If the war should come, might not California seek a protectorate under Great Britain? It seemed possible, even likely—and a French or a Prussian protectorate was not inconceivable. The State Department learned that small native movements for independence and other movements for a foreign protectorate showed themselves from time to time. That was ominous—and there was something else. We were preparing to face and force the Oregon question. Might not Great Britain actually seize California, to strengthen both her military and her diplomatic position in Oregon? Plenty of sober minds besides Polk's thought she might, and behind that fear was one which the new nation had inherited in 1785 and as far back as there had been white men in America, the dread that Europe might set a limit to our development. It was playing its last stand now, continentally at least, and in fact there had ceased to be any basis whatever for it. A British government which was eager to settle the Oregon question and promote free trade with the United States had no designs on California. Nevertheless Polk's anxiety was genuine and understandable.

*     *     *     *     *

Polk appears to have been willing to fight for "all of Oregon" when he was elected but by Inauguration Day he was not so sure. Closer thought about Mexico had cooled Polk down but among the people the momentum of campaign emotions was not easily braked. Orators who had twisted the lion's tail on the stump went on twisting it in Congress, the press could not be called off, and the electorate which had been told that Oregon was ours up to 54°40′ kept on clamoring for 54°40′. Rhetoric had succeeded much too well, the British press was roaring back, and Polk was already embarrassed. His inaugural address delicately receded from the campaign. Our title, he said, was "clear and unquestionable." What title? "Our title to the country of Oregon." Not to the campaign slogan, "all of Oregon." The difference was big enough to let a weasel through.

It was not wide enough for the British press, however, nor even for the Peel government. That government had readily abandoned its intrigues in Texas as soon as annexation was accomplished. It was doing its best to negotiate a tariff agreement with the United States. It had one Irish problem on its hands and, as the potato crop began to fail, foresaw that it would soon have another one. As a little-England government, it had no dialectical desire for Oregon. Furthermore, it had a sheaf of recent reports which added up to the double conclusion that the Americans had established themselves in Oregon beyond any hope of getting them out and that Oregon was certainly not worth fighting for. (Just for good measure, as soon as it had negotiated a settlement it got another report from an investigating commission which had had to live under canvas, had found the country insufficiently supplied with hot water for bathing, and wanted nothing whatever to do with Oregon.) But the torchlight procession and campaign oratory over here had roused the hair-trigger contempt of the English for Cousin Jonathan, the late provincial. There was a popular uproar which the government could not disregard. The right questions were asked in Parliament and there was a bustle of activity in naval ports.

This badly frightened James Buchanan, the gentleman politician who had the greatest possible shrewdness but no backbone whatever. It also salted Polk's ideas with realism. A President who had already sent to Mexico stipulations likely to be unacceptable and had arranged to occupy California with a small and antique navy, if the stipulation should prove unacceptable, would find himself inconvenienced if he had to fight a skirmish with the mistress of the seas. In this clearer state of mind, he saw that relations with Great Britain had drifted into a crisis and must not be allowed to drift any longer. He moved to settle them. The campaign pledge of 54°40′ could be avoided by pointing out that the President was bound to renew the offers of his predecessors. They had all tried to compromise the conflicting claims with the 49th parallel, which was the boundary from the Great Lakes to the continental divide. So through the summer of '45 Polk tried to negotiate a settlement at the 49th parallel. But Pakenham, the British minister, not only understood the powerful leverage of the intensifying Mexican crisis, but in the natural course of things was bound at first by the traditional policy of his country: when an opponent offers concessions, you can get bigger ones by holding out. Pakenham would not close for 49°.

British firmness threw Buchanan into a panic and from then on he was for appeasement, though his attitude swung in a small arc as he maneuvered his most abiding interest, a nomination to the Supreme Court as a step toward the Presidency. He felt that negotiations could be continued only if Pakenham's demands were met, that anything else would mean war. Polk was not frightened, and Pakenham's adroitness had made him mad. He saw that the minister was playing diplomatics by the textbook, and he too knew the rules. So in late August of '45 he forced the timorous Secretary of State to notify Pakenham that, following the refusal of Her Majesty's government to accept the compromise, the President no longer felt himself bound by the policy of his predecessors and from now on would not be interested in any offer short of the whole of Oregon, up to 54°40′. When Pakenham promptly tried to reopen with a bid for 49°, provided only that the President would openly invite the concession, Buchanan all but wept with relief. The President was not interested, and he remained uninterested through the autumn, while the press of both countries screamed. Then on December 2, in his message to Congress, he played his ace. When the conflicting claims to Oregon had been stabilized *in statu quo*, both countries had accepted a joint right of occupation. This "joint occupancy" had been renewed ten years later but the treaty provided that it could be ended on formal notification one year in advance. In his message to Congress, Polk asked that the one year's notice be sanctioned now. He went on to advise that American legal jurisdiction be extended over Americans in Oregon (as they had been vehemently demanding for more than two years), and that land grants be made at the expiration of the stated year. He summarized his efforts to settle the controversy, rehearsed the British refusals to compromise, repudiated the British claim to the territory north of the Columbia River, and took occasion to restate the Monroe Doctrine at such length that, acquiring additional point from Texas and California, it began to develop the binding force it has been exercising ever since. And he said that we had "reached a period when the national rights in Oregon must either be abandoned or firmly maintained." Also that "they cannot be abandoned without a sacrifice of honor and interest."

\*     \*     \*     \*     \*

On January 5, 1846, a resolution to terminate the joint occupation of Oregon was introduced in the Senate, and now all the forces were committed, all the movements were under way, from here on there could be no turning back. Buchanan's alarm had steadily increased and he warned the President that the country, which was supporting 54°40′ with a sustained roar, would not support it. And on January 4, Representative Black of South Carolina, as perturbed as Buchanan, had called at the White House to say that the war fever of the Western Congressmen had alarmed the following of Mr. Calhoun, who would therefore vote against termination. He pleaded with the President to recede from his stand. Polk replied to Mr. Black

> that the only way to treat John Bull was to look him straight in the face; that I considered a bold & firm course on our part the pacific one; that if Congress faultered or hesitated in their course, John Bull would immediately become arrogant and more grasping in his demands & that such had been the history of the Brittish Nation in all their contests with other Powers for the last two hundred years.

One goal to the President. Polk had reached bedrock in British-American relations. It may be said that he not only looked John Bull in the face but struck him in the head with a blunt instrument, but he had the right idea. While Buchanan trembled and a second thought began perceptibly to sober Congress and the press, he tranquilly waited for England to settle on his original terms. He prepared one of the ingenuities that enable Presidents to back down without losing face. When John Bull was ready to accept 49°, Polk would, he decided, invoke a clause of the Constitution which it is usually the first concern of the administration to avoid. He would submit the anticipated offer to the Senate, not for its "consent" but for its "advice." By that time developments in Mexico could be counted on to put the Senate in a mood to advise the compromise.

So his diary is untroubled throughout January. His days are broken by the office seekers, "more importunate than meritorious," whom the uncomplicated Republic had not yet dared to bar from the executive office. He sits for his portrait to Mr. Healy, sent by France to immortalize both him and Old Hickory. Very bored, he conscientiously spends two hours at the Jackson Day banquet, his party's annual debauch of oratory. He attends the Presbyterian Church with Mrs. Polk and their nieces, but is scrupulous to honor Justice Catron by attending Catholic services on one Sunday. He wins two skirmishes with the Senate, over appointments.

Another skirmish develops serious trouble when the Senate rejects his nomination of George W. Woodward as Associate Justice of the Supreme Court. At first the villain responsible seems to be Mr. Cameron of Pennsylvania, who may have been piqued by Polk's failure to appoint Mr. John M. Read. But Polk had unanswerable reasons for not appointing him. Mr. Read was once a Federalist and it is the President's duty to protect the purity of our judicial institutions. Polk records an observation: he has never seen a Federalist who professed to change his opinions later than the age of thirty who did not revert to "broadly Federal and latitudinarian" opinions as soon as he received a life appointment. Presently, however, the carefully begotten rumors of Washington inform the President that not Mr. Cameron swayed the Senate but Mr. Buchanan: the city hears that the Secretary of State is going to get the appointment. So there is intrigue in the Cabinet— and perhaps that explains Buchanan's timidity. And clearly Buchanan is violating the pledge he signed before his appointment, to which Polk made all the Cabinet sign their names, not to use his office to advance himself toward the Presidency. Polk's integrity is affronted: if it shall prove that Buchanan has worked against Woodward's appointment, he will dismiss him. Buchanan glooms like Hamlet at Cabinet meetings, then sulks and opposes frivolous or capricious objections to the Oregon policy. Now the rumors begin to hint that he will break with the administration and resign. But "Mr. Buchanan will find that I cannot be forced to act against my convictions, and that if he chooses to retire I will find no difficulty in administering the Government without his aid."

\* \* \* \* \*

April produced the President's triumph. Final word came from Slidell on the seventh that Paredes had refused to receive him, and the Cabinet had moved so steadily that Polk found no opposition in it to the strongest measures—to war with Mexico. However, he would not recommend them to Congress just yet, for the Oregon question was at last coming to a head. Congress must now reach a decision, and could not like the necessity. The administration drove its forces with whip, spur, and nosebag. Mr. Polk believed that he could best control the Northern members with patronage, whereas with Southerners the appeal to principle was better. But the best talent of the Whigs was opposition, Polk's own party was half a dozen factions precariously held together, and both parties were looking not only at Oregon and Great Britain but two years ahead. Neither 49° nor 54°40', his diary noted in disgust, meant so much to even the Democratic Senators as '48 and the election.

Mr. Calhoun was trying to find leverage in Polk's proposal for a secret fund to buy a treaty from Mexico. He blew hot and cold and persisted in mentioning it inadvertently when he called to suggest that the way out of the Oregon impasse was to have the foreign ambassadors propose a negotiation—which was suggesting that Polk admit defeat. The Whigs liked the tactics that circumstances had imposed on them; they would not dissent from Termination, which the country obviously wanted, but, to make sure of their position if it should beget trouble, they would put the entire responsibility for it on the President. Enough Democrats had factional axes to grind to help out, and as the debates reached climax, that was the shape it began to take.

The House resolution instructed the President to "cause notice to be given" to Great Britain. The Senate resolution advised negotiation in its preamble and declared merely that the President was "authorized at his discretion" to give the notice—a much weaker platform for him to dive from. The Senate resolution was passed first, on April 16, and went to the House for concurrence. The House amended it so that the vital clause read that the President was "authorized and directed," and here for an anxious moment the whole thing seemed likely to stall. The first objective of the administration was imperiled for, Polk believed, the Senate was so divided on factional cleavage lines that it would, if given a chance, gladly let the resolution perish. His journal filled with intense, precise resentments, he hurried out the party chiefs in both Houses, sent his Cabinet cracking down, and labored with his own full strength. He yielded to the inevitable and let the Senate throw out the word "directed," thus losing his last chance to present Termination as the united will of the country, and there he dug his heels in. His all-out effort succeeded. The House accepted the Senate's modification and on April 23 the resolution "to abrogate the convention of 1827" passed both Houses. Polk signed it the next day, the notice of termination had already been prepared, and on April 28 Polk sealed it with the Great Seal of the United States and sent it by special packet to the sovereign of Great Britain. Joint Occupation of Oregon was over and Mr. Calhoun, the Whigs, and whoever might be interested, would now see who was bluffing.

It was a great victory. The President had put through the first of his measures, and he was confident that it would do the job, that Great Britain was the party running a bluff. The administration felt very good indeed but its exhilaration was premature. For though the hidden realities had not come to the surface during the Oregon debate they were on their way up, the inner tensions had been increased and half revealed, the opposition had found a tactic, and pressures were rising that must soon explode. He had won handsomely but he had almost lost, his party was breaking up and the wind was rising. One trouble with decisions is that they necessitate other decisions.

But, his Oregon position carried and the "Brittish" notified, he could turn to Mexico with a tranquil and cunning mind. We see him on April 30 amazed and touched by a delegation from the new school for the blind, twenty or thirty exhibiting their pitiful accomplishment, one "a female named Bridgman who had been taught by signs with the hands and fingers to understand and communicate ideas and to write." Polk's victorious month ended with that curiously symbolical note but it was five days earlier, on the twenty-fifth, three days before he dispatched the joint resolution, that it reached its climax. On April 25, after telling the Cabinet that the notice would go to Victoria in person on May 1, he announced that it was time to deal with Mexico. We must treat all nations alike, great or small, Great Britain had the gauntlet now and here was Mexico: Mr. Polk favored "a bold and firm course." The Cabinet understood and the Secretary of State spoke the right phrase: the President should recommend a declaration of war. "The other members of the Cabinet did not dissent, but concurred in the opinion that a message to Congress should be prepared and submitted to them in the course of the next week." Very well. The President would outline the points to be presented, and Mr. Buchanan would please collect the materials and sketch out a message.

That was April 25. On the same day the fuse that was burning at the Rio Grande reached powder.

\*    \*    \*    \*    \*

The marine band played in June dusk on the White House lawn, and here were dispatches from Minister McLane saying that Her Majesty's government would propose to settle the Oregon boundary at 49°. So the administration faced an embarrassment. The President, however, had prepared an exit: to submit the proposal, if it should come, for the advice of the Senate and thus escape the odium of having to withdraw from the extreme position. The levy and supply of armies for the Southern excursion made it all too clear that the extreme position would have to be abandoned, that the British offer would have to be accepted. But it was also clear that the oratory for 54°40' was going to be remembered.

The Cabinet agreed that the exit would have to be used. Except that Mr. Polk was by now completely surrounded by candidates for '48, and the strangest belligerence had Mr. Buchanan. Having for a full year protested, moaned, and all but wept at the President's firmness in the matter, having pleaded for the amelioration of many dispatches, having held out for 49° from the beginning and once demanded that Great Britain be given anything more that she might ask, he now held out for 54°40' and would bleed for it as gallantly as General Cass. He was ranging ahead to the national convention of '48 and the delegations of disappointed Western states, as the President immediately understood. Polk wrote that Buchanan's about-face "excited" him: he meant that it made him tearing mad, reasonably enough. His patience held for a day or two, then he loosed his formidable rage on his Secretary of State, who collapsed like a punctured bladder and would accept 49°.

Pakenham, the British Minister, drove up to the White House and made the expected proposal. Polk duly forwarded it to the Senate, where the warhawks bellowed with outraged anger. But for one thing Thomas Hart Benton's erudite analysis had convinced his colleagues, and for another, even a warhawk had to admit that one war at a time was enough. After two days of debate, the Third War with Great Britain became just something that *Niles' Register* had asked questions about in January, we were not going to twist the lion's tail, and the warhawks could muster just twelve votes against thirty-eight. Senator Allen of Ohio, however, had meant the orations that had annoyed Herman Melville: on the spot he resigned as chairman of the Committee on Foreign Relations.

The vote of June 12 was to instruct the President to accept 49°. Three days later Mr. Buchanan and Mr. Pakenham signed the convention that settled the Oregon question forever. . . . At this point it is wholesome to recall once more the rates of communication, since they governed the management of armies as well as the tidings of peace. The convention was signed on June 15. At once an express left Washington to notify the Oregonians that they were American citizens after all and need not, as some of them were at that moment proposing to do, commit a Bear Flag maneuver against the Hudson's Bay Company. It went to Vera Cruz and followed in Gillespie's tracks across enemy soil to Mazatlán. The first boat out was bound to China by way of the Sandwich Islands, and at Honolulu the dispatch was put on board the bark *Fawn*, which crossed the bar at the mouth of the Columbia on November 12. Five months after the signing of the convention, the *Fawn*'s supercargo was rowed to shore with the great news. He was nine days behind unofficial dispatches from Honolulu on the *Toulon*.

Mr. Polk had now achieved the first of his four objectives. But at some cost. Allen had become an enemy of the administration, so had Hannegan (he was almost incoherent, in fact, applying polysyllabic but barbed epithets to the President who had let him down), and the support of such men as Cass, Atchison, and Jarnegan could no longer be counted on for anything. The internal tensions of the Democracy had been stepped up still farther, nearer the breaking point.

\* \* \* \* \*

The sole practical preparation for war that had been made was the order for Commodore Sloat to seize the California ports if he should learn that war with Mexico had broken out. There had been some conversations between department heads and the appropriate committees of Congress. They had anticipated a war with Great Britain, however, and little action had come from them. Although Polk and his Cabinet had envisaged the possibility of war with Mexico from March 4, 1845, on to May, 1846, they had done nothing to prepare for it. They suffered the illusions of a nation that had not fought a war since 1814, had fought foreign wars only with the navy, and had never fought a war of conquest. They expected the irresistible sharpshooters of Yorktown and New Orleans to spring to arms: in Robert Dale Owen's phrase, "two companies of Kentucky rifles" could do the job. In June of '46 the Americans were springing to arms all right, far more of them than could be used, but no one had any idea what to do with them.

The army had no general staff to plan campaigns. It did have a military genius, Major General Winfield Scott. But Scott made no plans in advance of the war, and his first act after its outbreak was to disqualify himself by an act of insubordination toward his commander in chief. Polk retired him from command for a time and would probably have done so anyway, for he thought that Scott was too "visionary and scientific"—that he knew too much about his business. Scott wanted to equip and train an army before trying to use it, whereas the President wanted quick victories and a short war and no nonsense about logistics or discipline, which were unnecessary. And as for Polk himself—in the preparation of grand strategy he had a small army on Mexico's northern frontier, some maps, and an overwhelming ignorance not only of the conditions under which armies must operate but of the country through which his particular armies must operate. By the grace of God and the ultimate return of Winfield Scott, this equipment served him very well indeed.

They were poor maps; if they had been good ones, probably even the amateur strategists would have been deterred. If their innocence had been tarnished by knowledge of the country they proposed to campaign across they might easily have lost the war.

They were, however, passably informed about the internal politics of Mexico. So a plan of strategy developed: part desire to make sure of California (the true begetter of the war), part the hope that no fighting would prove necessary, and part a notion that the northern provinces would revolt. . . . From the Atlantic westward, these were Tamaulipas, Nuevo Leon, Coahuila, Chihuahua, and, on the Pacific, Sonora. North of these and a special problem were New Mexico and California. All the northern provinces were supposed to be ready to rebel against the federalist government of Mexico. Demonstrations had, in fact, occurred in some of them; Santa Anna had called attention to the shaky loyalty of Nuevo Leon and Tamaulipas; at the outbreak of war disturbances in Sonora were reported and they were expected to spread to Chihuahua.

So Polk decided to occupy the northern provinces and hold on, meanwhile blockading the seaports. That might do the job—with the assistance of a bribe fund, Santa Anna, civil war, and the luck of the American arms. Tamaulipas had already been invaded when Taylor occupied Matamoros. Just beyond the end of its southern coastline was Tampico, the second largest port of Mexico. Commodore Conner of the blockading squadron was ordered to occupy it; he did so and Taylor, after bungling his instructions to support Conner, finally sent some troops. As for Nuevo Leon and Coahuila, it was natural to expect Taylor to attend to them, for whether he should move overland or up the Rio Grande they would be square in his path. Eventually they were both occupied, when Taylor took Monterey and Worth, back in the army with his grievances and his goose quills, took Saltillo.

So much was obvious, and Mr. Polk's gaze moved across his map to Chihuahua. (Always remember that this province was the principal market of the Santa Fe trade.) The volunteers who were pouring in so fast would be concentrated at three places, the mouth of the Rio Grande, New Orleans, and somewhere in Texas, say San Antonio. On the map a mere forefinger would reach from San Antonio to the city of Chihuahua, the capital of the province. Good: we will take Chihuahua. So General John Ellis Wool, a veteran but neither senile nor a letter writer, was ordered to lead an expedition against it down that finger-length of paper from San Antonio. Wool, an excellent officer, cold, a martinet, undertook the job but it proved impossible. After great expense, a waste of material, transport, and supplies, after a dangerous waste of time and dispersion of force, and after much hardship unnecessarily inflicted on green troops, the expedition failed. Wool had to cross not a map but a countryside—and it detoured him in a vast arc so that, when he was recalled, he was little nearer Chihuahua than he had been at San Antonio.

The Chihuahua expedition was preposterous and a failure. The expedition against the special case, New Mexico, was little less preposterous as a military conception but it did not fail. It was Polk's own ewe lamb; he had been thinking about it as far back as he had been thinking about New Mexico. And he had the assistance of knowledgeful realists, Benton and a large part of Benton's constituency, those who were interested in the Santa Fe trade. The Western press had been advising such an expedition for months, and there were those at hand who knew how to get it started.

On May 13, the day when Polk signed the war proclamation, the governor of Missouri was called upon to supply a thousand mounted volunteers (he had anticipated the summons and already had the machinery working), and Colonel Stephen Watts Kearny, commanding the First Dragoons at Fort Leavenworth, was ordered to protect the freight caravans understood to be en route to Santa Fe. But it was, or immediately became, clear to

Polk that New Mexico was the true key to California and by May 16 the protection of the Santa Fe trade had become the conquest of New Mexico. Kearny was put in command of the volunteers being raised in Missouri and ordered to undertake another of Mr. Polk's bloodless conquests. (The President was supporting it with diplomacy, hoped to support it with bribes, and called in specialists in the Catholic religion to organize a propaganda arm.) By May 30, the conquest of New Mexico had become the conquest of California. Kearny (given discretionary power—apparently because he was not known to be a Whig) was ordered to organize New Mexico after he had occupied it, to determine whether he could reach California this year, and if he thought that he could, to do so. Thus the conception of an ambitious and potentially decisive campaign was fully developed in seventeen days.

It looked simple when you studied the map. It turned out to be almost as simple as it looked.

*        *        *        *        *

Through the summer President Polk was forced sometimes to remember that he had a war on. The necessity, which was national, greatly irked the head of the Democratic Party, which had gone local. He had his Oregon Settlement and his Independent Treasury now, and while Congress heaved and rippled with dissents he was trying to force through his bill for the reduction of the tariff of '42. It was vehemently opposed. Polk scented corruption and his resentment flowed steadily in his diary. He had to compromise with the Democratic ironmasters of Pennsylvania, though he told them their state was agricultural. The compromise got the bill passed but the November elections were to show that he had lost Pennsylvania. He had lost New York, too, though no one yet understood why.

Those November elections were never out of anyone's mind. Polk had gloomy apprehensions when he vetoed not only a bill for the repayment of the French Spoliation claims, the sustenance of an ancient lobby, but also that checking account of Congressmen, the rivers and harbors bill. The activity of pressure groups for various candidates grew obscene, but was only one part of the political turmoil. All summer long Mr. Buchanan yearned to be a Justice of the Supreme Court, as a further step toward the White House, but shrank from the fight he would surely have to make to be confirmed. Every angle and shadow of this appointment had to be considered in relation to the pressure groups. Polk was embarrassed in his maneuvers but on the whole relieved when Buchanan decided to stand pat and keep the State Department. He got little other relief. Few Democrats measured up to his standard of selfless subordination, none had a passion for anonymity, the party press was fractious, the Whig press was in full cry, revenues fell off when the tariff reduction took effect, the Treasury found no brokers who would take a war loan, and Congress, boiling and bucking toward adjournment, was not so much in rebellion as in a coma. It would have been a bad time for any administration, it was disastrous for a war administration.

But something had to be done about the war and it seemed to be up to Polk. No one had a plan but slowly, haphazardly, under pressure of events, politics, and chance, one began to form by accretion. Bile spurted in the President's diary at what he took to be a conspiracy—anything was a conspiracy that did not square with his ideas. There was Taylor. Since the engagements which he spelled "Palialito" and "Resacka," Taylor had apparently wanted to do nothing whatever. . . . The victor sat in his attakapas pantaloons under a tent fly and grew great. He wrote to his son-in-law Dr. Wood that "I greatly fear that the [any further] campaign will be a failure which will break down the individual who conducts it," but he summoned publicity to prevent the breakage. He established the friendliest relations with newspaper correspondents, who knew copy when they saw it. Brave, benignant, stupid, as common as your Uncle Bill, he dealt gently with the excesses of volunteers, assuring them that whoever might be responsible for disease, inaction, and bad food, Old Rough and Ready was not. While the political brigadiers kept a stream of letters going home where they would do the most good, Taylor also enlarged his correspondence. Bliss, his chief of staff, corrected the spelling, Taylor being of the opinion that, in our perfected system, a President did not need spelling or much else.

Polk foresaw Taylor's candidacy even before Taylor did and it made him furious. He could get neither plans nor information from Taylor, who had none. His hard mind bogged in the softness of what cannot be called Taylor's intelligence. He saw that Taylor, who unhappily could win battles, intended to carry out orders, not plan campaigns. Polk had no orders to give him—and the worst was that any campaign he might conceive for Taylor would only glorify the Whig candidate. There was no alternative to Taylor but Winfield Scott, the head of the army, and Scott was doubly damned. Not only was he a Whig and a perennial candidate, but he had opposed Polk's ideas. What was worse, he insisted on preparing to fight before fighting. He had warned Polk that it would take at least till fall to create an effective army. That proved his ignorance of political necessities or else meant a Whig plot to discredit the administration. He wanted to drill troops, arm them, work out logistic problems, gather shipping and transport—in short, he was scientific and visionary. He would not do. Polk longed to turn the war over to one of the Democratic orators whom he had made brigadiers. Any of them would have done, say Shields, who was lately of the Land Office, or Judge Quitman, who was a leading Mason, or Robert Patterson, who had nominated Jackson for the Presidency, or the venal Gideon Pillow, who claimed to have made Polk President. His favorite, however, was William Orlando Butler, who was probably the best military man of the lot. But the Cabinet had to inform him that he could not entrust the war to amateurs, and in his simple fear that votes would be lost the republic was saved. Polk gave in but went on despising Whigs and military science and by election time would achieve the most preposterous military suggestion ever made by a President.

It was Scott who kept the war going—Scott, and Jesup, the Quartermaster General, and Marcy, the Secretary of War. In a shambles of ignorance, inefficiency, graft, and political intrigue, they somehow got a prodigious job done. They turned loose a gigantic productivity and got some of it under control. Troops were raised, arms and munitions were manufactured, transport was achieved. It cost the Treasury hugely, the waste was incalculable, the failures were innumerable, but the job was done. And Scott, who was a soldier, was thinking toward the military end. He kept his temper, he wrote no more damaging letters, he began to make headway. He bade a friend "imitate the example of that heathen who touched his hat to the fallen statue of Jupiter, saying 'Who knows but that he may be replaced upon his pedestal?' "

Polk's secret war developed, the affair of Santa Anna. From Havana the great brigand was directing the efforts of his conspirators to undermine the Paredes government in his fatherland. They were succeeding. As early as January Paredes had written, "Order is precarious, peace insecure, and the nation, in the midst of the anarchy which consumes it and the chaos which surrounds it, moves toward dissolution and the fear of death." It had got steadily worse. His associates were either treacherous to him personally, café-table intellectuals, or grafters. He himself was honest and patriotic but stupid and given to drink. There were few revenues. The army had magnificent uniforms, incomplete equipment, and no pay. Besides, it was far from loyal. Various provinces were in chronic revolt, one was declaring itself independent, full-scale revolution was ready to break out. Paredes and such assistants as he could get dealt badly with the increasing anarchy—and had against them, in Havana, the master of treachery who was also the idol of the people, or of some of them. By mid-July Santa Anna had Mexico ready to long for some more of his liberation.

And Polk, who had agents in Mexico encouraging anarchy, now sent a messenger to inquire whether the earlier arrangement still held. On Santa Anna's word, it did. The brigand was going to reappear as a Liberator and, with the assistance of the United States, would deliver his unhappy country from the tyranny of its monarchists. When he returned to power he would accept Polk's offer to suspend hostilities. He would make a treaty ceding enough land to indemnify the United States for its war expenses. (Here, as elsewhere in Polk's dream, the United States was to pay for the ceded territory. In other words, the indemnity was to consist of the profit following a rise in real estate.) He would assist in determining a permanent boundary and make sure that the harbor of San Francisco was north of it. In order to preserve the appearance of coercion, which his bemused but patriotic countrymen would require, he suggested that the ports of Vera Cruz and Tampico be occupied. (By this time Polk had also got round to thinking of them.) He assured the messenger that the army of occupation would find the climate healthy. And he ended with a solicitous reminder: let the President see to it that the personal publicity of Santa Anna in the American press was conducted in the most favorable terms.

Good! The President renewed his undercover arrangements. He got to work again on the secret Executive fund of two million dollars that was to buy a treaty by underwriting the pay of the Mexican army. And in the serene belief that he had arranged a peace for the warring countries, he ordered Commodore Conner to pass the Liberator through the blockade. He had bought his gold brick.

The Liberator acted. On August 3 Vice President Bravo, Santa Anna's man, overthrew Paredes, and the garrison of Vera Cruz and other parts of the army made a *pronunciamento*. This ceremony, a tradition, consisted of a formal announcement, accompanied by oratory and salutes, that someone else had bought the army or was expected to buy it. Its symbolic value was considerable and even in the disaffected northern provinces detachments put their new loyalty on record. On August 8 Santa Anna left Havana on the steamship *Arab*. On August 16, under the arranged chaperonage of a captain of the British Navy, who reported to Conner that she carried no contraband, the *Arab* passed the blockade and anchored at Vera Cruz. In demonstrations of wild enthusiasm—gunfire, confetti, and a blizzard of engraved resolutions—Santa Anna landed and began a progress of state to his hacienda at Jalapa.

Napoleon was back and as much unity as Mexico was capable of answered his return. He told his countrymen that he desired no political power but hoped only to drive the invader from Mexican soil. He notified Mr. Polk that the American proposals for an armistice and the negotiation of peace could be considered only by the Mexican Congress, which would not meet till December. Then with the superhuman energy that was his one valuable characteristic he began transforming the pressed soldiery from a mob to an army.

President Polk had been as shrewd as possible and American diplomacy had achieved a triumph.

\* \* \* \* \*

Nothing is more fragile than the secrets of diplomacy. Rumors of Polk's deal with Santa Anna had reached the army, as we have seen. They also traveled across the United States, gathering picturesqueness as they spread. Before Santa Anna landed in Mexico the Whig press was airing them. They temporarily cured the schizophrenia of the Whigs, who on the one hand had had to denounce the war and on the other had had to praise the valor of those who were fighting it. In the public mind they mingled with other rumors, especially those which magnified the army opposing Taylor and anticipated for him disasters that were in no danger of occurring. There were casualty lists now, also: the dead and wounded of the first battles, of the guerilla raids, of the camp fevers. By August a discouragement typical of this stage of all our wars had undermined the enthusiasm of May. And finally, Henry Thoreau's laborious thinking at Walden Pond had been prophetic of his countrymen. A good many had caught up with Thoreau, with Theodore Parker, and with Hosea Bigelow. What, Hosea had asked on June 17,

*Wut*'ll make ye act like freemen?
*Wut*'ll git your dander riz?

. . . As early as July 9 the Baltimore *American*, a Whig sheet, had learned, it said, what portions of Mexico the administration intended to seize as the spoils of war. The rest of the party press was soon publishing the *American*'s findings. To wit: all Mexico to the line of Tampico; all California; parts of Jalisco, Guadalahara (meaning Guanajuato), and Zacatecas; all of Sonora, Durango, San Luis Potosi, "New Leon," Chihuahua, Coahuila, and Tamaulipas.

It must be said flatly: no such plan was in anyone's mind. Immediately after the declaration of war jubilant cries had gone up from the most extreme expansionists, eagle-screamers like Walter Whitman, and a few who would have been members of the slave conspiracy if there had been a slave conspiracy—cries which welcomed all Mexico to the liberation of the United States. Sometimes they added in the Central American states, sometimes the rest of the hemisphere. They had, however, soon subsided. Such a conquest was obviously impossible and few Americans knew enough foreign geography to have clear ideas about it. Toward the end of the war, when strains had been quadrupled, a desire to seize all or a great part of Mexico would awaken again, but in August of '46 none contemplated and few desired it. The most extreme expansionist in official life was Walker, the Secretary of the Treasury, and he said nothing. Polk himself wanted what he had always wanted, New Mexico and California. He carefully left the door open for further expansion, repeatedly telling his diary and his callers that "perhaps something more" was not unlikely, but that was a contingency, not a plan, and it hinged on a simple calculation of the costs of war.

Nevertheless, by August the expeditions against Santa Fe, Chihuahua, and California had notified everyone, if nothing else had, that this was a war of conquest. The United States was going to acquire a lot of land. Nearly everybody wanted that land but now there was no way to avoid thinking about it. Implications, relationships, began to force their way into consciousness.

At the beginning of August Congress, which would adjourn in ten days, was in one of the angry, resentful moods that always precedes a re-forming of the lines. Mr. Polk, detecting candidacies in every move it made, was stubbornly following out his plans. On the third he vetoed the seasonal pork, the rivers and harbors bill. On the fourth the House tried and failed to pass the bill over his veto. And on the fourth also he sent to a Senate which had lost its pork his proposal for a secret appropriation of two million dollars.

Once more, here is what Polk intended by this step in his deal with Santa Anna. Mexico owed citizens of the United States a considerable sum, duly adjudicated. Mexico had no money and could pay only by ceding land. Santa Anna, Polk thought, would make the cession. But no Mexican government could make such a cession unless it kept the support of the army. To keep that support, Santa Anna would have to pay the army, but Mexico had no revenue. The two million dollars, an advance on the ultimate payment in full, would enable Santa Anna to pay the army, conciliate his country, and actually make the cession of New Mexico and California which in turn would enable Polk to end his war. This, Polk thought, was a simple, straightforward way to peace. Nobody could have been more honest in that belief. Or more blind.

The proposal went to the Senate in Executive (secret) Session. At once it focused much opposition, resentment, and maneuvering that had been aimless. Polk and his whips worked hard, but in the bars and boarding houses where the unofficial steering committees met there was a flurry of purposeful preparation. Heads got together, expedients suggested themselves, and here was a big chance. The Whigs had him in a vise and would not vote his appropriation unless he also asked it of the House—which was equivalent to making it public and giving the show away. Polk refused to give in, worked furiously, had to give in. The money was asked of the House as an appropriation for foreign negotiations.

(*Voted:* to adjourn at noon of August 10.)

On August 8 Polk went to the Vice President's room in the Capitol, to sign the miscellaneous bills that drop out of the machine in quantity at the end of a session. The day wore on. Polk heard that a bill appropriating two million dollars for "extraordinary expenses" originating in the intercourse between the United States and foreign nations had been introduced in the House. He did not promptly learn what followed, but he began to hear that the gentlemen of the Congress were celebrating the imminent adjournment. "Several members . . . were much excited by drink," Mr. Polk, a temperate man, disapproved, and of course Daniel Webster was one of them. The President left the Capitol at eleven-thirty.

A little before 7 P.M., in the House Chamber, lamplit, moist with the terrible still heat of August in Washington. About a hundred people in the spectators' gallery, among them the majestic commander of the armies, General Scott, in dress uniform. Several speakers rose to defend the President's request, or to suspect it in Whig sneers. Mr. Winthrop of Massachusetts was specific: he felt a dilemma like the one that had forced him to vote for war, and he was sure that the President was asking Congress to sanction an increase of Southern territory, slave territory. Mr. Grider of Kentucky succeeded him. Then Mr. Wilmot of Pennsylvania, who had been busy during the five o'clock recess, stood up. Mr. David Wilmot, Democrat, in his first term, who had been wholly orthodox in his conduct so far, so orthodox that, alone of his delegation, he had supported Mr. Polk's tariff reduction.

(August 8, 1846. Taylor's army had occupied Mier, beyond Camargo, but had not started for Cerralvo on the road to Monterrey. Kearney's Dragoons stayed in camp on the Canadian River, while Doniphan's First Missouri and the artillery came down from the Raton to the parched New Mexico plain. Twenty-five miles out from Bent's Fort Susan Magoffin, just alive, saw no blade of grass but "with anxious eyes and heart to gain first the long wished luxury" saw her first "false ponds" or mirages. Francis Parkman, on his way south from Fort Laramie to the Pueblo, was in camp with Bisonette, had heard from an Indian that there was war with Mexico, and made a note on "the gross indecency" of some Indian names. Frémont started north with his captured mules from San Diego to join Stockton, who was preparing to take Los Angeles. Bryant had come out of the Salt Desert into the greasewood barrens west of it, and on this day saw grass again and cottonwoods, and with a lifting heart reached the Humboldt. There came to Fort Hall, where Boggs and Thornton were camped, one Jesse Applegate, a famous man, bringing word of a better route to the settlements in Oregon. At Fort Leavenworth the Mormon Battalion was getting equipment. At a crossing of the Weber River, near the mouth of Echo Canyon, the Donner party had sent James Frazier Reed ahead to find a road where no road was. Anxiously awaiting his return, they could ponder a message from Lansford Hastings which told them that the way he had chosen for them to travel to Great Salt Lake could not, he found, be traveled. . . . But Mr. Wilmot is speaking in the House.)

Speaking about the President's request. Mr. Wilmot says that he did not think this a war of conquest when he voted for it and does not think it one now. He will support the President, but just why does the President want this money? Since we will not pay for land we claim to be ours, that is up to the Rio Grande, there must be an intention to acquire more land. Mr. Wilmot approves our acquiring territory on the Pacific, including the Bay of San Francisco, by purchase or negotiation. But he is opposed to the extension of the peculiar institution. Slavery existed in Texas, so Mr. Wilmot accepted it there. But if, now, free territory comes in (and Mexico was free soil) God forbid that we shall plant the peculiar institution in it.

Mr. Wilmot, not being an orator, speaks easily, clearly, quietly. He moves an amendment to the bill:—

> *Provided:* That as an express and fundamental condition to the acquisition of any territory from the Republic of Mexico by the United States, by virtue of any treaty which may be negotiated between them, and to the use by the Executive of the moneys herein appropriated, neither slavery nor involuntary servitude shall ever exist in any part of said territory, except for crime, whereof the party shall first be duly convicted.

This is the Wilmot Proviso. It fastened the slavery question to Polk's request for two million dollars for the purchase of territory.

At 8:20 P.M., Saturday, August 8, it fell, not explosively, into a House which was disorganized, inattentive, and in some degree drunk. The Southern nerves were lax; only a feeble opposition could be improvised, though a whisper ran through the city, the gallery filled, and the Secretary of State, the Postmaster General, and the Secretary of the Navy hurried into the lobby to watch the maneuvering. After the customary substitutes and motions, the Proviso was amended to apply specifically to a treaty of peace. Then the House passed the bill and adjourned into cavernous heat.

On Monday, August 10, the Senate took up the House bill, an hour short of noon, and Lewis of Alabama moved to strike out the Proviso. Over Sunday something of its importance had been realized, groups had met hurriedly, angry plans had been formulated. But time was inexorable: the First Session of the Twenty-ninth Congress would end at twelve noon— and the House clock was seven minutes faster than the Senate's. Senator John Davis of Massachusetts got the floor, began to talk, and would not yield. It is not known whether he intended to let the bill come to vote in the last minute—Lewis' motion would surely have passed—or whether he intended to talk it to death. At any rate, while the clock was still short of twelve, word came that the House had adjourned. Mr. Davis was still talking but Mr. Atchison, the president pro tem, declared the Senate adjourned.

Polk was furious. He considered the Proviso "a mischievous & foolish amendment," to be explained as factional intrigue only. He wrote in his journal, altogether honestly, "What connection slavery had with making peace with Mexico it is difficult to conceive." He shared that difficulty with his kind and with, it is certain, a majority of his countrymen. But the limitations of his tight, shrewd mind show nakedly in that sentence, and that particular kind of limitation had now been started toward oblivion. His blindness was his country's evasion, and evasion was now going to end. Slavery was out of the closet, and it was going to stay out. By December the nation would be rocking in the storm which was to last nineteen years. David Wilmot, safeguarding the conquests of his party's war President, had made A. Lincoln President of the United States.

⋘⋗ ⋖⋙

THE *1850's were a time of political disintegration. The Whigs had nominated and elected Zachary Taylor in 1848 but at a price from which they never recovered: the permanent disaffection of the Conscience Whigs. "General Taylor!—I will be paralyzed before I will consent to vote for a candidate whose political doctrines are unknown," raged one Massachusetts Whig, "or for one who covets territory for increasing the slave power either by the increase of slaves or the addition of slave states to the Union." The struggle to incorporate into the structure of a major political party the commitment to "Free Soil" had opened. The implications of the impending political struggle were first made evident when the newly elected House of Representatives assembled in December of 1849. No party commanded a clear majority with which to elect a speaker and as a result the House could not organize. For three weeks debate raged, as factions jockeyed for power and place, until more than one dispassionate observer concluded the House was little more than "a cave of political winds." When on De-*

*cember 22, 1849, after sixty-three ballots, Howell Cobb finally eked out election, it was obvious that a major upheaval impended between the sections.*

The issue was joined when California's petition for statehood reached the floor of Congress. The long-stilled "fire bell in the night," of which Jefferson had written fearfully in 1820, again began to ring clamorously and would not be finally stilled until civil war had wracked the nation. California was intertwined with the expectations of both North and South in the territories. Northerners, at least a goodly proportion of them, insisted they were to be free; and Southerners, at least the more radical of them, proclaimed with Robert Toombs of Georgia "that if by your legislation you seek to drive us from the territories of California and New Mexico . . . , I am for disunion." But in the White House, Zachary Taylor, a blunt old Unionist, made it clear he would not back down under intimidation, and assuming that California would vote to be free, he refused to make bargains to advance the interest of slavery elsewhere as a precondition of the Golden State's admission. Nor did he express enthusiasm for organizing the New Mexico territory prior to the application of its inhabitants. As for the extension of the Missouri Compromise line to the Pacific, the Louisiana slaveholder in the White House was dead set against such accommodations.

In the resulting debate, the great figures of the past and the future arose to state their opposition or support for seeking a compromise solution. A dying Calhoun called for concessions to the South and warned, that in their absence: "We would be blind not to perceive, in that case, that your real objects are power and aggrandizement, and infatuated not to act accordingly." Daniel Webster made an impassioned plea for Union, only to have the poet Whittier lament "the soul" from Webster "has fled." But it remained for William Seward, a new Northern voice, to proclaim "a higher law than the Constitution," specifically the divine law which enjoined the extension of slavery.

The final spokesman of the past to rise was Henry Clay, who embraced compromise. Time and again, although rebuffed on all sides, he worked to compose an omnibus compromise acceptable to all. But his grip was loosening, his time of leadership was fast passing, and when Taylor suddenly on July 9, 1850, died, removing an unflinching enemy of compromise, Clay proved incapable of composing the necessary combinations to assure settlement. To his assistance came the young Stephen A. Douglas, Senator from Illinois, destined to dominate the politics of the oncoming decade, to serve as the broker of compromise. By mid-September of 1850, the proposals were law: California was a free state; the boundary of Texas and New Mexico was fixed and the federal government paid Texas in return $10 million and assumed $5 million in Texas debts; both the New Mexico and Utah territories were organized and the future of slavery in both were left to the territorial residents; the slave trade was suppressed in the District of Columbia; and a reinvigorated federal fugitive slave act was passed. The Compromise of 1850 had been passed and a decade of sectional peace was bought.

*But the price proved high. In 1852, the last Whig candidate, Winfield Scott, went down to overwhelming defeat at the hands of the Democrat Franklin Pierce. It was the twilight of the Whiggery; it was reprieve for the Democracy. The Compromise had solved nothing, it had merely delayed the impending crisis.*

*James Ford Rhodes (1848-1926) came to history when almost forty, after a successful career as a manufacturer. Although without much technical training, he produced (1892-1906) a seven-volume study of American history between 1850 and 1877. It was a narrative account which aimed, in Rhodes' own words, "to get rid so far as possible of all preconceived notions and theories" and to let the facts speak for themselves. His assumption was simple: the accumulation of facts, like those in science, would reveal the hidden but constant structure of history. As it was, Rhodes pursued a will-o'-the-wisp; he wrote a detailed history to which historians would return for fact but not interpretation.*

# HISTORY OF THE UNITED STATES
# FROM THE COMPROMISE OF 1850

## by James Ford Rhodes

It is now my intention to narrate the proceedings of the national conventions of the Democratic and Whig parties, two bodies which assembled with a fresher mandate from the people than had the representatives in Congress. The Democratic convention was held on June 1st at Baltimore, and the prominent candidates were Cass, Douglas, Buchanan, and Marcy. Cass was now nearly seventy years old, but temperate habits and a regular life had preserved his constitutional vigor. A son of New England, his education had been mainly acquired in the academy of Exeter, N.H., his native place. In early life he came West, and as governor of Michigan territory from 1813 to 1831 his administration of affairs was marked with intelligence and energy. His experience during this term of office with the British stationed in Canada, who constantly incited the Indians to wage war on the settlers of the Northwest, caused him to imbibe a hatred of England which never left him, and whose influence is traceable throughout his public career. He held the war portfolio under Jackson, later was Minister to France, and had now for several years represented Michigan in the Senate. His anglophobia and his readiness to assert vigorous principles of American nationality made him popular in the Northwest. He tried a solution of the slavery question in the Nicholson letter, written a few months before he was selected as the candidate of the Democratic party in 1848. In this letter he invented the doctrine which afterwards became widely known as the doctrine of popular sovereignty. He maintained that Congress should let the people of the territories regulate their internal concerns in their own way; and that in regard to slavery the territories should be put upon the same basis as the States.

Douglas was only thirty-nine years old: remarkably young to aspire to the highest office in the State. Clay had reached the age of forty-seven when he became a candidate for the presidency, and Webster was forty-eight when he began to dream that it might be his lot to reach the desired goal. Douglas was a son of New England, and, like many New England boys, worked on a farm in the summer and attended school in the winter. By the time he was twenty, he had wrought for two years at a trade, had completed the classical course at an academy, and had begun the study of law. He then went to Illinois, and before he had attained his majority was admitted to the bar; he became a member of the legislature at twenty-three, a Supreme judge at twenty-eight, a representative in Congress at thirty, and a senator at thirty-three.

Douglas's first political speech gained him the title of the "Little Giant"; the name was intended to imply the union of small physical with great intellectual stature. Yet he was not a student of books, although a close observer of men. He lacked refinement of manner; was careless of his personal appearance, and had none of the art and grace that go to make up the cultivated orator. John Quincy Adams was shocked at his appearance in the House, where, as the celebrated diary records, in making a speech he raved, roared, and lashed himself into a heat with convulsed face and frantic gesticulation. "In the midst of his roaring, to save himself from choking, he stripped off and cast away his cravat, unbuttoned his waistcoat, and had the air and aspect of a half-naked pugilist." But Douglas took on quickly the character of his surroundings, and in Washington society he soon learned the ease of a gentleman and acquired the bearing of a man of the world. He was a great friend to the material development of the West, and especially of his own State, having broad views of the future growth of his section of country. He vied with Cass in his dislike of England. He believed in the manifest destiny of the United States. He thought that conditions might arise under which it would become our bounden duty to acquire Cuba, Mexico, and Central America. He was called the representative of young America, and his supporters antagonized Cass as the candidate of old-fogyism. His adherents were aggressive, and for months had made a vigorous canvass on his behalf. A Whig journal ventured to remind Douglas that vaulting ambition overleaps itself, but added, "Perhaps a little judge never read Shakespeare, and does not think of this."

James Buchanan was born in Pennsylvania in 1791. He had a fair school and college education, studied law, soon acquired a taste for politics, was sent to the legislature, served as representative in Congress ten years, and was elected three times senator. In the Senate he distinguished himself as an ardent supporter of President Jackson. He was Secretary of State under Polk, but since the close of that administration had remained in private life. He was a gentleman of refinement and of courtly manners.

Marcy was a shrewd New York politician, the author of the phrase "To the victors belong the spoils." He had been judge, United States senator, and three times governor. He held the war portfolio under Polk, but his conduct of the office had not added to his reputation, for it had galled the administration to have the signal victories of the Mexican war won by Whig generals, and it was currently believed that the War Minister had shared in the endeavor to thwart some of the plans of Scott and Taylor. Always an honored citizen of New York, it has seemed fitting that the highest mountain-peak in the State by bearing his name should serve as a monument to his memory.

The hall in which the convention met at Baltimore was one of the largest in the country; it could accommodate five thousand people. There was then nothing like the outside pressure on the delegates which is seen now at every one of these national conventions when the nomination is contested; but the city thronged with people, and it was apparent that the friends of Douglas had mustered in full force. On the evening of the first day an immense meeting took place in Monument Square, where an enthusiastic crowd listened to eloquent speakers. The first two days of the convention were occupied in organization and in confirmation of the two-thirds rule. It was decided to make the nomination before the adoption of the platform. This action did not by any means portend differences in agreeing upon a declaration of principles, but rather showed the desire of delegates to settle the important affair first. Owing to the confident feeling that this year's nomination was equivalent to an election, the contest became exceedingly animated.

A year previous Clay had serious doubts of the success of his own party, and, regarding it as nearly certain that a Democrat would be elected in 1852, he hoped that the nomination would fall to Cass, whom he considered quite as able as Buchanan, and much more honest and sincere.

On the first ballot Cass had 116, Buchanan 93, Marcy 27, Douglas 20, and all the other candidates 25 votes. The number necessary to a choice was 188. Cass had 75 from the free, and 41 from the slave, States; Buchanan, 32 from the free, and 61 from the slave, States; while Douglas had only two votes from the South. The interest centred in these three candidates. Their names and the announcement of their votes never failed to bring prolonged applause. The voting began on the third day of the convention, and seventeen ballots were that day taken. Douglas gained considerably at the expense of Cass, but it looked improbable that any of the three favorites could secure the nomination, which seemed likely to go to a dark horse. The merits of several others were canvassed, and among them Franklin Pierce. On the fourth day Douglas steadily increased until the twenty-ninth ballot, when the votes were: for Cass, 27; for Buchanan, 93; for Dougas, 91; and for no other candidate more than 26. On the morning of the fifth day, on the call of the States for the thirty-fourth ballot, the Virginia delegation retired for consultation, and coming back cast the fifteen votes of their State for Daniel S. Dickinson, of New York. This was received with favor.

Dickinson was a delegate; he immediately took the floor and said: "I came here not with instructions, but with expectations stronger than instructions, that I would vote for and endeavor to procure the nomination of that distinguished citizen and statesman, General Lewis Cass." After saying he highly appreciated the compliment paid him by "the land of Presidents, the Ancient Dominion," he declared, emphatically: "I could not consent to a nomination here without incurring the imputation of unfaithfully executing the trust committed to me by my constituents—without turning my back on an old and valued friend. Nothing that could be offered me— not even the highest position in the government, the office of President of the United States—could compensate me for such a desertion of my trust."

On the next ballot, Virginia cast her fifteen votes for Franklin Pierce, and at that time Cass reached his greatest strength, receiving 131. As the weary round of balloting continued, Pierce gained slowly, until, on the forty-eighth trial, he received 55, while Cass had 73, Buchanan 28, Douglas 33, and Marcy 90. On the forty-ninth ballot there was a stampede to Pierce, who received 282 votes to 6 for all others. The convention nominated William R. King, of Alabama, for Vice-President, and then adopted a platform. Its vital declarations were: "The Democratic party of the Union . . . will abide by, and adhere to, a faithful execution of the acts known as the compromise measures settled by the last Congress—the act for reclaiming fugitives from service or labor included; which act, being designed to carry out an express provision of the Constitution, cannot with fidelity thereto be repealed, nor so changed as to destroy or impair its efficiency. The Democratic party will resist all attempts at renewing in Congress, or out of it, the agitation of the slavery question, under whatever shape or color the attempt may be made."

The platform was adopted with but few dissenting voices. When the resolution endorsing the compromise measures was read, applause resounded from all sides; many delegates demanded its repetition; it was read over again, and a wild outburst of enthusiasm followed. There was no question that while the delegates had differed widely in regard to men, they were at one in desiring this resolution, a vital and popular article of Democratic faith.

Franklin Pierce, of New Hampshire, was now in his forty-eighth year. He had in his boyhood drunk in patriotic principles from his father, an old Revolutionary soldier, at whose hearthstone the fellow-veterans were always welcome, and whose greatest joy was to revive in common with these the sentiments which had animated them in 1776. Pierce was graduated from Bowdoin College, Maine, and afterwards became a lawyer. The prominent position which his father occupied in the Democratic party in the State was a help to the son's political advancement. He served in the legislature four years, went to Congress as representative at twenty-nine, and became United States senator at thirty-three, being the youngest man in the Senate. He resigned before the expiration of his term, and, coming home, devoted himself with diligence to the practice of his profession. He was a good lawyer and a persuasive advocate before a jury. He declined the position of Attorney-General offered him by Polk, the appointment of United States senator, and the nomination for governor by his own political party. He enlisted as a private soon after the outbreak of the Mexican war, but, before he went to Mexico, was commissioned as brigadier-general, and served under Scott with bravery and credit. He was a strong supporter of the compromise measures. An eloquent political speaker, graceful and attractive in manner, his integrity was above suspicion, and he was also deeply religious. He had not the knack of making money, and the fact received favorable mention that while long in public life, and later enjoying a good income from his profession, he had not accumulated ten thousand dollars.

Such was the man who had been chosen by the reunited Democratic party to lead it on to assured victory. It could only be said that he was a respectable lawyer, politician, and general, for he had tried all three callings, and in none of them had he reached distinction. There can be no better commentary on the fact that he was not a man of mark than the campaign biography written by his life-long friend, Nathaniel Hawthorne. The gifted author, who had woven entrancing tales out of airy nothings, failed, when he had his bosom friend and a future President for a subject, to make an interesting narrative. The most graceful pen in America, inspired by the truest friendship, labored painfully in the vain endeavor to show that his hero had a title to greatness; and the author, conscious that his book was not valuable, never consented to have the "Life of Pierce" included in a collected edition of his works.

Yet the book, in truthfulness and sincerity, was a model for a campaign life. Hawthorne would not set down one word that he did not believe absolutely true. Pierce evidently wished to appear before the public in his real character, for otherwise, knowing this quality of honesty in his friend, he would not have requested Hawthorne to write the biography, but would have been content with the fulsome panegyric that had already appeared. The author in his preface apologizes for coming before the public in a new occupation; but "when a friend, dear to him almost from boyish days, stands up before his country, misrepresented by indiscriminate abuse on the one hand, and by aimless praise on the other," it is quite proper "that he should be sketched by one who has had opportunities of knowing him well, and who is certainly inclined to tell the truth." The idea one gets of Pierce from the little book of one hundred and forty pages is that he was a gentleman of truth and honor, and warmly loved his family, his State, and his country. Having the inward feelings of a gentleman, he lacked not the external accomplishments; his fine physical appearance was graced by charming manners. It is quite certain that Pierce did not desire the nomination; even if his sincerity in his letter of January 12th be doubted, the statement of Hawthorne is conclusive. It is possible he shrank from public life on account of an unfortunate weakness, or that he did not wish to expose the feeble health of his wife to the social demands entailed by the position.

The nomination of Pierce was a complete surprise to the country. With the mass of the Democratic party, astonishment was mixed with indignation that the leaders who had borne the brunt of partisan conflict should be passed over for one whose history must be attentively studied, in order to know what he had done to merit the great honor. Yet the nomination was not the spontaneous affair which it seemed, for the candidature of Pierce had been carefully nursed and his interests were in competent hands. The idea of putting him forward originated early in the year among the New England Democrats, who deemed it quite likely that Cass, Douglas, and Buchanan would fail to secure the coveted prize. The favorite son of New Hampshire was eligible, as the State had been steadfastly Democratic, and Pierce was undoubtedly the most available man in New England. Several conferences were held to decide upon a plan of action, and it was determined that New Hampshire should not present his name nor vote for him until some other State had started the movement. Pierce was privy to much of this negotiation, and it is said that the delicate matter of his excessive conviviality was talked over with him, and that he promised to walk circumspectly should he become President. At all events, a letter written by him a few days before the convention shows a change of feeling from his expression of January in regard to the nomination; and if his personal objections still remained, they were overruled in the interest of the New Hampshire and New England Democracy. Pierce promptly accepted the nomination, "upon the platform adopted by the convention, not because this is expected of me as a candidate, but because the principles it embraces command the approbation of my judgment, and with them I believe I can safely say there has been no word nor act of my life in conflict."

The Whig convention met at Baltimore June 16th, in the same building that the Democrats had used, and it was noticed that greater taste had presided over the decoration of the hall than two weeks before. Among the delegates were many able and earnest men. Choate and Ashmun, of Massachusetts, Dayton, of New Jersey, and Clayton, of Delaware, were well known; and among those who afterwards gained distinction were Fessenden, of Maine, Dawes, of Massachusetts, Evarts, of New York,

The candidates for the presidential nomination were Webster, Fillmore, and General Scott; but the delegates differed in regard to the platform as well as in their preferences for men, and whether the Fugitive Slave law should be declared a finality was almost as important a question as who should be the nominee. There were more strangers in the city than at the time of the Democratic convention, and the outside pressure in favor of Webster was strong; but it was apparent to cool observers that the chances of success were for Scott. Fillmore had a large number of delegates pledged to him, for his friends had used unsparingly in his favor the patronage of the government, yet had effected little at the North; his supporters were almost entirely from the South, where he was, moreover, popular on account of his vigorous execution of the Fugitive Slave act. Clay, likewise, had declared for Fillmore. Constant demonstrations in favor of each of the three candidates were made in the form of processions headed by noisy bands, and evening meetings addressed by eulogistic orators. The leaders of the party and managers of the several candidates were constantly in conference, seeking to win outside support for their man.

The platform which was submitted on Friday, the third day of the convention, had the approval of the delegates from the South, of Webster's friends, and of Webster himself. The important resolution declared that the compromise acts, "the act known as the Fugitive Slave law included, are received and acquiesced in by the Whig party of the United States as a settlement in principle and substance of the dangerous and exciting questions which they embrace. . . . We insist upon their strict enforcement . . . and we deprecate all further agitation of the question thus settled." Rufus Choate rose to advocate this resolution. His appearance was striking; tall, thin, of a rich olive complexion, his face was rather that of an Oriental than an American. Raven locks hanging over a broad forehead, and piercing dark eyes, complete the picture. He had represented Massachusetts in the Senate, but his greatest triumphs had been won in the forum. His speech this day was the first example of that brilliant convention-oratory which animates and excites the hearers, and its beauty and power may still be felt when the issue that inspired this impassioned oration is dead. He said: "Why should we not engage ourselves to the finality of the entire series of measures of compromise? . . . The American people know, by every kind and degree of evidence by which such a truth ever can be known, that these measures, in the crisis of their time, saved this nation. I thank God for the civil courage which, at the hazard of all things dearest in life, dared to pass and defend them, and 'has taken no step backward.' I rejoice that the healthy morality of the country, with an instructed conscience, void of offence towards God and man, has accepted them. Extremists denounce all compromises ever. Alas! do they remember such is the condition of humanity that the noblest politics are but a compromise, an approximation—a type—a shadow of good things—the buying of great blessings at great prices? Do they forget that the Union is a compromise, the Constitution—social life—that the harmony of the universe is but the music of compromise, by which the antagonisms of the infinite Nature are composed and reconciled? Let him who doubts— if such there be—whether it were wise to pass these measures, look back and recall with what instantaneous and mighty charm they calmed the madness and anxiety of the hour! How every countenance, everywhere, brightened and elevated itself! How, in a moment, the interrupted and parted currents of fraternal feeling reunited! Sir, the people came together again as when, in the old Roman history, the tribes descended from the mount of Secession—the great compromise of that Constitution achieved—and flowed together behind the eagle into one mighty host of reconciled races for the conquest of the world. Well, if it were necessary to adopt these measures, is it not necessary to continue them? . . . Why not, then, declare the doctrine of their permanence? In the language of Daniel Webster, 'Why delay the declaration? Sink or swim, live or die, survive or perish, I am for it.' "

Few Americans have surpassed Choate in burning eloquence. He was a scholar, a student of words, and a master of language. The exuberance of his vocabulary was poured out through a voice of marvellous richness; dramatic gestures gave a point to his words, and he swayed that great audience as a reed is shaken with the wind. The enthusiastic and excited demonstrations of delight as Choate sat down displeased Botts, of Virginia, who was for Scott, and he took the orator to task for the attempt to excite enthusiasm for a particular candidate, when the ostensible object was to advocate the platform. This gave Choate the opportunity to name his candidate in a most felicitous way: "Ah, sir," he said, "what a reputation that must be, what a patriotism that must be, what a long and brilliant series of public services that must be, when you cannot mention a measure of utility like this but every eye spontaneously turns to, and every voice spontaneously utters, that great name of Daniel Webster!" If a vivid and appropriate speech could have changed the tide of that convention, Choate would have been rewarded by the success of the man whom he venerated and loved. A delegate from Ohio objected to the crucial resolution, and he spoke for an influential body of delegates, but the platform as a whole was adopted by a vote of 227 to 66. The nays were all from the North, and all were supporters of Scott.

The convention was now ready to ballot. Fillmore and Webster were of course in full sympathy with the platform, and it now became an important question—was Scott satisfied with the Fugitive Slave law? He was the candidate of the Seward Whigs, and many strong anti-slavery men were enthusiastic in his favor; yet to be nominated he must have Southern votes, and carry Southern States to be elected. Goaded to it by an insinuation of Choate, Botts, before the vote on the platform was taken, produced a letter from Scott which could be interpreted to mean that he was a strong friend of the compromise measures.

On the first ballot Fillmore had 133, Scott 131, and Webster 29 votes. Webster had votes from all the New England States except Maine, and six votes outside of New England; but from the South, none. Fillmore received all the votes from the South except one given to Scott by John Minor Botts, of Virginia. Scott had all the votes from the North except those given to Webster and sixteen to Fillmore. For fifty ballots there was no material change; thirty-two votes were the highest number Webster reached. On the fiftieth ballot, Southern votes began to go to Scott, and on the fifty-third he had enough of them to secure the nomination, the ballot standing: Scott, 159; Fillmore, 112; Webster, 21. In the Whig convention a majority nominated.

\*    \*    \*    \*    \*

Franklin Pierce, the youngest man who up to this time had taken the presidential oath, was inaugurated March 4th, 1853. The ceremony was more imposing than usual, and was witnessed by the largest number of strangers who had ever gathered in Washington to assist at the installation of a new chief magistrate. When he took the oath he did not, as is ordinary, use the word "swear," but accepted the constitutional alternative which permitted him to affirm that he would faithfully execute the office of President of the United States. Nor did he kiss the Book, after the Southern fashion, but laid his left hand upon the Bible and held his right hand aloft, having previously bared his head to the falling snow. He did not read the address, but spoke without manuscript or notes in a clear and distinct voice, with a graceful manner. The inaugural was a well-turned literary composition, delivered by an effective speaker, and made a striking impression upon the many auditors. He began: "My countrymen! It is a relief to feel that no heart but my own can know the personal regret and bitter sorrow over which I have been borne to a position so suitable for others rather than desirable for myself." This was an allusion to the sudden taking-away of his only living child, a bright boy of thirteen, by a railroad accident which happened in the early part of January. The boy, to whom Pierce was devotedly attached, was travelling with his father and mother, when his brains were dashed out before their eyes. Some Whig journals criticized this allusion as being a trick of the orator to awaken personal interest before proceeding to unfold his public policy; but the people who heard the words felt only sympathy for the handsome young President who thus frankly disclosed his private grief, knowing that he would gladly resign the most glittering of earthly prizes if only his son might have been restored to him.

The President hinted strongly that during his term of office it might be his part to add Cuba to the common country. "The policy of my administration," he said, "will not be controlled by any timid forebodings of evil from expansion. Indeed, it is not to be disguised that our attitude as a nation, and our position on the globe, render the acquisition of certain possessions, not within our jurisdiction, eminently important for our protection."

He affirmed the principle of the Monroe doctrine. He intimated that the Whigs should be turned out of the offices to make room for Democrats. Yet he was not hampered by promises made before nomination or election; he had no "implied engagements to ratify," so that in the disposal of patronage he should not be subject to the dictation of the politicians. "I acknowledge," he declared, "my obligations to the masses of my countrymen, and to them alone."

He made a vigorous appeal for the Union, holding that the compromise measures of 1850 were strictly constitutional, and should be "unhesitatingly carried into effect." While the Fugitive Slave act was not mentioned by name, everybody knew that this expression meant that the President would vigorously enforce that law, as it was the only part of the compromise on which executive action was now needed.

The enthusiastic cheers and noise of the cannon which greeted the President when he closed his address was typical of the joy of Democrats all over the country on their restoration to power. In truth, they had always felt, since the first election of Jackson, that the duty of administering the government belonged rightfully to them, and that in their hands only were the interests of the whole people properly protected. Aristocratic cabals and money combinations certainly fared better at the hands of the Whigs, but a party whose support was largely derived from those elements did not, the Democrats thought, deserve popular success. The Whigs had twice elected a President, but it was by means of the trick of playing upon the universal fancy for military prestige. It was now the general Democratic feeling that the installation of Pierce into office was a restoration simply of the power and patronage justly due the Democrats.

The inaugural was well received; it was generally satisfactory to the business interests. The disposition always exists on the part of the successful party to hail their new chief as a paragon of wisdom or virtue; nor, in the first days of the administration, do the defeated party bear rancor, but are willing to look on with charity, feeling that the new President deserves a fair chance. Especially was this the case when Franklin Pierce took the reins of government. He was very popular on election day, and so overpowering had been his success that he was still more popular on the day of his inauguration. If the general acclaim augured well for the prosperity of the new administration, few Presidents have started with auspices so favorable. Yet the anti-slavery Whigs, and a few anti-slavery Democrats whose principles were stronger than their desire to see the old party cemented, could not but tremble for their country when they saw in this cautious exposition of principle and announcement of programme that the President, whose hold on the people was apparently so powerful, did not regard human slavery as an evil, but was anxious to acquire more slave territory. It did not allay their apprehensions when he said that the new territory should be obtained "with a view to obvious national interest and security, and in a manner entirely consistent with the strictest observance of national faith"; for the intrigue by which Texas was annexed was too fresh in their minds. It was patent that the Southern men who composed the slavery propaganda, while strictly honorable in private life, were ready to use any means to extend the influence of their dear institution. It was a prime article of Southern faith that Texas had been honorably acquired; and if one were a true Democrat, he must believe the war with Mexico to have been just and holy.

A mere reading of the inaugural was sufficient to give rise to a suspicion that in President Pierce the Southern leaders had found a man who would do their bidding; but had one known what was going on in the inner councils of the party, the feeling would have been more than a suspicion. In the month following the election, Pierce had written a letter to Buchanan asking suggestions and advice, to which the Pennsylvania statesman was glad to respond fully and freely. He pointed out where lay the path of glory. "The foreign affairs of the government," he wrote, "and especially the question of Cuba, will occupy the most conspicuous place in your administration. I believe that Cuba can be acquired by cession upon honorable terms, and I should not desire to acquire it in any other manner. The President who shall accomplish this object will render his name illustrious, and place it on the same level with that of his great predecessor, who gave Louisiana to the Union."

Pierce, shortly after his election, sent a message to John A. Dix, of New York, requesting a personal interview. When Dix repaired to Concord he was offered, in the most cordial manner, the position of Secretary of State under the new administration, the President-elect assuring him that he would be especially desirable and gratifying. But when this became known to the party leaders, the extreme Southern politicians and the pro-slavery New York Democrats protested earnestly against the appointment, on account of Dix's connection with the Free-soil party in 1848, when he had been their candidate for governor. Thereupon a second interview between Pierce and Dix took place, and, as it was quite evident that the President-elect desired to be relieved of his obligation, Dix at once released him.

Far different was the treatment of Jefferson Davis, who early received an offer of the position of Secretary of War. He at first declined the appointment, but Pierce was so earnest in his solicitations that Davis came to Washington the day after the inauguration, and was finally prevailed upon to accept the position. This appointment, highly satisfactory to the Southern states-rights men, and in the main agreeable to the South, was particularly distasteful to the Union party in Mississippi. One frequently heard the remark in the North that Davis was the only member of the cabinet who had opposed the compromise measures of 1850. The difference in the treatment of Dix and of Davis, both of whom had similar personal claims on Pierce, was evidence that the extreme Southern faction of the party would receive more consideration than the Northern Democrats who were tinctured with Free-soilism.

The cabinet nominations were not sent to the Senate until three days after the inauguration. The President appointed William L. Marcy, of New York, Secretary of State; James Guthrie, of Kentucky, Secretary of the Treasury; Jefferson Davis, of Mississippi, Secretary of War; James C. Dobbin, of North Carolina, Secretary of the Navy; Robert McClelland, of Michigan, Secretary of the Interior; James Campbell, of Pennsylvania, Postmaster-General; and Caleb Cushing, of Massachusetts, Attorney-General.

The courteous action of Dix in permitting Pierce to retract the offer of the State portfolio did not relieve him of all embarrassment in regard to the leading position in the cabinet. Desirous of giving this place to a New York man, he was perplexed by the bitter factional contest among the Democrats of that State. Although all differences had been sunk during the Presidential canvass, the split which started in 1848 opened again as soon as the party gained the signal victory, and, while no principle seemed to be at stake, the fight was earnest for proper recognition in the distribution of the offices. It is undeniable that a few among those who were called Free-soilers remained true to their former declarations; but most of them were becoming merged in the faction called "Softs," whose endeavor was to unite the warring elements of the party in order to control elections, and who after 1848 became the link of connection between the Free-soilers and the "Hunkers" or "Hards," as the regular Democrats were called. Dix was a "Soft," with Free-soil antecedents; while Marcy, though the chief of the "Softs," had been directly opposed to the Free-soil movement. To satisfy the greatest number was the aim of the President, to whom this problem became the subject of serious thoughts and many councils; and although the whole cabinet, as finally announced, was published in the newspapers one week before the inauguration, Pierce did not really decide who should be his Secretary of State until he had actually been one day in office, for up to the morning of March 5th that portfolio had not been offered to Marcy.

Marcy was the best-known man in the cabinet; he was an adroit politician; his intellectual qualities were solid rather than brilliant, but he had a strong mind and honest purposes. Jefferson Davis and Caleb Cushing also brought to the council board talents of a high order.

The first appearance of Davis in national public life was in the House of Representatives at the age of thirty-seven. He was fortunate in having a liberal training that made him well fitted for the political arena. A graduate of West Point, he had served as lieutenant in the Blackhawk and other Indian wars. He then resigned his commission and for eight years, from the age of twenty-seven to thirty-five, he lived in retirement on his cotton plantation, superintending the work in the manner common to the Southern planter, but for the most part devoting himself to a systematic course of reading and study, for which his taste amounted to a passion. When he quitted the life of a recluse to engage in the affairs of State he was a man of culture, well read in the classical writers of England, and deeply versed in political history and political economy.

# V

# *Union on Trial*

No *region of the United States has commanded greater attention than the South, and no period of its history has fascinated historians more than the antebellum period, the four decades before the Civil War. This interest is heightened by the historian's awareness that he is dealing with a doomed society, one that in the words of a novelist has "Gone With the Wind." A goodly portion of the treatment of the region's history has dealt inordinately with the occasional few great plantations and the life that revolved around them. There according to a half-myth, a genteel life existed, one that permitted the existence of a gentry who in its highest moments infused life into a vanishing cavalier tradition. But as more than one contemporary sojourning in the South discovered, "I found that the South one reads and hears of is altogether different from the one that one sees and becomes acquainted with."*

*This was a simple acknowledgment that in the vast domain of the Cotton Kingdom, there existed wide diversities. The white-pillared plantation mansions existed, but most Southerners, even the planter, lived in either rough log dwellings or unpainted clapboard farmhouses. The staple crops of cotton, tobacco, rice, and sugar which provided the props of the Southern economy and the occasional great fortunes dominated the life of the region. The few cities and the numerous market towns serviced the huge bulk of these crops, but most Southerners remained rural. And these plain folk, often living in the still-virgin pinelands, measured their wealth in scrawny herds of cattle and hogs. To all but the most acute observer, they maintained themselves at a subsistence level of life.*

*The Southern railroad system as it grew before the war had a curiously fragmented character. It was designed to service the movement of the primary staple cotton to water transportation. Little in the way of organized industry existed, although as Lewis C. Gray,* History of Agriculture in the Southern United States to 1860 *(1933), noted, every plantation was, in fact, an agricultural factory. And Southern reformers, concerned by the obvious evidence that their section was being outstripped by the North, and also dismayed at the region's dependence on the North and Europe for its manufactured goods, agitated for increased industrialization. The Southerner persisted in investing a disproportionate share of his capital in land and slaves, diverting funds that some historians have argued might better have been employed elsewhere.*

*The omnipresent Negro slaves set the South apart before the war. Their value mitigated the worst possible excesses of a system which defined the slave as property. So long as the Negro represented a capital investment,* the white planter preferred to use white labor, particularly that of Irish immigrants, for the more dangerous tasks. When one planter was asked why he used German and Irish labor to drain a malarial swamp, he answered directly, "It is dangerous work and the Negro's life is too valuable to be risked at it." Nonetheless, more than one Southerner commented on the brutalizing effects of slavery. "We cannot compete with the planters of Alabama and Mississippi in a wild and destructive system," one South Carolinian protested, "by which even they have sunk under embarrassment and ruin, . . . [by] exhausting their soil and preventing the natural increase of slaves by a reckless system of pushing and driving." The corrosive impact of slavery upon Southern society gave it despite all its cavalier pretensions a seamy side, one which did not escape the view either of visitors or of their fellow Americans who lived in the free states. Southerners aware of this disapproval drew about them a defensive perimeter which as the nation moved toward Civil War resembled ever more sharply a closed society.

William E. Dodd (1869-1940), Southern born, devoted his academic career to Southern history. He recognized a distinctive Southern nationality in existence before the Civil War, one that further distinguished the antebellum South. Although a productive scholar, little of his work has stood the test of time. It is characterized by errors of fact and unsupportable conclusions. Even his The Cotton Kingdom which contemporaries viewed as "masterful" has not survived the test of time. His work does represent a pioneer venture into the understanding of Southern history, and he took care to emphasize the implicit danger of black slavery to the freedom of the white workingman. He never deviated from the proposition that "there can be no political democracy where economic democracy fails." During his long academic career at the University of Chicago, he took an active interest in public affairs, and after his retirement from Chicago in 1933, he served as Ambassador to Germany between 1933 and 1938, at which point as Hitler consolidated his power, Dodd stopped being an historian and became instead a maker of history.

# THE COTTON KINGDOM

## by William E. Dodd

The region which in the middle of the last century was known as the Cotton Kingdom extended a distance of more than a thousand miles from South Carolina to the neighborhood of San Antonio, Texas. The breadth of this country, from north to south, ranged from two hundred miles in Carolina and Texas to six or seven hundred miles in the Mississippi Valley. The land on which cotton could be easily grown measured perhaps as much as four hundred thousand square miles in 1850, if we count Texas, Arkansas, and Florida, which were then, however, yielding only small crops. Large areas in the lower South were not suited to cotton culture, although they contributed to the cotton kingdom other economic resources of no small value. The pine barrens of South Carolina, Georgia, Alabama, Mississippi, and Louisiana could produce immense quantities of lumber; and the hills and mountains of the two Carolinas, Georgia and Alabama supplied a large portion of the grain and the whisky consumed on the plantations.

The cotton belt is a well-watered country with an annual rainfall almost twice as great as that of Illinois or New York. Moreover the snows of the lower Appalachians which lie upon the densely wooded highlands and towering mountains during half the year are carried off through the eastern half of the cotton country by numerous rivers whose average volume is as great as that of the Susquehanna or the Ohio. In addition to these large streams of water there are thousands of smaller rivers, rising among the hills and struggling through the marshes of the low country, which enrich the land and furnish unsurpassed facilities for transportation. In lower South Carolina and Georgia the network of navigable waters brings every parish into touch with Charleston or other coast towns. Farther west the Chattahoochee, the Tombigbee, the Yazoo, the Mississippi itself, the Red, the Sabine, the Trinity, the Brazos, and the Colorado form systems of communication which make it easy to market all sorts of crops—particularly cotton, which can be hauled profitably a hundred miles to the river wharves. It is thus a fact of great importance in the study of the lower South that the larger part of the cotton region, somewhat like the tobacco region of colonial times, is within easy reach of Atlantic or Gulf ports.

The soil of the cotton belt, though not so fertile as that of the upper Mississippi valley, was exceedingly productive. In South Carolina and Georgia it had a reddish hue like that of the Virginia up-country; in Alabama and Mississippi it was dark like that of the prairie region of the Middle West; and everywhere it was soft and easily tillable. It produced corn as readily as cotton, but wheat did not thrive on so loose and open a soil. The seasons were so long that two or often three crops of vegetables were raised in a year, with the warm sun and abundant rains as the benevolent allies of the farmer. Peas, potatoes, beans, and fruit could be grown so quickly and abundantly that the problem of subsistence during the Civil War, for example, was much simpler than in any of the European countries fighting in the Great War.

But before the cotton-planters overran the country during the two decades preceding the beginning of this story, this area was virgin country and, with the exception of certain prairie districts, was covered with dense forests, while its river-bottoms were still tangled, impenetrable swamps. And even as late as 1860 the clearing of new lands was a large part of the planter's work. This was done by cutting away the brambles and dense undergrowth and then "deadening" the larger trees by a process of belting or taking away the bark near the ground and thus preventing further growth. This clearing of the forests let the sunlight fall upon the soil and enabled the planter to produce his first crop at a minimum of expense. But the tall, dead trees, from which the winds tore off branches and strewed them over the ground, gave the countryside a somber, despoiled appearance, and seemed the skeletons of the monarchs of the forest crying aloud against the desecration of nature and the sheer waste of the finest timber in the world.

The immediate profits of cotton-growing were so much more easily realized than the remote rewards of conservation that the spoliation of timber-lands continued with a ruthlessness unparalleled elsewhere in the world. Men became hardened to this work until the felling of trees became a pastime; and when there was nothing else for slaves to do, they were sent to the "new grounds" to cut timber and burn logs with the idea that older land would soon need to be abandoned and the new be added to the arable fields. West of South Carolina the land was bought at government sales at a dollar and a quarter an acre or was even seized without the formality of a purchase by squatters who entered the public domain, built their cabins, cleared patches of land, and then defied the Federal officials to oust them. The ease with which one might raise a crop of cotton and the relatively large returns which it brought drew men of all classes to the lower South. Thousands of square miles of rich lands within easy distance of navigable rivers gave the people of the region a sense of new opportunity, a feeling that the world belongs to him who can exploit it, and a restless craving for a new life and wide acres—all of which influenced profoundly not only the lower South but the whole course of American history. Between 1820 and 1850 almost anything seemed possible to the enterprising man of the cotton country.

Until 1830 Indian tribes held immense tracts in Georgia, Alabama, and Mississippi. The Cherokees, the Creeks, the Choctaws, and the Chickasaws counted many thousand warriors; they dwelt upon good cotton lands and, what was worse, they had been taught many of the arts of civilization by the Federal Government and had been encouraged to become orderly citizens of the United States. This policy tended to make of the Indian a permanent holder of his land; and in many, many instances these "wards of the nation" had become owners of good homes, masters of slaves, and successful cotton-planters.

The planters of Georgia first, and later those of the other States who coveted these lands with a covetousness unimagined by the kingly exploiter of Naboth's vineyard in ancient times, vowed that the Indians should not be allowed to develop settled, civilized communities. Since the planters were represented in Congress and the natives had recourse only to executive protection, the contest was most unequal; and, when President Jackson gave the Indians over to the tender mercies of their enemies, there was no help for them. The planters had their way, and the Indian lands were rapidly converted into cotton plantations. Pretty cottages and squalid wigwams, fertile fields and wild hunting-grounds, Negro slaves, horses, and farming implements all had to be sacrificed without any other reparation than doles of money and such lands as the Indian could settle beyond the Red River.

Having secured the vast area of land, the planters had then to obtain the labor requisite to cultivate their new acres. Between the close of the second war with England and the annexation of Texas this problem solved itself. On the river-bottoms of Maryland, Virginia, and North Carolina, or in the counties which bordered on the Piedmont region of those States, there were more than a million slaves whose numbers doubled every twenty years. Since the demand for tobacco had not greatly increased since 1800, there was no profitable employment for these growing hordes of blacks. The owner of slaves in this region could not move to the up-country west of the Blue Ridge, for there were no roads or canals by which to transport the wheat and corn which would be his chief crops in the new country. If he went still farther west to Kentucky or Missouri, he found tobacco-growing already well past the stage of profitable employment of slaves. There were left the wide prairies of Indiana and Illinois, but as the laws of those States did not recognize slavery the well-to-do Southerner could not go there except at the sacrifice of the larger part of his property.

The slaveholder of the older South might emigrate to the lower South, taking his Negroes with him, or he might sell his servants and eke out a living for himself and his family on the old homestead. It was a hard choice, but it could not well be avoided. Thousands emigrated and added their numbers and wealth to the cotton belt; other thousands sold their slaves and thus added to the increasing volume of labor needed to clear the forests and grow the cotton crops of the lower South. Year after year masters and slaves found their way to the new economic El Dorado, and year after year the influence and power of the planters became more evident to the rest of the country.

In the tobacco country or among the foothills of the older South another and larger class of people found that society was fast hardening around them and was compelling them to take subordinate social stations. They likewise emigrated, and many, very many, of them went to the Northwest, where they "took up" lands and raised just enough grain and pork to sustain their families. Even more of them went to Alabama and Mississippi, where they obtained a small tract of land, bought a Negro with their first crop of cotton, and set up as planters "on the make." These pioneers became the most resolute and uncompromising of all the enemies of the Indians and the most ardent advocates of the institution of slavery.

Thus practically the whole increase of the slave and the white population in the older South was emigrating and most of it was going to the new cotton region. In some counties of the seaboard States, such as Virginia, the population decreased by half in one or two decades, and everywhere the lands and houses of well-to-do people declined in value. Jefferson's magnificent home sold in 1820 for about $3000; Madison struggled manfully but in vain to avoid disposing of his family servants; and John Randolph talked about running away from his plantation to avoid bankruptcy. What was the reason for this state of affairs?

Old Virginia and her neighbors were caught between the upper and the nether economic millstones. Disavow it as they would, their most profitable product was the slave who could be sold. Negroes alone increased in value. It is no wonder that statesmen of the older South saw in this traffic a means of rehabilitating their declining commonwealths.

The census of 1850 gives the lower South, including Arkansas, 2,137,000 white people and 1,841,000 blacks, nearly all of whom were slaves—a total population of nearly 4,000,000. The great majority of whites lived in countries where slavery had little influence; and nearly all the slaves lived in the cotton belt, that is, in the districts within easy reach of the rivers. The upbuilding of this region had been accomplished almost entirely within thirty years, and the period of rapid growth and change had now come to a close.

Practically all the produce of these lower Southern States was exported. Their cotton sold in 1850 for $102,000,000; their sugar, for $14,800,000; and their rice, for $2,600,000—a total of $119,400,000. The exports of the whole country were only $203,000,000 in 1850, but while the larger part of these exports thus originated in the cotton States, less than a fourth of all the imports came through Southern ports. Charleston, for example, exported from $8,000,000 to $10,000,000 worth of goods each year, but imported scarcely over $2,000,000. The balance of trade was also against Mobile and other Southern cities. But because nearly half the people of the Cotton States were property, the per capita wealth of the planter was much greater than that of the Easterner; and, notwithstanding the most unfavorable balance of trade against his section, he made great display of his wealth.

Rapidly increasing wealth makes one hunger the more for still greater wealth and a wider area for one's operations. Even before the Indians had all moved across the Mississippi, the planters began a most vigorous campaign for the annexation of Texas. From New Orleans, Vicksburg, and Natchez, from Mobile and Montgomery, even from Charleston and Savannah, adventurous men and prospective planters hurried into the disputed region, took up lands, and began the cultivation of cotton and the importation of slaves from the older South. They were winning for the United States a new and promising empire. With equal zest and enthusiasm men from Tennessee, Kentucky, and Missouri hastened to join their Southern brethren and to help them wrest the coveted province from the hand of Mexico. The Revolution of 1836 brought independence to the Republic of Texas and eventually annexation to the American Union, through a coalition of Southern and Western party groups. The Mexican War followed, and still other vast areas of land were annexed to the United States. What cotton-planters wanted, Congress somehow found a way to grant.

Nor was the case wholly different in the greater matter of the national tariff. When, in 1828, the South and the West united to place Jackson in the President's chair, it was definitely understood that the "tariff of abominations" was to be abolished or greatly reduced. The exigencies of national politics caused Jackson to falter and delay. South Carolina allowed the new President four years to make up his mind. When he was still uncertain in 1832, that State proceeded to nullify the offensive national statute; the President then threatened war; South Carolina thereupon paused; but the outcome was the definite abandonment of the higher tariff policy in favor of the lower rates of the compromise tariff of 1833. Every South Carolinian thought that the planters had once again had their way; and South Carolinians were scattered over all the cotton States.

If ever people were taught to believe themselves invincible in politics, it was the people of the cotton country during the two decades which preceded 1850. A vast region of rich cotton lands had been rapidly opened up to them; the natives had been driven beyond the distant Red River; a new State embracing more than two hundred and fifty thousand square miles had been annexed; and the protective tariff policy by which Eastern manufacturers sought to possess the American markets free from competition had been abandoned. Why then might not the gentleman of the lower South boast of his growing riches and of his control of national affairs?

The lower South had been and still was an outwardly irreligious, dram-drinking, and dueling section. The French priests had built a compact religious community in and about New Orleans, but they had not pushed this work up the rivers and out into the great stretches of country where plantation life was dominant. Nor was their easygoing moral system entirely adapted to the needs of rural life. The cathedral church, the monastery, and the parochial schools filled the round of the priest's life and duties. The saving of souls in distant plantations was not his especial concern. Dueling and card-playing and horse-racing were not beyond the range of his own interests; why should he stir up a crusade against them? The faith of the Roman Catholic Church was, therefore, comparatively stagnant in the lower South. Aside from a few churches in Louisiana and Charleston, firmly established parishes in Mobile, and a diocese in Florida, this branch of the Christian Church had not become a force in the planter civilization.

If the founders of the Roman Catholic Church in the lower South were content to let the planters go their own way and to confine their activities to the larger towns, the builders of the Church of England were no more enterprising. They established their churches in Charleston, Savannah, and other towns, and set up chapels of ease in the outlying parishes—half-way houses, as it were, to the true church in the city—but they were not consumed with zeal to save the lost souls of the hordes of men who filled up the back country. Gambling and horse-racing and card-playing were to the Anglican clergy what they were to the Catholic priests, a means of hastening weary hours away. Even dueling among vestrymen of high standing was not to them one of the crimes to be denounced from the pulpit. They condoned slavery at first and later proclaimed it God's way of saving the souls of the heathen. Good sermons were indeed read on Sabbath days in the churches of Charleston and the other cities, and many charities occupied the attention of the Episcopalians of the lower South; but these gentle ministrations did not affect the red-blooded men and women who were building in the open country the foundations of a great section of the American Union.

Men of the cotton country might live freely, might partake of the joys of this world, and might even deny the fundamentals of the Christian faith without feeling that everlasting penance must be done in the world to come. Nor was there great religious or social scruple if aristocratic blood ran in Negro veins or if fine young gentlemen kept halfbreed mistresses. Only one must not bring one's hybrid offspring to Mardi Gras or seat them with the family in the cathedral church in New Orleans or St. Michael's in Charleston. Men drank the best and oldest wines of France till they were wholly drunk; they built the best of theaters and engaged troupes of actors from England whose reputations for immorality would have scandalized all New England; they even lured assemblies of clergymen to witness their races and take chances on their steeds. There was thus an un-Puritan and continental sort of life in the older communities of the young cotton kingdom which was in time wholly to disappear.

Another vanishing social group consisted of the high English gentry whose grandfathers had been received at the Court of St. James in the days of the Georges or who had chased the famous Blackbeard or who had even turned sea-robbers themselves. They, too, had made their fortunes in the unsettled eighteenth century; but in the decades which preceded 1850 they were fast disappearing from among the increasing number of cotton-planters. They had spread themselves over the lands of South Carolina, built their houses far inland, and mingled their blood with people of less aristocratic mold. The Pinckneys, the Rhetts, and the Petigrus were merged into the new aristocracy of the country, although they still owned houses in Charleston, held pews in the oldest churches, and made a fetish of their St. Cecilia Society, into whose sacred precincts unhallowed feet seldom dared to tread. By the middle of the century it was not so much the State of South Carolina that drew out the loyalty and devotion of the planter aristocracy; the building of a new economic and social order based on an enlarged planter group occupied men's thoughts and purposes in much the same way that the spread of *Kultur* has become the mission of the Pan-German party of our day. South Carolina contributed most to the making of that lower South which was to dominate so large a part of the national thought in the two decades before the Civil War.

An important racial element was contributed to the life of South Carolina by the French Huguenots of high intellectual endowment and even literary culture whose ancestors had driven in family coaches and had read good books for three generations. Unsurpassed in commercial pursuits, they heaped up fortunes which made their names known on both sides of the Atlantic during the Revolution and the decades which followed the adoption of the Federal Constitution. But aristocratic groups seldom maintain themselves. The Huguenots were fast merging into the planter-lawyer class, and when cotton became king in the South, their quaint accent was about all that remained to mark them as a race apart.

In New Orleans were old French families dating back to the days of the *Grand Monarque* himself, who had houses on St. Charles, Royal, or Toulouse Street, owned plantations on the river or offices on Canal Street, and attended French opera in the evening. Their wealth was invested in slaves or sugar or cotton; their quaint old coaches were seen along the Strand or the Esplanade; and their children took dancing lessons with French masters who showed both young and old what was good form in France.

So many Spaniards had come into the colony during the Spanish rule and so many English royalists from Revolutionary America that society was wonderfully mixed in New Orleans. All nationalities, including Germans and Italians, entered into the life of the lower Mississippi. And there were many creoles with the blood of several races in their veins. Octoroons and half-breeds and pure blacks made up the free Negro population, which had a life of its own unlike that in any other city in the country. Some Negroes were gentlemen with a standing amongst other gentlemen which would scandalize good Southerners of today. In New Orleans as in Charleston, there were Negro owners of slaves who played a considerable part in the civil life, were among the stanchest defenders of slavery as an institution, and were bitterly opposed to all who talked of setting free their slaves.

Outwardly New Orleans was the most European of all American cities in 1850, and its music, literature, and manners were European quite as much as American. But the tone was changing. Hillhouse and Story, Slocomb and Eustis, were names of families that did not remind one of either France or Spain. And there were many street names that bespoke the influence of the Yankees who had long ruled the city with a strange lack of reverence for old things and old times. New Orleans was definitely passing from the epoch of Catholic and fur-trading supremacy to that of Protestantism and cotton. Dr. Clapp, the great Boston preacher, and General Gaines, the hero of many battles, were the visible evidences of a new era; yet it must be recognized that French influence contributed much that was valuable to the plantation system.

The hills of North Carolina, Virginia, and Tennessee reared thousands and tens of thousands of plain, poor folk who made the bone and sinew of the lower South. They knew nothing of the gentle ways of Charleston or of the French manners of New Orleans. They built their cabins all over the up-country from what is now Charlotte to Atlanta; they overran northern Alabama and the Tombigbee Valley; and they "took up" lands in Mississippi and Louisiana. It was they who made by far the larger part of the new country. While the older Virginians brought with them their slaves and their good middle-class manners, and while the gentry of Charleston and New Orleans boasted of their families and their culture, these people adhered firmly to their stern Presbyterian faith or to the warmer religious emotionalism of the Baptists and Methodists.

To be sure, many of these settlers from the poorer districts of the older South were not saints or of the stuff of which saints are made, but there were enough of the earnest and devout to make the salt for the saving of the whole social lump. Slowly these elements were merged with the older order, learned somewhat of the elegance and form which made the Carolina and Louisiana stocks so attractive, and contributed the largest element to the new society which the world always associates with cotton and slavery.

For the moment a good deal of the religious inheritance from Jonathan Edwards, Whitefield, and Wesley, which the "new light" preachers had delivered to the poorer white people of the South, was lost in the migration to the cotton country. The frontier has always been indifferent to formal religion. The free life of the forest, the conflict with the Indians, and the struggle with nature tended to make men forget the catechism and the hymnal. Nor did the easy-going manners of the older planters, the horses, the hounds, and the illicit loves with squaws and Negro women, stiffen the backbone of personal morality. An affair of honor, a duel which always followed the slightest insult among men of family, was attractive to men who were just climbing to the higher rungs of the social ladder; and where law and social solidarity developed slowly these newer men quickly learned to defend themselves, to be the avengers of their own and their family's wrongs. Every man carried his weapon in his pocket and he was not slow to use it. Public gatherings were not the safest places for men of hot tempers.

And where the weather at all seasons was open, court days, barbecues, and even religious gatherings, not infrequently were the scenes of encounters between gentlemen and of fisticuffs between men of lower degrees. Feuds and lawsuits were engendered and prolonged to the great satisfaction of lawyers and hangers-on of the courts. To these occasions of legal conflict were added the myriad suits about land titles and preemption claims which gave sustenance to a host of attorneys. Where money came easily it went easily. Sergeant Prentiss, a New England lawyer-orator of the first importance in the cotton kingdom, received a fee of $50,000 for the conduct of a single case in the Supreme Court of Mississippi; and Reuben Davis became a state-wide hero in the defense of an acknowledged murderer.

As one reviews these elements and forces that entered into the make-up of the lower South in 1850, it becomes plain that this was a region of immense potentiality. Its great waterfalls might run the wheels of many thousand industrial plants, if Southerners ever turned their minds in the direction of manufacturing. Its fertile lands might feed cattle enough to supply the whole national demand for meat. Its harbors were ample for large fleets of ocean-going vessels. The people who had rushed in, dispossessed the native Indians, cleared the lands, become planters, established commonwealths, and sent spokesmen to Congress, were native Americans, with rare exceptions. They were tobacco farmers from the older South, poor whites from all the Atlantic States, Carolina gentlemen, French settlers in Louisiana, and Scotch-Irish farmers from the mountain districts of Pennsylvania, Maryland, and Virginia. The German element, which had formed so large a part of the Southern population at the time of the Revolution, could be detected only in proper names here and there and in an occasional *Verein*. Their language, manners, and religion had nearly everywhere given way to the dominant Anglo-Saxon civilization. The lower South was a region of vast opportunity but of wavering democratic faith; it was a region of American traditions, except in its growing devotion to slavery. If its political and social leaders would succeed in uniting all its groups, in moderating its growing ambitions, and in educating its great mass of illiterate people, it must of necessity become one of the greatest sections of the United States and dictate to a large extent the course of national history. Would these conditions be adequately met? Was it possible for the planters to develop the wisest counsels?

The amalgamation of the various elements and forces of the population which composed the cotton States in 1850 was strikingly paralleled by the rapid concentration of economic power in three or four thousand families who lived on the best lands and received three-fourths of the returns from the yearly exports. Two-thirds of the white people of the South had no connection with slavery and received only a very small part of the returns of the community output. A thousand families received over $50,000,000 a year, while all the remaining 666,000 families received only about $60,000,000. While these figures do not show such extreme concentration of wealth in a few hands as the facts of our own day disclose, they do nevertheless reveal a dangerous tendency.

Though there was some discontent even in the South at this menace of concentrated wealth, no effort was made to limit the size of men's fortunes. The tendency was to divide the great numbers of slaves owned by one master into plantation groups of something like a hundred each. A thousand acres of land and a hundred slaves made a unit which was regarded as the most productive; but one man might own ten such units and never be made to bear inheritance or super-taxes. The Hairstons owned as many as 1700 slaves distributed over plantations in Virginia, Alabama, and Mississippi; Howell Cobb of Georgia was pointed out as the master of a thousand Negroes; while the Aikens of South Carolina and Joseph Davis (brother of Jefferson Davis) of Mississippi were counted as millionaires.

There was something factitious about the growing wealth of the great masters. The number of slaves owned was believed to be an index of wealth. The greater the number of slaves one owned, the greater one's riches; and the number of slaves increased rapidly, even in the cotton belt. As fortune would have it, the price of cotton tended to rise during the period of 1845 to 1860. This rise in prices added a hundred per cent to the value of land, and it also added nearly a hundred per cent to the value of each slave. A cotton-planter had only to be a kind master and a reasonably good manager, or employ good overseers, and he could not avoid the rapid accumulation of wealth. He simply grew rich.

The rising price of cotton naturally increased the output of the plantations and gave the owners of slaves a sense of security which they had not known in the older South for fifty years. Between 1850 and 1860 the annual cotton crop increased from 2,500,000 to 5,000,000 bales, and thus more than doubled the wealth of the planters. What exaggerated the situation was the fact that these huge crops did not meet the demands of European and New England mills. Thus every way one turned, the fortunes of the cotton-growers increased and the difficulties of regulating or limiting the evil of slavery increased. Here seems to be an illustration of the saying that prosperity is quite as unfortunate in its effects as poverty.

Every year added to the wealth of him who had and seemed to take away from him who had not. A healthy Negro man was worth in 1845 about $750; in 1860 the same slave, although fifteen years older, was worth in the market a third more, and a young Negro man or woman readily sold for $1500. There was no help for it. Economic laws concentrated the wealth of the South in the cotton region. Owners of slaves, as we have already seen, did not like to sell their servants, but they did sell them under these circumstances, and there was a constant stream of unwilling slave emigration from the tobacco country to the lower South. Cotton proved to be the irresistible magnet. It was doubtless these conditions which moved Lincoln to make his remarkable statement of 1854 that he did not know what to do about slavery: "I surely will not blame them for not doing what I should not know how to do myself. If all earthly power were given me, I should not know what to do as to the existing institution."

But while the great planters were undoubtedly absorbing a disproportionate part of the wealth of the South, and while economic conditions were daily making more difficult the problem of the statesman who really loved the country, much if not most of this outward wealth found its way out of the cotton region. Leading Southern towns exported annually three or four times as much as they imported. New York, on the other hand, imported twice as much as she exported. Each year $100,000,000 worth of foreign goods came into the United States through her custom-house, while only $50,000,000 worth went out that way. The same thing was true of Philadelphia and Boston. The cotton-planters, with their wide-spread fields and their troops of Negro laborers, were buying the bulk of their goods in the North and selling the whole of their output either to Europe or to the North at prices fixed in the world market. The merchants of New York, Boston, and Philadelphia thus reaped enormous profits.

In the realm of finance and banking there was a still stronger limitation upon the concentration of the profits of the cotton industry in the lower South. Men were chiefly interested in supplying their daily necessities from their own plantations, and the only commercial goods which they used were purchased from the North. As a result the planters paid little attention to matters of banking and credit. Although New Orleans was one of the greatest exporting cities in the country, the amount of money on deposit in her banks was insignificant. Less than a third of the returns on the cotton which annually left her docks ever found place in her financial institutions. On the other hand, New York or Philadelphia always had on deposit more money than the total value of her exports. What was true of New Orleans was true of the cotton belt as a whole. Though the cotton, rice, and sugar of the South sold for $119,400,000 in 1850, the total bank deposits of the region amounted to only some $20,000,000. Ten years later, when the value of the crops had increased to more than $200,000,000, less than $30,000,000 was deposited in the banks of the cotton and sugar belt.

Nor was it different in the matter of loans or specie or banking capital. While agricultural production was concentrated in the comparatively small area where cotton could be grown and the returns all seemed to be going to the planters, the evidence is conclusive that far the greater part of the proceeds was left in the hands of those who supplied the South with its necessaries and its luxuries. The earnings of the slave plantations were thus consumed by tariffs, freights, commissions, and profits which the Southerners had to pay. Southern towns were only marts of trade, not depositories of the crops of surrounding or distant areas. Thus while the planters monopolized the cotton industry, drew to themselves the surplus of slaves, and apparently increased their wealth enormously, they were really but custodians of these returns, administrators of the wealth of Northern men who really ultimately received the profits of Southern plantations and Southern slavery.

If some planters saw this dangerous tendency and sought frantically to check it, the majority of men were oblivious of it and endeavored to emulate the delusive riches of the great planters. The small farmer, the tenant, and the piney-woods squatter, so well described by Frederick Law Olmsted, all contributed to the power and prestige of the industrial leaders. They produced but little surplus—a bale of cotton, a little fresh beef or pork, poultry and eggs. This produce they carried on ox-carts or rickety wagons drawn by poverty-stricken horses to the nearest plantation towns and bought in exchange a New England bonnet for the wife, New England shoes for the husband and sons, or a little coffee or molasses for the family table. Although these people rarely became members of the privileged order, they were closely bound to it, tributary in their small way to the great planter aristocracy.

Another class of Southerners contributed in similar manner to the master group. They were the so-called "crackers" or "hill-Billies" of northern Georgia and north-central Alabama, and the poorer whites who dwelt on the semibarren lands which the planters refused to cultivate or had worn out by their reckless methods of cultivation. They sometimes owned a few slaves, made a score of bales of cotton, and raised some wheat and corn for the planter market. Their net returns amounted to $100 or $200 per year and their homes bore a somewhat better aspect than did the cabins of the piney-woods people. The great majority of Southern whites belonged to these classes. They lived on the poorer lands in the cotton belt—on the hills that border the lower reaches of the Appalachian Mountains or on the sandy ridges of Louisiana and Texas. They were the inarticulate masses. Sometimes, as in the case of Andrew Johnson, twice Governor of Tennessee, or Joseph E. Brown of Georgia, the inveterate enemy of Jefferson Davis during the Civil War, they might rise to power and influence, but the great masses of them could hardly hope to see better days.

Like the piney-woods men, the farmers and tenants of the hills were all dependents of their greater neighbors, willing hangers-on of a system which, if they but knew it, could give them no promise of better things. The reasons for this dependency were two: many of these ne'er-do-wells were but the distant cousins of the rich, the cast-offs of the fast-growing cotton aristocracy; many others were prospective planters, hopeful that they or their sons might migrate to some new cotton region with a little store of savings, preempt a tract of government land, buy a slave or two, and set up as planters. It was from such classes in Virginia or the Carolinas that many, if not the majority, of the great cotton-planters had come. The lower South was as yet too big for these farmers and tenants to entertain and nurse the hopeless envy that cankers our own industrial life. They were not altogether contented: but they were far from dangerous. Moreover the planters were a democratic folk in their manners. They were too near the poor in point of time and descent to hold their heads as high as their social prestige might have tempted them to. They endeavored consciously to make and keep friends with their poorer neighbors—for these neighbors had the ballot. They were the "freemen" to whom every returning member of Congress must make his appeal against Yankee tariffs and Yankee abolitionists; and their votes had made possible the annexation of Texas and the war with Mexico, by which the power and even the riches of the planters had been greatly increased. The lower South was a social unit except for the poor slaves, of whom our knowledge comes only through the writings of his master.

The two millions of blacks on whose sturdy shoulders this kingdom of cotton was securely fastened were inexorably bound to the system. Willingly or unwillingly, they increased its solidarity and lent enchantment to the life of the planter. They boasted of the limitless lands of their masters, of the incomparable horses of "ol' massa," of the riches of "ol' massa's" table and the elegancies of "ol' massa's great house." What their inmost thoughts were is not likely ever to be known. They certainly produced the greater part of the cotton and sugar of the South; they disliked the whites who did not own slaves; and they were even more cordially disliked by those same whites. And this mutual dislike tended to fasten the bonds of slavery more closely and to prevent any rift between the planters and their less fortunate white brethren by keeping the slaves loyal to their masters and by deterring the poor whites from sympathizing with any abolitionist movement. Every class of Southern society, therefore, was disposed to lend power and influence to the owner of great plantations, save only a bare remnant of mountaineers who were too remote to feel the kinship of the masters or the racial antipathies between lowland whites and blacks.

❧ ☙

TRAVELERS *to America in the mid-nineteenth century were invariably struck by the contradiction of a society that preached equality for all and kept its black folk enslaved. They were not alone in their unease. "You ought . . . to appreciate how much the great body of the Northern people do crucify their feelings," Abraham Lincoln wrote a Southern friend, "in order to maintain their loyalty to the constitution and the Union." The source of their pain had been succinctly expressed by the great Illinoisan when he said earlier, "You know I dislike slavery, . . . a thing which has . . . the power of making me miserable." Even as he made his confession, Lincoln acknowledged the Southern right to own slaves. But where such sentiments prevail, it is reasonable to assume that an appeal to have done with the source of such pain will have, at least potentially, a wide audience. Such an appeal took shape in 1832 with the founding of the New England Anti-Slavery Society and in 1833 with the organization of the American Anti-Slavery Society. Their membership called for the immediate emancipa-*

*tion as a duty of conscience. In a short time, they would set forth the ex-
istence of a "higher law," superior to man-made law, founded in the divine
order, and subject only to the restriction of the individual conscience.*

*William Lloyd Garrison in his first edition of the* Liberator *published
on January 1, 1831, set the tone when in his famous manifesto he declared,
"I will be as harsh as truth, and as uncompromising as justice." Any doubt
about where he stood on slave masters was settled when he declared: "God,
and the angels, and the devil, and the universe know that they are without
excuse." Within the popular Protestant sects, ministers such as the great
revivalist Charles G. Finney denounced the institution and the churches that
tolerated it. "Let Christians of all denominations meekly but firmly come
forth, and pronounce their verdict, . . . let them give forth and write
of the head and front of this great abomination,* SIN!" *Finney appealed; and
in the wake of such appeals, by 1836, the Methodist Church was on its way
to breaking up along sectional lines, as would also the Baptist and Presbyterian professions.*

*The abolitionists were but a corporal guard, yet by 1840, they espoused
political action through the Liberty Party, and in 1844, their vote was believed to have given New York and the election to Polk. When in 1848, the
Liberty Party fused into the Free Soil Party, they added to their support
dissident Democrats who thought the South blocked the aspirations of
Northerners, Whigs whose conscience would not allow them to support a
slaveowner, and others who saw in the promise of free soil opportunity
unhampered by slavery. Whatever their motives, they set in motion the
organization of "a new agency,* the party of Freedom," *its purpose to guide
the rising tide of public opinion against Slavery.*

*Aware that they were a minority, they nonetheless persisted in denounc-
ing unjust laws, not hesitating to declare as Charles Sumner did of the
Fugitive Slave Act of 1850, "I* AM BOUND TO DISOBEY THIS ACT." *When the
Kansas-Nebraska Act was passed, seeming to place as it did slavery on an
equal footing with freedom in the territories, they issued an appeal that
destroyed the Whiggery and rocked the Democracy to its foundations.
In 1856, a newly assembled Republican party called for the confinement
of slavery, and in 1859, John Brown launched his raid on Harpers Ferry.
And when he went before a Virginia court to hear his end by hanging
decreed, Old Brown did not protest his fate; instead he bound it up with
"His despised poor" and prepared to "mingle my blood further with the
blood of my children and with the blood of millions in this slave country
whose rights are disregarded by wicked, cruel and unjust enactments." It
was as Herman Melville noted, "The Portent . . . the meteor of the war."
A year later, Abraham Lincoln was elected President, and the abolitionist
crusade was little more than two years from its goal—emancipation of the
slave.*

*Albert Bushnell Hart (1854-1943), who taught at Harvard between
1883 and 1926, gained his greatest fame as editor of the first* American
Nation *series. Its twenty-eight volumes are a landmark in collective
scholarship. That of Hart made no bones about the error of slavery or the*

*worth of the abolitionist crusade; it gave the traditional Northern view
of the subject, and as such gives testimony to the sentiment of much of
the North on the eve of Civil War.*

# SLAVERY AND ABOLITION, 1831-1841

## *by Albert Bushnell Hart*

The defenders of slavery were many, and made up for their lack of
literary prestige by the liveliness of their feeling. Some foreign visitors, especially Sir Charles Lyell, condoned slavery; and some northern ministers
were enthusiastic champions, especially the Reverend Nehemiah Adams, of
Boston, on the basis of a brief visit to Savannah. Within the south the
cudgels were taken up for slavery by leaders of every kind. The southern
clergymen almost without exception defended the system. There was hardly
a college president or professor who would not enter the lists in behalf of
slavery, and Chancellor Harper, of the College of South Carolina, was one
of a group of contributors, including Simms, the literary man, Dew, a
college professor, and Hammond, a public man, who joined in a semi-
official defence of slavery entitled *The Pro-Slavery Argument*. State governors, like McDuffie, of South Carolina, joined in the conflict, and legislatures
adopted long, defensive reports.

In the discussion the south had a technical advantage in that not a single
southern public man of large reputation and influence failed to stand by
slavery; while from the northern ranks some, like Webster, stifled their
natural objections; others, like Cass, "Northern men with Southern principles," ranged themselves alongside their southern brothers in an open defence of slavery.

The first argument in favor of slavery was that it was an institution
traceable to the very roots and origins of society, "a principal cause of
civilization. Perhaps . . . the sole cause." Aristotle recognized and approved
slavery; the Romans had slavery, and it was the cause of their prosperity.
The Jews had slavery under a system closely resembling that of the south.
Hagar was a slave, "and the angel of the Lord said unto her, Return to thy
mistress, and submit thyself under her hands." Against the objection that
the mediaeval Catholic church was resolute against slavery was set the
authority of some of the church fathers. Had not England admitted vil-
leinage? Did not the philosopher Locke permit slavery in his model Constitution for the Carolinas? That Greece and Rome had perished in spite of
their system of slavery; that England had for centuries disavowed both
chattel and villein servitude; that by 1830 all Europe, except Russia, had rid
itself of serfdom, took away the force of this argument of precedent, which
is put forth chiefly by learned and casuistical writers.

The argument of the authority of the Scriptures was living, vital, and very
effectual; for the Reformation habit of referring all cases of moral conduct

to the Bible was almost universal in the United States. The advocates and
the opponents of total abstinence, of woman's rights, of imprisonment for
debt, of instrumental music in churches, of theatres, dipped into that great
sea and fished out "proof-texts" which were triumphantly held to be conclusive. It was undeniable that both the Old and the New Testament mentioned, legislated on, and did not expressly condemn slavery; that though
the word "slave" appears in but two places in the King James version, the
word "servant" frequently refers to slaves. The Tenth Commandment
forbids the coveting of "his man-servant, nor his maid-servant." The Jews
were allowed to buy "bondmen and bondmaids. Moreover, of the children
of the strangers that do sojourn among you, of them shall ye buy." "If his
master have given him a wife, and she have borne him sons or daughters;
the wife and her children shall be her master's." "If a man smite his servant,
or his maid, with a rod, and he die under his hand; he shall be surely
punished. Notwithstanding, if he continue a day or two, he shall not be
punished: for he is his money." In these and some similar passages were found
Scriptural sanction for the purchase, sale, and extreme punishment of slaves,
and even for the separation of families, in the United States of America.

Another Scriptural argument, a thousand times repeated, goes back to the
unseemly behavior of Ham, youngest son of Noah and father of Canaan;
when the old patriarch "drank of the wine, and was drunken." And he said,
"Cursed be Canaan; a servant of servants shall he be unto his brethren. And
he said, Blessed be the Lord God of Shem; and Canaan shall be his servant."
If Shem was the ancestor of the Anglo-Saxons, if Canaan was the ancestor of
the Africans, was it not a Q. E. D. that African slavery was not only allowed,
but divinely ordained and commanded? In a generation ignorant of any
theory of the Aryan race, and still little troubled by the damnation of un-
regenerate infants, such a curse upon unborn generations for a technical
fault of a remote ancestor seemed not unreasonable.

The New Testament also contained passages highly encouraging to the
slaveholders, such as, "Let every man abide in the same calling wherein he
was called." "Servants, be obedient to them that are your masters according
to the flesh, with fear and trembling, in singleness of your heart, as unto
Christ." "Let as many servants as are under the yoke count their own masters
worthy of all honor." And most comfortable of all was St. Paul's appeal to
Philemon to receive Onesimus (asserted to be a fugitive slave), who had
"departed for a season, . . . not now as a servant, but above a servant, a
brother beloved, specially to me."

That both Old and New Testaments recognized the existence of slavery
when they were written, and nowhere instituted direct commands against it,
was absolutely irrefutable; but the anti-slavery people quoted Scripture
against Scripture. They argued that the references to slavery in the Old
Testament were precisely like those to polygamy; and if slavery was justified
because of Hagar's children, concubinage was equally justified. There were
also passages in the Old Testament bidding the master to set his bondsman
free after seven years, and against man-stealing. Were not the Jews them-

selves, after four hundred years of slavery in Egypt, conducted into freedom by a divinely appointed leader? As for Onesimus, Paul speaks of him as a "brother" and a "beloved brother"—not a useful comparison for a slave-owner.

The most telling counter-argument was always the general spirit of Christ and the apostles. How could slavery be made to fit with the injunction, "Go ye into all the world, and preach the gospel to every creature"; with the appeal to "be kindly affectioned one to another with brotherly love; in honor preferring one another." If Abraham was a slave-holder, Christ was not; and His message was to the poorest and lowliest of His time. The very fact that the Christian people of the south in general admitted that the slaves had souls to be saved or lost, that they were admitted to baptism, to church membership, even in the white churches, made it difficult to set the Negro apart as subject to the curses and the admonitions of the Bible, but not entitled to its promises, its comforts, or its principles of equality in the sight of God, that "no respecter of persons."

Another group of arguments was based upon the character of the Negro, and led to inconsistencies not easy to reconcile. "By what right is it," asked Chancellor Harper, "that man exercises dominion over the beasts of the field? . . . The savage can only be tamed by being enslaved or by having slaves"; and he proceeds to demonstrate that the African Negro is, at best, an inferior variety of the human race. This inferiority was at great length argued on physical grounds: the Negro brain is lighter in proportion to his weight; his skin has an extra quantity of pigment; he has a long head, unusual proportions, woolly hair; his features are brutal; his vocal organs incapable of pronouncing white folks' language; he has an animal odor—such are the arguments repeated by writer after writer.

The Negro's intellectual inferiority was equally set up against him, though few southern writers went to the extent of saying "none has given evidence of an approach to even mediocrity of intellectual excellence." That ignorant slaves were inferior to educated masters was self-evident; the materials were not at hand for so complete a judgment as to whether they were in all cases inferior to ignorant white people; and it was difficult to maintain that no person having Negro blood was capable of intellectual effort. The difficulty with the argument of mental inferiority, as also with most of the Scriptural arguments, was that they applied equally to inferior white races or to inferior members of the Anglo-Saxon race.

The literature of the subject is full of descriptions of the favorable effect of slavery upon the Negro: slavery brought him out of savagery into the elevating influences of civilization, from heathendom into the light of salvation; it gave him care and medical advice in illness, and saved him from the mysterious diseases of the jungle. The Negroes "are undergoing the very best education which it is possible to give. . . . They are in the course of being taught habits of regular and patient industry"; slavery brought him into intimate personal relations with the white people, and even into warm friendships and affections with the master's family. "When I was a boy," says

Pollard, "I esteemed Tom to be the best friend I had in the world. . . . I had a great boyish fondness for him, gave him coppers, stole biscuits for him from the table, bought him a primer and taught him to read."

On good plantations there was indeed little suffering and much enjoyment. The owner was often a patriarch whose counsel and sympathy were freely sought by the slaves, to settle their disputes and to reconcile quarrels. To see the master come back was one of the great pleasures in distant and neglected plantations. The slaves were free from the responsibility of choosing their careers or insuring their own support. They had to be fed and clothed when northern laborers were thrown out of work by hard times, and they were cared for in sickness and in old age. So much did this happy state of things please the slave-holders that sometimes they wished it might be extended to the white people. "If some superior power should impose on the laborious poor of some other country—this as their unalterable condition—you shall be saved from the torturing anxiety concerning your own future support and that of your children."

If the ordinary slave was expected to be happy, much more the fortunate Negroes who were placed in positions of responsibility—the butler, the family cook, the old nurse, beloved and kissed by generations of white children—people who had the profoundest pride in "our family." These were the Negroes seen handsomely dressed on the streets of the cities, engaging in subscription assemblies, or even holding a little property recognized by the master as their own. A few such specially trusted slaves were actually managers of the master's estates, though a white overseer was always present.

With regard to the argument of the good of the Negro, two questions must be asked: were the Negroes really happy? and how far was happiness an evidence that slavery was a good thing for them? Upon the first point the evidence is overwhelming that many slaves were as well fed and housed as the poor whites of the neighborhood, and were unconscious of serious injustice. Even when torn from their kindred and sold to the dreaded "down river," the Negroes quickly recovered their cheerfulness. When the advocates of slavery insisted that their slaves were better off than agricultural laborers and factory operatives in England or even in the northern states, they could be contradicted. It was a time of misery and degradation in the factory population of England, and parliamentary inquiries revealed horrors which led to immediate reforms of the worst abuses; these evils served as a text for the south, but the reforms were not imitated.

The condition of the slave, in comparison with the free labor of the north, may be gauged by two lines of evidence: they were certainly no better off than the poor whites of that day, who were, and still are, far inferior in comfort to what the memory of man knows to have been the ordinary conditions of working-men in the north at that time. This indirect argument is confirmed by the testimony of Olmstead, a farmer, an employer of labor, and an economist, who asserts that hired laborers in the north could not be induced to remain a day in the conditions of the slaves on the best plantations. If the slaves were all happy and contented, it was a fair question why they desired to be free. It was, after all, an odd kind of happiness which no free Negro sought, and against which white men would have fought to their last breath.

Perhaps a more candid argument was the good of the white man. Slavery caused a larger production than could be had by any other form of labor; slavery was favorable to the increase of wealth, partly by emphasizing the sacredness of vested property, partly because slaves, unlike white laborers, were wealth, exchangeable from hand to hand, and partly because slavery favored the accumulation of capital in a few intelligent hands. That other countries and other states were prosperous without slavery, and had greater accumulations, was neither understood nor recognized by the south. Certainly the profits of slavery, down to 1860, built up very few fortunes, even measured in slaves; and neighboring parts of states of equal fertility, such as Kentucky and Ohio, or Maryland and Pennsylvania, showed a superiority of northern wealth of every sort, which is hard to account for on any other theory than a better type of labor. Whatever the advantages of slavery to the white race, they were not shared by the poor whites, who had no part in the annual produce of slavery, and for whose education and improvement nothing was spent out of that surplus; while they were exposed to the widespread contempt for labor with the hands, and to the degradation brought about by the nearness of a subject and immoral race.

The south was not a mercenary community, and was probably more affected by the argument of social well-being than by the argument of profit. It was generally believed in the south that slavery was necessary to relieve the whites from the danger of labor in a hot climate, and still more from the degradation of manual labor of any kind. Slavery also, by its discipline and the out-door habits of the whites, fostered a military spirit and thus provided for the maintenance of order and for future defence. Hints were not wanting that the masterful race might even organize a Negro army officered by white men which would be a protection against exterior enemies.

Slavery was also supposed to be favorable to the manners and breeding of the white race, and it was a notable fact that southerners who visited England were commonly received on better terms than northern gentlemen, while in the midst of all that was noxious in slavery there bloomed the lovely and hardy flower of southern womanhood. The seduction of white women was almost unknown in a society where black women were so easily accessible; and the whole force of society was brought to bear to protect white girls from the dark and earthly sides of life. On the plantations the mistresses were often springs of bounty, kindness, and genuine affection for the slaves.

The evil effects of slavery on young men even southern writers could not deny, for from childhood upward they were exposed to the basest temptations to temper and to morals. A state of things in which a boy expected and received the unquestionable obedience of every slave on the plantation was not favorable to self-control or moderation. The south abounded in brawls and homicides. The poor whites were often quarrelsome and murderous, and even in the highest circles affrays and duels were frequent. That slavery was the sole reason why so many of the Negroes, both male and female, were unchaste was a criticism that could not be sustained; but that slavery magnified the evil influences on the blacks and whites was so self-evident that a witness above cavil says: "We may and do acknowledge our guilt in the south, but not as slaveholders."

Another line of argument was that slavery was absolutely necessary for the safety of the whites. The fear of insurrection has been discussed elsewhere. One of the most frequent arguments in favor of slavery was the example of the fitful and disturbed republic of Haiti, which was accepted as proof positive that the Negroes, if set free, would never permit their masters to live, and that they could not maintain a civilized community of their own. Yet this argument was thought compatible with the theory that slavery was a necessary condition of a genuine republican government—for the masters. Thus Hammond, after paying his respects to the "nowhere accredited dogma of Mr. Jefferson that 'all men are born equal,'" argues that in the south the slave-holders "are both educated and independent in their curcumstances, while those who unfortunately are not so (that is, the poor whites), being still elevated far above the mass, are higher toned and more deeply interested in preserving a stable and well-ordered government."

The time even came when slavery was defended, not as a system that might, by an effort, be explained or justified, and still less as an institution that must remain simply because it was ineradicable, though that argument was sometimes heard. John C. Calhoun said, in his seat in the Senate, February 6, 1837: "But let me not be understood as admitting even by implication that the existing relations between the two races in the slave-holding states is an evil;—far otherwise, I hold it to be a good, as it had thus far proved to be to both." This was the theory eventually settled upon by practically the entire reasoning south. From this position the corollary naturally followed that so good a system ought to be extended into the northern states to replace the dangerous and destructive principle of political equality and universal suffrage. For example, in 1858, Senator Hammond said of the Mississippi Valley: "We own the most of that valley; . . . those who have settled above us, are now opposed to us, another generation will tell a different tale. They are ours by every law of nature. Slavery will go over every foot of this valley." Another corollary was that if slavery were endangered through the union of free and slave-holding states, the union must give way. "Come what may," wrote Hammond, in 1845, "we are firmly resolved that our system of domestic slavery shall stand."

\*       \*       \*       \*       \*

The arguments against slavery during this period were substantially the same as those used by the later abolitionists, and turned mainly on natural right, Christianity, humanity, the bad effects on the southern whites, and the injury to the whole Union. The argument of natural right was in accord with the text of all the slave-state constitutions and of the principles of government in the south. If there were any "inalienable" rights, property in man was impossible; to exclude Negroes from the principles of the Declaration of Independence they must be looked on as something else than men; and, therefore, pro-slavery writers sometimes abjured the Declaration of Independence as false and unthinkable. Human rights were expanding both in content and extent: Anglo-Saxons were being relieved from the arbitrary control of employers and jailers, and the alien was admitted to both the old and the new privileges. To hold that men could be excluded from the beneficent principles of free government because they were inferior to other men was a doctrine which struck at the basis of free government in America.

The anti-slavery argument from Christianity appealed to the principles of Christianity. Who was to shut the Negro out from the Golden Rule, from the glorious message of the gospel, from the building up of his own character through the grace of God? It was hard to escape from the dilemma that if the Negro was a hopeless pagan, incapable of civilization and of the Christian virtues, his presence was an unspeakable curse to the community; and if he was a man who could respond to the divine truths, who made the white man his keeper?

Africa might perhaps be held responsible for the low morals of the slave; but it was a fair argument that slavery denied both Christianity and civilization when it broke up families. To say that Negroes "are themselves both perverse and comparatively indifferent about this matter, . . . the Negroes forming those connections, knowing the chances of their premature dissolution," was to admit the damaging charge that slave life paralyzed the natural family instincts even of the savage.

The cruelty of slavery was also an unfailing argument; from the southern newspapers themselves, from every-day advertisements, from the reports of travellers, incidents could be gleaned which sickened and appalled the reader. The rejoinder that cruelties occurred constantly in northern institutions, such as jails, poor-houses, and orphan-asylums, was not conclusive; in the northern states public sentiment was watchful, and nobody felt that the whipping of defenceless people was necessary for the preservation of society.

Anti-slavery people took exceptions to the restrictions, legal and practical, on the intellectual improvement of the Negro, and to the cynical defences of those restrictions.

The anti-slavery argument covered not only the slaves, but the white men. It criticized the imperiousness of the master, the demoralizing effect of the relations of the sexes, the setting-up of the great slave-holding families as the head of social and political life, the effect on the poor whites of the degradation of labor. In the national government the influence of the great slave-holders was paramount during the whole period from 1815 to 1860. Of the five northern presidents—John Quincy Adams, Van Buren, Fillmore, Pierce, and Buchanan—not one stood against the pro-slavery men while in office. No recognized abolitionist and few out-and-out anti-slavery men, after 1840, were appointed to a foreign mission or a consulate, or a collectorate or important postmastership, or to the federal bench. In Congress, the southerners, by their abilities, their long terms of service, their habit of standing together, and their success in holding a part of the northern men, almost always had their will.

The most telling argument against slavery in the long-run was that it did not pay. Inasmuch as it did pay some people, as the wealth of the south increased from decade to decade, it was hard to make anybody believe that slavery was really a drain on the community. The census of 1850, the accumulated materials in journals like *Niles' Register* and *De Bow's Review*, and the criticisms of Olmsted brought out the fact that the south was gaining wealth slowly, and that in value of land, value of crops, value of buildings, miles of railroad, and extent of shipping, and also in schools, journals, and other evidences of intellectual growth, had fallen behind the rest of the Union. The anti-slavery people were sure that the only reason was that the north had free labor and the south had slave labor. The experience of the last forty years has shown that slavery was not a complete explanation. The Negro could not be made as efficient as the intelligent, well-rewarded, and productive labor of the north simply by setting him free. The south was equally mistaken in insisting that slavery was the only thing that made the Negro efficient; it was clinging to a cast-iron and rigid system which America had outgrown.

*In March, 1861, Mary Chesnut, a South Carolinian, turned to a visiting Englishwoman, as they passed a slave auction block, and said: "If you can stand that, no other Southern thing need choke you." The simple fact is that for somewhat more than two hundred years, the fate of the black man in America was to be defined under law as property, on a level with, as Lincoln once noted, "Hogs." It meant the black man, woman, or child—and these were generally defined as anyone with one-sixteenth Negro blood—lived utterly at the mercy of their owners. "Men and women are punished when their masters and mistresses are brutes, not when they do wrong," Mary Chesnut confided in her diary. She went on to draw a brutal indictment of the peculiar institution, the euphemism used by antebellum contemporaries to describe slavery. "Under slavery," she raged, "we live surrounded by prostitutes, yet an abandoned [white] woman is sent out of a decent house. Who thinks any worse of a Negro or mulatto woman for being a thing we can't name? God forgive us, but ours is a monstrous system, a wrong and an iniquity! Like the patriarchs of old, our men live all in one house with their wives and their concubines; and the mulattoes one sees in every family partly resemble the white children. Any lady is ready to tell you who is the father of all the mulatto children in everybody's household but her own." The ultimate indictment of slavery is that it meant the enslavement often of one's own children.*

*Whatever the law might define as the status of the slave, he was a human. No matter how tight the controls, there always existed the chance that they might seek to break the laws confining them. To reduce that possibility to a minimum, the Southerner, never fully free from the fear of a black insurrection, inflicted swift retribution for the smallest infraction. He also assumed the innate inferiority of the Negro, a condition that somehow made any brutality inflicted seem less inhumane. It was assumed that nothing could change the black's nature except "the lash, which is a great institution for stretching Negroes' skin and making them grow good." When Denmark Vesey resorted to conspiracy in 1822, Charleston swiftly reacted, although the proof was minimal and almost exclusively hearsay, and executed by hanging 35 suspected conspirators. A strand of terror underlay the system, the blacks kept in check with the lash and the whites using it with alacrity lest their bondsmen get out of hand.*

*Slavery gave a white man the right to a black man's labor; it was organized, legalized theft. It converted a living body into a source of income for the owner and a fund of capital that could be drawn upon by sale. The very nature of the institution precluded anything but the most elemental family life. To come to grips with the monstrous thing that slavery is has, until recently, been beyond the American historian. To face it fully is to come to grips with the most massive failure of American democracy. To avoid the task, historians have generally settled for some manner of apology. No historian is more typical of this tendency than Ulrich B. Phillips (1877-1934). Georgia born, a prolific producer of works on Southern history, he viewed the plantation as "a school constantly training and controlling pupils who were in a backward state of civilization." He further contended, "On the whole the plantations were the best schools yet invented for the mass training of that sort of inert and backward people which the bulk of the American Negroes represented." Unfortunately, for Phillip's analogy, the plantation school made no provision for graduation into freedom. Nor did his use of plantation records, pioneer though it might have been, preclude serious criticism, for as Richard Hofstadter noted, the plantations used were unrepresentative and, as a consequence, the portrait of slavery drawn emerged as flawed. And adding to the limitations of his approach was his underlying belief that what was at stake in the South was the preservation of its "Historic Civilization" from "Africanization and ensavagement." Phillips did draw attention to the humanizing tendencies of plantation racial relations, and he did define how Southerners of the plantation tradition differ from other Americans on race. "It is characteristic of Southerners in the plantation tradition," he wrote, "that they disesteem Negroes in the mass while esteeming them individually, whereas the rest of the world is inclined to dislike them individually while tending to champion their cause in the mass." There is a germ of truth in that judgment.*

# AMERICAN NEGRO SLAVERY

## by Ulrich Bonnell Phillips

Typical planters though facile in conversation seldom resorted to their pens. Few of them put their standards into writing except in the form of instructions to their stewards and overseers. These counsels of perfection, drafted in widely separated periods and localities, and varying much in detail, concurred strikingly in their main provisions. Their initial topic was usually the care of the slaves. Richard Corbin of Virginia wrote in 1759 for the guidance of his steward: "The care of negroes is the first thing to be recommended, that you give me timely notice of their wants that they may be provided with all necessarys. The breeding wenches more particularly you must instruct the overseers to be kind and indulgent to, and not force them when with child upon any service or hardship that will be injurious to them, . . . and the children to be well looked after, . . . and that none of them suffer in time of sickness for want of proper care." P. C. Weston of South Carolina wrote in 1856: "The proprietor, in the first place, wishes the overseer most distinctly to understand that his first object is to be, under all circumstances, the care and well being of the negroes. The proprietor is always ready to excuse such errors as may proceed from want of judgment; but he never can or will excuse any cruelty, severity or want of care towards the negroes. For the well being, however, of the negroes it is absolutely necessary to maintain obedience, order and discipline, to see that the tasks are punctually and carefully performed, and to conduct the business steadily and firmly, without weakness on the one hand or harshness on the other." Charles Manigault likewise required of his overseer in Georgia a pledge to treat his negroes "all with kindness and consideration in sickness and health." On J. W. Fowler's plantation in the Yazoo-Mississippi delta from which we have seen . . . such excellent records of cotton picking, the preamble to the rules framed in 1857 ran as follows: "The health, happiness, good discipline and obedience, good, sufficient and comfortable clothing, a sufficiency of good, wholesome and nutritious food for both man and beast being indispensably necessary to successful planting, as well as for reasonable dividends for the amount of capital invested, without saying anything about the Master's duty to his dependents, to himself, and his God, I do hereby establish the following rules and regulations for the management of my Prairie plantation, and require an observance of the same by any and all overseers I may at any time have in charge thereof."

Joseph A. S. Acklen had his own rules printed in 1861 for the information of applicants and the guidance of those who were employed as his overseers. His estate was one of the greatest in Louisiana, his residence one of the most pretentious, and his rules the most sharply phrased. They read in part: "Order and system must be the aim of everyone on this estate, and the maxim strictly pursued of a time for everything and everything done in its time, a place for everything and everything kept in its place, a rule for everything and everything done according to rule. In this way labor becomes easy and pleasant. No man can enforce a system of discipline unless he himself conforms strictly to rules. . . . No man should attempt to manage negroes who is not perfectly firm and fearless and [in] entire control of his temper."

James H. Hammond's "plantation manual" which is the fullest of such documents available, began with the subject of the crop, only to subordinate it at once to the care of the slaves and outfit: "A good crop means one that is good taking into consideration everything, negroes, land, mules, stock, fences, ditches, farming utensils, etc., etc., all of which must be kept up and improved in value. The effort must therefore not be merely to make so many cotton bales or such an amount of other produce, but as much as can be made without interrupting the steady increase in value of the rest of the property. . . . There should be an increase in number and improvement in condition of negroes."

For the care of the sick, of course, all these planters were solicitous. Acklen, Manigault and Weston provided that mild cases be prescribed for by the overseer in the master's absence, but that for any serious illness a doctor be summoned. One of Telfair's women was a semi-professional midwife and general practitioner, permitted by her master to serve blacks and whites in the neighborhood. For home needs Telfair wrote of her: "Elsey is the doctoress of the plantation. In case of extraordinary illness, when she thinks she can do no more for the sick, you will employ a physician." Hammond, however, was such a devotee of homeopathy that in the lack of an available physician of that school he was his own practitioner. He wrote in his manual: "No negro will be allowed to remain at his own house when sick, but must be confined to the hospital. Every reasonable complaint must be promptly attended to; and with any marked or general symptom of sickness, however trivial, a negro may lie up a day or so at least. . . . Each case has to be examined carefully by the master or overseer to ascertain the disease. The remedies next are to be chosen with the utmost discrimination; . . . the directions for treatment, diet, etc., most implicitly followed; the effects and changes cautiously observed. . . . In cases where there is the slightest uncertainty, the books must be taken to the bedside and a careful and thorough examination of the case and comparison of remedies made before administering them. The overseer must record in the prescription book every dose of medicine administered." Weston said he would never grudge a doctor's bill, however large; but he was anxious to prevent idleness under pretence of illness. "Nothing," said he, "is so subversive of discipline, or so unjust, as to allow people to sham, for this causes the well-disposed to do the work of the lazy."

Pregnancy, childbirth and the care of children were matters of special concern. Weston wrote: "The pregnant women are always to do some work up to the time of their confinement, if it is only walking into the field and staying there. If they are sick, they are to go to the hospital and stay there until it is pretty certain their time is near." "Lying-in women are to be attended by the midwife as long as is necessary, and by a woman put to nurse them for a fortnight. They will remain at the negro houses for four weeks, and then will work two weeks on the highland. In some cases, however, it is necessary to allow them to lie up longer. The health of many women has been ruined by want of care in this particular." Hammond's rules were as follows: "Sucklers are not required to leave their homes until sunrise, when they leave their children at the children's house before going to field. The period of suckling is twelve months. Their work lies always within half a mile of the quarter. They are required to be cool before commencing to suckle—to wait fifteen minutes at least in summer, after reaching the children's house before nursing. It is the duty of the nurse to see that none are heated when nursing, as well as of the overseer and his wife occasionally to do so. They are allowed forty-five minutes at each nursing to be with their children. They return three times a day until their children are eight months old—in the middle of the forenoon, at noon, and in the middle of the afternoon; till the twelfth month but twice a day, missing at noon; during the twelfth month at noon only. . . . The amount of work done by a suckler is about three fifths of that done by a full hand, a little increased toward the last. . . . Pregnant women at five months are put in the sucklers' gang. No plowing or lifting must be required of them. Sucklers, old, infirm and pregnant receive the same allowances as full-work hands. The regular plantation midwife shall attend all women in confinement. Some other woman learning the art is usually with her during delivery. The confined woman lies up one month, and the midwife remains in constant attendance for seven days. Each woman on confinement has a bundle given her containing articles of clothing for the infant, pieces of cloth and rag, and some nourishment, as sugar, coffee, rice and flour for the mother."

The instructions with one accord required that the rations issued to the Negroes be never skimped. Corbin wrote, "They ought to have their belly full, but care must be taken with this plenty that no waste is committed." Acklen, closely followed by Fowler, ordered his overseer to "see that their necessities be supplied, that their food and clothing be good and sufficient, their houses comfortable; and be kind and attentive to them in sickness and old age." And further: "There will be stated hours for the negroes to breakfast and dine (in the field), and those hours must be regularly observed. The manager will frequently inspect the meals as they are brought by the cook—see that they have been properly prepared, and that vegetables be at all times served with the meat and bread." At the same time he forbade his slaves to use ardent spirits or to have such about their houses. Weston wrote: "Great care should be taken that the negroes should never have less than their regular allowance. In all cases of doubt, it should be given in favor of the largest quantity. The measure should not be struck, but rather heaped up over. None but provisions of the best quality should be used." Telfair specified as follows: "The allowance for every grown negro, however old and good for nothing, and every young one that works in the field, is a peck of corn each week and a pint of salt, and a piece of meat, not exceeding fourteen pounds, per month. . . . The suckling children, and all other small ones who do not work in the field, draw a half allowance of corn and salt. . . . Feed everything plentifully, but waste nothing." He added that beeves were to be killed for the negroes in July, August and September. Hammond's allowance to each working hand was a heaping peck of meal and three pounds of bacon or pickled pork every week. In the winter, sweet potatoes were issued when preferred, at the rate of a bushel of them in lieu of the peck of meal; and fresh beef, mutton or pork, at increased weights, were to be substituted for the salt pork from time to time. The ditchers and drivers were to have extra allowances in meat and molasses. Furthermore, "Each ditcher receives every night, when ditching, a dram [jigger] consisting of two-thirds whiskey and one-third water, with as much asafoetida as it will absorb, and several strings of red peppers added in the barrel. The dram is a large wine-glass full. In cotton picking time when sickness begins to be prevalent, every field hand gets a dram in the morning before leaving for the field. After a soaking rain all exposed to it get a dram before changing their clothes; also those exposed to the dust from the sheller and fan in corn shelling, on reaching the quarter at night; or anyone at any time required to keep watch in the night. Drams are not given as rewards, but only as medicinal. From the second hoeing, or early in May, every work hand who uses it gets an occasional allowance of tobacco, about one sixth of a pound, usually after some general operation, as a hoeing, plowing, etc. This is continued until their crops are gathered, when they can provide for themselves." The families, furthermore, shared in the distribution of the plantation's peanut crop every fall. Each child was allowed one third as much meal and meat as was given to each field hand, and an abundance of vegetables to be cooked with their meat. The cooking and feeding was to be done at the day nursery. For breakfast they were to have hominy and milk and cold corn bread; for dinner, vegetable soup and dumplings or bread; and cold bread or potatoes were to be kept on hand for demands between meals. They were also to have molasses once or twice a week. Each child was provided with a pan and spoon in charge of the nurse.

Hammond's clothing allowance was for each man in the fall two cotton shirts, a pair of woolen pants and a woolen jacket, and in the spring two cotton shirts and two pairs of cotton pants, with privilege of substitution when desired; for each woman six yards of woolen cloth and six yards of cotton cloth in the fall, six yards of light and six of heavy cotton cloth in the spring, with needles, thread and buttons on each occasion. Each worker was to have a pair of stout shoes in the fall, and a heavy blanket every third year. Children's cloth allowances were proportionate and their mothers were required to dress them in clean clothes twice a week.

In the matter of sanitation, Acklen directed the overseer to see that the negroes kept clean in person, to inspect their houses at least once a week and especially during the summer, to examine their bedding and see to its being well aired, to require that their clothes be mended, "and everything attended to which conduces to their comfort and happiness." In these regards, as in various others, Fowler incorporated Acklen's rules in his own, almost verbatim. Hammond scheduled an elaborate cleaning of the houses every spring and fall. The houses were to be completely emptied and their contents sunned, the walls and floors were to be scrubbed, the mattresses to be emptied and stuffed with fresh hay or shucks, the yards swept and the ground under the houses sprinkled with lime. Furthermore, every house was to be whitewashed inside and out once a year; and the negroes must appear once a week in clean clothes, "and every negro habitually uncleanly in person must be washed and scrubbed by order of the overseer—the driver and two other negroes officiating."

As to schedules of work, the Carolina and Georgia lowlanders dealt in tasks; all the rest in hours. Telfair wrote briefly: "The negroes to be tasked when the work allows it. I require a reasonable day's work, well done—the task to be regulated by the state of the ground and the strength of the negro." Weston wrote with more elaboration: "A task is as much work as the meanest full hand can do in nine hours, working industriously. . . . This task is never to be increased, and no work is to be done over task except under the most urgent necessity; which over-work is to be reported to the proprietor, who will pay for it. No negro is to be put into a task which (he) cannot finish with tolerable ease. It is a bad plan to punish for not finishing tasks; it is subversive of discipline to leave tasks unfinished, and contrary to justice to punish for what cannot be done. In nothing does a good manager so much excel a bad as in being able to discern what a hand is capable of doing, and in never attempting to make him do more." In Hammond's schedule the first horn was blown an hour before daylight as a summons for work-hands to rise and do their cooking and other preparations for the day. Then at the summons of the plow driver, at first break of day, the plowmen went to the stables whose doors the overseer opened. At the second horn, "just at good daylight," the hoe gang set out for the field. At half past eleven the plowmen carried their mules to a shelter house in the fields, and at noon the hoe hands laid off for dinner, to resume work at one o'clock, except that in hot weather the intermission was extended to a maximum of three and a half hours. The plowmen led the way home by a quarter of an hour in the evening, and the hoe hands followed at sunset. "No work," said Hammond, "must ever be required after dark." Acklen contented himself with specifying that "the negroes must all rise at the ringing of the first bell in the morning, and retire when the last bell rings at night, and not leave their houses after that hour unless on business or called." Fowler's rule was of the same tenor: "All hands should be required to retire to rest and sleep at a suitable hour and permitted to remain there until such time as it will be necessary to get out in time to reach their work by the time they can see well how to work."

Telfair, Fowler and Hammond authorized the assignment of gardens and patches to such slaves as wanted to cultivate them at leisure times. To prevent these from becoming a cloak for thefts from the planter's crops, Telfair and Fowler forbade the growing of cotton in the slaves' private patches, and Hammond forbade both cotton and corn. Fowler specifically gave his negroes the privilege of marketing their produce and poultry "at suitable leisure times." Hammond had a rule permitting each work hand to go to Augusta on some Sunday after harvest; but for some reason he noted in pencil below it: "This is objectionable and must be altered." Telfair and Weston directed that their slaves be given passes on application, authorizing them to go at proper times to places in the neighborhood. The negroes, however, were to be at home by the time of the curfew horn about nine o'clock each night. Mating with slaves on other plantations was discouraged as giving occasion for too much journeying.

"Marriage is to be encouraged," wrote Hammond, "as it adds to the comfort, happiness and health of those who enter upon it, besides insuring a greater increase. Permission must always be obtained from the master before marriage, but no marriage will be allowed with negroes not belonging to the master. When sufficient cause can be shewn on either side, a marriage may be annulled; but the offending party must be severely punished. Where both are in wrong, both must be punished, and if they insist on separating must have a hundred lashes apiece. After such a separation, neither can marry again for three years. For first marriage a bounty of $5.00, to be invested in household articles, or an equivalent of articles, shall be given. If either has been married before, the bounty shall be $2.50. A third marriage shall be not allowed but in extreme cases, and in such cases, or where both have been married before, no bounty will be given."

"Christianity, humanity and order elevate all, injure none," wrote Fowler, "whilst infidelity, selfishness and disorder curse some, delude others and degrade all. I therefore want all of my people encouraged to cultivate religious feeling and morality, and punished for inhumanity to their children or stock, for profanity, lying and stealing." And again: "I would that every human being have the gospel preached to them in its original purity and simplicity. It therefore devolves upon me to have these dependants properly instructed in all that pertains to the salvation of their souls. To this end whenever the services of a suitable person can be secured, have them instructed in these things. In view of the fanaticism of the age, it behooves the master or overseer to be present on all such occasions. They should be instructed on Sundays in the day time if practicable; if not, then on Sunday night." Acklen wrote in his usual peremptory tone: "No negro preachers but my own will be permitted to preach or remain on any of my places. The regularly appointed minister for my places must preach on Sundays during daylight, or quit. The negroes must not be suffered to continue their night meetings beyond ten o'clock." Telfair in his rules merely permitted religious meetings on Saturday nights and Sunday mornings. Hammond encouraged his negroes to go to church on Sundays, but permitted no exercises on the plantation beyond singing and praying. He, and many others, encouraged his negroes to bring him their complaints against drivers and overseers, and even against their own ecclesiastical authorities in the matter of interference with recreations.

Fighting among the negroes was a common bane of planters. Telfair prescribed: "If there is any fighting on the plantation, whip all engaged in it, for no matter what the cause may have been, all are in the wrong." Weston wrote: "Fighting, particularly amongst women, and obscene or abusive language, is to be always rigorously punished."

"Punishment must never be cruel or abusive," wrote Acklen, closely followed by Fowler, "for it is absolutely mean and unmanly to whip a negro from mere passion and malice, and any man who can do so is utterly unfit to have control of negroes; and if ever any of my negroes are cruelly or inhumanly treated, bruised, maimed or otherwise injured, the overseer will be promptly discharged and his salary withheld." Weston recommended the lapse of a day between the discovery of an offense and the punishment, and he restricted the overseer's power in general to fifteen lashes. He continued:

"Confinement (not in the stocks) is to be preferred to whipping; but the stoppage of Saturday's allowance, and doing whole task on Saturday, will suffice to prevent ordinary offences. Special care must be taken to prevent any indecency in punishing women. No driver or other negro is to be allowed to punish any person in any way except by order of the overseer and in his presence." And again: "Every person should be made perfectly to understand what they are punished for, and should be made to perceive that they are not punished in anger or through caprice. All abusive language or violence of demeanor should be avoided; they reduce the man who uses them to a level with the negro, and are hardly ever forgotten by those to whom they are addressed." Hammond directed that the overseer "must never threaten a negro, but punish offences immediately on knowing them; otherwise he will soon have runaways." As a schedule he wrote: "The following is the order in which offences must be estimated and punished: 1st, running away; 2d, getting drunk or having spirits; 3d, stealing hogs; 4th, stealing; 5th, leaving plantation without permission; 6th, absence from house after horn-blow at night; 7th, unclean house or person; 8th, neglect of tools; 9th, neglect of work. The highest punishment must not exceed a hundred lashes in one day, and to that extent only in extreme cases. The whip lash must be one inch in width, or a strap of one thickness of leather 1½ inches in width, and never severely administered. In general fifteen to twenty lashes will be a sufficient flogging. The hands in every case must be secured by a cord. Punishment must always be given calmly, and never when angry or excited." Telfair was as usual terse: "No negro to have more than fifty lashes for any offence, no matter how great the crime." Manigault said nothing of punishments in his general instructions, but sent special directions when a case of incorrigibility was reported: "You had best think carefully respecting him, and always keep in mind the important old plantation maxim, viz: 'never to threaten a negro,' or he will do as you and I would when at school—he will run. But with such a one, . . . if you wish to make an example of him, take him down to the Savannah jail and give him prison discipline, and by all means solitary confinement, for three weeks, when he will be glad to get home again. . . . Mind then and tell him that you and he are quits, that you will never dwell on old quarrels with him, that he has now a clear track before him and all depends on himself, for he now sees how easy it is to fix 'a bad disposed nigger.' Then give my compliments to him and tell him that you wrote me of his conduct, and say if he don't change for the better I'll sell him to a slave trader who will send him to New Orleans, where I have already sent several of the gang for misconduct, or their running away for no cause." In one case Manigault lost a slave by suicide in the river when a driver brought him up for punishment but allowed him to run before it was administered.

As to rewards, Hammond was the only one of these writers to prescribe them definitely. His head driver was to receive five dollars, the plow driver three dollars, and the ditch driver and stock minder one dollar each every Christmas day, and the nurse a dollar and the midwife two dollars for every actual increase of two on the place. Further, "for every infant thirteen months old and in sound health, that has been properly attended to, the mother shall receive a muslin or calico frock."

"The head driver," Hammond wrote, "is the most important negro on the plantation, and is not required to work like other hands. He is to be treated with more respect than any other negro by both master and overseer. . . . He is to be required to maintain proper discipline at all times; to see that no negro idles or does bad work in the field, and to punish it with discretion on the spot. . . . He is a confidential servant, and may be a guard against any excesses or omissions of the overseer." Weston, forbidding his drivers to inflict punishments except at the overseer's order and in the presence, described their functions as the maintenance of quiet in the quarter and of discipline at large, the starting of the slaves to the fields each morning, the assignment and supervision of tasks, and the inspection of "such things as the overseer only generally superintends." Telfair informed his overseer: "I have no driver. You are to task the negroes yourself, and each negro is responsible to you for his own work, and nobody's else."

Of the master's own functions Hammond wrote in another place: "A planter should have all his work laid out, days, weeks, months, seasons and years ahead, according to the nature of it. He must go from job to job without losing a moment in turning round, and he must have all the parts of his work so arranged that due proportion of attention may be bestowed upon each at the proper time. More is lost by doing work out of season, and doing it better or worse than is requisite, than can readily be supposed. Negroes are harassed by it, too, instead of being indulged; so are mules, and everything else. A halting, vacillating, undecided course, now idle, now overstrained, is more fatal on a plantation than in any other kind of business—ruinous as it is in any."

In the overseer all the virtues of a master were desired, with a deputy's obedience added. Corbin enjoined upon his staff that they "attend their business with diligence, keep the negroes in good order, and enforce obedience by the example of their own industry, which is a more effectual method in every respect than hurry and severity. The ways of industry," he continued, "are constant and regular, not to be in a hurry at one time and do nothing at another, but to be always usefully and steadily employed. A man who carries on business in this manner will be prepared for every incident that happens. He will see what work may be proper at the distance of some time and be gradually and leisurely preparing for it. By this foresight he will never be in confusion himself, and his business, instead of a labor, will be a pleasure to him." Weston wrote: "The proprietor wishes particularly to impress upon the overseer the criterions by which he will judge of his usefullness and capacity. First, by the general well-being of all the negroes; their cleanly appearance, respectful manners, active and vigorous obedience; their completion of their tasks well and early; the small amount of punishment; the excess of births over deaths; the small number of persons in hospital; and the health of the children. Secondly, the condition and fatness of the cattle and mules; the good repair of all the fences and buildings, harness, boats, flats and ploughs; more particularly the good order of the banks and

trunks, and the freedom of the fields from grass and volunteer [rice].
Thirdly, the amount and quality of the rice and provision crops. . . . The
overseer is expressly forbidden from three things, viz.: bleeding, giving spirits
to any negro without a doctor's order, and letting any negro on the place
have or keep any gun, powder or shot." One of Acklen's prohibitions upon
his overseers was: "Having connection with any of my female servants will
most certainly be visited with a dismissal from my employment, and no
excuse can or will be taken."

Hammond described the functions as follows: "The overseer will never
be expected to work in the field, but he must always be with the hands when
not otherwise engaged in the employer's business. . . . The overseer must
never be absent a single night, nor an entire day, without permission previously obtained. Whenever absent at church or elsewhere he must be on the
plantation by sundown without fail. He must attend every night and morning at the stables and see that the mules are watered, cleaned and fed, and
the doors locked. He must keep the stable keys at night, and all the keys,
in a safe place, and never allow anyone to unlock a barn, smoke-house or
other depository of plantation stores but himself. He must endeavor, also,
to be with the plough hands always at noon." He must also see that the
negroes are out promptly in the morning, and in their houses after curfew,
and must show no favoritism among the negroes. He must carry on all experiments as directed by the employer, and use all new implements and
methods which the employer may determine upon; and he must keep a full
plantation diary and make monthly inventories. Finally, "The negroes must
be made to obey and to work, which may be done, by an overseer who
attends regularly to his business, with very little whipping. Much whipping
indicates a bad tempered or inattentive manager, and will not be allowed."
His overseer might quit employment on a month's notice, and might be discharged without notice. Acklen's dicta were to the same general effect.

As to the relative importance of the several functions of an overseer, all
these planters were in substantial agreement. As Fowler put it: "After taking
proper care of the negroes, stock, etc., the next most important duty of the
overseer is to make, if practicable, a sufficient quantity of corn, hay, fodder,
meat, potatoes and other vegetables for the consumption of the plantation,
and then as much cotton as can be made by requiring good and reasonable
labor of operatives and teams." Likewise Henry Laurens, himself a prosperous planter of the earlier time as well as a statesman, wrote to an overseer
of whose heavy tasking he had learned: "Submit to make less rice and keep
my negroes at home in some degree of happiness in preference to large
crops acquired by rigour and barbarity to those poor creatures." And to
a new incumbent: "I have now to recommend to you the care of my
negroes in general, but particularly the sick ones. Desire Mrs. White not
to be sparing of red wine for those who have the flux or bad loosenesses;
let them be well attended night and day, and if one wench is not sufficient
add another to nurse them. With the well ones use gentle means mixed with
easy authority first—if that does not succeed, make choice of the most
stubborn one or two and chastise them severely but properly and with

mercy, that they may be convinced that the end of correction is to be amendment." Again, alluding to one of his slaves who had been gathering the pennies of his fellows: "Amos has a great inclination to turn rum merchant. If his confederate comes to that plantation, I charge you to discipline him with thirty-nine sound lashes and turn him out of the gate and see that he goes quite off."

The published advice of planters to their fellows was quite in keeping with these instructions to overseers. About 1809, for example, John Taylor, of Carolina, the leading Virginian advocate of soil improvement in his day, wrote of the care and control of slaves as follows: "The addition of comfort to mere necessaries is a price paid by the master for the advantages he will derive from binding his slave to his service by a ligament stronger than chains, far beneath their value in a pecuniary point of view; and he will moreover gain a stream of agreeable reflections throughout life, which will cost him nothing." He recommended fireproof brick houses, warm clothing, and abundant, varied food. Customary plenty in meat and vegetables, he said, would not only remove occasions for pilfering, but would give the master effective power to discourage it; for upon discovering the loss of any goods by theft he might put his whole force of slaves upon a limited diet for a time and thus suggest to the thief that on any future occasion his fellows would be under pressure to inform on him as a means of relieving their own privations. "A daily allowance of cyder," Taylor continued, "will extend the success of this system for the management of slaves, and particularly its effect of diminishing corporal punishments. But the reader is warned that a stern authority, strict discipline and complete subordination must be combined with it to gain any success at all."

Another Virginian's essay, of 1834, ran as follows: Virginia negroes are generally better tempered than any other people; they are kindly, grateful, attached to persons and places, enduring and patient in fatigue and hardship, contented and cheerful. Their control should be uniform and consistent, not an alternation of rigor and laxity. Punishment for real faults should be invariable but moderate. "The best evidence of the good management of slaves is the keeping up of good discipline with little or no punishment." The treatment should be impartial except for good conduct which should bring rewards. Praise is often a better cure for laziness than stripes. The manager should know the temper of each slave. The proud and high spirited are easily handled: "Your slow and sulky negro, although he may have an even temper, is the devil to manage. The negro women are all harder to manage than the men. The only way to get along with them is by kind words and flattery. If you want to cure a sloven, give her something nice occasionally to wear, and praise her up to the skies whenever she has on anything tolerably decent." Eschew suspicion, for it breeds dishonesty. Promote harmony and sound methods among your neighbors. "A good disciplinarian in the midst of bad managers of slaves cannot do much; and without discipline there cannot be profit to the master or comfort to the slaves." Feed and clothe your slaves well. The best preventive of theft is plenty of pork. Let them have poultry and gardens and fruit trees to attach them to their houses and promote amenability. "The greatest bar to good discipline in Virginia is the number of grog shops in every farmer's neighborhood." There is no severity in the state, and there will be no occasion for it again if the fanatics will only let us alone.

An essay written after long experience by Robert Collins, of Macon, Georgia, which was widely circulated in the 'fifties, was in the same tone: "The best interests of all parties are promoted by a kind and liberal treatment on the part of the owner, and the requirement of proper discipline and strict obedience on the part of the slave. . . . Every attempt to force the slave beyond the limits of reasonable service by cruelty or hard treatment, so far from extorting more work, only tends to make him unprofitable, unmanageable, a vexation and a curse." The quarters should be well shaded, the houses free of the ground, well ventilated, and large enough for comfort; the bedding and blankets fully adequate. "In former years the writer tried many ways and expedients to economize in the provision of slaves by using more of the vegetable and cheap articles of diet, and less of the costly and substantial. But time and experience have fully proven the error of a stinted policy. . . . The allowance now given per week to each hand . . . is five pounds of good clean bacon and one quart of molasses, with as much good bread as they require; and in the fall, or sickly season of the year, or on sickly places, the addition of one pint of strong coffee, sweetened with sugar, every morning before going to work." The slaves may well have gardens, but the assignment of patches for market produce too greatly "encourages a traffic on their own account, and presents a temptation and opportunity, during the process of gathering, for an unscrupulous fellow to mix a little of his master's produce with his own. It is much better to give each hand whose conduct has been such as to merit it an equivalent in money at the end of the year; it is much less trouble, and more advantageous to both parties." Collins further advocated plenty of clothing, moderate hours, work by tasks in cotton picking and elsewhere when feasible, and firm though kindly discipline. "Slaves," he said, "have no respect or affection for a master who indulges them over much. . . . Negroes are by nature tyrannical in their dispositions, and if allowed, the stronger will abuse the weaker, husbands will often abuse their wives and mothers their children, so that it becomes a prominent duty of owners and overseers to keep peace and prevent quarrelling and disputes among them; and summary punishment should follow any violation of this rule. Slaves are also a people that enjoy religious privileges. Many of them place much value upon it; and to every reasonable extent that advantage should be allowed them. They are never injured by preaching, but thousands become wiser and better people and more trustworthy servants by their attendance at church. Religious services should be provided and encouraged on every plantation. A zealous and vehement style, both in doctrine and manner, is best adapted to their temperament. They are good believers in mysteries and miracles, ready converts, and adhere with much pertinacity to their opinions when formed." It is clear that Collins had observed plantation negroes long and well.

Advice very similar to the foregoing examples was also printed in the form of manuals at the front of blank books for the keeping of plantation records; and various planters described their own methods in operation as based on the same principles. One of these living at Chunnennuggee, Alabama, signing himself "N.B.P.," wrote in 1852 an account of the problems he had met and the solutions he had applied. Owning some 150 slaves, he had lived away from his plantation until about a decade prior to this writing; but in spite of careful selection he could never get an overseer combining the qualities necessary in a good manager. "They were generally on extremes; those celebrated for making large crops were often too severe, and did everything by coercion. Hence turmoil and strife ensued. The negroes were ill treated and ran away. On the other hand, when he employed a good-natured man there was a want of proper discipline; the negroes became unmanageable and, as a natural result, the farm was brought into debt." The owner then entered residence himself and applied methods which resulted in contentment, health and prolific increase among the slaves, and in consistently good crops. The men were supplied with wives at home so far as was practicable; each family had a dry and airy house to itself, with a poultry house and a vegetable garden behind; the rations issued weekly were three and a half pounds of bacon to each hand over ten years old, together with a peck of meal, or more if required; the children in the day nursery were fed from the master's kitchen with soup, milk, bacon, vegetables and bread; the hands had three suits of working clothes a year; the women were given time off for washing, and did their mending in bad weather; all hands had to dress up and go to church on Sunday when preaching was near; and a clean outfit of working clothes was required every Monday. The chief distinction of this plantation, however, lay in its device for profit sharing. To each slave was assigned a half-acre plot with the promise that if he worked with diligence in the master's crop the whole gang would in turn be set to work his crop. This was useful in preventing night and Sunday work by the negroes. The proceeds of their crops, ranging from ten to fifty dollars, were expended by the master at their direction for Sunday clothing and other supplies. On a sugar plantation visited by Olmsted a sum of as many dollars as there were hogsheads in the year's crop was distributed among the slaves every Christmas.

～⸰⸱⸰～

JOHN C. CALHOUN *has provoked different descriptions from the historians. For one historian he was the "cast-iron man," for another an "opportunist," and for even another "The Marx of the Master Class." His major biographer, Charles M. Wiltse, in a three-volume work traces the South Carolinian's journey from "nationalist" to "nullifier" to "sectionalist." And as Wiltse notes, the shifts had their roots in the changing circumstances of his home state South Carolina. It was in this state and, in particular, in its Charleston metropolis that the cutting edge of disunionist sentiment was hewn razor sharp. All of Calhoun's political speculations and his political maneuverings fall into perspective when examined against the needs of the Palmetto State.*

*The root of South Carolina's problems has usually been designated as economic, a conclusion that has been reinforced by the strength of the state's protest against the tariff. And there is ample evidence that the up-state cotton planters found the competition of the newer lands in Alabama and Mississippi paricularly hard. This is not the whole story, for as a young historian, William W. Freehling, has recently noted the tidewater rice regions knew a large prosperity. Economic conditions are not adequate to explain the state's response. John C. Calhoun put his finger on the key when he declared, "The difficulty is in the diversity of the races. So strongly drawn is the line between the two in consequence, and so strengthened by the force of habit and education, that it is impossible for them to exist to-gether in the community, where their numbers are so nearly equal as in the slaveholding states, under any other relation than that which now exists." The problem was doubly acute in a state like South Carolina where the slaves outnumbered whites by a proportion of about 58 to 42 percent. It is hardly surprising to find that the state's authorities took a dim view of any criticism of slavery. Within the state, the need to guard against Negro in-subordination was deemed "paramount to all laws, all treaties, all constitu-tions." Such precedence arose "from the supreme and permanent law of self-preservation." The difficulty of maintaining an homogeneity of view on slavery arose when attacks were launched from outside the state. It was this aspect of abolitionism that struck the deepest chord of fear within the Cotton Kingdom.*

*To secure the South against an attack upon its peculiar institution, Calhoun insisted that the states as prior to the federal government possessed sovereign power, and that the purpose of the Washington government was to meet specific needs, and an effort to exceed these bounds could be met by a state's nullifying a federal act which exceeded the limited power assigned the central government. Underscoring his sense of the federal power was a sharp awareness that the South fell steadily behind the North. He meant to circumscribe the rights of a majority to impose its will upon a minority, and he made the powerful point that the Federal Constitution was hedged around with restraints on majority decision. Once he had vested minority rights with negative sovereignty, he set into motion increasingly strong Southern demands for a federal government which would actively defend slavery as an absolute good. And from there, it was a small step to George Fitzhugh's perverse declaration: "Liberty for the few—Slavery, in every form, for the mass!"*

*Charles Edward Merriam (1874-1953) combined a career in political sci-ence and history and took particular care to emphasize the interrelationship between the practical and theoretical in politics. Between 1900 and 1940, he taught Political Science at the University of Chicago while finding much time for public service on both the local and national level.*

# A HISTORY OF AMERICAN POLITICAL THEORIES

## by Charles Edward Merriam

The finally accepted statement of the states-rights doctrine was made by the great political philosopher of the South, John C. Calhoun. The work in which his ideas are most systematically expressed is, *A Disquisition on Government*, accompanied by *A Discourse on the Constitution and Government of the United States*, one of the ablest treatises on political theory that appeared in the first half of the last century. This, taken in connection with the numerous public utterances of Calhoun, affords a basis for the study of his political philosophy.

An analysis will first be made of his theory of nullification, and then of the doctrine of secession with which he is associated. The inquiry is directed in the first place, then, to the general attitude of Calhoun toward the fundamental question of the origin of the political society.

Calhoun condemned in no uncertain terms the time-honored hypothesis of a precivil "state of nature" and the origin of government by means of a contract. This had been the theory of the revolutionists in the seventeenth and eighteenth centuries, and continued to be the prevailing American doctrine even in the nineteenth. In fact, this hypothesis of an original "state of nature" and the contractual character of government had been one of the leading principles of "the Fathers"; the theory of contract had even been extended from individuals to the relations between the states; it was recognized in many of the state constitutions; adopted by men of all parties, aristocrats as well as democrats; and was generally accepted as the correct theory of the origin of political institutions. In the politics of Calhoun, however, there was no place for the assumptions of the *Naturrecht* philosophy, and he had no sympathy with this interpretation of the nature of government. The "state of nature" he regarded as a mere fiction, an unwarrantable hypothesis. "Instead of being the natural state of man, it is, of all conceivable states, the most opposed to his nature, most repugnant to his feelings, and most incompatible with his wants. His natural state is the social and political."

Government is not artificial and unnatural, but perfectly natural in the sense that it is necessary to the development and perfection of human powers. Government is not a matter of choice, depending for its origin and continuance on the caprice of the individual; on the contrary, it is a primary necessity of man, and, "like breathing, it is not permitted to depend on our volition." There are, reasons Calhoun, two fundamental elements in the constitution of man: one the selfish, the other the social instinct or tendency. Of these two, however, the stronger is the selfish tendency, and as a consequence, there arises conflict between individuals which must be in some way controlled. The instrument by means of which this control is effected is government—a necessity arising out of the essential nature of man. *Society* is necessary to man; *government* is necessary to society. But government itself contains the germ of evil, and must in its turn be controlled or balanced. To this end is erected a *constitution* intended to hold in check the destructive tendencies found in government. This constitution bears the same relation to government that government bears to society; as government restrains the selfish tendencies of the individual, so the constitution checks the selfish tendencies of the government. There is this difference to be noted, however, that government is of divine origin, whereas the constitution is a human device and construction. There *must* be a government; there *may* be a constitution.

The organization of the constitution Calhoun regards as one of the greatest of political problems. How can the government be given the powers necessary and yet be restrained from oppressing the members of the society? Calhoun's answer to this perennial problem is that there must be created an *organism* "by which resistance may be systematically and peaceably made on the part of the ruled to oppression and abuse of power on the part of the rulers." This result may be effected by establishing the responsibility of the rulers to the ruled through the exercise of the right of suffrage—the primary principle in the establishment of constitutional government. Yet this alone is inadequate to afford the necessary protection; "it only changes the seat of authority, without counteracting, in the least, the tendency of the government to oppression and abuse of its powers." We are still confronted by the imminent danger that the majority of the electors will prove to be tyrannical and oppress the weaker minority as intolerably as the most irresponsible government.

Calhoun enters, therefore, on a vigorous polemic against the despotism of the majority. He asserts that the tendency of the majority is to assume all the rights belonging to the people. Although only a fraction, they assume to be and act as the whole people; while on the other hand, the minority is treated as if it were nothing at all. Again, Calhoun points out the probability that great political parties will arise, that their organization will become increasingly centralized, and that continually stricter party discipline will prevail. Offices will come to be regarded as the legitimate reward of the victorious party, while recognition of other than partisans will be excluded. Party strife will become fiercer and fiercer as it becomes more factional, and will finally result in an appeal to force and the establishment of absolute government.

Nor is there any way by which this inherent tendency may be effectively restrained. It may be urged that a sufficient check is found in the power of public opinion to keep party spirit within reasonable limits. But to this Calhoun is not ready to assent. He concedes the great strength of public sentiment, particularly that of modern times in its highly developed form, but does not consider it even yet as an effective barrier against the tendencies of the majority. Public opinion itself may be just as despotic as the majority party, just as radical and unreasonable, and consequently just as uncertain a defender of the rights of the minority. Nor are constitutional restrictions or the separation of powers of sufficient force against the majority. All restrictions must be interpreted, all requirements carried out, by the prevailing party. The minority is helpless and must submit to any adjustment of constitutional balances that may commend itself to the majority.

The "tyranny of the majority" is, then, one of the fundamental propositions in the theory of Calhoun. Majority rule is always liable to abuse at the hands of a party, an interest, or a section, which interprets constitutional law, determines public opinion, arrogates to itself the right and privilege properly belonging only to the whole people. With dramatic power Calhoun pictures the inevitable advance of majority encroachment and aggression. Application of this principle is made in reference to the question of taxation. Under the operation of the numerical majority, says Calhoun, a party or section obtaining power may easily abuse and oppress another section found in the minority. Taxes may be levied by the majority section, which burden chiefly the minority section; not only this, but these taxes are actually returned by the minority to the majority, virtually bounties paid by the weaker to the stronger party. The case in point was that of the protective tariff, which he considered was levied for the benefit of the North at the expense of the South. It seemed to him, therefore, an excellent illustration of the "majority tyranny" upon which so much emphasis had been laid.

In place of the dangerous, "*numerical* majority," Calhoun presents his doctrine of the "*concurrent* majority." "All constitutional governments," says Calhoun, "take the sense of the community by its parts, each through its appropriate organ." On the other hand, those governments in which power is centred in an individual or a body of individuals, even including the majority, may be regarded as absolute governments. The principle upon which they rest is, in last analysis, force, in contrast to the principle of constitutional governments, which is that of compromise. Under the "concurrent" or "constitutional" majority system this principle of compromise will be made effective by giving "each interest or portion of the community a negative on the others." Without a "concurrent majority" there can be no negative; without a negative there can be no constitution. Calhoun declares that "it is this negative power—the power of preventing or arresting the action of the government—be it called by what term it may—veto, interposition, nullification, check, or balance of power—which, in fact, forms the Constitution." The positive power makes the *government*, but the negative power makes the *constitution*. The essence of the "concurrent majority" is, then, the veto power granted to the various separate interests. Governmental action is conditioned, not upon the consent of a majority of *individuals*, but upon that of various *interests*.

The advantages of such a system are presented with great enthusiasm. With a "concurrent majority" there will be a greater degree of attachment to the state than is otherwise possible. Attention will be attracted not so much to party as to country. The government will not discriminate against any one interest or group, and hence there will be no violent resentments and animosities provoked as under the rule of the absolute majority. Consequently there will result a higher development of "common devotion." Politically and morally there must follow, according to Calhoun, loftier standards of conduct under this regime of compromise than under that of force. Moreover, under this system there may be obtained a higher degree of liberty. Government will be effectually restrained from arbitrary and oppressive conduct by the veto power of the various interests, and thus political freedom will be guaranteed. In any other government, indeed, liberty can be little more than a name; the "constitutional majority" alone makes it a reality. By the same logic, civilization and progress are fostered by the system of compromise, for under it are secured liberty and harmony —two great factors in civilized development. On the whole, Calhoun would conclude that the "organism" known as the "concurrent" or "constitutional" majority is eminently adapted to realize the great ends of government included under the protection and perfection of society.

Two objections may be raised against the proposed system, Calhoun concedes; namely, its complexity and its ineffectiveness. To the first of these he replies that the simplest of all governments are absolute and that all free governments are of necessity complex in their structure. Hence this style of argument applies to the whole philosophy and practice of free government, which he does not consider it necessary to defend. Nor is the objection to the effectiveness of the proposed system regarded as serious. Calhoun maintains that in times of real stress the compromise principle is not unfavorable to the passage of necessary measures, and that any policy agreed upon is far more enthusiastically supported than if compelled by force. Obedience will be rendered, not from a selfish or sectional motive, but from a higher sense of obligation to country. An analogy to the compromise principle is discovered in the unanimity required of a jury before decisive action can be taken. As circumstances lead the jurors to a unanimous decision, so the far more imperious necessities of government will lead to a compromise and agreement in the affairs of state. Historical illustrations of the compromise are afforded by the experience of Poland with the *liberum veto*, by the Confederacy of the Six Nations, the Patricians and Plebeians in Rome, the Lords and Commons in England, and by the United States, if the original intention of the Fathers were carried out.

It is now evident that Calhoun's argument all leads up to the defence of a particular theory of public law in the United States. "Concurrent" or "constitutional" majority is simply the prolegomena to nullification. The individual states of the Union are to enjoy a veto on the proceedings of the general government, thus establishing the principle of action through the concurrent instead of the numerical majority. A state may reject any measure of the general government regarded as inconsistent with the terms of the Constitution; may, in other words, nullify the proposed action of the federal government. If three-fourths of the states support the action of the government, the nullifying state must either yield or withdraw from the Union. Thus a constitutional means of defence is possessed by each state; there is no possibility of tyrannical conduct on the part of the "numerical majority"; and the action of the "concurrent majority" is assured. Nullification, in Calhoun's eyes, was not only a theory of the relation of the states to the Union, but it was a theory of constitutional government in general; founded not merely in the particular system of the United States, but equally essential in the framework of any free constitution.

In South Carolina for example, he points out, representation in the legislature is distributed on the basis of property, population, and territory. Representation in the senate is based on election districts, and thus gives to the southern part of the state the predominance in that body; the house is based on property and population, thus giving the northern part of the state the majority there. As the governor, the judges, and all important officers are elected by the legislature, there is established an equilibrium between the sections. "Party organization," says Calhoun, "party discipline, party proscription, and their offspring, the spoils principle, have been unknown to the state." The same principle and similar methods might well be introduced, he thinks, into other states and there be followed by like beneficent results.

As already stated, nullification as conceived by Calhoun was not simply a theory of the American Union, but a fundamental doctrine of free government. Whether the political theory of nullification was chronologically or only logically antecedent to the constitutional theory of nullification, is a matter which need not here be discussed; the important fact is that in the developed thought of Calhoun, the "concurrent majority" was declared to be a vital element in constitutional government.

The next object of inquiry is Calhoun's statement of the doctrine of secession. The germ of this theory is found in Calhoun's conception of the nature of sovereignty. In the early years of the Republic it had been generally believed that in the United States there existed a divided sovereignty. The states were sovereign in certain matters, the national government sovereign in certain others, and each was supreme in its proper sphere. If any ultimate sovereign was thought of, it was the people as contrasted with the government.

Calhoun, however, was wholly intolerant of any theory of divided sovereignty. To him this was logically impossible and contradictory. He reasoned that in its very nature sovereignty must be indivisible. "To divide is to destroy it"; sovereignty must be one, or it is not at all. There can be no state partly sovereign and partly non-sovereign; there can be no association composed of half-sovereign states on the one hand, and a half-sovereign government on the other. The vital principle of the state, its life and spirit, cannot be sundered; it must remain one and indivisible. Thus in Calhoun's doctrine, all compromise was rejected, and the doctrine of the indivisibility of sovereignty presented in its clearest and most striking light.

Applying this argument to the nature of the Union, Calhoun asserted that the states were originally sovereign, and that they had never yielded up their sovereignty. They could not surrender a part and retain another part, but they must either have given up all, or have retained all; the states must be fully sovereign or fully subject. This was the alternative which Calhoun urged with relentless logic. Given the original sovereignty of the states, and the indivisibility of sovereignty, either the states must be sovereign communities and the United States a mere agent, or the United States must be sovereign and the states wholly subordinate. In Calhoun's theory there was no opportunity given for a division of the field between the states and the Union; such a compromise was excluded. It is true, he concedes, that the central government enjoys the right to exercise sovereign powers, but it does not have the true sovereignty from which these powers are only emanations. The central government acts as a sovereign, but it is not a sovereign. It wears the robes of authority only by sufferance of the legitimate owner, the states.

To the central government there are delegated by the states certain attributes of sovereignty, such as the war power, the taxing power, the power to coin money; but these powers do not constitute sovereignty. In Calhoun's theory these attributes of sovereignty may be divided, and the supreme authority itself remain unimpaired. Thus the states do not surrender the sovereignty; they merely forego the exercise of certain of its attributes, and these are liable to recall at any moment by the state from which derived. In fact, neither federal nor state *government* is supreme, for there is a determining power back of both. One must distinguish, he maintains, between the constitution-making power and the law-making power; the former alone is sovereign, and to its act is due the formation and organization of the government. The constituent power in any state concedes both to the state government and to the national government certain powers or attributes of sovereignty; but as it may recall the power granted to the state government, so with equal right it may recall the authority delegated to the central government. Throughout this process the sovereign power remains intact. The practical conclusion which he draws is, naturally, that the states may at any time rightfully assert their sovereign prerogative and withdraw from the Union.

It is further important to notice how, on Calhoun's basis, he differentiated the United States from a league or confederacy. What line of demarcation could he draw between the political organization under the Articles of Confederation and that effected under the Constitution? Calhoun declared that the main difference between these two types of association consisted in the fact that the Confederacy lacked one essential feature of the "Republic," namely, a fixed and stable government. The so-called "government" of a confederacy is "nearly allied to an assembly of diplomats," meeting to determine certain policies, and then leaving their execution largely to the several parties to the agreement. "Our system is the first that ever substituted a *government* in lieu of such bodies. This, in fact, constitutes its peculiar characteristic. It is new, peculiar, and unprecedented." Among the changes involved in the passage from Confederacy to "Republic" was, in the first place, a change in the source from which power was derived. The Confederacy obtained its authority from the state governments; the "Republic" from the sovereign communities themselves. The Confederacy was a mere league between governments; the "Republic" is a "more perfect union" between sovereign communities. Another point of difference is that in the "Republic" there is needed a much more careful specification and enumeration of powers than was required in the Confederacy, where the states themselves were immediately concerned in the administration. Furthermore, under the Confederacy the state governments were superior to the central government, which was merely their agent; but in the "Republic" the federal and the state governments are equals and coordinates. Both are inferior in rank to the constitutional convention of the state which gives them life. Lastly, there was a change in the method of executing the commands of the central government. The Confederacy acted through the states; the "Republic" is authorized to act directly upon individuals.

The difference, then, between the "Republic," or a federal system, and a "nation" must be sought, not in the character of the powers exercised, but in the basis upon which they rest. It matters not how large the power of the federal government; if that power may be recalled by the states, the federal government is subordinate and they are sovereign. The federal government may have possession; the states have ownership; and they may at any time evict their tenant, or any one of the states may claim its share of the estate.

Of the influence of Calhoun there is no question. He was easily the first in rank among the theorists of his school, and his ideas dominated the South. His political theories became the dogma of the particularistic party; they were pressed with the most rigid and unyielding logic, and led straight to the trial of arms in the Civil War. After the close of this struggle, the theory of states-rights was again stated by such authorities as Jefferson Davis, Alexander H. Stephens, and Bernard J. Sage, but little was added to what had already been said by Calhoun. His doctrines still stand as the most perfect formulation of the particularistic idea which played so large a part in the first two generations of the life of the Republic.

The nationalist theory of the Union, like the particularistic doctrine, did not develop immediately on the establishment of the Constitution. The first great champion of the cause was Daniel Webster, who contributed more to the strengthening of Union sentiment than any other one man. Webster's theory, however, was constitutional in nature, rather than philosophic. He attempted to show from the language of the Constitution itself, without much discussion of philosophic or historic considerations, that the Union was formed by a contract between individuals which resulted in the establishment of a supreme law and government, and that the states as such were not concerned in this agreement. "The people of the United States" he understood to mean the people of the whole Union, and not of the several states. The Union is not merely a compact between states to form a new Confederacy, but an agreement between individuals to form a national government. "It is established," said he, "by the people of the United States. It does not say by the people of the several states. It is as all the people of the United States that they established the Constitution." Thus the Constitution of the United States was formed just as any state constitution; namely, by means of an agreement between individuals.

But a state constitution, although created originally by an agreement between individuals, was not regarded as a contract, but as a *law*. It was created by an agreement, but when that agreement was once made, there came into being a law proper. To use an analogy from private law, the agreement has become an "executed contract." "When the people agree to erect a government," said Webster, "and actually erect it, the thing is done, and the agreement is at an end. The compact is executed, and the end designed by it is attained." The same argument was made by Story, who urged that a constitution falls under the definition of law as laid down by the eminent authority, Blackstone. "It is," said he, "a rule of action prescribed by the supreme power in the state, regulating the rights and duties of the whole community. It is a rule, as distinguished from a temporary or sudden order—permanent, uniform, and universal. It is also called a rule to distinguish it from a compact or agreement, for a contract is a promise proceeding from us, law is a command directed to us."

On this basis it was denied that the Constitution of the United States could be regarded as a contract, and the assertion made that it must be considered as a law in the strict and proper sense of the term. It is, in fact, the supreme law of the land, and carries with it the very highest degree of obligation. The Union is not a mere treaty relation which may be denounced at will, but an agreement as obligatory and indissoluble as the social contract on which the whole fabric of society rests. Hence a state has no more right to question the authority and supremacy of the Constitution than a citizen of Massachusetts has to question the constitution of that state; not even as much right, for the Constitution of the United States is the supreme law of the whole society. The individual may exert the original right of revolution, but he has no legal right to resist the constituted authorities of the nation.

Webster's doctrine was, then, that the Union is not a treaty relation between sovereign states, as Calhoun argued, or a contract between states by which the sovereignty of the contracting parties is diminished, as Madison contended; but it is a *law*, resting on a social contract between individuals, and in which the states as such had no part. The Constitution is a government ordained and established by the people of the United States. In the expressive language of Webster, the Union is, "the association of the people under a constitution of government, uniting their highest interests, cementing their present enjoyments, and blending in an indivisible mass all their hopes for the future."

Although reasoning with great skill and eloquence from the strict letter of the Constitution, it is evident that Webster's real power did not come from his constitutional arguments as such. The very question over which he and Calhoun fought was whether the Union should be regarded and interpreted from the standpoint of constitutional law or of international law. If the states were never sovereign or had yielded up their sovereignty, then Webster's contention, that secession is an unconstitutional act, was valid. But to Calhoun, who looked upon the Union as, in ultimate analysis at least, a treaty between sovereign states, secession could not be regarded as unconstitutional, but at the worst as a breach of international law. The discussion, as they carried it on, amounted to an argument over the legality of an act, with one of the parties denying the existence of the law under which such validity was contested. Webster wished to make a purely legal argument on the question of legal sovereignty. Calhoun declined to make it purely a legal question, but at the same time disregarded the matter of fact.

When we consider the social and economic forces on which political forms are based, Webster had the stronger position, and for this reason. Calhoun was continually looking backward to a state of things that once perhaps may have existed, and he failed to observe that every year was carrying him farther away from his premise. The fatal flaw in his argument was that, even granting his cherished hypothesis that the states were originally sovereign, it did not follow that they would continue to possess that fullness of power forever. On the other hand, Webster's hypothesis was looking to the future tense, and every year of nationalizing conditions was therefore strengthening his contention. The great weight of his argument was due to the fact that even if his interpretation of "We, the people" was denied, it did not follow that his conclusions were not sound. His power as a controversialist really came, not from the strength of his constitutional arguments as such, but from the fact that he followed a great current of public sentiment, springing from the impulse of nationality. He had with him the reasoned and unreasoned forces of an ethnic and geographic unity struggling toward self-expression.

*≈§ §≈*

BETWEEN *1846 and 1861, the primary business of American politicians was to find a way to put at rest the question of slavery in the territories. It proved an insurmountable problem. The Wilmot Proviso had proven eminently attractive in the North; to counteract it, in December of 1847, Lewis B. Cass had set forth the doctrine of popular sovereignty which would leave the decision of slavery or no slavery to the residents of the territory. Stephen A. Douglas incorporated it into the Compromise of 1850 when he formulated the Utah and New Mexico Enabling Acts. Except for the Fugitive Slave Act, the Compromise's provisions stirred little controversy, and by 1854, debates over the issues raised in 1850 had practically ceased.*

*Then suddenly, in one legislative act, all the controversy awoke to renewed and vigorous life. That act was the Kansas-Nebraska Act. It disrupted the political scene and set the stage for the birth of the Republican party. It convinced Northerners that a slave plot was afoot to roll back the march of freedom, and no less thoroughly convinced Southerners that Northern abolitionists intended to destroy slavery everywhere and expose the South to rapine, plunder, and murder. It put an almost unknown Abraham Lincoln on the road to the White House, and no less certainly barred the same route to the act's author, Stephen A. Douglas. The vast consequences that flowed from the act have left historians wondering why*

*Douglas chose to introduce the bill and why its effects were so disruptive.*

*No single explanation has proven sufficient to account for its effects. But it is safe to say that Douglas intended his act as a response to the real need for organization of the territory. He acceded to pressure to extend the principle of popular sovereignty to the new territories and, by so doing, abrogated the Missouri Compromise. It gave the Free-Soil congressional faction an opportunity to arrange the "bill as a gross violation of a sacred pledge; as a criminal betrayal of precious rights; as part and parcel of an atrocious plot." The substance of this charge found its way into the official Republican rhetoric and after the war underscored the "court" or "victor's" view of the history leading up to conflict. It left Douglas under a shadow that was not challenged until the appearance of Allen Johnson's* Stephen A. Douglas *(1908), which treated him as a sincere believer in popular sovereignty as the only equitable solution of a divisive sectional issue. Subsequently, other historians emphasized the Douglas desire to open a route for a transcontinental railroad, the complex internecine war which racked the Democracy, or his statesmanship.*

*P. Orman Ray (1875-    ) entered the fray with the publication of his dissertation in 1909; in it he emphasized a complex of political rivalries, particularly those in adjacent Missouri. Most critics feel that he overstated the role of Missouri politics but he set in motion a view of Douglas less as author of events and more as a broker trying to work out a political solution acceptable to all. His failure to find an adequate resolution of the crisis revealed how deep the gulf was that divided the nation. It brought into existence a Solid South and an almost as Solid North. Only in the great border region did the politics of moderation survive. As for Douglas, his effort destroyed him. And in Kansas, a rehearsal for conflict opened that portended the larger strife of a bare half decade later.*

# THE REPEAL OF THE MISSOURI COMPROMISE

## by P. Orman Ray

On December 5, 1853, the day on which the 33d Congress opened, Senator A. C. Dodge of Iowa gave notice of his intention to introduce a bill for the organization of a territorial government for Nebraska, which he did introduce on the fourteenth. The bill was immediately referred to the Committee on Territories of which Mr. Douglas was the chairman as well as the most prominent and influential member. In the House a Nebraska bill, practically the duplicate of Senator Dodge's bill, was introduced by Hon. J. G. Miller of Missouri on the twenty-second of December, and immediately referred to the Committee on Territories of which Hon. W. A. Richardson of Illinois was chairman.

The real significance of these facts has been missed by historians who, approaching the origin of the Repeal through the pages of the *Congressional*

*Globe,* have been unduly impressed with the prominent part played by Senator Douglas. They have assumed that it originated with a Senator who had spent the summer and early autumn of 1853 in Europe, and had returned to Washington only a month before Congress met; and who has left good evidence that the reopening of the slavery agitation in connection with Nebraska Territory was unexpected by him three weeks before Congress convened. Whereas the fact is that the questions involved in the Nebraska territorial movement were forced upon the attention of the committees of which Mr. Douglas and his colleague in the House were the chairmen, possibly against their will and apparently without much foreknowledge on the part of Senator Douglas, by representatives of the two States most deeply interested.

It is not strange that a great degree of mystery should heretofore seem to have surrounded the repeal of the time-honored Missouri Compromise. The difficulty has been to get behind the scenes and discover what was going on in and around the halls of Congress between the fifth of December, and the twenty-third of January. The pages of the *Congressional Globe* record only results. Of the processes by which those results are achieved, there is seldom any record. Politicians, as well as the Almighty, often "move in a mysterious way" their "wonders to perform." One cannot expect, in the nature of the case, to get much evidence of what was occurring in the corridors and committee rooms at the Capitol, and at the lodgings of Senators and Representatives. Nevertheless we are not left entirely in the dark. One source of information little used by previous writers sheds considerable light upon what was taking place outside the Senate Chamber and the Hall of Representatives. Upon the testimony of the "Washington Correspondents" of the great newspapers of the day, it must be admitted, implicit reliance for accuracy cannot be placed; but in the absence of contradicting evidence, their testimony may be entitled to greater weight than would otherwise be the case. Especially will this be true if their testimony fits with surprising exactness into the facts presented in the preceding chapters.

"Notice has been given in Congress of the introduction of a bill for the creation of a territorial government for Nebraska," wrote "Fairfax," the Washington Correspondent of the Richmond *Enquirer* within a week after the opening of Congress. To "Fairfax" it was plain that Congress would witness a renewal of the slavery agitation as a direct result of political conditions in Missouri.

> This subject [he went on to say] is one of great interest and will create much feeling. The freesoilers led on by Mr. Benton will make every effort to hasten on a territorial organization, hoping thereby to be able to exclude slavery from it. This gentleman announced some time ago in Missouri that Nebraska was open for settlement. . . . The facts relating to the matter should be understood and the objects of Mr. Benton and those who act with him cannot be mistaken. To prevent the Southerners from carrying their property into Nebraska, to have another free State touching the slave State of Missouri, to influence

the next August elections in Missouri, and the presidential campaign of
1856: these are the objects of Mr. Benton and his freesoil allies.

Writing ten days later the same Correspondent again called attention to
the subject of Nebraska and to Mr. Atchison's attitude:

> . . . The President of the Senate, Mr. Atchison, *is pledged by his
> speeches before the people of Missouri to move the repeal of the law
> prohibiting slavery in the Territory north of the parallel of 36° 30'*. He
> will oppose the Nebraska territorial bill and insist upon the admission of
> slavery into the Territory, if it be established at all, both on the original
> constitutional ground, and also upon the ground that it would be
> prejudicial to the interests of Missouri to be surrounded by a cordon
> of free States. Mr. Douglas will soon report the Nebraska bill and we
> shall witness a renewal thereupon of slavery agitation. In fine as long
> as slavery exists it will be a subject of political or religious or sectional
> or philanthropic agitation. Let it be known that at all events the great
> feature of the opening of the 33d Congress is the slavery discussion and
> that too in a House remarkable beyond its predecessors for men of ex-
> perience and moderation and general ability.

Even the distant *Missouri Republican* had its Correspondent at Washington.

> Old Bullion was not so far out [he wrote] when he said slavery and
> Nebraska would be the questions of the session. The proceedings in
> respect to the Territories are yet somewhat vague and indefinite but
> *some very interesting and important propositions have been laid before
> the Committee by the outsiders who assume to regulate their deliber-
> ations;* and from the present aspect of this subject, I am inclined to
> think that the freesoilers have rather caught a Tartar with this Nebraska
> question and don't know what to do with him. It is well known that
> Mr. Atchison, Col. Manypenny and the conservatives on the question
> that lies under and beyond the organization of Nebraska were willing
> to waive the agitation this winter. . . . Now, however, the ball is
> opened. The freesoilers have set forth their program, which is "Nebraska
> immediately if not sooner."

It is not an unwarranted inference from this communication that some
pressure was being brought to bear upon the Committee on Territories—
which, so far as practical legislation was concerned, meant Mr. Douglas—to
report the Nebraska bill in such a form that it would bear a direct relation
to the political situation in Missouri. Indeed one might very reasonably expect that such pressure would be brought to bear on Senator Douglas. We
have seen that the Nebraska territorial question was bound to and did come
before the Committee on Territories when Congress met. Senator Douglas
was thus obliged to act, and to act either with the conservative, slavery-
restrictionist element in the Democratic party, or with the radical, pro-
slavery wing. He himself declared afterwards that he had been no "volun-

teer" in the matter: "I have been Chairman of the Committee on Territories for the past ten years," he said, "and it was my duty to act in this matter and bring forward this bill. *I was no volunteer in this matter. It devolved upon me as a duty*." Whence came this outside pressure and what were the considerations which determined with which wing of the party he would cooperate?

Some time after the Repeal, Senator Atchison claimed that he came to Washington with pledges to the people of Missouri hardly cold upon his lips to support a Nebraska territorial bill on condition that it should repeal the Missouri Compromise. He therefore desired to be chairman of the Committee on Territories when the Nebraska bill was to be introduced, with the object, one may fairly assume, of obtaining full credit in Missouri for his efforts in this direction. With this purpose in mind, Mr. Atchison claimed to have had an interview with Senator Douglas at which he informed Mr. Douglas of what he desired, the introduction of a bill for Nebraska like the one he had promised to vote for, and that he would like to be chairman of the Committee on Territories in order to introduce such a measure. If he could get that position, he would immediately resign as President *pro tempore* of the Senate. Mr. Douglas, according to Atchison's story, requested time to consider the matter, saying that if, at the expiration of a given time, he could not introduce such a bill as Senator Atchison proposed and which would at the same time accord with his own sense of right and justice to the South, he would resign as chairman of the Committee in Democratic caucus, and exert his influence to get Atchison appointed.

No good reason exists for rejecting the foregoing claim of Senator Atchison. There is nothing in it which is improbable, or unreasonable. On the contrary it was most natural in view of Senator Atchison's obvious interest in the subject. If, to his personal interest, the further fact be added that Atchison and Douglas were close friends, that Douglas entertained a strong dislike of Benton, that within the two years preceding Douglas on more than one occasion had gone over into Missouri to aid the Atchison faction against Benton, the probability of Atchison seeking the cooperation of Mr. Douglas at this critical moment becomes almost a certainty.

Assuming that Atchison sought to influence Senator Douglas, it is easy to see how powerful an appeal he could make for the incorporation into Dodge's Nebraska bill, when in Douglas's committee, of a clause which in effect should repeal the Compromise restriction. It is fair to argue that Senator Atchison's political necessity might have been so presented as to appear as Douglas's great political opportunity. In the first place, by championing the Repeal Mr. Douglas would be assisting a political and personal friend in dire straits. Furthermore, he would be placing the radical wing of the Southern Democracy under obligation to himself, and thus would very materially increase his chances of obtaining the presidential nomination in 1856. The principle of popular sovereignty would afford ground upon which the rank and file of the factions in Missouri might unite in harmony, since each faction had but recently declared in favor of that method of deciding the "vexed" question; and this would enhance the popularity of the measure in other portions of the West. Ready at hand was a plausible justification for attaching the repeal feature to the Nebraska bill; Democratic newspapers had already interpreted the Compromise of 1850 as applicable to Nebraska. Loyalty to that Compromise as thus interpreted could be made a test of political orthodoxy in New York where the party was suffering from serious internal dissensions. Moreover, to this basis for the Repeal objections from either of the two national parties would be forestalled by the doctrine of supersedure, for both parties stood committed to the finality of the Compromise of 1850. If, in addition to this, it be conceded that Mr. Douglas was a sincere believer in the dogma of popular sovereignty, it requires no abnormal imagination to conceive how effectively a personal and political friend could have appealed to Mr. Douglas to assume official responsibility for the Repeal. In a word, it might have been presented as a turning point in Senator Douglas's political career. One path seemed to lead to the highest political reward, the realization of his presidential aspirations. The other seemed to involve resignation from the chairmanship of the Committee on Territories, in those years perhaps the most prominent, Committee in the Senate, with a consequent loss of prestige in both the West and the South. Even to a less "practical" politician than Mr. Douglas the appeal might well prove irresistible. That Senator Douglas should have hesitated and weighed the consequences was most natural, for clearly the situation marked a crisis of which he must have been fully conscious.

Senator Atchison did not arrive in Washington until late in November, and whatever conversation upon this subject he may have had with Mr. Douglas doubtless occurred in December and probably during the three weeks after the Walker and Lanphier letter and while the Dodge bill was in the hands of Douglas's committee. Toward the end of that period it began to leak out that something unusual was under consideration. The Correspondent of the Baltimore *Sun* wrote:

> . . . The Senate Committee on Territories has it [the Nebraska bill] under consideration and will probably report in favor of the organization of more than one territorial government. A plan has been proposed also to avoid the opposition to the bill which has been threatened by Mr. Atchison in his addresses to the people of Missouri. Some means will be adopted for the prevention of the threatened revival of the slavery question in this bill.

About the same time the Correspondent of the Charleston *Courier* had evidently been admitted to inside information, for he wrote to his paper:

> The speeches of Senator Atchison in Missouri pledge him and his constituents mutually to raise a storm here against the slavery restriction when the subject of Nebraska Territory shall come up. That the question is certain to come off I have heard from all quarters. I have conversed with some members of the Senate committee on territories, however, and they think they will be able to give the bill a form which

will suit all parties in relation to the admission of slaves. *They will put the project on the basis of the Compromise of 1850,* as applicable to the Territories of New Mexico and Utah. . . .

By the fourth of January, Senator Douglas seems to have reached a decision. On that day he reported back to the Senate the Nebraska bill introduced by Senator Dodge. It had made no reference to the subject of slavery; but it now carried important amendments relating to that subject and was accompanied by a special report of an unusual nature. The amendments constituted a new section:

> *Section 21. And be it further enacted,* That in order to avoid all misconstruction, it is hereby declared to be the true intent and meaning of this act, so far as the question of slavery is concerned, to carry into practical operation the following propositions and principles established by the compromise measures of 1850, to-wit:
>
> *First:* That all questions pertaining to slavery in the Territories and in the new States to be formed therefrom, are to be left to the decision of the people residing therein, through their appropriate representatives.
>
> *Second:* That "all cases involving title to slaves," and "questions of personal freedom," are referred to the adjudication of the local tribunals, with the right of appeal to the Supreme Court of the United States.
>
> *Third:* That the provisions of the Constitution and laws of the United States, in respect to fugitives from service, are to be carried into faithful execution in all the "organized Territories," the same as in the States.

In the report which accompanied the bill, and of which Mr. Douglas was probably the author, the Committee took occasion to commend to the Senate the principal amendments to the Dodge bill upon the ground that by those amendments:

> The principles established by the compromise measures of 1850, so far as they are applicable to territorial organizations, are proposed to be affirmed and carried into practical operation within the limits of the new Territory.

The Committee then went on to state what they regarded as having been the object and intent of the Compromise measures of 1850:

> In the judgment of your Committee, those measures were intended to have a far more comprehensive and enduring effect than the mere adjustment of the difficulties arising out of the recent acquisitions of Mexican territory. They were designed to establish certain great principles, which would not only furnish adequate remedies for existing evils, but, in all time to come, avoid the perils of a similar agitation, by withdrawing the question of slavery from the halls of Congress and the political arena, and committing it to the arbitrament of those who were immediately interested in, and alone responsible for its consequences.

With a view to making their action conform to what they regarded as the settled policy of the Government, "sanctioned by the approving voice of the American people," the Committee

> deemed it their duty to incorporate and perpetuate, in their territorial bill, the principles and the spirit of . . . [the compromise] measures.

The discussion of the bill then went over until the twenty-third of January. In the meantime, however, Senator Archibald Dixon of Kentucky, a Whig who was serving out the unexpired term of Henry Clay, gave notice that when the bill should come up for consideration he would offer an amendment, in the form of an added section, providing that the Missouri Compromise restriction upon slavery

> shall not be so construed as to apply to the Territory contemplated by this act, or to any other Territory of the United States; but that the citizens of the several States and Territories shall be at liberty to take and hold their slaves within any of the Territories of the United States, or of the States to be formed therefrom, as if the said . . . [prohibition] had never been passed.

In other words, Senator Dixon, although a Whig, proposed to apply to this new Nebraska Territory the simon-pure Calhoun doctrine, which Senator Atchison had been supporting in Missouri.

On the twenty-third of January, Mr. Douglas called up the Nebraska bill, and for the Committee on Territories, reported a substitute bill for the one reported on January 4. This new bill divided the territory described in the earlier bill and provided for the organization of the two Territories, Kansas and Nebraska. The bill, henceforth known as the Kansas-Nebraska bill, contained the following section:

> Section 14. . . . The Constitution, and all laws of the United States which are not locally inapplicable, shall have the same force and effect within the said Territories as elsewhere in the United States, except the eighth section of the act preparatory to the admission of Missouri into the Union, approved March 6, 1820, *which was superseded by the principles of the legislation of 1850, commonly called the compromise measures, and is declared inoperative.*

Historians have been somewhat puzzled by the fourth of January report, by the Dixon amendment, and by the substitution of a bill creating two Territories and expressly repealing the Missouri Compromise.

If we take into consideration the difficult problem confronting Senator Douglas after the opening of Congress, his natural hesitation before committing himself to the solution which the interests of Senator Atchison demanded, and the desire of the Iowa Delegate, Hadley D. Johnson, for two Territories, the puzzle becomes simplified.

It is not unfair to regard the fourth of January bill and report as in the nature of an experiment. Mr. Douglas has now decided to pursue the course desired by the Senator from Missouri. Just which consideration was decisive, it is impossible to say. But having reached a decision Mr. Douglas may well have been troubled with serious doubts as to the best method of formulating the legislation necessary to effect the Repeal. He would naturally take the greatest pains to choose language as mild, as plausible as possible, and not likely to provoke the hostility of the anti-slavery wing of his party. The Repeal must be disguised under the most carefully selected phraseology in order to avoid, if possible, a renewal of the slavery agitation. The bill must be made acceptable to all parties; and so he attempts a compromise. Hence the extraordinary pains betrayed in this extraordinary report to gloss over the real significance of what was being done; hence the mild and circumlocutory phraseology. Mr. Douglas is feeling his way, endeavoring to ward off agitation. The bill and report of January 4 constitute a vain attempt to accomplish the Repeal by a sort of compromise measure based upon an analogy between the divergent views in 1850 regarding the status of slavery under Mexican law in the territory acquired from Mexico, and the divergent views in 1854 regarding the validity of the Missouri Compromise prohibition of slavery in the territory acquired from France.

His efforts were in vain. The anti-slavery leaders at once took alarm. The pro-slavery leaders were dissatisfied at the ambiguous language. And so Senator Dixon, another friend of Senator Atchison, gave notice of his amendment repealing the Missouri Compromise in the most explicit terms. There is no evidence upon the point, but it is not unreasonable to suppose that Mr. Atchison or his friends may, for the purpose of influencing Mr. Douglas, have instigated this action by Senator Dixon, who, although a Whig, when it came to slavery, "knew no Whiggery and knew no Democracy." It would be shrewd politics to startle Senator Douglas, to make him apprehensive that his political thunder was to be stolen, and by a Whig! If therefore he wished to turn the Repeal to his own political profit there must be no ambiguous hedging, no measure the legal effect of which could be open to question. At any rate, there is evidence that Senator Douglas was disconcerted by Senator Dixon's manoeuvre. This convinced him that the radicals were determined to push the Repeal whether with or without his help, and that if he was to make political capital out of it, the time had arrived, at least so far as the language of the bill was concerned, to come out boldly, unreservedly and unequivocally in support of the Repeal. So within a week after Senator Dixon's notice Mr. Douglas reported the substitute, or Kansas-Nebraska bill, of January 23, repealing the Missouri Compromise in terms clear and unmistakable, and so satisfactory to the radical Senator Dixon that he withdrew his amendment. By the twenty-third of January, therefore, the Rubicon is crossed: henceforth there must be no retreating, no equivocating, if Mr. Douglas expected to gain anything. That he met the whirlwind of wrath which ensued as successfully as he did is perhaps the best commentary upon his courage and cleverness as a politician and his ability as a debater and popular orator.

But before committing himself finally and irrevocably to the Repeal,

Mr. Douglas and those more personally interested in the success of the measure realized the essential importance of securing the support of the Administration. In the week between the Dixon amendment and the twenty-third of January, this support was secured. The account of the way in which it was brought about as told by the Correspondent of the New York *Herald* is not only interesting but significant for the prominence which it gives to Senator Atchison in accomplishing the desired result; also, as will appear later, for the prominence given to the names of Senators Hunter and Mason of Virginia.

> . . . The Cabinet was in session all day yesterday and to a late hour in the evening discussing the merits of the Nebraska bill and the amendment proposed by Senator Dixon. . . . The result of the Cabinet deliberations yesterday has been an agreement to have an amendment offered in the Senate by way of compromise adding to the 21st section of the Nebraska bill a proviso to the effect that the rights of persons and property shall be subject only to the restrictions and limitations imposed by the Constitution of the United States and the acts giving governments, to be adjusted by a decision of the Supreme Court of the United States. . . .

Writing on the twenty-third of January, the day on which the Kansas-Nebraska bill was substituted, the same Correspondent said:

> The past twenty-four hours have witnessed a complete somersault of the President and Cabinet on the Nebraska matter. In order to understand the whole matter we must give a brief narrative. The amendment which was sent you yesterday was submitted by Mr. Breckenridge of Kentucky and Mr. Phillips of Alabama to Judge Douglas, who, it was understood, was prepared with an amendment declaring the Missouri Compromise inoperative. The same amendment he offered today. Mr. Douglas stated that he had no particular objections to the Cabinet amendment, if the South would consent to accept it; for he considered his bill as originally reported in fact amounting to an abrogation of the Missouri Compromise. The gentlemen then called upon several leading men, Messrs. *Atchison, Mason, Hunter,* [the italics are mine] and others, and discovered that the Cabinet amendment would not go down at all. This fact having been communicated to the President, he begged his friends to get the leading members together for consultation yesterday [Sunday]. The result of this consultation was an agreement that the amendment presented today by Judge Douglas should be agreed upon and the South would resist any other amendment upon the bill. [Here the amendment is quoted.] . . . It will be seen that it does not use the word "repeal" . . . but substitutes the words "supersedes" and "inoperative." This is done to avoid the opposition of the ultra Southern men who contend that the Missouri law is unconstitutional and who would therefore refuse to "repeal" an unconstitutional enactment, a mere quibble of course as to words.
>
> Mr. *Atchison, Hunter, Mason,* Douglas, Bright, Breckenridge, Phillips, and perhaps some others, accordingly repaired yesterday afternoon to

the White House to see the President, and tell him the result of their deliberations. The President, however, having probably heard of his supreme court amendment, told the gentlemen that he had "religious scruples about discussing the subject on Sunday." The gentlemen did not appreciate the difference between the propriety of the President directing them to discuss the matter, Sunday though it was, and his joining in the discussion himself, then stated *through Mr. Atchison,* that if the President declined to discuss the proposition, they would take it for granted that he favored it and would regard the amendment abrogating the Missouri Compromise as an Administration measure. Upon this the President spoke and after sundry gyrations, agreed that the bill should be reported, and said the Administration would then take ground. The gentlemen left with the understanding that the Administration would take ground in its favor.

On the second of April the Correspondent of the *Missouri Republican* wrote:

> . . . The assent and support of Gen. Pierce had been obtained before the bill was introduced and when it was afterwards thought necessary to change its phraseology, Pierce was again consulted and drew the amendment by which the Missouri act was to be "superseded." It was thought advisable by *Douglas and Atchison* to induce the President to commit himself in this manner in order to avoid risk of his withdrawing his countenance after the battle should be joined. They therefore insisted upon this course, and Pierce with great good nature complied. With the famous clause repealing the Missouri Compromise in his own hand-writing Gen. Pierce cannot recant his promise nor refuse the assistance of his Democratic bodyguard in the House to support and carry it where that sort of strength was most required and where he alone could command it.

Outside the Senate Chamber Senator Atchison was evidently playing an active and important part in bringing about the Repeal; and this illustrates the importance of looking beyond the pages of the *Congressional Globe* to discover the real history of the repeal of the Missouri Compromise. From the *Globe* it might be inferred that Senator Atchison had little to do with the Repeal, since he took almost no part in the debate upon the Kansas-Nebraska bill. The *Globe* indicates that he made only two very brief speeches and that these speeches were not directed to the principal topic of debate but to the Clayton amendment whereby aliens were to be excluded from political privileges in the new Territories. His silence however is not at all inconsistent with the idea that he exerted a powerful influence in shaping this piece of legislation. It may in part be explained by the fact that as President *pro tempore* of the Senate after the death of Vice-President King, Mr. Atchison as presiding officer could hardly be expected to, and as a matter of fact did not, participate in debate as actively as many other Senators. Furthermore it is not always the talkers, the debaters of the House or Senate who are the most influential members of Congress. Atchison and

Benton, for example, were representatives of two types of men to be found in every deliberative body. The former preferred the less conspicuous but not less potent and more difficult role of influencing legislation through personal appeals. Benton chose the more conspicuous stage of the speech-maker. As Senator Atchison, with Benton in mind, truly said: "stormy speeches and bills full of attractive promises the people can be made to know all about; but the unknown labor in committee and in Congress necessary to command success by making measures understood, the people . . . cannot be made fully to appreciate."

On the sixth of February, the bill then being under consideration in the Senate, Mr. Douglas moved to amend the substitute bill reported on the twenty-third of January, by striking out from Section 14 the words, "which was superseded by," and inserting in their place the words, "which is inconsistent with." The clause will then provide, said Mr. Douglas,

"that the Constitution and laws not locally inapplicable shall have the same force in the Territory as elsewhere, except the eighth section of the Missouri act, 'which is inconsistent with the principles of the legislation of 1850, commonly called the compromise measures, and is hereby declared inoperative.' This is the express idea conveyed in the original words, but I prefer to make it plainer."

Considerable discussion followed as to the relative merits of the two phrases, "superseded by" and "inconsistent with," in which Senators Cass and Stuart of Michigan, Badger of North Carolina, and Walker of Wisconsin, participated. The matter then went over until the next morning. In the meantime Senator Douglas had an opportunity to take counsel with the friends of the bill, and when the Senate reconvened the next day Mr. Douglas had perfected his amendment. He rose and stated that he had drawn an amendment which he believed would meet the approbation of the friends of the bill. He therefore moved to amend the fourteenth section by striking out the words,

> . . . which [the Missouri Compromise act] was superseded by the principles of the legislation of 1850, commonly called the compromise measures, and is hereby declared inoperative,

and inserting the words,

> . . . which, being inconsistent with the principle of non-intervention by Congress with slavery in the States and Territories, as recognized by the legislation of 1850, commonly called the compromise measures, is hereby declared inoperative and void, it being the true intent and meaning of this act not to legislate slavery into any territory or state, nor to exclude it therefrom; but to leave the people thereof perfectly free to form and regulate their domestic institutions in their own way, subject only to the Constitution of the United States.

"I move that amendment *with the general concurrence of the friends of the measure*," said Mr. Douglas: "It will apply to both Territories." The amendment was adopted on the fifteenth of February.

With this vote it was in fact determined that the Missouri Compromise should be repealed as Senator Atchison had suggested. But so far as the official record shows, Stephen A. Douglas and not Mr. Atchison was the author of the Repeal.

⋙ ⋘

THE *erosion of established authority is a gradual process; it often occurs imperceptibly and it is only from the perspective of distance that the process can be discerned. The eruption of political discontent let loose by the Kansas-Nebraska Act revealed how advanced was the disintegration of the old federal system. The Kansas Territory created by the act exposed the depth of sectional alienation. Into the distracted territory poured men bent on making Kansas free and men no less bent on making it slave. They were joined by adventurers who thought they discerned a fortune in the virgin lands or, more disreputably, planned to exploit the absence of effective law enforcement to indulge in safe horse thievery or less attractive enterprises. Kansas fused morality and private gain, both sufficiently sharp-edged to give the territory its contemporary description as Bloody Kansas.*

*In the ravines of Kansas and upon its plains, men were trained in guerrilla warfare, or so one of the first biographers of John Brown claimed. But, as James C. Malin demonstrated in* John Brown and the Legend of Fifty-six *(1942), Brown did not originally intend to do more in Kansas than settle upon the land in the hope of getting a new start. Once in Kansas, Brown's antipathy to slavery interlaced his private expectations, and his key role in the Potawatomie massacre of five "pro-slavery" men when combined with his later role at Harpers Ferry thoroughly obscured Brown's original motives. In the aftermath of Civil War, as the awesome price exacted by it stood revealed, the actors in the tragedy took to explaining the justice of their actions. The narrow self-seeking rivalries, the petty piques, all those actions which make men lesser than angels were forgotten, and only the moral imperative was left to be remembered. And Kansas, where all things were obscure, the mass murder at Potawatomie, for that was what it was, fused into a legend of a prophet come to free the downtrodden, a man who had been heard to mutter at a New England Anti-Slavery Convention in 1859, "These men are all talk; what is needed is action—action!"*

*Unwittingly, Stephen A. Douglas had created an arena in which the first sounds of fratricidal warfare were heard; within Kansas, on its still largely empty plains, men of whom John Brown was the most spectacular example revealed how profound a separation existed within the American people. James Buchanan desperately struggled to pacify Kansas, but he failed, and when he did he had irreparably divided his party, destroying the last national political agent. For Abraham Lincoln Kansas posed the question of the future: "Welcome, or unwelcome, agreeable, or disagreeable, whether this shall be an entire slave nation, is the issue before us."*

*Theodore C. Smith (1871-1961), long Woodrow Wilson Professor of American History and Government at Williams College, devoted his scholarly career to a study of the political impact of slavery. His study of political abolitionism as embodied in the Liberty and Free Soil parties, although dated, still remains the basic source on the subject.*

# PARTIES AND SLAVERY, 1850-1859

## by Theodore Clarke Smith

The immediate result of the Kansas-Nebraska act was to revolutionize parties in the north; but its ultimate outcome was to lead the country to the verge of civil war by creating an intense rivalry in the territory which it opened to settlement. When the bill passed, the general opinion was that while Nebraska would develop into a free community, Kansas was practically assured as a slave state; for its geographical position marked it out as the field for immigration from Missouri, the lower Mississippi Valley, and Kentucky and Tennessee, rather than from the states to the north of the Ohio River. Although the southern leaders did not initiate the repeal of the Missouri Compromise, they gladly welcomed the apparently undoubted opportunity to gain an additional slave state to counterbalance California in the Senate. The first settlers in Kansas came from western Missouri, and before the end of 1854 many of them took up claims along the Missouri and Kansas rivers, founding the little towns of Kickapoo, Leavenworth, and Atchison, and bringing a few slaves with them. "Popular sovereignty," as established by Douglas, seemed to mean exactly what the southern leaders desired.

But the indignation among northern men over the opening of Kansas and Nebraska to slave-holders now led to an entirely unforeseen attempt to turn the principle of "popular sovereignty" against the south itself, by securing a majority of anti-slavery settlers in Kansas, the very region conceded to the slave-holders. Even before the passage of the bill, steps were taken which led to the formation of a New England Emigrant Aid Society, organized by Eli Thayer, of Worcester, and largely supported by Amos Lawrence and others of the wealthiest and most prominent men of Massachusetts. The purpose of the corporation was to assist the emigration of genuine settlers—not necessarily abolitionists or even anti-Nebraska men—who were unwilling to see Kansas made into a slave state; the society did not enlist men as recruits, but was ready to assist applicants by loaning capital for mills and hotels and by furnishing supplies and transportation. In the summer of 1854 the first band of northern settlers reached Kansas, and others soon followed. With them, although not under the auspices of the society, came other immigrants from New York and the states of the "Old Northwest," looking for farms in the fertile valleys of the Kansas and its tributaries. Soon a new community, holding aloof from the Missourian settlements, was planted near the town of Lawrence, named in honor of the principal patron of the Emigrant Aid Society, and the country became aware that the settlement of the territory was taking on an unusual and ominous form.

This "invasion" of Kansas by northern immigrants brought sharply to the front one of the many hazy points in Douglas's "popular sovereignty." When, under the law, was the decision to be made regarding the existence of slavery? Must it be postponed till a state constitution was framed, or could it be made at any earlier time? The full southern theory, announced by Calhoun as early as 1847, and held by most southerners in 1854, was that there could be no interference with slavery by either Congress or the territorial legislature, no community except a state being competent to make a decision. Douglas would not commit himself on this point, but a very general impression prevailed in the north that the principle of popular or "squatter sovereignty" would permit the inhabitants of a territory to decide the point for themselves as soon as they chose. All saw, northern and southern men alike, that in default of any positive protection of slavery by law, actual control of the territorial government by anti-slavery men would effectually prevent Kansas from ever becoming a slave state.

This danger was perceived as soon as the organized eastern emigration began, and a thrill of indignation ran through Missouri and the entire south. The actual purpose of the Emigrant Aid Society was wholly misunderstood, and the extent of its operations exaggerated beyond all measure. It was believed to be a corporation with unbounded resources, formed for the purpose of holding Kansas by force, sending out hordes of mercenaries, mostly abolitionists, enemies of God and man, provisioned, and armed to the teeth to seize Kansas from legitimate southern emigrants. They are "a band of Hessian mercenaries," said a committee of Missourians, in an address to the people of the United States. "To call these people emigrants is a sheer perversion of language. They were not sent to cultivate the soil. . . . They have none of the marks of the old pioneers. If not clothed and fed by the same power which has effected their transportation they would starve. They are hirelings—an army of hirelings. . . . They are military colonies of reckless and desperate fanatics."

The sense of unfairness and unjust aggression which the operations of the Emigrant Aid Society, as seen through these distorted rumors, excited in the south, was as keen in its way as the northern indignation had been over the repeal of the slavery restriction. The Missourians and southerners in general felt that the attempt to settle Kansas with northern emigrants was a direct effort to take from them what was rightfully theirs, and they were at once driven into a counter-effort to defeat this aggression by controlling the territorial government from the start in the interests of slavery. The contest thus begun not only convulsed Kansas, but speedily shook the country from end to end.

The first open conflict between the opposing forces came in the autumn of 1854. The territorial governor, appointed by Pierce to carry the Kansas-Nebraska act into effect, was Andrew H. Reeder, a Pennsylvania Democrat, who announced his entire willingness to see Kansas become a slave state, a man of an excitable temperament, wholly unprepared and to a large degree unfitted for the task which he found thrust upon him. No sooner had he arrived and named November 29 for the election of a territorial delegate than the storm broke. On that day over sixteen hundred armed men from the western counties of Missouri, who had been organized in "Blue Lodges" for the purpose of making Kansas a slave state, marched into the territory under the leadership of United States Senator Atchison, and cast votes for Whitfield, a former Indian agent and a southerner, as territorial delegate. Owing possibly to the general confusion in the region, as well as to his desire to avoid trouble, Reeder raised no objection to this illegality; nor did the House hesitate to admit Whitfield to a seat in December, 1854, and the Missourian invasion, although known in the east, aroused little comment in the whirl of the Republican and Know-Nothing campaign.

During the winter of 1854-1855, the Missourians appealed to the south to prevent the swamping of the slave-holders in Kansas by a flood of New England abolitionists. More money, more settlers and arms must be supplied if Kansas was to be kept as a slave state. "Two thousand slaves actually in Kansas," urged B. F. Stringfellow, a Missouri leader, "will make a slave state out of it. Once fairly there nobody will disturb them." By the spring of 1855 the excitement in Missouri had become intense, and when Reeder ordered the election of a territorial legislature for March 30, it was felt that the decisive moment was at hand. Although a census of the territory, taken in February, 1855, showed that out of a total of 8601 inhabitants more than half came from the south, and less than seven hundred came from New England, the Missourians felt it would not do to leave anything to chance. On the election day, at least five thousand armed and organized men, led by Atchison, Stringfellow, and others, invaded the territory, took possession of the polls in nearly every district, overawed or drove away the election judges, and cast 6307 ballots. The northern immigrants, most of them utterly unused to violence, and all unprepared for such a performance, were too astounded and alarmed to make any effective protest; and when Reeder was called upon to declare the returns he found himself surrounded by Missourians, while he had scarcely any independent supporters.

Had Reeder possessed the courage to declare the entire election fraudulent, the history of the territory and of the country might have been different; but he did no more than to throw out returns from seven contested districts, and gave certificates of election to the remaining members, who, when they met as a legislature, promptly unseated the seven Free-Soilers. Kansas was thus organized with a legislature composed wholly of pro-slavery men, and the south scored the first success in the contest. The victory was won, however, by fraud and violence, and the whole theory of peaceful "popular sovereignty" vanished into thin air.

Very significant were the different ways in which the two sections regarded this election. Upon the people of the north it produced an impression of horror and disgust. "The impudence of this attempt," said Greeley, "is paralleled only by its atrocity. . . . If a man can be found in the Free

State to counsel the surrender of Kansas to the Slave power, he is a coward and a slave in soul." In the south, on the contrary, it was universally regarded as an act of justifiable self-defence against the unfair encroachments of the north; one invasion had simply been answered by another one in behalf of the right. In no clearer way could the differing standards of the north and the south be contrasted.

To the unfortunate Reeder now fell the duty of co-operating as governor with the legislature chosen by the "Border Ruffians," as the Missourians began to be called. First he showed by his conduct what a revolution had been worked by his six months' experience in his views regarding slavery and slave-holders, for in returning to Washington to consult the president, he made a speech in Pennsylvania which told the story of the election in detail. When he reached Washington he found himself the object of a growing southern dislike and suspicion. His failure to oppose the northern invaders, his refusal to co-operate with the Missourians, and still more his letters and speeches, earned him in southern eyes the epithets of "incompetent," "corrupt," "traitor," and "scoundrel."

Reeder found Pierce much disturbed by the growing excitement in the south over Kansas affairs, and unable or unwilling to give him any support. He showed so plainly that he would welcome Reeder's resignation that the governor offered to do so, provided Pierce would give him a written statement approving his conduct; but this Pierce dared not do. After fruitless interviews, Reeder returned to Kansas, with the eyes of the whole country upon him, but sure that his official career was to be a short one. The territorial legislature met in July, at Pawnee, a town without inhabitants, according to contemporary accounts, where Reeder had taken up a quantity of land. The governor's message was conciliatory, but the legislature disregarded him utterly, and, in spite of his indignant protest, adjourned to another settlement, Shawnee Mission, on the Missouri border, where it proceeded to enact a set of laws which won immediate notoriety. Regardless of the Calhoun theory of the impotence of a mere territorial legislature over slavery, it passed statutes to establish and protect the institution in the territory, adopting for the purpose the text of the Missouri slave code.

The principal statute, entitled "An act to punish offences against slave property," inflicted the death penalty for inciting a slave insurrection; death or ten years at hard labor for aiding a slave to escape; and two years at hard labor for denying "by speaking or writing," or by printing or introducing any printed matter, "the right of persons to hold slaves in this territory." The last section also was noteworthy. "No person," it ran, "who is conscientiously opposed to holding slaves or who does not admit the right to hold slaves in this territory, shall sit as jurors on the trial of any prosecution for any violation of any of the sections of this act." The news of this legislation intensified the rising anger of the north. "This will suffice," said the *Tribune*, "if enforced, to hang nearly every anti-slavery man in the territory. . . . And upheld we presume it will be." Reeder remained in office but a short time, being removed on August 15, nominally because of land speculation and "lack of sympathy with the people," but everybody knew that it was owing to his refusal to adapt himself to the pro-slavery Democrats.

By this time the country was aware that a new and serious "Kansas question" was shaping itself. The anti-slavery indignation of the north, which had dwindled in the winter of 1855, now rapidly revived at what appeared the violent and ruthless determination on the part of the Missourians to make Kansas slave territory with or without law, justice, or a majority of voters. The south, equally aroused, was now thoroughly committed to the effort to defeat the lawless invasions of the northerners, and raised a universal voice of approval over the Missourian exploits. The Georgia Democratic convention of June 5, 1855, resolved, "That we sympathize with the friends of the slavery cause in Kansas in their manly efforts to maintain their rights and the interests of the southern people, and that we rejoice at their recent victories over the paid adventurers and Jesuitical horde of northern abolitionism . . . that the deep interest taken by the people of Missouri . . . is both natural and proper, and that it is their right and duty to extend to their southern brethren in the territory every legitimate and honorable sympathy and support."

In the summer of 1855 the situation in Kansas was further complicated by the sudden action of the northern settlers, who had hitherto played a passive part. Led by Dr. Charles Robinson, an aggressive, cool-headed politician, an agent of the Emigrant Aid Society, who had been in California in 1849, the northerners determined to give a new demonstration of "popular sovereignty" by repudiating the territorial legislature as illegal and seeking admission to the Union under a state constitution. At the same time they prepared to meet force with force in case the "Border Ruffians" again invaded the territory. Rifles and ammunition were sent for, the men were drilled, and "Jim" Lane, a reckless, volatile man from Indiana, with little soundness of judgment but with great natural oratorical ability, became the military chief. During September and October several mass conventions organized a "Free State party" and provided for a constitutional convention, which met duly at Topeka, October 23, comprising only delegates elected by the Free State settlers, and drew up the "Topeka Constitution" prohibiting slavery. It is worthy of note that the convention also submitted to popular vote, simultaneously with the constitution, an ordinance prohibiting the entrance of Negroes, free or slave, into the state, a fact indicating how far from abolitionist the northern settlers were. During this time occurred the regular election of a territorial delegate; but the Free State men conducted a separate election of their own, and unanimously sent Reeder to contest the seat to which Whitfield had been re-elected by all the pro-slavery votes.

This policy of the northern settlers stirred the southern element to lively indignation and contempt. The whole south regarded the Free State movement as a trick by which the "abolitionists," defeated in the election of the territorial legislature, sought none the less to gain control of the region. Missourians began to utter threats of violence, and when Shannon of Ohio, the new governor, arrived on the scene, he found the situation growing daily more menacing. Shannon, a Douglas Democrat, favorably disposed to the southern claim for Kansas, easily accepted the pro-slavery view that the Topeka constitution was a revolutionary proceeding, and in his inaugural address clearly showed that he meant to oppose the northerners. He even presided at a meeting at Leavenworth where the pro-slavery sympathizers organized themselves into a "Law-and-Order party" to oppose the treasonable plans of the Free State people, and in a speech declared "The President is behind you!"

By this time it was evident that "popular sovereignty" was producing serious consequences. There were two communities in the same territory, living in separate towns and governed by separate laws. The slightest event might cause a collision, for the Missourians were true frontiersmen, habituated to the ready use of knife or gun and only waiting for a pretext to "clean out the abolition crowd." Cases of brawls and shooting became frequent. Finally, in late November, just before the time set by the Free State men for a vote upon their constitution, an episode occurred which nearly brought on civil war. A Free State man who had been arrested by Sheriff Jones, a red-hot Missourian, for uttering threats against a pro-slavery murderer, was freed by a band of northerners and taken to Lawrence. Without further delay the infuriated sheriff sent word to Missouri, and later, as an after-thought, to Shannon; and at once about fifteen hundred excited "Border Ruffians" swarmed into the territory, to be joined by the pro-slavery, territorial, "Law-and-Order" millitia. The town of Lawrence was found, however, to be surrounded by earthworks, behind which lay several hundred Free State men armed in part with the dreaded Sharps rifles, and the invading force hesitated to attack. This gave time for the cooler heads on each side to work for peace; and finally Shannon, upon visiting the scene, saw that the Free State town had done nothing in the eye of the law to call for any such attack, and drew up a sort of treaty of peace. The Missourians withdrew in great disgust and freely announced that they were simply biding their time.

After this bloodless affair, somewhat absurdly called the "Wakarusa War," the Free State party carried through the rest of its programme undisturbed, except by a few brawls and shooting affrays. The Topeka constitution was ratified on December 15, and the ordinance excluding Negroes adopted, and on January 15, 1856, a governor and a legislature were elected. On March 4 the Topeka legislature met, and, following the cautious advice of Robinson, the governor, made no attempt for the moment to assume jurisdiction over the pro-slavery settlements, but adopted a memorial to Congress asking for admission to the Union, and adjourned until the summer to await events.

Such was the astounding result of a year and a half of "popular sovereignty" in Kansas. The organized immigration from New England; the Missourian retort of fraud and intimidation; the illegal voting, and the extreme pro-slavery action of the Shawnee Mission legislature were utterly beyond the imagination of the senators and representatives who passed the bill in 1854. On the other hand, the attempted imitation of California by the Free State men, involving a defiance of the territorial authorities and an ignoring of nearly one-half of the actual inhabitants of the territory, was a total surprise to the eastern anti-Nebraska men. The settlers in Kansas, without direction from any quarter, took affairs into their own hands, and created a political situation as exciting as the original Kansas question, and far more ominous. The time had come when the federal government could not avoid taking a hand. The rival organizations, the contesting delegates, and the imminent danger of war between the factions forced Congress and the president to act. When the thirty-fourth Congress, chosen in the months of political upheaval, met in December, 1855, the attention of the whole country was focussed upon the struggle for control of the territory, and sectional passions were deeply involved.

While the course of events in Kansas was leading, through violence and illegality, to the verge of civil war, national political organization was also passing through a crisis. The question before the country after the election of 1854 was whether an anti-slavery party should win the support of northern voters, or whether the old Whig party, comprising southern as well as northern members, should be revived under some new form. As the sudden anger over the repeal of the Missouri Compromise died away, and the issue of the control of the territorial government did not for a year come before Congress, old political traditions tended to draw men into organizations which claimed to be national rather than sectional, and which avoided the old danger of arousing the south and endangering the stability of the Union.

These feelings worked strongly against the Republican party in the year 1855, and aided a vigorous effort, which now began, to create a successor to the old Whig party through the expansion of the Know-Nothings into a national organization. The national council of November, 1854, adopted a new Union oath which placed the order on much the same basis as the "Union-saving" compromisers of 1850 and 1851. "You will discourage and denounce," it ran, "any attempt coming from any quarter . . . to destroy or subvert it or to weaken its bonds, . . . and you will use your influence to procure an amicable adjustment of all political discontents or differences which may threaten its injury or overthrow. You do further promise and swear that you will not vote for any one . . . whom you know or believe to be in favor of a dissolution of the Union . . . or who is endeavoring to produce that result."

This action paved the way for others besides anti-slavery and anti-foreign enthusiasts to enter the organization; and in the winter and spring of 1855 councils were formed all over the United States, honey-combing the local Republican or anti-Nebraska coalitions of the west with a Know-Nothing oath-bound membership, and practically absorbing the entire southern Whig body.

By the spring of 1855 the wildest claims were made for the order; it was said to have a sworn enrollment of over a million voters and to be able to control every city and nearly every state in the Union. The spring elections turned over Rhode Island, New Hampshire, and Connecticut into the hands of the Know-Nothings, and thus gave color to these assertions; but the Virginia campaign in May, 1855, showed that in the south the Know-Nothings were merely the Whigs under a new name. Henry A. Wise, the Democratic candidate for governor, made a powerful canvass of the state and was successful, after a savage contest, by a ten thousand majority. Thenceforward the extravagant claims for the Know-Nothings were discounted, but although it was seen that it could not revolutionize the south, its control of the north was not yet disproved.

By this time, however, two obstacles to the triumphant progress of the Know-Nothing party were becoming visible. In the first place, the attitude of its northern and southern members was fundamentally different on slavery matters. The New England Know-Nothings were anti-slavery men, who had joined the society in order to strike at the Pierce administration; and when they gained control of a state they enacted laws to obstruct the return of fugitive slaves, passed resolutions denouncing the repeal of the Missouri Compromise, and elected anti-slavery men to the United States Senate. But the southern Know-Nothings, although old Whigs, and strongly Unionist, were equally pro-slavery, and the chief ground of attack against them by the southern Democrats was not so much their secret and proscriptive platform as the fact of their being in the same order with the New England Americans. "Know-Nothingism," said a Virginia Democratic address, "has its origin and growth in those quarters of the Union where Abolitionism is most powerful. . . . Every election in which Northern Know-Nothingism has triumphed has inured to the benefit of Abolitionism. . . . We appeal to Southern men, without distinction of party, to ponder the consequences before they cooperate with this organization." The danger of sectional difficulty in the new Union party was visible almost as soon as it was created.

The other weakness of the new party lay in the fact that it was almost without strong leaders. Except in the northernmost slave states, where such men as Clayton, of Delaware, and Bell, of Tennessee, gave it some support, the conservative Whigs who might have been in sympathy with its nonsectional and Unionist aspirations recoiled in disgust from its riotous and proscriptive character and its secret machinery. Such men as Winthrop and Choate, of Massachusetts, representing the Webster tradition, were entirely out of sympathy with it. In the south, such influential men as Stephens and Toombs, of Georgia, and Benjamin, of Louisiana, went squarely over to the Democratic party. "I know of but one class of people," said Stephens, "that I look upon as dangerous to the country. . . . This class of men at the North, of which the Massachusetts, New Hampshire and Connecticut legislatures are but samples, I consider as our worst enemies; and to put them down I will join as political allies, now and forever, all true patriots at the North and South, whether native or adopted. . . . Their very organization is not only anti-American, anti-Republican, but at war with the fundamental law of the Union and therefore revolutionary in its character."

The abler anti-slavery leaders at the North in like manner held aloof from the movement. Seward, Chase, and Sumner refused to countenance the party, and Greeley, in the *Tribune*, openly scoffed at it, declaring, in a phrase which became permanently attached to it, that "it would seem as devoid of the elements of permanence as an anti-Cholera or anti-Potato-rot party would be." Almost the only strong leader in the north was Wilson, of Massachusetts, a sincere anti-slavery man whose political career showed boldness, shrewdness, and a light regard of party ties. Using the Know-Nothing party simply as a means to secure the redemption of Massachusetts from the "Cotton Whigs," and bring about his own election to the Senate, he was entirely willing to destroy it in the interests of the anti-slavery cause. Left, then, to the management of men new to public life or drawn from the ranks of minor politicians, the party showed no efficient leadership.

When the national council of the order met, in June, 1855, at Philadelphia, the differences between northern and southern Know-Nothings led to a sharp contest over the attitude of the body upon slavery in the territories. Anti-Catholic and anti-foreign declarations were unanimously accepted; but it took days of hot debate before the council, by a vote of 80 to 59, could adopt the following resolution: "Pretermitting any opinion upon the power of Congress to establish or prohibit slavery in the territories, it is the sense of this National Council that Congress ought not to legislate on the subject of slavery within the territories of the United States, and that any interference by Congress with slavery as it exists in the District of Columbia would be . . . a breach of the National faith." From this time on the order stood committed to the familiar policy of expressly conciliating the south.

By this time the practical identity of the Know-Nothing, or American party, as it now styled itself, with the Whigs was manifest in membership and character. A year of pretence at mystery had exhausted the efficacy of that device, and when the proceedings of the national council were reported, unchecked, to newspapers day by day, it was evident that the oaths, grips, passwords, and ritual had ceased to serve their purpose. From this time the state organizations ordinarily held open conventions and went before the voters as the "American party," although in popular language the name Know-Nothing lingered on. In the elections of 1855 the southern Know-Nothings carried Maryland, Kentucky, and Texas, and cast a respectable minority in other states; in the extreme west, also as a pro-slavery party, they carried California; but in the north, although they carried New York—where the irreconcilable "Hard" and "Soft" Democrats still ran separate tickets—their vote fell off badly in Massachusetts and Pennsylvania, for not even the repudiation of the troublesome twelfth section of the Philadelphia platform could hold anti-slavery members.

The Republicans also lost ground, being unable to gain in the states where the Know-Nothings were strong. Their only victory was in Ohio, which elected Chase governor over both a Democratic competitor and a candidate supported by Whigs and Know-Nothings. At the expense of these two parties the Democrats profited, making a bold campaign in every state, denouncing the sectionalism of the Republicans and the proscriptive aims of the Americans. They carried five southern states, and regained Pennsylvania, Wisconsin, and Maine, the last through Whig assistance. On the whole, the year ended with the political future still doubtful. It looked very much as if the old situation had returned, with the Know-Nothings occupying the place of the Whigs, the Republicans standing as an enlarged Free Soil party, and the Democrats likely to maintain themselves against a divided opposition.

But by this time the rising excitement over the situation in Kansas began to influence the situation. The enthusiasm of the people of the north for the Free State cause in Kansas resembled that of a country at the beginning of a war. Newspapers were crowded with inflammatory editorials, articles, and extracts from letters of northern emigrants describing acts of violence and cruelty. Public meetings were held everywhere, in which speakers made urgent appeals for volunteers, subscriptions, and arms for Kansas. One such, at New Haven, Connecticut, attained national fame. After an address by Henry Ward Beecher, fifty rifles were subscribed for to fit out a party of emigrants sent under the auspices of the Congregationalist clergy and church-members of the city. Beecher's advocacy of the use of Sharps rifles by the Kansas settlers led to their being termed "Beecher's Bibles" by friend and foe.

On the other side, the south was thrilled with anger and alarm. Atchison, of Missouri, made urgent appeal for southern aid, reiterating that the future of the institution of slavery was bound up in the outcome of the contest for Kansas. "If Kansas is abolitionized," he wrote, "Missouri ceases to be a slave state, New Mexico becomes a free state, California remains a free state; but if we secure Kansas as a slave state, Missouri is secure, New Mexico and southern California, if not the whole of it, becomes a slave state; in a word, the prosperity or ruin of the whole south depends on the Kansas struggle." In response to such appeals, an agitation for money and men spread over the south, with public meetings, fiery speeches, subscriptions, and the raising of companies of emigrants. Attempts were even made in the Alabama and Georgia legislatures to pass acts offering state aid to Kansas emigrants.

Yet, although southern feeling was deeply stirred, the results of this agitation did not equal those of the simultaneous northern propaganda; and the only important reinforcement provided in the winter of 1856 was a company of less than three hundred men raised by Colonel Buford, of Alabama, largely at his own personal expense. This force, which went unarmed, in deference to a proclamation of President Pierce, set forth from Montgomery with gifts of Bibles, amid prayers and enthusiastic popular sympathy; but upon its arrival in the territory it was immediately armed as part of the territorial militia. By the end of February it was clear that the coming spring would find men swarming into Kansas, with what results no one could foresee.

In the midst of this increasing excitement, the ill-fated American party tore itself to pieces upon the unavoidable issue. The first proof of its fatal weakness appeared in a contest for the speakership of the House of Representatives, which delayed the conduct of all public business from the meeting of Congress in December, 1855, until the end of February, 1856. The regular administration Democrats numbered only seventy-five in place of the one hundred and fifty-nine who controlled the previous Congress, and their candidate was Richardson. The opposition, elected in the political whirlwind of 1854, was too heterogeneous to combine. The largest single group comprised about one hundred and seventeen Americans, leaving about forty "straight" Republicans and a number of independents. But of the Know-Nothing plurality, only about forty could be held together in support of Fuller, of Pennsylvania, the avowedly American candidate. Nearly all the rest joined the Republicans in voting for Banks, of Massachusetts, who had just abandoned the Know-Nothing party for the Republican. For weeks, running into months, the tripartite struggle went on, in an irregular running debate, mainly on the Kansas issue, interrupted with ballotings for speaker.

January 12, 1856, the three candidates explained their views. Banks insisted that Congress had both the power and the duty to prohibit slavery in the territories; Fuller denied that either Congress or the territorial legislature had any power except to protect slavery; while Richardson stood on Douglas's ground that, whether Congress had the right to prohibit slavery or not, it rested with the territorial government to afford protection. Incessant attempts at coalition between Democrats and southern Know-Nothings, and between Republicans and all other anti-Nebraska men, were fruitless. The House in exhaustion voted to elect by a plurality, and Banks was chosen, February 2, by 103 votes to 100 for Aiken, of South Carolina. This victory ended a long period of suspense; the defeated southerners acquiesced in the result, and the House was finally ready for business.

A few days later the Know-Nothing party, shattered as a congressional group, also broke into pieces as a political organization. February 18 a national council of the order met at Philadelphia, modified the party platform by striking out the objectionable twelfth section, and inserting a clause which demanded congressional non-interference with "domestic and social affairs" in a territory, and condemned the Pierce administration for reopening sectional agitation by the repeal of the Missouri Compromise. No such attempt to befog the issue could prevent a crisis when the nominating convention of the American party assembled four days later in the same place. The anti-slavery northern members refused to be bound by the platform just adopted by the order, and demanded that no candidates be nominated who were not in favor of interdicting slavery north of 36°30' by congressional action. When this proviso was laid on the table, at once a score of members withdrew. The next day the convention nominated ex-President Fillmore, the man who had signed the fugitive-slave law, with Donelson, of Tennessee, for vice-president. Thereupon more members seceded and joined the earlier bolters in a call for a national convention of all "Americans opposed to the establishment of slavery in any of the territory which was covered by the Missouri Compromise," at New York in June. Plainly the American party as a national organization was bankrupt. Sectional passions were too strong to enable men from north and south to stand on a common platform ignoring slavery, and the party was moribund before it was two years old.

On the same day with the American convention, the first Republican national convention met at Pittsburgh, under a call from the state committees of nine states, but with delegates present from twenty-three. The proceedings were full of enthusiasm, for the leaders felt that with ordinary prudence and adequate organization their party might absorb all the dissatisfied Know-Nothings and follow up its victory in the speakership contest with one in the coming presidential election. Resolutions were adopted looking to a thorough political organization; a national committee was appointed, one of whose members was Governor Robinson, of Kansas; and a national nominating convention was called for June 17. On the Kansas question, the party took the full Free State position by demanding the admission of the territory as a state under the Topeka constitution.

By the end of February, 1856, the results of the Kansas excitement were visible in the definite failure of the American party and the practical certainty that the Republican party would take its place in the north. The presidential election was to be contested by a northern sectional party, long dreaded by all conservatives; and the outcome must depend largely on the course of events in Kansas and the way in which Congress and the administration dealt with them. The situation was highly critical, increasing in tension with every week.

&#x2E3E; &#x2E3F;

IN *1858, two prospective candidates for the Presidency of the United States —Stephen A. Douglas and Abraham Lincoln—vied for the Senate seat from Illinois. In the course of it, both candidates met in seven debates, during the course of which the relative merits of free soil and popular sovereignty were argued. Douglas did not hesitate to exploit the racial issue, charging Lincoln with a "belief that the Negro was made his equal." His Republican opponent, fully aware of the depth of racist sentiments in the United States, promptly disavowed any intention of making the Negro the social or political equal of white men. But Lincoln took particular care to emphasize that the black man should have the right to the fruits of his own labor. "All I ask for the Negro is that if you do not like him," Lincoln argued, "let him alone." He added, "If God gave him but little, that little let him enjoy." Douglas eked through to victory, but he did so with a party divided; Buchanan, unwilling to forgive Douglas' stubborn defense of popular sovereignty during the Lecompton Constitution debate, threw the full federal patronage in support of a third candidate. It marked an irreconcilable split within the Democratic party that would not heal.*

*When the Democratic convention convened at Charleston, South Carolina, the Southerners demanded explicit protection of slavery in the territories and an abandonment of popular sovereignty. Douglas' spokesman flatly warned the assembled Southerners, "Gentlemen of the South, you mistake us—you mistake us—we will not do it." What seemed apparent from the outset of the convention had finally happened. "The South has driven the Northern Democracy to the wall, and now insists upon protection of slavery in the Territories," one astute observer noted. To accede to such a demand would result in "the political execution of every Northern Democrat, and the total destruction of the Democratic party." The Charleston Convention ended in deadlock and breakup.*

*At Chicago, the Republican convention, where William H. Seward was the front runner, settled instead for the seemingly more moderate Lincoln. The campaign and election that followed were really two separate elections. In the North, the race was between Lincoln and Douglas, and in the South, it was between John C. Breckinridge, the Southern Democratic candidate, and John Bell, the Union Party choice. The result was foregone, Lincoln with less than 40 percent of the total vote swept the Northern electoral vote; even if all the opposition's 60 percent plus had been cast for a single candidate, the electoral result would not have been changed. Ironically, what Calhoun had feared, Northern electoral dominance, had come to pass, but with a twist: it was a minority decision.*

*Once elected Lincoln maintained a silence as first South Carolina and then six of the other Deep South states seceded. When he did speak it was to make it crystal clear that he would tolerate no extension of slavery into the territories. "You think slavery is right and ought to be extended; while we think it is wrong and ought to be restricted. That I suppose is the rub," he wrote to Alexander H. Stephens, as the old republic fell apart. The long journey to a rendezvous with irrepressible conflict was almost complete.*

*Arthur Charles Cole (1886-     ), long a professor of history at the University of Illinois and Brooklyn College, centered his scholarship on the Old South and the era leading to Civil War. His work on the Whig party in the South remains a basic source, one which, along with his study of the irrepressible conflict, provides points of departure for further research.*

# THE IRREPRESSIBLE CONFLICT, 1850-1865

## by Arthur Charles Cole

Throughout the presidential campaign of 1860 powerful forces of Northern capital were arrayed against the candidacy of the Illinois rail splitter. Conservative fears seemed borne out early in November when the news came of the suspension of the oldest banking house in Baltimore. "The panic of 1860 has commenced in earnest," commented a New York journal. "This state of things is the harbinger of what may be expected in case Lincoln should be elected. . . . The merchants of New York should give heed to those signs of the times, and strive, with might and main, for the success of the Union ticket." The belated meeting on November 5 of a group of New York merchants favorable to Lincoln's election was a rather equivocal demonstration of Wall Street support. The Illinois standard-bearer was privately under powerful pressure from the commercial and manufacturing interests of New England "to barter away the moral principle involved in this contest, for the commercial gain of a new submission to the South." As in 1856, funds were poured into Pennsylvania, the pivotal state. August Belmont and other Democratic Wall Street bankers gave generously of their means to save Pennsylvania and the nation from a political revolution. Old-

line politicians in the Republican ranks, like Thurlow Weed, admitted that
Pennsylvania had been lost in 1856 only because the Democrats had expended fifty thousand dollars more than the Republicans were able to raise.
Now the latter left no stone unturned, even collecting funds from the
beneficiaries of the New York City railroad franchises.

The Republican victory on election day seemed a great blow to American
prosperity. Trade with the South reached a complete standstill: the wheels
of industry ceased for the moment to turn: securities at the stock exchange
went topsy-turvy: money became excessively stringent as the banks, fearful
of another panic, called in their loans. The future was dark and uncertain.
Was the economic development of the nation to be sacrificed to maudlin
sentimentality and blind fanaticism? This was the question upon the lips of
conservative men of affairs.

The moneyed interests of the North, hysterical at the thought of secession, favored preserving the Union at any price, particularly since disunion
was likely to be accompanied by the forfeiture of Southern debts. There
was owing upon the books of Northern merchants and bankers a Southern
debt of two or three hundred millions of dollars: nor was there any evidence
of a disposition to pay those obligations as they fell due. Indeed, as Southerners beheld the utter terror of Northern creditors at the specter of repudiation, disunion began to offer even greater attractions than mere relief from
long-continued economic exploitation and a time-worn crusade. Journals
like the *Clayton* (Alabama) *Banner* advanced the argument that it was
"*treason to the South to pay money*, or in any way *encourage*, aid or abet
the transfer to the hostile section of so important a weapon of attack and
defense." Many were induced to favor a general "smash-up" that would
wipe out their liabilities to Northern creditors.

Northern argument that the South was not really in earnest, that talk of
disunion was an ancient brand of bluff and braggadocio, and that repudiation could easily be met by confiscation of Southern property in the free
states did not relieve these fears. Loudly in petitions and mass meetings the
"doughface" spokesmen of Northern capital begged for the acceptance of
a scheme of compromise that would satisfy the South and save the Union.
Lincoln was never quite sure until he entered office that the Eastern leaders
even of his own party could be kept from yielding to such entreaties. When
in due course the lower tier of Southern states effected their withdrawal
from the Union and Lincoln assumed the reins of administration at the
most trying time in the nation's history, "the upper world of millionaire
merchants, bankers, contractors, and great traders" rejoiced that the Republicans were at length suffering "for their success."

Lincoln's election, indeed, inaugurated a revolution which played havoc
with many existing institutions, political, social and economic. But the brunt
of the upheaval fell upon the states that had taken their stand for a static,
agrarian civilization in which the institution of chattel slavery held the place
of paramount importance. Some Southerners consoled themselves with the
thought that they were of the blood of a master race, a noble Norman
stock not to be crushed by Northern Puritans of vulgar Saxon origin. They

repudiated all thought of brotherhood with the Yankees: this was no frat-ricidal war but a renewal of the hereditary hostility between the "two races engaged." Let not the "Saxonized naw-worm" bring his taint to the soil of the South. Others, like Senator Wigfall of Texas, accepted as compliment and not reproach the description of their section as a primitive but civilized agricultural community. If, they claimed, it lacked not only a commercial marine, manufacturing and the mechanic arts but also any real cities, litera-ture or even press, it was by choice. In such an atmosphere, of course, the plantation system and the institution of chattel slavery might flourish, al-though then only with the reins of power in the hands of its ardent ex-ponents and champions. But amid the whirl and rush of modern industrial civilization its doom was certain.

*　　*　　*　　*　　*

The political "revolution" of 1860, which sent Abraham Lincoln to the White House, transferred to the North the reins of power previously held to a surprising degree by Southern men and Southern sympathizers. South-ern conservatives could see no serious menace in the mere fact of Lincoln's election and counseled patience unless some overt hostile act were taken. Extremists, on the other hand, like the editors of the *Charleston Mercury*, proclaimed the direct consequences to Southern rights and Southern honor and declared their unwillingness to believe or accept any assurances that might come from the president-elect. Southerners generally, including Alexander H. Stephens, were alarmed that the triumphant party had made the subject of slavery the "central idea" in a platform of principles which aimed "to put the institutions of nearly half of the States, under the ban of public opinion and national condemnation."

After long contemplation of sufferings from economic discrimination, they had become acutely sensitive to what Senator Judah P. Benjamin in 1856 called "the incessant attack of the Republicans, not simply on the in-terests, but on the feelings and sensibilities of a high-spirited people by the most insulting language, and the most offensive epithets." Much of the ag-gressiveness of the "chivalry" politicians of the fifties was the result of the effort to compensate for this wounded pride. "Southern honor" was at stake; in its behalf there could be no excess of zeal. Therefore little exact analysis needed to be made of the alleged menace to slavery. The fire eaters preferred what the *Nashville Republican Banner* at first derided as "subli-mated abstractions," although when the issue of state "coercion" was raised in April, 1861, the same editorial pen found vent in similar fulminations.

Contemporary assertion of the constitutional right of peaceful secession was one of the commonest of these abstractions. The doctrine was written into formal pronouncements. According to this argument the burden of responsibility for an armed clash would rest upon the North. But Southern champions were not unwilling to face the serious possibility of conflict. For a decade "The Sword" had been toasted in South Carolina as "The arbiter of national disputes. The sooner it is unsheathed in maintaining Southern rights, the better." "No nation has ever yet matured its political growth without the stern and searing experience of civil war," William H. Trescott had declared in 1850. "If war does come," added Edward B. Bryan, "it will be an open, rigorous and determined war, between two great nations; the one defending all that is sacred, the other the Lord knows what." Those who cradled the Southern Confederacy were therefore more than mere closet philosophers.

The day of compromise passed despite the active efforts of its advocates in and out of Congress. Determined to preserve the prosperity which depended upon the continued cooperation of the South, financiers of New York, Boston and Philadelphia supplemented the conservative politicians in their efforts to quell Northern sectionalism. But large and imposing Union meetings, and even a general tendency toward greater moderation in the North, were not enough to quiet the storm that had been loosed.

The winter of 1860-1861 witnessed the secession of the lower tier of seven slave states. A month and more of anxious waiting after Lincoln's inauguration ended in war being precipitated by the events in Charleston Harbor. There, after a futile resistance, the little federal garrison at Fort Sumter surrendered to a Southern force. As this news flashed through Dixie the people went wild with joy. Processions of singing and shouting revelers marched up and down the streets; later the celebration was adjourned to clubs, restaurants, bars and taprooms. It seemed a favorable omen that one little state could successfully defend the sacredness of her soil; how then could the North—even with the seventy-five thousand volunteers for which Lincoln now called—expect to subjugate a united South? Under this impelling logic and in view of reiterated hostility to any attempt at state coercion, the upper tier of states—Virginia, Tennessee, Arkansas and North Carolina—successively arrayed themselves on the side of Southern independence.

Secessionists had early made ready to defend their rights by force. Military preparedness had been a matter of serious concern in the crisis of 1850-1851. Military education then took on a more serious aspect. Literary institutions like La Grange College were converted into military academies. Virginia Military Institute at Lexington, under patrons like Professor Jackson whose sturdiness was to win him the name of "Stonewall," became second in reputation only to West Point. In the excitement following John Brown's raid Virginia and near-by regions were put "on a war footing."

During the presidential campaign, in anticipation of Lincoln's election, companies of "minute men" were formed in South Carolina; blue-cockaded recruits drilled and paraded in the principal centers of the state. With the news of the "Black Republican" victory organizations of "minute men" also appeared in New Orleans and other cities while efforts were made to transform into effective military units the militia that had existed largely on paper. Orders for weapons and munitions were placed with dealers in New York and New England as well as in Baltimore. These developments, together with movements to boycott other Northern goods and to expel suspicious Northerners, stirred the popular pulse and created something of a mob spirit that the advocates of secession promptly capitalized. The news of the South Carolina ordinance of secession was hailed by noisy salutes and enthusiastic demonstrations which brought new recruits. Confederate flags were flung from private dwellings and public buildings, even in states that had not yet seceded. Home guards were organized in nearly every city or town, ready to act upon rumors of incendiary fires and servile insurrection which the existing nervous tension bred. In some communities the secretly organized "chivalry leaders" varied their excited discussions with target practice, using as a mark a board roughly hewn into the shape of a man and designated as "Old Abe." Meantime the state legislatures gave legal authorization for properly equipped military forces.

The celebration of the Sumter victory was followed by more serious tasks. War had to be made in earnest if the Southern Confederacy was to take its place in the family of nations. Previously there had been idle talk, even in Richmond, of a grand march on the capital at Washington. Now it was urged that Southern hearth and home be safeguarded against "the invading hosts of the damned Abolitionists." President Jefferson Davis called for one hundred thousand troops, later for four times that number. Volunteers poured into the recruiting offices from plantation homes and yeoman farms. Clumsy yokels as well as sleek, dandyish youths with long, flowing locks enlisted in the ranks to fight the battles of Southern chivalry. Within a year half the eligible male population had responded to the appeal to arms.

In six months the South had achieved an apparent unity out of the diversity of sentiment that had prevailed at the time of secession. Most of those who had urged that the sectional fight should be continued within the Union had acquiesced in the separatist decision of their respective states. The conservative planter who still shook his head and quietly lamented the passing of better days was left undisturbed in his rural isolation, but the zealous Union man quickly felt the adverse judgment of the community, visited upon him perhaps by vigilance committees and other emissaries of King Mob. In due time conscription and exile reduced the numbers of both types; some Louisiana Unionists even preferred refuge in the swamps to involuntary service in the Confederate army. Of those who remained at home many kept silent, hoping to escape the penalties of disloyalty to the Confederacy.

Throughout the war the mountain fastnesses and valleys of "Alleghania," centering around western North Carolina, northern Alabama, and eastern Tennessee, formed the chief stronghold of the Unionists. This was an isolated region of little cotton culture and slaveholding where a mild antislavery sentiment had earlier cropped out. There, spokesmen like George W. Lane and R. S. Tharin of Alabama and Andrew Johnson, "Parson" Brownlow, and the Reverend N. G. Taylor of Tennessee openly defied the "cotton nobility." Others when forced into "secesh" service took their vows "from the teeth out." In communities torn by dissension the Union sympathizers awaited the succor of the federal army; meantime their ranks were depleted by refugee migration to Northern states, by enlistments in the Union forces, and by the ravages of a guerrilla warfare which they waged mountain-style with their Confederate neighbors.

Lurid tales were recounted in Northern parts of the maltreatment and sufferings of these loyalist dissenters. In eastern Tennessee both sides intermittently harassed and abused their opponents and at times burned, pillaged and murdered. Two or three thousand local Union noncombatants were said to have suffered martyrdom. In 1863 James Longstreet's hungry army cleared the country of its food supplies; when it retreated before A. E. Burnside's forces, starvation and destitution stared the rejoicing Unionists in the face. Only generous contributions from the North rescued the unfortunate from their plight.

The fighting Union bushwhackers of Alleghania furnished a striking contrast to the mild-mannered Quaker brethren of the North Carolina meeting and other conscientious objectors whom the Southern authorities tried to recruit despite their well-known gospel of peace in war time. Their conscientious scruples and their generally Union sympathies were often put to the most severe test. That none suffered complete martyrdom at the hands of the military authorities they felt could only be attributed to the protection of an "overruling Providence." Under the injunction to feed the hungry and clothe the naked, even neutral Quakers often gave aid and shelter to Unionist refugees and escaped federal prisoners. The latter also encountered Union men who were secretly organized, sometimes despite their acceptance of Confederate service, to assist in passing on such fugitives along an "underground railroad" to friendly hands and to eventual safety within the Union lines.

As has been said, certain venerable and distinguished sons of the South like James L. Petigru of South Carolina and Judge Garnett Andrews, a large Georgia slaveholder, refused to have any part in the war that they opposed and were left unmolested out of respect for their gray hairs or because they were regarded as amiable and harmless dotards. Younger blood, however, was given no choice. Under the circumstances many preferred to fight for the Union. The advancing federal armies brought Northern state recruiting agents who operated in active rivalry to credit the new recruits to their own commonwealths, sometimes offering bounties greater than those available to their own citizens. In the course of the struggle nearly three hundred thousand white Union soldiers were enrolled from the slave states. The border states and Tennessee were especially generous in this respect while even Alabama furnished over two thousand white recruits. Some of these had seen service in the Confederate forces but, like Jeremiah Clemens who had been a major general in the Alabama militia, had experienced a change of heart and welcomed an opportunity to change sides.

But a year of war, with little in the way of definite accomplishment, dulled the enthusiasm of many for participating on either side of the struggle. Yet the Southern forces that had suffered and fought in trench and camp sorely needed reenforcement. Accordingly, in April, 1862, despite their strong state-rights predilections, the legislative representatives of the Confederacy adopted a policy of conscription which, amended in September, rendered liable to draft all able-bodied males between the ages of eighteen and forty-five. Numerous exemptions were authorized, including state and Confederate officials and persons engaged in war industries or in what were deemed essential occupations. Under these arrangements many continued to evade military service. By one device or another, including in some cases self-imposed physical disabilities, probably one hundred and fifty thousand persons were exempted from active military service in the area east of the Mississippi River.

Professions like teaching—when twenty or more pupils were under tutelage—acquired new popularity even with those who had previously scorned the art of the pedagogue. The privileged status of apothecaries resulted in shops that boasted of "a few empty jars, a cheap assortment of combs and brushes, a few bottles of 'hair dye' and 'wizard oil' and other Yankee nostrums": soon they anticipated their modern counterpart in having even greater resemblance to variety stores or produce depots. Some found no way out except through the employ of substitutes. Here was a profitable field for brokers, as the market price of a soldier soon mounted to fifteen hundred dollars and three thousand dollars: professional misfits and deserters found their places as raw materials of the trade. Under the "twenty-nigger" clause many slaveholders escaped for a time the hardships of camp and battle-field while resenting any suggestion that this was "a rich man's war and a poor man's fight." It was estimated in September, 1864, that "over 100,000 landed proprietors and most of the slaveholders are now out of the ranks," a condition which, though doubtless exaggerated, caused ominous mutterings to reverberate through the Confederacy. In due time the government remedied the more flagrant abuses and in the last year of the war the manpower of the South was more effectively mobilized. The government maintained in active service a fighting machine that averaged about four hundred thousand men. Probably a grand total of well over a million served under the Stars and Bars in the course of the bloody struggle.

The Confederate soldiery did not, however, constitute an altogether enthusiastic fighting force. Caste barriers were felt to exist not only between officers and privates—with an often "shameful disregard" of the humble musket bearer by those in authority—but also among the rank and file where the sensitive exemplar of chivalry chafed at having to share the lot of rough, uncouth countrymen. The latter, conscious that those who had no direct stake in slavery constituted three fourths of the defenders of the Confederacy, in turn resented the implied superiority. Smoldering class hatred sometimes flared up on the arrival of rumors that wealthy exempts at home were "grinding the faces of the poor with their extortions and their speculations." There were increased mutterings against the conscript officers of the "Jeff Davis Secession Aristocracy."

Those who fought in the ranks were clad in a great variety of colors and costumes; but the bright plumage of many an original outfit soon disappeared in the ruck of war and weather. Replacements came from a multitude of sources. Many were glad to don captured federal uniforms even though at the grave risk of being mistakenly shot by Confederate bullets. The increasingly used gray uniform was often of a tobacco or butternut-colored homespun which, when a little rusty, seemed "the ugliest imaginable style of dress." From the beginning there was a shortage of overcoats and blankets while the supply of shoes was never adequate. Lee's army crossed the Potomac in the late summer of 1862 with thousands of his men *"barefooted, blanketless,* and *hatless!"* If Southern sympathizers in Maryland considered joining the Confederate cause, the impulse was thoroughly routed by the appearance of this Falstaffian horde. The real tragedy of these ragged troops, however, came with the onset of bitter winter weather.

Hunger constantly menaced the gaunt recruits of Dixie. Regular rations were scant enough from the start and, because of the poor management of the commissariat, often failed of delivery. After the spring of 1863 reduced allotments became a necessity. The generosity of the country people often supplied the deficiency and shipments from home sometimes broke prolonged fasts just when starvation seemed at hand. Raids upon Union supply centers and foraging also supplemented local stores. The Confederate cavalry, to which no beef was issued over a period of eighteen months and more, subsisted chiefly on corn, with an especial fondness for roasting ears in season.

In other particulars as well the Confederate forces suffered from inadequate arrangements for their health and physical well-being. Many of the better trained city physicians promptly enlisted and were given commissions for active service. On the other hand, in the rural areas anyone who possessed a small stock of medicines, a few recipes and a knowledge of how to bleed a patient was accepted as a military doctor. For a time the Confederates rejoiced that the Yankees were the chief sufferers as the malarial mosquitoes fought for their Southern homeland. But in the fall of 1862 yellow fever decimated the population of Wilmington and smallpox soon raged violently in the Confederate capital. Supplies of quinine and other necessary medicines threatened to fail despite some success in smuggling from the North and through the blockade. The Confederate government established laboratories to relieve the shortage and was fortunate in being able to enlist the services of the Le Contes in the laboratories at Columbia, South Carolina, which became the chief local source of supply.

After a battle all the doctors who could be spared from cities like Richmond hurried off to the field. For miles around every dwelling served as a hospital. In Richmond public buildings and even tobacco factories sheltered the sick and wounded, sometimes to a total of thirty thousand and more. Overworked army surgeons became hardened to the neglect which they were often powerless to correct. In general, little attention was directed to the most elementary sanitary precautions. To be sure, many an angel of mercy appeared among the volunteer nurses; Sally Tompkins, the Florence Nightingale of the South, was commissioned captain for her unwearied ministrations. But the South never developed an elaborate civilian volunteer organization to parallel the Sanitary and Christian Commissions of the North.

With all the hardships of field and camp and with the enemy penetrating farther and farther into Dixie, the drain of desertion impaired the strength of the Southern legions. The urge to desert was not a matter of simple disloyalty. Ill-fed, barefoot, homesick and war-weary soldiers could not have been expected to maintain a satisfactory morale. Discontent made rapid headway. Backcountry farmers and mountain yeomen increasingly resented the mandates that issued from the ruling class of the black belt. Often under the impelling need of their families for food and clothing they fled to the rescue. At times they sought relief from military routine in swamp and forest or mountain fastness. There, in desperate bands, they resisted the efforts of the Confederate authorities to hunt them down. Some sought the enemies' lines to taste the more generous treatment of federal generals. In all, at least two hundred thousand deserters were lost to the Confederate ranks. Desertion it was which virtually undermined the conscription policy of the Southern Confederacy.

An effective mobilization of all the available resources of the Southland was never attained. War materials and supplies were the obvious first need. Every type of weapon was promptly turned to account. The recruit usually appeared for service with a nondescript gun or revolver; even double-barreled shotguns were equipped for service with bayonets. The first extensive munition supply came from the federal forts and arsenals which were taken over following secession. Though one hundred and fifteen thousand stands of arms had been sent for storage in Southern arsenals in the spring of 1860 by Secretary of War Floyd, most of these were condemned muskets, as were those he sold to various Southern states after Lincoln's election. The Confederate leaders made haste upon the secession of Virginia to seize the United States arms factory at Harper's Ferry, but the federal commander destroyed the arsenal and most of the machinery in the armory building before abandoning it. Throughout the war Southern victories in the field usually involved the capture of arms and ammunition needed to replenish scanty supplies.

In the placing of orders for arms and munitions in Europe Southern purchasing agents were for some time favored over their Northern rivals. Even after the increasing effectiveness of the blockade made difficult the delivery of foreign purchases, the Confederate authorities used the leverage of cotton sales to compel blockade runners to include a proper share of war materials in their cargoes. For adequate supplies, however, emphasis had more and more to be laid upon local factories that the war brought into existence or into greater importance. Richmond, with the Tredegar works and other plants, became an important center from which a line of ordnance works was established by 1863 reaching into the Lower South. Selma, Alabama, like the Columbus and Augusta section of Georgia, witnessed an important development of munition manufacturing. Powder factories— some private and some government institutions—were set up all over the South, the most important being the government plant at Augusta. With infinite ingenuity and resource the ordnance department under General Josiah Gorgas, a native of Pennsylvania, was soon able to meet the demands made upon it, so that shortages in the field were due largely to the problem of distribution rather than of supply. When the dearth of metals threatened to curtail production, the South responded to the stirring appeal of General P. G. T. Beauregard to spare the church and plantation bells that they might be molded into cannon. In the same way copper kettles, brass door-knobs, lead and old iron implements were contributed. The rails of the horse-car street railroad in Richmond were sacrificed for the manufacture of armor for a gunboat.

The war, particularly the shutting out of foreign goods by the blockade, made a necessity out of the oft-proclaimed virtue of Southern self-sufficiency. As new ventures in iron, textile, glass and paper production were launched, loyal Southerners chose to believe that their economic problems were finding a solution. A cheerful optimism prevailed in official and un-official circles until well into the war. With the editor of the *Richmond Enquirer* they believed that this would "deprive the hated Yankee man and the hyena Yankee woman of their immemorial market." "Augusta drills," "Atlanta shirtings" and "Graniteville sheetings" set the standard in textiles. Although cotton operatives were exempted from military duty, the head of the Graniteville mills soon complained that Congress allowed only a seventy-five-per-cent profit. The products of the paper mills were usually very crude and rough, though newspaper publishers rejoiced when they found even this supply adequate for their most economical needs.

In the later years of the war the success of the Union arms greatly re-duced the number of Southern factories. Northern generals were not un-aware of the contribution they might make along these lines toward the throttling of the South. General W. T. Sherman not only burned the cotton factories at Rosswell, Georgia, but—quite unnecessarily, it would seem—transported the four hundred young women operatives beyond the Ohio in order to make certain that production would not be resumed in that vicinity. This unfortunate instance of the deportation of innocent and help-less females seems to have been overlooked by historians of American war-fare.

The effective mobilization of the South's material resources depended in large part upon the adequacy of its transportation system. The railroads consisted mainly of short lines operated under a particularism that prevented them from achieving the effective military co-ordination that was secured in the North. Rolling stock and trackage deteriorated rapidly under the heavy wartime traffic, nor was it possible to develop an adequate replace-ment by local efforts. Not a single bar of railroad iron was rolled in the Confederacy during the war. The rails of less important lines were some-times torn up to serve a greater need and Confederate troops often covered their retreat by the wholesale destruction of tracks and bridges. This was supplemented by the havoc wrought by the Union armies. In particular, Sherman's soldiers were past masters in this work, burning the ties and fences to heat the rails which they then wrapped around a tree trunk or a telegraph pole and transformed into "hair-pins" and "cork-screws." The federals captured eleven locomotives at Vicksburg which, after being over-hauled and repainted, were christened "General Grant," "Abraham Lin-coln" and the like. One of the most daring exploits of the war was the attempt of a group of twenty-four young Union raiders in northern Georgia under J. J. Andrews to cut the line of the Memphis and Charleston Railroad, an attempt which ended in a bold but unsuccessful effort to run off with a Confederate railroad train. With such a multitude of handicaps it was manifestly impossible for the railroads to play their proper role of not only guaranteeing adequate supplies, but also of equalizing the varying degrees of plenty and shortage that often existed in different parts of "rebeldom."

The people of Dixie, fighting for hearth and home, were prepared to make their many sacrifices to the cause of Southern independence. Yet they did not achieve—or at least maintain—that high degree of unity and morale which was essential to a successful revolution.

&

AND *the war came. Not exactly the war that everyone had expected: one that would last a brief season and like a summer storm fade away as swiftly as it billowed up. Instead, it lasted four full seasonal cycles to end in April as it had begun in April. Between the beginning and the end, the original intent of the war to restore "the Union as it was" changed to the more comprehensive intention to destroy slavery. Lincoln had originally been "anxious and careful that the inevitable conflict" for the restoration of the Union would "not degenerate into a violent and remorseless revolutionary struggle." But as the war deepened in its intensity, and as the national self-mutilation exacted a bloodier price, Lincoln recognized that "the dogmas of the quiet past, are inadequate to the stormy present." In a time of revolutionary upheaval, when precedent is nonexistent, only a consummate effort, he believed, to disenthrall oneself from the confines of the past could save the country.*

*To achieve this end, the North had to accept that nothing short of total independence would satisfy the South. Once Northerners understood the paramount Southern objective, they also realized that the stake was nothing less than the Union. The polar stars of the two protagonists were at diametrically opposite points, and as each pursued their opposed goals the rift that divided them grew wider until no dialogue was possible. Instead the stakes of the conflict steadily escalated until its only end was the destruction of one or the other of the belligerents. Nothing short of a total war in which the difference between soldier and civilian faded and the target encompassed a whole people could bring the Southern Confederacy down into ruins and force its surrender.*

*Before the war had drained the South of the means to continue resistance, somewhere between 750,000 and 1,250,000 Southerners had borne arms, and no less than 2,000,000 Northerners had entered the fray. In fields stretching from Shiloh, Antietam, Bull Run, Gettysburg, the Wilderness, Spotsylvania, Cold Harbor, Chickamauga, Atlanta and those numberless other names that can still stir uncooled memories, no less than 619,000 Americans died. When the guns fell silent a border drawn in blood separated Ameri-*

*cans in heart if not in fact. Within a single country, there dwelt side by side two people: one the conqueror and the other the conquered. Out of this division, as Woodrow Wilson believed, the task of creating a single American nationality emerged, one which a century later is not yet complete.*

*Bruce Catton (1899-     ), long a reporter on various newspapers, and briefly a federal employee, has written the most colorful and readable history of the Army of the Potomac. It captures through its numerous references to contemporary diaries, memoirs, letters, and the other written debris of a vanished generation the flavor of a tragedy. The sounds, smell, pain, hopes, joys, despair, and anxiety are all there. All that is missing is an awareness of the utter futility of it all. But then Americans have never really felt at ease with the Civil War except when it is presented as a pageant which as the English critic Matthew Arnold concluded "made American history interesting." The Civil War marked the greatest failure of American democracy. It brought the republic of the Founding Fathers to a fundamental crisis that could be resolved only on the battlefield, and it left a legacy of division between the sections that is only now beginning reluctantly to fade.*

# MR. LINCOLN'S ARMY

## by Bruce Catton

The rowboat slid out on the Potomac in the hazy light of a hot August morning, dropped down past the line of black ships near the Alexandria wharves, and bumped to a stop with its nose against the wooden side of a transport. Colonel Herman Haupt, superintendent of military railroads, a sheaf of telegrams crumpled in one hand, went up the Jacob's ladder to the deck—clumsily, as was to be expected of a landsman, but rapidly, for he was an active man—and disappeared into a cabin. A moment later he returned, and as he came down the ladder he was followed by a short, broad-shouldered, sandy-haired man, deeply tanned by the sun of the Virginia peninsula, with thin faint lines of worry between his eyes: Major General George Brinton McClellan, commander of the Army of the Potomac, which had been coming up from the south by water for a week and more and which at the moment was scattered all the way from Alexandria to the upper Rappahannock, most of it well out of the general's reach and all of it, as he suspected, soon to be out from under his authority.

There was an air about this youthful general—an air of far-off bugles, and flags floating high, and troops cheering madly, as if the picture of him which one hundred thousand soldiers had created had somehow become real and was now an inseparable part of his actual appearance. He could look jaunty and dapper after a day in the saddle, on muddy roads, in a driving rainstorm; like a successful politician, he lived his part, keeping himself close to the surface so that every cry and every gesture of the men who adored him called him out to a quick response that was none the less genuine for being completely automatic. It was impossible to see him, in his uniform with the stars on his shoulders, without also seeing the army—"my army," he called it proudly almost as if it were a personal possession, which was in a way the case: he had made it, he had given it shape and color and spirit, and in his mind and in the minds of the men he commanded the identification was complete.

He sat in the stern of the rowboat, beside the superintendent of military railroads, and he was silent as the boat went back upstream to the landing. The docks and the river front were a confusion of steamboats and barges and white-topped wagons and great stacks of boxed goods and equipment, and the quaint little town itself was lost in a restless, lounging concourse of soldiers: loose fringes of a moving army, convalescents and strays and detailed men, and here and there a regiment moving off with cased flags at route step toward some outlying camp. From this same town the general had set out, nearly five months ago, to take his army down to the swamps and forests below Richmond and win the war; he had known in his heart that he was destined to save the country, and the army had gone forth with unstained uniforms and gleaming rifle barrels, and with proud flags that had never touched the ground.

But nothing had worked quite the way he had expected. The Army of the Potomac, made in his own image, had spent some months on the Virginia peninsula—that long neck of land which runs southeast between the James and the York rivers, and which the army remembered as composed chiefly of mud, mosquitoes, and steaming heat, with a great tangle of gloomy forests infested by lean and hairy men with rifles who uttered shrill, nerve-splitting screams as they came forward endlessly to the attack. The luck of the army and the general had been all bad. Many battles had been fought, and while no great defeat had been suffered there had been a weary retreat from in front of Richmond to a dismal camp far down the river. The general considered that this retreat had been a masterful accomplishment, but the government considered it sheer disaster, and it was trying now—in August 1862—to strike the southern Confederacy with another instrument.

This new instrument, as McClellan was frank to state, had been poorly chosen. Scattered fragments of commands had been swept together and entrusted to a self-confident soldier from the Western armies, General John Pope, and Pope had been sent down into Virginia overland, following the line of the Orange and Alexandria Railroad to the Rappahannock River. Leaving McClellan and his army to swelter in their camp on the James, the rebels had promptly concentrated against Pope's army and had been giving him a bad time of it—so bad, indeed, that McClellan's army was now being pulled back to Washington and was being forwarded to Pope by bits and pieces. McClellan was not being sent forward with it; and this morning, as he passed through the sprawling base of supplies, where white door fronts of the colonial era looked down on muddy streets churned by endless wagon trains, it seemed likely that he would presently be a general without an army.

The general went with the colonel to the colonel's office. They were both West Pointers, and when the war broke out they had both been railroad men, and they could talk the same language. As soon as they were seated Haupt gave McClellan such news as he had. None of it was good. Seen thus, from behind the lines, the war was untidy, misdirected, discouraging.

Enemy forces, said Haupt, were across the railroad line at Manassas Junction. It had been thought at first that these were merely a handful of roving cavalry—cavalry had descended on the railroad a few days earlier, farther down the line at Catlett's—but it was beginning to be clear now that they were more important than that. A New Jersey brigade had gone forward to restore the situation and had run into rifle and artillery fire too heavy to come from any cavalry; had, as a matter of fact, been most distressingly cut to pieces. Two Ohio infantry regiments were holding on where the railroad crossed Bull Run, but they were obviously in grave danger and would probably have to come back. Confederates apparently were either on or near the railroad this side of them, between Bull Run and Alexandria; the bridge over Pohick Creek near Burke's Station, only thirteen miles out, was rumored to have been burned, and the telegraph line had been cut. Nor was it just the two Ohio regiments that were in peril. The seizure of Manassas Junction meant that General Pope was out of forage for his horses and rations for his men.

Colonel Haupt did not know where Pope was, and it seemed that the War Department did not know either. It was bombarding Haupt with inquiries and had evidently developed the jitters—McClellan saw a wire complaining that there had been "great neglect and carelessness" on the Manassas plain. To McClellan that seemed obvious. He did not admire General Pope, either as a man or as a soldier, and his present prospect of forwarding his own troops to Pope at a time when Pope's position was unknown and the road leading in his direction was blocked by rebel soldiers was not one that McClellan could think about with any pleasure.

Clearly, this was no time for an army commander or a superintendent of military railroads to sit holding his thumbs. With the plight of Pope's army and the dire fix of those two Ohio regiments Colonel Haupt had no direct concern, except that it was up to him to get the railroad back in working order so that these and other troops could be fed, supplied, and, if necessary, transported; and for this he had a plan of action, which he now asked McClellan to approve. A wrecking and construction train, ready to go forward and repair damaged tracks and bridges, was standing on a siding with steam up. Also ready was a freight train loaded with forage and rations. Haupt proposed to send out ahead of these a train of flatcars carrying a battery of field artillery and a few hundred sharpshooters. This could go as far as the condition of the track permitted, and the guns and riflemen could then advance by road and clear out such rebel marauders as might be in the vicinity. The wrecking train could then get the bridges repaired in short order—Haupt kept a stock of prefabricated bents and stringers on hand, ready for just such emergencies as this, and if they had to, his construction gangs could build a bridge with timber from torn-down farmhouses along the right of way—and when that had been done the supply trains could be leapfrogged through with subsistence for Pope's army.

The thin lines between McClellan's eyes deepened slightly and he shook his head slowly. He could not approve the plan. It would be attended with risk. Haupt was primarily a railroad man; any kind of expedient was all right, for him, if it just gave him a chance to put his track gangs on the job and get the line opened up again. Also, there was not, inherently, any very great difference between a rebel army and a spring freshet on a Pennsylvania mountain river—both broke up a railroad, and when the damage had been done one went out and fixed it as quickly as possible. But McClellan's mind was full of the mischances that can befall troops which are incautiously thrust out into enemy territory; he repeated that he could not approve. Haupt was irritated. All military operations, he said, were attended with risk, as far as he could see, and the risk here did not seem to be excessive. Surely, if the advance guard were properly handled, nothing very disastrous could happen. The trains could be kept safely in the rear while the skirmishers went forward. If the enemy were found in force, the men could retire to their train and the whole expedition could quickly be brought back out of harm's way.

McClellan shook his head again. The situation was too obscure. Enemy troops, possibly in very substantial numbers, appeared to be between Pope's army and Washington; the first thing to do was to arrange the troops actually present in such a way that the capital itself would be safe. Then preparations could be made for an advance in force. Meanwhile— the general had grown pale beneath his tan and appeared genuinely un- well—did the colonel have any brandy and water? The colonel did. McClellan took it and seemed revived, borrowed a scratch pad, and wrote a telegram to the War Department, reporting that he was ashore in Alexandria and describing the situation as he had found it. Then he de- parted.

Left to himself, Haupt fumed and pondered, and wished that he had not succeeded in finding McClellan at all. Earlier in the morning he had telegraphed his proposal to General Henry W. Halleck, commander, under the President, of the armies of the United States. Halleck, who never made a decision himself if it could possibly be passed along to someone else, had replied: "If you can see Gen. McClellan, consult him. If not, go ahead as you propose." Haupt had now seen General McClellan and he wished he hadn't; if he had only missed him, the expedition could be under way by now.

Although he had been trained as a soldier—he had been graduated from West Point in 1835, in the same class with George Gordon Meade—Haupt was essentially a civilian. Resigning his commission shortly after graduation, he had gone into railroad work, had built a good part of the Juniata division of the Pennsylvania Railroad, and had become, successively, division superintendent and chief engineer for that line. He had been brought into the army, somewhat against his will, as a railroad and construction expert, and he was admired in high places. President Lincoln liked to tell about the marvelous bridge Haupt had built "out of beanpoles and cornstalks" down on the Aquia Creek line out of Fredericksburg. Haupt actually belonged in the next century; as it was, in the Civil War most generals failed to appreciate him. He was used to direct action, and generals irritated him. His present job gave them many occasions to do this, and they never seemed to miss a chance. Three days ago, for example, Haupt had bestirred himself to assemble trains to send General Joe Hooker's division forward to Pope. He got the trains lined up, Hooker's troops were at hand ready to go aboard, but Hooker himself had vanished—presumably to seek the fleshpots in Washington. Haupt telegraphed to his good friend and brother railroad man, P. H. Watson, Assistant Secretary of War. Back came Watson's reply.

"General Hooker was in Alexandria last night, but I will send to Willard's and see if he is there. I do not know any other place that he frequents. Be as patient as possible with the generals; some of them will trouble you more than they do the enemy."

That was a judgment with which Haupt was ready to agree. He had no sooner got Hooker out of his hair than General Samuel D. Sturgis got into it. Sturgis showed up with a division of troops, demanding immediate transportation to the front. To make sure that his request for transportation got top priority Sturgis had moved his soldiers out and had seized the railroad—or that part of it which lay within his reach, which was enough to tie up the entire line—swearing that no trains would go anywhere until his division had been moved. Haupt tried to reason with him, but it was no go—Haupt was a colonel and Sturgis was a general, and Sturgis would not listen. Sturgis had the rank and he had the soldiers, and for the moment he had the railroad, too, and no temporary colonel was going to tell him what to do.

Haupt had had to go through that sort of thing before. General Pope had had similar ideas when he first took command in northern Virginia, announcing that his own quartermaster would control the movement of railroad cars just as he ran the wagon trains, and informing Haupt that his function was to do as he was told. Within two weeks the line had got into such a snarl that no trains could move in any direction. Pope came to see that it took a railroad man to run a railroad—he could get a point now and then if it was obvious enough, could John Pope, for all his bluster—and he was glad to hand the road back to Colonel Haupt; particularly so since Haupt by this time had got from the Secretary of War an order giving him complete and unqualified control over the railroad and everything on it, regardless of the orders any army commander might issue. Haupt, therefore, was ready to take Sturgis in his stride; but Sturgis had troops and guns and swore he would use them. Furious, Haupt telegraphed Halleck, getting in return a bristling order which specifically authorized him, in the name of the general-in-chief, to put Sturgis under arrest if there was any more funny business. Haupt summoned Sturgis to his office. Sturgis came, rather elevated with liquor, accompanied by his chief of staff.

Haupt showed Halleck's order and explained that he was getting all sorts of troops and supplies forward to General Pope and that Sturgis would simply have to wait his turn. Sturgis was not impressed, and he somehow got the idea that the order Haupt was exhibiting had been issued by General Pope.

"I don't care for John Pope one pinch of owl dung," said Sturgis solemnly—a sentiment which had its points but was hardly germane. Patiently Haupt explained: this order was not from Pope, it was from Halleck, who held the power to bind and to loose. Sturgis shook his head and repeated his judgment of Pope, savoring the sentence as if the thought had been bothering him for a long time. Haupt fluttered the order at him and went over it a third time. Sturgis, his needle stuck in one groove, repeated:

"I don't care for John Pope—"

His chief of staff tugged at his sleeve to stop him, and hastily and earnestly whispered in his ear. Sturgis blinked, finally got the point, and rose to his feet ponderously.

"Well, then," he said—with what, all things considered might be called owlish dignity, "*take* your damned railroad."

So that had been settled, and Sturgis had awaited his turn. But the episode had tied up the railroad for the better part of a day and had canceled the movement of four troop trains. Haupt was more than ready to agree with Assistant Secretary Watson about the generals.

Anyway, that was over. Now there was the problem of reopening Pope's supply line. Pope's soldiers must be getting hungry; and besides, with the outer end of the line gone, the Alexandria yards were clogged with loaded freight cars that had no place to go. Across the river, in Washington, the Baltimore and Ohio was complaining that boxcars consigned to Pope's army were filling the tracks on Maryland Avenue, the available B. & O. engines were too heavy to go over the Long Bridge; would Colonel Haupt please send an engine over from Alexandria and get them, so that the B. & O. could go on with its regular work? This Haupt could by no means do, having more cars in Alexandria now than he could handle. The B. & O. needled the War Department, which sent plaintive messages; and the day wore on, and the situation did not improve. Haupt reflected that he was, after all, in charge of the railroad, and that somewhere off to the southwest there was an army that greatly needed supplies. He determined to go ahead on his own hook. After dark he sent a message to McClellan—who by now had established his headquarters on shore—notifying him that at four in the morning he would start his construction train forward, followed by the subsistence train. Would McClellan at least let him have two hundred soldiers to go along as train guard? If the men did not report, Haupt added, the trains would go ahead without them.

He got no answer. At midnight he gave up on McClellan, got on his horse, and set out to appeal to the first general he saw—any general, just so long as he had a few troops to spare and was willing to loan a few of them to help open a vital railway line.

By good luck the first general Haupt found was Winfield Scott Hancock, a brigade commander in the Army of the Potomac, recently back from the peninsula, where in spite of the fact that his brigade had not had too much fighting to do he had somehow marked both it and himself as men who would be very useful indeed before the war was over. Late as it was, Hancock had only just gone to bed. He liked to do all his paper work around midnight and had a habit, whenever he encountered a report that was in any way faulty, of having the author hauled out of bed at once and brought to brigade headquarters to receive a dressing-down that was usually loud enough to arouse the nearby regiments. This trait was a trial to Hancock's staff, but it meant that most reports by now were letter-perfect before they ever reached the general.

Hancock was a direct actionist, who both looked and acted like a soldier—a burly, handsome man, who somehow managed always to be wearing a clean white shirt even when the army had been in the field for weeks, and who, in an army where the officers were notably profane, was outstanding for the vigor, range, and effectiveness of his cursing. His men liked to tell how, at the battle of Williamsburg, he had galloped up, outdistancing his staff, to order his troops to the charge—"the air was blue all around him," one of them recalled admiringly. There was a great breezy vigor and bluffness about the man. Earlier in the war, when his brigade was still in training, his men had taken to killing and eating the sheep of farmers near camp, and Hancock had determined to stop it. One afternoon, riding the lines near his camp, he had seen a knot of soldiers in a meadow, bending over the body of a sheep. Putting his horse to the fence, he galloped up, shouting mightily, and the men of course scattered—all except one who tarried too long and whom Hancock, flinging himself from his saddle, seized with strong hands.

"Now, you scoundrel, don't tell me you didn't kill that sheep—I saw you with my own eyes!" roared the general. Just then the sheep, not yet knifed, realized that it was no longer being held and sprang to its feet and scampered nimbly away. Hancock stared at the rocketing sheep, looked blankly at the quaking soldier in his hands—and then threw his head back and made the meadow ring with shouts of laughter.

It was this Hancock whom Haupt found on his midnight quest for troops. Hancock heard his story and immediately detailed the men for him, and early in the morning Haupt's trains went lurching off into Virginia. By ten in the morning Haupt was notified that the bridge near Burke's Station had been rebuilt. He also learned that enemy troops were still somewhere in the vicinity of Manassas in very great strength; the head of the construction gang had been told that Lee himself was with them. A little later trains came steaming back from Fairfax Station loaded with wounded men.

For the moment this was all the news there was. Haupt's line of track went off into the darkness where moved shadowy forces made large by rumor. For all anyone knew, Lee and his whole army might be between Pope and Washington. McClellan picked up a report that 120,000 Confederates were moving toward Arlington and the Chain Bridge, bent on the capture of Washington and Baltimore. Halleck sagely remarked that the thing to be afraid of at that moment was the danger that rebel cavalry might dash forward by night and enter the city—"rebel cavalry" in those days being terrifying words, since the plowhands and mechanics whom the Federals were earnestly trying to turn into cavalrymen were no match at all for Jeb Stuart's incomparable troopers.

McClellan sent four infantry regiments out to the works at Upton's and Munson's hills, covering the main highway in from Centreville, and instructed them to hold the lines there at all hazards. The two divisions of Franklin's army corps, just disembarked, loitered about Alexandria waiting for orders; Halleck and McClellan agreed that they ought to go forward to aid Pope, but nobody knew quite where Pope was to be found, and anyway, Franklin had no horses to pull his artillery and no wagon train to carry food and ammunition, and there seemed to be no cavalry at hand to scout the road for him. Haupt darkly remarked to himself that a march of twenty-five miles would put Franklin in the fortified lines at Centreville, which would surely be within reaching distance of Pope, and felt that Franklin's men could carry on their backs enough food and ammunition to take them that far. Besides, Haupt seriously doubted that there was anything hostile this side of Centreville which could hurt a whole army corps. But nobody asked Haupt's opinion, McClellan and Halleck began to bicker fruitlessly about the advance, and Franklin's troops stayed where they were.

The next day was August 29, and outposts reported hearing the rumble of gunfire from beyond Centreville. Somewhere off in the outer darkness the armies apparently had collided. Later in the day Haupt was able to confirm this. Sitting at the end of the railway telegraph line, he got a message from Pope himself—in Centreville, by now—and Pope seemed to be in good spirits, reporting that he was engaged with sixty thousand Confederates, that Joe Hooker was driving them handsomely, and that McDowell and Sigel were cutting off the enemy's retreat. McClellan ordered Franklin to move forward, telling him: "Whatever may happen, don't allow it to be said that the Army of the Potomac failed to do its utmost for the country"—a remark which is a complete tip-off to the strange jealousies, rivalries, and antagonisms that were besetting the high command just then. The troops started to move that morning. Franklin remaining behind in an attempt to get supply wagons, of which he finally rounded up a scant twenty; then McClellan began to have second thoughts, wired Halleck that he did not think Franklin's men were in shape to accomplish much if they ran into serious resistance along the road, and finally ordered Franklin to halt at Annandale, seven miles out. Haupt had his railroad open as far as the Bull Run Bridge and was pushing supplies forward as fast as the trains could move.

As far as Haupt could see, things were on the mend. Pope was in touch with Washington and with his supply line again, his wagons were moving the stores up from Fairfax Station to Centreville, and the fighting seemed to be going favorably. But on the following day the luckless railroad man entered into a full-fledged nightmare, which was visited on him by order of the Secretary of War, Mr. Edwin M. Stanton.

Stanton, with his pudgy, bustling figure, his scraggly beard, and his hot little eyes, was prone to disastrous impulses when the going got tough, and he gave way to one on the thirtieth of August, 1862. Late the night before, Pope reported having fought a heavy battle in which he had lost ten thousand men and the enemy twice that many. The Confederates, he assured the Secretary, were in full retreat and he was about to pursue with vigor, which was all to the good. But Stanton, reflecting on those ten thousand casualties—plus the rebel wounded, who must be tended for humanity's sake—suddenly concluded that the wounded would never in the world be cared for unless he departed swiftly from regular channels, and he immediately departed therefrom with restless energy. He publicly issued an invitation to government clerks, private citizens, and all and sundry to volunteer as nurses and stretcher-bearers for the wounded out beyond Centreville. Simultaneously he ordered Haupt to stop whatever he was doing and prepare to transport this volunteer brigade to the field at once. (He also rounded up all the hacks and carriages he could find in Washington and sent them off to Centreville by road, but that did not affect Haupt; it just clogged the highway that Pope's men had to use.) Shortly thereafter scores and hundreds of civilians began to pour into Alexandria demanding transportation. Most of them were drunk, and those who were not were carrying bottles of whisky and obviously would be drunk before very long.

Haupt's head swam at the thought of dumping this howling mob down on a battlefield. Orders were orders, to be sure, but he was enough of an army man to know that there are ways and ways of rendering obedience. He delayed the train as long as he could; then, when he finally sent it off, he wired the officer in command at Fairfax Station to arrest all who were drunk. Also, he thought himself that while he had been ordered to take this mob out he had not been ordered to bring it back, so as soon as the train had been unloaded he had it hauled back to Alexandria.

"Those who were sober enough straggled off as soon as it was light enough to see, and wandered around until all whisky and provisions became exhausted, when they returned to the station to get transportation back," Haupt wrote later. "In this, most of them were disappointed."

It seemed cruel, he added, to make these people walk all the way back to Washington in the rain, but it was better to do that than to ignore the wounded; besides, his opinion of the volunteer nurses was not high— "generally it was a hard crowd and of no use whatever on the field." He learned later that some of the men bribed army ambulance drivers to leave the wounded and carry the civilians back to Washington.

And as this affair began to be straightened out the news from the front abruptly became worse. Having announced that he had won a great victory, Pope was slow to report bad news, but the news came trickling back anyway. One of the first to get the drift was General Jacob Cox, an Ohioan who had gone to the lines at Upton's Hill in command of the four regiments McClellan had sent out to hold the ground "at any hazard." On the morning of August 30, Cox saw the ambulances coming in from Centreville, accompanied by the walking wounded. These were men who had left the field the night before, and their impression was that they had won the battle and that the enemy was in retreat. Cox noticed that the sound of the firing, which he had been hearing all the previous day, was not nearly so loud. Adding that to the reports from the wounded men, he assumed that Pope was pursuing the foe and that the gunfire came from rear-guard actions—an assumption which Pope himself held until he finally reached the point where further delusion was impossible. During the afternoon, however, Cox could hear that the sound of the firing was getting louder—much louder and much heavier, with long, sustained, reverberating rolls of gunfire in which the individual shots could no longer be distinguished. Toward evening the pathetic parade of wounded was coming in greater numbers. It was accompanied by stragglers, and by dark the evidence of a disastrous defeat was all too visible. The spirits of the soldiers in the camps around Alexandria, which had been raised mightily by the early report of a victory, began to sag, and the provost marshal notified the War Department that he needed more men if he was to preserve order— "we are being overrun with straggling officers and men." The colonel of the 55th New York Infantry, landing at the Alexandria wharves next morning, noted an air of great depression as soon as he stepped ashore. Nobody knew just what had happened, but all sorts of rumors were afloat; he found the word "treason" being used freely.

Treason: betrayal, treachery, a will to lose when the means to win are at hand; a dark, frightening word, coming up out of the shadows, carrying fear and distrust and panic unreason with it, so that the visible enemies in gray and butternut off toward the Bull Run Mountains seemed less to be feared than those who might be standing, all unsuspected, at one's elbow. The word was used everywhere: in the President's Cabinet, in the War Department, in the tents of the generals, and—most disastrously of all—in the ranks of the tired army that was plodding back toward Washington. All of the disillusionment which began when the army was repulsed before Richmond, all of the sudden war-weariness which had come so soon to a land that had been long at peace, all of the bewilderment felt by men who saw themselves striking ineffectually at targets that mysteriously shifted and dissolved as one struck—all of this, welling up in the hearts of men who had done their best to no avail, began to find expression in that word. There had been betrayal: of high hopes and noble purposes, of all the army meant to itself and to the country. The country had suffered more than a defeat. What was happening now was the beginning of disintegration.

In the end it would become an army of legend, with a great name that still clangs when you touch it. The orations, the brass bands and the faded flags of innumerable Decoration Day observances, waiting for it in the years ahead, would at last create a haze of romance, deepening spring by spring until the regiments and brigades became unreal—colored-lithograph figures out of a picture-book war, with dignified graybeards bemused by their own fogged memories of a great day when all the world was young and all the comrades were valiant.

But the end of August in the year 1862 was not the time for the taking a distant and romantic view of things. The Army of the Potomac was not at that moment conscious of the formation of legends; it was hungry and tired, muddy and ragged, sullen with the knowledge that it had been shamefully misused, and if it thought of the future at all it was only to consider the evil chances which might come forth during the next twenty-four hours. It was in a mood to judge the future by the past, and the immediate past had been bad. The drunken generals who had botched up supply lines, the sober generals who had argued instead of getting reinforcements forward, the incredible civilians who had gone streaming out to a battlefield as to a holiday brawl, the incompetents who thought they were winning when they were losing were symbols of a betrayal that was paid for in suffering and humiliation by the men who were discovering that they had enlisted to pay just such a price for other men's errors.

The army had developed a high spirit down on the peninsula in spite of its troubles; a certain cockiness, even, a feeling that it knew of no other soldiers who were quite as good, plus a deep certainty that there was no general anywhere who could be trusted as much as its own commander, General McClellan. But this spirit was dissolving and the certainty was being mocked; and as it plodded on toward the fortified lines at Alexandria it was on the verge of ceasing to be an army at all. Men drifted off through the fields or formed little knots about campfires in the woods and farmyards. The winding columns on the roads stretched as they moved, the head of each column moving just a little faster than the tail. There was no panic, as there had been a year earlier after the first fight at Bull Run, when what had been thought to be an army simply melted into a frantic mob. Save for a bad hour or so at the Bull Run Bridge on the night of August 30, there had been no headlong rush to get away. But the miracle of the spirit which takes thousands of young men, ties them together in strange self-forgetfulness, and enables them to walk steadfastly and without faltering into the certainty of pain and death was wearing very thin. Bickerings and blunderings had sapped its power; where the men went now they went sullenly and only because they must. It would take little more to cause the men to realize that "must" had force only so long as they consented to it.

The army had been gay when it went out. The point that is so easy to overlook nowadays, when all of the illusions about war have been abraded to dust, is that those young men went off to war eagerly and with light hearts, coveting the great adventure which they blithely believed lay just ahead. They went to war because they wanted to go, every man of them, and the obvious fact that in their innocence they did not have the remotest idea what the reality was going to be like does not change the fact. The bounty jumpers and the drafted men had not yet appeared. This was the army of the nation's youth, consciously trying to live up to its own conception of bravery, convinced that a soldier marched forward into high romance; an army with banners that postured pathetically and sincerely as it followed its own boyish vision.

That posturing was of the very essence of the army's spirit, and it caused things to happen that could not happen in the armies of today. We read, for instance, of the father and son who enlisted together in a regiment of Massachusetts infantry. In the fighting at Bull Run the son was killed, and a comrade took the news to the father in the midst of the action. "Well," said the father grimly, "I would rather see him shot dead, as he was, than see him run away." And there is a glimpse of a New York regiment holding the line in another battle under heavy fire. The colonel of an adjoining regiment came over to report that this New York outfit was an especial target because its colors were being held too high: lower them a bit and the fire wouldn't be so costly. The colonel of the New York regiment— himself the most conspicuous target of all, riding slowly back and forth on horseback in rear of his men, who were lying behind a rail fence— looked at the waving flag and said: "Let it wave high. It is our glory." Then there was the colonel of another New York regiment, mortally wounded in a charge, who ordered his men to lift him and prop him up against a tree facing the firing. This done, at whatever cost in pain to the dying man, he said faintly: "Tell Mother I died with my face to the enemy"—and, the message duly noted, died.

The spirit of the first campaign these soldiers made comes down to us in a journal written by young Captain George Freeman Noyes, a pea-green but ardent officer on General Abner Doubleday's staff, who found himself making a night march up the Rappahannock when Pope was concentrating his army against Stonewall Jackson early in August. Wrote Captain Noyes:

> And so over a heavily-wooded, rolling country, through roads arched with foilage, the moonlight filling them with fantastic shapes and shadows, we pursued our romantic way. The peculiar quiet of the hour, and the weird influence of the forest scenery, with patches of moonlight flung in here and there among the prevailing shadow, every

turn of the road seemingly a narrow pass over which giant and grotesque trees stood guard to oppose our progress, added mystic significance to those reflections which our anticipated battle naturally awakened. No longer Yankee soldiers of the nineteenth century, we were for the nounce knights of the ancient chivalry.

Those fanciful old ideas about the glory of a waving flag, the shame of running from danger, the high importance of dying with one's face to the foe—since that war they have come to seem as out of date as the muzzle-loaders that were used for weapons in those days. The American soldier of later, more sophisticated eras may indeed die rather than retreat, and do it as courageously as any, but he never makes a song about it or strikes an attitude. His heroism is without heroics, and fine phrases excite his instant contempt, because he knows even before he starts off to war that fine phrases and noble attitudes and flags waving in death's own breeze are only so many forms of a come-on for the innocent; nor does he readily glimpse himself as a knight of the ancient chivalry. But in the 1860s the gloss had not been worn off. Young men then went to war believing all of the fine stories they had grown up with; and if, in the end, their disillusion was quite as deep and profound as that of the modern soldier, they had to fall farther to reach it.

The fall was acutely painful, and it was taking place rapidly in the late summer of 1862. The easiest way to see what was going on—in the soldier's emotions, and in the war itself—is to follow briefly the career of the Black Hat Brigade, which was to become famous.

This outfit was made up of the 2nd, 6th, and 7th Wisconsin regiments and the 19th Indiana—Western troops in an army predominantly of Easterners—and it was assembled in Fredericksburg in the spring and put under the command of young John Gibbon, lately jumped to a brigadier's commission from his position as captain of regular artillery. Gibbon was a West Pointer—a lean, sharp-nosed, bearded man with a habit of blunt speech, who was quietly sorry to have to leave his guns and his tough regulars, where he felt at home, for infantry and volunteers, where he felt strange. He had served on the Western plains under Albert Sidney Johnston before the war; came from North Carolina, had three brothers in the Confederate Army, but for his part had elected to stand by the Union.

Rather to his surprise, he found that he liked his new command, and he wrote that all the men needed was discipline and drill to make first-class soldiers: a judgment that was to be vindicated, for these Westerners turned out to be fighters as good as any the army ever possessed. Gibbon applied the drill and discipline, discovered that volunteers were unlike regulars— praise and the promise of reward were more effective than the fear of punishment which the regulars required—and to tone up their morale he saw to it that they were outfitted, beyond regulations, with black felt hats and white gaiters; hence their nickname, the Black Hat Brigade.

The first combat veterans the boys encountered—Shields's division, down

from the Shenandoah Valley after a bloody fight with Stonewall Jackson—
jeered at them for bandbox soldiers, but the Westerners retorted that they
would rather wear leggings than be lousy like some people, and anyway,
they liked their own natty appearance. Like all new troops in that army,
when they started cross-country marching in the hot summer they threw
coats and blankets in the nearest ditches, knowing that they could draw
new ones, and no questions asked, from the regimental quartermasters.
This pained Gibbon's regular-army soul, and he forced the company commanders to receipt for the issue of clothing thereafter, and compelled them
to make regular returns on the requisitions, under penalty of drawing no
pay. The brigade carried its coats and blankets henceforward: a thing which
caused muttering at first, but morale was high and Gibbon made the men
feel like soldiers, and the muttering died away.

So far the war had been a romantic frolic for these boys. They liked to
remember the period of training around Washington, when they had been
camped along a stream on the far side of which were home-state neighbors,
the 5th Wisconsin. The 5th belonged to General Hancock's brigade, and
Hancock had a bull voice that could be heard halfway to Richmond, and
the 5th was commanded by a Colonel Cobb, very much of a leading citizen
back home but strictly an amateur soldier here like all the rest of them.
One day when Hancock was drilling his brigade Colonel Cobb got mixed
up and took his regiment off the wrong way in some evolution, and the
delighted Wisconsin boys across the river could hear Hancock roar:
"Colonel Cobb! Where in the damnation are you going with your battalion?" Thereafter, as long as they were neighbors, it struck the Black
Hat Brigade as amusing to go down to the riverbank in the still of the
evening and chant in unison: "Colonel Cobb! Where in the damnation are
you going with your battalion?"

They had worked out a gag for rainy days, when it was too muddy to
drill and all hands were snuggled under their pup tents trying to keep dry
and were afflicted by boredom. Some private possessed of a great voice
would sing out: "When our army marched down to Bull Run, what did
the big bullfrog say?" And hundreds of men would croak: Big thing! Big
thing! ("Big thing" was Civil War slang for any notable event or achievement—a great battle, promotion to a corporal's chevrons, a two-week
furlough, the theft of a crock of apple butter, or anything else worth
talking about.) Then the leader would call: "And when our army came
back from Bull Run, what did the little frogs say?" To which the answer
in unmelodious screeching trebles, was: "Run, Yank! Run, Yank!" And to
close it, the question was: "What does the Bully Sixth say?" The answer,
in deep pinewoods bass: "Hit 'em again! Hit 'em again!"

The whole brigade took a queer, perverse pride in the regimental band
of the 6th Wisconsin—not because it was so good, but because it was so
terrible. It was able to play only one selection, something called "The
Village Quickstep," and its dreadful inefficiency (the colonel referred to
it in his memoirs as "that execrable band") might have been due to the
colonel's quaint habit of assigning men to the band not for musical ability

but as punishment for misdemeanors—or so, at least, the regiment stoutly believed. The only good thing about the band was its drum major, one William Whaley, who was an expert at high and fancy twirling of his baton. At one review, in camp around Washington, the brigade had paraded before McClellan, who had been so taken with this drum major's "lofty pomposity" (as a comrade described it) that he took off his cap in jovial salute—whereupon the luckless Whaley, overcome by the honor, dropped his baton ignominiously in the mud, so that his big moment became a fizzle.

At the end of July the brigade moved out of its camp at Fredericksburg and tramped up the Rappahannock to join Pope—the same movement which led Captain Noyes to see knights of the ancient chivalry marching along the moonlit roads. The men were impatient. They belonged to General Irvin McDowell's corps, and they had been sorely disappointed because orders to go to Richmond and join McClellan's forces there had been canceled at the last minute. Now they looked ahead to action, for it was believed that Pope would plunge at once into battle. Reaching the point of concentration, they did a great deal of marching and counter-marching and heard the rumble of artillery duels from afar, and once or twice long-range shells fell among them, but they got into no fighting. And finally they found themselves, with the three other brigades in the division of General Rufus King, trudging off to the northeast on the Warrenton turnpike, heading in the direction of Centreville. Along the way they captured their first prisoner—a straggler from Stonewall Jackson's corps, who had had his fill of fighting and surrendered willingly enough, but who was an authentic armed rebel for all that. This lanky soldier looked with interest at the full packs carried by Gibbon's boys and remarked: "You uns is like pack mules—we uns is like race horses. All Old Jackson gave us was a musket, a hundred rounds, and a gum blanket, and he druv us like hell."

The men did not know exactly where they were going, but they understood vaguely that Old Jackson was somewhere up ahead; it looked as if they would get into a sure-enough fight this time, and their spirits rose. To be sure, if they were being hurried into action their course was obstructed by numerous mix-ups. They had got into Warrenton at dusk, hungry, their rations exhausted, and were met by General McDowell in person, who regretted that they could not have any supper but ordered them to move out on the turnpike at once: this was a forced march, no time to draw rations, they had to keep moving. So they started on, found the road blocked by stalled wagon trains, and made a supperless bivouac two miles from Warrenton. The next day they were led down a country lane and thrown into line of battle on some deserted farm, and held there for several hours in complete solitude, before they were recalled and taken back to the main highway; and there they were halted again, to butcher some of their beef cattle and make a leisurely meal. But the men had been soldiers long enough to understand that that sort of thing just went with army life, and their enthusiasm was undimmed. At last, after an afternoon

in which they had heard occasional sputters of musket fire far ahead,
they went tramping along the pike a mile or two out of the little hamlet
of Gainesville, the brigade well closed up, General Gibbon riding at the
head, a mile of empty road in front and behind separating it from the
rest of the division. It was getting on toward sunset, and the trees on the
left of the road were casting long cool shadows. A regimental band was
playing a quickstep—one hopes, somehow, that it was the band of the
6th Wisconsin—and the boys were enjoying the war.

The road led straight ahead, like a white dusty arrow, and General
Gibbon trotted on in advance to the top of a little rise, where he pulled up
to see if he could see anything of the leading brigade. It had vanished, and
Gibbon glanced off to the west, to the left of the road. The ground was
more or less open there, and it rose in a long, gentle slope; and as Gibbon
looked he saw several slim columns of horse-roving cavalry, most likely,
he told himself—come trotting out of a grove on the hillside, half a mile
away. He was just beginning to speculate whether this cavalry was Federal
or Confederate when all the little columns swerved simultaneously, presenting their flanks. At sight of this familiar maneuver something clicked in the
mind of this young general who had always been a gunner: that wasn't
cavalry at all, it was field artillery going into battery!

Gibbon sent an aide galloping back to the rear of the column to bring
up the brigade artillery—Battery B, 4th U.S., the one Gibbon himself had
commanded before he became a brigadier of infantry. The aide had hardly
started when six shells came screaming over the road, to burst in the woods
off to the right. The colonels of the four infantry regiments, without waiting for orders, swung their men into line facing to the west and got them
off the road and had them lie down under cover of a low bank. Battery B
came clattering madly up the pike in a cloud of dust, while another salvo
from the hostile battery crashed into the treetops. As he cantered into a
field west of the road to post the guns Gibbon noticed with approval
that his soldiers, although they had been taken completely by surprise,
did not seem to be nervous. Perhaps half a dozen men, out of more than
eighteen hundred present, had scurried hastily off into the woods when the
first shells came over, but they were coming back now with shamefaced
grins to rejoin their comrades. Battery B came up, the men tore down a
rail fence to make a gateway, and the guns went lumbering into the field
beside Gibbon, swinging around and unlimbering with the sure precision
of the regulars. In a moment counterbattery fire had been opened.

Up to this point nothing had been seen of the enemy but his six guns.
The natural supposition was that they were horse artillery attached to Jeb
Stuart's cavalry, engaged in cavalry's favorite practice of harassing infantry
on the march. The logical thing to do was to shake a line of infantry out to
chase the guns away, and this—after a quick study of the ground in front—
Gibbon proceeded to do. The 2nd Wisconsin and 19th Indiana moved
forward from behind the protecting bank, broke through a little belt of
bushes and scrub trees, and started out across the field to make the rebel
battery cease and desist. The whole thing was done with earnest care,

just as it had been done on the drill ground so many times: colonel and
lieutenant colonel of each regiment full of business, carefully sighting
the lines of direction, sending guides forward, fussing mightily about
alignment, trying their level best to do it all regular army style—doing it
just a little self-consciously, one gathers, because General Gibbon came
riding over from the guns to watch, and the general was a regular, and
this was the first time under fire. The lines were formed presently and
the men went forward, a fringe of skirmishers in advance, and they came
to the top of a low ridge. The Confederate artillery suddenly ceased firing,
and a line of gray-clad skirmishers rose from the grass in front of the
guns and began a pop-pop of small-arms fire. Then, from the woods beyond, a great mass of Confederate infantry emerged, coming down the
slope to give the Westerners their first trial by combat, red battle flags
with the starred blue cross snapping in the evening breeze—Stonewall
Jackson's men, whose measured conviction it was that they could whip
any number of Yankees at any time and place, and whose record gave
them tolerably good reason for the belief.

And a long, tearing crackle of musketry broke over the shadowed field,
and the Wisconsin and Indiana boys learned what it was like to fight.
Gibbon, who had thought he was quelling impudent horse artillery, went
spurring back to bring up his other two regiments, couriers galloped down
the road to ask for help from the other brigades, and presently the 6th
Wisconsin came up to take position at the right of the line. Many years
later its colonel recalled with pride the military precision with which his
regiment deployed for action under fire. Gibbon threw the 7th Wisconsin
in where the 2nd was fighting, and the battle was on.

It was a strange battle—a straightaway, slam-bang, stand-up fight with
no subtleties and no maneuvering, no advancing and no retreating. Some
of the Confederates found cover around a little farmhouse, and the 6th
Wisconsin got some protection because the ground sagged in an almost
imperceptible little hollow right where it was posted, so that most of the
bullets that came its way went overhead. But for the most part the men
did not seek cover—did not even lie down on the ground, which was the
way many fire fights took place in those days, but simply stood facing
each other in even, orderly ranks, as if they were on parade awaiting inspection, and volleyed away at the murderous range of less than one
hundred yards.

On the right, Battery B fired rapidly and accurately, and some other
brigade had brought another battery into action off on the left, and before
long General Doubleday sent up the 56th Pennsylvania and the 76th New
York—virgin regiments, like those of Gibbon—to join in the fight; and
this amazing combat of two dress-parade battle lines at point-blank range
sent its echoes resounding across the Manassas plain, while a dense cloud
of acrid smoke went rolling up the evening sky. Years later General Gibbon
remarked that he heard, that evening, the heaviest musket fire he heard during the entire war.

The fight lasted for an hour and a half. When it ended both sides were exactly where they were when it began, except that a Confederate brigade which tried a flanking movement around the Federal right had got tangled up in a ravine full of underbrush, in the smoky dusk, and couldn't find its way out, while the 19th Indiana had been edged off to the left rear to cope with what looked like a flank attack from that direction. Gibbon was proud of the way his Hoosiers managed this maneuver while under fire. Toward evening, with the Confederate fieldpieces out of action, Stuart's incredible artillerist, John Pelham, brought a section of guns up to within seventy paces of Gibbon's line and opened fire, without any visible effect whatever except to add to the total of killed and maimed.

Night came at last, mercifully, and put an end to it, the rival battle lines slowly drew apart, and, as General Gibbon wrote, "everything except the groans of the wounded quieted down." The Black Hat boys could call themselves veterans now; they had had their baptism of fire—baptism by total immersion, one might say. The 2nd Wisconsin—which, over the length of the war, was to win the terrible distinction of having a higher percentage of its total enrollment killed in action than any other regiment in the United States Army—had taken 500 men into this fight and left 298 of them dead or wounded on the field; it got a leg on the record that evening. The 7th Wisconsin and the 19th Indiana had lost nearly as heavily. The 6th Wisconsin had been lucky by comparison, losing 72 men out of 504 engaged. A regimental historian wrote later that to the end of the war this brigade was always ready for action, "but we were never again eager."

All in all, more than a third of the Federal soldiers who went into action that evening had been shot. Over on the Confederate side, though the Federals didn't know it at the time, the story was about the same. The famous Stonewall brigade had lost 33 percent of its numbers, the 21st Georgia had lost 173 out of 242 in action, and two division commanders had gone down, one of them the famous General Dick Ewell. Next morning one of Jeb Stuart's staff officers came out to take a casual look at the scene of action. "The lines were well marked by the dark rows of bodies stretched out on the broom-sedge field, lying just where they had fallen, with their heels on a well-defined line," he wrote. "The bodies lay in so straight a line that they looked like troops lying down to rest. On each front the edge was sharply defined, while towards the rear it was less so. Showing how men had staggered backward after receiving their death blow."

The Federals drew a line of battle in the woods next to the turnpike, sent out parties to bring in as many of the wounded as possible, established crude field hospitals under the trees, and in general tried to catch their breath. A staff officer, coming up the pike from the rear, found a campfire blazing in the road, with the generals grouped around it, staff officers seated outside the inner circle, orderlies holding the reins of saddled horses still farther out, the firelight gleaming on tanned faces, a ribbon of wood smoke climbing up out of the glow to disappear in the arching branches above. The brigadiers were assembled and the division commander, General King, who had been taken ill that afternoon and had had to seek shelter back at Gainesville and so had not been present during the fight, came up to join them, weak and pale. His division was part of McDowell's corps, but nobody could find McDowell, who had ridden off in midafternoon to seek General John Pope in the vicinity of Manassas and who, it developed later, had got completely lost in the woods and found neither Pope nor anyone else until the next day. Since neither King nor McDowell had been around while the fighting was going on, the battle had really been fought under nobody's direction—except Gibbon's and he was responsible only for his own brigade. Now that the generals were in council nobody knew quite what to do, for King's original orders were to march to Centreville, and it was painfully obvious that before he could do that he would have to drive Stonewall Jackson out of the way, which was clearly too much of a task for any single division.

In the end it was agreed that the command had better withdraw in the direction of Manassas Junction, which lay several miles to the east, and it was so ordered. Sometime after midnight the tired troops withdrew and tramped silently off down a country road in the blackness, all the gay banter of their earlier marches quite forgotten; and in a cloudy dawn they dropped down in a field near Manassas to get a little sleep, while the staff hurried off to try to find Pope, McDowell, or somebody who could tell them what the brigade was supposed to do next.

The soldiers didn't get much sleep. Orders came in presently: Fitz-John Porter and his V Corps from the Army of the Potomac were coming up and would be backtracking along the road toward Gainesville, and King's division—now commanded by General John Hatch, for King's illness had put him out—would go with them. So the men drew up in marching order by the roadside, and pretty soon the head of Porter's corps came along, marching with an indefinable swagger even in the informal route step of the cross-country hike, and the young Westerners cheered mightily in boyish hero worship—this was the Army of the Potomac, these were veterans of the fabulous fighting around Richmond, McClellan's men were joining Pope's, and everything would be all right now.

Porter's men received the cheers with high disdain. They included a solid division of regulars, plus some volunteer regiments which had acquired much esprit de corps, which means that they looked down on practically all soldiers who did not belong to their own outfit. They had taken the worst the Confederates had to give at Gaines's Mill, and at Malvern Hill they had seen the furious Southern assault waves break up in a swirling foam of bloody repulse on the hard rock of massed artillery and rifle fire, and their immeasurable contempt for John Pope was quite broad enough to include all of his troops. They called out loftily: "Get out of the way, straw-feet—we're going to go up to show you how to fight." ("Straw-foot" was the Civil War term for rookie. The idea was that some of the new recruits were of such fantastic greenness that they did not know the left foot from the right and hence could not be taught to keep time properly or to step off on the left foot as all soldiers should. The drill sergeants, in desperation, had finally realized that these green country lads did at least

know hay from straw and so had tied wisps of hay to the left foot and straw
to the right foot and marched them off to the chant of "Hay-foot, straw-
foot, hay-foot, straw-foot." Hence: straw-foot—rookie, especially a dumb
rookie.) Gibbon's boys were hurt—after last evening they felt entitled to
join any brotherhood whose entry fee was courage under fire—and they
yelled back: "Wait until you've been where we've been—that'll take some
of the slack out of your pantaloons"; but they still admired those hard
veterans and were glad to be with them. After a while they swung into
column and followed the V Corps along the road, heading back toward
what they had just marched away from—perfectly ready to fight again,
but not hankering for it any longer.

*Two theatres of war commanded the attention of both belligerents during
the first twenty-seven months of the struggle. One was the Mississippi Valley and the other Northern Virginia. The key to the former was Vicksburg
while that of the latter was Richmond. In both theatres the men who led
the Union and the Confederate armies earned their spurs. When on July 4,
1863, Vicksburg fell to Grant, the second scene of operations shifted eastward to Chattanooga and Georgia beyond. Yet, until mid-war, the South
although inferior in resources and war-making potential had the upper hand.
It was not until the second stage of the war beginning with Gettysburg that
the Northern preponderance proved strong enough to overwhelm Southern
resistance.*

*The original Southern advantage consisted of a more effective immediate
mobilization of its means of war and its superior military leadership. From
the beginning of the war, the South had a clear awareness of its objective:
independence. The North sought, at least in the beginning, to return to a
federal system that the South had found intolerable. It is not surprising that
at first the full mobilization of Northern potential was kept in check; the
original northern aim of restoration of "The Union as it was" confined the
scope of necessary attack. Only when the target became the whole Southern
society did the destructive might of the North prove unbeatable.*

*Beyond a doubt, the Southern military leadership, drawing heavily as it
did upon the officers who deserted the Federal Army when war commenced,
were originally superior to that of the North. In the East, Union General
George B. McClellan, no matter what his defects as a battlefield general,
proved an organizational genius who forged the Army of the Potomac.
This army endured the mishandling of Pope, Burnside, and Hooker to find
first in Meade and then in Grant the leadership that led it to victory. The
Confederate Army of Northern Virginia led first by Joseph E. Johnston and
then by Robert E. Lee developed a secondary leadership in men like Stonewall Jackson, Jeb Stuart, James Longstreet, and A. P. Hill who gave élan to
Confededate leadership. In the West, the North steadily developed a superior*

*generalship. When faced with a war without precedent, Ulysses S. Grant, William Tecumseh Sherman, and Philip Sheridan improvised tactics and strategy. They also learned to fight a war which, as Sherman explained it, aimed ". . . to whip the rebels, to humble their pride, to follow them to their inmost recesses, and make them fear and dread us." Terror as an instrument of war had been incorporated into the Northern arsenal. When the Northern leadership trained in the West combined with the instrument of war formed by McClellan, the Confederate armies were harried to death. Grant hung onto Lee's forces like a bulldog and Sherman plunged through the South devastating everything in his path.*

*The war in the West was a war of magnificent maneuver and sweeping marches; the war in the East was played out in a narrow arena largely confined until the final year of war to the barely one-hundred-mile-wide corridor that separated Washington from Richmond. It was here that the greatest of Southern generals revealed his genius and his patrician remoteness. No one who ever met Robert E. Lee quite succeeded in breaking through his reserve, and yet on the battlefield, this general revealed a willingness to gamble that converted battles such as Chancellorsville into military masterpieces. It was as if the aloof general needed the stimulation of battle to reveal his hidden fire. But as he confessed shortly before his surrender to a colleague: "I have never believed we could, against the gigantic combination for our subjugation, make good in the long run our independence. . . ." This absence of hope was, however, irrelevant, for, Lee added, "But such considerations really made with me no difference. We had, I was satisfied, sacred principles to maintain and rights to defend, for which we were in duty bound to do our best, even if we perished in the endeavor."*

*Most of Lee's generalship was devoted to maintaining a defensive posture which, if it were successful, would wear the North down and finally compel its recognition of Southern independence. Only twice did he feel strong enough to challenge the North with an actual invasion of its territory. Both that at Antietam and Gettysburg terminated in his repulse after staggering losses for both sides. In the single day's fight of September 17, 1862, at Antietam, combined losses totaled 26,134 out of some 127,160 engaged. In the three days of fighting at Gettysburg between July 1 and 3, 1863, total casualties reached 51,112 out of 158,343 men in the field. In both instances, Southern losses exceeded by a considerable number those of their opponent. Given the inferior manpower resources of the South, such a struggle could not long be sustained. After Gettysburg, Lee retired to a defensive position from which he did not budge until war's end.*

*Douglas Southall Freeman (1886-1953), Virginia born, held a doctorate in history from Johns Hopkins, but followed a career as editor of the Rich-mond* News-Letter. *He complemented this occupation with a distinguished career as historian and biographer. His four-volume biography of Robert E. Lee won a Pulitzer Prize in 1934. When read in combination with his three-volume study of* Lee's Lieutenants *(1942-1944), it is tantamount to a definitive history of the Army of Northern Virginia. Upon his death he was at work on the sixth volume of a projected eight-volume biography of*

*George Washington. As the first president of the Society of American His-*
*torians, he emphasized the writing of history as literature, an emphasis that*
*still is central to the operation of the society. His sense of history as a branch*
*of literature accounts for the fact that he was one of the few historians*
*among the fifty members of the American Academy of Arts and Letters.*

# R. E. LEE: A BIOGRAPHY

## *by Douglas Southall Freeman*

Over the hills from Cashtown, along a road he had never travelled before,
Lee galloped toward Gettysburg like a blinded giant. He did not know
where the Federals were, or how numerous they might be. Ewell—and
doubtless Hill also—he had cautioned not to bring on a general engagement
with a strong adversary until the rest of the infantry came up, but with no
cavalry to inform him, he could not tell what calamity he might invite by
advancing at all, or what opportunity he might lose by advancing cautiously.
Never had he been so dangerously in the dark.

Louder and nearer was the sound of the artillery. Soon, to his regret and
surprise, infantry volleys in a spiteful staccato added their treble to the bass
of the guns. Smoke was now visible on the horizon, swept by the breeze into
a long cloud. At 2 o'clock, when he still was about three miles from Gettysburg, he came into the open country and found Pender's division deployed.
In the distance, action was visible. He turned into a grassy field on the left
of the road and found a position that commanded a good view. Quickly
putting binoculars to his eyes he studied the gray and green panorama before him. A cultivated ridge, long and wide and broken only by a few rail
fences and patches of woodland, led down to Willoughby Run. Beyond that
little stream the ground rose to another ridge on which stood conspicuously
a Lutheran seminary with a cupola. Over this ridge to the east at an elevation about fifty feet below that of the ground on which Lee stood, was
Gettysburg. South and southeast of the town, dimly discernible, were dan-
gerous-looking hills and ridges.

Lee's eyes could not have lingered long on their vague outlines, because
his glasses must have fixed themselves quickly on the smoke that was rising
on either side of the Chambersburg road where it crossed Willoughby Run.
Evidently there had been an attack and a repulse. The artillery was blazing
away, and Heth's division was apparently forming on a front about a mile
in length. Two of Heth's brigades were in bad order. Beyond them, across
the run, where the smoke from the Union batteries was swelling, must be
the Federal infantry—and how strong? That was the question Lee's anxious
mind instantly fashioned: Was it a heavy force or merely a detached unit,
sent to guard the Gettysburg crossroads? The guns did not seem very numerous, but the infantry fire came from a front at least as long as Heth's. That
was ominous.

Soon Lee's presence on the field became known, and officers began to bring him news. Heth had sent forward two of his brigades, Archer's and Davis's, during the morning. They had pushed forward vigorously and had driven the enemy back. Later the Federals had attacked them in heavy force and, about an hour before Lee arrived, had compelled them to retire. Part of Archer's brigade had been cut off, and Archer himself had been captured. Heth was now resting his men in line of battle preparatory to attacking again with his entire division, and Hill had directed Pender to support him.

Finding their opponents out of range, the Federal infantry had halted and had ceased firing. The artillery exchange was slowing down. As Lee rode closer to the lines he was still so uncertain of the strength of the opposing troops and so anxious not to bring on a general engagement until his whole army was concentrated, that had there not been a sudden stir north of Gettysburg about 3 o'clock he would probably have forbidden an advance. The enemy began to move out troops in that direction; the right of the Federal line that faced Hill was drawn in; firing commenced briskly. Soon from the woods above Gettysburg a long gray line of battle emerged. It was Rodes's division of Ewell's corps, marching under orders to join Lee at Gettysburg. Having heard the sound of Hill's engagement, Rodes had taken advantage of the cover on the ridge and was coming up almost on the right flank of the forces that had been engaged with Hill. It could not have happened more advantageously if this chance engagement had been a planned battle!

The Federals rallied quickly to this new threat. As they deployed to meet Rodes's attack, he had to change direction somewhat to the right. In doing this his left brigade, Doles's, shifted to confront a column that had started northward from the town as if to turn Rodes's left. Doles thus became detached from the rest of the command. O'Neal's brigade on his right thereupon lost direction and was scattered. The attack against the flank of the troops facing Hill had, therefore, to be delivered by two brigades, Daniel's and Iverson's, with Ramseur's in reserve. The details of all this could not be seen, of course, from Lee's position, but it was soon apparent that Rodes was having hard fighting, in the face of stubborn resistance, and was not advancing rapidly.

General Heth rode up to Lee. "Rodes," said he, "is heavily engaged; had I not better attack?"

"No," said Lee, reasoning that little was to be gained and much was to be risked by committing himself to the offensive with only part of his forces. "No, I am not prepared to bring on a general engagement today—Longstreet is not up."

But the very gods of war seemed to wear gray that hot afternoon. Rodes had not been long in action when smoke began to rise still farther to the eastward and guns from that quarter added their roar. Early's division of Ewell's corps had arrived on Rodes's left and was driving the Federals who had been threatening Doles's flank. At precisely the right place, and at exactly the right moment, a third blow was being delivered. Everything was working perfectly. The hard-beset Federals formed a right angle now, their left running from south to north, and their right from west to east. Opposite their left was Heth, with two of his four brigades unscathed and with Pender's fresh division in reserve. At the angle in the line Rodes was hammering hard. On the Federal right, Early's veterans were thundering. With Pender it would be easy to outflank the Federal left, and with Early to turn their right.

As quickly as the situation changed with the arrival of Early, Lee's decision was reversed. So fair an opportunity was not to be lost. The orders flashed quickly—let Heth go forward; bring up Pender at once. It was a miniature Second Manassas! Before night Confederate independence might be closer to reality.

The men in the ranks were as willing as their commander. With a rebel yell that echoed weirdly over the Pennsylvania hills, Heth's brigades swept eastward. Shifting their advance somewhat toward the right, Pender's troops moved across the ridge, joined with Heth, and charged irresistibly over Willoughby Run. Rodes pressed on; Early swept everything before him. In forty-five minutes the battle was over. The Federals were routed and had been hurled back toward the ridges south and east of Gettysburg. The town was in Early's hands. Nearly 5000 bewildered prisoners were being herded on the field. Almost as many dead and wounded lay on the ground. A doubtful morning had ended in a smashing victory. The campaign of invasion could not have had a more auspicious opening.

Riding hurriedly forward across Willoughby Run and up the next ridge, Lee halted near the point where the Chambersburg turnpike comes down from the ridge. Here he had a closer view of the ground to which it was to be assumed the enemy would retreat. Half a mile away, at his feet, lay the town of Gettysburg. South of it was a high cleared hill that seemed to dominate a series of ridges that spread from it to the east and to the south. Toward this hill, in confused and demoralized masses, the defeated Federals were retreating. On the hill were blue infantry reserves and artillery. Some of Hill's guns were at once ordered up by Lee to open on these troops. If more than this could be done—if the ground could be seized at once and the Federals driven from it—the Confederates would control the whole position. Could this be accomplished without bringing on the general engagement that Lee was anxious to avoid until the entire army was up? Hill, who was unhappily sick, reported that the Federals had fought with unusual tenacity and that his own men were exhausted and disorganized. Prisoners had been taken from two Federal corps—the I and the XI—and they stated that the whole Union army was moving on Gettysburg.

Ewell, then, must undertake the advance. As Lee did not know the condition of Ewell's men or the strength of the hill from the northern approach, he did what he always did with his corps commanders in like circumstances: he issued discretionary orders. Sending Ewell an account of what he saw, he told him it was only necessary to "push those people" to get possession of the hill, and he suggested that Ewell do so, if practicable, without committing the whole army to battle.

Soon after this message was sent by Major Walter H. Taylor, General Longstreet rode up. General Lee pointed out to him the enemy's position, and while he was engaged with other military duties, Longstreet made a careful survey of the front with his field-glasses. The two were, at the time, on a long hill, Seminary Ridge, that fell away to the east and then rose again to the road that led from Gettysburg to Emmitsburg. East of this road was rolling land parallel to Seminary Ridge and about three miles in length. At its southern end was an eminence of some 600 feet known as Round Top. Northeast of this, at a little distance, was a second hill, slightly lower, styled Little Round Top. At the northern end of the ridge was a high cleared position, on part of which was the burial ground of the town, which gave its name to the hill and to the ridge—an ominous name, fated soon to be all too apt, Cemetery Hill, Cemetery Ridge. From where Lee and Longstreet stood, they could see that the high ground continued eastward and southeastward from Cemetery Hill, reaching another height called Culp's Hill. The whole of the opposite ridge was, therefore, a fishhook with the shank running from south to north and with the point to the southeast. Round Top was at the end of the shank of the hook, the loop, so to speak, where the line might be joined. Cemetery Ridge was the shank, Cemetery Hill the beginning of the bend, and Culp's Hill the point. Gettysburg was directly north of the bend. It was a most formidable position, distant an average of about 1400 yards from Seminary Ridge, which, in turn, afforded excellent ground for a defensive battle.

Longstreet studied the terrain closely by the side of the chief with whom there had not been a ripple of disagreement since they had entered Pennsylvania; but when Longstreet put down his glasses and turned to Lee, it was to assert his innate self-confidence and his faith in the plan he had formulated, ere he left Virginia, for offensive strategy and defensive tactics. Without waiting, apparently, for Lee to ask his opinion, he declared the field ideal for the course on which he had set his heart. "All we have to do," he later quoted himself as saying in substance, "is to throw our army around by their left, and we shall interpose between the Federal army and Washington. We can get a strong position and wait, and if they fail to attack us we shall have everything in condition to move back tomorrow night in the direction of Washington, selecting beforehand a good position into which we can put our troops to receive battle next day. Finding our object is Washington or that army, the Federals will be sure to attack us. When they attack, we shall beat them, as we proposed to do before we left Fredericksburg, and the probabilities are that the fruits of our success will be great."

This was rather remarkable language for a subordinate to address to the commanding general, ten minutes after his arrival on the field of battle, and when he had not been advised of the strength of the enemy. It was, moreover, a proposal that involved great risks. Meade presumably was moving from the direction of Washington, but how close he was and how fully concentrated, Lee did not know and could not ascertain in the absence of his cavalry. The Southern army had been compelled to advance cautiously to Gettysburg, and had been more than fortunate in finding and in driving the enemy there. To have led the army blindly around the Federal left "would have been wildly rash." The surest hope of victory, the best defensive, was to attack the two corps immediately in front, as soon as a sufficient force for the purpose could be brought up. To delay and to manoeuvre was to gamble with ruin.

Lee therefore answered Longstreet at once: "If the enemy is there, we must attack him."

Longstreet retorted sharply: "If he is there, it will be because he is anxious that we should attack him—a good reason, in my judgment, for not doing so." And he proceeded to argue his point.

Lee said little more but displayed not the slightest intention of changing his plan of attacking the enemy at the earliest possible moment, before the whole of the Army of the Potomac could be brought up.

At some stage of the discussion Colonel A. L. Long returned from a reconnaissance Lee had ordered him to make in front of Cemetery Hill. Long reported that the position seemed to be occupied in considerable force, with some troops behind a stone fence near the crest, and with others on the reverse slope. An attack, he said, would be hazardous and doubtful of success. About the same time, Lieutenant James Power Smith arrived with a message from Ewell. He probably had passed Taylor as the latter was hurrying to the commander of the Second Corps with Lee's orders to take Cemetery Ridge if practicable. Ewell, said Smith, desired him to inform the commander that General Rodes and General Early believed they could take Cemetery Hill if they were supported on the right, and that, "it would be well if Lee occupied at once the higher ground in front of our right, which seemed to command the Cemetery Hill."

"I suppose," Lee answered, "this is the higher ground to which these gentlemen refer," and, pointing to the front, he handed Smith his field-glasses. "You will find that some of those people are there now."

After Smith had looked, Lee went on. "Our people are not yet up, and I have no troops with which to occupy this higher ground."

Then he turned to Longstreet with a question that officer had not previously given him opportunity of asking: Where on the road were the troops of the First Corps? But Longstreet was angry because his counsel had been rejected, and he was not disposed to be communicative. McLaws's division, he said, was about six miles away, but beyond that he was indefinite and noncommittal.

Lee urged him to bring his corps up as rapidly as possible, and turning to Smith gave him this message to Ewell: Smith was to tell Ewell that Lee did not then have troops to support him on the right, but that Lee wished Ewell to take Cemetery Hill if it was possible. He added that he would ride over to see Ewell very shortly.

Longstreet did not like this either. Although the troops about whose position he was so vague were those on whom Lee would naturally rely for an assault on the western flank of Cemetery Hill, Longstreet argued—then or before this time—that if Lee intended to attack, he should do so immediately.

Lee explained again his reasons for not making the attack at once and expressed regret that the non-arrival of Imboden at Chambersburg had forced him to leave Pickett's division there. A general assault must wait until the arrival of at least McLaws's and Hood's divisions of the First Corps.

Longstreet had no more to say, thinking that Lee might later change his mind and make no attack, and presently "Old Pete" rode off. It was now about 5:30 P.M. Firing had ceased along the whole front. Major Taylor had returned and had reported the delivery of Lee's message to Ewell, but there was no sign of any effort on the part of Ewell to storm Cemetery Hill. To ascertain precisely the state of affairs on the front of the Second Corps, Lee rode over to Gettysburg and soon found Ewell and Rodes together. In the arbor back of a little house north of the town on the Carlisle road, he sat down with them to hear their reports.

\* \* \* \* \*

Was the plan understood? It was. Had aught been omitted in preparation? Neither Hill nor Longstreet knew of anything—at least Longstreet did not think to tell Lee that he had not inquired whether the artillery still had enough ammunition for a long cannonade. Lee folded up his map, the three rose from the fallen log where they had seated themselves, and, mounting once again, they rode each to his station. The commanding general was still confident; Hill was alert but had none of the immediate responsibility of the assault on him; Longstreet was close to black dismay. "He knew," Longstreet subsequently said of Lee, "that I did not believe that success was possible; that care and time should be taken to give the troops the benefit of positions and the grounds; and he should have put an officer in charge who had more confidence in his plan." But of this he said nothing to Lee. For the supreme effort of all his warring, Lee had to act through a sullen, despairing lieutenant.

There was a momentary flurry as a troop of Federal cavalry rode into the rear of Hood's division, but this was quickly over. A battery of horse artillery was put into the Emmitsburg pike to protect the flank against further incursions by mounted troops, and the last preparations were complete.

The time had come to give the order for the bombardment. Longstreet could not bring himself to do it. Instead, he wrote Colonel Alexander: "If the artillery fire does not have the effect to drive off the enemy or greatly demoralize him, so as to make our effort pretty certain, I would prefer that you should not advise Pickett to make the charge. I shall rely a great deal upon your judgment to determine the matter and shall expect you to let Gen. Pickett know when the moment offers." Then Longstreet went off in the woods and lay down—to think of some method of assisting the attack, as he affirmed, but as Colonel Fremantle thought, to go to sleep.

Alexander was of the bravest of the brave, but he was unprepared to assume the responsibility he felt his chief was trying to unload on him. As soon as he received Longstreet's note, he replied, in substance:

"I will only be able to judge of the effect of our fire on the enemy by his return fire, as his infantry is little exposed to view and the smoke will obscure the field. If, as I infer from your note, there is any alternative to this attack, it should be carefully considered before opening our fire, for it will take all the artillery ammunition we have left to test this one, and if the result is unfavorable we will have none left for another effort. And even if this is entirely successful, it can only be so at a very bloody cost."

Aroused to receive this message, Longstreet drafted an answer as follows:

"Colonel: The intention is to advance the infantry if the artillery has the desired effect of driving the enemy's off, or having other effect such as to warrant us in making the attack. When that moment arrives advise Gen. Pickett and of course advance such artillery as you can use in aiding the attack."

This paper reached Alexander at a time when General A. R. Wright was with him. "What do you think of it?" he asked Wright.

"The trouble is not in going there," his fellow-Georgian answered. "I was there with my brigade yesterday. There is a place where you can get breath and re-form. The trouble is to stay there after you get there, for the whole Yankee army is there in a bunch."

Alexander sought out Pickett, who was calm and confident, and then sent back this brief note to Longstreet:

"General: when our fire is at its best, I will advise General Pickett to advance."

The silence on the field was now almost complete. Directly opposite the Confederate line a little group of Federal officers were sitting about on the ground, after a late breakfast, smoking and wondering whether Meade had been correct when he had said early in the morning that if Lee attacked at all that day it would be against the centre, because he had tried on both flanks and had failed. The Federal infantry were huddled behind the stone wall that ran along the ridge, or were blistering in the tall grass in front of the wall, where the first line had been formed.

The Southern infantry were idling under cover. They had ceased their usual banter, because the rumor had spread among them that they were to be called to charge over the rim of the hill that cut off their view of the Federal position, but in the memory of old triumphs, and in their unshakable faith in the leadership of Lee, they were as confident as ever they had been. All Pickett's fifteen regiments were Virginians, some of them among the earliest volunteers. They were fresh and had done no severe fighting since Sharpsburg. Trimble's ten regiments, Pender's former command, were from North Carolina, as good troops as that state had sent to the front. Two of Pettigrew's brigades were of A. P. Hill's famous old "light division," Virginians, Tennesseans, and Alabamians, but both these units were small and both were under colonels. One of them, Mayo's, was in bad condition. Pettigrew's two remaining brigades were Davis's Mississippians and his own North Carolinians. They were new to the Army of Northern Virginia, but they had caught the contagion of its morale. Wilcox's old brigade of five Alabama regiments had been tested on many a field.

Thus, in the forty-seven regiments of the column of attack, about 15,000 men, there were to be nineteen regiments from Virginia, fourteen from North Carolina, seven from Alabama, four from Mississippi, and three from

Tennessee. If Perry were employed in support, three Florida regiments would be added; if Perrin were called in, he would lead the five South Carolina regiments that had been McGowan's and previously Gregg's famous brigade. And if Wright were needed, his Georgians would be ready again. Every Southern state east of the Mississippi was, or might be, represented in the assault—the Army of Northern Virginia at its best, a cross-section of the Confederacy, city dwellers and the sons of great planters, men from the tidal waters and from the hungry mountains, scholars and illiterates, the inheritors of historic names and the unrenowned sons of the poor. Hungry, athirst, dirty, they waited under the noonday sun whose fiery course was to decide whether America was to be two nations.

One o'clock in the stately house in Richmond where Davis, sick and anxious, looked up expectantly for a telegram from Lee whenever a knock came at his door; noon along the Mississippi, as Pemberton with heavy heart was penning a letter asking terms of General Grant for the surrender of Vicksburg; tea time in London, and a sealed letter on the desk of John Bigelow, telling Secretary Seward he was satisfied that Lee's invasion of Pennsylvania had been made in concert with J. A. Roebuck's proposal in the House of Commons that Her Majesty's government enter into negotiations with foreign powers for the recognition of the Confederacy. Almost on the hour, the silence of the fields around Gettysburg was broken by a gun on the Emmitsburg road. Before men had time to shape the question that rose in every mind, the echo of another cannon swelled from the same position. It was the agreed signal for the opening of the bombardment.

Instantly the gunners all along the line sprang to their loaded pieces, and in another moment the roar of the massed batteries shook the ridge. Orders were to fire in salvoes, and as the guns were discharged together, the concussion told of a coming terror that would make men long for the lesser dangers of Gaines's Mill and of Sharpsburg. Two or three miles away, waiting teamsters heard the windows rattle as if assailed by a sudden storm. The firing was a little high for the stone wall behind which the Federal infantry were huddled, but as the exploding shells struck the ridge they hurled the earth into the air and shattered rocks that flew in fragments as deadly as the iron itself. Soon the Federal batteries opened, eighteen guns from the very grove Pickett was to charge, and up and down a line that lengthened until a front of fully two miles was blazing in answer. On their high trajectory, round shells could be plainly seen for the whole of their flight, but the rifled shells were visible only when they tumbled. Soon the smoke and the dust obscured the target and darkened the sun. Save for the odor and the long, sulphurous strata above the denser clouds, the scene resembled the centre of some furious thunderstorm. Now the Confederate shell found a caisson, and as its contents exploded with a roar and a flash of flame, the artillerists raised a yell that was plainly heard by the Federals. Now, in return, a Union missile struck in the waiting ranks of the infantry, and the stretcher-bearers rushed in to carry out the wounded, the men who never saw the other side of the hill.

Twenty minutes of this maddening bombardment, and the ammunition of some of the Confederate batteries was half gone, with no diminution in the Federal fire. Alexander felt, by this time, that there was little hope of silencing the enemy's fire and he reasoned that unless the infantry moved soon, the artillery would not be able to cover its advance. He scratched off this note to Pickett:

"General: If you are to advance at all, you must come at once or we will not be able to support you as we ought. But the enemy's fire has not slackened materially and there are still 18 guns firing from the cemetery."

Behind Alexander's position, between the artillery and in the infantry, Longstreet rode at a walk, looking neither to right nor to left. In front of Armistead's and Garnett's brigades, the chaplains came out and, kneeling, offered prayers amid a knot of bareheaded boys.

"This is a desperate thing to attempt," Garnett said to Armistead.

"It is," stout-hearted old Armistead answered, "but the issue is with the Almighty, and we must leave it in His hands."

Presently, after a shell had hit a nearby tree, Armistead calmly pulled off a splinter and exhibited it to the men. "Boys," said he, "do you think you can go up under that? It is pretty hot out there."

There was a confident answer, but presently, when a rabbit sprang from the bushes and leaped rapidly toward the rear, a gaunt Virginian voiced the feelings of thousands when he cried: "Run, ole hahr; if I was an ole hahr I would run, too." The wounded were more numerous; a fragment of a bursting shell had struck down Colonel W. R. Aylett of the Fifty-fourth Virginia. It was harder waiting under that fire than it would be in making the assault.

Suddenly, through a rift in the smoke, Alexander saw Federal batteries withdrawing from the vicinity of the little grove. At the same instant the Federal fire began to fall off. It was now or never. On a bit of paper, Alexander scrawled to Pickett:

"For God's sake come quick. The 18 guns have gone. Come quick or my ammunition will not let me support you properly."

A messenger dashed off through the smoke with the paper.

Pickett, at that moment, was in receipt of Alexander's previous dispatch. He read it and without a word passed it on to Longstreet, who had dismounted. Longstreet scrutinized it, but gave no order.

"General," said Pickett, anxiously, "shall I advance?"

Still no answer from Longstreet. He turned and looked away, and then, as if the effort cost him his very heart's blood, slowly nodded his head.

Pickett shook back his long hair, and saluted. "I am going to move forward, sir," he said, and galloped off.

About that same time, a shell fell close to the ordnance train, which was parked near at hand. Fearing for the safety of all the ammunition the army had to replenish the gaping caissons, General Pendleton ordered the wagons to the rear and, a little later, recalled four of the nine eleven-pounder howitzers that Alexander had not been able to employ in the bombardment but had intended to use in following up the advance. Major Richardson, left in charge of the other howitzers, moved them also, to get them out of the line of fire. Alexander must have been notified promptly of this, for when Long-street rode to him after Pickett had left, Alexander told him that the how-itzers were gone and that the ammunition of all the batteries was running low.

"Go and stop Pickett where he is," Longstreet said sharply, "and replenish your ammunition."

"We can't do that, sir," Alexander said. "The train has but little. It would take an hour to distribute it, and meanwhile the enemy would improve the time."

"I do not want to make this charge," Longstreet said slowly and with deep emotion. "I do not see how it can succeed. I would not make it now but that General Lee has ordered it and is expecting it." With that he stopped, but he did not send word to Lee of the state of his ammunition. Lee received no intimation from any source that it was nearly exhausted.

The Confederate artillerists paused now, for the infantry had to pass through the batteries. The Federal guns continued for a few minutes and then they, too, reserved their fire. Three hundred yards behind Alexander's batteries, the infantrymen realized that their time had come. Soon Pickett galloped up, as debonair as if he had been riding through the streets of Richmond under the eye of his affianced. "Up, men," he called, "and to your posts! Don't forget today that you are from old Virginia!" Almost at the same moment, on the crest, Pettigrew called to Marshall, "Now, Colonel, for the honor of the good Old North State, forward."

General Garnett, buttoned to the neck in an old blue overcoat, and much too ill to take the field, mounted his great black horse and rode out in front of his column as it sprang into line. Kemper on his charger took position in advance of his willing regiments. Armistead, who was to support these two brigadiers, turned his horse's head and came up to the color-sergeant of the Fifty-third Virginia. "Sergeant," he cried, "are you going to put those colors on the enemy's works today?"

"I will try, sir, and if mortal man can do it, it shall be done!"

Then Armistead took off his hat, put it on the point of his sword and shouted in a voice that had never failed to reach the farthest man in his brigade, "Attention, Second battalion, the battalion of direction! Forward, guide centre! March!" And turning his horse, he went on ahead of them, his white head a mark for the bullets that were soon to fly.

Now the skirmish line was in the open; now Garnett and Kemper rode out. Behind Kemper was Colonel Eppa Hunton of the Eighth Virginia on his horse, and behind Garnett was mounted Colonel Lewis Williams of the First, both of them too sick to walk but neither of them willing to be left behind. All the other officers, by Pickett's orders, were afoot. And now the front brigades, except Davis's and Mayo's, were emerging from the woods. The front was oblique because of the greater distance Pettigrew had to cover, and there was a gap between Garnett's left and Fry's right. Once clear of the woods, at a word of command, the whole line was dressed until it was almost perfect in its formation. Nineteen battle flags were in sight, their red deepened by the sunlight, and the array seemed overpowering, but, as the smoke had lifted, those who looked on the right could see that the flank of Kemper was separated by almost half a mile from the left of McLaws— as if inviting an enfilade fire in its advance, or a counterattack should it fail. From the left, the sight was one to make men catch their breath. Far beyond that flank, in Gettysburg, Rodes's soldiers called out to the Federal surgeons: "There go the men who will go through your damned Yankee line for you!" Lee saw it all, and the sight that stirred him most was that of the bandages on the heads and arms of some of Pettigrew's Carolinians. They had been wounded in the battle of July 1, and had been mustered back into the ranks by their commander, along with all the cooks and extra-duty men.

Davis had come out of the woods by this time, as had Mayo's brigade, lagging on his left. Soon the supporting line was visible, too—Armistead on the right, then Lowrance, then Lane on the left—and twenty-five more battle flags were visible. Armistead's left overlapped Lowrance's right at the start, but this was quickly rectified, and the whole swept forward at common time, Armistead's men with their arms at right shoulder. Each unit moved as if the distance had been taped and marked for a grand review.

Two hundred yards forward and scarcely a shot. Kemper, moving sharply toward the left, was across the double fence at Spangler's lane. Garnett's men, with scarcely a stir in their alignment, were negotiating the post-and-rail fence in their front and were sweeping through a lesser obstruction as if it were not there. Then, as if awakened from a dream, the Federal artillerists opened—not with the weakened fire that the supposed withdrawal of eighteen guns had led the Confederates to anticipate, but with the full fury of massed guns. The blast was concentrated on Pickett, because Pettigrew was not yet within effective range. The shells tore gaps in the line; flags began to go down; behind the advancing ranks, dead and writhing men littered the ground. But the charge continued at the same measured pace, with scarcely the fire of a single Southern musket.

Soon the skirmishers were brought to a stand at the post-and-plank fences along the Emmitsburg road. They disputed this barrier with the Federal skirmishers, who held their own until the main Confederate line was within one hundred yards. Then the enemy fell back. Openings were made in the stubborn fence, but as the men made for these, they crowded together and offered a mark that the Federal gunners reached again and again. Once beyond the second fence on the eastern side of the road, Pickett's men were halted, and the line was drawn again with care. Armistead was close behind now, the flanks of Garnett's and of Archer's brigades had met, and Pettigrew's two right brigades, though they had been forced to cross a number of farm fences, had kept their formation admirably. Davis had caught up, but Mayo's brigade was falling behind more and more. All Pettigrew's units were now under artillery fire and were suffering heavily.

Up the hill now and at double time! Kemper swings still farther to the left, up a little swale, and his flank is bare to the enemy's bullets. More colors go down; hundreds of men have fallen. Still the formation is excellent, and the front is heavy enough to cover the 250 yards that separate the Confederate right from the wall. Here is the Federal advanced line already, hidden in the tall grass. It fires and flees. A flash of flame, a roar, and the Federal infantry behind the stone wall has opened with their volley. From the right, a small Union command is tearing Kemper's flank. Garnett, still on that rearing black horse, is shouting to his men; the rebel yell rolls up the ridge in answer to the Federal challenge; Garnett is charging bayonets; the Union artillery has stopped its blasts on the right but is still pouring canister into Pettigrew. Only a hundred yards for Pickett now, hardly more for Pettigrew. Fry's brigade has almost been absorbed by the commands on its right and left. Armistead is on the heels of Garnett and Kemper; Lowrance and Lane are fighting across the field in the rear of Pettigrew through bursting shell.

"Fire!" cries Garnett, and his men for the first time pull trigger.

"Fire!" Kemper echoes, and his troops send a volley against the wall at the same instant that their high, furious yell breaks out. Armistead had ridden back so that his line can fire, and his horse is down. There goes his volley; on the left, where the stone wall is farther up the ridge and higher, the Federal infantry have opened on Pettigrew.

Twenty-five yards—only twenty-five to the barrier in Garnett's front. The grimy faces of the Federal infantry can be seen where the smoke lifts for an instant in front of the wall. But the lines are all in confusion now. Fry's men are mingled with Garnett's, Marshall's right is piling up on Garnett's left. Garnett is down, dead, and his horse is racing back toward the Confederate lines, a great gash in his shoulder; Kemper has fallen; the line is melting away on the right and on the left. Still the dauntless men rush upward. The Virginians and some of the Tennesseans and Carolinians are at the stone fence, and on their left the rest of Marshall's brigade is rushing into the open ground at the angle and fighting on to the wall, eighty yards farther eastward. Armistead is up now, at the low barrier, his sword is high, and his hat, pierced by the point of his sword, is down to the hilt of his blade. His voice is ringing out above the din "Follow me!" Over the wall then, with the bayonet, and on to the crest of the hill! About 100 men of five brigades follow him into the melee, with butt and thrust, but they fall at every step. In the angle, Marshall's men press on. The enemy is all around them. Where are the thousands who marched in that proud line from the woods? Where are the flags and where the supports? The right is in the air; they are bluecoats firing over there, not Confederates. And on the left— more Federals. The place is a death-trap—are there no officers to tell one what to do? In the front are the enemy's batteries; Armistead lies yonder among the guns, forty yards within the wall, his left hand on a cannon, his right still grasping his sword. Davis has reached the wall and has recoiled, broken; Mayo's men have failed; the left has melted away. Lowrance and Lane are in the angle, but they are only a fragment. Are there no reinforcements to drive the victory home? Wilcox is advancing on the right and that is Perry's little brigade beside him, but they have lost direction. Instead of following Kemper's turn they are moving straight on—to annihilation if they continue. A few batteries have advanced, but their fire is weak and erratic. No support; no succor! In the angle and beyond the wall, there is nothing to do but to struggle with those thickening masses of Federals. Here and there an officer is calling out "Steady, men"; pistols are being used against muskets; Captain M. P. Spessard yonder has stopped to take a last look at his dying son and then has sprung over the wall, and is fighting with his bare sword in a hand-to-hand struggle with Federal infantrymen. That color-sergeant is using his flag staff as a lance; the flag of the Eleventh North Carolina has gone down again and again, and now Captain Francis Bird is carrying it and rallying his men; the survivors, unconsciously crowding around the standards, are stumbling over the bodies of the dead; every minute sees the struggling remnants thinned.

From the right there is a rush and a volley; on the left the Federals loose an overwhelming blast of musketry; in front, they stand stubbornly behind the wall at the angle and on the crest. The column is surrounded—there is no escape except in abandoning the heights, won with so much blood and valor. Every man for himself! Uplifted hands for the soldier whose musket has been struck down, a white handkerchief here, a cry of "I surrender," and for the rest—back over the wall and out into the field again. The assault has failed. Men could do no more!

❧ ☙

THE limits upon Confederate resources became steadily more apparent after Gettysburg. Lee notified a somber Jefferson Davis in February of 1864, "We are not in a condition, & never have been in my opinion, to invade the enemy's country with a prospect of permanent benefit." What he did not realize was that Union forces possessed the power to strike simultaneously in Virginia and Georgia. Already Lincoln had surrendered to Grant as general-in-chief the task of devising the grand strategy which would bring the Confederacy to its knees. At the heart of Grant's plan was a simple intention, the armies of the East and West should work in tandem so as to tie down all Confederate forces and deprive the South of the opportunity to shift manpower to threatened points. It meant in effect that no point in the South should be free of envelopment. For all purposes, when the spring of 1864 opened, the whole South had been made into a beleaguered fortress.

Lee had been accustomed to repulsing Federal forces with ease; the technique was simple, inflict upon them heavy losses and the Army of the Potomac would spend weeks and often months licking its wounds. Now he would face Grant who had instructed his lieutenants, "Lee's army will be your objective point. Wherever Lee goes, there you will go also." No less emphatic directions went to Sherman as he launched his invasion of Georgia. For the remainder of the war, Lee and his men would know no rest. The three-day Battle of the Wilderness, May 5-7, 1864, would inflict 17,666 casualties upon Federal forces, but unlike previous battles, Grant chose not to withdraw but raced Lee's army to Spotsylvania where at "the Bloody Angle," in savage trench fighting, "rank after rank was riddled by shot and shell and bayonet-thrusts, and finally sank, a mass of torn and mutilated corpses." An additional *10,920* Union troops fell casualty to the battle, and as in the Wilderness, Southern losses are uncertain, for one sign of the developing collapse of the Confederacy was the breakdown of its records. The culminating battle of the month-long campaign came at Cold Harbor on June *3* when more than *7,000* Federal troops fell in a matter of minutes to a savage Confederate cross fire. After that, the war around Richmond settled down into a routine of siege. Union losses in the previous six weeks of fighting approached *70,000* as opposed to about *40,000* for the Confederates. But there was a significant difference; Grant could replace his losses and Lee could not do more than scrape the bottom of the barrel. All that was left were boys and aged men.

Sherman, too, pursued his enemy with unrelenting ruthlessness, but he also directed increasingly the weight of war against civilians. When he entered Atlanta, he expelled its entire civilian population, reasoning rightly that they would tax further already sagging Confederate resources, and when he abandoned the city, he put it to the torch as he had Jackson and Meridian, Mississippi, and as he would to Columbia, South Carolina. So as Grant pinned down Lee in the environs of Richmond, Sherman led the Federal Army of the West eastward and then northward until as spring of *1865* broke, he stood barely two hundred miles from Richmond. Lee had finally been brought to bay. On April *2, 1865,* he finally abandoned Richmond, a goodly portion of which would be leveled by fire, and seven days later, at Appomattox, he surrendered. For all practical purposes, the war was over. It was Palm Sunday; five days later, on Good Friday, an assassin's bullet crashed into Lincoln's brain—the next day, as morning broke, Lincoln joined the more than *600,000* men who had died in the war to save the Union.

John G. Nicolay (*1832-1902*), Bavarian born, passed most of his life in the United States. Between *1859* and *1865*, after abandoning a newspaper career, he served as Lincoln's secretary with John Hay. After Lincoln's death, he served for a time as American consul at Paris, and then as marshal of the United States Supreme Court. He wrote with Hay a ten-volume biography of Abraham Lincoln (*1890*) and was one of the co-editors of Lincoln's Complete Works.

# ABRAHAM LINCOLN: A HISTORY

## by John G. Nicolay and John Hay

From the hour of Mr. Lincoln's reëlection the Confederate cause was doomed. The cheering of the troops which greeted the news from the North was heard within the lines at Richmond and at Petersburg; and although the leaders maintained their attitude of defiance, the impression rapidly gained ground among the people that the end was not far off. The stimulus of hope being gone, they began to feel the pinch of increasing want. Their currency had become almost worthless. In October, a dollar in gold was worth thirty-five dollars in Confederate money. With the opening of the new year the price rose to sixty-dollars, and, despite the efforts of the Confederate treasury, which would occasionally rush into the market and beat down the price of gold ten or twenty per cent a day, the currency gradually depreciated until a hundred for one was offered and not taken. It was natural for the citizens of Richmond to think that monstrous prices were being extorted for food, clothing, and supplies, when in fact they were paying no more than was reasonable. To pay a thousand dollars for a barrel of flour was enough to strike a householder with terror, but ten dollars is not a famine price. High prices, however, even if paid in dry leaves, are a hardship when dry leaves are not plentiful; and there was scarcity even of Confederate money in the South.

At every advance of Grant's lines a new alarm was manifested in Richmond, the first proof of which was always a fresh rigor in enforcing the conscription laws and the arbitrary orders of the frightened authorities. After the capture of Fort Harrison, north of the James, squads of guards were sent into the streets with directions to arrest every able-bodied man they met. It is said that the medical boards were ordered to exempt no one capable of bearing arms for ten days. Human nature will not endure such a strain as this, and desertion grew too common to punish.

As disaster increased, the Confederate government steadily lost ground in the confidence and respect of the Southern people. Mr. Davis and his councilors were doing their best, but they no longer got any credit for it. From every part of the Confederacy came complaints of what was done, demands for what was impossible to do. Some of the States were in a condition near to counter-revolution. A slow paralysis was benumbing the limbs of the insurrection, and even at the heart its vitality was plainly declining. The Confederate Congress, which had hitherto been the mere register of the President's will, now turned upon him. On January 19 it passed a resolution making Lee general-in-chief of the army. This Mr. Davis might have borne with patience, although it was intended as a notification that his meddling with military affairs must come to an end. But far worse was the bitter necessity put upon him as a sequel to this act, of reappointing General Joseph E. Johnston to the command of the army which was to resist Sherman's victorious march to the north. Mr. Seddon, rebel Secretary of War, thinking his honor impugned by a vote of the Virginia delegation in Congress, resigned. Warnings of serious demoralization came daily from the army, and disaffection was so rife in official circles in Richmond that it was not thought polite to call public attention to it by measures of repression.

It is curious and instructive to note how the act of emancipation had by this time virtually enforced itself in Richmond. The value of slave property was gone. It is true that a slave was still occasionally sold, at a price less than one tenth of what he would have brought before the war, but servants could be hired of their nominal owners for almost nothing—merely enough to keep up a show of vassalage. In effect, any one could hire a Negro for his keeping—which was all that anybody in Richmond, black or white, got for his work. Even Mr. Davis had at last become docile to the stern teaching of events. In his message of November he had recommended the employment of forty thousand slaves in the army—not as soldiers, it is true, save in the last extremity—with emancipation to come.

On December 27, Mr. Benjamin wrote his last important instruction to John Slidell, the Confederate commissioner in Europe. It is nothing less than a cry of despair. Complaining bitterly of the attitude of foreign nations while the South is fighting the battles of England and France against the North, he asks: "Are they determined never to recognize the Southern Confederacy until the United States assent to such action on their part?" And with a frantic offer to submit to any terms which Europe might impose as the price of recognition, and a scarcely veiled threat of making peace with the North unless Europe should act speedily, the Confederate Department of State closed its four years of fruitless activity.

Lee assumed command of all the Confederate armies on February 9. His situation was one of unprecedented gloom. The day before he had reported that his troops, who had been in line of battle for two days at Hatcher's Run, exposed to the bad winter weather, had been without meat for three days. A prodigious effort was made, and the danger of starvation for the moment averted, but no permanent improvement resulted. The armies of the Union were closing in from every point of the compass. Grant was every day pushing his formidable left wing nearer the only roads by which Lee could escape; Thomas was threatening the Confederate communications from Tennessee; Sheridan was riding for the last time up the Shenandoah valley to abolish Early; while from the south the redoubtable columns of Sherman were moving northward with the steady pace and irresistible progress of a tragic fate.

A singular and significant attempt at negotiation was made at this time by General Lee. He was so strong in the confidence of the people of the South, and the government at Richmond was so rapidly becoming discredited, that he could doubtless have obtained the popular support and compelled the assent of the Executive to any measures he thought proper for the attainment of peace. From this it was easy for him and for others to come to the wholly erroneous conclusion that General Grant held a similar relation to the government and people of the United States. General Lee seized upon the pretext of a conversation reported to him by General Longstreet as having been held with General E. O. C. Ord under an ordinary flag of truce for the exchange of prisoners, to address a letter to Grant, sanctioned by Mr. Davis, saying he had been informed that General Ord had said General Grant would not decline an interview with a view "to a satisfactory adjustment of the present unhappy difficulties by means of a military convention," provided Lee had authority to act. He therefore proposed to meet General Grant "with the hope that . . . it may be found practicable to submit the subjects of controversy . . . to a convention of the kind mentioned"; professing himself "authorized to do whatever the result of the proposed interview may render necessary."

Grant at once telegraphed these overtures to Washington. Stanton received the despatch at the Capitol, where the President was, according to his custom, passing the last night of the session of Congress, for the convenience of signing bills. The Secretary handed the telegram to Mr. Lincoln, who read it in silence. He asked no advice or suggestion from any one about him, but, taking up a pen, wrote with his usual slowness and precision a despatch in Stanton's name, which he showed to Seward, and then handed to Stanton to be signed and sent. The language is that of an experienced ruler, perfectly sure of himself and of his duty:

"The President directs me to say that he wished you to have no conference with General Lee, unless it be for capitulation of General Lee's army, or on some minor or purely military matter. He instructs me to say that you are not to decide, discuss, or confer upon any political questions. Such questions the President holds in his own hands, and will submit them to no military conferences or conventions. Meanwhile you are to press to the utmost your military advantages."

Grant answered Lee that he had no authority to accede to his proposition, and explained that General Ord's language must have been misunderstood. This closed to the Confederate authorities the last avenue of hope of any compromise by which the alternative of utter defeat or unconditional surrender might be avoided.

Early in March, General Lee visited Richmond for conference with Mr. Davis on the measures to be adopted in the crisis which he saw was imminent. He had never sympathized with the slight Congress had intended to put upon Mr. Davis when it gave him supreme military authority, and continued to the end to treat his President as commander-in-chief of the forces. There is direct contradiction between Mr. Davis and General Lee as to how Davis received this statement of the necessities of the situation. Mr. Davis says he suggested immediate withdrawal from Richmond, but that Lee said his horses were too weak for the roads in their present condition, and that he must wait. General Lee, on the other hand, is quoted as saying that he wished to retire behind the Staunton River, from which point he might have indefinitely protracted the war, but that the President overruled him. Both agreed, however, that sooner or later Richmond must be abandoned, and that the next move should be to Danville.

But before he turned his back forever upon the lines he had so stoutly defended, Lee resolved to dash once more at the toils by which he was surrounded. He placed half his army under the command of General John B. Gordon, with orders to break through the Union lines at Fort Stedman and take possession of the high ground behind them. A month earlier Grant had foreseen some such move on Lee's part, and had ordered General Parke to be prepared to meet an assault on his center, and to have his commanders ready to bring all their resources to bear on the point in danger, adding: "With proper alacrity in this respect, I would have no objection to seeing the enemy get through." This characteristic phrase throws the strongest light both on Grant's temperament, and on the mastery of his business at which he had arrived. Under such generalship, an army's lines are a trap into which entrance is suicide.

The assault was made with great spirit at half-past four on the morning of March 25. Its initial success was due to a singular cause. The spot chosen was a favorite point for deserters to pass into the Union lines, which they had of late been doing in large numbers. When Gordon's skirmishers, therefore, came stealing through the darkness, they were mistaken for an unusually large party of deserters, and they overpowered several picket-posts without firing a shot. The storming party, following at once, took the trenches with a rush, and in a few minutes had possession of the main line on the right of the fort, and, next, of the fort itself. It was hard in the semi-darkness to distinguish friends from foes, and for a time General Parke was unable to make headway; but with the growing light his troops advanced from every direction to mend the breach, and, making short work of the Confederate detachments, recaptured the fort, opening a cross-fire of artillery so withering that few of the Confederates could get back to their own lines. This was, moreover, not the only damage the Confederates suffered. Humphreys and Wright, on the Union left, rightly assuming that Parke could take care of himself, instantly searched the lines in their front to see if they had been essentially weakened to support Gordon's attack. They found they had not, but in gaining this knowledge captured the enemy's intrenched picket-lines in front of them, which, being held, gave inestimable advantage to the Union army in the struggle of the next week.

Grant's chief anxiety for some time had been lest Lee should abandon his lines; but though burning to attack, he was delayed by the same bad roads which kept Lee in Richmond, and by another cause. He did not wish to move until Sheridan had completed the work assigned him in the Shenandoah valley and joined either Sherman or the army at Petersburg. On March 24, however, at the very moment Gordon was making his plans for next day's sortie, Grant issued his order for the great movement to the left which was to finish the war. He intended to begin on the twenty-ninth, but Lee's desperate dash of the twenty-fifth convinced him that not a moment was to be lost. Sheridan reached City Point on the twenty-sixth. Sherman came up from North Carolina for a brief visit next day. The President was also there, and an interesting meeting took place between these famous brothers in arms and Mr. Lincoln; after which Sherman went back to Goldsboro, and Grant began pushing his army to the left with even more than his usual iron energy.

It was a great army—the result of all the power and wisdom of the government, all the devotion of the people, all the intelligence and teachableness of the soldiers themselves, and all the ability which a mighty war had developed in the officers. In command of all was Grant, the most extraordinary military temperament this country has ever seen. The numbers of the respective armies in this last grapple have been the occasion of endless controversy. As nearly as can be ascertained, the grand total of all arms on the Union side was 124,700; on the Confederate side, 57,000.

Grant's plan, as announced in his instructions of March 24, was at first to despatch Sheridan to destroy the South Side and Danville railroads, at the same time moving a heavy force to the left to insure the success of this raid, and then to turn Lee's position. But his purpose developed from hour to hour, and before he had been away from his winter headquarters one day, he gave up this comparatively narrow scheme, and adopted the far bolder plan which he carried out to his immortal honor. He ordered Sheridan not to go after the railroads, but to push for the enemy's right rear, writing him: "I now feel like ending the matter. . . . We will act all together as one army here, until it is seen what can be done with the enemy."

On the thirtieth, Sheridan advanced to Five Forks, where he found a heavy force of the enemy. Lee, justly alarmed by Grant's movements, had despatched a sufficient detachment to hold that important crossroads, and taken personal command of the remainder on White Oak Ridge. A heavy rainstorm, beginning on the night of the twenty-ninth and continuing more than twenty-four hours, greatly impeded the march of the troops. On the thirty-first, Warren, working his way toward the White Oak road, was attacked by Lee and driven back on the main line, but rallied, and in the afternoon drove the enemy again into his works. Sheridan, opposed by Pickett with a large force of infantry and cavalry, was also forced back, fighting obstinately, as far as Dinwiddie Court House, from which point he hopefully reported his situation to Grant at dark. Grant, more disturbed than Sheridan himself, rained orders and suggestions all night to effect a concentration at daylight on that portion of the enemy in front of Sheridan; but Pickett, finding himself out of position, silently withdrew during the night, and resumed his strongly intrenched post at Five Forks. Here Sheridan followed him on April 1, and repeated the successful tactics of his Shenandoah valley exploits so brilliantly that Lee's right was entirely shattered.

This battle of Five Forks should have ended the war. Lee's right was routed; his line had been stretched westward until it broke; there was no longer any hope of saving Richmond, or even of materially delaying its fall. But Lee apparently thought that even the gain of a day was of value to the Richmond government, and what was left of his Army of Northern Virginia was still so perfect in discipline that it answered with unabated spirit every demand made upon it. Grant, who feared Lee might get away from Petersburg and overwhelm Sheridan on the White Oak road, directed that an assault be made all along the line at four o'clock on the morning of the second. His officers responded with enthusiasm; and Lee, far from dreaming of attacking the day before, made what hasty preparations he could to resist them.

It is painful to record the hard fighting which followed. Wright, in his assault in front of Forts Fisher and Walsh, lost eleven hundred men in fifteen minutes of murderous conflict that made them his own; and other commands fared scarcely better, Union and Confederate troops alike displaying a gallantry distressing to contemplate when one reflects that, the war being already decided, all this heroic blood was shed in vain. The Confederates, from the Appomattox to the Weldon road, fell slowly back to their inner line of works; and Lee, watching the formidable advance before which his weakened troops gave way, sent a message to Richmond announcing his purpose of concentrating on the Danville road, and made preparations for the evacuation which was now the only resort left him.

Some Confederate writers express surprise that General Grant did not attack and destroy Lee's army on April 2; but this is a view, after the fact, easy to express. The troops on the Union left had been on foot for eighteen hours, had fought an important battle, marched and countermarched many miles, and were now confronted by Longstreet's fresh corps behind formidable works, while the attitude of the force under Gordon on the south side of the town was such as to require the close attention of Parke. Grant, anticipating an early retirement of Lee from his citadel, wisely resolved to avoid the waste and bloodshed of an immediate assault on the inner lines of Petersburg. He ordered Sheridan to get upon Lee's line of retreat; sent Humphreys to strengthen him; then, directing a general bombardment for five o'clock next morning, and an assault at six, gave himself and his soldiers a little of the rest they had so richly earned and so seriously needed.

He had telegraphed during the day to President Lincoln, who was still at City Point, the news as it developed from hour to hour. Prisoners he regarded as so much net gain; he was weary of slaughter, and wanted the war ended with as little bloodshed as possible; and it was with delight that he summed up on Sunday afternoon: "The whole captures since the army started out gunning will not amount to less than twelve thousand men, and probably fifty pieces of artillery."

Lee bent all his energies to saving his army and leading it out of its untenable position on the James to a point from which he could effect a junction with Johnston in North Carolina. The place selected for this purpose was Burkeville, at the crossing of the South Side and Danville roads, fifty miles southwest from Richmond, whence a short distance would bring him to Danville, where the desired junction could be made. Even yet he was able to cradle himself in the illusion that it was only a campaign that had failed, and that he might continue the war indefinitely in another field. At nightfall all his preparations were completed, and dismounting at the mouth of the road leading to Amelia Court House, the first point of rendezvous, where he had directed supplies to be sent, he watched his troops file noiselessly by in the darkness. By three o'clock the town was abandoned; at half-past four it was formally surrendered. Meade, reporting the news to Grant, received orders to march his army immediately up the Appomattox; and divining Lee's intentions, Grant also sent word to Sheridan to push with all speed to the Danville road.

Thus flight and pursuit began almost at the same moment. The swift-footed Army of Northern Virginia was racing for its life, and Grant, inspired with more than his habitual tenacity and energy, not only pressed his enemy in the rear, but hung upon his flank, and strained every nerve to get in his front. He did not even allow himself the pleasure of entering Richmond, which surrendered to Weitzel early on the morning of the third.

All that day Lee pushed forward toward Amelia Court House. There was little fighting except among the cavalry. A terrible disappointment awaited Lee on his arrival at Amelia Court House on the fourth. He had ordered supplies to be forwarded there, but his half-starved troops found no food awaiting them, and nearly twenty-four hours were lost in collecting subsistence for men and horses. When he started again on the night of the fifth, the whole pursuing force was south and stretching out to the west of him. Burkeville was in Grant's possession; the way to Danville was barred; the supply of provisions to the south cut off. He was compelled to change his route to the west, and started for Lynchburg, which he was destined never to reach.

It had been the intention to attack Lee at Amelia Court House on the morning of April 6, but learning of his turn to the west, Meade, who was immediately in pursuit, quickly faced his army about and followed. A running fight ensued for fourteen miles, the enemy, with remarkable quickness and dexterity, halting and partly intrenching themselves from time to time, and the national forces driving them out of every position; the Union cavalry, meanwhile, harassing the moving left flank of the Confederates, and working havoc on the trains. They also caused a grievous loss to history by burning Lee's headquarters baggage, with all its wealth of returns and reports. At Sailor's Creek, a rivulet running north into the Appomattox, Ewell's corps was brought to bay, and important fighting occurred; the day's loss to Lee, there and elsewhere, amounting to eight thousand in all, with several of his generals among the prisoners. This day's work was of incalculable value to the national arms. Sheridan's unerring eye appreciated the full importance of it, his hasty report ending with the words: "If the thing is pressed, I think that Lee will surrender." Grant sent the despatch to President Lincoln, who instantly replied:

"Let the thing be pressed."

In fact, after nightfall of the sixth, Lee's army could only flutter like a wounded bird with one wing shattered. There was no longer any possibility of escape; but Lee found it hard to relinquish the illusion of years, and as soon as night came down he again began his weary march westward. A slight success on the next day once more raised his hopes; but his optimism was not shared by his subordinates, and a number of his principal officers, selecting General Pendleton as their spokesman, made known to him on the seventh their belief that further resistance was useless, and advised surrender. Lee told them that they had yet too many men to think of laying down their arms, but in answer to a courteous summons from Grant sent that same day, inquired what terms he would be willing to offer. Without waiting for a reply, he again put his men in motion, and during all of the eighth the chase and pursuit continued through a part of Virginia green with spring, and until then unvisited by hostile armies.

Sheridan, by unheard-of exertions, at last accomplished the important task of placing himself squarely on Lee's line of retreat. About sunset of the eighth, his advance captured Appomattox Station and four trains of provisions. Shortly after, a reconnaissance revealed the fact that Lee's entire army was coming up the road. Though he had nothing but cavalry, Sheridan resolved to hold the inestimable advantage he had gained, and sent a request to Grant to hurry up the required infantry support; saying that if it reached him that night, they "might perhaps finish the job in the morning." He added, with singular prescience, referring to the negotiations which had been opened: "I do not think Lee means to surrender until compelled to do so."

This was strictly true. When Grant replied to Lee's question about terms, saying that the only condition he insisted upon was that the officers and men surrendered should be disqualified from taking up arms again until properly exchanged, Lee disclaimed any intention to surrender his army, but proposed to meet Grant to discuss the restoration of peace. It appears from his own report that even on the night of the eighth he had no intention of giving up the fight. He expected to find only cavalry before him next morning, and thought his remnant of infantry could break through while he himself was amusing Grant with platonic discussions in the rear. But on arriving at the rendezvous he had suggested, he received Grant's courteous but decided refusal to enter into a political negotiation, and also the news that a formidable force of infantry barred the way and covered the adjacent hills and valley. The marching of the Confederate army was over forever, and Lee, suddenly brought to a sense of his real situation, sent orders to cease hostilities, and wrote another note to Grant, asking an interview for the purpose of surrendering his army.

The meeting took place at the home of Wilmer McLean, in the edge of the village of Appomattox, on April 9, 1865. Lee met Grant at the threshold, and ushered him into a small and barely furnished parlor, where were soon assembled the leading officers of the national army. General Lee was accompanied only by his secretary, Colonel Charles Marshall. A short conversation led up to a request from Lee for the terms on which the surrender of his army would be received. Grant briefly stated them, and then wrote them out. Men and officers were to be paroled, and the arms, artillery, and public property turned over to the officer appointed to receive them.

"This," he added, "will not embrace the side-arms of the officers, nor their private horses or baggage. This done, each officer and man will be allowed to return to their homes, not to be disturbed by United States authority so long as they observe their parole and the laws in force where they may reside."

General Grant says in his "Memoirs" that up to the moment when he put pen to paper he had not thought of a word that he should write. The terms he had verbally proposed were soon put in writing, and there he might have stopped. But as he wrote a feeling of sympathy for his gallant antagonist came over him, and he added the extremely liberal terms with which his letter closed. The sight of Lee's fine sword suggested the paragraph allowing officers to retain their sidearms; and he ended with a phrase he evidently had not thought of, and for which he had no authority, which practically pardoned and amnestied every man in Lee's army—a thing he had refused to consider the day before, and which had been expressly forbidden him in the President's order of March 3. Yet so great was the joy over the crowning victory, and so deep the gratitude of the government and people to Grant and his heroic army, that his terms were accepted as he wrote them, and his exercise of the Executive prerogative of pardon entirely overlooked. It must be noticed here, however, that a few days later it led the greatest of Grant's generals into a serious error.

Lee must have read the memorandum with as much surprise as gratification. He suggested and gained another important concession—that those of the cavalry and artillery who owned their own horses should be allowed to take them home to put in their crops; and wrote a brief reply accepting the terms. He then remarked that his army was in a starving condition, and asked Grant to provide them with subsistence and forage; to which he at once assented, inquiring for how many men the rations would be wanted. Lee answered, "About twenty-five thousand"; and orders were given to issue them. The number turned out to be even greater, the paroles signed amounting to twenty-eight thousand two hundred and thirty-one. If we add to this the captures made during the preceding week, and the thousands who deserted the failing cause at every by-road leading to their homes, we see how considerable an army Lee commanded when Grant "started out gunning."

With these brief and simple formalities, one of the most momentous transactions of modern times was concluded. The Union gunners prepared to fire a national salute, but Grant forbade any rejoicing over a fallen enemy, who, he hoped, would be an enemy no longer. The next day he rode to the Confederate lines to make a visit of farewell to General Lee. They parted with courteous good wishes, and Grant, without pausing to look at the city he had taken, or the enormous system of works which had so long held him at bay, hurried away to Washington, intent only upon putting an end to the waste and burden of war.

A very carnival of fire and destruction had attended the flight of the Confederate authorities from Richmond. On Sunday night, April 2, Jefferson Davis, with his cabinet and their more important papers, hurriedly left the doomed city on one of the crowded and overloaded railroad trains. The legislature of Virginia and the governor of the State departed in a canal-boat toward Lynchburg; and every available vehicle was pressed into service by the frantic inhabitants, all anxious to get away before their capital was desecrated by the presence of "Yankee invaders." By the time the military left, early next morning, a conflagration was already under way. The rebel Congress had passed a law ordering government tobacco and other public property to be burned. General Ewell, the military commander, asserts that he took the responsibility of disobeying the law, and that they were not fired by his orders. However that may be, flames broke out in various parts of the city while a miscellaneous mob, inflamed by excitement and by the alcohol which had run freely in the gutters the night before, rushed from store to store, smashing in the doors and indulging all the wantonness of pillage and greed. Public spirit was paralyzed, and the whole fabric of society seemed crumbling to pieces, when the convicts from the penitentiary, a shouting, leaping crowd of parti-colored demons, overcoming their guard, and drunk with liberty, appeared upon the streets, adding their final dramatic horror to the pandemonium.

It is quite probable that the very magnitude and rapidity of the disaster served in a measure to mitigate its evil results. The burning of seven hundred buildings, comprising the entire business portion of Richmond, warehouses, manufactories, mills, depots, and stores, all within the brief space of a day, was a visitation so sudden, so unexpected, so stupefying, as to overawe and terrorize even wrong-doers, and made the harvest of plunder so abundant as to serve to scatter the mob and satisfy its rapacity to quick repletion.

Before a new hunger could arise, assistance was at hand. General Weitzel, to whom the city was surrendered, taking up his headquarters in the house lately occupied by Jefferson Davis, promptly set about the work of relief; organizing efficient resistance to the fire, which, up to this time, seems scarcely to have been attempted; issuing rations to the poor, who had been relentlessly exposed to starvation by the action of the rebel Congress; and restoring order and personal authority. That a regiment of black soldiers assisted in this noble work must have seemed to the white inhabitants of Richmond the final drop in their cup of misery.

Into the capital, thus stricken and laid waste, came President Lincoln on the morning of April 4. Never in the history of the world did the head of a mighty nation and the conqueror of a great rebellion enter the captured chief city of the insurgents in such humbleness and simplicity. He had gone two weeks before to City Point for a visit to General Grant, and to his son, Captain Robert Lincoln, who was serving on Grant's staff. Making his home on the steamer which brought him, and enjoying what was probably the most satisfactory relaxation in which he had been able to indulge during his whole presidential service, he had visited the various camps of the great army in company with the general, cheered everywhere by the loving greetings of the soldiers. He had met Sherman when that commander hurried up fresh from his victorious march, and after Grant started on his final pursuit of Lee the President still lingered; and it was at City Point that he received the news of the fall of Richmond.

Between the receipt of this news and the following forenoon, but before any information of the great fire had reached them, a visit was arranged for the President and Rear-Admiral Porter. Ample precautions were taken at the start. The President went in his own steamer, the *River Queen*, with her escort, the *Bat*, and a tug used at City Point in landing from the steamer. Admiral Porter went in his flag-ship, the *Malvern*, and a transport carried a small cavalry escort and ambulances for the party. But the obstructions in the river soon made it impossible to proceed in this fashion. One unforeseen accident after another rendered it necessary to leave behind even the smaller boats, until finally the party went on in Admiral Porter's barge, rowed by twelve sailors, and without escort of any kind. In this manner the President made his advent into Richmond, landing near Libby Prison. As the party stepped ashore they found a guide among the contrabands who quickly crowded the streets, for the possible coming of the President had been circulated through the city. Ten of the sailors, armed with carbines, were formed as a guard, six in front and four in rear, and between them the President. Admiral Porter, and the three officers who accompanied them walked the long distance, perhaps a mile and a half, to the center of the town.

The imagination can easily fill up the picture of a gradually increasing crowd, principally of Negroes, following the little group of marines and officers, with the tall form of the President in its center; and, having learned that it was indeed Mr. Lincoln, giving expression to joy and gratitude in the picturesque emotional ejaculations of the colored race. It is easy also to imagine the sharp anxiety of those who had the President's safety in charge during this tiresome and even foolhardy march through a city still in flames, whose white inhabitants were sullenly resentful at best, and whose grief and anger might at any moment culminate against the man they looked upon as the incarnation of their misfortunes. But no accident befell him. Reaching General Weitzel's headquarters, Mr. Lincoln rested in the mansion Jefferson Davis had occupied as President of the Confederacy, and after a day of sightseeing returned to his steamer and to Washington, to be stricken down by an assassin's bullet, literally "in the house of his friends."

⋙ ⋘

WHEN *the war was ending, Walt Whitman reported a conversation between two soldiers in which one told the other he had seen the monument to John C. Calhoun in Charleston, South Carolina. When he finished, the other veteran said: "I have seen Calhoun's monument. That you saw is not the real monument. But I have seen it. It is the desolated, ruined south; nearly the whole generation of young men between seventeen and thirty destroyed or maim'd; all the old families used up—the rich impoverish'd, the plantations cover'd with weeds, the slaves unloos'd and become the masters, and the name of southerner blacken'd with every shame—all that is Calhoun's real monument." It was a graphic synopsis of the Southern reality. Total war had culminated in total defeat.*

*The future of the South presented the nation with a major problem. From the very beginning of the war, it had been agreed that secession was an impossibility but it was also obvious that millions of Southerners were in open rebellion against the federal authority, and as such were guilty of treason. As the war continued, Congress passed a number of acts which inflicted monetary losses, deprivation of civil rights, and imprisonment as prospective punishment upon those who had rebelled. The President possessed the power to pardon those who were willing to take the oath of allegiance. Lincoln also set to work restoring the states when ten percent of its citizenry eligible to vote in 1860 took the oath. Congress quickly responded with a demand that no less than fifty percent of the eligible voters take the oath. The makings of a major conflict between Executive and legislature existed but Lincoln promptly indicated that he saw his plan of restoration was but one of many possible plans. Most certainly, given Lincoln's fundamentally politic inclinations, he would not have pressed the struggle to the breaking point with Congress.*

*The death of Lincoln created a different situation. His successor Andrew Johnson was a pro-Union Southerner and a Democrat. His whole political career had been built upon his role as an "outsider," in which he was always at odds with the establishment. His vindictive policies as war governor of occupied Tennessee had led those Republicans who wanted to punish the rebellious South to assume that in him they had an ally. But once he was in the Presidency, Johnson set to work restoring the Southern states as quickly as possible. When Congress reconvened in December of 1865, they were greeted by newly elected Southern congressmen. Their response was simple: they refused to seat them. The Republican congressional leadership revealed its intention to guarantee the Negro his civil rights and to extend the life of the Freedmen's Bureau, an agency which had been established to provide relief and legal aids for the newly emancipated freedman. When Johnson vetoed both efforts, legislative warfare broke out between the Republican-controlled Congress and an Executive bent upon restoring the Democratic party.*

*In the struggle that ensued, Congress finally prevailed. It divided the South into military districts and made a precondition of its readmission the ratification of the Fourteenth Amendment. To complete its triumph, Congress in 1868 subjected Johnson to the humiliation of impeachment. They failed to convict by a single vote. The last thing the defeated South needed at war's end had occurred: it had become the victim of partisan politics. The memory of that experience would dominate Southern politics for generations to come.*

*William A. Dunning (1857-1922), a graduate of Columbia University, taught at his alma mater from 1886 until his death. His major field of interest was Reconstruction with a particular emphasis upon the constitutional issues at stake. He took a hostile view of the Republican legislative leadership but generally avoided excessive praise or condemnation. He seemed to take the view that the events should be permitted to speak for themselves. His own work, therefore, has a detachment and judiciousness which still makes it useful. What controversy has erupted over Dunning and his interpretations relates largely to the school of students associated with his name. A goodly number of his students at Columbia concentrated upon state studies of Reconstruction. Such works as Walter L. Fleming,* The Civil War and Reconstruction in Alabama *(1905), C. Mildred Thompson,* Reconstruction in Georgia *(1915), and James W. Garner,* Reconstruction in Mississippi *(1901) are basic to our understanding of the South during Reconstruction. They are, however, flawed by a set of assumptions which treats the Negro as obviously inferior to the white. They also accept as self-evident that all Southern whites were victims of the hard times of Reconstruction, neatly neglecting the extent to which many often prominent*

*Southerners had collaborated with, if not actively participated in, Recon-*
*struction governments. It is probably fair to conclude that Dunning was*
*larger in his racial views than his students, at least those of Southern origin.*

# RECONSTRUCTION,
## POLITICAL AND ECONOMIC, 1865-1877

### by William Archibald Dunning

Flagrant war ended, as it had begun, when Congress was not in session, and when the executive department of the government, therefore, must assume all the responsibility of dealing with the new situation. The man who took up the exercise of the chief executive power on April 15, 1865, was not the man whom any important element of the people in either North or South would have deliberately chosen for the task. Andrew Johnson had been nominated for the vice-presidency at Baltimore, in 1864, under the influence of two ideas which pervaded the convention—namely, that the Republican party had given up its identity and become merged in the Union party; and that the Union Party was not sectional, but included South as well as North in its membership. Borr in North Carolina, a resident during all his mature life of Tennessee, and an unfaltering supporter throughout his public career of the ante-bellum Democracy, Mr. Johnson, on the ticket with Lincoln, served excellently as a symbol of the party transformation which the war had effected; but few of the party which elected him vice-president would have judged it wise to intrust the difficult task of reconstruction to a man whose antecedents were southern, slave-holding, and ultra-state-rights Democratic; while the northern Copperheads and the southern secessionists alike regarded him with all the scorn which is excited by an apostate.

The new president was not, however, of a temperament to be affected by, even if conscious of, the consternation which his accession to power produced. The same integrity of purpose, force of will, and rude intellectual force, which had raised him from the tailor's bench in a mountain hamlet to leadership in Tennessee, sustained him when he confronted the problems of the national administration. He felt in reference to the future just as he had felt as to the past when, at the simple ceremony of his induction into the presidency, he had said: "The duties have been mine, the consequences are God's." The complacent self-sufficiency which was manifest in this, as in very many other of his public addresses, was, however, a quality of speech rather than of character in the new president. Positive, aggressive, and violent in controversy, fond of the fighting by which his convictions must be maintained, he nevertheless, in the formation of his opinions on great questions of public policy, was as diligent as any man in seeking and weighing the views of all who were competent to aid him.

The first six weeks of Johnson's administration were dominated by the emotions which the assassination of his predecessor excited in all parts of the land. At Washington affairs fell largely under the direction of the secretary of war, whose total loss of self-control in the crisis contributed to intensify the panicky and vindictive feeling that prevailed. The idea that leading Confederates were concerned in Booth's plot not only led to the offer of large rewards for the capture of Jefferson Davis, Jacob Thompson, Clement C. Clay, and others, but also strengthened the hands of those who were demanding that the conquered people as a whole should receive harsh treatment. Mr. Johnson himself had, in the fierce days of his struggle for the Union cause in Tennessee, repeatedly proclaimed his belief that the leaders of secession should receive severe punishment. In the first weeks of his presidency this policy was emphasized by the iteration and reiteration as was his habit, of the pregnant phrases: "Treason is a crime and must be made odious"; "Traitors must be punished." As the hot pursuit of the scattered and fleeing Confederate leaders brought more and more of them into the hands of the troops, it seemed as if the great drama of secession was about to end in a series of executions for treason. Even the surrendered and paroled generals were marked for exemplary punishment, especially Robert E. Lee, lawyers advising the President that the immunity guaranteed by the terms of surrender ceased with the end of the war.

When, however, the excitement caused by the assassination of Mr. Lincoln subsided, and the suspicions that Davis and his associates had been concerned in the deed were seen by sane minds to be unfounded, conservative northern sentiment began to show alarm at the vindictive course to which the president seemed tending. General Grant met the suggestion of Lee's arrest with so peremptory a negative as to render impossible further proceedings on that line. Moreover, the general atmosphere of the White House at Washington was quite different from that of the state-house at Nashville, and the advice which was given to Mr. Johnson by most of his constitutional advisers was of another quality than that which he had been wont to receive from the embittered and revengeful Unionists of Tennessee. He had gladly retained all the members of Mr. Lincoln's cabinet, and in them he found persisting that distaste for proscription which Booth's victim had made no attempt to conceal. Especially was this feeling manifest after the return of Seward to duty in May; for the secretary of state harbored no resentments in politics, and the weight of his influence could not have failed, under the circumstances, to be very great. Accordingly, though many prominent Confederates were kept in strict confinement, and were treated in some cases with much more rigor and harshness than was necessary, the policy of bringing them to trial and punishment gradually was abandoned.

That Mr. Johnson willingly gave up this policy in the case of Jefferson Davis is more than doubtful. But the obstacles in the way of any procedure that offered the slightest hope of conviction assumed a formidable character from the outset. From every influential quarter in the North came, as soon as hostilities had ceased, urgent demands that military tribunals should be suppressed and that the administration of justice should be left to the ordinary courts. Nevertheless, the conspirators associated with John Wilkes Booth were tried and convicted in June by a military commission. Public opinion, under the tension of the great tragedy, condoned this proceeding, though there was some criticism of it. Wirz, the Confederate commander at Andersonville, charged with the abuse and murder of Union prisoners, was brought to the gallows November 10 by the same sort of tribunal; in this case the procedure was questioned, if not strongly condemned, by all conservative men. That such a method should be employed in the case of Davis or other distinguished prisoners, civilian or military, became impossible as soon as public opinion assumed its normal calmness. On the other hand, every project that was suggested for securing a conviction of these men before a civil court was rejected as either unconstitutional or impracticable by the best legal advice that the administration could procure.

The prisoners of state who were put in rigorous confinement under the influence of the demand for harsh treatment included Jefferson Davis and Alexander H. Stephens, president and vice-president of the defunct Confederacy, Reagan, Seddon, Campbell, and Mallory, of the late Confederate cabinet, half a dozen of the state governors under the Confederacy, and a number of other prominent men. While these political leaders were being made to feel the bad, and expect the worst, consequences of failure in civil war, the military forces of both conquered and conquering sections were being dissolved and blended in the general population. Within four days after the surrender of Lee's army recruiting was suspended in the North. As the other Confederate organizations successively made their submission, and it became clear that no prolongation of the struggle was to be feared, plans for the reduction of the military establishment were put in operation in every direction.

The efficiency of the machinery of the war department under Secretary Stanton was as well exhibited in this process as it had been in the progress of hostilities. First in importance of the tasks undertaken was the mustering out of the great volunteer army, amounting in April to about one million men. Of these over eight hundred thousand had, by November 15, been transported to their homes, paid off, and returned to civil life. At the same time the production and purchase of supplies were stopped, and vast stocks of material were disposed of. Between April 20 and November 8, 1865, the quartermaster-general's bureau sold property amounting to $13,357,345. From 128,840 horses and mules was realized $7,500,000; 83 locomotives and 1009 cars brought $1,500,000; 2500 buildings were vacated and ordered sold; and 83,887 wage-earners were discharged by that bureau alone.

Throughout the summer and autumn of 1865 the railway and steamboat lines were full of returning soldiers. Into every hamlet, however remote, came sooner or later some bearer of personal experience in the great conflict, now seeking to assume or resume the vocation of civil life. The "old soldier" became a significant social type, and left a clear impress on the popular life and character of the time. It is difficult to detect, however, any economic influence of the great and sudden change in the North during the middle of 1865. The abrupt transfer of nearly a million able-bodied men from destructive to productive occupation, with the simultaneous curtailment and extinction of many large industries, might have been expected to make itself conspicuously felt in business and finance. But hardly a ripple was manifest on the placid surface of economic life. The readjustment of forces proceeded so peacefully as to leave no sign.

Doubtless no small influence in the placidity of the North was attributable to the absence of anything like such a condition in the South. Nothing could be more striking than the difference between the prosperous and cheerful *milieu* to which the northern soldier returned and the hopeless conditions which greeted his late antagonist of the South. While the veterans of Grant's and Sherman's armies were being transported to their homes with every provision for their comfort that forethought could suggest, those who had followed Lee and Johnson were slowly and painfully making their way, chiefly on foot, through ravaged and poverty stricken regions that offered them little cheer save the benedictions of the inhabitants. Some one hundred and seventy-four thousand surrendered Confederate soldiers were paroled by the Union authorities, and over sixty thousand were discharged from northern prison camps during the summer. These men represented in a great measure the most useful elements of the population, but the situation which they found when they reached their homes was, as a rule, destitute of all opportunity for usefulness. Capital, labor, currency—all were either lacking or so transformed as to require unfamiliar methods of employment. Many an officer whose word had in March been law for a thousand men was in May toiling as the humblest manual laborer, in order to procure the little United States currency that would command the necessities of life for his family.

In those regions where any cotton had escaped the ravages of war the high price of this commodity offered an attractive promise of financial salvation to the lucky owners. But marketing the cotton was difficult and often impossible in the disorganized condition of the country; and, moreover, the title to much of it was, under the new rigorously applied war legislation of Congress, subject to dispute. Treasury agents and army officers were very active in seizing all that could in any way be made to bear the taint of service, either actual or promised, to the Confederate cause. Extensive fraudulent operations of corrupt officials and rapacious speculators wrested from the owners much that was free from such taint. And, finally, the tax of three cents per pound, which confronted any one who got his cotton safely through these other perils, cut down materially his much-needed proceeds.

It was felt on all hands that the most effective means of promoting the revival of the South, and putting it in the way of sustaining its population, would be the prompt removal of the restrictions on trade which the war had involved. Accordingly the president began this process immediately on the cessation of hostilities, and continued it as rapidly as conditions seemed to warrant. As early as April 29, 1865, he ordered the discontinuance of restrictions on domestic trade in all parts of the rebel territory east of the Mississippi River, so far as that territory was within the Union military lines. By proclamations of May 22 and June 13 this removal of restrictions was made general east of the Mississippi save as to contraband of war; and on June 24 the trans-Mississippi region was put on the same footing. As to foreign commerce, the blockade established by President Lincoln was rescinded by proclamation of June 23, and on July 1 all the ports of the South were thrown open to trade, except in contraband, which remained under prohibition till August 29.

When the barriers were thus thrown down which had made intercourse between the two sections for four years illegal, there was a wide-spread resumption of both social and business relations between the people who had so recently been enemies. Not without hesitation, suspicion, awkwardness, and desperate efforts to avoid those dangerous topics which were uppermost in all men's minds, old friendships were renewed, old connections were looked up with a view to re-establishment. Not a few southerners came promptly North to find opportunities which they despaired of ever seeing in their own section, and which well-disposed northern acquaintances were not slow to put in their way. The most pronounced movement, however, was from North to South, under the operation of the commercial instinct. A host of traders kept up with, or far preceded, the opening of railways and steamer lines into the long-closed regions. Many capitalists also sought in the conquered and stricken country profitable investment for their wealth. Especially inviting seemed the cotton plantations which could now be bought at ridiculously low prices from their resourceless owners. Sharp-witted officers and even privates in the Union armies, having noted the opportunities in neighborhoods which their duties made familiar, sent their friends or returned themselves to take advantage of their observations. The experience of this first body of northern immigrants proved almost uniformly unfortunate, despite the exceptionally low prices which they paid for their land. Their failure was largely due to unfamiliarity with the peculiarities of the crop which they sought to raise. Other causes contributed greatly, however, to render their success impossible, and among these were the social and political conditions under which they were obliged to live.

The disbandment of the great armies, and the restoration of intercourse between the sections, was only a little step towards a general peace basis. Civil government had yet to be instituted in the conquered region, and the status of the freedmen had to be fixed on some clear foundation of law. Pending the establishment of civil government under some plan of reconstruction, the preservation of order and the supervision of such fragments of local administrative machinery as still existed were entirely in the hands of the United States army. Each of the lately hostile states constituted a military department, whose commander, with headquarters at the capital or chief town, controlled affairs through garrisons and properly distributed posts. During the summer of 1865 the need of considerable bodies of troops everywhere disappeared. Isolated crimes, such as inevitably accompany war and social disorganization, were often reported, and in some regions bands of outlaws operating on a large scale required suppression; but in general that part of the people who had sustained the Confederacy fully acknowledged their subjugation, and made no sign of opposition to the power which was over them.

Nevertheless, in one important respect resentment did take on a serious aspect among the whites. As the withdrawal of troops to be mustered out proceeded, the forces remaining in the South showed an ever-increasing proportion of Negro regiments. The use of these troops was due in part to the fact that their desire to leave the service was, to say the least, not urgent, while the opposite was generally the case with the white volunteers; and in part to a deliberate purpose to emphasize the completeness of the catastrophe which the war had brought upon the South. Protests against the presence of the black troops began very early from the southern whites, and the demoralizing effects of such garrisons, and especially of small posts in rural districts, where discipline was not the most rigorous, became more and more evident as time went on.

Side by side with the general authority exercised by the department commanders, and gradually supplanting it in importance, was the jurisdiction and far-reaching control assumed by the Freedmen's Bureau. This institution was created by an act of March 3, 1865, to give unity and central organization to the various conflicting systems which had grown up for the care of the freedmen during the war. Under the provisions of the act the bureau was to have charge of all matters pertaining to refugees, freedmen, and abandoned lands in states which had been the theatre of war. Through a commissioner, assistant commissioners, superintendents, and local agents, the interests of the former slaves (for it was this class that the act was chiefly intended to provide for) were to be looked after wherever the power of the United States extended. When the Confederacy collapsed practically the whole territory in which slavery had existed became thus the field for the operations of the bureau. During the summer of 1865 its organization was completed and its influence became promptly manifest both in the South, where its agents assumed a conspicuous place in the work of social readjustment, and in the North, where the reports of its activities contributed much to shape public opinion on the serious political issues which were impending.

The most general summary of the functions assumed by the bureau shows how intimate its connection was with the movement assumed by the bureau reorganization. It assigned abandoned land to the freedmen and promoted the acquisition of other lands by lease or purchase; it supervised the charitable relief and educational enterprises which were being carried on among the blacks; it exercised jurisdiction over controversies in which freedmen were involved, either with one another or with the whites; it took charge of family relations among the blacks, and strove to create a sense of the sanctity of marriage where such an idea had but a shadowy, if any, existence, finally, and most important to all, it took cognizance of all arrangements through which the whites sought to secure the labor of the freedmen, guaranteed the latter against any suggestion of slavery, and saw to it that the laborer would not be the victim of oppression, either as to the kind and duration of his labor or as to the amount of his wages. The bureau assumed, in short, a general guardianship of the emancipated race, and, backed by the paramount military force of the United States, undertook to play a determining role in the process of reorganizing southern society.

The orders and instructions issued by General Howard, the head of the bureau, for carrying out this comprehensive programme, were characterized almost uniformly by moderation and good judgment. Much the same may be said of the directions that emanated from the assistant commissioners for their respective states, though here in some cases a tendency appeared to lecture the southern whites on the sinfulness of slavery and on their general depravity, and to address to the freedmen pious homilies and moral platitudes obviously above their intelligence, and designed for the latitude of New England and the Western Reserve. Assistant Commissioner Whittlesey, of North Carolina, for example, solemnly informed the white men of that state that "the school house, the spelling book and the Bible will be found better preservers of peace and good order than the revolver and the bowie knife"; and General Saxton assured the freedmen of South Carolina, Georgia, and Florida that "labor is ennobling to the character and, if rightly directed, brings to the laborer all the comforts and luxuries of life," that "falsehood and theft should not be found in freedom—they are the vices of slavery," and that "cotton is a regal plant and the more carefully it is cultivated, the greater will be the crop."

While such vagaries were rare among the higher officials, the local agents, whose function it was to apply the general policy of the bureau to concrete cases, displayed, of course, the greatest diversity of spirit and ability. It was from these lower officials that the southern whites formed their general estimate of the character and value of the institution, while the people of the North were guided more by the just and practical policy outlined in the orders from headquarters. However much tact and practical good sense the local agent was able to bring to the performance of his delicate duties, he in most cases, being a northern man, was wholly unable to take a view of the situation that could make him agreeable to the whites of the neighborhood. He saw in both freedman and former master qualities which the latter could never admit. Hence the working of the bureau, with its intrusion into the fundamental relationships of social life, engendered violent hostility from the outset on the part of the whites. The feeling was enhanced by the conduct of the ignorant, unscrupulous, and deliberately oppressive agents who were not rare. As soon, therefore, as it became established, the bureau took the form, to the southern mind, of a diabolical device for the perpetuation of the national government's control over the South, and for the humiliation of the whites before their former slaves.

The bureau, however, was by the terms of the law but a transitional institution, limited in its existence to one year after the end of the war. Its functions were not well correlated by the law with those of the regular military authority, and at first the two species of armed rule caused some confusion in the process of social rehabilitation. Before the situation was cleared up a third species of authority was installed in every state by the President's policy of restoring civil government. This policy, which was to become the centre of so terrible a political storm, must now be examined in detail.

In confronting the problem of restoring civil governments in the South, President Johnson was under no necessity of devising a solution. That already applied by Lincoln in three of the states was ready to the hand of his successor. Indeed, the draught of a proclamation for instituting the process of restoration in the other states had been submitted by Secretary Stanton to the cabinet, and was discussed in the last meeting before the assassination. Accordingly, Johnson took up the work at the precise point where Lincoln had left it. First, in order to dispose of the idea that the state governments which had exercised authority under the Confederacy might be permitted to continue their functions, the military commanders were ordered to prevent any attempt of the old legislatures to meet, and such of the governors as could be caught, including Brown, of Georgia, Clark, of Mississippi, Magrath, of South Carolina, Vance, of North Carolina, and Watts, of Alabama, were consigned to prison. This left only military government in seven of the rebel states. As to Virginia, an executive order of President Johnson, dated May 9, 1865, formally recognized Francis H. Peirpoint as governor of the state; and without formal declarations governors Brownlow, of Tennessee, Wells, of Louisiana, and Murphy, of Arkansas, the official heads of the organizations created under Lincoln's administration and with his aid, were assumed to be the chiefs of legitimate governments, and were encouraged to extend their authority throughout the territory included within their respective state limits.

Having thus provided for the four commonwealths which were far advanced on the road to restoration, Johnson proceeded to carry out Lincoln's project for the remaining seven. The new conditions produced by the end of hostilities gave occasion for some slight modifications of the amnesty programme. Attorney-General Speed having furnished an opinion that a new proclamation was necessary to supersede those of Mr. Lincoln, Johnson's substitute was issued on May 29, 1865. The oath which it prescribed as a condition of pardon differed from Lincoln's in requiring an unqualified instead of a qualified pledge to support all laws and decrees touching slavery; and it excepted from the privilege of the amnesty six classes of persons in addition to those excepted by Lincoln, the most significant of the new classes being that of persons worth twenty thousand dollars or more.

On the same day the reorganization of North Carolina was begun by a proclamation appointing W. W. Holden provisional governor, and directing him to assemble a constitutional convention of delegates chosen by the loyal part of the people of the state, and to exercise all powers necessary to enable that part of the people to organize a republican form of government such as the United States might constitutionally guarantee. The test of loyalty prescribed was the taking of the oath embodied in the amnesty proclamation. Only such persons as should have taken that oath might participate, either as electors or as elected, in the process of reorganization, and, moreover, only such as were qualified voters under the laws of the state that had been in force immediately before the pretended secession.

The only feature of this project which excited much discussion among the advisers of the president, official and other, was that fixing the qualifications for voting. Radical senators and representatives insistently urged the importance of including the freedmen in the reorganizing electorates, and the cabinet was evenly divided on this question. Chief Justice Chase, who travelled during May along the whole Atlantic coast from Washington to Key West, sent back a stream of letters representing that both the conditions and the opinions that obtained in the South favored reorganization through Negro suffrage. But Johnson had none of the brilliant illusions that beset the chief-justice and the other radicals as to the political capacity of the blacks, and he lacked, moreover, the audacity of conception which found constitutional warrant for a determination of suffrage qualifications by executive decree. His decision, therefore, was for leaving the reorganization to the old white electorate. The possibility and the desirability of a later extension of the suffrage by degrees to the freedmen, through action of the new state governments themselves, he did not question.

The North Carolina proclamation, in addition to its directions for the organization of a state government, embodied formal commands to the Federal heads of departments to resume the performance of their duties within the limits of the state: the treasury was to begin the collection of taxes; the post-office was to renew its service; and the district courts and marshals were to take up the administration of justice. Side by side, thus, with the military authority of the United States was to be put in operation, as fast as the offices could be manned, the regular processes of civil government so far as these fell within the Federal sphere.

At intervals from June 13 to July 13 proclamations identical in tenor with that affecting North Carolina named provisional governors and re-established the Federal administration in the remaining six states of the Confederacy. The provisional governors, as soon as they were installed in power, proceeded first to revive the local administrative authorities, which had been dormant since the suppression of the old state government. County and municipal officials who had ceased to act when the United States troops took possession of a state were ordered to resume their functions, taking the amnesty oath as a part of their qualification. Next the provisional governor took the necessary steps for the election and assembling of a constitutional convention. The first of these bodies to complete its work was that of Mississippi, which adjourned August 24, and the last to finish was that of Texas, on April 6, 1866; all the other conventions held their sessions during September and October, 1865.

The first function of these conventions was to signify by formal public acts the acceptance by the respective states of the results of the war. Through the provisional governors it was ascertained what the president would regard as an adequate expression of such acceptance. Following the suggestions thus procured, the conventions first declared the invalidity of the ordinances of secession, South Carolina and Georgia by repealing, Florida by annulling, and the rest by proclaiming null and void the obnoxious acts. Next slavery was declared abolished forever. Finally, the state debts contracted in aid of the war against the United States government were repudiated, except in South Carolina. Having performed these essential duties, the conventions made such modifications in the old state constitutions as the new situation required, and then adjourned *sine die*, leaving to the legislatures, for which provision was duly made, the task of further promoting the social reorganization. During October and November elections were held in most of the states, and governors and legislatures under the new constitutions were chosen. The legislatures, when they met—as they did very promptly in most cases—were confronted with the suggestion, scarcely less imperative than a command, that they ratify the Thirteenth Amendment. This requirement also was satisfied by all except Mississippi. By the end of the year the provisional governors had been relieved of their offices in all the states but Texas, and the civil governments that had been organized under their direction were in the full exercise of their functions.

This restoration of self-government was not, however, accompanied as yet by the withdrawal of military authority. December 1 the President revoked the suspension of the writ of *habeas corpus* for all the United States except the states of the former Confederacy, Kentucky, the District of Columbia, and the territories of Arizona and New Mexico. On April 2, 1866, he formally declared the rebellion at an end in all the seceded states except Texas. When the process of reorganization had at last been completed in that state, the president proclaimed, August 20, 1866, the complete restoration of peace, order, tranquillity, and civil authority throughout the United States.

🙚 🙘

THE *trouble with the writing of Reconstruction history is that it has largely been approached in the spirit of partisanship. The aftermath of war is rarely a pleasant experience. The very nature of conflict is that it disrupts established patterns of government and institutions. If nothing else, the job of rebuilding the destroyed cities, farms, railroads and other destroyed properties would have proven a massive task. But the defeat of the Confederacy brought with it the overthrow of a whole social system. Almost four million slaves found themselves freedmen, often without property and with only the slimmest of notions about the meaning of their freedom. Their former white masters were often as destitute and desperate to find some way to survive. Perhaps a government which set out to govern with an even hand might have been able to do justice to both; one thing is certain, both black and white Southerners badly needed help.*

*White Southerners were psychologically incapable of coming to grips with the new order of things. To find that their conquerors insisted that the Negro receive his just due, given the general belief in black inferiority,* seemed a perverse determination to inflict humiliation upon a defeated foe. Southerners, and it might be added most historians, found it impossible to believe that some Northerners sincerely believed in the justice of giving the black man in both North and South civil equality. But Southerners were not without legitimate complaint, for as one militant civil rights worker, Thomas Wentworth Higginson, noted, Northerners exposed their hypocrisy when they decreed "that the Negro should be a man at the South, to spite the white man, but not . . . that he should be a man at the North, when it offends their prejudices." Civil rights as an act of retribution are hardly likely to survive once the will to punish has passed.

It was no less true that white Southerners were hypersensitive to their defeat. "Have we suffered all—have our brave men fought so desperately and died so nobly for this?" lamented one Southern girl. She went on to raise the tragic cry of all defeated people: "For four years there has been throughout this broad land little else than the anguish of anxiety—the misery of sorrow over dear ones sacrificed—for nothing!" It is not surprising that many Southerners hated the Yankee more bitterly than ever before. To learn to live with their defeat proved more than a white could bear; only by un-doing its worse consequences could it be made tolerable.

Faced with black participation in voting, the whites translated it into a time of intolerable corruption. No doubt, corruption existed, but much-needed expenditures to restore wartime destruction and provide educational facilities made by Reconstruction legislatures were translated into proof of not only corrupt government but of black ineptitude. Southerners con-veniently forgot that except for a brief interlude in South Carolina, no branch of a Southern legislature ever passed under complete Negro control. Nor did they remember the extent to which white Southerners joined these governments. The participation of Northern whites, no matter what their motive, was explained by reference to the carpetbag. Northerners they equated with thieves. In the end, the myth of Black Reconstruction entered into the baggage of the Southern Democrats as they struggled to regain their sectional ascendancy as fully as that of the Bloody Flag provided a rallying point for Republicans. The subject of Reconstruction had fallen captive to partisanship and as the Negro historian W. E. B. Dubois (1868-1963) demonstrated, so had the historian.

George Fort Milton (1895-1955) complemented his career as editor of the Chattanooga News with a career as a historian. He concentrated his at-tention on the period between 1850 and 1877 and in a trilogy beginning with Eve of Conflict: Stephen A. Douglas and the Needless War (1934) and ending with the Age of Hate indicted the Northern authors of Civil War and Reconstruction. It provides an excellent Southern view of a disabling experience.

# THE AGE OF HATE
# ANDREW JOHNSON AND THE RADICALS

*by George Fort Milton*

Only a few seconds after the gavels sounded the death knell of the Thirty-Ninth Congress, they struck again to call the Fortieth Congress into being. "Thanks to the firmness of the Northern people and the follies of Andrew Johnson," the *Nation* declared, the personnel of the new Congress was substantially that of its predecessor. Although in strict fact there was hardly a minute's interval between the two sessions, all the forms of organization of a new legislative body were carefully complied with. The opening was full of color. The galleries were so crowded that the members' cloakrooms were opened to the ladies, and the staid Congressional sofas were quickly filled with billowing loveliness. The initial scenes of the new session were faintly reminiscent of those which had marked the beginning of the preceding one: Edward McPherson, Thad Stevens' clerk, called the roll, omitting the names of the Southern members—save that now the members from Tennessee were called—and James Brooks, the minority leader, a melancholy, scholarly looking man, somewhat resembling Charles Sumner in appearance, made a protest which he knew would go unheeded.

No attention was paid to Brooks' objection to the organization of the House with ten States absent. "Smiler" Colfax was immediately reelected speaker and the new members from the Northern States went forward to take the oath. Among them was a new representative from Massachusetts, elected by the voters of a Congressional district in which he did not live, none other than Benjamin F. Butler, the "Hero of Fort Fisher," now as blatant in his Radicalism as any in the House. His visage startled those unaccustomed to it. "Make the best you can of it," wrote a correspondent who witnessed his induction into the House, "it is a terrible face; it looks like a pirate's—a strong, unscrupulous, cruel face, a low wide head, the crossed eyes, the hatchety Roman nose, the thin lips, make a combination powerful and pitiless." Aside from the addition of Ben Butler, the House leadership was substantially the same as before. But it was a leadership which caused the *Nation* a little later to remark that "this is not a time to legislate under the guidance of . . . persons who are more anxious for victory than for either truth or justice."

There were many changes in the personnel of the new Senate and, without exception, they were favorable to the Radicals. The President's staunch Pennsylvania friend, Edgar Cowan, had dropped out, and Simon Cameron had taken his place, the change reducing the number of Johnson Republicans in the Senate to four. Two Democratic Senators, McDougall of California and Nesmith of Oregon, had been defeated, reducing the Democrats to seven, of whom only two came from the North. Several of the more Conservative Republicans had been replaced with extremists: Harris of New York had given way to Roscoe Conkling, "with his Saxon curls"; Foster, president *pro tem* of the Senate in the last Congress, had been replaced by Ferry. Drake, one of Missouri's most ferocious impeachers, had taken the place of Brown of that State. James S. Harlan, late of the President's Cabinet, had been elected to the Senate by the Radical Iowa legislature. Oliver P. Morton, once a supporter of Johnson, now a fugleman for the Radicals, and soon to be Thad Stevens' successor as the autocrat of Congress, entered the Senate. From Kansas came a meek looking little man named Ross, the successor of Johnson's friend, Jim Lane, who had committed suicide. Nebraska's two new Senators were "men of the right sort," Ben Wade pledged. By these shifts, the Radical roll in the Senate had grown to forty-two, an overwhelming majority.

With Foster's departure, the Senate had to elect another of its members president *pro tempore*. At 10:30 on Monday morning, the retiring Senator bade farewell to his associates, who proceeded forthwith to the election of his successor. The changing temper of the majority was indicated by the choice they made. No longer did such men as Fessenden or Trumbull appeal to them. For, with all their active Radicalism, both Fessenden and Trumbull were men of conscience and of high standards of public duty. In December, 1865, at the beginning of the Thirty-Ninth Congress, had Foster not been elected, majority choice would have fallen upon the able senators from Maine or Illinois; but by the summer of 1866, the Radical temper had changed and Gideon Welles made note that the Radical program was "to make Wade president of the Senate, then to impeach the President."

In March, 1867, the Radical Senators saw even more clearly the possibility of a new president in the White House, and they picked Ben Wade of Ohio—"Bluff Ben"—for the job. "You know I am not a parliamentarian," Wade warned them. They knew it full well, but they had not picked the Ohio Radical for a parliamentarian. They had picked him because if there were to be a new president in the White House before March 4, 1869, they wanted him to be one of their own.

Although Wade had served in the Senate for a dozen years or more, his mien and character could appeal only to men ready to win their way by any means. His appearance, though less startling than that of Ben Butler, was sufficiently rough. His head was "most savage," his forehead high and steep; shaggy eyebrows beetled from a "perceptive brow." He had a "rough-hewn" nose, a mouth resolute and dogged, a broad and "immovable" chin. By his election, the *Independent* declared, "the Senate has honored itself"; but the country felt otherwise, as did many of the Conservative Republicans in both Houses. The idea got abroad that Ben Wade was even more unfit for the presidency than was Andrew Johnson, and his election as president *pro tem* was to deliver a body blow to the first attempt at impeachment.

The first sitting of this new Congress continued until March 30, the time being occupied with the debate and passage of a Supplementary Reconstruction Act. No sooner had the first one been passed, vetoed and re-enacted over the presidential negative than the Radicals determined to amend a fatal defect in the law. The processes by which States should secure their readmission into the Union had been set forth in the initial measure with great particularity, but either by inattention or design the framers of the bill had failed to provide for the initiation of the processes. No one was charged with the duty or clothed with the power to take the first step, the election of delegates to a constitutional convention of the State. The Military Reconstruction Act carefully prescribed the constituencies which were to select the new constitution-makers and the qualifications of the members, but it failed to indicate the authority which should call the convention or supervise the election of its members.

This lapse was probably the result of design rather than of negligence. Many in the Thirty-Ninth Congress were unwilling that the Southern States be coerced against their will into adopting these processes, but desired that such terms be held out to the South as a "boon" which the South could accept or reject. Furthermore, a substantial group of the Radicals was not anxious for the South to adopt the steps for readmission. They were quite willing for military rule to continue—so long as it did, Radical control of Congress would not be challenged—and they thought, with probable truth, that the South would prefer bayonet to Negro rule.

But the new Congress had a different tone. More Radical than the old one, its majority was determined that something be done at once towards restoring the Union. As soon as it had been organized, steps were taken to repair the omission of initiating authority in the first Reconstruction bill. The result was the supplementary Military Reconstruction Act, which directed the district commanders to have a complete registration of the qualified voters of each State made before the first of September of that year. They were next directed to fix a day for the election of delegates to the state constitutional conventions and otherwise to arrange for the initiation of the steps provided for in the original act.

One new, distinct addition was made to the prescribed steps by which a State could secure a new constitution. The majority of votes cast for holding a convention was to be ignored unless a majority of all registered voters should have voted in the election. Similarly, no state constitution should be considered as having been ratified unless at least half of all the registered voters should have taken part in the ratification election.

The House gave but two hours to this measure, putting a gag on debate, apparently "because it loves to apply the gag to Democrats." But the Senate took a week for debate, and the bill did not finally pass until Tuesday, March 19. It then became necessary for the Radicals to remain in session until the Constitutional time given the President for approving or disapproving measures should elapse. Since the Radicals had no especial further business to press through, the wait for the inevitable veto passed rather slowly. The House desultorily debated a project to accord government aid to the destitute of the South, irrespective of their attitude during the war. In this discussion an exciting colloquy took place which was to influence the fortunes of the President.

John A. Bingham of Ohio was supporting the bill; during his advocacy, he wandered over to the Democratic side of the House, and Ben Butler taunted him that he had "got over on the other side not only in body but in spirit." Enraged at this palpable hit, Bingham assailed the General in scathing terms. "It does not become a gentleman who recorded his vote fifty times for Jefferson Davis, the arch-traitor in this rebellion, as his candidate for President of the United States, to undertake to damage this cause by attempting to cast an imputation either upon my integrity or my honor. I repel with scorn and contempt any utterance of that sort from any man, whether he be the Hero of Fort Fisher not taken or of Fort Fisher taken."

But Butler was in nowise at a loss for a crushing reply. "I have never concealed that before the war, I . . . voted fifty-seven times for Jefferson Davis for President," he told the House. "I thought him the representative man of the South, and I hoped by his nomination to prevent threatened disunion. . . . The difference between me and the honorable gentleman from Ohio is this: While Jefferson Davis was in the Union, a Senator of the United States, and claiming to be a friend of the Union, I supported him; but now he (Bingham) supports him when he is a traitor."

Butler next referred to his own war record. Bingham had had the bad taste "to attack me for the reason that I could not do any more injury to the enemies of my country. I agree to that. I did all I could, the best I could, . . . and because I could not do more, I feel exceedingly chagrined. . . . But the only victim of that gentleman's prowess that I know of was an innocent woman hung upon the scaffold, one Mrs. Surratt. And I can sustain the memory of Fort Fisher if he and his present associates can sustain him in shedding the blood of a woman tried by a military commission, and convicted without sufficient evidence. . . ."

Driven wild by this sudden blow beneath the belt, Bingham lost control of himself and responded almost in gibberish—so much so that a few days later, he asked leave to revise his remarks for the record. When he did so, Butler returned to the charge, expanding his indictment of Bingham.

The Hero of Fort Fisher adverted at great length to Booth's Diary, which had just been uncovered by the Judiciary Committee. He was exercised over the leaves which had been torn from it, which, he contended, must have contained evidence of a startling nature; the same hands which had suppressed the Diary thus far might have torn the pages from it to suppress the evidence contained. By all means this document should have been produced at the trial of Payne, Herold, Atzerodt and Mrs. Surratt, he charged, for it proved two things: First, that Booth's original plot had been to abduct President Lincoln, and only at the last moment had it been changed from kidnaping to murder. Therefore, "if Mrs. Surratt did not know of the change of purpose, there is no evidence that she knew in any way of the assassination. Second, the people of the country had a right to know every bit of evidence available as to the assassination conspiracy, so as to find who were all the accomplices of Booth; to find who it was that changed Booth's purpose from capture to assassination; who it was that could profit by assassination who could not profit by capture and abduction of the President; who it was expected by Booth would succeed to Lincoln if the knife made a vacancy."

"Who spoliated that book?" Butler asked dramatically, "who suppressed that evidence? Who caused an innocent woman to be hung when he had in his pocket the diary that states at least what was the idea and purpose of the main conspirator in the case?" Butler quoted Booth's statement that he proposed to return to Washington and give himself up "and clear myself from this great crime." How then, asked Butler, could Booth clear himself: "By disclosing his accomplices? Who were they? Who spoliated this book after it got into the hands of the government, if it was not spoliated before?" He sought to imply the answer to his questions: Andrew Johnson had been Booth's accomplice and had mutilated the Diary in order to suppress the evidence of his own guilt.

Upon the utterance of this charge, Bingham returned to the encounter, this time as a defender of the President. "Such a charge," he said, "is only fit to come from a man who lives in a bottle and is fed with a spoon."

Congress did not have to wait the expected ten days for the Presidential veto. On March 23 Andrew Johnson returned the Supplementary Military Reconstruction bill with his disapproval. The general tone of his message was that of the veto of the original act, but to the Radicals, it was "one of the strangest messages ever written." One striking paragraph read:

"When I contemplate the millions of our fellow citizens of the South, with no alternative left but to impose upon themselves this fearful and untried experiment of complete Negro enfranchisement—and white disfranchisement, it may be, almost as complete—or submit indefinitely to the rigor of martial law, without a single attribute of freemen, deprived of all the sacred guarantees of our Federal Constitution, and threatened with even worse wrongs, if any worse are possible, it seems to me that their condition is the most deplorable to which any people can be reduced."

Neither House paid any attention to the veto, not even according it the distinction of angry remonstrance, but immediately passed the bill over the veto. With this action the business of the session was concluded. But the Members of Congress were by no means agreed as to the fashion in which and the date to which they should adjourn.

Blaine wished the recess to be from March 26 to November 11, but Ben Butler objected strenuously to a seven months' suspension. He recalled that in ordering this March session of the new Congress, the previous one had declared "that Andrew Johnson was a bad man, and that this House and the Senate should sit here and take care of his acts." Furthermore, impeachment should not be postponed eight months. Blaine responded that the public was not anxious for impeachment. The question had already been settled in the negative. With this, Old Thad turned his scorn upon Maine's Representative, asserted that the growing reluctance to impeach arose from Ben Wade's selection by the Senate, and declared that Blaine had told the House, "there will be no impeachment by this Congress; we would rather have the

President than the scalawags of Ben Wade." Blaine hotly denied this, main-taining that he had said that Fessenden was a safer man for President, while Stevens angrily reiterated his charge.

The Senate, too, was divided on adjournment. Trumbull wished to sus-pend until the constitutional date in December. But Sumner and other ex-treme Radicals were vehemently opposed to this. "Our President is a bad man," said Sumner, "search history and I am sure that you will find no ruler who, during the same short space of time, has done so much mischief to his country . . . and now, I ask, can Congress quietly vote to go home and leave this bad man without hindrance of any kind?" Senator Nye declared that the Supreme Court might hold the Reconstruction measures unconstitutional the very next month. Where would Congress then be, unable to meet this situation until its reassembly in December?

After much controversy the two Houses finally agree to adjourn until the first Wednesday in July, "when the roll shall be called and the presiding officer of each House shall inform the presiding officer of the other whether or not a quorum is present, and if a quorum of the two Houses shall not have appeared, they shall adjourn the two Houses without day." Thereupon Congress adjourned.

During these difficult days in Congress, the President had not been inactive. The passage of the original Military Reconstruction bill had imposed several important executive duties upon him. Even though he deemed the measure a gross violation of the Constitution, he still felt it his duty to undertake its enforcement, until the Supreme Court should have declared it a contraven-tion of the Federal charter.

Questions of the construction and interpretation of the initial Military Reconstruction act quickly came before the Cabinet. Exactly what were the power and jurisdiction of the military governors and department com-manders to be put over the Southern States? If the President must enforce an unconstitutional law, Welles early hinted to him that it was most impor-tant to pick the right men for military governors. After several such hints, it became apparent that Johnson intended to make one further effort to trust Stanton; Welles was alarmed when he saw that the President was consulting only Grant and Stanton about the governorships, and predicted "he will have trouble." At the Cabinet of March 12 Johnson said nothing on the subject, but took the Secretary of War aside for a private talk for a quarter of an hour, at the close of which "Stanton was unusually jubilant, . . . and could not suppress his feelings." On the next day the list was announced in the newspapers, this publication being the first hint of the personnel to several Members of the Cabinet. "The slime of the serpent," Welles felt, "is over them all." It might not have been easy to find five men among the army generals in whom to put confidence, Father Gideon agreed, but in yielding to Stanton the President had named two undependable, men, particularly hostile to him: Sickles to command the two Carolinas, and Sheridan for Louisiana and Texas.

Late in March, Cabinet asperities over the proper interpretation of the acts of Congress were lessened because of the interest in the political campaign in progress in Connecticut. It was beginning to be suspected that the sentiment of the voters of the North was not nearly so Radical as had been indicated by the 1866 election. At a by-election in Iowa, a Johnson candidate won by a majority of over 500 votes, and George H. Parker of Davenport telegraphed, "We are indebted to the uncompromising firmness of the President for this result." If the Connecticut outcome were to bear out the tendency observable in Iowa, the assault of Congress on the South might be checked.

The Radicals were intensely anxious over this New England test. On March 21 the *Independent* fulminated editorially: "If Connecticut shall vote the wrong way on the first of April, she will reincite Andrew Johnson to further usurpations, and reanimate the Rebellion to further defiance. A vote cast for the Democratic party of Connecticut is a plaudit to Jefferson Davis and a laurel to General Lee."

The Radicals made the usual charges that the Johnson men "spent money like water." In any event, the result of the election was a Conservative triumph up and down the line. The Democratic candidate for governor, James E. English, was elected by a handsome majority, and the voters of the Nutmeg State strongly disapproved the admission of Negroes to the ballot box. The *Independent* entitled its editorial on the outcome "O! Backsliding Connecticut," and reflected sadly that "the States that now need reconstruction are the Northern."

The result created a sensation in Washington, bringing confusion to the Radicals and joy to the White House. Johnson interpreted it as the harbinger of the "inevitable doom" of the Radicals. With mock generosity, the *Independent's* Washington correspondent declared, "Everybody will excuse the President for excessive delight, for it is the first crumb of comfort he has had since he turned traitor."

The attention of the country now turned to two judicial involvements. These were the release on bail of Jefferson Davis, and the unavailing attempt of Southern State governments to bring the Military Reconstruction Acts before the Supreme Court for adjudication by that body.

The President of the late Confederate States had been incarcerated at Fortress Monroe since the summer of 1865. Why had he not been put on trial for treason? This question had been raised again and again in and out of Congress, but President Johnson had not been responsible for the delay. Repeatedly he had sought to have Davis brought to the bar of justice. The government had hired eminent counsel to take charge of the case, with William M. Evarts as the principal. An indictment had been returned by the Federal Grand Jury sitting at Norfolk, but Chief Justice Chase remained unwilling to hold circuit court in Richmond, and both the United States attorney at Richmond and Mr. Evarts were unwilling to bring Davis to trial before District Judge Underwood when the Chief Justice was not sitting with him.

In the meantime Northern sentiment toward Davis had become more forgiving. Charles O'Conor, perhaps the most eminent member of the New York bar, had volunteered to act as Davis' counsel. Conover's trial and conviction had proved that Davis' implication in the plot to assassinate Lincoln had been on perjured testimony, and public sentiment reacted in his behalf. Dr. Craven's account of Jefferson Davis' prison life, showing how harshly the Confederate president had been treated, caused the North further to relent. Horace Greeley, John A. Andrew, Senator Henry Wilson and other Radicals began to advocate better treatment for Jefferson Davis. The President and the Attorney-General had insisted all along that humanity be practiced in his incarceration while the strict letter of the law be observed at the trial.

Late in April, 1867, Judge Underwood of Richmond determined to bring Davis to the bar. On May 7 Stanton submitted to the Cabinet a letter which L. H. Chandler, United States Attorney for Virginia, had written the War Department asking for "an order upon the commandant at Fortress Monroe, directing him to surrender Jefferson Davis to the United States Marshal, or his deputies, upon any process which may issue from the Federal Court." When the President inquired, "Well, Mr. Secretary, what recommendation have you to make in this case?" Stanton replied, "I have no recommendation to make." After Stanton's evasion of responsibility, Johnson directed the application to be returned to the Secretary of War, "who will at once issue the order requested by District-Attorney Chandler."

Stanton "is playing the same old trick," the President told Colonel Moore that evening. "If it had not been for the influence of the War Department with this damned extreme gang during the past session, . . . all this trouble would long since have been brought to a close."

At any rate, on May 13, Jefferson Davis was brought into court at Richmond, entering on the arm of General Burton. Charles O'Conor was there to conduct his case, and Mr. Evarts was on hand to represent the government. When the case was called, it was announced that the government was not ready, whereupon O'Conor asked that the prisoner be admitted to bail. Judge Underwood questioned whether the offense of treason was bailable. No objection being made by the government, the judge gave his opinion that, as the indictment had been returned under the act of 1862, the court could use its discretion as to whether the offense was or was not bailable. He held that it was bailable and set the bond at $100,000.

Waiting in the court room were Horace Greeley and a number of other distinguished Northern citizens. The editor of the New York *Tribune*, whose excoriation of Davis while President had been unsparing, was now preaching universal amnesty as well as universal suffrage, and he had come to Richmond to sign Jefferson Davis' bond. Along with him were Augustus Schell and fourteen other wealthy and distinguished men. After the document had been signed, the judge announced: "The marshal will discharge the prisoner." This was done amid "deafening applause, huzzas and waving of hats." A Radical newspaper correspondent declared that the ovation expressed the city's heart, "jubilant and defiant." After an informal levee, the President of the late Confederate States made his way to Canada, where he remained until the next episode in the attempt to try him for treason took place in 1868.

While Horace Greeley had signed Davis' bond, his act by no means represented the general attitude of the Radicals. The *Independent* denounced the act with "regret, indignation and scorn." Greeley was made to feel Radical anger, for the circulation of the *Tribune* diminished by many thousands almost over night, and the sale of Greeley's "American Conflict" shrank suddenly to a negligible amount. After the "arch-criminal of all times" had been admitted to bail, the languid proceedings of impeachment investigation flared up in fitful vigor, only to die down again when it became apparent from the testimony of Stanbery, Evarts, Judge Underwood, the United States Attorney and others that President Johnson had been about the only man consistently desirous that Davis be tried.

Another legal measure which attracted great public attention was the attempt of Provisional Governors Sharkey of Mississippi and Jenkins of Georgia to bring the Military Reconstruction Acts before the Supreme Court. With the passage of the two acts the Southern people were appalled at the prospect before them. It was hard for them to realize that the North was determined to exclude intelligence from Southern governments and to enforce the rule of the most ignorant class upon those unhappy States. The President apparently was impotent. The Northern voters had not listened to his appeal. But there remained a third department of the government, the judicial. It was no Radical body. Its decisions in the Milligan, Garland and Cummings cases afforded a faint hope that there was still a Constitution in the land. Before giving up in black despair, the South would appeal to the Supreme Court.

On April 5 Governor Sharkey, Alexander H. Garland and Robert J. Walker, representing the State of Mississippi, asked leave to file a plea to have the Supreme Court perpetually enjoin Andrew Johnson from "executing or in any manner carrying out" the Reconstruction Acts. On the same day the President brought the matter before the Cabinet, and Stanbery was instructed to appear before the Supreme Court and object to the Mississippi motion—"Sharkey's new rebellion," a Radical journal termed it—on the ground that the President, as representative of the United States, could not be sued. Doubtless the Radicals were somewhat surprised to find Andrew Johnson's attorney-general appearing before the high court and endeavoring to prevent the judicial overthrow of these last measures which Andrew Johnson himself had gravely reprehended as unconstitutional. But the Tennessee tailor-politician was just the man to do his duty, no matter what anguish of heart it cost him.

Senator Trumbull appeared as special counsel for the government. Stanbery made a forcible presentation of the government's position, Charles O'Conor argued the Mississippi motion and the court took the matter under advisement.

Before its decision was handed down, Provisional Governor Jenkins of Georgia made similar application to the Court. On April 10 Jenkins issued an address to the people of his State, pointing out that of the three departments of the Federal Government, two were in direct antagonism regarding the constitutionality of the Military Reconstruction measures. There yet remained, however, the third department, the judicial, "the great conservator of the supremacy of the Constitution, whose decrees, unlike the executive veto, cannot be overridden by the Congress. That court has not yet spoken. Should it be found in accordance with the executive, this usurpation will be arrested." Jenkins avoided Mississippi's error by seeking to enjoin, not the President, but the Secretary of War, the General of the Army, and the Department Commander assigned to the Georgia command.

Unhappily for the Southern people, the Supreme Court was unwilling to accept jurisdiction in either of these applications. On April 15 an unanimous court, the Chief Justice speaking, denied the Mississippi petition, lack of jurisdiction being given as the cause. In May the Georgia petition was also rejected. Prudence rather than judicial judgment seems to have influenced the court's determination in these two cases. In the Mississippi case Chase gave this explanation: "The Congress is the Legislative Department of the government. The President is the Executive Department. Neither can be restrained in its action by the Judicial Department; though the acts of both, when performed, are, in proper case, subject to its cognizance." The Chief Justice pointed out the "impropriety" of such interference as had been sought by limning its possible consequences. "Suppose the plea filed and the injunction prayed be allowed," he recited. "If the President refuses obedience, it is needless to observe that the court is without power to enforce its process. If, on the other hand, the President complies with the order of the court and refuses to execute the acts of Congress, is it not clear that a collision may occur between the executive and legislative departments of the government? May not the House of Representatives impeach the President for such refusal? In that case could this court interfere, in behalf of the President, thus endangered by compliance with its mandate, and restrain by injunction the Senate of the United States from sitting as a court of impeachment?"

The court had refused to take jurisdiction in the Mississippi case because no question of person or property was involved, the only matter at issue being the rights of putative governments. As soon as its decision had been announced, Mississippi's counsel made desperate efforts to be permitted to amend their application so that they could involve person or property in the case and thus meet the Supreme Court's definition of the types of cases it felt properly to be within the province of its decision. The application was reargued and, by a four to four decision, Justice Grier being absent, the plea was disallowed.

Thus the South's last hope to prevent the forcible imposition of Negro domination had proven vain. The President had been unable to stop the Radical onslaught, and the Supreme Court, fearful of its own fate, appeared unwilling to interpose its protecting hand between the Radicals and the prostrate South. "We have fallen on evil times," lamented ex-President Buchanan. "What is to become of the Supreme Court of the United States?" And the Radicals mixed their exultation and relief with warnings; Congress would find the means "to carry out its purposes if the Supreme Court puts itself in the way"; the Court had better beware "the risk of amputation!"

Long before the Supreme Court dismissed the Southern petitions, the President began to have trouble with his district commanders in the South. His unwisdom in allowing Stanton to name the men assigned to the five military districts quickly became apparent. Eight days after assuming command of the fifth district, Sheridan, under his own interpretation of his powers as granted by the Reconstruction Act, abruptly removed A. S. Herron, Attorney-General of the State of Louisiana; J. S. Monroe, Mayor of New Orleans, and Edwin Abell, Judge of the First District Court of that city. A few days later he removed the Board of Levee Commissioners. When questioned by Washington about these summary actions, Sheridan almost insolently contended that he had the right and power to remove whomsoever he saw fit without authorization by the President. In Alabama, General Pope had removed the Mayor of Mobile, and there was trouble under way in Georgia.

After a series of such episodes, McCulloch, Secretary of the Treasury, could contain himself no longer. Early in May he went to the President to tell him bluntly, face to face, that he had brought his troubles on himself. His hesitating course was responsible for the Administration's evil days. He had retained in his Cabinet a man "notoriously opposed to his Administration, a man who from the beginning had been an embarrassment; that there was never any free interchange of opinion when that member was present. . . . Yet in many of the important measures and movements, that false member had a controlling voice and often was the only person consulted." McCulloch thrust the instance of the selection of the military governors up to the President, selections "made without consultation with any Member of the Cabinet, save the false and unfaithful one." Johnson listened to McCulloch's reproaches and agreed that the Secretary of the Treasury was right. But this was all.

None the less, Andrew Johnson pushed ahead on the task ahead of him, examining with the most careful detail every one of the multifarious problems presented. The President was acutely dissatisfied with conditions in the internal revenue bureau of the Treasury Department. This unit had at its head Commissioner Rollins, an arrant Radical, and its conduct was a source of great scandal under Lincoln, Johnson and Grant. Secretary McCulloch was peculiarly blind to Rollins' treachery to the President and to the frauds of the Federal Revenue being committed by the Commissioner's subordinates. The President asked again and again for reform, but McCulloch consistently defended the Bureau. On May 6 he wrote Johnson: "If there be honest men in the country, they are at the head of the office of Internal Revenue. Great demoralization pervades the country and great frauds are being unquestionably committed upon our revenue, particularly . . . in the illicit distribution of liquor. But I assure you that earnest efforts are being made to prevent them."

In this same month came an invitation which must have seemed to the harassed Chief Executive an opportunity for temporary escape from the heart-breaking problems of the Presidency. A monument to Jacob Johnson was to be unveiled at Raleigh on June 4, and Governor Jonathan Worth invited the President to be present at these exercises and to attend the commencement of the University of North Carolina at Chapel Hill. Mayor Dallas Haywood of Raleigh also urged the President to visit his birthplace. On May 22 Johnson answered: "I accept the invitation of my native city to be her guest and, deeply grateful for the respect in which they hold my father's memory, will be present."

Another invitation, this one to take part in the dedication of the great Masonic building in Boston, came to the President. Remembering the sad experiences of the Swing Around the Circle, his apprehensive friends sought to restrain him and, on May 24, Thomas Ewing wrote: "Do not, I pray you, go to Boston. The occasion is not a propitious one. There are yet anti-Masons as well as Masons. . . . Besides, there will be fifty lying scamps dogging at your heels who will circulate more fresh slander than can be corrected in six months.

"Your proposed trip to Raleigh is well, the occasion warrants it [but] I hope you will meddle not at all with politics, even in private conversation, and let all who honestly or dishonestly inquire as to your opinions and purposes find them in your official papers. Foolish friends and crafty enemies will publish their version of what you say, alike to your injury. . . . He who is a President must in his intercourse with the public forget that he is a man."

Fortunately, Ewing's apprehensions as to untoward incidents on these presidential journeys proved unfounded. Johnson greatly enjoyed them both and was treated with great respect by the public.

Upon his return to Washington from Raleigh, the vexing problems of Reconstruction again imperatively presented themselves. On June 10 General Sickles sent the President his views of the responsibility of commanders. "I regard these States," he wrote, "as having been placed under your control as commander-in-chief by Congress, which assume that the United States have paramount and exclusive jurisdiction. Your control as commander-in-chief is exercised through district commanders appointed by yourself. These commanders are subject to your orders. You may revoke or suspend any order they give. You may control their action by general or particular instructions. You may relieve or supersede them."

About this time Sickles' suspension of execution of an order of a civil court aroused the Southern Conservatives to fever heat, and drew an opinion from Attorney-General Stanbery that the General's procedure was illegal and an usurpation.

On June 19, smarting under Stanbery's sharp words, Sickles asked to be relieved from the command of his department and demanded a court of inquiry on his conduct, that "I may vindicate myself from the accusations of the Attorney-General." But the General did not secure his wish. The President, who disliked him, and remarked, concerning him, "A conceited cuckold is an abomination in the sight of God," liked neither his Carolina conduct nor his attempts to embarrass the Administration. Accordingly he directed the General to retain command and declined to order the court of inquiry.

About this same time Sheridan went a step further and removed Governor Wells of Louisiana from office. This aroused even greater furore through the South, and on June 20, General J. B. Steedman telegraphed the President from New Orleans that "want of respect for Governor Wells personally alone represses an expression of indignation felt by all honest and sensible men at the unwarranted usurpation of General Sheridan in removing the civil officers of Louisiana. It is believed here that you will reinstate Wells. He is a bad man and has no influence. I believe General Sheridan made the removal to embarrass you, believing the feeling at the North would sustain him. My conviction is that on account of the bad character of Wells and Monroe, you ought not to reinstate any who have been [ousted] because you cannot reinstate any without reinstating all. But you ought to prohibit the exercise of this power in the future."

In view of such impetuous proceedings on the part of the military commanders, the President determined to do what he could to assuage the asperities of the Reconstruction Acts by careful administration. He made a written request of Attorney-General Stanbery for that officer's considered and careful legal opinion as to the meaning of the Reconstruction Acts. On May 24 Stanbery had furnished his views on the Reconstruction Acts' provisions regarding qualification of voters in the Southern States. On June 12 he supplemented this first opinion with one of considerably greater length dealing with this and other phases of the Acts.

On June 18 the President brought the whole matter before the Cabinet. Stanbery proposed that a record be kept of the ensuing Cabinet deliberations and that the vote of each member on each point be recorded. Wells looked askance at this new departure, but the President, "nervous and apprehensive," was anxious to have a written record of this important discussion.

At the outset, Welles said that the Reconstruction Acts were "so abominable, so flagrantly unconstitutional, that I do not feel inclined to have anything to do with them." His chief objection to Stanbery's opinion was that the Attorney-General had endeavored to raise an edifice with no foundation; he had sought so to interpret the Reconstruction Act as to enable the South to endure it. Indeed, Stanbery "had done more for popular rights, under a law which despotically deprived the people of their undoubted guaranteed rights, than I had supposed possible."

The Secretary of the Navy considered the President in an extraordinary and embarrassing position; he had sworn to support the Constitution and had also taken oath to see the laws faithfully executed. The two were incompatible. When Johnson had appointed military governors, he had done all that could be expected of him. But now that the governors disagreed and sought instruction, he had quite properly asked the law officer of the government for his opinion. But let it be sent out merely as the Attorney-General's construction and not as a binding order. In this Welles agreed with Stanton, whose temper and attitude during the four days' debate—indeed, from the very moment of the passage of the Tenure-of-Office Act over the veto Stanton had prepared for the President—had become surly, rude and overbearing. The Secretary of War insisted that Congress had intended to strike down civil government in the South and to establish military dominion, and that the President had no right or authority to temper the process.

On June 19 the President submitted a list of nineteen interrogatories which he had prepared, remarking as he did so upon "the necessity for uniformity of opinion in the Cabinet." Stanton objected to any such mode of procedure, demanding time for written answers. The Attorney-General answered that the questions were very plain and such as he himself could answer at once. Seward and McCulloch said they were ready. Still protesting, Stanton yielded, but first read a paper he had written the night before, disclosing his Radical attitude toward the acts. Though his paper was condemned by every one of his associates, he did not reply. Then the Attorney-General began the interrogatories. Of the nineteen questions, twelve produced no dissent. On the seven remaining—and they were the important ones—all members agreed except Stanton, who dissented from each, at times with insolence.

The President wished to know if the power was vested in him "to see that the Reconstruction Acts are faithfully executed," and all but Stanton answered yes. But the latter referred to "the limitations and qualifications . . . of the Act of Congress." Another question was whether the President had the right of supervision over the military commanders, and whether they were bound to perform their duties in conformity with his instruction. All answered affirmatively save Stanton, who declared that "the duties assigned to the military commanders . . . are specifically entrusted to them, and they are not bound to perform these duties in conformity with his (the President's) instruction unless they are in accordance with the Acts of Congress."

Johnson desired to know whether unlimited power had been given the military commanders "to abolish, modify, control or supersede the laws of the State," to which question all responded in the negative except Stanton, who said that "the military authority is paramount," and that a commanding general "has unlimited power to abolish, modify, control or supersede the State law." It was all too apparent that the attitude of subservient submissiveness which he had displayed prior to the Tenure-of-Office Act had been hypocritical. Stanton had at last removed his mask.

None the less, Johnson determined to issue Stanbery's rulings to the military commanders, and after some dispute as to the form of the preamble, a draft was adopted, reciting that several commanders had sought instructions, that the Acts and the Attorney-General's opinions thereon "have been carefully considered by the President in conference with the heads of the respective departments" and that the President "has concluded that the following is the correct and practical interpretation of the acts . . . and directs the same to be transmitted to the said commanders for their information, in order that there may be uniformity in the execution of the said acts."

The important portion of Stanbery's opinion concerned the registration of voters. The Attorney-General gave the South all the leeway the strict letter of the law allowed. Whenever an applicant for registration as a voter took the oath prescribed by the Supplementary Reconstruction Act, Stanbery ruled, "his name must go on the registry. The Board of Registrations cannot enter upon the inquiry whether he has sworn truly or falsely."

This opinion angered and alarmed the Radicals, who immediately began to agitate for quorums to be present in July in both Houses of Congress to annihilate the Attorney-General's views. General Sheridan telegraphed from New Orleans to Grant: "Mr. Stanbery's interpretation is practically . . . opening a broad macadamized road for perjury and fraud to travel on." "The little fellow" gave out for publication this dispatch, highly disrespectful to the President. The latter resented it keenly, and rumors began to be bruited about that Sheridan was to be removed. These led the *Independent* to declare that "the people would throw a thousand Andrew Johnsons into the sea sooner than permit one Phil Sheridan to walk the plank."

With the publication of this opinion, Radical demand for the July session of Congress became so insistent that there was no doubt that quorums would be present when the designated July date arrived. Some of the Radicals affected surprise that "the President would do so stupid a thing as to interfere with the successful operation of the Reconstruction Act." But the extremists in both Houses of Congress set to work with a vengeance to annihilate the opinion given by the Attorney-General.

In the House debate, Ben Butler startled the Radicals by informing them that "in the opinion of some of the ablest lawyers of the country, some of the points in Mr. Stanbery's opinion were well taken." Therefore, he argued, the act which Congress now would pass "must be made so distinct and so clear that misinterpretation of it would be impossible."

The bill finally enacted conformed to Butler's specifications. It authorized the commanders of the military districts, in so many words, to suspend or remove any official in the "pretended governments" of the "Rebel States" and to fill vacancies thus created. These acts were to be reviewed not by the President but by the General of the Army. Such removals were not merely permissive but mandatory. It was made the duty of the district commanders to oust "all disloyal persons."

This measure reached the President on July 14, and on July 19 he returned it with his veto. Even Andrew Johnson's patience was approaching a breaking point. Congress had had the insolence to declare that none of the officers or military commanders should "be bound in his action by any opinion of any civil officer of the United States," a direct endeavor to remove all authority from the President. In his message, Andrew Johnson spoke sternly about this new usurpation of executive authority by Congress.

"Within a period of less than a year, the legislation of Congress has attempted to strip the Executive Department of some of its essential powers. The Constitution, and the oath provided in it devolve upon the President the power and duty to see that the laws are faithfully executed. The Constitution, in order to carry out this power, gives him the choice of agents, and makes them subject to his control and supervision. But in the execution of these laws the constitutional obligation upon the President remains, but the power to exercise that constitutional duty is effectually taken away. The military commander is, as to the power of appointment, made to take the place of the President, and the General of the Army the place of the Senate; and any attempt on the part of the President to assert his own constitutional powers may, under pretense of law, be met by official insubordination. It is to be feared that these military officers, looking to the authority given by these laws, rather than to the letter of the Constitution, will recognize no authority but the commander of the district and the General of the Army."

Nor was this all. While he remained President, he informed Congress, and "whilst the obligation rests upon me to see that all the laws are faithfully executed, I can never willingly surrender that trust or the powers given for its execution. I can never give my assent to be made responsible for the faithful execution of the laws, and at the same time surrender that trust, and the powers which accompany it, to any other officer, high or low, or to any number of executive officers."

When the Radicals promptly repassed the bill over the veto, these sentences gave rise to excited comment. Here was further proof that the President was a bad man, an enemy of the country, who must be impeached.